Summary of Financial Ratios
Short-Term Liquidity Ratios

1. $\text{Current Ratio} = \dfrac{\text{Current Assets}}{\text{Current Liabilities}}$

2. $\text{Quick Ratio} = \dfrac{\text{Cash + Short-Term Investments + Receivables}}{\text{Current Liabilities}}$

3. $\text{Cash Ratio} = \dfrac{\text{Cash + Short-Term Investments}}{\text{Current Liabilities}}$

4. $\text{Operating Cash Flow Ratio} = \dfrac{\text{Cash Flows from Operating Activities}}{\text{Current Liabilities}}$

Debt Management Ratios

5a. $\text{Times Interest Earned (Accrual Basis)} = \dfrac{\text{Operating Income}}{\text{Interest Expense}}$

5b. $\text{Times Interest Earned (Cash Basis)} = \dfrac{\text{Cash Flows from Operations + Income Tax Payments + Interest Payments}}{\text{Interest Payments}}$

6. $\text{Long-Term Debt to Equity Ratio} = \dfrac{\text{Long-Term Debt (including current portion)}}{\text{Total Equity}}$

7. $\text{Debt to Equity Ratio} = \dfrac{\text{Total Liabilities}}{\text{Total Equity}}$

8. $\text{Long-Term Debt to Total Assets Ratio} = \dfrac{\text{Long-Term Debt (including current portion)}}{\text{Total Assets}}$

9. $\text{Debt to Total Assets Ratio} = \dfrac{\text{Total Liabilities}}{\text{Total Assets}}$

Asset Efficiency Ratios

10. $\text{Accounts Receivable Turnover Ratio} = \dfrac{\text{Net Credit Sales or Net Sales}}{\text{Average Accounts Receivable}}$

11. $\text{Inventory Turnover Ratio} = \dfrac{\text{Cost of Goods Sold}}{\text{Average Inventory}}$

12. $\text{Asset Turnover Ratio} = \dfrac{\text{Net Sales}}{\text{Average Total Assets}}$

Profitability Ratios

13. $\text{Gross Profit Percentage} = \dfrac{\text{Gross Profit}}{\text{Net Sales}}$

14. $\text{Operating Margin Percentage} = \dfrac{\text{Income from Operations}}{\text{Net Sales}}$

15. $\text{Net Profit Margin Percentage} = \dfrac{\text{Net Income}}{\text{Net Sales}}$

16. $\text{Return on Assets} = \dfrac{\text{Net Income} + [\text{Interest Expense} \times (1 - \text{Tax Rate})]}{\text{Average Total Assets}}$

17. $\text{Return on Equity} = \dfrac{\text{Net Income}}{\text{Average Equity}}$

Stockholder Ratios

18. $\text{Earnings per Share (EPS) Ratio} = \dfrac{\text{Net Income} - \text{Preferred Dividends}}{\text{Average Number of Common Shares Outstanding}}$

19. $\text{Return on Common Equity} = \dfrac{\text{Net Income}}{\text{Average Common Equity}}$

20. $\text{Dividend Yield Ratio} = \dfrac{\text{Dividends per Common Share}}{\text{Closing Market Price per Share for the Year}}$

21. $\text{Dividend Payout Ratio} = \dfrac{\text{Common Dividends}}{\text{Net Income}}$

22. $\text{Stock Repurchase Payout Ratio} = \dfrac{\text{Common Stock Repurchases}}{\text{Net Income}}$

23. $\text{Total Payout Ratio} = \dfrac{\text{Common Dividends + Common Stock Repurchases}}{\text{Net Income}}$

Dupont Analysis

24. $\text{Return on Equity} = \dfrac{\text{Net Income}}{\text{Sales}} \times \dfrac{\text{Sales}}{\text{Average Total Assets}} \times \dfrac{\text{Average Total Assets}}{\text{Average Equity}}$

FIFTH EDITION

FINANCIAL ACCOUNTING

The Cornerstone of Business Decision Making

JAY S. RICH
Illinois State University

JEFFERSON P. JONES
Auburn University

LINDA A. MYERS
University of Tennessee-Knoxville

Australia • Brazil • Canada • Mexico • Singapore • United Kingdom • United States

Financial Accounting: The Cornerstone of Business Decision Making, **Fifth Edition**
Jay S. Rich, Jefferson P. Jones, and Linda A. Myers

Senior Vice President, Higher Education Product Management: Erin Joyner

Product Director: Jason Fremder

Senior Product Manager: Matthew Filimonov

Product Manager: Melody Sorkhabi

Content Development Manager: Andrea Meyer

Senior Content Manager: Tricia Hempel

Product Assistant: Matt Schiesl

Executive Marketing Manager: Nathan R. Anderson

Marketing Coordinator: Sean Messer

Senior Digital Delivery Lead: Jessica Robbe

Production Service: Lumina Datamatics, Inc.

Design: Chris Doughman

Intellectual Property:
Analyst: Ashley Maynard
Project Managers: Carly Belcher, Betsy Hathaway

For product information and technology assistance, contact us at
Cengage Customer & Sales Support, 1-800-354-9706.

For permission to use material from this text or product, submit all requests online at **www.cengage.com/permissions.**
Further permissions questions can be emailed to
permissionrequest@cengage.com.

Microsoft Excel® and PowerPoint® are registered trademarks of Microsoft Corporation. © 2017 Microsoft.

The financial statements are included for illustrative and education purposes only. Nothing herein should be construed as financial advice.

Library of Congress Control Number: 2017942575

ISBN: 978-0-357-13269-2

Cengage
200 Pier 4 Boulevard
Boston, MA 02210
USA

Cengage is a leading provider of customized learning solutions with employees residing in nearly 40 different countries and sales in more than 125 countries around the world. Find your local representative at:
www.cengage.com.

To learn more about Cengage platforms and services, register or access your online learning solution, or purchase materials for your course, visit **www.cengage.com.**

Printed in the United States of America
Print Number: 01   Print Year: 2020

This book is dedicated to our students—past, present, and future—who are at the heart of our passion for teaching.

BRIEF CONTENTS

The fifth edition of Financial Accounting: The Cornerstone of Business Decision Making

We have been teaching financial accounting for decades. We love it and believe that financial accounting is one of the most important courses in the business curriculum. As it is one of the first business courses students take, we work to share our love and enthusiasm for the material and to show each student that accounting is both *exciting* and *relatable* to their current life, as well as to their future—regardless of their major.

We wrote this book because there was no other book available that helped us balance between a couple of critical and often contradictory goals—creating a solution that will both help students read and study *and* also attract majors to the field by demonstrating the best aspects of accounting.

Here's our approach:

We wanted to create a solution that helps students read and study. Many—if not most—students have poor study habits. They often also have unrealistic beliefs about how much studying is needed for success in accounting. As a result, they show up unprepared. We help overcome this problem using a variety of strategies:

- **All examples within the fifth edition are consistent in format**. Providing students with complete information and clear, step-by-step solutions helps build confidence and is a resource that students will reference continually throughout the course.

EXAMPLE 1.1   USING THE FUNDAMENTAL ACCOUNTING EQUATION

On January 1, Gundrum Company reported assets of $125,000 and liabilities of $75,000. During the year, assets increased by $44,000 and stockholders' equity increased by $15,000.

Required:

1. What is the amount reported for stockholders' equity on January 1?

2. What is the amount reported for liabilities on December 31?

Solution:

1. Stockholders' equity on January 1 is $50,000. This amount is calculated by rearranging the fundamental accounting equation as follows:

$$\text{Assets} = \text{Liabilities} + \text{Stockholders' Equity}$$

$$\$125,000 = \$75,000 + \text{Stockholders' Equity}$$

$$\text{Stockholders' Equity} = \$125,000 - \$75,000 = \underline{\mathbf{\$50,000}}$$

2. At December 31, liabilities are $104,000. This amount is computed by adding the change to the appropriate balance sheet elements and then rearranging the fundamental accounting equation as follows:

$$\text{Assets} = \text{Liabilities} + \text{Stockholders' Equity}$$

$$(\$125,000 + \$44,000) = \text{Liabilities} + (\$50,000 + \$15,000)$$

$$\text{Liabilities} = (\$125,000 + \$44,000) - (\$50,000 + \$15,000)$$

$$= \$169,000 - \$65,000 = \underline{\mathbf{\$104,000}}$$

- Using our text and the integrated examples, you won't need to spend as much valuable class time teaching "how"; you can instead focus on "why."

- **Author-created "office hours"–style Show Me How (SMH) videos** walk students through solving a similar (but not identical) activity. These videos are linked to Many of the most assigned exercises within the homework and can be reviewed on a student's own time in the Adaptive Study Plan. Because these are author-created videos, the Show Me How videos cover the conceptual roots behind the problem but are careful not to give away the answer. It is important that students learn by doing the work.

- **The Adaptive Study Plan (ASP) in CengageNOWv2** is a turnkey preclass assignment allowing you to assign a self-paced module that reviews a chapter's learning objectives. In addition, students may access the ASP on their own time to study and review.

What's New in 5e?

We wanted to create a financial accounting solution that would illustrate the best aspects of accounting. Students often have preconceived notions that accounting is boring or irrelevant. We want to show that accounting is attractive and exciting. Here is how we tackled this challenge in a fresh way:

- **A focus on why accounting is important.** Right from the start, we strive to explain why accounting matters to students, and why it is relevant for *all* majors. This is carried throughout the narrative. We don't just explain "how"; we also explain "why." We've found that students learn better when they know why.

- **Earlier introduction to detailed financial statements (e.g., the multistep income statement)** allows for earlier discussions of why accounting is important and how it can be used. Students can start reading and using actual annual reports (10Ks) earlier.

- **A new supplement to Chapter 1 on Reading a Company's Annual Report and Form 10-K** introduces students to the contents of an annual report and Form 10-K. It describes what information can be found in each section and also briefly discusses earning announcements and non-GAAP reporting.

- **New annual report problems for every chapter.** A library of hundreds of author-created and fully algorithmic real-world annual report problems allows you to assign students annual report problems (on well-known companies such as Home Depot and Lowe's) without worrying about students copying their answers from one another.

We also always want to provide up-to-date content that you need to teach the way you want. Additional updates include the following:

- **A new appendix on data analytics** provides an introductory-level summary of what data analytics is and how it can be used to answer accounting questions. A series of exercises allows students to practice using data analytics techniques.

- **New: Analytics cases.** Students need to understand how data may be used to make decisions; however, it is critical that they also understand the underlying accounting issue. Integrated Analytics cases help students learn Excel or Tableau and Analytics, as they also reinforce accounting skills such as the Aging of Accounts method. The authors' goal was to create cases that you can't effectively use without knowing the underlying accounting.

  - New PowerPoints, with a more interactive focus

  - Updated test banks

  - Updated ASP quizzing

  - Additional Excel Online problems

  - Many new Tell Me More videos

Close the Gap

Between Homework and Exam Performance

with **CengageNOWv2**

We've talked with hundreds of accounting instructors across the country, and we are learning that online homework systems have created a new challenge in the accounting course.

We are hearing that students perform well on the homework but poorly on the exam, which leads instructors to believe that students are not truly learning the content, but rather are memorizing their way through the system.

CengageNOWv2 better prepares students for the exam by providing an online homework experience that is similar to what students will experience on the exam and in the real world.

Read on to see how CengageNOWv2 helps close this gap.

Closing the gap, one step at a time.

CengageNOWv2 (CNOWv2) is a powerful course management and online homework tool that helps students succeed in introductory accounting.

Here's how CNOWv2 can help you and your students:

Building business skills. Excel, Analytic, and other business skills are important, but there is a lot to cover in the Introductory Accounting course. CNOWv2 allows you to expose students to Excel and data analytics without requiring you to teach these topics.

- **The Excel Online problem type** seamlessly integrates Excel and algorithmically generates data sets into the classroom. Because it is online, all students will have the same version. You won't have to accommodate the hassles of differing versions and platforms.

- In addition, accompanying **Show Me How** videos on every Excel Online problem mean that you do not need to worry about teaching Excel. CNOWv2 walks students through how to solve a similar assignment.

- **Analytics cases.** Students need to understand how data may be used to make decisions; however, it is critical that they also understand the underlying accounting issue. Integrated Analytics cases help students learn Excel or Tableau and Analytics as they also reinforce accounting skills such as the Aging of Accounts method. The authors' goal was to create cases that you can't effectively use without knowing the underlying accounting.

Reading and interpreting 10K information. It is critical that students learn not just how to create accounting information but also how to use that information. Notably, all students (even the nonmajors) will be able to read and interpret an annual report or 10K and make some simple decisions.

- **Annual report problems.** A library of hundreds of author-created and fully algorithmic real-world annual report problems allow you to assign students annual report problems (on well-known companies such as Home Depot and Lowe's) without worrying about students copying their answers from one another.

The "10 o'clock at night" problem. Experience and usage data reveal that students typically complete homework at times when their instructors are not available to help. As a result, they get stuck and frustrated and give up. CNOWv2 has integrated tools to help students overcome this common roadblock.

- **Show Me How problem demonstration videos** walk students through how to solve a similar (but not identical) activity. These author-created videos are linked to hundreds of items within the homework and may also be reviewed on a student's own time in the Adaptive Study Plan.

Because these are author-created videos, the Show Me How videos cover the conceptual roots behind the problem but are careful not to give away the answer. It's important that students learn by doing the work.

In addition, the Show Me How videos are also available in new assignable (but ungraded) video assignments.

Chapter 1, Learning Objective 4: Show Me How: Transactions
Chapter 1, Learning Objective 4: Show Me How: Accounting equation V3
Chapter 1, Learning Objective 4: Show Me How: Effect of transactions on accounting equation
Chapter 1, Learning Objective 4: Show Me How: Nature of transactions
Chapter 1, Learning Objective 4: Show Me How: Transactions (Acct Eq)

- **Adaptive Feedback** in Blanksheet of Paper items provides custom feedback that is truly adaptive. Where many platforms provide generic feedback, CNOWv2's Adaptive Feedback gives feedback based on the exact entry that a student makes.

- **Check My Work Feedback** is available with all homework items in CNOWv2 and supplements Adaptive Feedback. This is generic feedback that is supplied to students when they click on "Check My Work."

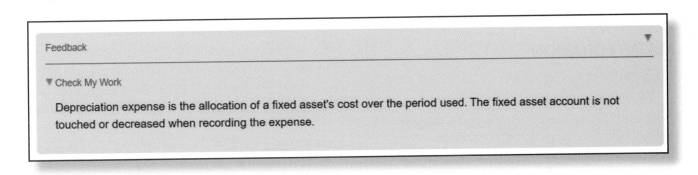

Students ace the homework but bomb the exam. Online homework is very popular in accounting, but students all too often try to game the system and guess their way through the homework. Then, when students get to the exam, they discover that they can't complete a journal entry or build a financial statement without the guidance and help of an online platform.

- **CNOWv2's Blanksheet of Paper problems** provide a much freer form and open environment without the drop-downs found in other systems. These items allow students to make mistakes and provide less handholding than traditional style activities.

- As these are purposely designed to be more challenging—and are generally all algorithmic—there is always a traditional drop-down style item if you would rather not assign a Blanksheet of Paper item.

Ensuring students show up to class and ready to learn. Accounting is a tough class. Students can't just show up to class and learn. They need to be exposed to the course material so that they (and you) can have a productive class.

- **The Adaptive Study Plan** is a turnkey preclass assignment that allows instructors to assign a self-paced module that reviews a chapter's learning objectives. In addition, students may access the ASP on their own time to study and review.

- Rest assured that your students will each have a unique class prep experience. The Adaptive Study Plan's quiz questions are drawn from pools. Each time students take the quiz, they will receive unique questions. There are pools of both qualitative and quantitative questions per learning objective. Additionally, the quantitative questions are algorithmic.

And that's not all...

You might also want to learn about the MindTap eReader, our LMS integration options, and more.

MindTap eReader. The MindTap eReader is the most robust digital reading experience available. Fully optimized for the iPad. Note-taking, highlighting, and more. Offline access to smartphones. The MindTap eReader also features ReadSpeaker®, an online text-to-speech application that vocalizes, or "speechenables," online educational content.

LMS INTEGRATION

CengageNOWv2 can be seamlessly integrated with most Learning Management Systems. Adopters will enjoy:

A Seamless User Experience—Access your Cengage resources seamlessly using only your LMS login credentials.

Simplified Registration Process—Get students up and running faster!

Content Customization and Deep Linking—Use our Content Selector to create a unique learning path for students that blends your content with Cengage activities, eText, and more within your LMS course.

Automatic Grade Synchronization*—Need to have your course grades recorded in your LMS gradebook? No problem. Simply select the activities you want synched, and grades will automatically be recorded in your LMS gradebook.

Accessibility. Cengage is committed to making its educational materials accessible to users of all abilities. We are steadily working to increase accessibility and create a full spectrum of usable tools, features, and choices that are accessible for users of all abilities. All new Cengage products and services are designed with accessibility in mind. In addition, the technology teams are constantly working toward the goal of optimizing the screen reader experience. With the latest release of CengageNOWv2:

- Images and graphics have been converted to HTML tables so that they can be read by screen readers.

- The assignment experience now offers proper heading structure to support easy navigation with assistive technology.

- CengageNOWv2 solutions offer high-contrast and well-structured HTML, which helps support screen reader interactivity.

- All videos are created with closed captioning and transcripts available for download.

- The MindTap eReader is HTML based and compatible with most screen reading assistive software. The eReader supports browser settings for high-contrast narrative text, variable font sizes, and multiple foreground and background color options.

For more information on accessibility, please visit www.cengage.com/accessibility.

SUPERIOR SUPPLEMENTS

SOLUTIONS MANUAL

Author-written and carefully verified multiple times to ensure accuracy and consistency with the text, the Solutions Manual contains answers to all Discussion Questions, Multiple-Choice Exercises, Brief Exercises, Exercises, Problem Sets and Cases that appear in the text. These solutions help you easily plan, assign, and efficiently grade assignments. All solutions are given in simplified Excel spreadsheets and also available in PDF format. The Solutions Manual is available electronically for instructors only on the password-protected portion of the text's website at http://login .cengage.com.

TEST BANK

Test Bank Content is delivered via Cengage Testing, Powered by Cognero, a flexible, online system that allows you to:

- Author, edit and manage test bank content
- Create multiple test versions in an instant
- Deliver tests from your LMS, from your classroom, or through CengageNOWv2
- Export Tests in Word Format

POWERPOINT® LECTURE SLIDES

The PowerPoint® slides have been revised to encourage lively classroom discussions.

COMPANION WEBSITE

This robust companion website provides immediate access to a rich array of teaching and learning resources—including the Solutions Manual and Power Points. Easily download the instructor resources you need from the password-protected, instructor-only section of the site.

CENGAGE.COM FREE STUDY TOOLS FOR STUDENTS

This robust product website provides immediate access to a rich array of interactive learning resources for students. Students should go to www.cengage.com and search by the author, title, or ISBN of the book at the top of the page. Cengage.com will lead students to the product page to access the free study resources.

ACKNOWLEDGMENTS AND THANKS

We would like to thank the following reviewers whose valuable comments and feedback helped shape and refine this edition:

Dawn P. Addington, *Central New Mexico Community College*

Elizabeth Ammann, *Lindenwood University*

Sandra H. Bitenc, *University of Texas at Arlington*

Duane M. Brandon, *Auburn University*

Rada Brooks, *University of California at Berkeley*

Esther S. Bunn, *Stephen F. Austin State University*

Gayle Chaky, *Dutchess Community College*

Chiaho Chang, *Montclair State University*

Dr. Michel Charifzadeh, *Reutlingen University*

Linda Christiansen, *Indiana University Southeast*

Lawrence Chui, *University of St. Thomas*

Tony Cioffi, *Lorain County Community College*

Rita Kingery Cook, *University of Delaware*

Joseph R. D'Agostin, *Fairfield University*

Dori Danko, *Grand Valley State University*

John M. Davis, *Ashland Community & Technology College*

Peggy DeJong, *Kirkwood Community College*

Andrew DeJoseph, *Nassau Community College*

Michael P. Dole, *Marquette University*

Carleton M. Donchess, *Bridgewater State University*

Emily L. Drogt, *Grand Valley State University*

Peter Dryden, *University of Ballarat*

Richard J. Dumont, *Post University*

James M. Emig, *Villanova University*

Steven Ernest, *Baton Rouge Community College*

Alan Falcon, *Loyola Marymount University*

Dr. James Falter, *Marietta College*

Jack Fatica, *Terra Community College*

Annette Fisher, *Glendale Community College*

Anthony B. Flores, *Allan Hancock College*

Umit Gurun, *University of Texas at Dallas*

Penny Nunn Hahn, *Henderson Community College*

Rosemary Hall, *Bellevue College*

Dr. Helmi Hammami, *Qatar University*

Sheila Handy, *East Stroudsburg University*

Michael Harkness, *University of Michigan*

Dennis Heiner, *College of Southern Idaho*

SueannHely, *West Kentucky Community & Technical College*

Joshua Herbold, *University of Montana*

Joan Van Hise, *Fairfield University*

David R. Honodel, *University of Denver*

Carol Hughes, *Asheville Buncombe Technical College*

Nelson Ildefonso, *Coastline Community College*

Matthew I. Isaak, *University of Louisiana at Lafayette*

Sharon S. Jackson, *Samford University*

Marianne James, *California State University, Los Angeles*

Gene E. A. Johnson, *Clark College, Vancouver*

Linda Jones, *Neosho County Community College*

Daniel J. Kerch, *Pennsylvania Highlands Community College*

Shirly A. Kleiner, *Johnson County Community College*

Dr. Trevor M. Knox, *Muhlenberg College*

Susan Kowalske, *Salem State University*

A. J. Kreimer, *Temple University*

Barbara Kren, *Marquette University*

Steven J. LaFave, *Augsburg College*

David Laurel, *South Texas College*

Dr. Wayne Lewis, *Hudson Valley Community College*

Linda Lindsay, *University of Lethbridge*

Joseph LiPari, *Montclair State University*

Nancy P. Lynch, *West Virginia University*

Susan A. Lynn, *University of Baltimore*

Jennifer Malfitano, *Delaware County Community College*

Carol Mannino, *Milwaukee School of Engineering*

Herb Martin, *Hope College*

Carmen Martorana Jr., *Medaille College*

Josephine Mathias, *Mercer County Community College*

Jeanine Metzler, *Northampton Community College*

Lorie D. Milam, *University of Texas at San Antonio*

Shawn Miller, *Lone Star College*

Laurel Bond Mitchell, *University of Redlands*

Norma R. Montague, *Wake Forest University*

Charles T. Moores, *University of Nevada, Las Vegas*

Donata Muntean, *Charles Sturt University*

Lisa Murawa, *Mott Community College*

Debra Nelson, *Kalamazoo Valley Community College*

David W. O'Bryan, *Pittsburg State University*

Glenn E. Owen, *Allan Hancock College*

Glenn Pate, *Palm Beach State College*

Sy Pearlman, *California State University*

Richard Persaud, *Miami Dade College*

Judy Peterson, *Monmouth College*

Brandis Phillips, *North Carolina AT&T State University*

Janice Pitera, *Broome Community College*

Dr. Ronald Premuroso, *University of Montana*

Eric Press, *Temple University*

Kristen Quinn, *Northern Essex Community College*

Glenn Rechtschaffen, *University of Auckland*

Howard Rockness, *University of North Carolina at Wilmington*

Dr. Robert E. Rosacker, *University of Wisconsin, La Crosse*

Paul A. San Miguel, *Western Michigan University*

Angels H. Sandberg, *Shorter University*

Susan D. Sandblom, *Scottsdale Community College*

Gail Sanderson, *Lebanon Valley College*

Christine Schalow, *University of Wisconsin, Stevens Point*

Lee Schiffel, *Valparaiso University*

Joseph Schubert, *Delaware Technical Community College*

Randy Serrett, *University of Houston*

Amy Genson Sheneman, *Grand Valley State University*

Lynn R. Smith, *Utah Valley University*

Steven H. Smith, *Western Washington University*

Nancy Snow, *University of Toledo*

Barbara Squires, *Corning Community College*

Tim Stein, *Baker College of Muskegon*

Ronald Strittmater, *North Hennepin Community College*

Joel M. Strong, *St. Cloud State University*

Daniel Taylor, *University of Pennsylvania*

Steve Teeter, *Utah Valley University*

Dr. Thiruvadi, *Morgan State University*

Robert C. Urell, *Irvine Valley College*

Al Wallace, *Owensboro Community & Technical College*

Sharon Walters, *Morehead State University*

Larry Watkins, *Northern Arizona University*

Robert Wesoloskie, *Elizabethtown College*

Denise White, *Austin Community College*

Terry Willyard, *Baker College*

Wendy Wilson, *Southern Methodist University*

Candace Witherspoon, *University of Kentucky*

Glenn Van Wyhe, *Pacific Lutheran University*

Yan Xiong, *California State University Sacramento*

We would also like to thank the following individuals for their careful verification of the textbook and all end-of-chapter materials:

Patty Worsham, *Norco College*

Tracy Newman, *M.S. Ed.*

Wendy Shanker, *Master of Management*

ABOUT THE AUTHORS

DR. JAY S. RICH is a Professor of Accounting at Illinois State University. He received his B.S., M.S., and Ph.D. from the University of Illinois. Prior to entering the Ph.D. program, he worked as an auditor at Price Waterhouse & Co. in Chicago and earned his CPA in 1985. He has published articles in *The Accounting Review, Auditing: A Journal of Practice & Theory, Accounting Horizons, Contemporary Accounting Research, Organizational Behavior and Human Decision Processes, Accounting Organizations and Society*, and others. He has also served on the editorial boards of *Auditing: A Journal of Practice & Theory* and *Current Issues in Auditing*. Dr. Rich has received both the Outstanding Dissertation Award and Notable Contribution to the Literature Award from the Audit Section of the American Accounting Association. He received the Outstanding Educator Award from the Illinois Society of CPAs in 2014. His primary teaching interest is financial accounting, and he has taught numerous courses at the undergraduate, masters, and doctoral levels. He is married and has three grown children. His outside interests include his family, travel, reading, and sports. He also repeatedly develops plans to exercise and diet at some point in the future. By all accounts, he is a master at grilling meat, a mediocre skier, and a shameful golfer.

DR. JEFFERSON P. JONES is an Associate Professor of Accounting in the School of Accountancy at Auburn University. He received his Bachelors in Accounting and Master of Accountancy degrees from Auburn University and his Ph.D. from Florida State University. His research interests focus on financial accounting, specifically investigating the quality of reported accounting information and accounting education. He has published articles in numerous journals, including *Advances in Accounting, Review of Quantitative Finance and Accounting, Issues in Accounting Education, International Journal of Forecasting, and The CPA Journal*. Professor Jones has received numerous teaching awards, including the Auburn University Beta Alpha Psi Outstanding Teaching Award (11 times); the Auburn University Outstanding Master of Accountancy Professor Teaching Award (five times), the Auburn University Outstanding Distance Master of Accountancy Teaching Award (three times); and the Auburn University College of Business McCartney Teaching Award. In addition, he has made numerous presentations around the country on research and pedagogical issues. He holds a CPA certificate in the state of Alabama (inactive) and is a member of the American Accounting Association, the American Institute of Certified Public Accountants (AICPA), and the Alabama Society of CPAs (ASCPA). He has had public accounting experience as an auditor for Deloitte & Touche. Professor Jones is also a coauthor of *Intermediate Accounting: Reporting & Analysis, 3e, Corporate Financial Accounting 16e, and Financial and Managerial Accounting 16e*. He is married, has two children, and enjoys playing golf and watching college football.

DR. LINDA A. MYERS is a Distinguished Professor of Accounting and holder of the Haslam Chair of Business at the University of Tennessee, Knoxville (UTK). She graduated from the University of Michigan and has published more than 40 peer-reviewed articles in *The Accounting Review, Journal of Accounting and Economics, Journal of Accounting Research, Contemporary Accounting Research, Review of Accounting Studies, and Accounting, Organizations and Society*, among others. She has also received the AAA's Notable Contribution to the Auditing Literature Award, the AAA's Financial Accounting and Reporting Section Best Paper Award, and the Financial Executives Research Foundation's Award for the Outstanding *Accounting Review* Article. Her research has been cited in the *New York Times* and *The Economist*, as well as by the Public Company Accounting Oversight Board and the U.S. Securities and Exchange Commission, and she has been quoted on National Public Radio's *Marketplace Business*. Professor Myers serves as an Editor at *Contemporary Accounting Research, Auditing: A Journal of Practice & Theory, Accounting Horizons, Journal of International Accounting Research, and CAFR*, as well as an Associate Editor at *Journal of Accounting, Auditing & Finance*, and on the Editorial Boards of *The Accounting Review* and *European Accounting Research*. She has taught financial accounting, managerial accounting, and Ph.D. seminars at McMaster University, University of Illinois, Texas A&M University, University of Arkansas, and UTK and currently serves as Director of the Ph.D. Program in Accounting at UTK. When she is not traveling around the globe, Professor Myers enjoys playing board games, cooking and entertaining, and spending time with her husband and her two children.

CONTENTS

CHAPTER 7

Operating Assets   398

CHAPTER 8

CHAPTER 9

CHAPTER 12

Financial Statement Analysis   690

APPENDIX 5

Financial Statement Information: The Kroger Co.   836

APPENDIX 6

Financial Statement Information: Sprouts Farmers Market, Inc.   848

1 Accounting and the Financial Statements

After studying Chapter 1, you should be able to:

1. Explain the nature of accounting.

2. Identify the forms of business organizations and the types of business activities.

3. Describe the relationships shown by the fundamental accounting equation.

4. Prepare a classified balance sheet and explain the information it communicates.

5. Prepare an income statement and explain the information it communicates.

6. Prepare the retained earnings statement and explain the information it communicates.

7. Identify the information communicated by the statement of cash flows.

8. Describe the relationships among the financial statements.

9. Explain the importance of ethics in providing useful financial information.

Andrej Sokolow/picture alliance/Getty Images

with Apple

In 1976, Steve Jobs and Steve Wozniak, the founders of **Apple Inc.**, began building personal computers in Jobs' parents' garage. Apple revolutionized the personal computer industry by making machines that were smaller, cheaper, user-friendly, and accessible to everyday consumers. As an industry leader, Apple appeared invincible. However, after a series of product failures, many analysts predicted the end of one of the computer industry's most prominent companies. With the introduction of revolutionary products such as the iMac, the iPod, the iTunes Store, and the iPhone, Apple has become the world's largest company by market value, with a stock price of over $300 per share at the beginning of 2020.

What type of information can help someone predict the successes (and failures) of a company like Apple? A good place to start is with a company's annual report (commonly referred to as Form 10-K). The accounting profession creates a valuable and essential economic resource—relevant and reliable financial information that people use to make important economic decisions that span a wide range of activities, including whether to invest in or loan money to a company. This financial information is provided in the form of financial statements—a summary of the results of a company's operations. The objective of this text is to help you read and interpret a company's annual report so that you can better use financial information to make important business decisions. Ultimately, your success in business will be influenced by how well you understand the accounting information contained in a company's annual report.

Source: Apple Inc. 2019 10-K.

3

WHY IS ACCOUNTING IMPORTANT?

Our economy is comprised of many different businesses. Some companies, such as **Apple Inc.**, focus on providing goods, which for Apple take many forms including desktop and laptop computers, iPads, iPhones, Apple Watches, and downloadable music. Other companies are primarily concerned with providing services. For example, **The Walt Disney Company** offers a variety of entertainment services from theme parks to motion pictures to streaming videos. While most entities, like Apple and Disney, exist in order to earn a profit, some are organized to achieve some other benefit to society (e.g., school districts exist to meet the educational needs of a community). Regardless of their objective, all entities use accounting to plan future operations, make decisions, and evaluate performance.

Accounting is an information system that identifies, measures, records, and communicates financial information about a company's business activities so decision-makers can make informed decisions. Without adequate information users will not be able to judge a business's economic opportunities and risks. Accounting is the "language of business" because it communicates information about the economic activities of a company that helps people make better decisions.

WHO USES ACCOUNTING INFORMATION

The demand for accounting information comes from both inside and outside the business and is summarized in Exhibit 1.1. Inside the business, managers use accounting information to help them plan and make decisions about the company. For example, managers use accounting information to help decide which actions to take, predict the consequences of their actions, and control the operations of the company. Accounting that is designed to meet the needs of internal users is called managerial accounting.

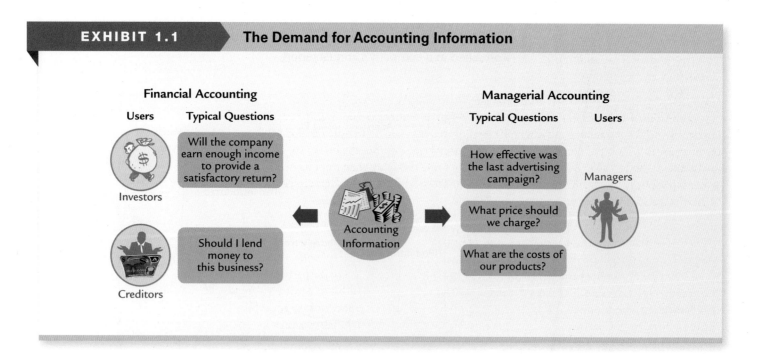

EXHIBIT 1.1   **The Demand for Accounting Information**

Outside the business, investors (owners) use accounting information to evaluate the future prospects of a company and decide where to invest their money. Creditors (lenders) use accounting information to evaluate whether to loan money to a company. Other external users include governmental agencies that use accounting information to determine taxes owed by companies, to implement regulatory objectives, and to make policy decisions; labor unions that are negotiating wage increases for its members; and financial analysts offering buy or sell recommendations to clients. Accounting information that satisfies the needs of external decision-makers is termed **financial accounting** and is the focus of this book.

The objectives of financial accounting involve providing decision-makers with information that assists them in assessing the amounts, timing, and uncertainties of a company's future cash flows. This information is provided through four basic financial statements: the balance sheet, the income statement, the retained earnings statement, and the statement of cash flows.

In this chapter, we will discuss the basic functioning of the accounting system within a business. We will address the following questions:

- What forms do businesses take?
- What are the basic business activities?
- How does the accounting system report these activities?
- How can decision-makers use the information provided by the accounting system?

Regardless of your major or future plans, knowledge of accounting and the ability to use accounting information will be critical to your success in business.

How will accounting affect my life?

ANSWER:
Accounting will impact many aspects of your daily life. The business that sells you goods or services uses accounting to keep track of how much money it received as well as the cost of operating the business. Calculating the amount of tax that is owed to the government requires accounting. When you invest your money, you should use accounting to understand a company's business and its prospects for the future. Plans that you make for the future often involve accounting to determine how much money you will need.

BUSINESSES: FORMS AND ACTIVITIES

OBJECTIVE 2
Identify the forms of business organizations and the types of business activities.

Accounting is an information system that identifies, measures, records, and communicates financial information about an accounting entity. An accounting entity is a business that has an identity separate from that of its owners and managers and for which accounting records are kept.

FORMS OF BUSINESS ORGANIZATION

This text emphasizes accounting for entities which take one of three forms: sole proprietorship, partnership, or corporation.

Sole Proprietorship A **sole proprietorship** is a business owned by one person. Sole proprietorships, which account for more than 70% of all businesses, are usually small, local businesses such as restaurants, photography studios, retail stores, or website developers. This organizational form is popular because it is simple to set up and gives the owner control over the business. While a sole proprietorship is an accounting entity separate from its owner, the owner is personally responsible for the debt of the business. Sole proprietorships can be formed or dissolved at the wishes of the owner.

Partnership A **partnership** is a business owned jointly by two or more individuals. Small businesses and many professional practices of physicians, lawyers, and accountants are often organized as partnerships. Relative to sole proprietorships, partnerships provide increased access to financial resources as well as access to the individual skills of each of the partners. The partnership entity does not pay taxes. Instead, each partner pays taxes at his or her individual rate. Similar to sole proprietorships, partnerships are accounting entities separate from the partners; however, the partners are jointly responsible for all the debt of the partnership.[1]

Corporation A **corporation** is a business organized under the laws of a particular state. A corporation, such as **Apple**, is owned by one or more persons called *stockholders*, whose

---

1 Many professional partnerships and multiple-owner businesses have been reorganized as *limited liability partnerships* (LLPs) or *limited liability corporations* (LLCs), which limit each partner's (owner's) liability to his or her investment in the partnership (business).

EXHIBIT 1.2 | **Forms of Business Organization**

Sole Proprietorship

- ⊕ Easily formed
- ⊕ Tax advantages
- ⊕ Controlled by owner
- ⊖ Personal liability
- ⊖ Limited life

Partnership

- ⊕ Access to the resources and skills of partners
- ⊕ Tax advantages
- ⊖ Shared control
- ⊖ Personal liability

Corporation

- ⊕ Easier to raise money
- ⊕ Easier to transfer ownership
- ⊕ Limited liability
- ⊖ More complex to organize
- ⊖ Higher taxes

---

ownership interests are represented by shares of stock. A primary advantage of the corporate form is the ability to raise large amounts of money (capital) by issuing shares of stock. Unlike a sole proprietorship or a partnership, a corporation is an "artificial person" and the stockholders' legal responsibility for the debt of the business is limited to the amount they invested in the business. In addition, shares of stock can be easily transferred from one owner to another through capital markets without affecting the corporation that originally issued the stock. The ability to raise capital by selling new shares, the limited legal liability of owners, and the transferability of the shares give the corporation an advantage over other forms of business organization. However, the requirements to form a corporation are more complex compared to the other forms of business organization. In addition, owners of corporations generally pay more taxes than owners of sole proprietorships or partnerships for two reasons:

- First, the corporate income tax rate is greater than the individual income tax rate.
- Second, a corporation's income is taxed twice—at the corporate level as income is earned, and at the individual level as earnings are distributed to stockholders. This is known as double taxation.

Exhibit 1.2 illustrates the advantages and disadvantages of each form of organization. While the combined number of sole proprietorships and partnerships greatly exceeds that

---

YOUDECIDE   Choice of Organizational Form

You are an entrepreneur who has decided to start a campus-area bookstore. In order to start your business, you have to choose among three organizational forms—sole proprietorship, partnership, or corporation. You have enough personal wealth to finance 40% of the business, but you must get the remaining 60% from other sources.

How does the choice of organizational form impact your control of the business and ability to obtain the needed funds?

The choice of organizational form can greatly impact many aspects of a business's operations. Each form has certain advantages and disadvantages that you should carefully consider.

- *Sole proprietorship:* A sole proprietorship would give you the most control of your business. However, you would be forced to obtain the additional 60% of funds

needed from a bank or other creditor. It is often difficult to get banks to support a new business.

- *Partnership:* If you choose to form a partnership, you would still have access to bank loans. In addition, you would also have the ability to obtain the additional funds from your partner or partners. In this situation, the partners would then have a 60% interest in the business, which may be an unacceptable loss of control.

- *Corporation:* If you choose to form a corporation, you could obtain the needed funds by issuing stock to investors. While a 60% interest may still be transferred to the stockholders, if the stock were widely dispersed among many investors, you might still retain effective control of the business with a 40% interest.

The choice of organizational form involves the consideration of many different factors.

of corporations, the majority of business in the United States is conducted by corporations. Therefore, this book emphasizes the corporate form of organization.

BUSINESS ACTIVITIES

Regardless of the form of a business, all businesses engage in activities that can be categorized as financing, investing, or operating activities. These activities are illustrated in Exhibit 1.3.

Business Activities

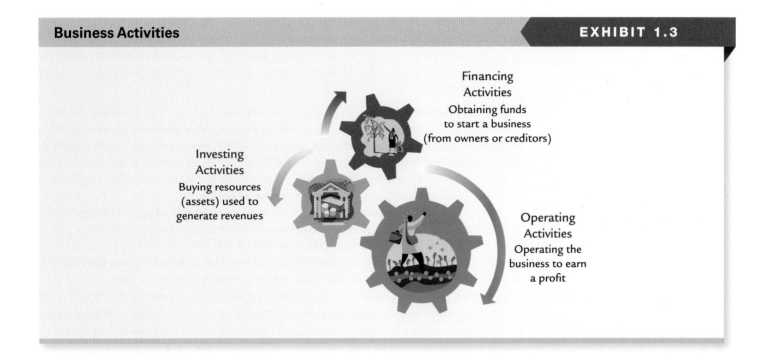

EXHIBIT 1.3

Financing Activities
Obtaining funds
to start a business
(from owners or creditors)

Investing Activities
Buying resources (assets) used to generate revenues

Operating Activities
Operating the business to earn a profit

Financing Activities A company's financing activities include obtaining the funds necessary to begin and operate a business. These funds come from either issuing stock or borrowing money. Most companies use both types of financing to obtain funds.

When a corporation borrows money from another entity such as a bank, it must repay the amount borrowed. The person to whom the corporation owes money is called a **creditor**. This obligation to repay a creditor is termed a **liability** and can take many forms. A common way for a corporation to obtain cash is to borrow money with the promise to repay the amount borrowed plus interest at a future date. Such borrowings are commonly referred to as *notes payable*. A special form of note payable that is used by corporations to obtain large amounts of money is called a *bond payable*.

In addition to borrowing money from creditors, a corporation may issue shares of stock to investors in exchange for cash. The dollar amount paid to a corporation for these shares is termed *common stock* and represents the basic ownership interest in a corporation. In a recent annual report, **Apple** reported it had issued 4,433,236,000 shares of common stock. The corporation is not obligated to repay the stockholder the amount invested; however, many corporations distribute a portion of their earnings to stockholders on a regular basis. These distributions are called *dividends*.

Creditors and stockholders have a claim on the **assets**, or economic resources, of a corporation. However, the claims on these resources differ. In the case of financial difficulty or distress, the claims of the creditors (liabilities) must be paid prior to the claims of the stockholders (called **stockholders' equity**). Stockholders' equity is considered a residual interest in the assets of a corporation that remain after deducting its liabilities.

Investing Activities Once a corporation has obtained funds through its financing activities, it buys assets (resources) that enable it to operate. For example, **Apple** recently reported $37,378 million in land, buildings, machinery, and equipment that it uses in its operations. A corporation may also obtain intangible assets that lack physical substance, such as copyrights and patents. The purchase and sale of the assets that are used in operations (commonly referred to as operating assets) are a corporation's investing activities.

Regardless of its form, assets are future economic benefits that a corporation controls. The assets purchased by a corporation vary depending on the type of business that the corporation engages in, and the composition of these assets is likely to vary across different companies and different industries. For example, in a recent annual report, property, plant, and equipment made up approximately 11% of **Apple**'s total assets. This is typical of many technology companies. In contrast, property, plant, and equipment made up 74.4% of the total assets of **Southwest Airlines**, a company that relies heavily on airplanes to produce revenue.

Operating Activities Once a corporation has acquired the assets that it needs, it can begin to operate. While different businesses have different purposes, they all want to generate revenue. **Revenue** is the increase in assets that results from the sale of products or services. For example, **Apple** recently reported sales revenue of $260,174 million. In addition to revenue, assets such as *cash, accounts receivable* (the right to collect an amount due from customers), *supplies,* and *inventory* (products held for resale) often result from operating activities.

To earn revenue, a corporation will incur various costs or expenses. **Expenses** are the cost of assets used, or the liabilities created, in the operation of the business. **Apple** reported expenses of $161,782 million related to the cost of iPhones, iPads, Apple Watches, and other products sold.

The liabilities that arise from operating activities can be of different types. For example, if a corporation purchases goods on credit from a supplier, the obligation to repay the supplier is called an *account payable*. In a recent annual report, **Apple** reported $46,236 million of accounts payable. Other examples of liabilities created by operating activities include *wages payable* (amounts owed to employees for work performed) and *income taxes payable* (taxes owed to the government).

The results of a company's operating activities can be determined by comparing revenues to expenses. If revenues are greater than expenses, a corporation has earned **net income**. If expenses are greater than revenues, a corporation has incurred a **net loss**.

OBJECTIVE 3

Describe the relationships shown by the fundamental accounting equation.

COMMUNICATION OF ACCOUNTING INFORMATION

A company's business activities are summarized and reported in a set of standardized reports called **financial statements**. The role of financial statements is to provide information that helps investors, creditors, and others make judgments that serve as the basis for the various decisions they make. Financial statements help answer questions such as those shown in Exhibit 1.4.

EXHIBIT 1.4	Questions Answered by Financial Statements

How well did the company perform during the year?

From what sources did a company's cash come and for what did the company use cash during the year?

What are the economic resources of the company and the claims against those resources?

How much better off is the company at the end of the year compared to the beginning of the year?

THE FOUR BASIC FINANCIAL STATEMENTS

Companies prepare four basic financial statements:

- The **balance sheet** reports the resources (assets) owned by a company and the claims against those resources (liabilities and stockholders' equity) at a specific point in time.
- The **income statement** reports how well a company has performed (revenues, expenses, and income) over a period of time.
- The **retained earnings statement** reports how much of the company's income was retained in the business and how much was distributed to owners over a period of time.[2]
- The **statement of cash flows** reports the sources and uses of a company's cash over a period of time.

These four financial statements are prepared and issued at the end of an accounting period. While the accounting period can be a year, companies may prepare financial statements for any point or period of time. Most companies prepare financial statements at the end of each month, quarter, and year to satisfy the users' needs for timely information. Note that the balance sheet is a point-in-time description, whereas the other financial statements are period-of-time descriptions that explain the business activities between balance sheet dates as shown in Exhibit 1.5.

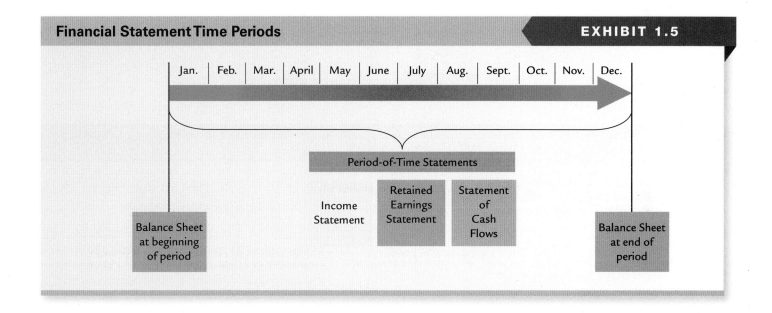

Financial Statement Time Periods   EXHIBIT 1.5

In order to make it easier to use financial statements over time and across companies, a common set of rules and conventions have been developed to guide the preparation of financial statements. These rules and conventions, called **generally accepted accounting principles (GAAP)**, were developed by several different organizations over a number of years. In the United States, the **Securities and Exchange Commission (SEC)** has the power to set accounting rules for publicly traded companies. However, the SEC has delegated this authority to the **Financial Accounting Standards Board (FASB)**. While the FASB

---

2 Information contained in the retained earnings statement is often included in a more comprehensive statement of changes in stockholders' equity, which describes changes in all components of stockholders' equity. This statement is presented in Chapter 10.

is the primary accounting standard setter in the United States, the FASB has been working closely with the **International Accounting Standards Board (IASB)** in its development of **international financial reporting standards (IFRS)**. While this text focuses on U.S. GAAP, major differences between U.S. GAAP and IFRS are discussed in Appendix 4 at the end of this text.

While financial statements prepared under GAAP provide the kind of information users want and need, the financial statements do not interpret this information. The financial statement user must use his or her general knowledge of business and accounting to interpret the financial statements as a basis for decision-making.

THE FUNDAMENTAL ACCOUNTING EQUATION

To understand financial statements, it is necessary that you understand how the accounting system records, classifies, and reports information about business activities. The **fundamental accounting equation** illustrates the foundation of the accounting system.

$$\text{Assets} = \text{Liabilities} + \text{Stockholders' Equity}$$

The fundamental accounting equation captures two basic features of any company. The left side of the accounting equation shows the assets, or economic resources of a company. The right side of the accounting equation indicates the claims on the company's assets. These claims may be the claims of creditors (liabilities) or they may be the claims of owners (stockholders' equity). The implication of the fundamental accounting equation is that a company's resources (its assets) must always be equal to the claims on those resources (its liabilities and stockholders' equity). EXAMPLE 1.1 illustrates this key relationship.

EXAMPLE 1.1   USING THE FUNDAMENTAL ACCOUNTING EQUATION

On January 1, Gundrum Company reported assets of $125,000 and liabilities of $75,000. During the year, assets increased by $44,000 and stockholders' equity increased by $15,000.

Required:
1. What is the amount reported for stockholders' equity on January 1?

2. What is the amount reported for liabilities on December 31?

Solution:
1. Stockholders' equity on January 1 is $50,000. This amount is calculated by rearranging the fundamental accounting equation as follows:

Assets = Liabilities + Stockholders' Equity

$125,000 = $75,000 + Stockholders' Equity

Stockholders' Equity = $125,000 − $75,000 = **$50,000**

2. At December 31, liabilities are $104,000. This amount is computed by adding the change to the appropriate balance sheet elements and then rearranging the fundamental accounting equation as follows:

Assets = Liabilities + Stockholders' Equity

($125,000 + $44,000) = Liabilities + ($50,000 + $15,000)

Liabilities = ($125,000 + $44,000) − ($50,000 + $15,000)

= $169,000 − $65,000 = **$104,000**

The fundamental accounting equation will be used to capture all of the economic activities recorded by an accounting system.

THE CLASSIFIED BALANCE SHEET

OBJECTIVE ◀ **4**
Prepare a classified balance sheet and explain the information it communicates.

The purpose of the balance sheet is to report the financial position of a company (its assets, liabilities, and stockholders' equity) at a specific point in time. The relationship between the elements of the balance sheet is given by the fundamental accounting equation:

$$\text{Assets} = \text{Liabilities} + \text{Stockholders' Equity}$$

Note that the balance sheet gets its name because the economic resources of a company (assets) must always equal, or be in balance with, the claims against those resources (liabilities and stockholders' equity).

The balance sheet is organized, or classified, to help users identify the fundamental economic similarities and differences between the various items within the balance sheet. These classifications help users answer questions such as:

- how a company obtained its resources
- whether a company will be able to pay its obligations when they become due

While companies often use different classifications and different levels of detail on their balance sheets, some common classifications are shown in Exhibit 1.6.

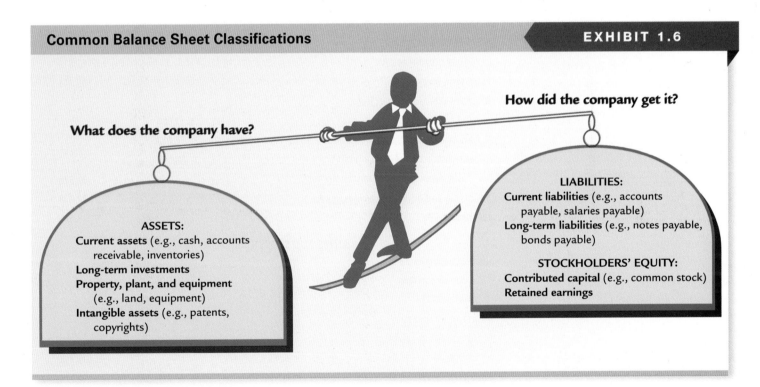

Common Balance Sheet Classifications

EXHIBIT 1.6

What does the company have?

ASSETS:
Current assets (e.g., cash, accounts receivable, inventories)
Long-term investments
Property, plant, and equipment (e.g., land, equipment)
Intangible assets (e.g., patents, copyrights)

How did the company get it?

LIABILITIES:
Current liabilities (e.g., accounts payable, salaries payable)
Long-term liabilities (e.g., notes payable, bonds payable)

STOCKHOLDERS' EQUITY:
Contributed capital (e.g., common stock)
Retained earnings

Let's examine the balance sheet classifications in more detail by looking at **Apple**'s balance sheet shown in Exhibit 1.7 (p. 12).

With regard to the heading of the financial statement, several items are of interest:

- *Company name:* The company for which the accounting information is collected and reported is clearly defined.
- *Financial statement type:* The title of the financial statement follows the name of the company.

- *Date:* The specific date of the statement is listed. **Apple** operates on a fiscal year that ends in September. A **fiscal year** is an accounting period that runs for 1 year. While many companies adopt a fiscal year that corresponds to the calendar year, others adopt a fiscal year that more closely corresponds with their business cycle.
- *Amounts:* **Apple** reports its financial results rounded to the nearest million dollars. Large companies often round the amounts presented for a more clear presentation. For Apple, the reported cash amount of $48,844 is actually $48,844,000,000.

EXHIBIT 1.7   **Classified Balance Sheet of Apple Inc.**

Apple Inc.
Balance Sheet
Sept. 28, 2019
(in millions of dollars)

ASSETS

Current assets:		
Cash	$ 48,844	
Marketable securities	51,713	
Accounts receivable, net	22,926	
Inventories	4,106	
Other current assets	35,230	
Total current assets		$ 162,819
Long-term investments		105,341
Property, plant, and equipment:		
Land and buildings	$ 17,085	
Machinery, equipment, and other	78,872	
Less: accumulated depreciation	(58,579)	
Total property, plant, and equipment		37,378
Intangible and other noncurrent assets		32,978
Total assets		$ 338,516

LIABILITIES AND STOCKHOLDERS' EQUITY

Current liabilities:		
Accounts payable	$46,236	
Other payable	37,720	
Unearned revenue	5,522	
Other current liabilities	16,240	
Total current liabilities		$ 105,718
Long-term liabilities		142,310
Total liabilities		$ 248,028
Stockholders' equity:		
Contributed capital	$45,174	
Retained earnings	45,898	
Other equity*	(584)	
Total stockholders' equity		90,488
Total liabilities and stockholders' equity		$ 338,516

*The ($584) million of other equity reported by Apple represents accumulated other comprehensive income. Accumulated other comprehensive income is discussed in Chapter 10.

Source: Apple Inc. 2019 10-K.

CURRENT ASSETS

The basic classification of a company's assets is between current and noncurrent items. **Current assets** consist of cash and other assets that are reasonably expected to be converted into cash within 1 year or one operating cycle, whichever is longer. The **operating cycle** of a company is the average time it takes a company to purchase goods, resell the goods, and collect the cash from customers. Because most companies have operating cycles less than 1 year, companies typically designate 1 year as the dividing line between current and noncurrent items. Common types of current assets are:

- Cash
- Marketable securities—short-term investments in the debt and stock of other companies as well as government securities
- Accounts receivable—the right to collect an amount due from customers
- Inventories—goods or products held for resale to customers
- Other current assets—a "catch-all" category that includes items such as prepaid expenses (advance payments for rent, insurance, and other services) and supplies

Current assets are listed on the balance sheet in order of liquidity or nearness to cash. That is, the items are reported in the order in which the company expects to convert them into cash.

NONCURRENT ASSETS

Assets that are not classified as current are classified as long-term or noncurrent assets. These include long-term investments; property, plant, and equipment; intangible assets; and other noncurrent assets.

Long-Term Investments Long-term investments are similar to short-term investments, except that the company expects to hold the investment for longer than 1 year. This category also includes land or buildings that a company is not currently using in operations. **Apple** reported long-term investments of $105,341 million.

Property, Plant, and Equipment Property, plant, and equipment represents the tangible, long-lived, productive assets used by a company in its operations to produce revenue. This category includes land, buildings, machinery, manufacturing equipment, office equipment, and furniture. **Apple** reported property, plant, and equipment of $37,378 million, representing 11% ($37,378 million ÷ $338,516 million) of its total assets. Property, plant, and equipment is originally recorded at the cost to obtain the asset. Because property, plant, and equipment helps to produce revenue over a number of years, companies assign, or allocate, a portion of the asset's cost as an expense in each period in which the asset is used. This process is called *depreciation*. The *accumulated depreciation* shown on Apple's balance sheet represents the total amount of depreciation that the company has expensed over the life of its assets. Because accumulated depreciation is subtracted from the cost of an asset, it is called a *contra-asset*. The difference between the cost and the accumulated depreciation is the asset's *book value* (or *carrying value*).

Intangible and Other Noncurrent Assets Intangible assets are similar to property, plant, and equipment in that they provide a benefit to a company over a number of years; however, these assets lack physical substance. Examples of intangible assets include patents, copyrights, trademarks, and goodwill.

Other noncurrent assets is a catch-all category that includes items such as deferred charges (long-term prepaid expenses) and other long-term miscellaneous items.

Next Level

Many classifications on the balance sheet are essentially subtotals. Is it really important to place accounts within the right category or is it enough to simply understand if they are assets, liabilities, or stockholders' equity?

ANSWER:
It is critical that you be able to identify accounts as assets, liabilities, or stockholders' equity accounts. However, the classifications are also important. Financial accounting is concerned with communicating useful information to decision-makers. These classifications provide decision-makers with information about the structure of assets, liabilities, and stockholders' equity that assists them in understanding a company's financial position.

CURRENT LIABILITIES

Current liabilities are closely related to current assets. **Current liabilities** consist of obligations that will be satisfied within 1 year or the operating cycle, whichever is longer. These liabilities can be satisfied through the payment of cash or by providing goods or services. **Current liabilities are typically listed in the order in which they will be paid** and include:

- Accounts payable—an obligation to repay a vendor or supplier for merchandise supplied to the company
- Salaries payable—an obligation to pay an employee for services performed
- Unearned revenue—an obligation to deliver goods or perform a service for which a company has already been paid
- Interest payable—an obligation to pay interest on money that a company has borrowed
- Income taxes payable—an obligation to pay taxes on a company's income

LONG-TERM LIABILITIES AND STOCKHOLDERS' EQUITY

Long-term liabilities are the obligations of the company that will require payment beyond 1 year or the operating cycle, whichever is longer. Common examples are:

- Notes payable—an obligation to repay cash borrowed at a future date
- Bonds payable—a form of an interest-bearing note payable issued by corporations in an effort to attract a large amount of investors

Stockholders' equity is the last major classification on a company's balance sheet. Stockholder's equity arises primarily from two sources:

- **Contributed capital**—the owners' contributions of cash and other assets to the company (includes the common stock of a company)
- **Retained earnings**—the accumulated net income of a company that has not been distributed to owners in the form of dividends

If a firm has been profitable for many years, and if its stockholders have been willing to forgo large dividends, retained earnings may be a large portion of equity. **Apple** reported approximately $45,898 million of retained earnings, representing approximately 51% of its total stockholders' equity.

Together, a company's liabilities and equity make up the **capital** of a business. **Apple** has debt capital, capital raised from creditors, of $248,028 million (total liabilities). Of this, $105,718 million comes from current creditors, while $142,310 million comes from long-term creditors. Apple's equity capital, which is the capital of the stockholders, is $90,488 million (total stockholders' equity).

PREPARING A CLASSIFIED BALANCE SHEET

Using the fundamental accounting equation and the common classifications of balance sheet items, a company will prepare its balance sheet by following five steps:

Step 1. Prepare a heading that includes the name of the company, the title of the financial statement, and the time period covered.

Step 2. List the assets of the company in order of their liquidity or nearness to cash. Use appropriate classifications. Add the assets and double underline the total.

Step 3. List the liabilities of the company in order of their time to maturity. Use appropriate classifications.

Step 4. List the stockholders' equity balances with appropriate classifications.

Step 5. Add the liabilities and stockholders' equity and double underline the total.

In general, only the first items in a column as well as any subtotals or totals have dollar signs. Also when multiple items exist within a classification, these items are grouped together in a separate column (to the left of the main column) and their total is placed in the main column. EXAMPLE 1.2 illustrates the steps in the preparation of a classified balance sheet.

EXAMPLE 1.2 PREPARING A CLASSIFIED BALANCE SHEET

Hightower Inc. reported the following account balances at December 31:

Inventories	$ 2,300	Accounts receivable	$ 4,200	Accounts payable	$ 3,750
Land	12,100	Cash	2,500	Common stock	14,450
Salaries payable	1,200	Equipment	21,000	Patents	2,500
Retained earnings	11,300	Accumulated depreciation	5,800	Notes payable, long-term	8,100

Required:
Prepare Hightower's balance sheet at December 31.

Solution:

Hightower Inc.		
Balance Sheet		Step 1
December 31		
ASSETS		
Current assets:		
Cash	$ 2,500	
Accounts receivable	4,200	
Inventories	2,300	
Total current assets		$ 9,000
Property, plant, and equipment:		
Land	$12,100	Step 2
Equipment	21,000	
Less: accumulated depreciation	(5,800)	
Total property, plant, and equipment		27,300
Intangible assets:		
Patents		2,500
Total assets		$38,800
LIABILITIES AND STOCKHOLDERS' EQUITY		
Current liabilities:		
Accounts payable	$ 3,750	
Salaries payable	1,200	
Total current liabilities		$ 4,950
Long-term liabilities:		Step 3
Notes payable		8,100
Total liabilities		$13,050
Stockholders' equity:		
Common stock	$14,450	
Retained earnings	11,300	Step 4
Total stockholders' equity		25,750
Total liabilities and stockholders' equity		$38,800	Step 5

USING BALANCE SHEET INFORMATION

The balance sheet conveys important information about the structure of assets, liabilities, and stockholders' equity, which is used to judge a company's financial health. For example, the relationship between current assets and current liabilities gives investors and creditors insights into a company's **liquidity**—the ability to pay obligations as they become due. Two useful measures of liquidity are *working capital* and the *current ratio*. Working capital and current ratios for a company are helpful when compared to other companies in the same industry. It is even more helpful to look at the trend of these measures over several years.

Working Capital **Working capital** is a measure of liquidity, computed as:

$$\text{Working Capital} = \text{Current Assets} - \text{Current Liabilities}$$

Because current liabilities will be settled with current assets, **Apple**'s working capital of $57,101 million ($162,819 million – $105,718 million) signals that it has adequate funds with which to pay its current obligations. Because working capital is expressed in a dollar amount, the information it can convey is limited. For example, comparing Apple's working capital to **Intel**'s working capital of $8,929 million would be misleading since Apple is $201,992 million larger (in terms of assets).

Current Ratio The **current ratio** is an alternative measure of liquidity that allows comparisons to be made between different companies and is computed as:

$$\text{Current Ratio} = \frac{\text{Current Assets}}{\text{Current Liabilities}}$$

For example, **Apple**'s current ratio of 1.54 ($162,819 million ÷ $105,718 million) can be compared with its competitors (e.g., Intel's current ratio is 1.40).[3] Apple's current ratio tells us that for every dollar of current liabilities, Apple has $1.54 of current assets. When compared to **Intel**, Apple is slightly more liquid.

 YOUDECIDE   **Assessing the Creditworthiness of a Prospective Customer**

You are the regional credit manager for Nordic Equipment Company. Thin Inc., a newly organized health club, has offered to purchase $50,000 worth of exercise equipment by paying the full amount plus 9% interest in 6 months. At your request, Thin provides the following figures from its balance sheet:

Current Assets		Current Liabilities	
Cash	$10,000	Accounts payable	$25,000
Accounts receivable	50,000	Notes payable	30,000
Supplies	4,000	Current portion of mortgage payable	18,000
Total	$64,000	Total	$73,000

Based on what you know about Thin's current assets and liabilities, do you allow the company to purchase the equipment on credit?

In making your decision, it is important to consider the relationship between a company's current assets and its current liabilities. Observe that Thin's current liabilities exceed current assets by $9,000 ($64,000 – $73,000) resulting in negative working capital. In addition, Thin's current ratio is 0.88 ($64,000 ÷ $73,000). By all indications, Thin is suffering from liquidity issues. Finally, there is no evidence presented that Thin's liquidity problem will improve. If Thin does fail to pay its liabilities, it is possible that the existing creditors could force Thin to sell its assets in order to pay off the debt. In such situations, it is possible that you will not receive the full amount promised. Unless Thin can demonstrate how it will pay its current short-term obligations, short-term credit should not be extended.

Allowing a company to purchase assets on credit requires evaluating the debtor's ability to repay the loan out of current assets.

---

3   Information for Intel was obtained from a recent *Form 10-K* of Intel.

THE INCOME STATEMENT

OBJECTIVE 5

Prepare an income statement and explain the information it communicates.

The income statement reports the results of a company's operations—the sale of goods and services and the associated cost of operating the company—for a given period. The long-term survival of a company depends on its ability to produce net income by earning revenues in excess of expenses. Income enables a company to pay for the capital it uses (dividends to stockholders and interest to creditors) and attract new capital necessary for continued existence and growth. Investors buy and sell stock and creditors loan money based on their beliefs about a company's future performance. The past income reported on a company's income statement provides investors with information about a company's ability to earn future income.

ELEMENTS OF THE INCOME STATEMENT

The income statement consists of two major items:

- Revenues and gains
- Expenses and losses

An income statement for **Apple** is presented in Exhibit 1.8.

Income Statement of Apple Inc.

EXHIBIT 1.8

Apple Inc. Income Statement For the fiscal year ended Sept. 28, 2019 (in millions of dollars)		
Revenues:		
Net sales	$260,174	
Interest and dividend income	4,961	
Other income	422	$ 265,557
Expenses:		
Cost of goods sold	$161,782	
Selling, general, and administrative expenses	18,245	
Research and development	16,217	
Interest expense	3,576	
Income taxes expense	10,481	(210,301)
Net income		$ 55,256

Source: Apple Inc. 2019 10-K.

Examining the heading of the income statement, notice that it follows the same general format as the balance sheet—it indicates the name of the company, the title of the financial statement, and the time period covered by the statement. However, the income statement differs from the balance sheet in that it covers a period of time instead of a specific date.

Revenues and Gains **Revenues** are the increase in net assets that result from the sale of products or services. Revenues can arise from different sources and have different names depending on the source of the revenue. *Sales revenue* (or *service revenue* for companies that provide services) arises from the principal activity of the business. For **Apple**, its sales revenue comes from sales of hardware (such as computers, iPhones, iPads, and Apple Watches), software (operating systems), peripheral products and accessories, digital content (such as iTunes store sales), and service and support (AppleCare and Apple Pay). Apple, like most other companies, recognizes sales revenue when it satisfies its obligation to its customer by transferring goods or performing services. This normally happens in the period that a sale occurs.

Gains are increases in net assets that occur from peripheral or incidental transactions. Thus, gains may be thought of as revenues from sources other than the sale of products or services. For example, Apple may recognize a gain when it sells one of its buildings. For simplicity, in this chapter, we will use the term "revenues" to refer to both revenues and gains.

Expenses and Losses   **Expenses** are the cost of resources used to earn revenues during a period. Expenses have different names depending on their function. **Apple**'s income statement in Exhibit 1.8 reports five different expenses:

- *Cost of goods sold* (often called *cost of sales*)—the cost to the seller of all goods sold during the accounting period.[4]
- *Selling, general, and administrative expenses*—the expenses that a company incurs in selling goods, providing services, or managing the company that are not directly related to production. These expenses include advertising expenses; salaries paid to salespersons or managers; depreciation on administrative buildings; and expenses related to insurance, utilities, property taxes, and repairs.
- *Research and development expense*—the cost of developing new products.
- *Interest expense*— expense incurred as a result of borrowing money from creditors. Interest is often referred to as the time value of money.
- *Income taxes expense*—the income taxes paid on the company's pretax income.

Losses are decreases in net assets that occur from peripheral or incidental transactions. Thus, losses may be thought of as expenses that are not associated with revenues. For example, a company may suffer a loss from flood damage. For simplicity, in this chapter, we will use the term "expenses" to refer to expenses and losses.

Net Income   Net income, or net earnings, is the difference between total revenues and expenses. **Apple** reported net income of $55,256 million ($265,557 million – $210,301 million). If total expenses are greater than total revenues, the company would report a net loss.

INCOME STATEMENT FORMATS

Companies prepare their income statements in one of two different formats: single-step income statements or multiple-step income statements.

Single-Step Income Statement   In a single-step income statement, there are only two categories: total revenues and total expenses. Total expenses are subtracted from total revenues in a *single step* to arrive at net income. The advantage of a single-step income statement is its simplicity.

PREPARING A SINGLE-STEP INCOME STATEMENT   The preparation of a single-step income statement involves four steps:

Step 1.   Prepare a heading that includes the name of the company, the title of the financial statement, and the time period covered.

Step 2.   List the revenues of the company, starting with sales revenue (or service revenue) and then listing other revenue items. Add the revenues to get total revenue.

Step 3.   List the expenses of the company, usually starting with cost of goods sold. Add the expenses to get total expenses.

Step 4.   Subtract the expenses from the revenues to get net income (or net loss if expenses exceed revenues). Double-underline net income.

---

4   We will discuss procedures for calculating cost of goods sold in Chapter 6.

In general, only the first items in a column as well as any subtotals or totals have dollar signs. Also when multiple items exist within a classification, these items are grouped together in a separate column (to the left of the main column) and their total is placed in the main column. EXAMPLE 1.3 shows how to prepare a single-step income statement.

EXAMPLE 1.3 PREPARING A SINGLE-STEP INCOME STATEMENT

Hightower Inc. reported the following account balances for the year ending December 31:

Cost of goods sold	$31,300	Interest expense	$ 540
Salaries expense	8,800	Sales revenue	50,600
Insurance expense	700	Depreciation expense	1,500
Interest income	1,200	Rent expense	2,100
Income taxes expense	2,000		

Required:

Prepare a single-step income statement for Hightower for the year ending December 31.

Solution:

Hightower Inc. Income Statement For the year ended December 31			
Revenues:			Step 1
Sales revenue	$50,600		
Interest income	1,200		Step 2
Total revenues		$ 51,800	
Expenses:			
Cost of goods sold	$31,300		
Salaries expense	8,800		
Rent expense	2,100		
Depreciation expense	1,500		Step 3
Insurance expense	700		
Interest expense	540		
Income taxes expense	2,000		
Total expenses		(46,940)	
Net income		$ 4,860	Step 4

Multiple-Step Income Statement A second income statement format is the *multiple-step income statement*. The multiple-step income statement organizes revenues and expenses into multiple categories. The resulting subtotals highlight important relationships between revenues and expenses that financial statement users find useful. A multiple-step income statement contains three important subtotals: gross margin, income from operations, and net income. A multiple-step income statement for **Apple** is shown in Exhibit 1.9.

| EXHIBIT 1.9 | Multiple-Step Income Statement for Apple Inc. |

Apple Inc.
Income Statement
For the fiscal year ended Sept. 28, 2019
(in millions of dollars)

Net sales	$ 260,174	
Cost of goods sold	(161,782)	
Gross margin		$ 98,392
Operating expenses:		
Research and development expense	$ 16,217	
Selling, general, and administrative expenses	18,245	
Total operating expenses		(34,462)
Income from operations		$ 63,930
Other income and expense:		
Interest and dividend income	$ 4,961	
Interest expense	(3,576)	
Other income	422	1,807
Income before income taxes		$ 65,737
Income taxes expense		(10,481)
Net income		$ 55,256

Source: Apple Inc. 2019 10-K.

GROSS MARGIN A company's **gross margin (or gross profit)** is calculated as:

$$\text{Gross Margin} = \text{Net Sales} - \text{Cost of Goods Sold}$$

Gross margin represents the initial profit made from selling a product, but it is *not* a measure of total profit because other operating expenses have not yet been subtracted. However, gross margin is closely watched by managers and other financial statement users. A change in a company's gross margin can give insights into a company's current pricing and purchasing policies, thereby providing insight into the company's future performance.

INCOME FROM OPERATIONS **Income from operations** is computed as:

$$\text{Income from Operations} = \text{Gross Margin} - \text{Operating Expenses}$$

Operating expenses are the expenses the business incurs in selling goods or providing services and managing the company. Operating expenses typically include research and development expenses, selling expenses, and general and administrative expenses. Income from operations indicates the level of profit produced by the principal activities of the company. **Apple** can increase its income from operations by either increasing its gross margin or decreasing its operating expenses.

NONOPERATING ACTIVITIES A multiple-step income statement reports nonoperating activities in a section which is frequently called *other income and expenses.* **Nonoperating activities** are revenues and expenses from activities other than the company's principal operations. They include gains and losses from the sale of equipment and other items that were not acquired for resale. For many companies, the most important nonoperating item is interest and investment income. Exhibit 1.10 lists some common nonoperating items.

Typical Nonoperating Items		**EXHIBIT 1.10**

  Other Revenues and Gains

Interest income on
investments
Dividend income from
investments in stock
of other companies
Rent revenue
Gains on disposal of
property, plant,
and equipment

  Other Expenses and Losses

Interest expense from loans
Losses from disposal
of property, plant,
and equipment
Losses from accidents or
vandalism
Losses from employee
strikes
Income taxes expense

NET INCOME Nonoperating items are subtracted from income from operations to obtain income before taxes. Income taxes expense is then subtracted to obtain net income. Regardless of whether a single-step or multiple-step format is used, notice that there is no difference in the amount of the revenue or expense items reported. That is, net income is the same under either format. The only difference is how the revenues and expenses are classified.

PREPARING A MULTIPLE-STEP INCOME STATEMENT The preparation of a multiple-step income statement involves five steps:

Step 1. Prepare a heading that includes the name of the company, the title of the financial statement, and the time period covered.
Step 2. Compute gross profit as the difference between net sales and cost of goods sold.
Step 3. Compute income from operations by subtracting operating expenses from gross profit.
Step 4. Compute income before income taxes by subtracting nonoperating activities from income from operations.
Step 5. Compute net income (or net loss) by subtracting income taxes expense from income before income taxes. Double-underline net income.

EXAMPLE 1.4 shows how to prepare a multiple-step income statement.

EXAMPLE 1.4   PREPARING A MULTIPLE-STEP INCOME STATEMENT

Hightower Inc. reported the following account balances for the year ending December 31:

Cost of goods sold	$31,300	Interest expense	$ 540
Salaries expense	8,800	Sales revenue	50,600
Insurance expense	700	Depreciation expense	1,500
Interest income	1,200	Rent expense	2,100
Income taxes expense	2,000		

Required:
Prepare a multiple-step income statement for Hightower for the year ending December 31.

CONTINUED

EXAMPLE 1.4   PREPARING A MULTIPLE-STEP INCOME STATEMENT (CONTINUED)

Solution:

Hightower Inc. **Income Statement** **For the year ended December 31**		
Sales revenue	$ 50,600	
Cost of goods sold	(31,300)	
Gross margin		$ 19,300
Operating expenses:		
Salaries expense	$ 8,800	
Rent expense	2,100	
Depreciation expense	1,500	
Insurance expense	700	
Total operating expenses		(13,100)
Income from operations		$ 6,200
Other income and expenses:		
Interest income	$ 1,200	
Interest expense	(540)	
Total other income and expenses		660
Income before income taxes		$ 6,860
Income taxes expense		(2,000)
Net income		$ 4,860

Step 1

Step 2

Step 3

Step 4

Step 5

USING INCOME STATEMENT INFORMATION

A company's ability to generate current income is useful in predicting its ability to generate future income. When investors believe that future income will improve, they will buy stock. Similarly, creditors rely on their judgments of a company's future income to make loans. Investors' and creditors' estimates of the future profitability and growth of a company are aided by a careful examination of how a company has earned its revenue and managed its expenses.

Net Profit Margin A useful measure of a company's ability to generate profit is its **net profit margin** (sometimes called return on sales). Net profit margin shows the percentage of profit in each dollar of sales revenue (or service revenue) and is computed as:

$$\text{Net Profit Margin} = \frac{\text{Net Income}}{\text{Sales (or Service) Revenue}}$$

This ratio provides an indication of management's ability to control expenses. Future income depends on maintaining (or increasing) market share while controlling expenses.

YOUDECIDE Assessing Future Profitability

You are looking to invest in one of two companies in the same industry—Graebel Inc. or Stanley Company. Your initial examination revealed that both companies reported the same amount of net income for 2024. Further analysis produced the following 5-year summary:

Graebel Inc.

	2020	2021	2022	2023	2024
Sales revenue	$625,000	$750,000	$820,000	$920,000	$1,000,000
Net income	$ 30,000	$ 36,000	$ 40,000	$ 45,000	$ 50,000
Profit margin	4.8%	4.8%	4.9%	4.9%	5.0%

Stanley Company

	2020	2021	2022	2023	2024
Sales revenue	$1,025,000	$975,000	$940,000	$1,020,000	$1,040,000
Net income	$ 51,000	$ 48,000	$ 46,000	$ 49,000	$ 50,000
Profit margin	5%	4.9%	4.9%	4.8%	4.8%

Which company is the better investment?

Investors seek those investments that will provide the largest return at the lowest risk. One factor associated with large returns is future profitability. Over the last 5 years, Graebel's sales and net income have steadily increased while Stanley's sales and net income have remained, on average, stable. Sales growth is an indicator of the possibility of increasing future income. Further, Graebel's increasing profit margin (compared to a decreasing profit margin for Stanley) indicates that Graebel is doing a better job at controlling its expenses relative to Stanley, enabling Graebel to earn more profit on each dollar of sales. While the future never can be predicted with certainty, the data suggest that, if current trends continue, Graebel will grow more rapidly than Stanley. Therefore, an investment in Graebel would probably yield the larger future return.

Accounting information can help you judge a company's potential for future profitability and growth.

RETAINED EARNINGS STATEMENT

OBJECTIVE

Prepare the retained earnings statement and explain the information it communicates.

The owners of a company contribute capital in one of two ways:

- directly, though purchases of common stock from the company
- indirectly, by the company retaining some or all of the net income earned each year rather than paying it out in dividends

As noted earlier, the income earned by the company but not paid out in the form of dividends is called retained earnings. The retained earnings statement summarizes and explains the changes in retained earnings during the accounting period.[5] The beginning balance in retained earnings is increased by net income earned during the year and decreased by any dividends that were declared. Exhibit 1.11 shows the retained earnings statement for **Apple**.

Notice the heading is similar to the heading for the income statement in that it covers a period of time instead of a specific date. In addition, **Apple** declared $14,129 million of dividends. While many companies, such as Apple, provide its stockholders with a return on their investment in the form of dividends, many growing companies choose not to pay dividends in order to reinvest its earnings and support future growth.

---

5 Some companies may choose to report a statement of stockholders' equity, which explains the changes in all of the stockholders' equity accounts. This statement is discussed more fully in Chapter 10.

EXHIBIT 1.11   Retained Earnings Statement for Apple Inc.

Apple Inc. Retained Earnings Statement For the fiscal year ended Sept. 28, 2019 (in millions of dollars)	
Retained earnings, Sept. 29, 2018	$ 70,400
Add: Net income	55,256
	$125,656
Less: Dividends declared	(14,129)
Other*	(65,629)
Retained earnings, Sept. 28, 2019	$ 45,898

*The other items deducted in Apple's retained earnings statement are related to repurchases of common stock and common stock issued under Apple's stock plans. These items are beyond the scope of this text.

Source: Apple Inc. 2019 10-K.

PREPARING A RETAINED EARNINGS STATEMENT

The preparation of the retained earnings statement involves four steps:

Step 1. Prepare a heading that includes the name of the company, the title of the financial statement, and the time period covered.

Step 2. List the retained earnings balance at the beginning of the period obtained from the balance sheet.

Step 3. Add net income obtained from the income statement.

Step 4. Subtract any dividends declared during the period. Double-underline the total, which should equal retained earnings at the end of the period as reported on the balance sheet.

The preparation of a retained earnings statement is detailed in EXAMPLE 1.5.

EXAMPLE 1.5   PREPARING A RETAINED EARNINGS STATEMENT

Hightower Inc. reported the following account balances for the year ending December 31:

Net income	$4,860	Retained earnings, Jan. 1	$ 9,440
Dividends declared	3,000	Retained earnings, Dec. 31	11,300

Required:
Prepare Hightower's retained earnings statement for the year ending December 31.

Solution:

Hightower Inc. Retained Earnings Statement For the year ended December 31		
		Step 1
Retained earnings, January 1	$ 9,440	Step 2
Add: Net income	4,860	Step 3
Less: Dividends declared	(3,000)	
Retained earnings, December 31	$11,300	Step 4

YOUDECIDE — Dividend Policy Decisions

You are the manager of a fast-growing software engineering firm. Over the last 5 years, your company has doubled the amount of its income every year. This tremendous growth has been financed through funds obtained from stockholders and cash generated from operations. The company has virtually no debt.

How would you respond to stockholders who have recently complained that the company's policy not to pay dividends is preventing them from sharing in the company's success?

Retained earnings can be an important source of financing for many companies. When companies feel that they have

profitable growth opportunities, they should reinvest the earnings in the business instead of paying out the amount to stockholders as dividends. The reinvestment of these funds should result in higher stock prices (and increased wealth for the stockholders) as the company grows. If the company chose to pay a dividend, it would be forced to either abandon the growth opportunities or finance them through some other, more costly method (e.g., issuing debt).

When management feels that the company has growth opportunities that will increase the value of the company, the reinvestment of earnings is usually preferable.

USE OF THE RETAINED EARNINGS STATEMENT

The retained earnings statement is used to monitor and evaluate a company's dividend payouts to its shareholders. For example, some older investors seek out companies with high dividend payouts so that they will receive cash during the year. Other investors are more interested in companies that are reinvesting a sufficient amount of earnings that will enable them to pursue profitable growth opportunities. Finally, creditors are interested in a company's dividend payouts. If a company pays out too much in dividends, the company may not have enough cash on hand to repay its debt when it becomes due.

STATEMENT OF CASH FLOWS

OBJECTIVE 7
Identify the information communicated by the statement of cash flows.

The last of the major financial statements, the statement of cash flows, describes the company's cash receipts (cash inflows) and cash payments (cash outflows) for a period of time. The statement of cash flows for **Apple** is shown in Exhibit 1.12.

Statement of Cash Flows

EXHIBIT 1.12

Apple Inc.
Statement of Cash Flows
For the fiscal year ended Sept. 28, 2019
(in millions of dollars)

Cash at the beginning of the year		25,913
Net cash provided from operating activities	$ 69,391	
Net cash used by investing activities	45,896	
Net cash used by financing activities	(90,976)	
Net change in cash		$ 24,311
Cash at the end of the year		$50,224

Source: Apple Inc. 2019 10-K.

ELEMENTS OF THE STATEMENT OF CASH FLOWS

Cash flows are classified into one of three categories:

- **Cash flows from operating activities**—any cash flows directly related to earning income. This category includes cash sales and collections of accounts receivable as well as cash payments for goods, services, salaries, and interest.
- **Cash flows from investing activities**—any cash flow related to the acquisition or sale of investments and long-term assets such as property, plant, and equipment. Note that the cash flows from investing activities of a healthy, growing business often reflect an excess of expenditures over receipts.
- **Cash flows from financing activities**—any cash flow related to obtaining capital of the company. This category includes the issuance and repayment of debt, common stock transactions, and the payment of dividends.

The preparation of the statement of cash flows will be discussed in Chapter 11.

USE OF THE STATEMENT OF CASH FLOWS

Because cash is the lifeblood of any company and is critical to success, the statement of cash flows can be an important source of information as users attempt to answer how a company generated and used cash during a period. Such information is helpful as users assess the company's ability to generate cash in the future. Creditors can use the statement of cash flows to assess the creditworthiness of a company. A company with healthy cash flow—particularly if it comes from operating activities—is in a good position to repay debts as they come due and is usually a low-risk borrower. Stockholders are also interested in the adequacy of cash flows as an indicator of the company's ability to pay dividends and to expand its business. The statement of cash flows is covered in more detail in Chapter 11.

OBJECTIVE 8

Describe the relationships among the financial statements.

RELATIONSHIPS AMONG THE STATEMENTS

At this point, it is important to notice the natural relationships of the four basic financial statements and the natural progression from one financial statement to another. The accounting period begins with a balance sheet. During the year, the company earns net income from operating its business. Net income from the income statement increases retained earnings on the retained earnings statement. Ending retained earnings is then reported in the stockholders' equity section of the balance sheet at the end of the accounting period. Finally, the statement of cash flows explains the change in cash during the year. These relationships are shown in Exhibit 1.13 (p. 27).

The relationships create linkages between the financial statements, referred to as **articulation** of the financial statements. The three key linkages are as follows:

- The income statement links the beginning and ending balance sheet through the retained earnings account. Therefore, the income statement can be viewed as explaining, through retained earnings, the change in the financial position during the year.
- The statement of stockholders' equity links the beginning and ending balances of equity in the balance sheet.
- The statement of cash flows links the beginning and ending balances of cash in the balance sheet.

Relationships Among the Financial Statements

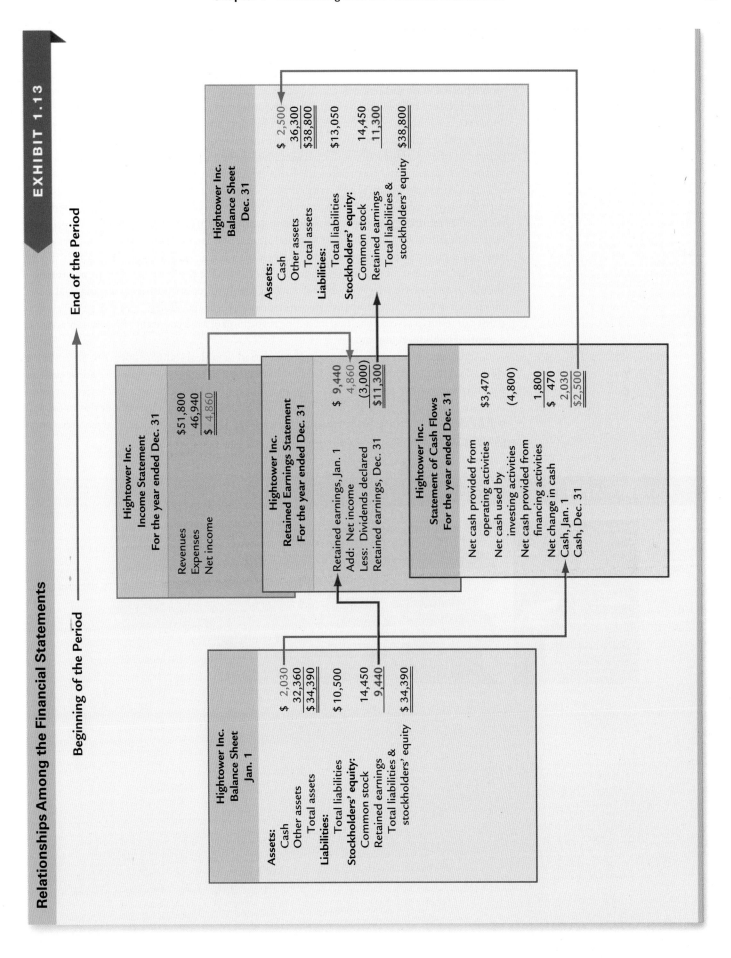

EXHIBIT 1.13

Beginning of the Period → End of the Period

Hightower Inc.
Balance Sheet
Jan. 1

Assets:	
Cash	$ 2,030
Other assets	32,360
Total assets	$34,390
Liabilities:	
Total liabilities	$10,500
Stockholders' equity:	
Common stock	14,450
Retained earnings	9,440
Total liabilities & stockholders' equity	$34,390

Hightower Inc.
Income Statement
For the year ended Dec. 31

Revenues	$51,800
Expenses	46,940
Net income	$ 4,860

Hightower Inc.
Retained Earnings Statement
For the year ended Dec. 31

Retained earnings, Jan. 1	$ 9,440
Add: Net income	4,860
Less: Dividends declared	(3,000)
Retained earnings, Dec. 31	$11,300

Hightower Inc.
Statement of Cash Flows
For the year ended Dec. 31

Net cash provided from operating activities	$3,470
Net cash used by investing activities	(4,800)
Net cash provided from financing activities	1,800
Net change in cash	$ 470
Cash, Jan. 1	2,030
Cash, Dec. 31	$2,500

Hightower Inc.
Balance Sheet
Dec. 31

Assets:	
Cash	$ 2,500
Other assets	36,300
Total assets	$38,800
Liabilities:	
Total liabilities	$13,050
Stockholders' equity:	
Common stock	14,450
Retained earnings	11,300
Total liabilities & stockholders' equity	$38,800

OBJECTIVE
Explain the importance of ethics in
providing useful financial information.

PROFESSIONAL ETHICS

For the economy to function effectively and efficiently, users must have faith that the information reported in financial statements is accurate and dependable. Accountants are often under intense pressure to apply the accounting standards to present a company in a favorable light. However, accountants serve the greater good of society and have an ethical responsibility to all the users who make decisions based on the financial information presented. Confidence that standards of ethical behavior will be maintained—even when individuals have incentives to violate those standards—is crucial to the financial reporting process.

The American Institute of Certified Public Accountants (AICPA), recognizing that its members have an obligation of self-discipline above and beyond the requirements of generally accepted accounting principles, has adopted a code of professional conduct which provides ethical guidelines for accountants in the performance of their duties. These ethical principles require accountants to serve the public interest with integrity. For example, auditors should fulfill their duties with objectivity, independence, and due professional care. In no situation should an auditor yield to pressure from management to report positively on financial statements that overstate the company's performance or prospects. Violation of these ethical standards can result in severe penalties, including revocation of an accountant's license to practice as a certified public accountant.

Acting ethically is not always easy. The violation of ethical standards may not always bring clear and direct penalties; however, it often has subtle and long-lasting negative consequences for individuals and companies. Because of the important role of accounting in society, accountants are expected to maintain the highest level of ethical behavior. Throughout this book, you will be exposed to ethical dilemmas that we urge you to consider. As you analyze these cases, consider the guidelines in Exhibit 1.14.

EXHIBIT 1.14   **Guidelines in Ethical Decision-Making**

YOUDECIDE Career Analysis

As you consider various career options, keep in mind that virtually every organization must have an accounting system. Thus, accountants are employed in a wide range of businesses, including private companies, public accounting firms, governments, and banks. To help you evaluate whether an accounting career is right for you, consider the following question:

What skills and character traits are required for accountants?

Accountants must have well-developed analytical skills and must be effective communicators, both verbally and in writing. Most accounting assignments—whether in business, government, or public accounting—are team assignments in which team members must be able to communicate effectively and work quickly and cooperatively to a solution.

As a profession, accounting requires a high level of academic study and is subject to professional competence requirements. Most members of public accounting firms, and many management accountants and consultants, are (or are in the process of becoming) Certified Public Accountants (CPAs). Other valuable professional certifications are the Certified Management Accountant (CMA), the Certified Internal Auditor (CIA), and the Certified Fraud Examiner (CFE) designations. All of these designations are designed to ensure that the accountants who offer their services are properly qualified and maintain a high level of personal integrity and ethical behavior.

While the career opportunities for accountants are virtually boundless, even if you choose a different career path, the knowledge and experience that you can gain from accounting will prove invaluable in your career.

Accountants must possess strong analytical and communication skills, demonstrate professional competency, and behave ethically.

LO1. Explain the nature of accounting.

KEY TAKEAWAYS

- Accounting is an information system that identifies, measures, records, and communicates financial information.
- The information is used both inside and outside of the business to make better decisions.
- Financial accounting focuses on the needs of external decision-makers.

KEY TERMS

Accounting, 4
Financial accounting, 5

LO2. Identify the forms of business organizations and the types of business activities.

KEY TAKEAWAYS

- The three forms of business organizations are as follows:
  - Sole proprietorship—owned by one person
  - Partnership—jointly owned by two or more individuals
  - Corporation—a separate legal entity organized under the laws of a particular state
- Regardless of the form of business, all businesses are involved in three activities:
  - Financing activities—obtaining funds (from either issuing stock or borrowing money) necessary to begin and operate the business
  - Investing activities—buying the assets that enable a business to operate
  - Operating activities—the activities of a business that generate a profit

KEY TERMS

Assets, 7
Corporation, 5
Creditor, 7
Expenses, 8
Liability, 7
Net income, 8

Net loss, 8
Partnership, 5
Revenue, 8
Sole proprietorship, 5
Stockholders' equity, 7

KEY TAKEAWAYS

- The fundamental accounting equation captures all of the economic activities recorded by an accounting system.
- The left side of the accounting equation shows the assets, or economic resources, of a company.
- The right side of the accounting equation shows the claims on the company's assets (liabilities or stockholders' equity).

LO3. Describe the relationships shown by the fundamental accounting equation.

KEY TERMS

Balance sheet, 9
Financial Accounting Standards Board
    (FASB), 9
Financial statements, 8
Fundamental accounting equation, 10
Generally accepted accounting principles
    (GAAP), 9
Income statement, 9

International Accounting Standards Board
    (IASB), 10
International financial reporting standards
    (IFRS), 10
Retained earnings statement, 9
Securities and Exchange Commission
    (SEC), 9
Statement of cash flows, 9

KEY CALCULATION

Assets = Liabilities + Stockholders' Equity

EXAMPLE

EXAMPLE 1.1 Using the fundamental accounting equation, page 10

KEY TAKEAWAYS

- A balance sheet reports the resources (assets) owned by a company and the claims against those resources (liabilities and stockholders' equity) at a specific point in time.
- In order to help users identify the fundamental economic similarities and differences between the various items on the balance sheet, assets and liabilities are classified as either current or noncurrent (long-term). Stockholders' equity is classified as either contributed capital or retained earnings.

LO4. Prepare a classified balance sheet and explain the information it communicates.

KEY TERMS

Capital, 14	Liquidity, 16
Contributed capital, 14	Long-term investments, 13
Current assets, 13	Long-term liabilities, 14
Current liabilities, 14	Operating cycle, 13
Current ratio, 16	Property, plant, and equipment, 13
Fiscal year, 12	Retained earnings, 14
Intangible assets, 13	Working capital, 16

KEY CALCULATIONS

Assets = Liabilities + Stockholders' Equity

Current Ratio = Current Assets ÷ Current Liabilities

Working Capital = Current Assets − Current Liabilities

EXAMPLE

EXAMPLE 1.2   Preparing a classified balance sheet, page 15

LO5. Prepare an income statement and explain the information it communicates.

KEY TAKEAWAYS

- The income statement reports how well a company has operated over a period of time and provides information about the future profitability and growth of a company.
- The income statement includes the revenues and expenses of a company, which can be reported in either a single-step or a multiple-step format.

KEY TERMS

Expenses, 18	Net profit margin, 22
Gains, 18	Nonoperating activities, 20
Gross margin (gross profit), 20	Operating expenses, 20
Income from operations, 20	Revenues, 17
Losses, 18	

KEY CALCULATIONS

Gross Margin = Net Sales − Cost of Goods Sold

Income from Operations = Gross Margin − Operating Expenses

Net Income = Revenues − Expenses

Net Profit Margin = Net Income ÷ Sales (or Service) Revenue

EXAMPLES

EXAMPLE 1.3	Preparing a single-step income statement, page 19
EXAMPLE 1.4	Preparing a multiple-step income statement, page 21

KEY TAKEAWAYS

- The retained earnings statement reports how much of a company's income was retained in a business and how much was distributed to owners for a period of time.
- The retained earnings statement provides users with insights into a company's dividend payouts.

LO6. Prepare the retained earnings statement and explain the information it communicates.

KEY CALCULATION

Ending Retained Earnings = Beginning Retained Earnings + Net Income − Dividends Declared

EXAMPLE

EXAMPLE 1.5	Preparing a retained earnings statement, page 24

KEY TAKEAWAYS

- The statement of cash flows reports the sources of a company's cash inflow and the uses of a company's cash over time.
- The statement of cash flows can be used to assess the creditworthiness of a company.

LO7. Identify the information communicated by the statement of cash flows.

KEY TERMS

Cash flows from financing activities, 26
Cash flows from investing activities, 26
Cash flows from operating activities, 26

LO8. Describe the relationships among the financial statements.

KEY TAKEAWAYS

- There is a natural relationship among the four basic financial statements, implying that financial statements are prepared in a particular order.
- Starting with the balance sheet at the beginning of the accounting period, financial statements are generally prepared in the following order: income statement, retained earnings statement, and balance sheet at the end of the period.

KEY TERM

Articulation, 26

LO9. Explain the importance of ethics in providing useful financial information.

KEY TAKEAWAYS

- The maintenance of a high ethical standard is necessary for users to have faith in the accuracy of financial statements, which is a key factor in the effective and efficient functioning of the economy.
- To make ethical decisions, you should recognize the ethical issue, analyze and consider the impact of your options, and make a decision that fulfills your ethical responsibilities.

REVIEW PROBLEM

Enderle Company reported the following account balances at December 31:

Equipment	$19,800	Sales revenue	$82,500	Interest expense	$ 1,200
Retained earnings, end of year	15,450	Accumulated depreciation	5,450	Retained earnings, beginning of year	10,300
Copyright	1,200	Cash	2,900	Depreciation expense	3,500
Accounts payable	5,500	Salaries expense	18,100	Cost of goods sold	52,000
Interest income	2,300	Common stock	11,500	Inventory	5,600
Bonds payable	10,000	Land	15,000	Income taxes expense	3,000
Dividends declared	1,850	Accounts receivable	3,700	Interest payable	300

Required:

1. Prepare Enderle's single-step income statement for the year ending December 31.
2. Prepare Enderle's retained earnings statement for the year ending December 31.
3. Prepare Enderle's balance sheet at December 31.

Solution:

1.

Enderle Company Income Statement For the year ended December 31		
Revenues:		
Sales revenue	$82,500	
Interest income	2,300	
Total revenues		$ 84,800
Expenses:		
Cost of goods sold	$52,000	
Salaries expense	18,100	
Depreciation expense	3,500	
Interest expense	1,200	
Income taxes expense	3,000	
Total expenses		(77,800)
Net income		$ 7,000

2.

Enderle Company Retained Earnings Statement For the year ended December 31	
Retained earnings, January 1	$10,300
Add: Net income	7,000
Less: Dividends declared	(1,850)
Retained earnings, December 31	$15,450

3.

Enderle Company Balance Sheet December 31		
ASSETS		
Current assets:		
Cash	$ 2,900	
Accounts receivable	3,700	
Inventory	5,600	
Total current assets		$12,200
Property, plant, and equipment:		
Land	$15,000	
Equipment	19,800	
Less: Accumulated depreciation	(5,450)	
Total property, plant, and equipment		29,350
Intangible assets:		
Copyright		1,200
Total assets		$42,750

(*Continued*)

LIABILITIES AND STOCKHOLDERS' EQUITY		
Current liabilities:		
Accounts payable	$ 5,500	
Interest payable	300	
Total current liabilities		$ 5,800
Long-term liabilities:		
Bonds payable		10,000
Total liabilities		$15,800
Stockholders' equity:		
Common stock	$11,500	
Retained earnings	15,450	
Total stockholders' equity		26,950
Total liabilities and stockholders' equity		$42,750

APPLYING KNOWLEDGE

DISCUSSION QUESTIONS

OBJECTIVE 1

1. Define *accounting*.

2. Why is there a demand for accounting information? Name six groups that create demand for accounting information about businesses, and describe how each group uses accounting information.

OBJECTIVE 2

3. What is an accounting entity?

4. Name and describe three different forms of business organization.

5. Name and describe the three main types of business activities.

6. Define the terms *assets, liabilities,* and *stockholders' equity*.

7. Define the terms *revenue* and *expense*. How are these terms related?

OBJECTIVE 3

8. Name and briefly describe the purpose of the four financial statements.

9. What types of questions are answered by the financial statements?

10. What is point-in-time measurement? How does it differ from period-of-time measurement?

OBJECTIVE 4

11. Write the fundamental accounting equation. Why is it significant?

12. What information is included in the heading of each of the four financial statements?

13. Define *current assets* and *current liabilities*. Why are current assets and current liabilities separated from noncurrent assets and long-term liabilities on the balance sheet?

14. Describe how items are ordered within the current assets and current liabilities sections on a balance sheet.

15. Name the two main components of stockholders' equity. Describe the main sources of change in each component.

OBJECTIVE 5

16. What equation describes the income statement?

17. How does the multiple-step income statement differ from the single-step income statement?

18. Explain the items reported on a retained earnings statement. **OBJECTIVE** 6

19. Name and describe the three categories of the statement of cash flows. **OBJECTIVE** 7

20. How is the retained earnings statement related to the balance sheet? How is the income statement related to the retained earnings statement? **OBJECTIVE** 8

21. Give an example of unethical behavior by a public accountant and describe its consequences. **OBJECTIVE** 9

MULTIPLE-CHOICE QUESTIONS

1-1 Which of the following statements is *false* concerning forms of business organization? **OBJECTIVE** 2
    a. A corporation has tax advantages over the other forms of business organization.
    b. It is easier for a corporation to raise large sums of money than it is for a sole proprietorship or partnership.
    c. A sole proprietorship is an easy type of business to form.
    d. Owners of sole proprietorships and partnerships have personal liability for the debts of the business while owners of corporations have limited legal liability.

1-2 Which of the following statements regarding business activities is true?
    a. Operating activities involve buying the long-term assets that enable a company to generate revenue.
    b. Financing activities include obtaining the funds necessary to begin and operate a business.
    c. Investing activities center around earning interest on a company's investments.
    d. Companies spend a relatively small amount of time on operating activities.

1-3 Which of the following is *not* one of the four basic financial statements? **OBJECTIVE** 3
    a. Balance sheet   c. Statement of cash flows
    b. Income statement   d. Auditor's report

1-4 What type of questions do the financial statements help to answer?
    a. Is the company better off at the end of the year than at the beginning of the year?
    b. What resources does the company have?
    c. For what did a company use its cash during the year?
    d. All of the above.

1-5 At December 31, Pitt Inc. has assets of $12,900 and liabilities of $6,300. What is the stockholders' equity for Pitt at December 31? **OBJECTIVE** 4
    a. $6,600   c. $18,100
    b. $6,300   d. $19,200

1-6 Which of the following is *not* shown in the heading of a financial statement?
    a. The title of the financial statement
    b. The name of the company
    c. The time period covered by the financial statement
    d. The name of the auditor

Use the following information for Multiple-Choice Questions 1-7 and 1-8:
At December 31, Marker reported the following items: cash, $7,500; inventory, $3,900; accounts payable, $5,900; accounts receivable, $3,100; common stock, $6,000; property, plant, and equipment, $10,500; interest payable, $1,600; retained earnings, $11,500.

1-7   Refer to the information for Marker above. What is the total of Marker's current assets?

a. $12,100   c. $14,500
b. $13,700   d. $25,000

1-8   Refer to the information for Marker above. What is Marker's stockholders' equity?

a. $7,500   c. $19,100
b. $17,500   d. $25,000

OBJECTIVE   **1-9**   Which of the following statements regarding the income statement is true?

a. The income statement provides information about the profitability and growth of a company.
b. The income statement shows the results of a company's operations at a specific point in time.
c. The income statement consists of assets, expenses, liabilities, and revenues.
d. Typical income statement accounts include sales revenue, unearned revenue, and cost of goods sold.

1-10   For the most recent year, Grant Company reported revenues of $182,300, cost of goods sold of $108,800, inventory of $8,500, salaries expense of $48,600, rent expense of $12,000, and cash of $12,300. What was Grant's net income?

a. $9,400   c. $21,400
b. $12,900   d. $24,900

OBJECTIVE   **1-11**   Which of the following statements concerning retained earnings is true?

a. Retained earnings is the difference between revenues and expenses.
b. Retained earnings is increased by dividends and decreased by net income.
c. Retained earnings represents accumulation of the income that has not been distributed as dividends.
d. Retained earnings is reported as a liability on the balance sheet.

OBJECTIVE   **1-12**   Which of the following sentences regarding the statement of cash flows is *false*?

a. The statement of cash flows describes the company's cash receipts and cash payments for a period of time.
b. The statement of cash flows reconciles the beginning and ending cash balances shown on the balance sheet.
c. The statement of cash flows reports cash flows in three categories: cash flows from business activities, cash flows from investing activities, and cash flows from financing activities.
d. The statement of cash flows may be used by creditors to assess the creditworthiness of a company.

(*Continued*)

BRIEF EXERCISES

Brief Exercise 1-13 Users of Financial Information

OBJECTIVE 1

Listed below are several users of accounting information and decisions that user may make.

User of Accounting Information		Decision
1. Manager	a.	Determines whether the company paid the proper amount of taxes.
2. Financial Analyst	b.	Decides if a factory is profitable or should be closed.
3. Investor	c.	Determines if a company will be able to repay its obligations.
4. Creditor	d.	Decides if the reported net income will cause the stock price to rise or fall.
5. Government	e.	Recommends to buy or sell a company's stock.

Required:

Indicate which user of accounting information is responsible for each of the decisions.

Brief Exercise 1-14 Forms of Business Organization

OBJECTIVE 2

Listed below are the forms of business organization and several related advantages or disadvantages.

Form of Business Organization		Advantage or Disadvantage
1. Sole proprietorship	a.	Most complex to organize
2. Partnership	b.	Owner(s) have personal responsibility for the debt of the organization
3. Corporation	c.	Access to the individual skills of each of the owners
	d.	Limited personal liability for the debt of the organization
	e.	Easier to raise large amounts of capital
	f.	The greatest percentage of businesses are organized in this manner
	g.	Owners generally pay higher taxes than owners of other forms of business organizations

Required:

Match each form of business organization with its respective advantage or disadvantage. (*Hint:* Some advantages or disadvantages may be related to more than one form of business organization.)

Brief Exercise 1-15 Business Activities

OBJECTIVE 2

Marni Restaurant Company engaged in the following transactions during March, its first month of operations.

a. Received $100,000 cash from the sale of stock.
b. Purchased $20,000 of inventory from J&J Wholesale Company.
c. Purchased $30,000 of kitchen equipment for its restaurants.
d. Obtained a $25,000 loan from First State Bank.
e. Sold $18,000 of food to customers.
f. Paid employee weekly salaries of $8,500.
g. Repaid $10,000 of principal relating to the loan in Item d.

(*Continued*)

Required:

For each of the above business activities, indicate whether it is an operating, investing, or financing activity.

OBJECTIVE 3

EXAMPLE 1.1

Brief Exercise 1-16 Using the Accounting Equation

At the beginning of the year, Morgan Company had total assets of $425,000 and total liabilities of $260,000.

Required:

Use the fundamental accounting equation to answer the following independent questions:

1. What is total stockholders' equity at the beginning of the year?
2. If, during the year, total assets increased by $73,000 and total liabilities increased by $32,000, what is the amount of total stockholders' equity at the end of the year?
3. If, during the year, total assets decreased by $52,000 and total stockholders' equity increased by $35,000, what is the amount of total liabilities at the end of the year?
4. If, during the year, total liabilities increased by $85,000 and total stockholders' equity decreased by $73,000, what is the amount of total assets at the end of the year?

OBJECTIVE 3

EXAMPLE 1.1

Brief Exercise 1-17 Using the Accounting Equation

Listed below are three independent scenarios.

Scenario	Assets	Liabilities	Equity
1	$ (a)	$42,000	$56,000
2	115,000	(b)	77,000
3	54,000	18,500	(c)

Required:

Use the fundamental accounting equation to find the missing amounts.

OBJECTIVE 4

EXAMPLE 1.2

Brief Exercise 1-18 Balance Sheet

Below are items that may appear on the balance sheet.

Item		Classification	
1.	Buildings	a.	Current assets
2.	Copyright	b.	Property, plant, and equipment
3.	Inventory	c.	Intangible assets
4.	Unearned service revenue	d.	Current liabilities
5.	Prepaid insurance	e.	Long-term liabilities
6.	Common stock	f.	Contributed capital
7.	Accounts payable	g.	Retained earnings
8.	Accounts receivable		
9.	Accumulated depreciation		
10.	Notes payable (due in 5 years)		
11.	Net income less dividends		
12.	Cash		

Required:

Match each item with its appropriate classification.

(Continued)

Brief Exercise 1-19 Balance Sheet

OBJECTIVE 4
EXAMPLE 1.2

An analysis of the transactions of Cavernous Homes Inc. yields the following totals at December 31: cash, $3,200; accounts receivable, $4,500; notes payable, $5,000; supplies, $8,100; common stock, $7,000; and retained earnings, $3,800.

Required:

Prepare a balance sheet for Cavernous Homes Inc. at December 31.

Brief Exercise 1-20 Income Statement

OBJECTIVE 5
EXAMPLE 1.3

An analysis of the transactions of Rutherford Company for the year ended December 31 yields the following information: sales revenue, $65,000; insurance expense, $4,300; interest income, $3,900; cost of goods sold, $28,800; salaries expense, $22,500; income taxes expense, $2,400; and loss on disposal of property, plant, and equipment, $1,200.

Required:

Prepare a single-step income statement.

Brief Exercise 1-21

OBJECTIVE 5
EXAMPLE 1.4

Refer to the information in Brief Exercise 1-20.

Required:

Prepare a multiple-step income statement.

Brief Exercise 1-22 Retained Earnings Statement

OBJECTIVE 6
EXAMPLE 1.5

Listed below are events that affect stockholders' equity.

a. Reported net income of $85,000.
b. Paid a cash dividend of $10,000.
c. Reported sales revenue of $120,000.
d. Issued common stock of $50,000.
e. Reported a net loss of $20,000.
f. Reported expenses of $35,000.

Required:

For each of the events, indicate whether it increases retained earnings (I), decreases retained earnings (D), or has no effect on retained earnings (NE).

Brief Exercise 1-23 Retained Earnings Statement

OBJECTIVE 6
EXAMPLE 1.4

Parker Company has a balance of $35,000 in retained earnings on January 1. During the year, Parker reported revenues of $82,000 and expenses of $55,000. Parker also paid a dividend of $8,000.

Required:

What is the amount of retained earnings on December 31?

Brief Exercise 1-24 Statement of Cash Flows

OBJECTIVE 7

Listed below are items that would appear on a statement of cash flows.

a. Cash received from customers
b. Cash paid for dividends
c. Cash received from a bank loan
d. Cash paid to suppliers
e. Cash paid to purchase equipment

(Continued)

Required:
Indicate in which part of the statement of cash flows each of the items would appear: operating activities (O), investing activities (I), or financing activities (F).

OBJECTIVE **Brief Exercise 1-25 Relationships Among the Financial Statements**

Listed below are three independent scenarios.

Scenario	Balance Sheet: Retained Earnings	Income Statement: Net Income	Balance Sheet: Retained Earnings
1.	$30,000	$25,000	$ (a)
2.	(b)	30,000	94,000
3.	50,000	(c)	70,000

Required:
Compute the missing amount in each row. Assume no withdrawals or dividends.

EXERCISES

OBJECTIVE **Exercise 1-26 Decisions Based on Accounting Information**

Decision-makers use accounting information in a wide variety of decisions including the following:
1. Deciding to lend money to a business
2. Deciding if an individual has paid enough in taxes
3. Deciding to place merchandise on sale in order to reduce inventory
4. Deciding to invest in a business
5. Deciding whether to demand additional benefits for employees
6. Deciding whether to recommend a client buy stock as an investment

Required:
Match each decision with one of the following decision-makers who is primarily responsible for the decision: a government (G), an investor (I), a labor union (U), business managers (M), a bank (B), or a financial analyst (FA).

OBJECTIVE 2 **Exercise 1-27 Forms of Business Organizations**

Listed below are definitions, examples, or descriptions related to business entities.
1. Owned by one person
2. Can make and sell goods (manufacturing)
3. Owned by more than one person
4. Can sell goods (merchandising)
5. Can provide and sell services
6. Legally, a separate entity from the owner(s)
7. A law firm owned by some of the employees who are each liable for the financial obligations of the entity
8. The Coca-Cola Company

Required:
1. For each of the three types of business entities (sole proprietorship, partnership, and corporation), select as many of the definitions, examples, or descriptions as apply to that type of entity.
2. **CONCEPTUAL CONNECTION** Explain the advantages and disadvantages of each type of business entity.

Exercise 1-28 Business Activities

OBJECTIVE ◀2

Listed below are various activities that companies engage in during a period.

a. Purchase of equipment
b. Payment of a dividend
c. Purchase of supplies
d. Sale of equipment
e. Sale of goods or services
f. Borrow money from a bank
g. Contribution of cash by owners

Required:
For each of the activities listed above, classify the activity as operating (O), investing (I), or financing (F).

Exercise 1-29 Business Activities

OBJECTIVE ◀2

 SHOW ME HOW

Bill and Steve recently formed a company that manufactures and sells high-end kitchen appliances. The following is a list of activities that occurred during the year.

a. Bill and Steve each contributed cash in exchange for common stock in the company.
b. Land and a building to be used as a factory to make the appliances were purchased for cash.
c. Machines used to make the appliances were purchased for cash.
d. Various materials used in the production of the appliances were purchased for cash.
e. Three employees were paid cash to operate the machines and make the appliances.
f. Running low on money, the company borrowed money from a local bank.
g. The money from the bank loan was used to buy advertising on local radio and television stations.
h. The company sold the appliances to local homeowners for cash.
i. Due to extremely high popularity of its products, Bill and Steve built another factory building on its land for cash.
j. The company paid a cash dividend to Bill and Steve.

Required:
Classify each of the business activities listed as an operating activity (O), an investing activity (I), or a financing activity (F).

Exercise 1-30 Accounting Concepts

OBJECTIVE ◀4 5 6

A list of accounting concepts and related definitions is presented below.

	Concept		Definition
1.	Revenue	a.	Owner's claim on the resources of a company
2.	Expense	b.	The difference between revenues and expenses
3.	Net income (loss)	c.	Increase in assets from the sale of goods or services
4.	Dividend	d.	Economic resources of a company
5.	Asset	e.	Cost of assets consumed in the operation of a business
6.	Liability	f.	Creditors' claims on the resources of a company
7.	Stockholders' equity	g.	Distribution of earnings to stockholders

Required:
Match each of the concepts with its corresponding definition.

OBJECTIVE ▶3▶   ## Exercise 1-31 The Fundamental Accounting Equation

Financial information for three independent cases is given below.

	Assets	Liabilities	Equity
1.	$116,200	$ (a)	$55,400
2.	212,600	145,900	(b)
3.	(c)	22,500	48,300

Required:
Compute the missing numbers in each case.

OBJECTIVE ▶4▶   ## Exercise 1-32 Balance Sheet Structure

The following accounts exist in the ledger of Higgins Company: accounts payable, accounts receivable, accumulated depreciation, bonds payable, building, common stock, cash, equipment, income taxes payable, inventory, notes payable (due in 5 years), prepaid insurance, retained earnings, trademarks, and wages payable.

Required:
1. Organize the above items into a properly prepared classified balance sheet.
2. **CONCEPTUAL CONNECTION** Which information might be helpful to assess liquidity?

OBJECTIVE ▶4▶

 SHOW ME HOW

Exercise 1-33 Identifying Current Assets and Liabilities

Dunn Sporting Goods sells athletic clothing and footwear to retail customers. Dunn's accountant indicates that the firm's operating cycle averages 6 months. At December 31, Dunn has the following assets and liabilities:

a. Prepaid rent in the amount of $8,500. Dunn's rent is $500 per month.
b. A $9,700 account payable due in 45 days.
c. Inventory in the amount of $46,230. Dunn expects to sell $38,000 of the inventory within 3 months. The remainder will be placed in storage and expected to be sold by November of the next year.
d. An investment in marketable securities in the amount of $1,900. Dunn expects to sell $700 of the marketable securities in 6 months. The remainder are not expected to be sold for 3 years.
e. Cash in the amount of $1,050.
f. An equipment loan in the amount of $60,000 due in 5 years. Interest of $4,500 is due in March of the next year ($3,750 of the interest relates to the current year, with the remainder relating to the first 3 months of the next year).
g. An account receivable from a local university in the amount of $2,850. The university has promised to pay the full amount in 3 months.
h. Store equipment at a cost of $9,200. Accumulated depreciation has been recorded on the store equipment in the amount of $1,250.

Required:
1. Prepare the current asset and current liability portions of Dunn's December 31, balance sheet.
2. Compute Dunn's working capital and current ratio at December 31.
3. **CONCEPTUAL CONNECTION** As an investor or creditor, what do these ratios tell you about Dunn's liquidity?

Exercise 1-34 Current Assets and Current Liabilities

Hanson Construction has an operating cycle of 9 months. On December 31, Hanson has the following assets and liabilities:

a. A note receivable in the amount of $1,500 to be collected in 6 months
b. Cash totaling $1,380
c. Accounts payable totaling $2,100, all of which will be paid within 2 months
d. Accounts receivable totaling $12,000, including an account for $7,000 that will be paid in 2 months and an account for $5,000 that will be paid in 18 months
e. Construction supplies costing $6,200, all of which will be used in construction within the next 12 months
f. Construction equipment costing $60,000, on which depreciation of $22,400 has accumulated
g. A note payable to the bank in the amount of $6,800 is to be paid within the next year

Required:
1. Calculate the amounts of current assets and current liabilities reported on Hanson's balance sheet at December 31.
2. **CONCEPTUAL CONNECTION** Comment on Hanson's liquidity.

Exercise 1-35 Depreciation

Swanson Products was organized as a new business on January 1. On that date, Swanson acquired equipment at a cost of $425,000, which is depreciated at a rate of $40,000 per year.

Required:
Describe how the equipment and its related depreciation will be reported on Swanson's income statement for its first year of operations and on its balance sheet at December 31 (the end of its first year of operations).

Exercise 1-36 Stockholders' Equity

On January 1, Mulcahy Manufacturing Inc., a newly formed corporation, issued 1,000 shares of common stock in exchange for $150,000 cash. No other shares were issued during the year, and no shares were repurchased by the corporation. On November 1, the corporation's major stockholder sold 300 shares to another stockholder for $50,000. The corporation reported net income of $37,500 for the year.

Required:
Prepare the stockholders' equity section of Mulcahy's balance sheet at December 31.

Exercise 1-37 Classified Balance Sheet

College Spirit sells sportswear with logos of major universities. At the end of the year, the following balance sheet account balances were available.

Accounts payable	$104,700	Income taxes payable	$ 11,400
Accounts receivable	6,700	Inventory	481,400
Accumulated depreciation	23,700	Long-term investment	110,900
Bonds payable	180,000	Notes payable, short-term	50,000
Cash	13,300	Prepaid rent (current)	54,000
Common stock	300,000	Retained earnings, Dec. 31	84,500
Furniture	88,000		

(Continued)

Required:

1. Prepare a classified balance sheet for College Spirit at December 31.
2. Compute College Spirit's working capital and current ratio at December 31.
3. **CONCEPTUAL CONNECTION** Comment on College Spirit's liquidity as of December 31.

OBJECTIVE   **Exercise 1-38 Classified Balance Sheet**

Jerrison Company operates a wholesale hardware business. The following balance sheet accounts and balances are available for Jerrison at December 31.

Accounts payable	$ 65,100	Equipment, data processing	$309,000
Accounts receivable	95,500	Income taxes payable	21,600
Accumulated depreciation (on building)	216,800	Interest payable	12,600
		Inventory	187,900
Accumulated depreciation (on data processing equipment)	172,400	Investments (long-term)	32,700
		Investments (short-term)	21,000
		Land	41,000
Accumulated depreciation (on trucks)	31,200	Notes payable (due in 6 months)	150,000
Bonds payable (due in 4 years)	200,000	Prepaid insurance (for 4 months)	5,700
Building (warehouse)	419,900	Retained earnings, Dec. 31	?
Cash	11,400	Salaries payable	14,400
Common stock	150,000	Trucks	106,100

Required:

1. Prepare a classified balance sheet for Jerrison at December 31.
2. Compute Jerrison's working capital and current ratio at December 31.
3. **CONCEPTUAL CONNECTION** If Jerrison's management is concerned that a large portion of its inventory is obsolete and cannot be sold, how will Jerrison's liquidity be affected?

OBJECTIVE   **Exercise 1-39 Balance Sheet Relationships**

Balance sheet information for Milton Company is as follows:

	Year 1	Year 2
Current assets	$ (a)	$ 25,000
Long-term liabilities	(b)	34,900
Intangible assets	10,400	9,200
Long-term investments	19,200	(f)
Property, plant, and equipment (net)	85,700	92,800
Current liabilities	14,500	12,300
Total assets	142,200	(g)
Retained earnings	56,900	67,000
Total liabilities	50,300	(h)
Contributed capital	(c)	(i)
Total stockholders' equity	(d)	(j)
Total liabilities and stockholders' equity	(e)	149,200

Required:

Compute the missing values (a)-(j). All the necessary information is provided. (*Hint:* It is not necessary to calculate your answers in alphabetical order.)

Exercise 1-40 Income Statement Structure

OBJECTIVE ◀ 5

The following accounts exist in the ledger of Butler Company: salaries expense, advertising expense, cost of goods sold, depreciation expense, interest expense, income taxes expense, sales revenue, and utilities expense.

Required:
1. Organize the above items into a properly prepared single-step income statement.
2. **CONCEPTUAL CONNECTION** What information would be helpful in assessing Butler's ability to generate future income?

Exercise 1-41 Single-Step Income Statement

OBJECTIVE ◀ 5

SHOW ME HOW

ERS Inc. maintains and repairs office equipment. ERS had an average of 10,000 shares of common stock outstanding for the year. The following income statement account balances are available for ERS for the year ended December 31.

Advertising expense	$24,200	Salaries expense	
Depreciation expense		(for administrative personnel)	$195,600
(on service van)	16,250	Service revenue	933,800
Income taxes expense	15,150	Supplies expense	66,400
Insurance expense	11,900	Utilities expense	26,100
Interest expense	10,100	Wages expense	
Rent expense	58,400	(for service technicians)	448,300

Required:
1. Prepare a single-step income statement for ERS.
2. **CONCEPTUAL CONNECTION** Compute net profit margin for ERS. If ERS is able to increase its service revenue by $100,000, what should be the effect on future income?
3. **CONCEPTUAL CONNECTION** Assume that ERS' net profit margin was 8.5% in the previous year. As an investor, what conclusions might you draw about ERS' future profitability?

Exercise 1-42 Multiple-Step Income Statement

OBJECTIVE ◀ 5

The following information is available for Bergin Pastry Shop for the year ended December 31.

Gross margin	$34,700
Income from operations	9,200
Income taxes expense (15% of income before taxes)	?
Interest expense	1,800
Net sales	85,300

Required:
Prepare a multiple-step income statement for Bergin for the year ended December 31.

Exercise 1-43 Income Statement

OBJECTIVE ◀ 5

SHOW ME HOW

The following information is available for Wright Auto Supply at December 31.

Cost of goods sold	$292,000	Rent expense	$21,000
Depreciation expense	31,250	Salaries (administrative)	33,800
Income taxes expense	32,520	Sales revenue	585,600
Interest expense	2,400	Wages expense (salespeople)	96,750

(Continued)

Required:

1. Prepare a single-step income statement for the year ended December 31.
2. Prepare a multiple-step income statement for the year ended December 31.
3. **CONCEPTUAL CONNECTION** Comment on the differences between the single-step and the multiple-step income statements.

 OBJECTIVE 6

SHOW
ME HOW

Exercise 1-44 Retained Earnings Statement

On January 1, Sherwood Company had retained earnings of $18,240. During the year, Sherwood had revenues of $837,400 and expenses of $792,100 and paid cash dividends in the amount of $38,650.

Required:

1. Determine the amount of Sherwood's retained earnings at December 31.
2. **CONCEPTUAL CONNECTION** Comment on Sherwood's dividend policy.

 OBJECTIVE 7

SHOW
ME HOW

Exercise 1-45 Statement of Cash Flows

Walters Inc. began operations on January 1. The following information relates to Walters' cash flows during the year.

Cash received from owners	$201,500	Cash paid to employees	
Cash paid for purchase of		for salaries	46,400
land and building	128,700	Cash paid for dividends to	
Cash paid for advertising	34,200	stockholders	37,500
Cash received from customers	139,800	Cash paid for supplies	28,700
Cash paid to purchase machine	$ 32,000		

Required:

1. Calculate the cash provided/used for each cash flow category.
2. **CONCEPTUAL CONNECTION** Comment on Walters' creditworthiness.

 OBJECTIVE 8

Exercise 1-46 Relationships Among the Financial Statements

On January 1, Zachary Corporation reported following amounts:

Cash	$ 20,400
Retained earnings	105,600

Zachary's accountant provided the following information that occurred during the year:

Revenues	$650,100	Cash inflow from operating activities	$ 892,250
Expenses	578,600	Cash outflow for investing activities	(990,300)
Dividends declared	30,000	Cash inflow from financing activities	108,400

Required:
Calculate the amount of cash and retained earnings as on December 31.

 OBJECTIVE 8

SHOW
ME HOW

Exercise 1-47 Relationships Among the Financial Statements

The following information for Kellman Inc. is available at the end of the year.

Total assets on Jan. 1	$82,400	Common stock on Jan. 1	$50,000
Total assets on Dec. 31	88,500	Common stock on Dec. 31	50,000
Total liabilities on Jan. 1	9,200	Net income for the year	19,500
Total liabilities on Dec. 31	11,300		

Required:
Calculate the amount of dividends declared reported on the retained earnings statement.

Exercise 1-48 Relationships Among the Financial Statements

OBJECTIVE ◀ 8

During the year, Moore Corporation declared and paid $20,000 of dividends. Moore's assets, liabilities, and common stock at the beginning and end of the year were:

	January 1	December 31
Total assets	$152,200	$171,800
Total liabilities	56,600	63,750
Common stock	60,000	60,000

Required:
Using the information provided, compute Moore's net income.

Exercise 1-49 Professional Ethics

OBJECTIVE ◀ 9

Ethical behavior is essential to the conduct of business activity. Consider each of the following business behaviors:

a. A manager prepares financial statements that grossly overstate the performance of the business.
b. A CPA resigns from an audit engagement rather than allow a business client to violate an accounting standard.
c. An internal auditor decides against confronting an employee of the business with minor violations of business policy. The employee is a former college classmate of the auditor.
d. An accountant advises his client on ways to legally minimize tax payments to the government.
e. A manager legally reduces the price of a product to secure a larger share of the market.
f. Managers of several large companies secretly meet to plan price reductions designed to drive up-and-coming competitors out of the market.
g. An accountant keeps confidential details of her employer's legal operations that would be of interest to the public.
h. A recently dismissed accountant tells competitors details about her former employer's operations as she seeks a new job.

Required:
Identify each behavior as ethical (E) or unethical (U).

PROBLEM SET A

OBJECTIVE ◀ 3

Problem 1-50A Applying the Fundamental Accounting Equation

On January 1, Huffer Corporation had total assets of $232,400, total liabilities of $94,200, common stock of $50,000, and retained earnings of $88,200. During the year, Huffer had net income of $51,750, declared and paid dividends of $10,000, and issued additional common stock for $15,000. Huffer's total assets on December 31 were $285,500.

Required:
Calculate the amount of liabilities that Huffer must have on December 31 in order for the balance sheet equation to balance.

OBJECTIVE 4 5 6 8 ▸   ## Problem 1-51A Accounting Relationships

Information for Beethoven Music Company is given below.

Total assets at the beginning of the year	$145,200	Equity at the beginning of the year $	(b)
Total assets at the end of the year	(a)	Equity at the end of the year	104,100
Total liabilities at the beginning of the year	92,600	Dividends paid during the year	(c)
		Net income for the year	77,500
Total liabilities at the end of the year	126,900	Revenues	554,800
		Expenses	(d)

Required:

Use the relationships in the balance sheet, income statement, and retained earnings statement to determine the missing values.

OBJECTIVE 5 ▸   ## Problem 1-52A Single-Step Income Statement

Powers Wrecking Service demolishes old buildings and other structures and sells the salvaged materials. During the year, Powers had $425,000 of revenue from demolition services and $137,000 of revenue from salvage sales. Powers also had $1,575 of interest income from investments. Powers incurred $243,200 of wages expense, $24,150 of depreciation expense, $48,575 of supplies expense, $84,000 of rent expense, $17,300 of miscellaneous expense, and $43,900 of income taxes expense.

Required:

Prepare a single-step income statement for Powers for the year ended December 31.

OBJECTIVE 5 ▸   ## Problem 1-53A Multiple-Step Income Statement

Cooper Merchandising reported the following items related to sales of goods to customers for the current year: sales revenue of $625,000 and cost of goods sold of $248,000. Cooper also reported $1,250 of interest income, $103,600 of wages expense, $12,150 of depreciation expense, $23,575 of supplies expense, $65,000 of rent expense, $8,300 of miscellaneous expense, and $32,500 of income taxes expense.

Required:

Prepare a multiple-step income statement for Cooper.

OBJECTIVE 4 5 6 8 ▸   ## Problem 1-54A Income Statement and Balance Sheet Relationships

Each column presents financial information taken from one of four different companies, with one or more items of data missing.

	Company			
Financial Statement Item	**Floyd**	**Slater**	**Wooderson**	**O'Bannion**
Total revenue	$ 125	$ 715	$ (e)	$ 2,475
Total expense	92	(c)	54	(g)
Net income (net loss)	(a)	184	18	(600)
Total assets	905	1,988	(f)	8,140
Total liabilities	412	(d)	117	2,280
Total equity	(b)	823	80	(h)

Required:

Use your understanding of the relationships among financial statements and financial statement items to determine the missing values (a–h).

Problem 1-55A Single-Step Income Statement and Balance Sheet

OBJECTIVE 4 5

The following information for Rogers Enterprises is available at December 31 and includes all of Rogers' financial statement amounts except retained earnings:

Accounts receivable	$72,920	Property, plant, and equipment	$ 90,000
Cash	13,240	Rent expense	135,000
Common stock (10,000 shares)	70,000	Retained earnings	?
Income taxes expense	12,800	Salaries expense	235,200
Income taxes payable	4,150	Salaries payable	14,800
Interest expense	16,000	Service revenue	463,500
Notes payable (due in 10 years)	25,000	Supplies	42,000
Prepaid rent (building)	31,500	Supplies expense	34,400

Required:

Prepare a single-step income statement and a classified balance sheet for the year ending December 31, for Rogers.

Problem 1-56A Multiple-Step Income Statement and Balance Sheet

OBJECTIVE 4 5

The following information for Moore Inc. is available as on December 31 and includes all of Moore's financial statement amounts except retained earnings:

Accounts receivable	$68,910	Property, plant, and equipment	$ 90,000
Cash	16,290	Rent expense	135,000
Common stock (10,000 shares)	70,000	Retained earnings	?
Cost of goods sold	$395,000	Salaries expense	235,200
Income taxes expense	8,600	Salaries payable	14,800
Income taxes payable	4,150	Sales revenue	863,500
Interest expense	16,000	Supplies	44,100
Interest income	2,000	Supplies expense	34,400
Notes payable (due in 10 years)	25,000		
Prepaid rent (building)	31,500		

Required:

Prepare a multiple-step income statement and a classified balance sheet for Moore for the year ending December 31.

Problem 1-57A Retained Earnings Statement

OBJECTIVE 6

Dittman Expositions has the following data available:

Dividends, declared, Year 1	$ 10,250	Retained earnings, Jan. 1, Year 1	$ 20,900
Dividends, declared, Year 2	12,920	Revenues, Year 1	407,500
Expenses, Year 1	382,100	Revenues, Year 2	451,600
Expenses, Year 2	418,600		

Required:

Prepare retained earnings statements for Year 1 and Year 2.

OBJECTIVE 6

Problem 1-58A Retained Earnings Statements

The table below presents the retained earnings statements for Bass Corporation for 3 successive years. Certain numbers are missing.

	Year 1	Year 2	Year 3
Retained earnings, beginning	$21,500	$ (b)	$33,600
Add: Net income	9,200	10,100	(f)
	$30,700	$ (c)	$ (g)
Less: Dividends declared	(a)	(d)	(3,900)
Retained earnings, ending	$27,200	$ (e)	$41,200

Required:

Use your understanding of the relationship between successive retained earnings statements to calculate the missing values (a–g).

OBJECTIVE 4 5 6

🔍 **SHOW ME HOW**

Problem 1-59A Income Statement, Retained Earnings Statement, and Balance Sheet

The following information relates to Ashton Appliances for the current year.

Accounts payable	$ 16,800	Income taxes expense	$ 16,650
Accounts receivable	69,900	Income taxes payable	12,000
Accumulated depreciation (building)	104,800	Insurance expense	36,610
Accumulated depreciation (furniture)	27,600	Interest expense	15,500
Bonds payable (due in 7 years)	192,000	Inventory	59,850
Building	300,000	Other assets	92,800
Cash	41,450	Rent expense (store equipment)	80,800
Common stock	243,610	Retained earnings, January 1	54,000
Cost of goods sold	511,350	Salaries expense	228,710
Depreciation expense (building)	11,050	Salaries payable	7,190
Depreciation expense (furniture)	12,000	Sales revenue	948,670
Furniture	130,000		

Required:

1. Prepare a single-step income statement, a retained earnings statement, and a properly classified balance sheet as of December 31.
2. Prepare a multiple-step income statement.
3. **CONCEPTUAL CONNECTION** How does the multiple-step income statement differ from the single-step income statement you prepared for Ashton?

OBJECTIVE 8

Problem 1-60A Stockholders' Equity Relationships

Data from the financial statements of four different companies are presented in separate columns in the table below. Each column has one or more data items missing.

	Company			
Financial Statement Item	Berko	Manning	Lucas	Corey
Equity, Jan. 1:				
Common stock	$50,000	$ 35,000	$ (i)	$ 15,000
Retained earnings	12,100	(e)	26,400	21,900
Total equity	$ (a)	$ 44,300	$ 66,400	$ 36,900
Net income (loss)	$ 7,000	$ (1,800)	$ 6,000	$ (m)
Dividends declared	2,000	0	(j)	1,400
Equity, Dec. 31:				
Common stock	50,000	35,000	55,000	15,000
Retained earnings	(b)	(f)	(k)	27,600
Total equity	$ (c)	$ (g)	$84,500	$ (n)
Total assets, Dec. 31	92,500	(h)	99,200	(o)
Total liabilities, Dec. 31	$ (d)	$14,800	$ (1)	$10,700

(Continued)

Required:

Use your understanding of the relationships among the financial statement items to determine the missing values (a–o).

Problem 1-61A Relationships Among Financial Statements

OBJECTIVE 3 8

Carson Corporation reported the following amounts for assets and liabilities at the beginning and end of a recent year.

	Beginning of Year	End of Year
Assets	$385,500	$420,250
Liabilities	152,800	156,600

Required:

Calculate Carson's net income or net loss for the year in each of the following independent situations:

1. Carson declared no dividends, and its common stock remained unchanged.
2. Carson declared no dividends and issued additional common stock for $40,000 cash.
3. Carson declared dividends totaling $15,000, and its common stock remained unchanged.
4. Carson declared dividends totaling $20,000 and issued additional common stock for $35,000.

PROBLEM SET B

Problem 1-50B Applying the Fundamental Accounting Equation

OBJECTIVE 3

On January 1, KJ Corporation had total assets of $525,700, total liabilities of $290,800, common stock of $100,000, and retained earnings of $134,900. During the year, KJ had net income of $205,500, paid dividends of $70,000, and issued additional common stock for $75,000. KJ's total assets at the end of the year were $710,100.

Required:

Calculate the amount of liabilities that KJ must have at the end of the year in order for the balance sheet equation to balance.

Problem 1-51B The Fundamental Accounting Equation

OBJECTIVE 4 5 6 8

Information for TTL Inc. is given below.

Total assets at the beginning of the year	$ (a)	Equity at the end of the year	$ (c)
Total assets at the end of the year	758,150	Dividends paid during the year	35,500
Total liabilities at the beginning of the year	368,200	Net income for the year	(d)
Total liabilities at the end of the year	(b)	Revenues	929,440
Equity at the beginning of the year	272,900	Expenses	835,320

Required:

Use the relationships in the balance sheet, income statement, and retained earnings statement to determine the missing values.

Problem 1-52B Single-Step Income Statement

OBJECTIVE 5

Parker Renovation Inc. renovates historical buildings for commercial use. During the year, Parker had $763,400 of revenue from renovation services and $5,475 of interest income from miscellaneous investments. Parker incurred $222,900 of wages expense, $135,000 of depreciation expense, $65,850 of insurance expense, $109,300 of utilities expense, $31,000 of miscellaneous expense, and $61,400 of income taxes expense.

(Continued)

Required:

Prepare a single-step income statement for Parker for the year ended December 31.

OBJECTIVE 5

Problem 1-53B Multiple-Step Income Statement

Lakas Company reported the following items related to sales of goods to customers for the current year: sales revenue of $425,000 and cost of goods sold of $178,400. Cooper also reported $620 of interest income, $850 of interest expense, $66,100 of wages expense, $11,590 of depreciation expense, $13,122 of supplies expense, $35,910 of rent expense, $8,800 of miscellaneous expense, and $23,200 of income taxes expense.

Required:

Prepare a multiple-step income statement for Lakas.

OBJECTIVE 4 5 6 8

Problem 1-54B Income Statement and Balance Sheet Relationships

Each column presents financial information taken from one of four different companies, with one or more items of data missing.

Financial Statement Item	Company			
	Crick	Pascal	Eiffel	Hilbert
Total revenue	$ 925	$ 533	$ (e)	$1,125
Total expense	844	(c)	377	(g)
Net income (net loss)	(a)	289	126	(340)
Total assets	709	1,810	(f)	3,150
Total liabilities	332	(d)	454	2,267
Total equity	(b)	950	98	(h)

Required:

Use your understanding of the relationships among financial statements and financial statement items to find the missing values (a–h).

OBJECTIVE 4 5

Problem 1-55B Income Statement and Balance Sheet

Ross Airport Auto Service provides parking and minor repair service at the local airport while customers are away on business or pleasure trips. The following account balances (except for retained earnings) are available for Ross Airport Auto Service at December 31.

Accounts payable	$ 17,200	Interest payable	$ 4,800
Accounts receivable	39,200	Inventory (repair parts)	6,100
Accumulated depreciation (equipment)	42,300	Investments (long term)	35,000
Cash	7,700	Notes payable (due in 7 years)	160,000
Common stock (20,000 shares)	100,000	Prepaid rent (3 months)	27,300
Depreciation expense (equipment)	12,450	Rent expense	103,500
Dividends	6,300	Retained earnings, Dec. 31	48,200
Equipment	270,800	Service revenue (parking)	232,600
Income taxes expense	2,700	Service revenue (repair)	198,500
Income taxes payable	1,100	Supplies expense (repair parts)	36,900
Interest expense	21,300	Wages expense	246,100
Interest income	4,100	Wages payable	12,500

Required:

Prepare a single-step income statement and a classified balance sheet for the year ended December 31.

(*Continued*)

Problem 1-56B Multiple-Step Income Statement and Balance Sheet

OBJECTIVE ◄ 4 5

The following information for Cheng Company is available as on December 31 and includes all of Wuhan's financial statement amounts except retained earnings:

Accounts receivable	$ 58,930	Prepaid rent (building)	8,500
Cash	14,275	Property, plant, and equipment	$ 105,000
Common stock (10,000 shares)	105,000	Rent expense	65,000
Cost of goods sold	$279,800	Retained earnings	?
Income taxes expense	6,000	Research and development expense	$ 12,700
Income taxes payable	2,850	Salaries expense	115,900
Insurance expense	$ 5,000	Salaries payable	11,400
Interest expense	8,450	Sales revenue	525,100
Gain on disposal of property,		Supplies	24,600
plant, and equipment	5,000	Supplies expense	14,400
Notes payable (due in 10 years)	15,000		
Patent	12,380		

Required:

Prepare a multiple-step income statement and a classified balance sheet for Cheng for the year ending December 31.

Problem 1-57B Retained Earnings Statement

OBJECTIVE ◄ 6

Magical Experiences Vacation Company has the following data available:

Dividends, declared, Year 1	$ 14,000	Retained earnings, Jan. 1, Year 1	$ 55,300
Dividends, declared, Year 2	16,000	Revenues, Year 1	221,900
Expenses, Year 1	188,500	Revenues, Year 2	325,400
Expenses, Year 2	250,800		

Required:

Prepare retained earnings statements for Year 1 and Year 2.

Problem 1-58B Retained Earnings Statements

OBJECTIVE ◄ 6

The table below presents the retained earnings statements for Dillsboro Corporation for 3 successive years. Certain numbers are missing.

	Year 1	Year 2	Year 3
Retained earnings, beginning	$ (a)	$19,500	$26,700
Add: Net income	11,100	(c)	9,500
	$ 26,900	$ (d)	$ (f)
Less: Dividends declared	(7,400)	(5,200)	(g)
Retained earnings, ending	$ (b)	$ (e)	$34,100

Required:

Use your understanding of the relationship between successive retained earnings statements to calculate the missing values (a–g).

OBJECTIVE ▶ 4 5 6 ▶

SHOW
ME HOW

Problem 1-59B Income Statement, Retained Earnings Statement, and Balance Sheet

McDonald Boat Company sells pleasure boats in southern Florida. The following account balances are available:

Accounts payable	$ 26,400	Interest expense	$ 99,400
Accounts receivable	268,700	Interest payable	18,000
Accumulated depreciation (building)	64,500	Land	875,000
Accumulated depreciation (equipment)	950,400	Rent expense	14,600
Bonds payable (due in 5 years)	2,000,000	Rent payable	2,400
Building	197,300	Retained earnings, Jan. 1	128,600
Cash	22,300	Sales revenue	1,932,300
Common stock (40,000 shares)	600,000	Supplies	9,800
Cost of goods sold	987,200	Supplies expense	89,100
Depreciation expense (building)	21,500	Utilities expense	131,300
Depreciation expense (equipment)	142,300	Wages expense	348,700
Dividends	25,300	Wages payable	21,600
Equipment	2,490,000		
Income taxes expense	21,700		

Required:

1. Prepare a single-step income statement, a retained earnings statement, and a classified balance sheet for the year ended December 31.
2. Prepare a multiple-step income statement.
3. **CONCEPTUAL CONNECTION** How would a multiple-step income statement be different from the single-step income statement you prepared for McDonald Marina?

OBJECTIVE ▶ 8 ▶

Problem 1-60B Stockholders' Equity Relationships

Data from the financial statements of four different companies are presented in separate columns in the table below. Each column has one or more data items missing.

	Company			
Financial Statement Item	**Stackhouse**	**Compton**	**Bellefleur**	**Merlotte**
Equity, January 1:				
Common stock	$45,000	$39,000	$ 80,000	$ 25,000
Retained earnings	18,800	15,300	6,900	(k)
Total equity	$63,800	$ (d)	$ 86,900	$ 38,900
Net income (loss)	$ (a)	$ 7,100	$ 9,700	$ (4,500)
Dividends declared	2,100	800	(h)	0
Equity, December 31:				
Common stock	45,000	39,000	80,000	25,000
Retained earnings	21,700	(e)	(i)	(1)
Total equity	$ (b)	$ (f)	$ 95,300	$ (m)
Total assets, December 31	(c)	88,200	113,400	(n)
Total liabilities, December 31	$14,400	$ (g)	$ (j)	$ 15,700

Required:

Use your understanding of the relationships among the financial statement items to determine the missing values (a–n).

Problem 1-61B Relationships Among Financial Statements

Leno Corporation reported the following amounts for assets and liabilities at the beginning and end of a recent year.

	Beginning of Year	End of Year
Assets	$256,500	$358,200
Liabilities	92,650	121,900

Required:

Calculate Leno's net income or net loss for the year in each of the following independent situations:

1. Leno declared no dividends, and its common stock remained unchanged.
2. Leno declared no dividends and issued additional common stock for $15,000 cash.
3. Leno declared dividends totaling $10,000, and its common stock remained unchanged.
4. Leno declared dividends totaling $12,000 and issued additional common stock for $20,000.

CASES

Case 1-62 Using Accounting Information

Jim Hadden is a freshman at Major State University. His earnings from a summer job, combined with a small scholarship and a fixed amount per term from his parents, are his only sources of income. He has a new MasterCard that was issued to him the week he began classes. It is spring term, and Jim finds that his credit card is "maxed out" and that he does not have enough money to carry him to the end of the term. Jim confesses that irresistible opportunities for spring term entertainment have caused him to overspend his resources.

Required:

Describe how accounting information could have helped Jim avoid this difficult situation.

Case 1-63 Analysis of Accounting Periodicals

The accounting profession is organized into three major groups: (a) accountants who work in nonbusiness entities, (b) accountants who work in business entities, and (c) accountants in public practice. The periodical literature of accounting includes monthly or quarterly journals that are written primarily for accountants within each of these groups.

Required:

1. Use your library and identify one journal published for each of the three professional groups. Identify the publisher of each journal and describe its primary audience.
2. Choose two of the three audiences you have just described. Briefly explain how members of one audience would benefit by reading a journal published primarily for members of the other audience.

Case 1-64 Career Planning

A successful career requires us to take advantage of opportunities that are difficult to fore-see. Success is also aided by having a plan or strategy by which to choose among career alternatives as they arise.

Required:

1. How do you want to be employed in 5 years, and what must you do to get there?
2. How do you want to be employed in 10 years, and what must you do to get there?

Case 1-65 Financial Statement Analysis

Agency Rent-A-Car Inc. rents cars to customers whose vehicles are unavailable due to accident, theft, or repair ("Wheels while your car heals"). The company has a fleet of more than 40,000 cars located at 700 offices throughout the United States and Canada. Its balance sheets at January 31, 2023, and January 31, 2022, contain the following information (all dollar amounts are stated in thousands of dollars):

	1/31/2023	1/31/2022
Assets		
Cash	$ 5,210	$ 4,125
Accounts receivable	28,100	32,891
Supplies	7,152	7,853
Property and equipment	281,152	285,130
Other assets	15,250	9,563
	$336,864	$339,562
Liabilities and Stockholders' Equity		
Accounts payable	$ 19,655	$ 35,483
Other noncurrent liabilities	144,680	168,260
Stockholders' equity	172,529	135,819
	$336,864	$339,562

Required:

1. What is the dollar amount of current assets and current liabilities at January 31, 2023? At January 31, 2022? What does this information tell you about the company's liquidity?
2. Assume that stockholders were paid dividends of $21,000 during 2023 and that there were no other changes in stockholders' equity except for net income. How much net income did the business earn during the year?

Case 1-66 Financial Statement Analysis

Reproduced on the following page are portions of the president's letter to stockholders and selected income statement and balance sheet data for the Wright Brothers Aviation Company. Wright Brothers is a national airline that provides both passenger service and package delivery service.

To Our Stockholders:

In 2023, the airline industry began to show some life. As fuel prices leveled and travelers showed an increased willingness to fly domestically, it was generally perceived that a gradual recovery was in place. The worldwide increase in the demand for air travel throughout the year translated into improved demand for the Company's services. In fact, revenues for both the passenger and package segments improved in every quarter of 2023. Most importantly, the Company started generating cash from operations in the last half of the year, and the passenger segments returned to generating profits in the third quarter...

With improved operating performance as the basis for negotiating a financial restructuring, the next critical step for the Company is to satisfactorily restructure its obligations in order to insure that the Company can operate effectively in the future. With that in mind, a strategic decision, albeit a difficult one, was made in February 2023—the Company filed for reorganization under Chapter 11 of the U.S. Bankruptcy Code...

	2023	2022	2021	2020	2019
Revenues:					
Passenger services	$ 141,343	$ 136,057	$ 354,246	$ 390,080	$ 337,871
Package services	35,199	60,968	145,940	203,675	202,615
Total revenues	176,542	197,025	500,186	593,755	540,486
Operating income	(54,584)	(92,613)	(16,663)	52,137	39,527
Net income (loss)	(182,647)	(340,516)	(67,269)	(14,553)	(22,461)
Current assets	123,553	134,009	183,268	193,943	209,944
Total assets	542,523	678,846	952,623	1,040,903	1,133,498
Current liabilities	698,583	641,645	542,640	129,369	120,960
Long-term debt	116,572	119,481	144,297	576,446	655,383
Stockholders' equity	(272,632)	(82,280)	265,686	335,088	357,155

Required:

1. What trends do you detect in revenues, operating income, and net income for the period 2019–2023?
2. What happened to working capital over the 2019–2023 period? To what do you attribute this result?
3. The price of Wright Brothers stock declined steadily throughout the 2019–2023 period. Do you consider this decline to be a reasonable reaction to the financial results reported? Why or why not?

Case 1-67 Professional Ethics

Professional ethics guide public accountants in their work with financial statements.

Required:

Why is ethical behavior by public accountants important to society? Be sure to describe the incentives that public accountants have to behave *ethically* and *unethically*.

Case 1-68 Ethical Issues

Lola, the CEO of JB Inc., and Frank, the accountant for JB Inc., were recently having a meeting to discuss the upcoming release of the company's financial statements. Following is an excerpt of their conversation:

(Continued)

Lola: These financial statements don't show the hours of hard work that we've put in to restore this company to financial health. In fact, these results may actually prevent us from obtaining loans that are critical to our future.

Frank: Accounting does allow for judgment. Tell me your primary concerns, and let's see if we can work something out.

Lola: My first concern is that the company doesn't appear very liquid. As you can see, our current assets are only slightly more than current liabilities. The company has always paid its bills—even when cash was tight. It's not really fair that the financial statements don't reflect this.

Frank: Well, we could reclassify some of the long-term investments as current assets instead of noncurrent assets. Our expectation is that we will hold these investments for several years, but we could sell them at any time; therefore, it's fair to count these as current assets. We could also reclassify some of the accounts payable as noncurrent. Even though we expect to pay them within the next year, no one will ever look close enough to see what we've done. Together these two changes should make us appear more liquid and properly reflect the hard work we've done.

Lola: I agree. However, if we make these changes, our long-term assets will be smaller and our long-term debt will be larger. Many analysts may view this as a sign of financial trouble. Isn't there something we can do?

Frank: Our long-term assets are undervalued. Many were purchased years ago and recorded at historical cost. However, companies that bought similar assets are allowed to record them at an amount closer to their current market values. I've always thought this was misleading. If we increase the value of these long-term assets to their market value, this should provide the users of the financial statements with more relevant information and solve our problem, too.

Lola: Brilliant! Let's implement these actions quickly and get back to work.

Required:
Describe any ethical issues that have arisen as the result of Lola and Frank's conversation.

Case 1-69 Research and Analysis Using the Annual Report

Obtain **Apple Inc.**'s 2019 annual report either through the "Investor Relations" portion of their website (do a web search for Apple investor relations) or go to www.sec.gov and click "Company Filings Search" under "Filings."

Required:
Answer the following questions:
1. On what date did Apple's fiscal year end? Was this date different from the previous year? If so, why?
2. How many years of balance sheet and income statement information does Apple present?
3. With regard to the balance sheet:
   a. What amounts did Apple report as total assets, liabilities, and stockholders' equity for 2019?
   b. Did the amounts reported as assets, liabilities, and stockholders' equity change over the last year? If so, by how much?
   c. What amounts were reported as current assets and current liabilities for the years presented?
   d. Provide an assessment of Apple's liquidity based on the information obtained in part b.

4. With regard to the income statement:
   a. What amounts did Apple report as revenues, expenses, and net income for 2019?
   b. Do you detect any trends with regard to revenues, expenses, or net income?
5. With regard to the statement of cash flows:
   a. What amounts did the company report for cash flow from operating activities, cash flow from investing activities, and cash flow from financing activities for 2019?
   b. How much cash did the company spend on purchasing PP&E in 2019?
6. With regard to management's discussion and analysis:
   a. What accounting policies and estimates does Apple consider critical? Where would these policies and estimates be described?
   b. What is management's opinion as to prospects for 2020?
7. Are the financial statements audited? If so, by whom?

Case 1-70 Comparative Analysis: Kroger versus Sprouts

Refer to the 10-K reports of Kroger and Sprouts that are available for download from the companion website at Cengage.com.

Required:

Answer the following questions:
1. Describe each company's business and list some of the more common products or brands sold by each company.
2. What is the fiscal year-end of Kroger? Of Sprouts? Why would you expect these to be similar?
3. With regard to the balance sheet:
   a. What amounts did each company report for total assets, liabilities, and stockholders' equity for its most recent fiscal year?
   b. What amounts were reported as current assets and current liabilities for each company's most recent fiscal year-end?
   c. Assess the liquidity of each company.
   d. Describe any other similarities and differences that you noticed between the two companies.
4. With regard to the income statement:
   a. What amounts did Kroger report as revenues, expenses, and net income for its most recent fiscal year-end?
   b. What amounts did Sprouts report as revenues, expenses, and net income for its most recent fiscal year-end?
   c. Compare any trends that you detect with regard to revenues, expenses, and net income.
5. What were the major sources and uses of cash for each company?

ANNUAL REPORT PROBLEM

HOME DEPOT

Download the 10-K for **Home Depot** from the companion website at Cengage.com.

Required:

1. What does Home Depot report for the following items for the most current fiscal year?
   a. Current assets
   b. Current liabilities
   c. Net sales
   d. Cost of goods sold
   e. Operating expenses

(Continued)

2. Assume that Home Depot projects the following:
   - Sales, cost of goods sold, and operating expenses will grow by 5% in the next fiscal year.
   - Current assets will increase by $1,000,000.
   - Current liabilities will increase by $2,000,000.

   Assume all other items remain unchanged from the prior year. Provide the next fiscal year's forecasted balances for current assets, current liabilities, net sales cost of goods sold, and operating expenses.

3. Answer the following questions:
   a. What is the company's exact name?
   b. What is Home Depot's common stock trading symbol?
   c. In what city is Home Depot's headquarters located?
   d. Calculate the Home Depot's forecasted current ratio (round to two decimal places).
   e. Calculate the Home Depot's forecasted gross margin (round to two decimal places).
   f. Calculate Home Depot's forecasted income from operations (round to two decimal places).

Note: *While the Annual Report problems in the textbook are static, when assigned in CNOW, these activities are algorithmic and the answers may vary from what appears in the Solutions Manual.*

CONTINUING PROBLEM

FRONT ROW ENTERTAINMENT

Cam and Anna met during their freshman year of college as they were standing in line to buy tickets to a concert. While waiting in line, the two shared various aspects of their lives. Cam, whose father was an executive at a major record label, was raised in New York. Some of his favorite memories were meeting popular musical artists—from the Rolling Stones to the Black Eyed Peas—as he accompanied his father on business trips. Anna, on the other hand, was born and raised in a small, rural town in southern Georgia. Her fondest childhood memories involved singing with her family, who often performed at county fairs and other small events. Even though they had different backgrounds, they felt an instant bond through their shared passion for music. Over the next couple of years, this friendship strengthened as they attended numerous concerts and other events together.

While on a road trip to see a new band during their senior year, Cam and Anna started discussing their future career plans. Both had an entrepreneurial spirit and were seeking a way to combine their majors in business with their passion for music. Cam had recently overheard his father discussing how many artists were unhappy with the current concert promoters. Anna had heard similar complaints from her cousin, whose band recently had their first top 25 hit. When Cam suggested that he and Anna form a concert promotion business, they both knew they had found the perfect careers.

Concert promoters sign artists, usually through the artists' agents, to contracts in which the promoter is responsible for organizing live concert tours. Typically, this includes booking the venue, pricing the tour, advertising the tour, and negotiating other services from local vendors. In general, the barriers to entry in the concert promotion industry are relatively low, with one of the more important items being forming a relationship with the various artists. Through their industry contacts (Cam's father, Anna's cousin), they felt that they could develop a client list relatively easily. A second major barrier would be to obtain the up-front cash necessary to promote the tour properly.

(Continued)

Since their friendship had started many years ago as they were trying to get front row seats, they decided to name their business Front Row Entertainment. With their first big decision made, it was time to get to work.

Required:

1. Discuss some of the typical business activities (financing, investing, and operating) that a business like Front Row Entertainment is likely to have. (*Hint:* You may want to perform an Internet search for concert promoters to obtain a better understanding of the industry.) Be sure to list some of the specific account names for assets, liabilities, stockholders' equity, revenues, and expenses that may arise from these activities.
2. Explain the advantages and disadvantages of the forms of business organization that Cam and Anna might choose for Front Row Entertainment. Which form would you recommend?
3. Cam and Anna will need to prepare financial statements to report company performance. What type of information does each financial statement provide? Be sure to describe the insights that each financial statement provides to users.

1s Reading a Company's Annual Report and Form 10-K

The U.S. Securities and Exchange Commission (SEC) requires companies that sell stock to the public to issue formal reports each year. These reports summarize their financial position and performance. The annual formal report that a company files with the SEC is called Form 10-K. Investors can access companies' Form 10-Ks from the SEC's website at www.sec.gov/edgar.shtml. In addition, some companies send annual reports to shareholders or post annual reports on their own company websites. These annual reports typically contain some or all of the information from the company's Form 10-K and can also contain additional information that management wants to share with parties outside of the company. This other information might include charts, graphs, or photos, and it could contain details about management's compensation, plans for new products, and other information that might be of interest to current or potential stockholders or lenders. This information could also be interesting to company suppliers and customers, competitors, financial analysts, and employees. Because 10-Ks are issued annually and because Form 10-K and the annual report contain similar information, many people refer to the 10-K as the annual report.

Each year, every publicly traded company issues a 10-K report. No two reports are exactly the same, but the SEC requires that all reports provide similar types of information.

All 10-Ks include the following four financial statements:

- Balance sheet
- Income statement
- Statement of changes in shareholders' equity
- Statement of cash flows

U.S. companies are required to prepare these financial statements according to a set of accounting standards, conventions, and rules known as Generally Accepted Accounting Principles, or GAAP.

A company's 10-K also includes the following:

- Notes to the financial statements
- Management's discussion and analysis (commonly known as an MD&A)
- Independent auditor's report

The notes provide details about the GAAP used by the company and about how the financial statement numbers were compiled; the MD&A provides management's discussion of the business and the financial statements; and the auditor's report contains an opinion from the independent auditor about whether the company's financial statements comply with GAAP.

Let's look at Activision Blizzard's 2019 annual report and Form 10-K as an example. The annual report posted on Activision Blizzard's website and the Form 10-K is available from the SEC's EDGAR website.

Activision Blizzard is one of the world's largest computer game publishers. Some of the company's most popular games are Call of Duty, World of Warcraft, and Candy Crush. According to page 34 of the annual report, in December 2019 alone, more than 409 million people played Activision Blizzard games.

WHAT'S IN THE ANNUAL REPORT?

Altogether, Activision Blizzard's 2019 annual report is 148 pages long and its Form 10-K is 164 pages long. Other than on the front and back cover, which feature characters from Activision Blizzard's games, the annual report contains no pictures. Instead, the company uses the annual report to provide financial statement users with the Form 10-K information that is required by the SEC and to present information about management's compensation plans.

The annual report is compiled by Activision Blizzard's managers, and the 10-K follows the rules set out by the SEC.

Letter to Shareholders The first page of the annual report contains a letter to shareholders. This letter is written jointly by Activision Blizzard's Chief Executive Officer (CEO), who is the person in the company's top management position, and the Chairman of the Board of Directors. The board of directors monitors the company's managers and represents the interests of shareholders. The letter to shareholders begins with an acknowledgment that COVID-19 is disrupting businesses around the world but explains that Activision Blizzard is well positioned because it provides entertainment remotely. The letter focuses on how the company is increasing its investment in its most popular games and is creating new mobile games. It is signed by the CEO and the Chairman of the Board.

Form 10-K The next section of Activision Blizzard's annual report contains its Form 10-K. The SEC requires every publicly traded company to issue a 10-K every year. There are strict rules about what information the company includes in the 10-K and about how to measure that information. Much of this book is about the rules that govern the measurement and disclosure of information in the 10-K.

The 10-K is organized into four parts. There are 15 required items, as outlined in the following textbox. Because every company must disclose all of the 15 items, reviewing the material in the textbox will help you to locate information in any company's 10-K.

PART I

Item 1—"Business" requires a description of the company's business, including its main products and services, what subsidiaries it owns, and what markets it operates in. This section may also include information about recent events, competition the company faces, regulations that apply to it, labor issues, special operating costs, or seasonal factors. This is a good place to start to understand how the company operates.

Item 1A—"Risk Factors" includes information about the most significant risks that apply to the company or to its securities. Companies generally list the risk factors in order of their importance. In practice, this section focuses on the risks themselves and not on how the company addresses those risks. Some risks may apply to the entire economy, some may apply only to the company's industry sector or geographic region, and some may be unique to the company.

Item 1B—"Unresolved Staff Comments" requires the company to explain certain comments on previously filed reports that it has received from the SEC staff if these comments have not been resolved after an extended period of time.

Item 2—"Properties" includes information about the company's significant physical properties, such as principal plants and mines.

Item 3—"Legal Proceedings" requires the company to include information about significant pending lawsuits or other legal proceedings, but not ordinary litigation.

Item 4—This item has no required information and is reserved by the SEC for future rulemaking.

PART II

Item 5—"Market for Registrant's Common Equity, Related Stockholder Matters and Issuer Purchases of Equity Securities" provides information about the company's equity securities, including market information, the number of shareholders, dividends, stock repurchases by the company, and similar information.

Item 6—"Selected Financial Data" provides certain financial information about the company for the past 5 years. You can find much more detailed financial information about the past 3 years in a separate section: **Item 8—"Financial Statements and Supplementary Data."**

Item 7—"Management's Discussion and Analysis of Financial Condition and Results of Operations" or MD&A gives the company's perspective on the business results from the last financial year. This section allows company management to tell its story in its own words. The MD&A presents:

- The company's operations and financial results, including information about the company's liquidity and capital resources and any known trends or uncertainties that could materially affect the company's results. This section may also discuss management's views of key business risks (like changing customer tastes, reliance on water or other natural resources, the need for adequate capital and exposure to changes in interest rates, or the effects of climate change) and what it is doing to address them.
- Material changes in the company's results compared to the prior year, as well as off-balance sheet arrangements and the company's contractual obligations.
- Critical accounting judgments, such as estimates and assumptions. These accounting judgments—and any changes from previous years—can have a significant impact on the numbers in the financial statements.

Item 7A—"Quantitative and Qualitative Disclosures about Market Risk" requires information about the company's exposure to market risk, including interest rate risk, foreign currency exchange risk, commodity price risk, and equity price risk. The company may discuss how it manages its market risk exposures.

Item 8—"Financial Statements and Supplementary Data" requires the company's audited financial statements. This includes the company's income statement (which is sometimes called the statement of earnings or the statement of operations), balance sheet, statement of cash flows, and statement of stockholders' equity. The financial statements are accompanied by notes that explain the information presented in the financial statements.

Item 9—"Changes in and Disagreements with Accountants on Accounting and Financial Disclosure" requires the company, if there has been a change in its external auditor, to discuss any disagreements it had with the former auditor. Many investors view this disclosure as a red flag.

Item 9A—"Controls and Procedures" includes information about the company's disclosure controls and procedures and its internal control over financial reporting.

Item 9B—"Other Information" includes any financial information that was required to be reported on a different form during the fourth quarter of the year covered by the 10-K but is not reported in the current 10-K.

PART III

Disclosures in this part (Items 10 through 14) are required in the 10-K, but most companies meet this requirement by providing the information in a separate document called a proxy statement. Companies provide this statement to their shareholders in connection with the annual meeting. If the information is provided through a proxy statement, the 10-K includes a statement saying that the information from the proxy statement is included by reference—in effect directing readers to go to the proxy statement to find the information. The proxy statement is typically filed a month or two after the 10-K so financial statement users do not have access to this information as quickly. For more information about proxy statements and shareholder voting in corporate elections, see the SEC's Spotlight on Proxy Matters. For information about how to find company proxy statements on the SEC's Electronic Data Gathering, Analysis and Retrieval (EDGAR) database, see https://www.sec.gov/fast-answers/answersproxyhtfhtm.html.

Item 10—"Directors, Executive Officers and Corporate Governance" requires information about the backgrounds and experience of the company's directors and executive officers, the company's code of ethics, and certain qualifications for directors and member of committees of the board of directors.

Item 11—"Executive Compensation" includes detailed disclosure about the company's compensation policies and programs as well as how much compensation was paid to the top executive officers of the company in the previous year.

Item 12—"Security Ownership of Certain Beneficial Owners and Management and Related Stockholder Matters" requires information about the shares owned by the company's directors, officers, and certain large shareholders, and about shares covered by equity compensation plans.

Item 13—"Certain Relationships and Related Transactions, and Director Independence" includes information about relationships and transactions between the company and its directors, officers, and their family members. It also includes information about whether each director is independent.

Item 14—"Principal Accountant Fees and Services" requires companies to disclose the fees they paid to their accounting firm for various types of services during the year.

PART IV

Item 15—"Exhibits and Financial Statement Schedules" requires a list of the financial statements and exhibits included as part of the Form 10-K. Many exhibits are required, including documents such as the company's bylaws, copies of its material contracts, and a list of subsidiaries.

There are two primary differences between the annual report that Activision Blizzard posted on its website and the 10-K that it filed with the SEC. The first difference is that the annual report includes the letter from management to shareholders. It is common for companies to include a letter to shareholders in their annual reports, but this letter is not part of the 10-K and is not audited by the company's independent auditors. The second difference is that the annual report includes many pages of "Exhibits" that provide details about the company's stock compensation plans and other personnel issues.

HIGHLIGHTS FROM FORM 10-K

PART 1 OF FORM 10-K

Part 1 of Activision Blizzard's 10-K is a 24-page, in-depth description of the business. This section of the 10-K discusses the company's strategic vision and its three reportable business segments: Activision Publishing, Inc.; Blizzard Entertainment, Inc.; and King Digital Entertainment. Activision develops games primarily for consoles such as PlayStation and Xbox, with its biggest game being Call of Duty; Blizzard develops games mainly for PCs, with its biggest game being World of Warcraft; and King develops games primarily for mobile platforms, with its biggest game being Candy Crush. This part of the 10-K also explains that the company earns revenue by selling four different types of products: full games, downloadable content, microtransactions, and subscriptions. Finally, Activision Blizzard outlines the risks that the company faces. These risks include that competitors will take market share, that the vast majority of revenue from microtransactions relies on a very small number of users, and that recruiting and retaining key personnel are critical given the competition for highly skilled programmers and engineers.

Monthly Active Users

We monitor monthly active users ("MAUs") as a key measure of the overall size of our user base. MAUs are the number of individuals who accessed a particular game in a given month. We calculate average MAUs in a period by adding the total number of MAUs in each of the months in a given period and dividing that total by the number of months in the period. An individual who accesses two of our games would be counted as two users. In addition, due to technical limitations, for Activision and King, an individual who accesses the same game on two platforms or devices in the relevant period would be counted as two users. For Blizzard, an individual who accesses the same game on two platforms or devices in the relevant period would generally be counted as a single user. In certain instances, we rely on third parties to publish our games. In these instances, MAU data is based on information provided to us by those third parties, or, if final data is not available, reasonable estimates of MAUs for these third-party published games.

The number of MAUs for a given period can be significantly impacted by the timing of new content releases, since new releases may cause a temporary surge in MAUs. Accordingly, although we believe that overall trending in the number of MAUs can be a meaningful performance metric, period-to-period fluctuations may not be indicative of longer-term trends. The following table details our average MAUs on a sequential quarterly basis for each of our reportable segments (amounts in millions):

	December 31, 2019	September 30, 2019	June 30, 2019	March 31, 2019	December 31, 2018	September 30, 2018
Activision	128	36	37	41	53	46
Blizzard	32	33	32	32	35	37
King	249	247	258	272	268	262
Total	409	316	327	345	356	345

Average MAUs increased by 93 million, or 29%, for the three months ended December 31, 2019, as compared to the three months ended September 30, 2019, primarily due to an increase in average MAUs for Activision driven by the Call of Duty franchise as a result of the October 2019 launches of *Call of Duty: Mobile* and *Call of Duty: Modern Warfare.*

Source: ACTIVISION BLIZZARD, INC., FORM 10-K

Management's Discussion and Analysis (MD&A) (Item 7)

Activision Blizzard's MD&A provides details about the company's business segments, business highlights, and how the company records revenue. Here, management provides details about the company's three segments. Investors and financial analysts care about how much of the company's revenue and income come from each segment because these segments have different risks and different potential for growth.

Activision Blizzard also provides information about how the Monthly Active User (MAU) count has changed over the past year, with the company gaining 53 million MAUs between December 2018 and December 2019.

Net Revenues by Platform

The following tables detail our net revenues by platform (amounts in millions):

		For the Years Ended December 31,		
	2019	2018	Increase/ (decrease)	% Change
Net revenues by platform:				
Console	$ 1,920	$ 2,538	$ (618)	(24)%
PC	1,718	2,180	(462)	(21)
Mobile and ancillary (1)	2,203	2,175	28	1
Other (2)	648	607	41	7
Total consolidated net revenues	$ 6,489	$ 7,500	$ (1,011)	(13)

(1) Net revenues from "Mobile and ancillary" include revenues from mobile devices, as well as non-platform-specific game-related revenues, such as standalone sales of toys and accessories.

(2) Net revenues from "Other" primarily includes revenues from our Distribution business and the Overwatch League.

Source: ACTIVISION BLIZZARD, INC., FORM 10-K

The company also provides information about revenue from each gaming platform. Here we can see that mobile games generate the greatest amount of revenue and that both console and PC games generated less revenue in 2019 than in 2018.

The Financial Statements and Supplementary Information (Item 8)

Item 8 in a Form 10-K is the financial statements and supplemental information. Supplemental information includes the Notes to the Consolidated Financial Statements and the Report of the Independent Registered Public Accounting Firm.

BALANCE SHEET Activision Blizzard provides balance sheets for the current and previous years. The column headings indicate that the left-hand column is for December 31, 2019, and the right-hand column is for December 31, 2018. By comparing the columns, financial statement users can see how the company's financial position changed during 2019. At the top of the balance sheet, is "(Amounts in millions, except share data)." This tells the reader that although the balance sheet displays a value for cash and cash equivalents of $5,794 at the end of 2019, the real amount is

ACTIVISION BLIZZARD, INC. AND SUBSIDIARIES
CONSOLIDATED BALANCE SHEETS
(Amounts in millions, except share data)

	At December 31, 2019	At December 31, 2018
Assets		
Current assets:		
Cash and cash equivalents	$ 5,794	$ 4,225
Accounts receivable, net of allowances of $132 and $190, at December 31, 2019 and December 31, 2018, respectively	848	1,035
Inventories, net	32	43
Software development	322	264
Other current assets	296	539
Total current assets	7,292	6,106
Software development	54	65
Property and equipment, net	253	282
Deferred income taxes, net	1,293	458
Other assets	658	482
Intangible assets, net	531	735
Goodwill	9,764	9,762
Total assets	$ 19,845	$ 17,890
Liabilities and Shareholders' Equity		
Current liabilities:		
Accounts payable	$ 292	$ 253
Deferred revenues	1,375	1,493
Accrued expenses and other liabilities	1,248	896
Total current liabilities	2,915	2,642
Long-term debt, net	2,675	2,671
Deferred income taxes, net	505	18
Other liabilities	945	1,167
Total liabilities	7,040	6,498
Commitments and contingencies (Note 23)		
Shareholders' equity:		
Common stock, $0.000001 par value, 2,400,000,000 shares authorized, 1,197,436,644 and 1,192,093,991 shares issued at December 31, 2019 and December 31, 2018, respectively	—	—
Additional paid-in capital	11,174	10,963
Less: Treasury stock, at cost, 428,676,471 shares at December 31, 2019 and December 31, 2018	(5,563)	(5,563)
Retained earnings	7,813	6,593
Accumulated other comprehensive loss	(619)	(601)
Total shareholders' equity	12,805	11,392
Total liabilities and shareholders' equity	$ 19,845	$ 17,890

The accompanying notes are an integral part of these Consolidated Financial Statements.

Source: ACTIVISION BLIZZARD, INC., FORM 10-K

$5,794 million or almost $6 billion. The company reports total assets of $19,845 million and more than half of this is Goodwill. Goodwill is an intangible asset that can be generated when one company buys or merges with another company. In this case, in 2008, Vivendi Games merged with Activision to form Activision Blizzard, and in 2016, the combined company purchased King. It is very uncommon for a company to have more than half of its assets in Goodwill, but transactions like these created a very large amount of Goodwill for the combined company, and now the majority of the company's value comes from the software that it uses to run its games.

The balance sheet also provides information about Activision Blizzard's liabilities and shareholders' equity. It's interesting to note that the par (or stated) value of the company's shares is $0.000001 or 1/10,000th of a penny per share. This is different from the market value or stock price, which is much higher. The balance sheet also indicates that the company has repurchased more than 400 million shares of its own stock from investors and is holding these in Treasury Stock. Total shareholders' equity is $12,805 million. It's the value of the assets ($19,845 million) less the value of the liabilities ($7,040 million).

ACTIVISION BLIZZARD, INC. AND SUBSIDIARIES
CONSOLIDATED STATEMENTS OF OPERATIONS
(Amounts in millions, except per share data)

	For the Years Ended December 31,		
	2019	2018	2017
Net revenues			
Product sales	$ 1,975	$ 2,255	$ 2,110
Subscription, licensing, and other revenues	4,514	5,245	4,907
Total net revenues	6,489	7,500	7,017
Costs and expenses			
Cost of revenues—product sales:			
Product costs	656	719	733
Software royalties, amortization, and intellectual property licenses	240	371	300
Cost of revenues—subscription, licensing, and other revenues:			
Game operations and distribution costs	965	1,028	984
Software royalties, amortization, and intellectual property licenses	233	399	484
Product development	998	1,101	1,069
Sales and marketing	926	1,062	1,378
General and administrative	732	822	745
Restructuring and related costs	132	10	15
Total costs and expenses	4,882	5,512	5,708
Operating income	1,607	1,988	1,309
Interest and other expense (income), net (Note 18)	(26)	71	146
Loss on extinguishment of debt	—	40	12
Income before income tax expense	1,633	1,877	1,151
Income tax expense	130	29	878
Net income	$ 1,503	$ 1,848	$ 273
Earnings per common share			
Basic	$ 1.96	$ 2.43	$ 0.36
Diluted	$ 1.95	$ 2.40	$ 0.36
Weighted-average number of shares outstanding			
Basic	767	762	754
Diluted	771	771	766

The accompanying notes are an integral part of these Consolidated Financial Statements.

Source: ACTIVISION BLIZZARD, INC., FORM 10-K

INCOME STATEMENT The next financial statement in Activision Blizzard's Form 10-K is called the "consolidated statements of operations." Consolidated means that a statement combines the financial statements of the separate businesses (Activision, Blizzard, and King). Statement of operations is another name for the income statement. In this statement, the company reports all of the revenues and expenses for the years ended December 31, 2019; December 31, 2018; and December 31, 2017. Revenue, which is the amount that Activision Blizzard earns from customers, is broken down into two components. In 2019, the company earned approximately $2 billion from sales of game disks and downloads, and it earned another $4.5 billion from items like the monthly subscription fees that customers pay to play its games.

The costs and expenses section tells readers that the company incurred costs of almost $4.9 billion for operating expenses (like producing and maintaining games, marketing, and administrative costs). It reported $1,503 million of net income and investors owned 767 million shares of stock. This means that Activision Blizzard's earnings per share (EPS) was $1.96 in 2019.

STATEMENT OF CHANGES IN SHAREHOLDERS' EQUITY The statement of changes in shareholders' equity shows how the shareholders' equity accounts changed from the beginning to the end of the year. Shareholders' equity increases when the company earns net income or issues new shares to investors and decreases when the company earns a loss, pays dividends, or buys back shares from investors. In this book, we use a simplified version of the statement of changes in shareholders' equity called the retained earnings statement. The retained earnings statement is a simplification because it reports changes in shareholders' equity from net income or net loss and from the payment of dividends, but it ignores changes in shareholders' equity from selling or buying back shares of stock.

In some years, shareholders' equity can also change because of changes in accounting rules or income tax rules or because the company merges with another company. In 2019, Activision Blizzard's employees were rewarded for good performance with new shares of stock and stock options, and this increased shareholders' equity.

Notice that the final column of Activision Blizzard's statement presents the total value of shareholders' equity. The number $11,392 represents the total shareholders' equity in millions as of December 31, 2018. During 2019, shareholders' equity changed because the company earned net income of $1,503 million (which is also the amount reported on the income statements), declared dividends of $283 million, and reported some other changes. The final value of total shareholders' equity as of December 31, 2019 is $12,805 million. This is equal to the amount of shareholders' equity reported on the December 31, 2019 balance sheet.

STATEMENT OF CASH FLOWS Activision Blizzard's final financial statement is the statement of cash flows. This statement contains three main sections: cash from operating activities, cash from investing activities, and cash from financing activities, as well as a reconciliation of the change in cash and cash equivalents during the year.

Cash from operating activities The first section provides information about how much cash the company received from selling its games and services, as well as how much cash it paid to make those games and to provide services. Activision Blizzard uses the indirect method to calculate cash from operating activities. Under this method, the company starts with net income and makes adjustments to subtract noncash revenue and expenses and to add back cash inflows and outflows that have not yet been recorded as revenue and expenses. Some of the larger adjustments are depreciation and amortization expenses, which initially decreased net income by $743 million but are added back to net income because they are not paid in cash. The other standard adjustments that Activision Blizzard made were for changes in noncash operating assets such as inventories and accounts receivable. Activision Blizzard also made large adjustments for deferred taxes and for the purchase of other businesses. Although these are important factors affecting Activision Blizzards' 2019 cash flows, they are beyond the scope of this book and are usually covered in an advanced accounting course or in a course on accounting for business combinations.

ACTIVISION BLIZZARD, INC. AND SUBSIDIARIES
CONSOLIDATED STATEMENTS OF CHANGES IN SHAREHOLDERS' EQUITY
For the Years Ended December 31, 2019, 2018, and 2017
(Amounts and shares in millions, except per share data)

	Common Stock		Treasury Stock		Additional Paid-In Capital	Retained Earnings	Accumulated Other Comprehensive Income (Loss)	Total Shareholders' Equity
	Shares	Amount	Shares	Amount				
Balance at December 31, 2016	1,174	$ —	(429)	$(5,563)	$ 10,442	$ 4,869	$ (629)	$ 9,119
Components of comprehensive income:								
Net income	—	—	—	—	—	273	—	273
Other comprehensive income (loss)	—	—	—	—	—	—	(9)	(9)
Issuance of common stock pursuant to employee stock options	11	—	—	—	178	—	—	178
Issuance of common stock pursuant to restricted stock units	2	—	—	—	—	—	—	—
Restricted stock surrendered for employees' tax liability	(1)	—	—	—	(54)	—	—	(54)
Share-based compensation expense related to employee stock options and restricted stock units	—	—	—	—	181	—	—	181
Dividends ($0.30 per common share)	—	—	—	—	—	(226)	—	(226)
Balance at December 31, 2017	1,186	$ —	(429)	$(5,563)	$ 10,747	$ 4,916	$ (638)	$ 9,462
Cumulative impact from adoption of new revenue accounting standard	—	—	—	—	—	88	3	91
Components of comprehensive income:								
Net income	—	—	—	—	—	1,848	—	1,848
Other comprehensive income (loss)	—	—	—	—	—	—	34	34
Issuance of common stock pursuant to employee stock options	5	—	—	—	98	—	—	98
Issuance of common stock pursuant to restricted stock units	2	—	—	—	—	—	—	—
Restricted stock surrendered for employees' tax liability	(1)	—	—	—	(93)	—	—	(93)
Share-based compensation expense related to employee stock options and restricted stock units	—	—	—	—	211	—	—	211
Dividends ($0.34 per common share)	—	—	—	—	—	(259)	—	(259)
Balance at December 31, 2018	1,192	$ —	(429)	$(5,563)	$ 10,963	$ 6,593	$ (601)	$ 11,392
Components of comprehensive income:								
Net income	—	—	—	—	—	1,503	—	1,503
Other comprehensive income (loss)	—	—	—	—	—	—	(18)	(18)
Issuance of common stock pursuant to employee stock options	4	—	—	—	105	—	—	105
Issuance of common stock pursuant to restricted stock units	2	—	—	—	—	—	—	—
Restricted stock surrendered for employees' tax liability	(1)	—	—	—	(58)	—	—	(58)
Share-based compensation expense related to employee stock options and restricted stock units	—	—	—	—	164	—	—	164
Dividends ($0.37 per common share)	—	—	—	—	—	(283)	—	(283)
Balance at December 31, 2019	1,197	$ —	(429)	$(5,563)	$ 11,174	$ 7,813	$ (619)	$ 12,805

The accompanying notes are an integral part of these Consolidated Financial Statements.

Source: ACTIVISION BLIZZARD, INC., FORM 10-K

Cash from investing activities The second section records the cash from buying and selling long-term investments. For example, the statement records cash outflows of $116 million for capital expenditures because the company purchased items like buildings, computers, and other equipment.

Cash from financing activities The final section relates to financing activities such as issuing stock, taking out loans, paying dividends, and paying back loans. In 2019, Activision Blizzard's biggest cash flow from financing was a cash outflow of $283 million to pay dividends to shareholders.

Total change in cash Summing up the cash provided by these three business activities leads to a total increase in cash during 2019 of $1,569 million. Adding this to the 2018 balance of $4.2 billion in cash yields a 2019 balance of $5.8 billion in cash. These ending balances can be found on the 2018 and 2019 balance sheets and are referred to as "cash and cash equivalents."

ACTIVISION BLIZZARD, INC. AND SUBSIDIARIES
CONSOLIDATED STATEMENTS OF CASH FLOWS
(Amounts in millions)

	For the Years Ended December 31,		
	2019	2018	2017
Cash flows from operating activities:			
Net income	$ 1,503	$ 1,848	$ 273
Adjustments to reconcile net income to net cash provided by operating activities:			
Deferred income taxes	(352)	(35)	(181)
Provision for inventories	6	6	33
Non-cash operating lease cost	64	—	—
Depreciation and amortization	328	509	888
Amortization of capitalized software development costs and intellectual property licenses (1)	225	489	311
Loss on extinguishment of debt	—	40	12
Share-based compensation expense (2)	166	209	176
Unrealized gain on equity investment (Note 10)	(38)	—	—
Other	51	7	40
Changes in operating assets and liabilities, net of effect from business acquisitions:			
Accounts receivable, net	182	(114)	(165)
Inventories	7	(5)	(26)
Software development and intellectual property licenses	(275)	(372)	(301)
Other assets	164	(51)	(97)
Deferred revenues	(154)	(122)	220
Accounts payable	31	(65)	85
Accrued expenses and other liabilities	(77)	(554)	945
Net cash provided by operating activities	1,831	1,790	2,213
Cash flows from investing activities:			
Proceeds from maturities of available-for-sale investments	153	116	80
Purchases of available-for-sale investments	(65)	(209)	(135)
Capital expenditures	(116)	(131)	(155)
Other investing activities	6	(6)	3
Net cash used in investing activities	(22)	(230)	(207)
Cash flows from financing activities:			
Proceeds from issuance of common stock to employees	105	99	178
Tax payment related to net share settlements on restricted stock units	(59)	(94)	(56)
Dividends paid	(283)	(259)	(226)
Proceeds from debt issuances, net of discounts	—	—	3,741
Repayment of long-term debt	—	(1,740)	(4,251)
Premium payment for early redemption of note	—	(25)	—
Other financing activities	—	(1)	(10)
Net cash used in financing activities	(237)	(2,020)	(624)
Effect of foreign exchange rate changes on cash and cash equivalents	(3)	(31)	76
Net increase (decrease) in cash and cash equivalents and restricted cash	1,569	(491)	1,458
Cash and cash equivalents and restricted cash at beginning of period	4,229	4,720	3,262
Cash and cash equivalents and restricted cash at end of period	$ 5,798	$ 4,229	$ 4,720

(1) Excludes deferral and amortization of share-based compensation expense.
(2) Includes the net effects of capitalization, deferral, and amortization of share-based compensation expense.

The accompanying notes are an integral part of these Consolidated Financial Statements.

Source: ACTIVISION BLIZZARD, INC., FORM 10-K

NOTES TO THE FINANCIAL STATEMENTS The next section of the 10-K contains the notes to the financial statements. This section provides details about how the financial statement numbers were calculated. For example, footnote 2 describes the significant accounting policies that Activision Blizzard used and includes items like a description of when the company recognizes subscription revenue.

In total, Activision Blizzard's 10-K contains 24 footnotes that provide details about many financial statement items including leases, depreciation, stock-based compensation, and income tax.

Subscription, Licensing, and Other Revenues

<u>Subscription Arrangements</u>

Subscription revenue arrangements are mostly derived from *World of Warcraft*, which is playable through Blizzard's servers and is generally sold on a subscription-only basis. Revenues associated with the sales of subscriptions are deferred until the subscription service is activated by the consumer and are then recognized ratably over the subscription period as the performance obligations are satisfied.

Revenues attributable to the purchase of *World of Warcraft* software by our customers, including expansion packs, are classified as "Product sales," whereas revenues attributable to subscriptions and other in-game revenues are classified as "Subscription, licensing, and other revenues."

Source: ACTIVISION BLIZZARD, INC., FORM 10-K

THE AUDITOR'S REPORT An independent accountant audits the company's annual financial statements. The auditor's report is a key part of the 10-K. Activision Blizzard's 10-K includes an audit opinion written by the accounting firm PricewaterhouseCoopers LLP (PwC). PwC is one of the four largest accounting firms in the world. Activision Blizzard's board of directors hired PwC to examine the company's 10-K and the underlying systems that the company used to prepare the financial statements. After examining Activision Blizzard's accounting system and 10-K, PwC wrote a report referred to as the auditor's report.

The auditor's report is important because external parties, including shareholders, lenders, and potential investors, cannot directly verify Activision Blizzard's financial statement information. For example, there is no way for outsiders to know whether Activision Blizzard really has $32 million worth of inventory or whether the accounts receivable really total more than $848 million. Before writing the audit report, PwC would have inspected the inventory, verified the accounts receivable, and collected information to verify the other financial statement numbers. This independent verification is called an audit, and a general description of the audit is summarized in PwC's audit report.

We conducted our audits in accordance with the standards of the PCAOB. Those standards require that we plan and perform the audits to obtain reasonable assurance about whether the consolidated financial statements are free of material misstatement, whether due to error or fraud, and whether effective internal control over financial reporting was maintained in all material respects.

Source: ACTIVISION BLIZZARD, INC., FORM 10-K

Most auditor's reports express an "unqualified opinion" that the financial statements fairly present the company's financial position in conformity with GAAP. If, however, an auditor expresses a "qualified opinion" or a "disclaimer of opinion," investors should look carefully at what prevented the auditor from expressing an unqualified opinion. PwC's report for Activision Blizzard states:

In our opinion, the consolidated financial statements referred to above present fairly, in all material respects, the financial position of the Company as of December 31, 2019 and 2018, and the results of its operations and its cash flows for each of the three years in the period ended December 31, 2019 in conformity with accounting principles generally accepted in the United States of America. Also in our opinion, the Company maintained, in all material respects, effective internal control over financial reporting as of December 31, 2019, based on criteria established in *Internal Control - Integrated Framework* (2013) issued by the COSO.

Source: ACTIVISION BLIZZARD, INC., FORM 10-K

For large companies, the independent auditor also reports on the company's internal controls over financial reporting. Investors should carefully evaluate any material weaknesses in the internal controls over financial reporting.

MANAGEMENT CERTIFICATIONS In addition, the Sarbanes-Oxley Act of 2002 requires the company's chief executive officer and chief financial officer to certify that the 10-K fairly presents the company's financial condition, results of operations, and cash flows in all material respects. These are called Sections 302 and 906 certifications, and you can usually find them in Exhibits 31 and 32.

SUMMARY

Altogether, annual reports and 10-Ks provide readers with a summary of the company's financial position and financial performance, as well as indications of its prospects for future financial performance. Information in the financial statements can help investors, lenders, suppliers, customers, and employees make informed decisions about their potential dealings with the company. The financial statements provide much of this information, but the other portions of the annual report and 10-K put the financial statements into perspective and provide financial statement users with a more complete picture.

Note that company management is responsible for preparing the 10-K and filing it with the SEC. Laws and regulations prohibit companies from making materially false or misleading statements in their 10-Ks. Likewise, companies are prohibited from omitting material information that is needed to make the disclosure not misleading.

The SEC neither prepares the 10-K nor vouches for its accuracy. Instead, the SEC sets the disclosure requirements, and SEC staff review company 10-Ks to monitor and enhance compliance with SEC requirements. All 10-Ks filed with the SEC are available to the public on the SEC's website from https://www.sec.gov/edgar.shtml

EARNINGS ANNOUNCEMENTS

Form 10-K is not investors' first source of information about the company's performance. Companies are required to file their 10-Ks with the SEC within 90 days of their year-ends, but most companies discuss their financial performance in press releases much earlier. These press releases are referred to as earnings announcements. They generally include information about the company's earnings and EPS, as well as management's narrative explaining the company's performance.

On February 6, 2020, Activision Blizzard announced its financial results for the fourth quarter (October through December) and for the full year 2019. The company reported revenues of almost $6.5 billion and EPS of $1.96 for the year. These numbers were calculated using GAAP. In addition, the company reported non-GAAP EPS of $2.31.

NON-GAAP EPS

As discussed previously, the audited financial statements are prepared using GAAP. Companies often provide a non-GAAP earnings number, in addition to the GAAP earnings number, in their earnings announcements. Non-GAAP means that the numbers were calculated in a way that does not conform to GAAP. You may also find non-GAAP financial measures in the 10-K. Companies are permitted to present non-GAAP measures, but they must clearly show how these numbers differ from the most comparable GAAP measures. As an investor, it is up to you to decide how much weight to place on non-GAAP measures.

Non-GAAP Earnings

These earnings often exclude revenues, expenses, gains, or losses that are required under GAAP. A common example would be excluding any losses that are unusual or are unlikely to occur in future periods. For example, companies might exclude losses due to earthquakes or other natural disasters, along with losses related to shut downs because of COVID-19. Non-GAAP earnings rarely include revenues, expenses, gains, or losses that are not allowed under GAAP. An example would be recognizing a gain that cannot be recorded in GAAP earnings until the following year.

Blizzard Activision's adjustments all exclude expenses that are required under GAAP. The earnings announcement includes a section explaining the difference between GAAP EPS and non-GAAP EPS. These differences occur because Blizzard Activision excludes some expenses related to employee stock options and the amortization of intangible assets. Excluding expenses increases reported earnings and EPS.

Activision Blizzards Quarter 4 and Full Year 2019 Earnings Announcement

Feb 6, 2020

Better-Than-Expected Q4 Results

SANTA MONICA, Calif.–(BUSINESS WIRE)–Feb. 6, 2020– Activision Blizzard, Inc. (Nasdaq: ATVI) today announced fourth-quarter and full year 2019 results.

"Our fourth quarter results exceeded our prior outlook for both revenue and earnings per share," said Bobby Kotick, Chief Executive Officer of Activision Blizzard. "Our recent Call of Duty® success illustrates the scale of our growth potential, as we expanded the community to more players in more countries on more platforms than ever before. With our strong content pipeline across our franchises and momentum in mobile, esports, and advertising, we look forward to continuing to delight our players, fans and stakeholders in 2020 and beyond."

Financial Metrics

(in millions, except EPS)	Q4			CY	
	2019	Prior Outlook*	2018	2019	2018
GAAP Net Revenues	$1,986	$1,812	$2,381	$6,489	$7,500
Impact of GAAP deferrals	*$722*	*$834*	*$454*	*($101)*	*($238)*
GAAP EPS	$0.68	$0.29	$0.89	$1.95	$2.40
Non-GAAP EPS	$0.62	$0.43	$0.90	$2.31	$2.72
Impact of GAAP deferrals	*$0.61*	*$0.72*	*$0.39*	*($0.06)*	*($0.12)*

* Prior outlook was provided by the company on November 7, 2019 in its earnings release.

For the year ended December 31, 2019, Activision Blizzard's net revenues presented in accordance with GAAP were $6.49 billion, as compared with $7.50 billion for 2018. GAAP net revenues from digital channels were $4.93 billion. GAAP operating margin was 25%. GAAP earnings per diluted share were $1.95, as compared with $2.40 for 2018. On a non-GAAP basis, Activision Blizzard's operating margin was 33% and earnings per diluted share were $2.31, as compared with $2.72 for 2018.

For the quarter ended December 31, 2019, Activision Blizzard's net revenues presented in accordance with GAAP were $1.99 billion, as compared with $2.38 billion for the fourth quarter of 2018. GAAP net revenues from digital channels were $1.44 billion. GAAP operating margin was 23%. GAAP earnings per diluted share were $0.68, as compared with $0.89 for the fourth quarter of 2018. On a non-GAAP basis, Activision Blizzard's operating margin was 30% and earnings per diluted share were $0.62, as compared with $0.90 for the fourth quarter of 2018.

Activision Blizzard generated $1.83 billion in operating cash flow for the year ended December 31, 2019, as compared with $1.79 billion for 2018. For the quarter, operating cash flow was $918 million, as compared with $999 million for the fourth quarter of 2018.

Please refer to the tables at the back of this press release for a reconciliation of the company's GAAP and non-GAAP results.

Source: U.S. Securities and Exchange Commission

Activision Blizzard is not alone in reporting non-GAAP earnings. In fact, 97% of companies in the S&P 500 reported non-GAAP measures of firm performance in 2017.[1] Why do companies report these non-GAAP numbers? The accounting firm Deloitte LLP provides several reasons. First, for some companies, management bonuses are calculated using non-GAAP numbers. Second, banks and other lenders might evaluate performance using non-GAAP numbers. Finally, in some cases, non-GAAP measures can provide a more accurate indication of company value.[2] Because the majority of non-GAAP adjustments increase reported earnings, it's important that financial statement users understand how these numbers are calculated.

Activision Blizzard's 2019 earnings announcement, which includes a discussion of non-GAAP earnings, can be downloaded from https://investor.activision.com/static-files/cefd71d2-d21f-4976-80ae-d8e8bacaff8d.

Non-GAAP Financial Measures: As a supplement to our financial measures presented in accordance with U.S. Generally Accepted Accounting Principles ("GAAP"), Activision Blizzard presents certain non-GAAP measures of financial performance. These non-GAAP financial measures are not intended to be considered in isolation from, as a substitute for, or as more important than, the financial information prepared and presented in accordance with GAAP. In addition, these non-GAAP measures have limitations in that they do not reflect all of the items associated with the company's results of operations as determined in accordance with GAAP.

Activision Blizzard provides net income (loss), earnings (loss) per share, and operating margin data and guidance both including (in accordance with GAAP) and excluding (non-GAAP) certain items. When relevant, the company also provides constant FX information to provide a framework for assessing how our underlying businesses performed excluding the effect of foreign currency rate fluctuations. In addition, Activision Blizzard provides EBITDA (defined as GAAP net income (loss) before interest (income) expense, income taxes, depreciation, and amortization) and adjusted EBITDA (defined as non-GAAP operating margin (see non-GAAP financial measure below) before depreciation). The non-GAAP financial measures exclude the following items, as applicable in any given reporting period and our outlook:

- expenses related to share-based compensation;

- the amortization of intangibles from purchase price accounting;

- fees and other expenses related to acquisitions, including related debt financings, and refinancing of long-term debt, including penalties and the write off of unamortized discount and deferred financing costs;

- restructuring and related charges;

- other non-cash charges from reclassification of certain cumulative translation adjustments into earnings as required by GAAP;

- the income tax adjustments associated with any of the above items (tax impact on non-GAAP pre-tax income is calculated under the same accounting principles applied to the GAAP pre-tax income under ASC 740, which employs an annual effective tax rate method to the results); and

- significant discrete tax-related items, including amounts related to changes in tax laws (including the Tax Cuts and Jobs Act enacted in December 2017), amounts related to the potential or final resolution of tax positions, and other unusual or unique tax-related items and activities.

In the future, Activision Blizzard may also consider whether other items should also be excluded in calculating the non-GAAP financial measures used by the company. Management believes that the presentation of these non-GAAP financial measures provides investors with additional useful information to measure Activision Blizzard's financial and operating performance. In particular, the measures facilitate comparison of operating performance between periods and help investors to better understand the operating results of Activision Blizzard by excluding certain items that may not be indicative of the company's core business, operating results, or future outlook. Additionally, we consider quantitative and qualitative factors in assessing whether to adjust for the impact of items that may be significant or that could affect an understanding of our ongoing financial and business performance or trends. Internally, management uses these non-GAAP financial measures, along with others, in assessing the company's operating results, and measuring compliance with the requirements of the company's debt financing agreements, as well as in planning and forecasting.

Source: U.S. Securities and Exchange Commission

---

[1]   https://blog.auditanalytics.com/long-term-trends-in-non-gaap-disclosures-a-three-year-overview/
[2]   https://www2.deloitte.com/us/en/pages/audit/articles/a-roadmap-to-non-gaap-financial-measures.html

Q 1s-1

Required:

Match each of the following descriptions with their location in the annual report.

Description		Location in the Annual Report
1. An integral part of the financial statements that helps to fulfill the accountant's responsibility for full disclosure of all relevant information	a.	Notes to the financial statements
	b.	Management's discussion and analysis (MD&A)
2. An opinion as to whether the financial statements fairly present the company's financial position and results of operations	c.	Independent auditor's report
	d.	Financial statements
3. The costs incurred to generate revenues		
4. A discussion and explanation of various items reported in the financial statements		
5. How the shareholders' equity account changed from the start to the end of the year		
6. Clarification or expansion upon the information presented in the financial statements		
7. The amounts of goodwill and other intangible assets owned by the company		
8. Details about how the amount of cash the company held changed during the year		

Solutions:

1. a. Notes to the financial statements
2. c. Independent auditor's report
3. d. Financial statements (income statement)
4. b. Management's discussion and analysis (MD&A)
5. d. Financial statements (statement of changes in shareholders' equity)
6. a. Notes to the financial statements
7. d. Financial statements (balance sheet)
8. d. Financial statements (statement of cash flows)

Q 1s-2

Wang Company's annual report includes the following items: financial statements, notes to the financial statements, management's discussion and analysis, and an independent auditor's report.

Required:

For each of the following items, where would you most likely find the information in the annual report?

1. A description of the risks associated with operating the company in an international market
2. Detailed information about the company's outstanding debt, including the interest rate and the maturity date
3. A description of the accounting methods used by the company
4. The total resources and claims to the resources of the company
5. A discussion of the sales trends
6. The amount of dividends paid to common stockholders

7. An opinion as to whether the financial statements are a fair presentation of the company's financial position and results of operations
8. The cost of operating the company over a period of time

Solutions:

1. Management's discussion and analysis
2. Notes to the financial statements
3. Notes to the financial statements
4. Financial statements (balance sheet)
5. Management's discussion and analysis
6. Financial statements (retained earnings statement)
7. Independent auditor's report
8. Financial statements (income statement)

MULTIPLE-CHOICE QUESTIONS

MC 1s-1 Who among the following uses financial statement data to make decisions?

a. Customers

b. Investors

c. Suppliers

d. All of these

MC 1s-2 Which section of the Form 10-K includes an analysis of the company's financial condition and performance?

a. Item 4—Submission of Matters to Vote
b. Item 5—Market for Common Stock
c. Item 6—Selected Financial Data
d. Item 7—Management's Discussion and Analysis

MC 1s-3 Corporations are required to disclose earnings per share on which of the following statements?

a. Statement of cash flows

b. Balance sheet

c. Income statement

d. All of these

MC 1s-4 A company's management is most likely to describe how earnings compare with expected earnings in which of the following?

a. Statement of cash flows

b. An earnings announcement

c. Income statement

d. All of these

MC 1s-5 Details about a company's stock-based compensation and the cost of leasing equipment are most likely to be found in which of the following?

a. Independent auditor's report

b. Earnings announcement

c. Notes to the financial statements

d. All of these

MC 1s-6 Cash that the company received from issuing debt would be reported on which of the following?

a. Statement of cash flows, under cash from financing
b. Income statement
c. Balance sheet
d. Statement of cash flows, under cash from operations

MC 1s-7 Which section of the Form 10-K provides readers with a basic understanding of the company's operations?

a. Item 1—Business

b. Item 2—Properties

c. Item 3—Legal Proceedings

d. Item 9A—Controls and Procedures

Solutions:

1. d
2. d
3. c
4. b
5. c
6. a
7. a

2

The Accounting Information System

After studying Chapter 2, you should be able to:

1 Describe the qualitative characteristics, assumptions, and principles that underlie accounting.

2 Explain the relationships among economic events, transactions, and the expanded accounting equation.

3 Analyze the effect of business transactions on the accounting equation.

4 Determine how debits and credits are used in the double-entry accounting system.

5 Prepare journal entries for transactions.

6 Explain why transactions are posted to the general ledger.

7 Prepare a trial balance and explain its purpose.

Angela Papuga/Getty Images Entertainment/Getty Images

EXPERIENCE FINANCIAL ACCOUNTING

with The Walt Disney Company

Tracing its roots to a cartoon studio in California, **The Walt Disney Company** has become one of the largest and most diversified media and entertainment companies in the world with goods and services that touch our lives every day. In 2019, Disney earned $69.57 billion in revenue, with the majority ($60.542 billion) coming from services and the remainder ($9.028 billion) from the sale of products. To better manage its business and report more useful information to users, Disney divides its operations into four business segments:

- Parks and Resorts—includes Disney's resorts and theme parks in Florida and California; experiences such as Disney Cruise Line, Adventures by Disney, and Disney Vacation Club; and the sale of licensed merchandise.
- Media Networks—operates the ABC television network as well as cable channels such as ESPN, Disney, Freeform, FX, and National Geographic. This segment also includes Disney's investments in other media businesses such as A+E Television Networks, which operates the A&E, HISTORY, and Lifetime cable channels.
- Studio Entertainment—produces live-action and animated motion pictures distributed under the Walt Disney Pictures, 20th Century Fox, Marvel, Lucasfilm, and Pixar banners, as well as musical recordings and live stage plays.
- Direct-to-Consumer and International—consists of streaming-based subscription services (Disney+, ESPN+, and Hulu) and international television networks and channels.

Exhibit 2.1 shows the year-over-year revenue growth of these four segments.

While Disney attributes a portion of its increased revenue to growth in its legacy operations (e.g., higher spending at theme parks and increased sales of its merchandise), the majority of the revenue growth is due to Disney's acquisition of 21st Century Fox and Hulu.

Companies like Disney rely on comprehensive accounting systems to capture, record, and report their various business activities. While the type of system depends on many factors such as the company's size and the volume of transactions it processes, most companies will use computerized accounting systems to efficiently provide information that is needed by the users of its financial statements. While Disney invests heavily in its accounting system, it recognizes that no system is foolproof. Therefore, financial accounting systems should be based on several key principles, including rigorous oversight by management and dedication to a system of internal controls that are designed to ensure the accuracy and reliability of the accounting records. With such a major emphasis on its accounting system, users of Disney's financial statements can feel confident that its business activities are recorded and reported properly.

EXHIBIT 2.1 ▸ **Year-Over-Year Revenue Growth**

Revenue by Business Segment
(amounts in millions)

OBJECTIVE

Describe the qualitative characteristics, assumptions, and principles that underlie accounting.

FUNDAMENTAL ACCOUNTING CONCEPTS

In the previous chapter, we described the typical business activities in which companies engage and how accounting systems report these activities through the financial statements. It's also important to understand the underlying concepts behind accounting systems. This chapter will discuss those concepts as well as the procedures that companies use to record information about business activities and how this information ultimately is transformed into financial statements. That is, you will see where the numbers on the financial statements actually come from. An understanding of these procedures is essential if you are to be an effective user of financial statements. As you review the financial statements, you are assessing a company's performance, cash flows, and financial position. To make those assessments, you need to be able to infer the actions of a company from what you see in the financial statements. That inference depends on your understanding of how companies transform the results of their activities into financial statements.

These transforming procedures are called the **accounting cycle**. The accounting cycle is an orderly process that is based on a series of steps and conventions. If the financial statements are to present fairly the effects of the company's activities, proper operation of the accounting cycle is essential. For example, if **Disney** failed to properly apply accounting procedures, it is likely that many of its business activities would be improperly recorded (if they were even recorded at all) and its financial statements would be seriously misstated.

In this chapter, we will begin the discussion of the accounting cycle and how the completion of each step of the accounting cycle moves the accounting system toward its end product—the financial statements. We will address the following questions:

- What concepts and assumptions underlie accounting information?
- How do companies record business activities?
- What procedures are involved in transforming information about business activities into financial statements?
- How do business activities affect the financial statements?

THE CONCEPTUAL FRAMEWORK

Generally accepted accounting principles (GAAP) rest on a conceptual framework of accounting. This framework flows logically from the fundamental objective of financial reporting: to provide information that is useful in making investment and credit decisions. The conceptual framework is designed to support the development of a consistent set of accounting standards and provide a consistent body of thought for financial reporting. An understanding of the conceptual framework should help you in understanding complex accounting standards by providing a logical structure to financial accounting; in other words, the concepts help to explain "why" accountants adopt certain practices. Exhibit 2.2 summarizes the characteristics of useful information as well as the underlying assumptions and principles that make up the conceptual framework and serve as the foundation of GAAP.

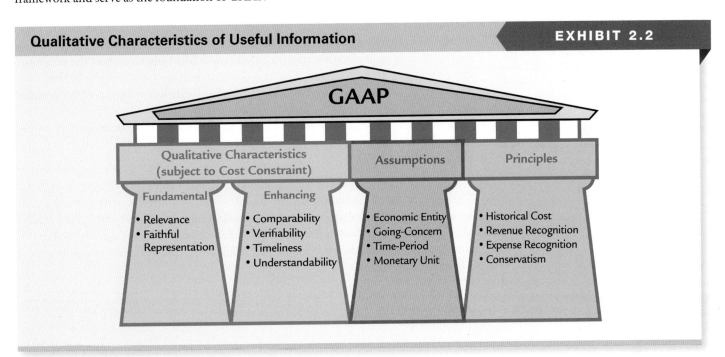

Qualitative Characteristics of Useful Information   **EXHIBIT 2.2**

QUALITATIVE CHARACTERISTICS OF USEFUL INFORMATION

Given the overall objective of providing useful information, the FASB has identified two fundamental characteristics that useful information should possess—relevance and faithful representation. The application of these criteria determines which economic events should be shown in the financial statements and how best to record these events.

- **Relevance:** Information is relevant if it is capable of making a difference in a business decision by helping users predict future events (*predictive value*) or providing feedback about prior expectations (*confirmatory value*). If the omission or misstatement of information could influence a decision, the information is said to be *material*. Therefore, materiality is also an aspect of relevance.
- **Faithful representation:** Accounting information should be a faithful representation of the real-world economic event that it is intending to portray. Faithfully represented information should be *complete* (includes all necessary information for the user to understand the economic event), *neutral* (unbiased), and *free from error* (as accurate as possible).

In applying these fundamental characteristics, the usual process is to identify the most relevant information and then determine if it can be faithfully represented. If so, the fundamental qualitative characteristics have been satisfied. If not, the process should be repeated with the next most relevant type of information.

In addition to the fundamental characteristics, four enhancing characteristics—comparability, verifiability, timeliness, and understandability—have been identified. These enhancing characteristics are considered complementary to the fundamental characteristics, and their presence should help determine the degree of the information's usefulness.

- **Comparability:** Comparable information allows external users to identify similarities and differences between two or more items. Information is useful when it can be compared with similar information about other companies or with similar information about the same company for a different time period. Included within comparability is consistency. **Consistency** can be achieved when a company applies the same accounting principles for the same items over time. Consistency can also be achieved when multiple companies use the same accounting principles in a single time period. Comparability should be viewed as the goal while consistency helps to achieve that goal.
- **Verifiability:** Information is verifiable when independent parties can agree on the measurement of the activity. When multiple independent observers can reach a general consensus, there is an implication that the information faithfully represents the economic event being measured.
- **Timeliness:** Information is timely if it is available to users before it loses its ability to influence decisions.
- **Understandability:** If users who have a reasonable knowledge of accounting and business can, with reasonable study effort, comprehend the meaning of the information, it is considered understandable.

Enhancing characteristics should be maximized to the extent possible.

These qualitative characteristics are bound by one pervasive constraint—the **cost constraint**. The cost constraint states that the benefit received from accounting information should be greater than the cost of providing that information. If the cost exceeds the benefit, the information is not considered useful. Exhibit 2.3 illustrates the qualitative characteristics of useful financial information.

EXHIBIT 2.3   **Qualitative Characteristics of Accounting Information**

Trade-offs are often necessary in evaluating these criteria. For example, the most relevant information may not be able to be faithfully represented. Similarly, changing economic situations may require a change in the accounting principle used. Such a change may decrease the comparability of the information presented. In these situations, the accountant must exercise judgment in determining the accounting principles that would produce the most useful information for the decision-maker. In all situations, accountants should follow a **full disclosure** policy. That is, any information that would make a difference to financial statement users should be revealed.

ASSUMPTIONS

The following four basic assumptions underlie accounting:

- **Economic entity assumption:** Under this assumption, each company is accounted for separately from its owners. For example, **Disney** does not record the personal transactions of Robert Iger, its former CEO and largest individual shareholder, in its financial statements.
- **Going-concern assumption:** This assumption states that a company will continue to operate long enough to carry out its existing commitments. Without this assumption, many of our accounting procedures could not be followed. This assumption is essential for valuing assets (future benefits) and liabilities (future obligations).
- **Time-period assumption:** This assumption allows the life of a company to be divided into artificial time periods so that net income can be measured for a specific period of time (e.g., monthly, quarterly, or annually). Without this assumption, a company's income could only be reported at the end of its life.
- **Monetary unit assumption:** This assumption requires that a company account for and report its financial results in monetary terms (such as U.S. dollar, euro, or Japanese yen). This assumption implies that certain nonmonetary items (such as brand loyalty or customer satisfaction) are not reported in a company's financial statements since they can't be measured in monetary terms.

PRINCIPLES

Principles are general approaches that are used in the measurement and recording of business activities. The four basic principles of accounting are: the historical cost principle, the revenue recognition principle, the expense recognition principle, and the conservatism principle.

- **Historical cost principle:** This principle requires that the activities of a company are initially measured at their cost—the exchange price at the time the activity occurs. For example, when **Disney** buys equipment used at one of its theme parks, it initially records the equipment at the cost paid to acquire it. Accountants use historical cost because it provides an objective and verifiable measure of the activity. However, the historical cost principle has been criticized because, after the date of acquisition, it does not reflect changes in market value. The Financial Accounting Standards Board (FASB), aware of this criticism, has been developing standards that use market values to measure certain assets and liabilities (such as investments in marketable securities) after the date of acquisition.
- **Revenue recognition principle:** This principle is used to determine when revenue is recorded and reported. Under this principle, revenue is to be recognized or recorded in the period in which a company satisfies its performance obligation or promise within a contract. Generally, this occurs when services are performed or goods are delivered to customers.
- **Expense recognition principle:** This principle requires that an expense be recorded and reported in the same period as the revenue that it helped generate. It is often referred to as the matching principle. This may or may not be in the same period that cash is paid. Together, the application of the revenue and expense recognition principles determine a company's net income. These two principles will be discussed in more detail in Chapter 3.
- **Conservatism principle:** This principle states that accountants should not overstate assets and income when they prepare financial statements. The idea behind this principle is that conservatism is a prudent reaction to uncertainty and offsets management's natural

 Next Level

Companies assume they are going concerns. Wouldn't the valuation of a company's assets be more relevant if this assumption were relaxed and the net assets valued at their current selling costs?

ANSWER:
Current selling costs are only relevant if the company intends to sell the assets in the near term. However, many assets (such as machinery or buildings) are used over long periods of time, and in these situations, the use of current selling prices would be of little value to financial statement users. In addition, the cost of obtaining current values for these assets would greatly outweigh the benefits received.

optimism about the company's future prospects. However, conservatism should not lead to biased financial information nor should it ever be used to justify the deliberate understatement of assets or income.

The application of these qualitative characteristics, assumptions, and principles is illustrated in EXAMPLE 2.1 .

EXAMPLE 2.1   APPLYLING THE CONCEPTUAL FRAMEWORK

Mario is faced with the following questions as he prepares the financial statements of DK Company:

1. Should the purchase of inventory be valued at what DK paid to acquire the inventory or at its estimated selling price?

2. Should information be provided that financial statement users might find helpful in predicting DK's future income?

3. Faced with a choice between two equally acceptable estimates, should Mario choose the one that results in the higher or the lower amount for net income?

4. Although DK is profitable, should the financial statements be prepared under the assumption that DK will go bankrupt?

5. Should DK's inventory be reported in terms of the number of units on hand or the dollar value of those units?

6. Should equipment leased on a long-term basis be reported as an asset (the economic substance of the transaction) or should it be reported as a rental (the form of the transaction)?

7. Should DK recognize revenue from the sale of its products when the sale is made or when the cash is received?

8. Should DK record the purchase of a vacation home by one of its shareholders?

9. Should DK report income annually to its shareholders or should it wait until all transactions are complete?

10. Should DK report salary expense in the period that the employees actually worked or when the employees are paid?

Required:
Which qualitative characteristic, assumption, or principle should Mario use in resolving the situation?

Solution:

1. Historical cost: The activities of a company (such as purchase of inventory) should be initially measured at the exchange price at the time the activity occurs.

2. Relevance: Material information that has predictive or confirmatory value should be provided.

3. Conservatism: When faced with a choice, accountants should avoid overstating assets or income.

4. Going-concern: In the absence of information to the contrary, it should be assumed that a company will continue to operate indefinitely.

5. Monetary unit: A company should account for and report its financial results in monetary terms.

6. Faithful representation: Information should portray the economic event that it is intending to portray completely, accurately, and without bias.

7. Revenue recognition: Revenue should be recognized when a company satisfies its performance obligation to a customer.

8. Economic entity: A company's transactions should be accounted for separately from its owners.

9. Time-period: The life of a company can be divided into artificial time periods so that income can be measured and reported periodically to interested parties.

10. Expense recognition: Expenses should be recorded and reported in the same period as the revenue it helped generate.

Given this conceptual foundation, we will now turn our attention to the process of recording information about business activities in the accounting system.

MEASURING BUSINESS ACTIVITIES: THE ACCOUNTING CYCLE

OBJECTIVE 2

Explain the relationships among economic events, transactions, and the expanded accounting equation.

The sequence of procedures used by companies to transform the effects of business activities into financial statements is called the accounting cycle. The accounting cycle is shown in Exhibit 2.4.

The Accounting Cycle

EXHIBIT 2.4

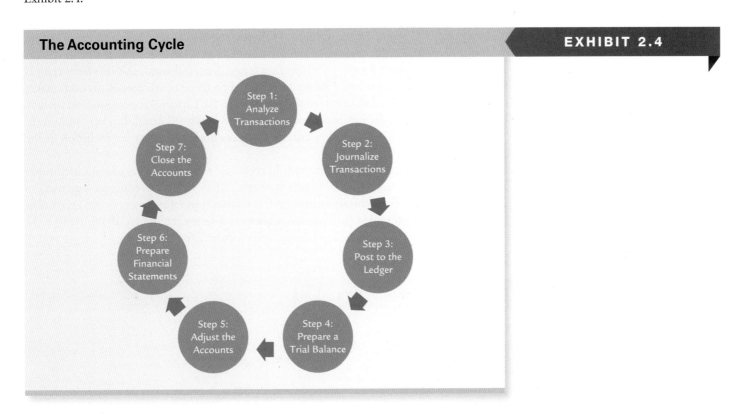

The steps in the accounting cycle are performed each period and then repeated. Steps 1 through 4 are performed regularly each period as business activities occur. We will discuss these four steps in this chapter. Steps 5 through 7 are performed at the end of a period and are discussed in Chapter 3.

ECONOMIC EVENTS

As we discussed in Chapter 1, a company engages in numerous activities that can be categorized as financing, investing, or operating activities. Each of these activities consists of different **events** that affect the company. Some of these events are *external* and result from exchanges between the company and another entity outside of the company. For example, when **Disney** issues common stock to investors, or sells a theme park ticket to a customer, it is engaging in an exchange with another entity. Other events are *internal* and result from the company's own actions. When Disney uses equipment in its operations, no other entity is involved; however, the event still has an impact on the company.

Accounting measures the effects of events that influence a company and incorporates these events into the accounting system which, ultimately, produces the financial statements. However, not every event that affects a company is recorded in the accounting records. In order for an event to be recorded, or recognized, in the accounting system, the items making up the event must:

- impact a financial statement element (asset, liability, stockholders' equity, revenue, expense, gain, or loss)
- faithfully represent the event

The first requirement usually is met when at least one party to a contract performs its responsibility according to the contract. For example, assume a buyer and seller agree upon the delivery of an asset and sign a contract. The signing of the contract usually is not recorded in the accounting system because neither party has performed its responsibility. Instead, recognition typically will occur once the buyer receives the asset or pays the seller, whichever comes first.

Even if the event impacts a financial statement element, a faithful representation of the event must be possible if it is to be recorded. An increase in travel or energy costs may adversely affect **Disney**'s future business. However, the effects of this cost increase cannot be faithfully represented, and the event will not be immediately recognized in the financial statements. Providing a measurement that is complete, unbiased, and free from error is important in accounting to avoid misleading users of financial statements. A decision-maker would find it extremely difficult, if not impossible, to use financial statements that include amounts that failed to faithfully represent what has actually occurred. It is very important to pay attention to the recognition criteria as you consider an event for inclusion in the accounting system.

An accounting transaction results from an economic event that causes one of the elements of the financial statements (assets, liabilities, stockholders' equity, revenues, or expenses) to change and that can be faithfully represented. A **transaction** refers to any event, external or internal, that is recognized in the financial statements. The process of identifying events to be recorded in the financial statements is illustrated in Exhibit 2.5.

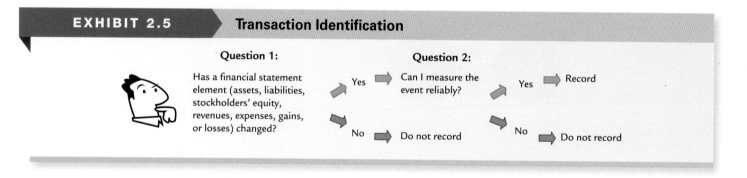

EXHIBIT 2.5   **Transaction Identification**

Question 1:

Has a financial statement element (assets, liabilities, stockholders' equity, revenues, expenses, gains, or losses) changed?

Yes → **Question 2:** Can I measure the event reliably?

No → Do not record

Yes → Record

No → Do not record

THE EXPANDED ACCOUNTING EQUATION

Because accounting is concerned with the measurement of transactions and their effect on the financial statements, a starting point in the measurement and recording process is the fundamental accounting equation:

$$\text{Assets} = \text{Liabilities} + \text{Stockholders' Equity}$$

Recall from Chapter 1 that:

- The two sides of the accounting equation must always be equal or "in balance" as a company conducts its business. Accounting systems record these business activities in a way that maintains this equality. As a consequence, every transaction has a two-part, or double-entry, effect on the equation.
- The balance sheet and the income statement are related through retained earnings. Specifically, net income (revenues minus expenses) increases retained earnings. Given this relationship, the fundamental accounting equation can be rewritten to show the elements that make up stockholders' equity.

With the expanded accounting equation shown in Exhibit 2.6, we are now ready to analyze how transactions affect a company's financial statements.

The Expanded Accounting Equation **EXHIBIT 2.6**

Assets = Liabilities + Stockholders' Equity

Assets = Liabilities + Contributed Capital + Retained Earnings

Assets = Liabilities + Contributed Capital + Beginning Retained Earnings + Revenues − Expenses − Dividends Declared

 YOUDECIDE **Recognition of Economic Events**

As you are analyzing the most recent financial statements of Big Oil (B&O) Company, you question if the company properly recorded an economic event. You know that B&O owns and operates several off-shore oil drilling platforms in the Gulf of Mexico. You also recall from news reports that a hurricane severely damaged two of the platforms, leading to a significant loss in revenue while the platforms were inactive. While you see evidence in the financial statements of the damage and repair to the platforms, you cannot find any evidence of the lost revenue in the financial statements.

Does the loss in revenue from the damaged oil platforms qualify for recognition in the financial statements?

To be recognized in the financial statements, the event must impact a financial statement element and be faithfully represented. While B&O may have been able to measure the loss in revenue, no financial statement element has been affected. While you may argue that this event affected revenue, revenue is an increase in assets resulting from the sale of products. Because the lost sales did not result in an inflow of assets, it is not considered revenue. In addition, expenses are defined as the cost of resources used to earn revenues. The lost revenue does not represent the use of resources and is therefore not an expense. Therefore, the lost revenue cannot be recognized in the financial statements.

Recognition of events in the financial statements requires analysis of whether the event impacted a financial statement element and can be faithfully represented.

STEP 1: ANALYZE TRANSACTIONS

OBJECTIVE 3

Analyze the effect of business transactions on the accounting equation.

Transaction analysis is the process of determining the economic effects of a transaction on the elements of the accounting equation. Transaction analysis usually begins with the gathering of *source documents* that describe business activities. Source documents can be internally or externally prepared and include items such as purchase orders, cash register tapes, and invoices that describe the transaction and monetary amounts involved. These documents are the beginning of a "trail" of evidence that a transaction was processed by the accounting system.

After gathering the source documents, accountants must analyze these business activities to determine which transactions meet the criteria for recognition in the accounting records. Once it is determined that a transaction should be recorded in the accounting system, the transaction must be analyzed to determine how it will affect the accounting equation. In performing transaction analysis, it is important to remember that the accounting equation must always remain in balance. Therefore, each transaction will have at least two effects on the accounting equation.

In summary, transaction analysis involves the following three steps:

Step 1. Write down the accounting equation (use either the basic or an expanded accounting equation).

Step 2. Identify the financial statement elements that are affected by the transaction.

Step 3. Determine whether the elements increased or decreased.

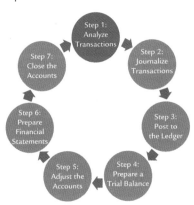

EXAMPLE 2.2 illustrates the basic process of transaction analysis.

EXAMPLE 2.2   PERFORMING TRANSACTION ANALYSIS

Luigi Inc. purchases a $3,000 computer from WorstBuy Electronics on credit, with payment due in 60 days.

Required:
Determine the effect of the transaction on the elements on the accounting equation.

Solution:
A computer is an economic resource, or asset, that will be used by Luigi in its business. The purchase of the computer increased assets and also created an obligation, or liability, for Luigi. Therefore, the effect of the transaction on the accounting equation is as follows:

Assets	=	Liabilities	+	Stockholders' Equity	
				Contributed Capital	+ Retained Earnings
+$3,000		+$3,000			

Note that the transaction analysis in Example 2.2 conformed to the two underlying principles of transaction analysis:

- There was a dual effect on the accounting equation.
- The accounting equation remained in balance after the transaction.

All transactions can be analyzed using a similar process.

To provide a further illustration of the effect of transactions on the accounting equation, consider the case of HiTech Communications Inc. HiTech is a newly formed corporation that operates an advertising agency that specializes in promoting computer-related products in the Cincinnati area. We show the effects of 13 transactions on HiTech's financial position during March, its first month of operations.

TRANSACTION 1: ISSUING COMMON STOCK

On March 1, HiTech sold 1,000 shares of common stock to several investors for cash of $12,000. The effect of this transaction on the accounting equation is:

Assets	=	Liabilities	+	Stockholders' Equity	
				Contributed Capital	+ Retained Earnings
+$12,000				+$12,000	

The sale of stock increases assets, specifically cash, and also increases stockholders' equity (contributed capital or common stock). Notice that there is a dual effect, and although both assets and equity change, the equality of the equation is maintained. The issuance of stock would be considered a financing activity.

TRANSACTION 2: BORROWING CASH

On March 2, HiTech raised additional funds by borrowing $3,000 from First Third Bank of Cincinnati. HiTech promised to pay the amount borrowed plus 8% interest to First Third Bank in 1 year. The financial effect of this transaction is:

Assets	=	Liabilities	+	Stockholders' Equity	
				Contributed Capital	+ Retained Earnings
+$3,000		+$3,000			

! Next Level

Why must the accounting equation always remain in balance?

ANSWER:
The accounting equation captures the business activities of a company. The left side of the accounting equation describes the economic resources, or assets, that the company has acquired. The right side of the equation describes the claims on these assets—either from creditors (liabilities) or from stockholders (stockholders' equity). Because all resources belong to either the creditors or the stockholders, the equation must balance.

This borrowing has two effects: the asset cash is increased and a liability is created. HiTech has an obligation to repay the cash borrowed according to the terms of the borrowing. Such a liability is called a note payable. Because this transaction is concerned with obtaining funds to begin and operate a business, it is classified as a financing activity.

TRANSACTION 3: PURCHASE OF EQUIPMENT FOR CASH

On March 3, HiTech purchased office equipment (such as computer equipment) from Micro-Center Inc. for $4,500 in cash. The effect of this transaction on the accounting equation is:

Assets	=	Liabilities	+	Stockholders' Equity	
				Contributed Capital	+	Retained Earnings
+$4,500					
−$4,500					

There is a reduction in cash (an asset) as it is spent and a corresponding increase in another asset, equipment. The purchased equipment is an asset because HiTech will use it to generate future revenue. Notice that this transaction merely converts one asset (cash) into another (equipment). Total assets remain unchanged and the accounting equation remains in balance. Because Transaction 3 is concerned with buying long-term assets that enable HiTech to operate, it is considered an investing activity.

TRANSACTION 4: PURCHASING INSURANCE

On March 4, HiTech purchased a 6-month insurance policy for $1,200 cash. The effect of this transaction on the accounting equation is:

Assets	=	Liabilities	+	Stockholders' Equity	
				Contributed Capital	+	Retained Earnings
+$1,200					
−$1,200					

There is a reduction in cash (an asset) as it is spent and a corresponding increase in another asset, prepaid insurance. The purchased insurance is an asset because the insurance will benefit future accounting periods. This type of asset is often referred to as a prepaid asset. Notice that, like Transaction 3, this transaction converts one asset (cash) into another (prepaid insurance). Total assets remain unchanged and the accounting equation remains in balance. Because Transaction 4 is concerned with the operations of the company, it is classified as an operating activity.

TRANSACTION 5: PURCHASE OF SUPPLIES ON CREDIT

On March 6, HiTech purchased office supplies from Hamilton Office Supply for $6,500. Hamilton Office Supply agreed to accept full payment in 30 days. As a result of this transaction, HiTech received an asset (supplies) but also incurred a liability to pay for these supplies in 30 days. The financial effect of this transaction is:

Assets	=	Liabilities	+	Stockholders' Equity	
				Contributed Capital	+	Retained Earnings
+$6,500		+$6,500			

A transaction where goods are purchased on credit is often referred to as a purchase "on account" and the liability that is created is referred to as an account payable. Because Transaction 5 is concerned with the operations of the company, it is classified as an operating activity.

TRANSACTION 6: PROVIDING SERVICES FOR CASH

On March 10, HiTech provided advertising services to Miami Valley Products in exchange for $8,800 in cash. Recall that revenue is recognized when a company satisfies its performance obligation to its customers. As an advertising company, providing advertising services is HiTech's primary obligation to its customer, Miami Valley Products. Therefore, this transaction results in an increase in assets (cash) and an increase in revenue.

Assets	=	Liabilities	+	Stockholders' Equity	
				Contributed Capital	+ Retained Earnings
+$8,800					+$8,800

As shown in Exhibit 2.6, *revenues increase retained earnings.* The dual effects (the increase in assets and the increase in retained earnings) maintain the balance of the accounting equation. Because Transaction 6 is concerned with the operations of the company, it is classified as an operating activity.

TRANSACTION 7: PROVIDING SERVICES ON CREDIT

On March 15, HiTech provided advertising services to the *Cincinnati Times* for $3,300. HiTech agreed to accept full payment in 30 days. When a company performs services for which they will be paid at a later date, this is often referred to as a sale "on account." Instead of receiving cash, HiTech received a promise to pay from the *Cincinnati Times*. This right to collect amounts due from customers creates an asset called an account receivable. Similar to the cash sale in Transaction 6, the credit sale represents revenue for HiTech because it has satisfied its performance obligation to the *Cincinnati Times* by providing the advertising service. The financial effect of this transaction is:

Assets	=	Liabilities	+	Stockholders' Equity	
				Contributed Capital	+ Retained Earnings
+$3,300					+$3,300

Note that the revenue is recognized when the service is provided, not when the cash is actually received. Because Transaction 7 is concerned with the operations of the company, it is classified as an operating activity.

TRANSACTION 8: RECEIPT OF CASH IN ADVANCE

On March 19, HiTech received $9,000 from the *Metropolis News* for advertising services to be completed in the next 3 months. Similar to Transaction 6, HiTech received cash for services. However, due to the revenue recognition principle, HiTech cannot recognize revenue until it has performed the advertising service. Therefore, the receipt of cash creates a liability for HiTech for the work that is due in the future. The effect of this transaction on the accounting equation is:

Assets	=	Liabilities	+	Stockholders' Equity	
				Contributed Capital	+ Retained Earnings
+$9,000		+$9,000			

The liability that is created by the receipt of cash in advance of performing the revenue-generating activities is called an unearned revenue. Because Transaction 8 is concerned with the operations of the company, it is classified as an operating activity.

TRANSACTION 9: PAYMENT OF A LIABILITY

On March 23, HiTech pays $6,000 cash for the supplies previously purchased from Hamilton Office Supply on credit (Transaction 5). The payment results in a reduction of an asset (cash) and the settlement of HiTech's obligation (liability) to Hamilton Office Supply. The financial effect of this transaction is:

Assets	=	Liabilities	+	Stockholders' Equity	
				Contributed Capital +	Retained Earnings
−$6,000		−$6,000			

As a result of this cash payment, the liability "Accounts Payable" is reduced to $500 ($6,500 − $6,000). This means that HiTech still owes Hamilton Office Supply $500. Notice that the payment of cash did not result in an expense. The expense related to supplies will be recorded as supplies are used. Because Transaction 9 is concerned with the operations of the company, it is classified as an operating activity.

TRANSACTION 10: COLLECTION OF A RECEIVABLE

On March 25, HiTech collected $3,000 cash from the *Cincinnati Times* for services sold earlier on credit (Transaction 7). The collection of cash increases assets. In addition, the accounts receivable (an asset) from the *Cincinnati Times* is also reduced. The financial effect of this transaction is:

Assets	=	Liabilities	+	Stockholders' Equity	
				Contributed Capital +	Retained Earnings
+$3,000					
−$3,000					

As a result of this cash payment, the *Cincinnati Times* still owes HiTech $300. Notice that the cash collection did not result in the recognition of a revenue. The revenue was recognized as the service was performed (Transaction 7). Because Transaction 11 is concerned with the operations of the company, it is classified as an operating activity.

TRANSACTION 11: PAYMENT OF SALARIES

On March 26 (a Friday), HiTech paid weekly employee salaries of $1,800. Remember from Chapter 1 that an expense is the cost of an asset consumed in the operation of the business. Because an asset (cash) is consumed as part of HiTech's normal operations, salaries are an expense. As shown in Exhibit 2.6, *expenses decrease retained earnings.* The effect of this transaction on the accounting equation is:

Assets	=	Liabilities	+	Stockholders' Equity	
				Contributed Capital +	Retained Earnings
−$1,800					−$1,800

Consistent with the expense recognition principle, *expenses are recorded in the same period as the revenue that it helped generate.* Because Transaction 10 is concerned with the operations of the company, it is classified as an operating activity.

TRANSACTION 12: PAYMENT OF UTILITIES

On March 30, HiTech paid its utility bill of $5,200 for March. Because an asset (cash) is consumed by HiTech as part of the operations of the business, the cost of utilities used during the month is an expense. The effect of this transaction on the accounting equation is:

Assets	=	Liabilities	+	Stockholders' Equity	
				Contributed Capital	+	Retained Earnings
−$5,200					−$5,200

Similar to the payment of salaries, utility expense is recorded as a decrease in retained earnings in the same period that it helped to generate revenue. Because Transaction 12 is concerned with the operations of the company, it is classified as an operating activity.

TRANSACTION 13: PAYMENT OF A DIVIDEND

On March 31, HiTech declared and paid a cash dividend of $500 to its stockholders. Dividends are not an expense. Dividends are a distribution of net income and are recorded as a direct reduction of retained earnings when they are declared. The effect of this transaction on the accounting equation is:

Assets	=	Liabilities	+	Stockholders' Equity	
				Contributed Capital	+	Retained Earnings
−$500					−$500

The payment of a dividend is classified as a financing activity.

OVERVIEW OF TRANSACTIONS FOR HITECH COMMUNICATIONS INC.

Exhibit 2.7 summarizes HiTech's transactions in order to show their cumulative effect on the accounting equation. The transaction number is shown in the first column on the left. Revenue and expense items are identified on the right. Notice that this summary reinforces the two key principles discussed earlier:

- Each transaction has a dual effect on the elements of the accounting equation.
- The accounting equation always remains in balance—the total change in assets ($29,100) equals the change in liabilities plus stockholders' equity ($29,100).

Transaction analysis can be used to answer many important questions about a company and its activities. Using the information in Exhibit 2.7, we can answer the following questions:

- *What are the amounts of total assets, total liabilities, and total equity at the end of March?* At the end of March, HiTech has total assets of $29,100, total liabilities of $12,500, and total equity of $16,600 ($12,000 of contributed capital plus $4,600 of retained earnings). These amounts for assets, liabilities, and stockholders' equity at the end of March would be carried over as the beginning amounts for April.

Summary of Transactions for HiTech Communications Inc.

EXHIBIT 2.7

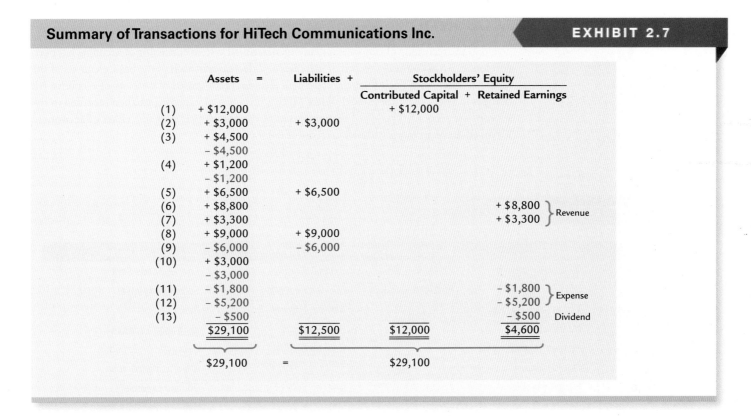

	Assets	=	Liabilities +	Stockholders' Equity	
				Contributed Capital +	Retained Earnings
(1)	+ $12,000			+ $12,000	
(2)	+ $3,000		+ $3,000		
(3)	+ $4,500				
	− $4,500				
(4)	+ $1,200				
	− $1,200				
(5)	+ $6,500		+ $6,500		
(6)	+ $8,800				+ $8,800 } Revenue
(7)	+ $3,300				+ $3,300
(8)	+ $9,000		+ $9,000		
(9)	− $6,000		− $6,000		
(10)	+ $3,000				
	− $3,000				
(11)	− $1,800				− $1,800 } Expense
(12)	− $5,200				− $5,200
(13)	− $500				− $500 Dividend
	$29,100		$12,500	$12,000	$4,600

$$\$29,100 \quad = \quad \$29,100$$

- *What is net income for the month?* Net income is $5,100, which represents the excess of revenues of $12,100 ($8,800 + $3,300) over expenses of $7,000 ($5,200 + $1,800). Notice that dividends are not included in income; instead they are included on the retained earnings statement.
- *How much cash was received during the month? How much was spent? How much cash does HiTech have at the end of the month?* During March, HiTech received a total of $35,800 in cash ($12,000 + $3,000 + $8,800 + $9,000 + $3,000) and spent a total of $19,200 ($4,500 + $1,200 + $6,000 + $1,800 + $5,200 + $500). At the end of the month, HiTech had cash on hand of $16,600 ($35,800 − $19,200).

The summary in Exhibit 2.7 can become quite cumbersome. For example, in order to determine the amount of cash that HiTech has at the end of the month, you may find it necessary to refer back to the actual transactions to determine which ones involved cash and which did not. In addition, what if an investor or creditor wanted to know not only net income but also the types of expenses that HiTech incurred? (For example, what was the dollar amount spent for salaries?) To answer these questions, more information is needed than the transaction summary provides. For a company like **Disney**, a spreadsheet such as the preceding one would prove inadequate to convey its financial information to investors and creditors. A better way to record and track information that is consistent with the preceding model is necessary. The solution is double-entry accounting.

DOUBLE-ENTRY ACCOUNTING

OBJECTIVE

Determine how debits and credits are used in the double-entry accounting system.

Double-entry accounting describes the system used by companies to record the effects of transactions on the accounting equation. The effects of transactions are recorded in accounts. Under double-entry accounting, each transaction affects at least two accounts. In this section, we will explore accounts and the process by which transactions get reflected in specific accounts.

ACCOUNTS

To aid in the recording of transactions, an organizational system consisting of accounts has been developed. An **account** is a record of increases and decreases in each of the basic elements of the financial statements. Each financial statement element is composed of a variety of accounts. All changes in assets, liabilities, stockholders' equity, revenues, or expenses are then recorded in the appropriate account. The list of accounts used by the company is termed a **chart of accounts**.[1] A typical list of accounts is shown in Exhibit 2.8.

EXHIBIT 2.8	Typical Accounts			
Assets	**Liabilities**	**Stockholders' Equity**	**Revenues and Gains**	**Expenses and Losses**
Cash	Accounts Payable	Common Stock	Sales Revenue	Cost of Goods Sold
Investments	Salaries Payable	Retained Earnings	Service Revenue	Salaries Expense
Accounts Receivable	Unearned Sales Revenue		Interest Income	Rent Expense
Inventory	Interest Payable		Rent Revenue	Insurance Expense
Land	Income Taxes Payable		Gain on Disposal of Property, Plant, & Equipment	Depreciation Expense
Buildings	Notes Payable			Advertising Expense
Equipment	Bonds Payable		Gain on Sale of Intangibles	Utilities Expense
Patent				Repairs & Maintenance Expense
Copyright				Property Taxes Expense
				Loss from Disposal of Property, Plant, & Equipment

Every company will have a different chart of accounts depending on the nature of its business activities. However, once a company selects which accounts will be used, all transactions must be recorded into these accounts. As the company engages in transactions, the transaction will either increase or decrease an account. The amount in an account at any time is called the *balance* of the account. For example, the purchase of equipment will increase the balance in the equipment account, whereas the disposal of equipment will decrease the balance of the equipment account. For financial reporting purposes, the balances of related accounts typically are combined and reported as a single amount, with amounts of individual accounts such as land, buildings, and machinery disclosed in the footnotes.

Although an account can be shown in a variety of ways, transactions are frequently analyzed using a **T-account**. The T-account gets its name because it resembles the capital letter T (see Exhibit 2.9). A T-account is a two-column record that consists of an account title and two sides divided by a vertical line—the left and the right side. The left side is referred to as the **debit** side and the right side is referred to as the **credit** side.

---

1 This textbook uses a simplified and standardized chart of accounts that can be found on the inside cover of the book and on page 128. Account titles for real company financial statements may vary. Common alternate account titles are introduced, as appropriate, when accounts are introduced.

Form of a T-Account

EXHIBIT 2.9

Title of Account

DEBIT | Debit (Left Side) | Credit (Right Side) | CREDIT

Note that the terms debit and credit simply refer to the left and the right side of an account. The left is always the debit side and the right is always the credit side. *Debit and credit do not represent increases or decreases.* (Increases or decreases to accounts are discussed in the next section.) Instead, debit and credit simply refer to *where* an entry is made in an account. The terms debit and credit will also be used to refer to the act of entering dollar amounts into an account. For example, entering an amount on the left side of an account will be called debiting the account. Entering an amount on the right side of an account is called crediting the account.

You may be tempted to associate the terms credit and debit with positive or negative events. For example, assume you returned an item that you purchased with a credit card to the local store and the store credited your card. This is generally viewed as a positive event since you now owe less money to the store. Or, if you receive a notice that your bank had debited your account to pay for service charges that you owe, this is viewed negatively because you now have less money in your account. Resist this temptation. In accounting, *debit means the left side of an account and credit means the right side of an account.*

DEBIT AND CREDIT PROCEDURES

Using the accounting equation, we can incorporate debits and credits in order to determine how balance sheet accounts increase or decrease. There are three steps in determining increases or decreases to a balance sheet account:

Step 1. Draw a T-account and label each side of the T-account as either debit (left side) or credit (right side).
Step 2. Determine the normal balance of an account. All accounts have a **normal balance**. While individual transactions will increase and decrease an account, it would be unusual for an account to have a nonnormal balance.
Step 3. Increases or decreases to an account are based on the normal balance of the account.

This procedure is shown in EXAMPLE 2.3 .

Next Level

On a bank statement, a credit to a person's account means the account has increased. Similarly, a debit means the account has decreased. Why don't credit and debit always mean "add" and "subtract"?

ANSWER:
From the bank's perspective, a person's account is a liability since the bank must pay cash on demand. Because liabilities have normal credit balances, a credit will increase the account and a debit will decrease the account. However, from an individual's perspective, cash is an asset which has a normal debit balance. Therefore, debits increase cash and credits decrease cash. It is critical to always look at the normal balance of an account before determining if a transaction increases or decreases an account.

EXAMPLE 2.3   DETERMINING INCREASES OR DECREASES TO A BALANCE SHEET ACCOUNT

The balance sheet is comprised of three fundamental accounts—assets, liabilities, and stockholders' equity. Stockholders' equity consists of contributed capital and retained earnings.

Required:
Determine how each of the five balance sheet accounts increases or decreases.

Solution:
- Because assets are located on the left side of the accounting equation, their normal balance is a debit. Therefore, debits will increase assets and credits will decrease assets.

- Because liabilities and stockholders' equity are on the right side of the accounting equation, their normal balance is a credit. Therefore, credits will increase liabilities and stockholders' equity while debits will decrease these accounts.

- As stockholders' equity accounts, both contributed capital and retained earnings have normal credit balances and are increased by credits and decreased by debits.

This is illustrated in the following T-accounts:

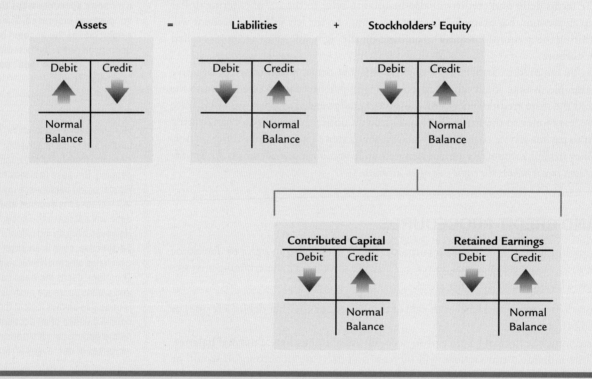

As we illustrated earlier in the chapter, every transaction will increase or decrease the elements of the accounting equation—assets, liabilities, and stockholders' equity. The direction of these increases and decreases must be such that the accounting equation stays in balance—the left side must equal the right side. In other words, *debits must equal credits*. This equality of debits and credits provides the foundation of double-entry accounting in which the two-sided effect of a transaction is recorded in the accounting system.

The same three-step procedure can be followed to determine increases or decreases in revenues, expenses, gains, losses, and dividends declared. EXAMPLE 2.4 demonstrates how increases and decreases in these accounts are recorded.

EXAMPLE 2.4 — DETERMINING INCREASES OR DECREASES TO REVENUES, EXPENSES, GAINS, LOSSES, AND DIVIDENDS DECLARED

The retained earnings account is affected by revenues, expenses, gains, losses, and dividends declared.

Required:

Determine how each of these five accounts increases or decreases.

Solution:

• Revenues and gains increase stockholders' equity through retained earnings. Therefore, revenues and gains have a normal credit balance. That means that credits will increase revenues and gains, while debits will decrease revenues and gains.

• Expenses and losses decrease stockholders' equity through retained earnings. Therefore, expenses and losses have a normal debit balance. That means that debits will increase expenses and losses, while credits will decrease expenses and losses.

• Dividends declared are defined as a distribution of retained earnings. Because dividends declared reduce retained earnings and stockholders' equity, dividends declared have a normal debit balance. That means that debits will increase dividends declared, while credits will decrease dividends declared.

These procedures are summarized below.

From Example 2.4, you should notice several items. First, revenues and gains have opposite effects on retained earnings than expenses and losses; therefore, revenues and gains have opposite normal balances than expenses and losses. Second, any change (increase or decrease) in revenue, expense, gain, loss, or dividends declared affects the balance of stockholders' equity. Specifically,

- an increase in a revenue or gain increases stockholders' equity
- a decrease in a revenue or gain decreases stockholders' equity
- an increase in an expense, loss, or dividends declared decreases stockholders' equity
- a decrease in an expense, loss, or dividends declared increases stockholders' equity

Finally, when revenues and gains exceed expenses and losses, a company has reported net income, which increases stockholders' equity. When revenues and gains are less than expenses and losses, a company has reported a net loss, which reduces stockholders' equity. These debit and credit procedures are summarized in Exhibit 2.10.

The important point from this analysis is that while debits are always on the left and credits are always on the right, the effect of a debit or credit on an account balance depends upon the normal balance of that account.

EXHIBIT 2.10   **Summary of Debit and Credit Procedures**

 YOUDECIDE   Inferring Activities from T-Accounts

As you examine the accounting records of Newton Inc., you notice that accounts receivable increased from $4,500 to $5,200 during the year and that credit sales were $65,800.

What was the amount of accounts receivable collected?

The primary activities that affect accounts receivable are the sale goods and services on credit (increases in accounts receivable) and the collection of cash related to these credit sales (decreases in accounts receivable). To help visualize the account activity, prepare a T-account as follows:

Accounts Receivable			
Beginning balance	4,500		
Credit sales	65,800	?	Cash collections
Ending balance	5,200		

Because you know the beginning and ending balances of accounts receivable and the amount of credit sales, you can determine the cash collections as:

$$\text{Cash collections} = \$4{,}500 + \$65{,}800 - \$5{,}200 = \mathbf{\$65{,}100}$$

An understanding of how business activities affect individual accounts can yield valuable insights into the economic events that occurred during a period.

STEP 2: JOURNALIZE TRANSACTIONS

OBJECTIVE 5 5

Prepare journal entries for transactions.

While it would be possible to record transactions directly into accounts, most companies enter the effects of the transaction in a journal using the debit and credit procedures described in the previous section. A **journal** is a chronological record showing the debit and credit effects of transactions on a company. Each transaction is represented by a **journal entry** so that the entire effect of a transaction is contained in one place. The process of making a journal entry is often referred to as journalizing a transaction. Because a transaction first enters the accounting records through journal entries, the journal is often referred to as the book of original entry.

A journal entry consists of three parts: (1) the date of the transaction, (2) the accounts and amounts to be increased or decreased, and (3) a brief explanation of the transaction. Each journal entry shows the debit and credit effects of a transaction on specific accounts. In preparing a journal entry, the following steps should be followed:

Step 1. Analyze the transaction using the procedures described in Example 2.2 (p. 90).

Step 2. Determine which accounts are affected.

Step 3. Prepare the journal entry using the debit and credit procedures in Examples 2.3 (p. 98) and 2.4 (p. 99). This process is illustrated in EXAMPLE 2.5.

EXAMPLE 2.5   MAKING A JOURNAL ENTRY

On January 1, Luigi Inc. purchases a $3,000 computer from WorstBuy Electronics on credit, with payment due in 60 days.

Required:
Prepare a journal entry to record this transaction.

Solution:
First, analyze the transaction using the procedures described in Example 2.2 (p. 90):

Assets	=	Liabilities	+	Stockholders' Equity		
				Contributed Capital	+	Retained Earnings
+$3,000		+$3,000				

Step 1

The purchase of a computer has increased the asset account "Equipment," which is recorded with a debit. In addition, a liability, "Accounts Payable," was created and the increase in this account is recorded with a credit.

Step 2

Date	Account and Explanation	Debit	Credit
Jan. 1	Equipment	3,000	
	Accounts Payable		3,000

Step 3

From the journal entry in Example 2.5, notice several items:

- The date of the transaction is entered in the Date column.
- For each entry in the journal, the debit (the account and amount) is entered first and flush to the left. If there were more than one debit, it would be entered directly underneath the first debit on the next line. The credit (the account and the amount) is written below the debits and indented to the right. The purpose of this standard format is to make it possible for anyone using the journal to identify debits and credits quickly and correctly.
- *Total debits must equal total credits.*

In some instances, more than two accounts may be affected by an economic event. When this occurs, a compound journal entry is created as illustrated in EXAMPLE 2.6.

EXAMPLE 2.6   MAKING A COMPOUND JOURNAL ENTRY

Luigi Inc. purchases a $3,000 computer from WorstBuy Electronics by paying $1,000 cash with the remainder due in 60 days.

Required:
Prepare a compound journal entry to record this transaction.

Solution:
First, analyze the transaction as follows:

Assets	=	Liabilities	+	Stockholders' Equity	
				Contributed Capital + Retained Earnings	Step 1
+$3,000		+$2,000			
−$1,000					

The purchase of this equipment increased the asset "Equipment," decreased the asset "Cash," and increased the liability "Accounts Payable." — Step 2

Luigi would make the following journal entry:

Date	Account and Explanation	Debit	Credit	
Jan. 1	Equipment	3,000		Step 3
	Cash		1,000	
	Accounts Payable		2,000	

Next Level

If all journal entries have equal debits and credits, how can mistakes or errors occur?

ANSWER:
Mistakes or errors could still occur when entire transactions are not recorded, transactions are recorded for the wrong amounts or in the wrong accounts, or transactions are not recorded in the proper accounting period. While journal entries provide a safeguard against errors and mistakes, it will not prevent them all.

The use of a journal helps prevent the introduction of errors in the recording of business activities. Because all parts of the transaction appear together, it is easy to see whether equal debits and credits have been entered. If debits equal credits for *each* journal entry, then debits equal credits for *all* journal entries. At the end of the period, this fact leads to a useful check on the accuracy of journal entries. However, if the wrong amounts or the wrong accounts are used, debits can still equal credits, yet the journal entries will be incorrect. Additionally, each entry can be examined to see if the accounts that appear together are logically appropriate.

ETHICAL DECISIONS When an error is discovered in a journal entry, the accountant has an ethical responsibility to correct the error (subject to materiality), even if others would never be able to tell that the error had occurred. For example, if an accountant accidentally records a sale of merchandise by crediting Interest Income instead of Sales Revenue, total revenue would be unaffected. However, this error could significantly affect summary performance measures such as gross margin (sales minus cost of goods sold) that are important to many investors. When material errors are discovered, they should be corrected, even if this means embarrassment to the accountant. ●

To provide a further illustration of recording transactions using journal entries, consider the case of HiTech Communications Inc. that was presented earlier in the chapter. For the remainder of the book, we will analyze each transaction and report its effects on the accounting equation in the margin next to the journal entry. Next, we identify the accounts that were affected by incorporating account titles into the transaction analysis model. Finally, we prepare the journal entry based on the analysis. You should always perform these steps as you prepare journal entries.

TRANSACTION 1: ISSUING COMMON STOCK

On March 1, HiTech sold 1,000 shares of common stock to several investors for cash of $12,000.

Date	Account and Explanation	Debit	Credit	Assets	=	Liabilities	+	Stockholders' Equity
March 1	Cash	12,000		▲				
	Common Stock		12,000					▲

TRANSACTION 2: BORROWING CASH

On March 2, HiTech raised additional funds by borrowing $3,000 on a 1-year, 8% note payable to First Third Bank of Cincinnati.

Date	Account and Explanation	Debit	Credit	Assets	=	Liabilities	+	Stockholders' Equity
March 2	Cash	3,000		▲				
	Notes Payable		3,000			▲		

TRANSACTION 3: PURCHASE OF EQUIPMENT FOR CASH

On March 3, HiTech purchased office equipment (computer equipment) from Micro Center Inc. for $4,500 in cash.

Date	Account and Explanation	Debit	Credit	Assets	=	Liabilities	+	Stockholders' Equity
March 3	Equipment	4,500		▲				
	Cash		4,500	▼				

TRANSACTION 4: PURCHASING INSURANCE

On March 4, HiTech purchased a 6-month insurance policy for $1,200 in cash.

Date	Account and Explanation	Debit	Credit	Assets	=	Liabilities	+	Stockholders' Equity
March 4	Prepaid Insurance	1,200		▲				
	Cash		1,200	▼				

TRANSACTION 5: PURCHASE OF SUPPLIES ON CREDIT

On March 6, HiTech purchased office supplies from Hamilton Office Supply for $6,500. Hamilton Office Supply agreed to accept full payment in 30 days.

Date	Account and Explanation	Debit	Credit	Assets	=	Liabilities	+	Stockholders' Equity
March 6	Supplies	6,500		▲				
	Accounts Payable		6,500			▲		

TRANSACTION 6: PROVIDING SERVICES FOR CASH

On March 10, HiTech provided advertising services to Miami Valley Products in exchange for $8,800 in cash.

Date	Account and Explanation	Debit	Credit	Assets	=	Liabilities	=	Stockholders' Equity
March 10	Cash	8,800		▲				
	Service Revenue		8,800					▲

TRANSACTION 7: PROVIDING SERVICES FOR CREDIT

On March 15, HiTech provided advertising services to the *Cincinnati Times* for $3,300. HiTech agreed to accept full payment in 30 days.

Date	Account and Explanation	Debit	Credit	Assets	=	Liabilities	+	Stockholders' Equity
March 15	Accounts Receivable	3,300		▲				
	Service Revenue		3,300					▲

TRANSACTION 8: RECEIPT OF CASH IN ADVANCE

On March 19, HiTech received $9,000 in advance for advertising services to be completed in the next 3 months.

Date	Account and Explanation	Debit	Credit	Assets	=	Liabilities	+	Stockholders' Equity
March 19	Cash	9,000		▲				
	Unearned Service Revenue		9,000			▲		

TRANSACTION 9: PAYMENT OF A LIABILITY

On March 23, HiTech pays $6,000 cash for the supplies previously purchased from Hamilton Office Supply (Transaction 5).

Date	Account and Explanation	Debit	Credit	Assets	=	Liabilities	+	Stockholders' Equity
March 23	Accounts Payable	6,000				▼		
	Cash		6,000	▼				

TRANSACTION 10: COLLECTION OF A RECEIVABLE

On March 25, HiTech collected $3,000 cash from the *Cincinnati Times* for services sold earlier on credit (Transaction 7).

Date	Account and Explanation	Debit	Credit	Assets	=	Liabilities	+	Stockholders' Equity
March 25	Cash	3,000		▲				
	Accounts Receivable		3,000	▼				

TRANSACTION 11: PAYMENT OF SALARIES

On March 26, HiTech paid employees their weekly salaries of $1,800 cash.

Date	Account and Explanation	Debit	Credit	Assets	= Liabilities +	Stockholders' Equity
March 26	Salaries Expense	1,800				▼
	Cash		1,800	▼		

TRANSACTION 12: PAYMENT OF UTILITIES

On March 30, HiTech paid its utility bill of $5,200 for March.

Date	Account and Explanation	Debit	Credit	Assets	= Liabilities +	Stockholders' Equity
March 30	Utilities Expense	5,200				▼
	Cash		5,200	▼		

TRANSACTION 13: PAYMENT OF A DIVIDEND

On March 31, HiTech declared and paid a cash dividend of $500 to its stockholders.

Date	Account and Explanation	Debit	Credit	Assets	= Liabilities +	Stockholders' Equity
March 31	Dividends Declared	500				▼
	Cash		500	▼		

YOU DECIDE   Detecting Journal Entry Errors

You have been asked to inspect a delivery company's journal. Upon doing so, you find the following entry related to the purchase of a truck:

Date	Account and Explanation	Debit	Credit
June 29	Equipment, Delivery Truck	11,000	
	Prepaid Rent		11,000

Is this journal entry correct?

Because delivery trucks cannot be exchanged for prepaid rent, you conclude that an error was made in preparing this journal entry. It's likely that the error was in the credit side of the entry. Instead of prepaid rent, the credit could be either to cash (if the purchase of the truck was for cash) or to note payable (if the purchase was on credit). Had the same data been entered directly into the accounts, this error would have been much more difficult to detect and correct.

The use of a journal helps prevent the introduction of errors in the recording of business activities.

STEP 3: POST TO THE LEDGER

OBJECTIVE 6

Explain why transactions are posted to the general ledger.

Because the journal lists each transaction in chronological order, it can be quite difficult to use the journal to determine the balance in any specific account. For example, refer to the journal entries shown earlier for HiTech Communications. What is the balance in cash at the end of the month? This relatively simple question is difficult to answer with the use of the journal.

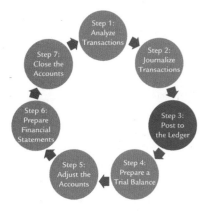

To overcome this difficulty, companies will use a general ledger to keep track of the balances of specific accounts. A **general ledger** is simply a collection of all the individual financial statement accounts that a company uses.[2] In a manual accounting system, a ledger could be as simple as a notebook with a separate page for each account. Ledger accounts are often shown using the T-account format introduced earlier.

The process of transferring the information from the journalized transaction to the general ledger is called **posting** and is illustrated in Exhibit 2.11. Posting is essentially copying the information from the journal into the ledger. Debits in the journal are posted as debits to the specific ledger account, and credits in the journal are posted as credits in the specific ledger account. To facilitate this process, most journals and ledgers have a column titled "Posting Reference." As the information is copied into the ledger, the number assigned to the account is placed in the "Posting Reference" column of the journal and the journal page number is placed in the "Posting Reference" column of the ledger.

EXHIBIT 2.11	The Posting Process for HiTech Communications Inc.

GENERAL JOURNAL

Page: 2

Date	Account and Explanation	Post. Ref.	Debit	Credit
Mar. 31	Dividends Declared	3900	500	
	Cash	1000		500

GENERAL LEDGER

Account: CASH

Account Number: 1000

Date	Explanation	Post. Ref.	Debit	Credit	Balance
Mar. 1	Issued stock	1	12,000		12,000
2	Borrowed from bank	1	3,000		15,000
3	Purchased equipment	1		4,500	10,500
4	Purchased insurance	1		1,200	9,300
10	Sold advertising services	1	8,800		18,100
19	Sold advertising services in advance	1	9,000		27,100
23	Paid accounts payable	1		6,000	21,100
28	Paid salaries	1		1,800	19,300
29	Collected receivable	2	3,000		22,300
30	Paid utilities	2		5,200	17,100
31	Paid dividend	2		500	16,600

This column provides a link between the ledger and journal that

- helps to prevent errors in the posting process
- allows you to trace the effects of a transaction through the accounting system

The general ledger accounts for HiTech are shown using T-accounts in Exhibit 2.12. The numbers in parentheses correspond to the transaction numbers.

---

2   Most companies supplement the general ledger with subsidiary ledgers that record "subaccounts" that make up the larger general ledger account. For example, a single account such as Accounts Receivable may appear in the general ledger; however, the accounts receivable for individual customers are usually contained in a subsidiary ledger. The general ledger account will equal the total balance of all the accounts in the subsidiary ledger for that account.

General Ledger Accounts of HiTech Communications (T-account view)   EXHIBIT 2.12

Assets

Cash

(T1)	12,000	4,500	(T3)
(T2)	3,000	1,200	(T4)
(T6)	8,800	6,000	(T9)
(T8)	9,000	1,800	(T11)
(T10)	3,000	5,200	(T12)
		500	(T13)
	16,600		

Accounts Receivable

(T7)	3,300	3,000	(T10)
	300		

Supplies

(T5)	6,500	
	6,500	

Prepaid Insurance

(T4)	1,200	
	1,200	

Equipment

(T3)	4,500	
	4,500	

Liabilities

Accounts Payable

(T9)	6,000	6,500	(T5)
		500	

Unearned Service Revenue

	9,000	(T8)
	9,000	

Notes Payable

	3,000	(T2)
	3,000	

Stockholders' Equity

Common Stock

	12,000	(T1)
	12,000	

Service Revenue

	8,800	(T6)
	3,300	(T7)
	12,100	

Salaries Expense

(T11)	1,800	
	1,800	

Utilities Expense

(T12)	5,200	
	5,200	

Dividends Declared

(T13)	500	
	500	

STEP 4: PREPARE A TRIAL BALANCE

OBJECTIVE 7

Prepare a trial balance and explain its purpose.

To aid in the preparation of financial statements, some companies will prepare a trial balance before they prepare financial statements. The **trial balance** is a list of all active accounts and each account's debit or credit balance. The accounts are listed in the order they appear in the ledger—assets first, followed by liabilities, stockholders' equity, dividends declared, revenues, and expenses. By organizing accounts in this manner, the trial balance serves as a useful tool in preparing the financial statements. The preparation of the trial balance for HiTech Communications is shown in EXAMPLE 2.7 .

EXAMPLE 2.7   PREPARING A TRIAL BALANCE

Refer to the general ledger for HiTech in Exhibit 2.12 (p. 107).

Required:
Prepare a trial balance for HiTech Communications Inc. at March 31.

Solution:

Account	Debit	Credit
HiTech Communications Inc.		
Trial Balance		
March 31		
Cash	$16,600	
Accounts Receivable	300	
Supplies	6,500	
Prepaid Insurance	1,200	
Equipment	4,500	
Accounts Payable		$ 500
Unearned Service Revenue		9,000
Notes Payable		3,000
Common Stock		12,000
Dividends Declared	500	
Service Revenue		12,100
Salaries Expense	1,800	
Utilities Expense	5,200	
	$36,600	$36,600

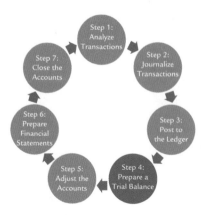

In addition, the trial balance is used to *prove the equality of debits and credits.* If debits did not equal credits, the accountant would quickly know that an error had been made. The error could have been in the journalizing of the transaction, the posting of the transaction, or in the computation of the balance in the ledger. However, a word of caution is necessary: a trial balance whose debits equal credits does *not* mean that all transactions were recorded correctly. A trial balance will not detect errors of analysis or amounts. Sometimes the wrong account is selected for a journal entry or an incorrect amount is recorded for a transaction. In other cases, a journal entry is omitted or entered twice. As long as both the debit and credit portions of the journal entry or posting reflect the incorrect information, the debit and credit totals in a trial balance will be equal.

KEY TAKEAWAYS

LO1. Describe the qualitative characteristics, assumptions, and principles that underlie accounting.

- The fundamental qualitative characteristics of accounting information are as follows:
  - Relevance—refers to whether information is capable of making a difference in the decision-making process. Relevant information is material and helps to predict the future or provides feedback about prior expectations.
  - Faithful representation—refers to whether information faithfully represents the economic event that it is intending to portray. Faithfully presented information should be complete, neutral, and free from error.
- The enhancing qualitative characteristics of accounting information are as follows:
  - Comparability—allows external users to identify similarities and differences between two or more items. Comparability includes the characteristic of consistency.
  - Verifiability—exists when independent parties can reach a consensus on the measurement of an activity.
  - Timeliness—available to users before the information loses its ability to influence decisions.
  - Understandability—ability of information to be comprehended (with reasonable effort) by users who have a reasonable knowledge of accounting and business.
- The four assumptions are as follows:
  - Economic entity—each company is accounted for separately from its owners.
  - Going-concern—a company will continue to operate long enough to carry out its commitments.
  - Time-period—allows the life of a company to be divided into artificial time periods.
  - Monetary unit—requires financial information to be reported in monetary terms.
- The four principles are as follows:
  - Historical cost—requires a business activity to be recorded at the exchange price at the time the activity occurs.
  - Revenue recognition—requires revenue to be recognized when a company satisfies its performance obligation to the customer.
  - Expense recognition—requires that expenses be recognized in the same period as the revenue that they helped generate; often called the matching principle.
  - Conservatism—requires assets and income to not be overstated.

KEY TERMS

Accounting cycle, 82
Comparability, 84
Conservatism principle, 85
Consistency, 84

Cost constraint, 84
Economic entity assumption, 85
Expense recognition principle, 85
Faithful representation, 83

EXAMPLE

EXAMPLE 2.1	Applying the conceptual framework, page 86

LO2. Explain the relationships among economic events, transactions, and the expanded accounting equation.

KEY TAKEAWAYS

- A company's business activities (operating, investing, and financing) consist of many different economic events that are external as well as internal to the company. Accounting attempts to measure the economic effects of these events. However, not all events are recognized, or recorded, in the accounting system.
- A transaction is an economic event that is recognized in the financial statements. An accounting transaction causes the elements of the accounting equation (assets, liabilities, contributed capital, retained earnings, revenues, or expenses) to change in a way that maintains the equality of their relationship.

KEY TERMS

Events, 87
Transaction, 88

KEY CALCULATIONS

Assets = Liabilities + Stockholders' Equity

Assets = Liabilities + Contributed Capital + Retained Earnings

Assets = Liabilities + Contributed Capital + Beginning Retained Earnings + Revenues – Expenses – Dividends Declared

KEY TAKEAWAYS

LO3. Analyze the effect of business transactions on the accounting equation.

- Transaction analysis is the process of determining the economic effects of a transaction on the elements of the accounting equation.
- Transaction analysis involves the following three steps:
  - Step 1: Write down the accounting equation (basic or expanded version).
  - Step 2: Identify the financial statement elements that are affected by the transaction.
  - Step 3: Determine whether the element increased or decreased.
- Each transaction will have a dual effect on the accounting equation, and the accounting equation will remain in balance after the effects of the transaction are recorded.

KEY TERM

Transaction analysis, 89

EXAMPLE

> **EXAMPLE 2.2**   Performing transaction analysis, page 90

KEY TAKEAWAYS

LO4. Determine how debits and credits are used in the double-entry accounting system.

- An account is a record of increases and decreases in a financial statement element. Each financial statement element is made up of a number of different accounts.
- All transactions are recorded into accounts.
- The final account balance, after all changes are recorded, is used to prepare the financial statements.
- The left side of an account is referred to as a debit. The right side of an account is referred to as a credit.
- All accounts have a normal balance, which is the positive account balance. Assets, expenses, and dividends declared have a normal debit balance. Liabilities, stockholders' equity, and revenues have a normal credit balance.
- Increases or decreases to an account are based on the normal balance of an account. Normal debit balance accounts (assets, expenses, losses, and dividends declared) are increased with debits and decreased with credits. Normal credit balance accounts (liabilities, stockholders' equity, revenues, and gains) are increased with credits and decreased with debits.

KEY TERMS

Account, 96
Chart of accounts, 96
Credit, 96
Debit, 96

Double-entry accounting, 95
Normal balance, 97
T-account, 96

EXAMPLES

EXAMPLE 2.3	Determining increases or decreases to a balance sheet account, page 98
EXAMPLE 2.4	Determining increases or decreases to revenues, expenses, gains, losses, and dividends declared, page 99

LO5. Prepare journal entries for transactions.

KEY TAKEAWAYS

- A journal entry represents the debit and credit effects of a transaction in the accounting records.
- A journal entry is prepared by following three steps:
  - Step 1: Analyzing the transaction
  - Step 2: Determining which accounts are affected
  - Step 3: Using debits and credits to record the effects of the transaction
- Journal entries are recorded in chronological order and consist of the date of the transaction, the accounts affected, the amount of the transaction, and a brief explanation.

KEY TERMS

Journal, 101
Journal entry, 101

EXAMPLES

EXAMPLE 2.5	Making a journal entry, page 101
EXAMPLE 2.6	Making a compound journal entry, page 102

LO6. Explain why transactions are posted to the general ledger.

KEY TAKEAWAYS

- To overcome the difficulty of determining account balances from transactions listed chronologically in the journal, information from the journal is transferred to the general ledger in a process called posting.
- As a result of posting, the general ledger accumulates the effects of the transactions into the individual financial statement accounts.

KEY TERMS

General ledger, 106
Posting, 106

KEY TAKEAWAYS

LO7. Prepare a trial balance and explain its purpose.

- The trial balance lists all active accounts, in the order in which they appear in the ledger, as well as each account's debit or credit balance.
- The trial balance is used to prove the equality of debits and credits and helps to uncover errors in journalizing or posting transactions.
- The trial balance serves as a useful tool in preparing the financial statements.

KEY TERM

Trial balance, 107

EXAMPLE

EXAMPLE 2.7   Preparing a Trial Balance, page 108

REVIEW PROBLEM

Boonville Delivery Service was recently formed to fill a need for speedy delivery of small packages. In December, its first month of operations, the following transactions occurred.

a. On December 1, Boonville sells common stock to several investors for $32,000.
b. On December 2, Boonville borrows $20,000 on a 1-year note payable from Warrick National Bank, to be repaid with 8% interest in 1 year.
c. On December 2, Boonville pays rent of $8,000 on its package sorting building for the current month.
d. On December 6, Boonville purchases $7,000 worth of office furniture by paying $1,400 in cash and signing a 1-year, 12% note payable for the balance.
e. On December 20, Boonville completes a delivery contract for Tornado Corporation and bills its customer $15,000.
f. On December 24, Boonville makes a rush delivery for $5,300 cash.
g. On December 28, Tornado pays the $15,000 owed from Transaction e.
h. On December 28, Boonville signs an agreement with BigTime Computers to accept and deliver approximately 400 packages per business day during the next 12 months. Boonville expects to receive $400,000 of revenue for this contract, but the exact amount will depend on the number of packages delivered.

i. On December 29, Boonville receives a $1,500 bill from Mac's Catering for miscellaneous services performed at a Christmas party Boonville held for its clients. (No previous entry has been made for this activity.)

j. On December 31, Boonville pays $2,600 cash in salaries to its secretarial staff for work performed in December.

k. On December 31, Boonville declares and pays dividends of $5,000 on its common stock.

Required:

1. Analyze and journalize the Transactions a through k.
2. Post the transactions to the general ledger.
3. Prepare the December trial balance for Boonville.

Solution:

1. **Analyzing and Journalizing Transactions**

    Transaction a: *Issuing Common Stock.*

Assets	=	Liabilities	+	Stockholders' Equity	
				Contributed Capital	+ Retained Earnings
Cash				Common Stock	
+$32,000				+$32,000	

Date	Account and Explanation	Debit	Credit
Dec. 1	Cash	32,000	
	Common Stock		32,000

Transaction b: *Borrowing Cash*

Assets	=	Liabilities	+	Stockholders' Equity	
				Contributed Capital	+ Retained Earnings
Cash		Notes Payable			
+$20,000		+$20,000			

Date	Account and Explanation	Debit	Credit
Dec. 2	Cash	20,000	
	Notes Payable		20,000

Transaction c: *Paying Rent*

Assets	=	Liabilities	+	Stockholders' Equity	
				Contributed Capital	+ Retained Earnings
Cash					Rent Expense
−$8,000					−$8,000

Date	Account and Explanation	Debit	Credit
Dec. 2	Rent Expense	8,000	
	Cash		8,000

Transaction d: *Purchasing Asset with Cash and Credit*

Assets	=	Liabilities	+	Stockholders' Equity	
				Contributed Capital +	Retained Earnings
Cash		Notes Payable			
−$1,400		+$5,600			
Furniture					
+$7,000					

Date	Account and Explanation	Debit	Credit
Dec. 6	Furniture	7,000	
	Cash		1,400
	Notes Payable		5,600

Transaction e: *Performing Services on Credit*

Assets	=	Liabilities	+	Stockholders' Equity	
				Contributed Capital +	Retained Earnings
Accounts Receivable					Service Revenue
+$15,000					+$15,000

Date	Account and Explanation	Debit	Credit
Dec. 20	Accounts Receivable	15,000	
	Service Revenue		15,000

Transaction f: *Performing Services for Cash*

Assets	=	Liabilities	+	Stockholders' Equity	
				Contributed Capital +	Retained Earnings
Cash					Service Revenue
+$5,300					+$5,300

Date	Account and Explanation	Debit	Credit
Dec. 24	Cash	5,300	
	Service Revenue		5,300

Transaction g: *Collecting an Account Receivable*

Assets	=	Liabilities	+	Stockholders' Equity	
				Contributed Capital +	Retained Earnings
Cash					
+$15,000					
Accounts Receivable					
−$15,000					

Date	Account and Explanation	Debit	Credit
Dec. 28	Cash	15,000	
	Accounts Receivable		15,000

Transaction h: *Signing of an Agreement to Provide Service*

This is an example of an important event that does not produce a journal entry at the time it occurs. There will be no recording of the transaction until one of the companies performs on its part of the contract (so, until Boonville provides the delivery service or BigTime Computers makes a payment to Boonville).

Transaction i: *Using Services*

Assets	=	Liabilities	+	Stockholders' Equity	
				Contributed Capital +	Retained Earnings
		Accounts Payable			Miscellaneous Expense
		+$1,500			−$1,500

Date	Account and Explanation	Debit	Credit
Dec. 29	Miscellaneous Expense	1,500	
	Accounts Payable		1,500

Transaction j: *Payment of Salaries*

Assets	=	Liabilities	+	Stockholders' Equity	
				Contributed Capital +	Retained Earnings
Cash					Salaries Expense
−$2,600					−$2,600

Date	Account and Explanation	Debit	Credit
Dec. 31	Salaries Expense	2,600	
	Cash		2,600

Transaction k: *Declaring and Paying a Cash Dividend*

Assets	=	Liabilities	+	Stockholders' Equity	
				Contributed Capital +	Retained Earnings
Cash					Dividends Declared
−5,000					−$5,000

Date	Account and Explanation	Debit	Credit
Dec. 31	Dividends Declared	5,000	
	Cash		5,000

2. **Posting of Transactions to the Ledger**

General Ledger of Boonville Delivery Service

Assets   **Liabilities**   **Stockholders' Equity**

Cash

(a)	32,000	8,000	(c)
(b)	20,000	1,400	(d)
(f)	5,300	2,600	(j)
(g)	15,000	5,000	(k)
	55,300		

Accounts Receivable

| (e) | 15,000 | 15,000 | (g) |
| | 0 | | |

Furniture

| (d) | 7,000 | | |
| | **7,000** | | |

Accounts Payable

| | | 1,500 | (i) |
| | | **1,500** | |

Notes Payable

		20,000	(b)
		5,600	(d)
		25,600	

Common Stock

| | | 32,000 | (a) |
| | | **32,000** | |

Dividends Declared

| (k) | 5,000 | |
| | **5,000** | |

Service Revenue

		15,000	(e)
		5,300	(f)
		20,300	

Salaries Expense

| (j) | 2,600 | |
| | **2,600** | |

Miscellaneous Expense

| (i) | 1,500 | |
| | **1,500** | |

Rent Expense

| (c) | 8,000 | |
| | **8,000** | |

3. **Preparing a Trial Balance**

Boonville Delivery Service
Trial Balance
December 31

Account	Debit	Credit
Cash	$55,300	
Accounts Receivable	0	
Furniture	7,000	
Accounts Payable		$ 1,500
Notes Payable		25,600
Common Stock		32,000
Dividends Declared	5,000	
Service Revenue		20,300
Rent Expense	8,000	
Salaries Expense	2,600	
Miscellaneous Expense	1,500	
	$79,400	$79,400

APPLYING KNOWLEDGE

DISCUSSION QUESTIONS

OBJECTIVE 1

1. What is the conceptual framework of accounting?
2. Identify the characteristics of useful information.
3. Discuss the trade-offs that may be necessary between the qualitative characteristics.
4. Distinguish between comparability and consistency.
5. Describe the constraint on providing useful information.
6. Identify the four assumptions that underlie accounting.
7. Discuss the four principles that are used to measure and record business transactions.

OBJECTIVE 2

8. Of all the events that occur each day, how would you describe those that are recorded in a firm's accounting records?
9. In order for a transaction to be recorded in a business' accounting records, the effects of the transaction must be faithfully represented. What is faithful representation, and why is it important?

OBJECTIVE 3

10. What is the basic process used in transaction analysis?
11. In analyzing a transaction, can a transaction only affect one side of the accounting equation? If so, give an example.
12. How do revenues and expenses affect the accounting equation?

OBJECTIVE 4

13. What is a T-account? Describe the basic components of any account.
14. Do you agree with the statement that "debits mean increase and credits mean decrease"? If not, what do debit and credit mean?
15. The words *debit* and *credit* are used in two ways in accounting: "to debit an account" and "a debit balance." Explain both usages of the terms *debit and credit.*
16. All accounts have normal balances. What is the normal balance of each of these accounts?
    - a. cash
    - b. sales
    - c. notes payable
    - d. inventory
    - e. retained earnings
    - f. salary expense
    - g. equipment
    - h. unearned revenue

OBJECTIVE 5

17. When a journal entry is made, what must be equal? Why?
18. Why is the term *double-entry* an appropriate expression for describing an accounting system?

OBJECTIVE 5 6

19. Can accounting transactions be directly recorded in the general ledger? If so, why do most companies initially record transactions in the journal?

OBJECTIVE 7

20. What kinds of errors will a trial balance detect? What kinds of errors will not be detectable by a trial balance?

OBJECTIVE 5 6 7

21. What are the initial steps in the accounting cycle and what happens in each step?

MULTIPLE-CHOICE QUESTIONS

2-1 Which of the following is *not* a benefit derived from the conceptual framework?   OBJECTIVE 1
   a. Supports the objective of providing information useful for making business and economic decisions.
   b. Provides a logical structure to aid in the understanding of complex accounting standards.
   c. Provides specific guidance on how transactions should be recorded.
   d. Supports the development of a consistent set of accounting standards.

2-2 Which of the following is *not* a characteristic of useful information?
   a. Comparability   c. Faithful representation
   b. Relevance   d. Conservatism

2-3 Information that provides feedback about prior expectations is:

	Relevant	**Faithfully Represented**
a.	Yes	Yes
b.	No	Yes
c.	Yes	No
d.	No	No

2-4 Relevant information possesses this quality:

	Freedom from Error	**Predictive Value**
a.	Yes	Yes
b.	No	Yes
c.	Yes	No
d.	No	No

2-5 Which of the following is *not* an assumption that underlies accounting?
   a. Historical cost   c. Time-period
   b. Economic entity   d. Going-concern

2-6 Which principle requires that expenses be recorded and reported in the same period as the revenue that it helped generate?
   a. Historical cost   c. Conservatism
   b. Revenue recognition   d. Expense recognition

2-7 Taylor Company recently purchased a piece of equipment for $2,000, which will   OBJECTIVE 2
   be paid within 30 days after delivery. At what point would the event be recorded in Taylor's accounting system?
   a. When Taylor signs the agreement with the seller
   b. When Taylor receives an invoice (a bill) from the seller
   c. When Taylor receives the asset from the seller
   d. When Taylor pays $2,000 cash to the seller

2-8 The effects of purchasing inventory on credit are to: OBJECTIVE 3
   a. increase assets and increase liabilities.
   b. increase assets and increase stockholders' equity.
   c. decrease assets and decrease stockholders' equity.
   d. decrease assets and decrease liabilities.

2-9 The effects of paying salaries for the current period are to:
   a. increase assets and increase stockholders' equity.
   b. increase assets and increase liabilities.
   c. decrease assets and decrease liabilities.
   d. decrease assets and decrease stockholders' equity.

2-10 Which of the following statements is *false*?   OBJECTIVE 4
   a. The left side of a T-account is called the credit side.
   b. All T-accounts have both a debit and a credit side.
   c. Transactions are frequently analyzed using a T-account.
   d. The amount in an account at any time is called the balance of the account.

2-11 Which of the following statements are true?
   I. Debits represent decreases, and credits represent increases.
   II. Debits must always equal credits.
   III. Assets have normal debit balances while liabilities and stockholders' equity have normal credit balances.
   a. I
   b. I and II
   c. II and III
   d. All of these are true.

2-12 Debits will:
   a. increase assets, expenses, and dividends declared.
   b. decrease liabilities, revenues, and dividends declared.
   c. increase assets, liabilities, revenues, expenses, and dividends declared.
   d. decrease assets, liabilities, revenues, expenses, and dividends declared.

OBJECTIVE 5

2-13 Which of the following statements are true?
   I. A journal provides a chronological record of a transaction.
   II. A journal entry contains the complete effect of a transaction.
   III. The first step in preparing a journal entry involves analyzing the transaction.
   a. I and II
   b. II and III
   c. I and III
   d. All of these are true.

OBJECTIVE 6

2-14 Posting:
   a. involves transferring the information in journal entries to the general ledger.
   b. is an optional step in the accounting cycle.
   c. is performed after a trial balance is prepared.
   d. involves transferring information to the trial balance.

OBJECTIVE 7

2-15 A trial balance:
   a. lists only revenue and expense accounts.
   b. lists all accounts and their balances.
   c. will help detect omitted journal entries.
   d. detects all errors that could be made during the journalizing or posting steps of the accounting cycle.

BRIEF EXERCISES

OBJECTIVE 1

EXAMPLE 2.1

Brief Exercise 2-16 Qualitative Characteristics

Seven statements are given below:

a. The two fundamental qualitative characteristics that information should possess are _____ and _____.
b. _____ is the characteristic that allows external users to identify similarities and differences between two or more items.
c. _____ is achieved when a company uses the same depreciation method from period to period.
d. _____ requires accounting information to be comprehensible to users who have a reasonable knowledge of business and economic activities and who are willing to study the information carefully.
e. When accounting information is complete, neutral, and free from error, it is said to be a _____ of the real-world economic event that it is intending to portray.
f. When multiple, independent parties can agree on the measurement of an activity, the information is said to be _____.
g. The characteristic of _____ is illustrated by a financial analyst needing information within the next week in order to make an investment decision.

Required:
Complete each of the statements with the appropriate qualitative characteristic.

Brief Exercise 2-17 Qualitative Characteristics

OBJECTIVE ◀ 1
EXAMPLE 2.1

Four statements are given below.

a. A financial item that may be useful to investors is not required to be reported because the cost of measuring and reporting this information is judged to be too great.
b. Timely information that is used to predict future events or provide feedback about prior events is said to possess this characteristic.
c. A quality of information that enables an analyst to evaluate the financial performance of two different companies in the same industry.
d. A trash can that is purchased for $10 is expensed even though it should be recorded as an asset because it will be used for many years.

Required:
Give the qualitative characteristic or constraint that is most applicable to each of the statements.

Brief Exercise 2-18 Assumptions

OBJECTIVE ◀ 1
EXAMPLE 2.1

Four common accounting practices are listed below:

a. Pewterschmidt Company values its inventory reported in the financial statements in terms of dollars instead of units.
b. Jim Trotter owns C&S Heating Company. In preparing the financial statements, Trotter makes sure that the purchase of a new truck for personal use is not included in C&S's financial statements.
c. Property, plant, and equipment is recorded at cost (minus any accumulated depreciation) instead of liquidation value.
d. Mueller Inc. prepares quarterly and annual financial statements.

Required:
Identify the accounting assumption that best describes each practice.

Brief Exercise 2-19 Accounting Principles

OBJECTIVE ◀ 1
EXAMPLE 2.1

Six statements are given below.

a. Quagmire Company recognizes revenue when the goods are delivered to a customer, even though cash will not be collected from the customer for 30 days.
b. Inventory, which was recently damaged by a flood, is reported at the lower of its cost or market value.
c. Moseley Inc. recorded land at its purchase price of $50,000. In future periods when the value of the land has increased, the land is still reflected in the financial statements at $50,000.
d. The cost paid for a delivery truck is recorded as an asset and expensed over the next 5 years as it is used to help generate revenue.
e. A company accepts $200 in December for services to be performed in January. The company recognizes revenue when the services are performed in January.
f. Mack Company purchases supplies in March. However, it does not expense the supplies until they are used in April.

Required:
Give the accounting principle that is most applicable to each of the statements.

Brief Exercise 2-20 Events and Transactions

OBJECTIVE ◀ 2

Several events are listed below.

a. Paid $30,000 for land.
b. Purchased office supplies for cash.
c. Performed consulting services for a client with the amount to be collected in 30 days.
d. Signed a contract to perform consulting services over the next 6 months.

(Continued)

Required:

For each of the events, identify which ones qualify for recognition in the financial statements. If an event does not qualify for recognition, explain why.

OBJECTIVE 3

EXAMPLE 2.2

Brief Exercise 2-21 Transaction Analysis

Four transactions are listed below.

a. Sold goods to customers on credit.
b. Collected amounts due from customers.
c. Purchased supplies on account.
d. Used supplies in operations of the business.

Required:

Prepare three columns labeled assets, liabilities, and stockholders' equity. For each of the transactions, indicate whether the transaction increased (+), decreased (−), or had no effect (NE) on assets, liabilities, or stockholders' equity.

OBJECTIVE 3

EXAMPLE 2.2

Brief Exercise 2-22 Transaction Analysis

Galle Inc. entered into the following transactions during January.

a. Borrowed $50,000 from First Street Bank by signing a note payable.
b. Purchased $25,000 of equipment for cash.
c. Paid $500 to landlord for rent for January.
d. Performed services for customers on account, $10,000.
e. Collected $3,000 from customers for services performed in Transaction d.
f. Paid salaries of $2,500 for the current month.
g. Declared and paid $800 dividend to stockholders.
h. Purchased $2,100 of supplies on credit.

Required:

Show the effect of each transaction using the following model.

				Stockholders' Equity		
Assets	=	Liabilities	+	Contributed Capital	+	Retained Earnings

OBJECTIVE 4

EXAMPLE 2.3

EXAMPLE 2.4

Brief Exercise 2-23 Debit and Credit Procedures

Refer to the accounts listed below.

a. Accounts Payable
b. Accounts Receivable
c. Retained Earnings
d. Service Revenue
e. Equipment

f. Common Stock
g. Salary Expense
h. Repair Expense
i. Cash
j. Notes Payable

Required:

For each of the accounts, complete the following table by entering the normal balance of the account (debit or credit) and the word increase or decrease in the debit and credit columns.

Account	Normal Balance	Debit	Credit

OBJECTIVE 5

EXAMPLE 2.5

EXAMPLE 2.6

Brief Exercise 2-24 Journalize Transactions

Galle Inc. entered into the following transactions during January.

a. January 1: Borrowed $50,000 from First Street Bank by signing a note payable.
b. January 4: Purchased $25,000 of equipment for cash.
c. January 6: Paid $500 to landlord for rent for January.
d. January 15: Performed services for customers on account, $10,000.
e. January 25: Collected $3,000 from customers for services performed in Transaction d.

f. January 28: Purchased land for $200,000 by paying $10,000 cash and obtaining a loan for the balance.

g. January 30: Paid salaries of $2,500 for the current month.

Required:
Prepare journal entries for the transactions.

Brief Exercise 2-25 Posting Journal Entries

OBJECTIVE 6
EXAMPLE 2.7

Listed below are selected T-accounts and their beginning balances for Galle Inc.

Cash	Accounts Receivable	Equipment	Notes Payable
12,000	6,300	5,000	0

Service Revenue	Salary Expense	Rent Expense
19,500	5,000	1,000

Required:
Post the journal entries from **Brief Exercise 2-24** to these accounts and compute the ending balance for each account.

Brief Exercise 2-26 Preparing a Trial Balance

OBJECTIVE 7
EXAMPLE 2.7

Listed below are the ledger accounts for Borges Inc. at December 31. All accounts have normal balances.

Service Revenue	$23,150	Dividends Declared	$ 1,500
Cash	12,850	Salaries Expense	4,300
Accounts Payable	2,825	Equipment	12,725
Common Stock	15,000	Accounts Receivable	5,700
Rent Expense	2,400	Advertising Expense	1,500

Required:
Prepare a trial balance for Borges at December 31.

EXERCISES

Exercise 2-27 Qualitative Characteristics

OBJECTIVE 1

Listed below are the fundamental and enhancing qualitative characteristics that make accounting information useful.

- Relevance
- Faithful representation
- Comparability
- Verifiability
- Timeliness
- Understandability

Required:
1. Match the appropriate qualitative characteristic with the statements below (items can be used more than once).
   a. When information is provided before it loses its ability to influence decisions, it has this characteristic.

(*Continued*)

b. When several accountants can agree on the measurement of an activity, the information possesses this characteristic.
c. If users can comprehend the meaning of the information, the information is said to have this characteristic.
d. If information confirms prior expectations, it possesses this characteristic.
e. If information helps to predict future events, it possesses this characteristic.
f. Freedom from bias is a component of this characteristic.
g. When several companies in the same industry use the same accounting methods, this qualitative characteristic exists.
h. Information that accurately portrays an economic event satisfies this characteristic.

2. **CONCEPTUAL CONNECTION** Explain the purpose of the conceptual framework.

OBJECTIVE

Exercise 2-28 Assumptions and Principles

Presented below are the four assumptions and four principles used in measuring and reporting accounting information.

Assumptions		Principles	
a.	Economic entity	e.	Historical cost
b.	Going-concern	f.	Revenue recognition
c.	Time-period	g.	Expense recognition
d.	Monetary unit	h.	Conservatism

Required:

Identify the assumption or principle that best describes each situation below.

1. Requires that an activity be recorded at the exchange price at the time the activity occurred.
2. Allows a company to report financial activities separate from the activities of the owners.
3. Implies that items such as customer satisfaction cannot be reported in the financial statements.
4. Specifies that revenue should only be recognized when a company has satisfied its performance obligation to a customer.
5. Justifies why some assets and liabilities are not reported at their value if sold.
6. Allows the life of a company to be divided into artificial time periods so accounting reports can be provided on a timely basis.
7. Is a prudent reaction to uncertainty.
8. Requires that expenses be recorded and reported in the same period as the revenue that it helped generate.

OBJECTIVE 2

Exercise 2-29 Events and Transactions

Several events are listed below.

a. Common stock is issued to investors.
b. An agreement is signed with a janitorial service to provide cleaning services over the next 12 months.
c. Inventory is purchased.
d. Inventory is sold to customers.
e. Two investors sell their common stock to another investor.
f. A 2-year insurance policy is purchased.

Required:

1. **CONCEPTUAL CONNECTION** For each of the events, identify which ones qualify for recognition in the financial statements.
2. **CONCEPTUAL CONNECTION** For events that do not qualify for recognition, explain your reasoning.

Exercise 2-30 Events and Transactions

OBJECTIVE 2

The following economic events related to K&B Grocery Store occurred during the year:

a. On February 7, K&B received a bill from Indianapolis Power and Light indicating that it had used electric power during January at a cost of $220; the bill need not be paid until March.

b. On February 15, K&B placed an order for a new cash register with NCR, for which $800 would be paid after delivery.

c. On February 21, the cash register ordered on February 15 was delivered. Payment was not due until March.

d. On February 22, the K&B store manager purchased a new passenger car for $35,000 in cash. The car is entirely for personal use and was paid for from the manager's personal assets.

e. On February 24, K&B signed a 2-year extension of the lease on the store building occupied by the store. Beginning with the March payment, the new lease required an increase in the monthly rental from $5,750 to $5,900.

f. On March 1, K&B paid $220 to Indianapolis Power and Light.

g. On March 5, K&B paid $5,900 to its landlord for March rent on the store building.

Required:

1. **CONCEPTUAL CONNECTION** Using the words "qualify" and "does not qualify," indicate whether each of the above events would qualify as a transaction and be recognized and recorded in the accounting system on the date indicated.

2. **CONCEPTUAL CONNECTION** For any events that did not qualify as a transaction to be recognized and recorded, explain why it does not qualify.

Exercise 2-31 Transaction Analysis

OBJECTIVE 3

The following events occurred for Parker Company.

a. Performed consulting services for a client in exchange for $2,900 cash.

b. Performed consulting services for a client on account, $1,650.

c. Paid $100,000 cash for land.

d. Purchased office supplies on account, $800.

e. Paid a $1,200 cash dividend to stockholders.

f. Paid $725 on account for supplies purchased in Transaction d.

g. Paid $1,500 cash for the current month's rent.

h. Collected $860 from client in Transaction b.

i. Stockholders invested $200,000 cash in the business.

Required:

1. Analyze the effect of each transaction on the accounting equation. For example, if salaries of $500 were paid, the answer would be "Decrease in stockholders' equity (expense) $500 and decrease in assets (cash) $500."

2. **CONCEPTUAL CONNECTION** For Event d, what accounting principle did you use to determine the amount to be recorded for supplies?

Exercise 2-32 Transaction Analysis

OBJECTIVE 3

Amanda Webb opened a home health care business under the name Home Care Inc. During its first month of operations, the business had the following transactions:

a. Issued common stock to Ms. Webb and other stockholders in exchange for $300,000 cash.

b. Paid $80,000 cash for a parcel of land on which the business will eventually build an office building.

c. Purchased supplies for $2,120 on credit.

(Continued)

d. Used the supplies purchased in Transaction c.

e. Paid rent for the month on office space and equipment, $1,200 cash.

f. Performed services for clients in exchange for $4,480 cash.

g. Paid salaries for the month, $2,200.

h. Paid $850 cash for advertising in the current month.

i. Paid $1,640 on account for supplies purchased in Transaction c.

j. Performed services for clients on credit in the amount of $1,910.

k. Paid a $400 dividend to stockholders.

Required:

Prepare an analysis of the effects of these transactions on the accounting equation of the business. Use the format below.

Assets	=	Liabilities	+	Stockholders' Equity	
				Contributed Capital	+	Retained Earnings

Exercise 2-33 Transaction Analysis and Business Activities

The accountant for Compton Inc. has collected the following information:

a. Compton purchased a tract of land from Jacobsen Real Estate for $875,000 cash.

b. Compton issued 2,000 shares of its common stock to George Micros in exchange for $125,000 cash.

c. Compton purchased a John Deere tractor for $86,000 on credit.

d. Michael Rotunno paid Compton $10,400 cash for services performed. The services had been performed by Compton several months ago for a total price of $12,000 of which Rotunno had previously paid $1,600.

e. Compton paid its monthly payroll by issuing checks totaling $36,250.

f. Compton declared and paid its annual dividend of $5,000 cash.

Required:

1. Prepare an analysis of the effects of these transactions on the accounting equation of the business. Use the format below.

Assets	=	Liabilities	+	Stockholders' Equity	
				Contributed Capital	+	Retained Earnings

2. Indicate whether the transaction is a financing, investing, or operating activity.

Exercise 2-34 Inferring Transactions from Balance Sheet Changes

Each of the following balance sheet changes is associated with a particular transaction:

a. Cash decreases by $22,000 and land increases by $22,000.

b. Cash decreases by $9,000 and retained earnings decreases by $9,000.

c. Cash increases by $100,000 and common stock increases by $100,000.

d. Cash increases by $15,000 and notes payable increases by $15,000.

Required:

CONCEPTUAL CONNECTION Describe each transaction listed above.

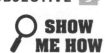

Exercise 2-35 Transaction Analysis

Goal Systems, a business consulting firm, engaged in the following transactions:

a. Issued common stock for $100,000 cash.

b. Borrowed $60,000 from a bank.

c. Purchased equipment for $42,000 cash.

d. Prepaid rent on office space for 6 months in the amount of $9,000.

e. Performed consulting services in exchange for $7,100 cash.

f. Performed consulting services on credit in the amount of $19,250.

g. Incurred and paid wage expense of $10,200.

h. Collected $13,500 of the receivable arising from Transaction f.

i. Purchased supplies for $1,680 on credit.

j. Used $1,100 of the supplies purchased in Transaction i.

k. Paid for all of the supplies purchased in Transaction i.

Required:

For each transaction described above, indicate the effects on assets, liabilities, and stockholders' equity using the format below.

Assets	=	Liabilities	+	Stockholders' Equity		
				Contributed Capital	+	Retained Earnings

Exercise 2-36 Transaction Analysis

OBJECTIVE ◄ 3

During December, Cynthiana Refrigeration Service engaged in the following transactions:

a. On December 3, Cynthiana sold a 1-year service contract to Cub Foods for $15,000 cash.

b. On December 10, Cynthiana repaired equipment of the A&W Root Beer Drive-In. A&W paid $1,500 in cash for the service call.

c. On December 10, Cynthiana purchased a new Chevy truck for business use. The truck cost $50,000. Cynthiana paid $8,500 down and signed a 1-year note for the balance.

d. Cynthiana received a $2,400 order of repair parts from Carrier Corporation on December 19. Carrier is expected to bill Cynthiana for $2,400 in early January.

e. On December 23, Cynthiana purchased 20 turkeys from Cub Foods for $500 cash. Cynthiana gave the turkeys to its employees as a Christmas gift.

Required:

For each transaction described above, indicate the effects on assets, liabilities, and stockholders' equity using the format below.

Assets	=	Liabilities	+	Stockholders' Equity		
				Contributed Capital	+	Retained Earnings

Exercise 2-37 Inferring Transactions from Balance Sheet Changes

OBJECTIVE ◄ 3

Each of the balance sheet changes below is associated with a particular transaction:

a. Equipment increases by $5,000 and cash decreases by $5,000.

b. Cash increases by $4,100 and stockholders' equity increases by $4,100.

c. Supplies increases by $400 and accounts payable increases by $400.

d. Supplies decreases by $250 and stockholders' equity decreases by $250.

Required:

CONCEPTUAL CONNECTION Describe each transaction listed above.

Exercise 2-38 Normal Balances and Financial Statements

OBJECTIVE ◄ 4

The following accounts are available for Haubstadt Shoe Works:

Accounts Payable	Advertising Expense
Accounts Receivable	Cash
Accumulated Depreciation (Equipment)	Common Stock

(Continued)

Cost of Goods Sold   Notes Payable
Depreciation Expense (Equipment)   Retained Earnings
Equipment   Sales Revenue
Interest Expense   Utilities Expense
Inventory

Required:

Using a table like the one below, indicate whether each account normally has a debit or credit balance and indicate on which of the financial statements (income statement, retained earnings statement, or balance sheet) each account appears.

Account	Debit	Credit	Financial Statement

OBJECTIVE 4

Exercise 2-39 Debit and Credit Effects of Transactions

Lincoln Corporation was involved in the following transactions during the current year:

a. Lincoln borrowed cash from the local bank on a note payable.
b. Lincoln purchased operating assets on credit.
c. Lincoln paid dividends in cash.
d. Lincoln purchased supplies inventory on credit.
e. Lincoln used a portion of the supplies purchased in Transaction d.
f. Lincoln provided services in exchange for cash from the customer.
g. A customer received services from Lincoln on credit.
h. The owners invested cash in the business in exchange for common stock.
i. The payable from Transaction d was paid in full.
j. The receivable from Transaction g was collected in full.
k. Lincoln paid wages in cash.

Required:

Prepare a table like the one shown below and indicate the effect on assets, liabilities, and stockholders' equity. Be sure to enter debits and credits in the appropriate columns for each of the transactions. Transaction a is entered as an example:

Assets	=	Liabilities	+	Stockholders' Equity	
				Contributed Capital	+ Retained Earnings
a. Increase		Increase			
(Debit)		(Credit)			

OBJECTIVE 4

Exercise 2-40 Debit and Credit Effect on Transactions

Jefferson Framers engaged in the following transactions:

a. Purchased land for $65,000 cash.
b. Purchased equipment for $26,400 in exchange for a 1-year, 8% note payable.
c. Purchased office supplies on credit for $1,200 from Office Depot.
d. Paid $20,000 principal plus $700 interest on a note payable.
e. Paid an account payable in the amount of $3,550.
f. Provided $61,300 of services on credit.
g. Provided $12,800 of services for cash.
h. Collected $26,910 of accounts receivable.
i. Paid $12,760 of wages in cash.
j. Issued common stock for $45,000 cash.

Required:

Using a table like the one below, enter the necessary information for each transaction. Enter the debits before the credits. Transaction a is entered as an example.

Transaction	Account	Increase/Decrease	Debit/Credit	Amount
(a)	Land	Increase	Debit	$35,200
	Cash	Decrease	Credit	$35,200

Exercise 2-41 Journalizing Transactions

OBJECTIVE ◄ 5

SHOW ME HOW

Kauai Adventures rents and sells surfboards, snorkeling, and scuba equipment. During March, Kauai engaged in the following transactions:

March   2   Received $51,500 cash from customers for rental.

3   Purchased on credit ten new surfboards (which Kauai classifies as inventory) for $180 each.

6   Paid wages to employees in the amount of $9,200.

9   Paid office rent for the month in the amount of $1,000.

12   Purchased a new Ford truck for $40,800; paid $1,000 down in cash and secured a loan from Princeville Bank for the $39,800 balance.

13   Collected a $1,050 account receivable.

16   Paid an account payable in the amount of $950.

23   Borrowed $10,000 on a 6-month, 8% note payable.

27   Paid the monthly telephone bill of $185.

30   Paid a monthly advertising bill of $1,550.

Required:

Prepare a journal entry for each of these transactions.

Exercise 2-42 Journalizing Transactions

OBJECTIVE ◄ 5

SHOW ME HOW

Remington Communications has been providing cellular phone service for several years. During November and December, the following transactions occurred:

Nov.   2   Remington received $2,200 for November phone service from Enrico Company.

6   Remington purchased $3,865 of supplies from Technology Associates on account.

10   Remington paid $6,220 to its hourly employees for their weekly wages.

15   Remington paid $3,865 to Technology Associates in full settlement of its account payable.

28   Remington paid $1,950 for utilities used during November.

30   Remington received a bill from Monticello Construction for $1,630 for repairs made to Remington's loading dock on November 15. Remington plans to pay the bill in early December.

Dec.   10   Remington paid $1,630 to Monticello Construction to settle the repair bill received on November 30.

Required:

1. Prepare a journal entry for each of these transactions.

2. **CONCEPTUAL CONNECTION** What accounting principle did you apply in recording the November 10 transaction?

Exercise 2-43 Transaction Analysis and Journal Entries

OBJECTIVE ◄ 5

SHOW ME HOW

Pasta House Inc. was organized in January. During the year, the transactions below occurred:

a. On January 14, Pasta House sold Martin Halter, the firm's founder and sole owner, 10,000 shares of its common stock for $8 per share.

b. On the same day, Bank One loaned Pasta House $45,000 on a 10-year note payable.

c. On February 22, Pasta House purchased a building and the land on which it stands from Frank Jakubek for $34,000 cash and a 5-year, $56,000 note payable. The land and building had appraised values of $30,000 and $60,000, respectively.

(Continued)

d. On March 1, Pasta House signed an $15,000 contract with Cosby Renovations to remodel the inside of the building. Pasta House paid $4,000 down and agreed to pay the remainder when Cosby completed its work.

e. On May 3, Cosby completed its work and submitted a bill to Pasta House for the remaining $11,000.

f. On May 20, Pasta House paid $11,000 to Cosby Renovations.

g. On June 4, Pasta House purchased restaurant supplies from Glidden Supply for $650 cash.

Required:

Prepare a journal entry for each of these transactions.

OBJECTIVE 4 5 6 7

Exercise 2-44 Accounting Cycle

Rosenthal Decorating Inc. is a commercial painting and decorating contractor that began operations in January. The following transactions occurred during the year:

a. On January 15, Rosenthal sold 500 shares of its common stock to William Hensley for $10,000.

b. On January 24, Rosenthal purchased $720 of painting supplies from Westwood Builders' Supply Company on account.

c. On February 20, Rosenthal paid $720 cash to Westwood Builders' Supply Company for the painting supplies purchased on January 24.

d. On April 25, Rosenthal billed Bultman Condominiums $12,500 for painting and decorating services performed in April.

e. On May 12, Rosenthal received $12,500 from Bultman Condominiums for the painting and decorating work billed in April.

f. On June 5, Rosenthal sent Arlington Builders a $9,500 bill for a painting job completed on that day.

g. On June 24, Rosenthal paid wages for work performed during the preceding week in the amount of $6,700.

Required:

1. Prepare a journal entry for each of the transactions.
2. Post the transactions to T-accounts.
3. Prepare a trial balance at June 30.

OBJECTIVE 7

Exercise 2-45 Preparing a Trial Balance Preparation

The following accounts and account balances are available for Badger Auto Parts at December 31:

Accounts Payable	$ 8,500		Income Taxes Payable	$ 3,600
Accounts Receivable	40,800		Interest Expense	6,650
Accumulated Depreciation (Furniture)	47,300		Interest Payable	1,800
Advertising Expense	29,200		Inventory	60,500
Cash	3,200		Notes Payable (Long-term)	50,000
Common Stock	100,000		Prepaid Rent	15,250
Cost of Goods Sold	184,300		Retained Earnings, January 1	15,900
Depreciation Expense (Furniture)	10,400		Sales Revenue	264,700
Furniture	128,000		Utilities Expense	9,700
Income Taxes Expense	3,800			

Required:

Prepare a trial balance. Assume that all accounts have normal balances.

Exercise 2-46 Preparing a Trial Balance

OBJECTIVE 7

The following trial balance that was prepared by the bookkeeper of Mason Company does not balance.

Mason Company
Trial Balance
December 31

	Debit	Credit
Cash		$20,000
Accounts Payable	$ 3,000	
Insurance Expense	1,500	
Supplies	1,200	
Accounts Receivable		10,300
Salaries Payable	1,900	
Notes Payable		3,100
Common Stock		10,000
Dividends		2,000
Retained Earnings	8,000	
Service Revenue	19,200	
Unearned Service Revenue	2,100	
Prepaid Insurance		1,900
Salaries Expense	9,500	
Supplies Expense		900
	$46,400	$48,200

Required:

Prepare a correct trial balance. Assume all accounts have normal balances.

Exercise 2-47 Effect of Errors on a Trial Balance

OBJECTIVE 7

The bookkeeper for Riley Inc. made the following errors:

a. A cash purchase of supplies of $348 was recorded as a debit to Supplies for $384 and a credit to Cash of $384.
b. A cash sale of $3,128 was recorded as a debit to Cash of $3,128 and a credit to Sales of $3,182.
c. A purchase of equipment was recorded once in the journal and posted twice to the ledger.
d. Cash paid for salaries of $5,270 was recorded as a debit to Salaries Expense of $5,270 and a credit to Accounts Payable of $5,270.
e. A credit sale of $7,600 was recorded as a credit to Sales Revenue of $7,600; however, the debit posting to Accounts Receivable was omitted.

Required:

Indicate whether or not the trial balance will balance after the error. If the trial balance will not balance, indicate the direction of the misstatement for any effected account (such as Cash will be overstated by $50).

PROBLEM SET A

Problem 2-48A Events and Transactions

OBJECTIVE 2 3

The accountant for Boatsman Products Inc. received the following information:

a. Boatsman sent its customers a new price list. Prices were increased an average of 3% on all items.
b. Boatsman accepted an offer of $150,000 for land that it had purchased 2 years ago for $130,000. Cash and the deed for the property are to be exchanged in 5 days.

(Continued)

c. Boatsman accepted $150,000 cash and gave the purchaser the deed for the property described in Item b.

d. Boatsman's president purchased 600 shares of the firm's common stock from another stockholder. The president paid $15 per share. The former stockholder had purchased the stock from Boatsman for $4 per share.

e. Boatsman leases its delivery trucks from a local dealer. The dealer also performs maintenance on the trucks for Boatsman. Boatsman received a $1,254 bill for maintenance from the dealer.

Required:

1. **CONCEPTUAL CONNECTION** Indicate whether or not each item qualifies as a transaction and should be recorded in the accounting system. Explain your reasoning.

2. **CONCEPTUAL CONNECTION** What accounting concept is illustrated by Item d?

OBJECTIVE 3 7

SHOW ME HOW

Problem 2-49A Analyzing Transactions

Luis Madero, after working for several years with a large public accounting firm, decided to open his own accounting service. The business is operated as a corporation under the name Madero Accounting Services. The following captions and amounts summarize Madero's balance sheet at July 31.

	Assets			=	Liabilities		+		Equity	
Cash	Accounts Receivable	+ Supplies		=	Accounts Payable	+ Notes Payable	+	Common Stock	+	Retained Earnings
8,000	15,900	4,100			2,500	4,000		12,000		9,500

The following events occurred during August.

a. Issued common stock to Ms. Garriz in exchange for $15,000 cash.
b. Paid $850 for first month's rent on office space.
c. Purchased supplies of $2,250 on credit.
d. Borrowed $8,000 from the bank.
e. Paid $1,080 on account for supplies purchased earlier on credit.
f. Paid secretary's salary for August of $2,150.
g. Performed accounting services for clients who paid cash upon completion of the service in the total amount of $4,700.
h. Used $3,180 of the supplies on hand.
i. Performed accounting services for clients on credit in the total amount of $1,920.
j. Purchased $500 in supplies for cash.
k. Collected $1,290 cash from clients for whom services were performed on credit.
l. Paid $1,000 dividend to stockholders.

Required:

1. Record the effects of the transactions listed above on the accounting equation. Use the format given in the problem, starting with the totals at July 31.

2. Prepare the trial balance at August 31.

Problem 2-50A Inferring Transactions from T-Accounts

OBJECTIVE ◄ 3 4 7

The following T-accounts summarize the operations of Chen Construction Company for July.

🔍 SHOW ME HOW

Assets

Cash

7/1	200		
7/2	1,000	150	7/5
7/7	2,500	700	7/9
7/11	150	750	7/14

Accounts Receivable

7/1	1,400	150	7/11

Supplies

7/1	750	
7/4	250	

Land

7/1	3,000	
7/9	700	

Liabilities

Accounts Payable

		1,100	7/1
7/5	150	250	7/4

Stockholders' Equity

Common Stock

	4,000	7/1
	1,000	7/2

Retained Earnings

		250	7/1
7/14	750	2,500	7/7

Required:

1. **CONCEPTUAL CONNECTION** Assuming that only one transaction occurred on each day (beginning on July 2) and that no dividends were paid, describe the transactions that most likely took place.
2. Prepare a trial balance at July 31.

Problem 2-51A Debit and Credit Procedures

OBJECTIVE ◄ 4

A list of accounts for Montgomery Inc. appears below.

Accounts Payable
Accounts Receivable
Accumulated Depreciation
Cash
Common Stock
Depreciation Expense
Equipment
Income Taxes Expense

Interest Expense
Land
Notes Payable
Prepaid Rent
Retained Earnings
Salaries Expense
Service Revenue
Supplies

Required:

Complete the table below for these accounts. The information for the first account has been entered as an example.

Account	Type of Account	Normal Balance	Increase	Decrease
Accounts Payable	Liability	Credit	Credit	Debit

(Continued)

OBJECTIVE

Problem 2-52A Journalizing Transactions

Monroe Company rents and sells electronic equipment. During September, Monroe engaged in the transactions described below.

Sept.		
	5	Purchased a Chevrolet truck for $38,900 cash.
	8	Purchased inventory for $4,200 on account.
	10	Purchased $1,250 of office supplies on credit.
	11	Rented sound equipment to a traveling stage play for $13,600. The producer of the play paid for the service at the time it was provided.
	12	Rented sound equipment and lights to a local student organization for a school dance for $2,400. The student organization will pay for services within 30 days.
	18	Paid employee wages of $4,750 that have been earned during September.
	22	Collected the receivable from the September 12 transaction.
	23	Borrowed $20,000 cash from a bank on a 3-year note payable.
	28	Issued common stock to new stockholders for $35,000.
	30	Paid a $3,250 cash dividend to stockholders.

Required:
Prepare a journal entry for each transaction.

OBJECTIVE 5 6

Problem 2-53A Journalizing and Posting Transactions

Cincinnati Painting Service Inc. specializes in painting houses. During June, its first month of operations, Cincinnati Painting engaged in the following transactions:

June	1	Issued common stock for $25,000.
	3	Purchased painting supplies from River City Supply for $1,675 on credit.
	8	Purchased a used truck from Hamilton Used Car Sales for $13,700, paying $1,500 down and agreeing to pay the balance in 6 months.
	14	Paid $4,230 to hourly employees for work performed in June.
	22	Billed various customers a total of $10,340 for June painting jobs.
	26	Received $6,100 cash from James Eaton for a house painting job completed and previously billed.
	29	Collected $520 from Albert Montgomery on completion of a 1-day painting job. This amount is not included in the June 22 bills.

Required:
1. Prepare a journal entry for each transaction.
2. Post the journal entries to the appropriate T-accounts.

OBJECTIVE 2 3 4 5
                                  6 7

Problem 2-54A The Accounting Cycle

Karleen's Catering Service provides catered meals to individuals and businesses. Karleen's purchases its food ready to serve from Mel's Restaurant. In order to prepare a realistic trial balance, the events described below are aggregations of many individual events during the year.

a. Common stock was issued for $22,000.
b. During the year, Karleen's paid office rent of $13,500.
c. Utilities expenses incurred and paid were $5,320.
d. Wages of $58,800 were earned by employees and paid during the year.
e. During the year, Karleen's provided catering services:

On credit	$128,200
For cash	18,650

f. Karleen's paid $59,110 for supplies purchased and used during the year.
g. Karleen's paid dividends in the amount of $3,500.
h. Karleen's collected accounts receivable in the amount of $109,400.

Required:

1. Analyze the events for their effect on the accounting equation.
2. Prepare journal entries. (*Note:* Ignore the date because these events are aggregations of individual events.)
3. Post the journal entries to the appropriate T-accounts.
4. Prepare a trial balance at December 31. Assume that all beginning account balances at January 1 are zero.

Problem 2-55A Comprehensive Problem

Western Sound Studios records and masters audio recordings of popular artists in live concerts. The performers use the recordings to prepare "live" songs for download. The following account balances were available at the beginning of the year:

Accounts Payable	$ 11,900
Accounts Receivable	384,000
Cash	16,300
Common Stock	165,000
Insurance Payable	1,000
Interest Payable	11,200
Notes Payable (Long-term)	100,000
Rent Payable (Building)	10,000
Retained Earnings, January 1	101,200

During the year, the following transactions occurred (the events described below are aggregations of many individual events):

a. Recording services in the amount of $994,000 were billed.
b. The accounts receivable at the beginning of the year were collected.
c. In addition, cash for $983,000 of the services billed in Transaction a was collected.
d. The rent payable for the building was paid. In addition, $48,000 of building rental costs was paid in cash. There was no rent payable or prepaid rent at year-end.
e. The insurance payable on January 1 was paid. In addition, $4,000 of insurance costs was paid in cash. There was no insurance payable or prepaid insurance at year-end.
f. Utilities expense of $56,000 was incurred and paid during the year.
g. Salaries expense for the year was $702,000. All $702,000 was paid during the year.
h. The interest payable at January 1 was paid. During the year, an additional $11,000 of interest was paid. At year-end no interest was payable.
i. Income taxes for the year in the amount of $19,700 were incurred and paid.

Required:

1. Establish a T-account for the accounts listed above and enter the beginning balances. Use a chart of accounts to order the T-accounts.
2. Analyze each transaction. Journalize as appropriate. (*Note:* Ignore the date because these events are aggregations of individual events.)
3. Post your journal entries to the T-accounts. Add additional T-accounts when needed.
4. Use the ending balances in the T-accounts to prepare a trial balance.

PROBLEM SET B

Problem 2-48B Events and Transactions

OBJECTIVE ◀ 2 3

The following list contains events that occurred during January at the local Ford dealer, Malcom Motors:

a. California Central University (CCU) signed a contract to purchase a fleet of Ford Crown Victoria vehicles from Malcom Motors at a total price of $200,000, payable to Malcom in two equal amounts on August 1 and September 1. The cars will be delivered to CCU during August.

(Continued)

b. The principal stockholder in Malcom Motors sold 10% of her stock in the company to John Lewis, the president of Malcom Motors, in exchange for $100,000 in cash.
c. Malcom Motors issued new stock to John Lewis in exchange for $50,000 in cash.
d. Malcom Motors owns the building it occupies; the company occupied the building during the entire month of January.
e. Malcom Motors owns land used for the storage of cars awaiting sale; the land was used by the company during the entire month of January.
f. Malcom Motors paid its lawyer $1,000 for services rendered in connection with the purchase agreement signed with California Central University.
g. Maintenance Management Company performed cleaning services for Malcom Motors during January under a contract that does not require payment for those services until March 1.

Required:
1. **CONCEPTUAL CONNECTION** Indicate whether each item qualifies as a transaction and should be recorded in the accounting system. Explain your reasoning.
2. **CONCEPTUAL CONNECTION** What concept is illustrated by Event b?

OBJECTIVE

Problem 2-49B Analyzing Transactions

Several years ago, Mary Emerson founded Emerson Consulting Inc., a consulting business specializing in financial planning for young professionals. The following captions and amounts summarize Emerson Consulting's balance sheet at January 1, the beginning of the current year:

Assets			=	Liabilities		+	Equity	
Cash	Accounts Receivable	Supplies		Accounts Payable	Notes Payable		Common Stock	Retained Earnings
3,000	6,600	4,800		500	1,000		10,000	2,900

During January, the following transactions occurred:

a. Issued common stock to a new stockholder in exchange for $12,000 cash.
b. Performed advisory services for a client for $3,850 and received the full amount in cash.
c. Received $925 on account from a client for whom services had been performed on credit.
d. Purchased supplies for $1,140 on credit.
e. Paid $875 on accounts payable.
f. Performed advisory services for $2,980 on credit.
g. Paid cash of $1,350 for secretarial services during January.
h. Paid cash of $800 for January's office rent.
i. Paid utilities used in January in the amount of $1,340.
j. Paid a dividend of $500.

Required:
1. Record the effects of the transactions listed above on the accounting equation for the business. Use the format given in the problem, starting with the totals at January 1.
2. Prepare the trial balance at January 31.

OBJECTIVE 3 4 7   **Problem 2-50B Inferring Transactions from T-Accounts**

The following T-accounts summarize the operations of Brilliant Minds Inc., a tutoring service, for April.

Assets

Cash

4/1	500	700	4/8
4/3	2,000	325	4/9
4/18	1,500	150	4/15
4/24	375		

Accounts Receivable

4/1	700	375	4/24

Supplies

4/1	900	140	4/11
4/15	150		

Equipment

4/1	1,200		
4/8	700		

Liabilities

Accounts Payable

4/9	325	625	4/1

Notes Payable

	2,000	4/3

Stockholders' Equity

Common Stock

	2,000	4/1

Retained Earnings

4/11	140	675	4/1
		1,500	4/18

Required:

1. **CONCEPTUAL CONNECTION** Assuming that only one transaction occurred on each day (beginning on April 3) and that no dividends were paid, describe the transaction that most likely took place.
2. Prepare a trial balance at April 30.

Problem 2-51B Debit and Credit Procedures

OBJECTIVE ◀ 3

A list of accounts for Montgomery Inc. appears below.

Accounts Payable	Income Taxes Payable
Accounts Receivable	Insurance Expense
Bonds Payable	Interest Expense
Building	Inventory
Cash	Investments
Common Stock	Retained Earnings
Copyright	Sales Revenue
Cost of Goods Sold	Unearned Revenue
Depreciation Expense	Utilities Expense
Income Taxes Expense	

Required:

Complete the table below for these accounts. The information for the first account has been entered as an example.

Account	Type of Account	Normal Balance	Increase	Decrease
Accounts Payable	Liability	Credit	Credit	Debit

Problem 2-52B Journalizing Transactions

OBJECTIVE ◀ 5

Monilast Chemicals engaged in the following transactions during December:

Dec.	2	Paid rent on office furniture, $1,200.
	3	Borrowed $25,000 on a 9-month, 8% note.

SHOW ME HOW

(*Continued*)

    7   Provided services on credit, $42,600.
    10   Purchased supplies on credit, $2,850.
    13   Collected accounts receivable, $20,150.
    19   Issued common stock, $50,000.
    22   Paid employee wages for December, $13,825.
    23   Paid accounts payable, $1,280.
    25   Provided services for cash, $13,500.
    30   Paid utility bills for December, $1,975.

Required:
Prepare a journal entry for each transaction.

OBJECTIVE

Problem 2-53B Journalizing and Posting Transactions

Findlay Testing Inc. provides water testing and maintenance services for owners of hot tubs and swimming pools. During September, the following transactions occurred:

Sept.   1   Issued common stock for $20,000.
    2   Purchased chemical supplies for $1,880 cash.
    5   Paid office rent for October, November, and December; the rent is $800 per month.
    8   Purchased $1,290 of advertising for September on account.
    13   Billed the city of Bellefontaine $2,100 for testing the water in the city's outdoor pools during September.
    18   Received $8,250 from Alexander Blanchard upon completion of overhaul of his swimming pool water circulation system. Since the job was completed and collected for on the same day, no bill was sent to Blanchard.
    25   Received $835 from the city of Bellefontaine for water testing that was previously billed.
    30   Recorded and paid September salaries of $3,970.

Required:
  1. Prepare a journal entry for each transaction.
  2. Post the journal entries to the appropriate T-accounts.

OBJECTIVE

Problem 2-54B The Accounting Cycle

Sweetwater Temporary Clerical Help Service opened for business in June. From the opening until the end of the year, Sweetwater engaged in the activities described below. So that a realistic trial balance can be prepared, the events described below are aggregations of many individual events.

  a. Sold 10,000 shares of common stock for $4.50 per share.
  b. Purchased office equipment from FurnitureMax Inc. for $18,710 cash.
  c. Received $112,880 from clients for services provided.
  d. Paid wages of $87,300.
  e. Borrowed $20,000 from the Bank of America on a 3-year note payable.
  f. Paid office rent of $10,200.
  g. Purchased office supplies on credit for $2,120 from Office Supply Inc.
  h. Paid $1,200 toward the payable established in Transaction g.
  i. Paid utility charges incurred during the year of $3,250.

Required:
  1. Analyze the events for their effect on the accounting equation.
  2. Prepare journal entries. (*Note:* Ignore the date because these events are aggregations of individual events.)
  3. Post the journal entries to T-accounts.
  4. Prepare a trial balance at December 31.

Problem 2-55B Comprehensive Problem

OBJECTIVE ◀ 2 3 4 5 6 7

Mulberry Services sells electronic data processing services to firms too small to own their own computing equipment. Mulberry had the following accounts and account balances as of January 1:

Accounts Payable	$ 14,000
Accounts Receivable	130,000
Cash	6,000
Common Stock	114,000
Interest Payable	8,000
Notes Payable (Long-term)	80,000
Prepaid Rent (Short-term)	96,000
Retained Earnings, January 1	16,000

During the year, the following transactions occurred (the events described below are aggregations of many individual events):

a. During the year, Mulberry sold $690,000 of computing services, all on credit.
b. Mulberry collected $570,000 from the credit sales in Transaction a and an additional $129,000 from the accounts receivable outstanding at the beginning of the year.
c. Mulberry paid the interest payable of $8,000.
d. Wages of $379,000 were paid in cash.
e. Repairs and maintenance of $9,000 were incurred and paid.
f. The prepaid rent at the beginning of the year was used during the year. In addition, $28,000 of computer rental costs were incurred and paid. There is no prepaid rent or rent payable at year-end.
g. Mulberry purchased computer paper for $13,000 cash in late December. None of the paper was used by year-end.
h. Advertising expense of $26,000 was incurred and paid.
i. Income tax of $10,300 was incurred and paid during the year.
j. Interest of $5,000 was paid on the long-term loan.

Required:

1. Establish a ledger for the accounts listed above and enter the beginning balances. Use a chart of accounts to order the ledger accounts.
2. Analyze each transaction. Journalize as appropriate. (*Note:* Ignore the date because these events are aggregations of individual events.)
3. Post your journal entries to T-accounts. Add additional T-accounts when needed.
4. Use the ending balances in the T-accounts to prepare a trial balance.

CASES

Case 2-56 Analysis of the Accounting Cycle

Susan Eel wants to sell you her wholesale fish store. She shows you a balance sheet with total assets of $150,000 and total liabilities of $20,000. According to the income statement, last year's net income was $40,000.

When examining the accounting records, you notice that several accounts receivable in the $10,000 to $15,000 range are not supported by source documents. You also notice that there is no source documentation to support the $30,000 balance in the building account and the $10,000 balance in the equipment account. Susan tells you that she gave the building and refrigeration equipment to the business in exchange for stock. She also says that she has not had time to set up and monitor any paperwork for accounts receivable or accounts payable.

(*Continued*)

Required:

1. What requirements for transaction recognition appear to have been ignored when the accounts receivable, building, and equipment were recorded?
2. What would be the effect on the financial statements if the values appearing in the balance sheet for accounts receivable, building, and equipment were overstated? What would be the effect if the accounts payable were understated?
3. Assuming that you would like to purchase the company, what would you do to establish a reasonable purchase price?

Case 2-57 Analysis of the Effects of Current Asset and Current Liability Changes on Cash Flows

You have the following data for Cable Company's accounts receivable and accounts payable at the end of the year:

Accounts receivable, January 1	$ 6,325
Sales made during the year on credit	93,680
Accounts receivable, December 31	7,950
Wages payable, January 1	4,960
Wage expense incurred during the year	49,510
Wages payable, December 31	3,625

Required:

1. **CONCEPTUAL CONNECTION** How much cash did Cable collect from customers during the year?
2. How would you classify cash collected from customers on the statement of cash flows?
3. How much cash did Cable pay for wages during the year?
4. How would you classify the cash paid for wages on the statement of cash flows?

Case 2-58 Ethical Issues

Kathryn Goldsmith is the chief accountant for Clean Sweep, a national carpet-cleaning service with a December fiscal year-end. As Kathryn was preparing the financial statements for Clean Sweep, she noticed several odd transactions in the general ledger for December. For example, rent for next January, which was paid in December, was recorded by debiting rent expense instead of prepaid rent. In another transaction, Kathryn noticed that the use of supplies was recorded with a debit to insurance expense instead of supplies expense. Upon further investigation, Kathryn discovered that the December ledger contained numerous such mistakes. Even with the mistakes, the trial balance still balanced.

Kathryn traced all of the mistakes back to a recently hired bookkeeper, Ben Goldsmith, Kathryn's son. Kathryn had hired Ben to help out in the accounting department over Christmas break so that he could earn some extra money for school. After discussing the situation with Ben, Kathryn determined that Ben's mistakes were all unintentional.

Required:

1. What ethical issues are involved?
2. What are Kathryn's alternatives? Which would be the most ethical alternative to choose?

Case 2-59 Research and Analysis Using the Annual Report

Obtain **Disney**'s 2019 annual report either through the "Investor Relations" portion of its website (do a web search for Disney investor relations) or go to www.sec.gov and click "Company Filings Search" under "Filings."

Required:

1. Determine the amounts in the accounting equation for the most recent year.
2. What is the normal balance for the following accounts?
   a. Receivables
   b. Accounts Payable
   c. Service Revenue
   d. Parks, Resorts, and Other Property
   e. Cost of Services
   f. Inventories
   g. Retained Earnings
3. Identify the additional account that is most likely involved when:
   a. Accounts Payable is decreased.
   b. Accounts Receivables is increased.
   c. Common Stock is increased.
   d. Wages Payable is increased.

Case 2-60 Comparative Analysis: Kroger versus Sprout

Refer to the 10-K reports of **Kroger** and **Sprout** that are available for download from the companion website at Cengage.com.

Required:

1. Determine the amounts in the accounting equation for the most current fiscal year for each company. Does the accounting equation balance?
2. Set up a T-account for Kroger's and Sprout's accounts receivable account and include the beginning and ending balances. Complete the T-account to reflect the sales and cash collections for the year for each company. Assume all sales are on account.
3. Prepare the journal entry to record the following two events for Kroger and Sprout. For simplicity, assume the event was recorded in a single journal entry on the last day of the company's fiscal year.
   a. What journal entry is necessary to record net sales for the current fiscal year? Assume that all sales were made on account.
   b. What journal entry is necessary to record cash collections from customers during the current fiscal year?

Case 2-61 Accounting for Partially Completed Events: a Prelude to Chapter 3

Ehrlich Smith, the owner of The Shoe Box, has asked you to help him understand the proper way to account for certain accounting items as he prepares his financial statements. Smith has provided the following information and observations:

a. A 3-year fire insurance policy was purchased at the beginning of the year for $2,400. Smith believes that a part of the cost of the insurance policy should be allocated to each period that benefits from its coverage.
b. The store building was purchased 8 years ago for $80,000. Smith expected then (as he does now) that the building will be serviceable as a shoe store for 20 years from the date of purchase. At the time of purchase, Smith estimated that he could sell the

(*Continued*)

property for $6,000 at the end of its serviceable life. He feels that each period should bear some portion of the cost of this long-lived asset that is slowly being consumed.

c. The Shoe Box borrowed $20,000 on a 1-year, 8% note that is due on September 1 next year. Smith notes that $21,600 cash will be required to repay the note at maturity. The $1,600 difference is, he feels, a cost of using the loaned funds and should be spread over the periods that benefit from the use of the loan funds.

Required:

1. Explain what Smith is trying to accomplish with the three items. Are his objectives supported by the concepts that underlie accounting?
2. Describe how each of the three items should be reflected in the current income statement and the December 31 balance sheet to accomplish Smith's objectives.

ANNUAL REPORT PROBLEM

HOME DEPOT

Download the 10-K for **Home Depot** from the companion website at Cengage.com.

Required:

1. What does Home Depot report for the following items?
   a. Total assets
   b. Total liabilities
2. Assume that Home Depot projects the following:
   - Assets are expected to increase by 12%.
   - Liabilities are projected to increase by 4%.

   Assume all other items remain unchanged from the prior year. Provide the next fiscal year's forecasted balances for total assets and total liabilities.

3. Answer the following questions:
   a. Compute the forecasted balance shareholders' equity based on the projections for assets and liabilities.
   b. What date would you expect Home Depot's next fiscal year to end?
   c. What accounting assumption supports the use of a fiscal year?
   d. Where does Home Depot discuss its revenue recognition policy?
   e. Who is Home Depot's auditor?
   f. What characteristic of useful information is most associated with the audit report?

Note: *While the Annual Report problems in the textbook are static, when assigned in CNOW, these activities are algorithmic and the answers may vary from what appears in the Solutions Manual.*

CONTINUING PROBLEM

FRONT ROW ENTERTAINMENT

After much consideration, Cam and Anna decide to organize their company as a corporation. On January 1, 2023, Front Row Entertainment Inc. begins operations. Due to Cam's family connections in the entertainment industry, Cam assumes the major responsibility for signing artists to a promotion contract. Meanwhile, Anna assumes the financial accounting and reporting responsibilities. The following business activities occurred during January:

Jan.   1   Cam and Anna invest $8,000 each in the company in exchange for common stock.

1	The company obtains a $25,000 loan from a local bank. Front Row Entertainment agreed to pay annual interest of 9% each January 1, starting in 2024. It will repay the amount borrowed in 5 years.
1	The company paid $1,200 in legal fees associated with incorporation.
1	Office equipment was purchased with $7,000 in cash.
1	The company pays $800 to rent office space for January.
3	A 1-year insurance policy was purchased for $3,600.
3	Office supplies of $2,500 were purchased from Equipment Supply Services. Equipment Supply Services agreed to accept $1,000 in 15 days with the remainder due in 30 days.
5	The company signs Charm City, a local band with a growing cult following, to a four-city tour that starts on February 15.
8	Venues for all four Charm City concerts were reserved by paying $10,000 cash.
12	Advertising costs of $4,500 were paid to promote the concert tour.
18	Paid $1,000 to Equipment Supply Services for office supplies purchased on January 3.
25	To aid in the promotion of the upcoming tour, Front Row Entertainment arranged for Charm City to perform a 20-minute set at a local festival. Front Row Entertainment received $1,000 for Charm City's appearance. Of this total amount, $400 was received immediately with the remainder due in 15 days. The festival took place on January 25.
25	Paid Charm City $800 for performing at the festival. *Note:* Front Row Entertainment records the fees paid to the artist in an operating expense account called Artist Fee Expense.
28	Due to the success of the marketing efforts, Front Row Entertainment received $3,800 in advance ticket sales for the upcoming tour.
30	The company collected $200 of the amount due from the January 25 festival.
30	Paid salaries of $1,200 each to Cam and Anna for the month of January.

Required:

1. Analyze and journalize the January transactions.
2. Post the transactions to the general ledger.
3. Prepare a trial balance at January 31, 2023.

TYPICAL CHART OF ACCOUNTS

ASSETS

Accounts Receivable
Accumulated Depletion
Accumulated
    Depreciation
Allowance for Doubtful
    Accounts
Allowance to Adjust
    Available-for-Sale
    Securities to Market
Allowance to Adjust
    Trading Securities to
    Market
Buildings
Cash
Copyright
Equipment
Finished Goods
    Inventory
Franchise
Furniture
Goodwill
Interest Receivable
Inventory
Investments
Investments—Available-
    for-Sale Securities
Investments—Equity
    Method
Investments—Trading
    Securities
Land
Leasehold Improvements
Natural Resources
Notes Receivable
Other Assets
Patent
Petty Cash
Prepaid Advertising
Prepaid Insurance
Prepaid Rent
Prepaid Repairs &
    Maintenance
Prepaid Security Services
Raw Materials Inventory
Rent Receivable
Supplies
Tax Refund Receivable
Trademark
Trucks
Work-in-Process Inventory

LIABILITIES

Accounts Payable
Bonds Payable
Capital Lease Liability
Charitable
    Contributions
Commissions Payable
Discount on Bonds
    Payable
Discount on Notes
    Payable
Dividends Payable
Excise Taxes Payable
Income Taxes Payable
Interest Payable
Lawsuit Payable
Lease Liability
Leased Assets
Medicare Taxes
    Payable
Notes Payable
Premium on Bonds
    Payable
Premium on Notes
    Payable
Property Taxes Payable
Rent Payable
Repair & Maintenance
    Payable
Royalties Payable
Salaries Payable
Sales Taxes Payable
Social Security Taxes
    Payable
Unearned Rent
    Revenue
Unearned Sales
    Revenue
Unearned Service
    Revenue
Unemployment Taxes
    Payable
Union Dues Payable
Utilities Payable
Wages Payable
Warranty Liability

STOCKHOLDERS' EQUITY

Accumulated Other
    Comprehensive
    Income
Additional Paid-In
    Capital—Common
    Stock
Additional Paid-In
    Capital—Preferred
    Stock
Additional Paid-In
    Capital—Treasury
    Stock
Common Stock
Preferred Stock
Retained Earnings
Treasury Stock
Unrealized Gain (Loss)
    on Available-for-Sale
    Securities

EQUITY-RELATED ACCOUNTS

Dividends
Income Summary

REVENUES/GAINS

Dividend Income
Interest Income
Investment Income—
    Equity Method
Rent Revenue
Sales Revenue
Service Revenue

Gain on Disposal of
    Property, Plant, &
    Equipment
Gain on Sale of
    Intangibles
Gain on Sale of
    Investments
Gain on Settlement of
    Lawsuit
Unrealized Gain (Loss) on
    Trading Securities

EXPENSES/LOSSES

Advertising Expense
Amortization Expense
Artist Fee Expense
Bad Debt Expense
Bank Service Charge
    Expense
Cash Over and Short
Commissions Expense
Cost of Goods Sold
Delivery Expense
Depreciation Expense
Income Taxes Expense
Insurance Expense
Interest Expense
Legal Expense
Medicare Taxes Expense
Miscellaneous Expense
Organizational Costs
Other Expense
Postage Expense
Property Taxes Expense

Purchase Allowances
Purchase Discounts
Purchase Returns
Purchases
Rent Expense
Repairs & Maintenance
    Expense
Research and
    Development Expense
Royalties Expense
Salaries Expense
Security Services Expense
Service Charge Expense
Social Security Taxes
    Expense
Supplies Expense
Transportation-In
Unemployment Taxes
    Expense
Utilities Expense
Wages Expense
Warranty Expense

Loss from Impairment
Loss on Disposal of
    Property, Plant, &
    Equipment
Loss on Sale of
    Intangibles
Loss on Sale of
    Investments

Note:

The Chart of Accounts for this edition of *Financial Accounting* has been simplified and standardized throughout all hypothetical in-chapter examples and end-of-chapter assignments in order to strengthen the pedagogical structure of the book. Account titles for real company financial statements will vary. Common alternate account titles are given in the textbook where the account is introduced, as appropriate, and real financial statement excerpts are included to help familiarize readers with alternate account titles.

When additional information is needed for an account title, it will be shown in parenthesis after the title [e.g., Accumulated Depreciation (Equipment), Excise Taxes Payable (State), Social Security Taxes Payable (Employer).]

This Chart of Accounts is listed alphabetically by category for ease of reference. However, accounts in the textbook and in real financial statements are listed in order of liquidity.

3 Accrual Accounting

After studying Chapter 3, you should be able to:

1. Explain the difference between cash-basis and accrual-basis accounting.

2. Explain how the time-period assumption, revenue recognition principle, and the expense recognition principle affect the determination of income.

3. Identify the kinds of transactions that may require adjustments at the end of an accounting period.

4. Prepare adjusting entries for accruals and deferrals.

5. Prepare financial statements from an adjusted trial balance.

6. Prepare closing entries.

7. List the steps in the accounting cycle.

8. (Appendix 3A) Prepare financial statement using a worksheet.

with FedEx®

FedEx began operations in 1973 with 14 jets that connected 25 U.S. cities. Some employees even used their own cars to deliver packages. As a pioneer of the hub and spoke model for overnight package delivery, FedEx is now the world's largest express transportation company with operations in over 220 countries. With more than 450,000 "team members," 681 aircraft, and 91,000 vehicles, FedEx connects markets that generate over 99% of the world's gross domestic product.

The end of the fiscal year, or accounting period, is a busy time as companies like FedEx make adjustments to the accounting information. Adjustments are necessary because a company's business activities often occur over several accounting periods. In a recent annual report, an excerpt of which is shown in Exhibit 3.1, FedEx's financial statements include many expenses that would not have been recognized without adjustments.

This sample of expenses, which doesn't include all the adjustments made, represents almost 13% of the total operating expenses that FedEx reported on its income statement. When FedEx recognized these expenses (except for depreciation and amortization), it also recorded a liability for them. These liabilities represented almost 56% of FedEx's current liabilities. The adjustment to recognize depreciation and amortization expense resulted in a decrease in assets of $3,353 million. Clearly, the failure to adjust for these expenses would significantly affect FedEx's financial statements.

Excerpt from FedEx's Financial Statements

EXHIBIT 3.1

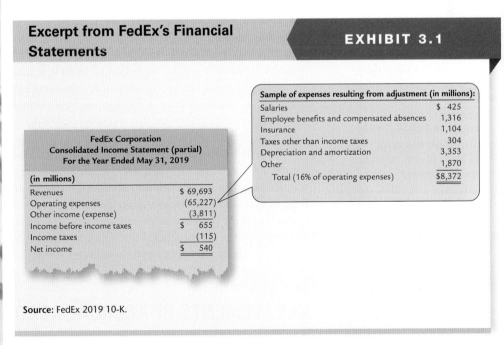

Sample of expenses resulting from adjustment (in millions):

Salaries	$ 425
Employee benefits and compensated absences	1,316
Insurance	1,104
Taxes other than income taxes	304
Depreciation and amortization	3,353
Other	1,870
Total (16% of operating expenses)	$8,372

FedEx Corporation
Consolidated Income Statement (partial)
For the Year Ended May 31, 2019

(in millions)	
Revenues	$ 69,693
Operating expenses	(65,227)
Other income (expense)	(3,811)
Income before income taxes	$ 655
Income taxes	(115)
Net income	$ 540

Source: FedEx 2019 10-K.

COMPLETING THE ACCOUNTING CYCLE

In the previous chapter, we examined how companies use the double-entry accounting system to record business activities that occur during the accounting period. However, accountants also make numerous adjustments at the end of accounting periods for business activities that occur over several accounting periods—activities like performing services for customers, renting office space, and using equipment. As shown with **FedEx**, these adjustments can be significant.

Why are so many business activities recognized in the accounts through adjustments rather than through the normal journal entry process described in Chapter 2? The illustrations used in Chapter 2 excluded activities that were still underway at the end of the accounting period. However, accrual accounting requires that any incomplete activities be recognized in the financial statements. This often requires estimates and judgments about the timing of revenue and expense recognition. The result is that accountants must adjust the accounts to properly reflect these partially completed business activities.

In this chapter, we will review the concepts that form the basis for adjustments and then complete the accounting cycle that was introduced in Chapter 2 by exploring the preparation and effects of adjusting journal entries, preparing financial statements from the adjusted accounts, and closing the accounts in order to prepare for the next accounting period. We will address the following questions:

- What is the difference between the cash basis and the accrual basis of accounting?
- What is the purpose of adjusting entries?
- What types of transactions require adjustment, and how are the adjustments recorded in the accounting system?
- Which accounts are closed at the end of the period, and why is this necessary?

ACCRUAL VERSUS CASH BASIS OF ACCOUNTING

If you were asked what your net income (revenues minus expenses) for the month was, what would you do? Most likely, you would go online and look at your bank activity for the month. You would then list the total of the deposits as revenue and the total of the withdrawals as expenses. The difference would be your net income. This method of accounting is called **cash-basis accounting**. Under cash-basis accounting, revenue is recorded when cash is received, regardless of when the goods are delivered or services are provided. Similarly, an expense is recorded when cash is paid, regardless of when it is actually incurred. Therefore, cash-basis accounting does not link recognition of revenues and expenses to the actual business activity but rather the exchange of cash. In addition, by recording only the cash effect of transactions, cash-basis financial statements may not reflect all of the assets and liabilities of a company at a particular date. For this reason, most companies do not use cash-basis accounting.

Accrual-basis accounting (also called *accrual accounting*) is an alternative to cash-basis accounting that is required by generally accepted accounting principles. Under accrual accounting, transactions are recorded when they occur. Accrual accounting is superior to cash-basis because it links income measurement to selling, the principle activity of the company. That is, revenue is recognized as the company satisfies its performance obligations by delivering goods or providing services; expenses are recognized when they are incurred. In contrast to cash-basis accounting, accrual accounting is a more complex system that records both *cash and noncash* transactions.

KEY ELEMENTS OF ACCRUAL ACCOUNTING

As shown in Exhibit 3.2, an accrual accounting system rests on three elements of the conceptual framework that were introduced in Chapter 2—the time-period assumption, the revenue recognition principle, and the expense recognition principle.

> **! Next Level**
>
> **Cash-basis accounting seems straightforward. Why complicate matters by introducing accrual accounting?**
>
> ANSWER:
> The objective of financial reporting is to provide information that is useful in making business and economic decisions. Most of these decisions involve predicting a company's future cash flows. The use of accrual accounting through the application of the revenue recognition and expense recognition principles links income recognition to the principal activity of the company, selling goods and services. Therefore, accrual accounting provides a better estimate of future cash flows than cash-basis accounting.

EXHIBIT 3.2

Key Elements of Accrual Accounting

TIME-PERIOD ASSUMPTION

Investors, creditors, and other financial statement users demand timely information from companies. For that reason, companies report their financial results for specific periods of time—a month, a quarter, or a year. The **time-period assumption** allows companies to artificially divide their operations into time periods so they can satisfy users' demands for information.

Companies frequently engage in activities that affect more than one time period. For example, **FedEx** often receives cash from a company to deliver products in one time period, although the actual delivery does not occur until a different time period. In addition, the aircraft and vehicles used by FedEx are purchased at a single point in time but are used over many years. To properly record the use of these aircraft and the providing of its service, accrual accounting requires that FedEx assign the revenues and expenses to the proper time period. This is quite often a difficult task and is guided by the revenue recognition and expense recognition principles.

THE REVENUE RECOGNITION PRINCIPLE

The **revenue recognition principle** determines when revenue is recorded and reported. Under this principle, revenue is recognized, or recorded, in the period in which a company satisfies its performance obligation, or promise within a contract. **A seller satisfies a performance obligation by transferring control of a promised good or service to a customer**. Control can be transferred from the seller to the buyer either at a point in time or over time.

To illustrate revenue recognition at a *point in time*, assume that on August 30, a customer purchases a gas grill from **Lowes**. When the customer leaves the store with the grill, the risks and rewards of ownership have been transferred from the seller to the buyer. At this point, revenue is considered to be earned. Exhibit 3.3 shows an excerpt from Lowes' revenue recognition policy.

Annual Report Excerpt: Lowes' Revenue Recognition Policy

EXHIBIT 3.3

Note 3: Revenue Recognition (in part)

Revenue from products primarily relates to in-store and online merchandise purchases, which are recognized at the point in time when the customer obtains control of the merchandise, which is at the time of in-store purchase or delivery of the product to the customer.

Source: Lowes 10-K.

However, control may also transfer to a customer *over time*. For example, assume that on March 29, **FedEx** picks up a computer from **Apple**'s distribution center and receives a cash payment of $30 to ship the computer to a customer. FedEx delivers the computer on April 2. On March 31, FedEx determines that the shipment is 60% of the way to its destination. Because FedEx has satisfied 60% of its performance obligation to deliver the computer, it can recognize $18 (60% × $30) of revenue in March. The remaining $12 of revenue will be recognized when FedEx completes the delivery in April. Exhibit 3.4 shows an excerpt of FedEx's revenue recognition policy.

EXHIBIT 3.4   **Annual Report Excerpt: FedEx's Revenue Recognition Policy**

Note 1: Summary of Significant Accounting Policies (in part)

REVENUE RECOGNITION. For transportation services, revenue is recognized over time as we perform the services in the contract because of the continuous transfer of control to the customer. Our customers receive the benefit of our services as the goods are transported from one location to another.

Source: FedEx 2019 10-K.

In both scenarios, notice that revenue is recognized when the performance obligation is satisfied, regardless of when cash is received.

THE EXPENSE RECOGNITION PRINCIPLE

Companies incur expenses for a variety of reasons. Sometimes expenses are incurred when an asset is used. In other instances, expenses are incurred when a liability is created. For example, FedEx incurs fuel expense as fuel is used to deliver packages. FedEx also incurs salary expense when employees work but are not paid immediately. The key idea is that **an expense is recorded when it is incurred, regardless of when cash is paid**.

Expense recognition is the process of identifying an expense with a particular time period. Under accrual accounting, expenses are recognized following the **expense recognition principle**, which requires that expenses be recorded and reported in the same period as the revenue that it helped to generate. Expenses for an accounting period should *include* only those costs used to earn revenue that was recognized in the accounting period. Expenses for an accounting period should *exclude* those costs used to earn revenue in an earlier period and those costs that will be used to earn revenue in a later period. Thus, the key to expense recognition is matching the expense with revenue.

CASH-BASIS VERSUS ACCRUAL-BASIS ACCOUNTING

In order to use the financial statements, it is important to understand how the revenue recognition and expense recognition principles affect the amounts reported. EXAMPLE 3.1 compares how the application of these principles results in accrual-basis income that differs from cash-basis income.

EXAMPLE 3.1 — APPLYING THE REVENUE RECOGNITION AND EXPENSE RECOGNITION PRINCIPLES

The state of Georgia hired Conservation Inc., a consulting company specializing in the conservation of natural resources, to explore options for providing water resources to the Atlanta metropolitan area. In November, Conservation incurred $60,000 of expenditures, on account, while investigating the water shortage facing the state. Conservation also delivered its recommendations and billed the state $100,000 for its work. In December, Conservation paid the $60,000 of expenses. In January, Conservation received the state's check for $100,000.

Required:

Calculate net income for November, December, and January using the following methods: (1) cash-basis accounting and (2) accrual-basis accounting.

Solution:

1. Cash-Basis Accounting: Under cash-basis accounting, revenue is recognized when cash is received and expense is recognized when cash is paid.

November		December		January	
Revenue	$0	Revenue	$ 0	Revenue	$100,000
Expense	0	Expense	60,000	Expense	0
Net income	$0	Net income	$(60,000)	Net income	$100,000
➡ Performed Service		➡ Paid Expenses		➡ Received Payment	

2. Accrual-Basis Accounting: Under accrual accounting, revenue is recognized when a company satisfies its performance obligation and expenses are matched with revenues.

November		December		January	
Revenue	$100,000	Revenue	$0	Revenue	$0
Expense	60,000	Expense	0	Expense	0
Net income	$ 40,000	Net income	$0	Net income	$0
➡ Performed Service		➡ Paid Expenses		➡ Received Payment	

By following the revenue recognition and expense recognition principles, net income was properly recognized in the period that the business activity occurred. In short, the difference between cash-basis and accrual-basis accounting is a matter of timing.

ETHICAL DECISIONS The revenue recognition and expense recognition principles have been abused in recent years. As companies strive to meet or exceed Wall Street expectations, management may be tempted to recognize revenue that has not yet been earned or to hide expenses that should be recognized. In recent years, the Securities and Exchange Commission (SEC) has conducted numerous investigations involving the abuse of both revenue and expense recognition. Some notable cases are listed in Exhibit 3.5.

While the actions summarized in Exhibit 3.5 were fraudulent and led to severe fines or jail time for many of the company executives, other innocent parties were also affected by these unethical actions. Stockholders, many of whom who had bought the stock at an inflated price, saw a significant drop in the stock's value after these actions were made public. In addition,

EXHIBIT 3.5   **Instances of Accounting Abuses**

Company	Action
Xerox	Used a variety of techniques (e.g., cookie-jar reserves, recognizing revenue prior to it being earned) to inflate income by approximately $1.5 billion. Xerox paid a $10 million fine, and six executives were ordered to pay $22 million.
Enron	Aggressively, and improperly, applied accounting rules to inflate revenue, misclassified loan transactions as sales, and used special purpose entities to hide its debt. The company went bankrupt, and several senior executives were criminally convicted.
HealthSouth	Systematically overstated its earnings in order to meet or exceed Wall Street earnings expectations. The total amount of the fraud was $4.6 billion. Fifteen executives, including five of the company's CFOs, pleaded guilty to fraud.
WorldCom	Improperly reduced operating expenses, which inflated income, by reversing (releasing) accrued liabilities and improperly classifying certain expenses as assets. Chief executive Bernard Ebbers was sentenced to 25 years in jail.
Bally Total Fitness	Recognized revenue on gym membership contracts before it was earned, and improperly delayed the recognition of expenses. In total, more than two dozen improprieties were discovered that caused stockholders' equity to be overstated by $1.8 billion. Bally's auditor paid $8.5 million to settle charges of improper auditing.

innocent employees lost their jobs as the companies struggled to deal with the fraud that occurred. When faced with an ethical dilemma to manipulate the recognition of revenue or expenses, a good rule of thumb is to make the decision that best portrays the economic reality of your company. ●

 YOUDECIDE   **Recognizing a Security Service Contract**

You are the chief financial officer of Secure Entry Inc., a security company, and it is your responsibility to develop the company's revenue and expense recognition policies. In April 2022, Secure Entry signed a 2-year contract with the Metropolis Stadium Authority (MSA) to provide security services at its stadium gates beginning in January 2023. Under the terms of the contract, MSA agrees to make 24 equal monthly payments to Secure Entry beginning in October 2022.

When should Secure Entry recognize revenue and expenses associated with the security contract?

To provide investors and creditors with the most useful information and be consistent with GAAP, you decide that Secure Entry should follow accrual accounting principles. Therefore, the contract should be initially recognized in October 2022, when MSA makes the first payment. At

that time, Secure Entry will record an increase in cash for the payment received and an equal increase in a liability (Unearned Revenue) to recognize that future services are owed. Secure Entry would not record the contract in its accounting system in April 2022 because the event does meet the recognition criteria discussed in Chapter 2.

Consistent with the revenue recognition principle, Secure Entry will recognize revenue each month, as services are performed, beginning in January 2023. Additionally, expenses related to the performance of security services should be matched against revenue from providing the security services and recognized monthly beginning in January 2023.

The proper recognition of revenues and expenses is critical in properly measuring and reporting income in the period that a business activity occurs.

ACCRUAL ACCOUNTING AND ADJUSTING ENTRIES

OBJECTIVE ◀ 3

Identify the kinds of transactions that may require adjustments at the end of an accounting period.

WHICH TRANSACTIONS REQUIRE ADJUSTMENT?

Many business activities continue for a period of time—for example, the use of rented facilities or interest incurred on borrowed money. Because entries in the accounting system are made at particular points in time rather than continuously, adjustments are needed at the end of an accounting period to record partially complete activities.[1] **Adjusting entries** are journal entries made at the end of an accounting period to record the completed portion of partially completed transactions. Adjusting entries are necessary to apply the revenue recognition and expense recognition principles and ensure that a company's financial statements include the proper amount for revenues, expenses, assets, liabilities, and stockholders' equity.

In EXAMPLE 3.2 , three representative transactions are described. The implication of the "length" of these transactions for recognition in the accounting system and for adjustment is discussed.

EXAMPLE 3.2 DETERMINING WHICH TRANSACTIONS REQUIRE ADJUSTMENT

ComputerTown sells computer equipment and provides computer repair service. Sales are typically made in cash or on account. Repairs are provided under service contracts, which customers purchase up front for a specified period of time (2, 3, or 5 years). Customers pay nothing when the computer is brought in for repair.

Required:

1. How should ComputerTown account for cash and credit sales of equipment?

2. How should ComputerTown account for repair services provided under service contracts?

3. How should ComputerTown account for the use of office supplies?

Solution:

1. Cash sales should be recorded as they occur and the equipment is delivered, often at a cash register that tracks total sales for the day. When orders are received from customers who want to purchase equipment on credit, the sale should be recorded when the equipment is delivered to the customer. In both situations, the sale is complete at a single point in time (the delivery of the equipment) and no adjusting entry is needed.

2. Repair service contracts are continuous activities that require an adjustment at the end of the accounting period. Revenue is recognized over time as the service is provided and should be recorded in proportion to the period of time that has passed since the contract became effective. The unexpired portion of the service contract should be recorded as a liability (unearned revenue) until the service is provided. Any expenses associated with the repair services should be recognized in the same period that service revenue is recognized (the expense recognition principle).

3. The use of supplies can be viewed as a sequence of individual activities. However, the preparation of documents required to keep track of each activity individually would be too costly. Instead, the use of supplies can be treated as a continuous transaction and recognized through an adjusting entry. Any supplies used will be reported as an expense, and the unused portion of supplies will be reported as an asset.

---

1 The distinction between business activities requiring adjustment and those that do not depend to some extent on our ability and willingness to keep track of activities. Some activities may occur so frequently or are so difficult to measure that no record of individual activities is maintained. In such cases, the sequence of individual activities becomes, for all intents and purposes, a continuous activity. For example, the use of office supplies is often treated as a continuous business activity because it is too costly to maintain a record of each time supplies are used.

Notice that in the second and third situations in Example 3.2, the preparation of adjusting entries is necessary to get the account balances properly stated and up to date. These end-of-period adjustments can have significant effects on a company's financial statements.

OBJECTIVE 4
Prepare adjusting entries for accruals and deferrals.

STEP 5: ADJUSTING THE ACCOUNTS

Adjustments are often necessary because timing differences exist between when a revenue or expense is recognized and cash is received or paid. These timing differences give rise to two categories of adjusting entries—accruals and deferrals. As shown in Exhibit 3.6, each category has two subcategories, resulting in four possible types of adjustments.

EXHIBIT 3.6   Types of Adjusting Entries

Accruals:
- **Accrued revenues:** Assets resulting from revenues that have been earned but for which no cash has yet been received
- **Accrued expenses:** Liabilities arising from expenses that have been incurred but not yet paid in cash

Deferrals:
- **Deferred (unearned) revenues:** Liabilities arising from the receipt of cash for which revenue has not yet been earned
- **Deferred (prepaid) expenses:** Assets arising from the payment of cash that have not been used or consumed by the end of the period

The purpose of all adjustments is to make sure revenues and expenses get recorded in the proper time period. As the revenue and expense balances are adjusted, asset and liability balances will be adjusted also. Therefore, **all adjusting entries will affect at least one income statement account and one balance sheet account. Cash is never affected by adjustments.**

A three-step procedure can be followed for making adjusting journal entries.

Step 1: Identify pairs of income statement and balance sheet accounts that require adjustment.
Step 2: Calculate the amount of the adjustment based on the amount of revenue that was earned or the amount of expense that was incurred during the accounting period.
Step 3: Record the adjusting journal entry.

This process is used for each of the four types of adjusting entries, as we will illustrate in the following sections.

ACCRUED REVENUES

Companies often engage in revenue-producing activities but are not paid until after the activities are complete. For example, **FedEx** has packages in transit at the end of an accounting period, meaning that FedEx has only partially completed its service. These transactions for which FedEx has satisfied its performance obligations but not received the cash are called **accrued revenues**. Another example of an accrued revenue is interest earned, but not yet received, on a loan. While interest is earned as time passes, the company only receives the cash related to interest periodically (e.g., monthly, semiannually, or annually). Therefore, an adjustment is necessary to record the amount of interest earned but not yet received.

For accrued revenues, an adjustment is necessary to record the revenue and the associated increase in a company's assets, usually a receivable. Exhibit 3.7 demonstrates the process necessary to record accrued revenues. Note that *the accrual of revenue is necessary because the performance obligation was satisfied prior to the receipt of cash.*

Next Level

Why don't adjusting entries involve cash?

ANSWER:
Cash receipts and cash payments are recorded when they occur at a specific point in time. Adjusting entries are concerned with applying the revenue recognition and expense recognition principles to continuous activities. Because revenue and expense recognition does not depend on cash receipt or cash payment, adjusting entries for continuous revenue and expense activities will not involve cash.

Accrued Revenues   **EXHIBIT 3.7**

The adjusting entry required to record accrued revenues is shown in EXAMPLE 3.3 .

EXAMPLE 3.3   RECORDING ACCRUED REVENUES

Assume that Porter Properties Inc., a calendar-year company, rented office space, to be occupied immediately, to the Tiger Travel Agency on November 1 for $5,000 per month. Porter requires Tiger Travel to make a rental payment at the end of every 3 months. No payment was made on November 1.

Required:

1. Prepare the adjusting journal entry necessary for Porter on December 31.

2. Prepare the entry necessary on January 31 to record the receipt of cash.

Solution:

1. **Step 1: Identify the accounts that require adjustment.** Consistent with the revenue recognition principle, Rent Revenue needs to be increased because Porter has satisfied its performance obligation by providing the office space. Because no payment was received, Porter would need to increase Rent Receivable to reflect their right to receive payment from Tiger Travel.

    Step 2: Calculate the amount of the adjustment. The amount of the adjustment would be calculated as:

    $5,000 per month × 2 months (office space occupied) = $10,000

    Step 3: Record the adjusting journal entry.

Date	Account and Explanation	Debit	Credit	Assets	= Liabilities +	Stockholders' Equity
Dec. 31	Rent Receivable	10,000		▲		
	Rent Revenue		10,000			▲

2. The amount of cash received is calculated as:

    $5,000 per month × 3 months (office space rented) = $15,000

Date	Account and Explanation	Debit	Credit	Assets	= Liabilities +	Stockholders' Equity
Jan. 31	Cash	15,000		▲		
	Rent Revenue		5,000			▲
	Rent Receivable		10,000	▼		

The $5,000 of Rent Revenue represents the 1 month of rent provided in January.

If the adjusting entry on December 31 was not made, assets, stockholders' equity, revenues, and income would be understated. The adjusting journal entry recognizes 2 months of revenue (November and December) in the accounting period in which the performance obligation was satisfied and updates the corresponding balance in Rent Receivable. Later, when cash is received, the remaining portion of the revenue is recognized and the receivable is reduced to reflect that it was paid. Consistent with the revenue recognition principle, revenue is recorded in the period in which the service is provided.

ACCRUED EXPENSES

Similar to the situation with accrued revenues, many companies incur expenses in the current accounting period but do not pay cash for these expenses until a later period. For example, Exhibit 3.1 showed that FedEx reported $425 million of salary expense related to services performed by FedEx employees but not paid as of the end of the year. This situation is quite common for operating costs such as payroll, taxes, utilities, rent, and interest. **Accrued expenses** are liabilities arising from expenses that have been incurred but not yet paid in cash.

For accrued expenses, an adjustment is necessary to record the expense and the associated increase in a company's liabilities, usually a payable. Exhibit 3.8 demonstrates the process necessary to record accrued expenses.

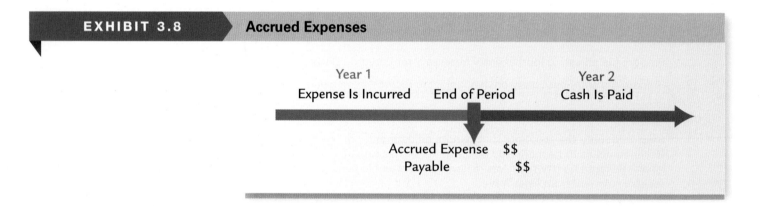

EXHIBIT 3.8 ▸ **Accrued Expenses**

Note that *the accrual of the expense is necessary because the expense was incurred prior to the payment of cash*. The adjusting entry required to record accrued expenses is shown in EXAMPLE 3.4.

EXAMPLE 3.4   RECORDING ACCRUED EXPENSES

Assume that Porter Properties Inc., a calendar-year company, paid its clerical employees every 2 weeks. Employees work 5 days a week for a total of 10 work days every 2 weeks. Total wages for 10 days is $50,000. Also assume that December 31 is 4 days into a 10-day pay period.

Required:

1.   Prepare the adjusting journal entry necessary for Porter on December 31.

2.   Prepare the entry necessary on January 10 to record the payment of salaries.

Solution:

1. **Step 1: Identify the accounts that require adjustment.** Salaries Expense needs to be increased because Porter has incurred an expense related to its employees working for 4 days in December. This expense needs to be matched against December revenues (an application of the expense recognition principle). Because no payment to the employees was made, Porter would need to increase Salaries Payable to reflect its obligation to pay its employees.

   Step 2: Calculate the amount of the adjustment. The amount of the adjustment would be calculated as:

   $50,000 biweekly salaries × (4 days/10 days) worked in 2 weeks = $20,000

   Step 3: Record the adjusting entry.

Date	Account and Explanation	Debit	Credit	Assets	=	Liabilities	+	Stockholders' Equity
Dec. 31	Salaries Expense	20,000						▼
	Salaries Payable		20,000			▲		

2. The amount of the salaries expense for the current year would be calculated as:

   $50,000 biweekly salaries × (6 days/10 days) worked in 2 weeks = $30,000

Date	Account and Explanation	Debit	Credit	Assets	=	Liabilities	+	Stockholders' Equity
Jan. 10	Salaries Expense	30,000						▼
	Salaries Payable	20,000				▼		
	Cash		50,000	▼				

If the adjusting journal entry on December 31 were not made, liabilities and expenses would be understated while income and stockholders' equity would be overstated. The adjusting journal entry recognizes the expense that was incurred during the accounting period and updates the balance in the corresponding liability. Later, when the cash is paid to the employees, the portion of the expense that was incurred in January is recognized and the previously created liability is reduced. Consistent with the expense recognition principle, expenses are recorded in the period that they were incurred.

DEFERRED (UNEARNED) REVENUES

Companies may collect payment for goods or services that it sells before it delivers those goods or services. For example, FedEx often collects cash for a package delivery prior to the actual performance of the delivery service. When the cash is collected, the revenue recognition is deferred, or delayed, until the service is performed. Transactions for which a company has received cash but not yet satisfied its performance obligations are called **deferred** (or **unearned**) **revenues**. Other examples of deferred revenues include rent received in advance, subscriptions received in advance, and tickets (e.g., for airlines, sporting events, concerts) sold in advance. In all of these situations, the receipt of cash creates a liability for the company to deliver goods or perform services in the future. The unearned revenue account delays, or defers, the recognition of revenue by recording the revenue as a liability until it is earned.

As the goods are delivered or the service is performed, an adjustment is necessary to reduce the previously recorded liability and to recognize the portion of the revenue that has been earned. The portion of revenue that has not been earned remains in the liability account, unearned revenue, until it is earned. Exhibit 3.9 demonstrates the process necessary to record deferred revenues.

EXHIBIT 3.9 ▸ Deferred (Unearned) Revenues

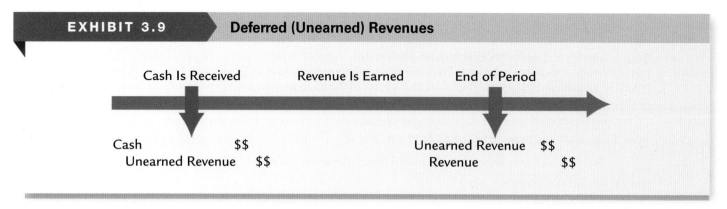

Note that *the deferral of revenue is necessary because the performance obligation was not sat-isfied at the time of cash receipt.* The adjusting entry recognizes the amount of revenue that has been earned from the time of cash receipt until the end of the accounting period. The adjusting entry required to adjust deferred revenues is shown in **EXAMPLE 3.5** .

EXAMPLE 3.5 ADJUSTING DEFERRED (UNEARNED) REVENUES

Assume that Porter Properties Inc., a calendar-year company, rented office space to the Tiger Travel Agency on November 1 for $5,000 per month. Porter requires Tiger Travel to make a rental payment every 3 months. If Tiger Travel pays its entire 3-month rental in advance, Porter has agreed to reduce the monthly rental to $4,500. Tiger Travel agrees and pays Porter $13,500 for 3 months' rental in advance.

Required:

1. Prepare the entry on November 1 to record the receipt of cash.

2. Prepare the adjusting journal entry necessary for Porter on December 31.

Solution:

1.

Date	Account and Explanation	Debit	Credit	Assets	=	Liabilities	+	Stockholders' Equity
Nov. 1	Cash	13,500		▲				
	Unearned Rent Revenue		13,500			▲		

2. **Step 1: Identify the accounts that require adjustment**. Rent Revenue needs to be increased because Porter has satisfied its performance obligation by providing the office space. Because a liability was previously recorded, Porter would need to decrease the liability, Unearned Rent Revenue, to reflect the decrease in their obligation to perform the service.

    Step 2: Calculate the amount of the adjustment. The amount of the adjustment would be calculated as:

    $4,500 per month × 2 months (office space rented) = $9,000

    Step 3: Record the adjusting entry.

Date	Account and Explanation	Debit	Credit	Assets	=	Liabilities	+	Stockholders' Equity
Dec. 31	Unearned Rent Revenue	9,000				▼		
	Rent Revenue		9,000					▲

If the adjusting entry on December 31 was not made, liabilities (Unearned Rent Revenue) would be overstated while stockholders' equity, revenue, and net income would be understated. The adjusting journal entry recognizes 2 months of revenue (November and December) in the accounting period in which it was earned and updates the corresponding balance in the liability, Unearned Rent Revenue. As a result of the adjusting entry, revenue is recorded in the period that a company satisfies its performance obligation.

DEFERRED (PREPAID) EXPENSES

Companies often acquire goods and services before they are used. These prepayments are recorded as assets called **deferred** (or **prepaid**) expenses. For example, **FedEx** reports prepaid expenses of $1,098 million on a recent balance sheet. Common prepaid expenses include items such as supplies, prepaid rent, prepaid advertising, and prepaid insurance. The purchases of buildings and equipment also are considered prepayments.

As the prepaid asset is used to generate revenue, an adjustment is necessary to reduce the previously recorded prepaid asset and recognize the related expense. The portion of the prepaid asset that has not been used represents the unexpired benefits and remains in the asset account until it is used. Therefore, expense recognition is delayed, or deferred, until the expense is incurred. Exhibit 3.10 demonstrates the process necessary to record deferred expenses.

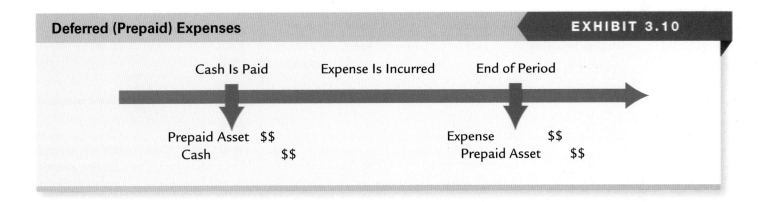

Deferred (Prepaid) Expenses

EXHIBIT 3.10

Note that *the deferral of the expense is necessary because the initial cash payment did not result in an expense*. Instead, an asset that provides future economic benefit was created. The adjusting entry recognizes the amount of expense that has been incurred from the time of the cash payment until the end of the accounting period. The adjusting entry required to adjust deferred expenses is shown in EXAMPLE 3.6.

EXAMPLE 3.6 ADJUSTING DEFERRED (PREPAID) EXPENSES

Assume that Porter Properties Inc., a calendar-year company, had $4,581 of office supplies on hand at the beginning of November. On November 10, Porter purchased office supplies totaling $12,365. The amount of the purchase was added to the Supplies account. At the end of the year, the balance in Supplies was $16,946 ($4,581 + $12,365). A count of office supplies on hand indicated that $3,263 of supplies remained.

Required:

1. Prepare the entry on November 10 to record the purchase of supplies.

2. Prepare the adjusting journal entry necessary for Porter on December 31.

CONTINUED

EXAMPLE 3.6   ADJUSTING DEFERRED (PREPAID) EXPENSES *(CONTINUED)*

Solution:

1.

Date	Account and Explanation	Debit	Credit	Assets	=	Liabilities	+	Stockholders' Equity
Nov. 10	Supplies	12,365		▲				
	Cash		12,365	▼				

2. **Step 1: Identify the accounts that require adjustment.** Supplies Expense needs to be increased because Porter has used office supplies during November and December. The use of the supplies would also decrease the asset, Supplies.

   Step 2: Calculate the amount of the adjustment. The amount of the adjustment would be calculated as:

   $16,946 (supplies available to be used) − $3,263 (supplies on hand) = $13,683

   This amount represents the cost of supplies used during November and December.

   Step 3: Record the adjusting entry.

Date	Account and Explanation	Debit	Credit	Assets	=	Liabilities	+	Stockholders' Equity
Dec. 31	Supplies Expense	13,683						▼
	Supplies		13,683	▼				

If the adjusting entry on December 31 was not made, assets, stockholders' equity, and net income would be overstated and expenses would be understated. The adjusting journal entry recognizes the expense incurred during November and December 2019 and updates the corresponding balance in the asset, Supplies. As a result of the adjusting entry, the expense is recorded in the period that it is incurred.

Depreciation While most deferred (prepaid) expenses are accounted for in a manner similar to that illustrated in Example 3.6, the purchase of long-lived assets such as buildings and equipment presents a unique situation. Recall from Chapter 1 that these types of assets are classified as property, plant, and equipment on the balance sheet. Because property, plant, and equipment helps to produce revenue over a number of years (instead of just one period), the expense recognition principle requires companies to systematically assign, or allocate, the asset's cost as an expense to each period in which the asset is used. This process is called **depreciation**. This concept and the methods used to compute depreciation expense are discussed in Chapter 7.

The depreciation process requires an adjustment to recognize the expense incurred during the period and reduce the long-lived asset. Depreciation expense represents the portion of the cost of the long-lived asset that is matched against the revenues that the asset helped to generate. A contra-account is used to reduce the amount of the long-lived asset. **Contra-accounts** are accounts that have a balance that is opposite of the balance in its related account. For long-lived asset, the contra-account is called accumulated depreciation. The adjusting entry to record depreciation is shown in EXAMPLE 3.7.

EXAMPLE 3.7 ADJUSTING FOR DEPRECIATION

Assume that Porter Properties purchased an office building on January 1 for $450,000. The depreciation expense on this building is $15,000 per year.

Required:
Prepare the adjusting journal entry necessary for Porter on December 31.

Solution:
Step 1: Identify the accounts that need adjustment. Depreciation Expense needs to be recorded because the building is used in operations. The building is decreased by increasing a contra-asset, accumulated depreciation.

Step 2: Calculate the amount of the adjustment. The amount of the adjustment is given as $15,000.

Step 3. Record the adjusting entry.

Date	Account and Explanation	Debit	Credit	Assets	=	Liabilities	+	Stockholders' Equity
Dec. 31	Depreciation Expense	15,000						▼
	Accumulated Depreciation		15,000	▼				

The purchase of a long-lived asset is essentially a long-term prepayment for the service that the asset will provide. For financial reporting purposes, the contra-account is deducted from the balance of the related asset account in the financial statements, and the resulting difference is known as the book value of the asset. The book value represents the unused portion of the long-lived asset. Exhibit 3.11 shows the financial statement presentation of the accumulated depreciation account for Porter Properties, assuming the asset has been used for 3 years.

Financial Statement Presentation of Accumulated Depreciation ◀ EXHIBIT 3.11

Porter Properties Inc. Balance Sheet December 31	
Assets:	
Current assets	$ 370,000
Property, plant, and equipment (net)	1,450,000
Other assets	80,000
Total assets	$ 1,900,000
Liabilities	$ 825,000
Equity	1,075,000
Total liabilities and equity	$ 1,900,000

Sample of accumulated depreciation presentation:

Building	$ 450,000
Less: Accumulated depreciation	(45,000)
Building (net)	$ 405,000

Notice that accumulated depreciation shows the total amount of depreciation taken in all years of the asset's life ($15,000 per year for 3 years). The use of the contra-account provides more information to users of the financial statements because it preserves both the original cost of the asset and the total cost that has expired to date.

SUMMARY OF FINANCIAL STATEMENT EFFECTS OF ADJUSTING ENTRIES

The effects of the adjustment process are summarized in Exhibit 3.12.

Adjusting entries are internal events that do not involve another company. The purpose of all adjustments is to make sure that revenues and expenses get recorded in the proper time period. As the revenue and expense balances are adjusted, asset and liability balances will be adjusted also.

EXHIBIT 3.12 ▶ **Effects of Adjusting Entries on the Financial Statements**

Type of Adjustment	Asset	Liability	Stockholders' Equity	Revenue	Expense
Accrued Revenue	▲		▲	▲	
Accrued Expense		▲	▼		▲
Deferred Revenue		▼	▲	▲	
Deferred Expense	▼		▼		▲

COMPREHENSIVE EXAMPLE

To provide a comprehensive example of the adjusting process, consider the trial balance of HiTech Communications that was introduced in Chapter 2 (see Exhibit 3.13). Upon review of the trial balance, the accountant for HiTech noted that the following accounts needed to be adjusted.

Adjustment 1: Accrued Revenue HiTech's accountant noted that HiTech had performed $1,500 of advertising services for which it had not yet billed the customer. Because the services had not yet been billed, no entry was made in the accounting system. However, HiTech must record the revenue that was earned during the accounting period, even though the cash flow will not occur until a later date. The adjusting entry to record this accrued revenue is:

Date	Account and Explanation	Debit	Credit	Assets	= Liabilities +	Stockholders' Equity
Mar. 31	Accounts Receivable	1,500		▲		
	Service Revenue		1,500			▲

Trial Balance

EXHIBIT 3.13

HiTech Communications Inc. Trial Balance March 31		
Account	**Debit**	**Credit**
Cash	$16,600	
Accounts Receivable	300	
Supplies	6,500	
Prepaid Insurance	1,200	
Equipment	4,500	
Accounts Payable		$ 500
Unearned Service Revenue		9,000
Notes Payable		3,000
Common Stock		12,000
Dividends Declared	500	
Service Revenue		12,100
Salaries Expense	1,800	
Utilities Expense	5,200	
Totals	$36,600	$36,600

! Next level

What is the relationship between the cash receipt or payment and the recognition of accruals or deferrals?

ANSWER:
When the revenue is earned or the expense is incurred **before** the associated cash flow occurs, an accrual adjusting entry is necessary. When the revenue is earned or the expense is incurred **after** the associated cash flow occurs, a deferral adjusting entry is necessary.

Adjustment 2: Accrual of Interest The note payable for $3,000 that HiTech signed on March 2 required it to pay interest at an annual rate of 8%. The formula for computing interest is:

$$\text{Interest} = \text{Principal} \times \text{Interest Rate} \times \text{Time}$$

The principal amount of the loan is usually the face value of the note. The interest rate is stated as an annual rate, and the time period is the fraction of a year that the note is outstanding. For HiTech, interest expense for March is computed as:

$$\text{Interest} = \$3,000 \times 8\% \times 1/12 = \underline{\$20}$$

Because interest expense has been incurred but the cash payment for interest will not occur until a later date, interest is an accrued expense that requires an increase to an expense account and an increase to a liability account. The adjusting entry to recognize accrued interest is:

Date	Account and Explanation	Debit	Credit	Assets	=	Liabilities	+	Stockholders' Equity
Mar. 31	Interest Expense	20						▼
	Interest Payable		20			▲		

Adjustment 3: Accrual of Salaries HiTech paid its weekly salaries on March 26 and properly recorded an expense (Transaction 10 from Chapter 2). Salaries are $360 per day. HiTech will not pay salaries again until April 2. However, employees worked on March 29, March 30, and March 31. Because employees have worked but will not be paid until a later date,

an adjustment is necessary to record the salaries incurred in March but not yet paid. Accrued salaries are $1,080 (3 days × $360 per day). The adjusting entry to recognize accrued salaries is:

Date	Account and Explanation	Debit	Credit	Assets	=	Liabilities	+	Stockholders' Equity
Mar. 31	Salaries Expense	1,080						▼
	Salaries Payable		1,080			▲		

Adjustment 4: Deferred (Unearned) Revenue HiTech's trial balance shows that a customer paid $9,000 in advance for services to be performed at a later date. This amount was originally recorded as a liability, Unearned Service Revenue. As HiTech performs services, the liability will be reduced and revenue will be recognized. Based on HiTech's analysis of work performed during March, it is determined that $3,300 of revenue has been earned. The adjusting entry to record this previously unearned revenue is:

Date	Account and Explanation	Debit	Credit	Assets	=	Liabilities	+	Stockholders' Equity
Mar. 31	Unearned Service Revenue	3,300				▼		
	Service Revenue		3,300					▲

Adjustment 5: Deferred (Prepaid) Expense—Supplies HiTech's trial balance shows a balance of $6,500 in the Supplies account. However, an inventory count at the close of business on March 31 determined that supplies on hand were $1,200. Because it was not efficient to record supplies expense during the period, HiTech must make an adjustment at the end of the period to record the supplies used during the period. It was determined that HiTech used $5,300 ($6,500 available to be used minus $1,200 not used) of supplies. The adjustment necessary to record the supplies used during March is:

Date	Account and Explanation	Debit	Credit	Assets	=	Liabilities	+	Stockholders' Equity
Mar. 31	Supplies Expense	5,300						▼
	Supplies		5,300	▼				

Adjustment 6: Deferred (Prepaid) Expense—Insurance HiTech's trial balance shows a balance of $1,200 in the Prepaid Insurance account related to a 6-month insurance policy purchased at the beginning of March. Because time has passed since the purchase of the insurance policy, the asset, Prepaid Insurance, has partially expired and an expense needs to be recognized. The expired portion of the insurance is $200 ($1,200 × 1/6). The adjustment necessary to record insurance expense is:

Date	Account and Explanation	Debit	Credit	Assets	=	Liabilities	+	Stockholders' Equity
Mar. 31	Insurance Expense	200						▼
	Prepaid Insurance		200	▼				

Adjustment 7: Depreciation HiTech's trial balance shows that $4,500 of equipment was purchased. Because this equipment is used to generate revenue, a portion of the cost of the equipment must be allocated to expense. HiTech computed depreciation expense as $125 per month. The adjustment necessary to record depreciation expense is:

Date	Account and Explanation	Debit	Credit	Assets	=	Liabilities	+	Stockholders' Equity
Mar. 31	Depreciation Expense	125						▼
	Accumulated Depreciation (Equipment)		125	▼				

The ledger for HiTech Communications, after posting of the adjusting journal entries, is shown in Exhibit 3.14.

General Ledger of HiTech Communications   **EXHIBIT 3.14**

Assets

Cash

16,600	
16,600	

Accounts Receivable

300	
(A1) 1,500	
1,800	

Supplies

6,500	
	5,300 (A5)
1,200	

Prepaid Insurance

1,200	
	200 (A6)
1,000	

Equipment

4,500	
4,500	

Accumulated Depreciation

	125 (A7)
	125

Liabilities

Accounts Payable

	500
	500

Notes Payable

	3,000
	3,000

Interest Payable

	20 (A2)
	20

Salaries Payable

	1,080 (A3)
	1,080

Unearned Service Revenue

	9,000
(A4) 3,300	
	5,700

Stockholders' Equity

Common Stock

	12,000
	12,000

Service Revenue

	12,100
	1,500 (A1)
	3,300 (A4)
	16,900

Salaries Expense

1,800	
(A3) 1,080	
2,880	

Utility Expense

5,200	
5,200	

Depreciation Expense

(A7) 125	
125	

Interest Expense

(A2) 20	
20	

Insurance Expense

(A6) 200	
200	

Supplies Expense

(A5) 5,300	
5,300	

Dividends Declared

500	
500	

Two major items should be apparent:

- *Adjusting entries affect one balance sheet account and one income statement account.* Without adjusting entries, the balances reported on both the balance sheet and the income statement would have been incorrect. If the adjustments were not recorded, HiTech would have understated revenue by $4,800 and understated expenses by $6,725.
- *Adjusting entries do not affect cash.*

YOUDECIDE   Financial Statement Effects of Adjusting Entries

You are considering investing in Get Fit Inc., a chain of gymnasiums and wellness facilities. As you are analyzing the financial statements to determine if Get Fit is a good investment, three items catch your attention:

- Get Fit requires customers to pay the first 6 months' membership fees at the time the customer joins one of its facilities. These fees are recorded as revenue at the time of cash receipt since the amount is nonrefundable.

- Get Fit paid for and distributed flyers to advertise its recent membership drive. Because these flyers will circulate and attract customers for approximately a year, Get Fit recorded the expenditures as prepaid advertising that will be expensed over the next year.

- Get Fit provides healthy snacks to its customers by charging their membership account. Get Fit records revenue at the end of the month when it bills customers, although customers do not pay until the next month.

Do you feel that Get Fit is properly recording the above transactions? If not, what is the effect on the financial statements?

First, the membership fees are a continuous activity that Get Fit is incorrectly treating as a point-in-time

activity. Because Get Fit has not yet provided a service to the customer, it has not yet been earned. Therefore, the membership fees should be initially recorded as unearned revenue. As the customers have use of the facility each month, an adjusting entry should be made to reduce unearned revenue and increase revenue. The fact that the fees are nonrefundable is irrelevant in deciding whether revenue should or should not be recognized. Second, because it is difficult to measure any future benefits associated with advertising costs, accountants take a conservative position and these costs should not be deferred; instead they should be expensed as incurred. Finally, Get Fit is appropriately recording an accrued revenue related to providing snacks. The fact that the customers do not pay until a later time period is not relevant in determining when the revenue is recorded.

If the above transactions had been properly recorded, Get Fit would have reported less revenue, higher expenses, and, therefore, lower net income. Financial statement users need to pay close attention to a company's policies with regard to revenue and expense recognition.

Adjusting entries can have a material impact on a company's reported revenues, expenses, and income.

OBJECTIVE 5
Prepare financial statements from an adjusted trial balance.

STEP 6: PREPARING THE FINANCIAL STATEMENTS

After a company has journalized and posted all of the adjusting entries, it updates the trial balance to reflect the adjustments that have been made. This trial balance is called an **adjusted trial balance**. Similar to the trial balance, the adjusted trial balance lists all of the active accounts and proves the equality of debits and credits. In addition, the adjusted trial balance is the primary source of information needed to prepare the financial statements. The adjusted trial balance for HiTech Communications is shown in Exhibit 3.15.

The financial statements can now be prepared using the balances obtained from the adjusted trial balance. As discussed in Chapter 1, the financial statements are interrelated. That is, there is a natural progression from one financial statement to another as the numbers in one financial statement flow into another financial statement. Because of this natural progression, financial statements are prepared in a particular order.

1. The income statement is prepared from the revenue and expense accounts.
2. Net income (obtained from the income statement) and dividends declared are used to prepare the retained earnings statement.
3. The balance sheet is prepared using the ending balance of retained earnings from the retained earnings statement.

Adjusted Trial Balance

EXHIBIT 3.15

HiTech Communications Inc. Adjusted Trial Balance March 31			
Account		Debit	Credit
Cash		$16,600	
Accounts Receivable		1,800	
Supplies		1,200	
Prepaid Insurance	Balance	1,000	
Equipment	Sheet	4,500	
Accumulated Depreciation (Equipment)	Accounts		$ 125
Accounts Payable			500
Unearned Service Revenue			5,700
Interest Payable			20
Salaries Payable			1,080
Notes Payable			3,000
Common Stock			12,000
Dividends Declared		500	
Service Revenue			16,900
Salaries Expense		2,880	
Utilities Expense	Income	5,200	
Depreciation Expense	Statement	125	
Interest Expense	Accounts	20	
Insurance Expense		200	
Supplies Expense		5,300	
Totals		$39,325	$39,325

 YOUDECIDE **Quality of Earnings**

Investors and other users often assess the quality of a company's earnings when analyzing companies. The quality of earnings refers to how well a company's reported earnings reflect the company's true earnings. High-quality earnings are generally viewed as permanent or persistent earnings that assist financial statement users in predicting future earnings and cash flows. Low-quality earnings are temporary or transitory earnings from one-time transactions or events that do not aid in predicting future earnings or cash flows. While there is no consensus on how best to measure earnings quality, research suggests that investors recognize differences in earnings quality and these differences affect a company's stock price.

How do adjusting entries influence the quality of earnings?

Because adjusting entries always effect amounts reported on the income statement, the estimates and judgments involved in making accruals and deferrals can have a significant impact on a company's income. Companies that make relatively pessimistic estimates and judgments are said to follow conservative accounting practices and are generally viewed as having earnings that are of higher quality. In contrast, many companies use relatively optimistic estimates and judgments and employ aggressive accounting practices. These companies are normally viewed as having a lower quality of earnings.

More conservative adjusting entries usually lead to better predictors of future earnings or cash flows and are viewed as contributing to higher earnings quality.

The financial statements are prepared using the steps illustrated in Examples 1.2, 1.3, and 1.4 (pages 10, 15, and 19). The financial statements of HiTech Communications and their interrelationship are shown in Exhibit 3.16.

EXHIBIT 3.16	Relationships Among the Financial Statements

HiTech Communications Inc.
Income Statement
For the month ended March 31

Service revenue		$ 16,900
Expenses:		
Supplies expense	$5,300	
Utilities expense	5,200	
Salaries expense	2,880	
Insurance expense	200	
Depreciation expense	125	
Interest expense	20	(13,725)
Net income		$ 3,175

HiTech Communications Inc.
Retained Earnings Statement
For the month ended March 31

Retained earnings, March 1	$ 0
Add: Net income	3,175
Less: Dividends Declared	(500)
Retained earnings, March 31	$ 2,675

HiTech Communications Inc.
Balance Sheet
March 31

ASSETS			LIABILITIES AND STOCKHOLDERS' EQUITY		
Current assets:			Current liabilities:		
Cash	$16,600		Accounts payable	$ 500	
Accounts receivable	1,800		Unearned service revenue	5,700	
Supplies	1,200		Interest payable	20	
Prepaid insurance	1,000		Salaries payable	1,080	
Total current assets		$20,600	Total current liabilities		$ 7,300
Property, plant, and equipment:			Long-term liabilities:		
Equipment	$ 4,500		Notes payable		3,000
Less: Accumulated depreciation	(125)		Total liabilities		$10,300
Total property, plant, and equipment		4,375	Stockholders' equity:		
			Common stock	$12,000	
			Retained earnings	2,675	
			Total stockholders' equity		14,675
Total assets		$24,975	Total liabilities and stockholders' equity		$24,975

STEP 7: CLOSING THE ACCOUNTS

OBJECTIVE 6
Prepare closing entries.

When we introduced the fundamental accounting equation in Chapter 1, we identified three kinds of balance sheet accounts: assets, liabilities, and stockholders' equity. These accounts are **permanent accounts** in that their balances are carried forward from the current accounting period to future accounting periods. We also identified five other accounts: revenues, gains, expenses, losses, and dividends declared. These accounts are used to collect the activities of only one period, so they are considered **temporary accounts**. The final step of the accounting cycle, closing the accounts, is done to:

- Transfer the effects of revenues, expenses, gains, losses, and dividends declared (the temporary accounts) to the permanent stockholders' equity account, Retained Earnings.
- Clear the revenue, expenses, gains, losses, and dividends declared (reduce their balances to zero) so they are ready to accumulate the business activities of the next accounting period. Without closing entries, the temporary accounts would accumulate the business activities of *all* accounting periods, not just the current time period.

The closing process is accomplished through a series of journal entries that are dated as of the last day of the accounting period. The closing process can be completed in a four-step procedure:

Step 1: Close revenues (and gains) to Retained Earnings.
Step 2: Close expenses (and losses) to Retained Earnings.
Step 3: Close Dividends Declared to Retained Earnings.

The closing process is illustrated in EXAMPLE 3.8 .

> **! Next level**
>
> **What would happen if we didn't make closing entries?**
>
> ___
>
> **ANSWER:**
> The closing process transfers temporary account balances (revenues, expenses, gains, losses, and dividends declared) to retained earnings. If the accounts were not closed, these amounts would not get properly reflected in stockholders' equity and the accounting equation wouldn't balance. In addition, the temporary accounts would accumulate amounts from different accounting periods, making it extremely difficult to determine the effect of business activities for a specific accounting period.

EXAMPLE 3.8   CLOSING THE ACCOUNTS

Porter Properties' general ledger shows the following balances as on December 31, the end of the year: Rent Revenue, $2,174,000; Salaries Expense, $1,300,000; Supplies Expense, $150,000; Interest Expense, $15,000; Insurance Expense, $20,000; Retained Earnings at the beginning of the year $1,135,000; and Dividends Declared, $5,000. All accounts have normal balances.

Required:
Prepare the closing entries for Porter at December 31.

Solution:
Step 1: Close revenues to Retained Earnings.

Date	Account and Explanation	Debit	Credit
Dec. 31	Rent Revenue	2,174,000	
	Retained Earnings		2,174,000

CONTINUED

EXAMPLE 3.8   CLOSING THE ACCOUNTS (CONTINUED)

Step 2: Close expenses to Retained Earnings.

Date	Account and Explanation	Debit	Credit
Dec. 31	Retained Earnings	1,485,000	
	Salaries Expense		1,300,000
	Supplies Expense		150,000
	Interest Expense		15,000
	Insurance Expense		20,000

Step 3: Close Dividends Declared to Retained Earnings.

Date	Account and Explanation	Debit	Credit
Dec. 31	Retained Earnings	5,000	
	Dividends Declared		5,000

Notice that revenues (and gains), which have a normal credit balance, are closed by debiting the revenue (or gain) account. Similarly, expenses (and losses), which normally have a debit balance, are closed by crediting the expense (or loss) accounts. After the first two journal entries, income for the period, $689,000 ($2,174,000 − $1,485,000), has been transferred to Retained Earnings. Thus, the beginning and ending balance sheets are linked through the closing process. This relationship is known as articulation of the financial statements. The closing process for Porter is illustrated in Exhibit 3.17.

EXHIBIT 3.17   The Closing Process

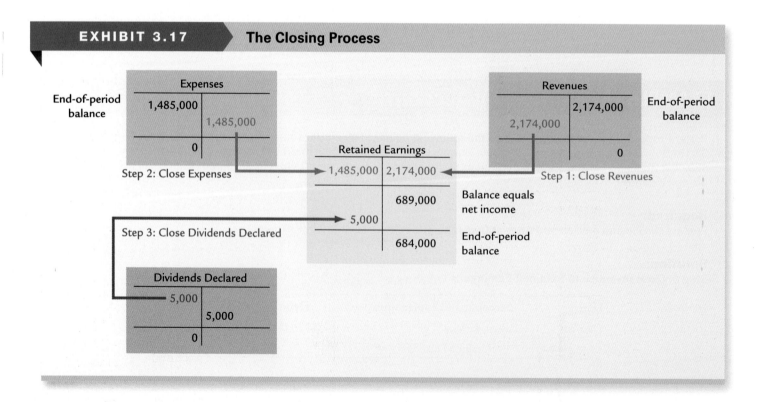

SUMMARY OF THE ACCOUNTING CYCLE

OBJECTIVE ◀ **7**

List the steps in the accounting cycle.

In Chapter 2, we introduced the accounting cycle as a sequence of procedures that transforms business activities into financial statements. The accounting cycle is shown in Exhibit 3.18.

The Accounting Cycle

EXHIBIT 3.18

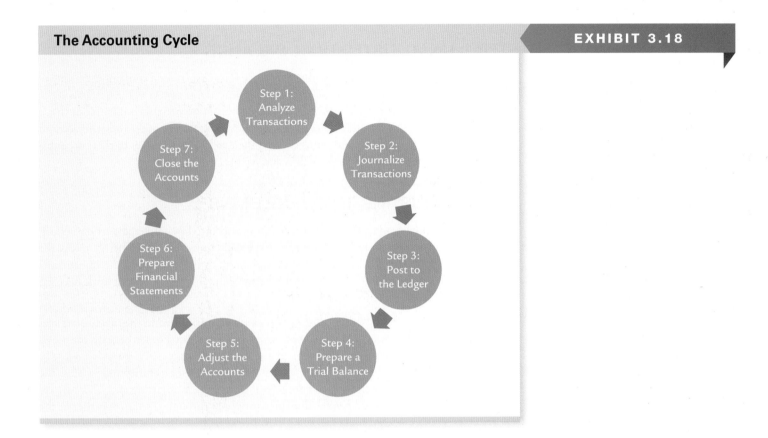

Notice that the accounting cycle begins with the analysis of transactions to determine which business activities are recognized in the accounting records and their effect on the fundamental accounting equation. Those activities that meet the recognition criteria are journalized and posted to the ledger. These three steps are repeated many times during an accounting period. The remaining steps of the accounting cycle are performed only at the end of the accounting period. For those transactions still underway at the end of the accounting period, the completed portion of the transaction is recognized with adjusting entries. Next, the financial statements are prepared. Finally, the temporary accounts—revenues, expenses, gains, losses, and dividends declared—are closed and their balances transferred to Retained Earnings. At this point, the income statement accounts have zero balances, and the balance sheet accounts all contain the correct beginning balances for the start of the next accounting period. The accounting cycle can begin again.

APPENDIX 3A: USING A WORKSHEET TO PREPARE FINANCIAL STATEMENTS

OBJECTIVE ◀ **8**

(Appendix 3A) Prepare financial statement using a worksheet.

Accountants often use an informal schedule called a **worksheet** to assist them in organizing and preparing the information necessary to perform the end-of-period steps in the accounting cycle—namely the preparation of adjusting entries, financial statements, and closing entries. The worksheet is not a financial statement but simply an organizational tool that summarizes the information generated by the accounting system and enables the accountant to check the information for completeness and consistency. While worksheets can be completed manually, most worksheets today are created in computer spreadsheets.

A typical worksheet is shown in Exhibit 3.19. This exhibit uses the information for HiTech Communications that was presented in Chapters 2 and 3.

The completion of the worksheet requires the following six steps.

STEP 1: UNADJUSTED TRIAL BALANCE

The worksheet starts with the unadjusted trial balance. The first column contains the listing of accounts used during the period in the same order as the accounts appear in the trial balance—the balance sheet accounts first followed by the income statement accounts. Note that a retained earnings account was added. Because this is the first month of operations, this account has a zero balance. The next two columns contain the unadjusted balances of these accounts and are totaled to ensure the equality of debits and credits.

STEP 2: ADJUSTING ENTRY COLUMNS

The next two columns contain the adjustments made to record the completed portion of business activities that remain underway at the end of the accounting period. Rather than take the time to make formal adjusting journal entries, the accountant typically enters the adjustments directly into the worksheet and then makes the formal journal entries after the worksheet has been completed. Two items should be noted:

- Adjustments often require the addition of accounts not included in the unadjusted trial balance. These additional accounts can be added, in no particular order, beneath the previous listing of accounts.
- Letters are typically used on a worksheet to identify the adjusting entries and to allow the accountant to easily match the debit and credit sides of each adjusting entry. The letters (a) through (g) correspond to the adjusting entries (1) through (7) shown earlier in the chapter.

The two columns are totaled to ensure the equality of debits and credits.

STEP 3: ADJUSTED TRIAL BALANCE

The next two columns represent an adjusted trial balance. The adjustments entered in columns D and E are added to or subtracted from the unadjusted balances in columns B and C. The two columns are totaled to ensure the equality of debits and credits. The adjusted trial balance is the basis for preparing the financial statements.

STEP 4: INCOME STATEMENT

The income statement balances are transferred to the income statement columns of the worksheet and the columns are totaled. The difference between the two columns is the net income or loss of the period. In Exhibit 3.19, HiTech reports its net income of $3,175 in the debit column of the income statement and the credit column of the retained earnings statement. This entry is made (1) to balance the two income statement columns and (2) to transfer net income to retained earnings.

STEP 5: RETAINED EARNINGS STATEMENT

The amounts for beginning retained earnings and dividends declared are transferred from the adjusted trial balance columns (columns F and G) to the retained earnings statement columns

Worksheet

EXHIBIT 3.19

HiTech Communications Inc.
Work Sheet
For the Month Ended March 31

Account Titles	Unadjusted Trial Balance Debit	Credit	Adjusting Entries Debit	Credit	Adjusted Trial Balance Debit	Credit	Income Statement Debit	Credit	Retained Earnings Statement Debit	Credit	Balance Sheet Debit	Credit
Cash	16,600				16,600						16,600	
Accounts Receivable	300		(a) 1,500		1,800						1,800	
Supplies	6,500			(e) 5,300	1,200						1,200	
Prepaid Insurance	1,200			(f) 200	1,000						1,000	
Equipment	4,500				4,500						4,500	
Accounts Payable		500				500						500
Unearned Revenue		9,000	(d) 3,300			5,700						5,700
Notes Payable		3,000				3,000						3,000
Common Stock		12,000				12,000						12,000
Retained Earnings, March 1		0				0				0		
Dividends	500				500				500			
Service Revenue		12,100		(a) 1,500 (d) 3,300		16,900		16,900				
Salaries Expense	1,800		(c) 1,080		2,880		2,880					
Utility Expense	5,200				5,200		5,200					
	36,600	36,600										
Interest Expense			(b) 20		20		20					
Interest Payable				(b) 20		20						20
Salaries Payable				(c) 1,080		1,080						1,080
Supplies Expense			(e) 5,300		5,300		5,300					
Insurance Expense			(f) 200		200		200					
Depreciation Expense			(g) 125		125		125					
Accumulated Depreciation (Equipment)				(g) 125		125						125
			11,525	11,525	39,325	39,325	13,725	16,900				
Net Income							(h) 3,175			(h) 3,175		
							16,900	16,900		3,175		
Retained Earnings, March 31									(i) 2,675			(i) 2,675
									3,175	3,175	25,100	25,100

(columns J and K). The columns are totaled and the difference is the amount of ending retained earnings. This amount is entered in the debit column of the retained earnings statement (to balance the two columns) and transferred to the credit column of the balance sheet as shown by letter (i).

STEP 6: BALANCE SHEET

The final portion of the worksheet is completed by transferring all the balance sheet account balances from the adjusted trial balance columns (columns F and G) to the balance sheet columns (columns L and M).

At this point, the worksheet provides all the necessary information to prepare the financial statements. The completed financial statements are shown in Exhibit 3.16 (p. 168).

REVIEW CENTER

KEY TAKEAWAYS

- Cash-basis and accrual-basis accounting are two alternatives for recording business activities in the accounting records.
- Under cash-basis accounting, revenues and expenses are recorded when cash is received or paid, regardless of when the revenues are earned or the expenses are incurred.
- Accrual-basis accounting links income measurement to the selling activities of a company by recognizing revenues and expenses when they occur.

KEY TERMS

Accrual-basis accounting, 148
Cash-basis accounting, 148

LO1. Explain the difference between cash-basis and accrual-basis accounting.

KEY TAKEAWAYS

- The revenue recognition principle states that revenue is recognized or recorded in the period in which a company satisfies its performance obligation, or promise within a contract.
  - A seller satisfies a performance obligation by transferring control of a promised good or service to a customer.
  - Control can be transferred from the seller to the buyer either at a point in time or over time.
- The expense recognition principle requires that expenses be recognized in the same period as the revenue they helped generate.
- The application of these two principles results in income being measured as the business activity occurs, regardless of when cash is received or paid.

KEY TERMS

Expense recognition principle, 150
Revenue recognition principle, 149
Time-period assumption, 149

LO2. Explain how the time-period assumption, revenue recognition principle, and the expense recognition principle affect the determination of income.

EXAMPLE

EXAMPLE 3.1	Applying the revenue recognition and expense recognition principles, page 151

L03. Identify the kinds of transactions that may require adjustments at the end of an accounting period.

KEY TAKEAWAYS

- Many business activities do not occur at a single point in time but continuously over time. Because entries in the accounting system are made at particular points in time, adjustments are needed at the end of an accounting period to record the completed portion of any partially completed activities.
- Adjusting entries apply the revenue recognition and expense recognition principles to ensure that a company's financial statements reflect the proper amount for revenues, expenses, assets, liabilities, and stockholders' equity.

KEY TERM

Adjusting entries, 153

EXAMPLE

EXAMPLE 3.2	Determining which transactions require adjustment, page 153

L04. Prepare adjusting entries for accruals and deferrals.

KEY TAKEAWAYS

- Adjusting entries are categorized as either accruals (accrued revenues and accrued expenses) or deferrals (deferred revenues and deferred expenses).
- Accruals occur when revenues have been earned or expenses have been incurred but no cash has been received or paid.
- Deferrals occur when cash has been received or paid prior to revenue being earned or the expense being incurred.

KEY TERMS

Accrued expenses, 156
Accrued revenues, 154
Contra-accounts, 160
Deferred (or unearned) revenues, 157
Deferred (or prepaid) expenses, 159
Depreciation, 160

EXAMPLES

KEY TAKEAWAYS

- An adjusted trial balance lists all of the active accounts and updates the trial balance to reflect the adjusting entries that have been made.
- The adjusted trial balance is the primary source of information needed to prepare the financial statements.
- Due to the interrelation between the financial statements, the income statement is prepared first, followed by the retained earnings statement, and the balance sheet.

KEY TERM

Adjusted trial balance, 166

KEY TAKEAWAYS

- Closing entries transfer the effects of revenues, expenses, gains, losses, and dividends declared to retained earnings.
- Closing entries clear the balances in revenues, expenses, gains, losses, and dividends declared (reduce their balances to zero) so that they are ready to accumulate the business activities of the next accounting period.

KEY TERMS

Permanent accounts, 169
Temporary accounts, 169

EXAMPLE

L05. Prepare financial statements from an adjusted trial balance.

L06. Prepare closing entries.

L07. List the steps in the accounting cycle.

KEY TAKEAWAYS

- During the accounting period, transactions are analyzed to determine their effect on the accounting equation.
- Transactions that meet the recognition criteria are then journalized in the general journal.
- Journal entries are posted from the general journal to the general ledger.
- A trial balance is prepared to summarize the effects of these transactions and check the equality of debits and credits.
- At the end of the accounting period, adjusting entries are prepared to recognize the completed portion of any partially completed business activities.
- The financial statements are prepared from the adjusted trial balance.
- The temporary accounts (revenues, expenses, gains, losses, and dividends declared) are closed to retained earnings.
- The accounting cycle repeats for the next accounting period.

L08. (Appendix 3A) Prepare financial statements using a worksheet.

KEY TAKEAWAYS

- A worksheet is an informal schedule that assists accountants in organizing and preparing the information necessary to perform the end-of-period steps in the accounting cycle.
- The worksheet begins with a trial balance and includes columns for adjusting entries, the adjusted trial balance, the income statement, the retained earnings statement, and the balance sheet.

KEY TERM

Worksheet, 171

REVIEW PROBLEM

Kenny's Laundry has one laundry plant and uses five rented storefronts on the west side of Indianapolis as its retail locations. At the end of the year (December 31), Kenny's had the following balances in its accounts before adjustment:

Cash	Accounts Receivable	Supplies
4,800	26,000	128,000

Land	Building	Accumulated Depreciation (Building)
124,400	249,000	36,000

Equipment		Accumulated Depreciation (Equipment)		Other Assets	
122,000			24,000	16,000	

Accounts Payable		Notes Payable (due in 6 years)		Unearned Service Revenue	
	8,000		120,000		12,000

Common Stock		Retained Earnings, January 1		Service Revenue	
	240,000		69,000		874,200

Rent Expense		Wages Expense		Insurance Expense	
168,000		431,000		14,000	

Salaries Expense		Interest Expense	
92,000		8,000	

An examination identified the following items that require adjustment:

a. Kenny's launders shirts for the service staff of a local car dealer. At the end of the year, the car dealer owes Kenny's $1,040 for laundry services that have been performed but will not be billed until early in the next year.
b. Kenny's supplies on hand at December 31 was $21,400.
c. Kenny's launders uniforms for a nearby McDonald's franchise. The franchisee pays Kenny's in advance for the laundry service once every 3 months. After examining the records, Kenny's accountant determines that the laundry has earned $8,400 of the $12,000 of unearned revenue.
d. Salaries in the amount of $1,500 are owed but unpaid and unrecorded.
e. Two months' interest at 8% on the note payable is owed but unpaid and unrecorded.
f. Depreciation expense for the building is $12,000.
g. Depreciation expense for the equipment is $24,000.
h. Income taxes expense of $5,200 is owed but unpaid and unrecorded.

Required:
1. Determine and record the adjusting entries at December 31 for Kenny's Laundry.
2. Post the effects of the adjustments to the proper accounts, and determine the account balances.
3. Prepare an income statement, retained earnings statement, and a balance sheet for Kenny's using the adjusted account balances.
4. Close the necessary accounts.

Solution:
1. The adjustments for Kenny's are as follows:

    a. The adjustment to record accrued revenue for services already provided is:

Date	Account and Explanation	Debit	Credit	Assets	= Liabilities	+ Stockholders' Equity
Dec. 31	Accounts Receivable	1,040		▲		
	Service Revenue		1,040			▲

(Continued)

b. The before adjustment balance in supplies is $128,000. Supplies actually on hand are $21,400. Supplies expense (used) is $106,600 ($128,000 − $21,400):

Date	Account and Explanation	Debit	Credit	Assets	=	Liabilities	+	Stockholders' Equity
Dec. 31	Supplies Expense	106,600						▼
	Supplies		106,600	▼				

c. The adjustment to record the amount of deferred (unearned) revenue earned for the year is:

Date	Account and Explanation	Debit	Credit	Assets	=	Liabilities	+	Stockholders' Equity
Dec. 31	Unearned Service Revenue	8,400				▼		
	Service Revenue		8,400					▲

d. The entry to record the accrual of salaries is:

Date	Account and Explanation	Debit	Credit	Assets	=	Liabilities	+	Stockholders' Equity
Dec. 31	Salaries Expense	1,500						▼
	Salaries Payable		1,500			▲		

e. Interest expense is $1,600 ($120,000 × 8% × 2/12). The entry to accrue interest expense is:

Date	Account and Explanation	Debit	Credit	Assets	=	Liabilities	+	Stockholders' Equity
Dec. 31	Interest Expense	1,600						▼
	Interest Payable		1,600			▲		

f. The entry to record depreciation expense for the building is:

Date	Account and Explanation	Debit	Credit	Assets	=	Liabilities	+	Stockholders' Equity
Dec. 31	Depreciation Expense (Building)	12,000						▼
	Accumulated Depreciation (Building)		12,000	▼				

g. The entry to record depreciation expense for the equipment is:

Date	Account and Explanation	Debit	Credit	Assets	=	Liabilities	+	Stockholders' Equity
Dec. 31	Depreciation Expense (Equipment)	24,000						▼
	Accumulated Depreciation (Equipment)		24,000	▼				

h. The adjustment for income taxes expense is:

Date	Account and Explanation	Debit	Credit	Assets	=	Liabilities	+	Stockholders' Equity
Dec. 31	Income Tax Expense	5,200						▼
	Income Taxes Payable		5,200			▲		

2. The adjusted account balances for Kenny's Laundry are shown in Exhibit 3.20.

Kenny's Laundry Adjusted Account Balances

EXHIBIT 3.20

Assets

Cash

4,800	

Accounts Receivable

26,000	
(a) 1,040	
27,040	

Supplies

128,000	106,600 (b)
21,400	

Land

124,400	

Building

249,000	

Accumulated Depreciation (Building)

	36,000
	12,000 (f)
	48,000

Equipment

122,000	

Accumulated Depreciation (Equipment)

	24,000
	24,000 (g)
	48,000

Other Assets

16,000	

Liabilities

Accounts Payable

	8,000

Notes Payable (due in 6 years)

	120,000

Interest Payable

	1,600 (e)
	1,600

Salaries Payable

	1,500 (d)
	1,500

Income Taxes Payable

	5,200 (h)
	5,200

Unearned Service Revenue

(c) 8,400	12,000
	3,600

Stockholders' Equity

Common Stock

	240,000

Retained Earnings, January 1

	69,000

Service Revenue

	874,200
	1,040 (a)
	8,400 (c)
	883,640

Rent Expense

168,000	

Wages Expense

431,000	

Insurance Expense

14,000	

Salaries Expense

92,000	
(d) 1,500	
93,500	

Interest Expense

8,000	
(e) 1,600	
9,600	

Supplies Expense

(b) 106,600	
106,600	

Depreciation Expense (Building)

(f) 12,000	
12,000	

Depreciation Expense (Equipment)

(g) 24,000	
24,000	

Income Taxes Expense

(h) 5,200	
5,200	

3. The income statement, statement of changes in retained earnings, and balance sheet for Kenny's Laundry are prepared from the adjusted account balances and appear in Exhibit 3.21.

EXHIBIT 3.21	**Financial Statements for Kenny's Laundry**

Kenny's Laundry
Income Statement
For the year ended December 31

Service revenue		$ 883,640
Less expenses:		
Wages expense	$431,000	
Rent expense	168,000	
Supplies expense	106,600	
Salaries expense	93,500	
Depreciation expense (equipment)	24,000	
Insurance expense	14,000	
Depreciation expense (building)	12,000	
Interest expense	9,600	
Income taxes expense	5,200	(863,900)
Net income		$ 19,740

Kenny's Laundry
Retained Earnings Statement
For the year ended December 31

Retained earnings, January 1	$69,000
Add: Net income	19,740
Less: Dividends Declared	0
Retained earnings, December 31	$88,740

Kenny's Laundry
Balance Sheet
December 31

ASSETS

Current assets:			
Cash		$ 4,800	
Accounts receivable		27,040	
Supplies		21,400	
Total current assets			$ 53,240
Property, plant, and equipment:			
Land		$124,400	
Building	$249,000		
Less: Accumulated depreciation	(48,000)	201,000	
Equipment	$122,000		
Less: Accumulated depreciation	(48,000)	74,000	
Total property, plant, and equipment			399,400
Other assets			16,000
Total assets			$468,640

LIABILITIES AND STOCKHOLDERS' EQUITY		
Current liabilities:		
Accounts payable	$ 8,000	
Salaries payable	1,500	
Interest payable	1,600	
Income taxes payable	5,200	
Unearned service revenue	3,600	
Total current liabilities		$ 19,900
Long-term liabilities:		
Notes payable (due in 6 years)		120,000
Total liabilities		$139,900
Stockholders' equity:		
Common stock	$240,000	
Retained earnings	88,740	
Total stockholders' equity		328,740
Total liabilities and stockholders' equity		$468,640

4. The entries to close the accounts are:

Date	Account and Explanation	Debit	Credit
Dec. 31	Service Revenue	883,640	
	Retained Earnings		883,640
31	Retained Earnings	863,900	
	Rent Expense		168,000
	Wages Expense		431,000
	Insurance Expense		14,000
	Salaries Expense		93,500
	Supplies Expense		106,600
	Depreciation Expense (Building)		12,000
	Depreciation Expense (Equipment)		24,000
	Interest Expense		9,600
	Income Tax Expense		5,200

APPLYING KNOWLEDGE

DISCUSSION QUESTIONS

1. How does accrual-basis net income differ from cash-basis net income?   **OBJECTIVE 1**
2. Explain when revenue may be recognized and give an example.   **OBJECTIVE 2**
3. What accounting concepts require that adjusting entries be employed?
4. What happens during the accounting cycle?   **OBJECTIVE 3**
5. Provide two examples of transactions that begin and end at a particular point in time and two examples of continuous transactions.
6. Why are adjusting entries needed?
7. Describe the recording of transactions that begin and end at a particular point in time and the recording of continuous transactions.

OBJECTIVE 4

8. For each of the four categories of adjusting entries, describe the business activity that produces circumstances requiring adjustment.

9. What is the difference between an *accrual* and a *deferral?*

10. Which type of adjustment will (a) increase both assets and revenues, (b) increase revenues and decrease liabilities, (c) increase expenses and decrease assets, and (d) increase both expenses and liabilities?

11. How is the amount for an interest expense (or interest revenue) adjustment determined?

12. Describe the effect on the financial statements when an adjustment is prepared that records (a) unrecorded revenue and (b) unrecorded expense.

OBJECTIVE 5

13. On the basis of what you have learned about adjustments, why do you think that adjusting entries are made on the last day of the accounting period rather than at several times during the accounting period?

OBJECTIVE 6

14. What is the purpose of closing entries?

15. Describe the three steps in the closing process.

16. Identify each of the following categories of accounts as temporary or permanent: assets, liabilities, equity, revenues, expenses, and dividends declared. How is the distinction between temporary and permanent accounts related to the closing process?

17. Why are only the balance sheet accounts permanent?

OBJECTIVE 7

18. List the seven steps in the accounting cycle in the order in which they occur and explain what occurs at each step of the accounting cycle.

OBJECTIVE 8

19. *(Appendix 3A)* What is the relationship between the accounting cycle and the worksheet?

20. *(Appendix 3A)* Describe the structure of the worksheet and the accounting information it contains.

MULTIPLE-CHOICE QUESTIONS

OBJECTIVE 1 2

3-1   Which of the following statements is true?
   a. Under cash-basis accounting, revenues are recorded when a company satisfies its performance obligations and expenses are recorded when incurred.
   b. Accrual-basis accounting records both cash and noncash transactions when they occur.
   c. Generally accepted accounting principles require companies to use cash-basis accounting.
   d. The key elements of accrual-basis accounting are the revenue recognition principle, the expense recognition principle, and the historical cost principle.

3-2   In December, Swanstrom Inc. receives a cash payment of $3,500 for services performed during December and a cash payment of $4,500 for services to be performed during the next month. Swanstrom also receives the December utility bill for $600 but does not pay this bill until January. For December, under the accrual basis of accounting, Swanstrom would recognize:
   a. $8,000 of revenue and $600 of expense.
   b. $8,000 of revenue and $0 of expense.
   c. $3,500 of revenue and $600 of expense.
   d. $3,500 of revenue and $0 of expense.

OBJECTIVE 3

3-3   Which transaction would require adjustment at December 31?
   a. The sale of merchandise for cash on December 30.
   b. Common stock was issued on November 30.
   c. Salaries were paid to employees on December 31 for work performed in December.
   d. A 1-year insurance policy (which took effect immediately) was purchased on December 1.

3-4 Which of the following statements is *false?*

a. Adjusting entries are necessary because timing differences exist between when a revenue or expense is recognized and cash is received or paid.

b. Adjusting entries always affect at least one revenue or expense account and one asset or liability account.

c. The cash account will always be affected by adjusting journal entries.

d. Adjusting entries can be classified as either accruals or deferrals.

3-5 Dallas Company loaned $10,000 to Ewing Company on December 1. Ewing will pay Dallas $720 of interest ($60 per month) in 1 year. Dallas's adjusting entry at December 31 is:

OBJECTIVE 4

a. Interest Expense............... 60

    Cash............................ 60

b. Cash................................ 60

    Interest Income.............. 60

c. Interest Receivable............... 60

    Interest Income................ 60

d. No adjusting entry is required.

3-6 Ron's Diner received the following bills for April utilities:

- Electricity: $625 received on April 29
- Telephone: $150 received on May 5

Both bills were paid in May 10. On the April balance sheet, Ron's Diner will report accrued expenses of:

a. $0.

b. $150.

c. $625.

d. $775.

3-7 In September, Golf World Magazine obtained $15,000 of subscriptions for 1 year of magazines and credited Unearned Sales Revenue. Delivery of the magazines will begin in October. At December 31, Golf World should make the following adjustment:

a. Debit Sales Revenue by $3,750 and credit Unearned Sales Revenue by $3,750.

b. Debit Unearned Sales Revenue by $3,750 and credit Sales Revenue by $3,750.

c. Debit Sales Revenue by $11,250 and credit Unearned Sales Revenue by $11,250.

d. Debit Unearned Sales Revenue by $11,250 and credit Sales Revenue by $11,250.

3-8 Hurd Inc. prepays rent every 3 months on March 1, June 1, September 1, and December 1. Rent for the 3 months totals $3,600. On December 31, Hurd will report Prepaid Rent of:

a. $0.

b. $1,200.

c. $2,400.

d. $3,600.

3-9 Which of the following statements is *incorrect* regarding preparing financial statements?

OBJECTIVE 5

a. The adjusted trial balance lists only the balance sheet accounts in a "debit" and "credit" format.

b. The adjusted trial balance is the primary source of information needed to prepare the financial statements.

c. The financial statements are prepared in the following order: (1) the income statement, (2) the retained earnings statement, and (3) the balance sheet.

d. The income statement and the balance sheet are related through the retained earnings account.

3-10 Reinhardt Company reported revenues of $122,000 and expenses of $83,000 on its income statement. In addition, Reinhardt declared and paid $4,000 of dividends during the year. On December 31, Reinhardt prepared closing entries. The net effect of the closing entries on retained earnings was a(n):

OBJECTIVE 6

a. decrease of $4,000.

b. increase of $35,000.

c. increase of $39,000.

d. decrease of $87,000.

OBJECTIVE 7

3-11 Which of the following is true regarding the accounting cycle?
   a. The accounts are adjusted after preparing the financial statements.
   b. Journal entries are made prior to the transaction being analyzed.
   c. The temporary accounts are closed after the financial statements are prepared.
   d. An adjusted trial balance is usually prepared after the accounts are closed.

BRIEF EXERCISES

OBJECTIVE 1

EXAMPLE 3.1

Brief Exercise 3-12 Accrual- and Cash-Basis Revenue

McDonald Music sells used CDs for $4.00 each. During the month of April, McDonald sold 7,650 CDs for cash and 13,220 CDs on credit. McDonald's cash collections in April included $30,600 for CDs sold for cash, $12,800 for CDs sold on credit during the previous month, and $29,850 for CDs sold on credit during April.

Required:
Calculate the amount of revenue recognized in April under (1) cash-basis accounting and (2) accrual-basis accounting.

OBJECTIVE 1

Brief Exercise 3-13 Accrual- and Cash-Basis Expenses

Speedy Delivery Company provides next-day delivery across the southeastern United States. During May, Speedy incurred $132,600 in fuel costs. Speedy paid $95,450 of the fuel cost in May, with the remainder paid in June. In addition, Speedy paid $15,000 in May to another fuel supplier in an effort to build up its supply of fuel.

Required:
Calculate the amount of expense recognized in May under (1) cash-basis accounting and (2) accrual-basis accounting.

OBJECTIVE 1

Brief Exercise 3-14 Accrual- and Cash-Basis Accounting

The following are several transactions for Halpin Advertising Company.

   a. Purchased $1,000 of supplies.
   b. Sold $5,000 of advertising services, on account, to customers.
   c. Used $250 of supplies.
   d. Collected $3,000 from customers in payment of their accounts.
   e. Purchased equipment for $10,000 cash.
   f. Recorded $500 depreciation on the equipment for the current period.

Required:
Identify the effect, if any, that each of the above transactions would have on net income under cash-basis accounting and accrual-basis accounting.

OBJECTIVE 2

Brief Exercise 3-15 Revenue Recognition Principle

Heartstrings Gift Shoppe sells an assortment of gifts for any occasion. During October, Heartstrings started a Gift-of-the-Month program. Under the terms of this program, beginning in the month of the sale, Heartstrings would select and deliver a random gift each month, over the next 12 months, to the person the customer selects as a recipient. During October, Heartstrings sold 25 of these packages for a total of $11,280 in cash.

Required:
For the month of October, calculate the amount of revenue that Heartstrings will recognize.

Brief Exercise 3-16 Expense Recognition (or Matching) Principle

OBJECTIVE 2
EXAMPLE 3.1

The following information describes transactions for Morgenstern Advertising Company during July:

a. On July 5, Morgenstern purchased and received $24,300 of supplies on credit from Drexel Supply Inc. During July, Morgenstern paid $20,500 cash to Drexel and used $18,450 of the supplies.
b. Morgenstern paid $9,600 to salespeople for salaries earned during July. An additional $1,610 was owed to salespeople at July 31 for salaries earned during the month.
c. Paid $2,950 to the local utility company for electric service. Electric service in July was $2,300 of the $2,950 total bill.

Required:
Calculate the amount of expense recognized in July under (1) cash-basis accounting and (2) accrual-basis accounting.

Brief Exercise 3-17 Revenue and Expense Recognition

OBJECTIVE 2
EXAMPLE 3.1

Lauhl Corporation provides janitorial services to several office buildings. During April, Lauhl engaged in the following transactions:

a. On April 1, Lauhl received $24,000 from Metro Corporation to provide cleaning services over the next 6 months.
b. On April 5, Lauhl purchased and received $8,500 of supplies on credit from Eagle Supply Company. During the month, Lauhl paid $5,000 to Eagle and used $1,300 of the supplies.
c. On April 20, Lauhl performed one-time cleaning services of $2,500 for Jones Company. Jones paid Lauhl the full amount on May 10.
d. On April 30, Lauhl paid employees wages of $3,400. An additional $850 was owed to employees for work performed in April.

Required:
Calculate the amount of net income that Lauhl should recognize in April under (1) cash-basis accounting and (2) accrual-basis accounting.

Brief Exercise 3-18 Identification of Adjusting Entries

OBJECTIVE 3
EXAMPLE 3.2

Singleton Inc. uses the accrual basis of accounting and had the following transactions during the year.

a. Merchandise was sold to customers on credit.
b. Purchased equipment to be used in the operation of its business.
c. A 2-year insurance contract was purchased.
d. Received cash for services to be performed over the next year.
e. Paid weekly employee salaries.
f. Borrowed money from First Bank by signing a note payable due in 5 years.

Required:
Identify and explain why each transaction may or may not require adjustment.

Brief Exercise 3-19 Accrued Revenue Adjusting Entries

OBJECTIVE 4
EXAMPLE 3.3

Powers Rental Service had the following items that require adjustment at year end.

a. Earned $9,880 of revenue from the rental of equipment for which the customer had not yet paid.
b. Interest of $650 on a note receivable has been earned but not yet received.

(Continued)

Required:
1. Prepare the adjusting entries needed at December 31.
2. What is the effect on the financial statements if these adjusting entries are not made?

OBJECTIVE 4

EXAMPLE 3.4

Brief Exercise 3-20 Accrued Expense Adjusting Entries

Manning Manufacturing Inc. had the following items that require adjustment at year end.

a. Salaries of $5,320 that were earned in December are unrecorded and unpaid.
b. Used $1,970 of utilities in December, which are unrecorded and unpaid.
c. Interest of $925 on a note payable has not been recorded or paid.

Required:
1. Prepare the adjusting entries needed at December 31.
2. What is the effect on the financial statements if these adjusting entries are not made?

OBJECTIVE 4

EXAMPLE 3.5

Brief Exercise 3-21 Deferred Revenue Adjusting Entries

Olney Cleaning Company had the following items that require adjustment at year end.

a. For one cleaning contract, $14,520 cash was received in advance. The cash was credited to Unearned Service Revenue upon receipt. At year end, $1,210 of the service revenue was still unearned.
b. For another cleaning contract, $9,840 cash was received in advance and credited to Unearned Service Revenue upon receipt. At year end, $3,280 of the services had been provided.

Required:
1. Prepare the adjusting journal entries needed at December 31.
2. What is the effect on the financial statements if these adjusting entries are not made?
3. What is the balance in Unearned Service Revenue at December 31 related to the two cleaning contracts?

OBJECTIVE 4

EXAMPLE 3.6

Brief Exercise 3-22 Deferred Expense Adjusting Entries

Best Company had the following items that require adjustment at year end.

a. Cash for equipment rental in the amount of $3,800 was paid in advance. The $3,800 was debited to prepaid rent when paid. At year end, $2,950 of the prepaid rent had expired.
b. Cash for insurance in the amount of $8,200 was paid in advance. The $8,200 was debited to prepaid insurance when paid. At year end, $1,850 of the prepaid insurance was still unused.
c. Supplies at the beginning of the year showed a balance of $2,000. Best purchased supplies of $16,200 during the year. At the end of the year, a physical count of supplies showed $4,125 of supplies on hand.

Required:
1. Prepare the adjusting journal entries needed at December 31.
2. What is the effect on the financial statements if these adjusting entries are not made?
3. What is the balance in prepaid rent, insurance expense, and supplies at December 31?

OBJECTIVE 4

EXAMPLE 3.7

Brief Exercise 3-23 Adjustment for Depreciation

LaGarde Company has a machine that it purchased for $125,000 on January 1. Annual depreciation on the machine is estimated to be $14,500.

Required:
1. Prepare the adjusting entry needed at the end of the year.
2. What is the book value of the machine reported on LaGarde's balance sheet at the end of the year?

Use the following information for Brief Exercises 3-24 through 3-27:
Sparrow Company had the following adjusted trial balance at December 31.

Sparrow Company Adjusted Trial Balance December 31		
Account	Debit	Credit
Cash	$ 3,150	
Accounts Receivable	5,650	
Prepaid Insurance	4,480	
Equipment	42,000	
Accumulated Depreciation (Equipment)		$ 24,000
Accounts Payable		2,800
Salaries Payable		4,450
Unearned Service Revenue		3,875
Common Stock		8,000
Retained Earnings		2,255
Dividends Declared	10,500	
Service Revenue		99,600
Salaries Expense	49,400	
Rent Expense	17,250	
Insurance Expense	2,200	
Depreciation Expense	4,950	
Income Taxes Expense	5,400	
Totals	$144,980	$144,980

Brief Exercise 3-24 Preparing an Income Statement

OBJECTIVE 5
EXAMPLE 1.3

Refer to the information for Sparrow Company above.

Required:
Prepare a single-step income statement for Sparrow.

Brief Exercise 3-25 Preparing a Retained Earnings Statement

OBJECTIVE 5
EXAMPLE 1.4

Refer to the information for Sparrow Company above.

Required:
Prepare a retained earnings statement for Sparrow.

Brief Exercise 3-26 Preparing a Balance Sheet

OBJECTIVE 5
EXAMPLE 1.2

Refer to the information for Sparrow Company above.

Required:
Prepare a classified balance sheet for Sparrow at December 31.

Brief Exercise 3-27 Preparing and Analyzing Closing Entries

OBJECTIVE 6
EXAMPLE 3.7

Refer to the information for Sparrow Company above.

Required:
1. Prepare the closing entries for Sparrow at December 31.
2. How does the closing process affect retained earnings?

OBJECTIVE **Brief Exercise 3-28 The Accounting Cycle**

Below are the steps of the accounting cycle.

Journalize transaction.
Prepare financial statements.
Prepare a trial balance.
Analyze transaction.
Adjust the account.
Close the accounts.
Post to the ledger.

Required:

List these steps of the accounting cycle in their proper order.

EXERCISES

OBJECTIVE **Exercise 3-29 Accrual- and Cash-Basis Expense Recognition**

The following information is taken from the accrual accounting records of Krueger Sales Company:

a. During January, Krueger paid $9,150 for supplies to be used in sales to customers during the next 2 months (February and March). The supplies will be used evenly over the next 2 months.
b. Krueger pays its employees at the end of each month for salaries earned during that month. Salaries paid at the end of February and March amounted to $4,925 and $5,100, respectively.
c. Krueger placed an advertisement in the local newspaper during March at a cost of $850. The ad promoted the pre-spring sale during the last week in March. Krueger did not pay for the newspaper ad until mid-April.

Required:

1. Under cash-basis accounting, how much expense should Krueger report for February and March?
2. Under accrual-basis accounting, how much expense should Krueger report for February and March?
3. **CONCEPTUAL CONNECTION** Which basis of accounting provides the most useful information for decision-makers? Why?

OBJECTIVE **Exercise 3-30 Revenue Recognition**

Each of the following situations relates to the recognition of revenue:

a. A store sells a gift card in December, which will be given as a Christmas present. The card is not redeemed until January.
b. A furniture store sells and delivers furniture to a customer in June with no payments and no interest for 6 months.
c. An airline sells an airline ticket and collects the fare in February for a flight in March to a spring break destination.
d. A theme park sells a season pass and collects the cash in January, which allows entrance into the park for an entire year.
e. A package delivery service delivers a package in October but doesn't bill the customer and receive payment until November.

Required:

CONCEPTUAL CONNECTION For each situation, indicate when the company should recognize revenue on an accrual basis.

Exercise 3-31 Revenue and Expense Recognition

OBJECTIVE ◀ 2

Electronic Repair Company repaired a high-definition television for Sarah Merrifield in June. Sarah paid $80 at the time of the repair and agreed to pay Electronic Repair $80 each month for 5 months beginning in July (the next month). Electronic Repair used $120 of supplies, which were purchased in May, to repair the television. Assume that Electronic Repair uses accrual-basis accounting.

Required:
1. In what month or months should revenue from this service be recorded by Electronic Repair?
2. In what month or months should the expense related to the repair of the television be recorded by Electronic Repair?
3. **CONCEPTUAL CONNECTION** Describe the accounting principles used to answer the above questions.

Exercise 3-32 Cash-Basis and Accrual-Basis Accounting

OBJECTIVE ◀ 1 2

⌕ SHOW
ME HOW

The records of Summers Building Company reveal the following information for the year.

a. Cash receipts (including $50,000 paid by stockholders in exchange for common stock) were $273,500.
b. Cash payments (including $8,000 of dividends declared and paid to stockholders) were $164,850.
c. Total selling price of services billed to customers was $201,700.
d. Salaries earned by employees were $114,250.
e. Cost of supplies used in operation of the business was $47,325.

Required:
1. Calculate Summers Building's net income on an accrual basis.
2. Calculate Summers Building's net income on a cash basis.
3. **CONCEPTUAL CONNECTION** Explain how cash-basis accounting allows for the manipulation of income.

Exercise 3-33 Revenue and Expense Recognition

OBJECTIVE ◀ 2

⌕ SHOW
ME HOW

Omega Transportation Inc., headquartered in Atlanta, Georgia, uses accrual-basis accounting and engaged in the following transactions:

- billed customers $3,580,000 for transportation services
- collected cash from customers in the amount of $2,479,000
- purchased fuel supplies for $1,655,000 cash
- used fuel supplies that cost $1,598,240
- employees earned salaries of $425,160
- paid employees $413,380 cash for salaries

Required:
Determine the amount of sales revenue and total expenses for Omega's income statement.

Exercise 3-34 Recognizing Expenses

OBJECTIVE ◀ 2

Treadway Dental Services gives each of its patients a toothbrush with the name and phone number of the dentist office and a logo imprinted on the brush. Treadway purchased 15,000 of the toothbrushes in October 2023 for $3,130. The toothbrushes were delivered in November and paid for in December 2023. Treadway began to give the patients the toothbrushes in February 2024. By the end of 2024, 4,500 of the toothbrushes remained in the supplies account.

Required:
1. How much expense should be recorded for the 15,000 toothbrushes in 2023 and 2024?
2. Describe how the 4,500 toothbrushes that remain in the supplies account will be handled in 2025.

OBJECTIVE

Exercise 3-35 Revenue Expense and Recognition

Carrico Advertising Inc. performs advertising services for several Fortune 500 companies. The following information describes Carrico's activities during the current year.

a. At the beginning of the year, customers owed Carrico $45,800 for advertising services performed during the previous year. During the current year, Carrico performed an additional $695,100 of advertising services on account. Carrico collected $708,700 cash from customers during the current year.

b. At the beginning of the year, Carrico had $13,350 of supplies on hand for which it owed suppliers $8,150. During the year, Carrico purchased an additional $14,600 of supplies on account. Carrico also paid $19,300 cash owed to suppliers for goods previously purchased on credit. Carrico had $2,230 of supplies on hand at the end of the year.

c. Carrico's operating and interest expenses were $437,600 and $133,400, respectively.

Required:

1. Calculate Carrico's income before taxes.
2. Calculate the ending balance of accounts receivable, the supplies used, and the ending balance of accounts payable.
3. **CONCEPTUAL CONNECTION** Explain the underlying principles behind why the three accounts computed in Requirement 2 exist.

OBJECTIVE

Exercise 3-36 Identification of Adjusting Entries

Conklin Services prepares financial statements only once per year using an annual accounting period ending on December 31. Each of the following statements describes an entry made by Conklin on December 31 of a recent year.

a. On December 31, Conklin completed a service agreement for Pizza Planet and recorded the related revenue. The job started in August.

b. Conklin provides weekly service visits to the local C.J. Nickel department store to check and maintain various pieces of computer printing equipment. On December 31, Conklin recorded revenue for the visits completed during December. The cash will not be received until January.

c. Conklin's salaried employees are paid on the last day of every month. On December 31, Conklin recorded the payment of December salaries.

d. Conklin's hourly wage employees are paid every Friday. On December 31, Conklin recorded as payable the wages for the first three working days of the week in which the year ended.

e. On December 31, Conklin recorded the receipt of a shipment of office supplies from Office Supplies Inc. to be paid for in January.

f. On December 31, Conklin recorded the estimated use of supplies for the year. The supplies were purchased for cash earlier in the year.

g. Early in December, Conklin was paid in advance by Parker Enterprises for 2 months of weekly service visits. Conklin recorded the advance payment as a liability. On December 31, Conklin recorded revenue for the service visits to Parker Enterprises that were completed during December.

h. On December 31, Conklin recorded depreciation expense on office equipment for the year.

Required:

Indicate whether each entry is an *adjusting entry* or a *regular journal entry,* and, if it is an adjusting entry, identify it as one of the following types: (1) revenue recognized before collection of cash, (2) expense recognized before payment of cash, (3) revenue recognized after collection of cash, or (4) expense recognized after payment of cash.

Exercise 3-37 Identification and Analysis of Adjusting Entries

OBJECTIVE ◀ 3

Medina Motor Service is preparing adjusting entries for the year ended December 31. The following items describe Medina's continuous transactions during the year:

a. Medina's salaried employees are paid on the last day of every month.
b. Medina's hourly employees are paid every other Friday for the preceding 2 weeks' work. The next payday falls on January 5 of the next year.
c. In November, Medina borrowed $600,000 from Bank One, giving a 9% note payable with interest due next March. The note was properly recorded.
d. Medina rents a portion of its parking lot to the neighboring business under a long-term lease agreement that requires payment of rent 6 months in advance on April 1 and October 1 of each year. The October 1 payment was made and recorded as prepaid rent.
e. Medina's service department recognizes the entire revenue on every auto service job when the job is complete. At December 31, several service jobs are in process.
f. Medina recognizes depreciation on shop equipment annually at the end of each year.
g. Medina purchases all of its office supplies from Office Supplies Inc. All purchases are recorded in the supplies account. Supplies expense is calculated and recorded annually at the end of each year.

Required:

Indicate whether or not each item requires an adjusting entry at December 31. If an item requires an adjusting entry, indicate which accounts are increased by the adjustment and which are decreased.

Exercise 3-38 Revenue Adjustments

OBJECTIVE ◀ 4

SHOW
ME HOW

Sentry Transport Inc. of Atlanta provides in-town parcel delivery services in addition to a full range of passenger services. Sentry engaged in the following activities during the current year:

a. In December, Sentry received $5,000 cash in advance from Rich's Department Store for an estimated 250 deliveries during the next 3 months. The entire amount was recorded as unearned revenue when received. During December, 110 deliveries were made for Rich's.
b. Sentry operates several small buses that take commuters from suburban communities to the central downtown area of Atlanta. The commuters purchase, in advance, tickets for 50 one-way rides. Each 50-ride ticket costs $500. At the time of purchase, Sentry credits the cash received to unearned revenue. At year end, Sentry determines that 10,160 one-way rides have been taken.
c. Sentry operates several buses that provide transportation for the clients of a social service agency in Atlanta. Sentry bills the agency in advance at the end of January, April, July, and October for the service to be performed over the next 3 months. The contract price is $7,500 for each 3-month period. Sentry properly recognizes revenue in the period in which the service is performed.
d. On December 23, Delta Airlines chartered a bus to transport its marketing group to a meeting at a resort in southern Georgia. The meeting will be held during the last week in January, and Delta agrees to pay for the entire trip on the day the bus departs. At year end, none of these arrangements have been recorded by Sentry.

Required:

1. Prepare adjusting entries at December 31 for these four activities.
2. **CONCEPTUAL CONNECTION** What would be the effect on revenue if the adjusting entries were not made?

OBJECTIVE 4

Exercise 3-39 Expense Adjustments

Faraday Electronic Service repairs stereos and DVD players. During the year, Faraday engaged in the following activities:

a. On September 1, Faraday paid Wausau Insurance $4,860 for its liability insurance for the next 12 months. The full amount of the prepayment was debited to prepaid insurance.
b. At December 31, Faraday estimates that $1,520 of utility costs are unrecorded and unpaid.
c. Faraday rents its testing equipment from JVC. Equipment rent in the amount of $1,440 is unpaid and unrecorded at December 31.
d. In late October, Faraday agreed to become the sponsor for the sports segment of the evening news program on a local television station. The station billed Faraday $4,350 for 3 months' sponsorship—November, December, and January—in advance. When these payments were made, Faraday debited prepaid advertising. At December 31, 2 months' advertising has been used and 1 month remains unused.

Required:
1. Prepare adjusting entries at December 31 for these four activities.
2. **CONCEPTUAL CONNECTION** What would be the effect on expenses if the adjusting entries were not made?

OBJECTIVE 4

Exercise 3-40 Prepayments, Collections in Advance

Greensboro Properties Inc. owns a building in which it leases office space to small businesses and professionals. During the year, Greensboro Properties engaged in the following transactions:

a. On March 1, Greensboro Properties paid $10,500 in advance to Patterson Insurance Company for 1 year of insurance beginning March 1. The full amount of the prepayment was debited to prepaid insurance.
b. On May 1, Greensboro Properties received $30,000 for 1 year's rent from Angela Cottrell, a lawyer and new tenant. Greensboro Properties credited unearned rent revenue for the full amount collected from Cottrell.
c. On July 31, Greensboro Properties received $240,000 for 6 months' rent on an office building that is occupied by Newnan and Calhoun, a regional accounting firm. The rental period begins on August 1. The full amount received was credited to unearned rent revenue.
d. On November 1, Greensboro Properties paid $4,500 to Pinkerton Security for 3 months' security services beginning on that date. The entire amount was debited to prepaid security services.

Required:
1. Prepare the journal entry to record the receipt or payment of cash for each of the transactions.
2. Prepare the adjusting entries you would make at December 31 for each of these items.
3. **CONCEPTUAL CONNECTION** What would be the total effect on the income statement and balance sheet if these entries were not recorded?

OBJECTIVE 4

Exercise 3-41 Prepayment of Expenses

JDM Inc. made the following prepayments for expense items during the year:

a. Prepaid building rent for 1 year on April 1 by paying $6,600. Prepaid rent was debited for the amount paid.
b. Prepaid 12 months' insurance on October 1 by paying $4,200. Prepaid insurance was debited.

c. Purchased $5,250 of office supplies on October 15, debiting supplies for the full amount. There were no office supplies on hand as of October 15. Office supplies costing $1,085 remain unused at December 31.

d. Paid $600 for a 12-month service contract for repairs and maintenance on a computer. The contract begins November 1. The full amount of the payment was debited to prepaid repairs and maintenance.

Required:

1. Prepare journal entries to record the payment of cash for each transaction.
2. Prepare adjusting entries for the prepayments at December 31.
3. **CONCEPTUAL CONNECTION** For all of the above items, assume that the accountant failed to make the adjusting entries. What would be the effect on net income?

Exercise 3-42 Adjustment for Supplies

OBJECTIVE ◀ 4

The downtown location of Chicago Clothiers purchases large quantities of supplies, including plastic garment bags and paper bags and boxes. At December 31, the following information is available concerning these supplies:

Supplies inventory, January 1	$ 4,150
Supplies inventory, December 31	5,220
Supplies purchased for cash during the year	12,690

All purchases of supplies during the year are debited to the supplies inventory.

Required:

1. What is the expense reported on the income statement associated with the use of supplies?
2. What is the proper adjusting entry at December 31?
3. By how much would assets and income be overstated or understated if the adjusting entry were not recorded?

Exercise 3-43 Adjusting Entries

OBJECTIVE ◀ 4

Allentown Services Inc. is preparing adjusting entries for the year ending December 31. The following data are available:

a. Interest is owed at December 31, on a 6-month, 8% note. Allentown borrowed $120,000 from NBD on September 1.

b. Allentown provides daily building maintenance services to Mack Trucks for a quarterly fee of $2,700 payable on the fifteenth of the month following the end of each quarter. No entries have been made for the services provided to Mack Trucks during the quarter ended December 31, and the related bill will not be sent until January 15 of the following year.

c. On January 1, the cost of office supplies on hand was $1,220. During the year, office supplies with a total cost of $6,480 were purchased from Office Depot and debited to office supplies inventory. On December 31, Allentown determined the cost of office supplies on hand to be $970.

d. On September 23, Allentown received a $7,650 payment from Bethlehem Steel for 9 months of maintenance services beginning on October 1. The entire amount was credited to unearned service revenue when received.

Required:

1. Prepare the appropriate adjusting entries at December 31.
2. **CONCEPTUAL CONNECTION** What would be the effect on the balance sheet and the income statement if the accountant failed to make the above adjusting entries?

OBJECTIVE 4

Exercise 3-44 Adjusting Entries

Reynolds Computer Service offers data processing services to retail clothing stores. The following data have been collected to aid in the preparation of adjusting entries for Reynolds Computer Service for the current year:

a. Computer equipment was purchased from IBM 3 years ago at a cost of $540,000. Annual depreciation is $132,500.

b. A fire insurance policy for a 2-year period beginning on September 1 was purchased from Good Hands Insurance Company for $12,240 cash. The entire amount of the prepayment was debited to prepaid insurance. (Assume that the beginning balance of prepaid insurance was $0 and that there were no other debits or credits to that account during the year.)

c. Reynolds has a contract to perform the payroll accounting for Dayton's Department Stores. On December 31, $5,450 of services have been performed under this contract but are unbilled.

d. Reynolds rents 12 computer terminals for $65 per month per terminal from Extreme Terminals Inc. At December 31, Reynolds owes Extreme Terminals for half a month's rent on each terminal. The amount owed is unrecorded.

e. Perry's Tax Service prepays rent for time on Reynolds' computer. When payments are received from Perry's Tax Service, Reynolds credits unearned rent revenue. At December 31, Reynolds has earned $1,810 for computer time used by Perry's Tax Service during December.

Required:
1. Prepare adjusting entries for each of the transactions.
2. **CONCEPTUAL CONNECTION** What would be the effect on the balance sheet and the income statement if the accountant failed to make the above adjusting entries?

OBJECTIVE 4

Exercise 3-45 Recreating Adjusting Entries

Selected balance sheet accounts for Gardner Company are presented below.

Prepaid Insurance		Wages Payable		Unearned Sales Revenue		Interest Receivable	
May 5 4,300			?		9,500 May 10	?	
	?			?			
1,250		5,400		2,250		825	

Required:
Analyze each account and recreate the journal entries that were made for the month of May. For deferrals, be sure to include the original journal entry as well as the adjusting journal entry.

OBJECTIVE 4

Exercise 3-46 Effect of Adjustments on the Financial Statements

VanBrush Enterprises, a painting contractor, prepared the following adjusting entries at year end:

a.	Wages Expense	2,550	
	Wages Payable		2,550
b.	Accounts Receivable	8,110	
	Service Revenue		8,110
c.	Unearned Service Revenue	5,245	
	Service Revenue		5,245
d.	Rent Expense	3,820	
	Prepaid Rent		3,820

Required:

1. Show the effect of these adjustments on assets, liabilities, equity, revenues, expenses, and net income.
2. **CONCEPTUAL CONNECTION** If these adjustments were made with estimates that were considered conservative, how would this affect your interpretation of earnings quality?

Exercise 3-47 Financial Statement Effects of Adjusting Entries

OBJECTIVE ◀4

When adjusting entries were made at the end of the year, the accountant for Parker Company did not make the following adjustments.

a. Wages of $2,900 had been earned by employees but were unpaid.
b. $3,750 of performance obligations had been satisfied but no cash was uncollected nor any revenue recorded.
c. $2,400 performance obligations had been satisfied. The customer had prepaid for this service and the amount was originally recorded in the Unearned Sales Revenue account.
d. $1,200 of insurance coverage had expired. Insurance had been initially recorded in the Prepaid Insurance account.

Required:

Identify the effect on the financial statements of the adjusting entries that were omitted.

Exercise 3-48 Preparing an Income Statement

OBJECTIVE ◀5

Oxmoor Corporation prepared the following adjusted trial balance.

 SHOW ME HOW

Oxmoor Corporation Adjusted Trial Balance December 31		
Account	**Debit**	**Credit**
Cash	$ 13,300	
Accounts Receivable	6,700	
Prepaid Rent	54,000	
Inventory	481,400	
Long-Term Investment	110,900	
Equipment	88,000	
Accumulated Depreciation		$ 23,700
Accounts Payable		111,700
Interest Payable		4,400
Note Payable (Short-term)		50,000
Bonds Payable		180,000
Common Stock		300,000
Retained Earnings, 1/1/2019		45,635
Dividends Declared	50,000	
Sales Revenue		583,900
Cost of Goods Sold	277,000	
Wages Expense	98,250	
Rent Expense	50,000	
Depreciation Expense	29,000	
Interest Expense	2,700	
Income Taxes Expense	38,085	
Totals	$1,299,335	$1,299,335

Required:

1. Prepare a single-step income statement for Oxmoor for the year ended December 31.
2. Prepare a multiple-step income statement for Oxmoor for the year ended December 31.

OBJECTIVE   **Exercise 3-49 Preparing a Retained Earnings Statement**

Refer to the unadjusted trial balance for Oxmoor Corporation in **Exercise 3-48**.

Required:

Prepare a retained earnings statement for Oxmoor for the year ended December 31.

OBJECTIVE   **Exercise 3-50 Preparing a Balance Sheet**

Refer to the unadjusted trial balance for Oxmoor Corporation in **Exercise 3-48**.

Required:

Prepare a classified balance sheet for Oxmoor at December 31.

OBJECTIVE   **Exercise 3-51 Preparation of Closing Entries**

On January 1, Grand Rapids Consulting Inc. had a retained earnings balance of $38,100 and reported the following accounts and balances at year end:

Sales Revenue	$162,820	Supplies Expense	$ 4,348
Salaries Expense	91,660	Income Taxes Expense	13,800
Rent Expense	11,250	Dividends (declared and paid)	8,400
Utilities Expense	8,415		

Required:

1. Prepare the closing entries made by Grand Rapids Consulting at December 31.
2. Prepare Grand Rapids Consulting's retained earnings statement.

OBJECTIVE 6   **Exercise 3-52 Preparing and Analyzing Closing Entries**

At December 31, the ledger of Aulani Company includes the following accounts, all having normal balances: Sales Revenue, $59,000; Cost of Goods Sold, $31,000; Retained Earnings, $20,000; Interest Expense, $3,200; Dividends (declared and paid), $5,000; Wages Expense, $8,000, and Interest Payable, $2,100.

Required:

1. Prepare the closing entries for Aulani at December 31.
2. How does the closing process affect Aulani's retained earnings?

OBJECTIVE 6   **Exercise 3-53 Preparation of Closing Entries**

James and Susan Morley recently converted a large turn-of-the-century house into a hotel and incorporated the business as Saginaw Enterprises. Their accountant is inexperienced and has made the following closing entries at the end of Saginaw's first year of operations:

Retained Earnings...	210,000	
Service Revenue...		177,000
Accumulated Depreciation..........................		33,000
Depreciation Expense....................................	33,000	
Income Taxes Expense..................................	8,200	
Utilities Expense...	12,700	
Wages Expense..	66,000	
Supplies Expense..	31,000	
Accounts Payable...	4,500	
Retained Earnings......................................		155,400
Dividends Declared..	3,200	
Retained Earnings......................................		3,200

Required:

1. Indicate what is wrong with the closing entries above.
2. Prepare the correct closing entries. Assume that all necessary accounts are presented above and that the amounts given are correct.
3. **CONCEPTUAL CONNECTION** Explain why closing entries are necessary.

Exercise 3-54 Preparation of a Worksheet *(Appendix 3A)*

OBJECTIVE

Unadjusted account balances at December 31 for Rapisarda Company are as follows:

Rapisarda Company Unadjusted Trial Balance December 31		
Account	**Debit**	**Credit**
Cash	$ 2,000	
Accounts Receivable	33,000	
Prepaid Rent	26,000	
Equipment	211,000	
Accumulated Depreciation (Equipment)		$ 75,000
Other Assets	24,000	
Accounts Payable		12,000
Note Payable (due in 10 years)		40,000
Common Stock		100,000
Retained Earnings, January 1		11,000
Service Revenue		243,000
Rent Expense	84,000	
Wages Expense	97,000	
Interest Expense	4,000	
Totals	$481,000	$481,000

The following data are not yet recorded:

a. Depreciation on the equipment is $18,350.
b. Unrecorded wages owed at December 31, 2019: $4,680.
c. Prepaid rent at December 31, 2019: $9,240.
d. Income taxes expense: $5,463.

Required:

Prepare a completed worksheet for Rapisarda Company.

PROBLEM SET A

Problem 3-55A Cash-Basis and Accrual-Basis Income

OBJECTIVE

George Hathaway, an electrician, entered into an agreement with a real estate management company to perform all maintenance of basic electrical systems and air-conditioning equipment in the apartment buildings under the company's management. The agreement, which is subject to annual renewal, provides for the payment of a fixed fee of $6,600 on January 1 of each year plus amounts for parts and materials billed separately at the end of each month. Amounts billed at the end of 1 month are collected in the next month. During the first

(Continued)

3 months (January, February, and March) of the year, George makes the following additional billings and cash collections:

	Billings for Parts and Materials	Cash Collected	Cash Paid for Parts and Materials	Cost of Parts and Materials Used
January	$280	$6,750*	$150	$160
February	0	250	185	170
March	320	0	290	300

* Includes $150 for parts and materials billed in December of the previous year.

Required:

1. Calculate the amount of cash-basis income reported for each of the first 3 months of the current year.
2. Calculate the amount of accrual-basis income reported for each of the first 3 months of the current year.
3. **CONCEPTUAL CONNECTION** Why do decision-makers prefer accrual-basis accounting?

OBJECTIVE 2

Problem 3-56A Revenue and Expense Recognition

Security Specialists performs security services for local businesses. During the year, Security Specialists performed $1,425,700 of security services and collected $1,445,000 cash from customers. Security Specialist's employees earned salaries of $82,350 per month. Security Services paid salaries of $980,200 cash for work performed. At the beginning of the year, there were $2,875 of supplies on hand. Supplies of $65,800 were purchased during the year, and $9,225 of supplies were on hand at the end of the year. Other general and administrative expenses incurred during the year were $26,500.

Required:

1. Calculate revenue and expenses for the year.
2. Prepare a single-step income statement for the year.
3. **CONCEPTUAL CONNECTION** Describe the accounting principles used to prepare the income statement.

OBJECTIVE 3 4

Problem 3-57A Identification and Preparation of Adjusting Entries

Kuepper's Day Care is a large daycare center in South Orange, New Jersey. The daycare center serves several nearby businesses as well as a number of individual families. The businesses pay $6,180 per child per year for daycare services for their employees' children. The businesses pay in advance on a quarterly basis. For individual families, daycare services are provided monthly and billed at the beginning of the next month. The following transactions describe Kuepper's activities during December:

a. On December 1, Kuepper borrowed $50,000 by issuing a 5-year, $50,000, 9% note payable.
b. Daycare service in the amount of $13,390 was provided to individual families during December. These families will not be billed until next January.
c. At December 1, the balance in unearned service revenue was $26,780. At December 31, Kuepper determined that $10,300 of this revenue was still unearned.
d. On December 31, the daycare center collected $40,170 from businesses for services to be provided in 2020.
e. On December 31, the center recorded depreciation of $1,875 on a bus that it uses for field trips.
f. The daycare center had prepaid insurance at December 1 of $3,600. An examination of the insurance policies indicates that prepaid insurance at December 31 is $3,000.
g. Interest on the $50,000 note payable (see Transaction a) is unpaid and unrecorded at December 31.

h. Salaries of $35,480 are owed but unpaid on December 31.

i. Supplies of disposable diapers on December 1 are $4,200. At December 31, the cost of diapers in supplies is $750.

Required:

1. Identify whether each transaction is an adjusting entry or a regular journal entry. If the entry is an adjusting entry, identify it as an accrued revenue, accrued expense, deferred revenue, or deferred expense.

2. Prepare the entries necessary to record the transactions above and on the previous page.

Problem 3-58A Preparation of Adjusting Entries

OBJECTIVE 4

Bartow Photographic Services takes wedding and graduation photographs. At December 31, the end of Bartow's accounting period, the following information is available:

a. All wedding photographs are paid for in advance, and all cash collected for them is credited to Unearned Service Revenue. Except for a year-end adjusting entry, no other entries are made for service revenue from wedding photographs. During the year, Bartow received $42,600 for wedding photographs. At year end, $37,400 of services had been performed. The beginning-of-the-year balance of Unearned Service Revenue was zero.

b. During December, Bartow photographed 225 members of the next year's graduating class of Shaw High School. The school has asked Bartow to print one copy of a photograph of each student for the school files. Bartow delivers these photographs on December 28 and will bill the school $5.00 per student in January of next year. Revenue from photographs ordered by students will be recorded as the orders are received during the early months of next year.

c. Equipment used for developing and printing was rented for $22,500. The rental term was for 1 year beginning on August 1 and the entire year of rent was paid on August 1. The payment was debited to Prepaid Rent.

d. Depreciation on the firm's building for the current year is $9,400.

e. Wages of $4,170 are owed but unpaid and unrecorded at December 31.

f. Supplies at the beginning of the year were $2,400. During the year, supplies costing $19,600 were purchased from Kodak. When the purchases were made, their cost was debited to Supplies. At year end, a physical inventory indicated that supplies costing $4,100 were on hand.

Required:

1. Prepare the adjusting entries for each of these items.

2. **CONCEPTUAL CONNECTION** By how much would net income be overstated or understated if the accountant failed to make the adjusting entries?

Problem 3-59A Effects of Adjusting Entries on the Accounting Equation

OBJECTIVE 4

Four adjusting entries are shown below.

a. Wages Expense..	3,410	
Wages Payable..		3,410
b. Accounts Receivable.................................	8,350	
Service Revenue...		8,350
c. Rent Expense...	2,260	
Prepaid Rent..		2,260
d. Unearned Service Revenue........................	5,150	
Service Revenue..		5,150

(Continued)

Required:

CONCEPTUAL CONNECTION Analyze the adjusting entries and identify their effects on the financial statement accounts. (*Note:* Ignore any income tax effects.) Use the following format for your answer:

Transaction	Assets	Liabilities	Common Stock	Retained Earnings	Revenues	Expenses

OBJECTIVE 4 5

SHOW ME HOW

Problem 3-60A Adjusting Entries and Financial Statements

You have the following unadjusted trial balance for Rogers Corporation at December 31:

Rogers Corporation Unadjusted Trial Balance December 31		
Account	Debit	Credit
Cash	$ 3,100	
Accounts Receivable	15,900	
Supplies	4,200	
Prepaid Rent	9,500	
Equipment	625,000	
Accumulated Depreciation		$ 104,000
Other Assets	60,900	
Accounts Payable		9,400
Unearned Service Revenue		11,200
Note Payable (due in 3 years)		50,000
Common Stock		279,500
Retained Earnings, January 1		37,000
Service Revenue		598,000
Wages Expense	137,000	
Rent Expense	229,000	
Interest Expense	4,500	
Totals	$1,089,100	$1,089,100

At year end, you have the following data for adjustments:

a. An analysis indicates that prepaid rent on December 31 should be $2,300.
b. A physical inventory shows that $650 of office supplies is on hand.
c. Depreciation is $35,250.
d. An analysis indicates that unearned service revenue should be $3,120.
e. Wages in the amount of $3,450 are owed but unpaid and unrecorded at year end.
f. Six months' interest at 8% on the note was paid on September 30. Interest for the period from October 1 to December 31 is unpaid and unrecorded.
g. Income taxes of $55,539 are owed but unrecorded and unpaid.

Required:
1. Prepare the adjusting entries.
2. Prepare a single-step income statement, a retained earnings statement, and a balance sheet using adjusted account balances.
3. **CONCEPTUAL CONNECTION** Why would you not want to prepare financial statements until after the adjusting entries are made?

Problem 3-61A Inferring Adjusting Entries from Account Balance Changes   OBJECTIVE ▸4

The following schedule shows all the accounts of Fresno Travel Agency that received year-end adjusting entries:

Account	Unadjusted Account Balance	Adjusted Account Balance
Prepaid Insurance	$ 23,270	$ 6,150
Prepaid Rent	3,600	2,100
Accumulated Depreciation	156,000	(a)
Wages Payable	0	6,750
Unearned Service Revenue	13,620	(b)
Service Revenue	71,600	78,980
Insurance Expense	0	(c)
Rent Expense	29,700	(d)
Depreciation Expense	0	12,500
Wages Expense	44,200	(e)

Required:
1. Calculate the missing amounts identified by the letters (a) through (e).
2. Prepare the five adjusting entries that must have been made to cause the account changes as indicated.

Problem 3-62A Preparation of Closing Entries and an Income Statement   OBJECTIVE ▸5 6

Round Grove Alarm Company provides security services to homes in northwestern Indiana. At year end (December 31), after adjusting entries have been made, the following list of account balances is prepared:

Accounts Payable	$ 23,250	Prepaid Rent	$ 4,750
Accounts Receivable	36,800	Rent Expense	27,600
Accumulated Depreciation (Equipment)	124,000	Retained Earnings, January 1	29,400
Common Stock	150,000	Salaries Expense	148,250
Depreciation Expense (Equipment)	45,300	Salaries Payable	12,600
Dividends Declared	6,000	Service Revenue	612,900
Equipment	409,500	Supplies	12,700
Income Taxes Expense	30,800	Supplies Expense	51,900
Income Taxes Payable	24,300	Utilities Expense	48,800
Interest Expense	4,800	Wages Expense	183,500
Notes Payable (due in 3 years)	34,000	Wages Payable	7,950
Other Assets	7,700		

Required:
1. Prepare closing entries for Round Grove Alarm.
2. Prepare a single-step income statement for Round Grove Alarm.

OBJECTIVE 4 5 6 7

Problem 3-63A Comprehensive Problem: Reviewing the Accounting Cycle

Tarkington Freight Service provides delivery of merchandise to retail grocery stores in the Northeast. At the beginning of the year (January 1), the following account balances were available:

Cash	$ 92,100	Accumulated Depreciation	
Accounts Receivable	361,500	(Equipment)	$ 580,000
Supplies	24,600	Land	304,975
Prepaid Advertising	2,000	Accounts Payable	17,600
Building	2,190,000	Wages Payable	30,200
Accumulated Depreciation		Notes Payable (due in 4 years)	1,000,000
(Building)	280,000	Common Stock	1,400,000
Equipment	795,000	Retained Earnings, January 1	462,375

During the year, the following transactions occurred:

a. Tarkington performed deliveries for customers, all on credit, for $2,256,700. Tarkington also made cash deliveries for $686,838.
b. There remains $286,172 of accounts receivable to be collected at December 31.
c. Tarkington purchased advertising of $138,100 during the year and debited the amount to prepaid advertising.
d. Supplies of $27,200 were purchased on credit and debited to the supplies account.
e. Accounts payable at the beginning of the year were paid early in January. There remains $5,600 of accounts payable unpaid at year end.
f. Wages payable at the beginning of the year were paid early in January. Wages were earned and paid during the year in the amount of $666,142.
g. During the year, Trish Hurd, a principal stockholder, purchased an automobile costing $42,000 for her personal use.
h. One-half year's interest at 6% annual rate was paid on the note payable on July 1.
i. Property taxes were paid on the land and buildings in the amount of $170,000.
j. Dividends were declared and paid in the amount of $25,000.

The following data are available for adjusting entries:

- Supplies in the amount of $13,685 remained unused at year end.
- Annual depreciation on the warehouse building is $70,000.
- Annual depreciation on the warehouse equipment is $145,000.
- Wages of $60,558 were unrecorded and unpaid at year end.
- Interest for 6 months at 6% per year on the note is unpaid and unrecorded at year end.
- Advertising of $14,874 remained unused at the end of the year.
- Income taxes of $482,549 related to the current year are unpaid at year end.

Required:
1. Post the beginning balances to T-accounts. Prepare journal entries for Transactions a through j and post the journal entries to T-accounts, adding any new T-accounts you need.
2. Prepare the adjustments and post the adjustments to the T-accounts, adding any new T-accounts you need.
3. Prepare a single-step income statement.
4. Prepare a retained earnings statement.
5. Prepare a classified balance sheet.
6. Prepare closing entries.
7. **CONCEPTUAL CONNECTION** Did you include Transaction "g" among Tarkington's journal entries? Why or why not?

Problem 3-64A Preparing a Worksheet *(Appendix 3A)*

OBJECTIVE 4 5 6 7 8

Marsteller Properties Inc. owns apartments that it rents to university students. At December 31, the following unadjusted account balances were available:

Cash	$ 4,600	Notes Payable (due in 2 years)	$2,000,000
Rent Receivable	32,500	Common Stock	1,500,000
Supplies	4,700	Retained Earnings, January 1	39,200
Prepaid Insurance	60,000	Rent Revenue	660,000
Land	274,000	Repairs & Maintenance Expense	73,200
Buildings	4,560,000	Advertising Expense	58,700
Accumulated Depreciation (Buildings)	1,015,000	Wages Expense	84,300
Other Assets	26,100	Utilities Expense	3,400
Accounts Payable	57,300	Interest Expense	90,000

The following information is available for adjusting entries:

a. An analysis of apartment rental contracts indicates that $3,800 of apartment rent is unbilled and unrecorded at year end.
b. A physical count of supplies reveals that $1,400 of supplies are on hand at December 31.
c. Annual depreciation on the buildings is $204,250.
d. An examination of insurance policies indicates that $12,000 of the prepaid insurance applies to coverage for 2019.
e. Six months' interest at 9% is unrecorded and unpaid on the notes payable.
f. Wages in the amount of $6,100 are unpaid and unrecorded at December 31.
g. Utilities costs of $300 are unrecorded and unpaid at December 31.
h. Income taxes of $5,738 are unrecorded and unpaid at December 31.

Required:

1. Prepare a worksheet for Marsteller Properties.
2. Prepare an income statement, a retained earnings statement, and a classified balance sheet for Marsteller Properties.
3. Prepare the closing entries.

PROBLEM SET B

Problem 3-55B Cash-Basis and Accrual-Basis Income

OBJECTIVE 1

Martin Sharp operates a lawn mower repair business. He maintains an inventory of repair parts that are purchased from a wholesale supplier. Martin's records show the following information for the first 3 months (January, February, and March) of the year.

	Cash Collected for Repair Work	Amounts Billed to Customers	Cash Payments to Supplier	Cost of Parts Used in Repairs
January	$3,200	$2,800	$1,165	$915
February	2,475	3,500	300	605
March	2,910	3,275	0	880

(Continued)

Required:

1. Ignoring expenses other than repair parts, calculate net income for each of the 3 months of the current year on a cash basis.
2. Ignoring expenses other than repair parts, calculate net income for each of the 3 months of the current year on an accrual basis.
3. **CONCEPTUAL CONNECTION** Why do decision-makers prefer accrual-basis accounting?

OBJECTIVE 2

Problem 3-56B Revenue and Expense Recognition

Aunt Bea's Catering Service provides catering service for special occasions. During the year, Aunt Bea performed $228,500 of catering services and collected $218,200 of cash from customers. Salaries earned by Aunt Bea's employees were $49,900. Aunt Bea paid employees $45,100. Aunt Bea had $1,200 of supplies on hand at the beginning of the year and purchased an additional $12,640 of supplies during the year. Supplies on hand at the end of the year were $2,820. Other selling and administrative expenses incurred during the year were $10,800.

Required:

1. Calculate revenue and expenses.
2. Prepare a single-step income statement.
3. **CONCEPTUAL CONNECTION** Describe the accounting principles used to prepare the income statement.

OBJECTIVE 3 4

Problem 3-57B Identification and Preparation of Adjusting Entries

Morgan Dance Inc. provides ballet, tap, and jazz dancing instruction to promising young dancers. Morgan began operations in January and is preparing its first monthly financial statements. The following items describe Morgan's transactions in January:

a. Morgan requires that dance instruction be paid in advance—either monthly or quarterly. On January 1, Morgan received $4,125 for dance instruction to be provided during the current year.
b. On January 31, Morgan noted that $825 of dance instruction revenue is still unearned.
c. On January 20, Morgan's hourly employees were paid $1,415 for work performed in January.
d. Morgan's insurance policy requires semiannual premium payments. Morgan paid the $3,000 insurance policy that covered the first half of the year in December of the previous year.
e. When there are no scheduled dance classes, Morgan rents its dance studio for birthday parties for $100 per two-hour party. Four birthday parties were held during January. Morgan will not bill the parents until February.
f. Morgan purchased $350 of office supplies on January 10.
g. On January 31, Morgan determined that office supplies of $85 were unused.
h. Morgan received a January utility bill for $770. The bill will not be paid until it is due in February.

Required:

1. Identify whether each transaction is an adjusting entry or a regular journal entry. If the entry is an adjusting entry, identify it as an accrued revenue, accrued expense, deferred revenue, or deferred expense.
2. Prepare the entries necessary to record the transactions above and on the previous page.

Problem 3-58B Preparation of Adjusting Entries

OBJECTIVE ◄ 4

West Beach Resort operates a resort complex that specializes in hosting small business and professional meetings. West Beach closes its fiscal year on January 31, a time when it has few meetings under way. At January 31, the following data are available:

a. A training meeting is under way for 16 individuals from Fashion Design. Fashion Design paid $4,500 in advance for each person attending the 10-day training session. The meeting began on January 28 and will end on February 6.

b. Twenty-one people from Northern Publishing are attending a sales meeting. The daily fee for each person attending the meeting is $280 (charged for each night a person stays at the resort). The meeting began on January 29, and guests will depart on February 2. Northern will be billed at the end of the meeting.

c. Depreciation on the golf carts used to transport the guests' luggage to and from their rooms is $11,250 for the year. West Beach records depreciation yearly.

d. At January 31, Friedrich Catering is owed $1,795 for food provided for guests through that date. This amount is unrecorded. West Beach classifies the cost of food as an "other expense" on the income statement.

e. An examination indicates that the cost of office supplies on hand at January 31 is $189. During the year, $850 of office supplies was purchased from Supply Depot. The cost of supplies purchased was debited to Office Supplies Inventory. No office supplies were on hand at the beginning of the year.

Required:

1. Prepare adjusting entries at January 31 for each of these items.
2. **CONCEPTUAL CONNECTION** By how much would net income be overstated or understated if the accountant failed to make the adjusting entries?

Problem 3-59B Effects of Adjusting Entries on the Accounting Equation

OBJECTIVE ◄ 4

Four adjusting entries are shown below.

a. Interest Expense............................	1,875	
Interest Payable...........................		1,875
b. Interest Receivable......................	1,150	
Interest Income..........................		1,150
c. Insurance Expense.......................	2,560	
Prepaid Insurance.......................		2,560
d. Unearned Rent Revenue.............	4,680	
Rent Revenue.............................		4,680

Required:

CONCEPTUAL CONNECTION Analyze the adjusting entries and identify their effects on the financial statement accounts. (*Note*: Ignore any income tax effects.) Use the following format for your answer:

Transaction	Assets	Liabilities	Common Stock	Retained Earnings	Revenues	Expenses

OBJECTIVE **4** **5**

 SHOW ME HOW

Problem 3-60B Adjusting Entries and Financial Statements

The unadjusted trial balance for Mitchell Pharmacy appears below.

Mitchell Pharmacy Unadjusted Trial Balance December 31		
Account	**Debit**	**Credit**
Cash	$ 3,400	
Accounts Receivable	64,820	
Inventory	583,400	
Prepaid Insurance	11,200	
Building	230,000	
Accumulated Depreciation		$ 44,000
Land	31,200	
Other Assets	25,990	
Accounts Payable		47,810
Notes Payable (due in 2 years)		150,000
Common Stock		600,000
Retained Earnings, January 1		41,200
Service Revenue		950,420
Wages Expense	871,420	
Interest Expense	12,000	
Totals	$1,833,430	$1,833,430

The following information is available at year end for adjustments:

a. An analysis of insurance policies indicates that $2,180 of the prepaid insurance is coverage for the next year.
b. Depreciation expense for the current year is $10,130.
c. Four months' interest at 10% is owed but unrecorded and unpaid on the note payable.
d. Wages of $4,950 are owed but unpaid and unrecorded at December 31.
e. Income taxes of $11,370 are owed but unrecorded and unpaid at December 31.

Required:
1. Prepare the adjusting entries.
2. Prepare a single-step income statement, a retained earnings statement, and a classified balance sheet using adjusted account balances.
3. **CONCEPTUAL CONNECTION** Why would you not want to prepare financial statements until after the adjusting entries are made?

OBJECTIVE **4**

Problem 3-61B Inferring Adjusting Entries from Account Balance Changes

The following schedule shows all the accounts of Eagle Imports that received year-end adjusting entries:

Account	Unadjusted Account Balance	Adjusted Account Balance
Prepaid Insurance	$ 15,390	$ (a)
Accumulated Depreciation	92,500	103,000
Interest Payable	0	(b)
Wages Payable	0	(c)

Account	Unadjusted Account Balance	Adjusted Account Balance
Unearned Service Revenue	$ 12,250	$ 2,620
Service Revenue	122,500	(d)
Insurance Expense	1,500	12,746
Interest Expense	1,125	5,300
Depreciation Expense	0	(e)
Wages Expense	24,200	41,800

Required:
1. Calculate the missing amounts identified by the letters (a) through (e).
2. Prepare the five adjusting entries that must have been made to cause the account changes as indicated.

Problem 3-62B Preparation of Closing Entries and an Income Statement

OBJECTIVE

Port Austin Boat Repair Inc. has entered and posted its adjusting entries for the current year. The following are selected account balances after adjustment:

Sales Revenue	$692,500	Insurance Expense	$94,300
Interest Income	7,600	Wages Payable	11,700
Accounts Payable	8,330	Utilities Expense	12,300
Wages Expense	405,300	Interest Expense	9,500
Accounts Receivable	65,000	Depreciation Expense (Equipment)	20,000
Supplies Expense	68,350	Accumulated Depreciation (Equipment)	75,000
Supplies	179,000	Income Taxes Expense	12,300
Prepaid Rent	7,200	Income Taxes Payable	8,300
Rent Expense	28,800	Dividends Declared	7,800
Unearned Sales Revenue	12,200		

Required:
1. Using the accounts and balances above, prepare the closing entries.
2. Prepare an income statement for Port Austin Boat Repair.

Problem 3-63B Comprehensive Problem: Reviewing the Accounting Cycle

OBJECTIVE

Wilburton Riding Stables provides stables, care for animals, and grounds for riding and showing horses. The account balances at January 1 (the beginning of the year) were:

Cash	$ 2,200	Accounts Payable	$ 23,700
Accounts Receivable	4,400	Income Taxes Payable	15,100
Supplies (Feed and Straw)	27,800	Interest Payable	2,700
Land	167,000	Wages Payable	14,200
Buildings	115,000	Notes Payable (due in 4 years)	60,000
Accumulated Depreciation (Buildings)	36,000	Common Stock	150,000
		Retained Earnings	55,200
Equipment	57,000		
Accumulated Depreciation (Equipment)	16,500		

(Continued)

During the year, the following transactions occurred:

a. Wilburton provided animal care services, all on credit, for $210,300. Wilburton rented stables to customers for $20,500 cash. Wilburton rented its grounds to individual riders, groups, and show organizations for $41,800 cash.

b. There remains $15,600 of accounts receivable to be collected at December 31.

c. Feed in the amount of $62,900 was purchased on credit and debited to the supplies account.

d. Straw was purchased for $7,400 cash and debited to the supplies account.

e. Wages payable at the beginning of the year were paid early in February. Wages were earned and paid during the year in the amount of $112,000.

f. The income taxes payable at the beginning of the year were paid early in April.

g. Payments of $73,000 were made to creditors for supplies previously purchased on credit.

h. One year's interest at 9% was paid on the note payable on July 1.

i. During the year, Jon Wilburton, a principal stockholder, purchased a horse for his wife, Jennifer, to ride. The horse cost $7,000, and Wilburton used his personal credit to purchase it. The horse is stabled at the Wilburtons' home rather than at the riding stables.

j. Property taxes were paid on the land and buildings in the amount of $17,000.

k. Dividends were declared and paid in the amount of $7,200.

The following data are available for adjusting entries:

- Supplies (feed and straw) in the amount of $30,400 remained unused at year end.

- Annual depreciation on the buildings is $6,000.

- Annual depreciation on the equipment is $5,500.

- Wages of $4,000 were unrecorded and unpaid at year end.

- Interest for 6 months at 9% per year on the note is unpaid and unrecorded at year end.

- Income taxes of $16,500 were unpaid and unrecorded at year end.

Required:

1. Post the beginning balances to T-accounts. Prepare journal entries for Transactions a through k and post the journal entries to T-accounts, adding any new T-accounts you need.

2. Prepare the adjustments and post the adjustments to the T-accounts, adding any new T-accounts you need.

3. Prepare a single-step income statement.

4. Prepare a retained earnings statement.

5. Prepare a classified balance sheet.

6. Prepare closing entries.

7. **CONCEPTUAL CONNECTION** Did you include Transaction i among Wilburton's journal entries? Why or why not?

OBJECTIVE 4 5 6 7 8

Problem 3-64B Preparing a Worksheet (Appendix 3A)

Flint Inc. operates a cable television system. At December 31, the following unadjusted account balances were available:

Cash	$ 2,000	Common Stock	$300,000
Accounts Receivable	89,000	Retained Earnings, January 1	14,700
Supplies	5,000	Dividends Declared	28,000
Land	37,000	Service Revenue	985,000
Building	209,000	Royalties Expense	398,000
Accumulated Depreciation (Building)	40,000	Property Taxes Expense	10,500
Equipment	794,000	Wages Expense	196,000
Accumulated Depreciation (Equipment)	262,000	Utilities Expense	34,000

Other Assets	19,700	Miscellaneous Expense	44,000
Accounts Payable	29,500	Interest Expense	15,000
Notes Payable (due in 4 years)	250,000		

The following data are available for adjusting entries:

a. At year end, $1,500 of office supplies remain unused.
b. Annual depreciation on the building is $20,000.
c. Annual depreciation on the equipment is $150,000.
d. The interest rate on the note is 8%. Four months' interest is unpaid and unrecorded at December 31.
e. At December 31, services of $94,000 have been performed but are unbilled and unrecorded.
f. Utility bills of $2,800 are unpaid and unrecorded at December 31.
g. Income taxes of $49,633 were unpaid and unrecorded at year end.

Required:
1. Prepare a worksheet for Flint.
2. Prepare a single-step income statement, a retained earnings statement, and a classified balance sheet for Flint.
3. Prepare the closing entries.

CASES

Case 3-65 Cash- or Accrual-Basis Accounting

Karen Ragsdale owns a business that rents parking spots to students at the local university. Karen's typical rental contract requires the student to pay the year's rent of $450 ($50 per month) on September 1. When Karen prepares financial statements at the end of December, her accountant requires that Karen spread the $450 over the 9 months that each parking spot is rented. Therefore, Karen can recognize only $200 of revenue (4 months) from each parking spot rental contract in the year the cash is collected and must defer (delay) recognition of the remaining $250 (5 months) to the next year. Karen argues that getting students to agree to rent the parking spot is the most difficult part of the activity so she ought to be able to recognize all $450 as revenue when the cash is received from a student.

Required:
Why do generally accepted accounting principles require the use of accrual accounting rather than cash-basis accounting for transactions like the one described here?

Case 3-66 Recognition of Service Contract Revenue

Zac Murphy is president of Blooming Colors Inc., which provides landscaping services in Tallahassee, Florida. On November 20, Mr. Murphy signed a service contract with Eastern State University. Under the contract, Blooming Colors will provide landscaping services for all of Eastern's buildings for a period of 2 years beginning on January 1, and Eastern will pay Blooming Colors on a quarterly basis beginning in January. Although the same amount of landscaping services will be rendered in every month, the contract provides for higher quarterly payments in the first year.

Initially, Mr. Murphy proposed that the revenue from the contract should be recognized when the contract is signed; however, his accountant, Sue Storm, convinced him that this would be inappropriate. Then Mr. Murphy proposed that the revenue should

(Continued)

be recognized in an amount equal to the cash collected under the contract. Again, Ms. Storm argued against his proposal, indicating that generally accepted accounting principles (GAAP) required recognition of an equal amount of contract revenue each month.

Required:

1. Give a reason that might explain Mr. Murphy's desire to recognize contract revenue earlier rather than later.
2. Put yourself in the position of Sue Storm. How would you convince Mr. Murphy that his two proposals are unacceptable and that an equal amount of revenue should be recognized every month?
3. If Ms. Storm's proposal is adopted, how would the contract be reflected in the balance sheets at the end of December prior to the services being provided. How would the contract be reflected in the balance sheet at January 31, after the first month of service is provided.

Case 3-67 Revenue Recognition

Melaney Parks purchased HealthPlus Fitness in January. Melaney wanted to increase the size of the business by selling 3-year memberships for $3,000, payable at the beginning of the membership period. The normal yearly membership fee is $1,500. Since few prospective members were expected to want to spend $3,000 at the beginning of the membership period, Melaney arranged for a local bank to provide a $3,000 installment loan to prospective members. By the end of the first year, 250 customers had purchased the 3-year memberships using the loan provided by the bank.

Melaney prepared her income statement for the first year of operations and included $750,000 ($3,000 × 250 members) as revenue because the club had collected the entire amount in cash. Melaney's accountant objected to the inclusion of the entire $750,000. The accountant argued that the $750,000 should be recognized as revenue as the club provides services for these members during the membership period. Melaney countered that memberships have been sold and the collection of the selling price has occurred. Therefore, she argues that all $750,000 is revenue in the year the cash is received.

Required:

1. Write a short statement supporting either Melaney or the accountant in this dispute.
2. Would your answer change if the $3,000 fee were nonrefundable? Why or why not?

Case 3-68 Applying the Expense Recognition Principle

Newman Properties Inc. completed construction of a new shopping center in July. During the first 6 months of the year while construction was being completed, Newman spent $550,000 for salaries, preparation of documents, travel, and other similar activities that was directly and incrementally associated with securing tenants (Macy's, Best Buy, and Office Depot) for the center. The center will open on August 1 with all its stores rented on 4-year leases. The rental revenue that Newman expects to receive from the current tenants is $8,500,000 per year for 4 years. The leases will be renegotiated at the end of the fourth year. The accountant for Newman wonders whether the $550,000 should be expensed in the current year or whether it should be initially recorded as an asset and matched against revenues over the 4-year lease term.

Required:

Write a short statement indicating why you support expensing the $550,000 in the current period or spreading the expense over the 4-year lease term.

Case 3-69 Adjusting Entries for Motion Picture Revenues

Link Pictures Inc. sells (licenses) the rights to exhibit motion pictures to theaters. Under the sales contract, the theater promises to pay a license fee equal to the larger of a guaranteed minimum or a percentage of the box office receipts. In addition, the contract requires the guaranteed minimum to be paid in advance. Consider the following contracts entered by Link during 2023:

a. Contract **A** authorizes a group of theaters in Buffalo, New York, to exhibit a film called Garage for 2 weeks ending January 7, 2024. Box office statistics indicate that first-week attendance has already generated licensing fees well in excess of the guaranteed minimum.

b. Contract **B** authorizes a chain of theaters in Miami, Florida, to exhibit a film called Blue Denim for a period of 2 weeks ending January 20, 2024. In most first-run cities, the film has attracted large crowds, and the percentage of box office receipts has far exceeded the minimum.

c. Contract **C** authorizes a chain of theaters in San Francisco to exhibit a film called Toast Points for a period of 2 weeks ending on December 12, 2023. The film is a "dog" and the theaters stopped showing it after the first few days. All prints of the film were returned by December 31, 2023.

The guaranteed minimum has been paid on all three contracts and recorded as unearned revenue. No other amounts have been received, and no revenue has been recorded for any of the contracts. Adjusting entries for 2023 are about to be made.

Required:

Describe the adjusting entry you would make at December 31, 2023, to record each contract.

Case 3-70 Effect of Adjusting Entries on Financial Statements (A Conceptual Approach)

Don Berthrong, the manager of the local Books-A-Million, is wondering how adjusting entries will affect his financial statements. Don's business has grown steadily for several years, and Don expects it to continue to grow for the next several years at a rate of 5–10% per year. Nearly all of Don's sales are for cash. Other than cost of goods sold, which is not affected by adjusting entries, most of Don's expenses are for items that require cash outflows (e.g., rent on the building, wages, utilities, and insurance).

Required:

1. Would Don's financial statement be affected significantly by adjusting entries?
2. Consider all businesses. What kinds of transactions would require adjustments that would have a significant effect on the financial statements? What kinds of businesses would be likely to require these kinds of adjustments?

Case 3-71 Research and Analysis Using the Annual Report

Obtain **FedEx Corporation**'s 2019 annual report either through the "Investor Relations" portion of their website (do a web search for FedEx investor relations) or go to www.sec.gov and click "Company Filings Search" under "Filings."

Required:

1. How does FedEx apply the revenue recognition principle?
2. With regard to the balance sheet and the income statement, what accounts may have required adjusting entries? Would these accounts require accruals or deferrals?
3. How much did FedEx owe its employees for services performed at the end of the 2019 fiscal year?

(Continued)

4. How much would FedEx credit to Retained Earnings when it closes its accounts for 2019? How much would be debited to Retained Earnings when it closes its accounts for 2019?

5. How much did FedEx report as income tax expense for 2019? How much did FedEx report as cash paid for taxes for 2019? Why are the amounts different and where does this difference get reported on FedEx's financial statements?

Case 3-72 Comparative Analysis: Kroger versus Sprouts

Refer to the 10-K reports of **Kroger** and **Sprouts** that are available for download from the companion website at Cengage.com.

Required:

1. Describe each company's revenue recognition policy. Is this policy consistent with the revenue recognition principle?

2. Which accounts on the balance sheet and income statement of each company may require adjusting entries? Would these accounts require accruals or deferrals?

3. How much would Kroger credit and debit to Income Summary for its most current fiscal year? How much would Sprouts credit and debit to Income Summary for its most current fiscal year?

4. Compare how much each company reported as income tax expense and as cash paid for taxes for the most recent year. Why are the amounts different, and where would this difference be reported on the financial statements?

ANNUAL REPORT PROBLEM

HOME DEPOT

Download the 10-K for **Home Depot** from the companion website at Cengage.com.

Required:

1. What does Home Depot report for the following accounts for the most current fiscal year?
   - Salaries payable
   - Deferred revenue
   - Accumulated depreciation

2. Assume that Home Depot projects the following:
   - Salaries payable will increase 2%
   - Deferred revenue will increase 4%
   - Accumulated depreciation will increase 3%

   Assume all other items remain unchanged from the prior year. Provide the forecasted balances for the next fiscal year for salaries payable, deferred revenue, and accumulated depreciation. Round your forecast to the nearest million dollars.

3. Assume that the unadjusted trial balance for the forecasted fiscal year reflects the following:
   - Salaries payable , $1,510
   - Deferred revenue, $1,823
   - Accumulated depreciation, $22,500

   Prepare the adjusting journal entries that Home Depot should make at year end.

4. Does Home Depot use the accrual basis or cash basis of accounting?

5. What type of accrual or deferral is Salaries Payable?

6. What type of account is Accumulated Depreciation?

7. What is an example of a deferred revenue account used by Home Depot?

Note: *While the Annual Report problems in the textbook are static, when assigned in CNOW, these activities are algorithmic and the answers may vary from what appears in the Solutions Manual.*

CONTINUING PROBLEM

FRONT ROW ENTERTAINMENT

Cam and Anna are very satisfied with their first month of operations. Their major effort centered on signing various artists to live performance contracts, and they had more success than they had anticipated. In addition to Charm City, they were able to use their contacts in the music industry to sign 12 other artists. With the tours starting in February, Cam and Anna were eager to hold their first big event. Over the next month, the following transactions occurred.

Feb. 1 Collected advance ticket sales of $28,400 relating to various concerts that were being promoted.
1 Paid $800 to rent office space in February.
2 Paid Equipment Supply Services $1,500, the balance remaining from the January 3 purchase of supplies.
6 Paid $30,150 to secure venues for future concerts. (These payments are recorded as Prepaid Rent.)
9 Received $325 related to the festival held on January 25.
12 Purchased $475 of supplies on credit from Equipment Supply Services.
15 Collected $3,400 of ticket sales for the first Charm City concert on the day of the concert.
15 Paid Charm City $9,000 for performing the February 15 concert. (*Remember*: Front Row records the fees paid to the artist in the Artist Fee Expense account.)
20 Collected advance ticket sales of $10,125 relating to various concerts that were being promoted.
21 Collected $5,100 of ticket sales for the second Charm City concert on the day of the concert.
21 Paid Charm City $12,620 for performing the February 21 concert.

At the end of February, Cam and Anna felt like their business was doing well; however, they decided that they needed to prepare financial statements to better understand the operations of the business. Anna gathered the following information relating to the adjusting entries that needed to be prepared at the end of February.

a. Two months of interest on the note payable is accrued. The interest rate is 9%.
b. A count of the supplies revealed that $1,825 of supplies remained on hand at the end of February.
c. Two months of the annual insurance has expired.
d. Depreciation related to the office equipment was $180 per month.
e. The rental of the venues for all four Charm City concerts was paid in advance on January 8. As of the end of February, Charm City has performed two of the four concerts in the contract.
f. An analysis of the unearned sales revenue account reveals that $8,175 of the balance relates to concerts that have not yet been performed.
g. Neither Cam nor Anna have received their salary of $1,200 each (total salary of $2,400) for February.
h. A utility bill of $435 relating to utility service on Front Row's office for January and February was received but not paid by the end of February.

(*Continued*)

Required:
1. Analyze and journalize the February transactions.
2. Set up T-accounts for each account, and post the transactions to the T-accounts. Be sure to use the balances computed in Chapter 2 as the beginning balances of the T-accounts.
3. Prepare a trial balance at February 28.
4. Prepare and post the adjusting entries needed at February 28.
5. By how much would net income be overstated or understated if the adjusting entries were not made?
6. Prepare a single-step income statement and a retained earnings statement for the 2-month period ending February 28. Prepare a classified balance sheet as of February 28.
7. Prepare the necessary closing entries.

The Accounting Cycle

Begin with the following account balances for University Street Parking Garage (assume all accounts have normal balances) at December 31, 2023:

Accounts payable	$ 16,700
Accounts receivable	39,200
Accumulated depreciation (equipment)	36,800
Cash	6,700
Common stock (20,000 shares)	100,000
Depreciation expense (equipment)	12,300
Dividends Declared	6,300
Equipment	269,500
Income taxes expense	2,700
Income taxes payable	1,100
Interest expense	16,500
Interest payable	0
Interest income	4,100
Inventory	4,900
Investments	35,000
Notes payable (due May 2, 2031)	160,000
Prepaid rent (4 months)	36,400
Rent expense	94,400
Retained earnings, January 1, 2023	43,000
Service revenue, parking	224,600
Service revenue, repair	208,100
Supplies expense	36,900
Wages expense	233,600
Wages payable	0

Required:

1. For the following transactions, provide the necessary adjusting entries and update the account balances to appropriately reflect these adjusting entries:

   a. University Street Parking rents space that requires a rental payment of $9,100 per month. University Street Parking has prepaid rent through March 31, 2024.

   b. At December 31, 2023, University Street Parking owes employees wages of $12,500.

   c. University Street Parking should have total depreciation expense on equipment for 2023 of $14,300.

   d. The note payable of $160,000 has an interest rate of 6.75%. University Street Parking has paid interest through October 31, 2023.

2. Prepare a properly classified income statement for 2023, retained earnings statement for 2023, and a properly classified balance sheet as of December 31, 2023, using the post-adjustment account balances.

4 Internal Control and Cash

After studying Chapter 4, you should be able to:

1. Describe the role of internal controls in managing a business.

2. Describe the five components of internal control.

3. Describe how businesses account for and report cash.

4. Describe how businesses control cash.

5. Describe the operating cycle and explain the principles of cash management.

EXPERIENCE FINANCIAL ACCOUNTING

with Berkshire Hathaway

As of early 2020, Warren Buffett's personal net worth was approximately $85.5 billion, making him the fourth richest person in the world (and that's after donating over $35 billion to charity). Buffett amassed this fortune through his company, Berkshire Hathaway. Berkshire's strategy is to invest in undervalued companies but have little or no involvement in their operations beyond approving who is on the management team. While Berkshire Hathaway has significant holdings in many, many companies, some notable investments are in GEICO, American Express, Costco, Kraft-Heinz, and Coca-Cola.

During the worst of the global financial crisis and its aftermath, Berkshire was a heavy investor, while others were selling. Buffett views down markets as an opportunity to buy because in the long run markets will go back up. Of course, this does not mean that in a down market every company's stock value will increase in the long run, but Buffett believes it provides a better opportunity to find undervalued stocks.

While the phrase "Cash Is King" is frequently quoted, the reality is that companies can have too much cash. This is because cash sitting in a bank account is not earning much, if any, return. Of course, companies, like families, need some cash to operate and protect themselves against emergencies. However, any surplus cash generated by operations should be (1) invested back into the company's operations to grow the company, (2) used to pay down debt, or (3) returned to the shareholders through dividends or stock repurchases. The best one of these three options depends on the company's investment opportunities and the amount and interest rate of the debt.

Berkshire's strategy is to stockpile large amounts of cash and wait for buying opportunities. Further, analysts and shareholders are tolerant of Berkshire Hathaway holding large amounts of cash, rather than returning that cash to shareholders. This is because they know Buffett is hunting for companies to buy and the investors were happy to leave their money in the hands of the most successful investor of our time. However, at the end of 2019, the U.S. stock market remained in its longest bull market (i.e., an up market, in which prices are rising) in history, which means undervalued stocks were more difficult to find. Consequently, since the beginning of the global financial crisis, Berkshire Hathaway's cash, cash equivalents, and short-term U.S. Treasuries have increased from approximately $25.5 billion at the end of 2008 to approximately $128 billion at the end of 2019 (see chart that follows).

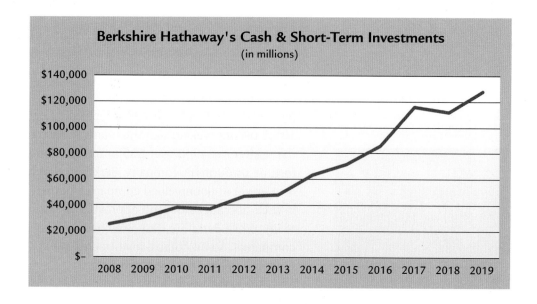

As Buffett and Berkshire Hathaway try to outwait this unprecedented bull market and find buying opportunities, analysts are beginning to question Berkshire's cash holdings by calling for cash to be returned to shareholders. In fact, Berkshire Hathaway seems to acknowledge this in its 2018 10-K by announcing that the Board of Directors has amended the stock repurchase program to allow Berkshire to "repurchase shares any time that Warren Buffett, Berkshire's Chairman of the Board and Chief Executive Officer, and Charlie Munger, Vice Chairman of the Board, believe that the repurchase price is below Berkshire's intrinsic value, conservatively determined" (p. K-29). As for dividends, Berkshire has not declared a cash dividend since 1967, but who knows what the future holds.

By the way, if your grandparents had invested $10,000 in Berkshire Hathaway on May 1, 1980, in January 2020 their holdings would have been worth over $12,500,000. Of course, we should point out that Warren Buffett himself would probably hate this anecdote because prudent investors should have sold some of their Berkshire holdings and invested them elsewhere to diversify their risk.

OBJECTIVE 1
Describe the role of internal controls in managing a business.

ROLE OF INTERNAL CONTROL

Except in very small businesses, top management delegates responsibility for engaging in business activities and recording their effects in the accounting system to other managers and employees. Management wants to make sure that these employees both:

- operate within the scope of their assigned responsibility
- act for the good of the business

To control employees' activities, management puts in place procedures that collectively are called the **internal control system**.

Internal control systems include all the policies and procedures established by top management and the board of directors to provide reasonable assurance that the company's objectives are being met in the following three areas (see the 3 columns in Exhibit 4.1):[1]

- Operations Objectives: effectiveness and efficiency of the entity's operations, including financial performance goals and safeguarding assets against loss.
- Reporting Objectives: reliability of reporting. They include internal and external financial and non-financial reporting.
- Compliance Objectives: compliance with applicable laws and regulations.

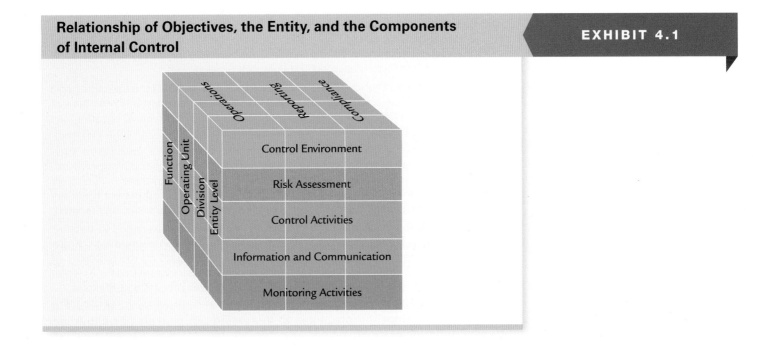

Relationship of Objectives, the Entity, and the Components of Internal Control

EXHIBIT 4.1

As such, internal control systems include many elements only indirectly related to our primary concern—the accounting system and financial statements. For example, policies and procedures concerning the extent and nature of research and development or advertising activities may have an important effect on the achievement of an entity's objectives but only indirectly affect its accounting system and financial statements.

Under the Sarbanes-Oxley Act of 2002, top management of publicly traded corporations have an increased responsibility for a system of internal controls that ensures the reliability of the financial statements. For example, the Act requires management to produce an internal control report. This report must acknowledge that management is responsible for establishing and maintaining an adequate internal control system and procedures for financial reporting and also that management has assessed the effectiveness of these controls. Further, the Act requires the principal executive and financial officers to certify that they are responsible for establishing and maintaining the system of internal control over financial reporting (see Exhibit 4.2). This certification was designed to prevent top management from denying knowledge or understanding of deceptive financial reporting as was tried in court by executives of **WorldCom**, among others.

---

1 The Committee of Sponsoring Organizations of the Treadway Commission (COSO), *Internal Control-Integrated Framework*, 2013.

| **EXHIBIT 4.2** | **Section 302 Certification by W. Rodney McMullen (CEO of The Kroger Co.) Taken from SEC Filings (Exhibit 31.1 of 10-K) for the Year Ended February 1, 2020** |

I, W. Rodney McMullen, certify that:

1. I have reviewed this annual report on Form 10-K of The Kroger Co.;

2. Based on my knowledge, this report does not contain any untrue statement of a material fact or omit to state a material fact necessary to make the statements made, in light of the circumstances under which such statements were made, not misleading with respect to the period covered by this report;

3. Based on my knowledge, the financial statements, and other financial information included in this report, fairly present in all material respects the financial condition, results of operations and cash flows of the registrant as of, and for, the periods presented in this report;

4. The registrant's other certifying officer and I are responsible for establishing and maintaining disclosure controls and procedures (as defined in Exchange Act Rules 13a-15(e) and 15d-15(e)) and internal control over financial reporting (as defined in Exchange Act Rules 13a-15(f) and 15d-15(f)) for the registrant and have:

    a) designed such disclosure controls and procedures, or caused such disclosure controls and procedures to be designed under our supervision, to ensure that material information relating to the registrant, including its consolidated subsidiaries, is made known to us by others within those entities, particularly during the period in which this report is being prepared;

    b) designed such internal control over financial reporting, or caused such internal control over financial reporting to be designed under our supervision, to provide reasonable assurance regarding the reliability of financial reporting and the preparation of financial statements for external purposes in accordance with generally accepted accounting principles;

    c) evaluated the effectiveness of the registrant's disclosure controls and procedures and presented in this report our conclusions about the effectiveness of the disclosure controls and procedures, as of the end of the period covered by this report based on such evaluation; and

    d) disclosed in this report any change in the registrant's internal control over financial reporting that occurred during the registrant's most recent fiscal quarter (the registrant's fourth fiscal quarter in the case of an annual report) that has materially affected, or is reasonably likely to materially affect, the registrant's internal control over financial reporting; and

5. The registrant's other certifying officer and I have disclosed, based on our most recent evaluation of internal control over financial reporting, to the registrant's auditors and the audit committee of the registrant's board of directors (or persons performing the equivalent functions):

    a) all significant deficiencies and material weaknesses in the design or operation of internal control over financial reporting which are reasonably likely to adversely affect the registrant's ability to record, process, summarize and report financial information; and

    b) any fraud, whether or not material, that involves management or other employees who have a significant role in the registrant's internal control over financial reporting.

Date: April 1, 2020

By:

W. Rodney McMullen

Chairman of the Board and Chief Executive Officer (principal executive officer)

Source: The Kroger Co. 2019, Exhibit 31.1 10-K.

In this chapter, we will examine the components of internal controls and demonstrate controls over cash, a company's most vulnerable asset. We will address the following questions:

- What are the five components of internal control?
- How are those controls applied to cash?
- How does the operating cycle affect cash?
- Why is cash management so important to a company?

COMPONENTS OF INTERNAL CONTROL

OBJECTIVE 2

Describe the five components of internal control.

The Committee of Sponsoring Organizations of the Treadway Commission (COSO) identified five components of an internal control system: the control environment, risk assessment, control activities, information and communication, and monitoring activities (see the 5 rows of Exhibit 4.1). Each component is crucial to meeting the company's objectives. These components are relevant to every level of a company's organizational structure including the overall entity and its subsidiaries or divisions (if any). In addition, any individual operating units, functions, or other subset defined by the organization would be subject to such internal control components (see the 3rd dimension of Exhibit 4.1).

CONTROL ENVIRONMENT AND ETHICAL BEHAVIOR

The foundation of the internal control system is the **control environment**—the collection of environmental factors that influence the effectiveness of control procedures. The control environment includes the following:

- philosophy and operating style of management
- personnel policies and practices of the business
- overall integrity, attitude, awareness, and actions of everyone in the business concerning the importance of control (commonly called the *tone at the top*)

An important feature of the control environment is recognizing that an individual employee's goals may differ from the goals of other individuals and the goals of the business. For example, when managers receive a bonus based on certain accounting numbers, like sales, they have been known to ship a large quantity of merchandise to customers right before year-end—even if the merchandise was not ordered (done by such companies as **Bausch and Lomb**, **IBM**, etc.). Although much of the merchandise was returned in the following year, sales targets for the current year were met and bonuses were paid.

Resolving these conflicting incentives in an ethical manner that promotes organizational objectives is highly dependent on the tone at the top. For example, hiring and firing practices that put zero tolerance on unethical behavior are increasingly common. Additionally, the Sarbanes-Oxley Act requires publicly traded corporations to establish formal procedures to receive, retain, and address any information that may affect the company's accounting or auditing. To comply with this requirement, companies have created ethics hotlines that allow employees to anonymously report unethical behavior. While this was an important step in empowering subordinates to report unethical behavior by their superiors, hotlines only address procedures to receive the information. Companies must also have procedures in place to make sure such information is never destroyed and that it is communicated to those with the power to resolve any issues, such as the board of directors and upper management.

ETHICAL DECISIONS Donna Jones has just been hired as an accounting clerk. One of her jobs is to summarize invoices presented for payment by various creditors. Once prepared, the summary is first inspected by Carmen Adams, the assistant controller to whom Donna reports, and then presented to Dick Stewart, the controller, for approval. After signing and approving the summary, Dick passes along the summary to his secretary, Nancy, who prepares and mails the checks.

During Donna's second week on the job, Carmen tells her that City Consulting Services Inc. will make trouble for the company unless paid immediately. She says, "Dick is rarely at his desk, and he and Nancy never look at signatures anyway. It would cost us at least another day for Dick to review and sign the summary. Just put the unsigned summary in the approved pile on Dick's desk, and Nancy will have the check in the mail by the end of the day."

Donna suspects that Carmen will give her a low performance rating if she refuses to follow these instructions, and she wants to do well on her first job. Further, she is quite sure that Dick and Nancy will not notice the omitted control procedure. On the other hand, Donna knows that the controller's approval is an important control procedure. Consider two possible endings for this story:

1. *Donna goes along with Carmen.* Every month, Carmen tells Donna that City Consulting Services needs to be paid immediately. Donna places the unauthorized summary on Dick's unoccupied desk. All goes well until the internal auditor runs a routine check on the credit ratings of the entities with which the company does business and discovers that City Consulting is nothing more than a bank account established by Carmen. Carmen is charged with fraud, and Donna's role is exposed in the public trial that follows. Donna is not charged in the case, but she loses her job and has great difficulty finding another comparable position.
2. *Donna refuses to go along with Carmen.* Donna receives a negative review from Carmen and is asked to leave the company. During an exit interview, Donna tells Dick why she believes Carmen gave her a negative review. Dick asks the internal audit department to follow up on City Consulting Services, at which time it is discovered to be a bank account established by Carmen. Carmen is charged with fraud. Dick contacts Donna saying, "After investigating your comments regarding Carmen's request, we have uncovered her scheme to defraud the company and would like you to return to the company."

Like Donna, most people in business face difficult ethical dilemmas from time to time. The effectiveness of internal control systems depends on the ethical tone set by management and the ethical awareness of all company personnel. ●

RISK ASSESSMENT

Risk assessment procedures (also called Enterprise Risk Management or ERM) are designed to identify, analyze, and manage **strategic risks** and **business process risks**.

Strategic Risks Strategic risks are possible threats to the organization's success in accomplishing its objectives and are *external* to the organization. These risks are often classified around industry forces such as competitors, customers, substitute products or services, suppliers, and threat of new competitors (these are known as Porter's Five Forces) or macro factors such as political, economic, social, and technological (also known as PEST factors).

Although entire courses are devoted to management of these strategic risks, the general idea is simple. For example, when **Amazon** was formed, **Barnes & Noble** was in the midst of high growth and was implementing cafes and music shops within supersized bookstores. Barnes & Noble was so deeply rooted in its "bricks-and-mortar" that it failed to respond to a technological factor: the Internet's transformation of the industry. By the time Barnesandnoble.com was launched, Amazon had secured the leading web presence for booksellers—a lead that Barnes & Noble has been unable to erode.

Business Process Risks Business processes are the *internal* processes of the company—specifically, how the company allocates its resources to meet its objectives. There are many business processes, but some of the more common ones are materials acquisition, production, logistics and distribution, branding and marketing, and human resources. The nature and relative importance of the business processes will vary from company to company based on their specific objectives. For example, **Dell** has adopted a low-cost provider objective. As such, it has concentrated on achieving operating efficiencies in order processing, production, and distribution. **Apple**, on the other hand, has adopted a product differentiation objective. This objective has led to an emphasis on product quality and continual research to develop better products with more features. As such, the risk assessment controls for these two companies will differ. Dell will be focused on monitoring inventory levels and production times, while Apple will focus on quality control and product development.

CONTROL ACTIVITIES

Control activities are the policies and procedures top management establishes to help ensure that its objectives are met. The control activities most directly related to the accounting system and financial statements vary widely from one business to another, but generally can be identified with one of the following five categories.

Clearly Defined Authority and Responsibility The *authority* to perform important duties is delegated to specific individuals, and those individuals should be held *responsible* for the performance of those duties in the evaluation of their performance. Among the designated duties of an individual may be the authority to perform specified types of activities for the business or to authorize others to execute such transactions. The clear delegation of authority and responsibility motivates individuals to perform well because they know they are accountable for their actions. For example, at **Wal-Mart** and other retailers, cashiers enter a code into the cash register and maintain responsibility for cash entering and leaving the register. At the end of their shift, a supervisor counts the money. Should the register have too much or too little cash, the cashier would clearly be responsible for the error.

Segregation of Duties Accounting and administrative duties should be performed by different individuals so that no one person prepares all the documents and records for an activity. This **segregation of duties** (also called *separation of duties*) reduces the likelihood that records could be used to conceal *irregularities* (intentional misstatements, theft, or fraud) and increases the likelihood that irregularities will be discovered. Segregation of duties also reduces the likelihood that unintentional record-keeping errors will remain undiscovered.

Although segregation of duties cannot eliminate the possibility of fraud, it does require people to work together. For example, movie theaters like **AMC** and **Showcase** require one employee to collect the cash and another employee to collect the tickets to admit the customer into the theater. If one person was responsible for collecting cash and admitting customers, this person could pocket the cash and let the customer in without issuing a ticket. In this case, the number of tickets issued would match up with the cash collected because no ticket was issued and the cash was pocketed. Instead, movie theaters have one person collect the cash and issue the ticket and a second person admit customers with tickets. Cash can still be pocketed, but the segregation of duties will require both employees to engage in the fraudulent scheme (we call this *collusion*) or the cash collected will not match the tickets collected.

Perhaps the most important aspect of segregation of duties is separating the record-keeping responsibility from the physical control of the assets. For example, if a customer pays $1,000, the employee who collects the $1,000 could easily steal some or all of the money if he or she has access to the accounting records. In this case, the employee could record that the money was paid and hide the fact that the money was not in the company accounts or record that some or all of the money was not paid and that the debt was "bad."

Adequate Documents and Records Accounting records are the basis for the financial statements and other reports prepared for managers, owners, and others both inside and outside the business. Summary records and their underlying documentation must provide information about specific activities and help in the evaluation of individual performance. For example, prenumbered shipping documents provide a basis for monitoring shipments of goods to customers. When warehouse employees receive a shipping document, they ship the goods. If the shipping documents were not prenumbered, a shipping document could be sent to the warehouse and later destroyed. Without the missing number in the sequence to signal a missing document, nobody would realize that the document was missing.

Safeguards over Assets and Records Both assets and records must be secured against theft and destruction. **Safeguarding** requires physical protection of the assets through, for example, fireproof vaults, locked storage facilities, keycard access, and anti-theft tags on merchandise. An increasingly important part of safeguarding assets and records is access controls for computers. Safeguards must be provided for computer programs and data files, which are more fragile and susceptible to unauthorized access than manual record-keeping systems. For example, access controls often mandate use of both alpha and numeric characters, may require password changes every few months, and increasingly require two-factor authentication in which access requires not only a password but also something that only the approved user can supply (e.g., a code texted to your phone number or a token). To illustrate, in July 2018 Google reported that by requiring all 85,000 employees to use a physical security key that they plug into a USB port (in addition to their username and password), there had been no successful phishing incidents on work-related accounts in more than a year.

Checks on Recorded Amounts Recorded amounts should be checked by an independent person to determine that amounts are correct and that they correspond to properly authorized activities. These procedures include clerical checks, reconciliations, comparisons of asset inspection reports with recorded amounts, computer-programmed controls, and management review of reports. For example, accounting records should be checked (or reconciled) to the bank statement and any discrepancies should be resolved immediately. Bank reconciliations are illustrated later in the chapter.

Such controls are effective at mitigating unintentional error, theft, and fraud. One of the elements typically cited in discussions of theft and fraud is opportunity. That is, persons committing theft or fraud believe they have the opportunity to "get away with it." Control activities are designed to prevent and detect theft and fraud by reducing employees' opportunity to conceal their actions. Yet, every year billions of dollars are lost to employee theft and fraud because effectively designed control activities are not followed.

INFORMATION AND COMMUNICATION

An internal control system will be unable to help a company achieve its objective unless adequate information is identified and gathered on a timely basis. Further, this information must be communicated to the appropriate employees in the organization. For example, consider a company like **Mercedes** that has a strategy of providing high-quality products. This company may gather information on the percentage of production that is rejected by quality control. If that percentage rises, it signals the possibility of problems in production (such as inferior material being used, poor training of new personnel, etc.). If such information is gathered and communicated, these problems can be addressed before the company's reputation for high quality is harmed. If, on the other hand, such information is not gathered and communicated, then management may not become aware of the problem until returns and complaints are made by dissatisfied customers. At this time, it may be too late to avoid damage to their reputation.

MONITORING

Monitoring is the process of tracking potential and actual problems in the internal control system. Monitoring is accomplished through normal supervising activities such as when a manager asks a subordinate how things are going. However, best practices for larger organizations suggest that an internal audit group help monitor the effectiveness of the internal control system. Monitoring the system of internal controls allows the organization to identify potential and actual weaknesses that could, if uncorrected, produce problems.

In fact, the Sarbanes-Oxley Act requires all publicly traded corporations to have an internal audit function that reports to the audit committee of the board of directors. The Act allows companies to outsource internal audit, but precludes the business that provides the (external) financial statement audit from performing internal audit services because it may impair the independence of the financial statement audit.

RELATIONSHIP BETWEEN CONTROL ACTIVITIES AND THE ACCOUNTING SYSTEM

The **accounting system** consists of the methods and records used to identify, measure, record, and communicate financial information about a business. Although we distinguish between the accounting system and the internal control system, the two are really one integrated system designed to meet the needs of a particular business. It is difficult to generalize the relationship between internal control activities and accounting systems because it directly depends on the objectives of a particular business. Consequently, the relationship is best explored through an example.

Consider Hendrickson Theaters Inc. which operates 10 movie theaters in a single city. All the theaters are rented, as are the projection equipment and concession facilities. Hendrickson's administrative offices, furnishings, and office equipment are also rented. The following chart of accounts indicates the structure of Hendrickson's accounting system:

Chart of Accounts for Hendrickson Theaters Inc.	
ASSETS	**REVENUES**
Cash	Admissions Revenue
Concessions Inventory	Concessions Revenue
Prepaid Rent	**EXPENSES**
LIABILITIES	Salaries Expense
Accounts Payable	Wages Expense
Salaries Payable	Cost of Concessions Sold
Wages Payable	Rent Expense (Movie)
EQUITY	Rent Expense (Theater)
Capital Stock	Rent (Equipment)
Retained Earnings	Rent (Office)
	Utilities Expense
	Advertising Expense
	Office Supplies Expense

Hendrickson's accountant makes journal entries daily for revenues, biweekly for wages, and monthly for the other expenses using general-purpose accounting software. Because Hendrickson has a relatively small number of accounts, its accounting system is quite simple. The portion of Hendrickson's accounting system related to revenues and the associated control activities are described in Exhibit 4.3.

| **EXHIBIT 4.3** | **Relationship Between the Accounting System and Control Procedures** |

Illustrations from the Internal Control Structure for Revenue and Cash for Hendrickson Theaters Inc.

Accounting System

Entries: Admissions and concessions revenues are recorded daily by increasing both cash and the appropriate revenue accounts.

Documentation: The cash register at each ticket booth and concession stand prepares a detailed list of cash transactions and a daily cash summary report. The daily summary reports from the 10 theaters are electronically transferred to the central office each night and are automatically summarized upon receipt. Each morning, the accountant generates a report and makes revenue entries in the computerized general ledger.

Reports: A variety of revenue analyses can be prepared on the computer system, including analyses by theater, movie, time of day, day of the week, and month.

Control Procedures

Authority and responsibility: Each theater manager is responsible for the control of cash in his or her theater, but the central office accountant makes all general ledger entries related to cash.

Segregation of duties: Maintenance of the general ledger is segregated from responsibility for local cash control. Ticket sellers and concession operators may assist in preparation of daily cash deposits, but the manager must check and sign deposit documents.

Documentation: Prenumbered admission tickets are dispensed by machine at each theater. The machine also prepares a report of the tickets issued each day, which is used by the theater manager to reconcile cash collected with the number of tickets sold.

Safeguards: The cash accumulates in each theater until the end of each day. However, when cash drawers reach a specified level, the cash register signals that a fixed amount of cash should be removed by the manager and placed in the theater's safe.

Checks: On an unannounced schedule, Hendrickson's accountant visits each theater and verifies cash receipts reported against the number of tickets issued. On these same visits, the accountant checks concession revenues against the amounts reported by inventorying concession supplies.

OBJECTIVE **3**

Describe how businesses account for and report cash.

ACCOUNTING AND REPORTING CASH

Cash includes not only currency and coins, but also savings and checking accounts and negotiable instruments like checks and money orders. When cash is received, a cash account is increased by a debit; and when cash is paid out, a cash account is decreased by a credit. Receipt and payment of cash are frequently accomplished by a check sent through the mail, a process that may require several days, and additional time may pass between receipt of the check and its deposit in the bank by the payee. Despite the fact that there may be a time lag between the issuance of a check and the actual transfer of funds, the accounting system treats payment by check in exactly the same way that it treats the transfer of currency. The receipt of either a check or currency is recorded by a debit to cash. Conversely, either the issue of a check or the payment of currency is recorded by a credit to cash.

Cash is reported on both the balance sheet and the statement of cash flows. The balance sheet typically reports the amount of cash and equivalents available at the balance sheet date, as shown in Exhibit 4.4. The statement of cash flows shows the sources and uses of cash during the year. The statement of cash flows will be discussed in more detail in Chapter 11.

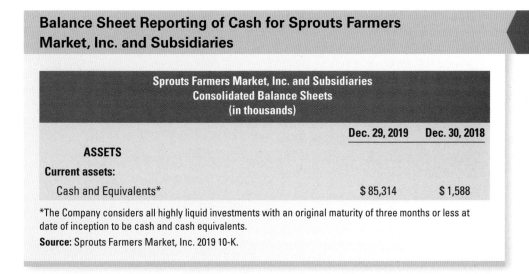

Balance Sheet Reporting of Cash for Sprouts Farmers Market, Inc. and Subsidiaries

EXHIBIT 4.4

Sprouts Farmers Market, Inc. and Subsidiaries Consolidated Balance Sheets (in thousands)		
	Dec. 29, 2019	**Dec. 30, 2018**
ASSETS		
Current assets:		
Cash and Equivalents*	$ 85,314	$ 1,588

*The Company considers all highly liquid investments with an original maturity of three months or less at date of inception to be cash and cash equivalents.

Source: Sprouts Farmers Market, Inc. 2019 10-K.

As explained in the notes to **Sprouts'** financial statements, **cash equivalents** include "all highly liquid investments with an original maturity of 3 months or less at date of inception." This is a standard definition and indicates that cash equivalents are both:

- easily convertible into known amounts of cash
- close enough to maturity that they are relatively insensitive to changes in interest rates

But why do companies bother to invest their cash in such short-term investments? The answer is that such investments earn a greater rate of return than cash sitting in a bank account. As shown in Exhibit 4.4, **Sprouts** had over $85,000,000 in cash and equivalents at December 29, 2019. If their investment strategy earns a mere 1% more than a bank account, they would earn an extra $850,000 in interest for the year (and their investment strategy almost certainly earns several percent more than a bank account).

CASH CONTROLS

OBJECTIVE 4

Describe how businesses control cash.

Internal controls are designed to protect all assets. But the more liquid an asset (i.e., the more easily it is converted into cash), the more likely it is to be stolen. In fact, an *Association of Certified Fraud Examiners'* fraud study suggested that 80% of all workplace frauds involved employee theft of company assets (i.e., embezzlement) and 90% of these thefts involved cash.[2] For example, casinos take in huge amounts of cash. At the **Mohegan Sun** casino in Connecticut, while counting cash, employees were required to wear jumpsuits with no pockets while supervisors observed them through one-way mirrors. That sounds like a good way to keep the counters from stealing cash; however, one employee shoved an estimated $600,000 under the elastic wristband of his jumpsuit over the course of his employment. He would take the money out of his sleeve and put it in his pockets during bathroom breaks. On the day he was caught, he had $97,300 in $100 bills. Now the casino uses transparent jumpsuits for its cash counters.

---

2 The other 20% includes such things as fraudulent financial statements.

Of course, casinos operate in a particularly difficult environment to control cash, but all companies must use internal control activities. As discussed, the following internal controls help businesses effectively control cash:

- The authority to collect, hold, and pay cash must be clearly assigned to specific individuals. Whenever feasible, cash-handling activities and cash record-keeping activities should be assigned to *different* individuals.
- Cash records should be examined often by an objective party as a basis for evaluating the performance of cash-handling activities.
- Controls should be supported by an appropriately designed record-keeping system.
- Cash should be safeguarded in vaults and banks.

Many of these controls are illustrated in the following YOU DECIDE.

 YOUDECIDE   **Internal Control over Cash in a Student Organization**

You are the treasurer of your sorority and have responsibility for collecting dues, depositing cash in the bank, writing all checks, maintaining accounting records, and preparing bank reconciliations and financial statements. After taking your financial accounting course, you realize that this is a clear violation of segregation of duties and mention this to your sorority president. She agrees, but says that segregation of duties is not nearly as important as simply finding someone willing to perform the treasurer's tasks.

What steps can you advise your student organization president to take to strengthen its internal control system?

You can advise the leader of your student organization to look into each of the following areas. A "no" answer to any question indicates a potential internal control weakness.

- *Is supporting documentation obtained from vendors whenever cash is paid or a liability is incurred?*
  The use of appropriate documentation assures the proper payment of bills and facilitates the appropriate accrual of liabilities on the year-end balance sheet.
- *Is every vendor invoice and all supporting documentation cancelled (e.g., by writing "Paid by check number 841 on November 29, 2023") at the time the check is written?*
  This action helps assure that duplicate payments are not made.
- *Does the organization's faculty advisor initial all checks written for amounts greater than some specified minimum (e.g., $500)?*
  This control reduces the possibility of unauthorized payments.

- *Are receipts of members' fees and dues deposited promptly (at least once a week)?*
  Prompt deposits help avoid misplacing receipts.
- *Does the organization have procedures to assist in the collection of membership dues?*
  Despite the mutual trust and friendship that are a part of most student organizations, uncollectible accounts can be a serious problem. The treasurer may need the assistance of formal procedures in collecting overdue accounts (e.g., placing sanctions on members who fail to pay).
- *Does the organization have an accounting policies and procedures manual?*
  Such a manual may be needed to prepare the year-end financial report in conformity with university and/or national governing body requirements.
- *Are complete minutes of all officers' meetings maintained?*
  The minutes should include (a) a listing of all changes in membership and officers, including the names of new members, (b) a schedule of dues that documents all financial obligations of members, (c) approval of payments, and (d) authorization of check signers. Including this information, along with descriptions of important decisions of the organization's governing body, documents all the important activities of the organization.

Businesses can effectively control cash with internal controls, which include guidelines for collecting, holding, and paying cash as well as keeping records and assigning individuals different responsibilities.

Although many of the cash controls with which you are most familiar (e.g., cash registers) might appear to be outside the accounting system, we will highlight three important areas where the accounting system interacts with the internal control system to strengthen cash controls:

- bank reconciliations
- cash over and short
- petty cash

RECONCILIATION OF ACCOUNTING RECORDS TO BANK STATEMENT

The use of a bank is one of the most important controls over cash. The bank duplicates the company's accounting by keeping their own accounting records of your account. Unfortunately, the bank's accounting records and company's accounting records often disagree because the transactions are not recorded at the same time (e.g., a company writes a check on January 18 and credits cash immediately; however, the bank will not debit your account until the check is presented to the bank—typically many days later). Therefore, to ensure that the accounting records are consistent with the bank's accounting records, any differences must be "reconciled." This process is called the **bank reconciliation**.

Periodically—usually once a month—the bank returns all checks processed during the period, together with a detailed record of the activity of the account. The document is a *bank statement*, which shows the beginning and ending account balance and the individual deposits and withdrawals recorded by the bank during the period. Basically, the bank statement is a copy of the bank's accounting records showing each customer the increases and decreases in their balances (see Exhibit 4.5, p. 232). Remember, a checking account is a liability for the bank (the bank owes you the balance). Therefore, deposits and other events that increase your bank account balance are labeled "credits" on the bank statement (because they increase the bank's liability to you), and withdrawals and other events that decrease your bank account balance are labeled "debits" (because they decrease the bank's liability to you).

Reconciliation of these separately maintained records serves two purposes:

- It serves a control function by identifying errors and providing an inspection of detailed records that deters theft.
- It serves a transaction detection function by identifying transactions performed by the bank, so the business can make the necessary entries in its records.

In general, differences between the cash account balance (see Exhibit 4.6, p. 233) and the bank statement balance develop from three sources:

- transactions recorded by the business, but not recorded by the bank in time to appear on the current bank statement
- transactions recorded by the bank, but not yet recorded by the business
- errors in recording transactions on either set of records

Transactions Recorded by the Business, but Not Yet Recorded by the Bank

There are generally two types of transactions recorded by the business, but not recorded by the bank in time to appear on the current statement: outstanding checks and deposits in transit.

Outstanding Checks An **outstanding check** is a check issued and recorded by the business that has not been "cashed" by the recipient of the check. The business has (properly) recorded the check as lowering its cash balance and the bank has (properly) not recorded the check as lowering the business's account balance because it has not been cashed. For example, when a check is written during December, but not cashed until January, the business's December 31 cash balance will be lower than its account balance on the December 31 bank statement.

Deposits in Transit A **deposit in transit** is an amount received and recorded by the business, but which has not been recorded by the bank in time to appear on the current bank statement. Deposits in transit cause the bank balance to be smaller than the business's cash account balance. Deposits in transit arise because many banks post any deposit received after 2:00 or 3:00 P.M. into their records on the next business day and because businesses often make deposits on weekends or holidays when the bank is not open for business, which could cause the deposit to appear on the next bank statement.

 Next Level

If a debit increases an asset and decreases a liability and a credit decreases an asset and increases a liability, why does the bank "credit" your account when you make a deposit and "debit" your account when you make a withdrawal?

ANSWER:
Because the "credit" and "debit" are from the bank's point of view. When you make a deposit, it actually increases the bank's liability to you—the bank now owes you more. When you make a withdrawal, it decreases the bank's liability to you.

EXHIBIT 4.5   **Bank Statement**

T	THIRD NATIONAL BANK	Account Statement
N	123 W. Main Street	
	Batavia, OH 45103	Statement Date:
B		August 31, 2023
	Member FDIC	

OHIO ENTERPRISES INC.   Account Number:
519 MAIN STREET   40056
BATAVIA, OH 45103

Previous Balance	Checks and Debits	Deposits and Credits	Current Balance
$7,675.20	$10,685.26	$7,175.10	$4,165.04

Checks and Debits			Deposits and Credits		Daily Balance	
Date	No.	Amount	Date	Amount	Date	Amount
8/3/23	1883	182.00			8/3/23	7,493.20
8/4/23	1884	217.26	8/4/23	2,673.10	8/4/23	9,949.04
8/6/23	1885	1,075.00			8/6/23	8,874.04
8/7/23	1886	37.50	8/7/23	4,500.00	8/7/23	13,336.54
8/10/23	1887	826.00			8/10/23	12,510.54
8/11/23	1888	50.00			8/11/23	12,460.54
8/12/23	1889	2,670.00				
8/12/23	1890	67.90			8/12/23	9,722.64
8/13/23	1891	890.00			8/13/23	8,832.64
8/14/23	1892	27.50			8/14/23	8,805.14
8/17/23	1893	111.00			8/17/23	8,694.14
8/18/23	DM	380.00			8/18/23	8,314.14
8/19/23	1894	60.00				
8/19/23	1895	510.00			8/19/23	7,744.14
8/20/23	1896	30.00			8/20/23	7,714.14
8/21/23	1897	1,600.00			8/21/23	6,114.14
8/24/23	1898	78.00			8/24/23	6,036.14
8/25/23	NSF	200.00			8/25/23	5,836.14
8/26/23	1899	208.80			8/26/23	5,627.34
8/27/23	1900	1,250.00			8/27/23	4,377.34
8/28/23	1902	175.00			8/28/23	4,202.34
8/31/23	1903	25.30	8/31/23 INT	2.00		
8/31/23	SC	14.00			8/31/23	4,165.04

Symbols:	CM Credit Memo	EC Error Correction	NSF Non-Sufficient Funds
	DM Debit Memo	INT Interest Earned	SC Service Charge

Reconcile your account immediately.

Transactions Recorded by the Bank, but Not Yet Recorded by the Business

Several types of transactions are recorded by the bank, but not yet recorded by the business, including service charges, non-sufficient funds checks, and debit and credit memos. After the reconciliation process, the business must make adjusting journal entries to record all the transactions that have been recorded by the bank but not yet recorded in the business's ledger cash account.

Service Charges **Service charges** are fees charged by the bank for services provided. Examples include annual or monthly maintenance, minimum balance, and foreign transaction fees. The amount of the fee is not known to the business (and therefore cannot be

T-Account for Cash, Prior to Reconciliation	EXHIBIT 4.6

Ohio Enterprises Inc.						
Cash						
Balance, 7/31/23	$6,200.94					
Date	Amount Deposited		Check Number	Check Amount	Check Number	Check Amount
8/1	$2,673.10		1886	$ 37.50	1896	$ 30.00
8/5	4,500.00		1887	826.00	1897	1,600.00
8/31	300.00		1888	50.00	1898	87.00
Total deposits	$7,473.10		1889	2,670.00	1899	208.80
			1890	67.90	1900	1,250.00
			1891	890.00	1901	93.00
			1892	27.50	1902	175.00
			1893	111.00	1903	25.30
			1894	60.00	1904	72.50
			1895	510.00	1905	891.00
			Total disbursements			$9,682.50
Balance, 8/31/23	$3,991.54					

recorded) until the bank statement is received. Bank service charges unrecorded by the business at the end of a month cause the bank balance to be smaller than the business's cash account balance.

Non-Sufficient Funds Checks A **non-sufficient funds (NSF) check** is a check that has been returned to the depositor because funds in the issuer's account are not sufficient to pay the check (also called a *bounced check*). The amount of the check was added to the depositor's account when the check was received; however, when the bank discovers the check cannot be paid, the amount of the NSF check is deducted from the account. This deduction is recorded by the bank before it is recorded by the business. NSF checks cause the bank balance to be smaller than the cash account balance.

Debit and Credit Memos A debit memo might result, for example, if the bank makes a prearranged deduction from the business's account to pay a utility bill. Debit memos recorded by the bank but not yet recorded by the business cause the bank balance to be smaller than the cash account balance. A credit memo could result if the bank collected a note receivable for the business and deposited the funds in the business's account. Credit memos recorded by the bank but not recorded by the business cause the bank balance to be larger than the cash account balance.

Errors The previous differences between the accounting records and bank account balances are the result of time lags between the recording of a transaction by the business and its recording by the bank. Errors in recording transactions represent yet another source of difference between a business's cash account balance and the bank balance. Errors are inevitable in any accounting system and should be corrected as soon as discovered. In addition, an effort should be made to determine the cause of any error as a basis for corrective action. Obviously, an intentional error designed to hide misappropriation of funds calls for quite different corrective action than does an error resulting from human fatigue or machine failure.

Performing a Bank Reconciliation To begin the reconciliation, start with the "cash balance from the bank statement" and the "cash balance from company records." These two balances are then adjusted as necessary to produce identical "adjusted cash balances" by following these steps:

Step 1. Compare the deposits on the bank statement to the deposits debited to the cash account. Any deposits debited to the cash account but not on the bank statement are likely deposits in transit, so look at a deposit slip to ensure that these amounts were actually deposited. Deposits in transit should be added to the "cash balance from the bank statement."

Step 2. Compare the paid (often called *cancelled*) checks that are electronically returned with the bank statement to the amounts credited to the cash account and the list of outstanding checks from prior months. Any checks credited to the cash account but not on the bank statement are likely outstanding checks. These amounts should be subtracted from the "cash balance from the bank statement."

Step 3. Look for items on the bank statement that have not been debited or credited to the cash account. These include bank service charges, interest payments, NSF checks, automatic payments (debit memos), and bank collections on behalf of the company (credit memos). Bank debits should be subtracted from the "cash balance from company records," while bank credits should be added to the "cash balance from company records." Of course, all these amounts should be verified.

Step 4. If the "adjusted cash balances" are still not the same, search for errors. The most common error is a "transposition" error in which, for example, a check is written for $823, but recorded as $283 (the 8 and 2 are transposed). In this case, the accounting records will show a $283 credit to the cash account, but the bank will show a $823 debit to the company's account. All errors made by the company must be added or subtracted from the "cash balance from company records." All errors made by the bank must be added or subtracted from the "cash balance from the bank statement."

This process is illustrated in EXAMPLE 4.1 .

EXAMPLE 4.1   PERFORMING A BANK RECONCILIATION

Refer to the bank statement in Exhibit 4.5 (p. 232) and the cash account in Exhibit 4.6 (p. 233). Recognize that the beginning balance was reconciled at the end of last month (July). Assume that this was performed correctly and all outstanding checks (numbers 1883, 1884, and 1885) and deposits in transit from July cleared during August.

Required:
1. Determine the adjustments needed by comparing the bank statement to the cash account.

2. Complete the bank reconciliation.

Solution:
Bank reconciliations help strengthen internal controls over cash by comparing the accounting records and the bank statement. This helps (1) identify errors, (2) deter theft, and (3) identify transactions performed by the bank so the business can make the necessary entries in its accounting records.

1. Four items in the cash account do not appear on the bank statement: the August 31 deposit (in transit), and checks 1901, 1904, and 1905 (outstanding). There is also an error. The amount posted to the cash account for check 1898 does not equal the amount cleared on the bank statement. The cancelled check on record was written for $78.00, not $87.00, so the error is on the company's records.

2.

Cash balance from bank statement		$ 4,165.04	Cash balance from company records		$3,991.54
Add: Deposit in transit (8/31)		300.00	Add:		
			Error in recording check 1898 (we recorded as $87, should be $78)	$ 9.00	
Less: Outstanding checks			Interest	2.00	11.00
1901	$ (93.00)				
1904	(72.50)				
1905	(891.00)	(1,056.50)	Less:		
Adjusted cash balance		**$3,408.54**	Service charge	$ 14.00	
			NSF check	200.00	
			Electric bill (Debit Memo)	380.00	(594.00)
			Adjusted cash balance		**$3,408.54**

Adjusted cash balances should equal.

If the person who writes the checks also performs the reconciliation, it is easier for him or her to cover up theft and fraud. Therefore, there are additional benefits when the bank reconciliation is performed by someone with no other responsibilities related to cash (the duties of reconciling cash and cash record keeping should be segregated).

Making Adjusting Entries as a Result of the Bank Reconciliation Once the bank reconciliation is completed, some adjustments to the accounting records may be necessary. No adjustments are necessary for outstanding checks or deposits in transit because the accounting records have correctly recorded these amounts. However, as shown in EXAMPLE 4.2, adjustments are necessary for any company errors or items such as bank charges or interest that the company does not find out about until receiving the bank statement.

EXAMPLE 4.2 MAKING ADJUSTING ENTRIES AS A RESULT OF THE BANK RECONCILIATION

Refer to the bank reconciliation performed in Example 4.1. Assume that all checks from this account were written to satisfy accounts payable.

Required:
Prepare the necessary adjusting journal entries.

Solution:
The bank reconciliation (see Example 4.1) identified (1) errors in the business's accounting records and (2) transactions performed by the bank that require entries to reflect the appropriate balances in the accounting records.

CONTINUED

Account and Explanation	Debit	Credit	Assets	= Liabilities +	Stockholders' Equity
Cash	9		▲		
Accounts Payable		9		▲	
Cash	2		▲		
Interest Income		2			▲
Bank Service Charge Expense	14				▼
Cash		14	▼		
Accounts Receivable	200		▲		
Cash		200	▼		
Utilities Expense	380				▼
Cash		380	▼		

CASH OVER AND SHORT

Another important control activity requires that cash receipts be deposited in a bank daily. At the end of each day, the amount of cash received during the day is debited to the cash accounts to which it has been deposited. The amount deposited should equal the total of cash register tapes. If it does not (and differences will occasionally occur even when cash-handling procedures are carefully designed and executed), the discrepancy is recorded in an account called **cash over and short**, as illustrated in EXAMPLE 4.3.

EXAMPLE 4.3   RECORDING CASH OVER AND SHORT

RSA has $20,671.12 prepared for deposit. However, the total of cash register tapes and other documents supporting the receipt of cash on that day is $20,685.14. Of that amount, $6,760.50 is from collections for accounts receivable and the remainder is cash sales.

Required:
Prepare the necessary journal entry to record today's cash receipts.

Solution:
Reconciling the cash in the register to the register tapes provides an important cash control by highlighting discrepancies. Investigation identifies causes of the discrepancy and permits appropriate corrective action to be taken.

Account and Explanation	Debit	Credit	Assets	= Liabilities +	Stockholders' Equity
Cash	20,671.12		▲		
Cash Over and Short	14.02				▼
Sales Revenue*		13,924.64			▲
Accounts Receivable		6,760.50	▼		

*$20,685.14 – $6,760.50

Observe that a cash *shortage* (as in Example 4.3) requires a debit to cash over and short, whereas a cash *overage* would require a credit.

One common source of cash over and short is errors in making change for cash sales. Significant amounts of cash over and short signal the need for a careful investigation of the causes and appropriate corrective action. Cash over and short is usually treated as an income statement account and is reported as a part of other expenses or other revenues.

PETTY CASH

Cash controls are more effective when companies pay with a check for the following reasons:

- Only certain people have the authority to sign the check. Those authorized to sign do not keep the accounting records and only sign the check with the proper documentation supporting the payment (e.g., evidence that the goods being paid for were properly ordered and received).
- Supporting documents are marked paid to avoid duplicate payment.
- Checks are prenumbered, which makes it easy to identify any missing checks.

However, issuing checks to pay small amounts is usually more costly than paying cash.[3] Therefore, a company may establish a **petty cash** fund to pay for items such as stamps or a cake for an employee birthday party. The petty cash fund is overseen by a petty cash custodian, who both pays for small dollar amounts directly from the fund and reimburses employees who have receipts for items they've bought with their own money. At the end of the month, the custodian submits all receipts (and other supporting documentation) to the company. After company personnel (other than the petty cash custodian) determine that the documents are authentic and that each transaction is supported by appropriate documentation, the custodian is given an amount to replenish the petty cash fund. The company then records the amounts spent in the accounting records. Because the custodian replenishes petty cash at the end of the month, the accounting records are appropriately updated each month. This process is illustrated in EXAMPLE 4.4.

Replenishment of petty cash may also occur during the month if the amount of petty cash available gets too low. However, to assure that all expenses are recorded in the appropriate accounting period, replenishment should occur at the end of the month or accounting period. As an additional control measure, a company should periodically verify its petty cash balances by counting the cash in the hands of custodians and comparing it to the custodian's petty cash record.

EXAMPLE 4.4 ACCOUNTING FOR PETTY CASH

On January 1, Oregon Industries establishes a petty cash fund of $500. On January 31, the petty cash custodian presents the following records of the month's transactions, together with related documents, and requests reimbursement:

Jan. 12	Hansen's Grocery (coffee)	$ 30
15	U.S. Post Office (postage)	70
17	Northwest Messenger (package delivery)	25
19	Office Depot (office supplies)	175
25	Mr. Strand, Controller (food for lunch meeting)	63
	Total	$363

After approving the expenses, the company issues a check to the custodian for $363.00 to replenish the fund.

CONTINUED

---

3 Checks cost money to print, mail, and process. Some estimate the cost of processing a check to be over $1. Therefore, banks have developed ways for businesses to transfer money without the use of paper checks. For example, most employees do not see an actual paycheck; instead, money is automatically deposited into their bank account. These are called electronic fund transfers (EFT). Use of EFTs is quite common and has become commonplace at the individual level through the use of debit cards.

EXAMPLE 4.4   ACCOUNTING FOR PETTY CASH (CONTINUED)

Required:

1. Prepare the journal entry to establish the petty cash fund on January 1.

2. Prepare the journal entry to record the replenishment of the fund on January 31.

3. Assuming the entry from Requirement 2 has been made, prepare the journal entry needed to increase the fund balance to $600.

Solution:

1. The petty cash fund is established when money is set aside for small expenditures.

Date	Account and Explanation	Debit	Credit	Assets	= Liabilities +	Stockholders' Equity
Jan. 1	Petty Cash	500.00		▲		
	Cash		500.00	▼		

2. The expenditures of petty cash are not recorded in the accounting records until the fund is replenished. The replenishment does not alter the balance of the petty cash fund (i.e., in this case the balance remains $500 as established in part 1).

Date	Account and Explanation	Debit	Credit	Assets	= Liabilities +	Stockholders' Equity
Jan. 31	Supplies	175.00		▲		
	Postage Expense	70.00				▼
	Delivery Expense	25.00				▼
	Miscellaneous Expense	93.00				▼
	Cash		363.00	▼		

3. After establishment of the petty cash fund (see part 1), the Petty Cash account is only debited or credited when the overall fund balance is increased or decreased, respectively.

Date	Account and Explanation	Debit	Credit	Assets	= Liabilities +	Stockholders' Equity
Jan. 31	Petty Cash	100.00		▼		
	Cash		100.00	▲		

We have spent considerable time discussing internal controls both in general and, over cash, in particular, for two reasons. First, internal controls are an integral part of the accounting system and business. Second, the accounting and reporting of cash is not that difficult. We will consider cash management strategies, but first we discuss the operating cycle because this affects the amount of cash needed.

OPERATING CYCLE

OBJECTIVE ◀ 5

Describe the operating cycle and explain the principles of cash management.

The **operating cycle** is the elapsed time between the purchase of goods for resale (or the purchase of materials to produce salable goods or services) and the collection of cash from customers (presumably a larger amount of cash than was invested in the goods sold). Although typically a year or less, the operating cycle can be as short as a few days for perishable goods or as long as many years for the production and sale of products such as timber or wine (see Exhibit 4.7).

The Operating Cycle	EXHIBIT 4.7

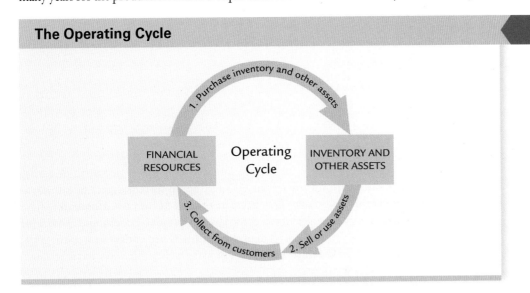

Consider the operating cycle for **H. H. Gregg**, a large appliance retailer that provides long-term financing for customers. Appliances remain in inventory for an average of 3 months before being sold. Most are sold on credit, and it takes an average of 12 months to collect the full amount of a sale. Thus, Gregg's operating cycle is 15 months, representing the average purchase-to-collection interval (3 months to sell plus 12 months to collect).

The length of the operating cycle influences the classification of assets and liabilities on balance sheets. In addition, the operating cycle plays an important role in the measurement of income. The length of the operating cycle also affects the amount of capital a business needs and the policies that govern its sales of goods and services, as the You Decide demonstrates.

✦ YOU DECIDE   Operating Cycle and Capital Requirements

You are the CFO of Tolland Gizmo. You sell, on credit, approximately 1,000 Gizmos per month at $10 per unit. In addition to the accounts receivable, you have an inventory of 200 Gizmos that were purchased at a cost of $6 per unit (a total inventory of $1,200) and $1,000 in cash. Currently, Tolland has 1 month's sales in accounts receivable and the following balance sheet:

ASSETS

Cash	$ 1,000
Inventory	1,200
Accounts receivable	10,000
Total	$12,200

LIABILITIES AND STOCKHOLDERS' EQUITY

Equity	$12,200
Total	$12,200

The sales force wants to lengthen the collection period of the accounts receivable to 3 months.

How would lengthening the collection period of the accounts receivable affect Tolland's financing requirements?

Tolland will now have higher financing costs because collection of the cash is delayed. This may require them to borrow additional money or forego spending the cash as quickly as possible. Presumably, the company would not allow its customers to take 3 months to pay unless compensated for doing so. Thus, Tolland will probably charge a higher price because of the extended payment terms.

Tolland's higher price to cover the increased financing costs it pays for a longer collection period will result in higher revenues.

CASH MANAGEMENT

With an understanding of the operating cycle, we now turn our attention to cash management strategies. As discussed, the activities of the operating cycle transform cash into goods and services and then back, through sales, into cash. This sequence of activities includes a continual process of paying and receiving cash. A company can significantly increase its net income through its cash management policies. At a high level, cash management principles entail the following:

- delaying payments to suppliers, so a company can earn as much interest on their cash as possible
- speeding up collection from customers in order to invest the cash sooner or reduce the need for additional financing
- earning the greatest return on any excess cash

We can follow these principles through the operating cycle.

BUYING INVENTORY

The first stage of the operating cycle is buying inventory. Money that is tied up in inventory sitting on the shelves is not earning any return. As such, an important aspect of cash management is to keep inventory levels low. This decreases the need for cash. Companies have made great strides in inventory management over the last few decades. For example, **Dell** went from holding approximately 11 weeks of sales in inventory in 1991 to under one week in 2001, while car companies such as **Toyota** time the delivery of parts such as windows and seats down to the minute.

PAYING FOR INVENTORY

The second stage of the operating cycle is paying for the inventory. As with all payments, a good cash management principle is to delay payments as long as possible while maintaining a good relationship with the payee. The longer a company keeps cash, the more interest it can collect. This may seem trivial, but consider a company like **Microsoft**. Its June 30, 2019, 10-K reveals approximately $8.6 billion in accounts payable. If Microsoft can earn 5% on this money, it will earn over to $1,178,000 per day in interest. You may practice this in your own lives if you wait until April 15 to pay any income taxes owed or pay your tuition on the last possible day.

SELLING INVENTORY

The third stage is selling the inventory, which often produces receivables. Good cash management suggests increasing the speed of receivable collections. This is an area that has become increasingly sophisticated over the last 20 years. In fact, many companies sell their receivables rather than wait for their customers to pay. Of course, they sell the receivables for less than they will receive (which represents interest and return for the buyer), but it also allows the company to receive the cash sooner and avoid hiring employees to service the receivables.

SHORT-TERM INVESTMENTS

Beyond delaying payments and speeding up collections, businesses try to keep their bank cash balances to a minimum because most bank accounts earn relatively small amounts of interest. Accordingly, short-term investments are purchased with temporary cash surpluses. The value and composition of short-term investment portfolios change continually in response to seasonal factors and other shifts in the business environment.

These investments will usually be liquidated (converted to cash through selling or maturity) before the business undertakes any significant short-term borrowing because the interest expense on short-term borrowings usually exceeds the return on short-term investments. Nonetheless, temporary shortages can result from the day-to-day ups and downs in the inflows and outflows of cash, as well as unforeseen needs for cash. A business with a good credit rating can borrow funds to resolve a temporary cash shortage. Such borrowings are frequently made under a line of credit, an agreement between the company and its bank in which the bank promises to lend the company funds up to a specified limit and at specified interest rates. The use of short-term investments as part of cash management is illustrated in the following You Decide.

 YOUDECIDE Cash Management

You are the treasurer at Ohio Wire, a medium-size manufacturer of cable and wire used in building and bridge construction. Since most construction is seasonal, Ohio Wire tends to have far more cash inflows during the summer months. Further, during the winter their cash outflows are often greater than their inflows.

How do you manage the excess cash accumulated during the summer months knowing that cash will be needed during the winter?

Ohio Wire will use its excess cash to make short-term investments. These investments should be able to be easily liquidated by winter when the cash will be needed. Some examples of such investments could be certificates of deposit, Treasury Bills, and short-term equity holdings. Further, most companies will have lines of credit at a bank. These arrangements allow the company to borrow any amount up to some limit with a phone call.

Investing excess cash in short-term investments allows companies to have immediate access to cash to cover temporary short falls, while minimizing borrowing costs.

Effective cash management ultimately requires some understanding of future cash flows. For example, if the company is planning to expand or pay off a loan, it must make sure it has the necessary cash on hand. If a company receives most of its cash for the year around the holidays, it must effectively manage the excess until the time it is needed. These projections are made as part of the budgeting process and are an integral part of managerial accounting courses.

LO1. Describe the role of internal controls in managing a business.

KEY TAKEAWAYS

- Internal control systems provide reasonable assurance that the company's objectives are being met in three areas:
  - Effectiveness and efficiency of operations
  - Reliability of financial reporting
  - Compliance with applicable laws and regulations

KEY TERM

Internal control system, 220

LO2. Describe the five components of internal control.

KEY TAKEAWAYS

- The internal control system includes the following:
  - The control environment
  - Risk assessment
  - Control activities
  - Information and communication
  - Monitoring
- Although we distinguish between the accounting system and the internal control system, the two are actually one integrated system designed to meet the needs of a particular business.

KEY TERMS

Accounting system, 227
Business process risks, 224
Control activities, 225
Safeguarding, 226
Segregation of duties, 225
Strategic risks, 224

LO3. Describe how businesses account for and report cash.

KEY TAKEAWAYS

- A cash account is debited when cash is received and credited when cash is paid out.
- Cash is reported on the balance sheet as the amount of cash and cash equivalents available on the balance sheet date.
- The statement of cash flows shows the sources and uses of cash during the accounting period.
- Cash equivalents are amounts that are easily convertible in to known amounts of cash and investments that are close to maturity.

KEY TERM

Cash equivalents, 229

KEY TAKEAWAYS

- Keeping control over cash is extremely difficult.
- It is important for the following:
  - Safeguarding cash
  - Adequately segregating the custody of cash from the authorization of payments and the accounting records
- Cash accounts include the following:
  - Cash in bank
  - Change funds
  - Petty cash
- Controls over these cash accounts include the following:
  - Bank reconciliations
  - Daily deposits and recording cash over and short amounts
  - Accounting procedures for petty cash funds

LO4. Describe how businesses control cash.

KEY TERMS

Bank reconciliation, 231
Cash over and short, 236
Deposit in transit, 231
Non-sufficient funds (NSF) check, 233
Outstanding check, 231
Petty cash, 237
Service charges, 232

EXAMPLES

Example 4.1	Performing a bank reconciliation, pages 234–235
Example 4.2	Making adjusting entries as a result of the bank reconciliation, pages 235–236
Example 4.3	Recording cash over and short, page 236
Example 4.4	Accounting for petty cash, pages 237–238

KEY TAKEAWAYS

- The operating cycle of the business starts when the business purchases inventory.
- When a business sells goods on credit, creating accounts receivable, cash is not replenished until the receivables are collected, which completes the operating cycle.
- Cash management is an important function at all companies because business is really a continuous cycle of paying and receiving cash.

LO5. Describe the operating cycle and explain the principles of cash management.

- Although aspects of cash management have become extremely sophisticated, basic strategies are as follows:
  - Keeping inventory levels low
  - Delaying payment of liabilities as long as possible
  - Speeding up collection of receivables
  - Investing idle cash to earn the greatest possible return while still being available when needed

KEY TERM

Operating cycle, 239

REVIEW PROBLEM

I. BANK RECONCILIATION

Fugazi Enterprises has the following information in its accounting records for their primary checking account:

Balance at April 30	$ 18,350
Checks written during May	114,700
Deposits during May	112,200

Fugazi's May bank statement contained the following information:

Balance per bank at April 30		$ 19,800
Credits during May:		
Deposits		109,600
Debits during May:		
Checks paid	$107,400	
Debit memo (May utilities)	8,000	
Bank service charge	80	115,480
Balance per bank at May 31		$ 13,920

The April bank reconciliation had deposits in transit of $850 and outstanding checks of $2,300. All these items cleared during May. These were the only reconciling items in April.

Required:

1. Prepare a bank reconciliation at May 31.
2. Prepare any adjusting entries necessary because of the bank reconciliation.

Solution:

1.

Cash balance from bank statement		$ 13,920
Add: Deposits in transit	$112,200 − ($109,600 − $850)*	3,450
Less: Outstanding checks	$114,700 − ($107,400 − $2,300)**	(9,600)
Adjusted cash balance		**$ 7,770**
Cash balance from company records Less:	($18,350 + $112,200 − $114,700)	$ 15,850
Debit memo (utilities)	$8,000	
Service charge	80	(8,080)
Adjusted cash balance		**$ 7,770**

*$112,200 was deposited during May, but the account was only credited for $109,600 during May. However, this $109,600 included $850 that was in transit at April 30, so only $108,750 ($109,600 − $850) of the May deposits were credited to the account.

**$114,700 in checks were written in May and $107,400 in checks cleared the bank during May. However, this $107,400 included $2,300 in checks that were outstanding from April, so only $105,100 ($107,400 − $2,300) in checks cleared that were written in May.

2.

Date	Account and Explanation	Debit	Credit	Assets	=	Liabilities	+	Stockholders' Equity
May 31	Utilities Expense	8,000						▼
	Bank Service Charge Expense	80						▼
	Cash		8,080	▼				

APPLYING KNOWLEDGE

DISCUSSION QUESTIONS

1. What is the purpose of an internal control system?

2. Internal control systems include policies and procedures to do what?

3. The Sarbanes-Oxley Act increased top management's responsibility for what?

4. What are the five components of internal control?

5. What is meant by "tone at the top"? Why is it so important to an effective system of internal controls?

6. What are strategic risks?

7. What are business process risks?

8. What are the five categories of control activities?

9. How do these control activities help protect a company against error, theft, and fraud?

10. How do control activities relate to the accounting system?

11. Why does a company give particular attention to internal controls for cash?

12. Why is it important to segregate the duties for handling cash from the duties for keeping the accounting records for cash?

13. Describe two advantages of performing reconciliations of the cash account to the balances on the bank statements.

14. Describe the potential sources of difference between a cash account and its associated bank statement balance.

15. What kinds of bank reconciliation items require the firm to make adjusting entries?

16. Describe how cash over and short can be used for internal control purposes.

17. Why do most companies have petty cash funds?

18. What are cash equivalents?

19. Why do companies invest their cash in short-term investments?

20. What is the operating cycle?

21. Describe the basic cash management principles.

22. Why do companies hold short-term investments?

OBJECTIVE 1

OBJECTIVE 2

OBJECTIVE 4

OBJECTIVE 3

OBJECTIVE 5

MULTIPLE-CHOICE EXERCISES

OBJECTIVE 1

4-1 What is the primary role of internal controls in managing a business?
a. To prevent cash from being stolen
b. To ensure that the financial statements are presented in such a manner as to provide relevant and reliable information for financial statement users and the company's creditors
c. To constrain subordinates' activities in order to prevent employees from deviating from the scope of their responsibilities and encouraging them to act in the best interest of the business
d. To encourage theft and to ensure that segregation of duties does not take place

4-2 Which of the following is *not* one of the three areas for which internal control systems are intended to provide reasonable assurance?
a. Reliability of financial reporting
b. Compliance with applicable laws and regulations
c. Effectiveness and efficiency of operations
d. Certification that the financial statements are without error

OBJECTIVE 2

4-3 Which of the following is *not* one of the five components of internal control?
a. Analysis of control procedures
b. Information and communication
c. Risk assessment
d. Control environment

4-4 Which of the following is *not* one of the five categories of control activities?
a. Checks on recorded amounts
b. Defalcation and financial reporting
c. Clearly defined authority and responsibility
d. Segregation of duties

4-5 The internal audit function is part of what element of the internal control system?
a. Control environment
b. Monitoring
c. Risk assessment
d. Control activities

4-6 Which of the following is *not* generally an internal control activity?
a. Establishing clear lines of authority to carry out specific tasks
b. Physically counting inventory in a perpetual inventory system
c. Reducing the cost of hiring seasonal employees
d. Limiting access to computerized accounting records

4-7 Allowing only certain employees to order goods and services for the company is an example of what internal control procedure?
a. Adequate documents and records
b. Clearly defined authority and responsibility
c. Safeguarding of assets and records
d. Checks on recorded amount

OBJECTIVE 4

4-8 Deposits made by a company but not yet reflected in a bank statement are called
a. deposits in transit.
b. debit memoranda.
c. credit memoranda.
d. None of the above.

4-9 Which one of the following would *not* appear on a bank statement for a checking account?
a. Deposits
b. Interest earned
c. Service charges
d. Outstanding checks

4-10 Which one of the following is *not* a cash equivalent?
a. 180-day note issued by a local or state government
b. 90-day U.S. Treasury bill
c. 60-day corporate commercial paper
d. 30-day certificate of deposit

4-11 The operating cycle is best described as the time between
   a. production and sale of inventory.
   b. the sale of inventory and collection of receivables.
   c. the formation of the company and the start of operations.
   d. purchase of goods for resale and collection of cash from customers.

OBJECTIVE ◀5

4-12 High level cash management strategies include
   a. bank reconciliations.
   b. cash over and short.
   c. petty cash.
   d. delaying payment for suppliers.

4-13 Effective cash management and control includes all of the following *except*
   a. the use of a petty cash fund.
   b. bank reconciliations.
   c. purchase of stocks and bonds.
   d. short-term investments of excess cash.

4-14 Cash management principles do *not* include
   a. earning the greatest return possible on excess cash.
   b. paying suppliers promptly.
   c. speeding up collection from customers.
   d. delaying payment of suppliers.

4-15 Which one of the following statements is true?
   a. Sound internal control practice dictates that cash disbursements should be made by check, unless the disbursement is very small.
   b. Petty cash can be substituted for a checking account to expedite the payment of all disbursements.
   c. Good cash management practices dictate that a company should maintain as large a balance as possible in its cash account.
   d. The person handling the cash should also prepare the bank reconciliation.

BRIEF EXERCISES

Brief Exercise 4-16 Role of Internal Control

OBJECTIVE ◀1

Internal controls play a crucial role in a business.

Required:
CONCEPTUAL CONNECTION Describe why internal controls are important. What are the potential consequences of an internal control failure?

Brief Exercise 4-17 Components of Internal Control

OBJECTIVE ◀2

The Committee of Sponsoring Organizations of the Treadway Commission (COSO) discussed five components of internal control.

Required:
Describe these five components of internal control.

Brief Exercise 4-18 Bank Reconciliation

OBJECTIVE ◀4

Firebird Corp. prepares monthly bank reconciliations of its checking account balance. The bank statement for February indicated the following:

Balance, February 28	$ 87,392
Service charge for February	100
Interest earned during February	875
NSF check from Valerie Corp. (deposited by Firebird)	630
Note ($12,000) and interest ($350) collected from a customer of Firebird's	12,350

(Continued)

Upon receiving the bank statement, Firebird's accountants analyzed its cash transactions for possible reconciling items between its cash balance per books and the bank statement:

Checking account balance per Firebird's books	$73,260
Outstanding checks as of February 28	6,440
Deposit in transit at February 28	4,785
Error in recording check 7853 issued by Firebird	18

The correct amount of check 7853 is $797. It was recorded as a cash disbursement of $779 by mistake. The check was issued to pay for merchandise purchases. The check appeared on the bank statement correctly.

Required:
1. Prepare a bank reconciliation schedule in proper form at February 28.
2. What is the amount of cash that should be reported on the February 28 balance sheet?

OBJECTIVE 4 ▶

Brief Exercise 4-19 Adjusting Entry from Bank Reconciliation

Koosh, a furniture company, made an error in recording a check received from a customer. Last month, Koosh's customer bought a table for $959. Upon receiving the check from the customer, Koosh entered the check as an increase of cash of $995.

Required:
Record the appropriate journal entry to correct the error.

OBJECTIVE 4 ▶

Brief Exercise 4-20 Adjusting Entry from Bank Reconciliation

Samba Corporation operates in an industry with high collectability issues. Recently, one of Samba's customers wrote a check for $235 for services performed. Samba's bank later informed Samba that its customer did not have cash available in his account to cover the $235 charge. As a result, Samba's bank assesses a $30 fee as the result of the NSF check received. Samba has not yet adjusted its books for the bank fee or the NSF check.

Required:
Record the appropriate journal entry to update Samba's books.

OBJECTIVE 4 ▶

Brief Exercise 4-21 Bank Reconciliation

Garrison Corporation was closing its books on May 31. Garrison's accountant prepared a bank reconciliation as of May 31 and has found the following possible reconciling items between its book balance and its cash balance per the bank:

Garrison's book balance	$76,940
Outstanding checks	550
Customer's NSF check returned by the bank	175
Interest earned on checking account	55

In the search for reconciling items, the accountant also discovered that Garrison made an error in recording a customer's check: the amount was recorded in cash receipts as $480; the bank recorded the amount correctly as $840.

Required:
What amount will Garrison report as its adjusted cash balance at May 31?

OBJECTIVE 4 ▶

Brief Exercise 4-22 Bank Reconciliation

Tosh Corp. prepares monthly bank reconciliations as part of its cash controls. Tosh's bank provided the following amount about Tosh's cash balance at the bank for during the month of April:

Balance, April 30	$86,250
Service charge for April	60
Note ($4,000) and interest ($205) collected for Tosh from a customer	4,205
Interest earned during April	110
NSF check from Orange Corp. (deposited by Tosh) for goods purchased on account	445

Tosh then analyzed its cash balance on its own set of books, revealing the following details:

Checking account balance per Tosh's books	$83,135
Deposit in transit at April 30	2,000
Outstanding checks as of April 30	1,350
Error in recording a check issued by Tosh. (Correct amount of the check is $549, but was recorded as a cash disbursement of $594. The check was issued to pay for merchandise originally purchased on account.)	45

Required:
1. Prepare a bank reconciliation at April 30 in proper form.
2. Record any necessary adjusting journal entries.

Brief Exercise 4-23 Cash Over and Short

OBJECTIVE ◀ 4

At the end of each day, Sparkle counts the cash in its cash registers. Sparkle then compares the physical amount of cash to the amount of cash that the register tape indicates should be in the cash drawer. On a recent day, Sparkle Company obtained the following data from its cash registers:

	Cash Sales per Register Tape	Cash in Register After Removing Opening Change
Register 1	$13,436.23	$13,432.57
Register 2	16,120.47	16,122.62
Register 3	12,871.12	12,868.48

Sparkle deposits its cash receipts in its bank account daily.

Required:
Prepare a journal entry to record these cash sales.

Brief Exercise 4-24 Cash Over and Short

OBJECTIVE ◀ 4

Milner Department Store has one cash register on which it performs daily cash counts. Recently, the cash count indicated that there was $9,218.47 in the register after deducting and removing the opening change amount of $50. However, the cash register tape reported sales in the amount of $9,217.85. Milner deposited its cash collected in its bank account.

Required:
Prepare a journal entry to record these cash collections.

Brief Exercise 4-25 Petty Cash Fund

OBJECTIVE ◀ 4

Cogsworth Inc. maintains a balance of $4,500 in its petty cash fund for routine purchases such as supplies. During the year, Cogsworth's employees paid for various office supplies and food purchases for office birthdays. As a result, Cogsworth's petty cash account has a balance of $432 on December 31. At the end of each year, Cogsworth replenishes the petty cash in full. Cogsworth classifies all petty cash transactions as miscellaneous expense.

Required:
What entry is made to record the replenishment of the petty cash fund?

OBJECTIVE 4 ▸ **Brief Exercise 4-26 Petty Cash with Change in Fund Balance**

Songbird Inc. maintains a petty cash fund with a balance of $2,225. During the month of September, Songbird's employees made routine expenses using cash from the petty cash fund totaling $1,005. At the end of September, Songbird replenishes the petty cash account, but it also decides to increase the fund balance to $2,400. Songbird classifies all petty cash transactions as miscellaneous expense.

Required:
What entry is made to record this activity?

OBJECTIVE 3 ▸ **Brief Exercise 4-27 Cash Reporting**

Blakely Industries has the following items:

Currency	$26,250
Customer checks that have not been deposited	700
U.S. government bonds that originally maturing in 3 months	13,000
U.S. government bonds that originally maturing in 12 months	14,000
Cash in saving and checking accounts	64,000
Certificates of deposits that originally maturing in 18 months	47,000

Required:
How much should Blakely report as cash and equivalents on its balance sheet?

OBJECTIVE 5 ▸ **Brief Exercise 4-28 Operating Cycle**

Businesses must decide whether to issue credit to customers.

Required:
CONCEPTUAL CONNECTION Describe how selling to customers on credit affects the operating cycle.

OBJECTIVE 5 ▸ **Brief Exercise 4-29 Cash Management**

Effective cash management is very important to the operating performance of a business.

Required:
CONCEPTUAL CONNECTION Explain the principles of cash management. Why might it be advantageous to delay paying suppliers?

EXERCISES

OBJECTIVE 1 2 ▸ **Exercise 4-30 Internal Control System**
Required:

A list of terms and a list of definitions and examples are presented below. Make a list numbered 1 through 5 and match the letter of the most directly related definition or example with the number of each term.

Term	Definition or Example
1. Strategic risk	a. A member of upper management was fired for violating the company's code of conduct.
2. Control environment	
3. Information and communication	b. The internal audit group is testing the operating effectiveness of various internal control activities.
4. Business process risk	c. Competitors begin offering extended warranty coverage on products.
5. Monitoring	d. Problems with our suppliers have resulted in lost sales because our stores were out of stock.
	e. Reports documenting problems with production are forwarded to management.

Exercise 4-31 Internal Control Terminology

OBJECTIVE ◄ 1 2

Required:

A list of terms and a list of definitions and examples are presented below. Make a list numbered 1 through 7 and match the letter of the most directly related definition or example with the number of each term.

Term	Definition or Example
1. Accounting controls	a. Company policy prevents accountants from handling cash.
2. Adequate documents and records	b. Company policy requires receiving reports to be made for all deliveries by suppliers.
3. Checks on recorded amounts	c. Cash deposits are reconciled with cash register records at the end of every day.
4. Effective personnel policies	d. This includes the accounting system, all policies and procedures of the business, and the environment in which they operate.
5. Internal control structure	e. Every evening, a jewelry store removes all items of merchandise valued at over $100 from its display.
6. Safeguards over assets and records	f. These are policies and procedures that govern the identification, measurement, recording, and communication of economic information.
7. Segregation of duties	g. Every new employee is required to spend 2 days in training courses to learn company policies.

Exercise 4-32 Classifying Internal Control Activities

OBJECTIVE ◄ 2

Required:

Match each of the control activities listed below with the most closely related type of control activity. Your answer should pair each of the numbers 1 through 10 with the appropriate letter.

Types of Control Activities
a. Adequate documents and records
b. Checks on recorded amounts
c. Clearly defined authority and responsibility
d. Safeguards over assets and records
e. Segregation of duties

Control Activities
1. Only the cashier assigned to the cash register is allowed to perform transactions.
2. Division managers are evaluated annually on the basis of their division's profitability.
3. Invoices received from outside suppliers are filed with purchase orders.
4. Employees with access to the accounting records are not permitted to open the mail because it contains many payments by check from customers.
5. The extent of access to the many segments of the company's computer system is tightly controlled by individual identification cards and passwords that change at regular intervals.
6. Each shipment to customers from inventory is recorded on a specially printed form bearing a sequential number; these forms are the basis for entries into the computer system, which makes entries to inventory records and produces periodic reports of sales and shipments.
7. At regular intervals, internal audit reviews a sample of expenditure transactions to determine that payment has been made to a bona fide supplier and that the related goods or services received and appropriately used.
8. A construction company stores large steel girders in an open yard surrounded by a 5-foot fence and stores welding supplies in a controlled-access, tightly secured concrete building.
9. Cash registers display the price of each item purchased to the customer as it is recorded and produce a customer receipt that describes each item and gives its price.
10. The person in the controller's office who prepares and mails checks to suppliers cannot make entries in the general ledger system.

OBJECTIVE

Exercise 4-33 Internal Control of Cash

Hannah Thatcher, a longtime employee of a local shoe store, is responsible for maintaining the company's cash records and for opening the daily mail, through which the company receives about 25% of its daily cash receipts. Virtually all cash received by mail is in the form of checks made payable to the company. Thatcher is also responsible for preparing deposits of currency and checks for the bank at the end of each day.

Required:

1. **CONCEPTUAL CONNECTION** Explain briefly how Thatcher might be able to steal some of the company's cash receipts.
2. **CONCEPTUAL CONNECTION** What internal control procedures would you recommend to prevent this theft?

OBJECTIVE

**SHOW
ME HOW**

Exercise 4-34 Cash Over and Short

Maestro Enterprises deposits the cash received during each day at the end of the day. Maestro deposited $47,845 on October 3 and $50,811 on October 4. Cash register records and other documents supporting the deposits are summarized as follows:

	10/3	10/4
Cash sales	$38,560	$43,170
Collections on account	8,380	7,655
Total receipts	$46,940	$50,825

Required:

1. Calculate the amount of cash over or cash short for each day.
2. Prepare the journal entry to record the receipt and deposit of cash on October 3.
3. Prepare the journal entry to record the receipt and deposit of cash on October 4.
4. **CONCEPTUAL CONNECTION** If you were the manager with responsibility over the cash registers, how would you use this information?

OBJECTIVE

**SHOW
ME HOW**

Exercise 4-35 Bank Reconciliation

Janie Corporation's bank statement for October reports an ending balance of $25,347, whereas Janie's cash account shows a balance of $23,963 on October 31. The following additional information is available:

a. A $765 deposit made on October 31 was not recorded by the bank until November.
b. At the end of October, outstanding checks total $2,334.
c. The bank statement shows bank service charges of $105 not yet recorded by the company.
d. The company erroneously recorded as $748 a check that it had actually written for $478. It was correctly processed by the bank.
e. A $350 check from a customer, deposited by the company on October 29, was returned with the bank statement for lack of funds.

Required:

1. Prepare the October bank reconciliation for Janie Corporation.
2. What amount will be reported as cash on the October 31 balance sheet?

OBJECTIVE

Exercise 4-36 Bank Reconciliation (Partial)

The cash account for Pitt Corporation contains the following information for June:

Cash balance, 5/31		$18,130
Cash received during June		42,650
		$60,780
Cash disbursements during June:		
Check 8255	$17,850	
Check 8256	22,375	
Check 8257	9,620	
Check 8258	2,735	52,580
Cash balance, 6/30		$ 8,200

The bank statement for April contains the following information:

Bank balance, 5/31		$34,525
Add: Deposits during June		42,650
		$77,175
Less: Checks paid during June:		
Check 8253	$ 1,720	
Check 8254	14,675	
Check 8255	17,850	
Check 8256	22,375	56,620
Bank balance, 6/30		$20,555

Required:

Assuming there were no deposits in transit at May 31 and that all outstanding checks at May 31 cleared during June, do the following:

1. Identify the outstanding checks at June 30.
2. Prepare the reconciliation of the bank and cash account balances at June 30.
3. Identify the outstanding checks at May 31.
4. Prepare the reconciliation of the bank and cash account balances at May 31.
5. **CONCEPTUAL CONNECTION** Why could you not perform the bank reconciliations without knowing that there were no deposits in transit on May 31 and that all outstanding checks at May 31 cleared during June?

Exercise 4-37 Bank Reconciliation

OBJECTIVE 4

Valentine Investigations has the following information for its cash account:

Balance, 1/31		$ 7,444
Deposits during February		106,780
Checks written during February		102,341

Valentine's bank statement for February contained the following information:

Balance per bank, 1/31		$ 8,910
Add: February deposits		104,950
		$ 113,860
Less:		
Checks paid in February	$(101,400)	
Bank service charge	(50)	
Debit memo (electric bill)	(800)	(102,250)
Balance per bank, 2/28		$ 11,610

A comparison of company records with the bank statement provided the following data:

	At 1/31	At 2/28
Deposits in transit	$2,750	$4,580
Outstanding checks	4,216	5,157

Required:

1. Prepare a bank reconciliation as of February 28.
2. Prepare adjusting entries for Valentine based on the information developed in the bank reconciliation.
3. What is the amount of cash that should be reported on the February 28 balance sheet?

Exercise 4-38 Bank Reconciliation

OBJECTIVE 4

Conway Company reported the following information:

Cash balance on balance sheet (12/31)	$22,066
Pre-reconciliation cash account balance (12/31)	23,916
Bank statement (12/31)	23,220

(Continued)

Bank service charges	$ 350
Bank debit memos (utility payments)	1,500
Deposits in transit (12/31)	9,160

Required:

1. Calculate the amount of outstanding checks as of December 31.
2. Prepare the adjusting entries that Conway must make at December 31.

OBJECTIVE **4**

Exercise 4-39 Adjusting Entries from a Bank Reconciliation

Hawk Enterprises identified the following items on its January reconciliation that may require adjusting entries:

a. A deposit of $1,190 was recorded in Hawk's accounting records, but not on the January 31 bank statement.
b. A check for $3,371 was outstanding at January 31.
c. Included with the bank statement was a check for $560 written by Eagle Corporation. The bank had, in error, deducted this check from Hawk's account.
d. Bank service charges were $375.
e. An NSF check written by one of Hawk's customers in the amount of $1,150 was returned by the bank with Hawk's bank statement. This customer was paying for merchandise originally purchased on account.

Required:

For each of these five items, prepare an adjusting entry for Hawk's journal, if any is required.

OBJECTIVE **4**

Exercise 4-40 Recording Petty Cash Account Transactions

During August, Peter Company engaged in the following transactions involving its petty cash fund:

a. On August 1, Peter Company established the petty cash fund by issuing a check for $1,250 to the fund custodian.
b. On August 4, the custodian paid $110 out of petty cash for freight charges on new equipment. This amount is properly classified as equipment.
c. On August 12, the custodian paid $145 out of petty cash for supplies. Peter expenses supplies purchases as supplies expense.
d. On August 22, the custodian paid $30 out of petty cash for express mail services for reports sent to the Environmental Protection Agency. This is considered a miscellaneous expense.
e. On August 25, the custodian filed a claim for reimbursement of petty cash expenditures during the month totaling $250.
f. On August 31, Peter issued a check for $285 to the custodian, replenishing the fund for expenditures during the month.

Required:

Prepare any journal entries required to record the petty cash account transactions that occurred during the month of August.

OBJECTIVE **3**

Exercise 4-41 Cash Reporting

Azul Industries has the following items:

Currency	$12,800
Customer checks that have not been deposited	830
Cash in saving and checking accounts	36,500
Certificates of deposits that originally matured in 18 months	46,000
U.S. government bonds that originally matured in 2 months	7,000
U.S. government bonds that originally matured in 12 months	12,000

Required:

How much should Azul report as cash and equivalents on its balance sheet?

Exercise 4-42 Components of Cash

The office manager for Stony Company had accumulated the following information at the end of a recent year:

Item	Amount
Accounts receivable	$22,470
Change for cash registers (currency and coin)	4,800
Amount on deposit in checking account (bank balance)	6,589
Amount on deposit in savings account (bank balance)	28,750
Balance in petty cash	500
Checks received from customers, but not yet deposited in bank	340
Checks sent by Stony to suppliers, but not yet presented at bank for payment	620
Deposits in transit	950
IOU from Richard Sandy, company president	10,000
Notes receivable	13,400
NSF check written by Liam Company	430
Prepaid postage	125

Required:

Calculate the total cash amount Stony will report on its balance sheet.

Exercise 4-43 Operating Cycle

Operations are often described as being cyclical in nature.

Required:

CONCEPTUAL CONNECTION Describe the cyclical nature of business activity.

Exercise 4-44 Operating Cycle

A list of businesses and a list of operating-cycle descriptions are presented below:

Business	Operating-Cycle Description
1. Tree nursery	a. Very short—customers typically pay cash, and inventory is often held less than 1 day.
2. Fast food restaurant	
3. Appliance store	b. A few months—merchandise is typically on hand for several weeks, and some customers may use credit.
4. Electric utility	
5. Clothing store	c. More than 1 year—merchandise may be in inventory for several months, and most customers will pay for purchases after 1 or 2 years.
	d. Several years—a number of years are required to prepare merchandise for sale. Customers probably pay cash for most items.
	e. A few months—customers pay monthly. The current assets used to provide customer services are consumed within a few months.

Required:

1. Match each business with a description of the operating cycle for that business.
2. **CONCEPTUAL CONNECTION** How does a longer operating cycle (such as Description c or d) change a company's financing needs relative to a shorter operating cycle (such as Description a)?

Exercise 4-45 Operating Cycle and Current Receivables

a. Dither and Sly are attorneys-at-law who specialize in federal income tax law. They complete their typical case in 6 months or less and collect from the typical client within 1 additional month.
b. Johnston's Market specializes in fresh meat and fish. All merchandise must be sold within one week of purchase. Almost all sales are for cash, and any receivables are generally paid by the end of the following month.

(Continued)

c. Mortondo's is a women's clothing store specializing in high-style merchandise. Merchandise spends an average of 7 months on the rack following purchase. Most sales are on credit, and the typical customer pays within 1 month of sale.

d. Trees Inc. grows Christmas trees and sells them to various Christmas tree lots. Most sales are for cash. It takes 6 years to grow a tree.

Required:

For each of the businesses described above, indicate the length of the operating cycle.

PROBLEM SET A

OBJECTIVE **1** **2**

Problem 4-46A Role of Internal Control

Internal control systems include policies and procedures designed to provide reasonable assurance that the corporation's objectives are being met in three areas: (a) effectiveness and efficiency of operations, (b) reliability of financial reporting, and (c) compliance with applicable laws and regulations. Like any other business, a grocery store uses internal control activities to meet their objectives in these three areas.

Required:

CONCEPTUAL CONNECTION Attempt to name a control for each area and describe how the control helps accomplish the store's objectives in these areas.

OBJECTIVE **2** **3**

Problem 4-47A Internal Control Procedures for Cash Receipts

Lee and Kim Cooper are planning to open and operate a clothing boutique in a newly developed subdivision. Lee and Kim are concerned that employees may try to pocket some of the cash collected from customers.

Required:

Identify some internal control procedures that could help ensure that no cash paid by customers is lost to theft.

OBJECTIVE **2** **3**

Problem 4-48A Internal Control for Cash

After comparing cash register tapes with inventory records, the accountant for Benning Convenience Stores is concerned that someone at one of the stores is not recording some of that store's cash sales and is stealing the cash from the unreported sales.

Required:

1. **CONCEPTUAL CONNECTION** Explain why a comparison of sales and inventory records would reveal a situation in which cash sales are not being recorded and cash from those sales is being stolen.
2. **CONCEPTUAL CONNECTION** Describe how an employee might be able to steal cash from sales.
3. **CONCEPTUAL CONNECTION** What internal control procedures would you recommend to make the theft you described in Requirement 2 more difficult?

OBJECTIVE **4**

Problem 4-49A Bank Reconciliation

SHOW
ME HOW

Shortly after July 31, Morse Corporation received a bank statement containing the following information:

Date		Checks			Deposits	Balance
6/30	Beg. balance					$ 7,107
7/1					$ 1,200	8,307
7/2		$ 620	$ 550	$ 344	12,500	19,293

(Continued)

7/3	35	8,100			11,158
7/5	311	97	4,000	9,100	15,850
7/9	4,500	790	286		10,274
7/12	34	7,100			3,140
7/15	634	1,880		7,000	7,626
7/19	3,780	414			3,432
7/24	1,492	649			1,291
7/29	350	1,486*		4,620	4,075
7/31	575	16**			3,484

*NSF check
**Bank service charge

July cash transactions and balances on Morse's records are shown in the following T-account:

Cash

Balance, 6/30	$ 6,758				
	Amount	Check	Check	Check	Check
Date	Deposited	Number	Amount	Number	Amount
7/1	$12,500	176	$8,100	186	$ 1,880
7/5	9,100	177	97	187	634
7/15	7,000	178	4,000	188	3,780
7/29	4,620	179	311	189	649
7/30	3,115	180	7,100	190	1,492
Total deposits	$36,335	181	4,500	191	52
		182	790	192	350
		183	34	193	575
		184	286	194	184
		185	414	195	1,022
Balance, 7/31	$ 6,843		Total disbursements		$36,250

Required:

1. Prepare a bank reconciliation for July.
2. Prepare the adjusting entries made by Morse Corporation as a result of this reconciliation process.
3. What amount is reported as cash on the balance sheet at July 31?

Problem 4-50A Bank Reconciliation

OBJECTIVE 4

Raymond Corporation received the following bank statement for the month of October:

Date		Checks			Deposits	Balance
9/30	Beg. balance					$ 4,831.50
10/2		$1,204.50			$2,970.18	6,597.18
10/4		43.80	$ 321.70			6,231.68
10/8		905.36				5,326.32
10/10		100.20	60.00	$38.11		5,128.01
10/13					4,000.00	9,128.01
10/14		290.45*				8,837.56
10/17		516.11	309.24			8,012.21
10/19		106.39	431.15	21.72	2,850.63	10,303.58
10/21		3,108.42				7,195.16
10/23		63.89				$ 7,131.27

(*Continued*)

Date	Checks		Deposits	Balance
10/25	290.00**	111.90		6,729.37
10/27	88.90			6,640.47
10/31	20.00***	1,308.77		5,311.70

*NSF check
**Debit memo (Rent Expense)
***Service charge

The cash records of Raymond Corporation provide the following information:

Date	Item	Debit	Credit	Balance
10/1	Balance from 9/30			$ 6,553.38
10/2	Check #1908		$ 321.70	6,231.68
10/5	Check #1909		905.36	5,326.32
10/6	Check #1910		100.20	5,226.12
10/6	Check #1911		60.00	5,166.12
10/7	Check #1912		38.11	5,128.01
10/12	Deposit #411	$4,000.00		9,128.01
10/15	Check #1913		516.11	8,611.90
10/16	Check #1914		309.24	8,302.66
10/17	Check #1915		431.15	7,871.51
10/17	Check #1916		21.72	7,849.79
10/18	Deposit #412	2,850.63		10,700.42
10/18	Check #1917		106.39	10,594.03
10/20	Check #1918		63.89	10,530.14
10/20	Check #1919		3,108.42	7,421.72
10/23	Check #1920		111.90	7,309.82
10/25	Check #1921		88.90	7,220.92
10/29	Check #1922		1,803.77	5,417.15
10/30	Check #1923		284.77	5,132.38
10/31	Check #1924		628.32	4,504.06
10/31	Deposit #413	3,408.20		7,912.26

The items on the bank statement are correct. The debit memo is for the payment by the bank of Raymond's office furniture rent expense for October.

Required:
1. Prepare a bank reconciliation. (*Hint*: There is one transposition error in the cash account.)
2. Prepare adjusting entries based on the bank reconciliation.
3. What amount is reported for cash in bank in the balance sheet at October 31?

OBJECTIVE 4

SHOW
ME HOW

Problem 4-51A Bank Reconciliation

The cash account of Dixon Products reveals the following information:

	Cash			
Balance, 4/30	11,800			
Deposits during May	37,600	41,620	Checks written during May	

The bank statement for May contains the following information:

Bank balance, 4/30		$ 11,750
Add: Deposits during May		37,250
		$ 49,000
Less: Checks paid during May	$(40,230)	
NSF check from Frolin Inc.	(190)	
Bank service charges	(40)	(40,460)
Bank balance, 5/31		$ 8,540

A comparison of detailed company records with the bank statement indicates the following information:

	At 4/30	At 5/31
Deposit in transit	$800	$1,150
Outstanding checks	750	2,140

The bank amounts are determined to be correct.

Required:
1. Prepare a bank reconciliation for May.
2. Prepare the adjusting entries made by Dixon as a result of the reconciliation process.
3. What amount is reported for cash on the balance sheet at May 31?

Problem 4-52A Recording Petty Cash Transactions

OBJECTIVE ◀ 4

Budding Products had a balance of $400 in cash in its petty cash fund at the beginning of November. The following transactions took place in November:

a. On November 1, the custodian paid $86 out of petty cash for new pens with Budding's newly designed logo prominently displayed. This is considered supplies expense.
b. On November 7, the custodian paid $138 out of petty cash for minor repairs to its equipment. This is a maintenance expense.
c. On November 9, the custodian paid $17 out of petty cash for transportation-in.
d. On November 15, the custodian paid $45 out of petty cash to have documents delivered to the accounting firm preparing the company's corporate tax return. This is considered an other expense.
e. On November 22, the custodian paid $91 out of petty cash to reimburse the Chief Financial Officer for costs he had incurred in traveling to the airport for an important international business conference. This is a travel expense.
f. On November 28, the custodian submitted receipts for the above expenditures and a check was drawn for the amount to replenish the fund.

Required:
Prepare any journal entries made by the corporation to record these transactions.

PROBLEM SET B

Problem 4-46B Role of Internal Control

OBJECTIVE ◀ 1 2

Internal control systems include policies and procedures designed to provide reasonable assurance that the corporation's objectives are being met in three areas: (a) effectiveness and efficiency of operations, (b) reliability of financial reporting, and (c) compliance with applicable laws and regulations. Like any other business, a bookstore uses internal control activities to meet its objectives in these three areas.

Required:
CONCEPTUAL CONNECTION Attempt to name a control for each area and describe how the control helps accomplish the store's objectives in these areas.

Problem 4-47B Internal Control Procedures for Cash Receipts

OBJECTIVE ◀ 2 3

Sean and Liz Kinsella are planning to open and operate a coffee shop on a university campus. Sean and Liz are concerned that part of the cash that customers pay for food might be kept by some of the store's employees.

(Continued)

Required:

CONCEPTUAL CONNECTION Identify some internal control procedures that could help ensure that all cash paid by customers is remitted to the business.

OBJECTIVE   **Problem 4-48B Internal Control for Cash**

After comparing cash register tapes with inventory records, the accountant for Good Times Music store is concerned that someone at one of the stores is not recording some of that store's cash sales and is stealing the cash from the unreported sales.

Required:

1. **CONCEPTUAL CONNECTION** Explain why a comparison of sales and inventory records would reveal a situation in which cash sales are not being recorded and cash from those sales is being stolen.
2. **CONCEPTUAL CONNECTION** Describe how an employee might be able to steal cash from sales.
3. **CONCEPTUAL CONNECTION** What internal control procedures would you recommend to make the theft you described in Requirement 2 more difficult?

OBJECTIVE   **Problem 4-49B Bank Reconciliation**

Shortly after July 31, Towanda Corporation received a bank statement containing the following information:

Date		Checks			Deposits	Balance
6/30	Beg. balance					$ 5,550
7/1					$ 300	5,850
7/2		$ 270	$ 150	$ 330	4,500	9,600
7/3		25	7,025			2,550
7/5		150	450	1,400	10,000	10,550
7/9		1,500	25	325		8,700
7/12		500	100			8,100
7/15		1,600	2,700		3,500	7,300
7/19		75	425			6,800
7/24		650	550			5,600
7/29			525*			5,075
7/31			25**			5,050

*NSF check (deposited in previous period, but withdrawn this period)
**Bank service charge

July cash transactions and balances on Towanda's records are shown in the following T-account:

Cash

Balance, 6/30	$ 5,550				
	Amount	Check	Check	Check	Check
Date	Deposited	Number	Amount	Number	Amount
7/1	$ 300	176	$ 270	186	$ 25
7/5	4,500	177	150	187	100
7/15	10,000	178	330	188	500
7/29	3,500	179	25	189	2,700
7/30	950	180	7,025	190	1,600
Total deposits	$19,250	181	150	191	75
		182	450	192	425
		183	1,400	193	550
		184	1,500	194	650
		185	325	195	275
Balance, 7/31	**$ 6,275**		Total disbursements		$18,525

Required:

1. Prepare a bank reconciliation for July.
2. Prepare the adjusting entries made by Towanda Corporation as a result of this reconciliation process.
3. What amount is reported as cash on the balance sheet at July 31?

Problem 4-50B Bank Reconciliation

OBJECTIVE ◀ 4

Donald Corporation received the bank statement shown below for the month of October:

Date		Checks			Deposits	Balance
9/30	Beg. balance					$ 5,205
10/2		$1,200			$2,950	6,955
10/4		50	$ 300			6,605
10/8		900				5,705
10/10		100	60	$35		5,510
10/13					4,000	9,510
10/14		300*				9,210
10/17		525	325			8,360
10/19		105	430	20	2,850	10,655
10/21		3,110				7,545
10/23		65				7,480
10/25		250**	110			7,120
10/27		90				7,030
10/31		25***	1,305			5,700

*NSF check
**Debit memo (Rent Expense)
***Service charge

The cash records of Donald Corporation provide the following information:

Date	Item	Debit	Credit	Balance
10/1	Balance from 9/30			$ 6,905
10/2	Check #1908		$ 300	6,605
10/5	Check #1909		900	5,705
10/6	Check #1910		100	5,605
10/6	Check #1911		60	5,545
10/7	Check #1912		35	5,510
10/12	Deposit #411	$4,000		9,510
10/15	Check #1913		525	8,985
10/16	Check #1914		325	8,660
10/17	Check #1915		430	8,230
10/17	Check #1916		20	8,210
10/18	Deposit #412	2,850		11,060
10/18	Check #1917		105	10,955
10/20	Check #1918		65	10,890
10/20	Check #1919		3,110	7,780
10/23	Check #1920		110	7,670
10/25	Check #1921		90	7,580
10/29	Check #1922		1,350	6,230
10/30	Check #1923		250	5,980
10/31	Check #1924		650	5,330
10/31	Deposit #413	3,300		8,630

(Continued)

The items on the bank statement are correct. The debit memo is for the payment by the bank of Donald's office furniture rent expense for October.

Required:
1. Prepare a bank reconciliation. (*Hint*: There is one transposition error in the cash account.)
2. Prepare adjusting entries based on the bank reconciliation.
3. What amount is reported for cash in bank on the balance sheet at October 31?

OBJECTIVE

Problem 4-51B Bank Reconciliation

SHOW ME HOW

The cash account of Mason Products reveals the following information:

Cash			
Balance, 4/30	10,100		
Deposits during May	39,600	40,000	Checks written during May

The bank statement for May contains the following information:

Bank balance, 4/30		$ 9,750
Add: Deposits during May		37,400
		$ 47,150
Less: Checks paid during May	$(38,500)	
NSF check from Higgins Inc.	(140)	
Bank service charges	(60)	(38,700)
Bank balance, 5/31		$ 8,450

A comparison of detailed company records with the bank statement indicates the following information:

	At 4/30	At 5/31
Deposit in transit	$900	$3,100
Outstanding checks	550	2,050

The bank amounts are determined to be correct.

Required:
1. Prepare a bank reconciliation for May.
2. Prepare the adjusting entries made by Mason Products as a result of the reconciliation process.
3. What amount is reported for cash on the balance sheet at May 31?

OBJECTIVE

Problem 4-52B Recording Petty Cash Transactions

Chicago Inc. had a balance of $1,200 in cash in its petty cash fund at the beginning of September. The following transactions took place in September:

a. On September 4, the custodian paid $90 out of petty cash for new stationery on which the company president's name appeared prominently. This is considered supplies expense.
b. On September 11, the custodian paid $225 out of petty cash for maintenance manuals for some equipment. This is a maintenance expense.
c. On September 15, the custodian paid $45 out of petty cash for transportation-in.
d. On September 23, the custodian paid $75 out of petty cash to have documents delivered to the lawyers who were defending the firm in a lawsuit. This is considered an other expense.
e. On September 27, the custodian paid $150 out of petty cash to reimburse the president for costs he had incurred when bad weather prevented the company jet from landing to pick him up after a meeting. This is a travel expense.
f. On September 30, the custodian submitted receipts for the above expenditures and a check was drawn for the amount to replenish the fund.

Required:
Prepare any journal entries made by the corporation to record these transactions.

CASES

Case 4-53 Ethics and Cash Controls

You have just been hired as a part-time clerk in a large department store. Each week you work three evenings and all day Saturday. Without the income provided by this job, you would be unable to stay in college. Charles Riley, the manager in the clothing department to which you are assigned, has worked for the store for many years. Managers receive both a salary and a commission on their sales.

Late one afternoon, just as you begin work, Mr. Riley is ringing up a purchase. You observe that the purchase consists of two expensive suits, a coat, and several pairs of trousers and that the customer declines Mr. Riley's offer to have the store's tailor do the alterations. After the customer departs with his merchandise and as Mr. Riley is departing for the evening, you say, "See you tomorrow." Mr. Riley gives a brief, barely audible response and departs for the evening.

As you return to the sales counter, you glance at the paper tape displayed through a small opening in the cash register that records all sales on an item-by-item basis. You have just completed the store course in register operation, so you are quite familiar with the register and the tape it produces. To your surprise, you note that the last sale consisted of just a single pair of trousers.

Required:

1. What do you conclude about this transaction?
2. What are the possible consequences for the store, for Mr. Riley, and for you personally of reporting your observations to Mr. Riley's superiors?
3. What are the possible consequences for the store, for Mr. Riley, and for you personally of *not* reporting your observations to Mr. Riley's superiors?
4. What would your decision be?

Case 4-54 The Operating Cycle

There are two retail stores in Millersburgh. One is a full-service store that typically sells on credit to its customers; the other is a smaller discount store that usually sells for cash. Full-service stores typically charge higher prices than discount stores for identical items.

Required:

1. Does the operating cycle suggest some economic reason for a portion of this price difference? Explain your answer.
2. **CONCEPTUAL CONNECTION** Can you think of other reasons why a full-service store might charge more than a discount store for the same merchandise?

Case 4-55 Internal Controls for Cash Disbursements

Campus Supply Store purchases merchandise on credit from a large number of suppliers. During the past 5 years, Campus's annual sales have grown from $100,000 to $1,500,000. A recent article in the local newspaper disclosed that an employee of another firm had been arrested for embezzling funds from his employer by diverting payments for purchases to his own bank account. Because of that article, the accountant for Campus has decided to examine Campus's procedures for purchases and payables.

Currently three different employees are authorized to order merchandise for the store. These employees normally complete paperwork provided by the suppliers' sales representatives, keeping a copy for their records. When the ordered merchandise arrives, whomever the delivery person can locate signs for the package. Bills are sent to the store by suppliers and are paid by Campus's accountant when due.

Required:

1. Indicate which general principles of internal control are violated by Campus's procedures for purchases and payables.
2. **CONCEPTUAL CONNECTION** Recommend procedures that would incorporate the five general categories of internal control where possible.

Case 4-56 Internal Controls for Collection of Receivables

Carolyn Furniture Galleries sells traditional furniture from two stores in St. Louis. Carolyn's credit terms allow customers to pay for purchases over 3 months with no finance charges. Carolyn's accountant has been responsible for approving customers for credit, recording cash received from customers in the accounting records, depositing cash collections in the bank, and following up on customers who are behind in their payments. Each month the accountant has prepared a report for Carolyn's president, indicating the cash collected, outstanding receivables, and uncollectible accounts.

Carolyn's president has been concerned about a significant increase in uncollectible accounts that began about 2 years ago, shortly after the current accountant was hired. Recently, a personal friend of Carolyn's president called. The caller had moved from St. Louis to Denver about 6 months ago. A month ago, the caller's new bank had refused a loan because a credit rating bureau in St. Louis had indicated that the caller had left bills unpaid at Carolyn Furniture. Carolyn's president knew that the caller had paid his account before leaving the community.

Carolyn's president called a detective agency and arranged for an investigation. Two weeks later, Carolyn's president was informed that the accountant had been spending much more money than his salary would warrant. Carolyn then called its auditor and arranged to have the accounting records for receivables and uncollectible accounts examined. This examination indicated that about $400,000 of cash had been stolen from the firm by the accountant. The accountant had identified customers who had moved and had recorded cash sales to continuing customers as credit sales in the accounts of the relocated customers. Carolyn's accountant had kept the cash received from the cash sales and had eventually written off the fictitious credit sales as uncollectible accounts. Without the accountant's knowledge, one of Carolyn's new employees had sent the names of the customers who had apparently defaulted on their accounts to the credit bureau.

Required:

CONCEPTUAL CONNECTION Identify the internal control weaknesses that permitted the accountant to steal the $400,000. Suggest internal control procedures that would make it difficult for someone else to repeat this theft.

Case 4-57 Cash Management

Hollis Corporation has the following budgeted schedule for expected cash receipts and cash disbursement.

Month	Expected Cash Receipts	Expected Cash Disbursements
July	$210,000	$200,000
August	280,000	210,000
September	230,000	190,000
October	160,000	180,000

Hollis begins July with a cash balance of $20,000, $15,000 of short-term debt, and no short-term investments. Hollis uses the following cash management policy:

a. End-of-month cash should equal $20,000 plus the excess of expected disbursements over receipts for the next month.
b. If receipts are expected to exceed disbursements in the next month, the current month ending cash balance should be $20,000.
c. Excess cash should be invested in short-term investments unless there is short-term debt, in which case excess cash should first be used to reduce the debt.
d. Cash deficiencies are met first by selling short-term investments and second by incurring short-term debt.

Required:

1. Calculate the expected buying and selling of short-term investments and the incurrence and repayment of short-term debt at the end of July, August, and September.
2. Discuss the general considerations that help accountants develop a cash management policy.

Case 4-58 Cash and Internal Controls

Identify a business with which you are familiar.

Required:

1. **CONCEPTUAL CONNECTION** Describe the ways in which it prevents theft of cash.
2. **CONCEPTUAL CONNECTION** Can you think of a way in which dishonest employees could circumvent the internal controls and steal cash?

Case 4-59 Researching and Analysis Using the Annual Report

Obtain **Microsoft's** June 30, 2019, 10-K either through the "Investor Relations" portion of its website (do a search for Microsoft investor relations) or go to www.sec.gov and click "Company Filings Search" under "Filings."

Required:

1. How much cash and equivalents and short-term investments did Microsoft hold as a percentage of total assets at the end of fiscal 2018 and 2019?
2. What is Microsoft's definition of a cash equivalent (see Note 1 under the "Financial Instruments" heading)? Does this appear consistent with other companies' definitions?
3. Look at Note 4 and specify how much of Microsoft's cash and cash equivalents balance is actually cash at the end of fiscal 2019. Other than cash, what items make up the cash and cash equivalent balance?
4. Locate the certifications required by the CEO and CFO under Section 302 of the Sarbanes-Oxley Act. (*Hint:* It is in Exhibits 31.1 and 31.2 at the end of the 10-K.) Who signed these certifications?

Case 4-60 Comparative Analysis: Kroger versus Sprout's Farmers Markets

Refer to the 10-K reports of **Kroger** and **Sprout's Farmers Markets** that are available for download from the companion website at Cengage.com.

(*Continued*)

Required:
1. How much cash and cash equivalents did Kroger and Sprouts hold as a percentage of total assets at the end of fiscal years 2018 and 2019?
2. **CONCEPTUAL CONNECTION** Describe the change in cash and cash equivalents as a percentage of total assets for Sprouts between 2018 and 2019. Speculate as to why this may have happened.
3. Locate the Auditor's Opinion on the effectiveness of internal controls over financial reporting and describe the steps the auditors took to audit the effectiveness of Kroger's and Sprouts's internal controls over financial reporting.

ANNUAL REPORT PROBLEM

HOME DEPOT

Download the 10-K for **Home Depot** that is available for download from the companion website at Cengage.com.

Required:
1. What does Home Depot report for the following accounts for the most current fiscal year?
   - Cash and cash equivalents
   - Short-term investments
   - Total assets
2. Assume that Home Depot projects the following:
   - Cash and cash equivalents will change by −1.0%.
   - Short-term investments will increase by 2%.
   - Total assets will increase by 4%.

   Assume that all other items remain unchanged from the prior year. Provide the next year's forecasted balances for the above accounts.
3. Which market risk factors are not listed in the 10-K?
4. Which section of the 10-K discusses internal control over financial reporting?
5. Who is responsible for maintaining Home Depot's internal control over financial reporting?
6. What type of opinion was given over internal control for financial reporting?

Note: *While the Annual Report problems in the textbook are static, when assigned in CNOW, these activities are algorithmic and the answers may vary from what appears in the Solutions Manual.*

CONTINUING PROBLEM

FRONT ROW ENTERTAINMENT

Over the next 2 months, Front Row Entertainment continued to enjoy success in signing artists and promoting their events. However, the increased business has put considerable stress on keeping timely and up-to-date financial records. In particular, both Cam and Anna are concerned with the accounting and management of the company's cash.

The tour promotion industry is a cash-intensive industry, normally requiring large prepayments to secure venues and arrange advertising. When the number of artists under contract was small, Cam and Anna developed a simple system to manage the company's cash. Normally, any cash received was put in a file cabinet in the company's office. If the amount appeared to be getting large, a deposit was made. Similarly, if a large check needed to be written, either Cam or Anna would check the balance in the checkbook.

If cash was not sufficient to cover the check, they'd get cash from the file cabinet and deposit the amount necessary to cover the check. However, with the increasing business, they would often forget to make deposits, causing several checks to be returned for non-sufficient funds. In addition, they were in the process of hiring additional office staff who would start work on May 1. They knew that leaving cash in a file cabinet would not be a good idea.

In order to obtain a better understanding of their cash position, Anna decides to perform a bank reconciliation—something she had failed to do since the company was started. According to the accounting records, the cash balance at April 30 was $7,495. Anna obtained the following information from Front Row's April bank statement and an analysis of canceled checks and deposits:

Balance per bank at April 30	$3,250
Deposits in transit at April 30	4,370
Outstanding checks as of April 30	1,160
Debit memo for April utilities	845
Bank service charge for April	50
Interest earned during April	450
NSF check from customer	590

Required:

1. **CONCEPTUAL CONNECTION** Discuss the purpose of an internal control system. How would the development of an internal control system benefit Front Row Entertainment? In your answer, be sure to highlight any problems that you noted with Front Row Entertainment's current system of accounting for cash.

2. Prepare a bank reconciliation for Front Row Entertainment for the period ending April 30, 2023.

3. Prepare any adjusting entries necessary because of the bank reconciliation.

4. **CONCEPTUAL CONNECTION** How did the failure to prepare a bank reconciliation affect the amounts reported on the previous financial statements?

5 Sales and Receivables

After studying Chapter 5, you should be able to:

1. Explain the criteria for revenue recognition.

2. Calculate net sales revenue.

3. Describe the principal types of receivables.

4. Record and properly present bad debt expense and the allowance for doubtful accounts.

5. Describe the cash flow implications of accounts receivable.

6. Record and properly present notes receivable from inception to maturity.

7. Describe internal control procedures for merchandise sales.

8. Analyze profitability and asset management using sales and receivables.

9. *(Appendix 5A)* Record and properly present receivables using the gross method.

Anutr Yossundara/Pond5

EXPERIENCE FINANCIAL ACCOUNTING

with Starbucks

Sales and cash flows are essential elements to any company's success. Consequently, investors and creditors carefully monitor a company's receivables to gain insight into the company's profitability and future cash flow. Investors and creditors expect companies to collect receivables relatively fast. This indicates that the company is efficient, because it is not "tying up" cash in receivables and has less risk of uncollectible accounts.

Analysts typically use the **accounts receivable turnover ratio** to compare companies' efficiency in collecting receivables. This ratio is calculated as follows:

Accounts Receivable Turnover = Net Sales ÷ Average Net Accounts Receivable

The following is the financial statement information needed to calculate the accounts receivable turnover for **Starbucks**.

(Amounts in millions)	2019	2018	2017
Receivables (net)	$ 879.2	$ 693.1	$870.4
Sales Revenue:			
Company-operated stores	21,544.4	19,690.3	
Licensed stores	2,875.0	2,652.2	
Foodservice	2,089.2	2,377.0	
Net Sales	**26,508.6**	**24,719.5**	

If an analyst makes the traditional turnover calculation with net sales in the numerator, Starbucks' would have an accounts receivable turnover ratio of 33.72 times per year for 2019 and 31.62 times per year for 2018. This is considerably higher (i.e., better) than the restaurant industry average of 26.43 times per year. However, it is always important to understand the company's business when computing any ratio. For example, these traditional ratios may be misleading for Starbucks, because its retail sales are primarily cash sales and its receivables arise almost entirely from licensing and foodservice activities. Therefore, to gain a clearer picture of Starbucks' receivables collection, analysts will often adjust the traditional accounts receivable turnover calculation by including only licensing and foodservice revenues in the numerator, as shown below:

2019: Accounts Receivable Turnover = ($2,875.0 + $2,089.2) ÷ (($879.2 + $693.1) ÷ 2) = 6.31

2018: Accounts Receivable Turnover = ($2,652.2 + $2,377.0) ÷ (($693.1 + $870.4) ÷ 2) = 6.43

Using the adjusted calculation, Starbucks turned its receivables over 6.31 and 6.43 times per year for 2019 and 2018, respectively. This means that Starbucks took 57.80 days on average (365/6.31) to collect accounts receivable in 2019 and 56.74 days in 2018. Over this two-year period, the speed of Starbucks' accounts receivable collection was relatively stable, but collection has slowed by approximately one day. Of course, the longer trend you have, the more you can learn about Starbucks' collection practices. If an analyst went back to 2012, he or she would discover that Starbucks' accounts receivable turnover has trended as shown in the following chart:

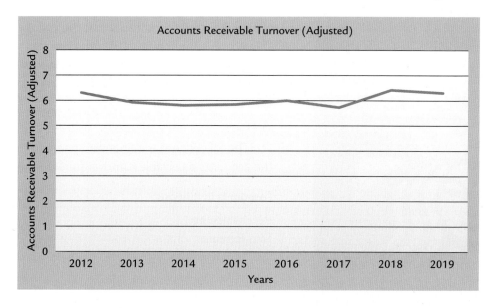

While Starbucks has not significantly improved its collection practices during this time period, it is good to see that collections are stable. This certainly would give analysts some confidence that there is little risk of emerging accounts receivable collections issues.

For many investors and creditors, revenue is the most scrutinized and important item reported in the financial statements. We will discuss two critical issues related to revenue: (1) the timing (e.g., is it revenue in 2022 or 2023) and (2) the appropriate amount of revenue to recognize.

OBJECTIVE

Explain the criterion for revenue recognition.

TIMING OF REVENUE RECOGNITION

As discussed in Chapters 1 and 2, companies typically make money by agreeing to provide a product to or perform a service for its customers in exchange for cash (or something else of value). Cash-basis accounting recognizes revenue in the period the cash is received (as on most individual tax returns). Accrual-basis accounting, on the other hand, recognizes revenue when the company's performance obligation is satisfied by transferring *control* of the promised good or service to the customer. The key concept is control. Control can pass either at a point in time or over time. While determining whether control passes over time or at a point in time can become complex, most of the time it is relatively straightforward and can be illustrated through the following examples.

Dick's Sporting Goods satisfies its performance obligation by letting you walk out of the store with the pair of shoes you just bought, thus giving you *control* of the shoes. Therefore, Dick's Sporting Goods recognizes revenue at the point of sale. For a service organization, the performance obligation is satisfied when the service is performed. For example, when **American Airlines** collects $450 in November for a flight to Mexico in March, it satisfies its performance obligation when the flight is provided in March. Therefore, American Airlines recognizes the revenue in March, when they provide the flight, not in November when the cash is collected.

However, sometimes revenue is recognized over time instead of at a point in time because control of the good or service is deemed to have passed over time. For example, if **Gold's Gym** collects $1,200 for a year-long membership in January, it is providing you with access to the gym each and every day. That is, each new day provides you with an additional benefit—it's up to you whether you take advantage of it! In this case, Gold's Gym should recognize $100 of revenue each month instead of $1,200 in January.

Revenue recognition for most sales transactions, like those in the previous paragraph, is relatively straightforward. Nevertheless, because some sales transactions can be complicated and businesses frequently attempt to recognize revenue too soon, the FASB has provided detailed guidance to "bring discipline" and, consequently, greater consistency to the revenue recognition process. However, we will leave discussion of these more complicated sales transactions for more advanced accounting courses and concentrate on the vast majority of the normal, everyday sales transactions. Specifically, service companies (such as airlines, accountants, lawn care services, etc.) recognize revenue in the period they provide the service to the customer, and sellers of goods recognize revenue in the period title passes to the customer.

ETHICAL DECISIONS Publicly traded corporations are under tremendous pressure to meet analyst targets for key financial-statement data, such as sales (and earnings per share). Many corporations, when faced with the reality of sales not meeting analysts' targets, resorted to a variety of practices to avoid such shortfalls. For example, **Bristol-Myers Squibb** was accused by the SEC of, among other things, "channel stuffing." In channel stuffing, companies ship more goods to a customer than the customer ordered near the end of a period. However, because sales are recognized at the time of shipment, all these sales are recorded in the current period. Of course, this practice will result in lower sales in the subsequent period when the customer returns the unwanted goods. ●

AMOUNT OF REVENUE RECOGNIZED

OBJECTIVE ◀ 2
Calculate net sales revenue.

The company should recognize revenue in the amount of consideration to which the company *expects* to receive in exchange for the goods or services provided. Typically, this is the cash received or the cash equivalent of the receivable. However, companies often induce customers to buy by modifying the terms of the sale. In this section, we discuss three modifications that affect the amount the company expects to collect: discounts, returns, and allowances.

SALES DISCOUNTS

To encourage prompt payment, businesses may offer a **sales discount**. This discount is a reduction of the normal selling price and is attractive to both the seller and the buyer. For the buyer, it is a reduction to the cost of the goods or services. For the seller, the cash is more quickly available and collection costs are reduced. For example, when cash is not available quickly, the seller may need to borrow money in order to pay its suppliers, employees, etc. The interest expense associated with borrowing money has a negative effect on net income.

Sales invoices use a standard notation to state discount and credit terms. For example, the invoice of a seller who expects payment in 30 days and offers a 2% discount if payment is made within 10 days would bear the notation 2/10, n/30. The notation n/30 indicates that the gross amount of the invoice (the full pre-discount amount) must be paid in 30 days. The notation 2/10 indicates that, if payment is made within the 10-day discount period, the amount owed is 2% less than the gross (pre-discount) amount of the invoice. This is referred to as the net price (e.g., net of the 2% discount). Of course, if payment is made after the end of the 10-day discount period, then the amount owed is equal to the gross (pre-discount) amount of the invoice.

Companies should record the revenue and associated receivable at the amount (gross or net) they expect to receive from the customer. For customers expected to take the discount, sales revenue should be recorded at the *net* amount. For customers not expected to pay in the discount period, sales revenue should be recorded at the *gross* amount. Because sales discounts typically offer terms that make it attractive to pay the net amount during the discount period (e.g., a 2% discount for paying 20 days early translates to a 36.5% annual rate of interest), conceptually a company should report sales revenue at a net price for most of its customers. We will illustrate the net method in EXAMPLE 5.1 and show the gross method in an appendix to this chapter.

EXAMPLE 5.1   RECORDING RECEIVABLES USING THE NET METHOD

On May 5, GCD Advisors billed Richardson's Wholesale Hardware $15,000 for consulting services provided during April. GCD offered terms of 2/10, n/30.

Required:

1. Prepare the journal entry to record the sale using the net method.
2. Prepare the journal entry assuming the payment is received on May 15 (within the discount period).
3. Prepare the journal entry assuming the payment is received on May 25 (after the discount period).

Solution:

1. When sales discounts are offered, the company should recognize revenue in the amount it *expects* to collect. Typically, this will be the net amount.

Date	Account and Explanation	Debit	Credit	Assets	= Liabilities +	Stockholders' Equity
May 5	Accounts Receivable*	14,700		▲		
	Sales Revenue*		14,700			▲

2.

Date	Account and Explanation	Debit	Credit	Assets	= Liabilities +	Stockholders' Equity
May 15	Cash*	14,700		▲		
	Accounts Receivable		14,700	▼		

3.

Date	Account and Explanation	Debit	Credit	Assets	= Liabilities +	Stockholders' Equity
May 25	Cash	15,000		▲		
	Accounts Receivable		14,700	▼		
	Sales Revenue**		300			▲

*$15,000 × 98%
**$15,000 × 2%

It is also important to monitor changes in how customers use sales discounts. For example, customers who stop taking sales discounts may be experiencing cash flow problems and therefore are potential credit risks. On the other hand, failure of a large number of customers to take discounts may indicate that an increase in the discount percentage is needed.

Finally, sales discounts must be distinguished from both trade and quantity discounts:

- A *trade discount* is a reduction in the selling price granted by the seller to a particular class of customers, for example, to customers who purchase goods for resale rather than for use.
- A *quantity discount* is a reduction in the selling price granted by the seller because selling costs per unit are less when larger quantities are ordered. This is why, for example, a 32-ounce soft drink does not cost double what a 16-ounce one costs at a restaurant.

For accounting purposes, the selling or invoice price is usually assumed to be the price after adjustment for the trade or quantity discounts; accordingly, trade and quantity discounts are not recorded separately in the accounting records.

SALES RETURNS AND ALLOWANCES

Occasionally, a customer will return goods as unsatisfactory. This is known as a **sales return**. In other cases, a customer will agree to keep goods that have minor defects, arrived late, or in some other way are rendered less valuable in return for a price reduction. It could be a service that was not completed on time, too. These are known as **sales allowances**. Sales returns and allowances should be recorded in the period of sale to correctly report sales revenue at the amount a company expects to collect. The problem is that for sales made near the end of the year, the return or allowance may not occur until the following period. Therefore, companies must estimate the amount of returns and allowances so that sales revenue can be reduced to their proper amounts. Sales returns will be discussed more fully in Chapter 6 when we introduce inventory, but we illustrate this concept with sales allowances in EXAMPLE 5.2 .

EXAMPLE 5.2   SALES ALLOWANCES

At year end, GCD Advisors has an Accounts Receivable balance of $1,000,000. Based on past experience, GCD Advisors estimates that allowances will be made for 0.2% of this balance.

The following January 18th, GCD grants an allowance of $1,500 to Metzler Enterprises as a result of a late shipment in December.

Required:

1. Calculate the amount of sales allowances GCD estimates will be made in the following year related to current year sales.
2. Prepare the adjusting journal entry to record the estimated sales allowances.
3. Prepare the journal entry to record GCD granting the allowance to Metzler Enterprises.

Solution:

1. $1,000,000 \times 0.002 = $2,000

2. Because the amount of revenue recognized should be the amount the company expects to collect, sales revenue for the current year should be reduced at the end of the period by the amount of estimated allowances.

Date	Account and Explanation	Debit	Credit	Assets	= Liabilities +	Stockholders' Equity
Dec. 31	Sales Revenue	2,000*				▼
	Returns and Allowances Liability		2,000		▲	

3. When allowances are made to specific customers, both the customers' receivable and the returns and allowances liability are reduced.

Date	Account and Explanation	Debit	Credit	Assets	= Liabilities +	Stockholders' Equity
Jan. 18	Returns and Allowances Liability	1,500			▼	
	Accounts Receivable		1,500	▼		

*$1,000,000 × 0.2%

If the bill has already been paid, the seller can either refund a portion of the purchase price and record a credit to cash or apply the allowance against future purchases by the customer by recording a credit to accounts receivable.

Management should look for unusual behavior in both sales revenue and sales returns and allowances. Often, significant changes in these accounts help to explain other changes in income statement or balance sheet accounts, as illustrated in the You Decide feature below.

YOUDECIDE   **Sales Returns and Allowances**

You are the Controller at Interplains Inc. Data for the past 4 years for sales revenue, sales returns and allowances, and net income are shown below.

	2020	2021	2022	2023
Sales revenue	$624,000	$653,000	$671,000	$887,000
Sales returns and allowances	6,100	6,400	6,300	14,800
Net income	30,000	29,000	31,500	12,200

What concerns are raised by the significant changes in sales revenue, sales returns and allowances, and net income in 2023?

Sales revenue, which had been relatively stable, increased by 32% in 2023. Often, significant growth in output is accompanied by quality assurance problems, as might be indicated by the 135% growth in sales returns and allowances. A check of production data might reveal the use of less highly trained workers or supervisors or might indicate that the current workforce is being worked heavily on overtime.

Further, notice the significant decrease in net income despite the large increase in sales revenue. When this happens, you must attempt to discover why. For example, when a firm becomes significantly more or less profitable, the attitude of the employees toward their work can change, causing changes in the quality of output. Some key employees may leave a firm with declining profitability, thus causing quality difficulties.

Significant changes in sales revenue, sales returns and allowances, and net income can indicate important changes or trends in the workforce or workflow and should be analyzed so that management can take appropriate action.

OBJECTIVE 3

Describe the principal types of receivables.

TYPES OF RECEIVABLES

Now that we've addressed the timing and measurement issues in revenue recognition, we will shift our attention to the accounting and analysis of the related receivables.

A receivable is money due from another business or individual. Receivables are typically categorized along three different dimensions:

- *Accounts Receivable or Notes Receivable:* A "note" is a legal document given by a borrower to a lender stating the timing of repayment and the amount (principal and/or interest) to be repaid. We discuss notes receivable later in the chapter. **Accounts receivable**, on the other hand, do not have a formal note. For example, while you likely signed a formal agreement to rent your apartment, you probably did not sign a formal agreement for your utilities.
- *Current or Noncurrent Receivables:* Although in practice both accounts and notes receivable are typically classified as current, accounts receivable are typically due in 30 to 60 days and do not have interest while notes receivable have interest and typically are due in anywhere from 3 to 12 months. Of course, if the due date is over 1 year, the note receivable typically will be classified as noncurrent.
- *Trade or Nontrade Receivables:* **Trade receivables** are due from customers purchasing inventory in the ordinary course of business while **nontrade receivables** arise from transactions not involving inventory (such as interest receivable or cash advances to employees).

OBJECTIVE 4

Record and properly present bad debt expense and the allowance for doubtful accounts.

ACCOUNTING FOR BAD DEBTS

We discussed the recognition of accounts receivable in the sales section, but an equally important concept is ensuring that the proper amount for accounts receivable is shown on the balance sheet. GAAP requires accounts receivable to be shown at their "net realizable value," which is the amount of cash the company expects to collect. Unfortunately, the amount of cash collected will almost never equal the total amount recognized in accounts receivable because some customers will not pay (e.g., a customer declares bankruptcy and ceases operations). When customers do not pay their accounts receivable, bad debts (also called uncollectible accounts) result. Although efforts are made to control bad debts, it is an expense of providing credit to customers. (The hope is that the increased business associated with providing credit will more than make up for the bad debts.)

As we saw in the previous section, sales revenues are reduced to reflect sales discounts as well as sales returns and allowances. Sales revenues are reduced in these situations because these transactions are the result of an action of the seller, such as acceptance of returned merchandise (a sales return) or price reductions offered to purchasers (sales discounts and allowances). Defaults on credit sales, on the other hand, arise from actions of the purchaser rather than the seller and, therefore, are not recorded as a reduction to revenue. If bad debts are not treated as a reduction to revenues, then they must be treated as expenses. And if they are expenses, the question arises as to when the expense should be recorded.

There are two methods to record **bad debt expense**: the direct write-off method and the allowance method.

DIRECT WRITE-OFF METHOD

The direct write-off method waits until an account is deemed uncollectible before reducing accounts receivable and recording the bad debt expense. As you recall, the expense recognition (or matching) principle requires expenses to be matched with the related revenues in the period in which the revenues are recognized on the income statement. Since accounts are often determined to be uncollectible in accounting periods subsequent to the sale period, the direct write-off method is inconsistent with the expense recognition principle and can only be used if bad debts are immaterial under GAAP.

ALLOWANCE METHOD

In the allowance method, bad debt expense is recognized in the period of sale, which allows it to be properly matched with revenues. The result is that bad debt expense is recognized before the actual default. Because defaults for the current period's sales have not yet occurred, the specific accounts receivable are not lowered; instead, an account is established to "store" the estimate until specific accounts are identified as uncollectible. This account is called **Allowance for Doubtful Accounts** as shown in EXAMPLE 5.3 .

Next Level

Why is the direct write-off method not GAAP?

ANSWER:
The direct write-off method fails to recognize the bad debt expense in the period it helped generate revenues, which is the period of sale, and does not show accounts receivable at net realizable value on the balance sheet.

EXAMPLE 5.3 ALLOWANCE FOR DOUBTFUL ACCOUNTS

At the end of the first year of operations, Hawthorne has an accounts receivable balance of $1,000,000. Although no customers have defaulted, Hawthorne estimates that $25,000 of that balance is uncollectible. At the end of the first year, Hawthorne would make the following adjusting entry:

Required:
1. Prepare the adjusting journal entry to record the uncollectible accounts.
2. How will Hawthorne's balance sheet report accounts receivable at December 31?

Solution:
1.

Date	Account and Explanation	Debit	Credit	Assets	= Liabilities +	Stockholders' Equity
Dec. 31	Bad Debt Expense	25,000				▼
	Allowance for Doubtful Accounts		25,000	▼		

2. Because no journal entry is made in the first period under the direct write-off method, Hawthorne's balance sheet would report the full $1,000,000 as accounts receivable at the end of the first year. Under the allowance method, however, accounts receivable would be presented as follows:

Accounts receivable	$1,000,000
Less: Allowance for doubtful accounts	(25,000)
Accounts receivable (net)	$ 975,000

When a specific account is ultimately determined to be uncollectible under the allowance method, it is *written off* by a debit to the allowance account and a credit to accounts receivable. This write-off removes the defaulted balance from the accounts receivable balance and from the estimate "storage" account—the allowance for doubtful accounts.

Under the allowance procedure, two methods commonly used to estimate bad debt expense are the *percentage of credit sales method* and the *aging method*.

PERCENTAGE OF CREDIT SALES METHOD The simpler of the two methods for determining bad debt expense is the **percentage of credit sales method**. Using past experience and management's views of how the future may differ from the past (for example, if credit policies change), it is possible to estimate the percentage of the current period's credit sales that will eventually become uncollectible. This percentage is multiplied by the total credit sales for the period to calculate the estimated bad debt expense for the period:

> Total Credit Sales × Percentage of Credit Sales Estimated to Default
> = Estimated Bad Debt Expense

The adjusting entry is then prepared to recognize the bad debt expense as shown in EXAMPLE 5.4 .

EXAMPLE 5.4   ESTIMATING BAD DEBT EXPENSE USING THE PERCENTAGE OF CREDIT SALES METHOD

Crimson Company has credit sales of $620,000 during the year and at the end of the year estimates that 1.43% of these credit sales will eventually default. Also, during the year, a customer defaults on a $524 balance related to goods purchased in the previous year. Prior to the write-off and the adjusting entry, Crimson's accounts receivable and allowance for doubtful accounts balances were $304,000 and $134 (credit), respectively.

Required:
1. Estimate the bad debt expense for the period.

2. Prepare the journal entry to record the write-off of the defaulted $524 balance.

3. Prepare the adjusting entry to record the bad debt expense for the year.

4. What is the net accounts receivable balance at the end of the year? How would this balance have changed if Crimson had not written off the $524 balance?

Solution:
1. The percentage of credit sales method is an Income Statement method used to estimate the ending balance in the income statement account—bad debt expense.

$$\$620,000 \times 0.0143 = \$8,866$$

2. When a customer defaults, the customer's receivable is lowered and the allowance for doubtful accounts is also lowered. Note that this journal entry has no effect on Net Accounts Receivable.

Date	Account and Explanation	Debit	Credit	Assets	= Liabilities +	Stockholders' Equity
Dec. 31	Allowance for Doubtful Accounts	524		▲		
	Accounts Receivable		524	▼		

3. The calculation in Part 1 estimated the *ending* balance of bad debt expense. This amount is also the adjustment because the balance before the adjustment is zero. This is usually the case for income statement accounts because they were closed at the end of the prior year.

Date	Account and Explanation	Debit	Credit	Assets	= Liabilities +	Stockholders' Equity
Dec. 31	Bad Debt Expense	8,866				▼
	Allowance for Doubtful Accounts		8,866	▼		

Bad Debt Expense

Preadjustment balance	0	
Adjustment	**8,866**	
Ending balance	8,866	

Allowance for Doubtful Accounts

		134	Beginning balance
Write-offs	524		
Preadjustment balance	390		
		8,866	**Adjustment**
		8,476	Ending balance

4.

	Year End	Assuming No Write-Off
Accounts receivable	$303,476*	$304,000
Less: Allowance for doubtful accounts	(8,476)**	(9,000)***
Net accounts receivable	$295,000	$295,000

*$304,000 − $524 = $303,476
**$134 − $524 + $8,866 = $8,476 (see T-account in Solution 3)
***T-account from Solution 3 without the $524 debit for the write-off

Note: Under the allowance method, the write-off of a specific account does not affect net accounts receivable.

Occasionally, accounts receivable that are written off are later partially or entirely collected. Suppose on February 5th of the following year, Crimson receives $25 of the $524 that was written off at the end of the previous year (see Requirement 2 of Example 5.4). Crimson would make the following entries:

Date	Account and Explanation	Debit	Credit	Assets	= Liabilities +	Stockholders' Equity
Feb. 5	Accounts Receivable	25		▲		
	Allowance for Doubtful Accounts		25	▼		
	Cash	25		▲		
	Accounts Receivable		25	▼		

Crimson's first entry reverses the appropriate portion of the write-off by restoring the accounts receivable and allowance for doubtful accounts balances. The second entry records the cash collection in the typical manner.

AGING METHOD Under the **aging method**, bad debt expense is estimated by determining the collectability of the accounts receivable rather than by taking a percentage of total credit sales. At the end of each accounting period, the individual accounts receivable are categorized by age.

Then an estimate is made of the amount expected to default in each age category based on past experience and expectations about how the future may differ from the past. As you may expect, the overdue accounts are more likely to default than the currently due accounts, as shown in the example below.

Accounts Receivable Age	Amount	Proportion Expected to Default	Amount Expected to Default
Less than 15 days	$190,000	1.0%	$1,900
16–30 days	40,000	4.0%	1,600
31–60 days	10,000	10.0%	1,000
Over 61 days	9,000	30.0%	2,700
	$249,000		$7,200

The total amount expected to default on year-end accounts receivable, $7,200 in the above example, is the amount that should be the ending balance in the allowance for doubtful accounts. Since the objective of the aging method is to estimate the ending balance in the allowance for doubtful accounts, any existing balance in the allowance account must be considered when determining the amount of the adjusting entry as shown in EXAMPLE 5.5.

EXAMPLE 5.5 ESTIMATING THE ALLOWANCE FOR DOUBTFUL ACCOUNTS USING THE AGING METHOD

On January 1, Sullivan Inc. has the following balances for accounts receivable and allowance for doubtful accounts:

Accounts receivable	$224,000 (debit)
Allowance for doubtful accounts	6,700 (credit)

During the year, Sullivan had $3,100,000 of credit sales, collected $3,015,000 of accounts receivable, and wrote off $60,000 of accounts receivable as uncollectible.

Required:
1. What is Sullivan's preadjustment balance in accounts receivable on December 31?

2. What is Sullivan's preadjustment balance in allowance for doubtful accounts on December 31?

3. Assuming Sullivan's analysis of the accounts receivable balance indicates that $7,200 of the current accounts receivable balance is uncollectible, by what amount will the allowance for doubtful accounts need to be adjusted?

4. What will be the ending balance in bad debt expense?

5. Prepare the necessary adjusting entry at year end.

Solution:

1.

Accounts Receivable			
Beginning balance	224,000		
Sales	3,100,000		
		3,015,000	Collections
		60,000	Write-offs
Preadjustment balance	249,000		

2.

Allowance for Doubtful Accounts				
		6,700	Beginning balance	
Write-offs	60,000			
Preadjustment balance	53,300			

3. The aging method is a balance sheet method and estimates the ending balance in the balance sheet account—allowance for doubtful accounts.

Allowance for Doubtful Accounts				
Preadjustment balance	53,300			
		60,500*	**Adjusting entry**	
		7,200**	Adjusted balance	

*Necessary adjustment to end up with an ending balance of $7,200.
**Estimate of ending balance determined by analyzing the receivables aging. This information was given in Requirement 3.

4. The preadjustment balance in bad debt expense is zero because all income statement accounts are closed to retained earnings at the end of the prior year.

Bad Debt Expense			
Preadjustment balance	0		
Adjustment	**60,500**		
Ending balance	60,500		

5.

Date	Account and Explanation	Debit	Credit	Assets	= Liabilities +	Stockholders' Equity
Dec. 31	Bad Debt Expense	60,500				▼
	Allowance for Doubtful Accounts		60,500	▼		

COMPARISON OF PERCENTAGE OF CREDIT SALES METHOD AND AGING METHOD The underlying difference between the percentage of credit sales method and the aging method is what is being estimated. The percentage of credit sales method is primarily concerned with appropriately estimating bad debt expense on the income statement. Because of the focus on the expense account, any existing balance in the allowance account is ignored when determining the amount of the adjusting entry. The aging method, on the other hand, is a balance sheet approach that analyzes the accounts receivable to estimate its net realizable value. This estimate provides the necessary ending allowance for doubtful accounts balance to report net accounts receivable at net realizable value.

BAD DEBTS FROM A MANAGEMENT PERSPECTIVE

Although bad debts result from actions of the purchaser (nonpayment), the amount of bad debt expense is influenced by the credit policies of the seller, as the You Decide feature below illustrates.

! Next Level

What are the conceptual and practical differences between the percentage of credit sales and aging methods?

ANSWER:
The percentage of credit sales method estimates the amount to be shown as bad debt expense on the income statement. The aging method estimates the amount to be shown as the allowance for doubtful accounts on the balance sheet. The preadjustment balance in these accounts must be adjusted so that the ending balance equals the respective estimates. However, because bad debt expense is an income statement account that is closed to retained earnings at the end of every period, its preadjustment balance should be zero. As such, the adjustment is equal to the estimate of the ending balance. The allowance for doubtful accounts, on the other hand, is a balance sheet account and will typically have an existing balance.

YOUDECIDE   Are Bad Debts Always Bad?

You are the owner/operator of Mt. Sterling Drug Company, a pharmaceutical wholesaler. In response to Mt. Sterling's "cash only" sales terms, competitors have attempted to lure business away by offering various incentives. Among these are credit terms whereby a customer typically has 30 to 60 days to pay for a purchase and receives a 1% to 2% discount for prompt payment (usually within 10 days of sale).

Which is worse, the potential bad debts that come with offering credit or the lost business from not offering credit?

There is no question that the inability to collect an account receivable is a serious problem. However, most wholesalers have come to accept bad debts as just another business expense. Certainly, no company would grant credit knowing that the specific customer will not pay for the goods purchased. Nonetheless, granting credit is a "necessary evil"—something that must be done to generate repeat business and maintain a competitive position.

An existing relationship with customers does not guarantee future business, especially if the customers can get a better deal elsewhere. Further, prudent screening of each customer's credit history should enable you to identify some of those who may have difficulty paying their accounts. Placing restrictions such as relatively low credit limits on these risky accounts or, in some cases, denying credit altogether should help keep bad debts to a minimum.

Suppose Mt. Sterling's gross margin is 30% of sales and that, as a result of the more liberal credit policy, sales increase by $100,000 and bad debts are limited to 3% of the new credit sales. Then Mt. Sterling's income from operations should increase by $27,000 (increased gross margin of $30,000 minus bad debt expense of $3,000), rather than decreasing.

When caution is used, most companies agree that the loss of business from not offering credit is more detrimental than the bad debt expenses incurred in doing so.

OBJECTIVE

Describe the cash flow implications of accounts receivable.

CASH MANAGEMENT PRINCIPLES RELATED TO ACCOUNTS RECEIVABLE

We now will focus on the cash management principles associated with accounts receivable.

FACTORING RECEIVABLES

In Chapter 4, we mentioned that a principle of cash management is increasing the speed of cash collection for receivables. An increasingly common practice is to **factor**, or sell, receivables. When receivables are factored, the seller receives an immediate cash payment reduced by the factor's fees. The factor, the buyer of the receivables, acquires the right to collect the receivables and the risk of uncollectibility. In a typical factoring arrangement, the sellers of the receivables have no continuing responsibility for their collection.

Factoring arrangements vary widely, but typically the factor charges a fee ranging from 1% to 3%. This fee compensates the factor for the time value of money (i.e., interest), the risk of uncollectibility, and the tasks of billing and collection. Large businesses and financial institutions frequently package factored receivables as financial instruments or securities and sell them to investors. This process is known as **securitization**. For example, **General Motors Acceptance Corporation (GMAC)** sells car loans to special financial institutions set up by investment banks. The financial institutions pay GMAC with funds raised from the sale of securities or notes, called certificates for automobile receivables (CARs). Banks use similar arrangements to package their credit card receivables into securities called certificates for amortizing revolving debts (CARDs).

CREDIT CARDS

Bank **credit cards**, such as **Visa** and **MasterCard**, are really just a special form of factoring. The issuer of the credit card (i.e., the bank) pays the seller the amount of each sale minus a service charge (on the date of purchase) and then collects the full amount of the sale from the buyer (at some later date).[1] For example, if a retail customer uses a **Citibank** Visa Card to pay $100 for a haircut, the salon would make the following entries assuming Citibank charges a 1.55% service charge:

Account and Explanation	Debit	Credit	Assets	= Liabilities +	Stockholders' Equity
Cash	98.45		▲		
Service Charge Expense	1.55				▼
Sales Revenue		100.00			▲

Although a 1.55% service charge may seem expensive, credit card sales provide sellers with a number of advantages over supplying credit directly to customers, including the following:

- Sellers receive the money immediately.
- Sellers avoid bad debts because as long as the credit card verification procedures are followed, the credit card company absorbs the cost of customers who do not pay.
- Recordkeeping costs decrease because employees are not needed to manage these accounts.
- Sellers believe that by accepting credit cards their sales will increase. For example, how many customers have driven away from a gas station that does not accept credit cards or even one that merely does not allow customers to pay at the pump?

Of course, many large retailers are willing to take on these costs to avoid the credit card service charge. For example, **Sears**, **Kohls**, **Target**, **Macy's**, and most other large retailers have internal credit cards. When these cards are used, the seller records it like any other accounts receivable and no service charge expense is incurred; however, they are accepting the risk of uncollectible accounts and the cost of servicing these accounts.

Nonbank credit cards, such as **American Express**, also result in a receivable for the seller because the issuer of the credit card (American Express) does not immediately pay the cash to the seller. American Express also charges a higher service charge to the seller. Consequently, sellers find American Express to be more costly than bank cards, such as **Visa** or **MasterCard**, which explains why many businesses do not accept American Express.

DEBIT CARDS

A **debit card** authorizes a bank to make an immediate electronic withdrawal (debit) from the holder's bank account. The debit card is used like a credit card except that a bank electronically reduces (debits) the holder's bank account and increases (credits) the merchant's bank account for the amount of a sale made on a debit card.

Debit cards appear to be somewhat disadvantageous to the card holder as transactions cannot be rescinded by stopping payment. Further, a purchase using a debit card causes an immediate reduction in a bank account balance, while a check written at the same time will require at least 1 or 2 days to clear, allowing the depositor to benefit from the additional money in the account until the check is presented at the bank for payment. However, debit cards offer significant advantages to banks and merchants in reduced transaction-processing costs. Thus, banks and merchants have incentive to design debit cards that minimize or eliminate the disadvantages and costs to card users.

NOTES RECEIVABLE

OBJECTIVE 6

Record and properly present notes receivable from inception to maturity.

Notes receivable are receivables that generally specify an interest rate and a maturity date at which any interest and principal must be repaid. Our discussion here is limited to simple notes that specify the repayment of interest and principal in a single payment on a given day (more complicated notes are described in Chapter 10).

---

1 The bank may also pay the full amount of the sale to the seller and then bill the service charge at the end of the period.

The amount lent is the **principal**. The excess of the total amount of money collected over the amount lent is called **interest**. For example, as shown in Exhibit 5.1, if **Caterpillar** lends $500,000 to a customer and is repaid $580,000 at some later date, then $80,000 of interest was collected.

EXHIBIT 5.1   **Principal and Interest in Loan Repayments**

Principal ($500,000)   Interest ($80,000)

Total Amount Collected ($580,000)

Interest can be considered compensation paid to the lender for giving up the use of resources for the period of a note (the time value of money). The interest rate specified in the note is an annual rate. Therefore, when calculating interest, you must consider the duration of the note using the following formula:

$$\text{Interest} = \text{Principal} \times \text{Annual Interest Rate} \times \text{Fraction of 1 Year}$$

For the example illustrated in Exhibit 5.1, what was the annual interest rate? The answer is that we have no way of knowing because the duration of the loan was not specified. If the duration of the loan was exactly 1 year, then the annual rate was 16%. If the duration was more (or less) than 1 year, however, then the annual rate is less (or more) than 16%.

Further, you will recall from Chapter 2 that expense and revenue recognition require that expenses and revenues be identified with specific accounting periods. If only 1 month of interest has been incurred by year end, an adjusting entry is required to recognize interest income and a corresponding interest receivable. Any remaining interest is recognized in subsequent periods.[2] The accounting for notes receivable is demonstrated in EXAMPLE 5.6.

---

2   Interest is, in fact, often computed in terms of days rather than months. Suppose, for example, that the 3-month note runs for 92 days (two 31-day months and one 30-day month). The total interest on the 92-day note would be $302.47 [($10,000)(0.12)(92/365)], and the first 31-day month's interest would be $101.92 [($10,000)(0.12)(31/365)]. Observe that daily interest complicates the arithmetic associated with interest calculations but does not alter the basic form of the calculations. To simplify interest computations, we will use monthly interest throughout the book.

EXAMPLE 5.6 ACCOUNTING FOR NOTES RECEIVABLE

Dover Electric Company purchased, on account, $50,000 of consulting services from Thomas Ltd. on November 1, 2023. The amount is due in full on January 1, 2024. Dover Electric is unable to pay the account by the due date and negotiates an extension with a 10% note in lieu of the unpaid account receivable.

Required:
1. Prepare Thomas's journal entries to record the sale on November 1, 2023, and the modification of payment terms on January 1, 2024.
2. How much interest will be paid if Dover Electric repays the note on (a) July 1, 2024, (b) December 31, 2024, or (c) March 31, 2025?
3. Prepare Thomas's adjusting entry to accrue interest on December 31, 2024, assuming the note is repaid on March 31, 2025.
4. Prepare Thomas's journal entries to record the cash received to pay off the note and interest on each of the three dates specified in Requirement 2.

Solution:

1.

Date	Account and Explanation	Debit	Credit	Assets	= Liabilities +	Stockholders' Equity
Nov. 1, 2023	Accounts Receivable	50,000		▲		
	Sales Revenue		50,000			▲

Date	Account and Explanation	Debit	Credit	Assets	= Liabilities +	Stockholders' Equity
Jan. 1, 2024	Notes Receivable	50,000		▲		
	Accounts Receivable		50,000	▼		

2. Interest = Principal × Annual Interest Rate × Fraction of 1 Year

(a) July 1, 2024:	(b) Dec. 31, 2024:	(c) March 31, 2025:
= $50,000 × 10% × (6/12)	= $50,000 × 10% × (12/12)	= $50,000 × 10% × (15/12)
= $2,500	= $5,000	= $6,250

3. Interest income is recognized in the period incurred.

Date	Account and Explanation	Debit	Credit	Assets	= Liabilities +	Stockholders' Equity
Dec. 31, 2024	Interest Receivable	5,000		▲		
	Interest Income		5,000			▲

4.

Date	Account and Explanation	Debit	Credit	Assets	= Liabilities +	Stockholders' Equity
July 1, 2024	Cash	52,500		▲		
	Notes Receivable		50,000	▼		
	Interest Income		2,500			▲

Date	Account and Explanation	Debit	Credit	Assets	= Liabilities +	Stockholders' Equity
Dec. 31, 2024	Cash	55,000		▲		
	Notes Receivable		50,000	▼		
	Interest Income		5,000			▲

Date	Account and Explanation	Debit	Credit	Assets	= Liabilities +	Stockholders' Equity
Mar. 31, 2025	Cash	56,250		▲		
	Notes Receivable		50,000	▼		
	Interest Receivable		5,000	▼		
	Interest Income		1,250			▲

Describe internal control procedures for merchandise sales.

INTERNAL CONTROL FOR SALES

Since sales revenues have a significant effect on a company's net income, internal control procedures must be established to ensure that the amounts reported for these items are correct. For sales revenues, these controls normally involve the following documents and procedures:

- Accounting for a sale begins with the receipt of a purchase order or some similar document from a customer. The order document is necessary for the buyer to be obligated to accept and pay for the ordered goods.
- Shipping and billing documents are prepared based on the order document. Billing documents are usually called *invoices*.
- A sale and its associated receivable are recorded only when the order, shipping, and billing documents are all present.

As illustrated in Exhibit 5.2, sales revenue should be recorded only when these three control documents are completed. When any of these three internal controls is not present, it is possible for valid sales to be unrecorded and for invalid sales to be recorded.

For sales returns and allowances, internal control procedures must be established that identify the conditions and documentation required before a sales return or a sales allowance can be recorded. These controls protect the firm from unwarranted reductions in revenues and receivables.

EXHIBIT 5.2   **Internal Controls for Recording Sales Revenue**

PURCHASE ORDER   No. R450

Richardson's Wholesale Hardware

Date: Sept. 1, 2023

To:

Bolt Manufacturing

QTY.	DESCRIPTION	PRICE	AMOUNT
30	Model No. SB100 snowblower	$500	$15,000

Ordered by: Jim Richardson

Jim Richardson

Purchase order number must appear on all shipments and invoice.

SHIPPING REPORT   No. B275

Bolt Manufacturing

Date: Sept. 1, 2023

To:

Richardson's Wholesale Hardware

QTY.	DESCRIPTION
30	Model No. SB100 snowblower

Purchase order: R450

INVOICE   No. B100

Bolt Manufacturing

Date: Sept. 1, 2023

Sold to:

Richardson's Wholesale Hardware

Purchase order: R450

QTY.	DESCRIPTION	PRICE	AMOUNT
30	Model No. SB100 snowblower	$500	$15,000

SUBTOTAL	$15,000
SALES TAX	0
SHIPPING & HANDLING	0
TOTAL DUE	$15,000

Date	Account and Explanation	Debit	Credit
Sept. 1	Accounts Receivable	15,000	
	Sales Revenue		15,000

ANALYZING SALES AND RECEIVABLES

OBJECTIVE 8▶

Analyze profitability and asset management using sales and receivables.

Analysts of the financial statements are extremely concerned with both sales and receivables.

SALES

Because sales revenue is such a key component of a company's success, analysts are interested in a large number of ratios that incorporate sales. Many of these ratios attempt to measure the return the company is earning on sales. These are called **profitability ratios**. For example, the ratios of income statement subtotals such as gross margin, operating income, and net income to sales are examined, but really any income statement subtotal deemed important can be of interest. The three most common ratios are gross profit margin, operating margin, and net profit margin:

$$\text{Gross Profit Margin} = \frac{\text{Gross Profit}}{\text{Net Sales}}$$

$$\text{Operating Margin} = \frac{\text{Operating Income}}{\text{Net Sales}}$$

$$\text{Net Profit Margin} = \frac{\text{Net Income}}{\text{Net Sales}}$$

Each of these ratios reveals information about a company's strategy and the competition it faces. For example, consider two large players in the retail industry—**Wal-Mart** and **Nordstrom**. Information available indicates that these two stores possess the following 5-year averages for these ratios:

	Wal-Mart	Nordstrom
Gross profit percentage	25.2%	36.1%
Operating margin percentage	4.39%	5.88%
Net profit margin percentage	2.4%	3.2%

Nordstrom's higher gross profit percentage suggests that Nordstrom is able to charge a premium on its merchandise. That is, Nordstrom follows a product differentiation strategy in which it tries to convince customers that its products are superior, distinctive, etc. **Wal-Mart**, on the other hand, is a low-cost provider who attempts to convince customers that it offers the lowest prices.

Analysts also like to look at the operating margin and net profit margin percentages to see how much is left from a sales dollar after paying for the product and all its operations. For these ratios, **Nordstrom** still retains a larger percentage of each sales dollar than **Wal-Mart**. How is it, then, that Wal-Mart makes so much money? It has a lot of sales dollars—its net sales revenue of $524.0 billion in 2019 is approximately 34 times greater than Nordstrom's $15.5 billion.

RECEIVABLES

Analysts are also concerned with asset management. Asset management refers to how efficiently a company is using the resources at its disposal. One of the most widely used asset management ratios is accounts receivable turnover:

$$\text{Accounts Receivable Turnover} = \frac{\text{Net Sales}}{\text{Average Net Accounts Receivable}}$$

This ratio provides a measure of how many times average trade receivables are collected during the period. In theory, net credit sales would be a much better numerator, but that figure is not normally disclosed. A higher number is better because it indicates that the company is more quickly collecting cash (through sales) from its inventory. As discussed in Chapter 4's section on cash management, this holds down borrowing costs and allows for a greater investment. Changes in this ratio over time are also very important. For example, a significant reduction in receivables turnover may indicate that management is extending credit to customers who are not paying.

Accounts receivable turnover for **Wal-Mart** and **Nordstrom** is:

	Wal-Mart	Nordstrom
Accounts receivable turnover	83.39	94.95

The average account receivables turnover for the Retail Industry is 80.86, so both Wal-Mart and Nordstrom are doing better than the industry average. That said, the retail industry is primarily a cash industry, because even when you pay with a credit card, the retailer receives cash immediately from the bank that owns the credit card. When the retailer uses an internal credit card, however, accounts receivable turnover will decrease because cash is not received until the customer pays their credit card bill. For example, Nordstrom's accounts receivable turnover was 11.54 prior to selling its credit card to TD Bank in 2015. EXAMPLE 5.7 illustrates the calculation of these ratios for Wal-Mart.

EXAMPLE 5.7   CALCULATING THE GROSS PROFIT MARGIN, OPERATING MARGIN, NET PROFIT MARGIN, AND ACCOUNTS RECEIVABLE TURNOVER RATIOS

The following information (in millions) is available for **Wal-Mart** for its fiscal year ending January 31, 2020:

Net sales	$523,964	Accounts receivable, 1/31/20	$6,284
Gross profit	129,359	Accounts receivable, 1/31/19	6,283
Operating income	20,568		
Net income	14,881		

Required:
Compute the (1) gross profit margin, (2) operating margin, (3) net profit margin, and (4) accounts receivable turnover for Wal-Mart for fiscal 2020.

Solution:

1.
$$\text{Gross Profit Margin Ratio} = \frac{\text{Gross Profit}}{\text{Net Sales}}$$
$$= \frac{\$129,359}{\$523,964} = 0.2469 \text{ or } 24.69\%$$

2.
$$\text{Operating Margin Ratio} = \frac{\text{Operating Income}}{\text{Net Sales}}$$
$$= \frac{\$20,568}{\$523,964} = 0.0393 \text{ or } 3.93\%$$

3.
$$\text{Net Profit Margin Ratio} = \frac{\text{Net Income}}{\text{Net Sales}}$$
$$= \frac{\$14,881}{\$523,964} = 0.0284 \text{ or } 2.84\%$$

4.
$$\text{Accounts Receivable Turnover Ratio} = \frac{\text{Net Sales}}{\text{Average Net Accounts Receivable}}$$
$$= \frac{\$523,964}{(\$6,284 + \$6,283) \div 2} = 83.39$$

APPENDIX 5A: RECORDING RECEIVABLES USING THE GROSS METHOD

OBJECTIVE 9

(Appendix 5A) Record and properly present receivables using the gross method.

As stated in earlier in the chapter, companies should record revenue at the amount they expect to receive from the customer. That is, a company should use the net method when the customer *is* expected to pay within the discount period and the gross method when the customer *is not* expected to pay within the discount period. While we expect this will result in the net method being the conceptually appropriate method for most customers, the gross method does have some practical advantages. For example, it simplifies communication with the customer because discussions are typically based on the gross amount. Regardless of the method used, the sales revenue reported on the income statement should reflect the amount expected to be collected from the customer. We will now illustrate the gross method using the same example used in Example 5.1.

On May 5, GCD Advisors billed Richardson's Wholesale Hardware $15,000 for consulting services provided during April. GCD offered terms of 2/10, n/30. If GDC uses the gross method, the following journal entry is made at the time of billing:

Date	Account and Explanation	Debit	Credit	Assets	= Liabilities +	Stockholders' Equity
May 5	Accounts Receivable	15,000		▲		
	Sales Revenue		15,000			▲

If, as anticipated, Richardson pays after the 10-day discount period (e.g., May 25), the following journal entry is made:

Date	Account and Explanation	Debit	Credit	Assets	= Liabilities +	Stockholders' Equity
May 25	Cash	15,000		▲		
	Accounts Receivable		15,000	▼		

If, however, Richardson were to pay within the 10-day discount period (e.g., May 15), the following journal entry would be made:

Date	Account and Explanation	Debit	Credit	Assets	= Liabilities +	Stockholders' Equity
May 15	Cash*	14,700		▲		
	Sales Revenue**	300				▼
	Accounts Receivable		15,000	▼		

*$15,000 × 98%
**$15,000 × 2%

It is important to note that sales revenues are reduced when the gross method is used and the discount is taken. This is conceptually similar to sales revenues being increased when the net method is used and the discount is not taken as shown in Example 5.1.

REVIEW CENTER

LO1. Explain the criterion for revenue recognition.

KEY TAKEAWAYS

- Revenue is recognized when the performance obligation has been satisfied.
- The performance obligation has been satisfied when delivery has occurred or services have been provided.

LO2. Calculate net sales revenue.

KEY TAKEAWAYS

- The appropriate amount of revenue to recognize is generally the cash received or the cash equivalent of accounts receivable.
- Companies often induce customers to buy by offering the following:
  - Sales discounts
  - Sales returns
  - Sales allowances
- Sales discounts are reductions of the normal selling price to encourage prompt payment.
- Sales returns occur when a customer returns goods as unsatisfactory.
- Sales allowances occur when a customer agrees to keep goods with minor defects if the seller reduces the selling price.
- Reductions in payments by customers due to discounts, returns, and allowances reduce sales revenue.

KEY TERM

Sales allowances, 273
Sales discount, 271
Sales returns, 273

EXAMPLES

| EXAMPLE 5.1 | Recording receivables using the net method, page 272 |
| EXAMPLE 5.2 | Sales allowances 273 |

LO3. Describe the principal types of receivables.

KEY TAKEAWAY

- Receivables are classified along three different dimensions:
  - Accounts and notes receivable
  - Trade and nontrade receivables
  - Current and noncurrent receivables

KEY TERMS

Accounts receivable, 274
Nontrade receivables, 274
Trade receivables, 274

KEY TAKEAWAYS

LO4. Record and properly present bad debt expense and the allowance for doubtful accounts.

- The primary issues in accounting for accounts receivable are when and how to measure bad debts (i.e., accounts that will not be paid).
- GAAP requires receivables to be shown at net realizable value on the balance sheet.
- The matching principle says that an expense should be recognized in the period in which it helps generate revenues.
- We must estimate and recognize bad debt expense in the period the sale is made—even though we do not know which accounts will be uncollectible.
- The estimate is made by using either of the following:
  - The percentage of credit sales method
  - The aging method
- The percentage of credit sales method estimates the bad debt expense directly.
- The aging method estimates the ending balance needed in the allowance for doubtful accounts, and bad debt expense follows.

KEY TERMS

Allowance for doubtful accounts, 275
Bad debt expense, 275
Percentage of credit sales method, 276
aging method, 277

KEY CALCULATIONS

Estimated Bad Debt Expense (*Percentage of Credit Sales Method*) =
Total Credit Sales × Percentage of Credit Sales Estimated to Default, 276

Estimated Bad Debt Expense (Aging Method), 276:
    Step 1: Amount Uncollectible by Age = Sales by Age Category (e.g., 31–60 days old) ×
        Percentage Estimated to be Uncollectible
    Step 2: Estimate of Ending Balance in Allowance = Sum of Amounts Uncollectible for All
        Age Categories
    Step 3: Bad Debt Expense = Estimate of Ending Balance in Allowance − Balance in
        Allowance Prior to Adjustment

EXAMPLES

EXAMPLE 5.3	Allowance for doubtful accounts, page 275
EXAMPLE 5.4	Estimating bad debt expense using the percentage of credit sales method, page 276–277
EXAMPLE 5.5	Estimating the allowance for doubtful accounts using the aging method, page 278–279

KEY TAKEAWAYS

LO5. Describe the cash flow implications of accounts receivable.

- Companies can increase the speed of cash collection on receivables by factoring, or selling, their receivables.
- The buyer of the receivables will charge a fee to compensate themselves for the time value of money, the risk of collectability, and the tasks of billing and collection.

- Receivables may be packaged as financial instruments or securities and sold to investors—called securitization.
- A special case of selling receivables is accepting credit cards like MasterCard and Visa.

KEY TERMS

Credit cards, 280
Debit card, 281
Securitization, 280
factor, 280

LO6. Record and properly present notes receivable from inception to maturity.

KEY TAKEAWAYS

- Notes receivable are recognized for the amount of cash borrowed or goods/services purchased.
- This initial amount is the principal amount of the note receivable.
- Any excess of amount repaid over principal is recognized as interest revenue in the period the interest was earned.

KEY TERMS

Interest, 282
Notes receivable, 281
Principal, 282

KEY CALCULATIONS

Interest = Principal × Annual Interest Rate × Fraction of 1 Year, 282

EXAMPLES

> **EXAMPLE 5.6**   Accounting for notes receivable, page 283

LO7. Describe internal control procedures for merchandise sales.

KEY TAKEAWAYS

- Since sales revenues have a significant effect on a company's net income, internal control procedures must be established to ensure that the amounts reported are correct.
- Typically, sales are not recorded until a three-way match is performed between the following:
  - The customer purchase order (which indicates that the customer wants the goods)
  - The shipping document (which indicates that the goods have been shipped to the customer)
  - The invoice (which indicates that the customer has been billed)

LO8. Analyze profitability and asset management using sales and receivables.

KEY TAKEAWAYS

- Because sales revenue is such a key component of a company's success, analysts are interested in a large number of ratios that incorporate sales.

- Many of these ratios attempt to measure how much the company is making on sales. These are called profitability ratios.
  - Gross profit margin
  - Operating margin
  - Net profit margin
- Analysts are also concerned with asset management—how efficiently a company is using the resources at its disposal.
- One of the most widely used asset management ratios is accounts receivable turnover.

KEY TERM

Profitability ratios, 285

KEY CALCULATIONS

Gross Profit Margin = Gross Profit ÷ Net Sales, 285
Operating Margin = Operating Income ÷ Net Sales, 285
Net Profit Margin = Net Income ÷ Net Sales, 285
Accounts Receivable Turnover = Net Sales ÷ Average Net Accounts Receivable, 285

EXAMPLES

EXAMPLE 5.7	Calculating the gross profit margin, operating margin, net profit margin, and accounts receivable turnover ratios, page 286

KEY TAKEAWAYS

LO9. (Appendix 5A) Record and properly present receivables using the gross method.

- Sales discounts are properly recorded in sales revenue using the gross method when the customer is not expected to pay within the discount period.
- If the customer does pay within the discount period, sales revenue should be decreased by the amount of the discount.

REVIEW PROBLEM

I. RECORDING SALES AND RECEIVABLES

Qwurk Productions performs graphic design services including designing and maintaining websites. The following activities occurred during 2023 and 2024:

11/1/23	Qwurk delivers a new logo to GCD Advisors and submits a bill for $2,000 with terms 2/10, n/30. Qwurk expects GCD to pay within the discount period.
11/15/23	Qwurk delivers an overall web concept to Mutare, which Mutare approves. Qwurk submits a bill for $1,000 with terms 2/10, n/30. Qwurk expects Mutare to pay within the discount period.
11/20/23	Qwurk delivers paper and envelopes incorporating the new logo to GCD Advisors and submits a bill for $200 with terms 2/10, n/30. Qwurk expects GCD to pay within the discount period.
11/22/23	Mutare pays for the 11/15 bill related to a new overall web concept.
11/25/23	GCD complains that the printing on much of the paper and envelopes is unacceptable. Qwurk offers to reduce the bill from $200 to $75. GCD accepts.
11/29/23	GCD pays for the 11/1 bill for a new logo and $75 for the 11/20 bill for paper and envelopes.
12/1/23	Qwurk installs a new website incorporating order fulfillment applications for Redbird Enterprises. Redbird signs a note to pay $20,000 plus 6% interest due on 7/1/20.
12/15/23	Qwurk writes off a $600 account receivable.

12/31/23	After performing an aging of its accounts receivable, Qwurk estimates that $2,000 of its accounts receivable will be uncollectible on a total balance of $600,000. The allowance for doubtful accounts has a credit balance of $300 prior to adjustment.
7/1/24	Redbird pays the note and interest in full.
12/31/24	At December 31, 2024, Qwurk estimates that $3,000 in allowances will be granted in 2025 that relate to services provided in 2024.

Required:

1. Provide the journal entry for November 1, 2023.
2. Provide the journal entry for November 15, 2023.
3. Provide the journal entry for November 20, 2023.
4. Calculate how much Mutare paid and provide the journal entry for November 22, 2023.
5. Provide the journal entry for November 25, 2023.
6. Calculate how much GCD paid and provide the journal entry for November 29, 2023.
7. Provide the journal entry for December 1, 2023.
8. Provide the journal entry for December 15, 2023.
9. Provide the necessary adjusting entries for December 31, 2023, to accrue interest on the note and adjust the allowance account.
10. What is the net realizable value of Qwurk's accounts receivable at December 31, 2023?
11. Calculate how much interest Redbird paid and provide the journal entry for July 1, 2024.
12. Provide the necessary adjustment for estimated returns and allowances.

Solution:

1.

Date	Account and Explanation	Debit	Credit		Assets	=	Liabilities	+	Stockholders' Equity
2023									
Nov. 1	Accounts Receivable	1,960			▲				
	Sales Revenue[a]		1,960						▲

2.

Date	Account and Explanation	Debit	Credit		Assets	=	Liabilities	+	Stockholders' Equity
2023									
Nov. 15	Accounts Receivable	980			▲				
	Sales Revenue[b]		980						▲

3.

Date	Account and Explanation	Debit	Credit		Assets	=	Liabilities	+	Stockholders' Equity
2023									
Nov. 20	Accounts Receivable	196			▲				
	Sales Revenue[c]		196						▲

[a]Gross amount	$ 2,000
Less: Discount ($2,000 × 2%)	(40)
Expected payment (net)	$ 1,960

[b]Gross amount	$ 1,000
Less: Discount ($1,000 × 2%)	(20)
Expected payment (net)	$ 980

[c]Gross amount	$ 200
Less: Discount ($200 × 2%)	(4)
Expected payment (net)	$ 196

4.

Date	Account and Explanation	Debit	Credit			
2023				Assets	= Liabilities +	Stockholders' Equity
Nov. 22	Cash[b]	980		▲		
	Accounts Receivable		980	▼		

5.

Date	Account and Explanation	Debit	Credit			
2023				Assets	= Liabilities +	Stockholders' Equity
Nov. 25	Sales Revenue	125				▼
	Accounts Receivable		125	▼		

6.

Date	Account and Explanation	Debit	Credit			
2023				Assets	= Liabilities +	Stockholders' Equity
Nov. 29	Cash[d]	2,075		▲		
	Accounts Receivable[e]		2,035	▼		
	Sales Revenue		40			▲

7.

Date	Account and Explanation	Debit	Credit			
2023				Assets	= Liabilities +	Stockholders' Equity
Dec. 1	Notes Receivable	20,000		▲		
	Sales Revenue		20,000			▲

8.

Date	Account and Explanation	Debit	Credit			
2023				Assets	= Liabilities +	Stockholders' Equity
Dec. 15	Allowance for Doubtful Accounts	600		▲		
	Accounts Receivable		600	▼		

9.

Date	Account and Explanation	Debit	Credit			
2023				Assets	= Liabilities +	Stockholders' Equity
Dec. 31	Interest Receivable[f]	100		▲		
	Interest Income		100			▲
	Bad Debt Expense	1,700				▼
	Allowance for Doubtful Accounts[g]		1,700	▼		

[d]Gross amount $ 2,000
Less: Discount (not allowed; paid after 10 days)   0
Total paid $ 2,000 + $75 = $2,075

[e]Accounts Receivable for 11/1 $ 1,960
Accounts Receivable for 11/20   75
Total $ 2,035

[f]$20,000 × 6% × 1/12

[g]Qwurk's estimate warrants a $2,000 credit balance. Because the account already has a $300 credit balance, a $1,700 credit is needed.

10. December 1, 2023:

Accounts receivable accounts	$600,000
Less: Allowance for doubtful accounts	(2,000)
Net realizable value	$598,000

Net accounts receivable are shown at net realizable value.

11. July 1, 2024:

$$\text{Interest paid} = \$20,000 \times 6\% \times 7/12$$
$$= \$700$$

Interest paid to Qwurk is for the period December 1, 2023, through July 1, 2024. However, the interest income for December 2023 was already recognized in 2023 (see journal entry in 9). Interest income of $600 will be recognized in 2024.

Account and Explanation	Debit	Credit	Assets	=	Liabilities	+	Stockholders' Equity
Cash	20,700		▲				
Interest Income		600					▲
Interest Receivable (from 9)		100	▼				
Notes Receivable		20,000	▼				

12.

Account and Explanation	Debit	Credit	Assets	=	Liabilities	+	Stockholders' Equity
Sales Revenue	3,000						▼
Returns and Allowances Liability		3,000			▲		

APPLYING KNOWLEDGE

DISCUSSION QUESTIONS

OBJECTIVE 1

1. When is revenue recognized?
2. When is a performance obligation satisfied?

OBJECTIVE 2

3. At what amount should sales revenue be recorded when sales discounts are present?
4. Why are sales discounts offered?
5. What are sales returns?
6. What are sales allowances? How do sales allowances differ from sales discounts?
7. What are trade discounts and quantity discounts?

OBJECTIVE 3

8. What are the principal types of receivables?

OBJECTIVE 4

9. Under the allowance method, why do we make an entry to record bad debt expense in the period of sale rather than in the period in which an account is determined to be uncollectible?

10. Why is the direct write-off method not GAAP?

11. What is the conceptual difference between the (1) percentage of credit sales and (2) aging methods of estimating bad debts?

12. What kind of account is *allowance for doubtful accounts*? What does it represent?

13. Why do companies issue credit when their past experience indicates that some customers will not pay?

14. How much interest will be due at maturity for each of the following interest-bearing notes?

	Principal	Months to Maturity	Annual Interest Rate
a.	$10,000	2	12%
b.	42,000	5	14
c.	18,000	4	13
d.	37,000	6	11

15. A business borrows $1,000, signing a note that requires repayment of the amount borrowed in two payments of $600 each, one at the end of each of the next two 6-month periods. Calculate the total interest on the note. What is the principal amount of the note?

16. A business borrows $1,000, signing a note that requires an interest rate of 12% per year and repayment of principal plus interest in a single payment at the end of 1 year. Calculate the total interest on the note. What is the amount of the single payment?

17. Describe what happens when receivables are factored.

OBJECTIVE 5

18. Accepting major credit cards requires the seller to pay a service charge. What advantages does the seller obtain by accepting major credit cards?

19. Why is interest typically charged on notes receivable, but not on accounts receivable?

OBJECTIVE 6

20. What documents must be present to trigger the recording of a sale (and associated receivable) in the accounting records?

OBJECTIVE 7

21. Describe the documents that underlie the typical accounting system for sales. Give an example of a failure of internal control that might occur if these documents were not properly prepared.

22. How may analyzing sales and receivables provide information about a firm's profitability?

OBJECTIVE 8

23. How may analyzing sales and receivables provide information about a firm's asset management?

MULTIPLE-CHOICE QUESTIONS

5-1 Food To Go is a local catering service. Conceptually, when should Food To Go recognize revenue from its catering service?

OBJECTIVE 1

    a. At the date the meals are served

    c. At the date the customer places the order

    b. At the date the invoice is mailed to the customer

    d. At the date the customer's payment is received

5-2 When is revenue from the sale of merchandise normally recognized?

    a. When the customer takes possession of the merchandise, if sold for cash, or when payment is received, if sold on credit

    b. When the customer pays for the merchandise

    c. Either on the date the customer takes possession of the merchandise or the date on which the customer pays

    d. When the customer takes possession of the merchandise

5-3 What does the phrase, "Revenue is recognized at the point of sale" mean?
 a. Revenue is recorded in the accounting records when the cash is received from a customer and reported on the income statement when sold to the customer.
 b. Revenue is recorded in the accounting records and reported on the income statement when goods are sold and delivered to the customer.
 c. Revenue is recorded in the accounting records when the goods are sold to a customer and reported on the income statement when the cash payment is received from the customer.
 d. Revenue is recorded in the accounting records and reported on the income statement when the cash is received from the customer.

5-4 On August 31, Montana Corporation signed a 4-year contract to provide services for Minefield Company at $30,000 per year. Minefield will pay for each year of services on the first day of each service year, starting on September 1. Using the accrual basis of accounting, when should Montana recognize revenue?
 a. On the first day of each year when the cash is received
 b. Equally throughout the year as services are provided
 c. On the last day of each year after the services have been provided
 d. Only at the end of the entire contract

OBJECTIVE 2

5-5 When should the net method be used to record sales revenue?
 a. Never—the gross method should always be used
 b. When the discount terms are favorable to the customer
 c. When the customer does not pay within the discount period
 d. When the customer is expected to pay within the discount period

5-6 On April 20, McLean Company provides lawn care services to Tazwell Corporation for $3,000 with terms 1/10, n/30. On April 28, Tazwell pays for half of the services provided, and on May 19 it pays for the other half. What is the total amount of cash McLean received?
 a. $3,000
 b. $2,700
 c. $2,985
 d. $2,970

OBJECTIVE 7

5-7 Which of the following statements concerning internal control procedures for merchandise sales is *not* correct?
 a. A sale and its associated receivable are recorded only when the order, shipping, and billing documents are all present.
 b. Shipping and billing documents are prepared based on the order document.
 c. Accounting for a sale begins with the receipt of a purchase order or some similar document from a customer.
 d. The order document is not necessary for the buyer to be obligated to accept and pay for the ordered goods.

OBJECTIVE 3

5-8 All of the following are ways in which receivables are commonly distinguished *except*
 a. collectible or uncollectible.
 b. trade or nontrade receivable.
 c. current or noncurrent.
 d. accounts or notes receivable.

OBJECTIVE 4

5-9 Which one of the following best describes the allowance for doubtful accounts?
 a. Cash flow account
 b. Income statement account
 c. Contra-account
 d. Liability account

5-10 If a company uses the direct write-off method of accounting for bad debts,
 a. it will report accounts receivable on the balance sheet at their net realizable value.
 b. it is applying the matching principle.
 c. it will reduce the Accounts Receivable account at the end of the accounting period for estimated uncollectible accounts.
 d. it will record bad debt expense only when an account is determined to be uncollectible.

5-11 Which of the following best describes the objective of estimating bad debt expense with the percentage of credit sales method?
a. To estimate the amount of bad debt expense based on an aging of accounts receivable
b. To determine the amount of uncollectible accounts during a given period
c. To estimate bad debt expense based on a percentage of credit sales made during the period
d. To facilitate the use of the direct write-off method

5-12 Which of the following best describes the concept of the aging method of receivables?
a. An accurate estimate of bad debt expense may be arrived at by multiplying historical bad debt rates by the amount of credit sales made during a period.
b. The precise amount of bad debt expense may be arrived at by multiplying historical bad debt rates by the amount of credit sales made during a period.
c. Estimating the appropriate balance for the allowance for doubtful accounts results in the appropriate value for net accounts receivable on the balance sheet.
d. Accounts receivable should be directly written off when the due date arrives and the customers have not paid the bill.

5-13 The aging method is closely related to the
a. income statement.
b. balance sheet.
c. statement of cash flows.
d. statement of retained earnings.

5-14 The percentage of credit sales approach is closely related to the
a. income statement.
b. balance sheet.
c. statement of retained earnings.
d. statement of cash flows.

5-15 The process by which firms package factored receivables as financial instruments or securities and sell them to investors is known as
a. credit extension.
b. bundling.
c. aging of accounts receivable.
d. securitization.

OBJECTIVE ◀ 5

5-16 Which one of the following statements is true if a company's collection period for accounts receivable is unacceptably long?
a. Cash flows from operations may be higher than expected for the company's sales.
b. The company may offer trade discounts to lengthen the collection period.
c. The company should expand operations with its excess cash.
d. The company may need to borrow to acquire operating cash.

5-17 Zenephia Corp. accepted a 9-month note receivable from a customer on October 1. If Zenephia has an accounting period which ends on December 31, when would it most likely recognize interest income from the note?
a. December 31 of the current year and June 30 of next year
b. October 1 of the current year
c. December 31 of the current year
d. June 30 of the following year

OBJECTIVE ◀ 6

5-18 The "principal" of a note receivable refers to
a. the amount of interest due.
b. the amount of cash borrowed.
c. the present value of the note.
d. the financing company that is lending the money.

5-19 Net profit margin percentage is calculated by
a. dividing operating income by (net) sales.
b. subtracting operating income from (net) sales.
c. dividing net income by (net) sales.
d. subtracting net income from (net) sales.

OBJECTIVE ◀ 8

OBJECTIVE 9 ▶ **5-20** *(Appendix 5A)* Under the gross method, the seller records discounts taken by the buyer
   a. at the time of sale.
   b. at the end of the period in question.
   c. never; discounts are irrelevant under the gross method.
   d. as a reduction to sales revenue.

BRIEF EXERCISES

OBJECTIVE 1
EXAMPLE 3.5

Brief Exercise 5-21 Service Revenue

H&R Wholesalers is a retailer providing low cost, bulk items to small companies. Companies must pay an annual membership fee of $100 to access H&R's warehouses. H&R received yearly membership fees from 420 companies on August 1.

Required:
At December 31, calculate the remaining amount of Unearned Revenue and the account balance of the Revenue account.

OBJECTIVE 1
EXAMPLE 3.5

Brief Exercise 5-22 Service Revenue

Bessie Milk Delivery provides weekly gourmet milk delivery to the residents of Moolawn. Bessie charges each customer $60 per week for its milk delivery, and it received advance payments for 1,800 weeks of milk delivery services in December. At December 31, three-fourths of the advance payments had been earned.

Required:
After the adjustments are recorded and posted at December 31, calculate what the balances will be in the Unearned Revenue and Revenue accounts?

OBJECTIVE 2
EXAMPLE 5.1

Brief Exercise 5-23 Sales Discounts Taken

Gordon's Grocers purchases bread from Buddy's Bread Company at $2.35 per loaf. Gordon's recently engaged in a customer service contract with Buddy's to purchase 26,000 loaves of Buddy's bread. Buddy offered credit to Gordon's at terms of 2/10, n/30. Buddy expects Gordon to pay within the discount period.

Required:
Prepare the journal entry to record the sale using the gross method. Then, prepare the journal entry assuming the payment is made within 10 days (within the discount period).

OBJECTIVE 2
EXAMPLE 5.1

Brief Exercise 5-24 Sales Discounts Not Taken

Assume the same information as in **Brief Exercise 5-41**: Gordon's Grocers purchases bread from Buddy's Bread Company at $2.35 per loaf. Gordon's engaged in a customer service contract to purchase 26,000 loaves of Buddy's bread. Buddy offered credit at terms of 2/10, n/30 and expects Gordon to pay within the discount period.

Required:
Prepare the journal entry assuming the payment is made after 10 days (after the discount period).

OBJECTIVE 4
EXAMPLE 5.4

Brief Exercise 5-25 Percentage of Credit Sales

Roeker Company provides information systems consultation services to large companies in the Chicagoland area. Due to a dip in the economy, Roeker has increased the percentage of credit sales which it believes will be uncollectible from 3.0% to 3.2% for the year. Roeker's consulting services provided revenues of $700,000 in 2023. During 2024, Roeker has write-offs of $750 related to goods purchased in 2023. Prior to the write-off for the $750 default, Roeker's accounts receivable and allowance for doubtful accounts balances were $480,000 and $232 (credit), respectively.

Required:

1. Prepare the journal entry to record the defaulted account.
2. Prepare the adjusting entry to record the bad debt expense for 2023.

Brief Exercise 5-26 Write-Off of Uncollectible Accounts

OBJECTIVE ◀ 4

EXAMPLE 5.4

Abel Enterprises had 30 customers utilizing its financial planning services in 2023. Each customer paid Abel $25,000 for receiving Abel's assistance. Abel estimates that 4.5% of its $750,000 credit sales in 2023 will be uncollectible. During 2024, Abel wrote off $3,300 related to services performed in 2023.

Required:

1. Prepare the journal entry to record the defaulted balance.
2. Prepare the adjusting entry to record the bad debt expense for 2023.

Brief Exercise 5-27 Aging Method

OBJECTIVE ◀ 4

EXAMPLE 5.5

On January 1, Hungryman Inc. has the following balances for accounts receivable and allowance for doubtful accounts:

Accounts Receivable	$1,280,000
Allowance for Doubtful Accounts (a credit balance)	44,000

During the year, Hungryman had $18,500,000 of credit sales, collected $17,945,000 of accounts receivable, and wrote off $60,000 of accounts receivable as uncollectible. At year end, Hungryman performs an aging of its accounts receivable balance and estimates that $52,000 will be uncollectible.

Required:

1. Calculate Hungryman's preadjustment balance in accounts receivable on December 31.
2. Calculate Hungryman's preadjustment balance in allowance for doubtful accounts on December 31.
3. Prepare the necessary adjusting entry for the year.

Brief Exercise 5-28 Aging Method

OBJECTIVE ◀ 4

EXAMPLE 5.5

Ingrid Inc. has strict credit policies and only extends credit to customers with outstanding credit history. The company examined its accounts and determined that at January 1, it had balances in Accounts Receivable and Allowance for Doubtful Accounts of $478,000 and $7,900 (credit), respectively. During the year, Ingrid extended credit for $3,075,000 of sales, collected $2,715,000 of accounts receivable, and had customer defaults of $4,280. Ingrid performed an aging analysis on its receivables at year end and determined that $6,800 of its receivables will be uncollectible.

Required:

1. Calculate Ingrid's balance in accounts receivable on December 31, prior to the adjustment.
2. Calculate Ingrid's balance in allowance for doubtful accounts on December 31, prior to the adjustment.
3. Prepare the necessary adjusting entry at year end.

Brief Exercise 5-29 Percentage of Credit Sales Method

OBJECTIVE ◀ 4

EXAMPLE 5.4

At December 31, Garner has a $15,000 credit balance in its allowance for doubtful accounts. Garner estimates that 3% of its credit sales for the year will eventually default. During the year, Garner had credit sales of $970,000.

Required:

Estimate the bad debt expense under the percentage of credit sales method.

OBJECTIVE

Brief Exercise 5-30 Collection of Amounts Previously Written Off

Hannah purchased a laptop computer from Perry Corp. for $1,500. Hannah's receivable has been outstanding for over 180 days, and Perry determines that the total amount is uncollectible and writes off all of Hannah's debt. Hannah later receives a windfall and pays the amount of her balance to Perry Corp.

Required:

Make the appropriate journal entries (if any) to record the receipt of $450 by Perry Corp.

OBJECTIVE

EXAMPLE 5.5

Brief Exercise 5-31 Accounts Receivable Balance

Hart Inc. began the year with $315,700 of accounts receivable. During the year, Hart sold a considerable amount of merchandise on credit and collected $2,427,000 of its credit sales. At the end of the year, the accounts receivable balance is $16,800 lower than the beginning balance.

Required:

Calculate the amount of credit sales during the period.

OBJECTIVE

EXAMPLE 5.5

Brief Exercise 5-32 Accounts Receivable Balance

XYZ Corp sells widgets to consumers for $20 each. Its beginning accounts receivable balance was $24,975, and it sold 12,376 widgets throughout the year. The total cash collections for the year amounted to $217,750.

Required:

Calculate the ending accounts receivable balance.

OBJECTIVE

EXAMPLE 5.5

Brief Exercise 5-33 Accounts Receivable Balance

Ray's beginning and ending accounts receivables balances are $147,990 and $142,720, respectively. Ray's sold $3,745,060 of merchandise, of which 50% was on credit.

Required:

Determine the amount of cash collections for the period.

OBJECTIVE

Brief Exercise 5-34 Accounting for Credit Card Sales

Jarrod's Meat Shop doubles as a butcher shop and a sandwich shop that sells to both individuals and a nearby hospital system. On a particular day, Jarrod's had cash sales of $450, credit sales of $600, sales on MasterCard of $657, and sales on Visa of $923. The sales on credit cards incur merchant charges of 1.6% for MasterCard and 1.9% for Visa.

Required:

Prepare a journal entry to record these sales.

Brief Exercise 5-35 Notes Receivable

Harrigan Enterprises utilizes Snoopy Systems to design and implement a cash management system. Due to Harrigan's cash management problems, it cannot currently pay for the system out of pocket. Snoopy chooses to extend a 6% note on January 1 for the $27,000 project cost.

Required:

1. Prepare Snoopy's journal entry to record the service performed on January 1.
2. Determine how much interest Snoopy will receive if the note is repaid on May 1.
3. Provide Snoopy's journal entry to record the cash received to pay off the note and interest on May 1.

Brief Exercise 5-36 Notes Receivable

OBJECTIVE 6

EXAMPLE 5.6

Crowne Cleaning provides cleaning services for Amber Inc., a business with four buildings. Crowne assigned different cleaning charges for each building based on the amount of square feet to be cleaned. The charges for the four buildings are $42,000, $37,000, $31,000, and $14,000. Amber secured this amount by signing a note bearing 8% interest on June 1.

Required:
1. Prepare the journal entry to record the sale on June 1.
2. Determine how much interest Crowne will receive if the note is repaid on December 1.
3. Prepare Crowne's journal entry to record the cash received to pay off the note and interest on December 1.

Brief Exercise 5-37 Ratio Analysis

OBJECTIVE 8

EXAMPLE 5.7

Dobby's income statement lists net sales of $179,000 and a gross margin of $111,000. All other expenses not included in the gross margin totaled $46,500.

Required:
1. Calculate Dobby's gross profit ratio.
2. Calculate Dobby's net profit margin ratio.

Brief Exercise 5-38 Ratio Analysis

OBJECTIVE 8

EXAMPLE 5.7

Willow Corporation sells upscale lamps to boutiques across the country. The average net trade accounts receivable for Willow is $780,000. In addition, the company has average net sales of $8,425,000.

Required:
Calculate Willow's accounts receivable turnover.

Brief Exercise 5-39 Ratio Analysis

OBJECTIVE 8

EXAMPLE 5.7

Watts Inc. specializes in imported goods, focusing particularly on food products. During the year, the company realized net sales of $9,700,000 and average net trade accounts receivable were $1,057,000. In the previous year, Watts had realized a net loss for the year in the amount of $20,000; however, extraordinary efficiency efforts in the current year increased net income by $445,000.

Required:
1. Calculate Watts' accounts receivable turnover for the current year.
2. Calculate Watts' net profit margin ratio for the current year.

Brief Exercise 5-40 *(Appendix 5A)* Sales Discounts

OBJECTIVE 9

Dave Gabel provides tax services for small businesses. This year's tax season has proved especially lucrative for Dave; he earned $65,000 for providing his services. Dave uses terms of 1/10, n/30 in billing his customers.

Required:
1. Prepare the necessary journal entries to record the sale, assuming Dave does not expect his customers to pay within the discount period.
2. Prepare the necessary journal entries to record collection of the receivable assuming the customer pays within 10 days.
3. Prepare the necessary journal entries to record collection of the receivable assuming the customer pays after 10 days.

Brief Exercise 5-41 *(Appendix 5A)* **Sales Discounts**

Ramsden Inc. provided consulting services with a gross price of $25,000 and terms of 2/10, n/30.

Required:

1. Prepare the necessary journal entries to record the sale under the gross method.
2. Prepare the necessary journal entries to record collection of the receivable, assuming the customer pays within 10 days.
3. Prepare the necessary journal entries to record collection of the receivable, assuming the customer pays after 10 days.

EXERCISES

OBJECTIVE

Exercise 5-42 Calculation of Revenue

Riggins Motors buys and sells used cars. Riggins made the following sales during January and February:

a. Six cars were sold to Taylor Taxi for a total of $146,000; the cars were delivered to Taylor on January 17. Taylor paid Riggins $50,000 on January 17 and the remaining $96,000 on February 12.

b. One car was sold to Street Classics for $28,000. The car was delivered to Street on January 25. Street paid Riggins on February 1.

Required:

Calculate the monthly revenue for Riggins for January and February.

OBJECTIVE

Exercise 5-43 Revenue Recognition

Volume Electronics sold a television to Sarah Merrifield on December 15. Sarah paid $100 at the time of the purchase and agreed to pay $100 each month for 5 months beginning January 15.

Required:

Determine in what month or months revenue from this sale should be recorded by Volume Electronics to ensure proper application of accrual accounting.

OBJECTIVE

Exercise 5-44 Calculation of Revenue from Cash Collection

Ranger Lawn Service provides mowing, weed control, and pest management services for a flat fee of $405 per lawn per month. During August, Ranger collected $11,050 in cash from customers, which included $1,500 for lawn care provided in July. At the end of August, Ranger had not collected from eight customers who had promised to pay in September when they returned from vacation.

Required:

Calculate the amount of Ranger's revenue for August.

OBJECTIVE

Exercise 5-45 Effects of Sales Discounts

Citron Mechanical Systems makes all sales on credit, with terms 1/15, n/30. During the year, the list price (prediscount) of services provided was $687,500. Customers paid $482,000 (list price) of these sales within the discount period and the remaining $205,500 (list price) after the discount period. Citron uses the net method of recording sales.

Required:

1. Compute the amount of sales that Citron recorded for the year.
2. Compute the amount of cash that Citron collected from these sales.
3. Assuming the net method was used for all sales, prepare a summary journal entry to record these sales and a second summary entry to record the cash collected.

Exercise 5-46 Sales and Sales Returns and Allowances

OBJECTIVE 2

Gold Enterprises had the following sales-related transactions on a recent day:

a. Billed customer $32,250 on account for services already provided.

b. Collected $6,105 in cash for services to be provided in the future.

c. The customer complained about aspects of the services provided in Transaction a. To maintain a good relationship with this customer, Gold granted an allowance of $1,600 off the list price. The customer had not yet paid for the services.

d. Gold provided the services for the customer in Transaction b. Additionally, Gold granted an allowance of $410 because the services were provided after the promised date. Because the customer had already paid, Gold paid the $410 allowance in cash.

SHOW ME HOW

Required:

1. Prepare the necessary journal entry (or entries) for each of these transactions.
2. **CONCEPTUAL CONNECTION** What concerns would Gold have assuming that the sales allowances for this period were significantly higher than in previous periods both in absolute terms and as a percentage of gross sales?

Exercise 5-47 Average Uncollectible Account Losses and Bad Debt Expense

OBJECTIVE 4

The accountant for Volunteer Company prepared the following data for sales and losses from uncollectible accounts:

Year	Credit Sales	Losses from Uncollectible Accounts*
2019	$ 883,000	$13,125
2020	952,000	14,840
2021	1,083,000	16,790
2022	1,189,000	16,850

* Losses from uncollectible accounts are the actual losses related to sales of that year (rather than write-offs of that year).

Required:

1. Calculate the average percentage of losses from uncollectible accounts for 2019 through 2022.
2. Assume that the credit sales for 2023 are $1,260,000 and that the weighted average percentage calculated in Requirement 1 is used as an estimate of losses from uncollectible accounts for 2023 credit sales. Determine the bad debt expense for 2023 using the percentage of credit sales method.
3. **CONCEPTUAL CONNECTION** Do you believe this estimate of bad debt expense is reasonable?
4. **CONCEPTUAL CONNECTION** How would you estimate 2023 bad debt expense if losses from uncollectible accounts for 2022 were $30,000? What other action would management consider?

Exercise 5-48 Bad Debt Expense: Percentage of Credit Sales Method

OBJECTIVE 4

Gilmore Electronics had the following data for a recent year:

Cash sales	$135,000
Credit sales	512,000
Accounts receivable determined to be uncollectible	9,650

The firm's estimated rate for bad debts is 2.2% of credit sales.

(Continued)

Required:

1. Prepare the journal entry to write off the uncollectible accounts.
2. Prepare the journal entry to record the estimate of bad debt expense.
3. If Gilmore had written off $3,000 of receivables as uncollectible during the year, how much would bad debt expense reported on the income statement have changed?
4. **CONCEPTUAL CONNECTION** If Gilmore's estimate of bad debts is correct (2.2% of credit sales) and the gross margin is 20%, by how much did Gilmore's income from operations increase assuming $150,000 of the sales would have been lost if credit sales were not offered?

OBJECTIVE 4

Exercise 5-49 Bad Debt Expense: Percentage of Credit Sales Method

Bradford Plumbing had the following data for a recent year:

Credit sales	$547,900
Allowance for doubtful accounts, 1/1 (a credit balance)	8,740
Accounts receivable, 1/1	42,340
Collections on account receivable	489,770
Accounts receivable written off	14,250

Bradford estimates that 2.7% of credit sales will eventually default.

Required:

1. Compute bad debt expense for the year (rounding to the nearest whole number).
2. Determine the ending balances in accounts receivable and allowance for doubtful accounts.

OBJECTIVE 4

Exercise 5-50 Bad Debt Expense: Aging Method

Glencoe Supply had the following accounts receivable aging schedule at the end of a recent year.

Accounts Receivable Age	Amount	Proportion Expected to Default	Allowance Required
Current	$310,500	0.005	$ 1,553
1–30 days past due	47,500	0.01	475
31–45 days past due	25,000	0.13	3,250
46–90 days past due	12,800	0.20	2,560
91–135 days past due	6,100	0.25	1,525
Over 135 days past due	4,200	0.60	2,520
			$11,883

The balance in Glencoe's allowance for doubtful accounts at the beginning of the year was $58,620 (credit). During the year, accounts in the total amount of $62,400 were written off.

Required:

1. Determine bad debt expense.
2. Prepare the journal entry to record bad debt expense.
3. If Glencoe had written off $90,000 of receivables as uncollectible during the year, how much would bad debt expense reported on the income statement have changed?

OBJECTIVE 4

Exercise 5-51 Aging Receivables and Bad Debt Expense

Perkinson Corporation sells paper products to a large number of retailers. Perkinson's accountant has prepared the following aging schedule for its accounts receivable at the end of the year.

Accounts Receivable Category	Amount	Proportion Expected to Default
Within discount period	$384,500	0.004
1–30 days past discount period	187,600	0.015
31–60 days past discount period	41,800	0.085
Over 60 days past discount period	21,400	0.200

Before adjusting entries are entered, the balance in the allowance for doubtful accounts is a *debit* of $480.

Required:
1. Calculate the desired postadjustment balance in Perkinson's allowance for doubtful accounts.
2. Determine bad debt expense for the year.

Exercise 5-52 Allowance for Doubtful Accounts

OBJECTIVE 4

At the beginning of the year, Kullerud Manufacturing had a credit balance in its allowance for doubtful accounts of $10,670, and at the end of the year it was a credit balance of $11,240. During the year, Kullerud made credit sales of $1,270,990, collected receivables in the amount of $1,240,830, and recorded bad debt expense of $42,550.

Required:
Compute the amount of receivables that Kullerud wrote off during the year.

Exercise 5-53 Collection of Amounts Previously Written Off

OBJECTIVE 4

SHOW ME HOW

Customer Rob Hufnagel owes Kellman Corp. $1,250. Kellman determines that the total amount is uncollectible and writes off all of Hufnagel's debt. Hufnagel later pays $350 to Kellman.

Required:
Make the appropriate journal entries (if any) to record the receipt of $350 by Kellman.

Exercise 5-54 Correcting an Erroneous Write-Off

OBJECTIVE 4

The new bookkeeper at Karlin Construction Company was asked to write off two accounts totaling $1,710 that had been determined to be uncollectible. Accordingly, he debited Accounts Receivable for $1,710 and credited Bad Debt Expense for the same amount.

Required:
1. Determine what was wrong with the bookkeeper's entry assuming Karlin uses the allowance method.
2. Give both the entry he should have made and the entry required to correct his error.

Exercise 5-55 Accounting for Notes Receivable

OBJECTIVE 6

SHOW ME HOW

On November 30, Tucker Products performed computer programming services for Thomas Inc. in exchange for a 5-month, $125,000, 9% note receivable. Thomas paid Tucker the full amount of interest and principal on April 30.

Required:
Prepare the necessary entries for Tucker to record the transactions described above assuming a December 31 year end.

Exercise 5-56 Recording Notes Receivable: Issuance, Payment, and Default

OBJECTIVE 6

SHOW ME HOW

Teatree Products permits its customers to defer payment by giving personal notes instead of cash. All the notes bear interest and require the customer to pay the entire note in a single payment 6 months after issuance. Consider the following transactions, which describe Teatree's experience with two such notes:
a. On October 31, Teatree accepts a 5-month, 8% note from Customer A in lieu of a $2,900 cash payment for services provided that day.
b. On February 28, Teatree accepts a 6-month, $3,200, 9% note from Customer B in lieu of a $3,200 cash payment for services provided on that day.
c. On March 31, Customer A pays the entire note plus interest in cash.
d. On August 31, Customer B pays the entire note plus interest in cash.

(Continued)

Required:

Prepare the necessary journal and adjusting entries required to record Transactions a through d in Teatree's records.

OBJECTIVE **Exercise 5-57 Internal Control for Sales**

Arrow Products is a mail-order computer software sales outlet. Most of Arrow's customers call on its toll-free phone line and order software, paying with a credit card.

Required:

CONCEPTUAL CONNECTION Explain why the shipping and billing documents are important internal controls for Arrow.

OBJECTIVE **Exercise 5-58 Ratio Analysis**

The following information was taken from Nash Inc.'s December 31st trial balances for this year and the previous year.

	This Year	Previous Year
Accounts receivable	$ 32,000	$ 39,000
Accounts payable	47,000	36,000
Sales	219,000	128,000
Sales returns	4,000	2,300
Retained earnings	47,000	16,000
Dividends declared and paid	5,000	1,000
Net income	36,000	9,000

Required:

1. Calculate the net profit margin and accounts receivable turnover for the this year. (*Note:* Round answers to two decimal places.)
2. How much does Nash make on each sales dollar?
3. How many days does the average receivable take to be paid (assuming all sales are on account)?

OBJECTIVE **Exercise 5-59 Ratio Analysis**

The following information was taken from Division Manufacturing's December 31st trial balances for this year and the previous year.

	This Year	Previous Year
Accounts receivable	$ 14,000	$ 17,000
Accounts payable	22,000	15,000
Cost of goods sold	158,000	124,000
Sales	346,000	239,000
Sales returns	17,000	10,000
Retained earnings	32,000	16,000
Dividends declared and paid	3,000	2,000
Operating income	25,000	18,000
Net income	19,000	18,000

Required:

1. Calculate the gross profit margin and operating margin percentage for this year. (*Note:* Round answers to two decimal places.)
2. Assuming that all of the operating expenses are fixed (or, won't change as sales increase or decrease), what will be the operating margin percentage if net sales increase by 30%?

Exercise 5-60 *(Appendix 5A)* Sales Discount Recorded at Gross

Nevada Company provided services with a list price of $48,500 to Small Enterprises with terms 2/15, n/45. Nevada records sales at gross.

Required:

1. Prepare the entries to record this sale in Nevada's journal.
2. Prepare the entry for Nevada's journal to record receipt of cash in payment for the sale *within* the discount period.
3. Prepare the entry for Nevada's journal to record receipt of cash in payment for the sale *after* the discount period.
4. Assume that Nevada's customer does not have the available cash to pay Nevada within the discount period. How much interest should the customer be willing to pay for a loan to permit them to take advantage of the discount period (assuming no additional costs to the loan)?

PROBLEM SET A

Problem 5-61A Revenue Recognition

Katie Vote owns a small business that rents computers to students at the local university for the 9-month school year. Katie's typical rental contract requires the student to pay the year's rent of $1,800 ($200 per month) in advance. When Katie prepares financial statements at the end of December, her accountant requires that Katie spread the $1,800 over the 9 months that a computer is rented. Therefore, Katie can recognize only $800 revenue (4 months) from each computer rental contract in the year the cash is collected and must defer recognition of the remaining $1,000 (5 months) to next year. Katie argues that getting students to agree to rent the computer is the most difficult part of the activity so she ought to be able to recognize all $1,800 as revenue when the cash is received from a student.

Required:

CONCEPTUAL CONNECTION Explain why GAAP require the use of accrual accounting rather than cash-basis accounting for transactions like the one described here.

Problem 5-62A Discount Policy and Gross Profit

Compton Audio sells MP3 players. During the year, Compton sold 1,750 units at an average of $225 per unit. Each unit costs Compton $150. At present, Compton offers no sales discounts. Compton's controller suggests that a generous sales discount policy would increase annual sales to 2,200 units and also improve cash flow. She proposes 5/10, n/30 and believes that 70% of the customers will take advantage of the discount.

Required:

1. If the controller is correct, determine how much the new sales discount policy would add to net sales and gross margin.
2. **CONCEPTUAL CONNECTION** Explain why the sales discount policy might improve cash flow.

Problem 5-63A Effects of Discounts on Sales and Purchases

Helmkamp Products sells golf clubs and accessories to pro shops. Gross sales for the year were $2,850,700 (Helmkamp's list price) on terms 2/15, n/45. Customers paid for $2,000,000 (Helmkamp's list price) of the merchandise within the discount period and the remaining $850,700 after the end of the discount period. Helmkamp expects its customers to pay within the discount period.

(Continued)

Required:

1. Determine how much cash was collected from sales.
2. Assuming all payments were received before year end, how much sales revenue will be reported on the income statement?

OBJECTIVE **Problem 5-64A Internal Control for Sales**

Yancy's Hardware has three stores. Each store manager is paid a salary plus a bonus on the sales made by his or her store. On January 5, 2024, Bill Slick, manager of one of the stores, resigned. Bill's store had doubled its expected December 2023 sales, producing a bonus for Bill of $6,000 in December alone. Charles Brook, an assistant manager at another store, was assigned as manager of Bill's store. Upon examination of the store's accounting records, Charles reports that the store's records indicated sales returns and allowances of $96,000 in the first 4 days of January 2024, an amount equal to about half of December 2023 sales.

Required:

1. **CONCEPTUAL CONNECTION** Explain what the large amount of sales returns and allowances suggest that Bill might have done.
2. **CONCEPTUAL CONNECTION** Determine how Yancy could protect itself from a manager who behaved as Bill likely did.

OBJECTIVE **Problem 5-65A Bad Debt Expense: Percentage of Credit Sales Method**

The Glass House, a glass and china store, sells nearly half its merchandise on credit. During the past 4 years, the following data were developed for credit sales and losses from uncollectible accounts:

Year of Sales	Credit Sales	Losses from Uncollectible Accounts*
2020	$197,000	$12,608
2021	202,000	13,299
2022	212,000	13,285
2023	273,000	22,274
Total	$884,000	$61,466

* Losses from uncollectible accounts are the actual losses related to sales of that year (rather than write-offs of that year).

Required:

1. Calculate the loss rate for each year from 2020 through 2023. (*Note:* Round answers to three decimal places.)
2. Determine whether there appears to be a significant change in the loss rate over time.
3. **CONCEPTUAL CONNECTION** If credit sales for 2024 are $400,000, determine what loss rate you would recommend to estimate bad debts. (*Note:* Round answers to three decimal places.)
4. Using the rate you recommend, record bad debt expense for 2024.
5. **CONCEPTUAL CONNECTION** Assume that the increase in The Glass House's sales in 2024 was largely due to granting credit to customers who would have been denied credit in previous years. How would this change your answer to Requirement 4? Describe a legitimate business reason why The Glass House would adopt more lenient credit terms.
6. **CONCEPTUAL CONNECTION** Using the data from 2020 through 2023, estimate the increase in income from operations in total for those 4 years assuming (a) the average gross margin is 25% and (b) 50% of the sales would have been lost if no credit was granted.

Problem 5-66A Aging Method Bad Debt Expense

OBJECTIVE 4

Cindy Bagnal, the manager of Cayce Printing Service, has provided the following aging schedule for Cayce's accounts receivable:

Accounts Receivable Category	Amount	Proportion Expected to Default
0–20 days	$ 86,550	0.01
21–40 days	19,400	0.06
41–60 days	10,250	0.12
Over 60 days	4,900	0.25
	$121,100	

Cindy indicates that the $121,100 of accounts receivable identified in the table does not include $4,600 of receivables that should be written off.

Required:

1. Journalize the $4,600 write-off.
2. Determine the desired postadjustment balance in allowance for doubtful accounts (round each aging category to the nearest dollar).
3. If the balance in allowance for doubtful accounts before the $4,600 write-off was a debit of $700, compute bad debt expense. Prepare the adjusting entry to record bad debt expense.

Problem 5-67A Determining Bad Debt Expense Using the Aging Method

OBJECTIVE 4

At the beginning of the year, Tennyson Auto Parts had an accounts receivable balance of $31,800 and a balance in the allowance for doubtful accounts of $2,980 (credit). During the year, Tennyson had credit sales of $624,300, collected accounts receivable in the amount of $602,700, wrote off $18,600 of accounts receivable, and had the following data for accounts receivable at the end of the period:

Accounts Receivable Age	Amount	Proportion Expected to Default
Current	$20,400	0.01
1–15 days past due	5,300	0.02
16–45 days past due	3,100	0.08
46–90 days past due	3,600	0.15
Over 90 days past due	2,400	0.30
	$34,800	

SHOW ME HOW

Required:

1. Determine the desired postadjustment balance in allowance for doubtful accounts.
2. Determine the balance in allowance for doubtful accounts before the bad debt expense adjusting entry is posted.
3. Compute bad debt expense.
4. Prepare the adjusting entry to record bad debt expense.

Problem 5-68A Accounting for Notes Receivable

OBJECTIVE 6

SHOW ME HOW

Yarnell Electronics sells computer systems to small businesses. Yarnell engaged in the following activities involving notes receivable:

a. On September 1, Yarnell sold a $10,000 system to Ross Company. Ross gave Yarnell a 6-month, 7% note as payment.
b. On December 1, Yarnell sold a $6,000 system to Searfoss Inc. Searfoss gave Yarnell a 9-month, 9% note as payment.

(Continued)

c. On March 1, Ross paid the amount due on its note.

d. On September 1, Searfoss paid the amount due on its note.

Required:

Prepare the necessary journal and adjusting entries for Yarnell Electronics to record these transactions assuming year end is December 31.

OBJECTIVE

Problem 5-69A Ratio Analysis

Selected information from Bigg Company's financial statements follows:

| | Fiscal Year Ended December 31 | | |
	2023	2022	2021
	(in thousands)		
Gross sales	$2,004,719	$1,937,021	$1,835,987
Less: Sales discounts	(4,811)	(4,649)	(4,406)
Less: Sales returns and allowances	(2,406)	(2,324)	(2,203)
Net sales	$1,997,502	$1,930,048	$1,829,378
Cost of goods sold	621,463	619,847	660,955
Gross profit	$1,376,039	$1,310,201	$1,168,423
Operating expenses	577,369	595,226	583,555
Operating income	$ 798,670	$ 714,975	$ 584,868
Other income (expenses)	15,973	(5,720)	(8,773)
Net income	$ 814,643	$ 709,255	$ 576,095

| | At December 31 | | |
	2023	2022	2021
	(in thousands)		
Accounts receivable	$201,290	$195,427	$182,642
Less: Allowance for doubtful accounts	(2,516)	(2,736)	(2,192)
Net accounts receivable	$198,774	$192,691	$180,450

Required:

1. Calculate the following ratios for 2022 and 2023: (a) gross profit margin, (b) operating margin, (c) net profit margin, and (d) accounts receivable turnover. (*Note:* Round answers to two decimal places.)

2. **CONCEPTUAL CONNECTION** For each of the first three ratios listed above, provide a plausible explanation for any differences that exist. (For example, why is the net profit margin higher or lower than it was the previous year?)

3. **CONCEPTUAL CONNECTION** Explain what each ratio attempts to measure. Make an assessment about Small Company based upon the ratios you have calculated. Are operations improving or worsening?

OBJECTIVE

Problem 5-70A *(Appendix 5A)* Sales Discounts

Cocoa Company regularly provides services to Yankee Supply with terms 1/15, n/30 and records sales at gross. During a recent month, the two firms engaged in the following transactions:

a. Cocoa provided services with a list price of $92,000.

b. Cocoa provided services with a list price of $27,000.

c. Yankee paid for the purchase in Transaction a within the discount period.

d. Yankee paid for the purchase in Transaction b after the discount period.

Required:

1. Prepare the journal entries for Cocoa to record the sales in Transactions a and b (make separate entries).
2. Prepare the journal entry to record the receipt of Yankee's payment in Transaction c.
3. Prepare the journal entry to record the receipt of Yankee's payment in Transaction d.
4. **CONCEPTUAL CONNECTION** What implied annual interest rate is Yankee incurring by failing to take the sales discount and, instead, paying the gross amount after 30 days?

PROBLEM SET B

Problem 5-61B Revenue Recognition

OBJECTIVE ◀ 1

Mary Wade owns a small business that rents parking spaces to students at the local university. Mary's typical rental contract requires the student to pay the year's rent of $720 ($60 per month) in advance. When Mary prepares financial statements at the end of December, her accountant requires that Mary spread the $720 over the 12 months that a parking space is rented. Therefore, Mary can recognize only $240 revenue (4 months) from each contract in the year the cash is collected and must defer recognition of the remaining $480 (8 months) to next year. Mary argues that getting students to agree to rent the parking space is the most difficult part of the activity so she ought to be able to recognize all $720 as revenue when the cash is received from a student.

Required:
CONCEPTUAL CONNECTION Explain why GAAP require the use of accrual accounting rather than cash-basis accounting for transactions like the one described here.

Problem 5-62B Discount Policy and Gross Profit

OBJECTIVE ◀ 2

Parker Electronics sells cell phones. During the year, Parker sold 1,500 units at an average of $500 per unit. Each unit cost Parker $350. At present, Parker offers no sales discounts. Parker's controller suggests that a generous sales discount policy would increase annual sales to 2,000 units and also improve cash flow. She proposes 3/15, n/20 and believes that 75% of the customers will take advantage of the discount.

Required:

1. If the controller is correct, determine how much the new sales discount policy would add to net sales and gross margin.
2. **CONCEPTUAL CONNECTION** Explain why the sales discount policy might improve cash flow.

Problem 5-63B Effects of Discounts on Sales and Purchases

OBJECTIVE ◀ 2

Smithson Products sells legal supplies to law firms. Gross sales for the year were $2,750,600 (Smithson's list price) on terms 3/10, n/30. Customers paid for $2,427,900 (Smithson's list price) of the merchandise within the discount period and the remaining $322,700 after the end of the discount period. Smithson records purchases and sales using the gross method to account for sales discounts.

Required:

1. Determine how much cash was collected from sales.
2. Assuming all payments were received before year end, how much sales revenue will be reported on the income statement?

OBJECTIVE 7

Problem 5-64B Internal Control for Sales

Johnson Tires has three stores. Each store manager is paid a salary plus a bonus on the sales made by his or her store. On January 5, 2024, Kevin Sampson, manager of one of the stores, resigned. Kevin's store had doubled its expected December 2023 sales, producing a bonus for Kevin of $7,000 in December alone. Jason Jones, an assistant manager at another store, was assigned as manager of Kevin's store. Upon examination of the store's accounting records, Jason reports that the store's records indicated sales returns and allowances of $124,000 in the first 4 days of January 2024, an amount equal to about half of December 2023 sales.

Required:
1. **CONCEPTUAL CONNECTION** Explain what the large amount of sales returns and allowances suggest that Kevin might have done.
2. **CONCEPTUAL CONNECTION** Determine how Johnson could protect itself from a manager who behaved as Kevin likely did.

OBJECTIVE 4

Problem 5-65B Bad Debt Expense: Percentage of Credit Sales Method

Kelly's Collectibles sells nearly half its merchandise on credit. During the past 4 years, the following data were developed for credit sales and losses from uncollectible accounts:

Year of Sales	Credit Sales	Losses from Uncollectible Accounts*
2020	$125,900	$10,007
2021	102,440	8,762
2022	131,120	9,849
2023	149,780	12,303
Total	$509,240	$40,921

* Losses from uncollectible accounts are the actual losses related to sales of that year (rather than write-offs of that year).

Required:
1. Calculate the loss rate for each year from 2020 through 2023. (*Note:* Round answers to three decimal places.)
2. Determine if there appears to be a significant change in the loss rate over time.
3. **CONCEPTUAL CONNECTION** If credit sales for 2024 are $182,000, explain what loss rate you would recommend to estimate bad debts. (*Note:* Round answers to three decimal places.)
4. Using the rate you recommend, record bad debt expense for 2024.
5. **CONCEPTUAL CONNECTION** Assume that the increase in Kelly's sales in 2024 was largely due to granting credit to customers who would have been denied credit in previous years. How would this change your answer to Requirement 4? Describe a legitimate business reason why Kelly's would adopt more lenient credit terms.
6. **CONCEPTUAL CONNECTION** Using the data from 2020 through 2023, estimate the increase in income from operations in total for those 4 years assuming (a) the average gross margin is 45% and (b) 20% of the sales would have been lost if no credit was granted (round to nearest dollar).

OBJECTIVE 4

Problem 5-66B Aging Method Bad Debt Expense

Carol Simon, the manager of Handy Plumbing, has provided the following aging schedule for Handy's accounts receivable:

Accounts Receivable Category	Amount	Proportion Expected to Default
0–20 days	$ 92,600	0.03
21–40 days	12,700	0.09
41–60 days	17,800	0.14
Over 60 days	2,100	0.30
	$125,200	

Carol indicates that the $125,200 of accounts receivable identified in the table does not include $9,400 of receivables that should be written off.

Required:

1. Journalize the $9,400 write-off.
2. Determine the desired postadjustment balance in allowance for doubtful accounts.
3. If the balance in allowance for doubtful accounts before the $9,400 write-off was a debit of $550, compute bad debt expense. Prepare the adjusting entry to record bad debt expense.

Problem 5-67B Determining Bad Debt Expense Using the Aging Method

OBJECTIVE 4

At the beginning of the year, Lennon Electronics had an accounts receivable balance of $34,800 and a balance in the allowance for doubtful accounts of $3,640 (credit). During the year, Lennon had credit sales of $891,420, collected accounts receivable in the amount of $821,400, wrote off $28,990 of accounts receivable, and had the following data for accounts receivable at the end of the period:

Accounts Receivable Age	Amount	Proportion Expected to Default
Current	$42,350	0.01
1–15 days past due	11,200	0.04
16–45 days past due	9,600	0.09
46–90 days past due	7,200	0.17
Over 90 days past due	5,480	0.30
	$75,830	

Required:

1. Determine the desired postadjustment balance in allowance for doubtful accounts (round amounts to nearest dollar for each aging category).
2. Determine the balance in allowance for doubtful accounts before the bad debt expense adjusting entry is posted.
3. Compute bad debt expense.
4. Prepare the adjusting entry to record bad debt expense.

Problem 5-68B Accounting for Notes Receivable

OBJECTIVE 6

Saracen Systems sells voice mail systems to small businesses. Saracen engaged in the following activities involving notes receivable (round to nearest dollar):

a. On October 1, Saracen sold an $12,000 system to Majors Company. Majors gave Saracen a 8-month, 8% note as payment.
b. On November 1, Saracen sold a $9,000 system to Hadley Inc. Hadley gave Saracen a 10-month, 10% note as payment.
c. On June 1, Majors paid the amount due on its note.
d. On September 1, Hadley paid the amount due on its note.

Required:

Prepare the necessary journal and adjusting entries for Saracen Systems to record these transactions assuming a December 31 year end.

OBJECTIVE ▶8   **Problem 5-69B Ratio Analysis**

Selected information from Small Company's financial statements follows.

| | Fiscal Year Ended December 31 | | |
	2023	2022	2021
	(in thousands)		
Gross sales	$1,663,917	$1,697,195	$1,714,167
Less: Sales discounts	(2,995)	(3,055)	(3,086)
Less: Sales returns and allowances	(2,496)	(2,546)	(2,571)
Net sales	$1,658,426	$1,691,594	$1,708,510
Cost of goods sold	881,876	891,027	860,512
Gross profit	$ 776,550	$ 800,567	$ 847,998
Operating expenses	482,050	496,958	487,214
Operating income	$ 294,500	$ 303,609	$ 360,784
Other income (expenses)	3,534	(3,036)	(1,804)
Net income	$ 298,034	$ 300,573	$ 358,980

| | At December 31 | | |
	2023	2022	2021
	(in thousands)		
Accounts receivable	$376,062	$365,109	$341,223
Less: Allowance for doubtful accounts	(8,461)	(71,926)	(5,971)
Net accounts receivable	$367,601	$293,183	$335,252

Required:

1. Calculate the following ratios for 2022 and 2023: (a) gross profit margin, (b) operating margin, (c) net profit margin, and (d) accounts receivable turnover. (*Note:* Round answers to two decimal places.)
2. **CONCEPTUAL CONNECTION** For each of the first three ratios listed above provide a plausible explanation for any differences that exist. (For example, why is the net profit margin higher or lower than it was the previous year?)
3. **CONCEPTUAL CONNECTION** Explain what each ratio attempts to measure. Make an assessment about Small Company based upon the ratios you have calculated. Are operations improving or worsening?

OBJECTIVE ▶9   **Problem 5-70B** *(Appendix 5A)* **Sales Discounts**

Spartan Inc. regularly provides services to Grieder Supply with terms 3/10, n/40 and records sales at gross. During a recent month, the two firms engaged in the following transactions:
a. Spartan sold merchandise with a list price of $250,000.
b. Spartan sold merchandise with a list price of $75,000.
c. Grieder paid for the purchase in Transaction a within the discount period.
d. Grieder paid for the purchase in Transaction b after the discount period.

Required:

1. Provide the journal entries for Spartan to record the sales in Transactions a and b (make separate entries).
2. Provide the journal entry to record the receipt of Grieder's payment in Transaction c.
3. Provide the journal entry to record the receipt of Grieder's payment in Transaction d.
4. **CONCEPTUAL CONNECTION** What implied annual interest rate is Grieder incurring by failing to take the sales discount and, instead, paying the gross amount after 40 days?

CASES

Case 5-71 Ethics and Revenue Recognition

Alan Spalding is CEO of a large appliance wholesaler. Alan is under pressure from Wall Street Analysts to meet his aggressive sales revenue growth projections. Unfortunately, near the end of the year he realizes that sales must dramatically improve if his projections are going to be met. To accomplish this objective, he orders his sales force to contact their largest customers and offer them price discounts if they buy by the end of the year. Alan also offered to deliver the merchandise to a third-party warehouse with whom the customers could arrange delivery when the merchandise was needed.

Required:

1. Do you believe that revenue from these sales should be recognized in the current year? Why or why not?
2. What are the probable consequences of this behavior for the company in future periods?
3. What are the probable consequences of this behavior for investors analyzing the current year financial statements?

Case 5-72 Recognition of Service Contract Revenues

Jackson Dunlap is president of New Miami Maintenance Inc., which provides building maintenance services. On October 15, 2023, Jackson signed a service contract with Western College, and Western made a down payment of $12,000. Under the contract, New Miami will provide maintenance services for all Western's buildings for a period of 2 years, beginning on January 1, 2024, and Western will pay New Miami $1,000 per month, beginning on January 31, 2024.

Initially, Jackson proposed that some portion of the revenue from the contract should be recognized in 2023; however, his accountant, Rita McGonigle, convinced him that this would be inappropriate. Then Jackson proposed that the revenue should be recognized in an amount equal to the cash collected under the contract in 2023. Again, Rita argued against his proposal, saying that GAAP required recognition of an equal amount of contract revenue each month.

Required:

1. Give a reason that might explain Jackson's desire to recognize contract revenue earlier rather than later.
2. Put yourself in Rita's position. How would you convince Jackson that his two proposals are unacceptable and that an equal amount of revenue should be recognized every month?
3. If Rita's proposal is adopted, how would the contract be reflected in the balance sheets at the end of 2023 and at the end of 2024?

Case 5-73 Revenue Recognition

Beth Rader purchased North Shore Health Club in June 2023. Beth wanted to increase the size of the business by selling 5-year memberships for $2,000, payable at the beginning of the membership period. The normal yearly membership fee is $500. Since few prospective members were expected to have $2,000, Beth arranged for a local bank to provide a $2,000 installment loan to prospective members. By the end of 2023, 250 customers had purchased the 5-year memberships using the loan provided by the bank.

(Continued)

Beth prepared her income statement for 2023 and included $500,000 as revenue because the club had collected the entire amount in cash. Beth's accountant objected to the inclusion of the entire $500,000. The accountant argued that the $500,000 should be recognized as revenue as the club provides services for these members during the membership period. Beth countered with a quotation from a part of "Generally Accepted Accounting Principles," *Accounting Research Bulletin 43, Chapter 1, Section A, No. 1:*

> *"Profit is deemed to be realized when a sale in the ordinary course of business is effected, unless the circumstances are such that collection of the sale price is not reasonably assured."*

Beth notes that the memberships have been sold and that collection of the selling price has occurred. Therefore, she argues that all $500,000 is revenue in 2023.

Required:

Write a short statement supporting either Beth or the accountant in this dispute.

Case 5-74 Sales Discount Policies

Consider three businesses, all of which offer price reductions to their customers. The first is an independently owned gas station located at a busy intersection in Cincinnati, Ohio, that offers a 3% discount for cash purchases of gasoline. The second is a large home improvement store located near an interstate exit in suburban Cleveland that offers building contractors terms of 3/10, n/45. And third is a clothing manufacturer and catalog retailer located in Columbus. Several times during each year, a catalog is distributed in which men's dress shirts are heavily discounted if purchased in lots of four or more.

Required:

1. What are the main objectives of the discount policies in each of the three businesses?
2. How does accounting information assist each business in achieving its discount policy objectives?

Case 5-75 Financial Analysis of Receivables

A chain of retail stores located in Kansas and Nebraska has requested a loan from the bank at which you work. The balance sheet of the retail chain shows significant accounts receivable related to its in-house credit card. You have been assigned to evaluate these receivables.

Required:

1. What questions concerning the quality of these receivables can you answer by analyzing the retailer's financial statements?
2. What additional questions would you raise, and what information would you request from the retailer to answer these questions?

Case 5-76 Income Effects of Uncollectible Accounts

The credit manager and the accountant for Goldsmith Company are attempting to assess the effect on net income of writing off $100,000 of receivables. Goldsmith uses the aging method of determining bad debt expense and has the following aging schedule for its accounts receivable at December 31:

Accounts Receivable Category	Amount	Proportion Expected to Default
Current	$2,980,400	0.004
1–30 days past due	722,600	0.035
31–60 days past due	418,500	0.095
Over 60 days past due	322,800	0.250
	$4,444,300	

The receivables being considered for write-off are all over 60 days past due.

Required:
1. Assume that the tax rate is 21%. What will be the effect on net income if the $100,000 is written off?
2. What data would you examine to provide some assurance that a company was not holding uncollectible accounts in its accounts receivable rather than writing them off when they are determined to be uncollectible?

Case 5-77 Research and Analysis Using the Annual Report

Obtain Whirlpool's Fiscal 2019 10-K (filed Feb. 11, 2020) through the "Investor Relations" portion of its website (do a web search for Whirlpool investor relations). Once at the Investor Relations section of the website, look for "SEC Filings" under the "FINANCIAL INFORMATION" header. When you see the list of all the filings, either filter for the "Annual Filings" or search for "10-K." Another option is to go to www.sec.gov and click "Company Filings Search" under "Filings."

Required:
1. Look at the "Accounts Receivable and Allowance for Doubtful Accounts" heading to Note 1 (Significant Accounting Policies). Do you think Whirlpool uses the percentage of credit sales method or the aging method to estimate bad debt expense?
2. Looking at the Balance Sheet, what was Whirlpool's allowance for doubtful accounts at December 31, 2018 and 2019?
3. Was a larger percentage of the gross accounts receivable considered uncollectible at fiscal year end 2018 or 2019?
4. Calculate Whirlpool's receivables turnover for fiscal 2018 and 2019 (Accounts Receivable, net, was $2,665 at the end of fiscal 2017). (*Note:* Round answers to two decimal places.) If the industry average for receivables turnover is 6.62, how do you evaluate their efficiency with receivables?
5. Calculate Whirlpool's gross profit margin, operating margin, and net profit margin for fiscal 2018 and 2019. (*Note:* Round answers to two decimal places.)
6. If the industry average for the gross profit margin is 28.12%, what sort of strategy do you think Whirlpool is pursuing?
7. Evaluate the trend of Whirlpool's operating margin and net profit margin and relate the trend to the industry averages of 10.42% and 7.81%, respectively.

Case 5-78 Comparative Analysis: Kroger versus Sprouts

Refer to the 10-K reports of **Kroger** and **Sprouts** that are available for download from the companion website at Cengage.com.

Required:

1. Look at Sprouts' Note 4 (Accounts Receivable). Based on this disclosure, what is the balance in the allowance for doubtful accounts for 2018 and 2019? Looking at Note 3 (Significant Accounting Policies) under the heading Accounts Receivable, when does Sprouts provide the allowance for doubtful accounts? Speculate as to why Sprouts accounts for the allowance for doubtful accounts in this manner.
2. What was Sprouts' allowance for doubtful accounts as a percentage of gross accounts receivable at the end of 2018 and 2019?
3. Using the balances reported on the balance sheets, what are Kroger's and Sprouts' receivables turnover for 2019? (*Note:* Round answer to two decimal places.)
4. Calculate Sprouts' gross profit margin for 2018 and 2019. (*Note:* Round answers to two decimal places.) What can you infer about the strategy pursued by these Sprouts based on this measure, assuming the industry average is around 23.4%?
5. Calculate Kroger's and Sprouts' operating margin for 2018 and 2019. (*Note:* Round answers to two decimal places.) Comment on these measures assuming the industry average is around 3.1%.
6. Calculate Kroger's and Sprouts' net profit margin for 2018 and 2019. (*Note:* Round answers to two decimal places.) Comment on these measures assuming the industry average is 2.2%.

ANNUAL REPORT PROBLEM

HOME DEPOT

Download the 10-K for **Home Depot** from the companion website at Cengage.com.

Required:

1. What does the company report for the following accounts for the most current fiscal year?
   - Net sales
   - Gross Profit
   - Operating income
   - Net income
   - Average Accounts receivable, net
2. Due to the building of new stores, the company expects the following:
   - Net sales and Gross Profit will increase by $6 billion.
   - Operating income will increase by $2 billion.
   - Net Income will increase by $750.
   - Average Accounts receivable is projected to be 2%– of sales.

   Provide the next year's forecasted balances for the above accounts.
3. Compute the forecasted accounts receivable turnover ratio (round to two decimal places).
4. Compute the forecasted gross profit margin (round to two decimal places).
5. Compute the forecasted operating margin (round to two decimal places).
6. Compute the forecasted net profit margin (round to two decimal places).
7. What type of business strategy does Home Depot use?

Note: *While the Annual Report problems in the textbook are static, when assigned in CNOW, these activities are algorithmic and the answers may vary from what appears in the Solutions Manual.*

CONTINUING PROBLEM

FRONT ROW ENTERTAINMENT

While Front Row Entertainment has had considerable success in signing artists and promoting concerts, Cam and Anna still had a few ideas to grow their business that they wanted to implement. One idea that they both agree on is to start an online fan "community" for each of their artists. By providing a more direct connection between the artists and their fans, each artist community would serve as an online fan club that should generate increased interest and attendance at the artists' concerts. In addition to marketing and promoting the artist, Front Row Entertainment could sell advertising space on these fan communities to companies interested in reaching the particular demographic that the artist attracts. Because the summer concert season is one of the busiest and most lucrative times of the year, Cam and Anna felt it was extremely important to get the fan communities in place prior to the beginning of the summer. Therefore, they engaged in the following selected transactions for the months of May and June:

May 1	Paid Web Design Inc. $8,500 to develop the fan websites. The fan websites were operational on May 10. Front Row charged this expenditure to other expense.
10	Front Row Entertainment sold $550 worth of advertising to Little John's Restaurant with terms 2/10, n/30. The advertising will randomly appear on the artists' websites throughout the month of May. Front Row expects Little John's to pay within the discount period.
15	Front Row Entertainment sold $450 worth of advertising to Sherwood Media with terms 2/10, n/30. The advertising related to an in-store DVD promotion that Sherwood was holding later in the month. Front Row expects Sherwood Media to pay within the discount period.
19	Front Row Entertainment received payment from Little John for the May 10 bill.
20	Sherwood Media informed Front Row that an error had been made on its advertisement. Sherwood's promotion was supposed to run from May 20 to May 25; however, the advertisement stated that the promotion would run from May 15 to May 25. Because the error was Front Row's fault, Front Row agreed to reduce the amount owed by $150.
June 1	Front Row Entertainment sold $750 worth of advertising to Big House Entertainment Company with terms 2/10, n/30. The advertising will randomly appear on the artists' websites throughout the month of June. Front Row expects Big House to pay within the discount period.
10	Sherwood paid Front Row the amount owed for the May 15 bill minus the allowance granted on May 20.
20	Front Row learns that Big House Entertainment has filed for bankruptcy, and it writes off the receivable from June 1st.

Over the next few months, the fan communities continue to grow in popularity, with more and more companies purchasing advertising space. By the end of 2023, Front Row reports the following balances:

Accounts receivable	$17,900
Allowance for doubtful accounts	250 (debit)
Credit sales	45,000

Required:

1. Prepare journal entries for the May and June transactions.
2. Prepare the adjusting entry required at December 31, 2023, with regard to bad debt under each of the following independent assumptions.
   a. Assume that Front Row performed an aging of its accounts receivable. Front Row estimates that $895 of its accounts receivable will be uncollectible.
   b. Assume that Front Row uses the percentage of credit sales method and estimates that 2% of credit sales will be uncollectible.

6

Cost of Goods Sold and Inventory

After studying Chapter 6, you should be able to:

1 Describe the types of inventories and how inventory costs flow through a company.

2 Explain how to record purchases and sales of inventory using a perpetual inventory system.

3 Apply the four inventory costing methods to compute ending inventory and cost of goods sold under a perpetual inventory system.

4 Analyze the financial reporting and tax effects of the various inventory costing methods.

5 Apply the lower of cost or net realizable value rule to the valuation of inventory.

6 Evaluate inventory management using the gross profit and inventory turnover ratios.

7 Describe how errors in ending inventory affect income statements and balance sheets.

8 (*Appendix 6A*) Explain how to record purchases of inventory using a periodic inventory system.

9 (*Appendix 6B*) Compute ending inventory and cost of goods sold under a periodic inventory system.

Sundry Photography/Shutterstock.com

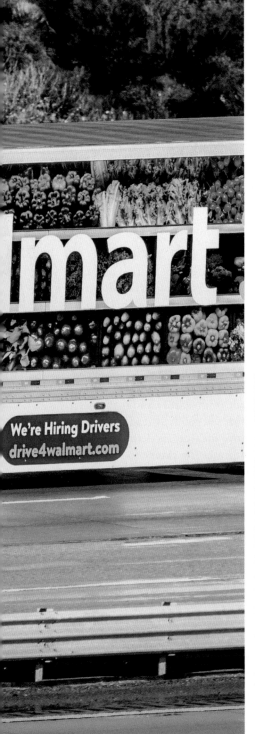

EXPERIENCE FINANCIAL ACCOUNTING

with Wal-Mart

Wal-Mart Stores, Inc., based in Bentonville, Arkansas, is one of America's largest public corporations with almost $524 billion in sales. Wal-Mart serves more than 265 million customers per week through 11,500 retail stores in 27 countries. Given the large volume of merchandise that is sold, Wal-Mart's profits depend heavily on the control and management of its inventory. After all, as shown in Exhibit 6.1, inventory makes up almost 72% of Wal-Mart's current assets.

For many companies, inventory is at the heart of the operating cycle and must be carefully managed and controlled. If a company doesn't have enough inventory on its shelves to meet customers' demand, it will lose sales. On the other hand, too much inventory will increase carrying costs, such as storage and interest costs, as well as increase the risk of obsolescence. Wal-Mart has long been recognized as a world leader in its effective use of technology to manage and control its inventory and distribution.

As you will see in this chapter, even though inventory is an asset, it can have a major impact on net income. That is because all inventory accounting systems allocate the cost of inventory between ending inventory and cost of goods sold. Therefore, the valuation of inventory affects cost of goods sold, which in turn affects net income. By managing and controlling its inventory, Wal-Mart has been able to tie up less of its money in inventory than its competitors, resulting in greater profits.

Composition of Wal-Mart's Current Assets

EXHIBIT 6.1

Wal-Mart Stores, Inc. Consolidated Balance Sheets (partial) January 31	
(in millions)	2020
ASSETS:	
Current assets:	
Cash and cash equivalents	$ 9,465
Receivables	6,284
Inventories	44,435
Prepaid expenses and other	1,622
Total current assets	$61,806

Cash · Inventories · Receivables · Prepaid expenses and other

Source: Wal-Mart Stores, Inc. 2020 10-K.

OBJECTIVE

Describe the types of inventories and
how inventory costs flow through
a company.

NATURE OF INVENTORY AND COST OF GOODS SOLD

Inventory represents products held for resale and is classified as a current asset on the balance sheet. The inventories of large companies like **General Electric**, **Procter and Gamble**, and **Wal-Mart** are composed of thousands of different products or materials and millions of individual units that are stored in hundreds of different locations. For other companies, inventories are a much less significant portion of their total assets. Exhibit 6.2 shows the relative composition of inventory for Wal-Mart and **Microsoft**.

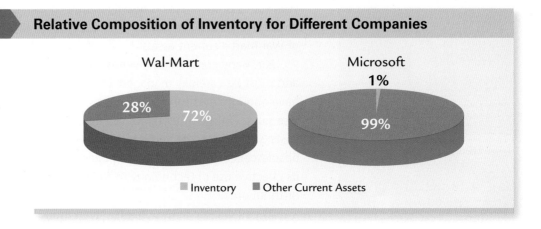

EXHIBIT 6.2 — Relative Composition of Inventory for Different Companies

For companies like **Wal-Mart**, these vast and varied inventories are at the heart of company operations and must be carefully controlled and accounted for. For example, one of Wal-Mart's key performance measures is the comparison of inventory growth to sales growth. In 2020, Wal-Mart's sales increased by 1.8% due to a variety of factors, including stronger U.S. sales. In response, it was able to increase its inventory by only 0.3%—an indication that Wal-Mart was effectively managing and controlling its inventory.

When companies like **Wal-Mart** sell their inventory to customers, the cost of the inventory becomes an expense called cost of goods sold. **Cost of goods sold** (or **cost of sales**) represents the outflow of resources caused by the sale of inventory and is the most important expense on the income statement of companies that sell goods instead of services. **Gross margin** (also called **gross profit**), a key performance measure, is defined as sales revenue minus cost of goods sold. Thus, gross margin indicates the extent to which the resources generated by sales can be used to pay operating expenses (selling and administrative expenses) and provide for net income. For 2020, Wal-Mart reported a gross margin of $129,359,000,000, calculated as:

$$\text{Revenue} - \text{Cost of Goods Sold} = \text{Gross Margin}$$
$$\$523,964,000,000 - \$394,605,000,000 = \$129,359,000,000 \ (24.7\% \text{ of revenue})$$

The cost of inventory has a direct effect on cost of goods sold and gross margin. To correctly interpret and analyze financial statements, one must understand inventory accounting. Accounting for inventories involves determining the cost of inventory through the use of one of several different inventory costing methods. In addition, GAAP allows certain departures from historical cost accounting for inventory. These choices that managers make affect the balance sheet valuation of inventory, the amount of reported net income, and the income taxes payable from year to year.

In this chapter, we will examine the process of accounting for inventory and cost of goods sold. We will address the following questions:

- What are the different types of inventory?
- What costs should be included in inventory?
- Which inventory system (perpetual or periodic) should be employed?
- How are inventory transactions recorded?
- How is ending inventory and cost of goods sold computed?
- What are the financial statement effects of the four alternative inventory costing methods?
- How does application of the lower of cost or net realizable value rule affect inventory valuation?

An understanding of inventory accounting will help in the analysis of financial statements as well as in managing a business.

TYPES OF INVENTORY AND FLOW OF COSTS

In previous chapters, we have discussed companies that sell services such as advertising agencies, delivery companies, repair companies, and accounting firms. For these companies, inventory plays a much smaller role. For example, **Facebook** doesn't even report an amount for inventory! Our focus in this chapter will be on companies that sell inventory. These companies are either merchandisers or manufacturers.

Merchandisers are companies (either retailers or wholesalers) that purchase inventory in a finished condition and hold it for resale without further processing.

- **Retailers** such as **Wal-Mart**, **Dillards**, and **Target** are merchandisers that sell directly to consumers.
- **Wholesalers** are merchandisers that sell to other retailers. For example, **McKesson** and **AmerisourceBergen** are wholesalers that supply pharmaceutical products to healthcare providers; **United Natural Foods** is a wholesaler that distributes natural, organic, and specialty foods to various retailers.

The inventory held by merchandisers is termed **merchandise inventory**. Merchandise inventory is an asset. When that asset is sold to a customer, it becomes an expense called cost of goods sold, which appears on the income statement. Wal-Mart's inventory disclosure, shown earlier in Exhibit 6.1 (p. 322), is an example of a typical disclosure made by a merchandising company.

Manufacturers are companies that buy and transform raw materials into a finished product, which is then sold. **Sony**, **Toyota**, and **Intel** are all manufacturing companies. Manufacturing companies classify inventory into three categories: raw materials, work-in-process, and finished goods.

- **Raw materials inventory** are the basic ingredients used to make a product. When these raw materials are purchased, the Raw Materials Inventory account is increased. As raw materials are used to manufacture a product, they become part of work-in-process inventory.
- **Work-in-process inventory** consists of the raw materials that are used in production as well as other production costs such as labor and utilities. These costs stay in this account until the product is complete. Once the production process is complete, these costs are moved to the Finished Goods Inventory account.
- **Finished goods inventory** represents the cost of the final product that is available for sale. When the finished goods inventory is sold to a customer, it becomes an expense called cost of goods sold, which appears on the income statement.

The inventory disclosure of **Intel**, shown in Exhibit 6.3, is an example of a typical disclosure made by a manufacturing company.

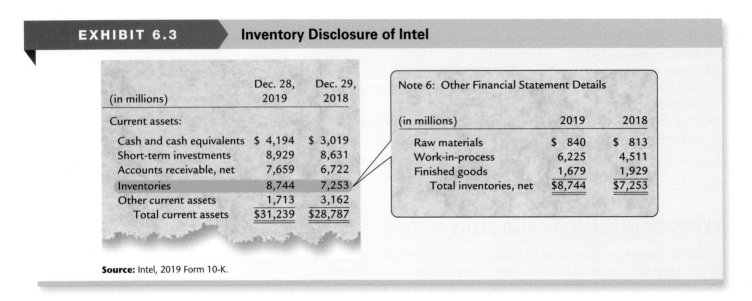

EXHIBIT 6.3	Inventory Disclosure of Intel

(in millions)	Dec. 28, 2019	Dec. 29, 2018
Current assets:		
Cash and cash equivalents	$ 4,194	$ 3,019
Short-term investments	8,929	8,631
Accounts receivable, net	7,659	6,722
Inventories	8,744	7,253
Other current assets	1,713	3,162
Total current assets	$31,239	$28,787

Note 6: Other Financial Statement Details

(in millions)	2019	2018
Raw materials	$ 840	$ 813
Work-in-process	6,225	4,511
Finished goods	1,679	1,929
Total inventories, net	$8,744	$7,253

Source: Intel, 2019 Form 10-K.

The relationship between the various inventory accounts and cost of goods sold is shown in Exhibit 6.4.

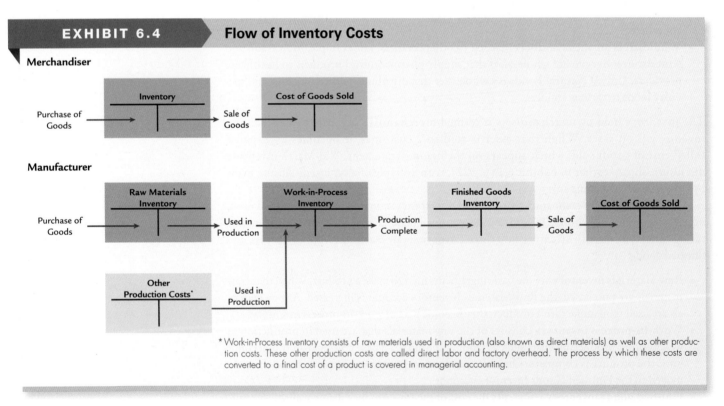

EXHIBIT 6.4	Flow of Inventory Costs

Merchandiser

Manufacturer

* Work-in-Process Inventory consists of raw materials used in production (also known as direct materials) as well as other production costs. These other production costs are called direct labor and factory overhead. The process by which these costs are converted to a final cost of a product is covered in managerial accounting.

Cost of goods sold is the cost to the seller of all inventory sold during the accounting period. Consistent with the expense recognition principle, cost of goods sold is recognized as an expense in the same period as the revenue from the sale of inventory is recognized.

COST OF GOODS SOLD MODEL

The relationship between cost of goods sold and inventory is given by the cost of goods sold model:[1]

	Beginning inventory
+	Purchases
=	Cost of goods available for sale
−	Ending inventory
=	Cost of goods sold

A company will start the year with an amount of inventory on hand called *beginning inventory*. During the year, any *purchases* of inventory are added to the inventory account. The sum of beginning inventory and purchases represents the **cost of goods available for sale**. The portion of the cost of goods available for sale that remains unsold at the end of the year is the company's *ending inventory* (the ending inventory for one period becomes the beginning inventory of the next period). The portion of the cost of goods available for sale that is sold becomes *cost of goods sold*. The cost of goods sold model is illustrated in Exhibit 6.5.

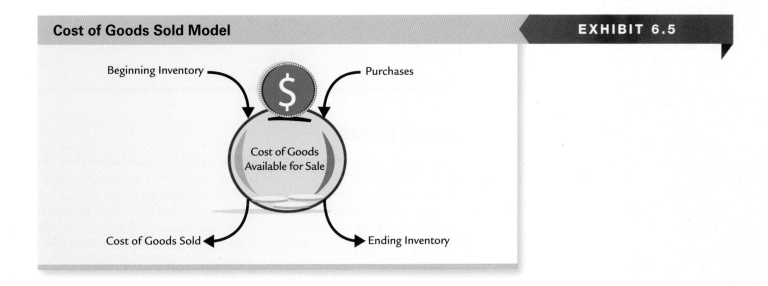

Cost of Goods Sold Model EXHIBIT 6.5

The determination of cost of goods sold requires an allocation of the cost of goods available for sale between ending inventory and cost of goods sold. Application of the cost of goods sold model is illustrated in EXAMPLE 6.1.

---

1 The concepts involved in accounting for inventories of manufacturers and merchandisers are similar. However, due to the complexities of accounting for manufacturing inventory, the remainder of the chapter will focus on merchandising companies.

EXAMPLE 6.1   APPLYING THE COST OF GOODS SOLD MODEL

Bargain Shops, a retail clothing store, had a beginning inventory of $26,000 on January 1. During the year, the company purchased goods from a supplier costing $411,000. At December 31, the cost of the unsold inventory was $38,000.

Required:
Compute cost of goods sold at December 31.

Solution:

	Beginning inventory	$ 26,000
+	Purchases	411,000
=	Cost of goods available for sale	$437,000
−	Ending inventory	(38,000)
=	Cost of goods sold	$399,000

The general structure of the cost of goods sold model can be rearranged to solve for any missing amount if the other three amounts are known. For example, if Bargain Shops did not know the cost of ending inventory but knew the cost of goods sold was $399,000, the company could determine ending inventory by rearranging the model as follows:

	Beginning inventory	$ 26,000
+	Purchases	411,000
=	Cost of goods available for sale	$ 437,000
−	Cost of goods sold	(399,000)
=	Ending inventory	$ 38,000

Next Level

Because all inventories ultimately get expensed as cost of goods sold, why aren't all costs recorded as cost of goods sold when they are incurred?

ANSWER:
Costs related to inventories are initially recorded in an inventory account to help a company achieve a proper matching of expenses with revenues. By recording costs in an inventory account, a company can delay the recognition of the expense until the goods are sold. If all inventory-related costs were expensed when incurred, users of financial statements would see a distorted picture of the company's profitability.

INVENTORY SYSTEMS

Because inventory is at the heart of the operating cycle for most wholesalers and retailers, the inventory accounting systems that track the level of inventory and record purchases and sales are particularly important. These systems provide the information needed to determine cost of goods sold and analyze inventory. In addition, these systems signal the need to purchase additional inventory or the need to make special efforts to sell existing inventory. They also provide information necessary to safeguard the inventory from misappropriation or theft. In short, these systems provide the information that managers need to manage and control inventory.

Companies use one of two types of inventory accounting systems—a perpetual inventory system or a periodic inventory system.

Perpetual Inventory System In a **perpetual inventory system**, balances for inventory and cost of goods sold are continually (perpetually) updated with each sale or purchase of inventory. This type of system requires that detailed records be maintained on a transaction-by-transaction basis for each purchase and sale of inventory. For example, every time that **Wal-Mart** purchases inventory from a supplier, it records this purchase directly in its inventory records. Similarly, when Wal-Mart makes a sale to a customer, it will not only record the sale (as illustrated in Chapter 5) but also update its inventory and cost of goods sold balances by decreasing inventory and increasing cost of goods sold. In other words, a perpetual inventory system records both the *revenue* and *cost* side of sales transactions.

With the volume of transactions that Wal-Mart has on a daily basis, this task may appear quite daunting. However, with the advent of "point of sale" cash register systems and optical bar code scanners, the implementation of perpetual inventory systems has become quite common. Some companies, such as Wal-Mart, are taking this idea a step further and using radio frequency identification (RFID) technology to track inventory. By attaching RFID tags to its inventory, Wal-Mart is able to more easily track inventory from its suppliers to the final customer, dramatically reducing inventory losses.

In a perpetual inventory system, the accounting system keeps an up-to-date record of both ending inventory and cost of goods sold at any point in time. However, a company that uses a perpetual system should still take a physical count of inventory at least once a year to confirm the balance in the inventory account. Any difference between the physical count of inventory and the inventory balance provided by the accounting system could be the result of errors, waste, breakage, or theft.

Periodic Inventory System   A **periodic inventory system** does not require companies to keep detailed, up-to-date inventory records. Instead, a periodic system records the cost of purchases as they occur (in an account separate from the inventory account), takes a physical count of inventory at the end of the period, and applies the cost of goods sold model to determine the balances of ending inventory and cost of goods sold. Thus, a periodic system only produces balances for ending inventory and cost of goods sold at the end of each accounting period (periodically). If a company using the periodic system needs to know the balance of inventory or cost of goods sold during a period, it must do either of the following:

- perform a physical count of inventory
- estimate the amount of inventory using an acceptable estimation technique

Comparison of Perpetual and Periodic Inventory Systems   Perpetual and periodic systems offer distinct benefits and any choice between the two inventory systems must weigh each system's advantages against its operating costs. The principal advantage of a periodic system is that it is relatively inexpensive to operate. Because perpetual systems require entering and maintaining more data than periodic systems, the additional costs can be quite substantial for a company with thousands of different items in inventory. However, with technological advances, this advantage is rapidly disappearing. The perpetual system has the advantage of making the balances of inventory and cost of goods sold continuously available. This provides management with greater control over inventory than it would have under a periodic inventory system. Providing managers with more timely information can be a significant and extremely valuable advantage in a competitive business environment. For example, much of **Wal-Mart**'s success has been attributed to its sophisticated inventory management and control system.

We will illustrate a perpetual inventory system in this chapter because of its growth and popularity in many different types of companies. A periodic inventory system is illustrated in Appendices 6A and 6B at the end of this chapter.

 YOUDECIDE   Just-in-Time Inventory Management

As the inventory manager for Goliath Inc., a large national merchandising company, it is your job to balance the costs of carrying inventory (e.g., finance costs, storage costs) against the costs of not meeting customer demand (e.g., the cost of lost sales). If Goliath can rely on its suppliers to deliver inventory on very short notice and in ready-to-use forms, very low inventory levels can be maintained. This approach to inventory management is called **just in time (JIT)** and is consistent with both minimizing inventory carrying costs and "out-of-stock" costs.

What information would you need to maintain a just-in-time inventory policy?

To synchronize the arrival of new inventory with the selling of the old inventory, you need detailed information about order-to-delivery times, receiving-to-ready-for-sale times, and inventory quantities. Delivery and make-ready times are used to control and minimize time lags between shipment of goods by suppliers and delivery to customers. In some retail stores, for example, merchandise arrives tagged, stacked, and ready for placement on the sales floor while in other retail stores several days may be required to get the merchandise ready for sale. Information on inventory quantities would also be useful as a signal to reorder a particular item of inventory. Perpetual inventory systems, which make inventory balances continuously available, can provide the needed information on inventory quantities.

Inventory management and control can lead to significant cost reductions and improved profitability.

OBJECTIVE

Explain how to record purchases and sales of inventory using a perpetual inventory system.

RECORDING INVENTORY TRANSACTIONS—PERPETUAL SYSTEM

The historical cost principle requires the activities of a company to be measured at their historical cost—the exchange price at the time the activity occurs. Applied to inventory, this principle implies that *inventory cost includes the purchase price of the merchandise plus any cost of bringing the goods to a salable condition and location.* Therefore, the cost of inventory will include the purchase price plus other "incidental" costs, such as freight charges to deliver the merchandise to the company's warehouse, insurance cost on the inventory while it is in transit, and various taxes. A company should stop accumulating costs as a part of inventory once the inventory is ready for sale.

ACCOUNTING FOR PURCHASES OF INVENTORY

Let's first take a look at how a merchandising company would account for inventory purchases. In a perpetual inventory system, the inventory account is used to record the costs associated with acquiring merchandise.

Purchases **Purchases** refers to the cost of merchandise acquired for resale during the accounting period. The purchase of inventory is recorded by increasing the inventory account. All purchases should be supported by a source document, such as an *invoice,* that provides written evidence of the transaction as well as the relevant details of the purchase. A typical invoice is shown in Exhibit 6.6. Note the various details on the invoice, such as the names of the seller and

---

EXHIBIT 6.6   **Sample Invoice**

Shoes Unlimited					INVOICE

We Care About Your Feet

301 College Street
Irvine, California 92612
Phone 800-555-2389 Fax 949-555-2300

INVOICE #256
DATE: Sept. 1

TO:

J. Parker Jones, Purchasing Manager
Brandon Shoes
879 University Blvd.
Auburn, Alabama 36830

SALESPERSON	P.O. NUMBER	REQUISITIONER	SHIPPED VIA	F.O.B. POINT	TERMS
E. Higgins	4895721	J. Parker Jones	UPS	Shipping Point	2/10, n/30

QUANTITY	DESCRIPTION	UNIT PRICE	TOTAL
100	Model No. 754 Athletic Running Shoe	$100	$10,000
	SUBTOTAL		$10,000
	SHIPPING & HANDLING		150
	TOTAL DUE		$10,150

the purchaser, the invoice date, the credit terms, the freight terms, a description of the goods purchased, and the total invoice amount.

The cost of purchases includes the effects of purchase discounts, purchase returns, and transportation charges.

Purchase Discounts As noted in Chapter 5, companies that sell goods on credit often offer their customers sales discounts to encourage prompt payment. From the viewpoint of the customer, such price reductions are called **purchase discounts**. The credit terms specify the amount and timing of payments. For example, credit terms of "2/10, n/30" mean that a 2% discount may be taken on the invoice price if payment is made within 10 days of the invoice date. This reduced payment period is known as the **discount period**. Otherwise, full payment is due within 30 days of the invoice date. If a purchase discount is taken, the purchaser reduces the inventory account for the amount of the discount taken, resulting in the inventory account reflecting the net cost of the purchase.

Generally, all available discounts should be taken. Failure to pay within the discount period is equivalent to paying interest for the use of money and can be quite expensive. For example, failure to take advantage of the 2% discount for credit terms of "2/10, n/30" is equivalent to an annual interest rate of 36.5%![2] Clearly, paying within the discount period is a good cash management policy.

Purchase Returns and Allowances Merchandise is inspected when received and may be tested in various ways before it becomes available for sale. The following issues may result in dissatisfaction with the merchandise:

- The wrong merchandise was delivered.
- The merchandise did not conform to specification.
- The merchandise was damaged or defective.
- The merchandise arrived too late at its destination.

If the purchaser is dissatisfied with the merchandise, it is frequently returned to the seller for credit or for a cash refund. The cost of merchandise returned to suppliers is called a **purchase return**. In some instances, the purchaser may choose to keep the merchandise if the seller is willing to grant a reduction of the purchase price. This situation is called a **purchase allowance**. Increases in purchase returns and allowances may signal deteriorating supplier relationships; thus, purchase returns are monitored very closely by purchasing managers. Because inventory was increased when the purchase was initially made, a purchase return or allowance is recorded by decreasing inventory.

Transportation Costs Transportation, or freight, costs are expenditures made to move the inventory from the seller's location to the purchaser's location. The proper recording of transportation costs depends upon whether the buyer or the seller pays for the transportation. Effectively, this question is the same as asking at what point the ownership of the inventory transfers from the seller to the buyer. The point at which ownership, or title, of the inventory changes hands depends on the shipping terms of the contract. The shipping terms can be either F.O.B. (free on board) shipping point or F.O.B. destination as illustrated in Exhibit 6.7.

- *F.O.B. shipping point:* If the shipping terms are **F.O.B. shipping point**, ownership of the inventory passes from the seller to the buyer at the shipping point. Under F.O.B. shipping point terms, the buyer normally pays the transportation costs, commonly termed **freight-in**.

---

2   This implied interest rate is computed as [365 days ÷ (30 days − 10 days)] × 2%. Notice that this formula uses a 20-day interest period computed as the days until final payment is due (30 days) minus the days in the discount period (10 days). This period can be adjusted to fit the specific credit terms of the transaction.

EXHIBIT 6.7   **Shipping Terms**

F.O.B. Shipping Point

F.O.B. Destination

> Ownership passes from the seller to the buyer when the goods are shipped.
> Buyer usually pays freight costs.
> Seller recognizes revenue at shipment.

> Ownership passes from the seller to the buyer when the goods are received.
> Seller usually pays freight costs.
> Seller recognizes revenue at delivery.

These costs are considered part of the total cost of purchases and the inventory account is increased. The seller would normally recognize revenue at the time of the shipment.

- *F.O.B. destination:* When the shipping terms are **F.O.B. destination**, ownership of the inventory passes when the goods are delivered to the buyer. Under F.O.B. destination shipping terms, the seller is usually responsible for paying the transportation costs, commonly termed **freight-out**. In this case, the transportation costs are not considered part of inventory; instead, the seller will expense these costs as a selling expense on the income statement. Revenue is not normally recognized until delivery of the goods has occurred.

Consigned Goods   Sometimes goods owned by one party are held and offered for sale by another. This arrangement is called a **consignment**. In a consignment, the seller (or *consignee*) earns a fee when the consigned goods are sold, but the original owner (or *consignor*) retains ownership of the goods. Manufacturers often use consignments to encourage large retailers, such as **Wal-Mart** and **Target**, to offer their products for sale. Retailers find these arrangements attractive because it enables them to reduce their investment in inventory. In consignment arrangements, the goods are not included in the seller's inventory.

ETHICAL DECISIONS   The proper determination of whether goods should or should not be considered part of the seller's inventory has created an ethical dilemma for some companies. With shipping terms of F.O.B. shipping point, managers may attempt to encourage customers to take delivery of more goods than are currently needed since such goods would generate revenue when the inventory is shipped. This practice, termed *channel stuffing*, effectively steals sales from the next period and distorts the results of the company's operations. The Securities and Exchange Commission (SEC) has closely examined transactions that were thought to be channel stuffing. For example, **Coca-Cola** paid $137.5 million due to channel stuffing allegations that allowed it to report artificially higher sales volumes to maintain a higher stock price. In addition, **Bristol-Myers Squibb** and **Monster Beverage** paid $150 million and $16.5 million, respectively, to settle allegations that included channel stuffing. ●

Recording Purchase Transactions   To summarize, the purchase price of inventory includes any cost of bringing the goods to a salable condition and location. Therefore, the inventory account is increased for the invoice price of a purchase as well as any transportation costs paid for by the buyer. Any purchase discounts, returns, or allowances reduce the inventory account. EXAMPLE 6.2 illustrates the journal entries required to record purchases of merchandise inventory.

Next Level

The purchase transactions that affect inventory seem complicated. Why go to all that trouble and effort when the periodic inventory system could be used?

ANSWER:

A perpetual inventory system requires a number of entries that directly affect inventory. While this system is certainly more complex than a periodic inventory system, the numerous entries provide management with up-to-date information that allows them to better manage and control their inventory.

EXAMPLE 6.2 RECORDING PURCHASE TRANSACTIONS IN A PERPETUAL INVENTORY SYSTEM

On September 1, Brandon Shoes purchased 50 pairs of hiking boots for $3,750 cash (or $75 a pair) and paid $150 of transportation costs. Also, on September 1, Brandon purchased 100 pairs of running shoes for $10,000; however, the seller paid the transportation costs of $300. The running shoes were purchased on credit with terms of 2/10, n/30. Brandon paid for one-half ($5,000) of the running shoes on September 10, within the discount period. After inspection, Brandon determined that running shoes costing $750 were defective and returned them on September 25. The remaining running shoes (cost of $4,250) were paid for on September 30.

Required:
Prepare the journal entries necessary to record the September transactions for Brandon Shoes.

Solution:

Date	Account and Explanation	Debit	Credit	Assets	= Liabilities +	Stockholders' Equity
Sept. 1	Inventory	3,750		▲		
	Cash		3,750	▼		
	(Purchased inventory for cash)					

Date	Account and Explanation	Debit	Credit	Assets	= Liabilities +	Stockholders' Equity
Sept. 1	Inventory	150		▲		
	Cash		150	▼		
	(Recorded payment of freight costs)					

Date	Account and Explanation	Debit	Credit	Assets	= Liabilities +	Stockholders' Equity
Sept. 1	Inventory	10,000		▲		
	Accounts Payable		10,000		▲	
	(Purchased inventory on credit)					

Date	Account and Explanation	Debit	Credit	Assets	= Liabilities +	Stockholders' Equity
Sept. 10	Accounts Payable	5,000			▼	
	Cash		4,900	▼		
	Inventory ($5,000 × 2%)		100	▼		
	(Recorded payment within the discount period)					

Date	Account and Explanation	Debit	Credit	Assets	= Liabilities +	Stockholders' Equity
Sept. 25	Accounts Payable	750			▼	
	Inventory		750	▼		
	(Returned defective running shoes)					

Date	Account and Explanation	Debit	Credit	Assets	= Liabilities +	Stockholders' Equity
Sept. 30	Accounts Payable	4,250			▼	
	Cash		4,250	▼		
	(Recorded payment outside the discount period)					

Note that the purchase of the hiking boots in Example 6.2 included the $150 of transportation costs (freight-in) because Brandon paid the freight. However, the purchase of the running shoes did not include freight costs because it was paid by the seller.

These journal entries illustrate that, under a perpetual inventory system, inventory is constantly updated with each purchase so that the net effect of purchases is reflected in the inventory account. The computation of net purchases for Brandon Shoes is summarized in Exhibit 6.8. Although the original invoice price was $13,750, the consideration of purchase discounts, returns, and transportation charges resulted in a much different value in the inventory account.

EXHIBIT 6.8 ▶ **Calculation of Net Purchases**

Invoice price of purchase	$13,750
Less: Purchase discounts	(100)
Purchase returns and allowances	(750)
Add: Transportation costs (freight-in)	150
Net cost of purchases	$13,050

ACCOUNTING FOR SALES OF INVENTORY

In addition to purchase transactions, merchandising companies must also account for the inventory effects of sales and sales returns. Because a perpetual inventory system is being used, the Merchandise Inventory account is also affected.

Sales As discussed in Chapter 5, a company recognizes sales revenue when it satisfies its performance obligations to a customer. The recording of sales revenue involves two journal entries:

- In the first journal entry, sales revenue is recognized.
- The second journal entry recognizes, consistent with the expense recognition principle, the cost of the goods related to the products that are sold. It also reduces the inventory account so that the perpetual inventory system will reflect an up-to-date balance for inventory.

Sales Returns and Allowances If a customer returns an item for some reason, the company will make an adjustment to decrease sales revenue for the amount of the return.[3] In addition, the company must make a second entry to decrease cost of goods sold and increase inventory to reflect the return of the merchandise.

Recording Inventory Effects of Sales Transactions The use of a perpetual inventory system requires that two journal entries be made for both sales and sales return transactions. These journal entries are illustrated in EXAMPLE 6.3.

In each of the transactions in Example 6.3, the external selling price of $120 per pair was recorded as Sales Revenue. The cost of goods sold (or inventory) portion of the transaction was recorded at the cost to Brandon Shoes of $100 per pair. Therefore, for each pair of shoes sold, Brandon Shoes made a gross margin of $20 ($120 − $100). The total cost of goods sold recognized by Brandon Shoes is $9,000 ($10,000 − $1,000). *In dealing with sales to customers, it is important to remember to record revenues at retail prices and to record expenses (and inventory) at cost.*

> **⚠ Next Level**
>
> Instead of making two entries to record a sale under a perpetual system, why not just make one entry for the net amount? Wouldn't gross margin be the same?
>
> **ANSWER:**
> A system could be developed that combines the two entries necessary to record a sale of inventory under a perpetual system; however, important information would be lost. If an entry were made to an account such as "Gross Margin" for the difference between sales revenue and cost of goods sold, no information would be provided on the total amount of revenues or cost of goods sold. This loss of information would be inconsistent with the purpose of financial reporting.

---

3 As shown in Chapter 5, an adjusting entry at the end of the year is necessary for expected returns that have not yet been made. If the return occurs before the adjusting entry is made, companies will reduce sales revenue at the time of the return.

EXAMPLE 6.3 RECORDING SALES TRANSACTIONS IN A PERPETUAL INVENTORY SYSTEM

On August 1, Brandon Shoes sold 100 pairs of football cleats to the local college football team for $12,000 cash (each pair of cleats was sold for $120 per pair). Brandon paid $10,000 (or $100 per pair) for the cleats from its supplier. On August 15, the local college football team returned 10 pairs of cleats for a cash refund of $1,200.

Required:

1. Prepare the journal entries to record the sale of the football cleats.

2. Prepare the journal entries to record the return of the football cleats.

Solution:

1.

Date	Account and Explanation	Debit	Credit	Assets	= Liabilities +	Stockholders' Equity
Aug. 1	Cash	12,000		▲		
	Sales Revenue		12,000			▲
	(Recorded sale to customer)					

Date	Account and Explanation	Debit	Credit	Assets	= Liabilities +	Stockholders' Equity
Aug. 1	Cost of Goods Sold	10,000				▼
	Inventory		10,000	▼		
	(Recorded cost of merchandise sold)					

2.

Date	Account and Explanation	Debit	Credit	Assets	= Liabilities +	Stockholders' Equity
Aug. 15	Sales Revenue	1,200				▼
	Cash		1,200	▼		
	(Recorded return of merchandise)					

Date	Account and Explanation	Debit	Credit	Assets	= Liabilities +	Stockholders' Equity
Aug. 15	Inventory	1,000		▲		
	Cost of Goods Sold		1,000			▲
	(Recorded cost of merchandise returned)					

You are a CPA auditing the financial statements of Henderson Electronics, a computer retailer located in Duluth, Georgia. Henderson's policy is to record a sales transaction when the merchandise is shipped to customers (F.O.B. shipping point). During the audit, you notice that 50 computers were sold to the Itasca County School District near the end of the year. Further investigation reveals that these 50 computers are still in Henderson's warehouse. James Henderson, the owner, tells you that the school district wanted to purchase the computers with funds from the district's current fiscal year, but couldn't take delivery because the computer labs at the various schools were under renovation. Therefore, Henderson billed the district and recorded a credit sale in the current year.

Was this transaction accounted for properly?

Because the company has an F.O.B. shipping point policy and the inventory had not been delivered, the computers are not considered sold in the current year. Therefore, the recording of the credit sale should not have been made, and the inventory should be included in Henderson's ending inventory. This type of transaction is commonly referred to as a "bill and hold" sale. Although it may be perfectly legal, such transactions have come under scrutiny by the SEC as a means for companies to improperly inflate sales revenue and should be carefully scrutinized.

The proper determination of whether goods should or should not be included in inventory impacts both the balance sheet and the income statement.

OBJECTIVE 3

Apply the four inventory costing methods to compute ending inventory and cost of goods sold under a perpetual inventory system.

COSTING INVENTORY

A key feature of the cost of goods sold model is that the determination of cost of goods sold requires an allocation of the cost of goods available for sale between ending inventory and cost of goods sold. If the prices paid for goods are constant over time, this allocation is easy to compute—multiply the cost per unit times the number of units on hand at year end (to determine the cost of ending inventory) or times the number of units sold (to determine the cost of goods sold).

For example, if Speigel Company began operations by purchasing 1,000 units of a single product for $24 each, total goods available for sale would be $24,000, calculated as:

$$\text{Inventory Available for Sale} \times \text{Cost per Unit} = \text{Goods Available for Sale}$$
$$1{,}000 \text{ units} \times \$24 = \$24{,}000$$

If 800 units were sold during the period, the cost of the remaining 200-unit ending inventory is $4,800:

$$\text{Ending Inventory} \times \text{Cost per Unit} = \text{Cost of Ending Inventory}$$
$$200 \text{ units} \times \$24 = \$4{,}800$$

Cost of goods sold is $19,200, calculated as:

$$\text{Units Sold} \times \text{Cost per Unit} = \text{Cost of Goods Sold}$$
$$800 \text{ units} \times \$24 = \$19{,}200$$

It makes no difference which of the 1,000 units remain in ending inventory because all units have the same cost ($24).

On the other hand, if the price paid for a good changes over time, the cost of goods available for sale may include units with different costs per unit. In such cases, the question arises: Which prices should be assigned to the units sold and which assigned to the units in ending inventory? For example, assume that Speigel Company purchased the same total of 1,000 units during a period at different prices:

Jan. 3	300 units purchased at $22 per unit	=	$ 6,600
Jan. 15	400 units purchased at $24 per unit	=	9,600
Jan. 24	300 units purchased at $26 per unit	=	7,800
	Cost of goods available for sale		$24,000

While the cost of goods available for sale is the same ($24,000), the cost of the 200-unit ending inventory depends on which goods remain in ending inventory. As illustrated by the cost of goods sold model discussed earlier, the cost assigned to ending inventory also affects the value of cost of goods sold.

	If ending inventory is made up of $22 per unit goods	**If ending inventory is made up of $26 per unit goods**
Ending inventory	$4,400	$5,200
	(200 units × $22/unit)	(200 units × $26/unit)
Cost of goods sold	$19,600	$18,800
	($24,000 − $4,400)	($24,000 − $5,200)

The determination of the value of ending inventory and cost of goods sold depends on management's choice of inventory system (perpetual or periodic) and method of allocating inventory costs.

INVENTORY COSTING METHODS

The inventory system (perpetual or periodic) determines *when* cost of goods sold is calculated—for every sales transaction or at the end of the period. An *inventory costing method* determines how costs are allocated to cost of goods sold and ending inventory. Although the assumption about how inventory costs flow could take many different forms, accountants typically use one of four inventory costing methods:

- specific identification
- first-in, first-out (FIFO)
- last-in, first-out (LIFO)
- average cost

Each of these four costing methods represents a different procedure for allocating the cost of goods available for sale between ending inventory and cost of goods sold. Only the specific identification method allocates the cost of purchases according to the *physical flow* of specific units through inventory. That is, specific identification is based on a *flow of goods* principle. In contrast, the other three methods—FIFO, LIFO, and average cost—are based on a *flow of cost* principle. When the FIFO, LIFO, or average cost methods are used, the physical flow of goods into inventory and out to the customers is generally unrelated to the flow of unit costs. *Generally accepted accounting principles do not require that the cost flow assumption be consistent with the physical flow of goods.*

Companies disclose their choice of inventory methods in a note to the financial statements. The 2019 annual report of **Wal-Mart** includes the following statement:

Notes to Consolidated Financial Statements

1. Summary of Significant Accounting Policies
Inventories.
The Company values inventories at the lower of cost or market—using the last-in, first-out ("LIFO") method for the Wal-Mart U.S. segment's inventories. The inventory at the Wal-Mart International segment is valued—using the first-in, first-out ("FIFO") method. The inventory at the Sam's Club segment is valued based on the weighted average cost LIFO method. At January 31, 2020, and January 31, 2019, the Company's inventories valued at LIFO approximated those inventories as if they were valued at FIFO.

Source: Wal-Mart Stores, Inc. 2019 Form 10-K.

Like many companies, **Wal-Mart** uses more than one method in determining the total cost of inventory. In general, LIFO and FIFO are the most widely used methods.

With the exception of specific identification, the inventory costing methods allocate cost of goods available for sale between ending inventory and cost of goods sold using the following process:

Step 1. Calculate the cost of goods available for sale *immediately prior* to any sale transaction.

Step 2. Apply the inventory costing method to determine ending inventory and cost of goods sold.

Step 3. Repeat Steps 1 and 2 for all inventory transactions during the period. The sum of the cost of goods sold computed in Step 2 is the cost of goods sold for the period. Ending inventory is the amount computed during the final application of Step 2 for the period.

To understand how inventory costing systems allocate costs (Step 2), it is useful to think of inventory as if it were a stack of separate layers, with each stack distinguished by the purchase price. Each time a purchase is made at a unit cost different from that of a previous purchase, a new layer of inventory cost is added to the stack. As inventory is sold, it is removed from the stack according to the cost flow assumption used. This process is illustrated in Exhibit 6.9 for the LIFO and FIFO methods.

EXHIBIT 6.9	Allocation of Inventory Costs

SPECIFIC IDENTIFICATION

The **specific identification method** determines the cost of ending inventory and the cost of goods sold based on the identification of the *actual* units sold and in inventory. This method does not require an assumption about the flow of costs but assigns cost based on the specific flow of inventory. It requires that detailed records of each purchase and sale be maintained so that a company knows exactly which items were sold and the cost of those items. Historically, this method was practical only for high-cost items with unique identifiers (e.g., serial numbers) that were sold in low numbers—for example, automobiles. With the introduction of bar coding, electronic scanners, and RFID, this method has become easier to implement, but its application is still relatively rare. The specific identification method is illustrated in EXAMPLE 6.4 .

EXAMPLE 6.4	APPLYING THE SPECIFIC IDENTIFICATION METHOD

Tampico Beachwear, a retail store specializing in beach apparel, has the following information related to purchases and sales of one of its more popular brand of shoes. (Each inventory layer is a different color.)

Date	Description	Units Purchased at Cost	Units Sold at Retail
Oct. 1	Beg. inventory	300 units @ $16 = $ 4,800	
3	Purchase 1	600 units @ $18 = $10,800	
8	Sale 1		800 units @ $30
15	Purchase 2	250 units @ $20 = $ 5,000	
20	Purchase 3	150 units @ $22 = $ 3,300	
25	Sale 2		300 units @ $30
		Goods available for sale:	Sales:
		1,300 units = $23,900	1,100 units = $33,000

The following is a schedule of those units that were sold during the month and those that remain in ending inventory at the end of the month:

Description	Units Sold	Units in Ending Inventory
Beginning inventory	300	—
Purchase 1	550	50
Purchase 2	170	80
Purchase 3	80	70
Total	1,100	200

Required:

1. Compute the cost of ending inventory at October 31 under the specific identification method.

2. Compute the cost of goods sold at October 31 under the specific identification method.

Solution:

1. Ending inventory is:

50 units @ $18	$ 900
80 units @ $20	1,600
70 units @ $22	1,540
200 units	$4,040

2. Cost of goods sold is:

300 units @ $16	$ 4,800
550 units @ $18	9,900
170 units @ $20	3,400
80 units @ $22	1,760
1,100 units	$19,860

Three items in Example 6.4 are of interest.

- *Cost of Goods Available for Sale:* The sum of ending inventory ($4,040) and cost of goods sold ($19,860) equals cost of goods available for sale ($23,900). The specific identification method, like all inventory costing methods, allocates the cost of goods available for sale between ending inventory and cost of goods sold.

- *Cost of Goods Sold:* Because there are usually far fewer units in ending inventory than in cost of goods sold, it is often easier to compute the cost of ending inventory and then find the cost of goods sold by subtracting ending inventory from cost of goods available for sale ($23,900 − $4,040 = $19,860).

- *Financial Statement Effects:* The determination of inventory cost affects both the balance sheet and the income statement. The amount assigned to ending inventory will appear on the balance sheet. The amount assigned to cost of goods sold appears as an expense on the income statement.

FIRST-IN, FIRST-OUT (FIFO)

The **first-in, first-out (FIFO) method** is based on the assumption that costs move through inventory in an unbroken stream, with the costs entering and leaving the inventory in the same order. In other words, *the earliest purchases (the first in) are assumed to be the first sold (the first out), and the more recent purchases are in ending inventory.* Every time inventory is sold, the cost of the earliest (oldest) purchases that make up cost of goods available for sale is allocated to cost of goods sold, and the cost of the most recent purchases is allocated to ending inventory. In many instances, this cost flow assumption is an accurate representation of the physical flow of goods. **Hewlett-Packard, Intel,** and **Chipotle** all use FIFO. In addition, grocery stores such as **Publix** use FIFO for their perishable items. EXAMPLE 6.5 illustrates the application of the FIFO method.

EXAMPLE 6.5   APPLYING THE FIFO INVENTORY COSTING METHOD

Tampico Beachwear, a retail store specializing in beach apparel, has the following information related to purchases and sales of one of its more popular brand of shoes. (Each inventory layer is a different color.)

Date		Description	Units Purchased at Cost	Units Sold at Retail
Oct.	1	Beginning inventory	300 units @ $16 = $ 4,800	
	3	Purchase 1	600 units @ $18 = $10,800	
	8	Sale 1		800 units @ $30
	15	Purchase 2	250 units @ $20 = $ 5,000	
	20	Purchase 3	150 units @ $22 = $ 3,300	
	25	Sale 2		300 units @ $30
			Goods available for sale:	Sales:
			1,300 units = $23,900	1,100 units = $33,000

Required:
Compute the cost of ending inventory and the cost of goods sold at October 31 using the FIFO method.

Solution:
Step 1: **Compute the cost of goods available for sale** *immediately prior* **to the first sale.** This produces an inventory balance of $15,600 ($4,800 + $10,800). Notice that this inventory balance is made up of two layers—a $16 layer and an $18 layer.

Step 2: **Apply FIFO to determine ending inventory and cost of goods sold.** The cost of goods available for sale is allocated between inventory (the most recent purchases) and cost of goods sold (the earliest purchases).

Date		Description	Cost of Goods Sold	Inventory Balance	
Oct.	1	Beginning inventory		300 × $16	= $ 4,800
	3	Purchase 1 (600 @ $18)		300 × $16 = $ 4,800 ⎱ 600 × $18 = $10,800 ⎰ = $15,600	
	8	Sale 1 (800 @ $30)	300 × $16 = $4,800 ⎱ 500 × $18 = $9,000 ⎰ = $13,800	100 × $18	= $ 1,800

Step 3: **Repeat Steps 1 and 2 for the remaining inventory transactions during the period.**

Date		Description	Cost of Goods Sold	Inventory Balance	
Oct.	8	Inventory on hand		100 × $18	= $ 1,800
	15	Purchase 2 (250 @ $20)		100 × $18 = $ 1,800 ⎱ 250 × $20 = $ 5,000 ⎰ = $ 6,800	

Date	Description	Cost of Goods Sold	Inventory Balance
20	Purchase 3 (150 @ $22)		100 × $18 = $1,800 ⎫
			250 × $20 = $5,000 ⎬ = $10,100
			150 × $22 = $3,300 ⎭
25	Sale 2 (300 @ $30)	100 × $18 = $1,800 ⎫	50 × $20 = $1,000 ⎫
		200 × $20 = $4,000 ⎬ = $ 5,800	150 × $22 = $3,300 ⎬ = **$ 4,300**
		Total **$ 19,600**	

The application of FIFO in Example 6.5 resulted in the following:

- Ending inventory reported on the balance sheet is $4,300.
- Cost of goods sold is $19,600 ($13,800 + $5,800).

Because the sum of ending inventory and cost of goods sold ($4,300 + $19,600) equals cost of goods available for sale ($23,900), Tampico could have also calculated cost of goods sold as the difference between cost of goods available for sale and ending inventory ($23,900 − $4,300).

LAST-IN, FIRST-OUT (LIFO)

The **last-in, first-out (LIFO) method** allocates the cost of goods available for sale between ending inventory and cost of goods sold based on the assumption that the most recent purchases (the last in) are the first to be sold (the first out). Under the LIFO method, *the most recent purchases (newest costs) are allocated to the cost of goods sold and the earliest purchases (oldest costs) are allocated to inventory.* Except for companies that stockpile inventory (e.g., piles of coal, stacks of hay, stacks of rock), this cost flow assumption rarely coincides with the actual physical flow of inventory. Companies such as **General Mills, Target,** and **Chevron** all use LIFO. EXAMPLE 6.6 illustrates the application of the LIFO method.

EXAMPLE 6.6 APPLYING THE LIFO INVENTORY COSTING METHOD

Tampico Beachwear, a retail store specializing in beach apparel, has the following information related to purchases and sales of one of its more popular brand of shoes. (Each inventory layer is a different color.)

Date	Description	Units Purchased at Cost	Units Sold at Retail
Oct. 1	Beginning inventory	300 units @ $16 = $ 4,800	
3	Purchase 1	600 units @ $18 = $10,800	
8	Sale 1		800 units @ $30
15	Purchase 2	250 units @ $20 = $ 5,000	
20	Purchase 3	150 units @ $22 = $ 3,300	
25	Sale 2		300 units @ $30
		Goods available for sale:	Sales:
		1,300 units = $23,900	1,100 units = $33,000

CONTINUED

EXAMPLE 6.6   APPLYING THE LIFO INVENTORY COSTING METHOD *(CONTINUED)*

Required:
Compute the cost of ending inventory and the cost of goods sold at October 31 using the LIFO method.

Solution:

Step 1: **Compute the cost of goods available for sale** *immediately prior* **to the first sale.** This produces an inventory balance of $15,600 ($4,800 + $10,800). Notice that this inventory balance is made up of two layers—a $16 layer and an $18 layer.

Step 2: **Apply LIFO to determine ending inventory and cost of goods sold.** The cost of goods available for sale is allocated between inventory (the earliest purchases) and cost of goods sold (the most recent purchases).

Date	Description	Cost of Goods Sold	Inventory Balance	
Oct. 1	Beginning inventory		300 × $16	= $4,800
3	Purchase 1 (600 @ $18)		300 × $16 = $4,800 600 × $18 = $10,800 }	= $15,600
8	Sale 1 (800 @ $30)	600 × $18 = $10,800 200 × $16 = $3,200 } = $14,000	100 × $16	= $1,600

Step 3: Repeat Steps 1 and 2 for the remaining inventory transactions during the period.

Date	Description	Cost of Goods Sold	Inventory Balance	
Oct. 8	Inventory on hand		100 × $16	= $1,600
15	Purchase 2 (250 @ $20)		100 × $16 = $1,600 250 × $20 = $5,000 }	= $6,600
20	Purchase 3 (150 @ $22)		100 × $16 = $1,600 250 × $20 = $5,000 150 × $22 = $3,300 }	= $9,900
25	Sale 2 (300 @ $30)	150 × $22 = $3,300 150 × $20 = $3,000 } = $6,300	100 × $16 = $1,600 100 × $20 = $2,000 }	= **$3,600**
		Total = **$20,300**		

The application of LIFO in Example 6.6 resulted in the following:

- Ending inventory reported on the balance sheet is $3,600.
- Cost of goods sold is $20,300, the sum of cost of goods sold during the period ($14,000 + $6,300).

Because the sum of ending inventory and cost of goods sold ($3,600 + $20,300) equals cost of goods available for sale ($23,900), Tampico could have also calculated cost of goods sold as the difference between cost of goods available for sale and ending inventory ($23,900 − $3,600).

AVERAGE COST

The **average cost method** allocates the cost of goods available for sale between ending inventory and cost of goods sold based on a weighted average cost per unit. This weighted average cost per unit is calculated after each purchase of inventory as:

$$\text{Weighted Average Cost per Unit} = \frac{\text{Cost of Goods Available for Sale}}{\text{Units Available for Sale}}$$

Because a new average is computed after each purchase, this method is often called the moving-average method. This weighted average cost per unit is then used to calculate ending inventory and cost of goods sold as:

$$\text{Ending Inventory} = \text{Units on Hand} \times \text{Weighted Average Cost per Unit}$$

$$\text{Cost of Goods Sold} = \text{Units Sold} \times \text{Weighted Average Cost per Unit}$$

The average cost method is used by companies such as **Office Depot, Microsoft,** and **Starbucks.** EXAMPLE 6.7 illustrates the application of the average cost method.

EXAMPLE 6.7 APPLYING THE AVERAGE COST INVENTORY COSTING METHOD

Tampico Beachwear, a retail store specializing in beach apparel, has the following information related to purchases and sales of one of its more popular brand of shoes. (Each inventory layer is a different color.)

Date	Description	Units Purchased at Cost	Units Sold at Retail
Oct. 1	Beginning inventory	300 units @ $16 = $ 4,800	
3	Purchase 1	600 units @ $18 = $10,800	
8	Sale 1		800 units @ $30
15	Purchase 2	250 units @ $20 = $ 5,000	
20	Purchase 3	150 units @ $22 = $ 3,300	
25	Sale 2		300 units @ $30
		Goods available for sale: 1,300 units = $23,900	Sales: 1,100 units = $33,000

Required:

Compute the cost of ending inventory and the cost of goods sold at October 31 using the average cost method. (*Note:* Use four decimal places for per-unit calculations and round all other numbers to the nearest dollar.)

Solution:

Step 1: Compute the cost of goods available for sale *immediately prior* to the first sale. This produces an inventory balance of $15,600 ($4,800 + $10,800) and inventory units of 900 (300 + 600).

Step 2: Apply the average cost method to determine ending inventory and cost of goods sold. The cost of goods available for sale is allocated between inventory and cost of goods sold using a weighted average cost per unit, calculated as:

$$\text{Weighted Average Cost per Unit} = \frac{\text{Cost of Goods Available for Sale}}{\text{Units Available for Sale}}$$

$$= \frac{\$15,600}{900 \text{ units}} = \$17.333 \text{ per unit}$$

CONTINUED

EXAMPLE 6.7   APPLYING THE AVERAGE COST INVENTORY COSTING METHOD *(CONTINUED)*

Date	Description	Cost of Goods Sold		Inventory Balance
Oct. 1	Beginning inventory		300 × $16	= $ 4,800 ($16.0000/unit)
3	Purchase 1 (600 @ $18)		300 × $16 = $ 4,800 ⎫ 600 × $18 = $10,800 ⎬	= $15,600 ($17.3333/unit)[a]
8	Sale 1 (800 @ $30)	800 × $17.3333 = $13,867	100 × $17.3333	= $ 1,733

[a] $15,600 ÷ 900 units = $17.3333/unit

Step 3: Repeat Steps 1 and 2 for the remaining inventory transactions during the period.

Date	Description	Cost of Goods Sold		Inventory Balance
Oct. 8	Inventory on hand		100 × $17.3333	= $ 1,733 ($17.3333/unit)[a]
15	Purchase 2 (250 @ $20)		100 × $17.3333 = $1,733 ⎫ 250 × $20.00 = $5,000 ⎬	= $ 6,733 ($19.2371/unit)[b]
20	Purchase 3 (150 @ $22)		350 × $19.2371 = $6,733 ⎫ 150 × $22.00 = $3,300 ⎬	= $10,033 ($20.0660/unit)[c]
25	Sale 2 (300 @ $30)	300 × $20.0660 = $ 6,020	200 × $20.0660	= $ 4,013
		Total = $19,887		

[b] $6,733 ÷ 350 units = $19.2371/unit

[c] $10,033 ÷ 500 units = $20.0660/unit

The application of the average cost method in Example 6.7 results in the following:

- Ending inventory reported on the balance sheet is $4,013.
- Cost of goods sold is $19,887, the sum of cost of goods sold during the period ($13,867 + $6,020).

Because the sum of ending inventory and cost of goods sold ($4,013 + $19,887) equals cost of goods available for sale ($23,900), Tampico could have also calculated cost of goods sold as the difference between cost of goods available for sale and ending inventory ($23,900 − $4,013).

The average cost method results in an allocation to ending inventory and cost of goods sold that is between the allocations produced by FIFO and LIFO.

OBJECTIVE 4

Analyze the financial reporting and tax effects of the various inventory costing methods.

ANALYSIS OF INVENTORY COSTING METHODS

Companies are free to choose among the four inventory costing methods, and the inventory accounting policy decisions that are made can have major effects on the financial statements. Proper management of these decisions, within the bounds of generally accepted accounting principles and good business ethics, can also affect the timing of income tax payments and the judgments of creditors, stockholders, and others. Therefore, it is important to understand the consequences of these accounting choices.

ILLUSTRATING RELATIONSHIPS: FINANCIAL STATEMENT EFFECTS OF ALTERNATIVE COSTING METHODS

Financial statement analysts frequently ask the hypothetical question, "How much would inventory and income have been if a different costing method had been used?" If the prices paid for purchased inventory are stable, all inventory costing methods will yield the same amounts for ending inventory and cost of goods sold. However, when purchase prices vary, the FIFO, LIFO, and average cost methods will produce different amounts for ending inventory, cost of goods sold and, therefore, income. To properly analyze financial statements, it is necessary to understand the impact of changing prices on inventories and income.

To illustrate, consider the inventory data for Tampico Beachwear, which had revenues for the period of $33,000 (1,100 units sold × $30 per unit) and operating expenses of $4,000 (assumed amount). This information and the related FIFO, LIFO, and average cost inventory calculations in Examples 6.5 through 6.7 produced the income statement amounts shown in Exhibit 6.10.

Financial Statement Effects of Alternative Inventory Costing Methods   EXHIBIT 6.10

Tampico Beachwear Condensed Income Statements For the month ending Oct. 31						
	FIFO		**LIFO**		**Average Cost**	
Sales		$33,000		$33,000		$33,000
Beginning inventory	$ 4,800		$ 4,800		$ 4,800	
Add: Purchases	19,100		19,100		19,100	
Cost of goods available for sale	$23,900		$23,900		$23,900	
Less: Ending inventory	(4,300)		(3,600)		(4,013)	
Cost of goods sold		19,600		20,300		19,887
Gross margin		$13,400		$12,700		$13,113
Operating expenses (given)		4,000		4,000		4,000
Income before taxes		$ 9,400		$ 8,700		$ 9,113
Income tax expense (30%)		2,820		2,610		2,734
Net income		$ 6,580		$ 6,090		$ 6,379

Notice that sales, purchases, and cost of goods available for sale are the same for each method. However, the changing purchase prices of each inventory layer result in different amounts for cost of goods sold, gross margin, and net income.

When purchase prices are rising, as they are in our example (remember that inventory cost went from $16 to $18 to $20 to $22), the FIFO method produces the highest cost for ending inventory, the lowest cost of goods sold, and, therefore, the highest gross margin (and net income) of the three methods. In contrast, the LIFO method produced the lowest cost for ending inventory, the highest cost of goods sold, and, therefore, the lowest gross margin (and net income) of the three methods. The average cost method produced amounts for inventory, cost of goods sold, and net income that fell between the FIFO and LIFO extremes. *When purchase prices are falling,* the situation is reversed. Exhibit 6.11 summarizes these relationships.

↑ Rising Purchase Prices

FIFO produces:
- Highest ending inventory
- Lowest cost of goods sold
- Highest income

LIFO produces:
- Lowest ending inventory
- Highest cost of goods sold
- Lowest income

↓ Falling Purchase Prices

FIFO produces:
- Lowest ending inventory
- Highest cost of goods sold
- Lowest income

LIFO produces:
- Highest ending inventory
- Lowest cost of goods sold
- Highest income

During periods of rising prices, we expect LIFO companies to report lower amounts for inventory cost and higher amounts for cost of goods sold than comparable FIFO companies. And during periods of falling prices, we expect LIFO companies to report higher amounts of inventory cost and lower amounts for cost of goods sold than comparable FIFO companies. Due to these effects, it can be argued that:

- LIFO results in the more realistic amount for income because it matches the most current costs, which are closer to the current market value, against revenue.
- FIFO results in the more realistic amount for inventory because it reports the most current costs, which are closer to the current market value, on the balance sheet.

INCOME TAX EFFECTS OF ALTERNATIVE COSTING METHODS

We have seen that in periods of rising prices, LIFO allocates the newest—and therefore highest—inventory purchase prices to cost of goods sold, resulting in a lower gross margin and lower net income. Therefore, in periods of rising prices, companies may choose LIFO because it produces the lowest current taxable income and the lowest current income tax payment. In Exhibit 6.10, LIFO produced income tax expense of $2,610 compared to income tax expense of $2,820 if FIFO had been used.

Of course, in the long run, all inventory costs will find their way to cost of goods sold and the income statement. Therefore, choosing LIFO to minimize current taxes does not avoid the payment of taxes; it merely postpones it, temporarily reducing the company's capital requirements for a period of time. The federal income tax code requires businesses that use LIFO for tax purposes to use LIFO for financial reporting purposes as well. This is known as the LIFO conformity rule.

ETHICAL DECISIONS   When managers select an inventory costing method, it may not always be in the best interest of the company. For example, in a period of rising prices, the owners of the company may prefer that a company use LIFO in order to reduce the taxes that must be paid. However, many management bonus plans are based on net income, and the use of FIFO would result in larger bonuses. If managers let the choice of inventory costing method be

Next Level

Why doesn't the FASB simply mandate the most conceptually correct inventory costing method instead of giving companies a choice between alternative methods?

ANSWER:
All inventory costing methods provide an allocation of the total dollar amount of goods available for sale between ending inventory and cost of goods sold. No one cost method is conceptually superior to any other. For example, LIFO actually achieves a better matching of current costs with current revenues on the income statement; however, the resulting balance sheet valuation can be quite misleading about the current market value of inventory on the balance sheet. Companies make the choice between inventory methods for a variety of reasons unique to their own situation.

guided solely by its effect on their compensation, the ethics of their behavior can certainly be questioned. ●

CONSISTENCY IN APPLICATION

Companies are free to choose whichever inventory costing method they prefer, regardless of whether the method matches the physical flow of goods. However, once a company adopts a particular costing method for an item, it must continue to use it consistently over time.[4] The consistent application of an accounting principle over time discourages changes in accounting methods from one period to another, even if acceptable alternative methods exist. This enhances the comparability and usefulness of accounting information. A change in accounting method may still be made; however, the effects of the change must be fully disclosed. The consistent application of accounting methods and the required disclosures of any accounting changes permit readers of financial statements to assume that accounting methods do not change over time unless specifically indicated.

YOU DECIDE Choosing Among Inventory Costing Methods

You are the owner and manager of Simply Fresh, a supermarket that specializes in selling fresh, organic food. You know that managing inventory is crucial to the company's success and that generally accepted accounting principles give you the freedom to choose between FIFO, LIFO, and average cost to report inventory and cost of goods sold.

What factors should you consider in selecting among the different inventory costing methods?

Three factors that should be considered are:

- *Actual physical flow of inventory:* Because most companies sell their oldest merchandise first, FIFO will give the closest approximation to the physical flow of inventory. However, GAAP does not require that the choice of inventory costing method be consistent with the physical flow of goods.

- *Financial statement effects:* During periods of rising prices, the use of FIFO will result in the highest cost for ending inventory, the lowest cost of goods sold, and the highest net income. These positive financial results may be desirable to satisfy stockholders who demand higher stock prices or meet lending agreements that are tied to financial performance. In addition, if management's bonus plan is tied to reported income, the use of FIFO may result in higher bonuses for management.

- *Tax benefits:* During periods of rising prices, the use of LIFO will result in lower income and possibly create significant tax savings for the company.

If financial statement users wish to make good decisions, it is important to understand the differences that result from management's choice of inventory method.

LOWER OF COST OR NET REALIZABLE VALUE RULE

OBJECTIVE **5**

Apply the lower of cost or net realizable value rule to the valuation of inventory.

The inventory accounting procedures described to this point have followed the historical cost principle—inventory is recorded in the firm's records at its historical purchase price (or cost). The price for which inventory items can be sold may decline because the goods have become obsolete, have been damaged, or have otherwise diminished in value. For example, clothes that have gone out of style due to changing fashions or seasons have declined in value. Similarly, technology companies experience rapid obsolescence due to quickly changing technologies. In cases where the selling price of inventory has dropped below its original cost, generally accepted accounting principles permit a departure from the historical cost concept.

---

4 All items of inventory need not be accounted for by the same costing method. Many companies use LIFO for a portion of inventory and FIFO or average cost for another portion of their inventory.

This departure from the historical cost principle is called the **lower of cost or net realizable value (LCNRV) rule**.[5] **Net realizable value** is computed as the estimated selling price less costs of disposal (e.g., selling expenses). Under LCNRV, if the net realizable value of a company's inventory is lower than its cost, the company reduces the amount recorded for inventory to its net realizable value. To apply LCNRV, a company must perform the following steps:

Step 1: Determine the cost of inventory using a costing method (e.g., specific identification, FIFO, or average cost)

Step 2: Establish the net realizable value of the inventory.

Step 3: Compare the net realizable value to historical cost (usually on an item-by-item basis) and value the inventory at the lower of the two amounts.

Step 4: If the value of the inventory computed in Step 3 is less than its cost, record a journal entry to reduce inventory to the lower amount.

The lower of net realizable value or historical cost is used as the cost for the inventory on the financial statements. A company must make an adjusting journal entry to record any reduction of the cost of inventory to market value. EXAMPLE 6.8 illustrates the application of the LCNRV rule.

EXAMPLE 6.8 VALUING INVENTORY AT LOWER OF COST OR NET REALIZABLE VALUE

MacKenzie Electronics prepared the following analysis of its inventory at December 31:

Product	Quantity	Historical Cost per Item	Selling Price per Item	Cost of Disposal per Item	Net Realizable Value per Item
75" LED HDTV	12	$1,000	$1,200	$100	$1,100
55" OLED TV	7	1,500	1,500	300	1,200
Wireless Soundbar	20	120	130	30	100

Required:

1. Determine the lower of cost or net realizable value for each item of inventory.

2. Prepare the journal entry needed on December 31 to value the inventory at lower of cost or net realizable value.

Solution:

1. The lower of cost or net realizable value analysis is shown below.

Product	Cost	Net Realizable Value	Lower of Cost or Net Realizable Value
75" LED HDTV	$12,000 (12 × $1,000)	$13,200 (12 × $1,100)	$12,000
55" OLED TV	10,500 (7 × $1,500)	8,400 (7 × $1,200)	8,400
Wireless Soundbar	2,400 (20 × $120)	2,000 (20 × $100)	2,000
	$24,900	$23,600	$22,400

---

5 The discussion in this section applies to companies that use the FIFO or average cost methods. Companies that use LIFO follow the lower of cost or market (LCM) rule where market value is defined as replacement cost. However, companies that use LIFO in a period of rising prices do not normally have lower of cost or market issues. The application of the LCM rule is discussed more fully in intermediate accounting texts.

2. Because the lower of cost or net realizable value of inventory is less than its cost, the inventory must be reduced by $2,500 ($24,900 − $22,400) as follows:

Date	Account and Explanation	Debit	Credit	Assets	= Liabilities +	Stockholders' Equity
Dec. 31	Cost of Goods Sold	2,500				▼
	Inventory		2,500	▼		

This entry reduces inventory and increases cost of goods sold in the period the selling price of the item declined.

The LCNRV rule is an application of the conservatism principle. The *conservatism principle* leads accountants to select the accounting methods or procedures that produce the lowest (most conservative) net income and net assets in the current period. Thus, accountants tend to recognize expenses and losses as early as possible and to recognize gains and revenues as late as possible. By conservatively valuing inventory, the LCNRV rule is designed to avoid overstating the current earnings and financial strength of a company by recognizing an expense in the period that there is a decline in the selling price of inventory rather than in the period that the inventory is sold.

! Next Level

If the Financial Accounting Standards Board (FASB) allows the value of inventory to be reduced to NRV when the NRV is less than cost, why can't the value of inventory be increased when the NRV is greater than cost?

ANSWER:
For the same reason that the conservatism principle allows inventory to be written down to NRV, it prevents inventory from being written up to NRV. Given uncertainty as to the actual future selling price of the inventory, a prudent reaction would be to avoid being overly optimistic about the company's future prospects. Overly optimistic projections of the future usually have far more serious negative consequences for people relying on the financial statements than do understatements.

YOUDECIDE An Ethical Dilemma Involving Overvalued Inventory

You are the controller for PC Location Inc., a retailer that operates six computer stores in the Chicago area. An analysis of year-end inventory reveals a large number of obsolete laptop computers that require a $180,000 write-down to net realizable value. When you inform the CEO of this issue, she reminds you that PC Location is currently negotiating with Second Chicago Bank to increase its long-term loan and the bank has asked to review PC Location's preliminary financial statements. The CEO asks you to delay recognizing the write-down until Second Chicago has seen the preliminary financial statements. "Let the auditors write down the inventory when they show up in February," she says. "That's what we pay them for."

What should you do in this situation?

If you agree to ignore the required LCNRV adjustment, the bank may decide to grant the loan on the basis of the misleading financial statements. But when they receive the audited financial statements several months later, an investigation will no doubt be launched, and you are likely to take the blame. The ethical course of action is for you to refuse to go along with the CEO. You should be prepared to support your adjustment and to argue the disastrous consequences of trying to mislead Second Chicago Bank. In addition, you should be prepared to present alternatives to proceeding with the new loan at this time. Of course, if you refuse to go along with the CEO, you may find yourself unemployed.

The application of judgment in accounting may lead to ethical dilemmas.

OBJECTIVE ⑥▶

Evaluate inventory management
using the gross profit and inventory
turnover ratios.

ANALYZING INVENTORY

Inventories are at the heart of many companies' operations and must be carefully controlled and accounted for. Two measures of how successful a company is at managing and controlling its inventory are the gross profit ratio and the inventory turnover ratio.

Gross Profit Ratio The **gross profit ratio** is calculated as:

$$\text{Gross Profit Ratio} = \frac{\text{Gross Profit}}{\text{Net Sales}}$$

This ratio is carefully watched by managers, investors, and analysts as a key indicator of a company's ability to sell inventory at a profit. In short, the gross profit ratio tells us how many cents of every dollar are available to cover expenses other than cost of goods sold and to earn a profit. An increasing gross profit ratio could signal that a company is able to charge more for its products due to high demand or has effectively controlled the cost of its inventory. A decrease in this ratio could signal trouble. For example, a company may have reduced its selling price due to increased competition or it is paying more for its inventory.

Inventory Turnover Ratio The **inventory turnover ratio** is calculated as:

$$\text{Inventory Turnover Ratio} = \frac{\text{Cost of Goods Sold}}{\text{Average Inventory}}$$

This ratio describes how quickly inventory is purchased (or produced) and sold. Companies want to satisfy the conflicting goals of having enough inventory on hand to meet customer demand while minimizing the cost of holding inventory (e.g., storage costs, obsolescence). Inventory turnover provides an indicator of how much of the company's funds are tied up in inventory. High inventory turnover ratios indicate that a company is rapidly selling its inventory, thus reducing inventory costs. Low inventory turnover reflects that the company may be holding too much inventory, thereby incurring avoidable costs or signaling that demand for a company's products has fallen. Financial statement users can also compute the **average days to sell inventory** as:

$$\text{Average Days to Sell Inventory} = \frac{365 \text{ days}}{\text{Inventory Turnover}}$$

EXAMPLE 6.9 illustrates the analysis of these performance measures for **Wal-Mart** and **Target**.

EXAMPLE 6.9   CALCULATING THE GROSS PROFIT AND INVENTORY TURNOVER RATIOS

The following information is available for **Wal-Mart** and **Target** for a recent fiscal year (all amounts in millions):

Account	Wal-Mart	Target
Net sales	$523,964	$77,130
Cost of goods sold	394,605	54,864
Gross profit	129,359	22,266
Inventory, Beginning of year	44,269	9,497
Inventory, End of year	44,435	8,992

Required:

1. Compute the gross profit ratio for Wal-Mart and Target.

2. Compute the inventory turnover ratio and the average days to sell inventory for Wal-Mart and Target.

Solution:

1. $\text{Gross Profit Ratio} = \dfrac{\text{Gross Profit}}{\text{Net Sales}}$

Wal-Mart	**Target**
$\dfrac{\$129,359}{\$523,964} = 0.247$, or 24.7%	$\dfrac{\$22,266}{\$77,130} = 0.289$, or 28.9%

2. $\text{Inventory Turnover Ratio} = \dfrac{\text{Cost of Goods Sold}}{\text{Average Inventory}}$

Wal-Mart	**Target**
$\dfrac{\$394,605}{(\$44,269 + \$44,435) \div 2} = 8.897$	$\dfrac{\$54,864}{(\$9,497 + \$8,992) \div 2} = 5.935$

$\text{Average Days to Sell Inventory} = \dfrac{365 \text{ days}}{\text{Inventory Turnover}}$

Wal-Mart	**Target**
$\dfrac{365}{8.897} = 41.0$ days	$\dfrac{365}{5.935} = 61.5$ days

As you can see in Example 6.9, consistent with their position as low margin retailers, both **Wal-Mart** and **Target** have gross profit ratios below that of companies like **Ralph Lauren**, which has a gross profit ratio of 61.6%. While Target generates a higher gross profit on each dollar of sales, Wal-Mart is able to more rapidly sell its inventory (approximately 20 days faster) than Target. This higher inventory turnover allows Wal-Mart to lower its cost of carrying inventory, which leads to higher income.

LIFO RESERVE ADJUSTMENTS

Analysts and other users often wish to compare companies that use different inventory costing methods. To assist in these comparisons, companies that use LIFO are required to report the amount that inventory would increase (or decrease) if the company had used FIFO. This amount is referred to as the **LIFO reserve**. The LIFO inventory value can be found as follows:

$$\text{LIFO Inventory Value} = \text{Reported FIFO Inventory} - \text{LIFO Reserve}$$

In addition, the effect on income can be found by examining the difference in the LIFO reserve. For example, **General Mills'** disclosure of its LIFO reserve is shown in Exhibit 6.12.

EXHIBIT 6.12   **LIFO Reserve Disclosure**

General Mills Inc. Notes to Consolidated Financial Statements Note 17: Supplemental Information (in part)		
(in millions)	May 26, 2019	May 27, 2018
Inventories, at FIFO	$1,772.8	$1,855.4
Excess of FIFO over LIFO	(213.5)	(213.2)
Inventories, at LIFO	$1,559.3	$1,642.2

Source: General Mills, Inc. 2019 Form 10-K.

This disclosure shows that inventories would have been $213.5 million higher under FIFO for the 2019 fiscal year. Analysts can adjust the inventory amount by substituting in the FIFO inventory values ($1,772.8 million and $1,855.4 million for fiscal years 2019 and 2018, respectively) for the LIFO values reported on the balance sheet. In addition, income would have been higher under FIFO by $0.3 million ($213.5 million − $213.2 million)—the difference between the LIFO reserve.

 YOUDECIDE   LIFO Liquidations

You are the purchasing manager for Tomlinson Health Management, an aggressively managed new business that provides pharmacy services to retirement communities, nursing homes, and small hospitals in a three-state area. In order to secure tax benefits, Tomlinson uses LIFO for most of its inventories. Tomlinson's business has become increasingly competitive in recent years, and the current year's income has fallen significantly. Avery Tomlinson, the principal stockholder and CEO, has instructed you to hold year-end inventories to the absolute minimum.

What could be Mr. Tomlinson's motivation to reduce inventories?

The LIFO inventory is composed of layers, each one representing a year's contribution to the inventory at the earliest purchase prices of that year. During a period of rising prices, the LIFO inventory will be made up of the relatively older costs trapped in the LIFO layers. If the quantity of inventory falls, some of these older costs, with relatively low unit prices, will be released to cost of goods sold. This produces a lower cost of goods sold, and higher income, than one computed at current FIFO prices.

Mr. Tomlinson may be engaging in the questionable practice of earnings management. Reducing inventories releases old, low-priced LIFO layers to the income statement, lowering cost of goods sold and raising net income. Of course, Tomlinson's act may also raise current income taxes and impair business operations due to insufficient quantities of inventory.

When analyzing inventory, it is important to understand how changing inventory levels affects the financial statements.

OBJECTIVE

Describe how errors in ending inventory affect income statements and balance sheets.

EFFECTS OF INVENTORY ERRORS

The cost of goods sold model describes the relationship between inventory and cost of goods sold. This relationship implies that the measurement of inventory affects both the balance sheet and the income statement. Even with recent technological advances, it is easy to make errors in determining the cost of the hundreds of items in a typical ending inventory. Incorrect counts, mistakes in costing, or errors in identifying items are common. Because the ending inventory of one period is the beginning inventory of the next period, errors in the measurement of ending inventory affect two accounting periods.

To illustrate the effect of an error in valuing ending inventory on the financial statements, consider the information in Exhibit 6.13. The "Correct" column shows the financial statements for Year 1 and Year 2 as they would appear if no error were made. The "Erroneous" column shows the financial statements for the 2 years as they would appear if the firm understated its ending inventory in Year 1 by $15,000. The "Error" column describes the effect of the error on each line of the statements.

Effect of an Inventory Error — EXHIBIT 6.13

(amounts in thousands)	Correct		Erroneous		Error*
Year 1 Financial Statements					
Income Statement (partial)					
Sales		$500		$500	
Cost of goods sold:					
Beginning inventory	$ 50		$ 50		
Purchases	250		250		
Cost of goods available for sale	$300		$300		
Less: Ending inventory	(60)		(45)		−$15
Cost of goods sold		240		255	+$15
Gross margin		$260		$245	−$15
Balance Sheet (partial)					
Inventory		$ 60		$ 45	−$15
Retained earnings		$100		$ 85	−$15
Year 2 Financial Statements					
Income Statement (partial)					
Sales		$600		$600	
Cost of goods sold:					
Beginning inventory	$ 60		$ 45		−$15
Purchases	290		290		
Cost of goods available for sale	$350		$335		−$15
Less: Ending inventory	(50)		(50)		
Cost of goods sold		300		285	−$15
Gross margin		$300		$315	+$15
Balance Sheet (partial)					
Inventory		$ 50		$ 50	
Retained earnings		180		180	

*A minus sign (−) indicates an understatement and a plus sign (+) indicates an overstatement.

The understatement of the ending inventory in Year 1 causes an overstatement of cost of goods sold in Year 1. Thus, gross margin for Year 1 is understated by $15,000. Ignoring income taxes, this error would then flow into both net income and retained earnings. However, the effect is not limited to Year 1. Because the ending inventory for Year 1 is the beginning inventory for Year 2, the beginning inventory for Year 2 is understated by $15,000. Assuming no other errors are made, this would lead to an understatement of cost of goods sold and an overstatement of gross margin (and net income) by $15,000. However, notice that when this flows into retained earnings, the understatement in Year 1 is offset by the overstatement in Year 2 so that retained earnings is correctly stated by the end of Year 2. This illustrates the self-correcting nature of inventory errors.

EXAMPLE 6.10 illustrates the analysis of inventory errors.

EXAMPLE 6.10   ANALYZING INVENTORY ERRORS

Dunn Corporation reported net income of $75,000 for Year 1. Early in Year 2, Dunn discovers that the December 31, Year 1, ending inventory was overstated by $6,000.

Required:
Determine the financial statement effects of the inventory errors for Year 1 and Year 2.

Solution:
For Year 1, assets (ending inventory) are overstated by $6,000. The overstatement of ending inventory causes an understatement of cost of goods sold (an expense) by $6,000. This error flows through to income and retained earnings (equity). Because the ending inventory for Year 1 is the beginning inventory for Year 2, the error has the opposite effects on income for Year 2. Assuming no other errors are made, the inventory error self-corrects and the Year 2 balance sheet is correctly stated. These effects are summarized below.

	Assets	Liabilities	Equity	Revenues	Expenses	Income
Year 1	$6,000 overstated	No effect	$6,000 overstated	No effect	$6,000 understated	$6,000 overstated
Year 2	No effect	No effect	No effect	No effect	$6,000 overstated	$6,000 understated

Even though inventory errors are self-correcting over two periods, it is still necessary to correct them in order to produce properly stated financial information for each period.

OBJECTIVE

Explain how to record purchases of inventory using a periodic inventory system.

APPENDIX 6A: PERIODIC INVENTORY SYSTEM

In a periodic inventory system, the inventory records are not kept continually, or perpetually, up to date. Instead, under a periodic inventory system, the inventory account is updated at the end of the period based on a physical count of the inventory on hand. The balance in the inventory account remains unchanged during the period. As purchase transactions occur, they are recorded in one of four temporary accounts:

- *Purchases:* The Purchases account accumulates the cost of the inventory acquired during the period.
- *Purchase Discounts:* The Purchase Discounts account accumulates the amount of discounts on purchases taken during the period.
- *Purchase Returns and Allowances:* The Purchase Returns and Allowances account accumulates the cost of any merchandise returned to the supplier or any reductions (allowances) in the purchase price granted by the seller.
- *Transportation-In:* The Transportation-In account accumulates the cost paid by the purchaser to transport inventory from suppliers.

The balances in these temporary accounts, along with the beginning and ending inventory balances obtained from the physical count of inventory, are used to compute cost of goods sold using the cost of goods sold model.

EXAMPLE 6.11 (p. 353) illustrates how to record purchase transactions in a periodic inventory system.

EXAMPLE 6.11 RECORDING PURCHASE TRANSACTIONS IN A PERIODIC INVENTORY SYSTEM

On September 1, Brandon Shoes purchased 50 pairs of hiking boots for $3,750 cash (or $75 a pair) and paid $150 of transportation costs. Also, on September 1, Brandon purchased 100 pairs of running shoes for $10,000; however, the seller paid the transportation costs of $300. The running shoes were purchased on credit with credit terms of 2/10, n/30. Brandon paid for one-half ($5,000) of the running shoes on September 10, within the discount period. After inspection, Brandon determined that running shoes costing $750 were defective and returned them on September 25. The remaining running shoes (cost of $4,250) were paid for on September 30.

Required:
Prepare the journal entries necessary to record the September transactions for Brandon Shoes.

Solution:

Date	Account and Explanation	Debit	Credit	Assets	= Liabilities +	Stockholders' Equity
Sept. 1	Purchases	3,750				▼
	Cash		3,750	▼		
	(Purchased inventory for cash)					

Date	Account and Explanation	Debit	Credit	Assets	= Liabilities +	Stockholders' Equity
Sept. 1	Transportation-In	150				▼
	Cash		150	▼		
	(Recorded payment of freight costs)					

Date	Account and Explanation	Debit	Credit	Assets	= Liabilities +	Stockholders' Equity
Sept. 1	Purchases	10,000				▼
	Accounts Payable		10,000		▲	
	(Purchased inventory on credit)					

Date	Account and Explanation	Debit	Credit	Assets	= Liabilities +	Stockholders' Equity
Sept. 10	Accounts Payable	5,000			▼	
	Cash		4,900	▼		
	Purchase Discounts ($5,000 × 2%)		100			▲
	(Recorded payment within the discount period)					

Date	Account and Explanation	Debit	Credit	Assets	= Liabilities +	Stockholders' Equity
Sept. 25	Accounts Payable (10 pairs × $75 per pair)	750			▼	
	Purchase Returns and Allowances		750			▲
	(Returned defective hiking boots)					

Date	Account and Explanation	Debit	Credit	Assets	= Liabilities +	Stockholders' Equity
Sept. 30	Accounts Payable	4,250			▼	
	Cash		4,250	▼		
	(Recorded payment outside of the discount period)					

Under either the periodic or the perpetual inventory system, the net cost of purchases (shown below) is the same.

Purchases	$13,750
Less: Purchase discounts	(100)
Purchase returns and allowances	(750)
Add: Transportation costs (freight-in)	150
Net cost of purchases	$13,050

Additionally, for sales transactions, there is no need to make a second journal entry to record the expense (and inventory) portion of a transaction. Instead, only the revenue portion is recorded as shown earlier in the text.

The differences between a periodic and perpetual inventory system are summarized in Exhibit 6.14.

EXHIBIT 6.14   **Perpetual versus Periodic Inventory Systems**

Activity	Perpetual System	Periodic System
Purchase	Inventory purchases are recorded in the *Inventory* account.	The costs of inventory purchases are recorded in the *Purchases* account.
Sale	When a sale is made, an entry is made to record the amount of sales revenue. *A second entry is made that increases the Cost of Goods Sold account and decreases the Inventory account.*	When a sale is made, an entry is made to record the amount of sales revenue only. *No entry is made to Cost of Goods Sold or Inventory.*
Costing ending inventory	At the end of the period, the *cost of ending* inventory is the balance in the Inventory account (which is verified by a physical count of inventory).	*The amount of ending inventory is determined at the end of the accounting by taking a physical count of inventory,* a procedure by which all items of inventory on a given date are identified and counted.
Determining cost of goods sold	Cost of goods sold for the period is the balance *in the Cost of Goods Sold account* at the end of the period.	Cost of Goods Sold is determined only at the end of the period by *applying the cost of goods sold model.*

OBJECTIVE
Compute ending inventory and cost of goods sold under a periodic inventory system.

APPENDIX 6B: INVENTORY COSTING METHODS AND THE PERIODIC INVENTORY SYSTEM

Regardless of whether a company uses a perpetual inventory system or a periodic inventory system, inventory costing methods are designed to allocate the cost of goods available for sale between ending inventory and cost of goods sold. Under a periodic inventory system, the inventory costing methods are applied *as if* all purchases during an accounting period take place prior to any sales of the period. While this is not a realistic assumption, it does simplify the computation of the ending inventory and cost of goods sold since only one allocation needs to be made, regardless of the number of purchases and sales. Given this assumption, the following steps can be applied to determine ending inventory and cost of goods sold:

Step 1. Calculate the cost of goods available for sale for the period.
Step 2. Apply the inventory costing method to determine ending inventory and cost of goods sold.

FIRST-IN, FIRST-OUT (FIFO)

Under the FIFO method, *the earliest purchases (the first in) are assumed to be the first sold (the first out) and the more recent purchases are in ending inventory.* EXAMPLE 6.12 illustrates the application of the FIFO method. Notice that this is the same information used to illustrate the inventory costing methods applied to a perpetual inventory system (Examples 6-5 through 6-7). However, the information on purchases is listed first and the sales can be combined because all purchases are assumed to occur prior to any sales.

EXAMPLE 6.12 APPLYING THE FIFO INVENTORY COSTING METHOD IN A PERIODIC INVENTORY SYSTEM

Tampico Beachwear, a retail store specializing in beach apparel, has the following information related to purchases and sales of one of its more popular brand of shoes. (Each inventory layer is a different color.)

Date		Description	Units Purchased at Cost	Units Sold at Retail
Oct.	1	Beginning inventory	300 units @ $16 = $ 4,800	
	3	Purchase 1	600 units @ $18 = $10,800	
	8	Sale 1		800 units @ $30
	15	Purchase 2	250 units @ $20 = $ 5,000	
	20	Purchase 3	150 units @ $22 = $ 3,300	
	25	Sale 2		300 units @ $30
			Goods available for sale:	Sales:
			1,300 units = $23,900	1,100 units = $33,000

Ending inventory is made up of 200 units (1,300 units available for sale − 1,100 units sold).

Required:
Compute the cost of ending inventory and the cost of goods sold at October 31 using the FIFO method.

Solution:
Step 1: Compute the cost of goods available for sale for the period ($23,900).

Step 2: Apply FIFO to determine ending inventory and cost of goods sold. The cost of goods available for sale is allocated between inventory (the most recent purchases) and cost of goods sold (the earliest purchases) as follows:

Ending Inventory			Cost of Goods Sold		
150 units × $22	=	$3,300	300 units × $16	=	$ 4,800
50 units × $20	=	1,000	600 units × $18	=	10,800
200 units		$4,300	200 units × $20	=	4,000
			1,100 units		$19,600

LAST-IN, FIRST-OUT (LIFO)

Under the LIFO method, *the most recent purchases (newest costs) are allocated to the cost of goods sold and the earliest purchases (oldest costs) are allocated to ending inventory.* EXAMPLE 6.13 illustrates the application of the LIFO method.

EXAMPLE 6.13 **APPLYING THE LIFO INVENTORY COSTING METHOD IN A PERIODIC INVENTORY SYSTEM**

Tampico Beachwear, a retail store specializing in beach apparel, has the following information related to purchases and sales of one of its more popular brand of shoes. (Each inventory layer is a different color.)

Date	Description	Units Purchased at Cost	Units Sold at Retail
Oct. 1	Beginning inventory	300 units @ $16 = $ 4,800	
3	Purchase 1	600 units @ $18 = $10,800	
8	Sale 1		800 units @ $30
15	Purchase 2	250 units @ $20 = $ 5,000	
20	Purchase 3	150 units @ $22 = $ 3,300	
25	Sale 2		300 units @ $30
		Goods available for sale: 1,300 units = $23,900	Sales: 1,100 units = $33,000

Ending inventory is made up of 200 units (1,300 units available for sale − 1,100 units sold).

Required:
Compute the cost of ending inventory and the cost of goods sold at October 31 using the LIFO method.

Solution:
Step 1: Compute the cost of goods available for sale for the period ($23,900).

Step 2: Apply LIFO to determine ending inventory and cost of goods sold. This cost of goods available for sale is allocated between inventory (the earliest purchases) and cost of goods sold (the most recent purchases) as follows:

Ending Inventory	Cost of Goods Sold		
200 units × $16 = **$3,200**	100 units × $16	=	$ 1,600
	150 units × $22	=	3,300
	250 units × $20	=	5,000
	600 units × $18	=	10,800
	1,100 units		**$20,700**

AVERAGE COST METHOD

Under the average cost method, the weighted average cost per unit is multiplied by:

- the number of units in ending inventory to determine the cost of ending inventory
- the number of units sold to determine cost of goods sold

This method is commonly referred to as the weighted average method. In contrast to the perpetual inventory system, the weighted average cost per unit is not continually calculated. Rather it is calculated based on the total cost of goods available for sale and the total units available for sale. EXAMPLE 6.14 illustrates the application of the average cost method.

EXAMPLE 6.14 APPLYING THE AVERAGE COST INVENTORY COSTING METHOD IN A PERIODIC INVENTORY SYSTEM

Tampico Beachwear, a retail store specializing in beach apparel, has the following information related to purchases and sales of one of its more popular brand of shoes. (Each inventory layer is a different color.)

Date		Description	Units Purchased at Cost	Units Sold at Retail
Oct.	1	Beginning inventory	300 units @ $16 = $ 4,800	
	3	Purchase 1	600 units @ $18 = $10,800	
	8	Sale 1		800 units @ $30
	15	Purchase 2	250 units @ $20 = $ 5,000	
	20	Purchase 3	150 units @ $22 = $ 3,300	
	25	Sale 2		300 units @ $30
			Goods available for sale: 1,300 units = $23,900	Sales: 1,100 units = $33,000

Ending inventory is made up of 200 units (1,300 units available for sale − 1,100 units sold).

Required:
Compute the cost of ending inventory and the cost of goods sold at October 31 using the average cost method.

(*Note:* Use four decimal places for per-unit calculations and round all other numbers to the nearest dollar.)

Solution:

Step 1: Compute the cost of goods available for sale for the period ($23,900).

Step 2: Apply the average cost method to determine ending inventory and cost of goods sold. First, compute a weighted average cost of the goods available for sale:

$$\text{Weighted Average Cost per Unit} = \frac{\text{Cost of Goods Available for Sale}}{\text{Units Available for Sale}}$$

$$= \$23,900 \div 1,300 \text{ units} = \textbf{\$18.3846 per unit}$$

Next, allocate the cost of goods available for sale ($23,900) between inventory and cost of goods sold using the average cost of the inventory as follows:

Ending Inventory	**Cost of Goods Sold**
200 units × $18.3846 = **$3,677**	1,100 units × $18.3846 = **$20,223**

Under all inventory costing methods, periodic inventory systems allocate the cost of purchased goods between cost of goods sold and ending inventory only at the end of the period. In contrast, the perpetual inventory system performs this allocation each time a sale is made. Because of this difference in the timing of cost allocations, the two systems usually yield different amounts for the cost of goods sold and ending inventory under both the LIFO and average cost assumptions. FIFO amounts, however, are always the same under both periodic and perpetual inventory systems.[6]

---

6 This occurs because FIFO always allocates the earliest items purchased to cost of goods sold, resulting in ending inventory being the latest items purchased. Under both the perpetual and periodic inventory systems, these are the same units of inventory at the same cost. Therefore, the timing of the cost allocation is irrelevant under FIFO.

REVIEW CENTER

LO1. Describe the types of inventories and how inventory costs flow through a company.

KEY TAKEAWAYS

- Merchandising companies hold one type of inventory—merchandise inventory.
- Manufacturing companies have three types of inventory: raw materials, work-in-process, and finished goods.
- When goods are purchased, the cost of the purchase is recorded in inventory (for merchandisers) or raw materials inventory (for manufacturers). During the production process, manufacturers record the cost (raw materials, labor, and overhead) in work-in-process and then transfer the cost to finished goods inventory when the product is complete.
- Once the product is sold, the cost is transferred out of the inventory account and into cost of goods sold.
- The relationship between inventory and cost of goods sold is described by the cost of goods sold model.

KEY TERMS

Cost of goods available for sale, 325

Cost of goods sold (cost of sales), 322

Finished goods inventory, 323

Gross margin (gross profit), 322

Inventory, 322

Manufacturers, 323

Merchandise inventory, 323

Merchandisers, 323

Periodic inventory system, 327

Perpetual inventory system, 326

Raw materials inventory, 323

Retailers, 323

Wholesalers, 323

Work-in-process inventory, 323

EXAMPLE

EXAMPLE 6.1   Applying the cost of goods sold model, page 326

KEY CALCULATIONS

Cost of Goods Available for Sale = Beginning Inventory + Net Purchases

Cost of Goods Sold = Beginning Inventory + Net Purchases − Ending Inventory

Gross Margin = Revenue − Cost of Goods Sold

KEY TAKEAWAYS

- In a perpetual inventory system, purchases of inventory are recorded by increasing the inventory account.
- If a purchase discount exists, inventory is reduced by the amount of the discount taken.
- When a purchased item is returned (purchase return) or a price reduction is granted by the seller (purchase allowance), the inventory item is reduced by the amount of the purchase return or allowance given.
- If transportation costs exist and the shipping terms are F.O.B shipping point, the transportation costs are considered part of the total cost of purchases, and the inventory account is increased.
- If transportation costs exist and the shipping terms are F.O.B. destination, the seller pays these costs and records them as a selling expense on the income statement.
- In a perpetual inventory system, sales require two entries that (1) record the sales revenue and (2) recognize the expense (cost of goods sold) associated with the decrease in inventory.
- If an item is later returned, two entries must be made—one that decreases sales revenue and a second that decreases cost of goods sold associated with the return of inventory.

LO2. Explain how to record purchases and sales of inventory using a perpetual inventory system.

KEY TERMS

Consignment, 330
Discount period, 329
F.O.B. destination, 330
F.O.B. shipping point, 329
Freight-in, 329

Freight-out, 330
Purchase allowance, 329
Purchase discounts, 329
Purchase return, 329
Purchases, 328

EXAMPLES

EXAMPLE 6.2	Recording purchase transactions in a perpetual inventory system, page 331	
EXAMPLE 6.3	Recording sales transactions in a perpetual inventory system, page 333	

KEY CALCULATION

Net Purchase = Invoice Price of Purchase − Purchase Discounts − Purchase Returns and Allowances + Transportation Costs (Freight-in)

KEY TAKEAWAYS

- The four inventory costing methods are specific identification; first-in, first-out (FIFO); last-in, first-out (LIFO); and average cost.
- The specific identification method determines the cost of ending inventory and the cost of goods sold based on the identification of the actual units sold and the units remaining in inventory.

LO3. Apply the four inventory costing methods to compute ending inventory and cost of goods sold under a perpetual inventory system.

- The other three inventory costing methods allocate cost of goods available for sale between ending inventory and cost of goods sold using the following process.
  - Step 1. Calculate the cost of goods available for sale *immediately prior* to any sales transaction.
  - Step 2. Apply the inventory costing method to determine ending inventory and cost of goods sold.
  - Step 3. Repeat Steps 1 and 2 for all inventory transactions during the period. The sum of the cost of goods sold computed in Step 2 is the cost of goods sold for the period. Ending inventory is the amount computed during the final application of Step 2 for the period.

KEY TERMS

Average cost method, 340
First-in, first-out (FIFO) method, 338
Last-in, first-out (LIFO) method, 339
Specific identification method, 336

EXAMPLES

EXAMPLE 6.4	Applying the specific identification method, page 336–337	
EXAMPLE 6.5	Applying the FIFO inventory costing method, page 338–339	
EXAMPLE 6.6	Applying the LIFO inventory costing method, page 339–340	
EXAMPLE 6.7	Applying the average cost inventory costing method, page 341–342	

KEY CALCULATIONS

Cost of Goods Sold = Units Sold × Weighted Average Cost per Unit

Ending Inventory = Units on Hand × Weighted Average Cost per Unit

Weighted Average Cost per Unit = Cost of Goods Available for Sale ÷ Units Available for Sale

LO4. Analyze the financial reporting and tax effects of the various inventory costing methods.

KEY TAKEAWAYS

- If the prices paid for purchased inventory are stable, all inventory costing methods will yield the same amounts for ending inventory and cost of goods sold.
- When purchase prices vary, FIFO, LIFO, and the average cost methods will produce different amounts for ending inventory, cost of goods sold, and, therefore, income.
- When prices are *rising*, the FIFO method produces the highest cost for ending inventory, the lowest cost of goods sold, and the highest gross margin (and net income).
- When prices are *rising*, the LIFO method produces the lowest cost for ending inventory, the highest cost of goods sold, and, therefore, the lowest gross margin (and net income) of the three methods. Because LIFO results in lower income, it results in the lowest income taxes.

- When purchase prices are *falling*, the situation is reverse.
- The average cost method produces amounts for inventory, cost of goods sold, and net income that fall between the FIFO and LIFO extremes.

KEY TAKEAWAYS

- If the net realizable value of inventory drops below its original cost, generally accepted accounting principles permit a departure from the historical cost concept.
- A company is allowed to reduce the amount recorded for inventory to its net realizable value, where net realizable value is computed as estimated selling costs less costs of disposal.
- This lower of cost or net realizable value (LCNRV) rule is an application of the conservatism principle.

KEY TERM

Lower of cost or net realizable (LCNRV) value, 346

EXAMPLE

EXAMPLE 6.8	Valuing inventory at lower of cost or net realizable value, page 346–347

LO5. Apply the lower of cost or net realizable value rule to the valuation of inventory.

KEY TAKEAWAYS

- Two useful measures of how successful a company is at managing and controlling its inventory are the gross profit ratio and the inventory turnover ratio.
- The gross profit ratio indicates how many cents of every dollar are available to cover expenses other than cost of goods sold and to earn a profit.
- The inventory turnover ratio describes how quickly inventory is purchased (or produced) and sold.

KEY TERMS

Average days to sell inventory, 348
Gross profit ratio, 348
Inventory turnover ratio, 348
LIFO reserve, 349

EXAMPLE

EXAMPLE 6.9	Calculating the gross profit and inventory turnover ratio, page 348–349

LO6. Evaluate inventory management using the gross profit and inventory turnover ratios.

KEY CALCULATIONS

$$\text{Average Days to Sell Inventory} = \frac{365 \text{ days}}{\text{Inventory Turnover}}$$

$$\text{Inventory Turnover Ratio} = \frac{\text{Cost of Goods Sold}}{\text{Average Inventory}}$$

$$\text{LIFO Inventory Value} = \text{Reported FIFO Inventory} - \text{LIFO Reserve}$$

LO7. Describe how errors in ending inventory affect income statements and balance sheets.

KEY TAKEAWAYS

- Inventory errors can arise for a number of reasons, including incorrect counts of inventory, mistakes in costing, or errors in identifying items.
- Because the ending inventory of one period is the beginning inventory of the next period, an error in the measurement of ending inventory will affect the cost of goods sold and net income of two consecutive periods.
- Inventory errors are self-correcting; therefore, the assets and stockholders' equity of only the first period are misstated (assuming no other errors are made).

EXAMPLE

EXAMPLE 6.10   Analyzing inventory errors, page 352

LO8. *(Appendix 6A)* **Explain how to record purchases of inventory using a periodic inventory system.**

KEY TAKEAWAYS

- In a periodic inventory system, purchases of inventory are recorded by increasing the purchases account.
- If a purchase discount exists, the purchases discount account is increased by the amount of the discount taken.
- When a purchased item is returned (purchase return) or a price reduction is granted by the seller (purchase allowance), the purchase returns and allowances account is increased by the amount of the purchase return or allowance given.
- If transportation costs exist and are paid by the purchaser, the transportation costs are considered part of the total cost of purchases and the purchases account is increased.

EXAMPLE

EXAMPLE 6.11   Recording purchase transactions in a periodic inventory system, page 353

KEY TAKEAWAYS

- Under a periodic inventory system, the inventory costing methods are applied as if all purchases during an accounting period take place prior to any sales of the period.
- Given this assumption, you will then apply the following steps:
  - Step 1. Calculate the cost of goods available for sale for the period.
  - Step 2. Apply the inventory costing method to determine ending inventory and cost of goods sold.

EXAMPLES

EXAMPLE 6.12	*(Appendix 6B)* Applying the FIFO inventory costing method in a periodic inventory system, page 355
EXAMPLE 6.13	*(Appendix 6B)* Applying the LIFO inventory costing method in a periodic inventory system, page 356
EXAMPLE 6.14	*(Appendix 6B)* Applying the average cost inventory costing method in a periodic inventory system, page 357

**LO9. *(Appendix 6B)*
Compute ending
inventory and cost of
goods sold under a
periodic inventory system.**

REVIEW PROBLEM

Sagamore Supplies, an office supply wholesale store, uses a perpetual inventory system. Sagamore recorded the following activity for one of its inventory accounts:

Date		Activity	Number of Units	Cost per Unit
Oct.	1	Beginning inventory	2,500	$16
	15	Purchase	5,100	$17
Nov.	3	Sale	5,900	
	20	Purchase	4,800	$18
Dec.	10	Sale	5,300	

Additional information on the purchases and sales is:

- All purchases were cash purchases.
- All sales were cash sales, and all inventory items were sold for $25 per unit.

Required:

1. Compute the cost of ending inventory and the cost of goods sold using the following methods: (a) FIFO, (b) LIFO, and (c) average cost.

2. Assume that Sagamore uses the FIFO inventory costing method. Prepare the journal entries to record the purchases and sales of inventory.

Solution:

1.

a. Under FIFO, the cost of ending inventory is $21,600, and cost of goods sold is $191,500 ($97,800 + $93,700).

(Continued)

Date		Description	Cost of Goods Sold	Inventory Balance	
Oct.	1	Beginning inventory		$2,500 \times \$16$	$= \$ 40,000$
	15	Purchase (5,100 @ $17)		$\left.\begin{array}{l} 2,500 \times \$16 = \$40,000 \\ 5,100 \times \$17 = \$86,700 \end{array}\right\}$	$= \$126,700$
Nov.	3	Sale (5,900 @ $25)	$\left.\begin{array}{l} 2,500 \times \$16 = \$40,000 \\ 3,400 \times \$17 = \$57,800 \end{array}\right\} = \$97,800$	$1,700 \times \$17$	$= \$ 28,900$

This is an interim calculation. Because the period is not over, these steps need to be repeated until the end of the accounting period.

Date		Description	Cost of Goods Sold	Inventory Balance	
Nov.	3	Inventory on hand		$1,700 \times \$17$	$= \$ 28,900$
	20	Purchase (4,800 @ $18)		$\left.\begin{array}{l} 1,700 \times \$17 = \$28,900 \\ 4,800 \times \$18 = \$86,400 \end{array}\right\}$	$= \$115,300$
Dec.	10	Sale (5,300 @ $25)	$\left.\begin{array}{l} 1,700 \times \$17 = \$28,900 \\ 3,600 \times \$18 = \$64,800 \end{array}\right\} = \underline{\mathbf{\$93,700}}$	$1,200 \times \$18$	$= \underline{\mathbf{\$ 21,600}}$

b. Under LIFO, the cost of ending inventory is $19,200, and cost of goods sold is $193,900 ($99,500 + $94,400).

Date		Description	Cost of Goods Sold	Inventory Balance	
Oct.	1	Beginning inventory		$2,500 \times \$16$	$= \$ 40,000$
	15	Purchase (5,100 @ $17)		$\left.\begin{array}{l} 2,500 \times \$16 = \$40,000 \\ 5,100 \times \$17 = \$86,700 \end{array}\right\}$	$= \$126,700$
Nov.	3	Sale (5,900 @ $25)	$\left.\begin{array}{l} 5,100 \times \$17 = \$86,700 \\ 800 \times \$16 = \$12,800 \end{array}\right\} = \$99,500$	$1,700 \times \$16$	$= \$ 27,200$

This is an interim calculation. Because the period is not over, these steps need to be repeated until the end of the accounting period.

Date		Description	Cost of Goods Sold	Inventory Balance	
Nov.	3	Inventory on hand		$1,700 \times \$16$	$= \$ 27,200$
	20	Purchase (4,800 @ $18)		$\left.\begin{array}{l} 1,700 \times \$16 = \$27,200 \\ 4,800 \times \$18 = \$86,400 \end{array}\right\}$	$= \$113,600$
Dec.	10	Sale (5,300 @ $25)	$\left.\begin{array}{l} 4,800 \times \$18 = \$86,400 \\ 500 \times \$16 = \$ 8,000 \end{array}\right\} = \underline{\mathbf{\$94,400}}$	$1,200 \times \$16$	$= \underline{\mathbf{\$ 19,200}}$

c. Under average cost, the cost of ending inventory is $21,183, and cost of goods sold is $191,917 ($98,359 + $93,558).

Date		Description	Cost of Goods Sold	Inventory Balance	
Oct.	1	Beginning inventory		$2,500 \times \$16$	$= \$ 40,000$ ($16/unit)
	15	Purchase (5,100 @ $17)		$\left.\begin{array}{l} 2,500 \times \$16 = \$40,000 \\ 5,100 \times \$17 = \$86,700 \end{array}\right\}$	$= \$126,700$ ($16.6711/unit)[a]
Nov.	3	Sale (5,900 @ $25)	$5,900 \times \$16.6711 = \$98,359$	$1,700 \times \$16.6711$	$= \$ 28,341$

[a] $126,700 ÷ 7,600 units = $16.6711/unit

This is an interim calculation. Because the period is not over, these steps need to be repeated until the end of the accounting period.

Date		Description	Cost of Goods Sold	Inventory Balance	
Nov.	3	Inventory on hand		$1,700 \times \$16.6711$	$= \$ 28,341$
	20	Purchase (4,800 @ $18)		$\left.\begin{array}{l} 1,700 \times \$16.6711 = \$28,341 \\ 4,800 \times \$18 \quad = \$86,400 \end{array}\right\}$	$= \$114,741$ ($17.6525/unit)[b]
Dec.	10	Sale 2 (5,300 @ $25)	$5,300 \times \$17.6525 = \underline{\mathbf{\$93,558}}$ $1,200 \times \$17.6525$		$= \underline{\mathbf{\$21,183}}$

[b] $114,741 ÷ 6,500 units = $17.6525/unit

2.

Date	Account and Explanation	Debit	Credit	Assets	=	Liabilities	+	Stockholders' Equity
Oct. 15	Inventory	86,700		▲				
	Cash		86,700	▼				

Date	Account and Explanation	Debit	Credit	Assets	=	Liabilities	+	Stockholders' Equity
Nov. 3	Cash	147,500		▲				
	Sales Revenue		147,500					▲

Date	Account and Explanation	Debit	Credit	Assets	=	Liabilities	+	Stockholders' Equity
Nov. 3	Cost of Goods Sold	97,800						▼
	Inventory		97,800	▼				

Date	Account and Explanation	Debit	Credit	Assets	=	Liabilities	+	Stockholders' Equity
Nov. 20	Inventory	86,400		▲				
	Cash		86,400	▼				

Date	Account and Explanation	Debit	Credit	Assets	=	Liabilities	+	Stockholders' Equity
Dec. 10	Cash	132,500		▲				
	Sales Revenue		132,500					▲

Date	Account and Explanation	Debit	Credit	Assets	=	Liabilities	+	Stockholders' Equity
Dec. 10	Cost of Goods Sold	93,700						▼
	Inventory		93,700	▼				

APPLYING KNOWLEDGE

DISCUSSION QUESTIONS

1. What are the differences between merchandisers and manufacturers?

OBJECTIVE **1**

2. Describe the types of inventories used by manufacturers and merchandisers.

3. Compare the flow of inventory costs between merchandisers and manufacturers.

4. What are the components of cost of goods available for sale?

5. How is cost of goods sold determined?

6. How do the perpetual and periodic inventory accounting systems differ from each other?

7. Why are perpetual inventory systems more expensive to operate than periodic inventory systems? What conditions justify the additional cost of a perpetual inventory system?

OBJECTIVE 2 ▶ 8. Why are adjustments made to the invoice price of goods when determining the cost of inventory?

9. Identify the accounting items for which adjustments are made to the invoice price of goods when determining the net cost of purchases.

10. Describe the difference between F.O.B. shipping point and F.O.B. destination.

11. Why do sales transactions under a perpetual inventory system require two journal entries?

OBJECTIVE 3 ▶ 12. Why do the four inventory costing methods produce different amounts for the cost of ending inventory and cost of goods sold?

13. The costs of which units of inventory (oldest or newest) are allocated to ending inventory or cost of goods sold using the FIFO, LIFO, and average cost methods?

OBJECTIVE 4 ▶ 14. If inventory prices are rising, which inventory costing method should produce the smallest payment for taxes?

15. How would reported income differ if LIFO rather than FIFO were used when purchase prices are rising? When purchase prices are falling?

16. How would the balance sheet accounts be affected if LIFO rather than FIFO were used when purchase prices are rising? When purchase prices are falling?

OBJECTIVE 5 ▶ 17. Why are inventories written down to the lower of cost or net realizable value?

18. What is the effect on the current period income statement and the balance sheet when inventories are written down using the lower of cost or net realizable value method? What is the effect on future period income statements and balance sheets?

OBJECTIVE 6 ▶ 19. What do the gross profit and inventory turnover ratios tell company management about inventory?

20. What is the LIFO reserve, and when is it used?

OBJECTIVE 7 ▶ 21. How does an error in the determination of ending inventory affect the financial statements of two periods?

OBJECTIVE 8 ▶ 22. *(Appendix 6A)* What accounts are used to record inventory purchase transactions under the periodic inventory system? Why aren't these accounts used in a perpetual inventory system?

OBJECTIVE 9 ▶ 23. *(Appendix 6B)* "For each inventory costing method, perpetual and periodic systems yield the same amounts for ending inventory and cost of goods sold." Do you agree or disagree with this statement? Explain.

MULTIPLE-CHOICE QUESTIONS

OBJECTIVE 1 ▶ **6-1** If beginning inventory is $20,000, purchases are $185,000, and ending inventory is $30,000, what is cost of goods sold as determined by the cost of goods sold model?

   a. $135,000   c. $195,000

   b. $175,000   d. $235,000

OBJECTIVE ◀ 2

6-2   Which of the following transactions would *not* result in an entry to the inventory
account in the buyer's accounting records under a perpetual inventory system?
a. Purchase of merchandise on credit
b. Return of merchandise to the supplier
c. Payment of a credit purchase of merchandise within the discount period
d. Payment of freight by the seller for goods received from a supplier

6-3   Briggs Company purchased $15,000 of inventory on credit with credit terms of 2/10,
n/30. Briggs paid for the purchase within the discount period. How much did Briggs
pay for the inventory?
a. $14,700   c. $15,000
b. $14,850   d. $15,300

6-4   Which of the following transactions would *not* result in an adjustment to the inventory
account under a perpetual inventory system?
a. Sale of merchandise for cash
b. Sale of merchandise on credit
c. Receipt of payment from a customer within the discount period
d. Return of merchandise by a customer

OBJECTIVE ◀ 3

6-5   U-Save Automotive Group purchased 10 vehicles during the current month. Two
trucks were purchased for $20,000 each, two SUVs were purchased for $31,000 each,
and six hybrid cars were purchased for $27,000 each. A review of the sales invoices
revealed that five of the hybrid cars were sold and both trucks were sold. What is the
cost of U-Save's ending inventory if it uses the specific identification method?
a. $89,000   c. $135,000
b. $129,000   d. $175,000

Use the following information for Multiple-Choice Questions 6-6 through 6-8:
Morgan Inc. has the following units and costs for the month of April:

	Units Purchased at Cost	Units Sold at Retail
Beginning inventory, April 1	1,200 units at $25	
Purchase 1, April 9	1,500 units at $28	
Sale 1, April 12		2,400 units at $45
Purchase 2, April 22	1,000 units at $30	

6-6   Refer to the information for Morgan Inc. above. If Morgan uses a perpetual inventory
system, what is the cost of ending inventory under FIFO at April 30?
a. $32,500   c. $63,600
b. $38,400   d. $69,500

6-7   Refer to the information for Morgan Inc. above. If Morgan uses a perpetual inventory
system, what is the cost of goods sold under LIFO at April 30?
a. $37,500   c. $63,600
b. $38,400   d. $64,500

6-8   Refer to the information for Morgan Inc. above. If Morgan uses a perpetual inventory
system, what is the cost of ending inventory under average cost at April 30?
(*Note:* Use four decimal places for per-unit calculations and round to the nearest
dollar.)
a. $35,838   c. $64,000
b. $38,000   d. $66,162

OBJECTIVE 4   **6-9**   When purchase prices are rising, which of the following statements is true?
a. LIFO produces a higher cost of goods sold than FIFO.
b. LIFO produces a higher cost for ending inventory than FIFO.
c. FIFO produces a lower amount for net income than LIFO.
d. Average cost produces a higher net income than FIFO or LIFO.

6-10   Which method results in a more realistic amount for income because it matches the most current costs against revenue?
a. FIFO   c. Specific identification
b. Average cost   d. LIFO

OBJECTIVE 5   **6-11**   Which of the following statements regarding the lower of cost or net realizable value (LCNRV) rule is true?
a. The LCNRV rule is an application of the historical cost principle.
b. When the selling price of inventory drops below the historical cost of inventory, an adjustment is made to decrease inventory to its net realizable value and decrease income.
c. If a company uses the LCNRV rule, there is no need to use a cost flow assumption such as FIFO, LIFO, or average cost.
d. When the selling price of inventory is above the historical cost of inventory, an adjustment is made to increase inventory to its net realizable value and increase income.

OBJECTIVE 6   **6-12**   Which of the following statements is true with regard to the gross profit ratio?
1. An increase in cost of goods sold would increase the gross profit rate (assuming sales remain constant).
2. An increase in the gross profit rate may indicate that a company is efficiently managing its inventory.
3. An increase in selling expenses would lower the gross profit rate.
a. 1   c. 1 and 2
b. 2   d. 2 and 3

6-13   An increasing inventory turnover ratio indicates that a company:
a. has reduced the time it takes to purchase and sell inventory.
b. is having trouble selling its inventory.
c. may be holding too much inventory.
d. has sold inventory at a higher profit.

OBJECTIVE 7   **6-14**   Ignoring taxes, if a company understates its ending inventory by $10,000 in the current year:
a. assets for the current year will be overstated by $10,000.
b. net income for the subsequent year will be overstated by $10,000.
c. cost of goods sold for the current year will be understated by $10,000.
d. retained earnings for the current year will be unaffected.

OBJECTIVE 8   **6-15**   *(Appendix 6A)* Which of the following statements is true for a company that uses a periodic inventory system?
a. The purchase of inventory requires a debit to Inventory.
b. The return of defective inventory requires a debit to Purchase Returns and Allowances.
c. The payment of a purchase within the discount period requires a credit to Purchase Discounts.
d. Any amounts paid for freight are debited to Inventory.

Use the following information for Multiple-Choice Questions 6-16 through 6-18:

Morgan Inc. has the following units and costs for the month of April:

	Units Purchased at Cost	Units Sold at Retail
Beginning inventory, April 1	1,200 units at $25	
Purchase 1, April 9	1,500 units at $28	
Sale 1, April 12		2,400 units at $45
Purchase 2, April 22	1,000 units at $30	

6-16 *(Appendix 6B)* Refer to the information for Morgan Inc. above. If Morgan uses a periodic inventory system, what is the cost of goods sold under FIFO at April 30?

a. $32,800

b. $38,400

c. $63,600

d. $69,200

OBJECTIVE 9

6-17 *(Appendix 6B)* Refer to the information for Morgan Inc. above. If Morgan uses a periodic inventory system, what is the cost of ending inventory under LIFO at April 30?

a. $32,800

b. $38,400

c. $63,600

d. $69,200

6-18 *(Appendix 6B)* Refer to the information for Morgan Inc. above. If Morgan uses a periodic inventory system, what is the cost of ending inventory under average cost at April 30? (*Note:* Use four decimal places for per-unit calculations and round all other numbers to the nearest dollar.)

a. $34,667

b. $35,838

c. $66,162

d. $67,333

BRIEF EXERCISES

Brief Exercise 6-19 Applying the Cost of Goods Sold Model

OBJECTIVE 1
EXAMPLE 6.1

Hempstead Company has the following data:

Item	Units	Cost
Inventory, January 1	940	$10,340
Purchases	4,510	49,610
Inventory, December 31	770	8,470

Required:

1. How many units were sold?
2. Using the cost of goods sold model, determine the cost of goods sold.

OBJECTIVE 1

EXAMPLE 6.1

Brief Exercise 6-20 Applying the Cost of Goods Sold Model

Milton Company reported beginning inventory of $60,000 on January 1. During the year, it purchased inventory of $625,000 and sold inventory for $950,000. A count of inventory at the end of the year determined that the cost of inventory on hand was $50,000.

Required:

1. What was Milton's cost of goods sold?
2. What is Milton's gross margin?

Use the following information for Brief Exercises 6-21 and 6-22:

Mathis Company and Reece Company use the perpetual inventory system. The following transactions occurred during the month of April:

a. On April 1, Mathis purchased merchandise on account from Reece with credit terms of 2/10, n/30. The selling price of the merchandise was $3,100, and the cost of the merchandise sold was $2,225.
b. On April 1, Mathis paid freight charges of $250 cash to have the goods delivered to its warehouse.
c. On April 8, Mathis returned $800 of the merchandise, which had originally cost Reece $500.
d. On April 10, Mathis paid Reece the balance due.

OBJECTIVE 2

EXAMPLE 6.2

Brief Exercise 6-21 Recording Purchase Transactions

Refer to the information for Mathis and Reece companies above.

Required:

1. Prepare the journal entry to record the April 1 purchase of merchandise and payment of freight by Mathis.
2. Prepare the journal entry to record the April 8 return of merchandise.
3. Prepare the journal entry to record the April 10 payment to Reece.

OBJECTIVE 2

EXAMPLE 6.3

Brief Exercise 6-22 Recording Sales Transactions

Refer to the information for Mathis and Reece companies above.

Required:

Prepare the journal entries to record these transactions on Reece's books. Assume that Reece uses the net method to record sales on account.

Use the following information for Brief Exercises 6-23 through 6-26:

Filimonov Inc. has the following information related to purchases and sales of one of its inventory items:

Date		Description	Units Purchased at Cost	Units Sold at Retail
June	1	Beginning inventory	200 units @ $10 = $2,000	
	9	Purchase 1	300 units @ $12 = $3,600	
	14	Sale 1		400 units @ $25
	22	Purchase 2	250 units @ $14 = $3,500	
	29	Sale 2		225 units @ $25

Brief Exercise 6-23 Inventory Costing: FIFO

OBJECTIVE 3
EXAMPLE 6.5

Refer to the information for Filimonov Inc. and assume that the company uses a perpetual inventory system.

Required:

Calculate the cost of goods sold and the cost of ending inventory using the FIFO inventory costing method.

Brief Exercise 6-24 Inventory Costing: LIFO

OBJECTIVE 3
EXAMPLE 6.6

Refer to the information for Filimonov Inc. and assume that the company uses a perpetual inventory system.

Required:

Calculate the cost of goods sold and the cost of ending inventory using the LIFO inventory costing method.

Brief Exercise 6-25 Inventory Costing: Average Cost

OBJECTIVE 3
EXAMPLE 6.7

Refer to the information for Filimonov Inc. and assume that the company uses a perpetual inventory system.

Required:

Calculate the cost of goods sold and the cost of ending inventory using the average cost method. (*Note:* Use four decimal places for per-unit calculations and round all other numbers to the nearest dollar.)

Brief Exercise 6-26 Effects of Inventory Costing Methods

OBJECTIVE 4
EXAMPLE 6.5, 6.6, 6.7

Refer to your answers for Filimonov Inc. in **Brief Exercises 6-23** through **6-25**.

Required:

1. In a period of rising prices, which inventory costing method produces the highest amount for ending inventory?
2. In a period of rising prices, which inventory costing method produces the highest net income?
3. In a period of rising prices, which inventory costing method produces the lowest payment for income taxes?
4. In a period of rising prices, which inventory method generally produces the most realistic amount for cost of goods sold? For inventory? Would your answer change if inventory prices were decreasing during the period?

Brief Exercise 6-27 Lower of Cost or Net Realizable Value

OBJECTIVE 5
EXAMPLE 6.8

The accountant for Murphy Company prepared the following analysis of its inventory at year end:

Item	Units	Cost per Unit	Net Realizable Value
RSK-89013	600	$38	$47
LKW-91247	420	47	40
QEC-57429	510	26	32

Required:

1. Compute the carrying value of the ending inventory using the lower of cost or net realizable value rule applied on an item-by-item basis.
2. Prepare the journal entry required to value the inventory at lower of cost or net realizable value.

OBJECTIVE 6

EXAMPLE 6.9

Brief Exercise 6-28 Inventory Analysis

Callahan Company reported the following information for the current year:

Net sales revenue	$280,000
Cost of goods sold	120,000
Beginning inventory	5,000
Ending inventory	10,000

Required:

1. Compute Callahan's (a) gross profit ratio, (b) inventory turnover ratio, and (c) average days to sell inventory. (Round all answers to two decimal places.)
2. Explain the meaning of each number.

OBJECTIVE 7

EXAMPLE 6.10

Brief Exercise 6-29 Inventory Errors

Haywood Inc. reported the following information for Year 1:

Beginning inventory	$ 25,000
Ending inventory	50,000
Sales revenue	1,000,000
Cost of goods sold	620,000

A physical count of inventory at the end of the year showed that ending inventory was actually $65,000.

Required:

1. What is the correct cost of goods sold and gross profit for Year 1?
2. Assuming the error was not corrected, what is the effect on the balance sheet at December 31 Year 1? At December 31, Year 2?

OBJECTIVE 8

EXAMPLE 6.11

Brief Exercise 6-30 *(Appendix 6A)* Recording Purchase Transactions

Mathis Company and Reece Company use the periodic inventory system. The following transactions occurred during the month of April:

a. On April 1, Mathis purchased merchandise on account from Reece with credit terms of 2/10, n/30. The selling price of the merchandise was $3,100, and the cost of the merchandise sold was $2,225.
b. On April 1, Mathis paid freight charges of $250 cash to have the goods delivered to its warehouse.
c. On April 8, Mathis returned $800 of the merchandise, which had originally cost Reece $500.
d. On April 10, Mathis paid Reece the balance due.

Required:

1. Prepare the journal entry to record the April 1 purchase of merchandise and payment of freight by Mathis.
2. Prepare the journal entry to record the April 8 return of merchandise.
3. Prepare the journal entry to record the April 10 payment to Reece.

Use the following information for Brief Exercises 6-31 through 6-33:
Filimonov Inc. has the following information related to purchases and sales of one of its inventory items:

Date	Description	Units Purchased at Cost	Units Sold at Retail
June 1	Beginning inventory	200 units @ $10 = $2,000	
9	Purchase 1	300 units @ $12 = S3,600	
14	Sale 1		400 units @ $25
22	Purchase 2	250 units @ $14 = $3,500	
29	Sale 2		225 units @ $25

Brief Exercise 6-31 *(Appendix 6B)* Inventory Costing Methods: Periodic FIFO

OBJECTIVE ◄ 9
EXAMPLE 6.12

Refer to the information for Filimonov Inc. and assume that the company uses a periodic inventory system.

Required:
Calculate the cost of goods sold and the cost of ending inventory using the FIFO inventory costing method.

Brief Exercise 6-32 *(Appendix 6B)* Inventory Costing Methods: Periodic LIFO

OBJECTIVE ◄ 9
EXAMPLE 6.13

Refer to the information for Filimonov Inc. and assume that the company uses a periodic inventory system.

Required:
Calculate the cost of goods sold and the cost of ending inventory using the LIFO inventory costing method.

Brief Exercise 6-33 *(Appendix 6B)* Inventory Costing Methods: Periodic Average Cost

OBJECTIVE ◄ 9
EXAMPLE 6.14

Refer to the information for Filimonov Inc. and assume that the company uses a periodic inventory system.

Required:
Calculate the cost of goods sold and the cost of ending inventory using the average cost method. (*Note:* Use four decimal places for per-unit calculations and round all other numbers to the nearest dollar.)

EXERCISES

Exercise 6-34 Applying the Cost of Goods Sold Model

OBJECTIVE ◄ 1

Wilson Company sells a single product. At the beginning of the year, Wilson had 150 units in stock at a cost of $8 each. During the year, Wilson purchased 825 more units at a cost of $8 each and sold 240 units at $13 each, 210 units at $15 each, and 335 units at $14 each.

Required:
1. Using the cost of goods sold model, what is the amount of ending inventory and cost of goods sold?
2. What is Wilson's gross margin for the year?

SHOW
ME HOW

Exercise 6-35 Applying the Cost of Goods Sold Model

The following amounts were obtained from the accounting records of Steed Company:

	Year 1	Year 2	Year 3
Beginning inventory	$ 9,600	(b)	(d)
Net purchases	(a)	$55,300	$51,100
Ending inventory	11,200	(c)	13,750
Cost of goods sold	44,500	49,800	(e)

Required:
Compute the missing amounts.

Exercise 6-36 Perpetual and Periodic Inventory Systems

Below is a list of inventory systems options.
a. Perpetual inventory system
b. Periodic inventory system
c. Both perpetual and periodic inventory systems

Required:
Match each option with one of the following:
1. Only revenue is recorded as sales are made during the period; the cost of goods sold is recorded at the end of the period.
2. Cost of goods sold is determined as each sale is made.
3. Inventory purchases are recorded in an inventory account.
4. Inventory purchases are recorded in a purchases account.
5. Cost of goods sold is determined only at the end of the period by subtracting the cost of ending inventory from the cost of goods available for sale.
6. Both revenue and cost of goods sold are recorded during the period as sales are made.
7. The inventory is verified by a physical count.

Exercise 6-37 Recording Purchases

Compass Inc. purchased 1,250 bags of insulation, on account, from Glassco Inc. The bags of insulation cost $5.50 each. Compass paid Turner Trucking $320 to have the bags of insulation shipped to its warehouse. Compass returned 50 bags that were defective and paid for the remainder. Assume that Compass uses the perpetual inventory system and that Glassco did not offer a purchase discount.

Required:
1. Prepare a journal entry to record the purchase of the bags of insulation.
2. Prepare the entry to record the payment for shipping.
3. Prepare the entry for the return of the defective bags.
4. Prepare the entry to record the payment for the bags kept by Compass.
5. What is the total cost of this purchase?

Exercise 6-38 Recording Purchases

Dawson Enterprises uses the perpetual system to record inventory transactions. Dawson had the following transactions in April:
a. On April 1, Dawson purchased merchandise on credit for $25,150 with terms 2/10, n/30.
b. On April 2, Dawson purchased merchandise on credit for $28,200 with terms 3/15, n/25.
c. On April 9, Dawson paid for the purchase made on April 1.
d. On April 25, Dawson paid for the merchandise purchased on April 2.

Required:
Prepare journal entries for these four transactions.

Exercise 6-39 Recording Purchases and Shipping Terms

OBJECTIVE 2

On May 12, Digital Distributors received three shipments of merchandise. The first was shipped F.O.B. shipping point, had a total invoice price of $142,500, and was delivered by a trucking company that charged an additional $8,300 for transportation charges from Digital. The second was shipped F.O.B. shipping point and had a total invoice price of $87,250, including transportation charges of $5,700 that were prepaid by the seller. The third shipment was shipped F.O.B. destination and had an invoice price of $21,650, excluding transportation charges of $1,125 paid by the seller. Digital uses a perpetual inventory system. Digital has not paid any of the invoices.

Required:

Prepare journal entries to record these purchases.

Exercise 6-40 Recording Sales and Shipping Terms

OBJECTIVE 2

🔍 **SHOW ME HOW**

Stanley Company shipped the following merchandise during the last week of December. All sales were on credit.

Sales Price	Shipping Terms	Date Goods Shipped	Date Goods Received
$5,460	F.O.B. shipping point	December 27	January 3
$3,800	F.O.B. destination	December 29	January 5
$4,250	F.O.B. destination	December 29	December 31

Required:

1. Compute the total amount of sales revenue recognized by Stanley in December.
2. **CONCEPTUAL CONNECTION** If Stanley included all of the above shipments as revenue, what would be the effect on Stanley's assets, liabilities, and stockholders' equity?

Exercise 6-41 Recording Purchase and Sales Transactions

OBJECTIVE 2

Raymond Company and Geeslin Company both use a perpetual inventory system. The following transactions occurred during the month of January:

Jan. 1   Raymond purchased $5,000 of merchandise on account from Geeslin with credit terms of 2/10, n/30. The cost of the merchandise was $3,750. Assume that Geeslin uses the net method to record sales discounts.

     8   Raymond returned $500 of the merchandise to Geeslin. The cost of the merchandise returned was $375.

    10   Raymond paid invoices totaling $3,000 to Geeslin for the merchandise purchased on January 1.

    30   Raymond paid Geeslin the balance due.

Required:

Prepare the journal entries to record these transactions on the books of Raymond and Geeslin.

Exercise 6-42 Recording Purchases and Sales

OBJECTIVE 2

Printer Supply Company sells computer printers and printer supplies. One of its products is a toner cartridge for laser printers. At the beginning of the year, there were 225 cartridges on hand that cost $62 each. During the year, Printer Supply purchased 1,475 cartridges at $62 each. After inspection, Printer Supply determined that 15 cartridges were defective and returned them to the supplier. Printer Supply also sold 830 cartridges at $95 each and sold an additional 710 cartridges at $102 each after a midyear selling price increase. Customers returned 20 of the cartridges that were purchased at $102 to Printer Supply for miscellaneous reasons. Assume that Printer Supply uses a perpetual inventory system.

(Continued)

Required:

1. Prepare summary journal entries to record the purchases, sales, and return of inventory. Assume that all purchases and sales are on credit but no discounts were offered.
2. What is the cost of ending inventory, cost of goods sold, and gross profit?

OBJECTIVE **Exercise 6-43 Inventory Costing Methods**

Tyler Company has the following information related to purchases and sales of one of its inventory items.

Date	Description	Units Purchased at Cost	Units Sold at Retail
Sept. 1	Beginning inventory	20 units @ $5	
10	Purchase	30 units @ $8	
20	Sales		40 units @ $15
25	Purchase	25 units @ $10	

Assume Tyler uses a perpetual inventory system.

Required:

1. Calculate ending inventory and cost of goods sold using the FIFO, LIFO, and average cost methods.
2. Which inventory costing method produces the highest amount for net income?
3. Which inventory costing method produces the lowest amount for taxes?
4. Which inventory costing method produces the highest amount for ending inventory?

OBJECTIVE   **Exercise 6-44 Inventory Costing Methods**

SHOW ME HOW

Crandall Distributors uses a perpetual inventory system and has the following data available for inventory, purchases, and sales for a recent year:

Activity	Units	Purchase Price (per unit)	Sale Price (per unit)
Beginning inventory	110	$7.10	
Purchase 1, Jan. 18	575	7.20	
Sale 1	380		$12.00
Sale 2	225		12.00
Purchase 2, Mar. 10	680	7.50	
Sale 3	270		12.00
Sale 4	290		12.50
Purchase 3, Sept. 30	230	7.70	
Sale 5	240		12.50

Required:

1. Compute the cost of ending inventory and the cost of goods sold using the specific identification method. Assume the ending inventory is made up of 40 units from beginning inventory, 30 units from Purchase 1, 80 units from Purchase 2, and 40 units from Purchase 3.
2. Compute the cost of ending inventory and cost of goods sold using the FIFO inventory costing method.
3. Compute the cost of ending inventory and cost of goods sold using the LIFO inventory costing method.
4. Compute the cost of ending inventory and cost of goods sold using the average cost inventory costing method. (*Note:* Use four decimal places for per-unit calculations and round all other numbers to the nearest dollar.)
5. **CONCEPTUAL CONNECTION** Compare the ending inventory and cost of goods sold computed under all four methods. What can you conclude about the effects of the inventory costing methods on the balance sheet and the income statement?

Exercise 6-45 Inventory Costing Methods

On June 1, Welding Products Company had a beginning inventory of 210 cases of welding rods that had been purchased for $88 per case. Welding Products purchased 1,150 cases at a cost of $95 per case on June 3. On June 19, the company purchased another 950 cases at a cost of $112 per case. Sales data for the welding rods are:

Date	Cases Sold
June 9	990
June 29	975

Welding Products uses a perpetual inventory system, and the sales price of the welding rods was $130 per case.

Required:

1. Compute the cost of ending inventory and cost of goods sold using the FIFO method.
2. Compute the cost of ending inventory and cost of goods sold using the LIFO method.
3. Compute the cost of ending inventory and cost of goods sold using the average cost method. (*Note:* Use four decimal places for per-unit calculations and round all other numbers to the nearest dollar.)
4. **CONCEPTUAL CONNECTION** Assume that operating expenses are $21,600 and Welding Products has a 30% tax rate. How much will the cash paid for income taxes differ among the three inventory methods?
5. **CONCEPTUAL CONNECTION** Compute Welding Products' gross profit ratio (rounded to two decimal places) and inventory turnover ratio (rounded to three decimal places) under each of the three inventory costing methods. How would the choice of inventory costing method affect these ratios?

Exercise 6-46 Financial Statement Effects of FIFO and LIFO

The chart below lists financial statement items that may be affected by the use of either the FIFO or LIFO inventory costing methods.

	FIFO	LIFO
Ending inventory		
Cost of goods sold		
Gross margin		
Income before taxes		
Payments for income taxes		
Net income		

Required:

CONCEPTUAL CONNECTION Assuming that prices are rising, complete the chart by indicating whether the specified item is (a) higher or (b) lower under FIFO and LIFO.

Exercise 6-47 Effects of Inventory Costing Methods

Jefferson Enterprises has the following income statement data available for the year:

Sales revenue	$828,600
Operating expenses	370,400
Interest expense	42,100
Income tax rate	34%

(*Continued*)

Jefferson uses a perpetual inventory accounting system and the average cost method. Jefferson is considering adopting the FIFO or LIFO method for costing inventory. Jefferson's accountant prepared the following data:

	If Average Cost Used	If FIFO Used	If LIFO Used
Ending inventory	$ 65,950	$ 78,500	$ 40,100
Cost of goods sold	399,050	386,500	424,900

Required:

1. Compute income before taxes, income taxes expense, and net income for each of the three inventory costing methods. (Round to the nearest dollar.)
2. **CONCEPTUAL CONNECTION** Why are the cost of goods sold and ending inventory amounts different for each of the three methods? What do these amounts tell us about the purchase price of inventory during the year?
3. **CONCEPTUAL CONNECTION** Which method produces the most realistic amount for net income? For inventory? Explain your answer.

Exercise 6-48 Inventory Costing Methods

Neyman Inc. has the following data for purchases and sales of inventory:

Date	Units	Cost per Unit
Beginning inventory	22	$400
Purchase 1, Feb. 24	130	370
Sale 1	145	
Purchase 2, July 2	180	330
Purchase 3, Oct. 31	90	250
Sale 2	265	

All sales were made at a sales price of $450 per unit. Assume that Neyman uses a perpetual inventory system.

Required:

1. Compute the cost of goods sold and the cost of ending inventory using the FIFO, LIFO, and average cost methods. (*Note:* Use four decimal places for per-unit calculations and round all other numbers to the nearest dollar.)
2. **CONCEPTUAL CONNECTION** Why is the cost of goods sold lower with LIFO than with FIFO?

OBJECTIVE

Exercise 6-49 Effects of FIFO and LIFO

Sheepskin Company sells to colleges and universities a special paper that is used for diplomas. Sheepskin typically makes one purchase of the special paper each year on January 1. Assume that Sheepskin uses a perpetual inventory system. You have the following data for the past 3 years:

Year 1

Beginning inventory	0 pages
Purchases	10,000 pages at $1.60 per page
Sales	8,500 pages

Year 2

Beginning inventory	1,500 pages
Purchases	16,200 pages at $2.00 per page
Sales	15,000 pages

Year 3

Beginning inventory	2,700 pages
Purchases	18,000 pages at $2.50 per page
Sales	20,100 pages

Required:

1. What would the ending inventory and cost of goods sold be for each year if FIFO is used?
2. What would the ending inventory and cost of goods sold be for each year if LIFO is used?
3. **CONCEPTUAL CONNECTION** For each year, explain the cause of the differences in cost of goods sold under FIFO and LIFO.

Exercise 6-50 Lower of Cost or Net Realizable Value

Meredith's Appliance Store has the following data for the items in its inventory at the end of the accounting period:

Item	Number of Units	Historical Cost per Unit	Selling Price per Unit	Disposal Costs
Window air conditioner	25	$180	$150	$45
Dishwasher	22	225	230	20
Refrigerator	35	420	450	25
Microwave	15	220	190	15
Washer (clothing)	28	180	260	40
Dryer (clothing)	18	210	275	50

Required:

1. Compute the carrying value of Meredith's ending inventory using the lower of cost or net realizable value rule applied on an item-by-item basis.
2. Prepare the journal entry required to value the inventory at lower of cost or net realizable value.
3. **CONCEPTUAL CONNECTION** What is the conceptual justification for valuing inventory at the lower of cost or net realizable value?

Exercise 6-51 Lower of Cost or Market

Shaw Systems sells a limited line of specially made products, using television advertising campaigns in large cities. At year end, Shaw has the following data for its inventory:

Item	Number of Units	Historical Cost per Unit	Selling Price per Unit	Disposal Costs
Phone	625	$ 24	$ 25	$ 5
Stereo	180	177	200	10
Electric shaver	215	30	31	3
MP3 alarm clock	450	26	27	2
Handheld game system	570	40	45	3

Required:

1. Compute the carrying value of the ending inventory using the lower of cost or net realizable value rule applied on an item-by-item basis.
2. Prepare the journal entry required to value the inventory at lower of cost or net realizable value.
3. **CONCEPTUAL CONNECTION** What is the impact of applying the lower of cost or net realizable value rule on the financial statements of the current period? What is the impact on the financial statements of a subsequent period in which the inventory is sold?

OBJECTIVE **6**

Exercise 6-52 Analyzing Inventory

The recent financial statements of McLelland Clothing Inc. include the following data:

Sales	$754,690
Cost of goods sold:	
Computed under FIFO	528,600
Computed under LIFO	555,000
Average inventory:	
Computed under FIFO	72,200
Computed under LIFO	45,800

Required:

1. Calculate McLelland's gross profit ratio (rounded to two decimal places), inventory turnover ratio (rounded to three decimal places), and the average days to sell inventory (assume a 365-day year and round to two decimal places) using the FIFO inventory costing method. Be sure to explain what each ratio means.
2. Calculate McLelland's gross profit ratio (rounded to two decimal places), inventory turnover ratio (rounded to three decimal places), and the average days to sell inventory (assume a 365-day year and round to two decimal places) using the LIFO inventory costing method. Be sure to explain what each ratio means.
3. **CONCEPTUAL CONNECTION** Which ratios—the ones computed using FIFO or LIFO inventory values—provide the better indicator of how successful McLelland was at managing and controlling its inventory?

OBJECTIVE **7**

Exercise 6-53 Effects of an Error in Ending Inventory

Waymire Company prepared the partial income statements presented below for 2023 and 2022.

	2023		2022	
Sales revenue		$ 538,200		$ 483,700
Cost of goods sold:				
Beginning inventory	$ 39,300		$ 32,100	
Purchases	343,200		292,700	
Cost of goods available for sale	$382,500		$ 324,800	
Ending inventory	(46,800)	335,700	(39,300)	285,500
Gross margin		$ 202,500		$ 198,200
Operating expenses		(167,200)		(151,600)
Income before taxes		$ 35,300		$ 46,600

During 2024, Waymire's accountant discovered that ending inventory for 2022 had been understated by $6,500.

Required:

1. Prepare corrected income statements for 2023 and 2022.
2. Prepare a schedule showing each financial statement item affected by the error and the amount of the error for that item (ignore the effect of income taxes). Indicate whether each error is an overstatement (+) or an understatement (−).

Exercise 6-54 *(Appendix 6A)* Recording Purchases

OBJECTIVE 8

Compass Inc. purchased 1,250 bags of insulation, on account, from Glassco Inc. The bags of insulation cost $5.50 each. Compass paid Turner Trucking $320 to have the bags of insulation shipped to its warehouse. Compass returned 50 bags that were defective and paid for the remainder. Assume that Compass uses the periodic inventory system.

Required:

1. Prepare a journal entry to record the purchase of the bags of insulation.
2. Prepare the entry to record the payment for shipping.
3. Prepare the entry for the return of the defective bags.
4. Prepare the entry to record the payment for the bags kept by Compass.
5. What is the total cost of this purchase?
6. **CONCEPTUAL CONNECTION** If you have previously worked **Exercise 6-37**, compare your answers. What are the differences? Be sure to explain why the differences occurred.

Exercise 6-55 *(Appendix 6A)* Recording Purchase and Sales Transactions

OBJECTIVE 8

The following transactions occurred during the month of January.

Jan. 1 Raymond purchased $5,000 of merchandise on account from Geeslin with credit terms of 2/10, n/30. The cost of the merchandise was $3,750. Assume that Geeslin uses the net method to record sales discounts.

8 Raymond returned $500 of the merchandise to Geeslin. The cost of the merchandise returned was $375.

10 Raymond paid invoices totaling $3,000 to Geeslin for the merchandise purchased on January 1.

30 Raymond paid Geeslin the balance due.

Assume that Raymond Company uses the periodic inventory system.

Required:

Prepare the journal entries to record these transactions on the books of Raymond Company.

Exercise 6-56 *(Appendices 6A and 6B)* Recording Purchases and Sales

OBJECTIVE 9 8

Printer Supply Company sells computer printers and printer supplies. One of its products is a toner cartridge for laser printers. At the beginning of the year, there were 225 cartridges on hand at a cost of $62 each. During the year, Printer Supply purchased 1,475 cartridges at $62 each, sold 830 cartridges at $95 each, and sold an additional 710 cartridges at $102 each after a midyear selling price increase. Printer Supply returned 15 defective cartridges to the supplier. In addition, customers returned 20 cartridges that were purchased at $102 to Printer Supply for various reasons. Assume that Printer Supply uses a periodic inventory system.

Required:

1. Prepare journal entries to record the purchases, sales, and return of inventory. Assume that all purchases and sales are on credit but no discounts were offered.
2. What is the cost of ending inventory, cost of goods sold, and gross profit?
3. **CONCEPTUAL CONNECTION** If you have previously worked **Exercise 6-42**, compare your answers. What are the differences? Be sure to explain why the differences occurred.

OBJECTIVE

Exercise 6-57 Inventory Costing Methods: Periodic Inventory

Tyler Company has the following information related to purchases and sales of one of its inventory items.

Date		Description	Units Purchased at Cost	Units Sold at Retail
Sept.	1	Beginning inventory	20 units @ $5	
	10	Purchase	30 units @ $8	
	20	Sales		40 units @ $15
	25	Purchase	25 units @ $10	

Assume that Tyler uses a periodic inventory system.

Required:

Calculate the cost of goods sold and the cost of ending inventory using the FIFO, LIFO, and average cost methods. (*Note:* Use four decimal places for per-unit calculations and round all other numbers to the nearest whole dollar.)

OBJECTIVE

Exercise 6-58 *(Appendix 6B)* Inventory Costing Methods: Periodic Inventory System

Jackson Company had 400 units in beginning inventory at a cost of $20 each. Jackson's 2019 purchases were:

Date	Purchases
Feb. 21	5,200 units @ $24 each
July 15	4,800 units @ $28 each
Sept. 30	8,500 units @ $30 each

Jackson uses a periodic inventory system and sold 18,500 units at $50 each during the year.

Required:

1. Calculate the cost of ending inventory and the cost of goods sold using the FIFO, LIFO, and average cost methods. (*Note:* Use four decimal places for per-unit calculations and round all other numbers to the nearest dollar.)
2. Prepare income statements through gross margin using each of the costing methods in Requirement 1.
3. **CONCEPTUAL CONNECTION** What is the effect of each inventory costing method on income?

OBJECTIVE

Exercise 6-59 *(Appendix 6B)* Inventory Costing Methods: Periodic Inventory System

The inventory accounting records for Lee Enterprises contained the following data:

Beginning inventory	1,400 units @ $12 each
Purchase 1, Feb. 26	2,400 units @ $16 each
Sale 1, March 9	2,300 units @ $27 each
Purchase 2, June 14	2,200 units @ $20 each
Sale 2, Sept. 22	1,900 units @ $29 each

Required:

1. Calculate the cost of ending inventory and the cost of goods sold using the FIFO, LIFO, and average cost methods. (*Note:* Use four decimal places for per-unit calculations and round all other numbers to the nearest dollar.)
2. **CONCEPTUAL CONNECTION** Compare the ending inventory and cost of goods sold computed under all three methods. What can you conclude about the effects of the inventory costing methods on the balance sheet and the income statement?

Exercise 6-60 *(Appendix 6B)* **Inventory Costing Methods: Periodic System** OBJECTIVE ◀ 9

Harrington Company had the following data for inventory during a recent year:

	Units	Cost per Unit	Total Cost
Beginning inventory	500	$ 9.00	$ 4,500
Purchase 1, Jan. 28	1,600	9.40	$15,040
Purchase 2, May 2	1,200	10.20	12,240
Purchase 3, Aug. 13	1,400	10.80	15,120
Purchase 4, Nov. 9	1,100	11.30	12,430
Total purchases	5,300		54,830
Goods available for sale	5,800		$59,330
Less: Sales	(5,240)		
Ending inventory	560		

Assume that Harrington uses a periodic inventory accounting system.

Required:

1. Using the FIFO, LIFO, and average cost methods, compute the ending inventory and cost of goods sold. (*Note:* Use four decimal places for per-unit calculations and round all other numbers to the nearest dollar.)
2. **CONCEPTUAL CONNECTION** Which method will produce the most realistic amount for income? For inventory?
3. **CONCEPTUAL CONNECTION** Which method will produce the lowest amount paid for taxes?

PROBLEM SET A

Problem 6-61A Applying the Cost of Goods Sold Model OBJECTIVE ◀ 1

The following amounts were obtained from the accounting records of Rabren Supply Company:

	Year 1		Year 2	
Net sales		$359,620		$423,150
Cost of goods sold:				
Beginning inventory	$36,800		(d)	
Purchases	(a)		301,600	
Goods available for sale	(b)		(e)	
Ending inventory	42,780		(f)	
Cost of goods sold		(c)		289,700
Gross margin		$116,450		(g)

Required:

Compute the missing amounts.

Problem 6-62A Recording Sale and Purchase Transactions OBJECTIVE ◀ 2

Alpharack Company sells a line of tennis equipment to retailers. Alpharack uses the perpetual inventory system and engaged in the following transactions during April, its first month of operations:

a. On April 2, Alpharack purchased, on credit, 360 Wilbur T-100 tennis rackets with credit terms of 2/10, n/30. The rackets were purchased at a cost of $30 each. Alpharack paid Barker Trucking $195 to transport the tennis rackets from the manufacturer to Alpharack's warehouse, shipping terms were F.O.B. shipping point, and the items were shipped on April 2.

(Continued)

b. On April 3, Alpharack purchased, for cash, 115 packs of tennis balls for $10 per pack.
c. On April 4, Alpharack purchased tennis clothing, on credit, from Designer Tennis Wear. The cost of the clothing was $8,250. Credit terms were 2/10, n/25.
d. On April 10, Alpharack paid for the purchase of the tennis rackets in Transaction a.
e. On April 15, Alpharack determined that $325 of the tennis clothing was defective. Alpharack returned the defective merchandise to Designer Tennis Wear.
f. On April 20, Alpharack sold 118 tennis rackets at $90 each, 92 packs of tennis balls at $12 per pack, and $5,380 of tennis clothing. All sales were for cash. The cost of the merchandise sold was $7,580.
g. On April 23, customers returned $860 of the merchandise purchased on April 20. The cost of the merchandise returned was $450.
h. On April 25, Alpharack sold another 55 tennis rackets, on credit, for $90 each and 15 packs of tennis balls at $12 per pack, for cash. The cost of the merchandise sold was $1,800.
i. On April 29, Alpharack paid Designer Tennis Wear for the clothing purchased on April 4 minus the return on April 15.
j. On April 30, Alpharack purchased 20 tennis bags, on credit, from Bag Designs for $320. The bags were shipped F.O.B. destination and arrived at Alpharack on May 3.

Required:

1. Prepare the journal entries to record the sale and purchase transactions for Alpharack during April.
2. Assuming operating expenses of $8,500 and income taxes of $1,180, prepare Alpharack's income statement for April.

OBJECTIVE **Problem 6-63A** **Inventory Costing Methods**

Anderson's Department Store has the following data for inventory, purchases, and sales of merchandise for December:

Activity	Units	Purchase Price (per unit)	Sale Price (per unit)
Beginning inventory	10	$8.00	
Purchase 1, Dec. 2	22	8.80	
Purchase 2, Dec. 5	26	9.05	
Sale 1, Dec. 7	19		$20.00
Sale 2, Dec. 10	25		20.00
Purchase 3, Dec. 12	12	9.80	
Sale 3, Dec. 14	20		20.00

Anderson's uses a perpetual inventory system. All purchases and sales were for cash.

Required:

1. Compute cost of goods sold and the cost of ending inventory using FIFO.
2. Compute cost of goods sold and the cost of ending inventory using LIFO.
3. Compute cost of goods sold and the cost of ending inventory using the average cost method. (*Note:* Use four decimal places for per-unit calculations.)
4. Prepare the journal entries to record these transactions assuming Anderson chooses to use the FIFO method.
5. **CONCEPTUAL CONNECTION** Which method would result in the lowest amount paid for taxes?

Problem 6-64A Inventory Costing Methods

OBJECTIVE ◀ 3 4 6

Gavin Products uses a perpetual inventory system. For Year 1 and Year 2, Gavin has the following data:

Activity	Units	Purchase Price (per unit)	Sale Price (per unit)
Year 1			
Beginning inventory	200	$ 9	
Purchase 1, Feb. 15	300	11	
Sale 1, Mar. 10	320		$25
Purchase 2, Sept. 15	500	12	
Sale 2, Nov. 3	550		25
Purchase 3, Dec. 20	150	13	
Year 2			
Sale 3, Apr. 4	200		25
Purchase 4, June 25	200	14	
Sale 4, Dec. 18	150		25

Required:

1. For each year, compute cost of goods sold, the cost of ending inventory, and gross margin using FIFO.
2. For each year, compute cost of goods sold, the cost of ending inventory, and gross margin using LIFO.
3. For each year, compute cost of goods sold, the cost of ending inventory, and gross margin using the average cost method. (*Note:* Use four decimal places for per-unit calculations and round all other numbers to the nearest dollar.)
4. **CONCEPTUAL CONNECTION** Which method would result in the lowest amount paid for taxes?
5. **CONCEPTUAL CONNECTION** Which method produces the most realistic amount for income? For inventory? Explain your answer.
6. **CONCEPTUAL CONNECTION** Compute Gavin's gross profit ratio and inventory turnover ratio under each of the three inventory costing methods. (*Note:* Round answers to two decimal places.) How would the choice of inventory costing method affect these ratios?

Problem 6-65A Lower of Cost or Net Realizable Value

OBJECTIVE ◀ 5

Sue Stone, the president of Tippecanoe Home Products, has prepared the following information for the company's television inventory at the end of the year:

Model	Quantity	FIFO Cost per Unit	Selling Price per Unit	Disposal Costs
T-260	15	$250	$480	$35
S-256	28	325	330	30
R-193	20	210	250	20
Z-376	15	285	290	40

Required:

1. Determine the carrying amount of the inventory using lower of cost or net realizable value applied on an item-by-item basis.
2. Prepare the journal entry required to value the inventory at lower of cost or net realizable value.
3. **CONCEPTUAL CONNECTION** What is the impact of applying the lower of cost or net realizable value rule on the financial statements of the current period? What is the impact on the financial statements of a subsequent period in which the inventory is sold?

OBJECTIVE **3** **5**

Problem 6-66A Inventory Costing and LCNRV

Ortman Enterprises sells a chemical used in various manufacturing processes. On January 1, Ortman had 5,000,000 gallons on hand, for which it had paid $0.50 per gallon. During the year, Ortman made the following purchases:

Date	Gallons	Cost per Gallon	Total Cost
Feb. 20	10,000,000	$0.52	$ 5,200,000
May 15	25,000,000	0.56	14,000,000
Sept. 12	32,000,000	0.60	19,200,000

During the year, Ortman sold 65,000,000 gallons at $0.75 per gallon (35,000,000 gallons were sold on June 29 and 30,000,000 gallons were sold on Nov. 22), leaving an ending inventory of 7,000,000 gallons. Assume that Ortman uses a perpetual inventory system. Ortman uses the lower of cost or net realizable value for its inventories, as required by generally accepted accounting principles.

Required:

1. Assume that the net realizable value of the chemical is $0.76 per gallon on December 31. Compute the cost of ending inventory using the FIFO and average cost methods, and then apply LCNRV. (*Note:* Use four decimal places for per-unit calculations and round all other numbers to the nearest dollar.)
2. Assume that the net realizable value of the chemical is $0.58 per gallon on December 31. Compute the cost of ending inventory using the FIFO and average cost methods, and then apply LCNRV. (*Note:* Use four decimal places for per-unit calculations and round all other numbers to the nearest dollar.)

OBJECTIVE **7**

Problem 6-67A Effects of an Inventory Error

The income statements for Graul Corporation for the 3 years ending in 20Y9 appear below.

	20Y9	20Y8	20Y7
Sales revenue	$ 4,643,200	$ 4,287,500	$ 3,647,900
Cost of goods sold	(2,475,100)	(2,181,600)	(2,006,100)
Gross margin	$ 2,168,100	$ 2,105,900	$ 1,641,800
Operating expense	(1,548,600)	(1,428,400)	(1,152,800)
Income from operations	$ 619,500	$ 677,500	$ 489,000
Other expenses	(137,300)	(123,600)	(112,900)
Income before taxes	$ 482,200	$ 553,900	$ 376,100
Income tax expense (34%)	(163,948)	(188,326)	(127,874)
Net income	$ 318,252	$ 365,574	$ 248,226

During 20Y9, Graul discovered that the 20Y7 ending inventory had been misstated due to the following two transactions being recorded incorrectly.

a. A purchase return of inventory costing $42,000 was recorded twice.
b. A credit purchase of inventory made on December 20 for $28,500 was not recorded. The goods were shipped F.O.B. shipping point and were shipped on December 22, 20Y7.

Required:

1. Was ending inventory for 20Y7 overstated or understated? By how much?
2. Prepare correct income statements for all 3 years.
3. **CONCEPTUAL CONNECTION** Did the error in 20Y7 affect cumulative net income for the 3-year period? Explain your response.
4. **CONCEPTUAL CONNECTION** Why was the 20Y9 net income unaffected?

Problem 6-68A *(Appendices 6A and 6B)* **Inventory Costing Methods**   OBJECTIVE ◄ 8 9

Spiegel Department Store has the following data for inventory, purchases, and sales of merchandise for December:

Activity	Units	Purchase Price (per unit)	Sale Price (per unit)
Beginning inventory	10	$8.00	
Purchase 1, Dec. 2	22	8.80	
Purchase 2, Dec. 5	26	9.05	
Sale 1, Dec. 7	19		$20.00
Sale 2, Dec. 10	25		20.00
Purchase 3, Dec. 12	12	9.80	
Sale 3, Dec. 14	20		20.00

Spiegel uses a periodic inventory system. All purchases and sales are for cash.

Required:

1. Compute cost of goods sold and the cost of ending inventory using FIFO.
2. Compute cost of goods sold and the cost of ending inventory using LIFO.
3. Compute cost of goods sold and the cost of ending inventory using the average cost method. (*Note:* Use four decimal places for per-unit calculations.)
4. Prepare the journal entries to record these transactions assuming Spiegel chooses to use the FIFO method.
5. **CONCEPTUAL CONNECTION** Which method would result in the lowest amount paid for taxes?
6. **CONCEPTUAL CONNECTION** Refer to **Problem 6-63A** and compare your results. What are the differences? Be sure to explain why the differences occurred.

Problem 6-69A *(Appendix 6B)* **Inventory Costing Methods**   OBJECTIVE ◄ 9

Jet Black Products uses a periodic inventory system. For Year 1 and Year 2, Jet Black has the following data:

Activity	Units	Purchase Price (per unit)	Sale Price (per unit)
Year 1			
Beginning inventory	200	$ 9.00	
Purchase 1, Feb. 15	300	11.00	
Sale 1, Mar. 10	320		$25.00
Purchase 2, Sept. 15	500	12.00	
Sale 2, Nov. 3	550		25.00
Purchase 3, Dec. 20	150	13.00	
Year 2			
Sale 3, Apr. 4	200		25.00
Purchase 4, June 25	200	14.00	
Sale 4, Dec. 18	150		25.00

All purchases and sales are for cash.

Required:

1. Compute cost of goods sold, the cost of ending inventory, and gross margin for each year using FIFO.
2. Compute cost of goods sold, the cost of ending inventory, and gross margin for each year using LIFO.
3. Compute cost of goods sold, the cost of ending inventory, and gross margin for each year using the average cost method. (*Note:* Use four decimal places for per-unit calculations and round all other numbers to the nearest dollar.)

(Continued)

4. **CONCEPTUAL CONNECTION** Which method would result in the lowest amount paid for taxes?

5. **CONCEPTUAL CONNECTION** Which method produces the most realistic amount for income? For inventory? Explain your answer.

6. **CONCEPTUAL CONNECTION** What is the effect of purchases made later in the year on the gross margin when LIFO is employed? When FIFO is employed? Be sure to explain why any differences occur.

7. **CONCEPTUAL CONNECTION** If you worked **Problem 6-64A**, compare your answers. What are the differences? Be sure to explain why any differences occurred.

PROBLEM SET B

OBJECTIVE   **Problem 6-61B Applying the Cost of Goods Sold Model**

The following amounts were obtained from the accounting records of Wachter Sports Products Inc.:

	Year 1		Year 2	
Net sales		(a)		$154,810
Cost of goods sold:				
Beginning inventory	(b)		(d)	
Purchases	104,250		(e)	
Goods available for sale	(c)		$127,500	
Ending inventory	6,940		(f)	
Cost of goods sold		104,730		(g)
Gross margin		$ 28,600		$ 38,980

Required:
Compute the missing amounts.

OBJECTIVE   **Problem 6-62B Recording Sale and Purchase Transactions**

Jordan Footwear sells athletic shoes and uses the perpetual inventory system. During June, Jordan engaged in the following transactions its first month of operations:

a. On June 1, Jordan purchased, on credit, 100 pairs of basketball shoes and 210 pairs of running shoes with credit terms of 2/10, n/30. The basketball shoes were purchased at a cost of $85 per pair, and the running shoes were purchased at a cost of $60 per pair. Jordan paid Mole Trucking $310 cash to transport the shoes from the manufacturer to Jordan's warehouse, shipping terms were F.O.B. shipping point, and the items were shipped on June 1 and arrived on June 4.

b. On June 2, Jordan purchased 88 pairs of cross-training shoes for cash. The shoes cost Jordan $65 per pair.

c. On June 6, Jordan purchased 125 pairs of tennis shoes on credit. Credit terms were 2/10, n/ 25. The shoes were purchased at a cost of $45 per pair.

d. On June 10, Jordan paid for the purchase of the basketball shoes and the running shoes in Transaction a.

e. On June 12, Jordan determined that $585 of the tennis shoes were defective. Jordan returned the defective merchandise to the manufacturer.

f. On June 18, Jordan sold 50 pairs of basketball shoes at $116 per pair, 92 pairs of running shoes for $85 per pair, 21 pairs of cross-training shoes for $100 per pair, and 48 pairs of tennis shoes for $68 per pair. All sales were for cash. The cost of the merchandise sold was $13,295.

g. On June 21, customers returned 10 pairs of the basketball shoes purchased on June 18. The cost of the merchandise returned was $850.

h. On June 23, Jordan sold another 20 pairs of basketball shoes, on credit, for $116 per pair and 15 pairs of cross-training shoes for $100 cash per pair. The cost of the merchandise sold was $2,675.

i. On June 30, Jordan paid for the June 6 purchase of tennis shoes minus the return on June 12.

j. On June 30, Jordan purchased 60 pairs of basketball shoes, on credit, for $85 each. The shoes were shipped F.O.B. destination and arrived at Jordan on July 3.

Required:

1. Prepare the journal entries to record the sale and purchase transactions for Jordan during June.

2. Assuming operating expenses of $5,300 and income taxes of $365, prepare Jordan's income statement.

Problem 6-63B Inventory Costing Methods

OBJECTIVE 2 3 4

Ein Company began operations in February. Ein's accounting records provide the following data for the remainder of the year for one of the items the company sells:

Activity	Units	Purchase Price (per unit)	Sale Price (per unit)
Beginning inventory	9	$58	
Purchase 1, Feb. 15	6	72	
Purchase 2, Mar. 22	8	80	
Sale 1, Apr. 9	10		$150
Purchase 3, May 29	9	86	
Sale 2, July 10	15		150
Purchase 4, Sept. 10	8	96	
Sale 3, Oct. 15	12		150

Ein uses a perpetual inventory system. All purchases and sales were for cash.

Required:

1. Compute cost of goods sold and the cost of ending inventory using FIFO.
2. Compute cost of goods sold and the cost of ending inventory using LIFO.
3. Compute cost of goods sold and the cost of ending inventory using the average cost method. (*Note:* Use four decimal places for per-unit calculations and round all other numbers to the nearest penny.)
4. Prepare the journal entries to record these transactions assuming Ein chooses to use the FIFO method.
5. **CONCEPTUAL CONNECTION** Which method would result in the lowest amount paid for taxes?

Problem 6-64B Inventory Costing Methods

OBJECTIVE 3 4 6

Terpsichore Company uses a perpetual inventory system. For Year 1 and Year 2, Terpsichore has the following data:

Activity	Units	Purchase Price (per unit)	Sale Price (per unit)
Year 1			
Beginning inventory	100	$45	
Purchase 1, Feb. 25	700	52	
Sale 1, Apr. 15	600		$90

(*Continued*)

Activity	Units	Purchase Price (per unit)	Sale Price (per unit)
Purchase 2, Aug. 30	500	56	
Sale 2, Nov. 13	600		90
Purchase 3, Dec. 20	400	58	
Year 2			
Sale 3, Mar. 8	400		90
Purchase 4, June 28	900	62	
Sale 4, Dec. 18	200		90

Required:

1. For each year, compute cost of goods sold, the cost of ending inventory, and gross margin using FIFO.
2. For each year, compute cost of goods sold, the cost of ending inventory, and gross margin using LIFO.
3. For each year, compute cost of goods sold, the cost of ending inventory, and gross margin using the average cost method. (*Note:* Use four decimal places for per-unit calculations and round all other numbers to the nearest dollar.)
4. **CONCEPTUAL CONNECTION** Which method would result in the lowest amount paid for taxes?
5. **CONCEPTUAL CONNECTION** Which method produces the most realistic amount for income? For inventory? Explain your answer.
6. **CONCEPTUAL CONNECTION** Compute Terpsichore's gross profit ratio and inventory turnover ratio under each of the three inventory costing methods. (*Note:* Round answers to two decimal places.) How would the choice of inventory costing method affect these ratios?

OBJECTIVE 5

Problem 6-65B Lower of Cost or Net Realizable Value

Kevin Spears, the accountant of Tyler Electronics Inc., has prepared the following information for the company's inventory at the end of the year:

Model	Quantity	FIFO Cost per Unit	Selling Price per Unit	Disposal Costs
RSQ535	30	$100	$150	$30
JKY942	52	140	160	35
LLM112	84	85	90	10
KZG428	63	105	145	17

Required:

1. Determine the carrying amount of the inventory using lower of cost or net realizable value applied on an item-by-item basis.
2. Prepare the journal entry required to value the inventory at lower of cost or net realizable value.
3. **CONCEPTUAL CONNECTION** What is the impact of applying the lower of cost or net realizable value rule on the financial statements of the current period? What is the impact on the financial statements of a subsequent period in which the inventory is sold?

OBJECTIVE 3 5

Problem 6-66B Inventory Costing and LCNRV

J&J Enterprises sells paper cups to fast-food franchises. On January 1, J&J had 5,000 cups on hand, for which it had paid $0.10 per cup. During the year, J&J made the following purchases and sales:

Date	Units	Cost per Unit	Total Cost
Feb. 20	100,000	$0.12	$12,000
May 15	57,000	0.14	7,980
Sept. 12	85,000	0.15	12,750

During the year, J&J sold 240,000 cups at $0.35 per cup (80,000 cups were sold on April 2 and 160,000 cups were sold on October 20), leaving an ending inventory of 7,000 cups. Assume that J&J uses a perpetual inventory system. J&J uses the lower of cost or net realizable value for its inventories, as required by generally accepted accounting principles.

Required:

1. Assume that the net realizable value of the cups is $0.38 per cup on December 31. Compute the cost of ending inventory using the FIFO and average cost methods, and then apply LCNRV. (*Note:* Use four decimal places for per-unit calculations and round all other numbers to the nearest dollar.)

2. Assume that the net realizable value of the cups is $0.12 per cup on December 31. Compute the cost of ending inventory using the FIFO and average cost methods, and then apply LCNRV. (*Note:* Use four decimal places for per-unit calculations and round all other numbers to the nearest dollar.)

Problem 6-67B Effects of an Inventory Error

OBJECTIVE 7

The income statements for Picard Company for the 3 years ending in 20Y6 appear below.

	20Y6	20Y5	20Y4
Sales revenue	$1,168,500	$ 998,400	$ 975,300
Cost of goods sold	(785,800)	(675,450)	(659,800)
Gross margin	$ 382,700	$ 322,950	$ 315,500
Operating expense	(162,500)	(142,800)	(155,300)
Income from operations	$ 220,200	$ 180,150	$ 160,200
Other expenses	(73,500)	(58,150)	(54,500)
Income before taxes	$ 146,700	$ 122,000	$ 105,700
Income tax expense (34%)	(49,878)	(41,480)	(35,938)
Net income	$ 96,822	$ 80,520	$ 69,762

During 20Y6, Picard discovered that the 20Y4 ending inventory had been misstated due to the following two transactions being recorded incorrectly:

a. Inventory costing $37,000 that was returned to the manufacturer (a purchase return) was not recorded. The items were included in ending inventory.

b. A credit purchase of inventory made on August 30, 20Y4, for $12,800 was recorded twice. The goods were shipped F.O.B. shipping point and were shipped on September 5, 20Y4.

Required:

1. Was ending inventory for 20Y4 overstated or understated? By how much?
2. Prepare correct income statements for all 3 years.
3. **CONCEPTUAL CONNECTION** Did the error in 20Y4 affect cumulative net income for the 3-year period? Explain your response.
4. **CONCEPTUAL CONNECTION** Why was the 20Y6 net income unaffected?

Problem 6-68B *(Appendices 6A and 6B)* Inventory Costing Methods

OBJECTIVE 8 9

Edwards Company began operations in February. Edwards accounting records provide the following data for the remainder of the year for one of the items the company sells:

Activity	Units	Purchase Price (per unit)	Sale Price (per unit)
Beginning inventory	9	$58	
Purchase 1, Feb. 15	6	72	
Purchase 2, Mar. 22	8	80	
Sale 1, Apr. 9	10		$150

(Continued)

Activity	Units	Purchase Price (per unit)	Sale Price (per unit)
Purchase 3, May 29	9	86	
Sale 2, July 10	15		150
Purchase 4, Sept. 10	8	96	
Sale 3, Oct. 15	12		150

Edwards uses a periodic inventory system. All purchases and sales were for cash.

Required:

1. Compute cost of goods sold and the cost of ending inventory using FIFO.
2. Compute cost of goods sold and the cost of ending inventory using LIFO.
3. Compute cost of goods sold and the cost of ending inventory using the average cost method. (*Note:* Use four decimal places for per-unit calculations and round all other numbers to the nearest dollar.)
4. Prepare the journal entries to record these transactions assuming Edwards chooses to use the FIFO method.
5. **CONCEPTUAL CONNECTION** Which method would result in the lowest amount paid for taxes?
6. **CONCEPTUAL CONNECTION** Refer to **Problem 6-63B** and compare your results. What are the differences? Be sure to explain why the differences occurred.

OBJECTIVE ▶9▶

Problem 6-69B *(Appendix 6B)* Inventory Costing Methods

Grencia Company uses a periodic inventory system. For Year 1 and Year 2, Grencia has the following data (assume all purchases and sales are for cash):

Activity	Units	Purchase Price (per unit)	Sale Price (per unit)
Year 1			
Beginning inventory	100	$45	
Purchase 1, Feb. 25	700	52	
Sale 1, Apr. 15	600		$90
Purchase 2, Aug. 30	500	56	
Sale 2, Nov. 13	600		90
Purchase 3, Dec. 20	400	58	
Year 2			
Sale 3, Mar. 8	400		90
Purchase 4, June 28	900	62	
Sale 4, Dec. 18	200		90

Required:

1. Compute cost of goods sold, the cost of ending inventory, and gross margin for each year using FIFO.
2. Compute cost of goods sold, the cost of ending inventory, and gross margin for each year using LIFO.
3. Compute cost of goods sold, the cost of ending inventory, and gross margin for each year using the average cost method. (*Note:* Use four decimal places for per-unit calculations and round all other numbers to the nearest dollar.)
4. **CONCEPTUAL CONNECTION** Which method would result in the lowest amount paid for taxes?
5. **CONCEPTUAL CONNECTION** Which method produces the most realistic amount for income? For inventory? Explain your answer.

6. **CONCEPTUAL CONNECTION** What is the effect of purchases made later in the year on the gross margin when LIFO is employed? When FIFO is employed? Be sure to explain why any differences occur.

7. **CONCEPTUAL CONNECTION** If you worked **Problem 6-64B**, compare your answers. What are the differences? Be sure to explain why any differences occurred.

CASES

Case 6-70 Inventory Valuation and Ethics

Mary Cravens is an accountant for City Appliance Corporation. One of Mary's responsibilities is developing the ending inventory amount for the calculation of cost of goods sold each month. At the end of September, Mary noticed that the ending inventory for a new brand of televisions was much larger than she had expected. In fact, there had been hardly any change since the end of the previous month when the shipments of televisions arrived. Mary knew that the firm's advertising had featured the new brand's products, so she had expected that a substantial portion of the televisions would have been sold.

Because of these concerns, Mary went to the warehouse to make sure the numbers were correct. While at the warehouse, Mary noticed that 30 of the televisions in question were on the loading dock for delivery to customers, and another, larger group of 200 sets were in an area set aside for sales returns. Mary asked Barry Tompkins, the returns supervisor, why so many of the televisions had been returned. Barry said that the manufacturer had used a cheap circuit board that failed on many of the sets after they had been in service for a week or two. Mary then asked how the defective televisions had been treated when the inventory was taken at the end of September. Barry said that the warehouse staff had been told to include in the ending inventory any item in the warehouse that was not marked for shipment to customers. Therefore, all returned merchandise was considered part of ending inventory.

Mary asked Barry what would be done with the defective sets. Barry said that they would probably have to be sold to a liquidator for a few cents on the dollar. Mary knew from her examination of the inventory data that all the returned sets had been included in the September inventory at their original cost.

Mary returned to the office and prepared a revised estimate of ending inventory using the information Barry Tompkins had given her to revalue the ending inventory of the television sets. She submitted the revision along with an explanatory note to her boss, Susan Grant. A few days later, Susan stopped by Mary's office to report on a conversation with the chief financial officer, Herb Cobb. Herb told Susan that the original ending inventory amount would not be revised. Herb said that the television sets in question had been purchased by his brother and adequate documentation existed to support the sale.

Required:

1. What would happen to cost of goods sold, gross margin, income from operations, and net income if the cost of the returned inventory had been reduced to its liquidation price as Mary had proposed?

2. What should Mary do now?

Case 6-71 Inventory Costing When Inventory Quantities Are Small

A number of companies have adopted a just-in-time procedure for acquiring inventory. These companies have arrangements with their suppliers that require the supplier to deliver inventory just as the company needs the goods. As a result, just-in-time companies keep very little inventory on hand.

Required:

1. Should the inventory costing method (FIFO or LIFO) have a material effect on cost of goods sold when a company adopts the just-in-time procedure and reduces inventory significantly?
2. Once a company has switched to the just-in-time procedure and has little inventory, should the inventory costing method (LIFO or FIFO) affect cost of goods sold?

Case 6-72 Inventory Purchase Price Volatility

At the beginning of the current year, Steel Technologies Inc. changed from the LIFO to the FIFO method for its inventory costing. Steel Technologies' annual report indicated that this change had been instituted because the price at which the firm purchased steel was highly volatile.

Required:

Explain how FIFO cost of goods sold and ending inventory would be different from LIFO when prices are volatile.

Case 6-73 The Effect of Reductions in Inventory Quantities

Hill Motor Company, one of the country's largest automobile manufacturers, disclosed the following information about its inventory in the notes to its financial statements:

Inventories are stated generally at cost, which is not in excess of net realizable value. The cost of inventory is determined by the last-in, first-out (LIFO) method. If the first-in, first-out (FIFO) method of inventory valuation had been used, inventory would have been about $2,519 million higher at December 31, 20Y9, and $2,668 million higher at December 31, 20Y8. As a result of decreases in inventory, certain inventory quantities carried at lower LIFO costs prevailing in prior years, as compared with costs of current purchases, were liquidated in 20Y9 and 20Y8. These inventory adjustments improved pretax operating results by approximately $134 million in 20Y9 and $294 million in 20Y8.

Required:

1. Explain why the reduction in inventory quantities increased Hill Motor Company's net income.
2. **CONCEPTUAL CONNECTION** If Hill Motor Company had used the FIFO inventory costing method, would the reduction in ending inventory quantities have increased net income?

Case 6-74 Errors in Ending Inventory

From time to time, business news will report that the management of a company has misstated its profits by knowingly establishing an incorrect amount for its ending inventory.

Required:
1. Explain how a misstatement of ending inventory can affect profit.
2. Why would a manager intent on misstating profits choose ending inventory to achieve the desired effect?

Case 6-75 Ethics and Inventory

An electronics store has a large number of computers that use outdated technology in its inventory. These computers are reported at their cost. Shortly after the December 31 year end, the store manager insists that the computers can be sold for well over their cost. But the store's accountant has been told by the sales staff that it will be difficult to sell these computers for more than half of their inventory cost.

Required:
1. Why is the store manager reluctant to admit that these computers have little sales value?
2. What are the consequences for the business of failing to recognize the decline in value?
3. What are the consequences for the accountant of participating in a misrepresentation of the inventory's value?

Case 6-76 Research and Analysis Using the Annual Report

Obtain **Wal-Mart**'s 2020 annual report either through the "Investor Relations" portion of its website (do a web search for Wal-Mart investor relations) or go to www.sec.gov and click "Company Filings Search" under "Filings."

Required:
1. What amount did Wal-Mart report for inventories in its consolidated balance sheets for their fiscal years that end in 2020?
2. What inventory valuation method does Wal-Mart use to determine the cost of its inventories? (*Hint:* You may need to refer to the notes to the consolidated financial statements.)
3. What amount did Wal-Mart report for cost of goods sold for the fiscal years ending in 2020, 2019, and 2018?
4. Compute the gross profit (rounded to one decimal place) and inventory turnover (rounded to two decimal places) ratios for the fiscal year ending in 2020. What do these ratios tell you?
5. Does Wal-Mart use the lower of cost or net realizable value rule to account for its inventory? Does it appear that Wal-Mart will write down its inventory to net realizable value?
6. What would be the effect on the financial statements if Wal-Mart were to overstate its inventory by 1%?

Case 6-77 Comparative Analysis: Kroger versus Sprouts

Obtain the 10-K reports of **Kroger** and **Sprouts** either through the "Investor Relations" portion of its website or go to www.sec.gov and click "Company Filings Search" under "Filings."

Required:

1. What amounts do Kroger and Sprouts report for inventories in their consolidated balance sheets at the end of the 2019 and 2018 fiscal years?
2. Do Kroger and Sprouts use the same method to value their inventories?
3. What amount does Kroger report for cost of goods sold for the 2017, 2018, and 2019 years? What amount does Sprouts report for cost of goods sold for the 2017, 2018, and 2019 fiscal years?
4. Compute the gross profit and inventory turnover ratios for the 2019 fiscal year. (*Note:* Round answers to two decimal places.) What do these ratios tell you about the success of each company in managing and controlling their inventory?
5. Do Kroger and Sprouts use the lower of cost or net realizable value rule to account for their inventories? By what amount have they written inventories down in the 2019 fiscal year?

ANNUAL REPORT PROBLEM

HOME DEPOT

Download the 10-K for **Home Depot** from the companion website at Cengage.com.

Required:

1. What does Home Depot report for the following accounts for the most current fiscal year?
   - Net sales
   - Beginning inventory
   - Cost of sales
   - Ending inventory
2. Assume that Home Depot projects the following:
   - Net sales and cost of goods sold will increase by 5% in the next fiscal year.
   - Purchases are expected to be 103% of cost of sales.

Assume all other items remain unchanged from the prior year. Provide the next year's forecasted balances for the following accounts:
   - Net sales
   - Purchases
   - Cost of sales
   - Beginning inventory
   - Ending inventory
3. What inventory costing method does Home Depot use to value its inventory?
4. Is the inventory costing more likely to increase earnings or decrease taxes relative to other inventory costing methods?
5. Compute the forecasted inventory turnover ratio (round to two decimal places).
6. How many days will it take to sell the inventory on hand? (Round to the nearest day.)
7. Compute the gross profit ratio (round to two decimal places).

Note: While the Annual Report problems in the textbook are static, when assigned in CNOW, these activities are algorithmic and the answers may vary from what appears in the Solutions Manual.

CONTINUING PROBLEM

FRONT ROW ENTERTAINMENT

In addition to developing online fan communities, Cam and Anna believe that they could increase Front Row Entertainment's revenue by selling live-performance DVDs at the concert. Front Row records the following activity between May and August 2023 for one of its artists:

Date	Activity	Number of Units	Cost per Unit
May 10	Purchase inventory	240	$8.25
25	Sale	180	
June 5	Purchase inventory	300	8.75
12	Sale	150	
July 5	Sale	135	
Aug. 8	Purchase inventory	190	9.25
20	Sale	110	

Front Row sells all of its DVDs for $15 each and uses a perpetual inventory system.

Required:

1. Compute ending inventory and cost of goods sold using the FIFO, LIFO, and average cost methods. (*Note:* Use four decimal places for per-unit calculations and round all other numbers to the nearest penny.)
2. Discuss the advantages and disadvantages of each method.
3. Assume that Front Row decides to use FIFO. Prepare the journal entries necessary to record the above transactions. Assume all purchases and sales were for cash.

7 Operating Assets

After studying Chapter 7, you should be able to:

1. Describe the accounting for operating assets.

2. Explain how the historical cost principle applies to recording the cost of a fixed asset.

3. Explain the concept of depreciation.

4. Compute depreciation expense using various depreciation methods.

5. Distinguish between capital and revenue expenditures.

6. Account for revisions in depreciation.

7. Describe the process of recording the disposal of a fixed asset.

8. Evaluate the use of fixed assets.

9. Describe the measurement and reporting of intangible assets.

10. Describe the measurement and reporting of natural resources.

11. *(Appendix 7A)* Describe the process of recording an impairment of a fixed asset.

ZikG/Shutterstock.com

EXPERIENCE FINANCIAL ACCOUNTING

with Verizon

With revenues exceeding $131 billion, **Verizon Communications, Inc.** is one of the world's leading providers of telecommunications services. Verizon boasts 10 million broadband and Fios video connections as well as almost 120 million subscribers to its wireless voice and data communication services. With users demanding enhanced data-carrying capabilities, higher transmission speeds, and increased multimedia capabilities, Verizon has chosen to use its network to differentiate itself from its competitors. As a result, Verizon has spent over $51 billion between 2017 and 2019 to maintain, upgrade, and expand its technology infrastructure. The results of these investments have led Verizon to claim that it operates the most reliable wireless network in the country, which has resulted in impressive growth in the number of subscribers to its wireless services. For a company like Verizon, effective management of its long-term operating assets (e.g., its wireless network) is essential for the generation of revenue and profit.

Verizon's strategy for success rests on two key premises that relate to its network. First, the network must provide reliable access to every location that its customers need to access. For a simple call home or in crises, customers must be able to count on Verizon's network to function effectively. Second, Verizon is committed to investing in new technology in order to maintain a high level of customer satisfaction and remain competitive. Without continual investment, Verizon knows it will lose customers. Consistent with these goals, Verizon spent $17.9 billion in 2019 related to the buildup, expansion, and upgrade of its network. These expenditures represent an asset on Verizon's balance sheet that will provide a future benefit in terms of growth in market share and profitability. By closely analyzing a company's expenditures on productive assets, you will be able to better assess the company's long-term productivity, profitability, and ability to generate cash flow.

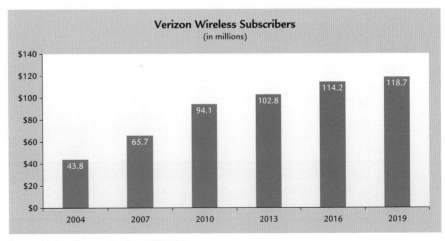

Verizon Wireless Subscribers
(in millions)

Year	Subscribers
2004	43.8
2007	65.7
2010	94.1
2013	102.8
2016	114.2
2019	118.7

Source: Verizon Communications 2019 10-K.

UNDERSTANDING OPERATING ASSETS

In this chapter, we will examine the measurement and reporting issues related to **operating assets**, which are the long-lived assets that are used by the company in the normal course of operations. Unlike inventory, operating assets are not sold to customers. Instead, operating assets are used by a company in the normal course of operations to generate revenue. They are usually held by a company until they are no longer of service. In other words, operating assets are held until their *service potential* has been exhausted. The typical operating asset is used for a period of 4 to 10 years, although some are held for only 2 or 3 years and others for as long as 30 or 40 years. Operating assets are divided into three categories:

- *Property, plant, and equipment (PP&E)*, often called *fixed assets* or *plant assets*, are operating assets that are tangible (e.g., can be seen and touched). They include, among other things, land, land improvements, buildings, and equipment.
- *Intangible assets*, which generally result from legal and contractual rights, do not have physical substance. They include patents, copyrights, trademarks, licenses, and goodwill.
- *Natural resources* are naturally occurring materials that have economic value. They include timberlands and deposits such as coal, oil, and gravel.

Operating assets represent future economic benefits, or service potential, that will be used in the normal course of operations. At acquisition, an operating asset is recorded at its cost, including the cost of acquiring the asset and the cost of preparing the asset for use (historical cost principle). These costs are said to be *capitalized*, which means that they are reported as long-term assets with a service potential of greater than 1 year. As the service potential of an operating asset declines, the cost of the asset is allocated as an expense among the accounting periods in which the asset is used and benefits are received (the expense recognition principle). This allocation is called *depreciation* for property, plant, and equipment assets, *amortization* for intangible assets, and *depletion* for natural resources.

Operating assets are often the most costly of the various types of assets acquired by an entity. For manufacturing companies, property, plant, and equipment frequently represents a major percentage of a manufacturing company's total assets. However, in other industries, such as computer software, operating assets may be a relatively insignificant portion of a company's assets. For many companies, depreciation, amortization, and depletion are also among the largest items of periodic expense. Exhibit 7.1 shows the percentages of operating assets in relation to total assets for various companies.

EXHIBIT 7.1   **Percentages of Operating Assets in Relation to Total Assets**

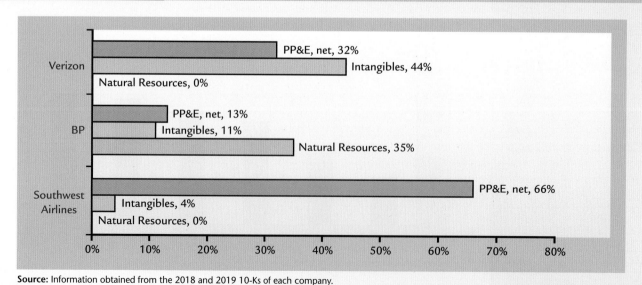

Source: Information obtained from the 2018 and 2019 10-Ks of each company.

For **Verizon**, operating assets (property, plant, and equipment plus intangible assets) comprise approximately 76% of its total assets. Fixed assets include the expenditures required to build, upgrade, and expand its wireless network. In addition, Verizon has significant investments in intangible operating assets, primarily licenses that provide Verizon with the exclusive right to use certain radio frequencies to provide wireless services. In contrast, companies such as **BP** (one of the largest oil companies in the world) have relatively more natural resources (oil and natural gas properties), while **Southwest Airlines'** operating assets are made up primarily of its airplanes. Information about a company's operating assets gives financial statement users insights into a company's ability to satisfy customer demands (productive capacity) and the effectiveness of management in using the company's assets to generate revenue. While the relative mix of operating assets may vary among companies, it is clear that the management of operating assets is critical to a company's long-term success.

In this chapter, we will discuss the measurement and reporting issues related to the initial acquisition, use, and disposition of operating assets. We will address the following questions:

- What is included in the cost of an operating asset?
- How should an operating asset's cost be allocated to expense?
- How should expenditures after acquisition be treated?
- How is the retirement of an operating asset recorded?

ACQUISITION OF PROPERTY, PLANT, AND EQUIPMENT

OBJECTIVE 2

Explain how the historical cost principle applies to recording the cost of a fixed asset.

Property, plant, and equipment are the tangible operating assets used in the normal operations of a company. These assets are tangible in the sense that they have a visible, physical presence in the company. Property, plant, and equipment includes:

- Land: the site of a manufacturing facility or office building used in operations[1]
- Land Improvements: structural additions or improvements to land (such as driveways, parking lots, fences, landscaping, lighting)
- Buildings: structures used in operations (factory, office, warehouse)
- Equipment: assets used in operations (machinery, furniture, automobiles)

It is important to note that land has an unlimited life and service potential and is not subject to depreciation. However, land improvements, buildings, and equipment have limited lives and limited service potential. Therefore, the cost of these assets is recorded in separate accounts and depreciated over the periods in which they are used to generate revenue.

MEASURING THE COST OF A FIXED ASSET

The cost of a fixed asset is any expenditure to acquire the asset and to prepare the asset for use. For example, the cost of a machine would be its purchase price (minus any discount offered) plus sales taxes, freight, installation costs, and the cost of labor and materials for trial runs that check its performance. Expenditures that are included as part of the cost of the asset are said to be *capitalized*. Exhibit 7.2 (p. 402) shows expenditures that are typically included as part of the cost of various types of property, plant, and equipment.

Expenditures that are *not* included as part of the cost of the asset are expensed immediately. Generally, recurring costs that benefit a period of time, not the asset's life, are

---

1 Land purchased for future use or as an investment is not considered part of property, plant, and equipment.

EXHIBIT 7.2   **Typical Costs of Acquiring Property, Plant, and Equipment**

Land

Cost includes:
• Purchase price
• Real estate commissions
• Delinquent property taxes
• Closing costs (attorney, title and survey fees)

• Clearing and grading costs
• Demolition of unwanted buildings, minus any salvage

Land Improvement

Cost includes:
• Purchase price
• Sales taxes
• Installation costs

Building

Cost includes:
• Purchase price
• Closing costs
• Architectural fees

• Cost of building permits
• Excavation costs
• Remodeling fees

Equipment

Cost includes:
• Purchase price
• Sales taxes
• Transportation costs

• Insurance during transportation
• Installation costs
• Cost of trial runs

expensed instead of capitalized. Unnecessary costs that do not increase an asset's usefulness (e.g., vandalism, damage during installation) are also expensed. Careful judgment should be exercised in determining which costs should be capitalized and which costs should be expensed.

ETHICAL DECISIONS The distinction between whether an expenditure should be capitalized or expensed can have dramatic consequences for a company's financial statements. **WorldCom**'s handling of this issue triggered one of the largest financial restatements in U.S. history. When WorldCom used the telecommunications lines of another company, it paid a fee which should have been expensed in the current period. By improperly capitalizing $3.8 billion of these costs, WorldCom was able to increase its income and its operating cash flow, thereby concealing large losses. ●

RECORDING THE COST OF A FIXED ASSET

The historical cost principle requires that a company record its fixed assets at the exchange price at the time the asset is purchased. When cash is paid in exchange for an asset, the amount of cash given, plus any other expenditure necessary to prepare the asset for use, becomes part of the historical cost of the acquired asset. In addition to cash purchases, companies often purchase fixed assets by issuing debt. In this situation, the asset is valued at the fair value of the liability on the date the asset is acquired. Interest paid on the debt is generally viewed as resulting from a financing decision rather than from the decision to acquire the asset. Therefore, interest on borrowed funds normally is not added to the purchase price of an asset.[2] EXAMPLE 7.1 illustrates the accounting procedures for the measurement and recording of the cost of a fixed asset.

Next Level

If a company did not record all of the costs necessary to acquire an asset and prepare it for use, what would be the effect on the financial statements?

ANSWER:
If costs were not recorded as an asset, these costs would be immediately expensed, which would lower income in the current period. By recording these costs as assets, the company delays the recognition of expense until the service potential of the asset is used.

---

2   For assets that require a long period of preparation for use, such as ships, large plants, or buildings, GAAP does permit the addition of interest to the cost of the asset. This topic is addressed in Intermediate Accounting.

EXAMPLE 7.1 RECORDING THE PURCHASE OF A FIXED ASSET FOR CASH OR DEBT

On June 29, Drew Company acquired a new automatic milling machine. Drew paid $20,000 in cash and signed a 1-year, 10% note for $80,000. Following the purchase, Drew incurred freight charges, on account, of $2,900 to ship the machine to its factory. After the machine arrived, Drew paid a contractor $5,300 cash for installation.

Required:
Prepare the journal entry to record the purchase of the equipment.

Solution:
All costs necessary to acquire the machine and prepare it for use, including freight and installation costs, are included in the cost of the machine. The cost of the machine is $108,200, computed as:

$$\$20{,}000 + \$80{,}000 + \$2{,}900 + \$5{,}300 = \underline{\$108{,}200}$$

Drew would make the following entry to record the machine:

Date	Account and Explanation	Debit	Credit	Assets	= Liabilities +	Stockholders' Equity
June 29	Equipment	108,200		▲		
	Cash ($20,000 + $5,300)		25,300	▼		
	Notes Payable		80,000		▲	
	Accounts Payable		2,900		▲	

When noncash consideration, such as land or stock, is given in exchange for an asset, the acquired asset is reported at the fair value of the consideration given or the fair value of the asset received, whichever is more clearly evident. EXAMPLE 7.2 shows the proper accounting for this situation.

EXAMPLE 7.2 RECORDING THE PURCHASE OF A FIXED ASSET FOR NONCASH CONSIDERATION

On April 9, Zhang Company acquired a new building in exchange for 5,000 shares of its own stock, which was selling for $50 per share.

Required:
Prepare the journal entry to record the purchase of the building.

Solution:

Date	Account and Explanation	Debit	Credit	Assets	= Liabilities +	Stockholders' Equity
April 9	Building	250,000		▲		
	Common Stock (5,000 × $50)		250,000			▲

YOUDECIDE   **The Purchase Decision**

You are the controller of Stanley Inc., a struggling manufacturing company that is experiencing cash flow problems. You are reviewing two proposals that would enable the company to obtain a piece of equipment that is critical to its operations. The first proposal would allow the company to purchase the equipment by signing a long-term note payable. The second proposal involves having the company rent the equipment.

What factors should you consider in making the decision of whether to purchase or rent the equipment?

Given the company's financial situation, renting the equipment may provide several advantages.

- Renting often requires little or no down payment, allowing a company with cash flow problems access to fixed assets that it would otherwise not be able to afford while freeing up cash for more immediate needs.
- Renting the equipment may protect the renter against obsolescence since the rented asset can be exchanged for a newer model at the end of the rental agreement.
- Rental agreements may provide the renter with an increased tax benefit.

However, renting also has disadvantages, such as interest rates that may be higher than normal long-term borrowing rates. In short, the decision to purchase or rent is a strategic decision that must be carefully considered.

Managers are often confronted with the decision to purchase or rent fixed assets. In fact, renting assets through leasing arrangements has become one of the more frequently used strategies for acquiring fixed assets.[3]

OBJECTIVE 3
Explain the concept of depreciation.

DEPRECIATION

We observed earlier that the cost of a fixed asset represents the cost of future benefits or service potential to a company. With the exception of land, this service potential declines over the life of each asset as the asset is used in the operations of the company. The expense recognition principle requires that the cost of a fixed asset be allocated as an expense among the accounting periods in which the asset is used and revenues are generated by its use. **Depreciation** is the process of allocating, in a systematic and rational manner, the cost of a tangible fixed asset (other than land) to expense over the asset's useful life.

The amount of depreciation expense is recorded each period by making the following adjusting journal entry:

Depreciation Expense	xxx	
Accumulated Depreciation		xxx

The amount of depreciation recorded each period, or **depreciation expense**, is reported on the income statement. **Accumulated depreciation**, which represents the total amount of depreciation expense that has been recorded for an asset since the asset was acquired, is reported on the balance sheet as a contra-asset. Accumulated depreciation is deducted from the cost of the asset to get the asset's **book value** (or **carrying value**). Exhibit 7.3 shows the disclosures relating to property, plant, and equipment and depreciation made by **Verizon** in its 2019 annual report.

Before continuing, it is critical to understand the following points:

- Depreciation is a *cost allocation process*. It is *not* an attempt to measure the fair value of the asset or obtain some other measure of the asset's value. In fact, the book value (cost minus accumulated depreciation) of an asset that is reported on a company's balance sheet is often quite different from the market value of the asset.
- Depreciation is *not* an attempt to accumulate cash for the replacement of an asset. Depreciation is a cost allocation process that does not involve cash.

---

3 Lease arrangements and their effects are discussed more fully in Chapter 9.

EXHIBIT 7.3

Excerpt from Verizon's Annual Report

Notes to Consolidated Financial Statements	
NOTE 5 Property, Plant, and Equipment:	
Land	$ 594
Buildings and equipment	31,216
Central office and other network equipment	152,733
Cable, poles, and conduit	52,658
Leasehold improvements	9,072
Work in progress	9,234
Furniture, vehicles, and other	10,227
	$ 265,734
Less: Accumulated depreciation	(173,819)
Property, plant, and equipment, net	$ 91,915

Source: Verizon Communications 2019 10-K.

INFORMATION REQUIRED FOR MEASURING DEPRECIATION

The following information is necessary in order to measure depreciation:

- cost of the fixed asset
- useful life (or expected life) of the fixed asset
- residual value (salvage value) of the fixed asset

Cost As discussed earlier in the chapter, the **cost** of a fixed asset is any expenditure to acquire the asset and to prepare the asset for use. In addition to cost, we also need to examine two other items—useful life and estimates of residual value—to measure depreciation. Exhibit 7.4 shows the relationship among the factors used to compute depreciation expense.

EXHIBIT 7.4

Components of Depreciation Expense

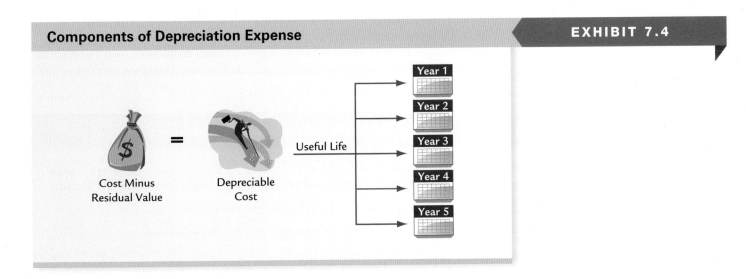

Useful Life The **useful life** of an asset is the period of time over which the company anticipates deriving benefit from the use of the asset.[4] The useful life of any fixed asset reflects

---

4 The useful life can be estimated in *service units* as well as in *units of time.* For example, an airline may choose to measure the useful life of its aircraft in hours of use rather than years.

both the physical capacities of the asset and the company's plans for its use. Many companies plan to dispose of assets before their entire service potential is exhausted. For example, major automobile rental companies typically use an automobile for only a part of its entire economic life before disposing of it. The useful life also is influenced by technological change. Many assets lose their service potential through obsolescence long before the assets are physically inoperable. As shown in Exhibit 7.5, **Verizon** uses an estimated useful life of 3 to 50 years for its fixed assets.

EXHIBIT 7.5   **Excerpt from Verizon's Annual Report**

Notes to Consolidated Financial Statements	
NOTE 5 Property, Plant, and Equipment	
	Lives (Years)
Land	—
Buildings and equipment	*7–45*
Central office and other network equipment	*3–50*
Cable, poles, and conduit	*7–50*
Leasehold improvements	*5–20*
Work in progress	—
Furniture, vehicles, and other	*3–20*

Source: Verizon Communications 2019 10-K.

Residual Value   The **residual value** (also called **salvage value**) is the amount of cash or trade-in consideration that the company expects to receive when an asset is retired from service. Accordingly, the residual value reflects the company's plans for the asset and its expectations about the value of the asset once its expected life with the company is over. A truck used for 3 years may have a substantial residual value, whereas the same truck used for 12 years may have minimal residual value. Residual value is based on projections of some of the same future events that are used to estimate an asset's useful life. Since depreciation expense depends on estimates of both useful life and residual value, depreciation expense itself is an estimate.

The cost of the asset minus its residual value gives an asset's **depreciable cost**. The depreciable cost of the asset is the amount that will be depreciated (expensed) over the asset's useful life.

 YOUDECIDE   **Impact of Depreciation Estimates**

You are a loan officer of the Prairie State Bank. The president of a ready-mix concrete company, Concrete Transit Company, has applied for a 5-year, $150,000 loan to finance his company's expansion. You have examined Concrete Transit's financial statements for the past 3 years and found the following:

	Year 3	Year 2	Year 1
Depreciation expense (calculated using the straight-line method)	$ 15,000	$ 15,000	$ 15,000
Income before taxes	$ 15,000	$ 17,000	$ 21,000
Depreciable assets (cost)	$470,000	$470,000	$470,000

Based on other customers in the same business that use the same depreciation method as Concrete Transit, you expected depreciation expense to be approximately 15% of the cost of the depreciable assets.

Should you make the loan?

Since Concrete Transit has similar assets and is using a similar depreciation method to its competitors, the most obvious reason for reporting a lower percentage of depreciation expense is that Concrete Transit is using different estimates of residual value and/or useful life than its competitors. As you will see in the next section, if higher estimates of residual value or useful life are used, depreciation expense will be lower and income will be higher. If you adjust Concrete Transit's depreciation expense to 15% of the cost of its depreciable assets,

depreciation expense will increase from $15,000 to $70,500 ($470,000 × 0.15) for each year. This would cause a decrease in income before taxes of $55,500 each year. These adjusted amounts suggest that Concrete Transit has been increasingly unprofitable. Given the difficulties it would likely have in making the required loan payments, the loan should not be made.

While most companies establish policies for depreciable assets that specify the estimation of useful lives and residual values, the measurement of depreciation expense (and income) ultimately relies on judgment.

DEPRECIATION METHODS

OBJECTIVE **4**

Compute depreciation expense using various depreciation methods.

The service potential of a fixed asset is assumed to decline with each period of use, but the pattern of decline is not the same for all assets. Some assets decline at a constant rate each year while others decline sharply in the early years of use and then more gradually as time goes on. For other assets, the pattern of decline depends on how much the asset is used each period. *Depreciation methods* are the standardized calculations required to determine periodic depreciation expense. The most common depreciation methods are:

- straight-line
- declining balance
- units-of-production

For any of these depreciation methods, the total amount of depreciation expense that has been recorded (accumulated depreciation) over the life of the asset will never exceed the depreciable cost (cost minus residual value) of the asset.

STRAIGHT-LINE METHOD

As its name implies, the **straight-line depreciation method** allocates an equal amount of an asset's cost to depreciation expense for each year of the asset's useful life. It is appropriate to apply this method to those assets for which an equal amount of service potential is considered to be used each period. The straight-line method is the most widely used method because it is simple to apply and is based on a pattern of declining service potential that is reasonable for many fixed assets.

The computation of straight-line depreciation expense is based on an asset's depreciable cost, which is the excess of the asset's cost over its residual value. Straight-line depreciation expense for each period is calculated by dividing the depreciable cost of an asset by the asset's useful life:

$$\text{Straight-Line Depreciation Expense} = \frac{(\text{Cost} - \text{Residual Value})}{\text{Expected Useful Life}}$$

Alternatively, some companies will calculate an annual rate at which the asset should be depreciated. The fraction, (1 ÷ Useful Life), is called the *straight-line rate*. Using the straight-line rate, a company would compute depreciation expense by multiplying the straight-line rate by the asset's depreciable cost. EXAMPLE 7.3 illustrates the computation of depreciation expense using the straight-line method.

Next Level

Why does the FASB allow companies to use different depreciation methods instead of requiring the use of a single depreciation method that would improve comparability?

ANSWER:
The depreciation method chosen by a company should capture the declining service potential of a fixed asset. Because assets are used differently, alternative methods are allowed so that the use of the asset can be better matched with the revenue it helped generate.

EXAMPLE 7.3   COMPUTING DEPRECIATION EXPENSE USING THE STRAIGHT-LINE METHOD

On January 1, Year 1, Morgan Inc. acquired a machine for $50,000. Morgan expects the machine to be worth $5,000 at the end of its 5-year useful life. Morgan uses the straight-line method of depreciation.

Required:

1. Compute the straight-line rate of depreciation for the machine.

2. Compute the annual amount of depreciation expense.

3. Prepare a depreciation schedule that shows the amount of depreciation expense for each year of the machine's life.

4. Prepare the journal entry required to record depreciation expense for the first year.

Solution:

1. $\text{Straight-Line Rate} = \dfrac{1}{\text{Useful Life}} = \dfrac{1}{5 \text{ years}} = \underline{\underline{20\%}}$

2. $\text{Straight-Line Depreciation Expense} = \dfrac{\$50,000 - \$5,000}{5 \text{ years}}$

$= \underline{\underline{\$9,000}} \text{ per year}$

Note: Depreciation expense may also be found by multiplying the straight-line rate (20%) by the asset's depreciable cost ($45,000).

3.

End of Year	Depreciation Expense	Accumulated Depreciation	Book Value
			$50,000
Year 1	$ 9,000	$ 9,000	41,000
Year 2	9,000	18,000	32,000
Year 3	9,000	27,000	23,000
Year 4	9,000	36,000	14,000
Year 5	9,000	45,000	5,000
	$45,000		

4.

Date	Account and Explanation	Debit	Credit	Assets	= Liabilities +	Stockholders' Equity
Dec. 31	Depreciation Expense	9,000				▼
	Accumulated Depreciation		9,000	▼		

Example 7.3 illustrates three important points:

- The straight-line depreciation method results in the recording of the same amount of depreciation expense ($9,000) each year, as shown in Exhibit 7.6.
- The contra-asset account, accumulated depreciation, increases at a constant rate of $9,000 per year until it equals the depreciable cost ($45,000).
- The book value of the machine (cost minus accumulated depreciation) decreases by $9,000 per year until it equals the residual value ($5,000) at the end of the asset's useful life.

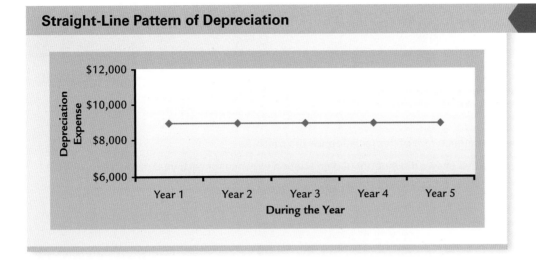

Straight-Line Pattern of Depreciation

EXHIBIT 7.6

DECLINING BALANCE METHOD

The **declining balance depreciation method** is an accelerated depreciation method that produces a declining amount of depreciation expense each period by multiplying the declining book value of an asset by a constant depreciation rate. It is called an accelerated method because it results in a larger amount of depreciation expense in the early years of an asset's life relative to the straight-line method. However, because the total amount of depreciation expense (the depreciable cost) must be the same under any depreciation method, accelerated methods result in a smaller amount of depreciation expense in the later years of an asset's life. The declining balance method is appropriate for assets that are subject to a rapid decline in service potential due to factors such as rapid obsolescence.

The declining balance depreciation rate is some multiple (m) of the straight-line rate:

$$\text{Declining Balance Rate} = (m) \times \text{Straight-Line Rate}$$

The multiple (m) is often 2, in which case the declining balance method is called the *double-declining-balance method.*[5]

Depreciation expense for each period of an asset's useful life equals the declining balance rate times the asset's book value (cost minus accumulated depreciation) at the beginning of the period as shown by the following equation:

$$\text{Declining Balance Depreciation Expense} = \text{Declining Balance Rate} \times \text{Book Value}$$

Because the declining balance method does not consider the residual value, it is possible that the calculated depreciation expense in the final year would cause the book value of the asset to fall below its residual value. An asset should not be depreciated below its residual value. Therefore, the final year of depreciation expense is computed as the amount needed to reduce the asset's book value to its residual value.

EXAMPLE 7.4 illustrates the computation of depreciation expense using the declining balance method.

---

5   In this text, a multiple of 2 is used for the declining balance method unless otherwise noted.

EXAMPLE 7.4   COMPUTING DEPRECIATION EXPENSE USING THE DECLINING BALANCE METHOD

On January 1, Year 1, Morgan Inc. acquired a machine for $50,000. Morgan expects the machine to be worth $5,000 at the end of its 5-year useful life. Morgan uses the double-declining-balance method of depreciation.

Required:

1. Compute the double-declining-balance rate of depreciation for the machine.

2. Prepare a depreciation schedule that shows the amount of depreciation expense for each year of the machine's life.

3. Prepare the journal entry required to record depreciation expense in the first year.

Solution:

1. $$\frac{1}{\text{Useful Life}} \times 2 = \frac{1}{5} \times 2 = \frac{2}{5} \text{ or } \underline{\underline{40\%}}$$

2.

End of Year	Depreciation Expense (Rate × Book Value)	Accumulated Depreciation	Book Value
			$50,000
Year 1	40% × $50,000 = $20,000	$20,000	30,000
Year 2	40% × $30,000 = 12,000	32,000	18,000
Year 3	40% × $18,000 = 7,200	39,200	10,800
Year 4	40% × $10,800 = 4,320	43,520	6,480
Year 5	1,480*	45,000	5,000
	$45,000		

*The amount needed to reduce the book value of the machine to its residual value ($6,480 − $5,000).

3.

Date	Account and Explanation	Debit	Credit		Assets	=	Liabilities	+	Stockholders' Equity
Dec. 31	Depreciation Expense	20,000							▼
	Accumulated Depreciation		20,000		▼				

Relative to the straight-line method, the double-declining-balance method results in the recognition of higher depreciation expense in the early years of the asset's life and lower depreciation expense in the later years of the asset's life, as shown in Exhibit 7.7.

EXHIBIT 7.7   Declining Balance Pattern of Depreciation

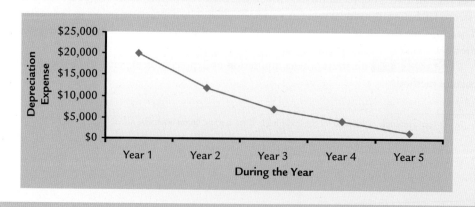

UNITS-OF-PRODUCTION METHOD

The two previous depreciation methods resulted in a pattern of expense that was related to the passage of time. However, when the decline in an asset's service potential is proportional to the usage of the asset and asset usage can be measured, depreciation expense can be computed using the **units-of-production depreciation method**. Usage is typically gauged by a measure of productive capacity (such as units produced, hours worked, or miles driven). An automobile is an example of an asset having service potential that usually declines with use, where usage is measured by the number of miles traveled.

To compute depreciation expense under the units-of-production method, the depreciation cost per unit is determined as shown in the equation:

$$\text{Depreciation Cost per Unit} = \frac{(\text{Cost} - \text{Residual Value})}{\text{Expected Usage of the Asset}}$$

Next, the depreciation cost per unit is multiplied by the actual usage of the asset:

$$\text{Units-of-Production Depreciation Expense} = \text{Depreciation Cost per Unit} \times \text{Actual Usage of the Asset}$$

An example of depreciation expense computed by the units-of-production method is shown in EXAMPLE 7.5.

EXAMPLE 7.5 COMPUTING DEPRECIATION EXPENSE USING THE UNITS-OF-PRODUCTION METHOD

On January 1, Year 1, Morgan Inc. acquired a machine for $50,000. Morgan expects the machine to be worth $5,000 at the end of its 5-year useful life. Morgan expects the machine to run for 30,000 machine hours. Morgan uses the units-of-production method of depreciation. The actual machine hours are:

Year	Machine Hours
Year 1	3,000
Year 2	9,000
Year 3	7,500
Year 4	4,500
Year 5	6,000

Required:

1. Compute the depreciation cost per machine hour.

2. Prepare a depreciation schedule that shows the amount of depreciation expense for each year of the machine's life.

3. Prepare the journal entry required to record depreciation expense in the first year.

Solution:

1. $\dfrac{\text{Depreciable Cost}}{\text{Estimated Usage}} = \dfrac{(\$50,000 - \$5,000)}{30,000 \text{ machine hours}} = \underline{\$1.50}$ per machine hour

CONTINUED

EXAMPLE 7.5   COMPUTING DEPRECIATION EXPENSE USING THE
UNITS-OF-PRODUCTION METHOD *(CONTINUED)*

2.

End of Year	Cost per Machine Hour	× Actual Usage	= Depreciation Expense	Accumulated Depreciation	Book Value
					$50,000
Year 1	$1.50	3,000	$ 4,500	$ 4,500	45,500
Year 2	1.50	9,000	13,500	18,000	32,000
Year 3	1.50	7,500	11,250	29,250	20,750
Year 4	1.50	4,500	6,750	36,000	14,000
Year 5	1.50	6,000	9,000	45,000	5,000
			$45,000		

3.

Date	Account and Explanation	Debit	Credit	Assets	= Liabilities +	Stockholders' Equity
Dec. 31	Depreciation Expense	4,500				▼
	Accumulated Depreciation		4,500	▼		
	(Record units-of-production depreciation expense)					

Note that when production varies widely and irregularly from period to period, the units-of-production method will result in an erratic pattern of depreciation expense, as shown in Exhibit 7.8.

EXHIBIT 7.8   **Units-of-Production Pattern of Depreciation**

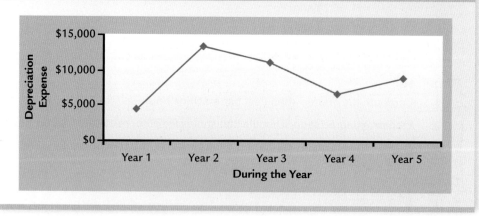

The units-of-production method does an excellent job of matching depreciation expense to usage of the asset. However, it is difficult to apply because it requires estimation of expected usage, which is more difficult than simply estimating useful life in years. Thus, it is less widely used than the other two depreciation methods.

CHOOSING BETWEEN DEPRECIATION METHODS

The three depreciation methods can be summarized as follows:

- The straight-line depreciation method produces a constant amount of depreciation expense in each period of the asset's life and is consistent with a constant rate of decline in service potential.
- The declining balance depreciation method accelerates the assignment of an asset's cost to depreciation expense by allocating a larger amount of cost to the early years of an asset's life. This is consistent with a decreasing rate of decline in service potential and a decreasing amount for depreciation expense.
- The units-of-production depreciation method is based on a measure of the asset's use in each period, and the periodic depreciation expense rises and falls with the asset's use. In this sense, the units-of-production depreciation method is based not on a standardized pattern of declining service potential but on a pattern tailored to the individual asset and its use.

Exhibit 7.9 compares the depreciation expense recorded by Morgan Inc. under each of the depreciation methods discussed. Note that the total amount of depreciation expense ($45,000) recognized by Morgan Inc. was the same under all three methods. This resulted in the asset having a book value of $5,000 at the end of its useful life. At this point, book value is equal to residual value. While the total depreciation expense for each method was the same, the yearly amounts of depreciation expense recognized were different.

Depreciation Patterns over Time

EXHIBIT 7.9

Year	Straight-Line	Double-Declining-Balance	Units-of-Production
Year 1	$ 9,000	$20,000	$ 4,500
Year 2	9,000	12,000	13,500
Year 3	9,000	7,200	11,250
Year 4	9,000	4,320	6,750
Year 5	9,000	1,480	9,000
Total	$45,000	$45,000	$45,000

Because each method is acceptable under GAAP, what factors does management use in selecting a depreciation method? Ideally, management should select the method that best matches the pattern of decline in service potential of the asset. This would result in the best matching of depreciation expense to the period in which the asset helped to generate revenue. However, in reality, other factors also help motivate this decision. For example, the simplicity and ease of application of the straight-line method is very appealing to management. In addition, the use of the straight-line method produces a higher reported income in the early years of an asset's life relative to the declining balance method. This higher income may increase management bonuses (which are often based on net income) and create a favorable impression to outside users which could result in higher stock prices. For these reasons, the straight-line method is the most popular depreciation method. However, once a depreciation method is chosen, that method should be consistently applied over time to enhance the comparability of the financial information.

ETHICAL DECISIONS The use of estimates in depreciation calculations presents an ethical issue for accountants. If an estimate is biased upward or downward, it can have significant financial statement impacts. For example, accountants may face pressures to increase the useful

 Next Level

If all depreciation methods result in the same amount being recorded as an expense over the life of the fixed asset, why would a financial statement user be concerned with the depreciation method chosen?

ANSWER:
The choice of depreciation method affects the amount recognized as an expense during each year of the fixed asset's life. Therefore, the company's reported income each year would be different based on the depreciation method chosen.

life of an asset beyond what is reasonable. This upwardly biased estimate of useful life decreases the amount of depreciation expense recorded and increases the company's net income. Accountants must resist these pressures and provide an unbiased estimate that faithfully portrays the service potential of the asset. ●

DEPRECIATION FOR PARTIAL YEARS

Fixed assets are purchased (or disposed of) at various times throughout the year. If the fixed asset is purchased (or disposed of) at the beginning or end of an accounting period, a full year of depreciation is recorded. If, however, the asset is purchased (or disposed of) during the accounting period, the expense recognition principle requires that depreciation be recorded only for the portion of the year that the asset was used to generate revenue.

To illustrate, consider an asset purchased on April 1 for $100,000, which is being depreciated using the straight-line method over 5 years with no residual value. For a full year (12 months), depreciation expense would be $20,000, calculated as:[6]

$$\frac{(\text{Cost} - \text{Residual Value})}{\text{Expected Usage Life}} = \frac{(\$100,000 - \$0)}{5 \text{ years}}$$

Because this asset was purchased in April, it was only depreciated for the partial year (9 months). Depreciation expense for the partial year would be $15,000, calculated as:

$$\$20,000 \times (9/12)$$

A full year of depreciation expense, $20,000, would be recorded for the next 4 years. Because a full year of depreciation was not taken in the year the asset was purchased, a partial year of depreciation (3 months) of $5,000 would need to be recorded in the final year of use to fully depreciate the asset. This is calculated as:

$$\$20,000 \times (3/12)$$

At this point, the asset would be fully depreciated.[7]

DEPRECIATION AND INCOME TAXES

A company can choose between the three depreciation methods discussed earlier as it prepares its financial statements, but the depreciation method used in preparing its tax return does not need to be the same. The Internal Revenue Code specifies which depreciation method a company should use to prepare tax returns. Tax depreciation rules are designed to stimulate investment in operating assets and, therefore, are not guided by the matching principle. Tax depreciation rules provide for the rapid (accelerated) expensing of depreciable assets, which lowers taxes. By bringing forward the bulk of depreciation expense, tax depreciation rules enable companies to save cash by delaying the payment of taxes. Most companies use the Modified Accelerated Cost Recovery System (MACRS) to compute depreciation expense for their tax returns, which is similar to the declining balance method. MACRS is not acceptable for financial reporting purposes.

---

6 Although acquisitions may occur *during* a month, for purposes of simplifying depreciation calculations, many companies follow the policy of substituting the date of the nearer first of the month for the actual transaction date. Thus, acquisitions on March 25 or April 9 would be treated as acquisitions on April 1 for purposes of calculating depreciation expense.

7 For the sake of simplicity, most examples, exercises, and problems in this book assume that asset purchases (and disposals) occur at the beginning of the accounting period.

YOUDECIDE Impact of Depreciation Method on Income

You are a financial analyst trying to assess the earnings performance and profitability of two companies, Cobine Inc. and Stabler Inc., which both began operations within the last year. Both companies report the same amount of income and are comparable in most every respect. However, one item catches your attention. While both companies report the same amount of property, plant, and equipment, Cobine reports a much smaller amount for depreciation expense. In the notes to the financial statements, Cobine indicates that it uses the straight-line depreciation method while Stabler uses the double-declining-balance depreciation method.

How does the difference in depreciation methods affect your assessment of the two companies?

When companies use different depreciation methods, significant variations may result in income although no real economic differences exist. All depreciation methods result in the same amount being expensed over the life of the asset; however, the amount expensed each year will differ.

Because its assets are relatively new, Cobine's use of the straight-line depreciation method will result in lower expense and higher income compared to Stabler, which uses the double-declining-balance method. However, if the company's fixed assets were relatively older, the situation will be reversed—the use of the accelerated depreciation method will result in lower expense and higher income relative to the straight-line method. In both cases, the differences in expense and income are merely the result of an accounting choice and reflect no real underlying economic differences between the two firms.

Financial statement users must be able to "see through" the financial statement effects of accounting choices and base their decision on the underlying economics of the business.

EXPENDITURES AFTER ACQUISITION

OBJECTIVE 5
Distinguish between capital and revenue expenditures.

In addition to expenditures made when property, plant, and equipment is purchased, companies incur costs over the life of the asset that range from ordinary repairs and maintenance to major overhauls, additions, and improvements. Companies must decide whether these expenditures should be capitalized (added to an asset account) or expensed (reported in total on the income statement).

REVENUE EXPENDITURES

Expenditures that do not increase the future economic benefits of the asset are called **revenue expenditures** and are expensed in the same period the expenditure is made. **Verizon**'s policy with regard to revenue expenditures, as disclosed in the notes to the financial statements, is shown below.

> *We charge the cost of maintenance and repairs, including the cost of replacing minor items not constituting substantial betterments, principally to Cost of Services as these costs are incurred.*
> **Source:** Verizon Communications 2019 10-K.

These expenditures maintain the level of benefits provided by the asset, relate only to the current period, occur frequently, and typically involve relatively small dollar amounts. An example of a revenue expenditure is the ordinary repair and maintenance of an asset.

CAPITAL EXPENDITURES

Expenditures that extend the life of the asset, expand the productive capacity, increase efficiency, or improve the quality of the product are called **capital expenditures**. Because these expenditures provide benefits to the company in both current and future periods, capital expenditures are added to an asset account and are subject to depreciation. These expenditures typically involve relatively large dollar amounts. Examples of capital expenditures include extraordinary or major repairs, additions, remodeling of buildings, and improvements (sometimes called betterments). For example, **Verizon** reported capital expenditures of approximately $17.9 billion related to the build-out, upgrade, and expansion of both its wired and wireless network capacity and the introduction of new technology.

Exhibit 7.10 summarizes different expenditures and how they would be accounted for.

EXHIBIT 7.10 ▶ **Types of Expenditures**

Type of Expenditure	Description	Examples	Accounting Treatment
Ordinary Repairs and Maintenance	Expenditures that keep an asset in normal operating condition	• Oil change for a truck • Painting of a building • Replacement of a minor part • Normal cleaning costs	*Expense* in the current period
Extraordinary or Major Repairs	Expenditures that extend the asset's useful life	• Overhaul or rebuilding of an engine • Fixing structural damage to a building	*Capitalize and depreciate* over the asset's remaining useful life
Additions	Adding a new or major component to an existing asset	• Adding a new wing to a building • Installing a pollution-control device on a machine	*Capitalize and depreciate* over the shorter of the remaining life of the asset or the addition
Improvements (or Betterments)	The replacement of a component of an asset with a better one that increases efficiency or productivity	• Replacing an old air conditioning unit with a more efficient one • Replacing a manual machine control with computer-controlled controls	*Capitalize and depreciate* over the improved asset's remaining useful life

---

Because it is often difficult to distinguish capital and revenue expenditures, managers must exercise professional judgment in deciding to capitalize or expense these costs. Many companies develop simple policies to aid them in making this decision. For example, a company may decide to expense all costs under $1,000.

OBJECTIVE 6 ▶
Account for revisions in depreciation.

REVISION OF DEPRECIATION

Depreciation expense is based on estimates of useful life and residual value. As new or additional information becomes available, a company will often find it necessary to revise its estimates of useful life, residual value, or both. The change of these estimates will result in a recalculation of depreciation expense. In addition, when a capital expenditure is made, it is also necessary for a company to recalculate its depreciation expense. In such situations, the company does not change previously recorded amounts related to depreciation. Instead, any revision of depreciation expense is accounted for in current and future periods.

To revise depreciation expense, the following steps are performed:

Step 1. Obtain the book value of the asset at the date of the revision of depreciation.
Step 2. Compute depreciation expense using the revised amounts for book value, useful life, and/or residual value.

 EXAMPLE 7.6 illustrates the accounting for a revision in depreciation.

EXAMPLE 7.6 REVISING DEPRECIATION EXPENSE

On January 1, Year 1, Parker Publishing Company bought a printing press for $300,000. Parker estimated that the printing press would have a residual value of $50,000 and a useful life of 10 years. Parker uses the straight-line depreciation method and the book value of the asset on December 31, Year 7, was $100,000. On January 1, Year 8, Parker paid $90,000 to add a digital typesetting component to the printing press. After the addition, the printing press is expected to have a remaining useful life of 6 years and a residual value of $10,000.

Required:

1. What is the book value of the printing press on January 1, Year 8?

2. What amount should Parker record for depreciation expense for Year 8?

Solution:

1. Because the digital typesetting component is a capital expenditure, the cost of the addition is added to the book value of the asset, resulting in a revised book value of $190,000 ($90,000 + $100,000).

2. Using the revised book value, the revised estimate of residual value, and the revised estimate of useful life, Parker would recognize depreciation expense in Year 8 of $30,000, calculated as:

$$\text{Depreciation Expense} = \frac{\$190,000 - \$10,000}{6 \text{ years}} = \underline{\$30,000} \text{ per year}$$

Note that only the current and future years are affected by this revision. Parker does *not* adjust the prior years' financial statements based on this new information. However, if the change in estimate is a material amount, it should be disclosed in the notes to the financial statements.

IMPAIRMENTS

Because depreciation is a cost allocation process and does not attempt to measure the fair value of the asset, the book value of an asset and the fair value of an asset may be quite different. When the fair value of the asset falls significantly below the book value of the asset, the asset may be impaired. An *impairment* is a permanent decline in the future benefit or service potential of an asset. The impairment may be due to numerous factors, including too little depreciation expense being recorded in previous years or obsolescence of the asset. If a fixed asset is impaired, a company should reduce the asset's book value to its fair value in the year the impairment occurs. The accounting for impairments is discussed more fully in Appendix 7A.

DISPOSAL OF FIXED ASSETS

Although companies usually dispose of fixed assets voluntarily, disposition may also be forced.

- **Voluntary disposal** occurs when the company determines that the asset is no longer useful. The disposal may occur at the end of the asset's useful life or at some other time. For example, obsolescence due to unforeseen technological developments may lead to an earlier than expected disposition of the asset.
- **Involuntary disposal** occurs when assets are lost or destroyed through theft, acts of nature, or by accident.

OBJECTIVE 7

Describe the process of recording the disposal of a fixed asset.

In either case, disposals rarely occur on the first or last day of an accounting period. Therefore, the disposal of property, plant, and equipment usually requires two journal entries:

1.   An entry to record depreciation expense up to the date of disposal.
2.   An entry to:

   • Remove the asset's book value (the cost of the asset and the related accumulated depreciation).
   • Record a gain or loss on disposal of the asset, which is computed as the difference between the proceeds from the sale and the book value of the asset.

Gains and losses on the disposal of property, plant, and equipment are normally reported as "other revenues or gains" or "other expenses and losses," respectively, and appear immediately after income from operations on a multiple-step income statement.

   Verizon's policy for recording disposals, as shown in the notes to its financial statements, is shown below.

> *When depreciable assets are retired or otherwise disposed of, the related cost and accumulated depreciation are deducted from the property, plant, and equipment accounts, and any gains or losses on disposition are recognized in income.*
> **Source:** Verizon Communications 2019 10-K.

   EXAMPLE 7.7   illustrates the accounting for the disposal of property, plant, and equipment.

EXAMPLE 7.7   RECORDING THE DISPOSITION OF PROPERTY, PLANT, AND EQUIPMENT

Pridgen Corporation sold a machine on July 1 for $22,000. The machine had originally cost $100,000. Accumulated depreciation at the beginning of the year (January 1) was $80,000. Depreciation expense from January 1 to July 1 was $5,000.

Required:

1.   Prepare the journal entry to record depreciation expense up to the date of disposal.

2.   Compute the gain or loss on disposal of the machine.

3.   Prepare the journal entry to record the disposal of the machine.

Solution:

1.

Date	Account and Explanation	Debit	Credit	Assets	= Liabilities +	Stockholders' Equity
July 1	Depreciation Expense	5,000				▼
	Accumulated Depreciation		5,000	▼		

2.

Proceeds from sale		$22,000
Less: Book value of asset sold:		
Cost	$100,000	
Accumulated depreciation ($80,000 + $5,000)	(85,000)	
Book value		15,000
Gain on disposal		$ 7,000

3.

Date	Account and Explanation	Debit	Credit	Assets	= Liabilities +	Stockholders' Equity
July 1	Cash	22,000		▲		
	Accumulated Depreciation	85,000		▲		
	Equipment		100,000	▼		
	Gain on Disposal of Property, Plant, and Equipment		7,000			▲

Note that Pridgen recorded depreciation expense up to the date of disposal. Once this journal entry is made, the book value is updated to reflect the increased accumulated depreciation. This revised book value is then used to compute the Gain on Disposal of Property, Plant, and Equipment, which appears in the "other revenues and gains" section of the income statement.

If Pridgen had received $12,000 for the asset, the following computation would be made:

Proceeds from sale		$12,000
Less: Book value of asset sold:		
Cost	$100,000	
Accumulated depreciation ($80,000 + $5,000)	(85,000)	
Book value		15,000
Loss on disposal of property, plant, and equipment		$ (3,000)

Because the proceeds from the sale were less than the book value, Pridgen would record a loss as follows:

Date	Account and Explanation	Debit	Credit	Assets	= Liabilities +	Stockholders' Equity
July 1	Cash	12,000		▲		
	Accumulated Depreciation	85,000		▲		
	Loss on Disposal of Property, Plant, and Equipment	3,000				▼
	Equipment		100,000	▼		

Pridgen would report the loss in the "other expenses and losses" section of the income statement.

YOU DECIDE Future Asset Replacement

You are considering a major investment in one of two long-haul trucking companies. Both companies are about the same size, travel competitive routes, and have similar net incomes. However, the balance sheets reveal a significant difference in the accumulated depreciation for the trucks as shown at right.

	Holt Company	Long Company
Trucks	$ 600,000	$ 550,000
Less: Accumulated depreciation	(138,000)	(477,000)
Book value	$ 462,000	$ 73,000

CONTINUED

YOUDECIDE **Future Asset Replacement** *(CONTINUED)*

What conclusions can you make regarding the future cash outflows each company will have to make for future asset replacements?

Assuming that the assets' estimates of useful life are consistent with their economic lives, the closer that accumulated depreciation is to historical cost, the older the assets and the more likely that they will have to be replaced. Long Company's assets are closer to being fully depreciated than those of Holt Company. Therefore, Long is more likely to make cash outflows for the replacement of its assets. Although more

information would be needed about Long in order to know the precise impact of the impending replacement, the comparison of the two accumulated depreciation amounts does provide you with valuable insights. While the recording of depreciation expense does not alter cash flow, accumulated depreciation signals the approaching future replacement of fixed assets, which usually requires cash.

A comparison of accumulated depreciation to historical cost can provide financial statement users with an approximation of the remaining life of the assets.

OBJECTIVE 8
Evaluate the use of fixed assets.

ANALYZING FIXED ASSETS

Because fixed assets are a major productive asset of most companies, it is useful to understand if the company is using these assets efficiently. In other words, how well is the company using its fixed assets to generate revenue? One measure of how efficiently a company is using its fixed assets is the **fixed asset turnover ratio**. It is calculated as:

$$\text{Fixed Asset Turnover Ratio} = \frac{\text{Net Sales}}{\text{Average Net Fixed Assets}}$$

The more efficiently a company uses its fixed assets, the higher the ratio will be.

In addition to the fixed asset turnover ratio, investors are also concerned with the condition of a company's fixed assets. Because older assets tend to be less efficient than newer assets, the age of a company's fixed assets can provide useful insights into the company's efficiency. The age of a company's fixed assets also can provide an indication of a company's capital replacement policy and assist managers in estimating future capital expenditures. A rough estimate of the **average age of fixed assets** can be computed as:

$$\text{Average Age of Fixed Assets} = \frac{\text{Accumulated Depreciation}}{\text{Depreciation Expense}}$$

EXAMPLE 7.8 illustrates the calculation of the fixed asset turnover ratio and the average age of fixed assets.

EXAMPLE 7.8   ANALYZING FIXED ASSET RATIOS

The following information was obtained from the financial statements of **Verizon** and **AT&T** for a recent year (all amounts in millions):

Account	Verizon	AT&T
Property, plant, and equipment, net, Jan. 1	$ 89,286	$131,473
Property, plant, and equipment, net, Dec. 31	91,915	130,128
Accumulated depreciation, Dec. 31	173,819	203,410
Net sales	131,868	181,193
Depreciation expense	16,682	28,217

Required:

1. Compute the fixed asset turnover ratio for Verizon and AT&T.

2. Compute the average age of Verizon's and AT&T's fixed assets as of December 31.

Solution:

1. $\text{Fixed Asset Turnover Ratio} = \dfrac{\text{Net Sales}}{\text{Average Net Fixed Assets}}$

Verizon	**AT&T**
$\dfrac{\$131,868}{\left[\dfrac{(\$89,286 + \$91,915)}{2}\right]} = \underline{1.46}$ times	$\dfrac{\$181,193}{\left[\dfrac{(\$131,473 + \$130,128)}{2}\right]} = \underline{1.39}$ times

2. $\text{Average Age of Fixed Assets} = \dfrac{\text{Accumulated Depreciation}}{\text{Depreciation Expense}}$

Verizon	**AT&T**
$\dfrac{\$173,819}{\$16,682} = \underline{10.42}$ years	$\dfrac{\$203,410}{\$28,217} = \underline{7.21}$ years

In Example 7.8, the fixed asset ratio tells us that for each dollar invested in fixed assets, **Verizon** generated sales of $1.46 while **AT&T** generated sales of $1.39. Thus, Verizon is more efficient in using its fixed assets to generate sales. In addition, Verizon's assets are, on average, 10.42 years old, while AT&T's assets are approximately 7.21 years old. Because Verizon's primary fixed asset is network equipment, which is depreciated between 3 and 50 years (see Exhibit 7.3 and Exhibit 7.5), this signals that Verizon will most likely be making significant capital expenditures over the next several years to replace its network equipment.

In addition to comparing a company's fixed asset turnover ratio with that of prior years and its competitors, it is necessary to gain an understanding of a company's operations to appropriately assess how efficiently a company is using its fixed assets. For example, **Verizon**'s fixed asset turnover may be lower than some of its competitors because it is currently spending large amounts to expand its network in anticipation of future sales. These expansion activities (which are capitalized in the current period) could depress Verizon's fixed asset turnover ratio.

INTANGIBLE ASSETS

OBJECTIVE 9

Describe the measurement and reporting of intangible assets.

Intangible operating assets, like tangible assets, represent future economic benefit to the company, but unlike tangible assets, they lack physical substance. Patents, copyrights, trademarks, leaseholds, organization costs, franchises, and goodwill are all examples of intangible assets. The economic benefits associated with most intangible assets are in the form of legal rights and privileges conferred on the owner of the asset. The economic value of a patent, for example, is the legal right to restrict, control, or charge for the use of the idea or process covered by the patent.

Because intangible assets lack physical substance, it is often easy to overlook their importance to the overall value of a company. Recent research suggests that between 60% and 80% of a company's market value may be tied to intangible assets. For many companies, intangible assets may be the most important asset it has. A pharmaceutical company such as **GlaxoSmithKline** could easily argue that the true value of the company lies with its intellectual capital and patents, not its tangible property, plant, and equipment. However, due to unique issues with intangibles (such as the highly uncertain nature of future benefits and the possibility of wide fluctuations in value), the value of many intangible assets is not adequately captured by current accounting standards. For example, GlaxoSmithKline's intangible assets, excluding goodwill, only make up approximately 39% of its total assets. As the value of intangible assets continues to be a key driver of company value, the measurement and evaluation of intangibles will certainly be a crucial issue.

ACQUISITION OF INTANGIBLE ASSETS

Intangible assets are recorded at cost, consistent with the historical cost principle. Similar to fixed assets, the cost of an intangible asset is any expenditure to acquire the asset and to prepare the asset for use.

For intangible assets purchased from outside the company, the primary element of the cost is the purchase price. Costs such as registration, filing, and legal fees are considered necessary costs and are capitalized as part of the intangible asset.

For internally developed intangible assets, the cost of developing the asset is expensed as incurred and normally recorded as **research and development (R&D) expense**. While expenditures for R&D may lead to intangible assets such as patents and copyrights, R&D is not an intangible asset. While many disagree with this position, current accounting standards require that all R&D be recorded as an expense. Exhibit 7.11 provides a listing of some typical intangible assets.

| **EXHIBIT 7.11** | **Common Types of Intangible Assets** |

Intangible Asset	Description	Cost Includes	Amortization
Patent	Right to manufacture, sell, or use a product. The legal life is 20 years from the date of grant.	Purchase price, registration fees, legal costs	Shorter of the economic life or legal life
Copyright	Right to publish, sell, or control a literary or artistic work. The legal life is life of author plus 70 years.	Purchase price, registration fees, legal costs	Shorter of the economic life or legal life
Trademark	Right to the exclusive use of a distinctive name, phrase, or symbol (e.g., the iPod name or the Nike "swoosh"). The legal life is 10 years but it can be renewed indefinitely.	Purchase price, registration fees, legal costs	Not amortized since it has an indefinite life; reviewed at least annually for impairment
Franchise	Exclusive right to conduct a certain type of business in some particular geographic area. Life of the franchise depends on specific terms of the franchise contract.	Initial cost paid to acquire the franchise	Shorter of the economic life or legal life
Goodwill	Unidentifiable intangible asset that arises from factors such as customer satisfaction, quality products, skilled employees, and business location. Goodwill is only recognized in business combinations.	The excess of the purchase price over the fair value of the identifiable net assets acquired in a business combination	Not amortized since it has an indefinite life; reviewed at least annually for impairment

Companies also incur significant costs such as legal fees, stock issue costs, accounting fees, and promotional fees when they are formed. It can be argued that these **organizational costs** are an intangible asset that provides a benefit to a company indefinitely. However, current accounting standards treat organizational costs as an expense in the period the cost is incurred.

SUBSEQUENT ACCOUNTING FOR INTANGIBLE ASSETS

Once an intangible asset is recorded, companies must determine if the asset has a finite life or an indefinite life. The cost of an intangible asset with a *finite life*, like the cost of a tangible asset, is allocated to accounting periods over the life of the asset to reflect the decline in service potential. This process is referred to as **amortization**. Most companies will amortize the cost of an intangible asset on a straight-line basis over the shorter of the economic or legal life of the asset. For example, a patent has a legal life of 20 years from the date it is granted. However, the economic advantage offered by a patent often expires before the end of its legal life as a result of other technological developments. Therefore, the shorter economic life should be used to amortize the cost of the patent.

If an intangible asset is determined to have an *indefinite life*, it is *not* amortized but is reviewed at least annually for impairment. EXAMPLE 7.9 illustrates the accounting for the acquisition and amortization of intangible assets.

EXAMPLE 7.9 ACCOUNTING FOR INTANGIBLE ASSETS

On January 1, King Company paid $40,000 cash to acquire a patent from Queen Company. The patent has 14 years of its legal life remaining. However, due to technological advancements, King estimates the patent will only provide benefits for another 10 years. In addition, King purchased a trademark from Queen for $60,000.

Required:

1. Prepare any journal entries necessary to record the acquisition of the patent and the trademark.

2. Compute the amortization expense for the patent and the trademark.

3. Prepare any adjusting journal entries necessary to record the amortization expense for the current year.

Solution:

1.

Date	Account and Explanation	Debit	Credit	Assets	= Liabilities +	Stockholders' Equity
Jan. 1	Patent	40,000		▲		
	Trademark	60,000		▲		
	Cash		100,000	▼		

2. $$\text{Patent Amortization} = \frac{\text{Cost} - \text{Residual Value}}{\text{Useful Life}} = \frac{\$40,000 - \$0}{10 \text{ years}} = \underline{\$4,000}$$

Trademark: Because the trademark has an indefinite life, no amortization is necessary.

3.

Date	Account and Explanation	Debit	Credit	Assets	= Liabilities +	Stockholders' Equity
Dec. 31	Amortization Expense	4,000				▼
	Patent		4,000	▼		

In Example 7.9, several items are of note:

- Most intangible assets do not have a residual value. Therefore, the cost that is being amortized is usually the entire cost of the intangible asset.
- King amortized the patent over the shorter of its remaining legal life (14 years) or its economic life (10 years). This is consistent with recognizing amortization expense over the period that the intangible asset is expected to provide benefits.
- King recorded the amortization expense by directly crediting the intangible asset, Patent. After the amortization expense is recorded, the book value of the patent is $36,000 ($40,000 – $4,000).
- Amortization expense is reported as operating expense on the income statement.

 YOUDECIDE   Measuring and Estimating the Dimensions of a Patent

You are the controller for Marietta Corporation, a research intensive company engaged in the design and sale of ceramic products. For the past year, half of Marietta's research staff has been engaged in designing a process for coating iron and steel with a ceramic material for use in high-temperature areas of automobile engines. The company has secured a patent for its process and is about to begin marketing equipment that uses the patented process. The assistant controller has argued that half of the year's cost of research activities should be assigned to the patent, including the salaries paid to researchers. Additionally, while Marietta expects the patented equipment to be a viable product for only 5 years, the assistant controller recommends that the patent should be amortized over its legal life of 20 years.

What is the impact of the assistant controller's recommendation, and how should you account for the patent?

If these costs were capitalized as part of the patent as the assistant controller recommended, current period assets and income would be overstated. In future periods, the higher recorded value of the intangible asset would result in an increase in amortization expense. While many analysts agree with the assistant controller that some research and development expenditures create an intangible asset, current accounting standards require that all research activities should be expensed when incurred.

If the patent were amortized over its legal life, the cost of the patent would be spread over 20 years, resulting in lower yearly amounts of amortization expense and higher income. However, accounting standards require that intangible assets be amortized over the shorter of their legal lives or their economic lives. Therefore, a relatively higher amortization expense should be recognized over the 5-year useful life of the patent.

Current accounting standards should be followed to avoid misstating the financial statements.

OBJECTIVE **10**

Describe the measurement and reporting of natural resources.

NATURAL RESOURCES

Natural resources, such as coal deposits, oil reserves, and mineral deposits, make up an important part of the operating assets for many companies. For example, **BP** has oil and gas properties of over $99 billion, representing approximately 35% of its total assets. Like intangible assets, natural resources present difficult estimation and measurement problems. However, natural resources differ from other operating assets in two important ways:

- Unlike fixed assets, natural resources are physically consumed as they are used by a company.
- Natural resources can generally be replaced or restored only by an act of nature. For example, timberlands are renewed by replanting and growth, but coal deposits and most mineral deposits are not subject to renewal.

The accounting for natural resources is quite similar to the accounting for intangible assets and fixed assets. At acquisition, all the costs necessary to ready the natural resource for separation from the earth are capitalized. At the time a company acquires the property on which a natural resource is located (or the property rights to the natural resource itself), only a small portion of the costs necessary to ready the asset for removal are likely to have been incurred. Costs such as sinking a shaft to an underground coal deposit, drilling a well to an oil reserve, or removing the earth over a mineral deposit can be several times greater than the cost of acquiring the property.

As a natural resource is removed from the earth, the cost of the natural resource is allocated to each unit of natural resource removed. This process of allocating the cost of the natural resource to each period in which the resource is used is called **depletion**. Depletion is computed by using a procedure similar to that for the units-of-production method of depreciation. First, a depletion rate is computed as:

$$\text{Depletion Rate} = \frac{\text{Cost} - \text{Residual Value}}{\text{Recoverable Units}}$$

Second, depletion is calculated by multiplying the depletion rate by the number of units of the natural resource recovered during the period:

$$\text{Depletion} = \text{Depletion Rate} \times \text{Units Recovered}$$

As the natural resource is extracted, the natural resource is reduced and the amount of depletion computed is added to inventory. As the inventory is sold, the company will recognize an expense (cost of goods sold) related to the natural resource. EXAMPLE 7.10 illustrates how to account for depletion of a natural resource.

EXAMPLE 7.10 ACCOUNTING FOR DEPLETION OF A NATURAL RESOURCE

Miller Mining Company purchased a 4,000-acre tract of land in southern Indiana for $12,000,000, on which it developed an underground coal mine. Miller spent $26,000,000 to sink shafts to the coal seams and otherwise prepare the mine for operation. Miller estimates that there are 10,000,000 tons of recoverable coal and that the mine will be fully depleted in 8 years. The land has a residual value of $500,000. During the year, 800,000 tons of coal were mined.

Required:

1. Compute the cost of the natural resource.

2. Compute the depletion rate.

3. How much depletion is taken during the year?

4. Prepare the journal entry necessary to record depletion and the related cost of goods sold.

Solution:

1. The cost of the natural resource includes all costs necessary to get the mine ready for use:

Cost	$12,000,000
Development/preparation costs	26,000,000
Cost	$38,000,000

2. $\text{Depletion Rate} = \dfrac{(\$38,000,000 - \$500,000)}{10,000,000 \text{ tons}} = \underline{\$3.75} \text{ per ton}$

3. $\text{Depletion} = \$3.75 \times 800,000 = \underline{\$3,000,000}$

4.

Date	Account and Explanation	Debit	Credit	Assets	= Liabilities +	Stockholders' Equity
Dec. 31	Inventory	3,000,000		▲		
	Accumulated Depletion		3,000,000	▼		

CONTINUED

EXAMPLE 7.10   ACCOUNTING FOR DEPLETION OF A NATURAL RESOURCE *(CONTINUED)*

Assuming all of the coal is sold in the year it is mined, the following entry should also be made:

Date	Account and Explanation	Debit	Credit	Assets	= Liabilities +	Stockholders' Equity
Dec. 31	Cost of Goods Sold	3,000,000				▼
	Inventory		3,000,000	▼		

In Example 7.10, the following items are of particular importance:

- Miller records depletion initially increasing an inventory account. As the coal is sold, inventory will be reduced and cost of goods sold will be recognized. Thus, the expense related to depletion will be matched with the revenue that is generated from the sale of the natural resource.
- Depletion increases the accumulated depletion account.[8] At December 31, Miller presents the coal mine among its assets in the balance sheet as shown in Exhibit 7.12.

EXHIBIT 7.12   Disclosure of Natural Resource by Miller Mining Company

Property, plant, and equipment:	
Land	$ 2,200,000
Equipment and machinery	19,800,000
Coal mine (cost of $38,000,000 minus accumulated depletion of $3,000,000)	35,000,000
Total property, plant, and equipment	$57,000,000

Companies will often incur costs for tangible fixed assets in connection with the use of a natural resource (such as buildings, equipment, roads to access the resource). Because the useful life of these assets is often limited by the life of the natural resource, these tangible assets should be depreciated using the units-of-production method on the same basis as the natural resource. However, if the assets have a life shorter than the expected life of the natural resource or will be used for the extraction of other natural resources, the assets should be depreciated over their own useful lives.

OBJECTIVE **11**

Describe the process of recording an impairment of a fixed asset.

APPENDIX 7A: IMPAIRMENT OF PROPERTY, PLANT, AND EQUIPMENT

An **impairment** is a permanent decline in the future benefit or service potential of an asset. The impairment may be due to numerous factors, including too little depreciation expense being recorded in previous years or obsolescence of the asset. A company is required to review an asset for impairment if events or circumstances lead the company to believe that an asset may

---

8   An alternative practice allowed by GAAP is to credit depletion directly to the asset account.

be impaired. Consistent with the principle of conservatism, if a fixed asset is impaired, a company should reduce the asset's book value to its fair value in the year the impairment occurs.

The impairment test consists of two steps:

Step 1. Existence: An impairment exists if the future cash flows expected to be generated by the asset are less than the asset's book value.

Step 2. Measurement: If an impairment exists, the impairment loss is measured as the difference between the book value and the fair value of the asset.

EXAMPLE 7.11 illustrates the accounting for an impairment.

EXAMPLE 7.11 — RECORDING AN IMPAIRMENT OF PROPERTY, PLANT, AND EQUIPMENT

Tabor Company acquired a machine for $150,000 several years ago. On January 1, when the machine has a book value of $60,000, Tabor believes that recent technological innovations may have led to an impairment in the value of the machine. Tabor estimates the machine will generate future cash flows of $50,000 and its current fair value is $42,000.

Required:

1. Determine if the machine is impaired as of January 1.

2. If the machine is impaired, compute the loss from impairment.

3. Prepare the journal entry to record the impairment.

Solution:

1. Step 1 of the impairment test is existence. The machine is impaired because the estimated future cash flows expected to be generated by the machine ($50,000) are less than the book value of the machine ($60,000).

2. Step 2 of the impairment test is measurement.

$$\text{Fair Value} - \text{Book Value} = \text{Loss from Impairment}$$
$$\$42,000 - \$60,000 = (\$18,000)$$

3.

Date	Account and Explanation	Debit	Credit	Assets	= Liabilities +	Stockholders' Equity
Jan. 1	Loss from Impairment	18,000				▼
	Equipment		18,000	▼		

LO1. Describe the accounting for operating assets.

KEY TAKEAWAYS

- Operating assets are the long-lived assets used by the company in the normal course of operations to generate revenue.
- Operating assets consist of three categories: property, plant, and equipment; intangible assets; and natural resources.
- Generally, operating assets are recorded at cost.
- As the service potential of the asset is used, the asset's cost is allocated as an expense (called depreciation, amortization, or depletion).

KEY TERM

Operating assets, 400

LO2. Explain how the historical cost principle applies to recording the cost of a fixed asset.

KEY TAKEAWAYS

- The cost of a fixed asset is any expenditure necessary to acquire the asset and to prepare the asset for use. This amount is generally the cash paid.
- If noncash consideration is involved, cost is the fair value of the asset received or the fair value of the asset given up, whichever is more clearly determinable.

KEY TERM

Property, plant, and equipment, 401

EXAMPLES

EXAMPLE 7.1	Recording the purchase of a fixed asset for cash or debt, page 403
EXAMPLE 7.2	Recording the purchase of a fixed asset for noncash consideration, page 403

LO3. Explain the concept of depreciation.

KEY TAKEAWAYS

- Depreciation is the process of allocating the cost of a tangible fixed asset to expense over the asset's useful life.
- Depreciation is not an attempt to measure fair value.
- Instead, depreciation is designed to capture the declining service potential of a fixed asset.
- Three factors are necessary to compute depreciation expense: cost, useful life, and residual value.

KEY TERMS

Accumulated depreciation, 404
Book value, 404
Carrying value, 404
Cost, 405
Depreciation, 404

Depreciable cost, 406
Depreciation expense, 404
Residual value, 406
Salvage value, 406
Useful life, 405

KEY CALCULATION

Depreciable Cost = Cost − Residual Value

KEY TAKEAWAYS

**LO4. Compute
depreciation expense
using various depreciation
methods.**

- The straight-line method allocates an equal amount of the asset's cost to each year
  of the asset's useful life by dividing the asset's depreciable cost (cost minus residual
  value) by the asset's useful life.
- The declining balance method is an accelerated method of depreciation that produces a declining amount of depreciation expense each period by multiplying the
  declining book value of an asset by a constant depreciation rate (computed as a multiple of the straight-line rate of depreciation).
- The units-of-production method recognizes depreciation expense based on the
  actual usage of the asset.

KEY TERMS

Declining balance depreciation method, 409
Straight-line depreciation method, 407
Units-of-production depreciation method, 411

KEY CALCULATIONS

Declining Balance Rate = $(m) \times$ Straight-Line Rate

Declining Balance Depreciation Expense = Declining Balance Rate $\times$ Book Value

$$\text{Depreciation Cost per Unit} = \frac{(\text{Cost} - \text{Residual Value})}{\text{Expected Usage of the Asset}}$$

$$\text{Straight-Line Depreciation Expense} = \frac{(\text{Cost} - \text{Residual Value})}{\text{Expected Useful Life}}$$

$$\text{Units-of-Production Depreciation Expense} = \text{Depreciation Cost per Unit} \times \text{Actual Usage of the Asset}$$

EXAMPLES

EXAMPLE 7.3	Computing depreciation expense using the straight-line method, page 408
EXAMPLE 7.4	Computing depreciation expense using the declining balance method, page 410
EXAMPLE 7.5	Computing depreciation expense using the units-of-production method, page 411–412

LO5. Distinguish between capital and revenue expenditures.

KEY TAKEAWAYS

- Revenue expenditures are expenditures that do not increase the future benefit of an asset and are expensed as incurred.
- Capital expenditures extend the life of the asset, expand productive capacity, increase efficiency, or improve the quality of the product. Capital expenditures are added to the asset account and are subject to depreciation.

KEY TERMS

Capital expenditures, 415
Revenue expenditures, 415

LO6. Account for revisions in depreciation.

KEY TAKEAWAYS

- When new or additional information becomes available, a company will revise its calculation of depreciation expense.
- A revision in depreciation will be recorded in current and future periods.

EXAMPLE

EXAMPLE 7.6	Revising depreciation expense, page 417

LO7. Describe the process of recording the disposal of a fixed asset.

KEY TAKEAWAYS

- When a fixed asset is disposed of (either voluntarily or involuntarily), a gain or loss is recognized.
- The gain or loss is the difference between the proceeds from the sale and the book value of the asset.
- The gain or loss is reported on the income statement as "other revenues or gains" or "other expenses and losses," respectively.

KEY TERMS

Involuntary disposal, 417
Voluntary disposal, 417

EXAMPLE

EXAMPLE 7.7 Recording the disposition of property, plant, and equipment, page 418–419

KEY TAKEAWAYS

LO8. Evaluate the use of fixed assets.

- The efficiency with which a company uses its fixed assets can be analyzed by using the fixed asset turnover ratio.
- The condition of a company's assets and insights into the company's capital replacement policy can be examined by computing the average age of fixed assets.

KEY TERMS

Average age of fixed assets, 420
Fixed asset turnover ratio, 420

KEY CALCULATIONS

$$\text{Fixed Asset Turnover Ratio} = \frac{\text{Net Sales}}{\text{Average Net Fixed Assets}}$$

$$\text{Average Age of Fixed Assets} = \frac{\text{Accumulated Depreciation}}{\text{Depreciation Expense}}$$

EXAMPLE

EXAMPLE 7.8 Analyzing fixed asset ratios, page 420–421

KEY TAKEAWAYS

LO9. Describe the measurement and reporting of fixed assets.

- Intangible assets are recorded at cost, which is any expenditure necessary to acquire the asset and prepare it for use.
- If the intangible asset has a finite life, it is amortized over the shorter of the economic or legal life of the asset.
- If the intangible asset has an indefinite life, it is not amortized but is reviewed at least annually for impairment.

KEY TERMS

Amortization, 423
Intangible operating assets, 421

Organizational costs, 422
Research and development (R&D) expense, 422

EXAMPLE

> **EXAMPLE 7.9**   Accounting for intangible assets, page 423

L10. Describe the measurement and reporting of natural resources.

KEY TAKEAWAYS

- The cost of natural resources is any cost necessary to acquire and prepare the resource for separation from the earth.
- As the natural resource is removed, the cost is allocated to each unit of the natural resource that is removed and recorded in an inventory account. This process is called depletion.
- Depletion is calculated using a procedure similar to the units-of-production depreciation method.

KEY TERMS

Depletion, 425
Natural resources, 424

KEY CALCULATIONS

$$\text{Depletion Rate} = \frac{\text{Cost} - \text{Residual Value}}{\text{Recoverable Units}}$$

$$\text{Depletion} = \text{Depletion Rate} \times \text{Units Recovered}$$

EXAMPLE

> **EXAMPLE 7.10**   Accounting for depletion of a natural resource, page 425–426

L11. (Appendix 7A) Describe the process of recording an impairment of a fixed asset.

KEY TAKEAWAYS

- Impairment exists when the future cash flows expected to be generated by an asset are less than the book value of the asset.
- An impairment loss, the difference between the book value and fair value of the asset, is recognized and the asset is reduced.

KEY TERM

Impairment, 426

KEY CALCULATION

Loss from Impairment = Fair Value − Book Value

EXAMPLES

EXAMPLE 7.11   Recording an impairment of property, plant, and equipment, page 427

REVIEW PROBLEM

The Carroll Company manufactures a line of cranes, shovels, and hoists, all of which are electronically controlled. During the year, the following transactions occurred:

a. On January 2, Carroll purchased a building by signing a note payable for $702,900. The building is expected to have a useful life of 30 years and a residual value of $3,900.

b. On January 3, Carroll purchased a delivery truck for $34,650 cash. The delivery truck is expected to have a useful life of 5 years and a $5,000 residual value.

c. Immediately after the acquisition of the truck, Carroll spent $5,350 on a new engine for the truck. After installing the engine, Carroll estimated that this expenditure increased the useful life of the truck to 8 years. The residual value is still expected to be $5,000.

d. In order to assure a coal supply for its heating plant, Carroll acquired a small operating coal mine for $1,980,000. Carroll estimated that the recoverable coal reserves at acquisition were 495,000 tons. Carroll's mine produced 40,000 tons of coal during the year.

e. Carroll purchased a patent on January 3 for $100,000. The patent has 12 years remaining on its legal life, but Carroll estimated its economic life to be 8 years. Carroll uses the straight-line amortization method.

Required:

1. Record the acquisition of the building and the delivery truck.

2. Prepare a depreciation schedule and record a full year's depreciation expense on the building (use the straight-line depreciation method) and on the truck (use the double-declining-balance depreciation method).

3. Compute and record depletion for the coal mine for the year.

4. Compute and record the amortization expense on the patent for the year on a straight-line basis.

5. Assume Carroll had sales of $8,800,000, fixed assets with an average net book value of $3,200,000, depreciation expense of $375,000, and accumulated depreciation of $2,062,500. Compute the fixed asset turnover ratio and the average age of the fixed assets. Comment on what the ratios mean.

Solution:

1. The cost of the building is $702,900 and is recorded as:

Date	Account and Explanation	Debit	Credit	Assets	=	Liabilities	+	Stockholders' Equity
Jan. 2	Buildings	702,900		▲				
	Notes Payable		702,900			▲		

The cost of the truck is $40,000 ($34,650 acquisition price + $5,350 from the overhaul of the engine). The purchase of the truck is recorded as:

Date	Account and Explanation	Debit	Credit	Assets	=	Liabilities	+	Stockholders' Equity
Jan. 3	Truck	40,000		▲				
	Cash		40,000	▼				

2. Depreciation on the items of property, plant, and equipment:

Building:

$$\text{Straight-Line Depreciation Expense} = \frac{\text{Cost} - \text{Residual Value}}{\text{Expected Life}}$$

$$= \frac{\$702,900 - \$3,900}{30 \text{ years}} = \underline{\$23,300} \text{ per year}$$

Date	Account and Explanation	Debit	Credit	Assets	=	Liabilities	+	Stockholders' Equity
Dec. 31	Depreciation Expense	23,300						▼
	Accumulated Depreciation		23,300	▼				

Truck:

Declining Balance Depreciation Expense = Declining Balance Rate × Book Value
Declining Balance Rate = (1/Useful Life) × 2 = (1/8) × 2 = 2/8, or 25%

Cost = $34,650 (from Transaction b) + $5,350 overhaul (from Transaction c)
    = $40,000

End of Year	Depreciation Expense	Accumulated Depreciation	Book Value
			$40,000
2019	25% × $40,000 = $10,000	$10,000	30,000

Date	Account and Explanation	Debit	Credit	Assets	=	Liabilities	+	Stockholders' Equity
Dec. 31	Depreciation Expense	10,000						▼
	Accumulated Depreciation		10,000	▼				

3. Depletion on the coal mine:

$$\text{Depletion Rate} = \frac{\text{Cost} - \text{Residual Value}}{\text{Recoverable Units}}$$

$$= \frac{\$1,980,000}{495,000} = \$4.00 \text{ per ton}$$

Depletion = Depletion Rate × Units Recovered
$$= \$4.00 \times 40,000 = \underline{\$160,000}$$

Date	Account and Explanation	Debit	Credit	Assets	=	Liabilities	+	Stockholders' Equity
Dec. 31	Inventory	160,000		▲				
	Accumulated Depletion		160,000	▼				

4. Amortization of the patent:

$$\text{Straight-Line Amortization Expense} = \frac{\text{Cost} - \text{Residual Value}}{\text{Expected Life}}$$

$$= \frac{\$100,000 - \$0}{8 \text{ years}}$$

$$= \underline{\$12,500 \text{ per year}}$$

Date	Account and Explanation	Debit	Credit	Assets	=	Liabilities	+	Stockholders' Equity
Dec. 31	Amortization Expense	12,500						▼
	Patent		12,500	▼				

5. The fixed asset turnover ratio is computed as its net sales divided by the average of its fixed assets. Carroll Company's fixed asset turnover ratio is 2.75 ($8,800,000/$3,200,000). This ratio describes how efficiently Carroll is using its fixed assets to generate revenue. The average age of fixed assets is computed as accumulated depreciation divided by depreciation expense. Carroll's fixed assets are approximately 5½ years old ($2,062,500/$375,000). For every dollar of fixed assets, Carroll is generating $2.75 of sales.

APPLYING KNOWLEDGE

DISCUSSION QUESTIONS

1. How do operating assets differ from nonoperating assets? What benefits do operating assets provide to the company?

   OBJECTIVE ◀ **1**

2. What are the classifications of operating assets? How do they differ from one another?

3. How does the cost concept affect accounting for operating assets? Under this concept, what is included in the cost of a fixed asset?

   OBJECTIVE ◀ **2**

4. How is the cost of a fixed asset measured in a cash transaction? In a noncash transaction?

(Continued)

5. What is the effect on the financial statements if a company incorrectly records an expense as an asset?

OBJECTIVE 3

6. How does the expense recognition principle affect accounting for operating assets?

7. What factors must be known or estimated in order to compute depreciation expense?

OBJECTIVE 4

8. How do the accelerated and straight-line depreciation methods differ?

9. What objective should guide the selection of a depreciation method for financial reporting purposes?

10. What objective should be of primary importance in the selection of a depreciation method for income tax reporting?

OBJECTIVE 5

11. What accounting concepts should be considered when evaluating the accounting for expenditures that are made for fixed assets after acquisition? Be sure to distinguish between revenue and capital expenditures.

OBJECTIVE 6

12. What is the proper accounting for depreciation when new or additional information becomes available that causes a company to change its estimates of useful life or residual value?

OBJECTIVE 7

13. How is the sale of equipment at an amount greater than its book value recorded? How would your answer change if the equipment is sold at an amount less than its book value?

OBJECTIVE 8

14. What information does the fixed asset turnover ratio and the average age of fixed assets provide users of financial statements?

OBJECTIVE 9

15. Describe the benefits that intangible assets provide to a company.

16. What factors should be considered when selecting the amortization period for an intangible asset?

OBJECTIVE 10

17. What basis underlies the computation of depletion?

OBJECTIVE 11

18. *(Appendix 7A)* What is an impairment of a fixed asset?

MULTIPLE-CHOICE QUESTIONS

OBJECTIVE 2

7-1 Anniston Company purchased equipment and incurred the following costs:

Purchase price	$68,500
Cost of trial runs	400
Installation costs	325
Sales tax	3,425

What is the cost of the equipment?
a. $68,500
b. $71,925
c. $72,250
d. $72,650

7-2 The cost principle requires that companies record fixed assets at:
a. fair value.
b. book value.
c. historical cost.
d. market value.

OBJECTIVE 3

7-3 When depreciation is recorded each period, what account is debited?
a. Depreciation Expense
b. Cash
c. Accumulated Depreciation
d. The fixed asset account involved

Use the following information for Multiple-Choice Questions 7-4 through 7-6:
Cox Inc. acquired a machine for $800,000 on January 1, Year 1. The machine has a salvage value of $20,000 and a 5-year useful life. Cox expects the machine to run for 15,000 machine hours. The machine was actually used for 4,200 hours in 2019 and 3,450 hours in 2020.

7-4 Refer to the information for Cox Inc. above. What would be the balance in the accumulated depreciation account at the end of the second year, if the straight-line method were used?

    a. $156,000   c. $312,000

    b. $160,000   d. $328,000

OBJECTIVE ◀ 4

7-5 Refer to the information for Cox Inc. above. What amount would Cox record as depreciation expense at December 31, Year 2, if the double-declining-balance method were used?

    a. $187,200   c. $195,200

    b. $192,000   d. $312,000

7-6 Refer to the information for Cox Inc. above. What amount would Cox record as depreciation expense for Year 1 if the units-of-production method were used (*Note:* Round your answer to the nearest dollar)?

    a. $179,400   c. $218,400

    b. $184,000   d. $224,000

7-7 Which of the following statements is true regarding depreciation methods?

    a. The use of a declining balance method of depreciation will produce lower depreciation charges in the early years of an asset's life compared to the straight-line depreciation method.

    b. Over the life of an asset, a declining balance depreciation method will recognize more depreciation expense relative to the straight-line method.

    c. The use of a declining balance method instead of the straight-line method will produce higher book values for an asset in the early years of the asset's life.

    d. The use of a higher estimated life and a higher residual value will lower the annual amount of depreciation expense recognized on the income statement.

7-8 Chapman Inc. purchased a piece of equipment which it depreciates on a straight-line basis. The useful life is 10 years and the residual value is estimated to be $12,000. Chapman's annual depreciation expense is $11,000. What was the original cost of the building?

    a. $98,000   c. $122,000

    b. $110,000   d. $134,000

7-9 Normal repair and maintenance of an asset is an example of what?

    a. Revenue expenditure

    b. Capital expenditure

    c. An expenditure that will be depreciated

    d. An expenditure that should be avoided

OBJECTIVE ◀ 5

7-10 Bradley Company purchased a machine for $34,000 on January 1. It depreciates the machine using the straight-line method over a useful life of 8 years and a $2,000 residual value. After using the machine for 2 years, Bradley revised its estimate of residual value to $1,000 and shortened the machine's useful life to 4 more years. What is the revised amount that Bradley should record for depreciation expense?

    a. $4,000   c. $6,000

    b. $5,750   d. $6,250

OBJECTIVE ◀ 6

OBJECTIVE 7

7-11   Jerabek Inc. sold one of its fixed assets that had a cost of $55,000 and accumulated depreciation of $35,000. What was the resulting gain or loss from the sale of the asset?
a. $5,000 loss
b. $5,000 gain
c. $15,000 loss
d. $15,000 gain

OBJECTIVE 8

7-12   Which of the following statements is true?
a. The fixed asset turnover ratio assists managers in determining the estimated future capital expenditures that are needed.
b. The average age of the fixed assets is computed by dividing accumulated depreciation by depreciation expense.
c. If net sales increases, the fixed asset turnover ratio will decrease.
d. A relatively low fixed asset turnover ratio signals that a company is efficiently using its assets.

OBJECTIVE 9

7-13   Which of the following is *not* an intangible asset?
a. Patent
b. Trademark
c. Research and development
d. Goodwill

7-14   Heston Company acquired a patent on January 1 for $75,000. The patent has a remaining legal life of 15 years, but Heston expects to receive benefits from the patent for only 5 years. What amount of annual amortization expense does Heston record related to the patent?
a. $5,000
b. $7,500
c. $15,000
d. $0—patents are not amortized.

OBJECTIVE 10

7-15   Howton Paper Company purchased $1,400,000 of timberland for its paper operations. Howton estimates that there are 10,000 acres of timberland, and it cut 2,000 acres in the current year. The land is expected to have a residual value of $200,000 once all the timber is cut. Which of the following is true with regard to depletion?
a. Depletion will cause Howton's timber inventory to increase.
b. Howton will record depletion expense of $280,000.
c. Howton's depletion rate is $140 per acre of timber.
d. Howton should deplete the timber at a rate of 20% (2,000 acres ÷ 10,000 acres) per year.

OBJECTIVE 11

7-16   (*Appendix 7A*) Murnane Company believes a machine that was originally purchased for $100,000 and has a current book value of $70,000 is impaired due to recent technological advances. Murnane expects the machine to generate future cash flow of $10,000 and has estimated the fair value of the machine to be $55,000. What is the loss from impairment?
a. $5,000
b. $15,000
c. $30,000
d. $45,000

BRIEF EXERCISES

OBJECTIVE 1

Brief Exercise 7-17 Understanding Operating Assets

Descriptions of operating assets are listed below.
a. Naturally occurring materials that have economic value
b. Tangible assets that can be seen and touched
c. Do not have physical substance
d. Depreciated over the accounting periods in which the asset is used and benefits are received
e. Generally result from legal and contractual rights

Required:

Identify the category of operating asset associated with each description as property, plant, and equipment; intangible assets; or natural resources.

Brief Exercise 7-18 Cost of a Fixed Asset

OBJECTIVE 2

EXAMPLE 7.1

Borges Inc. recently purchased land to use for the construction of its new manufacturing facility and incurred the following costs: purchase price, $125,000; interest charges, $500; real estate commissions, $9,500; delinquent property taxes, $1,800; closing costs, $3,500; and clearing and grading of the land, $12,800.

Required:

Determine the cost of the land.

Brief Exercise 7-19 Acquisition Cost

OBJECTIVE 2

EXAMPLE 7.1

Desert State University installed a HD video board with an invoice price of $5,000,000 in its football stadium. Desert State paid an additional $100,000 of delivery and installation costs relating to this board. Because this is one of the largest boards in the world, Desert State also installed ten 5-ton air conditioning units at a total cost of $120,000 to keep the board cool in the desert heat.

Required:

Determine the cost of the video board.

Brief Exercise 7-20 Acquisition Cost

OBJECTIVE 2

EXAMPLE 7.2

Cox Company recently purchased a machine by issuing 1,000 shares of stock selling for $20 per share. In addition to the purchase price, Cox incurred the following costs related to the machine: freight charges, $800; special foundation for machine, $400; and installation costs, $1,100.

Required:

Determine the cost of the machine.

Brief Exercise 7-21 Depreciation Concepts

OBJECTIVE 3

Listed below are concepts and terminology related to depreciation.

Concepts	Terminology
1. The period of time over which the company anticipates deriving benefit from the use of the asset	a. Depreciation
2. The cost of the asset minus its accumulated depreciation	b. Accumulated depreciation
3. The total amount of depreciation expense that has been recorded for an asset since the asset was acquired	c. Book value
	d. Useful life
4. The amount of cash or trade-in consideration that the company expects to receive when an asset is retired from service	e. Residual value
5. A process of cost allocation, not an attempt to measure the fair value of an asset	

Required:

Match each concept with the related terminology.

> *Use the following information for Brief Exercises 7-22 through 7-24:*
> Irons Delivery Inc. purchased a new delivery truck for $45,000 on January 1, 2023. The truck is expected to have a $3,000 residual value at the end of its 5-year useful life.

OBJECTIVE 4
EXAMPLE 7.3

Brief Exercise 7-22 Straight-Line Depreciation

Refer to the information for Irons Delivery Inc. above. Irons uses the straight-line method of depreciation.

Required:

Prepare the journal entry to record depreciation expense for 2023 and 2024.

OBJECTIVE 4
EXAMPLE 7.4

Brief Exercise 7-23 Declining Balance Depreciation

Refer to the information for Irons Delivery Inc. above. Irons uses the double-declining-balance method of depreciation.

Required:

Prepare the journal entry to record depreciation expense for 2023 and 2024.

OBJECTIVE 4
EXAMPLE 7.5

Brief Exercise 7-24 Units-of-Production Depreciation

Refer to the information for Irons Delivery Inc. above. Irons uses the units-of-production method of depreciation. Irons expects the truck to run for 160,000 miles. The actual miles driven in 2023 and 2024 were 40,000 and 36,000, respectively.

Required:

Prepare the journal entry to record depreciation expense for 2023 and 2024.

OBJECTIVE 5

Brief Exercise 7-25 Expenditures After Acquisition

Listed below are several transactions:
a. Paid $80 cash to replace a minor part of an air conditioning system.
b. Paid $40,000 to fix structural damage to a building.
c. Paid $8,000 for monthly salaries.
d. Paid $12,000 to replace a manual cutting machine with a computer-controlled machine.
e. Paid $1,000 related to the annual painting of a building.

Required:

Classify each transaction as either a revenue expenditure, a capital expenditure, or neither.

OBJECTIVE 6
EXAMPLE 7.6

Brief Exercise 7-26 Revision of Depreciation

On January 1, Slade Inc. purchased a machine for $90,000. Slade depreciated the machine with the straight-line depreciation method over a useful life of 10 years, using a residual value of $4,000. After using the machine for 2 years, a major overhaul, costing $35,000, was made. After the overhaul, the machine's residual value is estimated to be $2,500, and the machine is expected to have a remaining useful life of 12 years.

Required:

Determine the annual depreciation expense after the overhaul.

OBJECTIVE 7
EXAMPLE 7.7

Brief Exercise 7-27 Disposal of an Operating Asset

Jolie Company owns equipment with a cost of $85,500 and accumulated depreciation of 76,200.

Required:

Prepare the journal entry to record the disposal of the equipment on April 9 assuming:
1. Jolie sold the equipment for $11,200 cash.
2. Jolie sold the equipment for $7,900 cash.

Brief Exercise 7-28 Analyzing Fixed Assets

OBJECTIVE ◀ 8

EXAMPLE 7.8

Pitt reported the following information for Year 1 and Year 2:

	Year 1	Year 2
Property, plant, and equipment, cost	$550,000	$ 550,000
Accumulated depreciation	170,000	220,000
Net sales		4,600,000
Depreciation expense		50,000

Required:

Compute Pitt's fixed asset turnover ratio and the average age of its fixed assets. (*Note:* Round all answers to two decimal places.)

Brief Exercise 7-29 Cost and Amortization of Intangible Assets

OBJECTIVE ◀ 9

EXAMPLE 7.9

On January 2, Frazier Company purchased a restaurant franchise for $85,000. The terms of the franchise agreement allowed Frazier to have exclusive rights to operate a restaurant under the "Simply Fried" brand name for the next 10 years.

Required:

Prepare any journal entries related to the franchise that Frazier should make during the year.

Brief Exercise 7-30 Natural Resources and Depletion

OBJECTIVE ◀ 10

EXAMPLE 7.10

Luper Company acquired a tract of land that contained iron deposits for $2,500,000. Luper spent $120,000 to access the iron ore. Luper estimates that 2,000,000 tons of ore will be extracted. The estimated value of the land after the ore is extracted is $100,000. During the current year, Luper extracts 150,000 tons of iron ore.

Required:

Compute the cost of the natural resource and the amount of depletion taken during the year.

Brief Exercise 7-31 *(Appendix 7A)* Impairment

OBJECTIVE ◀ 11

Listed below is information related to three assets reported in the financial statements of Grant Company:

Asset	Book Value	Estimated Future Cash Flows	Fair Value
a. Building	$180,000	$200,000	$190,000
b. Equipment	50,000	45,000	40,000
c. Furniture	15,000	16,000	13,000

Required:

For each scenario, indicate whether the asset has been impaired and, if so, the amount of the impairment loss that should be recorded.

EXERCISES

Exercise 7-32 Balance Sheet Presentation

OBJECTIVE ◀ 1

Listed below are items that may appear on a classified balance sheet.

1. Land
2. Amounts due from customers
3. Office building
4. Truck
5. Goods held for resale
6. Amounts owed to suppliers
7. Patent
8. Timberland
9. Land held as investment
10. Goodwill

(Continued)

Required:

Indicate whether each item is included as an operating asset on a classified balance sheet. If the item is an operating asset, indicate whether the item is property, plant, and equipment; an intangible asset; or a natural resource as well as the cost allocation process used (depreciation, amortization, or depletion). If the item is not an operating asset, indicate the proper balance sheet classification.

 OBJECTIVE **1**

Exercise 7-33 Balance Sheet Classification

Micro-Technologies Inc., a computer manufacturer, has the following items on its balance sheet—office furniture delivery truck, patent, computer assembly machine, building, memory chips.

Required:

Indicate the proper balance sheet classification of each item and the cost allocation process used (depreciation, amortization, depletion).

 OBJECTIVE **2**

Exercise 7-34 Acquisition Cost

Items that may relate to property, plant, and equipment follow:

1. Purchase price of a machine
2. Delinquent property taxes at the time of purchase
3. Interest on debt used to purchase equipment
4. Sales taxes paid on purchase of equipment
5. Costs to install a machine
6. Ordinary repairs to equipment
7. Cost to remodel a building
8. Architectural fees paid for design of a building
9. Cost of training employees to run equipment
10. Transportation costs to have furniture delivered

Required:

CONCEPTUAL CONNECTION Determine whether each item is included as part of the cost of property, plant, and equipment. For any item excluded from the cost of property, plant, and equipment, explain why the item was excluded.

OBJECTIVE **2**

Exercise 7-35 Cost of a Fixed Asset

Laurel Cleaners purchased an automatic dry cleaning machine for $165,000 from TGF Corporation on April 1. Laurel paid $25,000 in cash and signed a 5-year, 10% note for $140,000. Laurel will pay interest on the note each year on March 31. Transportation charges of $4,250 for the machine were paid by Laurel. Laurel also paid $1,500 for the living expenses of the TGF installation crew. Solvent, necessary to operate the machine, was acquired for $1,000. Of this amount, $800 of the solvent was used to test and adjust the machine.

Required:

1. Compute the cost of the new dry cleaning machine.
2. **CONCEPTUAL CONNECTION** Explain why you excluded any expenditures from the cost of the dry cleaning machine.

OBJECTIVE **2**

Exercise 7-36 Cost of a Fixed Asset

Colson Photography Service purchased a new digital imaging machine on April 15 for $11,200. During installation Colson incurred and paid in cash the following costs:

Rental of drill	$ 150
Electrical contractor	1,300
Plumbing contractor	785

Colson also paid $160 to replace a bracket on the digital imager that was damaged when one of Colson's employees dropped a box on it while it was being installed.

Required:

1. Determine the cost of the digital imaging machine.
2. **CONCEPTUAL CONNECTION** Explain why you included or excluded the $160 bracket replacement cost.

Exercise 7-37 Cost of Fixed Assets

OBJECTIVE ▸2

SHOW ME HOW

Mooney Sounds, a local stereo retailer, needed a new store because it had outgrown the leased space it had used for several years. Mooney acquired and remodeled a former grocery store. As a part of the acquisition, Mooney incurred the following costs:

Cost of grocery store	$277,400	Wire and electrical supplies	$ 4,290
Cost of land (on which the		New doors	6,400
grocery store is located)	83,580	New windows	3,850
New roof for building	74,000	Wages paid to workers for remodeling	12,500
Lumber used for remodeling	23,200	Additional inventory purchased for	
Paint	515	grand opening sale	45,300

Required:

1. Determine the cost of the land and the building.
2. **CONCEPTUAL CONNECTION** If management misclassified a portion of the building's cost as part of the cost of the land, what would be the effect on the financial statements?

Exercise 7-38 Cost and Depreciation

OBJECTIVE ▸2 4

SHOW ME HOW

On January 1, Quick Stop, a convenience store, purchased a new soft-drink cooler. Quick Stop paid $15,380 cash for the cooler. Quick Stop also paid $750 to have the cooler shipped to its location. After the new cooler arrived, Quick Stop paid $222 to have the old cooler dismantled and removed. Quick Stop also paid $1,020 to a contractor to have new wiring and drains installed for the new cooler. Quick Stop estimated that the cooler would have a useful life of 8 years and a residual value of $500. Quick Stop uses the straight-line method of depreciation.

Required:

1. Prepare any necessary journal entries to record the cost of the cooler.
2. Prepare the adjusting entry at the end of the year to record depreciation expense on the new cooler.
3. What is the book value of the cooler after the adjusting entry is made?
4. **CONCEPTUAL CONNECTION** If Quick Stop had used a useful life of 12 years and a residual value of $800, how would this effect annual depreciation expense and the book value of the cooler at the end of the year?

Exercise 7-39 Characteristics of Depreciation Methods

OBJECTIVE ▸3

Below is a common list of depreciation methods and characteristics related to depreciation.

Depreciation Methods

a. Straight-line depreciation method
b. Declining balance depreciation method
c. Units-of-production depreciation method when actual units produced increases over the life of the asset

Characteristics

1. Results in depreciation expense that decreases over the life of the asset.
2. Results in depreciation expense that increases over the life of the asset.
3. Allocates the same amount of cost to each period of a depreciable asset's life.
4. Calculated by multiplying a *constant* depreciation rate by depreciable cost.

(Continued)

5. Calculated by applying a *constant* depreciation rate to the asset's book value at the beginning of the period.
6. Results in lowest income taxes in early years of the asset's life.
7. Consistent with the matching principle.

Required:

Match one or more of the depreciation methods with each characteristic.

Exercise 7-40 Depreciation Methods

On January 1, 2023, Loeffler Company acquired a machine at a cost of $200,000. Loeffler estimates that it will use the machine for 4 years or 8,000 machine hours. It estimates that after 4 years the machine can be sold for $20,000. Loeffler uses the machine for 2,100 and 1,800 machine hours in 2023 and 2024, respectively.

Required:

Compute depreciation expense for 2023 and 2024 using the (1) straight-line, (2) double-declining-balance, and (3) units-of-production methods of depreciation.

Exercise 7-41 Depreciation Methods

Berkshire Corporation purchased a copying machine for $8,700 on January 1, 2023. The machine's residual value was $425 and its expected life was 5 years or 2,000,000 copies. Actual usage was 480,000 copies the first year and 400,000 the second year.

Required:

1. Compute depreciation expense for 2023 and 2024 using the (a) straight-line method, (b) double-declining-balance method, and (c) units-of-production method.
2. For each depreciation method, what is the book value of the machine at the end of 2023? At the end of 2024?
3. **CONCEPTUAL CONNECTION** Assume that Berkshire uses the double-declining-balance method of depreciation. What is the effect on assets and income relative to if Berkshire had used the straight-line method of depreciation instead of the double-declining-balance method of depreciation?

Exercise 7-42 Depreciation Methods

Clearcopy, a printing company, acquired a new press on January 1. The press cost $173,400 and had an expected life of 8 years or 4,500,000 pages and an expected residual value of $15,000. Clearcopy printed 675,000 pages during the year.

Required:

1. Compute depreciation expense using the (a) straight-line method, (b) double-declining- balance method, and (c) units-of-production method.
2. What is the book value of the machine at the end of the year under each method?

Exercise 7-43 Depreciation Methods

Quick-as-Lightning, a delivery service, purchased a new delivery truck for $45,000 on January 1, 2023. The truck is expected to have a useful life of 10 years or 150,000 miles and an expected residual value of $3,000. The truck was driven 15,000 miles in 2023 and 13,000 miles in 2024.

Required:

1. Compute depreciation expense for 2023 and 2024 using the (a) straight-line method, (b) double-declining-balance method, and (c) units-of-production method.
2. For each method, what is the book value of the machine at the end of 2023? At the end of 2024?
3. **CONCEPTUAL CONNECTION** If Quick-as-Lightning used an 8-year useful life or 100,000 miles and a residual value of $1,000, what would be the effect on (a) depreciation expense and (b) book value under each of the depreciation methods?

Exercise 7-44 Inferring Original Cost

OBJECTIVE ◄ 4

Barton Construction Company purchased a piece of heavy equipment on January 1, which it is depreciating using the straight-line method. The equipment's useful life is 5 years and its residual value is $5,000. Barton recorded annual depreciation expense of $44,000.

Required:

Determine the original cost of the equipment.

Exercise 7-45 Choice Among Depreciation Methods

OBJECTIVE ◄ 4

Walnut Ridge Production Inc. purchased a new computerized video-editing machine at a cost of $450,000. The system has a residual value of $64,000 and an expected life of 5 years.

Required:

1. Compute depreciation expense, accumulated depreciation, and book value for the first 3 years of the machine's life using the (a) straight-line method and (b) double-declining-balance method.
2. Which method would produce the largest income in the first, second, and third years of the asset's life?
3. **CONCEPTUAL CONNECTION** Why might the controller of Walnut Ridge Production be interested in the effect of choosing a depreciation method? Evaluate the legitimacy of these interests.

Exercise 7-46 Capital versus Revenue Expenditure

OBJECTIVE ◄ 5

Warrick Water Company, a privately owned business, supplies water to several communities. Warrick has just performed an extensive overhaul on one of its water pumps. The overhaul is expected to extend the life of the pump by 10 years. The residual value of the pump is unchanged. You have been asked to determine which of the following costs should be capitalized as a part of this overhaul. Those costs not capitalized should be expensed.

Element of Cost	Classification and Explanation
New pump motor	
Repacking of bearings (performed monthly)	
New impeller (rotating component of a pump)	
Painting of pump housing (performed annually)	
Replacement of pump foundation	
New wiring (needed every 5 years)	
Installation labor, motor	
Installation labor, impeller	
Installation labor, wiring	
Paint labor (performed annually)	
Placement of fence around pump*	

* A requirement of the Occupational Safety and Health Administration that will add to maintenance costs over the remaining life of the pump.

Required:

CONCEPTUAL CONNECTION Classify each cost as part of the overhaul or as an expense. Be sure to explain your reasoning for each classification.

OBJECTIVE 5

Exercise 7-47 Expenditures After Acquisition

The following expenditures were incurred during the year:

a. Paid $4,000 for an overhaul of an automobile engine.
b. Paid $20,000 to add capacity to a cellular phone company's wireless network.
c. Paid $200 for routine maintenance of a manufacturing machine.
d. Paid $10,000 to remodel an office building.
e. Paid $300 for ordinary repairs

Required:

1. Classify the expenditures as either capital or revenue expenditures.
2. **CONCEPTUAL CONNECTION** If management improperly classified these expenditures, what would be the impact on the financial statements?

OBJECTIVE 6

Exercise 7-48 Revision of Depreciation

On January 1, the Kelley Company ledger showed a building with a cost of $250,000 and related accumulated depreciation of $96,000. The depreciation resulted from using straight-line depreciation with a useful life of 20 years and no residual value. On this date, Kelley determined that the building had a remaining useful life of 16 years and a residual value of $14,000.

Required:

Determine the depreciation expense for the year.

OBJECTIVE 6

Exercise 7-49 Revision of Depreciation

On January 1, 2021, Blizzards-R-Us purchased a snow-blowing machine for $125,000. The machine was expected to have a residual value of $12,000 at the end of its 5-year useful life. On January 1, 2023, Blizzards-R-Us concluded that the machine would have a remaining useful life of 6 years with a residual value of $3,600.

Required:

1. Determine the revised annual depreciation expense for 2023 using the straight-line method.
2. **CONCEPTUAL CONNECTION** How does the revision in depreciation affect the Blizzards-R-Us financial statements?

OBJECTIVE 5 6

Exercise 7-50 Expenditures After Acquisition

Roanoke Manufacturing placed a robotic arm on a large assembly machine on January 1. At that time, the assembly machine was expected to last another 3 years. The following information is available concerning the assembly machine.

Cost, assembly machine	$750,000
Accumulated depreciation, Jan. 1	480,000

The robotic arm cost $225,000 and was expected to extend the useful life of the machine by 3 years. Therefore, the useful life of the assembly machine, after the arm replacement, is 6 years. The assembly machine is expected to have a residual value of $120,000 at the end of its useful life.

Required:

1. Prepare the journal entry necessary to record the addition of the robotic arm.
2. Compute the revised amount of depreciation expense for the machine using the straight-line method, and prepare the necessary journal entry.
3. What is the book value of the machine at December 31?
4. **CONCEPTUAL CONNECTION** What would have been the effect on the financial statements if Roanoke had expensed the addition of the robotic arm?

Exercise 7-51 Expenditures After Acquisition and Depreciation

OBJECTIVE 5 6

Eastern National Bank installed a wireless encryption device in January 2019. The device cost $120,000. At the time the device was installed, Eastern estimated that it would have an expected life of 8 years and a residual value of $10,000. By 2022, the bank's business had expanded and modifications to the device were necessary. At the beginning of 2023, Eastern spent $35,000 on modifications for the device. Eastern estimates that the new expected life of the device (from January 2023) is 6 years and the new residual value is $4,000. Eastern uses the straight-line method of depreciation. Had Eastern not modified the device, it estimates that processing delays would have caused the bank to lose at least $50,000 of business per year.

Required:

1. Compute the accumulated depreciation for the device at the time the modifications were made (4 years after acquisition).
2. What is the book value of the device before and after the modification?
3. What will be annual straight-line depreciation expense for the device after the modification?
4. **CONCEPTUAL CONNECTION** The bank's president notes, "Since the after-modification, depreciation expense exceeds the before-modification depreciation expense. This modification was a poor idea." Comment on the president's assertion.

Exercise 7-52 Disposal of Fixed Asset

OBJECTIVE 7

Perfect Auto Rentals sold one of its cars on January 1. Perfect had acquired the car 2 years earlier for $23,400. At acquisition, Perfect assumed that the car would have an estimated life of 3 years and a residual value of $3,000. Assume that Perfect had properly used the straight-line depreciation method in previous years.

Required:

1. Prepare the journal entry to record the sale of the car assuming the car sold for (a) $9,800 cash, (b) $7,500 cash, and (c) $11,500 cash.
2. How should the gain or loss on the disposition (if any) be reported on the income statement?

Exercise 7-53 Disposal of Fixed Asset

OBJECTIVE 7

Pacifica Manufacturing retired a computerized metal stamping machine on December 31, 2023. Pacifica sold the machine to another company and did not replace it. The following data are available for the machine:

Cost (installed), Jan. 1, 2018	$880,000
Residual value estimated on Jan. 1, 2018	60,000
Estimated life as of Jan. 1, 2018	10 years

The machine was sold for $225,000 cash. Pacifica uses the straight-line method of depreciation.

Required:

1. Prepare the journal entry to record depreciation expense for 2023.
2. Compute accumulated depreciation at December 31, 2023.
3. Prepare the journal entry to record the sale of the machine.
4. **CONCEPTUAL CONNECTION** Explain how the disposal of the fixed asset would affect the 2019 financial statements. Ignore income taxes.

OBJECTIVE 3 4 5 7

Exercise 7-54 Depreciation and Disposal of Fixed Assets

Stanley Company reported the following information regarding its equipment:

Account	Amount
Equipment, Jan. 1	$745,120
Equipment, Dec. 31	831,410
Accumulated depreciation, Jan. 1	224,350
Accumulated depreciation, Dec. 31	257,690
Capital expenditures	148,735
Accumulated depreciation on equipment sold	50,320
Cash received for equipment sold	14,150

Required:

1. What journal entry did Stanley make to record depreciation expense?
2. What journal entry did Stanley make to record the disposal of the equipment?

OBJECTIVE 8

Exercise 7-55 Analyze Fixed Assets

Tabor Industries is a technology company that operates in a highly competitive environment. In 2020, management had significantly curtailed its capital expenditures due to cash flow problems. Tabor reported the following information for 2023:

- Net fixed assets (beginning of year), $489,000
- Net fixed assets (end of year), $505,000
- Net sales, $1,025,000
- Accumulated depreciation (end of year), $543,000
- Depreciation expense, $126,000

An analyst reviewing Tabor's financial history noted that Tabor had previously reported fixed asset turnover ratios and average age of its assets as follows:

	2018	2019	2020	2021	2022
Fixed asset turnover	2.48	2.45	2.74	2.57	2.33
Average age of assets (years)	1.81	1.79	1.94	2.81	3.74

During this time frame, the industry average fixed asset turnover ratio is 2.46 and the industry average age of assets is 1.79 years.

Required:

1. Compute Tabor's fixed asset turnover ratio for 2023.
2. Compute the average age of Tabor's fixed assets for 2023.
3. **CONCEPTUAL CONNECTION** Comment on Tabor's fixed asset turnover ratios and the average age of the fixed assets.

OBJECTIVE 9

Exercise 7-56 Acquisition and Amortization of Intangible Assets

TLM Technologies had these transactions related to intangible assets during the year.

Jan. 2	Purchased a patent from Luna Industries for $175,000. The remaining legal life of the patent is 15 years, and TLM expects the patent to be useful for 8 years.
Jan. 5	Paid legal fees in a successful legal defense of the patent of $90,000.
June 29	Registered a trademark with the federal government. Registration costs were $4,000. TLM expects to use the trademark indefinitely.
Sept. 2	Paid research and development costs of $478,200.

Required:

1. Prepare the journal entries necessary to record the transactions.
2. Prepare the entries necessary to record amortization expense for the intangible assets.
3. What is the balance of the intangible assets at the end of the year?

Exercise 7-57 Balance Sheet Presentation

OBJECTIVE 1 3 4 8 9

The following information relates to the assets of Westfield Semiconductors as of December 31. Westfield uses the straight-line method for depreciation and amortization.

Asset	Acquisition Cost	Expected Life	Residual Value	Time Used
Land	$104,300	Infinite	$100,000	10 years
Building	430,000	25 years	30,000	10 years
Machine	285,000	5 years	10,000	2 years
Patent	80,000	10 years	0	3 years
Truck	21,000	100,000 miles	3,000	44,000 miles

SHOW ME HOW

Required:

Use the information above to prepare the property, plant, and equipment and intangible assets portions of a classified balance sheet for Westfield.

Exercise 7-58 Amortization of Intangibles

OBJECTIVE 9

On January 1, Boulder Investments Inc. acquired a franchise to operate a Burger Doodle restaurant. Boulder paid $225,000 for a 10-year franchise and incurred organization costs of $15,000.

Required:

1. Prepare the journal entry to record the cash payment for the franchise fee and the organization costs.
2. Prepare the journal entry to record the annual amortization expense at the end of the first year.

Exercise 7-59 Depletion of Natural Resources

OBJECTIVE 10

Brandon Oil Company recently purchased oil and natural gas reserves in a remote part of Alaska for $1,850,000. Brandon spent $10,000,000 preparing the oil for extraction from the ground. Brandon estimates that 108,000,000 barrels of oil will be extracted from the ground. The land has a residual value of $20,000. During the year, 15,000,000 barrels are extracted from the ground.

Required:

Calculate the amount of depletion taken in the current year. (*Note:* Use two decimal points for calculations.)

Exercise 7-60 Depletion Rate

OBJECTIVE 10

SHOW ME HOW

Oxford Quarries purchased 45 acres of land for $185,000. The land contained stone that Oxford will remove from the ground, finish, and then sell as facing material for buildings. Oxford spent $435,000 preparing the quarry for operation. Oxford estimates that the quarry contains 55,000 tons of usable stone and that it will require 6 years to remove all the usable stone once quarrying begins. Upon completion of quarrying, Oxford estimates that the land will have a residual value of $11,150. During the current year, Oxford extracted 8,500 tons of stone.

Required:

1. Compute the depletion rate per ton.
2. Prepare the journal entry to record the extraction of the stone.

Exercise 7-61 Depletion of Timber

OBJECTIVE 10

Bedford Ridge Development purchased a 5,000-acre tract of forested land in southern Georgia. The tract contained about 1,650,000 pine trees that, when mature, can be used for utility poles. Bedford paid $800 per acre for the timberland. The land has a residual value of $107 per acre when all the trees are harvested. During the year, Bedford harvested 180,000 trees.

(Continued)

Required:
1. Compute the depletion per tree.
2. Prepare the journal entry to record the harvesting of the trees.

OBJECTIVE **11**

Exercise 7-62 *(Appendix 7A)* Impairment

On January 1, 2016, the Key West Company acquired a pie-making machine for $75,000. The machine was expected to have a useful life of 10 years with no residual value. Key West uses the straight-line depreciation method. On January 1, 2023, due to technological changes in the bakery industry, Key West believed that the asset might be impaired. Key West estimates the machine will generate net cash flows of $12,000 and has a current fair value of $10,000.

Required:
1. What is the book value of the machine on January 1, 2023?
2. Compute the loss related to the impairment.
3. Prepare the journal entry necessary to record the impairment of the machine.

PROBLEM SET A

OBJECTIVE **1**

Problem 7-63A Financial Statement Presentation of Operating Assets

Olympic Acquisitions Inc. prepared the following post-closing trial balance at December 31:

	Debit	Credit
Cash	$ 5,400	
Accounts Receivable	16,200	
Supplies	25,800	
Land	42,350	
Buildings	155,900	
Equipment	278,650	
Truck	31,100	
Franchise	49,600	
Goodwill	313,500	
Natural Resources	94,600	
Accounts Payable		$ 4,250
Accumulated Depreciation (Buildings)		112,000
Accumulated Depreciation (Equipment)		153,000
Accumulated Depreciation (Truck)		16,300
Wages Payable		6,850
Interest Payable		7,125
Income Taxes Payable		12,125
Notes Payable (due in 8 years)		185,550
Common Stock		304,500
Retained Earnings		211,400
Totals	$1,013,100	$1,013,100

Required:

Prepare a classified balance sheet for Olympic at December 31. (*Note:* Olympic reports the three categories of operating assets in separate subsections of assets.)

Problem 7-64A Cost of a Fixed Asset

OBJECTIVE ▸ 2

Mist City Car Wash purchased a new brushless car-washing machine for one of its bays. The machine cost $41,700. Mist City borrowed the purchase price from its bank on a 1-year, 8% note payable. Mist City paid $975 to have the machine transported to its place of business and an additional $200 in shipping insurance. Mist City incurred the following costs as a part of the installation:

Plumbing	$2,150
Electrical	1,125
Water (for testing the machine)	20
Soap (for testing the machine)	10

During the testing process, one of the motors became defective when soap and water entered the motor because its cover had not been installed properly by Mist City's employees. The motor was replaced at a cost of $640.

Required:

1. Compute the cost of the car-washing machine.
2. **CONCEPTUAL CONNECTION** Explain why any costs were excluded from the cost of the machine.

Problem 7-65A Depreciation Methods

OBJECTIVE ▸ 3 4

Hansen Supermarkets purchased a radio frequency identification (RFID) system for one of its stores at a cost of $190,000. Hansen determined that the system had an expected life of 8 years (or 50,000,000 items scanned) and an expected residual value of $12,000.

Required:

1. Determine the amount of depreciation expense for the first and second years of the system's life using the (a) straight-line and (b) double-declining-balance depreciation methods.
2. If the number of items scanned the first and second years were 6,100,000 and 5,600,000, respectively, compute the amount of depreciation expense for the first and second years of the system's life using the units-of-production depreciation method.
3. Compute the book values for all three depreciation methods as of the end of the first and second years of the system's life.
4. **CONCEPTUAL CONNECTION** What factors might management consider when selecting among depreciation methods?

Problem 7-66A Depreciation Schedules

OBJECTIVE ▸ 3 4

Wendt Corporation acquired a new depreciable asset for $94,000. The asset has a 4-year expected life and a residual value of zero.

Required:

1. Prepare a depreciation schedule for all 4 years of the asset's expected life using the straight-line depreciation method.
2. Prepare a depreciation schedule for all 4 years of the asset's expected life using the double-declining-balance depreciation method.
3. **CONCEPTUAL CONNECTION** What questions should be asked about this asset to decide which depreciation method to use?

Problem 7-67A Expenditures After Acquisition

OBJECTIVE ▸ 3 4 5

Pasta, a restaurant specializing in fresh pasta, installed a pasta cooker 3 years ago at a cost of $12,400. The cooker had an expected life of 5 years and a residual value of $900 when installed. As the restaurant's business increased, it became apparent that renovations would be necessary so the cooker's output could be increased. After 3 years of use, Pasta spent $8,200 to install

(Continued)

new heating equipment and $4,100 to add pressure-cooking capability. After these renovations, Pasta estimated that the remaining useful life of the cooker was 10 years and that the residual value was now $1,500.

Required:

1. Compute 1 year's straight-line depreciation expense on the cooker before the renovations.
2. Assume that 3 full years of straight-line depreciation expense had been recorded on the cooker before the renovations were made. Compute the book value of the cooker immediately after the renovations were made.
3. Compute 1 year's straight-line depreciation expense on the renovated cooker.

OBJECTIVE `5`

Problem 7-68A Repair Decision

Clermont Transit operates a summer ferry service to islands in the Ohio River. Farmers use the ferry to move farming equipment to and from the islands. Clermont's ferry is in need of repair. A new engine and steering assembly must be installed, or the Coast Guard will not permit the ferry to be used. Because of competition, Clermont will not be able to raise its rates for ferry service if these repairs are made. Costs of providing the ferry service will not be decreased if the repairs are made.

Required:

1. Identify the factors that Clermont should consider when evaluating whether or not to make the repairs.
2. **CONCEPTUAL CONNECTION** Since the revenue rate cannot be increased and costs will not be decreased if the repairs are made, can the cost of the repairs be capitalized? Why or why not?

OBJECTIVE `7`

Problem 7-69A Disposition of Fixed Assets

In order to provide capital for new hotel construction in other locations, Wilton Hotel Corporation has decided to sell its hotel in Pierre, South Dakota. Wilton auctions the hotel and its contents on October 1 with the following results:

Land	$600,000
Building	225,000
Furniture	120,000

Wilton's accounting records reveal the following information about the assets sold:

Asset	Acquisition Cost	Accumulated Depreciation
Land	$ 55,000	
Building	350,000	$155,000
Furniture	285,500	133,000

Required:

1. Prepare a separate journal entry to record the disposition of each of these assets.
2. **CONCEPTUAL CONNECTION** Explain how the disposals of the fixed assets above would affect the current period financial statements.

OBJECTIVE `9` `10`

Problem 7-70A Natural Resource and Intangible Accounting

McLeansboro Oil Company acquired a small oil company with only three assets during a recent year. The assets were acquired for $1,350,000 cash.

Asset	Fair Value	Expected Life
Oil	$1,125,000	55,000 barrels
Land	78,000	Indefinite
Equipment	62,000	550,000 barrels

Required:

1. Prepare the entry to record this acquisition in McLeansboro's journal. (*Hint:* Record the cost in excess of fair value as goodwill.)
2. If McLeansboro pumps and sells 11,000 barrels of oil in 1 year, compute the amount of depletion.
3. Prepare journal entries to record depletion for the 11,000 barrels of oil pumped and sold.
4. **CONCEPTUAL CONNECTION** Is the goodwill amortized? Explain your reasoning.
5. **CONCEPTUAL CONNECTION** Why are the land and the equipment capitalized separately from the oil well?

Problem 7-71A Accounting for Intangible Assets

OBJECTIVE ◀ 9

On January 1, 2017, Technocraft Inc. acquired a patent that was used for manufacturing semiconductor-based electronic circuitry. The patent was originally recorded in Technocraft's ledger at its cost of $1,780,000. Technocraft has been amortizing the patent using the straight-line method over an expected economic life of 10 years. Residual value was assumed to be zero. Technocraft sued another company for infringing on its patent. On January 1, 2024, Technocraft spent $50,000 on this suit and won a judgment to recover the $50,000 plus damages of $200,000. The sued company paid the $250,000.

Required:

1. Compute and record amortization expense on the patent for 2023 (prior to the lawsuit).
2. Prepare the necessary journal entry on January 1, 2024, to record the expenditure of $50,000 to defend the patent.
3. Prepare the journal entry to record the award of $250,000 on January 1, 2024.
4. Indicate the entry you would have made had Technocraft lost the suit. (*Note:* Assume that the patent would be valueless if Technocraft had lost the suit.)
5. **CONCEPTUAL CONNECTION** What are the financial statement effects of capitalizing or expensing the cost of defending the patent?

PROBLEM SET B

Problem 7-63B Financial Statement Presentation of Operating Assets

OBJECTIVE ◀ 1

Athens Inc. prepared the following post-closing trial balance at December 31:

	Debit	Credit
Cash	$ 3,325	
Accounts Receivable	27,975	
Prepaid Insurance	8,350	
Land	21,150	
Buildings	305,520	
Equipment	126,310	
Patent	9,970	
Goodwill	42,400	
Natural Resources	134,800	
Accounts Payable		$ 7,775
Accumulated Depreciation (Buildings)		101,950
Accumulated Depreciation (Equipment)		47,875
Unearned Revenue		9,825
Interest Payable		3,625
Income Taxes Payable		17,150
Notes Payable (due in 10 years)		170,000
Common Stock		125,000
Retained Earnings		196,600
Totals	$679,800	$679,800

(*Continued*)

Required:

Prepare a classified balance sheet for Athens at December 31. (*Note:* Athens reports the three categories of operating assets in separate subsections of assets.)

OBJECTIVE ▶2▶ **Problem 7-64B Cost of a Fixed Asset**

Metropolis Country Club purchased a new tractor to be used for golf course maintenance. The tractor cost $64,200. Metropolis borrowed the purchase price from its bank on a 1-year, 7% note payable. Metropolis incurred the following costs:

Shipping costs	$925
Shipping insurance	180
Calibration of cutting height	75

Required:
1. Compute the cost of the tractor.
2. **CONCEPTUAL CONNECTION** Explain why any costs were excluded from the cost of the tractor.

OBJECTIVE ▶3▶ ▶4▶ **Problem 7-65B Depreciation Methods**

Graphic Design Inc. purchased a state-of-the-art laser engraving machine for $65,200. Graphic Design determined that the system had an expected life of 10 years (or 1,500,000 items engraved) and an expected residual value of $8,200.

Required:
1. Determine the amount of depreciation expense for the first and second years of the machine's life using the (a) straight-line and (b) double-declining-balance depreciation methods.
2. If the number of items engraved the first and second years was 120,000 and 135,000, respectively, compute the amount of depreciation expense for the first and second years of the machine's life using the units-of-production depreciation method.
3. Compute the book values for all three depreciation methods as of the end of the first and second years of the system's life.
4. **CONCEPTUAL CONNECTION** What factors might management consider when selecting among depreciation methods?

OBJECTIVE ▶3▶ ▶4▶ **Problem 7-66B Depreciation Schedules**

Dunn Corporation acquired a new depreciable asset for $135,000. The asset has a 5-year expected life and a residual value of zero.

Required:
1. Prepare a depreciation schedule for all 5 years of the asset's expected life using the straight-line depreciation method.
2. Prepare a depreciation schedule for all 5 years of the asset's expected life using the double-declining-balance depreciation method.
3. **CONCEPTUAL CONNECTION** What questions should be asked about this asset to decide which depreciation method to use?

OBJECTIVE ▶3▶ ▶4▶ ▶5▶ **Problem 7-67B Expenditures After Acquisition**

Murray's Fish Market, a store that specializes in providing fresh fish to the Nashville, Tennessee, area, installed a new refrigeration unit 2 years ago at a cost of $27,500. The refrigeration unit has an expected life of 8 years and a residual value of $500 when installed. As the fish market's business increased, it became apparent that renovations were necessary so that the capacity of the refrigeration unit could be increased. After 2 years of use, Murray's spent $18,785 to install an additional refrigerated display unit (that was connected to the original unit) and replace the refrigeration coils. After this addition and renovation, Murray's Fish Market estimated that the remaining useful life of the original refrigeration unit was 12 years and that the residual value was now $1,000.

Required:

1. Compute 1 year's straight-line depreciation expense on the refrigeration unit before the addition and renovations.
2. Assume that 2 full years of straight-line depreciation expense were recorded on the refrigeration unit before the addition and renovations were made. Compute the book value of the refrigeration unit immediately after the renovations were made.
3. Compute 1 year's straight-line depreciation expense on the renovated refrigeration unit. Round your answer to the nearest dollar.

Problem 7-68B Remodeling Decision

OBJECTIVE 5

Ferinni Company operates a travel agency out of a historic building in Smalltown. Ferinni's CEO believes that the building needs to be remodeled in order to reach a wider customer base. The CEO proposes building a new entry that would be adjacent to Main Street in order to attract more foot traffic. The current entry faces a parking deck at the rear of the building and is easily overlooked by customers. The new entry will require the rearrangement of several offices inside the building. Because of competition from Internet travel sites, Ferinni will not be able to raise rates for its travel service after the remodeling is made.

Required:

1. Identify the factors that Ferinni should consider when evaluating whether to remodel the building.
2. **CONCEPTUAL CONNECTION** Since the revenue rate cannot be increased, can the cost of the remodeling be capitalized? Why or why not?

Problem 7-69B Disposition of Operating Assets

OBJECTIVE 7

Salva Pest Control disposed of four assets recently. Salva's accounting records provided the following information about the assets at the time of their disposal:

Asset	Cost	Accumulated Depreciation
Pump	$ 6,200	$ 4,800
Truck	18,600	17,500
Furniture	4,200	3,850
Chemical testing apparatus	6,800	4,000

The truck was sold for $2,450 cash, and the chemical testing apparatus was donated to the local high school. Because the pump was contaminated with pesticides, $500 in cash was paid to a chemical disposal company to decontaminate the pump and dispose of it safely. The furniture was taken to the local landfill.

Required:

1. Prepare a separate journal entry to record the disposition of each of these assets.
2. **CONCEPTUAL CONNECTION** Explain how the disposals of the fixed assets would affect the current period financial statements.

Problem 7-70B Natural Resource and Intangible Accounting

OBJECTIVE 9 10

On January 1, Mudcat Gas Inc. purchased a small natural gas company with two assets—land and natural gas reserves—for $158,000,000. The fair value of the land was $1,500,000 and the fair value of the natural gas reserves was $155,250,000. At that time, estimated recoverable gas was 105,000,000 cubic feet.

(*Continued*)

Required:

1. Prepare the entry to record this acquisition in Mudcat's journal. (*Hint:* Record any cost in excess of fair value as goodwill.)
2. If Mudcat recovers and sells 2,500,000 cubic feet in a year, compute the depletion. Round your answer to the nearest dollar.
3. Prepare journal entries to record annual depletion at the end of the year for the 2,500,000 cubic feet of natural gas recovered and sold. For purposes of this entry, assume the depletion and sale are recorded at December 31.
4. **CONCEPTUAL CONNECTION** Is the goodwill amortized? Explain your reasoning.
5. **CONCEPTUAL CONNECTION** Why is the land capitalized separately from the natural gas reserves?

OBJECTIVE

Problem 7-71B Accounting for Intangible Assets

Blackford and Medford Publishing Company own the copyrights on many top authors. On January 5, Blackford and Medford acquired the copyright on the literary works of Susan Monroe, an underground novelist in the 1960s, for $825,000 cash. Due to a recent resurgence of interest in the 1960s, the copyright has an estimated economic life of 5 years. The residual value is estimated to be zero.

Required:

1. Prepare a journal entry to record the acquisition of the copyright.
2. Compute and record the annual amortization expense for the copyright.

CASES

Case 7-72 Ethics, Internal Controls, and the Capitalization Decision

James Sage, an assistant controller in a large company, has a friend and former classmate, Henry Cactus, who sells computers. Sage agrees to help Cactus get part of the business that has been going to a large national computer manufacturer for many years. Sage knows that the controller would not approve a shift away from the national supplier but believes that he can authorize a number of small orders for equipment that will escape the controller's notice. Company policy requires that all capital expenditures be approved by a management committee; however, expenditures under $2,000 are considered expenses and are subject to much less scrutiny. The assistant controller orders four computers to be used in a distant branch office. In order to keep the size of the order down, he makes four separate orders over a period of several months.

Required:

1. What are the probable consequences of this behavior for the company? For the assistant controller?
2. Describe internal control procedures that would be effective in discouraging and detecting this kind of behavior.

Case 7-73 Management's Depreciation Decision

Great Basin Enterprises, a large holding company, acquired North Spruce Manufacturing, a medium-sized manufacturing business, from its founder who wishes to retire. Despite great potential for development, North Spruce's income has been dropping in recent years. Great Basin has installed a new management group (including a new controller, Christie Carmichael) at North Spruce and has given the group 6 years to expand and revitalize the operations. Management compensation includes a bonus based on net income generated by the North Spruce operations. If North Spruce does not show considerable improvement by the end of the sixth year, Great Basin will consider selling it. The new management immediately makes significant investments in new equipment but finds that new revenues develop slowly. Most of the new equipment will be replaced in 8 to 10 years. To defer income taxes to the maximum extent, Ms. Carmichael uses accelerated depreciation methods and the minimum allowable "expected lives" for the new equipment, which average 5 years. In preparing financial statements, Ms. Carmichael uses the straight-line depreciation method and expected lives that average 12 years for the new equipment.

Required:

1. Why did the controller compute depreciation expense on the financial statements as she did?
2. What are the possible consequences of the controller's decision on the amount of depreciation expense shown on the financial statements if this decision goes unchallenged?

Case 7-74 Effect of Estimates of Life and Residual Value on Depreciation Expense

Hattiesburg Manufacturing purchased a new computer-integrated system to manufacture a group of fabricated metal and plastic products. The equipment was purchased from Bessemer Systems at a cost of $550,000. As a basis for determining annual depreciation expense, Hattiesburg's controller requests estimates of the expected life and residual value for the new equipment. The engineering and production departments submit the following divergent estimates:

	Engineering Department Estimates	Production Department Estimates
Expected life	10 years	8 years
Residual value	$90,000	0

Before considering depreciation expense for the new equipment, Hattiesburg Manufacturing has net income in the amount of $250,000. Hattiesburg uses the straight-line method of depreciation.

Required:

1. Compute a full year's depreciation expense for the new equipment, using each of the two sets of estimates.
2. Ignoring income taxes, what will be the effect on net income of including a full year's depreciation expense based on the engineering estimates? Based on the production estimates?
3. If a business has a significant investment in depreciable assets, the expected life and residual value estimates can materially affect depreciation expense and therefore net income. What might motivate management to use the highest or lowest estimates? How would cash outflows for income taxes be affected by the estimates?

Case 7-75 Research and Analysis Using the Annual Report

Obtain **Verizon Communications, Inc.**'s 2019 annual report either through the "Investor Relations" portion of its website (do a web search for Verizon Communications investor relations) or go to www.sec.gov and click "Company Filings Search" under "Filings."

Required:

1. What method of depreciation does Verizon use? What are the typical useful lives of Verizon's operating assets?
2. What is the cost of Verizon's property, plant, and equipment on December 31, 2019? List the major components of Verizon's property, plant, and equipment.
3. What amount of accumulated depreciation is associated with property, plant, and equipment as of December 31, 2019?

(Continued)

4. Refer to the statement of cash flows:
   a. What is the amount of depreciation and amortization expense reported for each of the last 3 years?
   b. How much did Verizon spend on the acquisition of operating assets (capital expenditures) in each of the last 3 years?
   c. How much property, plant, and equipment was disposed of in 2019? (*Hint:* Also refer to the balance sheet.)
   d. Is the change in depreciation and amortization expense consistent with the pattern of capital expenditures observed? Why or why not?
5. What is the change in accumulated depreciation for the most recent year? Is this change explained by the depreciation and amortization expense reported? If not, what other items might cause accumulated depreciation to change?
6. Describe Verizon's capital expenditure plans for the future. (*Hint:* Refer to the Management Discussion and Analysis section.)
7. Explain Verizon's accounting policy with regard to intangible assets. (*Hint:* Refer to Note 1.)
8. List the types of intangible assets that Verizon possesses. What is Verizon's largest intangible asset?

Case 7-76 Comparative Analysis: Kroger versus Sprouts

Refer to the 10-K reports of **Kroger** and **Sprouts** that are available for download from the companion website at Cengage.com.

Required:
1. With regard to depreciation methods:
   a. What depreciation method does Kroger use? What depreciation method does Sprouts use?
   b. What are the typical useful lives of each company's operating assets?
   c. What effect will the useful lives have on the company's financial statements?
2. Refer to the statement of cash flows:
   a. What is the amount of depreciation and amortization expense that each company reported for the 3 years presented?
   b. How much did each company spend on the acquisition of operating assets (capital expenditures) in each of the last 3 years?
   c. Is the change in depreciation and amortization expense consistent with the pattern of capital expenditures observed? Why or why not?
3. Compute the fixed asset turnover and the average age of fixed assets for each company for 2016. What conclusions can you draw from these ratios?

ANNUAL REPORT PROBLEM

HOME DEPOT

Download the 10-K for **Home Depot** from the companion website at Cengage.com.

Required:
1. What amounts does Home Depot report for the following accounts for the most current fiscal year?
   - Land
   - Buildings
   - Equipment
   - Other PP&E
   - Accumulated depreciation
   - Net property, plant, and equipment
   - Sales
2. Assume that Home Depot projects the following:
   - Investment in property, plant, and equipment is expected to grow by 10% in the next fiscal year.

- Accumulated depreciation and amortization will increase at a similar rate.
- Net sales are expected to increase 2%.

Assume all other items remain unchanged from the prior year. Provide the next year's forecasted balances for Land, Buildings, Equipment, Other PP&E, Accumulated Depreciation, Net Property, Plant, and Equipment, and Sales.

3. Answer the following for the next fiscal year:

    a. What depreciation method is used?

    b. Assuming a useful life of 10 years and no residual value, what is the forecasted amount of depreciation expense?

    c. What is the estimated life of Home Depot's buildings?

    d. What is the forecasted fixed asset turnover ratio? Round to two decimal places.

    e. What is the forecasted average age of fixed assets? Round to two decimal places.

    f. What is forecasted depreciation expense as a percentage of net sales? Round to two decimal places.

Note: *While the Annual Report problems in the textbook are static, when assigned in CNOW, these activities are algorithmic and the answers may vary from what appears in the Solutions Manual.*

CONTINUING PROBLEM

FRONT ROW ENTERTAINMENT

After a successful first year, Cam and Anna decide to expand Front Row Entertainment's operations by becoming a venue operator as well as a tour promoter. A venue operator contracts with promoters to rent the venue (which can range from amphitheaters to indoor arenas to nightclubs) for specific events on specific dates. In addition to receiving revenue from renting the venue, venue operators also provide services such as concessions, parking, security, and ushering services. By vertically integrating their business, Cam and Anna can reduce the expense that they pay to rent venues. In addition, they will generate additional revenue by providing services to other tour promoters.

After a little investigation, Cam and Anna locate a small venue operator that owns The Chicago Music House, a small indoor arena with a rich history in the music industry. The current owner has experienced severe health issues and has let the arena fall into a state of disrepair. However, he would like the arena to be preserved and its musical legacy to continue. After a short negotiation, on January 1, 2024, Front Row purchases the venue by paying $10,000 in cash and signing a 15-year, 10% note for $380,000. In addition, Front Row purchases the right to use the "Chicago Music House" name for $25,000 cash.

During the month of January 2024, Front Row incurred the following expenditures as they renovated the arena and prepared it for the first major event scheduled for February.

Jan. 5 Paid $21,530 to repair damage to the roof of the arena.
  10   Paid $45,720 to remodel the stage area.
  21   Purchased concessions equipment (e.g., popcorn poppers, soda machines) for $12,350.

Renovations were completed on January 28, and the first concert was held in the arena on February 1. The arena is expected to have a useful life of 30 years and a residual value of $35,000. The concessions equipment will have a useful life of 5 years and a residual value of $250.

Required:

1. Prepare the journal entries to record the acquisition of the arena, the concessions equipment, and the trademark.

2. Prepare the journal entries to record the expenditures made in January.

3. Compute and record the depreciation for 2024 (11 months) on the arena (use the straight-line method) and on the concessions equipment (use the double-declining-balance method). Round all answers to the nearest dollar.

4. Would amortization expense be recorded for the trademark? Why or why not?

Integrating Asset Accounting

Obtain **Apple**'s fiscal year 2019 10-K (filed October 31, 2019) either from the "Investor Relations" portion of its website (do a web search for "Apple Investor Relations") or from www.sec.gov by clicking "Company Filings Search" under "Forms."

Required:

Using Apple's 10-K, answer the following questions:

1. Looking at Note 1 (*Summary of Significant Accounting Policies*), how does Apple define cash equivalents?

2. Looking at the "Report of Independent Registered Public Accounting Firm," supplying an opinion on Apple's internal controls over financial reporting (p. 58 of the 10-K), what was the auditor's opinion regarding the effectiveness of Apple's internal control over financial reporting? What criteria were used to evaluate the effectiveness of these controls?

3. What were Apple's accounts receivable turnovers (rounded to two decimal places) in 2018 and 2019? (Accounts receivable were $17,874 million at the end of 2017.) Assuming the industry average for 2019 was 8.22 times per year, describe Apple's relative efficiency with its accounts receivable.

4. What were Apple's inventory turnovers (rounded to two decimal places) in 2018 and 2019? (Inventories were $4,855 million at the end of 2017.) Assuming the industry average for 2017 was 20.24 times per year, describe Apple's relative efficiency with its inventory.

5. Describe the trend in Apple's accounts receivable and inventory turnover.

6. How many days' sales does Apple have in receivables and inventory for 2018 and 2019? (When added together, this is its operating cycle.) (*Note:* Round all answers to two decimal places.)

7. **CONCEPTUAL CONNECTION** Assuming 10% interest, how much interest expense did Apple incur due to its lengthening operating cycle (remember that the numbers are in millions)?

8. What were Apple's gross profit, operating margin, and net profit ratios in 2019? (*Note:* Round answers to two decimal places.) Assuming industry averages for 2019 were 27.57%, 7.87%, and 4.76%, respectively, describe Apple's profitability.

9. Looking at Note 1 (*Summary of Significant Accounting Policies*), what method of depreciation does Apple use? What is the range of useful life for internally used software? Do you think this useful life is appropriate?

8

Current and Contingent Liabilities

After studying Chapter 8, you should be able to:

1 Explain liability recognition and measurement criteria.

2 Identify the kinds of activities that produce current liabilities and prepare journal entries for these activities.

3 Describe contingent liabilities and the alternatives for their recognition and measurement.

4 Calculate warranty liabilities and warranty expense and prepare the necessary journal entries.

5 Analyze short-term liquidity using information contained in the current liabilities section.

EXPERIENCE FINANCIAL ACCOUNTING

with Starbucks

Investors and creditors assess the risk that a company will be unable to pay its current liabilities as they come due. Failure to pay current liabilities can lead to suppliers refusing to sell needed inventory or supplies, employees leaving because they fear the company is failing, among other problems. Consequently, even companies with good business models can be forced into bankruptcy by its inability to pay its current obligations, often termed a "liquidity crisis" or "short-term credit crunch."

A classic example of a liquidity crisis is a run on a bank. Recognize that one of a bank's obligations is the money they owe to their customers through checking and savings accounts. When depositors begin to lose faith in a bank, they will rush to withdraw their money. However, the bank does not have everyone's money sitting around in a vault; instead, the bank has loaned depositors' money to others (presumably at a higher interest rate than savings and checking accounts return).

To assess the risk that a company will be unable to pay its current liabilities (i.e., its short-term liquidity risk), financial statement users will examine the sufficiency of cash generated from current assets and operations as well as the company's availability to raise cash through additional borrowings. **Starbucks'** current liabilities represent obligations to (a) suppliers (accounts payable), (b) employees, landlords, taxing authorities, shareholders, etc. (accrued liabilities), (c) customers (stored value card liability), and (d) long-term creditors (current portion of long-term debt), among others.

Starbucks Corp.
Consolidated Balance Sheets (Partial)
(in millions)

	Sept. 29, 2019	Sept. 30, 2018	Oct. 1, 2017	Oct. 2, 2016
Current assets:				
Cash and cash equivalents	$ 2,686.6	$ 8,756.3	$ 2,462.3	$ 2,128.8
Short-term investments	70.5	181.5	228.6	134.4
Accounts receivable, net	879.2	693.1	870.4	768.8
Inventories	1,529.4	1,400.5	1,364.0	1,378.5
Prepaid expenses and other current assets	488.2	1,462.8	358.1	347.4
Total current assets	**5,653.9**	**12,494.2**	**5,283.4**	**4,757.9**

(*Continued*)

Current liabilities:

Accounts payable	$ 1,189.7	$ 1,179.3	$ 782.5	$ 730.6
Accrued liabilities	1,753.7	1,752.5	1,934.5	1,999.1
Insurance reserves	–	–	215.2	246.0
Accrued payroll and benefits	664.6	656.8	–	–
Income taxes payable	1,291.7	102.8	–	–
Stored value card liability	1,269.0	1,642.9	1,288.5	1,171.2
Current portion of long-term debt	–	349.9	–	399.9
Total current liabilities	**6,168.7**	**5,684.2**	**4,220.7**	**4,546.8**
Current ratio (Current assets/ Current liabilities)	**0.92**	**2.20**	**1.25**	**1.05**

Note 9: Debt (excerpt)

Our $2.0 billion unsecured 5-year revolving credit facility and $1.0 billion unsecured 364-day credit facility are available for working capital, capital expenditures and other corporate purposes, including acquisitions and share repurchases.

Both credit facilities contain provisions requiring us to maintain compliance with certain covenants. As of September 29, 2019, we were in compliance with all applicable covenants. No amounts were outstanding under our credit facility as of September 29, 2019.

The current liabilities of approximately $6.17 billion make up roughly 24% of the company's total liabilities at the end of fiscal 2019. Further, Starbucks's current ratio is 0.92, indicating that they do not have sufficient current assets to cover their current liabilities. And, when this current ratio is compared with the current ratio of 2.20, 1.25, and 1.05 in the previous three years, we are right to be concerned with Starbucks's short-term solvency. However, in addition to examining the liquidity ratios, such as the current ratio, financial-statement users may also look at Starbucks's ability to obtain additional short-term financing should it face a credit crunch. Note 9 to the financial statements indicates that Starbucks can access $3.0 billion of unsecured financing from various banks by simply asking for the financing (they compensate these banks for this option, but it's there). With cash and short-term investments approaching $2.7 billion and significant borrowing capacity, Starbucks appears to be well positioned to meet its short-term obligations.

CURRENT AND CONTINGENT LIABILITIES

Chapters 4–7 explained accounting and reporting for assets. Now we will move to the other side of the balance sheet and discuss liabilities and equity, which are the sources of cash and other financial resources used to acquire assets. We begin by examining liabilities.

Finding potential creditors, arranging attractive credit terms, structuring borrowings with lenders, and arranging to have enough cash coming in to pay the liabilities as they come due are several of the most important managerial functions. The result of liability management and the accounting recognition, measurement, and reporting issues for those activities appears in the liabilities portion of the balance sheet. The information provided by **Live Nation Entertainment** in its 2019 balance sheet is typical:

Live Nation Entertainment Consolidated Balance Sheets (Partial) (in thousands) December 31, 2019	
LIABILITIES AND STOCKHOLDER'S EQUITY	
	2019
Current liabilities:	
Accounts payable, client accounts	$ 1,005,888
Accounts payable	100,237
Accrued expenses	1,391,486
Deferred revenue	1,391,032
Current portion of long-term debt, net	37,795
Current portion of operating lease liabilities	121,950
Other current liabilities	59,211
Total current liabilities	$ 4,107,599
Long-term debt, net	3,271,262
Long-term operating lease liabilities	1,374,481
Long-term deferred income taxes	178,173
Other long-term liabilities	130,648

Source: Live Nation 2019 10-K.

Naturally, existing and potential investors and creditors also find this information useful when they want to know about the obligations management has assumed.

In this chapter and the next we discuss the three kinds of business obligations: current liabilities, contingent liabilities, and long-term debt. Current liabilities are those obligations that are (1) expected to be retired with existing current assets or creation of new current liabilities and (2) due within 1 year or one operating cycle, whichever is longer. All other liabilities are considered long-term. Contingent liabilities can be either current or long-term, but they are "iffy" in two ways. They may or may not turn into actual obligations and, for those contingencies that do become obligations, the timing and amount of the required payment is uncertain. In this chapter we focus on current and contingent liabilities and address the following questions:

- When are liabilities recognized?
- How are liabilities measured?
- What kinds of activities produce current liabilities and how are they recorded in the accounting records?
- What are contingent liabilities and how are they recorded in the accounting records?
- How do you measure and record warranty liabilities?

RECOGNITION AND MEASUREMENT OF LIABILITIES

OBJECTIVE

Explain liability recognition and measurement criteria.

Liabilities are probable future sacrifices of economic benefits. These commitments, which arise from activities that have already occurred, require the business to transfer assets or provide services to another entity sometime in the future. For example, an account payable arises from a transaction in which the business receives goods or services in return for a cash payment at some future time.

Within this general definition, liabilities have a wide variety of characteristics, as shown in Exhibit 8.1:

EXHIBIT 8.1   **Characteristics of Liabilities**

Payment of cash:
Although liabilities frequently require the payment of cash, some may require the transfer of assets other than cash or the performance of services.

Certainty:
Although the exact amount and timing of future payments are usually known, for some liabilities they may not be.

Legal enforceability:
Although many liabilities are legally enforceable claims, some may represent merely *probable* claims.

Payment recipient:
Although liabilities usually identify the entity to be paid, the definition does not exclude payment to as yet unidentified recipients.

Thus, the future outflow associated with a liability may or may not involve the payment of cash, may or may not be known with certainty, may or may not be legally enforceable, and may or may not be payable to a known recipient.

RECOGNITION OF LIABILITIES

Most liabilities are recognized when goods or services are received or money is borrowed. When a liability depends on a future event (i.e., a **contingent liability**), such as the outcome of a lawsuit, recognition depends on how likely the occurrence of the event is and whether a good estimate of the payment amount can be made. If the future payment is judged to be less than likely to occur or the payment is not estimable, the obligation should not be recognized. Such obligations may require disclosure in footnotes to the financial statements, as explained later in this chapter.

MEASUREMENT OF LIABILITIES

We all know that when you owe money you typically pay interest. That is, if you borrow $100 at 10% interest, when you pay it back 1 year later you must repay $110:

$$\text{Total Payment} = \text{Principal} + (\text{Principal} \times \text{Interest Rate} \times \text{Period})$$
$$= \$100 + (\$100 \times 10\% \times 12/12)$$

Sometimes companies will appear to give you a 0% interest loan. For example, furniture and electronics retailers frequently advertise "no interest, no money down for 12 months" or similar terms. Of course, we know this really means that the "interest" is included in the sales price because no business is going to truly provide 0% interest.

In theory, the amount of the liability reported on the balance sheet should not include any interest that has not yet occurred. For example, on a balance sheet prepared 6 months after borrowing the $100 at 10% interest described above, you should report a liability of $105:

$$\$100 + (\$100 \times 10\% \times 6/12)$$

However, many liabilities are more like your credit card or utilities bill. For example, you might owe your power company $150 for the use of electricity during September. You likely do not receive this bill until sometime during October, and you do not have to pay it until near the end of November. Further, there appears to be no interest because you owe $150 whether you pay the bill when you receive it in October or wait until the November due date.

Despite the apparent lack of interest, theoretically interest exists. Consequently, in theory we should calculate the interest on such liabilities. For example, if we made a balance sheet at the end of September, then a liability for the power company should be calculated to exclude the theoretical interest included in the $150 payment at the end of November (i.e., 2 months' interest at the market rate). Fortunately, we ignore the interest for most current liabilities because the amount of interest is relatively small (i.e., "immaterial" as accountants say). So most current liabilities are simply recorded and reported at the total amount owed, as we will see in the next section.

CURRENT LIABILITIES

Current liabilities are obligations that require the firm to pay cash or another current asset, create a new current liability, or provide goods or services within the longer of 1 year or one operating cycle. Since most firms have operating cycles shorter than 1 year, the 1-year rule usually applies.

Some firms combine their current liabilities into a very short list, while others provide considerable detail. Exhibit 8.2 compares the current liabilities sections of the balance sheets for two airlines—**Southwest** and **UAL** (**United Airlines**). Although it's reasonable to assume that

OBJECTIVE 2

Identify the kinds of activities that produce current liabilities and prepare journal entries for these activities.

Current Liability Sections from Two Balance Sheets   **EXHIBIT 8.2**

Southwest Airlines Co.
Consolidated Balance Sheets
(in millions)

LIABILITIES AND SHAREHOLDERS' EQUITY

	December 31,	
	2019	2018
Current liabilities:		
Accounts payable	$1,574	$1,416
Accrued liabilities	1,749	1,749
Current operating lease liabilities	353	–
Air traffic liability	4,457	4,134
Current maturities of long-term debt	819	606
Total current liabilities	$8,952	$7,905

Source: Southwest Airlines Co. 2019 10-K.

United Continental Holdings, Inc.
Consolidated Balance Sheets
(in millions)

	December 31,	
	2019	2018
LIABILITIES AND SHAREHOLDERS' EQUITY		
Current liabilities:		
Advance ticket sales	$ 4,819	$ 4,381
Accounts payable	2,703	2,363
Frequent flyer deferred revenue	2,440	2,286
Accrued salaries and benefits	2,271	2,184
Current maturities of long-term debt	1,407	1,230
Current maturities of finance leases	46	123
Current maturities of operating leases	686	719
Other	566	553
	$14,938	$13,839

Source: United Continental Holdings, Inc. 2019 10-K.

both airlines have similar types of current liabilities, Southwest combines its into a relatively short list while UAL provides more detail. Further, UAL orders its individual current liabilities more or less from largest to smallest (with "other" at the end), while Southwest appears to order its current liabilities in the order in which the liabilities will be paid (order of liquidity).

In the sections that follow, we will briefly describe how various types of current liabilities arise and the principles that underlie their recognition, measurement, and reporting.

ACCOUNTS PAYABLE

An **account payable** arises when a business purchases goods or services on credit. It is really just the flip side of an account receivable—when you have a payable, the business you owe has a receivable. Credit terms generally require that the purchaser pay the amount due within 30 to 60 days and seldom require the payment of interest. Accounts payable do not require a formal agreement or contract. For example, your account with the power company usually does not require you to sign a formal contract.

You may recall from Chapter 5 that accounts receivable have some valuation issues related to estimating bad debts. Accounts payable, on the other hand, have no such issues. They are measured and reported at the total amount required to satisfy the account, which is the cost of the goods or services acquired. For example, if Game Time Sporting Goods buys and receives running shoes on May 15, 2023, for which it pays its supplier $2,000 on June 15, 2023, it would need to make the following journal entries:

Date	Account and Explanation	Debit	Credit	Assets	=	Liabilities	+	Stockholders' Equity
May 15	Inventory	2,000		▲				
	Accounts Payable		2,000			▲		
June 15	Accounts Payable	2,000				▼		
	Cash		2,000	▼				

ACCRUED LIABILITIES

Unlike accounts payable, which are recognized when goods or services change hands, **accrued liabilities** are recognized by adjusting entries at the end of a period. They usually represent the completed portion of activities that are in process. For example, Green Landscaping pays wages of $10,000 (or $1,000 per work day) to its employees every other Friday. The standard entry is:

Date	Account and Explanation	Debit	Credit	Assets	=	Liabilities	+	Stockholders' Equity
Dec. 20	Wages Expense	10,000						▼
	Cash		10,000	▼				

What happens, however, when December 31 falls on the Tuesday before the Friday payday? In this case, the expense for the 7 days that have already been worked (5 days from last week and Monday and Tuesday of this week) must be recognized in the proper period. Additionally, because the work has been performed but the employees have not yet been paid, Green Landscaping has a liability to its employees. As such, on December 31 Green would make the following adjusting entry:

Date	Account and Explanation	Debit	Credit	Assets	= Liabilities +	Stockholders' Equity
Dec. 31	Wages Expense	7,000				▼
	Wages Payable		7,000		▲	

Further, when Green pays $10,000 to its employees on January 3, pay for 3 days is an expense of the current year (Wednesday, January 1 through Friday, January 3) and 7 days' pay retires the Wages Payable from December 31:

Date	Account and Explanation	Debit	Credit	Assets	= Liabilities +	Stockholders' Equity
Jan. 3	Wages Expense	3,000				▼
	Wages Payable	7,000			▼	
	Cash		10,000	▼		

This sort of process is used for a wide variety of activities that are completed over time. For example, taxes are paid on April 15 based on the previous year's net income. As such, on December 31 an adjusting entry will match the appropriate income taxes expense to the current year and set up a liability (income taxes payable) that will be paid off by April 15. The same logic applies to similar situations, such as property taxes and interest expense.

NOTES PAYABLE

A **note payable** typically arises when a business borrows money or purchases goods or services from a company that requires a formal agreement or contract (like when you sign a loan contract to buy a car). This formal agreement or contract is what distinguishes the note payable from an account payable. The agreement typically states the timing of repayment and the amount (principal and/or interest) to be repaid. Notes payable typically mature anywhere from 3 to 12 months, but it can be longer (if its maturity is greater than 12 months, it will be classified as a long-term liability). These longer maturities explain why creditors are more likely to impose interest on notes payable than with accounts payable.

Notes Payable When Borrowing from a Bank Notes payable normally specify the amount to be repaid indirectly, by stating the amount borrowed (the principal) and an interest rate. These notes are called *interest-bearing notes* because they explicitly state an **interest rate**. The maturity amount of an interest-bearing note is not stated explicitly but is determined from the interest rate, the principal amount, and the maturity date.

When a business borrows using a short-term, interest-bearing note, the transaction is recorded at the amount borrowed. This is illustrated in EXAMPLE 8.1.

EXAMPLE 8.1 RECORDING NOTES PAYABLE AND ACCRUED INTEREST

Korsgard Auto Parts borrowed $100,000 from a bank on October 1, 2023, at 10% interest. The interest and principal are due on October 1, 2024.

Required:

1. Prepare the required journal entry on October 1, 2023.

2. Prepare the adjusting journal entry on December 31, 2023.

3. Prepare the journal entry (or entries) on October 1, 2024.

CONTINUED

EXAMPLE 8.1   RECORDING NOTES PAYABLE AND ACCRUED INTEREST (CONTINUED)

Solution:

1. When a business transfers assets (or provides services) to another entity at some point in the future for activities that have already occurred, a liability must be recognized.

Date	Account and Explanation	Debit	Credit	Assets	=	Liabilities	+	Stockholders' Equity
Oct. 1, 2023	Cash	100,000		▲				
	Notes Payable		100,000			▲		

2. Interest expense must be recognized (accrued) in the period it helped generate revenues, which is not necessarily the period the interest is paid.

Date	Account and Explanation	Debit	Credit	Assets	=	Liabilities	+	Stockholders' Equity
Dec. 31, 2023	Interest Expense	2,500*						▼
	Interest Payable		2,500			▲		

3. The cash payment retires the liability (including interest). Note that 9 months of interest are recognized in 2024, which represents the interest from January 1st through October 1st.

Date	Account and Explanation	Debit	Credit	Assets	=	Liabilities	+	Stockholders' Equity
Oct. 1, 2024	Notes Payable	100,000				▼		
	Interest Expense	7,500**						▼
	Interest Payable	2,500				▼		
	Cash		110,000	▼				

*$100,000 × 10% × 3/12
**$100,000 × 10% × 9/12

Exhibit 8.3 illustrates the financial statement effects of the transactions recorded in Example 8.1. Notice that the interest payment of $10,000 is recorded as interest expense of $2,500 in 2023 and $7,500 in 2024.

EXHIBIT 8.3   Effect of Borrowing Money on the Annual Income Statement and Balance Sheet

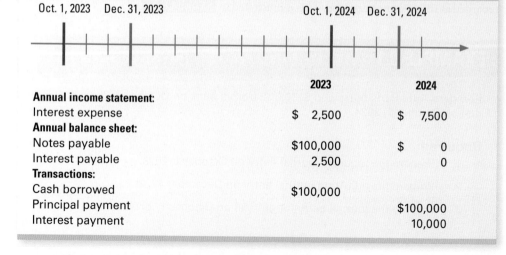

	2023	2024
Annual income statement:		
Interest expense	$ 2,500	$ 7,500
Annual balance sheet:		
Notes payable	$100,000	$ 0
Interest payable	2,500	0
Transactions:		
Cash borrowed	$100,000	
Principal payment		$100,000
Interest payment		10,000

Notes Payable from a Payment Extension

In addition to short-term borrowings, notes payable are often created when a borrower is unable to pay an account payable in a timely manner. In this case, the borrower is typically granted a payment extension, but the creditor requires that a formal note be signed to impose interest. As discussed, a current liability can be retired through creation of a new current liability. Rolling an account payable into a short-term note payable would be an example of this.

Assume that on March 8, 2023, Gibson Shipping orders $25,000 of packing materials from Ironman Enterprises on account. This amount is due on May 15, 2023. Gibson would need to make the following journal entry:

Date	Account and Explanation	Debit	Credit	Assets	= Liabilities +	Stockholders' Equity
Mar. 8	Supplies	25,000		▲		
	Accounts Payable		25,000		▲	

On May 15, Gibson cannot make the $25,000 payment and asks Ironman for a payment extension. Assuming Ironman grants the extension on the condition that Gibson signs a note that specifies 7% interest beginning on May 15, 2023, with a due date of November 15, 2023, Gibson would make the following journal entry:

Date	Account and Explanation	Debit	Credit	Assets	= Liabilities +	Stockholders' Equity
May 15	Accounts Payable	25,000			▼	
	Notes Payable		25,000		▲	

Finally, on November 15, 2023, when Gibson pays the amount in full, the journal entry would be as follows:

Date	Account and Explanation	Debit	Credit	Assets	= Liabilities +	Stockholders' Equity
Nov. 15	Notes Payable	25,000			▼	
	Interest Expense	875*				▼
	Cash		25,875	▼		

*$25,000 × 7% × 6/12

YOUDECIDE Making Short-Term Credit Decisions

You are a commercial loan officer at National City Bank. Hydraulic Controls, a local manufacturer of hydraulic clutch assemblies for compact foreign and domestic automobiles, would like to borrow money using a short-term note. The following data are available on Hydraulic's current liabilities, current assets, sales revenue, and net income (loss) for the past 3 years:

Item	2023	2022	2021
Accounts payable	$ 174,000	$ 146,000	$ 104,000
Short-term notes payable	332,000	291,000	291,000
Income taxes payable	0	43,000	50,000
Total current liabilities	$ 506,000	$ 480,000	$ 445,000
Total current assets	485,000	546,000	611,000
Sales revenue	5,047,000	5,293,000	5,538,000
Net income (loss)	(10,000)	89,000	130,000

Hydraulic Controls asks its bank to increase its short-term notes payable by $100,000.

CONTINUED

YOU DECIDE   Making Short-Term Credit Decisions (CONTINUED)

Should you approve a short-term note payable for Hydraulic?

To determine whether to extend additional credit to Hydraulic, you should consider the following:

- *How will the short-term notes be repaid?* The short-term notes would be repaid from current assets. But decline in the amount of current assets relative to current liabilities suggests that even the present amount of current liabilities may not be payable with the resources currently available.

- *What might be causing the recent increases in current liabilities and decreases in current assets?* Because profitability is declining, the firm may not be able to borrow from outside sources or secure cash from operations. Therefore, it may be drawing down current assets and increasing current liabilities to provide capital.

The decline in profitability, the trend in the ratio of current assets to current liabilities, and the present excess of current liabilities over current assets suggest that it would be unwise to extend additional credit at this time.

CURRENT PORTION OF LONG-TERM DEBT

The current portion of long-term debt is the amount of long-term debt principal that is due within the next year. At the end of each accounting period, the long-term debt that is due during the next year is reclassified as a current liability (see Exhibit 8.2, p. 467). Since the reclassification of most long-term debt as current does not usually change the accounts or amounts involved, journal entries are not required. In some cases, long-term debt that is due within the next year will be paid with the proceeds of a new long-term debt issue. Remember that current liabilities must be retired with existing current assets or creation of new current liabilities—a new long-term debt issue is creation of a new *long-term*, not current, liability. When such refinancing is expected, the maturing obligation is not transferred to current liabilities but is left as a long-term debt.[1]

OTHER PAYABLES

So far we have discussed accounts payable, accrued liabilities, and notes payable. However, businesses will have other current liabilities that do not fall into these categories. We will discuss some of the most common situations that can give rise to these other payables.

Sales Tax   At the time of a sale, most retail businesses collect **sales taxes**, usage taxes, or excise taxes for various state, local, and federal taxing authorities. These taxes, although collected as part of the total selling price, are not additions to revenue. Instead, they are money collected from the customer for the governmental unit levying the tax. These tax collections are liabilities until they are paid to the taxing authority. For example, businesses typically must remit sales tax collected to the state every quarter. EXAMPLE 8.2 illustrates the accounting for sales tax.

EXAMPLE 8.2   RECORDING LIABILITIES AT THE POINT OF SALE

During the first quarter of 2024, McLean County Tire sold, on credit, 1,250 truck tires at $180 each plus State of Illinois sales tax of 7% and City of Bloomington municipal taxes of 1%. These taxes are paid to the appropriate taxing authority each quarter.

Required:
Prepare the journal entry to record (1) first quarter sales and (2) payment of taxes to the appropriate taxing authority.

---

1   We discuss long-term liabilities in more detail in Chapter 9.

Solution:

1. The law often requires companies to collect taxes from customers. These represent liabilities because the company does not get to keep these tax collections.

Date	Account and Explanation	Debit	Credit	Assets	= Liabilities +	Stockholders' Equity
Mar. 31	Accounts Receivable	243,000		▲		
	Sales Revenue		225,000*			▲
	Sales Taxes Payable (State)		15,750**		▲	
	Sales Taxes Payable (City)		2,250***		▲	

*1,250 tires × $180
**1,250 tires × $180 × 7%
***1,250 tires × $180 × 1%

2. Taxes collected from customers are paid to the taxing authority periodically (typically quarterly). The liability is retired when the taxes are paid.

Date	Account and Explanation	Debit	Credit	Assets	= Liabilities +	Stockholders' Equity
Apr. 10	Sales Taxes Payable (State)	15,750			▼	
	Sales Taxes Payable (City)	2,250			▼	
	Cash		18,000	▼		

Withholding and Payroll Taxes Businesses are required to withhold taxes from employees' earnings and to pay taxes based on wages and salaries paid to employees. These **withholding** and **payroll taxes** are liabilities until they are paid to the taxing authority. Note that there are really two sources for these taxes: employees and employers.

EMPLOYEES Employees must pay certain taxes that are "withheld" from their paycheck. This is the difference between gross pay and net pay. The business does not have any rights to this money; instead, as with sales tax, they must pay these amounts to the proper authority. The standard withholdings are federal, state, and possibly city or county income taxes, as well as Social Security and Medicare. Employees may also have amounts withheld for such things as retirement accounts (e.g., 401-K), parking, and health insurance, among other things, but these are not taxes.

EMPLOYERS The business itself must pay certain taxes based on employee payrolls. These amounts are not withheld from employee pay; they are additional amounts that must be paid over and above gross pay. For example, employers match employee contributions to Social Security and Medicare (together these are called FICA). That is, if you have $400 withheld from your paycheck for Social Security, your employer pays the federal government $800 related to your employment. Employers also pay federal and state unemployment taxes (these are used to fund unemployment benefits) based on their history of firing employees (because fired employees are eligible to collect unemployment benefits). Finally, employers do have other costs—typically called fringe benefits—associated with employees, but these are not taxes. Examples of fringe benefits include employer contributions to retirement accounts and health insurance. Exhibit 8.4 shows the obligations most U.S. businesses pay in taxes or withhold from employee earnings. EXAMPLE 8.3 illustrates the accounting for these obligations.

EXHIBIT 8.4 | **Employer Payroll Taxes and Withheld Earnings**

Private industry employers (which excludes state and local government employers) break down as follows as of September 2019:

- Wages & Salaries, $24.38 (70.1%)
- Legally Required (FICA, etc.), $2.68 (7.7%)
- Insurance Benefits, $2.78 (8.0%)
- Paid Leave, $2.50 (7.2%)
- Retirement & Savings, $1.31 (3.8%)
- Supplemental Pay, $1.12 (3.2%)

Total Compensation per hour, $34.77 (100.0%)

Source: Bureau of Labor Statistics; news release USDL 19-2195, December 18, 2019.

EXAMPLE 8.3   RECORDING PAYROLL TAXES

Assume that McLean County Tire's hourly employees earned $48,500 in the pay period ending March 31. Federal income taxes withheld are $10,185. Additionally, a 3% state unemployment tax and an 0.8% federal unemployment tax are required to be paid by employers.

Required:

1. Prepare the journal entry related to the gross pay earned by employees (assume no employees have reached their annual Social Security limit of $137,700 for 2020).
2. Prepare the journal entry related to the payroll taxes on top of gross pay.

Solution:

1. The law requires companies to withhold certain taxes from employees' pay. Once withheld, these amounts are liabilities until paid to the taxing authority. The wages expense debit in this journal entry represents the employees' *gross pay*, while the credit to cash is the employees' *net (or take-home) pay*.

Date	Account and Explanation	Debit	Credit	Assets	= Liabilities +	Stockholders' Equity
Mar. 31	Wages Expense	48,500.00				▼
	Federal Income Taxes Withholding Payable		10,185.00		▲	
	Social Security Taxes Payable (Employee)		3,007.00[a]		▲	
	Medicare Taxes Payable (Employee)		703.25[b]		▲	
	Cash		34,604.75	▼		

2. Employers not only withhold taxes from employees' gross pay but also pay taxes over and above gross pay. These amounts also represent liabilities until paid to the taxing authority.

Date	Account and Explanation	Debit	Credit	Assets	= Liabilities +	Stockholders' Equity
Mar. 31	Federal Unemployment Taxes Expense	388.00				▼
	State Unemployment Taxes Expense	1,455.00				▼
	Social Security Taxes Expense	3,007.00				▼
	Medicare Taxes Expense	703.25				▼

[a] $48,500 × 6.2%
[b] $48,500 × 1.45%

Date	Account and Explanation	Debit	Credit	Assets	=	Liabilities	+	Stockholders' Equity
Mar. 31	Federal Unemployment Taxes Payable		388.00[c]			▲		
	State Unemployment Taxes Payable		1,455.00[d]			▲		
	Social Security Taxes Payable (Employer)		3,007.00[e]			▲		
	Medicare Taxes Payable (Employer)		703.25[f]			▲		

[c] $48,500 × 0.8%
[d] $48,500 × 3%
[e] $48,500 × 6.2%
[f] $48,500 × 1.45%

Note: The $48,500.00 payroll is (1) smaller than the total expense of $54,053.25 (i.e., the sum of expenses from both journal entries) and (2) larger than the $35,574.75 cash paid (i.e., net pay) to employees. In other words, the actual cost of an employee is more than his or her gross pay.

 # YOUDECIDE Full-Time Employee or Consultant?

You are the HR manager of Berndt Chocolates. The marketing department wants to hire a full-time employee at an annual salary of $52,000. They argue that this will save the company money because Berndt will no longer have to pay an outside marketing consultant approximately $65,000 per year to do the same job.

What factors should you consider in deciding whether to hire the full-time employee?

Businesses often make the decision of whether to hire a full-time employee or pay a consultant. Of course, the primary concern is which person will perform the function better, but there are other factors to consider. Hiring a consultant can provide several advantages. First, a full-time employee will incur costs in addition to salary. For example, assuming federal and state unemployment tax rates totaling 3.5% for a full-time employee earning $52,000, Berndt's payroll taxes will increase as follows:

Employer Payroll Taxes	Cost
OASDI (Social Security at 6.2%)	$3,224
Medicare (at 1.45%)	754
Federal and state unemployment (at 3.5%)	1,820
Total employer payroll taxes	$5,798

Further, most companies have fringe benefits such as health insurance, life insurance, retirement contributions, and bonuses. Assuming these fringe benefits are 30% of the employee's annual salary, this employee would cost $73,398 [$52,000 + $5,798 + ($52,000 × 30%)] per year. Second, it is much easier and less costly to decrease or eliminate consultants than full-time employees.

Aside from qualifications, the costs of federal and state taxes and benefits should be considered when deciding whether to hire full-time employees.

Unearned Revenues **Unearned revenue** is the liability created when customers pay for goods or services in advance. In such instances, the amount of the prepayment is a liability for the seller. This liability is discharged either by providing the goods or services purchased (at which time revenue is recognized) or by refunding the amount of the prepayment.[2] EXAMPLE 8.4 illustrates the accounting for unearned revenues.

---

2   If the goods or services are not provided, the seller may also be liable for legal damages. The amount of such damages would be recorded as an expense.

EXAMPLE 8.4   RECORDING UNEARNED REVENUES

Ron's Cajun Connection sells $100,000 of gift cards in December 2023. These gift cards may be redeemed at any time; however, they expire on December 31, 2024. During 2024, $98,875 of gift cards are redeemed.

Required:

1. Prepare the journal entry related to the sale of gift cards.

2. Prepare the journal entry related to redemption of the gift cards.

3. Prepare the journal entry related to the expiration of the remaining gift cards.

Solution:

1. When customers pay for goods or services in advance, the business recognizes a liability.

Date	Account and Explanation	Debit	Credit	Assets	=	Liabilities	+	Stockholders' Equity
Dec. 2023	Cash	100,000		▲				
	Unearned Sales Revenue		100,000			▲		

2. The revenue is recognized when the customer gains control of the asset redeemed with the gift card. When control of the asset passes to the customer, the performance obligation is satisfied. These entries are made individually as each gift card is received.

Date	Account and Explanation	Debit	Credit	Assets	=	Liabilities	+	Stockholders' Equity
During 2024	Unearned Sales Revenue	98,875				▼		
	Sales Revenue		98,875					▲

3. Although Ron's Cajun Connection does not gain control of an asset when gift cards expire, the performance obligation is satisfied because of the terms of the gift card. Note, this journal entry would be made individually as each gift card is redeemed.

Date	Account and Explanation	Debit	Credit	Assets	=	Liabilities	+	Stockholders' Equity
Dec. 31, 2024	Unearned Sales Revenue	1,125				▼		
	Sales Revenue		1,125					▲

Next Level

Why is a liability recognized when a customer prepays for a good or service (i.e., an unearned revenue)?

ANSWER:

Liabilities are probable future sacrifices of economic benefits, which arise from activities that have already occurred. Because the business here will provide the goods or services purchased by the customer at a future point, the prepayment is a liability. Further, the prepayment is not recognized as revenue because the performance obligation has not been satisfied.

A similar *long-term* liability, called *customer deposits*, is recorded when customers make advance payments or security deposits that are not expected to be earned or returned soon enough to qualify as current liabilities.

Example 8-4 demonstrates that revenue will not be recognized until the performance obligation is satisfied. Here, the performance obligation is not satisfied until the goods or services are provided. The National Retail Federation reports that approximately $30 billion in gift cards were purchased last holiday season. This is how all these stores account for gift cards.

CONTINGENT LIABILITIES

OBJECTIVE 3

Describe contingent liabilities and the alternatives for their recognition and measurement.

Measurement of the liabilities described so far was not affected by uncertainties about the amount, timing, or receipt of future asset outflows. However, such uncertainties exist. In financial accounting, a contingency is an ". . . existing condition, situation, or set of circumstances involving uncertainty" as to possible gain or loss.

A contingent liability is not recognized in the accounts unless both of the following are true:

- the event on which it is contingent is probable
- a reasonable estimate of the loss can be made

If the contingent event is almost certain to occur, reliable measurement of the liability is usually possible, so recognition is appropriate. For example, contingent liabilities arising from product warranties and pensions are recognized because previous experience allows for reliable measurements to be made. On the other hand, if occurrence of the contingent event is not probable or reliable measurement of the obligation is impossible, the potential obligation is not recorded as a liability. Instead, as shown in Exhibit 8.5, it may be disclosed in footnotes to the financial statements.

Recognition of Contingent Liabilities   **EXHIBIT 8.5**

	A Reasonable Estimate Can Be Made	No Reasonable Estimate Can Be Made
Probable	Make a journal entry to record the liability.	No journal entry is made: disclose information in a footnote to the financial statements.
Reasonably Possible	No journal entry is made: disclose information in a footnote to the financial statements.	No journal entry is made: disclose information in a footnote to the financial statements.
Remote	Neither record as a liability nor disclose in a footnote to the financial statements.	Neither record as a liability nor disclose in a footnote to the financial statements.

Lawsuits filed against a business are a classic example of contingent liabilities. Such legal proceedings have the potential to be very important. Consider Apple's lawsuits against Samsung for patent infringement and Samsung's countersuits against Apple. In different jurisdictions around the globe, these two companies were involved in over 50 lawsuits with billions of dollars in potential damages. While Samsung is a Korean company that follows Korean IFRS, Apple files an annual 10-K with the SEC. Exhibit 8.6 shows an excerpt from Apple's Note 10 to their fiscal year 2017 Financial Statements. After the close of fiscal year 2017, the final two cases were decided in Apple's favor, with Apple being awarded $120 million in November 2017 pertaining to Apple's iOS slide-to-unlock patent and $539 million in May 2018 pertaining to Apple's design and utility patents related to the iPhone.

Most large companies are party to multiple lawsuits at any point in time. Estimating when a loss is probable and determining a reasonable estimate requires information from the attorneys, but businesses rarely record a contingent liability prior to the jury deciding against them. We've probably all heard of such lawsuits as when Stella Liebeck sued **McDonald's** in 1992. Liebeck spilled coffee while removing the lid to add sugar, burning her legs. She suffered third degree burns over 6% of her body. McDonald's could have settled the case for $20,000, but they refused. Liebeck ultimately was awarded $200,000 in compensatory damages and $2.7 million in punitive damages.[3]

---

3 Liebek's compensatory damages were reduced to $160,000 because she was found to be 20% at fault.

> ### EXHIBIT 8.6   Disclosure of Contingencies
>
> **Excerpt from Note 10 to the Financial Statements[1]**
>
> **Contingencies** The Company is subject to various legal proceedings and claims that have arisen in the ordinary course of business and that have not been fully adjudicated, as further discussed in Part I, Item 1A of this Form 10-K under the heading "Risk Factors" and in Part I, Item 3 of this Form 10-K under the heading "Legal Proceedings." In the opinion of management, there was not at least a reasonable possibility the Company may have incurred a material loss, or a material loss in excess of a recorded accrual, with respect to loss contingencies for asserted legal and other claims. However, the outcome of litigation is inherently uncertain. Therefore, although management considers the likelihood of such an outcome to be remote, if one or more of these legal matters were resolved against the Company in a reporting period for amounts in excess of management's expectations, the Company's consolidated financial statements for that reporting period could be materially adversely affected.
>
> *Apple Inc. v. Samsung Electronics Co., Ltd., et al.*
>
> On August 24, 2012, a jury returned a verdict awarding the Company $1.05 billion in its lawsuit against Samsung Electronics Co., Ltd. and affiliated parties in the United States District Court, Northern District of California, San Jose Division. On March 6, 2014, the District Court entered final judgment in favor of the Company in the amount of approximately $930 millio. On May 18, 2015, the U.S. Court of Appeals for the Federal Circuit affirmed in part, and reversed in part, the decision of the District Court. As a result, the Court of Appeals ordered entry of final judgment on damages in the amount of approximately $548 million, with the District Court to determine supplemental damages and interest, as well as damages owed for products subject to the reversal in part. Samsung paid $548 million to the Company in December 2015, which was included in net sales in the Consolidated Statement of Operations. On December 6, 2016, the U.S. Supreme Court remanded the case to the U.S. Court of Appeals for the Federal Circuit for further proceedings related to the $548 million in damages. On February 7, 2017, the U.S. Court of Appeals for the Federal Circuit remanded the case to the District Court to determine what additional proceedings, if any, are needed. On October 22, 2017, on remand from the U.S. Supreme Court, the District Court ordered a new trial on damages.
>
> ---
> 1   Taken from Apple's Form 10-K for the period ended September 30, 2017.

Next Level

Accounts receivable have a contingent loss related to bad debts. A group of customers owes money (the accounts receivable); however, there is uncertainty about whether the customers will pay. How do we account for this contingency and why do we account for it in this way?

ANSWER:

As discussed in Chapter 5, companies typically use an estimate of uncollectible receivables to recognize "bad debt expense" and value the accounts receivable at net realizable value through a credit to the "allowance for doubtful accounts." This is done because it is probable that amounts will be uncollectible and this amount is reasonably estimated (generally based on past experience). So, although bad debt expense does not produce a liability (instead, it reduces an asset), the accounting for this contingency is consistent with contingent liabilities.

The accounting question becomes: When is a liability (and corresponding expense) recorded? Proper matching suggests that the expense would be recorded at the time Liebeck spilled the coffee. However, at this time, the loss was contingent. Since the liability and expense were not recorded until it was deemed probable that **McDonald's** would lose the lawsuit and a reasonable estimate could be made, McDonald's did not record a liability for this amount until they lost the lawsuit.

Of course, the likelihood that a contingent event will occur may change over time. A contingent liability that should not be recorded or disclosed at one time may need to be recorded or disclosed later because the facts and circumstances change. This frequently happens to contingent liabilities arising from litigation.

ETHICAL DECISIONS The contingent liability rules create an interesting ethical dilemma in lawsuits. Consider the fictional case of a class action lawsuit being filed against Giant Pharmaceuticals by patients who used one of Giant's best selling drugs. Company attorneys believe it is probable that Giant will settle the lawsuit for approximately $3 billion. However, if Giant were to recognize a $3 billion liability and expense, the plaintiff attorneys would likely refuse to settle for less. After all, what would you think if you were on the jury and the defendants' attorney showed you Giant's financial statements, explained the contingency rule, and said, "See, even Giant thinks it's probable that they will lose this lawsuit and pay damages of $3 billion." As you might expect, companies are extremely reluctant to record expenses and liabilities related to lawsuits for this reason or to even disclose that a loss is probable. Is this ethical? It probably isn't ethical, but it is an area that all parties seem to allow. As such, users of the financial statements cannot place too much reliance on the lack of expenses and liabilities related to lawsuits. ●

WARRANTIES

OBJECTIVE ◄ 4

Calculate warranty liabilities and warranty expense and prepare the necessary journal entries.

When goods are sold, the customer is often provided with a warranty against certain defects. A **warranty** usually guarantees the repair or replacement of defective goods during a period (ranging from a few days to several years) following the sale.

The use of parts and labor to satisfy warranty claims may occur in the accounting period in which the sale is made, but it is also likely to occur in some subsequent accounting period. Expense recognition requires that all expenses required to produce sales revenue for a given period be recorded in that period. Since warranty costs are sales-related, they must be recorded in the sales period. And since all warranty costs probably have not been incurred by the end of the sales period, they must be estimated. Businesses are likely able to make reasonable estimates of their warranty costs based on past experience.

The recognition of warranty expense and (estimated) warranty liability is normally recorded by an adjustment at the end of the accounting period. As warranty claims are paid to customers or related expenditures are made, the liability is reduced. EXAMPLE 8.5 illustrates the accounting for warranties.

EXAMPLE 8.5   RECORDING WARRANTY LIABILITIES

Nolan Electronics offers a 12-month warranty on all its computers. Nolan estimates that one computer of each 2,000 sold will require warranty service and that the average warranty claim will cost Nolan $155.

Required:

1. Prepare the journal entry to recognize warranty expense and associated liability, assuming Nolan sells 3,000,000 computers during 2023, for which no warranty work has yet been performed.

2. Prepare the journal entry for warranty repairs, assuming that in January 2024, Nolan gives $10,400 cash and parts costing $8,300 to its dealers for warranty repairs.

Solution:

1. Future warranty expenses must be recognized in the period of sale because that is the period the warranty helped generate revenues. The sale of a product with a warranty also creates an obligation to perform any future warranty work.

$$(3,00,000 \text{ computers sold}) \times \left(\frac{1 \text{ failure}}{2,000 \text{ sold}} \right) \times \left(\frac{\$155}{1 \text{ failure}} \right) = \$232,500$$

Date	Account and Explanation	Debit	Credit	Assets	= Liabilities +	Stockholders' Equity
Dec. 31, 2023	Warranty Expense	232,500				▼
	Warranty Liability		232,500		▲	

2. As the warranty work is performed, the liability is retired.

Date	Account and Explanation	Debit	Credit	Assets	= Liabilities +	Stockholders' Equity
Jan. 2024	Warranty Liability	18,700			▼	
	Cash		10,400	▼		
	Parts Inventory		8,300	▼		

Note: The income statement effect of warranties (activity in the equity column) occurs when goods are sold. Payments or other asset outflows associated with the satisfaction of warranty claims do not affect the income statement.

Exhibit 8.7 shows the footnote related to product warranties from the Notes to GE's 2019 Financial Statements. Note from this disclosure that GE estimated $713 million of new warranty liabilities in 2019 and incurred $715 million of warranty costs. Also note that actual warranty claims do not exactly equal the business's estimate, although they are unusually close in 2019. This results in adjustments (called "other changes" in the disclosure) being needed to get to the appropriate ending balance.

EXHIBIT 8.7   ▶   **Excerpt from Note 23 to the Financial Statements**

PRODUCT WARRANTIES

We provide for estimated product warranty expenses when we sell the related products. Because warranty estimates are forecasts that are based on the best available information, mostly historical claims experience, claims costs may differ from amounts provided. An analysis of changes in the liability for product warranties follows.

(in millions)	2019	2018	2017
Balance at January 1	$ 2,192	$ 2,103	$ 1,743
Current-year provisions	713	945	929
Expenditures	(715)	(788)	(708)
Other changes	(26)	(69)	139
Balance at December 31	$ 2,165	$ 2,192	$ 2,103

OBJECTIVE

Analyze short-term liquidity using information contained in the current liabilities section.

ANALYZING CURRENT LIABILITIES

Both investors and creditors are interested in a company's liquidity—that is, its ability to meet its short-term obligations. Failure to pay current liabilities can lead to suppliers refusing to sell to the company and employees leaving. As such, even companies with good business models can be forced into bankruptcy by their inability to pay current liabilities.

The following ratios are often used to analyze a company's ability to meet its current obligations:

$$\text{Current Ratio} = \frac{\text{Current Assets}}{\text{Current Liabilities}}$$

$$\text{Quick Ratio} = \frac{(\text{Cash} + \text{Marketable Securities} + \text{Accounts Receivable})}{\text{Current Liabilities}}$$

$$\text{Cash Ratio} = \frac{(\text{Cash} + \text{Marketable Securities})}{\text{Current Liabilities}}$$

$$\text{Operating Cash Flow Ratio} = \frac{\text{Cash Flows from Operating Activities}}{\text{Current Liabilities}}$$

The first three ratios compare all or parts of current assets to current liabilities. The logic is that current liabilities need to be paid over approximately the same time frame that current assets are turned into cash. "Acceptable" current ratios vary from industry to industry, but the thought is that current assets must exceed current liabilities (which implies a current ratio > 1) to be able to meet current obligations. In fact, the general rule of thumb appears to be that a current ratio greater than 2 is appropriate.

However, the second and third ratios recognize that some current assets are harder to liquidate. Both the quick and cash ratio exclude inventories because including inventories assumes that sales will be made. The quick ratio assumes that accounts receivable are liquid.

This is true when customers have low credit risk and pay in relatively short amounts of time. Of course, such an assumption is not true for all industries. For example, consider the financial crisis of 2008 when many creditors discovered that the mortgage debt that represented receivables for the creditors was far more likely to be uncollectible than they had been led to believe. Consequently, the use of the cash ratio may be more appropriate in these cases.

Operating cash flow, on the other hand, looks at the ability of cash generated from operating activities to meet current obligations. As with the current ratio, the operating cash flow ratio assumes that sales will continue into the future. EXAMPLE 8.6 illustrates the analysis of current liabilities.

EXAMPLE 8.6   CALCULATING LIQUIDITY RATIOS

Consider the following information from the homebuilding operations of **Lennar Corporation**, the largest homebuilder in that nation by total revenues, as of November 30, 2019 (in thousands):

Current liabilities	$2,970,134	Receivables	$ 329,124
Cash & equivalents	1,200,832	Inventories	17,776,507
Marketable securities	0	Cash flows from operating activities	1,482,343

Required:
Calculate the following: (1) current ratio, (2) quick ratio, (3) cash ratio, and (4) operating cash flow ratio.

Solution:

1. The current ratio recognizes that current liabilities are paid over approximately the same time frame that current assets are turned into cash. A ratio below 1 indicates that current assets are insufficient to meet current obligations.

$$\text{Current ratio: } \frac{\$1,200,832 + \$0 + \$329,124 + \$17,776,507}{\$2,970,134} = 6.50$$

2. The quick ratio removes inventories from the numerator of the current ratio. The quick ratio can be used when uncertainty exists regarding the ability of the company to sell its inventories.

$$\text{Quick ratio: } \frac{\$1,200,832 + \$0 + \$329,124}{\$2,970,134} = 0.52$$

3. The cash ratio removes both inventories and receivables from the numerator of the current ratio. Not only does it recognize that the inventories may not be sold (as in the quick ratio), but it also recognizes that there may be difficulty in collecting the receivables.

$$\text{Cash ratio: } \frac{\$1,200,832 + \$0}{\$2,970,134} = 0.40$$

4. The operating cash flow ratio looks at the ability of cash generated from operation to meet current obligations.

$$\text{Operating cash flow ratio: } \frac{\$1,482,343}{\$2,970,134} = 0.50$$

Note: Most of the information to calculate these ratios can also be found on the balance sheet (except for cash flows from operating activities, which is on the statement of cash flows).

In isolation, the current ratio in Example 8.6 appears very strong. For most industries, a current ratio greater than six is very rare. However, a vast majority of Lennar's current assets are inventories (unsold homes). In strong real estate markets, new homes can sell quite fast, but when a real estate slump hits, such homes can remain unsold for long periods of time. During the 2007 real estate market slump, for example, home builders experienced much slower sales. A few home builders even resorted to selling homes at a loss to generate needed cash.

The quick ratio and cash ratio in Example 8.6 show that **Lennar** cannot meet its current obligations with its cash reserves alone, which means Lennar must sell inventory to meet its current obligations. Further, Lennar's cash flows from operations cannot meet its current obligations. However, if we look more closely at the Operating Activities section of the Statement of Cash Flows, we see that cash flows from operations would have been over $2,000,000 if inventories hadn't grown. The question is why have inventories grown? Is it because business is good and Lennar is expanding or because business is bad and they are unable to sell their inventory? These are the questions that must be answered when analyzing a company.

REVIEW CENTER

KEY TAKEAWAYS

- Most liabilities are recognized in exchange for goods and services or the borrowing of money.
- In theory, the amount reported on the balance sheet should not include interest that has not yet accrued.
- For nearly all current liabilities, unaccrued interest is deemed immaterial, so most current liabilities are simply recorded and reported at the total amount due.

KEY TERMS

Contingent liability, 466
Liabilities, 465

LO1. Explain liability recognition and measurement criteria.

KEY TAKEAWAYS

- Current liabilities are obligations to outsiders who require the firm to pay cash or another current asset or provide goods or services within the longer of 1 year or one operating cycle.
- Current liabilities are the result of many common transactions such as the following:
  - Purchasing goods or services on credit (i.e., accounts payable)
  - The completed portion of activities that are in process at the end of the period such
  - Sales tax collected from customers
  - Payroll taxes such as taxes withheld from employees and Social Security
  - Notes payable
  - Goods or services paid for in advance by customers (i.e., unearned revenues)
  - The portion of long-term debt due within the year

LO2. Identify the kinds of activities that produce current liabilities and prepare journal entries for these activities.

KEY TERMS

Accounts payable, 468
Accrued liabilities, 468
Current liabilities, 467
Interest rate, 469
Note payable, 469

Payroll taxes, 473
Sales taxes, 472
Unearned revenue, 475
Withholding taxes, 473

EXAMPLES

EXAMPLE 8.1	Recording notes payable and accrued interest, page 469–470
EXAMPLE 8.2	Recording liabilities at the point of sale, page 472–473
EXAMPLE 8.3	Recording payroll taxes, page 474–475
EXAMPLE 8.4	Recording unearned revenues, page 476

LO3. Describe contingent liabilities and the alternatives for their recognition and measurement.

KEY TAKEAWAYS

- A contingent liability is an obligation whose amount, timing, or recipient depends on future events.
- A contingent liability is not recognized in the accounts unless the event on which it is contingent is probable (likely to occur) and a reasonable estimate of the liability can be made.
- If occurrence of the contingent event is not probable or reliable measurement of the obligation is impossible, the potential obligation is not recorded as a liability but may be disclosed in the footnotes.

KEY TERM

Contingent liabilities, 466

LO4. Calculate warranty liabilities and warranty expense and prepare the necessary journal entries.

KEY TAKEAWAYS

- Since warranties help generate sales, the estimated future cost of servicing the warranty must be recorded in the sales period (this is an example of the matching principle).
- Matching the costs servicing the warranty to the sales period is done by expensing the estimate of the future cost of servicing the warranty and creating a liability.
- As warranty claims are paid to customers or related expenditures are made, the estimated liability is reduced.

KEY TERM

Warranty, 479

EXAMPLE

EXAMPLE 8.5   Recording warranty liabilities, page 479

LO5. Analyze short-term liquidity using information contained in the current liabilities section.

KEY TAKEAWAYS

- Both investors and creditors are interested in a company's liquidity—that is, its ability to meet its short-term obligations.
- Failure to pay current liabilities can lead to suppliers refusing to sell needed inventory and employees leaving.
- Even companies with good business models can be forced into bankruptcy by their inability to pay current liabilities.

- Common ratios used to analyze a company's ability to meet its current obligations are as follows:
    ◦ Current ratio
    ◦ Quick ratio
    ◦ Cash ratio
    ◦ Operating cash flow ratio

KEY CALCULATIONS

Current Ratio = Current Assets ÷ Current Liabilities, 480
Quick Ratio = (Cash + Marketable Securities + Accounts Receivable) ÷ Current Liabilities, 480
Cash Ratio = (Cash + Marketable Securities) ÷ Current Liabilities, 480
Operating Cash Flow Ratio = Cash Flows from Operating Activities ÷ Current Liabilities, 480

EXAMPLE

> **EXAMPLE 8.6**   Calculating liquidity ratios, page 481

REVIEW PROBLEM

RECORDING CURRENT LIABILITIES AND CALCULATING THE CURRENT RATIO

ABC Co. has the following balances in its accounts as of the beginning of the day on December 31 (this is not all of the accounts):

Account	Debit	Credit
Accounts payable		$ 100,000
Accounts receivable	$150,000	
Cash	75,000	
Interest payable		0
Inventory	270,000	
Long-term notes payable		1,000,000
Other current assets	60,000	
Other current liabilities		45,000
Sales taxes payable		10,000
Short-term notes payable		0
Unearned revenues		30,000

The following additional information is *not* reflected in these balances:

a. On December 1, ABC bought equipment for $200,000 with a short-term note payable bearing 12% interest. ABC has not made any journal entries related to this transaction.

b. On December 31, ABC accepted delivery of $30,000 of inventory. ABC has not yet paid its suppliers.

(Continued)

c. Customers prepaid $10,600 related to services ABC will perform next year. This price included 6% state sales tax.

d. Gross salaries and wages in the amount of $20,000 are paid. Assume all employees are below the Social Security maximum, 5.4% state unemployment taxes and 0.8% federal unemployment taxes are paid on $3,225.81 of wages, and $2,500 of federal income taxes are withheld from employees.

Required:

1. Prepare the necessary journal entries for Items a–d.
2. Determine the current ratio before accounting for the additional information.
3. Determine the current ratio after accounting for the additional information.
4. Explain why ABC's current ratio deteriorated so badly.

Solution:

1. The necessary journal entries for each item are as follows:

a.

Date	Account and Explanation	Debit	Credit	Assets	=	Liabilities	+	Stockholders' Equity
Dec. 1	Equipment	200,000		▲				
	Short-term Notes Payable		200,000			▲		

b.

Date	Account and Explanation	Debit	Credit	Assets	=	Liabilities	+	Stockholders' Equity
Dec. 31	Inventory	30,000		▲				
	Accounts Payable		30,000			▲		

ABC must also accrue interest on December 31.

Date	Account and Explanation	Debit	Credit	Assets	=	Liabilities	+	Stockholders' Equity
Dec. 31	Interest Expense[a]	2,000						▼
	Interest Payable		2,000			▲		

c.

Date	Account and Explanation	Debit	Credit	Assets	=	Liabilities	+	Stockholders' Equity
Dec. 31	Cash	10,600		▲				
	Unearned Revenue		10,000			▲		
	Sales Taxes Payable (State)		600			▲		

d.

Date	Account and Explanation	Debit	Credit	Assets	=	Liabilities	+	Stockholders' Equity
Dec. 31	Wages Expense	20,000						▼
	Social Security Taxes Payable (Employee)[b]		1,240			▲		
	Medicare Taxes Payable (Employee)[c]		290			▲		
	Federal Income Taxes Withholding Payable		2,500			▲		
	Cash		15,970	▼				

[a] $200,000 × 12% × 1/12
[b] $20,000 × 6.2%

Date	Account and Explanation	Debit	Credit	Assets	= Liabilities +	Stockholders' Equity
Dec. 31	Social Security Taxes Expense	1,240.00				▼
	Medicare Taxes Expense	290.00				▼
	State Unemployment Taxes Expense[d]	174.19				▼
	Federal Unemployment Taxes Expense[e]	25.81				▼
	Social Security Taxes Payable (Employer)		1,240.00		▲	
	Medicare Taxes Payable (Employer)		290.00		▲	
	State Unemployment Taxes Payable[d]		174.19		▲	
	Federal Unemployment Taxes Payable[e]		25.81		▲	

[c]$20,000 × 1.45%
[d]$3,225.81 × 5.4%
[e]$3,225.81 × 0.8%

2. Before accounting for the additional information:

Current assets:	
Cash	$ 75,000
Accounts receivable	150,000
Inventory	270,000
Other current assets	60,000
Total current assets	$555,000
Current liabilities:	
Accounts payable	$100,000
Interest payable	0
Sales taxes payable	10,000
Short-term notes payable	0
Unearned revenues	30,000
Other current liabilities	45,000
Total current liabilities	$185,000

Current Ratio = $555,000/$185,000 = 3.0

3. After accounting for the additional information:

		Debit		Credit	
Current assets:					
Cash	$ 75,000	$10,600 (c)	$ 15,970 (d)		$ 69,630
Accounts receivable	150,000				150,000
Inventory	270,000	30,000 (b)			300,000
Other current assets	60,000				60,000
Total current assets					$579,630
Current liabilities:					
Accounts payable	100,000		30,000 (b)		$130,000
Interest payable	0		2,000 (b)		2,000
Sales taxes payable	10,000		600 (c)		10,600
Short-term notes payable	0		200,000 (a)		200,000
Unearned revenues	30,000		10,000 (c)		40,000
Other current liabilities	45,000		5,760 (d)*		50,760
Total current liabilities					$433,360

* $1,240 + $290 + $2,500 + $1,240 + $290 + $174.19 + $25.81 = $5,760

Current Ratio = $579,630/$433,360 = 1.34

4. The primary cause of the deterioration of ABC's current ratio is the addition of the short-term note payable related to the equipment. This transaction almost doubled the current liabilities, but current assets were unaffected by the addition of equipment. Another way to think about this is that ABC financed long-term operational assets with short-term financing.

APPLYING KNOWLEDGE

DISCUSSION QUESTIONS

OBJECTIVE 1

1. What are liabilities?
2. How is the amount of a liability measured?
3. When are most liabilities recognized?

OBJECTIVE 2

4. What are current liabilities? Provide some common examples.
5. Describe at least two ways in which current liabilities are frequently ordered on the balance sheet.
6. What is the difference between an account payable and a note payable?
7. What sort of transaction typically creates an account payable?
8. What do we mean by accrued liabilities? Provide some common examples.
9. What type of transaction typically creates a note payable?
10. Why is interest ignored when valuing accounts payable?
11. How is interest computed on an interest-bearing short-term note?
12. When would debt that must be repaid within the next year be classified as long-term instead of current?
13. Provide examples of payroll taxes that are paid by the employee through reduction of their gross pay. Provide some examples of payroll taxes that are paid by the employer.
14. Why do unearned revenues and customers' deposits qualify as liabilities?

OBJECTIVE 3

15. What are contingent liabilities? Provide an example.
16. When is a contingency recognized as a liability?

OBJECTIVE 4

17. Why is the liability for warranties recognized when products are sold rather than when the warranty services are performed?

OBJECTIVE 5

18. Describe the circumstances under which the current, quick, and cash ratios, respectively, are more appropriate measures of short-term liquidity than the other ratios.
19. Describe the differences between the current, quick, and cash ratios. Which one is the most conservative measure of short-term liquidity?
20. How does the rationale for the operating cash flow ratio differ from the rationale for the current, quick, and cash ratios?

MULTIPLE-CHOICE QUESTIONS

OBJECTIVE 1

8-1   Liabilities are recognized in exchange for
a. borrowing money.   c. goods.
b. services.   d. all of these.

8-2   When reporting liabilities on a balance sheet, in theory, what measurement should be used?
a. Present value of the present outflow   c. Future value of the present outflow
b. Present value of the future outflow   d. Future value of the future outflow

> *Use the following information for Multiple-Choice Questions 8-3 and 8-4:*
> Kinsella Seed borrowed $200,000 on October 1, 2023, at 10% interest. The interest and principal are due on October 1, 2024.

8-3 Refer to the information for Kinsella Seed above. What journal entry should be recorded on December 31, 2023?

    a. Debit Interest Expense 5,000; credit Interest Payable 5,000.
    b. Debit Interest Payable 5,000; credit Interest Expense 5,000.
    c. Debit Interest Receivable 20,000; credit Interest Expense 20,000.
    d. No entry is necessary.

OBJECTIVE 2

8-4 Refer to the information for Kinsella Seed above. What journal entry should be made with respect to the interest payment on October 1, 2024?

    a. Debit Interest Expense 15,000; debit Interest Payable 5,000; credit Cash 20,000.
    b. Debit Interest Expense 15,000; credit Cash 15,000.
    c. Debit Cash 20,000; credit Interest Expense 15,000; credit Interest Payable 5,000.
    d. Debit Interest Expense 20,000; credit Cash 20,000.

8-5 Which of the following is *not* a current liability?

    a. Accounts payable
    b. Unearned revenue
    c. Sales taxes payable
    d. Bonds payable due in 5 years

8-6 Which of the following is *not* an example of an accrued liability?

    a. Accounts payable
    b. Interest payable
    c. Wages payable
    d. Property taxes payable

8-7 Kramerica Inc. sold 350 oil drums to Thompson Manufacturing for $75 each. In addition to the $75 sale price per drum, there is a $1 per drum federal excise tax and a 7% state sales tax. What journal entry should be made to record this sale?

    a. Debit Accounts Receivable 28,438; credit Sales Revenue 28,438.
    b. Debit Accounts Receivable 26,250; credit Sales Revenue 26,250.
    c. Debit Accounts Receivable 26,250; debit Taxes Expense 2,188; credit Excise Taxes Payable (Federal) 350; credit Sales Taxes Payable (State) 1,838; credit Sales Revenue 26,250.
    d. Debit Accounts Receivable 28,438; credit Excise Taxes Payable (Federal) 350; credit Sales Taxes Payable (State) 1,838; credit Sales Revenue 26,250.

8-8 All of the following represent taxes commonly collected by businesses from customers *except*

    a. City sales taxes
    b. Federal excise taxes
    c. Unemployment taxes
    d. State sales taxes

8-9 Payroll taxes typically include all of the following *except*

    a. Social Security taxes
    b. Federal excise taxes
    c. Medicare taxes
    d. Federal unemployment taxes

8-10 When a credit is made to federal income taxes withholding payable account related to taxes withheld from an employee, the corresponding debit is made to

    a. Wages Expense.
    b. Taxes Expense.
    c. Taxes Payable.
    d. Cash.

8-11 When should a contingent liability be recognized?

    a. When a reasonable estimation can be made
    b. When the contingent liability is probable
    c. neither a nor b
    d. a and b

OBJECTIVE 3

8-12 Which of the following is true?
   a. No journal entries or footnotes are necessary if the probability of a contingent liability is remote.
   b. A contingent liability should always be recorded in the footnotes to the financial statements.
   c. A contingent liability should always be recorded within the financial statements.
   d. A company can choose to record a contingent liability either within its financial statements or in the footnotes to the financial statements.

8-13 ABC Advisors is being sued by a former customer. ABC's lawyers say that it is possible, but not probable, that the company will lose the lawsuit and the trial should last approximately 18 more months. Should ABC lose, they will most likely have to pay approximately $750,000. How should this lawsuit be reported in the financial statements?
   a. Current liability of $750,000 and Expense of $750,000
   b. Long-term liability of $750,000 and Expense of $750,000
   c. No disclosure is required.
   d. No effect on the balance sheet or income statement, but described in the footnotes.

OBJECTIVE

8-14 Warranty expense is
   a. recorded as it is incurred.   c. capitalized as a warranty asset.
   b. recorded in the period of sale.   d. None of these.

8-15 To record warranties, the adjusting journal entry would be
   a. a debit to Warranty Liability and a credit to Warranty Expense.
   b. a debit to Warranty Expense and a credit to Warranty Liability.
   c. a debit to Warranty Expense and a debit to Cash.
   d. a debit to Warranty Liability and a credit to Cash.

OBJECTIVE 5

8-16 How is the current ratio calculated?
   a. Current Assets/Current Liabilities
   b. Cash Flows from Operating Activities/Current Liabilities
   c. (Cash + Marketable Securities)/Current Liabilities
   d. (Cash + Marketable Securities + Accounts Receivable)/Current Liabilities

8-17 How is the cash ratio calculated?
   a. Current Assets/Current Liabilities
   b. Cash Flows from Operating Activities/Current Liabilities
   c. (Cash + Marketable Securities)/Current Liabilities
   d. (Cash + Marketable Securities + Accounts Receivable)/Current Liabilities

8-18 Which of the following transactions would cause the current ratio to increase (assuming the current ratio is currently greater than 1)?
   a. Purchased inventory on credit
   b. Purchased property, plant, and equipment for cash
   c. Received money from a customer related to an accounts receivable
   d. Paid off a payable

BRIEF EXERCISES

OBJECTIVE

Brief Exercise 8-19 Accounts Payable

On June 18, Stanton Electronics purchased, on credit, 1,700 TV sets for $525 each. Stanton plans to resell these TVs in its store. Stanton paid the supplier on July 31.

Required:
Prepare the necessary journal entry (or entries) on June 18 and July 31.

Brief Exercise 8-20 Accounts and Notes Payable

On April 15, Champion Industries buys $1,340,000 of inventory on credit. On May 31, Champion approaches its supplier because it cannot pay the $1,340,000. The supplier agrees to roll the amount into a note due on November 30 with 12% interest.

Required:

Prepare the necessary journal entries from April 15 through payment on November 30.

OBJECTIVE 2

EXAMPLE 8.1

Brief Exercise 8-21 Issuing Notes Payable

On August 31, Merryweather International borrows $385,000 from Chase Bank with a 9-month, 7% note.

Required:

What journal entry is made at Merryweather's year-end, December 31?

OBJECTIVE 2

EXAMPLE 8.1

Brief Exercise 8-22 Notes Payable

Essential Company, which manufactures steel tubing and casing for automobile production, borrowed $450,000 on January 1 to finance the purchase of a new piece of machinery with new heating technology. The terms of Essential's note dictate that it is a 8-month, 10%, interest-bearing note.

Required:

1. Record the borrowing transaction.
2. Record the repayment transaction.

OBJECTIVE 2

EXAMPLE 8.1

Brief Exercise 8-23 Accrued Interest

On July 1, Brimley Company issued a note with First National Bank with terms of 2 years and 10% interest to finance its inventory purchase of 1,000 plasma televisions with a list price of $2,750 each.

Required:

What adjusting entry should Brimley make at December 31?

OBJECTIVE 2

EXAMPLE 8.1

Brief Exercise 8-24 Accrued Interest

On March 1, the Applewood Corporation wanted to purchase a $175,000 piece of equipment, but Applewood was only able to furnish $60,000 of its own cash to purchase the equipment. Applewood borrowed the remainder of the $175,000 from the People's National Bank on a 2-year, 6% note.

Required:

If the company keeps its records on a calendar year, what adjusting entry should Applewood make on December 31?

OBJECTIVE 2

EXAMPLE 8.1

Brief Exercise 8-25 Accrued Property Taxes

Annual property taxes covering the preceding 12 months are always paid on July 1. Lou Inc. is always assessed $11,000 property taxes.

Required:

Given this information, determine the adjusting journal entry that Lou must make on December 31.

OBJECTIVE 2

Brief Exercise 8-26 Accrued Income Taxes

Nolan Inc. had taxable income of $400,000 for the year. Its effective tax rate is 35%. Nolan pays its income taxes the following April 15th.

OBJECTIVE 2

(Continued)

Required:

1. Given this information, determine the adjusting journal entry that Nolan must make on December 31st.
2. Prepare the journal entry to record the tax payment on April 15th.

OBJECTIVE 2 **Brief Exercise 8-27 Accrued Wages**

Natalie's Bakery pays its 20 hourly employees every Friday. Each of Natalie's employees earns a wage of $10 per hour and works 35 hours per week, spread evenly from Monday through Sunday. During the current year, December 31 falls on a Tuesday.

Required:

Given this information, determine the adjusting journal entry that Natalie's Bakery must make on December 31.

OBJECTIVE 2 **Brief Exercise 8-28 Accrued Wages**

Aqua company employs a part-time staff of 40 employees, each earning $15 per hour and working 35 hours per week. Employees work 5 days per week, Monday through Friday, and are paid weekly on Fridays. The appropriate journal entry was recorded at the end of the accounting period, Wednesday, April 30.

Required:

What journal entries are made on Wednesday, April 30, and Friday, May 2?

OBJECTIVE 2 **Brief Exercise 8-29 Accrued Wages**

Employees earn $2,500 per day, work 5 days per week, Monday through Friday, and get paid every Friday. The previous payday was Friday, March 22, and the accounting period ends on Monday, March 31.

Required:

What is the ending balance in the wages payable account on March 31?

OBJECTIVE 2 **Brief Exercise 8-30 Accrued Wages and Payment of Payroll**

Hansen Legal offices are open Monday through Friday, and Hansen pays employees salaries of $35,000 every other Friday. During the current year, December 31 falls on a Wednesday, and the next payday is January 7.

Required:

Given this information, determine the adjusting journal entry that Hansen must make on December 31 as well as the journal entry to record the payment of the payroll on January 7.

OBJECTIVE 2 **Brief Exercise 8-31 Sales and Excise Tax**

EXAMPLE 8.2

Betty's Antique Shop, a shop specializing in antiques from the 19th century, recently sold a chair from the Civil War era for $60,000 on account. The state sales tax is 5%, and there is a $400-per-antique federal excise tax.

Required:

Provide the journal entry to record the sale.

OBJECTIVE 2 **Brief Exercise 8-32 Sales Tax**

EXAMPLE 8.2

Grey's Furniture sold 50 couches to Shepherd Inc. for $980 each plus an additional state sales tax of 8%. Shepherd Inc. purchased on credit.

Required:

Provide the journal entry to record the sale (round to nearest penny).

Brief Exercise 8-33 Payroll Taxes

OBJECTIVE ◀ 2

EXAMPLE 8.3

Sid's Grocery Store has 100 employees who earn a wage of $18.75 per hour. Each of Sid's employees has worked a total of 160 hours over the month of July. At the time of recording July's monthly payroll, the following amounts have been withheld:

Federal income tax	$30,000
State income tax	8,000
Social Security	18,600
Medicare	4,350
Charitable contributions	1% of gross pay
Union dues	1% of gross pay

Also, the unemployment tax rate is 2% and applies to all but $30,000 of the gross payroll.

Required:
1. What is the amount of net pay recorded by Sid's?
2. Make the journal entries to record the payroll.

Brief Exercise 8-34 Payroll Taxes

OBJECTIVE ◀ 2

EXAMPLE 8.3

Champaign Inc., a company that provides educational consulting services to large universities across the nation, has a gross payroll of $25,000 for the pay period. The entire payroll is subject to Social Security and Medicare taxes. Champaign must also withhold $2,400 in federal income tax from the employees and pay state unemployment tax of $75. Assume the entire payroll is eligible for Social Security and Medicare at standard rates.

Required:
Provide the necessary journal entries for Champaign to record these payroll taxes (round to nearest penny).

Brief Exercise 8-35 Payroll Taxes

OBJECTIVE ◀ 2

EXAMPLE 8.3

It's the Tooth Dental works to provide high-quality pediatric dental services in a fun-loving environment for children. During December, It's the Tooth Dental employees earned $90,000 in wages. Social Security applied to $86,000 of these wages, while Medicare applies to all $90,000 at standard rates. Federal and state income taxes withheld were $1,100 and $500, respectively.

Required:
Provide the necessary journal entries for It's the Tooth Dental to record this activity.

Brief Exercise 8-36 Unearned Sales Revenue

OBJECTIVE ◀ 2

EXAMPLE 8.4

Cory's Carpet Cleaning normally charges $99 to clean one room of carpeting. During the holiday season, Cory offers a promotion to clean the customer's carpet 15 times at a discounted rate if the customer pays $720 in advance.

Required:
Make the journal entry to record the following transactions.
1. A customer's prepayment of $720
2. Cory's cleaning of the carpet one time

Brief Exercise 8-37 Unearned Rent Revenue

OBJECTIVE ◀ 2

EXAMPLE 8.4

First American Property Management leases commercial properties and expects its clients to pay rent on a monthly basis. A new client signs a 3-year lease with a yearly rent of $285,000 and agrees to pay the first 3 months in advance.

(Continued)

Required:

Make the journal entry to record the following transactions.

1. The customer's prepayment of 3 months' rent
2. The necessary adjusting entry after 1 month has passed

OBJECTIVE **3**   **Brief Exercise 8-38   Contingent Liabilities**

Many companies provide warranties with their products. Such warranties typically guarantee the repair or replacement of defective goods for some specified period of time following the sale.

Required:

CONCEPTUAL CONNECTION Why do most warranties require companies to make a journal entry to record a liability for future warranty costs?

OBJECTIVE **3**   **Brief Exercise 8-39   Contingent Liabilities**

SLC Electronics is the plaintiff in a class action lawsuit. Their attorney has written a letter that it is now extremely likely that SLC will lose the lawsuit and be forced to pay $3,000,000 in damages.

Required:

Prepare the necessary journal entry. If no entry is required state "none." Any recognition will be to Other Expense and Lawsuit Payable.

OBJECTIVE **4**
EXAMPLE 8.5

Brief Exercise 8-40   Warranties

Lee Electronics, a franchise of electronics stores located in small towns throughout the United States, sold 450 32-inch televisions for $575 each. The televisions carry an attached 3-year warranty for repairs. Lee Electronics estimates that repair costs will average 2% of the total selling price.

Required:

1. How much is recorded in the Warranty Liability account as a result of selling the televisions during the year, assuming no warranty service has yet been performed?
2. Provide the necessary adjusting entry at December 31.

OBJECTIVE **4**
EXAMPLE 8.5

Brief Exercise 8-41   Warranties

Barry's Party Warehouse provides wholesale party equipment and materials to Party Shops. Barry's Party sold 46 bounce houses at $29,000 each. The bounce houses carry a 4-year warranty for defects. Barry's estimates that repair costs will average 2% of the total selling price. The estimated warranty liability at the beginning of the year was $25,000. Claims of $23,000 were actually incurred during the year to honor warranties.

Required:

What was the balance in the Estimated Warranty Liability account at the end of the year?

OBJECTIVE **5**
EXAMPLE 8.6

Brief Exercise 8-42   Liquidity Ratios

JRL's financial statements contain the following information:

Cash	$400,000	Accounts payable	$575,000
Accounts receivable	800,000	Accrued expenses	180,000
Inventory	950,000	Long-term debt	900,000
Marketable securities	115,000		

(Continued)

Required:
1. What is its current ratio?
2. What is its quick ratio?
3. What is its cash ratio?
4. Discuss JRL's liquidity using these ratios.

Brief Exercise 8-43 Liquidity Ratios

OBJECTIVE 5
EXAMPLE 8.6

SJM's financial statements contain the following information:

Cash	$2,725,000	Accounts payable	$3,275,000
Accounts receivable	3,050,000	Accrued expenses	1,700,000
Inventory	3,950,000	Long-term debt	9,100,000
Marketable securities	1,725,000		

Required:
1. What is the current ratio?
2. What is the quick ratio?
3. What is the cash ratio?
4. Discuss SJM's liquidity using these ratios.

EXERCISES

Exercise 8-44 Accrued Wages

OBJECTIVE 2

Rising Stars Gymnastics pays its hourly employees every Saturday. The weekly payroll for hourly employees is $5,000, and the employees' hours are spread evenly from Monday through Saturday. During the current year, December 31 falls on a Wednesday.

Required:
Given this information, determine the adjusting journal entry that Rising Stars must make on December 31.

Exercise 8-45 Recording Various Liabilities

OBJECTIVE 2

Grove Hardware had the following transactions that produced liabilities during the year:
a. Purchased merchandise on credit for $50,000. (*Note:* Assume a periodic inventory system.)
b. Year-end wages of $22,000 were incurred, but not paid. Related federal income taxes of $2,200, Social Security of $1,364 (employee portion), and Medicare taxes of $320 were withheld from employees.
c. Year-end estimated income taxes payable, but unpaid, for the year were $37,350.
d. Sold merchandise on account for $2,160, including state sales taxes of $90. (*Note:* Assume a periodic inventory system.)
e. Employer's share of Social Security and Medicare taxes for the period were $1,364 and $320, respectively.
f. Borrowed cash under a 120-day, 7%, $20,000 note.

Required:
Prepare the entry to record each of these transactions (treat each transaction independently).

OBJECTIVE

Exercise 8-46 Recording Various Liabilities

Plymouth Electronics had the following transactions that produced liabilities during the year:

a. Purchased merchandise on credit for $80,000. (*Note:* Assume a periodic inventory system.)

b. Year-end wages of $40,000 were incurred, but not paid. Related federal income taxes of $13,000 and Medicare taxes of $580 were withheld. Employee wages are all above the Social Security maximum, so only Medicare was paid.

c. Year-end estimated income taxes payable, but unpaid, for the year were $113,615.

d. Sold merchandise on account for $3,636, including state sales taxes of $180. (*Note:* Assume a periodic inventory system.)

e. Employer's share of Medicare taxes for the period was $580. The taxes will be paid at a later date.

f. Borrowed cash under a 180-day, 8%, $155,000 note.

Required:

Prepare the entry to record each of these transactions (treat each transaction independently).

Exercise 8-47 Reporting Liabilities

Morton Electronics had the following obligations:

a. A legally enforceable claim against the business to be paid in 3 months.

b. A guarantee given by a seller to a purchaser to repair or replace defective goods during the first 6 months following a sale.

c. An amount payable to Bank One in 10 years.

d. An amount to be paid next year to Citibank on a long-term note payable.

Required:

CONCEPTUAL CONNECTION Describe how each of these items should be reported in the balance sheet.

Exercise 8-48 Accounts Payable

Sleek Ride, a company providing limo services, has a December 31 year-end date. For Sleek Ride, the following transactions occurred during the first 10 days of June:

a. Purchased, on credit, space for classified advertisements in the *New York Times* for $1,950. The advertising was run the day the space was purchased.

b. Purchased office supplies from Office Max on credit in the amount of $475.

c. One of Sleek Ride's sales staff signed a $20,000 contract to provide exclusive limo services for a large company for the remainder of the month. The salesperson's commission is 10% of service revenue. The commission will be paid July 10. (*Note:* Concern yourself only with the commission.)

d. Received electric bill for May. The bill is $4,200 and is due on June 15.

e. Received a bill for $970 from Harry's Auto. Harry's repaired 10 limos for Sleek Ride in late May. Payment is due on June 18.

Required:

Prepare journal entries for the above transactions.

Exercise 8-49 Accrued Liabilities

Charger Inc. had the following items that require adjusting entries at the end of the year.

a. Charger pays its employees $5,000 every Friday for a 5-day work week. This year December 31 falls on a Wednesday.

b. Charger earned income of $800,000 for the year for tax purposes. Its effective tax rate is 35%. These taxes must be paid by April 15 of next year.

c. Charger borrowed $280,000 with a note payable dated August 1. This note specifies 6%. The interest and principal are due on March 31 of the following year.

d. Charger's president earns a bonus equal to 10% of income in excess of $650,000. Income for the year was $800,000. This bonus is paid in May of the following year and any expense is charged to wages expense.

Required:

Prepare the adjusting journal entries to record these transactions at the end of the current year.

Exercise 8-50 Accrued Liabilities

OBJECTIVE ▸2

TJ Tile had the following items that require adjusting entries at the end of the year.

a. TJ pays payroll of $212,000 every other Friday for a 2-week period. This year the last payday is Friday, December 26. (*Note:* The work week is Monday through Friday.)

b. TJ purchased $295,000 of tile on July 1 with a note payable requiring 10% interest. The interest and principal on this note are due within 1 year. As of December 31, TJ had not made any principal or interest payments.

c. TJ's earned income is $800,000 for the year for tax purposes. Its effective tax rate is 21%. These taxes must be paid by April 15 of next year.

Required:

Prepare the adjusting journal entries to record these transactions at the end of the current year.

Exercise 8-51 Sales Tax

OBJECTIVE ▸2

Far and Wide Broadband provides Internet connection services to customers living in remote areas. During February 2020, it billed a customer a total of $295,000 before taxes. Weston also must pay the following taxes on these charges:

a. State of Kansas sales tax of 6%

b. Federal excise tax of 0.2%

c. State of Kansas use tax of 0.4%

Required:

Assuming Far and Wide collects these taxes from the customer, what journal entry would Far and Wide make when the customers pay their bills?

Exercise 8-52 Payroll Accounting and Discussion of Labor Costs

OBJECTIVE ▸2

Blitzen Marketing Research paid its weekly and monthly payroll on January 31. The following information is available about the payroll:

Item	Amount
Monthly salaries	$237,480
Hourly wages	585,000
FICA:	
Social Security (both employee and employer)	6.20%
Medicare (both employee and employer)	1.45%
Withholding for federal income taxes	$108,500
Federal unemployment taxes	1,200
State unemployment taxes	4,000

Blitzen will pay both the employer's taxes and the taxes withheld on April 15.

Required:

1. Prepare the journal entries to record the payroll payment and the incurrence of the associated expenses and liabilities. (*Note:* Round to nearest penny.)

2. What is the employees' gross pay? What amount does Blitzen pay in excess of gross pay as a result of taxes? (*Note:* Provide both an absolute dollar amount and as a percentage of gross pay, rounding to two decimal places.)

3. How much is the employees' net pay as a percentage of total payroll related expenses? (*Note:* Round answer to two decimal places.)

4. **CONCEPTUAL CONNECTION** If another employee can be hired for $60,000 per year, what would be the total cost of this employee to Blitzen?

Exercise 8-53 Unearned Revenue

Jennifer's Landscaping Services signed a $400-per-month contract on November 1 to provide plant-watering services for Lola Inc.'s office buildings. Jennifer's received 4 months' service fees in advance on signing the contract.

Required:
1. Prepare Jennifer's journal entry to record the cash receipt for the first 4 months.
2. Prepare Jennifer's adjusting entry at December 31.
3. **CONCEPTUAL CONNECTION** How would the advance payment [account(s) and amount(s)] be reported in Jennifer's balance sheet? How would the advance payment [account(s) and amount(s)] be reported in Lola's balance sheet?

Exercise 8-54 Recognition and Reporting of Contingent Liabilities

A list of alternative accounting treatments is followed by a list of potential contingent liabilities.

Alternative Accounting Treatments
a. Estimate the amount of liability and record.
b. Do not record as a liability but disclose in a footnote to the financial statements.
c. Neither record as a liability nor disclose in a footnote to the financial statements.

Potential Contingent Liabilities
1. Income taxes related to revenue included in net income this year but taxable in a future year
2. Potential costs in future periods associated with performing warranty services on products sold this period
3. Estimated cost of future services under a product warranty related to past sales
4. Estimated cost of future services under a product warranty related to future sales
5. Estimated cost of pension benefits related to past employee services that has yet to be funded
6. Potential loss on environmental cleanup suit against company; a court judgment against the company is considered less than probable but more than remotely likely
7. Potential loss under class-action suit by a group of customers; during the current year, the likelihood of a judgment against the company has increased from remote to possible but less than probable
8. Potential loss under an affirmative action suit by a former employee; the likelihood of a judgment against the company is considered to be remote
9. Potential loss from a downturn in future economic activity
10. Loss from out-of-court settlement of lawsuit that is likely to occur toward the end of next year

Required:
Match the appropriate alternative accounting treatment with each of the potential contingent liabilities listed above. Your answer should list the numbers 1 through 10 and, next to each number, the letter of the appropriate accounting treatment.

Exercise 8-55 Warranties

Kim's Athletics sells bicycles and other sports and athletic equipment. Sales and expected warranty claims for the year are as follows:

Item	Unit Sales	Expected Warranty Claims for Warranty Period	Cost per Claim
Mountain bikes	625	5 claims per 100 sold	$40
Racing bikes	150	1 claims per 15 sold	90
Snowboards	400	2 claim per 40 sold	35

Required:
1. Prepare the entry to record warranty expense for Kim's for the year.
2. **CONCEPTUAL CONNECTION** Why does Kim's have to record a liability for future warranty claims?

Exercise 8-56 Ratio Analysis

OBJECTIVE ◀ 5

SHOW
ME HOW

Intel Corporation provided the following information on its balance sheet and statement of cash flows (in millions):

Current liabilities	$ 22,310	Inventories	$ 8,744
Cash and equivalents	4,194	Other current assets	1,713
Marketable securities	1,082	Cash flows from operating activities	33,145
Receivables	7,659		

Required:

1. Calculate the (a) current ratio, (b) quick ratio, (c) cash ratio, and (d) operating cash flow ratio. (*Note:* Round answers to two decimal places.)
2. **CONCEPTUAL CONNECTION** Interpret these results.
3. **CONCEPTUAL CONNECTION** Assume that Intel, as a requirement of one of its loans, must maintain a current ratio of at least 1.50. Given the large amounts of cash and marketable securities, how could Intel accomplish this on December 31 (be specific as to dollar amounts)?

PROBLEM SET A

Problem 8-57A Payable Transactions

OBJECTIVE ◀ 2

Richmond Company engaged in the following transactions:

a. Purchased $160,000 of supplies from ABC Supplies on February 16. Amount due in full on March 31.
b. Paid for 25% of the purchased merchandise (Transaction a) on February 26.
c. On March 31, negotiated a payment extension with ABC for the remainder of the balance from the February 16 purchase by signing a 1-year, 10% note.
d. Borrowed $300,000 on a 10-month, 8% interest-bearing note on April 30.
e. Purchased $78,000 of merchandise on June 4. Amount due in full on June 30.
f. Paid for the purchased merchandise (Transaction e) on June 24.
g. Received from Haywood Inc. on August 19, a $22,000 deposit against a total selling price of $220,000 for services to be performed for Haywood.
h. Paid quarterly installments of Social Security and Medicare and individual income tax withholdings, as shown below, on October 15. The Social Security and Medicare were previously recorded as expenses during the quarter and the amounts paid represent both the employee and employer shares (50% each):

Social Security taxes withheld	$185,000
Medicare taxes withheld	43,266
Federal income taxes withheld	319,000

i. On December 15, Richmond completed the services ordered by Haywood on August 19. Haywood's remaining balance of $198,000 is due on January 31.

Required:

1. Prepare journal entries for these transactions.
2. Prepare any adjusting entries necessary at December 31.

Problem 8-58A Payroll Accounting

OBJECTIVE ◀ 2

Reed Enterprises has the following data available for its April 30 payroll:

Wages earned	$615,000*
Federal income taxes withheld	110,105

* All subject to Social Security and Medicare matching and withholding of 6.2% and 1.45%, respectively.

(Continued)

Federal unemployment taxes of 0.75% and state unemployment taxes of 0.80% are payable on $545,200 of the wages earned.

Required:

1. Compute the amounts of taxes payable and the amount of wages that will be paid to employees. Then prepare the journal entries to record the wages earned and the payroll taxes. (*Note:* Round to the nearest penny.)
2. **CONCEPTUAL CONNECTION** Reed would like to hire a new employee at a salary of $70,000. Assuming Social Security and Medicare taxes are as described earlier in the problem (with unemployment taxes paid on the first $12,000) and fringe benefits (e.g., health insurance, retirement) are 25% of gross pay, what will be the total cost of this employee for Reed?

Problem 8-59A Note Payable and Accrued Interest

Fairborne Company borrowed $600,000 on an 8%, interest-bearing note on October 1, 2023. Fairborne ends its fiscal year on December 31. The note was paid with interest on May 1, 2024.

Required:

1. Prepare the entry for this note on October 1, 2023.
2. Prepare the adjusting entry for this note on December 31, 2023.
3. Indicate how the note and the accrued interest would appear in the balance sheet at December 31, 2023.
4. Prepare the entry to record the repayment of the note on May 1, 2024.

Problem 8-60A Interest-Bearing Note Replacing an Unpaid Account Payable

Conti Products owed $80,000 on account for inventory purchased on December 1, 2024. Conti uses a perpetual inventory system and has a fiscal year that ends on December 31. Conti was unable to pay the amount owed by the March 1, 2025, due date because of financial difficulties. On March 1, 2025, Conti signed a 4-month, $80,000, 6% interest-bearing note. This note was repaid with interest on July 1, 2025.

Required:

1. Prepare the entry recorded on December 1, 2024.
2. Prepare the adjusting entry recorded on December 31, 2024.
3. Prepare the entry recorded on March 1, 2025.
4. Prepare the entry recorded on July 1, 2025.

Problem 8-61A Excise Taxes

Reagan Gas provides gas utilities to a wide area of eastern Illinois. During the month of May, it billed 36,000 of its residential customers located in the town of Moline a total of $3,295,000 for electricity (this is considered revenue). In addition, Reagan is required to collect the following taxes:

a. State excise tax: A tax of $5.00 per customer plus 3% of billing used to fund the Illinois Energy Commission
b. Federal excise tax: A tax of $0.45 per customer plus 0.2% of billing used to fund the Federal Energy Commission

Required:

1. Determine how much Reagan will bill these customers in total for the month of May.
2. Prepare the entry to record the billing of these amounts.
3. Prepare the entry to record the collection of these amounts.
4. Prepare the entry to record the payment of the state excise taxes to the appropriate governmental unit.

Problem 8-62A Unearned Revenue and Customer Deposits

OBJECTIVE ▶ 2

On November 20, 2023, Green Bay Electronics agreed to manufacture and supply 750 electronic control units used by Wausau Heating Systems in large commercial and industrial installments. On that date, Wausau deposited $250 per unit upon signing the 3-year purchase agreement, which set the selling price of each control unit at $1,000. Green Bay's inventory cost is $225 per unit. No units were delivered during 2023. The first 200 units will be delivered in 2024, 300 units will be delivered during 2025, and the remaining units will be delivered during 2026. Assume Green Bay uses a perpetual inventory system, and Wausau pays in cash upon delivery of units for amounts not covered by the deposit.

Required:

1. **CONCEPTUAL CONNECTION** Prepare the entry by Green Bay to record receipt of the deposit during 2023. How would the deposit be reported in the financial statements at the end of 2023?
2. **CONCEPTUAL CONNECTION** Prepare the entry by Green Bay to record the delivery of 200 units during 2024. How would the deposit be reported in the financial statements at the end of 2024?
3. Prepare the entry by Green Bay to record the delivery of 300 units during 2025.

Problem 8-63A Warranties

OBJECTIVE ◀ 4

Marshall Repairs and Detailing has recently opened its doors to provide quality auto repair services. To encourage business, Marshall offers a 9-month warranty on all repairs. The following data are available for the year:

Transmissions repaired	2,350
Expected frequency of warranty claims	0.08 per repair
Actual warranty claims	$32,700
Beginning balance for estimated warranty liability	$34,500
Estimated cost of each warranty claim	$ 240

Assume that warranty claims are paid in cash.

Required:

1. Compute the warranty expense for the year.
2. Prepare the entry to record the payment of the warranty claims for the year.
3. **CONCEPTUAL CONNECTION** What is the balance in the estimated warranty liability account at December 31? Why has the balance in the warranty liability account changed from the beginning of the year?

Problem 8-64A Ratio Analysis

OBJECTIVE ◀ 5

Consider the following information taken from GER's financial statements:

	September 30 (in thousands)	
	2024	2023
Current assets:		
Cash and cash equivalents	$ 1,274	$ 6,450
Receivables	30,071	16,548
Inventories	31,796	14,072
Other current assets	4,818	2,620
Total current assets	$67,959	$39,690
Current liabilities:		
Current portion of long-term debt	$ 97	$ 3,530
Accounts payable	23,124	11,228
Accrued compensation costs	5,606	1,929
Accrued expenses	9,108	5,054
Other current liabilities	874	777
Total current liabilities	$38,809	$22,518

(Continued)

Also, GER's operating cash flows were $12,829 and $14,874 in 2024 and 2023, respectively. *Note:* Round all answers to two decimal places.

Required:

1. Calculate the current ratios for 2024 and 2023.
2. Calculate the quick ratios for 2024 and 2023.
3. Calculate the cash ratios for 2024 and 2023.
4. Calculate the operating cash flow ratios for 2024 and 2023.
5. **CONCEPTUAL CONNECTION** Provide some reasons why GER's liquidity may be considered to be improving and some reasons why it may be worsening.

PROBLEM SET B

OBJECTIVE ▶2▶ **Problem 8-57B Payable Transactions**

Daniels Company engaged in the following transactions:

a. Purchased $25,000 of merchandise from XYZ Supplies on January 26. Amount due in full on February 28.
b. Paid for 40% of the purchased merchandise (Transaction a) on February 26.
c. On February 28, negotiate a payment extension with XYZ for the remainder of the balance from the January 26 purchase by signing a 1-year, 8% note.
d. Borrowed $300,000 on an 8-month, 9% interest-bearing note on July 31.
e. Purchased $150,000 of merchandise on August 2. Amount due in full on September 30.
f. Paid for the purchased merchandise (Transaction e) on September 28.
g. Received from Martel Inc. on October 4, a $40,000 deposit against a total selling price of $400,000 for services to be performed for Martel.
h. Paid quarterly installments of Social Security, Medicare, and individual income tax withholdings, as shown below, on October 10. The Social Security and Medicare were previously recorded as expenses during the quarter and the amounts paid represent both the employee and employer shares (50% each).

Social Security taxes withheld	$280,000
Medicare taxes withheld	65,484
Federal income taxes withheld	730,000

i. On December 15, Daniels completed the services ordered by Martel on October 4. Martel's remaining balance of $360,000 is due on January 31.

Required:

1. Prepare journal entries for these transactions.
2. Prepare any adjusting entries necessary at December 31.

OBJECTIVE ▶2▶ **Problem 8-58B Payroll Accounting**

McLaughlin Manufacturing has the following data available for its March 31 payroll:

Wages earned	$1,250,000*
Federal income taxes withheld	180,600

* All subject to Social Security and Medicare matching and withholding at 6.2% and 1.45%, respectively.

Federal unemployment taxes of 0.50% and state unemployment taxes of 0.80% are payable on the first $1,000,000.

Required:

1. Compute the taxes payable and wages that will be paid to employees. Then prepare the journal entries to record the wages earned and the payroll taxes. (*Note:* Round to the nearest penny.)

(Continued)

2. **CONCEPTUAL CONNECTION** McLaughlin Manufacturing would like to hire a new employee at a salary of $80,000. Assuming Social Security and Medicare taxes are as described earlier in the problem (with unemployment taxes paid on the first $7,000) and fringe benefits (e.g., health insurance, retirement, etc.) are 28% of gross pay, what will be the total cost of this employee for McLaughlin?

Problem 8-59B Note Payable and Accrued Interest

OBJECTIVE ▸ 2

Ellsworth Enterprises borrowed $425,000 on an 8%, interest-bearing note on September 30, 2024. Ellsworth ends its fiscal year on December 31. The note was paid with interest on March 31, 2025.

Required:

1. Prepare the entry for this note on September 30, 2024.
2. Prepare the adjusting entry for this note on December 31, 2024.
3. Indicate how the note and the accrued interest would appear on the balance sheet at December 31, 2024.
4. Prepare the entry to record the repayment of the note on March 31, 2025.

Problem 8-60B Interest-Bearing Note Replacing an Unpaid Account Payable

OBJECTIVE ▸ 2

Monte Cristo Products, which uses a perpetual inventory system, owed $770,000 on account for inventory purchased on November 1, 2024. The company's fiscal year ends on December 31. Monte Cristo was unable to pay the amount owed by the February 1 due date because of financial difficulties. On February 1, 2025, it signed a $770,000, 12% interest-bearing note. This note was repaid with interest on September 1, 2025.

Required:

1. Prepare the entry recorded on November 1, 2024.
2. Prepare the adjusting entry recorded on December 31, 2024.
3. Prepare the entry recorded on February 1, 2025.
4. Prepare the entry recorded on September 1, 2025.

Problem 8-61B Excise Taxes

OBJECTIVE ▸ 2

Yossarian Power Corporation provides electricity to a wide area of eastern Maine. During the month of March, it billed 3,000 of its residential customers located in the town of Maryville a total of $393,000 for electricity. In addition, Yossarian Power is required to collect the following taxes:

a. State excise tax: A tax of $3.50 per customer plus 2% of billing used to fund the Maine Energy Commission
b. Federal excise tax: A tax of $0.50 per customer plus 0.15% of billing used to fund the Federal Energy Commission

Required:

1. Determine how much Yossarian Power will bill these 3,000 customers in total for the month of March.
2. Prepare the entry to record the billing of these amounts.
3. Prepare the entry to record the collection of these amounts.
4. Prepare the entry to record the payment of the state excise taxes to the appropriate governmental unit.

Problem 8-62B Unearned Revenue and Customer Deposits

OBJECTIVE ▸ 2

On December 10, 2023, Kool-Air Solutions agreed to manufacture and supply 800 refrigerators used by Vandelay Industries. Vandelay deposited $150 per unit upon signing the 3-year purchase agreement, which set the selling price of each refrigerator at $950. Kool-Air's inventory cost is $425 per unit. No units were delivered during 2023. During 2024, 175 units will be delivered; during 2025, 325 units will be delivered; and during 2026, the remaining units will be delivered. Assume Kool-Air uses a perpetual inventory system and Vandelay pays in cash upon delivery of units for amounts not covered by the deposit.

(Continued)

Required:

1. **CONCEPTUAL CONNECTION** Prepare the entry by Kool-Air to record receipt of the deposit during 2023. How would the deposit be reported in the financial statements at the end of 2023?
2. **CONCEPTUAL CONNECTION** Prepare the entry by Kool-Air to record the delivery of 175 units during 2024. How would the deposit be reported in the financial statements at the end of 2024?
3. Prepare the entry by Kool-Air to record the delivery of 325 units during 2025.

OBJECTIVE 4

SHOW ME HOW

Problem 8-63B Warranties

Montague Auto Repair specializes in the repair of foreign car transmissions. To encourage business, Montague offers a 6-month warranty on all repairs. The following data are available for the year:

Transmissions repaired	4,500
Expected frequency of warranty claims	0.09 per repair
Actual warranty claims	$110,000
Beginning balance for estimated warranty liability	$ 25,000
Estimated cost of each warranty claim	$ 250

Assume that warranty claims are paid in cash.

Required:

1. Compute the warranty expense for the year.
2. Prepare the entry to record the payment of warranty claims for the year.
3. **CONCEPTUAL CONNECTION** What is balance in the warranty liability account at December 31? Why has the balance in the warranty liability account changed from the beginning of the year?

OBJECTIVE 5

Problem 8-64B Ratio Analysis

Consider the following information taken from Chicago Water Slide's (CWS's) financial statements:

	September 30 (in thousands)	
	2023	**2022**
Current assets:		
Cash and cash equivalents	$ 2,548	$12,900
Receivables	60,142	33,096
Inventories	63,592	28,144
Other current assets	9,636	5,240
Total current assets	$135,918	$79,380
Current liabilities:		
Current portion of long-term debt	$ 194	$ 7,060
Accounts payable	46,248	22,456
Accrued compensation costs	11,212	3,858
Accrued expenses	18,216	10,108
Other current liabilities	1,748	1,554
Total current liabilities	$ 77,618	$45,036

Also, CWS's operating cash flows were $25,658 and $29,748 in 2023 and 2022, respectively. *Note:* Round all answers to two decimal places.

Required:

1. Calculate the current ratios for 2023 and 2022.
2. Calculate the quick ratios for 2023 and 2022.
3. Calculate the cash ratios for 2023 and 2022.
4. Calculate the operating cash flow ratios for 2023 and 2022.
5. **CONCEPTUAL CONNECTION** Provide some reasons why CWS's liquidity may be considered to be improving and some reasons why it may be worsening.

CASES

Case 8-65 Ethics and Current Liabilities

Many long-term loans have contractual restrictions designed to protect the lender from deterioration of the borrower's liquidity or solvency in the future. These restrictions (typically called loan covenants) often take the form of financial-statement ratio values. For example, a lending agreement may state that the loan principal is immediately due and payable if the current ratio falls below 1.2. When borrowers are in danger of violating one or more of these loan covenants, pressure is put on management and the financial accountants to avoid such violations.

Jim is a second year accountant at a large publicly traded corporation. His boss approaches him and says,

> "Jim, I know why we increased our warranty liability, but it puts our current ratio in violation of a loan covenant with our bank loan. I know the bank will pass on it this time, but it's a big hassle to get the waiver. I just don't want to deal with it. I need you to reduce our estimate of warranty liability as far as possible."

Required:

1. How would lowering the estimate of warranty liability affect the current ratio?
2. How should Jim respond to his boss?
3. Given that Jim's employer is a publicly traded corporation, what safeguards should be at Jim's disposal?

Case 8-66 Short-Term Borrowing with Restrictions

Rocky Mountain Products has a line-of-credit agreement with Norwest Bank that allows it to borrow up to $100,000 at any given time provided that Rocky Mountain's current assets always exceed its current liabilities by the principal amount of the outstanding loan. If this requirement is violated, the entire loan is payable immediately; thus Rocky Mountain is very careful to fulfill the requirement at all times. All loans under this line of credit are due in 1 month and bear interest at a rate of 1% per month. On January 1, Rocky Mountain has current assets of $150,000 and current liabilities of $92,000; hence, the excess of current assets over current liabilities is $58,000. Rocky Mountain's current liabilities at January 1 include a short-term loan under the line of credit of $35,000 due on February 1.

Required:

1. Prepare the journal entry to record the borrowing of $35,000 on January 1. By how much did this transaction increase or decrease the excess of current assets over current liabilities?
2. Assume that Rocky Mountain used the entire amount of the loan to purchase inventory. Prepare the journal entry to record the purchase. (*Note:* The company uses a perpetual inventory system.) By how much did this purchase increase or decrease the excess of current assets over current liabilities?
3. Without violating the loan restriction, how much more could Rocky Mountain borrow under its line of credit on January 1 to invest in inventory? To invest in new equipment? Explain.

Case 8-67 Research and Analysis Using the Annual Report

Obtain **Costco**'s 2019 annual report (filed October 11, 2019) either through the "Investor Relations" portion of its website (do a web search for Costco investor relations) or go to www.sec.gov and click "Company Filings Search" under "Filings."

Required:

1. What are Costco's total current liabilities for 2019?
2. How much of its current liabilities is the current portion of all long-term liabilities?
3. Item 3 in the 10-K discusses legal proceedings. Costco references Note 10 of the Notes to Consolidate Financial Statements in Item 8 (this is the "Commitments and

(Continued)

Contingencies" Note). Based on the information in Note 10, do you believe that Costco is a defendant in any lawsuits? If so, do you believe that Costco has recognized a contingent liability related to these current legal proceedings?

4. Calculate Costco's current ratio for 2018 and 2019. (*Note:* Round answers to two decimal places.)
5. Discuss Costco's short-term liquidity based on the values and trends of the current ratio.
6. Calculate Costco's quick ratio and cash ratio for 2018 and 2019. (*Note:* Round answers to two decimal places.)
7. Discuss the implications of these ratios when evaluating Costco's short-term liquidity.
8. Calculate Costco's operating cash flows ratio. (*Note:* Round answer to two decimal places.)
9. Discuss the implications of this ratio when evaluating Costco's short-term liquidity.

Case 8-68 Comparative Analysis: Kroger versus Sprouts

Refer to the 10-K reports of **Kroger** and **Sprouts** that are available for download from the companion website at Cengage.com.

Required:

1. Kroger (Note 13, Commitments and Contingencies) has a note discussing contingencies. What three categories of contingencies does the note disclose? With respect to the contingencies resulting from Litigation, when does Kroger make a provision (i.e., accrue a liability) related to the contingency? How large does Kroger believe such provisions are in total?
2. Sprouts has a note providing detail on its accrued liabilities. Locate the note and provide the amount of its self-insurance liability as of December 29, 2019.
3. Calculate Kroger's and Sprouts' current ratios for 2018 and 2019. (*Note:* Round answers to two decimal places.)
4. Compare Kroger's and Sprouts' short-term liquidity based on the values and trends of the current ratios.
5. Calculate Kroger's and Sprouts' quick ratios and cash ratios for 2018 and 2019. For Kroger's, count "Store deposits in-transit" as cash. These amounts are primarily funds deposited to the Kroger's bank accounts for which it does not have immediate access—a majority of these amounts are related to sales paid for with credit cards and checks. (*Note:* Round answers to two decimal places.)
6. Compare the values and trends of these ratios when evaluating Kroger's and Sprouts' short-term liquidity.
7. Calculate Kroger's and Sprouts' operating cash flows ratios for 2018 and 2019. (*Note:* Round answers to two decimal places.)
8. Compare Kroger's and Sprouts' short-term liquidity based on the values and trends of the operating cash flows ratio.

ANNUAL REPORT PROBLEM

HOME DEPOT

Download the 10-K for **Home Depot** from the companion website at Cengage.com.

Required:

1. What does the company report for the following accounts:
   - Cash
   - Short-term investments
   - Accounts receivable
   - Inventory
   - Other current assets
   - Accounts payable

(Continued)

- Other current liabilities
- Cash flow from operations
2. Assume that the company projects the following:
   - Current assets will increase by 8%
   - Accounts payable will increase by 12%
   - Other current liabilities are expected to grow by 5%.
   - Cash flow from operations is expected to decrease by 1%

Assume all other items remain unchanged from the prior year. Provide the next year's forecasted balances for the above accounts.
3. Compute the forecasted current ratio?
4. Compute the forecasted quick ratio?
5. Compute the forecasted cash ratio?
6. Calculate the forecasted operating cash flow ratio?
7. Does the company report any contingent liabilities due to lawsuits?

Note: *While the Annual Report problems in the textbook are static, when assigned in CNOW, these activities are algorithmic and the answers may vary from what appears in the Solutions Manual.*

CONTINUING PROBLEM

FRONT ROW ENTERTAINMENT

Front Row has the following selected balances at the February 28, 2024:

Account	Debit	Credit
Cash	$12,480	
Accounts receivable	3,900	
Inventory	20,380	
Other current assets	31,000	
Accounts payable		$ 8,640
Interest payable		375
Sales taxes payable		1,200
Unearned sales revenue		26,100
Other current liabilities		8,300

The following information is *not* reflected in these balances:
a. On February 28, 2024, Front Row accepted delivery of $5,325 of live-performance DVDs from the supplier. Front Row has not yet paid the supplier.
b. On February 1, Front Row purchased $8,000 of equipment for its Chicago Music House venue by issuing a 1-year note payable bearing 10% interest. Front Row has not made any journal entries related to this transaction and should accrue for this at month's end. (*Note:* Round any calculations to the nearest dollar.)
c. Front Row collected $3,745 of advance ticket sales related to an upcoming concert. This price included 7% state sales tax.
d. Amanda Wilson was paid $2,000 in wages to update and monitor the online fan communities. Federal and state unemployment taxes are $16 and $108, respectively. All of Amanda's wages are subject to Social Security and Medicare at the normal rates. In addition, $375 of federal income taxes were withheld. (*Note:* Round any calculations to the nearest dollar.)

In addition, several individuals were injured during a concert in February when they pushed past security and rushed the stage. A personal injury lawsuit was filed against Front Row in the amount of $250,000. After investigating the incident and consultation with legal counsel, it was determined that the likelihood of a judgment against Front Row is remote.

Required:
1. Prepare the necessary journal entries for Transactions a through d. (*Note:* Round all calculations to the nearest dollar.)
2. Determine the current ratio before and after the additional information (round to 2 decimal places).
3. How should this contingent event be recorded?

9 Long-Term Liabilities

After studying Chapter 9, you should be able to:

1. Describe debt securities and the markets in which they are issued.

2. Record and properly present long-term debt at the time of issuance.

3. Use the straight-line method to record premium/discount amortization and properly present long-term debt.

4. Use the effective interest rate method to record premium/discount amortization and properly present long-term debt.

5. Calculate the after-tax cost of financing with debt and explain financial leverage.

6. Describe short- and long-term leases.

7. Analyze long-term solvency using information related to long-term liabilities.

8. (Appendix 9A) Calculate the market price of long-term debt using present value techniques.

Nieuwland Photography/Shutterstock.com

EXPERIENCE FINANCIAL ACCOUNTING

with American Airlines

American Airlines Group (AAL) is the parent company of **American Airlines**, **AMR Eagle**, and **AmericanConnection** airlines. These airlines serve more than 365 destinations in 61 countries and average nearly 6,800 flights per day with approximately 940 airplanes. In 2019, AAL had revenues of over $45.7 billion and total assets of almost $60 billion. However, AAL also has long-term debt and pension obligations (including current portions) of $30.4 billion.

Companies use long-term debt, along with issuing stock (see Chapter 10), as a way to finance and expand their operations. One measure used to evaluate the mix of debt and equity financing is the long-term debt to equity ratio. A ratio above 1.0 indicates that liabilities are greater than stockholders' equity. According to **Reuters Finance**, the long-term debt to equity ratio for the airline industry is 1.35. Compare this with the pharmaceutical industry that has an average long-term debt to equity ratio of 0.12. Why do airlines have so much more debt than pharmaceutical companies?

Industries that use property, plant, and equipment (PP&E) to generate revenues (such as airlines and hotels) typically have higher debt than industries that use intangible assets (such as pharmaceuticals and software). There are a number of reasons for this, but one is that PP&E is readily transferable to creditors in the event of financial distress, so creditors are more receptive to lending at lower rates.

There is a long history of finance research investigating the optimal mix of debt and equity financing because there are advantages and disadvantages for both. Factors affecting the optimal mix are difficult to quantify.

Relatively large amounts of long-term debt are not necessarily bad. Although more long-term debt means more interest expense, interest expense has the advantage of being tax deductible, unlike dividends paid to stockholders. Another advantage is that creditors do not share in the profits of the company, while stockholders do. Thus, if the borrowed money creates a return that is greater than the interest expense on the debt, the stockholders benefit. This is the concept of leverage. We will discuss this concept more in Chapter 12.

Long-term debt generally refers to obligations that extend beyond 1 year. Bonds, long-term notes, debentures, and capital leases belong in this category of liabilities. Exhibit 9.1 shows **Whirlpool**'s long-term debt obligations.[1]

EXHIBIT 9.1   **Excerpt from Whirlpool's 2019 10-K (Note 4)**

NOTE 7 FINANCING ARRANGEMENTS	December 31	
	2019	2018
	Millions of dollars	
Senior note—2.40%, maturing 2019	$ —	$ 250
Term Loan—1.00%, maturing 2019	—	687
Senior note—0.625%, maturing 2020	561	572
Senior note—4.85%, maturing 2021	300	300
Senior note—4.70%, maturing 2022	300	300
Senior note—3.70%, maturing 2023	250	250
Senior note—4.00%, maturing 2024	300	300
Senior note—3.70%, maturing 2025	350	350
Senior note—1.25%, maturing 2026	556	567
Senior note—1.10%, maturing 2027	667	681
Senior note—1.75%, maturing 2029	692	—
Senior note—5.15%, maturing 2043	249	250
Senior note—4.50%, maturing 2046	496	496
Other, net	(22)	(10)
	$4,699	$4,993
Less current maturities	559	947
Total long-term debt	$4,140	$4,046

Source: Whirlpool Corporation, 2019 10-K.

On the balance sheet, long-term debt is typically reported as a single number. The more detailed list, like this one for **Whirlpool**, is usually included in the notes to the financial statements.

Notice that **Whirlpool** subtracted current maturities (just before the bottom line) from the rest of its long-term debt. The difference ($4,140 for 2019) is the amount included as long-term debt on the balance sheet. As we noted in Chapter 8, long-term debt that is due to mature over the next year is reported as a current liability. For simplification, we will disregard the reclassification of long-term debt as current liabilities throughout this chapter.

---

[1] We use the term debt instead of *liabilities* in this chapter because this is the term used in real financial statements.

BONDS PAYABLE AND NOTES PAYABLE

OBJECTIVE 1

Describe debt securities and the markets in which they are issued.

When a company borrows money from a bank, it typically signs a formal agreement or contract called a "note." Frequently, notes are also issued in exchange for a noncash asset such as equipment. Collectively, we refer to these notes as **notes payable**. Larger corporations typically elect to issue bonds instead of notes. A **bond** is a type of note that requires the issuing entity to pay the face value of the bond to the holder when it matures and usually to pay interest periodically at a specified rate.[2] A bond issue essentially breaks down a large debt (large corporations frequently borrow hundreds of millions of dollars) into smaller chunks (usually $1,000) because the total amount borrowed is too large for a single lender. For example, rather than try to find a single bank willing (and able) to lend $800,000,000 at a reasonable interest rate, corporations typically find it easier and more economical to issue 800,000 bonds with a $1,000 face value. However, the concept behind the way we account for notes and bonds is identical (the only difference is the account title—either "Bonds Payable" or "Notes Payable"), and analysts typically do not distinguish between the two. As such, the terms have come to be used somewhat interchangeably.

All such contracts require the borrower to repay the **face value** (also called **par value** or **principal**). Typically the face value is repaid at **maturity**, which is a specified date in the future. However, some contracts require the principal to be repaid in, for example, monthly installments. These contracts typically require equal payments to be made each period. A portion of each payment is interest and a portion is principal. Car, student, and home loans are examples of installment loans.

Most debt contracts also require that the borrower make regular interest payments. Historically, interest payments were made when a bondholder detached a coupon from the debt contract and mailed it to the company on the interest payment date. These obligations are called *coupon notes, coupon debentures*, or *coupon bonds*, and the required interest payments are *coupon payments*. The terminology for coupons is still used today, but now the payments are automatically sent to the registered bondholder.

The amount of each interest payment can be calculated from the face amount, the interest rate, and the number of payments per year, which are all stated in the debt contract. (The **interest rate** identified in the contract goes by various names, including **stated rate**, **coupon rate**, and **contract rate**.) Recall the formula for calculating interest:

$$\text{Face Value} \times \text{Interest Rate} \times \text{Time (in years)}$$

To illustrate, consider a contract with a face value of $1,000, a stated interest rate of 8%, and semiannual interest payments. For this $1,000 note, the amount of each semiannual interest payment is $40:

$$\$1,000 \times 8\% \times 6/12 = \$40$$

TYPES OF BONDS

In practice, bonds also differ along a number of other dimensions, as illustrated in Exhibit 9.2 (p. 512).

Secured Bonds A **secured** bond has some collateral pledged against the corporation's ability to pay. For example, **mortgage bonds** are secured by real estate. In this case, should the borrower fail to make the payments required by the bond, the lender can take possession of (repossess) the real estate that secures the bond. The real estate provides "security" for the lender in case the debt is not paid. Bonds are also frequently secured by the stocks or bonds of other corporations and, in theory, can be secured by anything of value.

---

2 Interest is generally paid semiannually. We use both semiannual and annual interest payments in the text to better illustrate interest amortization.

EXHIBIT 9.2	Long-Term Debt Terms
Notes/Bonds	Debt instruments that require borrowers to pay the lender the face value and usually to make periodic interest payments.
Face Value/Par Value/Principal	Amount of money the borrower agrees to repay at maturity. Date on which the borrower
Maturity Date	agrees to pay the creditor the face (or par) value.
Stated/Coupon/Contract Rate	Rate of interest paid on the face (or par) value. The borrower pays the interest to the creditor each period until maturity.
Market/Yield Rate	Market rate of interest demanded by creditors. This is a function of economic factors and the creditworthiness of the borrower. It may differ from the stated rate.
Secured Bonds	Secured debt provides collateral (such as real estate or another asset) for the lender. If the borrower fails to make the payments required by the debt, the lender can take steps to "repossess" the collateral.
Unsecured/Debenture Bonds	Debt that does not have collateral is unsecured. Unsecured bonds typically are called debenture bonds.
Junk Bonds	Unsecured bonds that are relatively risky and, therefore, pay a high rate of interest to compensate the lender for the added risk.
Callable Bonds	Bonds that give the borrower the option to pay off the debt prior to maturity. Borrowers typically exercise this option when the interest being paid on the debt is substantially greater than the current market rate of interest.
Convertible Bonds	Bonds that give the lender the option to convert the bond into other securities—typically shares of common stock. Lenders will typically exercise this option when the value of the shares of common stock is more attractive than the interest and principal payments supplied by the debt instrument.

Unsecured Bonds Most bonds, however, are **unsecured**. These are typically called **debenture bonds**. In this case, there is no collateral; instead, the lender is relying on the general credit of the corporation. What this means is that should the borrower go bankrupt, any secured bondholders will get their collateral before the unsecured bondholders receive a single penny. That is, unsecured bondholders are the last lenders to be paid in bankruptcy (only the stockholders follow).

You may have heard of the term **junk bonds**. These are unsecured bonds where the risk of the borrower failing to make the interest and/or principal payments is relatively high. Why would anyone lend money under such circumstances? Because they receive a high enough rate of interest to compensate them for the risk.

Callable Bonds **Callable bonds** give the borrower the right to pay off (or call) the bonds prior to their due date. The borrower typically "calls" debt when the interest rate being paid is much higher than the current market conditions. This is similar to homeowners "refinancing" to obtain a lower interest rate on their home mortgage.

Convertible Bonds **Convertible bonds** allow the bondholder to convert the bond into another security—typically common stock. Convertible bonds will specify the conversion ratio. For example, each $1,000 bond may be convertible into 20 shares of common stock. In this case, bondholders will convert when the value of the 20 shares becomes more attractive than the interest payments and repayment of the $1,000 principal.

SELLING NEW DEBT SECURITIES

Borrowing, through the use of notes or bonds, is attractive to businesses as a source of money because the relative cost of issuing debt (the interest payments) is often lower than the cost of issuing equity (giving up ownership shares). Businesses may sell bonds directly to institutions such as insurance companies or pension funds. However, bonds are frequently sold to the public through an underwriter. Underwriters generate a profit either by offering a price that is slightly less than the expected market price (thereby producing a profit on resale) or by charging the borrower a fee.

Underwriters examine the provisions of the instrument (secured or unsecured, callable or not callable, convertible or not convertible), the credit standing of the borrowing business, and the current conditions in the credit markets and the economy as a whole to determine the **market rate** of interest (or **yield**) for the bond. The yield may differ from the stated rate because the underwriter disagrees with the borrower as to the correct yield or because of changes in the economy or creditworthiness of the borrower between the date of setting the stated rate and the date of issue.

As shown in Exhibit 9.3, there are three possible relationships between the stated interest rate and yield: (1) they can be equal, (2) the yield can be less than the stated rate, or (3) the yield can be greater than the stated rate. If the yield is equal to the stated rate, the bonds sell for the face value, or par. If the yield is less than the stated rate, the bonds represent particularly good investments because the interest payments are higher than market. In this case, the demand for such bonds will bid the selling price up above face value. When this happens, bonds are said to sell at a **premium**. On the other hand, if the yield is greater than the stated rate of interest, the below market interest payments will drive the selling price below the face value, in which case, the bond would sell at a **discount**.

Next Level

Why is the market value of bonds not always equal to their face value?

ANSWER:
If, for example, the stated rate of interest is higher than the market rate of interest, the bonds represent particularly good investments. As such, the demand for such bonds will bid the price up above face value. On the other hand, if the stated rate of interest is lower than the market rate of interest, the lack of demand for such bonds will bid the market price below face value.

The Relationships Between Stated Interest Rate and Yield		**EXHIBIT 9.3**

Bonds Sold at	Yield Compared to Stated Rate	Interest over the Life of the Bonds
Premium (Above Par)	Yield < Stated Rate	Interest Expense < Interest Paid
Par	Yield = Stated Rate	Interest Expense = Interest Paid
Discount (Below Par)	Yield > Stated Rate	Interest Expense > Interest Paid

---

 YOUDECIDE Fixed versus Variable-Rate Debt

You are the CFO of Carmean Corp. Carmean has decided to borrow $100,000,000 to finance expansion plans. One option is to issue 20-year bonds with a fixed rate of 8%. Carmean's investment bankers believe these will sell for par. Another option is to issue 20-year bonds with a variable rate of 1-year LIBOR (London Interbank Offered Rate) plus 4.5%. For the first year, this will result in a 6.5% rate, but the rate will be adjusted annually.

What types of things should you consider in making the decision about which borrowing option is best for Carmean?

Borrowers must trade off the potential benefit of lower rates with the risk of the rate increasing in the future. In fact, risk is what the difference in rates is all about. With a fixed rate, the lender bears all the risk of changing rates. Specifically, if fixed rates increase dramatically, the

lender is stuck with a below market return. Admittedly, if rates were to drop, the lender has an above market return, but this uncertainty is the definition of risk. With a variable rate, on the other hand, the borrower bears the risk (and rewards) of changing rates. The shift of risk from the lender to the borrower is why the lender is willing to accept a lower rate initially.

Borrowers must consider terms of the contract, such as how frequently the rate is adjusted, the length of the loan, limits on how much the rate can increase each year, or how high the rate can go, etc. Additionally, the borrower must consider its ability to handle increased interest payments should the rate adjust up.

In this case, Carmean should only opt for the lower variable rate if the company can absorb the higher interest payments should the rate adjust up.

ACCOUNTING FOR LONG-TERM DEBT

The accounting for notes and bonds is conceptually identical. Keep in mind that, in the bond and note examples that follow, everything would stay the same if we substituted the word *note* for *bond* and vice versa.

There are three basic cash flows for which the issuing corporation must account:

- issuance: the cash received when the bonds are issued (the issue or selling price)
- interest: the interest payments
- repayment: the repayment of the principal (or face value)

Assume that a corporation issues bonds with a total face value of $500,000, with a stated rate of 6.5% payable annually, and the principal is due in 5 years. Exhibit 9.4 depicts all three cash flows.

EXHIBIT 9.4	**Cash Flows for a Bond**

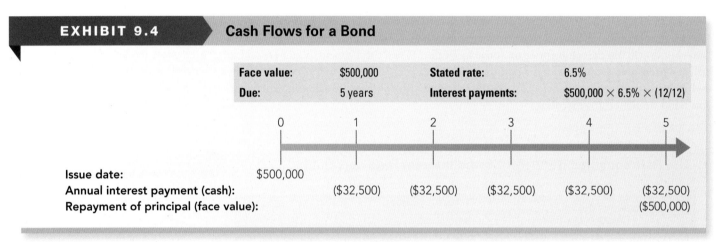

RECORDING ISSUANCE

The market price for debt is typically quoted as a percentage of face value. For example, if $100,000 face value bonds are issued at 103, their selling price is 103% of face value, or $103,000. Any amount paid above the face value is called a *premium*. In this case, a $3,000 premium was paid. If the bond is issued below face value, this difference is called a *discount*. For example, if these $100,000 face value bonds were issued at 96, there would be a $4,000 discount.

At the time of issue, the borrower records the face value of the bonds in a bond payable account and records any premium or discount in a separate account called Premium on Bonds Payable or Discount on Bonds Payable. The premium and discount accounts are called "valuation" accounts because they affect the value at which the liability is shown on the balance sheet. That is, as shown in Exhibit 9.5, both the premium and discount accounts are netted with bonds payable on the balance sheet, so on the date of issue the book value of the bonds payable is equal to the market value.

EXHIBIT 9.5	**Balance Sheet Presentation**

EXAMPLE 9.1 illustrates recording the issuance of bonds.

EXAMPLE 9.1   RECORDING THE ISSUANCE OF BONDS

On January 1, Vampatella Co. issued $100,000 face value of bonds, with a stated rate of 8%, due in 5 years with interest payable annually on December 31.

Required:
Prepare the journal entries assuming the bonds sell (1) for par, (2) for 103, and (3) for 96.

Solution:
1. When bonds are issued, they are valued on the balance sheet at their issue price by putting the face (or par) value in the bonds payable account and recording any premium or discount in a separate valuation account.

Date	Account and Explanation	Debit	Credit	Assets	=	Liabilities	+	Stockholders' Equity
Jan. 1	Cash	100,000		▲				
	Bonds Payable		100,000			▲		

2.

Date	Account and Explanation	Debit	Credit	Assets	=	Liabilities	+	Stockholders' Equity
Jan. 1	Cash (100,000 × 103%)	103,000		▲				
	Bonds Payable		100,000			▲		
	Premium on Bonds Payable		3,000			▲		

3.

Date	Account and Explanation	Debit	Credit	Assets	=	Liabilities	+	Stockholders' Equity
Jan. 1	Cash (100,000 × 96%)	96,000		▲				
	Discount on Bonds Payable	4,000				▼		
	Bonds Payable		100,000			▲		

RECOGNIZING INTEREST EXPENSE AND REPAYMENT OF PRINCIPAL

OBJECTIVE 3

Use the straight-line method to record premium/discount amortization and properly present long-term debt.

Recognizing repayment of the principal at maturity is trivial. Recall that the principal amount repaid is equal to the face value of the note. This is also the amount that was originally credited to the note or bond payable. As such, you merely need to debit the note or bond payable and credit the cash.

Recognizing the interest expense, on the other hand, is a bit more challenging because, conceptually, any premium received or discount granted by the borrower should be offset against future interest payments. In our examples above, when the bonds were issued at par (face value) the amount of cash received when issued was equal to the amount to be repaid at maturity. When the bonds were issued at a premium, the amount of cash received when issued was $103,000 ($3,000 greater than the face value), but only the face value ($100,000) is repaid at maturity. The $3,000 difference represents an effective reduction of the amount of interest paid to the borrower. In contrast, when the bonds were issued at a discount, the amount of cash received was $96,000 ($4,000 less than the face value), but the entire face value ($100,000) must be repaid at maturity. The additional $4,000 effectively represents additional interest.

Next Level

Why are premiums and discounts on bonds payable amortized to Interest Expense?

ANSWER:
Discounts occur when the stated rate of interest is below the market rate of interest. In this case, lenders lend less than the face value to the borrower but are repaid the entire face value at maturity. This difference between the amount lent and the amount repaid conceptually represents an additional interest payment to compensate the lender for accepting a below market interest rate. Similarly, premiums occur when the stated rate of interest is above the market rate of interest. In this case, lenders lend more than the face value to the borrower but are only repaid the face value at maturity. This difference represents a prepayment of interest by the lender to compensate the borrower for providing above market interest payments.

When an obligation extends over several interest periods, the amount of interest associated with each period also must be determined. **Interest amortization** is the process used to determine the amount of interest to be recorded in each of the periods the liability is outstanding.[3] This allocation has two parts:

- actual interest payment made to the lender during the period
- amortizing any premium or discount on the bond

INTEREST AMORTIZATION METHODS

Although the interest payment made to the lender during the period is always a component of the period's interest expense, there are two methods for amortizing any premium or discount:

- The **effective interest rate method** is based on compound interest calculations. Interest expense for the period is always the yield (the effective interest rate) times the carrying (or book) value of the bonds at the beginning of the period.
- The **straight-line method**, on the other hand, represents a simple approximation of effective interest amortization. Equal amounts of premium or discount are amortized to interest expense each period.

Although the effective interest rate method is GAAP, the straight-line method may be used if it produces approximately the same numerical results as the effective interest rate method. Frequently, the two methods do, in fact, produce quite similar results.

THE STRAIGHT-LINE METHOD

We will now discuss how interest expense is allocated to the various accounting periods using the straight-line method for:

- debt with regular interest payments sold at their face or par value
- debt with regular interest payments sold for more (a premium) or less (a discount) than the face or par value

DEBT WITH REGULAR INTEREST PAYMENTS SOLD AT PAR

When debt is sold at par, there is no premium or discount to amortize. In this case, the interest expense reported on the income statement is equal to the interest payment(s) made to the creditor during the period. This situation typically happens when a business borrows from a single creditor. In this case, the two parties can easily agree on a stated rate that equals the appropriate yield. EXAMPLE 9.2 illustrates how interest expense is recorded in this case.

EXAMPLE 9.2   RECORDING INTEREST EXPENSE FOR BONDS SOLD AT PAR

On January 1, 2024, Vampatella Co. issued $100,000 of 8% bonds at par. These bonds are due in 5 years with interest payable annually on December 31.

Required:
1. Calculate the interest payment made on December 31 of each year.

2. Prepare the journal entries necessary to recognize (a) the interest expense on December 31, 2024–2028, and (b) the repayment of the loan principal on December 31, 2028.

---

3   The same interest amortization procedures used by borrowers to account for liabilities are also used by lenders to account for the corresponding assets.

Solution:

1. The interest payment on December 31 of each year will be:

$$\$100,000 \times 8\% \times 12/12 = \$8,000$$

2. Any premium or discount is amortized over the life of the bond (or note) and netted with the interest payment to provide interest expense. However, when bonds are issued at par, there is no premium or discount to amortize, so the only component of interest expense is the interest paid to the lender for the period.

a.

Date	Account and Explanation	Debit	Credit	Assets	= Liabilities +	Stockholders' Equity
Dec. 31, 2024–2028	Interest Expense	8,000				▼
	Cash		8,000	▼		

b.

Date	Account and Explanation	Debit	Credit	Assets	= Liabilities +	Stockholders' Equity
Dec. 31, 2028	Bonds Payable	100,000			▼	
	Cash		100,000	▼		

Note, from Example 9.2, that the interest expense recorded is equal to the cash paid to the lender when the bond is issued at par.

DEBT WITH REGULAR INTEREST PAYMENTS SOLD AT A PREMIUM OR DISCOUNT

As mentioned previously, the sale of a bond at a discount or premium affects the borrower's interest expense. This is because total interest expense is the difference between the payments to the lenders and the amount received by the borrowing business. Let us compare a $1,000,000, 10%, 5-year bond contract with semiannual interest payments that are sold at a $10,000 discount (99% of par) with the same issue sold at a $20,000 premium (102% of par).

	Bond Sold at a Discount	Bond Sold at a Premium
Face amount payment at maturity	$1,000,000	$1,000,000
Interest payments (10% at $50,000 each)	500,000	500,000
Total payments to lenders	$1,500,000	$1,500,000
Less: Proceeds at issue	(990,000)	(1,020,000)
Total interest expense over life of bond	$ 510,000	$ 480,000

For the discounted bond, total interest expense ($510,000) exceeds interest payments ($500,000) by $10,000. For the bond issued at a premium, total interest expense ($480,000) is $20,000 less than the cash interest payments ($500,000).

This total interest expense is spread over the life of the bond. For the 10%, $1,000,000 bond sold at 99, interest expense would be $51,000 per 6-month interest period:

$$\frac{\$510,000}{10} = \$51,000 \text{ per 6-month interest period}$$

Another way of calculating this would be as:

Interest paid	$50,000
Amortization of discount (10,000/10 periods)	1,000
Total interest expense per period	$51,000

In fact, amortization tables like those in Examples 9.3 and 9.4 (page 520) are used to help calculate these amounts. Although such tables aren't really necessary when using the straight-line method for amortizing bond discount or premium, they are extremely helpful when the effective interest rate method is used, as is shown later in the chapter.
EXAMPLE 9.3 shows how to record interest expense when the bond is issued at a discount.

EXAMPLE 9.3   RECORDING INTEREST EXPENSE FOR BONDS SOLD AT A DISCOUNT USING THE STRAIGHT-LINE METHOD

On January 1, 2024, Franzen Inc. issues 5-year, $100,000,000, 8% bonds at 99 ($99,000,000). The discount at the time of the sale is $1,000,000. Interest is paid semiannually on June 30 and December 31.

Required:

1. Prepare the journal entry to record the issuance of the bonds on January 1, 2024.

2. Calculate the amount of discount that will be amortized each semiannual period.

3. Calculate the amount of interest expense for each semiannual period.

4. Complete an amortization table for each of the 10 semiannual periods.

5. Prepare the journal entries necessary to (a) recognize the interest expense on June 30 and December 31, 2024–2028, and (b) record the repayment of the loan principal on December 31, 2028.

Solution:

1. When bonds are issued, they are valued on the balance sheet at their issue price by putting the face (or par) value in the bonds payable account and recording any premium or discount in a separate valuation account.

Date	Account and Explanation	Debit	Credit	Assets	= Liabilities +	Stockholders' Equity
Jan. 1, 2024	Cash	99,000,000		▲		
	Discount on Bonds Payable	1,000,000			▼	
	Bonds Payable		100,000,000		▲	

2. Any premium or discount on the sale of a bond is amortized over the life of the bond—in this case, evenly each period.

$$\text{Discount Amortization} = \frac{\text{Total Discount}}{\text{Number of Interest Periods}} = \frac{\$1,000,000}{10 \text{ periods}} = \underline{\$100,000 \text{ per period}}$$

3. The amount of discount amortized each interest period effectively increases the interest expense recognized for the period. This is because the discount on the issue of the bonds (i.e., when bonds are issued for $99,000,000, but $100,000,000 is paid back at maturity) essentially represents additional interest being paid by the borrower.

$$\begin{aligned} \text{Interest Expense} &= \text{Interest Payment} + \text{Discount Amortization} \\ &= (\$100,000,000 \times 8\% \times 6/12) + \$100,000 \\ &= \$4,000,000 + \$100,000 \\ &= \underline{\$4,100,000} \end{aligned}$$

4. Such tables help organize the information to calculate the amount of discount to amortize and interest expense to recognize. Such tables are not really necessary with straight-line amortization of the discount, but they do help with effective interest method of amortizing discounts and premiums (shown later in the chapter).

Semiannual Period	Cash Payment (Credit)	Interest Expense (Debit)	Discount on Bonds Payable (Credit)	Discount on Bonds Payable Balance	Carrying Value
At issue				$1,000,000	$ 99,000,000
1	$4,000,000	$4,100,000	$100,000	900,000	99,100,000
2	4,000,000	4,100,000	100,000	800,000	99,200,000
3	4,000,000	4,100,000	100,000	700,000	99,300,000
4	4,000,000	4,100,000	100,000	600,000	99,400,000
5	4,000,000	4,100,000	100,000	500,000	99,500,000
6	4,000,000	4,100,000	100,000	400,000	99,600,000
7	4,000,000	4,100,000	100,000	300,000	99,700,000
8	4,000,000	4,100,000	100,000	200,000	99,800,000
9	4,000,000	4,100,000	100,000	100,000	99,900,000
10	4,000,000	4,100,000	100,000	0	100,000,000

Note: The discount on bonds payable is amortized to $0 at maturity.

5. Any discount (or premium) is amortized over the life of the bond (or note) and netted with the interest payment to provide interest expense. Because the discount is amortized with a credit, the effect is to increase interest expense above the amount of cash paid.

	Date	Account and Explanation	Debit	Credit	Assets	= Liabilities +	Stockholders' Equity
a.	June 30/Dec. 31	Interest Expense	4,100,000				▼
		Cash		4,000,000	▼		
		Discount on Bonds Payable		100,000		▲	

	Date	Account and Explanation	Debit	Credit	Assets	= Liabilities +	Stockholders' Equity
b.	Dec. 31, 2028	Bonds Payable	100,000,000			▼	
		Cash		100,000,000	▼		

Carrying Value over the Life of a Bond Issued at a Discount

EXHIBIT 9.6

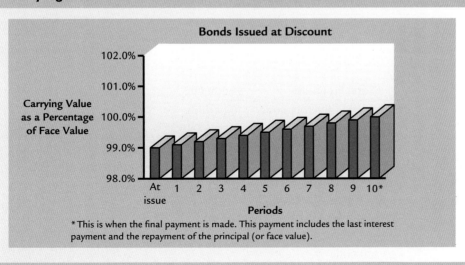

Bonds Issued at Discount

*This is when the final payment is made. This payment includes the last interest payment and the repayment of the principal (or face value).

Exhibit 9.6 (p. 519) illustrates how the carrying value of the bond shown in Example 9.3 moves closer to face value. In fact, the carrying value will be the face value at maturity because the discount balance will be $0 (i.e., it will be completely amortized). Notice that the beginning carrying value is 99% of the face value. This indicates that although the 8% stated rate is below market yield, it is only slightly below—8.25%.

EXAMPLE 9.4 shows how things change when the bond is issued at a premium.

Exhibit 9.7 illustrates how the carrying value of the bond shown in Example 9.4 declines over time due to the premium amortization. Notice that the beginning carrying value is 102% of the face value. This indicates that the 8% stated rate is slightly above market yield—7.51%. Notice that in this case, the carrying value is the face value of the bond plus the premium because both the bond payable and the premium have credit balances. Further, as the premium is amortized, the premium balance declines and the carrying value moves closer to face value.

EXAMPLE 9.4   RECORDING INTEREST EXPENSE FOR BONDS SOLD AT A PREMIUM USING THE STRAIGHT-LINE METHOD

On January 1, 2024, Ames Inc. issues 5-year, $100,000,000, 8% bonds at 102 ($102,000,000). The premium at the time of the sale is $2,000,000. Interest is paid semiannually on June 30 and December 31.

Required:

1. Prepare the journal entry to record the issuance of the bonds on January 1, 2024.

2. Calculate the amount of premium that will be amortized each semiannual period.

3. Calculate the amount of interest expense for each semiannual period.

4. Complete an amortization table for the 10 semiannual periods.

5. Prepare the journal entry necessary to (a) recognize the interest expense on June 30 and December 31, 2024–2028, and (b) record the repayment of the loan principal on December 31, 2028.

Solution:

1. When bonds are issued, they are valued on the balance sheet at their issue price by putting the face (or par) value in the bonds payable account and recording any premium or discount in a separate valuation account.

Date	Account and Explanation	Debit	Credit	Assets	=	Liabilities	+	Stockholders' Equity
Jan. 1, 2024	Cash	102,000,000		▲				
	Bonds Payable		100,000,000			▲		
	Premium on Bonds Payable		2,000,000			▲		

2. Any premium or discount on the sale of a bond is amortized over the life of the bond—in this case, evenly each period.

$$\text{Premium Amortization} = \frac{\text{Total Premium}}{\text{Number of Interest Periods}} = \frac{\$2,000,000}{10 \text{ periods}} = \underline{\$200,000}$$

3. The amount of premium amortized each interest period effectively decreases the interest expense recognized for the period. This is because the premium on the issue of the bonds (i.e., when bonds are issued for $102,000,000, but $100,000,000 is paid back at maturity) essentially represents the lender refunding a portion of the interest being paid.

$$\begin{aligned}
\text{Interest Expense} &= \text{Interest Payment} - \text{Premium Amortization} \\
&= (\$100,000,000 \times 8\% \times 6/12) - \$200,000 \\
&= \$4,000,000 - \$200,000 \\
&= \underline{\$3,800,000}
\end{aligned}$$

4. Such tables help organize the information to calculate the amount of discount or premium to amortize and interest expense to recognize.

Semiannual Period	Cash Payment (Credit)	Interest Expense (Debit)	Premium on Bonds Payable (Debit)	Premium on Bonds Payable Balance	Carrying Value
At issue				$2,000,000	$102,000,000
1	$4,000,000	$3,800,000	$200,000	1,800,000	101,800,000
2	4,000,000	3,800,000	200,000	1,600,000	101,600,000
3	4,000,000	3,800,000	200,000	1,400,000	101,400,000
4	4,000,000	3,800,000	200,000	1,200,000	101,200,000
5	4,000,000	3,800,000	200,000	1,000,000	101,000,000
6	4,000,000	3,800,000	200,000	800,000	100,800,000
7	4,000,000	3,800,000	200,000	600,000	100,600,000
8	4,000,000	3,800,000	200,000	400,000	100,400,000
9	4,000,000	3,800,000	200,000	200,000	100,200,000
10	4,000,000	3,800,000	200,000	0	100,000,000

Note: The premium on bonds payable is amortized to $0 at maturity.

5. Any premium (or discount) is amortized over the life of the bond (or note) and netted with the interest payment to provide interest expense. Because the premium is amortized with a debit, the effect is to decrease interest expense below the amount of cash paid.

	Date	Account and Explanation	Debit	Credit				
					Assets	**= Liabilities**	**+**	**Stockholders' Equity**
a.	June 30/Dec. 31	Interest Expense	3,800,000					▼
		Premium on Bonds Payable	200,000			▼		
		Cash		4,000,000	▼			
					Assets	**= Liabilities**	**+**	**Stockholders' Equity**
b.	Dec. 31, 2028	Bonds Payable	100,000,000			▼		
		Cash		100,000,000	▼			

Carrying Value over the Life of a Bond Issued at a Premium

EXHIBIT 9.7

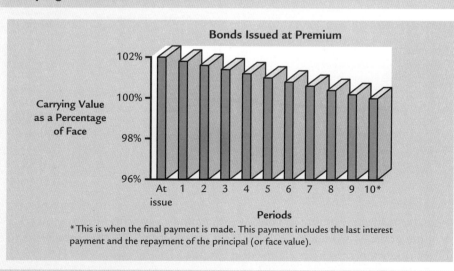

Bonds Issued at Premium

Carrying Value as a Percentage of Face

Periods

*This is when the final payment is made. This payment includes the last interest payment and the repayment of the principal (or face value).

ACCRUING INTEREST

In the previous discussion, interest payments were made on the last day of the period—December 31. This is frequently not the case in the real world. Assume that on August 31, 2023, Nadel Communications borrows $120,000,000 on a 3-year, 7% note. The note requires annual interest payments (each equal to 7% of $120,000,000) and repayment of the principal plus the final year's interest at the end of the third year. This borrowing would be recognized in Nadel's accounts as:

Date	Account and Explanation	Debit	Credit	Assets	=	Liabilities	+	Stockholders' Equity
Aug. 31, 2023	Cash	120,000,000		▲				
	Notes Payable		120,000,000			▲		

Since no interest payment is made at Nadel's year end (December 31), interest must be accrued for the period. Interest expense for the 4-month period from September to the end of December is $2,800,000 ($120,000,000 × 0.07 × 4/12). That means interest expense for the 8-month period from January to the end of August is $5,600,000 ($120,000,000 × 0.07 × 8/12). Nadel would recognize interest expense and the payment of interest on this note during 2023 through 2026 as:

Date	Account and Explanation	Debit	Credit	Assets	=	Liabilities	+	Stockholders' Equity
Dec. 31	Interest Expense	2,800,000						▼
	Interest Payable		2,800,000			▲		
Aug. 31	Interest Expense	5,600,000						▼
	Interest Payable	2,800,000				▼		
	Cash		8,400,000	▼				
Aug. 31, 2026	Notes Payable	120,000,000				▼		
	Cash		120,000,000	▼				

Observe that although Nadel's note involves multiple payments extending over 3 years, recognition of the borrowing and its repayment are very similar to the procedure used for short-term, interest-bearing notes illustrated in Chapter 8.

YOUDECIDE — Financial Statement Effects of Refinancing

You are the CFO of Global Industries. Eight years ago, Global issued $100,000,000 of bonds that yielded 11%. Global's borrowing costs are currently 9%. If Global were to refinance the debt, interest payments would drop by $2,000,000 per year.

Should Global refinance? How would the refinancing affect net income?

Unlike debt at a bank (such as a car loan or home mortgage), bonds are not paid off by merely repaying the principal; instead, bonds must be repurchased in the market at their fair market value. To illustrate, assume these bonds were issued at par. This means that their fair value was $100,000,000 on the date of issue. However, the fair value is $100,000,000 only when the market rate of interest is 11% (such as at issue) and on the maturity date (because no interest payments remain). If market rates fall below the 11% yield, the fair value of the debt will increase because the lenders will demand a premium to sell the above-market interest payments of 11%.

Accordingly, to refinance, Global must pay more than $100,000,000. This premium, coupled with the additional costs of refinancing, will more than offset the decrease in interest payments.

As for the effect on net income, because typically the carrying value of the existing debt is its amortized cost, not its fair market value, refinancing typically results in a gain or loss on refinancing being recognized. In this case, Global will pay more than the $100,000,000 carrying value of the bonds. The amount of this premium will be a loss on Global's income statement, thus lowering net income.

In this case, Global should only consider the cash flow implications. Specifically, Global should refinance if the present value of the interest saved exceeds the costs of refinancing. In reality, however, management also considers the financial-statement effects of the transaction, although any loss on refinancing does not affect the cash flows.

THE EFFECTIVE INTEREST RATE METHOD: RECOGNIZING INTEREST EXPENSE AND REPAYMENT OF PRINCIPAL

 OBJECTIVE 4

Use the effective interest rate method to record premium/discount amortization and properly present long-term debt.

The straight-line and effective interest rate methods are identical when a bond is issued at par because there are no premiums or discounts to amortize. Further, even when premiums or discounts exist, the *total* interest expense over the life of the bonds is identical regardless of the amortization method used. However, the interest expense allocated to the individual accounting periods differs because premiums and discounts are amortized in different manners.

Under the effective interest rate method, the amortization of premiums and discounts results in the interest expense for each accounting period being equal to a constant percentage of the bond book value (also called *carrying value*). That is, the interest expense changes every period, but the effective interest rate on the bond book value is constant. The straight-line method, on the other hand, has a constant interest expense each period, but the effective interest rate on the bond book value changes every period.

To use the effective interest method, you must distinguish between the cash interest payments being made, which are calculated as:

Face Value × Stated Rate × Time (in years)

and the effective interest expense being recorded, which is calculated as:

Carrying Value × Yield Rate × Time (in years)

This difference is so important it requires emphasis. Interest payments are calculated with face value and the stated rate of interest. These payments are the contracted cash payments for interest and therefore are the same each period. Interest expense, under the effective rate method, is calculated by using the Carrying Value (Face Value − Discount Balance or Face Value + Premium Balance) and the yield, or market rate, of interest.

Next Level

Is the total amount of interest expense over the life of the bond higher when we use straight-line amortization or the effective interest rate method?

ANSWER:
Neither—the total amount of interest expense is identical under both methods. What changes is the interest expense allocated to each period (see Exhibit 9.8).

EXAMPLE 9.5 illustrates how discounts are amortized under the effective interest rate method.

EXAMPLE 9.5 — RECORDING INTEREST EXPENSE FOR BONDS SOLD AT A DISCOUNT USING THE EFFECTIVE INTEREST RATE METHOD

On January 1, 2024, Brannigan Co. issued $1,000,000 of 8% bonds, due in 5 years with interest payable annually on December 31. The market rate of interest is 9%. Assume the bond was issued at $961,103. This was calculated using time value of money concepts [see Example 9.8 (p. 537) in Appendix 9A for the calculation].

Required:

1. Complete an amortization table for each of the five annual periods.

2. Prepare the journal entry necessary to (a) recognize the interest expense on December 31, 2024 and 2025, and (b) record the repayment of the loan principal on December 31, 2028.

Solution:

1. Such tables help organize the information to calculate the amount of discount to amortize and interest expense to recognize.

Annual Period	Cash Payment[a] (Credit)	Interest Expense[b] (Debit)	Discount on Bonds Payable[c] (Credit)	Discount on Bonds Payable Balance	Carrying Value[d]
At issue				$38,897	$961,103
Dec. 31, 2024	$80,000	$86,499	$6,499	32,398	967,602
Dec. 31, 2025	80,000	87,084	7,084	25,314	974,686
Dec. 31, 2026	80,000	87,722	7,722	17,592	982,408
Dec. 31, 2027	80,000	88,417	8,417	9,175	990,825
Dec. 31, 2028	80,000	89,175	9,175	0	1,000,000

[a] Cash Payment = Face Value × 8% (stated rate) × 12/12 = $80,000

[b] Interest Expense = Carrying Value × 9% (market rate or yield) × 12/12

[c] Change in Discount Balance = Interest Expense − Cash Payment

[d] New Carrying Value = Previous Carrying Value + Change in Discount on Bonds Payable Balance

2. Any discount (or premium) is amortized over the life of the bond (or note) and netted with the interest payment to provide interest expense. Because the discount is amortized with a credit, the effect is to increase interest expense above the amount of cash paid.

	Date	Account and Explanation	Debit	Credit	Assets	= Liabilities +	Stockholders' Equity
a.	Dec. 31, 2024	Interest Expense	86,499				▼
		Cash		80,000	▼		
		Discount on Bonds Payable		6,499		▲	
	Dec. 31, 2025	Interest Expense	87,084				▼
		Cash		80,000	▼		
		Discount on Bonds Payable		7,084		▲	
b.	Dec. 31, 2026	Bonds Payable	1,000,000			▼	
		Cash		1,000,000	▼		

As in the straight-line method, recording interest expense for bonds issued at a premium is the mirror image of bonds issued at a discount. EXAMPLE 9.6 illustrates how premiums are amortized under the effective interest rate method.

EXAMPLE 9.6 RECORDING INTEREST EXPENSE FOR BONDS SOLD AT A PREMIUM USING THE EFFECTIVE INTEREST RATE METHOD

On January 1, 2024, Cutler Co. issued $1,000,000 of 8% bonds, due in 5 years with interest payable annually on December 31. The market rate of interest is 7%. Assume the bond was issued at $1,041,002 [see Example 9.8 (p. 533) in Appendix 9A for the calculation].

Required:

1. Complete an amortization table for each of the five periods.

2. Prepare the journal entry necessary to (a) recognize the interest expense on December 31, 2024 and 2025, and (b) record the repayment of the loan principal on December 31, 2028.

Solution:

1. Such tables help organize the information to calculate the amount of premium to amortize and interest expense to recognize.

Annual Period	Cash Payment[a] (Credit)	Interest Expense[b] (Debit)	Premium on Bonds Payable[c] (Debit)	Premium on Bonds Payable Balance	Carrying Value[d]
At issue				$41,002	$1,041,002
Dec. 31, 2024	$80,000	$72,870	$7,130	33,872	1,033,872
Dec. 31, 2025	80,000	72,371	7,629	26,243	1,026,243
Dec. 31, 2026	80,000	71,837	8,163	18,080	1,018,080
Dec. 31, 2027	80,000	71,266	8,734	9,346	1,009,346
Dec. 31, 2028	80,000	70,654	9,346	0	1,000,000

[a] Cash Payment = Face Value × 8% (stated rate) × 12/12 = $80,000

[b] Interest Expense = Carrying Value × 7% (market rate or yield) × 12/12

[c] Change in Premium Balance = Cash Payment − Interest Expense

[d] New Carrying Value = Previous Carrying Value − Change in Premium on Bonds Payable Balance

2. Any premium (or discount) is amortized over the life of the bond (or note) and netted with the interest payment to provide interest expense. Because the premium is amortized with a debit, the effect is to decrease interest expense below the amount of cash paid.

	Date	Account and Explanation	Debit	Credit	Assets	=	Liabilities	+	Stockholders' Equity
a.	Dec. 31, 2024	Interest Expense	72,870						▼
		Premium on Bonds Payable	7,130				▼		
		Cash		80,000	▼				
	Dec. 31, 2025	Interest Expense	72,371						▼
		Premium on Bonds Payable	7,629				▼		
		Cash		80,000	▼				
b.	Dec. 31, 2028	Bonds Payable	1,000,000				▼		
		Cash		1,000,000	▼				

Next Level

Why is the effective interest rate method GAAP?

ANSWER:
The effective interest rate method does a better job of expense recognition by more accurately allocating, or matching, the time value of money to the proper period. Under the effective interest rate method, the interest expense is equal to market rate of interest (or yield) at issue on the bond book value. This makes sense because market forces will ensure that the creditor receives the market rate of return on the investment.

Note that the interest expense using the straight-line method is the same each period. In contrast, the interest expense using the effective interest method results in a different amount each period. This is because the interest expense is based on a constant *rate.* This rate is applied to the remaining carrying value of the bonds each period. Exhibit 9.8 illustrates how the carrying value of the bonds is different between the straight-line and effective interest methods for both a premium and a discount.

INSTALLMENT DEBT

Instead of paying off the principal at maturity, some debt requires a portion of the principal to be paid off each period (usually monthly), along with some interest. Classic installment debt payments are home mortgages or car payments. Installment debt payments are the same each period, but the portion that is considered interest changes because the outstanding principal balance is changing. To illustrate, consider buying a car for $30,000, at 4.2% annual interest, and 48 monthly payments. In this case, each monthly payment would be $680.06. After 48 payments, you would have paid a total of $32,642.87 ($680.06 × 48). This means you would have paid $2,642.87 of interest and $30,000 of principal. However, the initial monthly payments would have a relatively high portion allocated to interest because your outstanding loan balance is relatively high. Your last few payments, on the other hand, would have a relatively low portion allocated to interest because your outstanding loan balance is relatively low.

EXHIBIT 9.8   **Long-Term Debt Carrying Value Using Straight-Line and Effective Interest Methods to Amortize Premium and Discount**

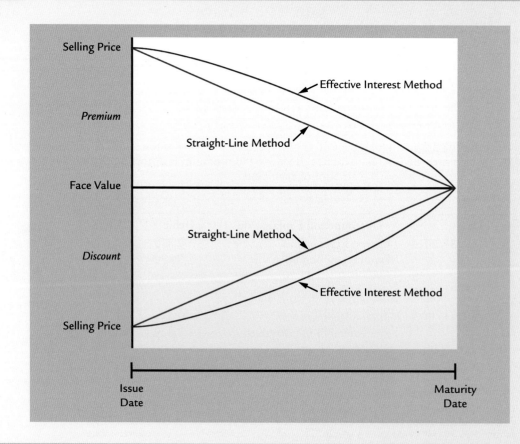

PROS AND CONS OF DEBT FINANCING

OBJECTIVE
Calculate the after-tax cost of financing with debt and explain financial leverage.

A business must weigh both the negative and positive aspects of debt financing in deciding whether or not to take the risk. This extremely complex decision is treated more fully in finance courses, but some general points follow.[4]

TAX DEDUCTIBLE INTEREST EXPENSE

A significant advantage of financing with debt rather than stock is the fact that the interest expense on debt is deductible for income tax purposes. Consider the case of Carmel Company, which issued $1,000,000 of 8% bonds that resulted in interest expense of $80,000 per year. The net cash outflow for Carmel's bonds is significantly less than $80,000, however, due to the effect of interest deductibility.

Since interest expense is deductible, taxable income is $80,000 less than it is without the bond issue. At the corporate rate of 21%, income taxes were reduced by $16,800 ($80,000 × 21%), yielding a net cash outflow for the bonds of $63,200 ($80,000 − $16,800). In other words, the cost of financing with bonds (or any other form of debt with tax-deductible interest payments) is the interest *net of income taxes*, which is determined using the following formula:

$$\text{Interest Net of Income Taxes} = (1 - \text{Tax Rate}) \times \text{Interest}$$
$$= (1 - 0.21) \times \$80,000$$
$$= \underline{\$63,200}$$

This results in an after-tax interest rate of 7.9% ($63,200/$800,000).

LEVERAGE

Another potential advantage of debt is that it fixes the amount of compensation to the lender. No matter how successful the firm is in using borrowed capital, its creditors receive only the return specified in the debt agreement (interest plus the face amount). Thus, if the borrowed capital generates income in excess of the interest on the debt, the firm's stockholders benefit. The use of borrowed capital to produce more income than needed to pay the interest on the debt is called **leverage**.

Under the right conditions, leverage has significant advantages. However, conditions also exist under which the use of leverage is disadvantageous. Exhibit 9.9 illustrates both conditions in which two companies—Carmel Company and Noblesville Inc.—have identical financial circumstances except that Carmel finances its operations with debt as well as stock; Noblesville carries no debt.

In 2022, favorable economic conditions allow Carmel to make the most of its leverage. Carmel's stockholders earn $4.11 per share, which includes an amount attributable to earnings in excess of the cost of borrowing. In contrast, Noblesville's stockholders earn only $3.16 per share in 2022. However, income from operations falls sharply in 2023. As a result, Carmel's stockholders earn only $0.95 per share compared with $1.05 per share for Noblesville's stockholders. Just as stockholders receive earnings in excess of the interest on debt, so they must bear the burden when the interest on debt exceeds earnings.

Next Level

How do credit cards calculate interest?

ANSWER:
Although terms vary from card to card, they all charge some percentage of our average balance for the period. If your card charges 1.5% of the average balance for the month and you have a $5,000 average balance, then interest charge would be $75. Interest of 1.5% may not sound that bad, but remember that this is per month. That equates to 18% per year (1.5% × 12 months). If all you do is pay the interest, you are not lowering your outstanding balance at all.

---

4 The following discussion explains the accounting concepts and procedures for debt used by borrowers. Although the concepts and procedures used by investors in debt securities are based on the same measurements and calculations, the reporting conventions are somewhat different. The most fundamental difference is that investors record debt acquired as assets rather than liabilities and record the interest as revenue rather than expense.

EXHIBIT 9.9	Effects of Financing with Debt			

	2022		2023	
	Carmel Company	Noblesville Inc.	Carmel Company	Noblesville Inc.
Balance sheet:*				
Assets	$3,000,000	$3,000,000	$3,000,000	$3,000,000
Bonds payable	$1,000,000	—	$1,000,000	—
Stockholders' equity	$2,000,000	$3,000,000	$2,000,000	$3,000,000
Number of common stock shares	100,000	150,000	100,000	150,000
Income statement:				
Income from operations	$ 600,000	$ 600,000	$ 200,000	$ 200,000
Interest expense (8%)	80,000	—	80,000	—
Income before taxes	$ 520,000	$ 600,000	$ 120,000	$ 200,000
Income taxes expense (21%)	109,200	126,000	25,200	42,000
Net income	$ 410,800	$ 474,000	$ 94,800	$ 158,000
Earnings per share	$ 4.11	$ 3.16	$ 0.95	$ 1.05

*Annual averages (assume that current liabilities are negligible).

INFLATION

A third advantage of financing with debt is that in periods of inflation, debt permits the borrower to repay the lender in dollars that have declined in purchasing power. For instance, based on changes in the consumer price index (CPI), $1,000,000 borrowed in 1988 and repaid in 2018 provided a lender with approximately 47% of the purchasing power of the amount loaned in 1988.

PAYMENT SCHEDULE

The primary negative attribute of debt is the inflexibility of the payment schedule. Debt requires specified payments to creditors on specified dates. If a payment is not made as scheduled, the borrower can be forced into bankruptcy. This attribute of debt makes it a more risky source of capital than equity. The larger the proportion of debt an entity uses to finance its capital needs, the greater the risk of default. As risk increases (because of a higher proportion of debt), the cost of the debt increases. At a certain point, the risk becomes so great that additional debt cannot be issued at any cost. For firms whose operational and competitive circumstances produce substantial fluctuations in earnings, even low levels of debt may be considered too risky.

Occasionally, a business finds that it is unable to make the interest or principal payments required by its long-term debt. If there is reason to expect that the firm will eventually be able to secure enough cash to make part of or all the required payments, creditors may permit a restructuring of the cash payment schedule. The amount at which the firm's liabilities are measured may or may not be changed by such a restructuring. In such cases, creditors must analyze the situation to ensure that they are better off than they would be if they forced a bankruptcy.

 OBJECTIVE 6
Describe short- and long-term leases.

LEASES

Many companies choose to **lease**, instead of purchase, some of their assets. While leasing can provide some advantages over purchasing that we will discuss shortly, let's first consider the substance of leasing. Long-term leases are very similar to purchasing. For example, what is the difference between buying a car and leasing car for 12 years? Whether you purchase or lease, you obtain substantially all the risks (e.g., repair costs) and benefits (e.g., driving it around) of using the car. Further, leases create an obligation to make the lease payments regardless of whether or not you use the asset. For example, if you sign an apartment lease for the following school year and then decide to study abroad next year, you are still responsible for the lease payment. You cannot simply notify the landlord that you will not be living there to avoid owing the lease payments.

A short-term lease, on the other hand, does seem fundamentally different from a purchase. For example, if you lease a car at the airport for three days while visiting another city, you are not obtaining substantially all of the risks and benefits of purchasing the car.

Accounting for leased assets reflects this underlying concept of whether you obtain the risks and benefits of ownership. Specifically, if the lease term is under one year, then no assets or liabilities are recognized on the balance sheet at the time the lease is signed (i.e., no journal entry is made when the lease is signed). Instead, as you have learned previously, you will record rent expense as you make the lease payments. However, if the lease term is one year or more, an asset and liability are recognized at the time the lease is signed. We'll leave the calculations on the amount to recognize for later courses. What is important is that an asset is debited to recognize the benefits that the leased asset will provide in the future and a liability is credited to recognize the obligation to make future lease payments.

What's interesting is that these lease accounting rules are very new. In fact, they began to take effect in fiscal years starting after December 15, 2018. Current rules allow companies to more easily avoid recognizing an asset or liability related to leases. In fact, a whole industry popped up around structuring leases to avoid recognizing the lease liability. However, *The Wall Street Journal* estimates that the new lease rules will result in an additional $2 trillion (not billion) of assets and liabilities being recognized on the balance sheet of American companies.[5] If the new leasing rules no longer permit companies to avoid recognizing an asset and liability when signing a lease, will companies stop leasing? While it is certainly possible that the leasing will be reduced, leasing does provide a number of other potential advantages over purchasing. For example,

1. *Less cash* is needed to sign a lease than to purchase an asset. Consider a restaurant opening its doors. If it were to buy the building and equipment, it would probably only be able to borrow about 80% of the purchase price; the other 20% would be a cash down payment. Most small businesses would have difficulty raising that much cash. Leases, on the other hand, often require no money down beyond 1 or 2 months' lease payment to serve as a security deposit or guarantee on paying the last month's rent.
2. Lease contracts offer *protection against obsolescence* and *flexibility*. Consider an asset, like computer equipment, that is anticipated to be replaced frequently. Many large companies lease rather than purchase their computer equipment so they can obtain faster and possibly more efficient computers without having the hassle of selling their old computers on a secondary market. Or, if the company's work force is subject to fluctuation, the number of computers it needs will also fluctuate. Leasing, once again, allows companies more flexibility in quickly increasing or decreasing the number of computers used.
3. Lease contracts can provide *lower cost financing* through tax advantages. While a discussion of the exact manner by which leasing can produce tax advantages is beyond the scope of this course, suffice it to say that companies may have significant tax advantages when leasing versus purchasing.

Because of these advantages, businesses will continue to lease assets.

---

5 Rapoport, M. November 12, 2015. "Coming to a Balance Sheet Near You: $2 Trillion in Leases." *The Wall Street Journal.*

OBJECTIVE

Analyze long-term solvency using information related to long-term liabilities.

RATIO ANALYSIS

Although long-term creditors are concerned with a company's short-term liquidity, they are primarily concerned with its long-term solvency. As such, long-term creditors focus on ratios that incorporate (1) long-term debt and (2) interest expense/payments.

The following ratios are often used to analyze a company's debt load:

$$\text{Debt to Equity} = \frac{\text{Total Liabilities}}{\text{Total Equity}}$$

$$\text{Debt to Total Assets} = \frac{\text{Total Liabilities}}{\text{Total Assets}}$$

$$\text{Long-Term Debt to Equity} = \frac{\text{Long-Term Debt (including current portion)}}{\text{Total Equity}}$$

The long-term debt to equity ratio is designed to look at the mix of debt and equity financing, as such it typically includes the current portion on long-term debt. For example, if the ratio is 1.00, then 50% of the company's financing comes from stockholders while the other 50% comes from creditors. However, over the last few decades borrowing arrangements have become more varied. Historically, when companies borrowed, they locked themselves into long-term debt contracts. Now many companies use short-term borrowing, such as revolving credit, as part of their financing plan. This has the advantage of allowing companies to more frequently adjust their levels of borrowing based on current conditions. The downside is that short-term credit exposes them to greater risk of interest rate changes. For example, when interest rates increase, short-term borrowers may be forced to refinance at these higher rates while long-term borrowers will be locked in at the lower rates. Of course, short-term borrowers can, and do, hedge these interest rate risks, but that is a topic for advanced accounting and finance courses.

Because it is increasingly common to use short-term debt financing, the debt to equity and debt to total asset ratios contain all debt. Although the denominators for these two ratios differ, they both give a sense of the extent to which a company is financed with debt. You can see this more clearly by remembering that Total Assets = Total Liabilities + Total Equity. Both ratios therefore measure the relative size of Total Liabilities in the accounting equation.

Other ratios focus a company's ability to make interest payments. These ratios are often called coverage ratios because they provide information on the company's ability to meet or cover its interest payments. The most common ratios focus on either accrual basis interest expense or the cash basis interest payment and are typically measured pretax because interest expense is tax deductible.

$$\text{Times Interest Earned (Accrual Basis)} = \frac{\text{Operating Income}}{\text{Interest Expense}}$$

$$\text{Times Interest Earned (Cash Basis)} = \frac{(\text{Cash Flows from Operations} + \text{Taxes Paid} + \text{Interest Paid})}{\text{Interest Paid}}$$

See **EXAMPLE 9.7** for an example of calculating these ratios and using them to analyze the long-term debt of a company.

Is it always better to have lower debt to equity, debt to total assets, and long-term debt to equity ratios?

ANSWER:

No. Debt provides opportunities for leverage. Think about it in this way—if you're guaranteed a return greater than your interest payments, it would not make sense to avoid borrowing. Of course, the reality is that while no returns are guaranteed, interest payments are unavoidable.

EXAMPLE 9.7 CALCULATING AND ANALYZING LONG-TERM DEBT RATIOS

Consider the following information from the 2019 10-Ks for **United Continental Holdings** (hereafter, UAL) and **Southwest Airlines** (in millions).

UAL			
Long-term debt (including current portion)	$14,552	Interest expense	$ 731
Total liabilities	41,080	Operating income	4,301
Total assets	52,611	Interest payments	648
Total equity	11,531	Cash flows from operations	6,909
		Income tax expense	905
		Income tax payments	29
Southwest Airlines			
Long-term debt (including current portion)	$ 2,665	Interest expense	$ 118
Total liabilities	16,063	Operating income	2,957
Total assets	25,895	Interest payments	88
Total equity	9,832	Cash flows from operations	3,987
		Income tax expense	657
		Income tax payments	779

Required:

1. Calculate the following ratios for both companies: (a) debt to equity, (b) debt to total assets, (c) long-term debt to equity, (d) times interest earned (accrual basis), and (e) times interest earned (cash basis).

2. Interpret these results.

Solution:

1. Investors and creditors are interested in a company's ability to meet its long-term obligations. Analysis of information about long-term liabilities and interest expense and payments provides such information.

Ratios	UAL	Southwest Airlines
a. debt to equity	$41,080 ÷ $11,531 = 3.56	$16,063 ÷ $9,832 = 1.63
b. debt to total assets	$41,080 ÷ $52,611 = 0.78	$16,063 ÷ $25,895 = 0.62
c. long-term debt to equity	$14,552 ÷ $11,531 = 1.26	$2,665 ÷ $9,832 = 0.27
d. times interest earned (accrual basis)	$4,301 ÷ $731 = 5.88	$2,957 ÷ $118 = 25.06
e. times interest earned (cash basis)	($6,909 + $29 + $648) ÷ $648 = 11.71	($3,987 + $779 + $88) ÷ $88 = 55.16

2. Southwest's solvency risk is clearly far lower than UAL's. Although UAL has a relatively high debt load, its operations are covering its interest payments. Southwest, on the other hand, has a relatively low debt load and can more easily make its interest payments.

   Not surprisingly, UAL is well below industry averages on most ratios while Southwest is an industry leader. These ratios are also reflected in their credit ratings. UAL has typically fluctuated between BB and BB—while Southwest has often ranged between A and A—(although it is currently BBB).

ETHICAL DECISIONS When evaluating a company's solvency, a major concern is whether all debt was properly recorded. Companies have long engaged in transactions designed to hide debt. Such transactions are typically called *off-balance-sheet financing.* Interestingly, many such transactions are legal and considered to be ethical by most. For example, as discussed previously, under current rules many companies structure their lease agreements to avoid being required to record an asset and liability related to the future lease obligation.

Because many financial-statement users view leases as unavoidable obligations, FASB now requires companies to report virtually all of its lease obligations on the face of the balance sheet. In 2019, **United Continental Holdings** (the parent company of United and Continental Airlines) reported long-term obligations (including current portions) under finance leases (i.e., the longer leases) and operating leases (i.e., the shorter leases) of $288 million and $5,632 million, respectively. If we capitalize these amounts, UAL's long-term debt to equity ratio goes from 1.26 (see solution to Example 9.7) to 1.78 [($14,552 + ($288 + $5,632) ÷ $11,531], an increase of over 41%.

Many companies also create other legal entities (called "special purpose entities" or SPEs) to "hide" debt. As with leases, such transactions are legal when certain rules are met involving outside investors. **Enron**, however, created some SPEs in which the documentation appeared to meet the outside investor rules to keep the debt off Enron's balance sheet. In hindsight, however, either unwritten side-agreements or complicated aspects of some of the contracts indicate that the debt should have been included on Enron's balance sheet. Keeping this debt off the balance sheet was important for Enron in maintaining its credit rating, but these unwritten side-agreements and complicated aspects of the contracts were necessary to attract outside investors. While virtually nobody considers structuring their leases to allow treatment as an operating lease to be unethical, the side-agreements and subterfuge used by Enron was not only unethical, but in many cases criminal. ●

OBJECTIVE 8

Calculate the market price of long-term debt using present value techniques.

APPENDIX 9A: PRICING LONG-TERM DEBT

Debt agreements create contractually defined cash flows for the lender. Specifically, lenders typically receive:

- periodic interest payments
- repayment of the loan principal at some future date (loan maturity)

To receive these cash flows, the lender must decide how much to lend. When you borrow from a bank or car dealer, this single lender will set the interest rate to reflect the desired market, or yield, rate. However, there are notable exceptions. For example, if you buy a car for $25,000 at 0.9% interest, does that mean the car dealer's yield is 0.9%? No, it really means that they would have been happy to sell you the car for something below $25,000, such as $24,250. In this case, the "extra" principal you repay ($25,000 − $24,250 = $750) represents interest.

Of course, similar situations happen to businesses, but by far the most common situation has to do with bonds because the stated rate of interest (e.g., 8%) on the bond does not provide the desired yield. As discussed, if the yield is above the stated rate, the bond will sell at a discount (e.g., 98), and if the yield is below the stated rate, it will sell at a premium (e.g., 103). But how are these prices determined?

Bonds are priced at the present value of the two future cash flows—the periodic interest payments provide an annuity, while the repayment of the principal is a lump sum. This calculation is shown in **EXAMPLE 9.8**.

EXAMPLE 9.8 DETERMINING THE MARKET VALUE OF A BOND

On January 1, 2024, Chu Co. issued $1,000,000 of 8% bonds, due in 5 years with interest payable annually on December 31.

Required:
1. Draw the cash flow diagram.
2. What is the market value of these bonds if sold to yield (a) 8%, (b) 9%, and (c) 7%?

Solution:
1. To calculate the market value of the bonds, you must understand the **amount** and **timing** of the cash flows associated with the bond.

PV = ?

$80,000 $80,000 $80,000 $80,000 $80,000
$1,000,000

2. Bonds are issued at the present value of future cash flows. The interest payments and repayment of the bond principal are the future cash flows. These amounts must be discounted at the market rate of interest (or yield).

  a. PV of interest payments   = Interest Payment × PV of an annuity, 5 periods, 8%
                          = $80,000 × 3.992710* = $319,417

  PV of principal payments = Principal Payment × PV of a single sum, 5 periods, 8%
                              = $1,000,000 × 0.680583* = $680,583

Market price of bonds = $319,417 + $680,583 = $1,000,000

---

*Although present and future value tables provided at the end of Appendix 3 (Exhibits A3.7, A3.8, A3.9, and A3.10) only show five decimal places, we have used factors to six decimal places in these calculations (and those that follow). Use of six decimal places allows the market price of the bond when issued at par to be calculated with no rounding error.

The market value of the bonds is below the $1,000,000 face value because the bond is paying 8% interest when the market expects a yield of 9%.

  b. PV of interest payments   = Interest Payment × PV of an annuity, 5 periods, 9%
                          = $80,000 × 3.889651 = $311,172

  PV of principal payments = Principal Payment × PV of a single sum, 5 periods, 9%
                              = $1,000,000 × 0.649931 = $649,931

Market price of bonds = $311,172 + $649,931 = $961,103

The market value of the bonds is above the $1,000,000 face value because the bond is paying 8% interest when the market expects a yield of 7%.

  c. PV of interest payments   = Interest Payment × PV of an annuity, 5 periods, 7%
                          = $80,000 × 4.100197 = $328,016

  PV of principal payments = Principal Payment × PV of a single sum, 5 periods, 7%
                              = $1,000,000 × 0.712986 = $712,986

Market price of bonds = $328,016 + $712,986 = $1,041,002

REVIEW CENTER

LO1. Describe debt securities and the markets in which they are issued.

KEY TAKEAWAYS

- Debt securities are issued in exchange for borrowed cash.
- In return for the borrowed cash, the borrower typically makes periodic interest payments and repays the face, or par, value at maturity.
- These securities may be placed directly with a creditor such as a bank or pension fund, or they may be more widely distributed with the help of an underwriter.

KEY TERMS

Bond, 511	Market rate, 513
Callable bonds, 512	Maturity, 511
Contract rate, 511	Mortgage bonds, 511
Convertible bonds, 512	Notes payable, 511
Coupon rate, 511	Par value, 511
Debenture bonds, 512	Premium, 513
Discount, 513	Principal, 511
Face value, 511	Secured, 511
Interest rate, 511	Stated rate, 511
Junk bonds, 512	Unsecured, 512
Long-term debt, 510	Yield, 513

KEY FORMULA

Interest Payment = Face Value × Interest Rate × Time (in years), 511

LO2. Record and properly present long-term debt at the time of issuance.

KEY TAKEAWAYS

- The issue price of long-term debt is typically quoted as a percentage of face value.
- At the time of issuance the borrower records the face value of the debt in bonds payable (or notes payable).
  - Any amount of cash received over the face value is credited to a premium.
  - Any amount of cash received under the face value is debited to a discount.
- The bonds payable (or notes payable) is netted with the premium or discount when reported on the balance sheet.

EXAMPLE

Example 9.1   Recording the issuance of bonds, page 515

KEY TAKEAWAYS

- In the straight-line method, equal amounts of premium or discount are amortized to interest expense each period.
- This results in a constant interest expense each period.
- Although GAAP requires use of the effective interest rate method, the straight-line method may be used if the results are not materially different from the effective interest rate method.

KEY FORMULA

Straight-line Method

Interest Expense = Interest Paid − Premium Amortization, 520

or

Interest Expense = Interest paid + Discount Amortization, 518

EXAMPLES

Example 9.2	Recording interest expense for bonds sold at par, page 516–517
Example 9.3	Recording interest expense for bonds sold at a discount using the straight-line method, page 518–519
Example 9.4	Recording interest expense for bonds sold at a premium using the straight-line method, page 520–521

KEY TAKEAWAYS

- GAAP requires the effective interest rate method to be used to amortize any premium or discount, unless the straight-line method is not materially different.
- Under this method, premiums and discounts are amortized in a manner that results in the interest expense for each accounting period being equal to a constant percentage of the bond book, or carrying, value.
- That is, the interest expense changes every period, but the effective interest rate on the bond book value is constant.
- This constant percentage is called the "yield" and represents the market rate of interest at the date of issue.

KEY FORMULA

Effective Interest Rate Method

Interest Expense = Carrying Value × Yield Rate × Time (in years), 523

LO3. Use the straight-line method to record premium/discount amortization and properly present long-term debt.

LO4. Use the effective interest rate method to record premium/discount amortization and properly present long-term debt.

EXAMPLES

Example 9.5	Recording interest expense for bonds sold at a discount using the effective interest rate method, page 524
Example 9.6	Recording interest expense for bonds sold at a premium using the effective interest rate method, page 525

LO5. Calculate the after-tax cost of financing with debt and explain financial leverage.

KEY TAKEAWAYS

- Since interest expense is deductible for tax purposes, the presence of interest expense lowers the taxes owed.
- The formula for the after-tax effect of interest expense is $(1 - \text{Tax Rate}) \times \text{Interest Expense}$.

KEY TERM

leverage, 527

LO6. Describe short- and long-term leases.

KEY TAKEAWAYS

- A long-term lease (i.e., lease term of 1 year or longer) is a noncancelable agreement that is, in substance, a purchase of substantial portion of the leased asset.
- Long-term leases must recognize an asset and liability at the time the lease is signed.
- Short-term leases (i.e., leases under 1 year) do not recognize an asset or liability at the time the lease is signed.
- This accounting treatment is a recent change to GAAP. Under previous rules, which will stay in effect until 2019, companies were able to avoid recognizing an asset or liability at the time of signing the lease for many long-term leases.
- Despite the rule change, leasing does provide many advantages over purchasing:
  - Less cash is needed for a down payment
  - There is better protection against obsolescence and more flexibility.
  - Cost of financing is lower.

LO7. Analyze long-term solvency using information related to long-term liabilities.

KEY TAKEAWAYS

- Although long-term creditors are concerned with a company's short-term liquidity, they are primarily concerned with its long-term solvency.
- Long-term creditors focus on ratios that incorporate the following:
  - Long-term debt
  - Interest expense/payments

KEY FORMULAS

Debt to Equity = Total Liabilities ÷ Total Equity, 530
Debt to Total Assets = Total Liabilities ÷ Total Assets, 530
Long-Term Debt to Equity = Long-Term Debt (including current portion) ÷ Total Equity, 530
Times Interest Earned (Accrual Basis) = Operating Income ÷ Interest Expense, 530
Times Interest Earned (Cash Basis) = (Cash Flows from Operations + Taxes Paid + Interest Paid) ÷ Interest Paid, 530

EXAMPLE

Example 9.7	Calculating and analyzing long-term debt ratios, page 531

KEY TAKEAWAYS

- Bonds are issued at the present value of future cash flows.
- The interest payments and repayment of the bond principal (or face value) are the future cash flows.
- These amounts must be discounted at the market rate of interest (or yield).

LO8. *(Appendix 9A)*
Calculate the market price of long-term debt using present value techniques.

EXAMPLE

Example 9.8	*(Appendix 9A)* Determining the market value of a bond, page 533

REVIEW PROBLEM

I. STRAIGHT-LINE METHOD

To finance a new hydroelectric plant, Midwest Electric issues $100,000,000 of 9%, 15-year bonds on January 1, 2024. The bonds pay interest semiannually on June 30 and December 31. Assume the market rate of interest on January 1, 2024, was above 9%.

Required:

1. Will the bonds be issued at par, a premium, or a discount? Why?
2. Describe the cash payments made by Midwest Electric.
3. Prepare the journal entry to record the bond issue assuming the bonds were issued at 91.
4. What is the amount of discount amortization per 6-month interest period assuming the bonds were issued at 91?
5. Complete an amortization table through June 30, 2026.
6. Prepare the journal entries for December 31, 2025, and June 30, 2026.
7. How will the bonds be shown on the December 31, 2025, balance sheet?
8. Prepare the journal entry to record the repayment of principal at maturity.

Solution:

1. The bonds will be issued at a discount (below par) because the stated rate is below the market rate. Thus, Midwest Electric will have to lower the price below face value to compensate creditors for accepting a below market interest payment.
2. The interest payments are made semiannually, so the interest payments are:

$$\$100,000,000 \times 9\% \times 6/12 = \underline{\$4,500,000}$$

There are 30 interest payments over the 15-year life of the bonds, so total interest payments are:

$$\$4,500,000 \times 30 = \underline{\$135,000,000}$$

At maturity, the face value of $100,000,000 is also repaid. Thus, total payments (interest plus principal) of $235,000,000 are made.

3.

Date	Account and Explanation	Debit	Credit	Assets	=	Liabilities	+	Stockholders' Equity
Jan. 1, 2024	Cash	91,000,000		▲				
	Discount on Bonds Payable	9,000,000				▼		
	Bonds Payable		100,000,000			▲		

4.   Discount Amortization $= \dfrac{\text{Total Discount}}{\text{Number of Interest Periods}}$

$= \dfrac{\$9,000,000}{30 \text{ periods}}$

$= \underline{\$300,000}$

5.

Semiannual Period	Cash Payment (Credit)	Interest Expense (Debit)	Discount on Bonds Payable (Credit)	Discount on Bonds Payable Balance	Carrying Value
At issue				$9,000,000	$91,000,000
06/30/24	$4,500,000	$4,800,000	$300,000	8,700,000	91,300,000
12/31/24	4,500,000	4,800,000	300,000	8,400,000	91,600,000
06/30/25	4,500,000	4,800,000	300,000	8,100,000	91,900,000
12/31/25	4,500,000	4,800,000	300,000	7,800,000	92,200,000
06/30/26	4,500,000	4,800,000	300,000	7,500,000	92,500,000

6.

Date	Account and Explanation	Debit	Credit	Assets	=	Liabilities	+	Stockholders' Equity
Dec. 31, 2025	Interest Expense	4,800,000						▼
	Cash		4,500,000	▼				
	Discount on Bonds Payable		300,000			▲		

Date	Account and Explanation	Debit	Credit	Assets	=	Liabilities	+	Stockholders' Equity
June 30, 2026	Interest Expense	4,800,000						▼
	Cash		4,500,000	▼				
	Discount on Bonds Payable		300,000			▲		

7.

Long-term liabilities:		
Bonds payable	$100,000,000	
Less: Discount on bonds payable	(7,800,000)	
Bonds payable (net)		92,200,000

8.

Date	Account and Explanation	Debit	Credit	Assets	=	Liabilities	+	Stockholders' Equity
Dec. 31, 2038	Bonds Payable	100,000,000				▼		
	Cash		100,000,000	▼				

II. EFFECTIVE INTEREST METHOD

To finance a new hydroelectric plant, Midwest Electric issues $100,000,000 of 9%, 15-year bonds on January 1, 2024. The bonds pay interest semiannually on June 30 and December 31. Assume the market rate of interest on January 1, 2024, was 10%.

Required:

1. Will the bonds be issued at par, a premium, or a discount? Why?
2. Describe the cash flows.
3. Using present value techniques, verify the bond issue price of $92,314,025. (*Note:* This requires the use of Appendix 9A (p. 532) and Appendix 3 (p. 798).
4. Prepare the journal entry to record the bond issue.
5. Complete an amortization table through June 30, 2026 (round to the nearest dollar).
6. Prepare the journal entries for December 31, 2025, and June 30, 2026.
7. How will the bonds be shown on the December 31, 2025, balance sheet?
8. Prepare the journal entry to record the repayment of principal at maturity.

Solution:

1. The bonds will be issued at a discount (below par) because the stated rate is below the market rate. Thus, Midwest Electric will have to lower the price below face value to compensate creditors for accepting a below market interest payment.
2. The interest payments are made semiannually, so the interest payments are:

$$\$100,000,000 \times 9\% \times 6/12 = \underline{\$4,500,000}$$

There are 30 interest payments over the 15-year life of the bonds, so total interest payments are:

$$\$4,500,000 \times 30 = \underline{\$135,000,000}$$

At maturity, the face value of $100,000,000 is also repaid. Thus, total payments (interest plus principal) of $235,000,000 are made.

3. The issue price is the present value of the cash flows:

PV of interest payments = Interest Payment $\times$ PV of an annuity, 30 semiannual periods, 5%
$$= \$4,500,000 \times 15.37245 = \underline{\$69,176,025}$$

PV of principal payments = Principal Payment $\times$ PV of a single sum, 30 semiannual periods, 5%
$$= \$100,000,000 \times 0.23138 = \underline{\$23,138,000}$$

Market price of bonds = \$69,176,025 + \$23,138,000 = \$92,314,025

4.

Date	Account and Explanation	Debit	Credit	Assets	=	Liabilities	+	Stockholders' Equity
Dec. 31, 2023	Cash	92,314,025		▲				
	Discount on Bonds Payable	7,685,975				▼		
	Bonds Payable		100,000,000			▲		

5.

Annual Period	Cash Payment (Credit)	Interest Expense (Debit)	Discount on Bonds Payable (Credit)	Discount on Bonds Payable Balance	Carrying Value
At issue				$7,685,975	$92,314,025
06/30/24	$4,500,000	$4,615,701	$115,701	7,570,274	92,429,726
12/31/24	4,500,000	4,621,486	121,486	7,448,788	92,551,212
06/30/25	4,500,000	4,627,561	127,561	7,321,227	92,678,773
12/31/25	4,500,000	4,633,939	133,939	7,187,288	92,812,712
06/30/26	4,500,000	4,640,636	140,636	7,046,652	92,953,348

6.

Date	Account and Explanation	Debit	Credit	Assets	=	Liabilities	+	Stockholders' Equity
Dec. 31, 2025	Interest Expense	4,633,939		▼				▼
	Cash		4,500,000					
	Discount on Bonds Payable		133,939			▲		

Date	Account and Explanation	Debit	Credit	Assets	=	Liabilities	+	Stockholders' Equity
June 30, 2026	Interest Expense	4,640,636		▼				▼
	Cash		4,500,000					
	Discount on Bonds Payable		140,636			▲		

7.

Long-term liabilities:
Bonds payable	$100,000,000	
Less: Discount on bonds payable	(7,187,288)	
Bonds payable (net)		92,812,712

8.

Date	Account and Explanation	Debit	Credit	Assets	=	Liabilities	+	Stockholders' Equity
Dec. 31, 2038	Bonds Payable	100,000,000		▼		▼		
	Cash		100,000,000					

APPLYING KNOWLEDGE

DISCUSSION QUESTIONS

OBJECTIVE 1

1. What is long-term debt?

2. What is the difference between a bond and a note? How do the accounting treatments differ?

3. What does the face (or par) value of a bond represent?

4. What is the maturity date of a bond?

5. What is the stated or coupon rate of a bond?

6. How does a bond's stated rate differ from its yield rate? Which one is used to calculate the interest payment?

7. How does a secured bond differ from an unsecured bond?

8. What does it mean if a bond is "callable"?

9. What does it mean if a bond is "convertible"?

10. What is a junk bond?

11. How is total interest for long-term debt calculated?

12. Describe the process that businesses follow to sell new issues of long-term debt.

13. Describe how the relationship between the stated rate and yield rate affect the price at which bonds are sold.

14. How are premiums and discounts presented on the balance sheet? **OBJECTIVE** ◄ 2

15. How do premiums and discounts on long-term debt securities affect interest expense? **OBJECTIVE** ◄ 3

16. What is the difference between the straight-line and effective interest rate methods of amortizing premiums and discounts?

17. How can there be interest expense each period for noninterest-bearing bonds if there are no interest payments?

18. Under the effective interest rate method, describe the difference in calculating the (a) interest payment and (b) interest expense for the period. **OBJECTIVE** ◄ 4

19. How does a firm "leverage" its capital structure? When is leverage advantageous? When is it disadvantageous? Who receives the advantage or bears the disadvantage of leverage? **OBJECTIVE** ◄ 5

20. Describe how recent rule changes will require leases to be accounted for beginning in 2019. **OBJECTIVE** ◄ 6

21. How do the old lease accounting rules differ from the new lease accounting rules?

22. *(Appendix 9A)* Describe how the bond issue price is calculated. **OBJECTIVE** ◄ 8

MULTIPLE-CHOICE QUESTIONS

9-1 Which of the following statements regarding bonds payable is true? **OBJECTIVE** ◄ 1
   a. Generally, bonds are issued in denominations of $100.
   b. When an issuing company's bonds are traded in the "secondary" market, the company will receive part of the proceeds when the bonds are sold from the first purchaser to the second purchaser.
   c. The entire principal amount of most bonds mature on a single date.
   d. A debenture bond is backed by specific assets of the issuing company.

9-2 Bonds are sold at a premium if the
   a. market rate of interest was more than the stated rate at the time of issue.
   b. market rate of interest was less than the stated rate at the time of issue.
   c. company will have to pay a premium to retire the bonds.
   d. issuing company has a better reputation than other companies in the same business.

9-3 If bonds are issued at 101.25, this means that
   a. a $1,000 bond sold for $1,012.50.
   b. a $1,000 bond sold for $101.25.
   c. the bonds sold at a discount.
   d. the bond rate of interest is 10.125% of the market rate of interest.

9-4 What best describes the discount on bonds payable account?
   a. A liability   c. A contra liability
   b. An asset   d. An expense

9-5 The premium on bonds payable account is shown on the balance sheet as
   a. a contra asset.   c. an addition to a long-term liability.
   b. a reduction of an expense.   d. a subtraction from a long-term liability.

9-6 When bonds are issued by a company, the accounting entry typically shows an **OBJECTIVE** ◄ 2
   a. increase in liabilities and a decrease in stockholders' equity.
   b. increase in assets and an increase in stockholders' equity.
   c. increase in liabilities and an increase in stockholders' equity.
   d. increase in assets and an increase in liabilities.

OBJECTIVE 3

9-7   Bower Company sold $100,000 of 20-year bonds for $95,000. The stated rate on the bonds was 7%, and interest is paid annually on December 31. What entry would be made on December 31 when the interest is paid? (Numbers are omitted.)

a. Interest Expense Cash

b. Interest Expense Bonds Payable Cash

c. Interest Expense Discount on Bonds Payable Cash

d. Interest Expense Discount on Bonds Payable Cash

9-8   Bonds in the amount of $100,000 with a life of 10 years were issued by the Roundy Company. If the stated rate is 6% and interest is paid semiannually, what would be the total amount of interest paid over the life of the bonds?

a. $120,000   c. $30,000

b. $60,000   d. $6,000

9-9   Sean Corp. issued a $40,000, 10-year bond, with a stated rate of 8%, paid semiannually. How much cash will the bond investors receive at the end of the first interest period?

a. $800   c. $3,200

b. $1,600   d. $4,000

OBJECTIVE 3 4

9-10   When bonds are issued at a discount, the interest expense for the period is the amount of interest payment for the period

a. plus the premium amortization for the period.

b. minus the premium amortization for the period.

c. plus the discount amortization for the period.

d. minus the discount amortization for the period.

9-11   When bonds are issued at a premium, the interest expense for the period is the amount of interest payment for the period

a. minus the premium amortization for the period.

b. plus the premium amortization for the period.

c. plus the discount amortization for the period.

d. minus the discount amortization for the period.

OBJECTIVE 4

9-12   Installment bonds differ from typical bonds in what way?

a. Essentially they are the same.

b. The entire principal balance is paid off at maturity for installment bonds.

c. Installment bonds do not have a stated rate.

d. A portion of each installment bond payment pays down the principal balance.

9-13   In 2019, Drew Company issued $200,000 of bonds for $189,640. If the stated rate of interest was 6% and the yield was 6.73%, how would Drew calculate the interest expense for the first year on the bonds using the effective interest method?

a. $189,640 × 8%   c. $200,000 × 8%

b. $189,640 × 6.73%   d. $200,000 × 6.73%

9-14   The result of using the effective interest method of amortization of the discount on bonds is that

a. the cash interest payment is greater than the interest expense.

b. the amount of interest expense decreases each period.

c. the interest expense for each amortization period is constant.

d. a constant interest rate is charged against the debt carrying value.

9-15   Serenity Company issued $100,000 of 6%, 10-year bonds when the market rate of interest was 5%. The proceeds from this bond issue were $107,732. Using the effective interest method of amortization, which of the following statements is true? Assume interest is paid annually.

a. Amortization of the premium for the first interest period will be $1,464.

b. Amortization of the premium for the first interest period will be $613.

c. Interest payments to bondholders each period will be $5,000.

d. Interest payments to bondholders each period will be $6,464.

9-16 Bonds are a popular source of financing because

    a. a company having cash flow problems can postpone payment of interest to bondholders.

    b. financial analysts tend to downgrade a company that has raised large amounts of cash by frequent issues of stock.

    c. bond interest expense is deductible for tax purposes, while dividends paid on stock are not.

    d. the bondholders can always convert their bonds into stock if they choose.

OBJECTIVE ◀ 5

9-17 Which of the following statements regarding the new accounting rules, which take effect in 2019, for leases is *false*?

    a. If the lease term is one year or longer, a liability must be recognized.

    b. If the lease term is less than one year, an asset must be recognized.

    c. The new lease accounting rules will result in more assets and liabilities being recognized on the balance sheet.

    d. Leasing will likely remain popular under the new lease accounting rules because leases do not require a large initial outlay of cash.

OBJECTIVE ◀ 6

9-18 Willow Corporation's balance sheet showed the following amounts: current liabilities, $5,000; bonds payable, $1,500; lease obligations, $2,300. Total stockholders' equity was $6,000. The debt to equity ratio is

    a. 1.47.   c. 0.83.

    b. 1.42.   d. 0.63.

OBJECTIVE ◀ 7

9-19 Kinsella Corporation's balance sheet showed the following amounts: current liabilities, $75,000; total liabilities, $100,000; total assets, $200,000. What is the long-term debt to equity ratio?

    a. 0.75   c. 0.25

    b. 0.375   d. 0.125

9-20 McLaughlin Corporation's balance sheet showed the following amounts: current liabilities, $75,000; total liabilities, $100,000; total assets, $200,000. What is the debt to total assets ratio?

    a. 2   c. 0.875

    b. 1   d. 0.50

9-21 *(Appendix 9A)* The bond issue price is determined by calculating the

    a. present value of the stream of interest payments and the present value of the maturity amount.

    b. future value of the stream of interest payments and the future value of the maturity amount.

    c. future value of the stream of interest payments and the present value of the maturity amount.

    d. present value of the stream of interest payments and the future value of the maturity amount.

OBJECTIVE ◀ 8

BRIEF EXERCISES

Brief Exercise 9-22 Reporting Long-Term Debt on the Balance Sheet

OBJECTIVE ◀ 2

EXAMPLE 9.1

Parky Corp. provides contracted home staging services to real estate agencies and their clients. Parky issued the following bonds in the current year:

a. 1,600 bonds with $1,000 face value, which the market has valued at $60,000 below its face value

b. 2,400 bonds with $1,000 face value, which the market has valued at $75,000 above its face value

Required:

Prepare the balance sheet presentation for these two bonds.

OBJECTIVE **2**
EXAMPLE 9.1

Brief Exercise 9-23 Issuance of Long-Term Debt

Natalie Corp. provides medical supplies to hospitals located in Western Washington and Oregon. This year, Natalie Corp. issued 8,000 bonds with a $1,000 face value. The nominal rate for each bond is 7%.

Required:

Prepare the necessary journal entries to record the issuance of these bonds assuming the bonds were issued (a) at par, (b) at 103, and (c) at 96.

OBJECTIVE **2**
EXAMPLE 9.1

Brief Exercise 9-24 Issuance of Long-Term Debt

Carrie Enterprises required an infusion of cash in order to purchase a large piece of equipment. To finance its equipment purchase, Carrie issued $4,100,000 of 9% bonds payable.

Required:

Prepare the necessary journal entries to record the issuance of the bonds assuming the bonds were issued (a) at par, (b) at 101, and (c) at 96.

OBJECTIVE **2**
EXAMPLE 9.1

Brief Exercise 9-25 Issuance of Long-Term Debt

H. Simpson Company is an entertainment company located in Springfield, IL. H. Simpson recently issued $200,000 of bonds to finance large expenditures for an upcoming television production. H. Simpson received cash of $194,620 upon the issuance of the bonds and plans to pay interest semiannually.

Required:

1. Prepare the necessary journal entry to record the issuance of the bonds.
2. Is the stated rate greater or less than the yield? How do you know?

OBJECTIVE **3**
EXAMPLE 9.2

Brief Exercise 9-26 Debt Issued at Par

On January 1, Desmond & Co. issued 4,000 bonds with a $1,000 par value at 100. The bonds have an 6% stated rate, pay interest on June 30 and December 31.

Required:

Prepare the journal entry(ies) to record the interest payment on June 30.

OBJECTIVE **3**
EXAMPLE 9.3

Brief Exercise 9-27 Debt Issued at a Discount (Straight Line)

On January 1, 2024, Drew Company issued 5-year bonds with a face value of $35,000,000 for $32,000,000. The stated rate of interest was 7% and interest is paid annually on December 31.

Required:

Prepare the necessary journal entry on December 31 at the end of the first year, assuming the straight-line method is followed.

OBJECTIVE **3**
EXAMPLE 9.3

Brief Exercise 9-28 Debt Issued at a Discount (Straight Line)

Use the information from **Brief Exercise 9-27**.

Required:

Prepare the amortization table for Drew Company's bonds (round to the nearest dollar).

OBJECTIVE **3**
EXAMPLE 9.4

Brief Exercise 9-29 Debt Issued at a Premium (Straight Line)

On January 1, 2024, Katia Crafts issued 80,000, 6-year bonds with $1,000 face value. External markets value the bonds at $840,000 more than face value. The stated rate of interest on Katia's bonds is 7%, and interest is paid annually on December 31.

Required:

Prepare the necessary journal entry on December 31, 2025, assuming the straight-line method is followed.

Brief Exercise 9-30 Debt Issued at a Premium (Straight Line)

OBJECTIVE ◀ 3

EXAMPLE 9.4

Use the information from **Brief Exercise 9-29**.

Required:

Prepare the amortization table for Katia Craft's bonds.

> *Use the following information for Brief Exercises 9-31 and 9-32:*
> Theodore Corporation decided to issue long-term debt in order to pay off its short-term obligations. On January 1, 2025, Theodore issued $850,000 in 8% bonds (payable on December 31, 2034) at 92. Interest is paid on June 30 and December 31. The market rate of interest is 10%.

Brief Exercise 9-31 Bonds Issued at a Discount (Effective Interest)

OBJECTIVE ◀ 4

EXAMPLE 9.5

Refer to the information for Theodore Corporation above.

Required:

Prepare the amortization table through December 31, 2026, using the effective interest rate method.

Brief Exercise 9-32 Bonds Issued at a Discount (Effective Interest)

OBJECTIVE ◀ 4

EXAMPLE 9.5

Refer to the information for Theodore Corporation above.

Required:

Prepare the journal entries for December 31, 2025 and 2026.

> *Use the following information for Brief Exercises 9-33 and 9-34:*
> Crafty Corporation received $472,088 of cash upon issuance of 500, $100 par value bonds. Each bond has a stated rate of 5% and will mature on December 31, 2030, 7 years after the issuance of the bonds. Interest is paid annually on December 31. The market rate of interest is 6%.

Brief Exercise 9-33 Bonds Issued at a Discount (Effective Interest)

OBJECTIVE ◀ 4

EXAMPLE 9.5

Refer to the information for Crafty Corporation shown above.

Required:

Prepare the amortization table using the effective interest rate method.

Brief Exercise 9-34 Bonds Issued at a Discount (Effective Interest)

OBJECTIVE ◀ 4

EXAMPLE 9.5

Refer to the information for Crafty Corporation shown above.

Required:

Prepare the journal entry for December 31, 2026 and 2027.

> *Use the following information for Brief Exercises 9-35 and 9-36:*
> Haley Industries issued $120,000 of 11%, 7-year bonds on January 1, 2024, with a $5,842 premium. Interest is paid annually on December 31. The market rate of interest is 10%.

Brief Exercise 9-35 Bonds Issued at a Premium (Effective Interest)

OBJECTIVE ◀ 4

EXAMPLE 9.6

Refer to the information above for Haley Industries.

Required:

Prepare the amortization table using the effective interest rate method.

OBJECTIVE 5

EXAMPLE 9.6

Brief Exercise 9-36 Bonds Issued at a Premium (Effective Interest)

Refer to the information shown above for Haley Industries.

Required:

Record the journal entries for December 31, 2025 and 2026.

OBJECTIVE 5

Brief Exercise 9-37 Cost of Debt Financing

Topple Corporation leases skyscrapers in cities throughout the world to large corporations. Topple's cost of debt financing is 9% and its tax rate is 21%.

Required:

Calculate the after-tax interest rate to two-tenths of 1%.

OBJECTIVE 5

Brief Exercise 9-38 Cost of Debt Financing

Crackle Company instituted an aggressive plan to lower its cost of financing over the next decade. Currently Crackle's cost of debt financing is 8%, its cost of equity financing is 14%, and its tax rate is 35%. Crackle currently has $2,500,000 of debt.

Required:

1. Calculate the after-tax cost amount of interest expense.
2. How does the tax effect of interest expense affect financial leverage?

OBJECTIVE 7

EXAMPLE 9.7

Brief Exercise 9-39 Ratio Analysis

Whitten Corporation's balance sheet shows the following amounts: current assets, $200,000; current liabilities, $80,000; bonds payable, $155,000; and lease obligations, $25,000. Total stockholders' equity is $120,000.

Required:

Calculate the debt to equity ratio. (*Note:* Round to two decimal places.)

OBJECTIVE 7

EXAMPLE 9.7

Brief Exercise 9-40 Ratio Analysis

Casey Corporation has $2,210,000 in total liabilities, $840,000 of which are current. Casey has $500,000 of cash and cash equivalents, $200,000 of other current assets, and $3,000,000 in property, plant, and equipment.

Required:

Calculate Casey's debt to equity ratio.

OBJECTIVE 7

EXAMPLE 9.7

Brief Exercise 9-41 Ratio Analysis

Trevor Corporation had $2,900,000 in total liabilities and $4,300,000 in total assets as of December 31. Trevor calculates that 40% of assets are designated as current, while $500,000 of Trevor's total liabilities are long-term.

Required:

Calculate Trevor's debt to assets ratio and its long-term debt to equity ratio. (*Note:* Round to two decimal places.)

OBJECTIVE 8

EXAMPLE 9.8

Brief Exercise 9-42 *(Appendix 9A)* Bond Issue Price

On January 1, Ruby Inc. issued 3,000 of $1,000 par value bonds with a stated rate of 6% and a 10-year maturity. Interest is payable semiannually on June 30 and December 31.

Required:

What is the issue price if the bonds are sold to yield 8%? (*Note:* Round to nearest dollar.)

Brief Exercise 9-43 *(Appendix 9A)* **Bond Issue Price**

OBJECTIVE ◄ 8

EXAMPLE 9.8

On January 2, Nelson Construction issued 3,500 of $1,000 par value bonds with a stated rate of 8%, maturing in 10 years. Interest is payable semiannually on June 30 and December 31.

Required:

What is the issue price if the bonds are sold to yield 6%? (*Note:* Round to nearest dollar.)

EXERCISES

Exercise 9-44 Issuing at Par, a Premium, or a Discount

OBJECTIVE ◄ 1 2

Dash Enterprises is planning to issue 1,500 bonds, each having a face amount of $1,000.

Required:

1. Prepare the journal entry to record the sale of the bonds at par.
2. Prepare the journal entry to record the sale of the bonds at a premium of $19,000.
3. Prepare the journal entry to record the sale of the bonds at a discount of $32,000.
4. **CONCEPTUAL CONNECTION** Assuming the stated rate is identical for the previous three scenarios, in which scenario is the market rate of interest (yield) highest? How do you know?

Exercise 9-45 Bond Premium and Discount

OBJECTIVE ◄ 1 2

Markway Inc. is contemplating selling bonds. The issue is to be composed of 750 bonds, each with a face amount of $1,000.

Required:

1. Calculate how much Markway is able to borrow if each bond is sold at a premium of $30.
2. Calculate how much Markway is able to borrow if each bond is sold at a discount of $10.
3. Calculate how much Markway is able to borrow if each bond is sold at 92% of par.
4. Calculate how much Markway is able to borrow if each bond is sold at 103% of par.
5. Assume that the bonds are sold for $975 each. Prepare the entry to recognize the sale of the 750 bonds.
6. Assume that the bonds are sold for $1,015 each. Prepare the entry to recognize the sale of the 750 bonds.

Exercise 9-46 Bonds with Annual Interest Payments

OBJECTIVE ◄ 2 3

Kiwi Corporation issued at par $420,000, 8% bonds on January 1, 2024. Interest is paid annually on December 31. The principal and the final interest payment are due on December 31, 2025.

Required:

1. Prepare the entry to recognize the issuance of the bonds.
2. Prepare the journal entry for December 31, 2024.
3. Prepare the journal entry to record repayment of the principal on December 31, 2025.
4. **CONCEPTUAL CONNECTION** How would the interest expense for 2024 change if the bonds had been issued at a premium?

Exercise 9-47 Issuance and Interest Amortization for Zero Coupon Note (Straight Line)

OBJECTIVE ◄ 2 3

Kerwin Company borrowed $10,000 on a 2-year, zero coupon note. The note was issued on January 1, 2024. The face amount of the note, $12,544, is to be paid at maturity on December 31, 2025.

Required:

1. Assuming straight line amortization, calculate the interest expense for 2024 and 2025.
2. Prepare the entries to recognize the borrowing, the first year's interest expense, and the second year's interest expense plus redemption of the note at maturity.

OBJECTIVE 2 3

Exercise 9-48 Interest Payments and Interest Expense for Bonds (Straight Line)

Swiss Inc. sold 15-year bonds with a total face amount of $1,800,000 and a stated rate of 8%. The bonds sold for $1,887,000 on January 1, 2024, and pay interest semiannually on June 30 and December 31.

Required:

1. Prepare the entry to recognize the sale of the bonds.
2. Determine the amount of the semiannual interest payment required by the bonds.
3. Prepare the journal entry made by Swiss at June 30, 2024, to recognize the interest expense and an interest payment.
4. Determine the amount of interest expense for 2024.
5. **CONCEPTUAL CONNECTION** If Swiss issued bonds with a variable interest rate, would you expect the market rate of interest (i.e., yield) to increase, decrease, or stay the same? Why?
6. **CONCEPTUAL CONNECTION** What should Swiss consider in deciding whether to use a fixed or variable rate?

OBJECTIVE 2 3

Exercise 9-49 Interest Payments and Interest Expense for Bonds (Straight Line)

On January 1, Harrington Corporation sold $385,000 of 15-year, 12% bonds. The bonds sold for $335,000 and pay interest semiannually on June 30 and December 31.

Required:

1. Prepare the journal entry to record the sale of the bonds.
2. Calculate the amount of the semiannual interest payment.
3. Prepare the entry for the first interest payment on June 30 to recognize the payment of interest and interest expense.
4. Calculate the annual interest expense for the first year.

OBJECTIVE 3

Exercise 9-50 Interest Payments and Interest Expense for Bonds (Straight Line)

On January 1, Perry Manufacturing issued bonds with a total face amount of $3,000,000 and a stated rate of 9%. Interest is payable annually on December 31.

Required:

1. Calculate the interest expense for the first year if the bonds were sold at par.
2. Calculate the interest expense for the first year if the bonds were sold at a premium and the straightline premium amortization is $12,000.
3. Calculate the interest expense for the first year if the bonds were sold at a discount and the straightline discount amortization is $33,000.

OBJECTIVE 3

Exercise 9-51 Completing a Debt Amortization Table (Straight Line)

Cagney Company sold $200,000 of bonds on January 1, 2024. A portion of the amortization table follows.

Period	Cash Payment (Credit)	Interest Expense (Debit)	Discount on Bonds Payable (Credit)	Discount on Bonds Payable Balance	Carrying Value
At issue				$8,000	$192,000
06/30/24	$12,000	$12,800	$800	7,200	192,800
12/31/24	12,000	12,800	800	6,400	193,600
06/30/25	?	?	?	?	?

Required:

1. Determine the stated interest rate on these bonds.
2. Calculate the interest expense and the discount amortization for the interest period ending on June 30, 2025.
3. Calculate the liability balance shown on a balance sheet after the interest payment is recorded on June 30, 2025.

Exercise 9-52 Using a Premium Amortization Table (Straight Line)

OBJECTIVE 3

For Dingle Corporation, the following amortization table was prepared when $400,000 of 5-year, 7% bonds were sold on January 1, 2024, for $420,000.

Period	Cash Payment (Credit)	Interest Expense (Debit)	Premium on Bonds Payable (Debit)	Premium on Bonds Payable Balance	Carrying Value
At issue				$20,000	$420,000
06/30/24	$14,000	$12,000	$2,000	18,000	418,000
12/31/24	14,000	12,000	2,000	16,000	416,000
06/30/25	14,000	12,000	2,000	14,000	414,000
12/31/25	14,000	12,000	2,000	12,000	412,000
06/30/26	14,000	12,000	2,000	10,000	410,000
12/31/26	14,000	12,000	2,000	8,000	408,000
06/30/27	14,000	12,000	2,000	6,000	406,000
12/31/27	14,000	12,000	2,000	4,000	404,000
06/30/28	14,000	12,000	2,000	2,000	402,000
12/31/28	14,000	12,000	2,000	0	400,000

Required:

1. Prepare the entry to recognize the issuance of the bonds on January 1, 2024.
2. Prepare the entry to recognize the first interest payment on June 30, 2024.
3. Determine what interest expense for this bond issue Dingle will report in its 2025 income statement.
4. Indicate how these bonds will appear in Dingle's December 31, 2027, balance sheet.

Exercise 9-53 Using a Discount Amortization Table (Straight Line)

OBJECTIVE 3

Panamint Candy Company prepared the following amortization table for $300,000 of 5-year, 9% bonds issued and sold by Panamint on January 1, 2025, for $285,000:

Period	Cash Payment (Credit)	Interest Expense (Debit)	Discount on Bonds Payable (Credit)	Discount on Bonds Payable Balance	Carrying Value
At issue				$15,000	$285,000
06/30/25	$13,500	$15,000	$1,500	13,500	286,500
12/31/25	13,500	15,000	1,500	12,000	288,000
06/30/26	13,500	15,000	1,500	10,500	289,500
12/31/26	13,500	15,000	1,500	9,000	291,000
06/30/27	13,500	15,000	1,500	7,500	292,500
12/31/27	13,500	15,000	1,500	6,000	294,000
06/30/28	13,500	15,000	1,500	4,500	295,500
12/31/28	13,500	15,000	1,500	3,000	297,000
06/30/29	13,500	15,000	1,500	1,500	298,500
12/31/29	13,500	15,000	1,500	0	300,000

Required:

1. Prepare the entry to recognize the sale of the bonds on January 1, 2025.
2. Prepare the entry to recognize the first interest payment on June 30, 2025.

(Continued)

3. Determine the interest expense for these bonds that Panamint will report on its 2027 income statement.
4. Indicate how these bonds will appear in Panamint's December 31, 2028, balance sheet.

OBJECTIVE

Exercise 9-54 Completing an Amortization Table (Straight Line)

Richter Corporation sold $1,000,000 face value of bonds at 104 on January 1, 2024. These bonds have a 7% stated rate and mature in 4 years. Interest is payable on June 30 and December 31 of each year.

Required:

1. Prepare a bond amortization table assuming straight-line amortization.
2. Prepare the journal entry for December 31, 2025.
3. Indicate how these bonds will appear in Richter's balance sheet at December 31, 2025.

OBJECTIVE 3

Exercise 9-55 Zero Coupon Bond

Johnson Company sold for $90,000 a $102,400, 2-year zero coupon bond on January 1, 2024. The bond matures on December 31, 2025.

Required:

1. Prepare the entry to record the issuance of the bond.
2. Prepare the adjusting entry to recognize 2024 interest expense.
3. Prepare the entry to recognize the 2025 interest expense and the repayment of the bond on December 31, 2025.

OBJECTIVE 3

Exercise 9-56 Zero Coupon Note

Crafty Cave Products borrowed $200,000 cash by issuing a 48-month, $246,660 zero coupon note on January 1, 2025. The note matures on December 31, 2027.

Required:

1. Prepare the entry to recognize the issuance of the note.
2. Prepare the adjustments to recognize 2025 and 2026 interest.
3. Prepare the entry to recognize 2027 interest and repayment of the note at maturity.

OBJECTIVE 4

Exercise 9-57 Note Interest Payment and Interest Expense (Effective Interest)

Jones Manufacturing sold $900,000 of 15-year, 7% notes for $822,186. The notes were sold on January 1, 2024, and pay interest semiannually on June 30 and December 31. The effective interest rate was 8%. Assume Jones uses the effective interest rate method.

Required:

1. Prepare the entry to record the sale of the notes.
2. Determine the amount of the semiannual interest payments for the notes.
3. Prepare the amortization table through 2025. (*Note:* Round to the nearest dollar.)
4. Prepare the entry for Jones' journal at June 30, 2024, to record the payment of 6 months' interest and the related interest expense.
5. Determine interest expense for 2025.

OBJECTIVE 4

Exercise 9-58 Bond Interest Payments and Interest Expense (Effective Interest)

On January 1, 2023, Hawthorne Corporation issued for $333,456, 7-year bonds with a face amount of $315,000 and a stated (or coupon) rate of 11%. The bonds pay interest annually and have an effective interest rate of 9%. Assume Hawthorne uses the effective interest rate method.

Required:

1. Prepare the entry to record the sale of the bonds.
2. Calculate the amount of the interest payments for the bonds.
3. Prepare the amortization table through 2024. (*Note:* Round to the nearest dollar.)
4. Prepare the journal entry for December 31, 2023, to record the payment of interest and the related interest expense.
5. Calculate the annual interest expense for 2023 and 2024.

Exercise 9-59 Completing a Bond Amortization Table (Effective Interest Rate Method)

OBJECTIVE 4

Cagney Company sold $200,000 of bonds on July 1, 2022. A portion of the amortization table appears below.

Period	Cash Payment (Credit)	Interest Expense (Debit)	Discount on Bonds Payable (Credit)	Discount on Bonds Payable Balance	Carrying Value
12/31/23	$9,000	$9,277	$277	$2,340	$197,660
06/30/24	9,000	9,290	290	2,050	197,950
12/31/24	?	?	?	?	?

Required:

1. Indicate the stated interest rate on these bonds.
2. Calculate the effective annual interest rate on these bonds. (*Note:* Round to the nearest 0.1%.)
3. Determine the interest expense and discount amortization for the interest period ending on December 31, 2024. (*Note:* Round to the nearest dollar.)
4. Determine the liability balance after the interest payment is recorded on December 31, 2024.

Exercise 9-60 Completing a Bond Amortization Table (Effective Interest Rate Method)

OBJECTIVE 4

MacBride Enterprises sold $200,000 of bonds on January 1, 2024. A portion of the amortization table appears below.

Period	Cash Payment (Credit)	Interest Expense (Debit)	Premium on Bonds Payable (Debit)	Premium on Bonds Payable Balance	Carrying Value
At issue				$6,457	$206,457
06/30/24	$9,000	$8,465	$535	5,922	205,922
12/31/24	9,000	8,443	557	5,365	205,365
06/30/25	9,000	8,420	580	4,785	204,785
12/31/25	?	?	?	?	?

Required:

1. Indicate the stated annual interest rate on these bonds.
2. Calculate the effective annual interest rate on these bonds. (*Note:* Round to the nearest 0.1%.)
3. Determine the interest expense and premium amortization for the interest period ending on December 31, 2025. (*Note:* Round to the nearest dollar.)
4. Determine when the bonds will mature.

> *Use the following information for Exercises 9-61 and 9-62:*
> Dandy Candy bought a delivery vehicle for $45,000 by issuing an 8% installment note on January. Dandy will make 12 monthly payments of $3,914.50 at the end of each month.

OBJECTIVE 4

Exercise 9-61 Installment Notes

Refer to the information for Dandy Candy shown above.

Required:

Prepare the amortization table using the effective interest rate method. (*Note:* Round to the nearest penny.)

OBJECTIVE 4

Exercise 9-62 Installment Notes

Refer to the information for Dandy Candy shown above.

Required:

Prepare the journal entries for the end of March and the end of April.

OBJECTIVE 4

Exercise 9-63 Installment Notes

ABC bank loans $250,000 to Yossarian to purchase a new home. Yossarian will repay the note in equal monthly payments over a period of 30 years. The interest rate is 12%.

Required:

If the monthly payment is $2,571.53, how much of the first payment is interest expense and how much is principal repayment? (*Note:* Round to the nearest cent.)

OBJECTIVE 3

Exercise 9-64 Noninterest-Bearing Bonds (Straight Line)

Dean Plumbing issues $1,000,000 face value, noninterest-bearing bonds on January 1, 2025. The bonds are issued at 65 and mature on December 31, 2028.

Required:

Assuming the straight-line amortization method is followed, prepare the journal entry on December 31, 2027.

OBJECTIVE 5

Exercise 9-65 Cost of Debt Financing

Stinson Corporation's cost of debt financing is 6%. Its tax rate is 20%.

Required:

Calculate the after-tax interest rate. (*Note:* Round answer to one decimal place.)

OBJECTIVE 5

Exercise 9-66 Cost of Debt Financing

Diamond Company's cost of debt financing is 10%. Its tax rate is 21%. Diamond has $3,000,000 of debt.

Required:

1. Calculate the after-tax cost amount of interest expense.
2. **CONCEPTUAL CONNECTION** How does the tax effect of interest expense affect financial leverage?

OBJECTIVE 7

Exercise 9-67 Ratio Analysis

Rising Stars Academy provided the following information on its balance sheet and statement of cash flows:

Long-term debt	$ 4,400	Interest expense	$ 398
Total liabilities	8,972	Net income	559
Total assets	38,775	Interest payments	432
Total equity	29,803	Cash flows from operations	1,015
Operating income	1,223	Income tax expenses	266
		Income taxes paid	150

Required:

1. Calculate the following ratios for Rising Stars: (a) debt to equity, (b) debt to total assets, (c) long-term debt to equity, (d) times interest earned (accrual basis), and (e) times interest earned (cash basis). (*Note:* Round answers to three decimal places.)
2. **CONCEPTUAL CONNECTION** Interpret these results.

Exercise 9-68 *(Appendix 9A)* Calculating Bond Issue Price

OBJECTIVE ◀ 8

On January 1, University Theatres issued $500,000 face value of bonds. The stated rate is 8%, and interest is paid semiannually on June 30 and December 31. The bonds mature in 15 years.

Required:

Calculate the price at which the bonds are issued assuming the market rate of interest is (a) 6% and (b) 10%.

PROBLEM SET A

Problem 9-69A Reporting Long-Term Debt

OBJECTIVE ◀ 2

Fridley Manufacturing's accounting records reveal the following account balances after adjusting entries are made on December 31, 2024:

Accounts payable	$ 62,500	Interest payable	$ 38,700
Bonds payable (9.4%, due in 2031)	800,000	Installment note payable (8%, equal	
Lease liability*	41,500	installments due 2025 to 2028)	120,000
Bonds payable (8.7%, due in 2027)	50,000	Notes payable (7.8%, due in 2029)	400,000
Deferred tax liability*	133,400	Premium on notes payable	
Discount on bonds payable		(7.8%, due in 2029)	6,100
(9.4%, due in 2031)	12,600	Note payable, 4% $50,000 face amount,	
Income taxes payable	26,900	due in 2030 (net of discount)	31,900

* Long-term liability

Required:

Prepare the current liabilities and long-term debt portions of Fridley's balance sheet at December 31, 2024. Provide a separate line item for each issue (do not combine separate bonds or notes payable), but some items may need to be split into more than one item.

Problem 9-70A Entries for and Financial Statement Presentation of a Note

OBJECTIVE ◀ 2 3

Augustine Corporation borrowed $150,000 from the J.P. Morgan Chase Bank on June 1, 2023, on a 3-year, 6.4% note. Interest is paid annually on May 31.

Required:

1. Record the borrowing transaction in Augustine's journal.
2. Prepare the adjusting entries made at December 31, 2023 and 2024.
3. Prepare the necessary journal entry to recognize the first interest payment on May 31, 2024.
4. Indicate how the note and associated interest would be presented in Augustine's December 31, 2024, balance sheet.
5. Prepare the necessary journal entries to record the repayment of the note and the last year's interest payment on May 31, 2026.

Problem 9-71A Preparing a Bond Amortization Table (Straight Line)

On January 1, 2025, Distel Company borrowed $102,700 by issuing 3-year, 9% bonds with a face amount of $100,000. Interest is paid annually on December 31.

Required:

Prepare an amortization table using the following column headings:

Period	Cash Payment (Credit)	Interest Expense (Debit)	Premium on Bonds Payable (Debit)	Premium on Bonds Payable Balance	Carrying Value

Problem 9-72A Note Computations and Entries (Straight Line)

On January 1, 2024, Sisek Company borrowed $800,000 with a 10-year, 9.75% note, interest payable semiannually on June 30 and December 31. Cash in the amount of $792,800 was received when the note was issued.

Required:

1. Prepare the necessary journal entry at January 1, 2024.
2. Prepare the necessary journal entry at June 30, 2024.
3. Prepare the necessary journal entry at December 31, 2024.
4. Determine the carrying amount of these notes at the end of the fifth year (December 31, 2028).

Problem 9-73A Preparing a Bond Amortization Table (Straight Line)

Edmonton-Alston Corporation issued 5-year, 9.5% bonds with a total face value of $700,000 on January 1 for $726,000. The bonds pay interest on June 30 and December 31 of each year.

Required:

1. Prepare an amortization table.
2. Prepare the entries to recognize the interest payments made on June 30 and December 31 of Year 1.

Problem 9-74A Preparing a Bond Amortization Table (Straight Line)

Sonoma Company, issued 5-year, 8.6% bonds with a total face value of $750,000 on January 1 for $711,450. The bonds pay interest on June 30 and December 31 of each year.

Required:

1. Prepare an amortization table.
2. Prepare the entries to recognize the bond issuance and the interest payments made on June 30 and December 31 of Year 1.

Problem 9-75A Preparing and Using an Amortization Table (Straight Line)

Girves Development Corporation has agreed to construct a plant in a new industrial park. To finance the construction, the county government issued $5,000,000 of 10-year, 4.75% revenue bonds for $5,125,000 on January 1, 2024. Girves will pay the interest and principal on the bonds. When the bonds are repaid, Girves will receive title to the plant. In the interim, Girves will pay property taxes as if it owned the plant. This financing arrangement is attractive to Girves, as state and local government bonds are exempt from federal income taxation and thus carry a lower interest rate. The bonds are attractive to investors, as both Girves and the county are issuers. The bonds pay interest semiannually on June 30 and December 31.

Required:

1. Prepare an amortization table through December 31, 2025, for these revenue bonds assuming straight-line amortization.

2. **CONCEPTUAL CONNECTION** Discuss whether or not Girves should record the plant as an asset after it is constructed.
3. **CONCEPTUAL CONNECTION** Discuss whether or not Girves should record the liability for these revenue bonds.

Problem 9-76A Noninterest-Bearing Note (Straight Line)

On January 1, 2024, Athena Corporation borrowed $110,000 cash on a $155,000, 24-month, 0% note. Athena uses the straight-line method of amortization.

Required:
1. Record the borrowing in Athena's journal.
2. Prepare the adjusting entry for December 31, 2024.
3. Prepare the entries to recognize the 2021 interest expense and repayment of the note on December 31, 2025.

Problem 9-77A Preparing an Amortization Table for Noninterest-Bearing Bonds (Straight Line)

On January 1, 2025, Georgetown Distributors borrowed $2,180,000 by issuing 4-year, zero coupon bonds. The face value of the bonds is $3,000,000. Georgetown uses the straight-line method to amortize any premium or discount.

Required:
Prepare an amortization table for these bonds, using the following column headings:

Period	Cash Payment (Credit)	Interest Expense (Debit)	Discount on Bonds Payable (Credit)	Discount on Bonds Payable Balance	Carrying Value

PROBLEM SET B

Problem 9-69B Reporting Long-Term Debt

Craig Corporation's accounting records reveal the following account balances after adjusting entries are made on December 31, 2023:

Accounts payable	$ 73,000	Interest payable	$ 33,400
Bonds payable (9.4%, due in 2028)	900,000	Installment note payable (9%, equal	
Lease liability*	30,000	installments due 2024 to 2034)	110,000
Bonds payable (8.3%, due in 2027)	60,000	Notes payable (7.8%, due in 2032)	350,000
Deferred tax liability*	127,600	Premium on notes payable	
Discount on bonds payable		(7.8%, due in 2032)	5,000
(9.4%, due in 2028)	11,900	3% note payable, $50,000 face	
Income taxes payable	28,100	amount, due in 2034	29,800

*Long-term liability

Required:
Prepare the current liabilities and long-term debt portions of Craig's balance sheet at December 31, 2023. Provide a separate line item for each issue (do not combine separate bonds or notes payable), but some items may need to be split into more than one item.

OBJECTIVE 2 3

Problem 9-70B Entries for and Financial Statement Presentation of a Note

Griddley Company borrowed $200,000 from the East Salvador Bank on February 1, 2023, on a 3-year, 8.6% note. Interest is paid annually on January 31.

Required:

1. Record the borrowing transaction in Griddley's journal.
2. Prepare the adjusting entries made at December 31, 2023 and 2024. (*Note:* Round to the nearest dollar.)
3. Prepare the necessary journal entry to recognize the first interest payment on January 31, 2024. (*Note:* Round to the nearest dollar.)
4. Indicate how the note and associated interest would be presented in Griddley's December 31, 2024, balance sheet.
5. Prepare the necessary journal entries to record the repayment of the note and the last year's interest payment on January 1, 2026. (*Note:* Round to the nearest dollar.)

OBJECTIVE 2 3

Problem 9-71B Preparing a Bond Amortization Table (Straight Line)

On January 1, 2024, Peacock Products borrowed $447,000 by issuing 3-year, 8% bonds with a face amount of $400,000. Interest is payable annually on December 31.

Required:

Prepare an amortization table using the following column headings. (*Note:* Round to the nearest dollar.)

Period	Cash Payment (Credit)	Interest Expense (Debit)	Premium on Bonds Payable (Debit)	Premium on Bonds Payable Balance	Carrying Value

OBJECTIVE 3

Problem 9-72B Note Computations and Entries (Straight Line)

On January 1, 2024, Benton Corporation borrowed $1,000,000 with 10-year, 8.75% note, interest payable semiannually on June 30 and December 31. Cash in the amount of $985,500 was received when the note was issued.

Required:

1. Prepare the necessary journal entry at January 1, 2024.
2. Prepare the necessary journal entry at June 30, 2024.
3. Prepare the necessary journal entry at December 31, 2024.
4. Determine the carrying amount of these notes at the end of the fifth year (December 31, 2028).

OBJECTIVE 3

Problem 9-73B Preparing a Bond Amortization Table (Straight Line)

Campton Company issued 5-year, 8.5% bonds with a total face value of $1,100,000 on January 1 for $1,175,000. The bonds pay interest on June 30 and December 31 of each year.

Required:

1. Prepare an amortization table
2. Prepare the entries to recognize the interest payments made on June 30 and December 31 of Year 1.

OBJECTIVE 3

Problem 9-74B Preparing a Bond Amortization Table (Straight Line)

Paddington Corporation issued 5-year, 7.8% bonds with a total face value of $800,000 on January 1 for $740,000. The bonds pay interest on June 30 and December 31 of each year.

Required:

1. Prepare an amortization table.
2. Prepare the entries to recognize the bond issuance and the interest payments made on June 30 and December 31 of Year 1.

Problem 9-75B Preparing a Bond Amortization Table (Straight Line) OBJECTIVE ▶3

Cook Construction has agreed to construct a factory in a new industrial park. To finance the construction, the county government issued $6,500,000 of 10-year, 4.75% revenue bonds for $6,950,000 on January 1, 2024. Cook will pay the interest and principal on the bonds. When the bonds are repaid, Cook will receive title to the factory. In the interim, Cook will pay property taxes as if it owned the factory. This financing arrangement is attractive to Cook, as state and local government bonds are exempt from federal income taxation and thus carry a lower interest rate. The bonds are attractive to investors, as both Cook and the county are issuers. The bonds pay interest semiannually on June 30 and December 31.

Required:
1. Prepare an amortization table through December 31, 2025, for these revenue bonds assuming straight-line amortization.
2. **CONCEPTUAL CONNECTION** Discuss whether or not Cook should record the factory as an asset after it is constructed.
3. **CONCEPTUAL CONNECTION** Discuss whether or not Cook should record the liability for these revenue bonds.

Problem 9-76B Noninterest-Bearing Note (Straight Line) OBJECTIVE ◀3

On January 1, 2024, Sorenson Financing Corporation borrowed $90,000 cash on a $110,300, 24-month, zero coupon note. Sorenson uses the straight-line method of amortization.

Required:
1. Record the borrowing in Sorenson's journal.
2. Prepare the adjusting entry for December 31, 2024.
3. Prepare the entries to recognize the 2025 interest expense and repayment of the note on December 31, 2025.

Problem 9-77B Preparing an Amortization Table for Noninterest-Bearing Bonds (Straight Line) OBJECTIVE ◀3

On January 1, 2024, Birch Inc. borrowed $2,500,000 by issuing 3-year, zero coupon bonds. The face value of the bonds is $2,680,000. Birch uses the straight-line method to amortize any premium or discount.

Required:
Prepare an amortization table for these bonds using the following column headings:

Period	Cash Payment (Credit)	Interest Expense (Debit)	Discount on Bonds Payable (Credit)	Discount on Bonds Payable Balance	Carrying Value

CASES

Case 9-78 Long-Term Debt and Ethics

You are the CFO of Diversified Industries. Diversified has suffered through 4 or 5 tough years. This has deteriorated its financial condition to the point that Diversified is in danger of violating two loan covenants related to its largest loan, which is not due for 12 more years. The loan contract states that if Diversified violates any of these covenants, the loan principal becomes immediately due and payable. Diversified would be unable to make this payment, and any additional loans taken to repay this loan would likely be at higher rates, forcing Diversified into bankruptcy. An investment banker suggests forming another entity (called "special purpose entities" or SPE) and transferring some debt to this SPE.

(Continued)

Structuring the SPE very carefully will have the effect of moving enough debt off Diversified's balance sheet to keep the company in compliance with all its loan covenants. The investment banker assures you that accounting rules permit such accounting treatment.

Required:

How do you react to the investment banker?

Case 9-79 Debt Covenants and Financial Reporting Standards

Debtholders receive note contracts, one for each note, that describe the payments promised by the issuer of the debt. In addition, the issuing corporation frequently enters a supplementary agreement, called a *note indenture*, with a trustee who represents the debtholders. The provisions or covenants of the indenture may place restrictions on the issuer for the benefit of the debtholders. For example, an indenture may require that the issuer's debt to equity ratio never rise above a specified level or that periodic payments be made to the trustee who administers a "sinking fund" to provide for the retirement of debt.

Consider Roswell Manufacturing's debt indenture, which requires that Roswell's debt to equity ratio never exceed 2:1. If Roswell violates this requirement, the debt indenture specifies very costly penalties, and if the violation continues, the entire debt issue must be retired at a disadvantageous price and refinanced. In recent years, Roswell's ratio has averaged about 1.5:1 ($15 million in total liabilities and $10 million in total stockholders' equity). However, Roswell has an opportunity to purchase one of its major competitors, Ashland Products. The acquisition will require $4.5 million in additional liabilities, but it will double Roswell's net income. Roswell does not believe that a stock issue is feasible in the current environment. The Financial Accounting Standards Board issued a new standard addressing accounting for post employment benefits, which is strongly supported by the Securities and Exchange Commission. Implementation of the new standard will add about $2 million to Roswell's long-term liabilities. Roswell's CEO, Martha Cooper, has written a strong letter of objection to the FASB. The FASB received similar letters from over 300 companies.

Required:

1. Write a paragraph presenting an analysis of the impact of the new standard on Roswell Manufacturing.
2. If you were a member of the FASB and met Martha Cooper at a professional meeting, how would you respond to her objection?

Case 9-80 Evaluating Leverage

Gearing Manufacturing Inc. is planning a $1,000,000 expansion of its production facilities. The expansion could be financed by the sale of $1,250,000 in 8% notes or by the sale of $1,250,000 in common stock, which would raise the number of shares outstanding from 50,000 to 75,000. Gearing pays income taxes at a rate of 30%.

Required:

1. Suppose that income from operations is expected to be $550,000 per year for the duration of the proposed debt issue. Should Gearing finance with notes or stock? Explain your answer.
2. Suppose that income from operations is expected to be $275,000 per year for the duration of the proposed debt issue. Should Gearing finance with notes or stock? Explain your answer.
3. Suppose that income from operations varies from year to year but is expected to be above $300,000, 40% of the time and below $300,000, 60% of the time. Should Gearing finance with notes or stock? Explain your answer.
4. As an investor, how would you use accounting information to evaluate the risk of excessive use of leverage? What additional information would be useful? Explain.

Case 9-81 Leverage

Cook Corporation issued financial statements at December 31 that include the following information:

Balance sheet at December 31:

Assets	$8,000,000
Liabilities	$1,200,000
Stockholders' equity (300,000 shares)	$6,800,000

Income statement for the year ended December 31:

Income from operations	$1,200,000
Less: Interest expense	(100,000)
Income before taxes	$1,100,000
Less: Income taxes expense (0.30)	(330,000)
Net income	$ 770,000

The levels of assets, liabilities, stockholders' equity, and operating income have been stable in recent years; however, Cook Corporation is planning a $1,800,000 expansion program that will increase income from operations by $350,000 to $1,550,000. Cook is planning to sell 8.5% notes at par to finance the expansion.

Required:

1. What earnings per share does Cook report before the expansion?
2. What earnings per share will Cook report if the proposed expansion is undertaken? Would this use of leverage be advantageous to Cook's stockholders? Explain.
3. Suppose income from operations will increase by only $150,000. Would this use of leverage be advantageous to Cook's stockholders? Explain.
4. Suppose that income from operations will increase by $200,000 and that Cook could also raise the required $1,800,000 by issuing an additional 100,000 shares of common stock (assume the additional shares were outstanding for the entire year). Which means of financing would stockholders prefer? Explain.

Case 9-82 Research and Analysis Using the Annual 10-K

Obtain **Marriott's** 2019 10-K through the "Investor Relations" portion of Marriott's website (do a web search for Marriott investor relations). Once at the Investor Relations part of the website, look for "SEC Filings." When you see the list of all the filings, either filter for the "Annual Filings" or search for "10-K" when you find the list of all SEC Filings.

Another option is to go to www.sec.gov and click "Company Filings Search" under "Filings."

Required:

1. What are Marriott's total liabilities for 2019?
2. How much of these liabilities are classified as long-term debt (not noncurrent liabilities, but classified as long-term debt)?
3. Look at Marriott's long-term debt footnote and answer the following questions:
   a. When does the debt that is still outstanding at December 31, 2019, with the highest effective interest rate mature?
   b. How much of the debt is maturing in each of the next 5 years (2020–2024)? How much is maturing in more than 5 years (2025 and beyond)?
   c. Marriott has a multicurrency revolving credit agreement. How much can it borrow under that agreement? How is the interest rate determined? When does this agreement expire?
4. Calculate and discuss Marriott's debt to equity and times interest earned (accrual basis) ratios.

Case 9-83 Comparative Analysis: Kroger versus Sprouts

Refer to the 10-K reports of **Kroger** and **Sprouts** that are available for download from the companion website at Cengage.com.

Required:

1. Look at Kroger's and Sprouts' footnotes. What is the highest interest rate Kroger has on its Senior Notes due through 2049 totaling $11,598 million? What is the most Sprouts can borrow on its Credit Agreement?
2. Calculate Kroger's and Sprouts' times interest earned (accrual) ratio for 2018 and 2019.
3. Calculate Kroger's and Sprouts' long-term debt to equity ratios for 2018 and 2019. Include the portion of finance leases combined with long-term debt on the balance sheet for simplicity. (*Note:* Round answers to two decimal places.)
4. Calculate Kroger's and Sprouts' debt to equity ratios for 2018 and 2019. (*Note:* Round answers to two decimal places.)
5. Calculate Kroger's and Sprouts' long-term debt to total assets ratios for 2018 and 2019. Include the portion of finance leases combined with long-term debt on the balance sheet for simplicity. (*Note:* Round answers to two decimal places.)
6. Calculate Kroger's and Sprouts' debt to total assets ratios for 2018 and 2019. (*Note:* Round answers to two decimal places.)
7. Comment on Kroger's and Sprouts' debt management.

ANNUAL REPORT PROBLEM

HOME DEPOT

Download the 10-K for **Home Depot** from the companion website at Cengage.com.

Required:

1. What does the company report for the following accounts for the most current fiscal year?
   - Total assets
   - Total liabilities
   - Long-term debt
   - Other long-term liabilities
   - Operating income
   - Interest expense
2. Assume that the company projects the following:
   - Total assets will increase by 5%.
   - Total liabilities will increase by 6%.
   - Long-term debt and interest expense will increase by 7%.
   - Operating Income will increase by $750 million.

   Assume all other items remain unchanged from the prior year. Provide the next year's forecasted balances for the above accounts.
3. What is the company's forecasted payment for leases?
4. Compute the forecasted debt to equity ratio (round to two decimal places).
5. Compute the forecasted debt to total assets ratio (round to two decimal places).
6. Compute the forecasted long-term debt to equity ratio (round to two decimal places).
7. Compute the forecasted time interest earned ratio on an accrual basis (round to two decimal places).
8. Is the company in a position to make interest payments on its debt?

Note: *While the Annual Report problems in the textbook are static, when assigned in CNOW, these activities are algorithmic and the answers may vary from what appears in the Solutions Manual.*

CONTINUING PROBLEM

FRONT ROW ENTERTAINMENT

In June 2024, Front Row Entertainment had the opportunity to expand its venue operations by purchasing five different venues. To finance this purchase, Front Row issued $1,500,000 of 6%, 5-year bonds on July 1, 2024. The bonds were issued for $1,378,300 and pay interest semiannually on June 30 and December 31.

Required:

1. Prepare the journal entry to record the bond issue at July 1, 2024.
2. Assume that Front Row uses the straight-line method of amortization.
   a. Prepare an amortization table through December 31, 2025.
      (*Note:* Round to the nearest dollar.)
   b. Prepare the journal entry required at December 31, 2024.
   c. How will the bonds be shown on the December 31, 2024, balance sheet?
3. Assume that Front Row uses the effective interest method of amortization and the annual market rate of interest was 8%.
   a. Prepare an amortization table through December 31, 2025. (*Note:* Round to the nearest dollar.)
   b. Prepare the journal entry required at December 31, 2024.
   c. How will the bonds be shown on the December 31, 2024, balance sheet?

10

Stockholders' Equity

After studying Chapter 10, you should be able to:

1. Describe common and preferred stock and their use in raising capital.

2. Record and properly present capital stock.

3. Record and properly present the distribution of assets to stockholders.

4. Describe the accounting issues related to retained earnings and accumulated other comprehensive income.

5. Analyze stockholder payout and profitability ratios.

Michael Nagle/Bloomberg/Getty Images

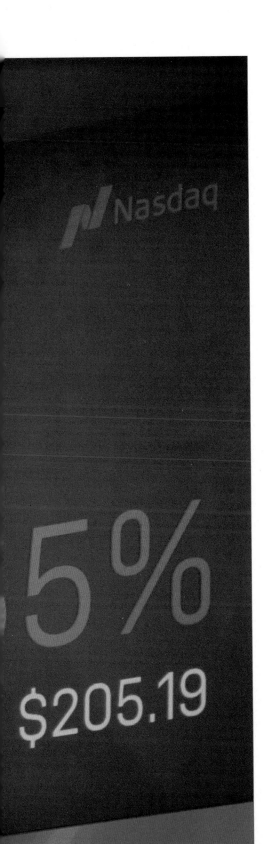

EXPERIENCE FINANCIAL ACCOUNTING

with Apple

How does **Apple** deliver a return to its investors? Like all companies, **Apple** is attempting to make money through its operations; it is just far more successful than are most companies at accomplishing this objective. As shown in Chart 1, **Apple** has generated over $604 billion in cash from its operations since 2007. Apple essentially has three choices of what to do with this cash. First, it can reinvest the cash in its operations through research and development, expansion, and so on. A company does this when it has investment options that will yield a sufficient return for shareholders. Second, a company can pay down its debt. This is a complicated choice affected by many factors, but at a high level, it occurs when the company views the interest rates on the debt as being unfavorable to the company. Third, cash can be returned to shareholders through dividends and stock repurchases. Dividends policy is determined by the Board of Directors, and dividends are generally paid when the company does not have sufficient investment options and any debt has relatively favorable terms. While stock repurchases also return cash to shareholders, such repurchases include the added element of creating treasury stock for the company. Consequently, in addition to providing a mechanism for returning cash to shareholders, stock repurchases also provide the company with a source of stock, for example, to issue to employees exercising stock options without diluting earnings per share (EPS).

Chart 1

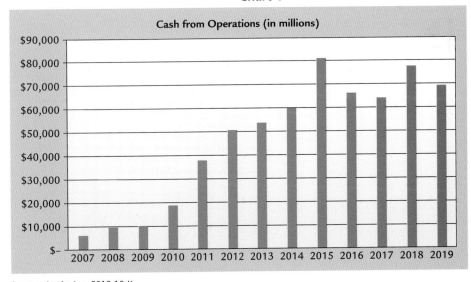

Cash from Operations (in millions)

Source: Apple, Inc. 2019 10-K

In the mid-1990s, **Apple** saw that profitability had declined in the computer segment due to increased price competition throughout the industry and a major investment was needed to reinvent itself. Consequently, its Board of Directors suspended dividends after October 1995 to, as stated in its 10-K for the year ended September 27, 1996, "…[initiate] programs to develop and market products and services more selectively targeted to education, home, and business segments." In July 1995, just prior to the suspension of dividends, Apple's common stock was selling for around $1.50 per share (adjusted for stock splits). By the following July, Apple's shares were down in the $0.50 range, where it stayed for a number of years.

Ultimately, as we all know, this investment led to the development of the iPod, iPhone, and iPad and, as shown in the chart, began to produce enormous amounts of cash. In fact, by 2012, Apple had no long-term debt and generated approximately $50 billion in cash from operations. While it did have attractive investment opportunities, it did not need $50 billion. Therefore, in July 2012, the Board of Directors began to pay dividends again and approved aggressive share repurchase programs. Since the Board of Directions made these policy decisions, Apple has paid over $88 billion in cash dividends and repurchased over $305 billion in common shares. As shown in Chart 2, this resulted in Apple's dividend payout (Common Dividends/Net Income) rising from 0.00% in 2011 to approximately 25% annually and its stock repurchase payout (Stock Repurchases/Net Income) rising from 0.00% in 2012 to between 60% and 122%. In every year since 2013, Apple has paid out over 87% of its net income to shareholders through dividends and stock repurchases. In fact, in 2014, 2018, and 2019, Apple's Total Payout (Dividend Payout + Stock Repurchase Payout) was over 140% of Net Income.

Chart 2

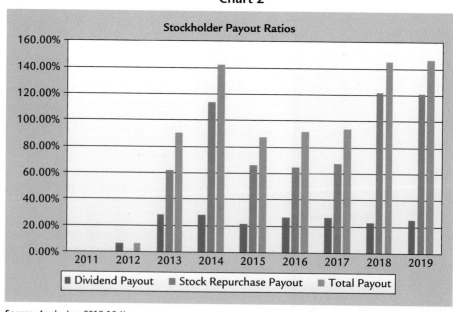

Source: Apple, Inc. 2019 10-K

And, just to make us all feel bad, if your parents had bought $1,000 of Apple stock in December 1998, when it was at its lowest price, it would now be worth around $762,000.

Stockholders' equity, which also is called **equity**, represents the owners' claims against the assets of a corporation after all liabilities have been deducted. As shown in the stockholders' equity section of Amazon's balance sheet in Exhibit 10.1, the stockholders' equity section of the balance sheet clearly identifies various elements of equity according to their source. The most common sources are (see Exhibit 10.1):

- capital stock—split between (1) preferred and common stock and (2) the associated additional paid-in capital
- retained earnings or deficit
- accumulated other comprehensive income
- treasury stock

In this chapter, we describe how common and preferred stock are used to raise capital for the corporation, discuss how corporations account for the various elements of stockholders' equity, and analyze stockholder payout and stockholder profitability using information contained in stockholders' equity.

Elements of Stockholders' Equity—Amazon.com, Inc.

EXHIBIT 10.1

Amazon.com, Inc. Stockholders' Equity section of Consolidated Balance Sheet (in millions) December 31, 2019		
	2018	**2019**
Stockholders' Equity		
Preferred stock, $0.01 par value:		
Authorized shares—500		
Issued and outstanding shares—none	—	—
Common stock, $0.01 par value:		
Authorized shares—5,000		
Issued shares—500 and 507		
Outstanding shares—477 and 484	5	5
Treasury stock, at cost	(1,837)	(1,837)
Additional paid-in capital	26,791	33,658
Accumulated other comprehensive loss	(1,035)	(986)
Retained Earnings	19,625	31,220
Total stockholders' equity	43,549	62,060

RAISING CAPITAL WITHIN A CORPORATION

OBJECTIVE

Describe common and preferred stock and their use in raising capital.

Recall from Chapter 1 that most large businesses are organized as corporations because incorporation increases the company's ability to raise cash (or capital) by easing the transfer of ownership and limiting the liability of owners. Ownership of a corporation is divided into a large number of equal parts or *shares*. Shares are owned in varying numbers by the owners of the corporation called **stockholders** or **shareholders**.

AUTHORIZATION TO ISSUE STOCK

Corporations are authorized, or *chartered*, in accordance with the provisions of state laws that govern the structure and operation of corporations. These laws differ from state to state, and a corporation can charter in any state. For instance, this excerpt from the cover sheet of Amazon's 10-K shows that although **Amazon** is headquartered in Seattle, Washington, it is chartered in Delaware, as are many corporations due to Delaware's favorable laws.

Amazon.com, Inc.
Cover Sheet from Form 10-K
December 31, 2019

UNITED STATES
SECURITIES AND EXCHANGE COMMISSION
Washington, D.C. 20549

FORM 10-K

(Mark One)

☒   ANNUAL REPORT PURSUANT TO SECTION 13 OR 15(d) OF THE SECURITIES EXCHANGE ACT OF 1934
For the fiscal year ended December 31, 2019

or

☐   TRANSITION REPORT PURSUANT TO SECTION 13 OR 15(d) OF THE SECURITIES EXCHANGE ACT OF 1934
For the transition period from   to   .

Commission File No. 000-22513

AMAZON.COM, INC.
(Exact name of registrant as specified in its charter)

Delaware	91-1646860
(State or other jurisdiction of incorporation or organization)	(I.R.S. Employer Identification No.)

410 Terry Avenue North
Seattle, Washington 98109-5210
(206) 266-1000
(Address and telephone number, including area code, of registrant's principal executive offices)

Securities registered pursuant to Section 12(b) of the Act:

Title of Each Class	Name of Each Exchange on Which Registered
Common Stock, par value $.01 per share	Nasdaq Global Select Market

Securities registered pursuant to Section 12(g) of the Act:
None

Although the provisions of incorporation laws vary from state to state, all states require persons who wish to form a corporation to apply to a prescribed state official for the issuance of a charter. The **corporate charter**, which is sometimes called the **articles of incorporation**, is a document that authorizes the creation of the corporation, setting forth its name and purpose and the names of the incorporators.

The typical corporate charter contains provisions that describe how stock may be issued by the corporation. First, it authorizes the corporation to issue stock in a limited number of classes. It also sets an upper limit on the number of shares that the corporation may issue in each class. And finally, it sets a lower limit on the amount for which each share must be sold.

Shares of stock are sold, or issued, when a corporation is formed. Additional shares may be issued later. The maximum number of shares the business may issue in each class of stock is referred to as the number of **authorized shares**. This must be distinguished from the number of **issued shares**, which is the number of shares actually sold to stockholders. A corporation rarely issues all of its authorized shares.

Corporations can buy back their own stock for reasons explained later in this chapter. Thus, the number of shares issued is further distinguished from the number of **outstanding shares**, which is the number of issued shares actually in the hands of stockholders. When firms reacquire their own stock, the reacquired shares are not considered to be outstanding. Exhibit 10.2 illustrates how the share quantities are determined.

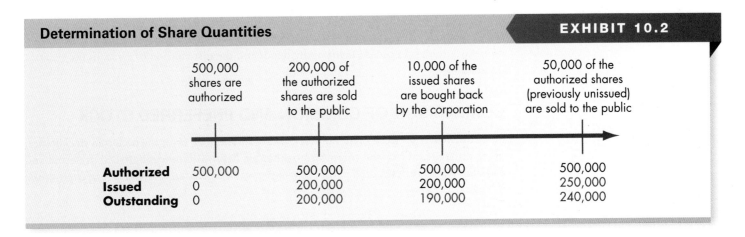

Determination of Share Quantities

EXHIBIT 10.2

	500,000 shares are authorized	200,000 of the authorized shares are sold to the public	10,000 of the issued shares are bought back by the corporation	50,000 of the authorized shares (previously unissued) are sold to the public
Authorized	500,000	500,000	500,000	500,000
Issued	0	200,000	200,000	250,000
Outstanding	0	200,000	190,000	240,000

These three share quantities—the number of shares authorized, issued, and outstanding—are reported for each class of stock on the balance sheet or in its accompanying notes.

COMMON STOCK

All classes of stock are designated as either common stock or preferred stock. These come with different financial benefits and provide different rights regarding the governance of the corporation. The primary rights for owners of **common stock** are

- voting in the election of the board of directors. You will recall that the board controls the operating and financial policies of the company.
- sharing in the profits and dividends of the company. We will talk more about this in the section on Dividends (p. 576).
- keeping the same percentage of ownership if new stock is issued (preemptive right).
- sharing in the distribution of assets in liquidation in proportion to their holdings. This is referred to as the "residual claim" because common stockholders are only paid after all creditors and preferred stockholders are paid in full (which is very rare in liquidation).

When you hear of someone who "made money by investing in stock," it is almost invariably through an investment in common stock. This is because, although the "residual claim" means common stockholders are only paid after the creditors and preferred stockholders are paid in full, it also means that common stockholders get *everything* that is left over after the creditors and preferred stockholders are paid in full. As such, the common stockholders receive the bulk of the financial gain from a profitable company through stock appreciation and dividends:

- *Stock appreciation:* The value of the stock increases above the price initially paid (of course, it is also possible that the stock's value decreases if the company is unprofitable—this is a risk of owning stock).
- *Dividends:* **Dividends** are payments to a company's stockholders from earnings. These payments are usually in the form of cash, but noncash assets and stock can also be given as dividends. Payment of dividends to common stockholders, however, depends on a company's alternatives. The company may elect to pay down debt or, if the company has growth opportunities, they may elect to keep (or retain) earnings to fund these investment options rather than pay dividends. In fact, many companies do not pay dividends to common stockholders.

PREFERRED STOCK

Preferred stock generally pays a regular dividend. In this regard, preferred stock is similar to debt, with the preferred stock dividend equating to interest payments. Additionally, the value of preferred stock, like the value of debt, is most closely tied to interest rate levels and the company's overall creditworthiness; the value of common stock, on the other hand, is most closely tied to the performance of the company. In this respect, preferred stock is a less risky investment than common stock. Preferred stockholders also receive priority over common stockholders in the payment of dividends and the distribution of assets in the event of liquidation.

COMPARISON OF COMMON AND PREFERRED STOCK

Some differences between preferred stock and common stock favor the preferred stockholder; other differences favor the common stockholder. Most differences between preferred and common stock are designated in the company's corporate charter and take one or more of the following forms:

- *Dividend preferences:* Preferred stock frequently requires that the issuing corporation pay dividends to preferred stockholders before paying dividends to common stockholders. Additionally, preferred dividends may be *cumulative and participating*, as explained on p. 581–582.
- *Conversion privileges:* Preferred stock may be convertible into common shares if the preferred stockholder elects to do so and certain conditions are satisfied. For example, each share of preferred stock might be convertible into, for example, 10 shares of common stock after a certain date.
- *Liquidation preferences:* If and when a corporation is dissolved, liquidating distributions are made to stockholders. Corporate charters frequently require the claims of preferred stockholders to be satisfied before those of common stockholders. Additionally, the charter may specify a liquidating amount for preferred shares.
- *Call provisions (redeemable):* The corporate charter may authorize or even require the corporation to repurchase (or redeem) any preferred shares that are sold. In such cases, the charter usually fixes the *call price* (the amount to be paid to the preferred stockholders) and specifies a date on or after which the shares may or must be repurchased. Note that this feature is similar to the repaying of the principal on a loan at the maturity date—particularly when the charter requires redemption at a specific date.
- *Denial of voting rights:* Most preferred stock does not confer voting rights, which means that preferred stockholders, unlike common stockholders, cannot vote at stockholders' meetings.

The first three characteristics of preferred stock are advantageous for preferred stockholders. The last two characteristics usually work in the interest of common stockholders.

Because of the relative advantages of different forms of stock, corporations are typically authorized by their charters to issue several classes of preferred stock and several classes of common stock, each with a different set of terms and provisions. A recent survey of a cross section of financial statements by the American Institute of Certified Public Accountants indicated that approximately 6% of the sampled companies had outstanding preferred stock, but all corporations have outstanding common stock. This excerpt from **Procter & Gamble's** 10-K illustrates how the different classes of stock are shown:

Classes of Stock for Procter & Gamble (amounts in millions)		
	2019	**2018**
Convertible Class A preferred stock, stated value $1 per share (600 shares authorized)	$928	$967
Nonvoting Class B preferred stock, stated value $1 per share (200 shares authorized)	—	—
Common stock, stated value $1 per share (10,000 shares authorized; issued: 2019—4,009.2, 2018—4,009.2)	4,009	4,009

Source: Procter & Gamble, Inc. 2019 10-K.

YOUDECIDE **Issuing Debt or Preferred Stock**

You are the CFO of Canova Manufacturing. Your company needs to raise capital to pursue an expansion project, but the company does not want to sell additional common stock.

What factors should you consider in deciding whether to issue debt or preferred stock?

In making your decision, it would be helpful to consider the following differences between debt and preferred stock.

Advantage of debt:

- Interest payments are tax deductible, while preferred dividends are not.

Advantages of preferred stock:

- Preferred stock is historically classified as equity, rather than debt, on the balance sheet. If Canova prefers to, or must, show lower debt totals, preferred stock is advantageous. For example, provisions of existing debt contracts may not allow Canova to issue additional debt.
- Preferred stock is less risky than debt because, unlike interest payments, missing a preferred dividend payment does not trigger bankruptcy. If Canova fears cash flow problems, this will be important.
- Companies with a history of operating losses typically do not pay income taxes. If Canova has these so-called net operating loss carryforwards, then debt no longer has the tax advantage.
- Preferred stock is generally sold to other corporations because these corporations do not pay taxes on the full amount of the dividends (i.e., there is a big tax break relative to receiving interest payments).

Although preferred stock and debt have many similarities, they have some important differences.

ACCOUNTING FOR ISSUANCE OF COMMON AND PREFERRED STOCK

OBJECTIVE ◀ 2

Record and properly present capital stock.

In examples in previous chapters, we recorded the contributions of stockholders in exchange for stock in a single account. In practice, however, cash or other assets (capital) contributed by stockholders is usually divided between two accounts, on the basis of the par value of the stock. **Par value** is an arbitrary monetary amount printed on each share of stock that establishes a minimum price for the stock when issued but does not determine its market value.[1] When a corporation receives more than par value for the newly issued stock, as it usually does (stock rarely sells for exactly its par value), the par value and the excess over par are recorded in separate accounts. The par value multiplied by the number of shares sold is recorded in an account that describes the type of stock—for example, common stock or preferred stock. If you refer back to Exhibit 10.1, you will see that on December 31, 2019, Amazon had 521 million shares issued with a par value of $0.01, which resulted in a balance of $5 million in *Common Stock*. The amount received in excess of the par value is recorded in an account called *Additional paid-in capital*. Exhibit 10.1 shows that Amazon had a balance of $33,658 million on December 31, 2019. These accounts are the first accounts shown in the stockholders' equity section of the balance sheet and taken together are known as **capital stock**. EXAMPLE 10.1 illustrates the accounting procedures for recording the sale of stock.

EXAMPLE 10.1   RECORDING THE SALE OF COMMON AND PREFERRED STOCK

Spectator Corporation is authorized to issue 1,000 shares of preferred stock with a 9% dividend rate and a par value of $20 per share and 50,000 shares of common stock with a par value of $2 per share. On January 2, 2019, Spectator issues 200 shares of preferred stock at $22 per share and 20,000 shares of common stock at $2.50 per share.

CONTINUED

---

1 The precise meaning of par value is established by securities laws that vary somewhat from state to state.

EXAMPLE 10.1   RECORDING THE SALE OF COMMON AND PREFERRED STOCK *(CONTINUED)*

Required:

1. How much cash did Spectator raise through its stock issuance?

2. Prepare the journal entries necessary to record the sale of common and preferred stock separately.

3. Prepare the stockholders' equity section of Spectator's balance sheet. (*Note:* Assume Spectator has yet to engage in any operations.)

Solution:

1.

Preferred stock ($22 × 200 shares)	$ 4,400
Common stock ($2.50 × 20,000 shares)	50,000
Total proceeds	**$54,400**

2. When companies sell stock, the resulting ownership claims are recorded in the Common Stock or Preferred Stock account at par with any amounts received in excess of par in Additional Paid-In Capital.

Date	Account and Explanation	Debit	Credit	Assets	= Liabilities +	Stockholders' Equity
Jan. 2	Cash	4,400		▲		
	Preferred Stock[a]		4,000			▲
	Additional Paid-In Capital—Preferred Stock[b]		400			▲
	Cash	50,000		▲		
	Common Stock[c]		40,000			▲
	Additional Paid-In Capital—Common Stock[d]		10,000			▲

[a] 200 shares × $20 par = $4,000
[b] 200 shares × ($22 − $20) = $400
[c] 20,000 shares × $2 par = $40,000
[d] 20,000 shares × ($2.50 − $2.00) = $10,000

3.

Stockholders' equity:		
Preferred stock, 9%, $20 par, 1,000 shares authorized, 200 shares issued and outstanding	$ 4,000	
Common stock, $2 par, 50,000 shares authorized, 20,000 shares issued and outstanding	40,000	
Additional paid-in capital:		
Preferred stock	400	
Common stock	10,000	
Total capital stock		$54,400
Retained earnings*		0
Total stockholders' equity		$54,400

*Note that retained earnings displays a zero balance because Spectator is a newly formed corporation.

STATED CAPITAL AND NO-PAR STOCK

The stock issued by Spectator Corporation carried a par value that represents the stated capital of the corporation. **Stated capital (legal capital)** is the amount of capital that, under law, cannot be returned to the corporation's owners unless the corporation is liquidated. Even when state law permits the issuance of **no-par stock** (stock without a par value), it frequently requires that no-par stock have a stated (legal) value, set by the corporation, in order to establish the corporation's stated or legal capital. Further, this is a relatively infrequent occurrence.

Stated value, like par value, is recorded separately in the *Common* (or *Preferred*) *Stock* account, while any excess paid over its stated value is recorded in *Additional Paid-In Capital—Common* (or *Preferred*) *Stock*.[2]

WARRANTS

A **stock warrant** is the right granted by a corporation to purchase a specified number of shares of its *common stock* at a stated price and within a stated time period. Corporations issue stock warrants in the following two situations:

- First, they may issue warrants along with bonds or preferred stock as an "equity kicker" to make the bonds or preferred stock more attractive. Such warrants often have a duration of 5 or more years.
- Second, they may issue warrants to existing stockholders who have a legal right to purchase a specified share of a new stock issue, in order to maintain their relative level of ownership in the corporation. Such warrants usually have a duration of less than 6 months.

OPTIONS

Corporations also grant employees and executives the right to buy stock at a set price as compensation for their services. These "rights" are called *stock options*. **Stock options** are frequently given to employees and executives as compensation for their services. For example, on March 1, 2022, an employer may give an executive the right to purchase 5,000 shares of the company's stock at $50 per share, that day's market price, anytime after March 1, 2024. If after the 2 years have elapsed the market price of the stock is higher than $50 (e.g., $62), the executive can purchase the 5,000 shares for $50 each and receive effective compensation of $60,000 [($62 − $50) × 5,000 shares]. Of course, if the price is lower than $50, the executive will not exercise the option.

ETHICAL DECISIONS The compensation expense recorded by a company when they grant stock options depends on many factors including the price at which employees can buy the stock (called the **exercise** or **strike price**) and the market value of the stock on the date of grant. As discussed, the strike price of the options and the market value of the stock are generally the same on the date of grant. However, during 2006, many companies came under investigation for "back dating" stock options. That is, companies waited to announce the granting of options and then picked the date in the past when the stock price was lowest. This maximized the value of each individual option to the employee.

This practice has been curtailed by the Sarbanes-Oxley Act, but in and of itself, this is not illegal. However, if on December 20 a company backdates options to May 1 (the lowest stock price of the year), the value of each option will be greater on December 20 than on May 1. As such, the company should calculate compensation expense using the market value of the stock on December 20. We will never know exactly how widespread the practice of backdating was,

Next Level

How do we account for stock issued in exchange for noncash assets or services (such as legal services in connection with incorporation)?

ANSWER:
The amount recorded should be the fair market value of the stock or the fair market value of the asset/service, whichever is more clearly determinable. In the case of a newly organized corporation, the fair market value of the asset/service is usually more clearly determinable. But in the case of established corporations with widely traded stock, the fair market value of the stock is more clearly determinable than the fair market value of the asset/service.

---

2   In some states, stated value functions exactly as does the par value of stock to identify the legal capital portion of total capital stock. However, in other states, legal capital is defined as the entire capital stock amount associated with the no-par stock. In these states, the entire capital stock amount is recorded in a single Common or Preferred Stock account.

but approximately 80 firms were initially the subject of an SEC probe and research estimates that 29.2% of firms backdated grants to top executives between 1996 and 2005.

Corporations elect to grant stock options for two primary reasons:

- First, stock options allow cash-poor companies to compete for top talent in the employee market. For example, market salary for a manager of systems quality and assurance may be $200,000 per year—well beyond the means of many start-up companies. However, such a person may agree to work for $100,000 per year and a significant number of stock options.
- Second, stock options are believed to better align the incentives of the employee with those of the owners. This concept is easy to understand with a bit of exaggeration. Employees would like to be paid millions of dollars a year to do nothing, while owners would like the employees to work hundreds of hours a week for free. Stock options help align these incentives because now an employee's personal wealth is tied to the success of the company's stock price—just like the owners. Knowledge of these uses of equity is important, but discussion of the complications of accounting for stock warrants and options is left for more advanced accounting courses.

 YOUDECIDE   Going Public

You are CEO of Georgian Inc., a successful manufacturer of electronic components for computer hardware. Georgian wishes to double its scale of operations in order to meet both existing and expected demand for its products. Georgian is a *privately held corporation*. High interest rates preclude Georgian from borrowing the necessary expansion capital, and its current owners are unable to invest significantly more capital at this time.

What effect will going public have on corporate control and expenses?

Raising enough capital to double the scale of operations will likely require giving away a substantial ownership interest. If the new owners are sufficiently well-organized

and cohesive, they could elect a majority of directors and control the company. On the other hand, if the new shares were purchased by a large number of investors with no organized interest in controlling Georgian, then effective control would remain in the hands of the original owners. Of course, the risk of losing control at some future time would still exist. Going public will also substantially increase the costs of financial reporting and corporate governance to comply with the requirements of the Sarbanes-Oxley Act of 2002.

Going public will most likely require giving up control of the company and will also increase expenses in order to comply with financial reporting standards.

OBJECTIVE
Record and properly present the distribution of assets to stockholders.

ACCOUNTING FOR DISTRIBUTIONS TO STOCKHOLDERS

As discussed, owners invest in corporations through the purchase of stock. Corporations can distribute cash to stockholders in the following ways:

- The corporation can repurchase the shares from owners.
- The corporation can issue dividends.

Historically, dividends were the most common method of distributing cash. Over recent years, however, repurchasing shares has become a more frequent method of cash distribution because it has tax advantages for stockholders relative to dividends.[3] First, dividends are paid to *all* stockholders, thus creating tax consequences for everyone. Stock repurchases, on the other hand, only trigger tax consequences for those stockholders who elect to sell their stock back to the company. Thus, if a stockholder does not want to incur tax consequences in the current

---

3   In fact, one study shows that the number of stock repurchases increased from 87 repurchases valued at $1.4 billion in 1988 to 1,570 repurchases valued at $222 billion in 1998 (Grullon, G. and D. Ikenberry. 2000. "What do we know about stock repurchases?" *Journal of Applied Corporate Finance.* Spring: 31–51).

year, he or she can elect not to sell the shares back to the company. Second, dividends have often been taxed at higher rates than gains from selling stock, although that is not currently the case.[4] Dividends do have the advantage of allowing stockholders to receive assets from the corporation without reducing their ownership share.

STOCK REPURCHASES (TREASURY STOCK)

When a corporation purchases its own previously issued stock, the stock that it buys is called **treasury stock**. Corporations purchase treasury stock for many reasons:

- to buy out the ownership of one or more stockholders
- to reduce the size of corporate operations
- to reduce the number of outstanding shares of stock in an attempt to increase earnings per share and market value per share
- to acquire shares to be transferred to employees under stock bonus, stock option, or stock purchase plans
- to satisfy the terms of a business combination in which the corporation must give a quantity of shares of its stock as part of the acquisition of another business
- to reduce vulnerability to an unfriendly takeover

The stock may be purchased on the open market, by a general offer to the stockholders (called a *tender offer*), or by direct negotiation with a major stockholder. If the objective of acquiring treasury stock is to reduce the size of corporate operations, the treasury shares may be retired after purchase. More frequently, however, repurchased stock is held in the corporation's treasury until circumstances favor its resale, or until it is needed to meet obligations of the corporation that must be satisfied with shares of its stock. Transactions in treasury stock, even very large ones, usually do not require stockholder approval.

Interestingly, some companies hold a relatively large portion of their issued shares in treasury. For example, at the end of 2019 **Coca-Cola Company** held approximately 39.2% of its shares in treasury at a repurchase cost of $52.2 billion (see Exhibit 10.3).

 Next Level

If a corporation buys the stock of another corporation and later sells that stock for a different price, a gain or loss is recorded on the income statement. However, when a corporation buys its own stock and later sells it for a different price, the income statement is not affected. Why is this?

ANSWER:
Transactions with a corporation's owners cannot be included on the income statement.

| Excerpt from Coca-Cola's 2019 10-K (Balance Sheet) | EXHIBIT 10.3 |

The following was included in the stockholders' equity section of Coca-Cola's 2019 balance sheet:

	Year ending December 31	
	2019	2018
The Coca-Cola Company Stockholders' Equity (in millions, except par value)		
Common stock, $0.25 par value; authorized 11,200 shares; issued 7,040 shares	1,760	1,760
Additional paid-in capital	17,154	16,520
Retained earnings	65,855	63,234
Accumulated other comprehensive income (loss)	(13,544)	(12,814)
Treasury stock, at cost 2,760 and 2,772 shares, respectively	(52,244)	(51,719)
Stockholders' equity attributable to shareowners of the Coca-Cola Company	**18,981**	**16,981**

Source: Coca-Cola Corporation, 2019 10-K.

---

4 Historically, dividends were taxed at ordinary income rates (e.g., similar to salaries and hourly wages), while gains from selling your stock (i.e., capital gains) were taxed at more favorable rates. This temporarily changed in 2003 as part of the *Jobs and Growth Tax Relief Reconciliation Act of 2003*. However, Congress made this change permanent and, at least for now, most dividends are taxed at the same rate as gains from selling stock.

Purchase   At first thought, one might consider recording the acquisition of treasury stock as an exchange of cash for an investment in stock (an exchange of one asset for another). However, that approach fails to recognize that the treasury stock is already represented by amounts in the corporation's equity accounts. Although the shares would represent an asset to another entity if it acquired them, they cannot represent an asset to the entity that issued them. Thus, the purchase of treasury stock is a reduction of equity rather than the acquisition of an investment. Instead of requiring a debit to an investment account, the reacquisition of treasury stock requires a debit for the amount paid to reacquire the stock to a contra-equity account, Treasury Stock. This interpretation is consistent with the provisions of most state incorporation laws, which prohibit the payment of dividends on treasury stock.[5]

Resale   If the treasury shares are reissued at some point in the future, the original cost of the shares is removed from the Treasury Stock account. Any excess of proceeds over the cost of the shares is not considered a gain because a corporation cannot generate income by buying and selling its own stock (income is reserved for transactions with nonowners); instead, a credit is made to a special paid-in capital account—*Additional Paid-In Capital—Treasury Stock*. If the treasury shares are sold for less than their cost, a debit is first made to "Additional Paid-In Capital—Treasury Stock." If the credit balance in Additional Paid-In Capital—Treasury Stock is not large enough to absorb the shortfall, then the unabsorbed debit reduces Retained Earnings. EXAMPLE 10.2 illustrates how to account for treasury stock.

EXAMPLE 10.2   ACCOUNTING FOR TREASURY STOCK

On July 1, Spectator Corporation repurchases 1,000 shares of its outstanding common stock for $15 per share. On September 15, Spectator sells 500 shares of treasury stock for $18 per share, and on December 1, Spectator sells 400 shares of treasury stock for $11 per share.

Required:

Prepare the journal entries to record (1) the purchase of treasury stock, (2) the sale of treasury stock on September 15, and (3) the sale of treasury stock on December 1.

Solution:

1. When purchasing its own previously issued stock, a corporation records a reduction to stockholders' equity by debiting treasury stock.

Date	Account and Explanation	Debit	Credit	Assets	=	Liabilities	+	Stockholders' Equity
July 1	Treasury Stock[a]	15,000		▼				▼
	Cash		15,000					

2. Any difference between the cost at which the treasury stock was purchased and the amount at which it is resold does not affect the income statement because these are transactions with owners. Instead, these differences affect stockholders' equity.

Date	Account and Explanation	Debit	Credit	Assets	=	Liabilities	+	Stockholders' Equity
Sept. 15	Cash[b]	9,000		▲				
	Treasury Stock[c]		7,500					▲
	Additional Paid-In Capital—							
	Treasury Stock[d]		1,500					▲

---

5   The method of accounting for treasury stock demonstrated here is called the *cost method*. This method is used by approximately 95% of the companies engaging in treasury stock transactions. An alternative method, called the *par value method,* is demonstrated in Intermediate Accounting courses.

3.   While additional paid-in capital treasury stock is used to account for differences between the cost at which the treasury stock was purchased and the amount at which it is resold, this account cannot have an overall debit balance. Instead, it can only be reduced (debited) to zero and any remainder is a debit to retained earnings.

Date	Account and Explanation	Debit	Credit	Assets	= Liabilities +	Stockholders' Equity
Dec. 1	Cash^e	4,400		▲		
	Additional Paid-In Capital—					
	Treasury Stock^f	1,500				▼
	Retained Earnings^g	100				▼
	Treasury Stock^h		6,000			▲

^{a} 1,000 shares × $15 = $15,000
^{b} 500 shares × $18 = $9,000
^{c} 500 shares × $15 = $7,500
^{d} 500 shares × ($18 − $15) = $1,500
^{e} 400 shares × $11 = $4,400
^{f} Additional Paid-In Capital—Treasury Stock can be debited in a journal entry, but the result of the journal entry cannot be a debit *balance* to the account. Thus, there is a limit of $1,500 due to the credit in Requirement 2.
^{g} Retained Earnings is debited if there is any remaining debit needed after Additional Paid-In Capital—Treasury Stock is zeroed out.
^{h} 400 shares × $15 = $6,000

Transfers among Stockholders We have been considering the effects on the equity accounts when a corporation buys or sells its own stock. However, treasury stock transactions constitute a special case. In general, the purchase or sale of stock after it is first issued does *not* alter the equity accounts of the issuing corporation, unless that corporation is itself the purchaser or seller. Although the issuing corporation's accounts do not change when shares are sold by one stockholder to another, the corporation's stockholder list must be updated. Large corporations usually retain an independent *stock transfer agent* to maintain their stockholder lists, which include the quantity and serial numbers of the shares held. Stock transfer agents also arrange for the transfer of certificates among stockholders and the issuance of new certificates to stockholders.[6]

Retirement of Treasury Shares Occasionally, treasury shares are permanently retired. That means these particular shares will no longer be traded. In such cases, the Common Stock account is debited for the par value of the stock and the Additional Paid-In Capital account is reduced for any excess of the purchase price of the treasury shares over par. If Spectator had retired the 1,000 shares it repurchased for $15/share in Example 10-2, it would have made the following entry assuming the par value of the stock was $2:

Date	Account and Explanation	Debit	Credit	Assets	= Liabilities +	Stockholders' Equity
July 1	Common Stock*	2,000				▼
	Additional Paid-In Capital—Common Stock	13,000				▼
	Cash		15,000	▼		

*1,000 shares × $2 = $2,000

---

6   Although the transfer of shares among stockholders does not affect the accounts of the issuing corporation, such transactions will require entries into the accounts of the buyers and sellers of the shares.

DIVIDENDS

A dividend is an amount paid by a corporation to a stockholder as a return on invested capital. Dividends represent distributions of accumulated net income. They are usually paid in cash but may also be paid in the form of noncash assets or additional shares of a corporation's own stock. All dividends, whatever their form, reduce retained earnings (see Exhibit 10.4).

EXHIBIT 10.4 ▶ **Dividends**

Dividends reduce Retained Earnings.

Cash dividends distribute cash to stockholders.

Stock dividends distribute additional shares to stockholders.

Stock splits transfer additional shares to stockholders without changing equity.

Cash Dividends Cash dividends are by far the most common form of dividend. The payment of a cash dividend is preceded by an official announcement or declaration by the board of directors of the company's intention to pay a dividend. The dividend declaration specifies the:

- **declaration date**—the date on which a corporation announces its intention to pay a dividend on common or preferred stock
- dollar amount of the dividend—usually stated as the number of dollars per share
- **date of record**—the date on which a stockholder must own one or more shares of stock in order to receive the dividend
- **payment date**—the date on which the dividend will actually be paid

Since the stock of most corporations is continually changing hands, it is necessary to set a date on which the ownership of shares is established as a basis for the payment of dividends. If a share of stock is sold between the date of record and the dividend payment date, the former owner of the share, rather than the new owner, receives the dividend. On the other hand, if a share of stock is sold between the declaration date and the date of record, the new owner, rather than the former owner, receives the dividend. The accounting for cash dividends is illustrated in EXAMPLE 10.3.

EXAMPLE 10.3   RECORDING CASH DIVIDENDS

The Kingsmill Corporation has issued 3,000 shares of common stock, all of the same class; 2,800 shares are outstanding and 200 shares are held as treasury stock. On November 15, Kingsmill's board of directors declares a cash dividend of $2.00 per share payable on December 15, to stockholders of record on December 1.

Required:
Prepare the journal entries at (1) the date of declaration, (2) the date of record, and (3) the payment.

Solution:

1. Dividends are not paid on treasury stock. Further, a liability is incurred on the date of declaration because the corporation has the legal obligation to pay after declaring the dividend.

Date	Account and Explanation	Debit	Credit	Assets	= Liabilities +	Stockholders' Equity
Nov. 15	Dividends Declared*	5,600				▼
	Dividends Payable		5,600		▲	

*Dividends declared are closed to Retained Earnings at the end of the period (2,800 shares × $2 = $5,600)

2. No journal entry is needed because the date of record is the date at which ownership is recorded to determine who will receive the dividend.

3.

Date	Account and Explanation	Debit	Credit	Assets	= Liabilities +	Stockholders' Equity
Dec. 15	Dividends Payable	5,600			▼	
	Cash		5,600	▼		

Dividend Policy The corporation's record of dividends and retained earnings provides useful information to:

- boards of directors and managers who must formulate a dividend policy
- stockholders and potential investors who wish to evaluate past dividend policies and assess prospects for future dividends

Historical records and long-term future projections of earnings and dividends are of particular interest to stockholders because the dividend policies of most large corporations are characterized by long-term stability. In other words, they are designed to produce a smooth pattern of dividends over time. For this reason, directors approach increases in the per-share dividend very cautiously and avoid decreases at all costs.

Liquidating Dividends When retained earnings has been reduced to zero, any additional dividends must come from capital stock. Such dividends are called **liquidating dividends** and must be charged first against additional paid-in capital, then the Common (or Preferred) Stock accounts. The payment of liquidating dividends usually accompanies the dissolution of the corporation and is regulated by various laws designed to protect the interests of creditors and other holders of nonresidual equity. Thus, the presence of significant liabilities will usually prevent, or at least require close monitoring of, liquidating dividends. Since these dividends are a return of paid-in capital, they are not taxed as income to the recipients.

Stock Dividends A cash dividend transfers cash from the corporation to its stockholders. In contrast, a **stock dividend** transfers shares of stock from the corporation to its stockholders—additional shares of the corporation's own stock. For each share outstanding, a fixed number of new shares is issued, and an amount of retained earnings is transferred to contributed capital accounts in a process known as *capitalization of retained earnings*. While a cash dividend reduces both total assets and total equity, a stock dividend alters neither total assets nor total equity. A stock dividend merely notifies investors that the equity section of the balance sheet has been rearranged.

The amount of retained earnings capitalized for each new share depends on the size of the stock dividend.

- *Small stock dividends* increase the number of outstanding shares by less than 25%; they are capitalized using the stock's market value just before the dividend.
- *Large stock dividends* increase the number of outstanding shares by 25% or more and are capitalized at par.

This is illustrated in EXAMPLE 10.4 .

EXAMPLE 10.4   RECORDING SMALL AND LARGE STOCK DIVIDENDS

On May 18, Arlington Corporation has 6,000,000 shares of $10 par common stock outstanding. This stock is currently trading at $12 per share.

Required:

1.   Determine how many new shares are issued and prepare the necessary journal entry assuming Arlington declares and pays a 5% stock dividend.

2.   Determine how many new shares are issued and prepare the necessary journal entry assuming Arlington declares and pays a 30% stock dividend.

Solution:

1.   Small stock dividends (<25%) are capitalized using the stock's market value on the date of declaration

$$6,000,000 \times 0.05 = 300,000 \text{ shares}$$

Account and Explanation	Debit	Credit	Assets	= Liabilities +	Stockholders' Equity
Dividends Declared*	3,600,000				▼
Common Stock**		3,000,000			▲
Additional Paid-In Capital—Common Stock		600,000			▲

2.   Large stock dividends (25%+) are capitalized at the stock's par value

$$6,000,000 \times 0.30 = \underline{1,800,000} \text{ shares}$$

Account and Explanation	Debit	Credit	Assets	= Liabilities +	Stockholders' Equity
Dividends Declared***	18,000,000				▼
Common Stock***		18,000,000			▲

*300,000 shares × $12 = $3,600,000
**300,000 shares × $10 = $3,000,000
***1,800,000 shares × $10 = $18,000,000

Note that the stock dividend merely transfers dollars from Retained Earnings to the Capital Stock accounts.

Although a stock dividend increases the *number* of shares held by each stockholder, it does not alter the *proportion* of shares held. For example, if an investor held 100,000 out of 2,000,000 outstanding shares before a 10% stock dividend, that investor would hold 110,000 out of 2,200,000 outstanding shares after the dividend. Thus the investor would hold 5% of the outstanding shares both before and after the stock dividend and would have a 5% claim on earnings and stockholders' equity both before and after:

$$\frac{100,000}{2,000,000} = \frac{110,000}{2,200,000} = \underline{\underline{0.05}}$$

Further, despite the popular belief to the contrary among stockholders and even some financial managers, research shows that neither stock dividends nor stock splits, which we will consider next, enhance the total market value of a corporation's outstanding common stock. Stock dividends should be distinguished from dividend plans that allow stockholders to choose between receiving a cash dividend and a share of stock with the equivalent current value. Such plans may enhance a stockholder's proportionate ownership and also avoid brokerage fees.

Stock Splits A stock split, like a stock dividend, increases the number of outstanding shares without altering the proportionate ownership of a corporation. Unlike a stock dividend, however, a stock split involves a *decrease* in the per-share par value (or stated value), with no capitalization of retained earnings. In other words, a **stock split** is a stock issue that increases the number of outstanding shares of a corporation without changing the balances of its equity accounts.

Consider a corporation that has 10,000 common shares outstanding with a par value of $30 per share. In a two-for-one stock split, stockholders will exchange each of their 10,000 original shares for two new shares; the number of shares will rise from 10,000 to 20,000; and the par value of each share will be reduced to $15 per share. The total par value of all stock will remain $300,000:

$$\$30 \times 10{,}000 \text{ shares} = \$15\ (\$30/2) \times 20{,}000\ (10{,}000 \times 2) \text{ shares} = \underline{\$300{,}000}$$

The split has the effect of distributing the par value over a larger number of shares.

Stock splits are used to reduce the per-share price of a stock. If nothing else changes, a two-for-one split should cut the market price of a stock in half. A corporation may wish to reduce the per-share price to encourage trading of its stock. The assumption is that a higher per-share price is an obstacle to purchases and sales of stock, particularly for small investors.

No entry is required to record a stock split because no account balances change. The changes in the par value and the number of outstanding shares are merely noted in the corporation's records.

While companies appear to split stock less frequently than in the past, to illustrate how companies use stock splits, look at the **Microsoft** data in Exhibit 10.5.

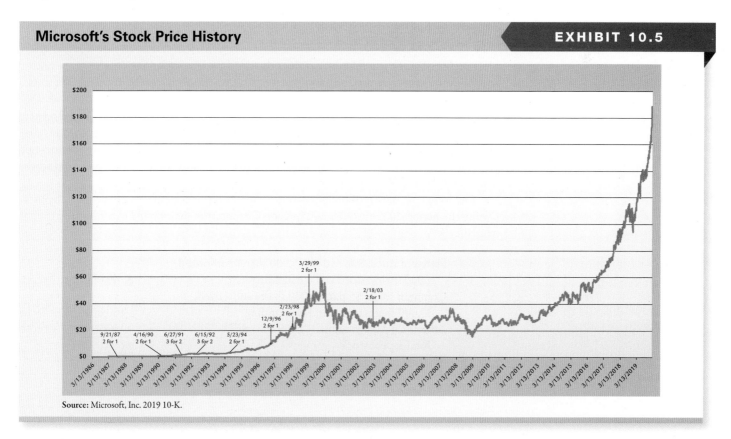

Microsoft's Stock Price History   **EXHIBIT 10.5**

Source: Microsoft, Inc. 2019 10-K.

Note that Microsoft stock has split nine times in its history. That means if you had owned 1,000 shares of Microsoft stock prior to September 21, 1987, and you never bought nor sold a single share, you would now have 288,000 shares:

$$1{,}000 \text{ shares} \times 2 \times 2 \times \frac{3}{2} \times \frac{3}{2} \times 2 \times 2 \times 2 \times 2 \times 2$$

These shares would have been worth approximately $53,380,800 in February 2020 (not to mention the quarterly dividends you would have received since mid-2004). Further, if we assume that splits have no effect on price, the price of a share of Microsoft stock during February 2020 (which was trading at around $185.35 per share), would have been approximately $53,380 per share if there had been no stock splits.

Not many individual investors can pay $53,380 per share, but two notable companies—**Berkshire Hathaway** (Warren Buffet's company) and **Google**—do not issue stock splits. As a consequence, during February 2020, a share of Google (Alphabet, Inc) stock was selling for approximately $1,521 per share, while Berkshire Hathaway Class A common was selling for approximately $340,000 per share. In fact, check to see what Berkshire Hathaway is selling for today by going to **Google Finance** or **Yahoo! Finance** and typing in "BRK.A."

Preferred Dividend Preferences While dividends on common stock are set by the corporation's board of directors, dividends on preferred stock are usually established as one of the terms of the issue. Most preferred stock issues fix their dividend rate as a percentage of the par value. For example, an 8% preferred share with a $100 par value has an annual dividend of $8 ($100 par × 8%). Of course, both preferred and common dividends are subject to various restrictions imposed by statute, corporate charter, terms of preferred stock issues, and contracts with bondholders and others.

Although preferred stockholders have no voting rights, they are "preferred" in the sense that corporations are required to pay dividends to them before paying dividends to common stockholders. Such dividend preferences can take three forms:

- current dividend preference
- cumulative dividend preference
- participating dividend preference

Most preferred stock issues grant a current dividend preference, and some also grant one or both of the other preferences, thereby further enhancing the likelihood of dividend payments.

Current Dividend Preference Preferred stock always has a **current dividend preference**, which provides that current dividends must be paid to preferred stockholders before any dividends are paid to common stockholders. However, the current dividend preference does not guarantee payment of preferred dividends. In lean years, both common and preferred stockholders may fail to receive dividends.

The following illustration demonstrates the impact of the current dividend preference. During the period 2022 through 2025, Cook Corporation maintained the following capital structure:

Preferred stock, 8%, $10 par, 5,000 shares authorized,	
4,000 shares issued and outstanding	$ 40,000
Common stock, $5 par, 50,000 shares authorized,	
30,000 shares issued and outstanding	150,000
Additional paid-in capital—common stock	60,000
Total capital stock	$250,000

Cook's board of directors determined the total dollar amount available for preferred and common dividends in each year from 2022 through 2025 as shown in the second column of the following schedule:

Year	Amount Available for Dividends	Dividends to Preferred	Dividends to Common
2022	$12,200	$3,200*	$9,000**
2023	7,000	3,200	3,800
2024	2,000	2,000	0
2025	0	0	0

*0.08 × $40,000 = $3,200
**$12,200 − $3,200 = $9,000

This schedule shows that the common dividend is any positive amount remaining after the full preferred dividend has been paid. If the total amount available for dividends is less than the full preferred dividend, the entire amount is paid to preferred stockholders.

Cumulative Dividend Preference Most preferred stock is cumulative. The **cumulative dividend preference** requires the eventual payment of all preferred dividends—both **dividends in arrears** and current dividends—before any dividends are paid to common stockholders. (Preferred stock dividends remaining unpaid for 1 or more years are considered to be in arrears.) In other words, no dividends can be paid to common stockholders until all prior and current preferred dividends have been paid. The cumulative dividend preference thus includes the current dividend preference. This is illustrated in EXAMPLE 10.5 .

EXAMPLE 10.5   CALCULATING CUMULATIVE PREFERRED DIVIDENDS

Jefferson Manufacturing has a single class of common stock and a single class of cumulative preferred stock. The cumulative preferred stock requires the corporation to pay an annual dividend of $6,500 to preferred stockholders. On January 1, 2023, Jefferson's preferred dividends were 1 year in arrears, which means that Jefferson declared neither preferred nor common dividends in 2022. From 2023 to 2025, Jefferson's board of directors determined they would be able to pay $9,000, $12,000, and $15,000, respectively.

Required:
Show how these anticipated payments will be split between preferred and common stockholders.

Solution:
The cumulative feature of preferred stock requires corporations to pay all current and unpaid prior-period dividends to preferred stockholders before paying any dividends to common stockholders.

Year	Amount Available for Dividends	Dividends to Preferred	Dividends to Common
2023	$ 9,000	$ 9,000*	$ 0
2024	12,000	10,500**	1,500**
2025	15,000	6,500	8,500

*The $9,000 dividend paid to preferred stockholders in 2023 removes the $6,500 in arrears from 2022, but leaves dividends in arrears at January 1, 2024, of $4,000—the excess of preferred dividends for 2022 and 2023 over the amount paid in 2023 [(2 × $6,500) − $9,000 = $4,000].

**The $10,500 dividend to preferred stockholders in 2024 pays the current preferred dividend ($6,500), removes the $4,000 in arrears, and leaves $1,500 to be paid to common stockholders ($12,000 − $6,500 − $4,000 = $1,500).

Dividends do not become a liability of a corporation until they have been declared by the board of directors. If preferred dividends in arrears have not been declared, they are not recorded as liabilities but are disclosed in a footnote to the financial statements.

Participating Dividend Preference   For some classes of preferred stock, dividends are not restricted to a fixed rate. Preferred stock that pays dividends in excess of its stated dividend rate is called *participating preferred stock*. Preferred stock that cannot pay dividends in excess of the current dividend preference plus cumulative dividends in arrears, if any, is called *nonparticipating preferred stock*.

The **participating dividend preference** provides that stockholders of participating preferred shares receive, in addition to the stated dividend, a share of amounts available for distribution as dividends to other classes of stock. Participating preferred stock may be either fully participating or partially participating:

- Fully participating preferred stock receives a share of *all* amounts available for dividends. Common stock is allocated a dividend at the same rate on par as the current dividend preference, and any remainder is divided between preferred and common stockholders—usually in proportion to the total par value of the two classes of stock.
- Partially participating preferred stock also receives a share of all amounts available for dividends, but the share is limited to a specified percentage of preferred par value.

 YOUDECIDE   Stock Repurchase or Dividend

You are the controller at Cohen Industries. The Board of Directors has decided to distribute $5,000,000 in excess cash to common stockholders.

In what ways can this distribution be accomplished? What factors should be considered when determining the best way?

You could either declare and pay a cash dividend or enter a stock repurchase plan. The primary difference between the two methods relates to tax consequences. First, while not currently the case, historically, the tax rate for dividends is higher than the rate on gains from selling stock. Second, while all common stockholders participate

in dividends and, thus, incur tax consequence, only those stockholders who choose to sell their stock back to Cohen will experience tax consequences. Additionally, you should consider the future of any such distributions to stockholders. Generally, companies do not like to lower dividends. Finally, you should consider the price of the stock. Stock repurchases are most attractive when you believe your stock to be undervalued.

Therefore, if this distribution is a one-time event, a stock repurchase would be the way to go; however, if excess cash is anticipated in future periods, instituting a cash dividend would make sense.

OBJECTIVE 4

Describe the accounting issues related to retained earnings and accumulated other comprehensive income.

ACCOUNTING FOR RETAINED EARNINGS AND ACCUMULATED OTHER COMPREHENSIVE INCOME

Retained earnings (or **deficit**) is the accumulated earnings (or losses) over the entire life of the corporation that has not been paid out in dividends. Generally, ending retained earnings is calculated with a simple formula:

	Beginning Retained Earnings
+	Net Income
−	Dividends
=	Ending Retained Earnings

RESTRICTIONS ON RETAINED EARNINGS

Under most corporate charters, the balance of a corporation's retained earnings represents an upper limit on the entity's ability to pay dividends. (Dividends cannot reduce retained earnings below zero.) A corporation's capacity to pay dividends may be further restricted by agreements with lenders, by the corporation's board of directors, and by various provisions of state law, as follows:

- An agreement between the corporation and bondholders may require that retained earnings never fall below a specified level so long as the bonds are outstanding.
- The firm's board of directors may set aside a portion of retained earnings and declare it unavailable for the payment of dividends. Such an action may be used to communicate to stockholders changes in dividend policy made necessary by expansion programs or other decisions of the board.
- State law may require that dividends not reduce retained earnings below the cost of treasury stock.

Restrictions of this sort are usually disclosed in footnotes to the financial statements to signify that the restricted amount is unavailable for dividends. In rare cases, a separate "reserve" account is established for the restricted portion of retained earnings. The reserve account is called either *Restricted Earnings* or *Appropriation of Retained Earnings*. The account title frequently indicates, quite specifically, the nature of the restriction or the appropriation, as, for example, "Restricted Retained Earnings under Agreements with Bondholders" or "Appropriation of Retained Earnings for Plant Expansion." When reserve accounts are used, Retained Earnings is reported on two or more lines in the equity section of the balance sheet (see Exhibit 10.6). One line is devoted to each restriction, and to "Unrestricted Retained Earnings" or "Unappropriated Retained Earnings."

Excerpt from Deere & Co. 2019 10-K

EXHIBIT 10.6

The following was included in the Capital Resources and Liquidity Note of **Deere & Co.**'s 2019 10-K:

Deere & Co. 2019 10-K

The credit agreements also require the equipment operations to maintain a ratio of total debt to total capital (total debt and stockholders' equity excluding accumulated other comprehensive income (loss)) of 65 percent or less at the end of each fiscal quarter. Under this provision, the company's excess equity capacity and retained earnings balance free of restriction at November 3, 2019, was $13,554 million.

Although Deere & Co. did not choose to show this restriction in the stockholders' equity portion of their balance sheet, if they had it would have appeared as follows:

STOCKHOLDERS' EQUITY (Partial)

	2019
Common stock, $1 par value (authorized—1,200,000,000 shares; issued—536,431,204 shares in 2019, at paid-in amount)	4,642
Common stock in treasury, 223,290,789 shares in 2019, at cost	(17,474)
Retained earnings:	
Restricted for credit agreement	16,298
Unrestricted	13,554
Total Retained Earnings	29,852

Source: Deer & Company, 2019 10-K.

Error Corrections and Prior Period Adjustments Errors in recording transactions can distort the financial statements. If errors are discovered and corrected before the closing process, then no great harm is done. However, if errors go undetected, then flawed financial statements are issued. No matter when they are discovered, errors must be corrected.

If an error resulted in a misstatement of net income, then correction may require a direct adjustment to retained earnings, called a **prior period adjustment**. To illustrate, suppose that Byrnes Corporation uses a computer program to calculate depreciation expense. In 2022, a programming error caused the 2022 depreciation expense to be understated by $16,000. The error was not discovered until August 2023; consequently, 2022 net income after income taxes (which are paid at a rate of 21%) was overstated by $12,640 [$16,000 × (1 − 0.21)]. The error correction would be recorded in August 2023 as follows:

Date	Account and Explanation	Debit	Credit	Assets	= Liabilities +	Stockholders' Equity
Aug. 2023	Retained Earnings	12,640				▼
	Tax Refund Receivable	3,360		▲		
	Accumulated Depreciation		16,000	▼		

Byrnes' retained earnings statement for 2023 incorporates the $12,640 prior period adjustment as follows:

Byrnes Corporation Retained Earnings Statement For the year ended December 31, 2023		
Retained earnings, January 1, 2023		$157,640
Less: Prior period adjustment:		
Correction of error in calculation of 2022		
depreciation expense (net of tax)		(12,640)
Retained earnings as adjusted, January 1, 2023		$145,000
Add: Net income for 2023		65,000
Less: Dividends declared in 2023:		
Cash dividend, preferred stock	$ (4,000)	
Stock dividend, common stock	(20,000)	
Total dividends declared		(24,000)
Retained earnings, December 31, 2023		$186,000

Notice that the adjustment is deducted from the beginning balance of retained earnings to produce an *adjusted* beginning balance.

Financial accounting standards define prior period adjustments in a way that specifically excludes adjustments arising from estimation errors and changes from one accounting principle to another. These changes are corrected by adjusting the related income accounts for the period in which they are discovered.

ACCOUNTING FOR ACCUMULATED OTHER COMPREHENSIVE INCOME

Financial accounting theory suggests that income represents the changes in the assets and liabilities of the company as a result of transactions with nonowners. However, over time the FASB has allowed the gains and losses from certain nonowner transactions to bypass the income statement and go directly to stockholders' equity. These instances are rare, and the transactions that produce them are somewhat complicated, but one example is unrealized gains and losses on investments classified as available-for-sale securities. To illustrate, if a company buys securities for $10,000 and at the end of the year those securities are worth $12,000, the company has a $2,000 unrealized gain (a gain or loss is realized when the share is actually sold). It seems logical

Next Level

Assume that a standard condition in a loan contract (called a *loan covenant*) requires a borrower to maintain retained earnings of $3,000,000 on a $500,000 loan. The borrower does not like this covenant and asks why it has to be there. What would you say?

ANSWER:
Loan covenants such as these are there to protect the lender from the borrower removing money from the company, then declaring bankruptcy, and never repaying the loan. For example, in the absence of this covenant, an unscrupulous borrower could borrow $500,000 from the bank then pay out all this cash to stockholders as dividends leaving little (or at least far less) collateral within the company.

that this gain would appear on the income statement, but FASB has ruled that these gains and losses, when the investment is classified as available-for-sale, are excluded from net income to reduce volatility due to fluctuations in fair value. At the same time, companies are required to include these gains and losses, along with net income in a measure called *comprehensive income.*

The FASB permits comprehensive income to be reported in one of two methods. The first method is a single statement approach in which both net income and comprehensive income are shown in the same statement. In this method, comprehensive income items will be added to or subtracted from net income to obtain total comprehensive income. The second method is a two-statement approach where total net income is shown on the first statement. That statement is followed by a statement of comprehensive income, which shows the components of comprehensive income and total comprehensive income. You can see an example of the two-statement approach in **Kroger**'s and **Sprouts Farmers Market**'s financial statements (pp. 824 and 836 of Appendices 4 and 5, respectively). A vast majority of companies use the two-statement approach.

Regardless of which option is used to disclose comprehensive income for the period, **accumulated other comprehensive income** is shown in the stockholders' equity section of the balance sheet. Accumulated other comprehensive income is the total of comprehensive income for all periods. By disclosing this information, companies communicate the changes in assets and liabilities resulting from all transactions with nonowners.

Although it is not a required statement, a majority of corporations traded on U.S. stock exchanges also provide a statement of stockholders' equity. This latter statement reconciles the beginning and ending balances for each of the elements of stockholders' equity changes.

EQUITY ANALYSIS

OBJECTIVE 5

Analyze stockholder payout and profitability ratios.

Stockholders want to understand the following:

- how the value of their shares of stock will change
- how the company will distribute any excess cash to stockholders

We all know that investors buy stock to increase their personal wealth. But how do stockholders use the financial statements to better understand these two dimensions?

STOCKHOLDER PROFITABILITY RATIOS

A primary driver of an increase in stock price is profitability. Profitability refers to the return that the company earns (in other words, its net income). However, the magnitude of the net income also matters because it shows how much had to be invested to earn the return. That is, would you rather earn $10 on a $100 investment or $20 on a $500 investment? Although the latter return is twice as large as the former, it also took an investment that was five times bigger. Assuming equal risk, etc., most investors would prefer to invest $100 to earn $10 because they then could use the extra $400 to invest somewhere else.

The two most common ratios used to evaluate stockholder profitability are return on common equity and earnings per share (EPS).

Return on Common Equity **Return on common equity** shows the growth in equity from operating activities. It is calculated as:

$$\text{Return on Common Equity} = \frac{\text{Net Income} - \text{Preferred Dividends}}{\text{Average Common Stockholder's Equity}}$$

Common stockholders' equity is calculated by taking total stockholders' equity and subtracting preferred stock.

Earnings per Share (EPS) **Earnings per share (EPS)** measures the net income earned by each share of common stock. It is calculated as:

$$EPS = \frac{\text{Net Income} - \text{Preferred Dividends}}{\text{Average Common Shares Outstanding}}$$

EXAMPLE 10.6 illustrates how to calculate stockholder profitability.

EXAMPLE 10.6   CALCULATING STOCKHOLDER PROFITABILITY RATIOS

Consider the following information from **Kroger**'s 2019 financial statements (all numbers in millions other than per-share amounts).

Common stock price (year end)	$28.99/share	Avg. common shares outstanding	799
Common dividends	$486	Dividends per common share	$0.62/share
Preferred dividends	$0	Net income (attributable to common	
Ending preferred stock	$0	shareholders)	$1,640
Ending total stockholders' equity	$8,573	Beginning preferred stock	$0
Purchases of treasury stock	$400	Beginning total stockholders' equity	$7,835

Required:
Calculate the following stockholder profitability ratios: (1) return on common equity and (2) EPS.

Solution:

1. $\text{Return on Common Equity} = \dfrac{\text{Net Income} - \text{Preferred Dividends}}{\text{Average Common Stockholder's Equity Outstanding}}$

    $= \dfrac{(\$1,640 - 0)}{[(\$7,835 - \$0) + (\$8,573 - \$0)] \div 2} = 19.99\%$

2. $\text{EPS} = \dfrac{\text{Net Income} - \text{Preferred Dividends}}{\text{Average Common Share Outstanding}} = \dfrac{(\$1,640 - \$0)}{799} = \$2.05$

STOCKHOLDER PAYOUT

Stockholders not only experience an increase in wealth through an increasing stock price, but may also receive cash, or a payout, from the company. The most common **stockholder payout** ratios relate to dividends. Dividend yield considers the ratio of dividends paid to stock price. This ratio is conceptually similar to an interest rate for debt:

$$\text{Dividend Yield} = \frac{\text{Dividends per Common Share}}{\text{Closing Market Price per Share for the Year}}$$

Another common dividend ratio calculates the proportion of dividends to earnings:

$$\text{Dividend Payout} = \frac{\text{Common Dividends}}{\text{Net Income}}$$

However, as discussed earlier, payouts to stockholders can also take the form of stock repurchases. As such, the stock repurchase payout ratio is:

$$\text{Stock Repurchase Payout} = \frac{\text{Common Stock Repurchases}}{\text{Net Income}}$$

By using these two ratios, stockholders can easily calculate the total payout:

$$\text{Total Payout} = \text{Dividend Payout} + \text{Stock Repurchase Payout}$$

Or, it can be calculated directly as:

$$\text{Total Payout} = \frac{\text{Common Dividends} + \text{Common Stock Repurchases}}{\text{Net Income (or Comprehensive Income)}}$$

EXAMPLE 10.7 illustrates how to calculate payout ratios.

EXAMPLE 10.7   CALCULATING STOCKHOLDER PAYOUT RATIOS

Consider the following information from **Kroger**'s 2019 financial statements (all numbers in millions other than per-share amounts).

Common stock price (year end)	$28.99/share	Avg. common shares outstanding	799
Common dividends	$486	Dividends per common share	$0.62/share
Preferred dividends	$0	Net income (attributable to common	
Ending preferred stock	$0	shareholders)	$1,640
Ending total stockholders' equity	$8,573	Beginning preferred stock	$0
Purchases of treasury stock	$400	Beginning total stockholders' equity	$7,835

Required:
Calculate the following stockholder payout ratios: (1) dividend yield, (2) dividend payout, (3) stock repurchase payout, and (4) total payout.

Solution:

1. $\text{Dividend Yield} = \dfrac{\text{Dividends per Common Share}}{\text{Common Stock Price}} = \dfrac{\$0.62}{\$28.99} = 2.14\%$

2. $\text{Dividend Payout} = \dfrac{\text{Common Dividends}}{\text{Net Income}} = \dfrac{\$486}{\$1,640} = 29.63\%$

3. $\text{Stock Repurchase Payout} = \dfrac{\text{Common Stock Repurchases}}{\text{Net Income}} = \dfrac{\$400}{\$1,640} = 24.39\%$

4. $\text{Total Payout} = \text{Dividend Payout} + \text{Stock Repurchase Payout} = 29.63\% + 24.39\% = 54.02\%$

Note: This can also be calculated directly as (Dividends + Stock Repurchases) ÷ Net Income.

INTERPRETING RATIOS

What do these stockholder profitability and payout ratios mean? The results of these ratios are usually used in two ways:

- *Compared over time to evaluate trends:* For example, in 2019 **Kroger**'s EPS was $2.05. This might be great news if EPS in 2018 were $1.15 or bad news if it were $4.25. In fact, EPS for 2017 and 2018 were $2.11 and $3.80, respectively. This means EPS increased by over 80% in 2018, but that increase was more than entirely lost in 2019. This is obviously concerning and worth investigating.
- *Compared to results for other companies in the industry:* For example, the 2019 return on common equity for **Kroger** was 19.99% and for **Sprouts Farmers Market** it was 25.55%. This makes Kroger's return on common equity of 19.99% look subpar. You can also look at industry averages. **Reuters** reports an industry average of 20.82%, so Kroger is slightly behind the industry average.

YOUDECIDE   Providing Shares for Employee Stock Options

You are the CFO of DTR Technology, a small, publicly traded software firm. Your stock price has increased by 120% over the last 2 years and is now at $22 per share. Of course, this is great news. However, one side effect is that DTR employees own approximately 750,000 stock options with an average exercise price of $5 per share.

What factors must be considered in handling the anticipated exercise of these options?

DTR could issue previously unissued shares and take in the exercise price, or $3,750,000 in total (750,000 × $5). Although this seems reasonable, very few companies follow this course of action. Instead, most companies engage in a stock repurchase plan. For example, **Microsoft** repurchased 150 million shares of stock in 2019 costing approximately $19.5 billion, at least partly because of their employee stock compensation plans. This is despite the fact that Microsoft stock closed fiscal year 2019 at $133.96, while the average exercise price of the nonvested options was $78.49. In other words, if Microsoft plans to buy back shares of stock for $133.96 per share while only receiving $78.49 per option exercised, they will lose $55.47 per share. Why does Microsoft buy back shares to either give away or sell at below market prices to employees when they could simply issue new shares? Microsoft, like most companies, chose to repurchase shares because issuing previously unissued shares will increase the number of shares outstanding, which will, in turn, decrease (or dilute) earnings per share.

For DTR, repurchasing shares on the open market to cover its 750,000 in options would cost $12,750,000 [750,000 options × ($22 − $5)], but would prevent earnings per share from being diluted.

REVIEW CENTER

LO1. Describe common and preferred stock and their use in raising capital.

KEY TAKEAWAYS

- Corporations sell both common stock and preferred stock to raise capital.
- Preferred stock generally guarantees a regular dividend and receives priority over common stock in the payment of dividends and distribution of assets in liquidation.
- Common stock has voting rights and receives all benefits not assigned to the preferred stockholders and creditors.
- Selling different classes of stock (with different features) attracts stockholders with diverse risk preferences and tax situations.

KEY TERMS

Articles of incorporation, 566
Authorized shares, 566
Common stock, 567
Corporate charter, 566
Dividends, 567
Equity, 565

Issued shares, 566
Outstanding shares, 566
Preferred stock, 567
Shareholders, 565
Stockholders, 565
Stockholders' equity, 565

LO2. Record and properly present capital stock.

KEY TAKEAWAYS

- Both preferred stock and common stock are generally recorded at par or stated value.
- Any extra consideration received is recorded as "additional paid-in capital."

KEY TERMS

Additional paid-in capital, 569
Capital stock, 569
Exercise (or strike) price, 571
No-par stock, 571

Par value, 569
Stated capital (legal capital), 571
Stock options, 571
Stock warrant, 571

EXAMPLE

EXAMPLE 10.1   Recording the sale of common and preferred stock, page 569–570

LO3. Record and properly present the distribution of assets to stockholders.

KEY TAKEAWAYS

- Assets are distributed to stockholders by either of the following:
  - Repurchasing their shares of stock
  - Paying dividends
- Generally, the cost of stock repurchases is recorded as a reduction in stockholders' equity (a debit to treasury stock).
- Typically, the corporation pays dividends with cash.
- Stock dividends and stock splits do not represent a payout to stockholders. These transactions have no effect on total stockholders' equity.
- Preferred stock generally has dividend preferences such as being cumulative or participating.

KEY TERMS

Cumulative dividend preference, 581
Current dividend preference, 580
Date of record, 576
Declaration date, 576
Dividends in arrears, 581
Liquidating dividends, 577

Payment date, 576
Participating dividend preference, 582
Stock dividend, 577
Stock split, 579
Treasury stock, 573

EXAMPLES

EXAMPLE 10.2	Accounting for treasury stock, page 574–575
EXAMPLE 10.3	Recording cash dividends, page 576–577
EXAMPLE 10.4	Recording small and large stock dividends, page 578
EXAMPLE 10.5	Calculating cumulative preferred dividends, page 581

LO4. Describe the accounting issues related to retained earnings and accumulated other comprehensive income.

KEY TAKEAWAYS

- Retained earnings represents the earnings that the corporation elects not to pay out in dividends.
- Ending retained earnings is calculated by adding net income and subtracting dividends to beginning retained earnings.
- Retained earnings can be restricted, which communicates to stockholders that this portion of retained earnings is not eligible for dividend payout.
- Certain nonowner transactions are not included on the income statement. These transactions are included in the Accumulated Other Comprehensive Income account in the stockholders' equity section of the balance sheet.

KEY TERMS

Accumulated other comprehensive income, 585
Prior period adjustment, 584
Retained deficit, 582
Retained earnings, 582

KEY CALCULATION

Ending Retained Earnings = Beginning Retained Earnings + Net Income − Dividends, p. 582

KEY TAKEAWAYS

LO5. Analyze stockholder payout and profitability ratios.

- Stockholders are primarily interested in two things:
  - Creation of value
  - Distribution of value
- Analysis of the stockholders' equity section of the balance sheet in conjunction with the statement of stockholders' equity allows stockholders to separate these concepts.

KEY TERMS

Earnings per share (EPS), 586
Return on common equity, 585
Stockholder payout, 586

KEY CALCULATIONS

Return on Common Equity = (Net Income − Preferred Dividends) ÷ Average Common Stockholders' Equity, 585

Earnings Per Share (EPS) = (Net Income − Preferred Dividends) ÷ Average Common Shares Outstanding, 586

Dividend Yield = Dividends per Common Share ÷ Common Stock Price, 586

Dividend Payout = Common Dividends ÷ Net Income, 586

Stock Repurchase Payout = Common Stock Repurchases ÷ Net Income, 586

Total Payout = Dividend Payout + Stock Repurchase Payout, 587

Total Payout (Direct) = (Common Dividends + Common Stock Repurchases) ÷ Net Income (or Comprehensive Income), 587

EXAMPLES

EXAMPLE 10.6   Calculating stockholder profitability ratios, page 586

EXAMPLE 10.7   Calculating stockholder payout ratios, page 587

REVIEW PROBLEM

STOCKHOLDERS' EQUITY

Grace Industries, a privately held corporation, has decided to go public. The current ownership group has 10,000,000 common shares (purchased at an average price of $0.50 per share) and the articles of incorporation authorize 50,000,000, $0.10 par, common shares and 1,000,000, 10%, $30 par, cumulative, preferred shares. On January 1, 2022, the public offering issues 8,000,000 common shares at $14 per share and 100,000 preferred shares at $33 per share.

On October 3, 2023, Grace Industries repurchases 750,000 common shares at $12 per share. After the repurchase, Grace's board of directors decides to declare dividends totaling $4,050,000 (no dividends were declared or paid in 2022). This dividend will be declared on November 15, 2023, to all stockholders of record on December 8, 2023. This dividend will be paid on December 23, 2023. On December 28, 2023, 100,000 of the treasury shares are reissued for $15 per share.

At December 31, 2023, Grace Industries has $12,000,000 of retained earnings and accumulated other comprehensive income of ($250,000).

Required:

1. Prepare the journal entry to record the January 1, 2022 issuance of the common and preferred stock.
2. Prepare the journal entry to record the October 3, 2023 stock repurchase.
3. Determine how much of the dividend will go to preferred stockholders.
4. Calculate what the dividends per common share will be.
5. Prepare the journal entry for the dividend declaration on November 15, 2023.
6. Prepare the journal entry on the date of record (December 8, 2023).
7. Prepare the journal entry on the dividend payment date (December 23, 2023).
8. Prepare the journal entry for the reissuance of treasury shares on December 28, 2023.
9. Prepare the stockholders' equity section of the balance sheet at December 31, 2023.

Solution:

1.

Date	Account and Explanation	Debit	Credit	Assets	=	Liabilities	+	Stockholders' Equity
Jan. 1, 2022	Cash[a]	3,300,000		▲				
	Preferred Stock[b]		3,000,000					▲
	Additional Paid-In Capital—Preferred Stock[c]		300,000					▲
	Cash[d]	112,000,000		▲				
	Common Stock[e]		800,000					▲
	Additional Paid-In Capital—Common Stock[f]		111,200,000					▲

[a]100,000 shares × $33 = $3,300,000
[b]100,000 shares × $30 par = $3,000,000
[c]100,000 shares × ($33 − $30) = $300,000
[d]8,000,000 shares × $14 = $112,000,000
[e]8,000,000 shares × $0.10 par = $800,000
[f]8,000,000 shares × ($14 − $0.10) = $111,200,000

2.

Date	Account and Explanation	Debit	Credit	Assets	= Liabilities +	Stockholders' Equity
Oct. 3, 2023	Treasury Stock*	9,000,000				▼
	Cash		9,000,000	▼		

*750,000 shares × $12 = $9,000,000

3. The preferred stock is cumulative, so the preferred stockholders must be paid their annual dividend for 2023 (the current year) and for 2022 (dividends in arrears).

> Preferred Dividends* $600,000

*100,000 shares × ($30 par × 10% × 2 years) = $600,000

4. The common stockholders receive any dividend remaining after the preferred dividend has been paid (because the preferred is not participating). Because common dividends are only paid to outstanding stock, the treasury shares must be subtracted from the issued shares. Remember that the ownership group owned 10,000,000 shares then issued 8,000,000 shares in the initial public offering.

$$\text{Common Dividends} = \frac{\$4{,}050{,}000 - \$600{,}000}{18{,}000{,}000 \text{ issued shares} - 750{,}000 \text{ treasury shares}} = \underline{\$0.20} \text{ per share}$$

5.

Date	Account and Explanation	Debit	Credit	Assets	= Liabilities +	Stockholders' Equity
Nov. 15, 2023	Dividends Declared*	4,050,000				▼
	Cash Dividends Payable		4,050,000		▲	

*Dividends Declared is closed to Retained Earnings.

6. No entry is necessary on the date of record.

7.

Date	Account and Explanation	Debit	Credit	Assets	= Liabilities +	Stockholders' Equity
Dec. 23, 2023	Cash Dividends Payable	4,050,000			▼	
	Cash		4,050,000	▼		

8.

Date	Account and Explanation	Debit	Credit	Assets	= Liabilities +	Stockholders' Equity
Dec. 28, 2023	Cash*	1,500,000		▲		
	Treasury Stock**		1,200,000			▲
	Additional Paid-In Capital—Treasury Stock		300,000			▲

*100,000 shares × $15 = $1,500,000
**100,000 shares × $12 = $1,200,000

9.   Stockholders' equity:

Preferred stock, 10%, $30 par, cumulative, 1,000,000 shares authorized, 100,000 shares issued and outstanding	$ 3,000,000[a]
Common stock, $0.10 par, 50,000,000 shares authorized, 18,000,000 shares issued, and 17,350,000 outstanding	1,800,000[b]
Additional paid-in capital:	
Preferred stock	300,000[c]
Common stock	115,200,000[d]
Treasury stock	300,000[e]
Total capital stock	$120,600,000
Retained earnings	12,000,000[f]
Less:	
Accumulated other comprehensive income	(250,000)[f]
Treasury stock (650,000 shares at cost)	(7,800,000)[g]
Total stockholders' equity	$124,550,000

[a] 100,000 shares issued at $30 par (see journal entry from 1).
[b] 18,000,000 shares issued at $0.10 par.
[c] 100,000 shares issued at $3 more than par ($33 selling price minus $30 par). See journal entry from 1.
[d] 10,000,000 shares issued to original ownership group at an average price of $0.50 per share ($0.40 per share in excess of par) plus 8,000,000 shares issued in IPO at $14 ($13.90 per share in excess of par).
[e] 100,000 treasury shares issued at $15 per share, which is $3 per share in excess of $12 cost (see journal entry from 8).
[f] Given in information.
[g] 750,000 shares repurchased at $12 per share minus 100,000 shares reissued.

APPLYING KNOWLEDGE

DISCUSSION QUESTIONS

OBJECTIVE 1

1. What does stockholders' equity represent?

2. What does a share of stock represent?

3. Why do corporations issue stock?

4. What is the difference between a privately and publicly held corporation?

5. What are authorized shares?

6. Why would the number of shares issued be different from the number of shares outstanding?

7. What are the benefits that common stockholders may receive?

8. How do common stock and preferred stock differ?

9. Discuss the similarities between preferred stock and debt.

10. Why do corporations utilize different forms of equity?

OBJECTIVE 3

11. Describe how cumulative preferred stock differs from noncumulative preferred stock.

12. How is a preferred stock dividend calculated?

OBJECTIVE 2

13. What balance sheet accounts are affected by the issuance of stock?

14. What is the difference between par value and stated value?

15. Why might a corporation grant stock options to employees in lieu of a higher salary?

16. What is a stock warrant? How are they used by corporations?

OBJECTIVE 3

17. Describe two ways corporations make payouts to stockholders.

18. What is treasury stock?

19. Give four reasons why a company might purchase treasury stock.

20. How would the purchase of treasury stock affect the stockholders' equity section of a corporation's balance sheet?

21. A corporation repurchases 10,000 shares of its common stock at $7 per share and later resells it for $11 per share. What is the effect on the income statement of this resell?

22. What entries are made (if any) at the declaration date, date of record, and date of payment for cash dividends?

23. Compare and contrast cash dividends and liquidating dividends.

24. Describe the effect of a cash versus a stock dividend on a company's stockholders' equity.

25. What is a stock dividend? How does it differ from a stock split?

26. What is the effect of a stock split on stockholders' equity account balances?

27. Explain each of the following preferred stock dividend preferences: (1) current dividend preference, (2) cumulative dividend preference, and (3) participating dividend preference.

28. Are dividends in arrears reported among the liabilities of the dividend-paying firm? If not, how are they reported, and why?

29. What are retained earnings?   **OBJECTIVE** ◀ 4

30. How may a corporation's retained earnings be restricted?

31. When are prior period adjustments used?

32. Distinguish between retained earnings and accumulated other comprehensive income.

33. Describe the statement of changes in stockholders' equity.

34. How are dividend payout and profitability ratios useful to investors?   **OBJECTIVE** ◀ 5

MULTIPLE-CHOICE QUESTIONS

10-1 Which of the following is *not* a component of stockholders' equity?   **OBJECTIVE** ◀ 1
   a. retained earnings
   b. net income
   c. loss on sale of equipment
   d. dividends payable

10-2 Which of the following statements is true?
   a. The outstanding number of shares is the maximum number of shares that can be issued by a corporation.
   b. The shares that are in the hands of the stockholders are said to be outstanding.
   c. It is very unlikely that corporations will have more than one class of stock outstanding.
   d. Preferred stock is stock that has been retired.

10-3 Authorized stock represents the:
   a. number of shares that are currently held by stockholders.
   b. number of shares that have been sold.
   c. number of shares that have been repurchased by the corporation.
   d. maximum number of shares that can be issued.

10-4 McKean Corporation authorized 500,000 shares of common stock in its articles of incorporation. On May 1, 100,000 shares were sold to the company's founders. However, on October 15, McKean repurchased 20,000 shares to settle a dispute among the founders. At this date, how many shares were issued and outstanding, respectively?
   a. 80,000 and 100,000
   b. 100,000 and 80,000
   c. 100,000 and 100,000
   d. 500,000 and 100,000

10-5   Harvey Corporation shows the following in the stockholders' equity section of its balance sheet: The par value of its common stock is $0.25 and the total balance in the Common Stock account is $50,000. Also noted is that 15,000 shares are currently designated as treasury stock. The number of shares *outstanding* is:

a. 185,000.

b. 196,250.

c. 200,000.

d. 215,000.

10-6   Ames Corporation repurchases 10,000 shares of its common stock for $12 per share. The shares were originally issued at an average price of $10 per share. Later it resells 6,000 of the shares for $15 per share and the remaining 4,000 shares for $17 per share. How much gain or loss should Ames report on its income statement as a result of these transactions?

a. $38,000 gain

b. $20,000 loss and $38,000 gain

c. $0

d. $20,000 loss

10-7   With regard to preferred stock,

a. its stockholders may have the right to participate, along with common stockholders, if an extra dividend is declared.

b. its issuance provides no flexibility to the issuing company because its terms always require mandatory dividend payments.

c. no dividends are expected by the stockholders.

d. there is a legal requirement for a corporation to declare a dividend on preferred stock.

OBJECTIVE ▶ 2   **10-8**   DAE Parts Shop began business on January 1. The corporate charter authorized issuance of 20,000 shares of $5 par value common stock and 5,000 shares of $10 par value, 5% cumulative preferred stock. DAE issued 12,000 shares of common stock at $25 per share on January 2. What effect does the entry to record the issuance of stock have on total stockholders' equity?

a. increase of $340,000

b. increase of $300,000

c. increase of $150,000

d. increase of $120,000

10-9   Thornwood Partners began business on January 1. The corporate charter authorized issuance of 75,000 shares of $1 par value common stock and 8,000 shares of $3 par value, 10% cumulative preferred stock. On July 1, Thornwood issued 20,000 shares of common stock in exchange for 2 years' rent on a retail location. The cash rental price is $3,000 per month, and the rental period begins on July 1. What is the correct entry to record the July 1 transaction?

a. Debit to Cash, $72,000; credit to Prepaid Rent, $57,600

b. Debit to Prepaid Rent, $72,000; credit to Common Stock, $72,000

c. Debit to Prepaid Rent, $72,000; credit to Common Stock, $20,000; credit to Additional Paid-In Capital—Common Stock, $52,000

d. Debit to Prepaid Rent, $72,000; credit to Common Stock, $60,000; credit to Additional Paid-In Capital—Common Stock, $12,000

OBJECTIVE ▶ 3   **10-10** A company would repurchase its own stock for all of the following reasons *except*:

a. it wishes to prevent unwanted takeover attempts.

b. it wishes to increase the earnings per share.

c. it believes the stock is overvalued.

d. it needs the stock for employee bonuses.

10-11 When a company purchases treasury stock, which of the following statements is true?

a. Dividends continue to be paid on the treasury stock.

b. It is no longer considered to be issued.

c. The cost of the treasury stock reduces stockholders' equity.

d. Treasury stock is considered to be an asset because cash is paid for the stock.

10-12 If a company purchases treasury stock for $6,000 and then reissues it for $5,000, the difference of $1,000 is:

a. a decrease in stockholders' equity.

b. a gain in stockholders' equity.

c. treated as a loss on the sale.

d. treated as a gain on the sale.

10-13 When a company retires its own common stock, the company must:

a. record a gain or loss depending on the difference between original selling price and repurchase cost.

b. decrease the Common Stock account balances by the original issue price.

c. get the approval of the state to do so.

d. issue a different class of stock to the former stockholders.

10-14 Which of the following should be considered when a company decides to declare a cash dividend on common stock?

a. the retained earnings balance only

b. the cash available and the retained earnings balance

c. the amount of authorized shares of common stock

d. the book value of the company's stock

10-15 When a company declares a cash dividend, which of the following is true?

a. Assets are decreased.

b. Assets are increased.

c. Stockholders' equity is increased.

d. Liabilities are increased.

10-16 What is the effect of a stock dividend on stockholders' equity?

a. Stockholders' equity is decreased.

b. Retained earnings is increased.

c. Additional paid-in capital is decreased.

d. Total stockholders' equity stays the same.

10-17 As a result of a stock split,

a. stockholders' equity is increased.

b. the stockholders have a higher proportionate ownership of the company.

c. the par value of the stock is changed in the reverse proportion as the stock split.

d. the market price of the outstanding stock is increasing because a split is evidence of a profitable company.

10-18 The balance of the $2.50 par value Common Stock account for Patriot Company was $240,000,000 before its recent 2-for-1 stock split. The market price of the stock was $50 per share before the stock split. What occurred as a result of the stock split?

a. The balance in the common stock account was increase to $480,000.

b. The balance in the retained earnings account decreased.

c. The market price of the stock dropped to approximately $25 per share.

d. The market price of the stock was not affected.

10-19 When a company declares a 3-for-1 stock split, the number of shares:

a. is reduced by one-third.

b. is reduced by one-third and the number of issued shares is tripled.

c. stays the same, but the number of issued shares triples.

d. triples.

10-20 Shea Company has 100,000 shares of 6%, $50 par value, cumulative preferred stock. In the prior year, no dividends were declared on preferred stock. This year, Shea was profitable and decided to pay dividends to stockholders of both preferred and common stock. If they have $750,000 available for dividends this year, how much could it pay to the common stockholders?

a. $750,000

b. $450,000

c. $150,000

d. $0

10-21 RVR Enterprises shows net income of $100,000 for 2023 and retained earnings of $500,000 on its December 31, 2023 balance sheet. During the year, RVR declared and paid $60,000 in dividends. What was RVR's retained earnings balance at December 31, 2022?

a. $400,000

b. $440,000

c. $460,000

d. $540,000

OBJECTIVE **4**

10-22 Comprehensive income:

a. includes transactions that affect stockholders' equity with the exception of those transactions that involve owners.

b. is considered an appropriation of retained earnings.

c. includes all transactions that are under management's control.

d. is the result of all events and transactions reported on the income statement.

10-23 FASB's concept of comprehensive income:

a. excludes the payment of dividends.

b. has a primary drawback because it allows management to manipulate the income figure to a certain extent.

c. requires that all transactions must be shown on the income statement.

d. allows items that are not necessarily under management's control, such as natural disasters, to be shown as an adjustment of retained earnings.

OBJECTIVE **5**

10-24 Garner Corporation issued $50,000 in common stock dividends. Its net income for the year was $250,000. What is Garner's dividend payout ratio?

a. 5

b. 2.5

c. 0.5

d. 0.2

BRIEF EXERCISES

OBJECTIVE **1**

Brief Exercise 10-25 Common Stock versus Preferred Stock

Corporations issue two general types of stock—common and preferred.

Required:

Describe the major differences between common and preferred stock.

OBJECTIVE **2**

Brief Exercise 10-26 Recording the Sale of Common and Preferred Stock

At the end of its first year of operations, Mulligan Corporation has outstanding shares of 104,000 common stock and 1,700 preferred stock. The State of Michigan authorized Mulligan to issue 3,000 shares of 8% preferred stock with a par value of $30 per share and 110,000 shares of common stock with a par value of $0.01 per share. Any common stock sold during the year had a selling price of $19.25 per share. Mulligan's preferred stock was issued at $53.00.

Required:

Prepare the journal entry to record any issuance of stock during the year.

OBJECTIVE **2**

EXAMPLE 10.1

Brief Exercise 10-27 Recording the Sale of Common Stock

Yellow Company, a food coloring manufacturer that provides its products to large processed-food corporations, issues 520,000 shares of common stock (par value $0.15) for $19 per share.

Required:

Prepare the necessary journal entry to record this transaction.

Brief Exercise 10-28 Calculating the Number of Shares Issued

OBJECTIVE ◀ 2
EXAMPLE 10.1

Chester Inc. issued shares of its $1.25 par value common stock for $14 per share. In recording the issuance of the stock, Chester credited the Additional Paid-In Capital—Common Stock account for $443,700.

Required:
How many shares were issued?

Brief Exercise 10-29 Accounting for Treasury Stock

OBJECTIVE ◀ 3
EXAMPLE 10.2

On August 19, Portland Corporation repurchases 2,600 shares of its outstanding common stock for $7 per share. On October 31, Portland sells 400 shares of treasury stock for $12 per share. Any additional sales of treasury stock during the year were sold for $5 per share. On December 31, Portland had no remaining treasury stock.

Required:
Prepare the necessary journal entries to record any transactions associated with treasury stock.

Brief Exercise 10-30 Accounting for Treasury Stock

OBJECTIVE ◀ 3
EXAMPLE 10.2

Big Ben Corporation provides travel planning services for large corporations across the world. On January 23, Big Ben Corporation repurchases $235,000 shares of its outstanding common stock for $18 per share. On May 19, Big Ben sells 111,500 shares of treasury stock for $10 per share. On November 1, Big Ben sells 75,000 shares of its treasury stock for $25 per share.

Required:
1. Prepare the necessary journal entries to record these transactions.
2. **CONCEPTUAL CONNECTION** How will these transactions affect Big Ben's income statement?

Use the following information for Brief Exercises 10-31 and 10-32:
Jumper Company purchases 185,000 shares of treasury stock for $17 per share.

Brief Exercise 10-31 Treasury Stock

OBJECTIVE ◀ 3
EXAMPLE 10.2

Refer to the information for Jumper Company above.

Required:
1. How will this transaction affect stockholders' equity?
2. How will this transaction affect net income?

Brief Exercise 10-32 Treasury Stock

OBJECTIVE ◀ 3
EXAMPLE 10.2

Refer to the information for Jumper Company above.

Required:
What is the appropriate journal entry to record the transaction?

Brief Exercise 10-33 Cash Dividends

OBJECTIVE ◀ 3
EXAMPLE 10.3

Teater Corporation issued 22,000 shares of common stock. At the beginning of the year, Teater held 9,000 shares of treasury stock, but it reissued 4,000 of those shares in November. On December 1, Teater's board of directors declares a cash dividend of $0.88 per share payable on December 20, to stockholders of record on December 15.

Required:
Prepare the appropriate journal entries for the date of declaration, date of record, and date of payment.

OBJECTIVE

EXAMPLE 10.3

Brief Exercise 10-34 Declaration of Cash Dividend

Redbird Corporation expected to pay its stockholders a dividend in January. The cash dividend of $62,000 was declared on December 31.

Required:

What is the appropriate journal entry, if any, to record this declaration on December 31?

OBJECTIVE

EXAMPLE 10.4

Brief Exercise 10-35 Stock Dividend

Augusta Corporation reported the following information: 50,000 shares of $4 par value common stock authorized, 42,000 shares common stock issued, 18,000 shares treasury stock.

Required:

1. What is the appropriate journal entry to record a 5% stock dividend if the market price of the common stock is $45 per share when the dividend is declared?
2. What is the appropriate journal entry to record a 27% stock dividend if the market price of the common stock is $45 per share when the dividend is declared?
3. **CONCEPTUAL CONNECTION** How do these transactions affect Augusta's total stockholders' equity?

OBJECTIVE

EXAMPLE 10.5

Brief Exercise 10-36 Preferred and Common Stock Dividends

Delafield Corporation has a single class of common stock and a single class of cumulative preferred stock. The cumulative preferred stock requires the corporation to pay an annual dividend of $14,000 to preferred stockholders. On January 1, 2023, Delafield's preferred dividends were 1 year in arrears. During the 3 years (2023–2025), Delafield's board of directors determined they would be able to pay $21,000, $23,000, and $26,000, respectively.

Required:

Show how these anticipated payments will be split between preferred and common stockholders.

Brief Exercise 10-37 Preferred Stock Dividends

OBJECTIVE

EXAMPLE 10.5

Eugene Corporation issued 25,000 shares outstanding of 6%, $5 par value, cumulative preferred stock. Eugene purchased 5,000 shares of its preferred stock to remain in its treasury. In 2021 and 2022, no dividends were declared on preferred stock. In 2023, Seashell had a profitable year and decided to pay dividends to stockholders of both preferred and common stock.

Required:

If Eugene has $75,000 available for dividends in 2023, how much could it pay to the common stockholders?

Use the following information for Brief Exercises 10-38 and 10-39:
Titanic Corporation's net income for the year is $450,000. On June 30, a $0.75 per-share cash dividend was declared for all common stockholders. Common stock in the amount of 38,000 shares was outstanding at the time. The market price of Titanic's stock at year end is $18 per share. Titanic had a $1,100,000 credit balance in retained earnings at the beginning of the year.

OBJECTIVE 4

Brief Exercise 10-38 Retained Earnings

Refer to the information for Titanic Corporation above.

Required:

Calculate the ending balance of retained earnings.

Brief Exercise 10-39 Retained Earnings

OBJECTIVE 4

Refer to the information for Titanic Corporation above. Assume that in July 31, Titanic discovered that prior year's depreciation was overstated by $75,000.

Required:

Prepare Titanic's retained earnings statement, assuming the prior year tax rate was 21%.

Brief Exercise 10-40 Stockholder Payout Ratios

OBJECTIVE 5

EXAMPLE 10.7

Super Duper Corporation had a string of successful years. Super Duper's executives wish to examine how its stockholders have been compensated for their contributed capital. The following information pertains to Super Duper Corporation:

Net income	$104,000
Dividends per common share	$1.50
Common shares	16,000
Purchases of treasury stock	$65,000
Common stock price	$25

Required:

Calculate the dividend yield, dividend payout, and total payout.

Brief Exercise 10-41 Stockholder Profitability Ratios

OBJECTIVE 5

EXAMPLE 10.6

The following information pertains to Capital Corporation:

Net income	$2,420,000
Average common equity	$18,250,000
Preferred stock, $10 par, 310,000	
issued, 10% cumulative	$3,100,000
Average common shares outstanding	675,000

Required:

Calculate the return on common equity and the earnings per share.

EXERCISES

Exercise 10-42 Accounting for Shares

OBJECTIVE 1

Kress Products' corporate charter authorized the firm to sell 800,000 shares of $10 par common stock. Kress sold 318,000 shares and reacquired 4,500 of those shares. The reacquired shares were held as treasury stock. Later Kress sold an additional 24,350 shares and purchased 8,200 more treasury shares.

Required:

Determine the number of issued and outstanding shares.

Exercise 10-43 Outstanding Stock

OBJECTIVE 1

Lars Corporation shows the following information in the stockholders' equity section of its balance sheet: The par value of common stock is $5, and the total balance in the Common Stock account is $225,000. There are 13,000 shares of treasury stock.

Required:

What is the number of shares outstanding?

> *Use the following information for Exercises 10-44 and 10-45:*
> Stahl Company was incorporated as a new business in January. The company is authorized to issue 600,000 shares of $2 par value common stock and 80,000 shares of 6%, $20 par value, cumulative preferred stock. In February, the company issued 75,000 shares of common stock for $15 per share and 5,000 shares of preferred stock for $25 per share. Net income for the year ended December 31 was $500,000.

OBJECTIVE

Exercise 10-44 Capital Stock

Refer to the information for Stahl Company above.

Required:

What is the amount of Stahl's total contributed capital at December 31?

OBJECTIVE

Exercise 10-45 Preparation of Stockholders' Equity Section

Refer to the information for Stahl Company above.

Required:

Prepare the stockholders' equity section of the balance sheet for Stahl Company.

OBJECTIVE

Exercise 10-46 Issuing Common Stock

Palan Products Inc. sold 46,750 shares of common stock to stockholders at the time of its incorporation. Palan received $48 per share for the stock.

Required:

1. Assume that the stock has a $16 par value per share. Prepare the journal entry to record the sale and issue of the stock.
2. Assume that the stock has a $9 stated value per share. Prepare the journal entry to record the sale and issue of the stock.
3. Assume that the stock has no par value and no stated value. Prepare the journal entry to record the sale and issue of the stock.
4. **CONCEPTUAL CONNECTION** How do the different par values affect total contributed capital and total stockholders' equity?

OBJECTIVE

Exercise 10-47 Issuing and Repurchasing Stock

Mohawk Company had the following transactions related to its common and preferred stock:

March 22	Sold 180,000 shares of $1 par common stock for $33 per share.
	Sold 1,500 shares of $5 par preferred stock at $11 per share.
November 9	Repurchased 25,000 shares of the common stock at $35 per share.

Required:
Prepare the journal entries for these transactions.

OBJECTIVE

Exercise 10-48 Prepare the Stockholders' Equity Section

Renee Corporation has the following stockholders' equity information:

	$5 Par Common	$10 Par Preferred
Additional paid-in capital	$2,250,000	$50,000
Shares:		
Authorized	750,000	40,000
Issued	300,000	8,000
Outstanding	250,000	8,000

Retained earnings is $1,837,000, and the cost of treasury shares is $1,200,000.

Required:

Prepare the stockholders' equity portion of Renee's balance sheet.

Exercise 10-49 Prepare the Stockholders' Equity Section

Wildcat Drilling has the following accounts on its trial balance.

OBJECTIVE ◀ 2

SHOW
ME HOW

	Debit	Credit
Retained Earnings		600,000
Cash	825,000	
Additional Paid-In Capital—Common		3,100,000
Additional Paid-In Capital—Preferred		400,000
Accounts Payable		345,000
Accounts Receivable	410,000	
Common Stock, $1 par		600,000
Preferred Stock, $10 par		340,000
Inventory	1,300,000	
Treasury Stock—Common (30,000 shares)	382,000	
Accumulated Other Comprehensive Income		70,000

Required:

Prepare the stockholders' equity portion of Wildcat's balance sheet.

Exercise 10-50 Interpret the Stockholders' Equity Section

Medici Inc. has the following stockholders' equity section of the balance sheet:

OBJECTIVE ◀ 2

Medici Inc.
Balance Sheet (Partial)

Stockholders' equity:		
Preferred stock, 100,000 shares authorized; 30,000		
issued and outstanding		$ 300,000
Common stock, 1,000,000 shares authorized;		
600,000 issued; 550,000 outstanding		1,200,000
Additional paid-in capital:		
Preferred stock	$ 90,000	
Common stock	4,800,000	
Total additional paid-in capital		4,890,000
Total capital stock		$6,390,000
Retained earnings		450,000
Accumulated other comprehensive income		22,000
Less: Treasury stock, at cost		(800,000)
Total stockholders' equity		$6,062,000

Required:

1. How many shares of preferred stock are authorized?
2. How many shares of common stock are outstanding?
3. What was the average selling price for the common stock when issued?
4. What was the average repurchase price for the treasury shares?
5. If the annual dividends on the preferred stock are $0.80 per share, what is the dividend rate on the preferred stock?

Exercise 10-51 Treasury Stock Transactions

Fritz Inc. had no treasury stock at the beginning of the year. During February, Fritz purchased 13,200 shares of treasury stock at $31 per share. In May, Fritz sold 5,500 of the treasury shares for $35 per share. In November, Fritz sold the remaining treasury shares for $22 per share.

Required:

Prepare journal entries for the February, May, and November treasury stock transactions.

Exercise 10-52 Cash Dividends on Common Stock

Berkwild Company is authorized to issue 2,000,000 shares of common stock. At the beginning of the year, Berkwild had 248,000 issued and outstanding shares. On July 2, Berkwild repurchased 4,610 shares of its common stock at $28 per share. On March 1 and September 1, Berkwild declared a cash dividend of $1.10 per share. The dividends were paid on April 1 and October 1.

Required:

1. Prepare the journal entries to record the declaration of the two cash dividends.
2. Prepare the journal entries to record the payment of the two dividends.
3. **CONCEPTUAL CONNECTION** Explain why the amounts of the two dividends are different.

Exercise 10-53 Cash Dividends on Common and Preferred Stock

Lemon Inc. has the following information regarding its preferred and common stock:

Preferred stock, $30 par, 12% cumulative; 300,000 shares authorized; 150,000 shares issued and outstanding

Common stock, $2 par; 2,500,000 shares authorized; 1,200,000 shares issued; 1,000,000 outstanding

At the beginning of the year, Lemon was 3 years in arrears on its preferred dividends. During the year, Lemon declared and paid dividends. As a result, the common stockholders received dividends of $0.45 per share.

Required:

1. What was the total amount of dividends declared and paid?
2. What journal entry was made at the date of declaration?

Exercise 10-54 Distribution to Stockholders

Owners invest in corporations through the purchase of stock.

Required:

CONCEPTUAL CONNECTION Describe two ways that corporations distribute assets to stockholders (without liquidating the company). Discuss their relative advantages and disadvantages.

Exercise 10-55 Stock Dividends

Crystal Corporation has the following information regarding its common stock: $10 par, with 500,000 shares authorized, 213,000 shares issued, and 183,700 shares outstanding.

Crystal declared and paid a 15% stock dividend when the market price of the common stock was $40 per share.

Required:

1. Prepare the journal entries to record declaration and payment of this stock dividend.
2. Prepare the journal entries to record declaration and payment assuming it was a 30% stock dividend.

Exercise 10-56 Stock Dividend

OBJECTIVE ◀ 3

The balance sheet of Cohen Enterprises includes the following stockholders' equity section:

Common stock, $1 par, 330,000 shares authorized,	
150,000 shares issued and outstanding	$150,000
Additional paid-in capital—common stock	341,800
Total capital stock	$491,800
Retained earnings	173,000
Total equity	$664,800

Required:

1. On April 15, when its stock was selling for $18 per share, Cohen Enterprises issued a small stock dividend. After making the journal entry to recognize the stock dividend, Cohen's total capital stock increased by $270,000. In percentage terms, what was the size of the stock dividend?

2. Ignoring the small stock dividend discussed in Requirement 1, assume that on June 1, when its stock was selling for $22 per share, Cohen issued a large stock dividend. After making the journal entry to recognize the stock dividend, Cohen's retained earnings decreased by $75,000. In percentage terms, what was the size of the stock dividend?

Exercise 10-57 Stock Split

OBJECTIVE ◀ 3

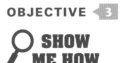

Birch Enterprises reported the following information: common stock, $3 par; 750,000 shares authorized; 400,000 shares issued and outstanding.

Required:

What is the typical effect of a 4-for-1 stock split on the information Birch Enterprises reports above? If the market value of the common stock is $600 per share when the stock split is declared, what would you expect the approximate market value per share to be immediately after the split?

Exercise 10-58 Stock Dividends and Stock Splits

OBJECTIVE ◀ 3

The balance sheet of Castle Corporation includes the following stockholders' equity section:

Common stock, $2 par, 80,000 shares authorized, 70,000	
shares issued and outstanding	$140,000
Additional paid-in capital—common stock	$363,400
Total capital stock	$503,400
Retained earnings	203,000
Total equity	$706,400

Required:

1. Assume that Castle issued 70,000 shares for cash at the inception of the corporation and that no new shares have been issued since. Determine how much cash was received for the shares issued at inception.

2. Assume that Castle issued 30,000 shares for cash at the inception of the corporation and subsequently declared a 2-for-1 stock split. Determine how much cash was received for the shares issued at inception.

3. Assume that Castle issued 67,000 shares for cash at the inception of the corporation and that the remaining 3,000 shares were issued as the result of stock dividends when the stock was selling for $63 per share. Determine how much cash was received for the shares issued at inception.

Exercise 10-59 Preferred Dividends

Eastern Inc.'s equity includes 8%, $25 par preferred stock. There are 100,000 shares authorized and 45,000 shares outstanding. Assume that Eastern declares and pays preferred dividends quarterly.

Required:

1. Prepare the journal entry to record declaration of one quarterly dividend.
2. Prepare the journal entry to record payment of the one quarterly dividend.

Exercise 10-60 Cumulative Preferred Dividends

Capital stock of Barr Company includes:

Common stock, $5 par, 650,000 shares outstanding	$3,250,000
Preferred stock, 15% cumulative, $60 par, 10,000 shares outstanding	600,000

As of December 31, 2024, 2 years' dividends are in arrears on the preferred stock. During 2025, Barr plans to pay dividends that total $360,000.

Required:

1. Determine the amount of dividends that will be paid to Barr's common and preferred stockholders in 2025.
2. If Barr paid $280,000 of dividends, determine how much each group of stockholders would receive.

OBJECTIVE 4

Exercise 10-61 Retained Earnings

Tigress Manufacturing had beginning retained earnings of $650,000. During the year, Tigress paid cash dividends of $70,000 to preferred stockholders and $55,000 to common stockholders. Net income for the year was $340,000.

Required:

1. Reproduce the Retained Earnings T-account for the year starting with the beginning balance.
2. Determine what Tigress's ending retained earnings is assuming that during the year it discovers that net income was overstated by $13,000 in prior years due to an error. The error was corrected and the current year's net income is correct.

Exercise 10-62 Retained Earnings

The December 31, 2024, comparative balance sheet of Smith Industries includes the following stockholders' equity section:

	2024	2023
Common stock, $2 par, 80,000 shares authorized, 60,000 shares issued and outstanding	$120,000	$120,000
Additional paid-in capital—common stock	371,800	371,800
Total capital stock	$491,800	$491,800
Retained earnings	173,000	116,000
Total equity	$664,800	$607,800

Required:

During 2024, Smith paid dividends of $0.50 per share. What was Smith's net income for 2024?

Exercise 10-63 Restrictions on Retained Earnings

At the end of the previous year, Longfellow Clothing had $226,700 of retained earnings, all unrestricted. During the current year, Longfellow earned net income of $92,000 and declared and paid cash dividends on common stock of $21,800. Additionally, Longfellow sold a bond issue with a covenant that required Longfellow to transfer from retained earnings to restricted retained earnings an amount equal to the principal of the bond issue, $50,000. At year end, Longfellow has 30,000 shares of $5 par common stock issued and outstanding. Additional paid-in capital—common stock is $236,500.

Required:

Prepare the stockholders' equity portion of Longfellow's year end balance sheet.

Exercise 10-64 Ratio Analysis

Consider the following information.

OBJECTIVE 5

SHOW ME HOW

Stock price	$55/share	Avg. common shares outstanding	850,000
Common dividends	$765,000	Dividends per common share	$0.90/share
Preferred dividends	$238,800	Net income	$15,485,000
2019 preferred stock	$6,162,000	2018 preferred stock	$5,299,000
2019 total stockholders' equity	$28,435,000	2018 total stockholders' equity	$25,483,000
Purchases of treasury stock	$120,000		

Required:

1. Calculate the stockholder payout ratios. (*Note:* Round answers to two decimal places.)
2. Calculate the stockholder profitability ratios. (*Note:* Round answers to two decimal places.)

Exercise 10-65 Ratio Analysis

OBJECTIVE 2

MJO Inc. has the following stockholders' equity section of the balance sheet:

MJO Inc.
Balance Sheet (Partial)

Stockholders' equity:		
Preferred stock, 100,000 shares authorized; 30,000		
issued and outstanding		$ 300,000
Common stock, 1,000,000 shares authorized; 600,000		
issued; 550,000 outstanding		1,200,000
Additional paid-in capital:		
Preferred stock	$ 90,000	
Common stock	4,800,000	
Total additional paid-in capital		4,890,000
Total capital stock		$6,390,000
Retained earnings		450,000
Accumulated other comprehensive income		22,000
Less: Treasury stock, at cost		(800,000)
Total stockholders' equity		$6,062,000

On the balance sheet date, MJO's stock was selling for $25 per share.

Required:

1. Assuming MJO's dividend yield is 1%, what are the dividends per common share?
2. Assuming MJO's dividend yield is 1% and its dividend payout is 20%, what is MJO's net income?

Exercise 10-66 Stockholders' Equity Terminology

A list of terms and a list of definitions or examples are presented below. Make a list of the numbers 1 through 12 and match the letter of the most directly related definition or example with each number.

Terms

1. stock warrant
2. date of record
3. par value
4. stock split
5. treasury stock
6. stock dividend

7. preferred stock
8. outstanding shares
9. authorized shares
10. declaration date
11. comprehensive income
12. retained earnings

Definitions and Examples

a. Capitalizes retained earnings.
b. Shares issued minus treasury shares.
c. Emerson Electric will pay a dividend to all persons holding shares of its common stock on December 15, even if they just bought the shares and sell them a few days later.
d. The accumulated earnings over the entire life of the corporation that has not been paid out in dividends.
e. Common Stock account balance divided by the number of shares issued.
f. The state of Louisiana set an upper limit of 1,000,000 on the number of shares that Gump's Catch Inc. can issue.
g. Shares that never earn dividends.
h. Any changes to stockholders' equity from transactions with nonowners.
i. A right to purchase stock at a specified future time and specified price.
j. A stock issue that requires no journal entry.
k. Shares that may earn guaranteed dividends.
l. On October 15, General Electric announced its intention to pay a dividend on common stock.

PROBLEM SET A

OBJECTIVE

Problem 10-67A Presentation of Stockholders' Equity

Green Line, a newly organized corporation, engaged in the following stockholders' equity activities:

a. Secured approval for a corporate charter that authorizes Green Line to sell 1,500,000, $2 par common shares and 200,000, $25 par preferred shares.
b. Sold 120,000 of the common shares for $9 per share.
c. Sold 65,000 of the preferred shares for $32 per share.
d. Repurchased 15,000 shares of the common stock at a cost of $11 per share.
e. Earned net income of $460,000.
f. Paid dividends of $52,000.

Required:

Prepare the stockholders' equity portion of Green Line's balance sheet after accounting for these activities.

Problem 10-68A Issuing Common and Preferred Stock

OBJECTIVE ◂ 2

Klaus Herrmann, a biochemistry professor, organized Bioproducts Inc. early this year. The firm will manufacture antibiotics using gene splicing technology. Bioproducts' charter authorizes the firm to issue 10,000 shares of 7%, $70 par preferred stock and 150,000 shares of $5 par common stock. During the year, the firm engaged in the transactions listed below.

a. Issued 50,000 common shares to Klaus Herrmann in exchange for $550,000 cash.
b. Sold 8,000 common shares to a potential customer for $12 per share.
c. Issued 4,000 shares of preferred stock to a venture capital firm for $85 per share.
d. Gave 100 shares of common stock to Margaret Robb, a local attorney, in exchange for Margaret's work in arranging for the firm's incorporation. Margaret usually charges $1,200 for comparable work.

Required:

Prepare a journal entry for each of these transactions.

Problem 10-69A Treasury Stock Transactions

OBJECTIVE ◂ 3

Hansen Inc. engaged in the following transactions during the current year:

a. Repurchased 13,000 shares of its own $1 par common stock for $14 per share on January 14.
b. Sold 2,000 treasury shares to employees for $6 per share on January 31.
c. Repurchased 3,000 more shares of the $1 par common stock for $16 per share on July 24.
d. Sold the remaining 11,000 shares from the January 14 purchase and 1,200 of the shares from the July 24 purchase to employees for $6.50 per share on August 1.

Required:

1. Prepare journal entries for each of these transactions.
2. **CONCEPTUAL CONNECTION** Determine what the effect on total stockholders' equity is for each of the four transactions.

Problem 10-70A Statement of Stockholders' Equity

OBJECTIVE ◂ 1 2

At the beginning of the year Haley Corporation had the following equity accounts and balances:

Common stock, $10 par	$800,000
Additional paid-in capital—common stock	200,000
Retained earnings	279,000

During the year Haley engaged in the following transactions involving its equity accounts:
a. Sold 5,000 shares of common stock for $19 per share.
b. Sold 1,200 shares of 12%, $50 par preferred stock at $75 per share.
c. Declared and paid cash dividends of $22,000.
d. Repurchased 1,000 shares of treasury stock (common) for $24 per share.
e. Sold 300 of the treasury shares for $26 per share.

Required:

1. Prepare the journal entries for Transactions a through e.
2. Net income for the year was $123,700. Prepare a statement of stockholders' equity at year end.

Problem 10-71A Common Dividends

OBJECTIVE ◂ 3

Fusion Payroll Service began the year with 1,200,000 authorized and 375,000 issued and outstanding $5 par common shares. During the year, Fusion entered into the following transactions:
a. Declared a $0.30 per-share cash dividend on March 10.
b. Paid the $0.30 per-share dividend on April 10.
c. Repurchased 8,000 common shares at a cost of $18 each on May 2.

(Continued)

d. Sold 1,500 unissued common shares for $23 per share on June 9.

e. Declared a $0.45 per-share cash dividend on August 10.

f. Paid the $0.45 per-share dividend on September 10.

g. Declared and paid a 5% stock dividend on October 15 when the market price of the common stock was $25 per share.

h. Declared a $0.50 per-share cash dividend on November 10.

i. Paid the $0.50 per-share dividend on December 10.

Required:

1. Prepare journal entries for each of these transactions. (*Note:* Round to the nearest dollar.)

2. Determine the total dollar amount of dividends (cash and stock) for the year.

3. **CONCEPTUAL CONNECTION** Determine the effect on total assets and total stockholders' equity of these dividend transactions.

OBJECTIVE 3

Problem 10-72A Stock Dividends and Stock Splits

Lance Products' balance sheet includes total assets of $587,000 and the following equity account balances at December 31:

Common stock, $2 par, 80,000 shares issued and outstanding	$160,000
Additional paid-in capital—common stock	24,000
Total capital stock	$184,000
Retained earnings	217,000
Total stockholders' equity	$401,000

Lance's common stock is selling for $12 per share on December 31.

Required:

1. How much would Lance Products have reported for total assets and retained earnings on December 31 if the firm had declared and paid a $15,000 cash dividend on December 31? Prepare the journal entry for this cash dividend.

2. How much would Lance have reported for total assets and retained earnings on December 31 if the firm had issued a 15% stock dividend on December 31? Prepare the journal entry for this stock dividend.

3. **CONCEPTUAL CONNECTION** How much would Lance have reported for total assets and retained earnings on December 31 if the firm had effected a 2-for-1 stock split on December 31? Is a journal entry needed to record the stock split? Why or why not?

OBJECTIVE 3

Problem 10-73A Preferred Dividends

Stevens Industries had the following preferred stock outstanding at the end of a recent year:

$5 par, 9%	12,000 shares
$10 par, 9%, cumulative	6,000 shares
$25 par, 10%, cumulative, convertible	9,000 shares
$50 par, 12%, nonparticipating	10,000 shares

Required:

1. Determine the amount of annual dividends on each issue of preferred stock and the total annual dividend on all four issues.

2. Calculate what the amount of dividends in arrears would be if the dividends were omitted for 1 year.

Problem 10-74A Ratio Analysis

OBJECTIVE ◀ 5

Consider the following information taken from the stockholders' equity section:

	(dollar amounts in thousands)	
	2024	**2023**
Preferred stock	$ 1,000	$ 1,000
Common stock, 334,328,193 and 330,961,869 shares issued in 2024 and 2023, respectively	3,343	3,310
Additional paid-in capital—common stock	766,382	596,239
Retained earnings	5,460,629	4,630,390
Accumulated other comprehensive (loss) income	(206,662)	58,653
Treasury stock (76,275,837 and 56,960,213 shares in 2024 and 2023, respectively) at cost	(3,267,955)	(2,205,987)
Total stockholders' equity	$ 2,756,737	$ 3,083,605

Additional Information (all numbers in thousands other than per-share information):	**2024**
Weighted average common shares outstanding	184,000
Price per share at year end	$105.45
Net income	$1,358,950
Preferred dividends	$100,000
Common dividends	$213,440
Common dividends per share	$1.16
Stock repurchases	$834,975

Required:

1. Calculate the following for 2024. (*Note:* Round answers to two decimal places.)

Stockholder Payout	**Stockholder Profitability**
Dividend yield	Return on common equity
Dividend payout	EPS
Total payout	
Stock repurchase payout	

2. **CONCEPTUAL CONNECTION** Assume 2023 ratios were:

Stockholder Payout	**Stockholder Profitability**
Dividend yield: 0.85%	Return on common equity: 34.26%
Dividend payout: 9.80%	EPS: $3.51
Total payout: 70.00%	
Stock repurchase payout: 60.20%	

and the current year industry averages are:

Stockholder Payout	**Stockholder Profitability**
Dividend yield: 0.76%	Return on common equity: 23.81%
Dividend payout: 12.35%	EPS: $1.23
Total payout: 48.37%	
Stock repurchase payout: 36.02%	

How do you interpret the company's payout and profitability performance?

PROBLEM SET B

Problem 10-67B Presentation of Stockholders' Equity

OBJECTIVE ◀ 1

Steven's Restorations, a newly organized corporation, engaged in the following stockholders' equity activities:

(Continued)

a. Secured approval for a corporate charter that authorizes Steven's to sell 1,000,000, $10 par common shares and 75,000, $100 par preferred shares.
b. Sold 480,000 of the common shares for $15 per share.
c. Sold 25,000 of the preferred shares for $105 per share.
d. Repurchased 2,000 shares of the common stock at a cost of $18 per share.
e. Earned net income of $107,000.
f. Paid dividends of $13,000.

Required:

Prepare the stockholders' equity portion of Steven's balance sheet after accounting for these activities.

OBJECTIVE   **Problem 10-68B Issuing Common and Preferred Stock**

Mallard Furniture recently became an incorporated furniture manufacturer after years of being run as a successful family business. Mallard's charter authorizes the firm to issue 10,000 shares of 8%, $25 par preferred stock and 50,000 shares of $2 par common stock. During the year, the company engaged in the following transactions:

a. Issued 25,000 common shares to Mallard's founding family in exchange for $140,000 cash.
b. Sold 5,000 common shares to a potential customer for $13 per share.
c. Issued 2,000 shares of preferred stock to a venture capital firm for $45 per share.
d. Gave 50 shares of common stock to Kelsey Kennedy, a local attorney, in exchange for Kelsey's help on a legal matter. Kelsey usually charges $1,500 for comparable work and this amount should be classified as a legal expense.

Required:

Prepare a journal entry for each of these transactions.

OBJECTIVE   **Problem 10-69B Treasury Stock Transactions**

Bentonite Adhesives Inc. engaged in the following transactions during the current year:

a. Repurchased 8,000 shares of its own $5 par common stock for $13 per share on January 14.
b. Sold 2,600 of the treasury shares to employees for $8 per share on January 31.
c. Repurchased 2,000 more shares of the $5 par common stock for $17 each on July 24.
d. Sold the remaining 5,400 shares from the January 14 purchase and 800 of the shares from the July 24 purchase to employees for $9 per share on August 1.

Required:

1. Prepare journal entries for each of these transactions.
2. **CONCEPTUAL CONNECTION** Determine the effect on total stockholders' equity for each of the four transactions.

OBJECTIVE   **Problem 10-70B Statement of Stockholders' Equity**

At the beginning of the year, Stanley Utilities Inc. had the following equity accounts and balances:

Common stock, $1 par	$4,500,000
Additional paid-in capital—common stock	1,375,000
Retained earnings	188,000

During the year Stanley Utilities engaged in the following transactions involving its equity accounts:

a. Sold 3,300 shares of common stock for $15 per share.
b. Sold 1,000 shares of 12%, $100 par preferred stock at $105 per share.
c. Declared and paid cash dividends of $8,000.
d. Repurchased 1,000 shares of treasury stock (common) for $38 per share.
e. Sold 400 of the treasury shares for $42 per share.

Required:

1. Prepare the journal entries for Transactions a through e.
2. Net income for the year was $87,000. Prepare a statement of stockholders' equity at year end.

Problem 10-71B Common Dividends

OBJECTIVE 3

Thompson Payroll Service began the year with 1,500,000 authorized and 820,000 issued and outstanding $8 par common shares. During the year Thompson entered into the following transactions:

a. Declared a $0.20 per-share cash dividend on March 24.
b. Paid the $0.20 per-share dividend on April 6.
c. Repurchased 13,000 common shares for the treasury at a cost of $12 each on May 9.
d. Sold 2,500 unissued common shares for $15 per share on June 19.
e. Declared a $0.40 per-share cash dividend on August 1.
f. Paid the $0.40 per-share dividend on September 14.
g. Declared and paid a 10% stock dividend on October 25 when the market price of the common stock was $15 per share.
h. Declared a $0.45 per-share cash dividend on November 20.
i. Paid the $0.45 per-share dividend on December 20.

Required:

1. Prepare journal entries for each of these transactions. (*Note*: Round to the nearest dollar.)
2. What is the total dollar amount of dividends (cash and stock) for the year?
3. **CONCEPTUAL CONNECTION** Determine the effect on total assets and total stockholders' equity of these dividend transactions.

Problem 10-72B Stock Dividends and Stock Splits

OBJECTIVE 3

Heller Company's balance sheet includes total assets of $3,872,000 and the following equity account balances at December 31:

Common stock, $5 par, 10,000 shares issued and outstanding	$ 95,000
Additional paid-in capital—common stock	162,000
Total capital stock	$257,000
Retained earnings	411,000
Total stockholders' equity	$668,000

Heller's common stock is selling for $23 per share on December 31.

Required:

1. Determine how much Heller's Products would have reported for total assets and retained earnings on December 31 if the firm had declared and paid a $22,000 cash dividend on December 31. Prepare the journal entry for this cash dividend.
2. Determine how much Heller would have reported for total assets and retained earnings on December 31 if the firm had issued a 12% stock dividend on December 31. Prepare the journal entry for this stock dividend.
3. **CONCEPTUAL CONNECTION** How much would Heller have reported for total assets and retained earnings on December 31, 2019, if the firm had effected a 2-for-1 stock split on December 31? Is a journal entry needed to record the stock split? Why or why not?

Problem 10-73B Preferred Dividends

OBJECTIVE 3

Steel Corporation had the following preferred stock outstanding at the end of a recent year:

$20 par, 9%	30,000 shares
$25 par, 10%, cumulative	15,000 shares
$100 par, 6%, cumulative, convertible	20,000 shares
$100 par, 8%, nonparticipating	8,000 shares

(Continued)

Required:

1. Determine the amount of annual dividends on each issue of preferred stock and the total annual dividend on all four issues.
2. Calculate what the amount of dividends in arrears would be if the dividends were omitted for 1 year.

OBJECTIVE ▶5▶

Problem 10-74B Ratio Analysis

Consider the following information taken from the stockholders' equity section:

	(dollar amounts in thousands)	
	2024	**2023**
Preferred stock	$ 1,000	$ 2,000
Common stock, 230,000,000 and 176,000,000 shares		
issued in 2024 and 2023, respectively	2,300	1,760
Additional paid-in capital—common stock	567,000	432,000
Retained earnings	4,604,600	3,700,000
Accumulated other comprehensive (loss) income	(454,600)	147,000
Treasury stock (37,000,000 and 19,000,000 shares in		
2024 and 2023, respectively) at cost	(1,750,000)	(975,000)
Total stockholders' equity	$ 2,970,300	$3,307,760

Additional Information (all numbers in thousands other than per-share information):	2024
Weighted average common shares outstanding	200,000
Price per share at year end	$58.30
Net income	$1,584,000
Preferred dividends	$50,000
Common dividends	$300,000
Common dividends per share	$1.50
Stock repurchases	$850,000

Required:

1. Calculate the following. (*Note*: Round answers to two decimal places.)

Stockholder Payout	Stockholder Profitability
Dividend yield	Return on common equity
Dividend payout	EPS
Total payout	
Stock repurchase payout	

2. **CONCEPTUAL CONNECTION** Assume last year's ratios were:

Stockholder Payout	Stockholder Profitability
Dividend yield: 2.31%	Return on common equity: 37.41%
Dividend payout: 13.65%	EPS: $6.12
Total payout: 78.59%	
Stock repurchase payout: 64.94%	

and the current year industry averages are:

Stockholder Payout	Stockholder Profitability
Dividend yield: 2.50%	Return on common equity: 44.44%
Dividend payout: 15.10%	EPS: $6.48
Total payout: 55.10%	
Stock repurchase payout: 40.00%	

How do you interpret the company's payout and profitability performance?

CASES

Case 10-75 Ethics and Equity

Roger and Gordon are middle managers at a large, publicly traded corporation. Roger tells Gordon that the company is about to sign an exclusive product distribution agreement with a small, publicly traded manufacturer. This contract will quadruple the manufacturer's revenue. Roger mentions to Gordon that the manufacturer's stock price will likely go "through the roof." Gordon says, "Maybe we should buy some stock."

Required:

1. Are Roger and Gordon being smart, being unethical but not breaking the law, or breaking the law?
2. How does the SEC monitor such activity?

Case 10-76 Stock Transactions and Ethics

Marilyn Cox is the office manager for DTR Inc. DTR constructs, owns, and manages apartment complexes. Marilyn has been involved in negotiations between DTR and prospective lenders as DTR attempts to raise $425 million to use to build apartments in a growing area of Tulsa. Based on her experience with past negotiations, Marilyn knows that lenders are concerned about DTR's debt to equity ratio. When the negotiations began, DTR had debt of $80 million and equity of $50 million. Marilyn believes that DTR's debt to equity ratio of 1.6 is probably the minimum that lenders will accept.

Marilyn is also aware that DTR issued $10 million of common stock to a long-time friend of the corporation's president in exchange for some land just before the negotiations with lenders began. The president's friend constructs and sells single-family homes. The land is in an area zoned only for single-family housing and would be an attractive site for single-family homes. Thus, the land is worth at least $10 million. However, DTR does not intend to build any single-family homes.

Required:

1. What would have been DTR's debt to equity ratio if the $10 million of stock had not been issued for the land?
2. If Marilyn believes that the $10 million stock issue was undertaken only to improve DTR's debt to equity ratio and that it will be reversed whenever the president's friend wants the land back or when DTR's debt to equity position improves, what should she do?

Case 10-77 Common and Preferred Stock

Expansion Company now has $2,500,000 of equity (100,000 common shares). Current income is $400,000 and Expansion Company needs $500,000 of additional capital. The firm's bankers insist that this capital be acquired by selling either common or preferred stock. If Expansion sells common stock, the ownership share of the current stockholders will be diluted because 20,000 more shares will be sold. If preferred stock is sold, the dividend rate will be 15% of the $500,000. Furthermore, the preferred stock will have to be cumulative, participating, and convertible into 20,000 shares of common stock.

Required:

Indicate whether Expansion should sell additional common or preferred stock, and explain the reasons for your choice.

Case 10-78 Leverage

Enrietto Aquatic Products' offer to acquire Fiberglass Products for $2,000,000 cash has been accepted. Enrietto has $1,000,000 of liquid assets that can be converted into cash and plans to either sell common stock or issue bonds to raise the remaining $1,000,000. Before this acquisition, Enrietto's condensed balance sheet and condensed income statement were as follows:

Enrietto Aquatic Products
Preacquisition Condensed Balance Sheet

Assets		Liabilities and Equity	
Assets	$20,000,000	Liabilities	$ 8,000,000
		Common stock, $10 par	6,000,000
		Retained earnings	6,000,000
		Total liabilities & stockholders' equity	$20,000,000

Enrietto Aquatic Products
Preacquisition Condensed Income Statement

Income from operations	$ 6,000,000
Less: Interest expense	(1,000,000)
Income before taxes	$ 5,000,000
Less: Income taxes expense (0.34)	(1,700,000)
Net income	$ 3,300,000

Enrietto's policy is to pay 60% of net income to stockholders as dividends. Enrietto expects to be able to raise the $1,000,000 it needs for the acquisition by selling 50,000 shares of common stock at $20 each or by issuing $1,000,000 of 20-year, 12% bonds. Enrietto expects income from operations to grow by $700,000 after Fiberglass Products has been acquired. (Interest expense will increase if debt is used to finance the acquisition.)

Required:

1. Determine the return on equity (net income/total equity) before the acquisition and for both financing alternatives (round percentages to two decimal places).
2. If Enrietto sells additional stock, what will be the cash outflow for dividends?
3. If Enrietto sells bonds, what will be the net cash outflows for new interest and for all dividends? (Remember that interest is tax-deductible.)
4. Assume that Enrietto sells stock and that none of the preacquisition stockholders buy any of the 50,000 new shares. What total amount of dividends will the preacquisition stockholders receive after the acquisition? How does this amount compare with the dividends they receive before the acquisition?
5. Which alternative is better for Enrietto's preacquisition stockholders?

Case 10-79 Research and Analysis Using the Annual Report

Obtain **Priceline.com**'s 2019 10-K (filed February 26, 2020) either through the "Investor Relations" portion of its website (do a web search for Priceline investor relations), or go to www.sec.gov and click "Company Filings Search" under "Filings."

Required:

1. What is the par value of the common stock and how many shares of common stock are authorized, issued, and outstanding at December 31, 2019?
2. What is Priceline.com's dividend policy? Why do you think they have this policy?
3. What is the common stockholders' equity at December 31, 2019 (in millions)?
4. How many shares of treasury stock were held at the end of 2019? What did they cost?
5. Calculate the dividend and stock repurchase payouts. (*Note:* Round answers to two decimal places and find common stock repurchases on the Statement of Cash Flows.)

6. Taking the weighted average of basic common shares outstanding from the EPS information at the bottom of the income statement, calculate the stockholder profitability ratios. (*Note:* While the financial statement amounts are in millions, the weighted average of basic common shares outstanding is given in thousands. You will need to adjust this number to millions.)

Case 10-80 Comparative Analysis: Kroger versus Sprouts Farmers Market

Refer to the 10-K reports of **Kroger** and **Sprouts Farmers Market** that are available for download from the companion website at Cengage.com.

Common Stock Price at fiscal year end:

	2019	2018
Kroger	$26.86	$28.07
Sprouts Farmers Market	19.69	22.98

Note: Round all answers to two decimal places. Numbers, other than per-share amounts, are in thousands.

Required:

1. What percentage of the total common shares issued has Kroger repurchased and retained as treasury shares at fiscal year end 2019? How many shares of common stock did Sprouts repurchase, how much did they spend on the share repurchases, and what did they do with the shares?
2. Calculate Kroger's and Sprouts' dividend yield and dividend payout for fiscal years 2018 and 2019. Use "Net earnings attributable to the Kroger Co." for Kroger instead of net income in the ratio calculations.
3. Calculate Kroger's and Sprouts' total payout and stock repurchase payout for fiscal years 2018 and 2019. Use "Net earnings attributable to the Kroger Co." for Kroger instead of net income in the ratio calculations.
4. Compare Kroger's and Sprouts' stockholder payouts based on the values and trends identified in these stockholder payout ratios.
5. Calculate Kroger's and Sprouts' return on common equity and EPS for fiscal years 2018 and 2019. When calculating EPS for Kroger, you will need to subtract $34 and $19 from Net Income for 2018 and 2019, respectively. These amounts are the combined distributed and undistributed earnings to participating securities as mentioned in the Earnings per Common Share footnote (Note 11) of Kroger's 2019 10-K. Such adjustments are very unusual but are necessary, in this case, to match up to EPS shown on the Income Statements. Do not subtract these amounts from Net Income when calculating return on common equity.
6. Compare the values and trends of these stockholder profitability ratios for Kroger and Sprouts.

ANNUAL REPORT PROBLEM

Download the 10-K for Lowes from the companion website at Cengage.com.

Required:

1. What does the company report for the following accounts for the most current fiscal year?
   - Common stockholders' equity
   - Common stock dividends
   - Preferred Stock dividends
   - Treasury stock
   - Net income
   - Common shares outstanding

(Continued)

2. What is the par value of the common stock?
3. a. How many common shares are authorized?
   b. How many common shares are issued?
4. Does the company have any preferred stock? If so, give the dollar amount.
5. Assume the company projects the following:
   - No common stock is planned to be issued but the company does plan to buy back 7 million shares at an average price of $92 per share.
   - Common stockholders' equity is expected to increase by 8%
   - Net income is expected to increase by 3%.
   - Common stock dividends are expected to increase by 2%.

   Assume all other items remain unchanged from the prior year. Provide the forecasted balances for the next fiscal year for the following accounts:
   - Common stockholders' equity
   - Common stock dividends
   - Preferred stock dividends
   - Treasury stock
   - Net income
   - Common shares outstanding
6. Compute the forecasted return on common equity (round to two decimal places).
7. Compute the forecasted earnings per share (round to two decimal places).
8. Compute the forecasted dividend payout (round to two decimal places).

Note: *While the Annual Report problems in the textbook are static, when assigned in CNOW, these activities are algorithmic and the answers may vary from what appears in the Solutions Manual.*

CONTINUING PROBLEM

FRONT ROW ENTERTAINMENT

After purchasing the five venues in June 2024, Front Row needed additional cash to renovate and operate these venues. While the company had successfully borrowed money before (from bank loans as well as from the issuance of bonds), it could not find a lender willing to invest in the business due to the large amount of debt that the company currently has on its balance sheet.

With debt financing out of the question, Front Row considers its other options. The name of an old college friend, Steve Trotter, immediately comes to Cam and Anna's mind. Steve has previous work experience in the retail industry and expressed a desire to manage Front Row's current merchandising operations (the sale of DVDs). His vision was to expand the operations to include apparel (t-shirts, hats, etc.) and other items (such as bobble-head dolls of the artists). In addition, several other family members have expressed an interest in investing in the company.

Front Row was authorized to issue 25,000 shares of its $1 par common stock. On January 1, 2023, it issued Cam and Anna 8,000 shares each for $1 per share. Front Row was also authorized to issue 20,000 shares of 8%, $50 par preferred stock. The following transactions occurred during the remainder of 2024.

June 15		Issued 2,000 shares of $1 par common stock to Steve for $20 per share.
July 1		Issued 3,000 shares of $50 preferred stock to family members for $75 per share.
	10	Repurchased 700 common shares at $16 per share.
Aug. 5		The board of directors declared a $25,000 dividend to all stockholders of record on August 31, 2024. The dividend will be paid on September 15, 2024.
Sept. 15		The $25,000 dividend was paid.
Dec. 15		300 of the treasury shares were reissued at $22 per share.

Front Row had $53,250 of retained earnings to be included in the December 31, 2024, balance sheet.

Required:

1. Prepare the journal entries to record the above transactions.
2. Prepare the stockholders' equity section of the balance sheet at December 31, 2024.

Integrating Accounting for Liabilities and Equity

Obtain Apple's fiscal year 2019 10-K (filed October 31, 2019) either from the "Investor Relations" portion of its website (do a web search for "Apple Investor Relations") or from www.sec.gov by clicking "Company Filings Search" under "Filings."

Required:

Using Apple's 10-K, answer the following questions (*Hint:* It may be easier to use the Word or the PDF file, and use the search feature within the program.):

1. Calculate Apple's current, quick, and cash ratios for 2018 and 2019. The industry averages for these ratios for 2019 were 1.72, 1.41, and 0.77, respectively. Comment on Apple's short-term liquidity.

2. Calculate Apple's debt to equity, long-term debt to equity, and times interest earned (accrual basis) for 2018 and 2019. The industry averages for these ratios for 2019 were 52.42%, 36.41%, and 13.83, respectively. You will need to read Note 4 to find the amount of interest expense. Comment on Apple's mix of debt and equity and long-term solvency.

3. Calculate Apple's return on equity for 2018 and 2019 (stockholders' equity for 2017 was $134,047 million). The industry average for 2019 was 15.26%. Comment on Apple's profitability.

4. Calculate Apple's dividend payout, stock repurchase payout, and total payout for 2018 and 2019. What are Apple's objectives with their dividend policy and stock repurchase plan (see the "Capital Return Program" portion of Item 7: Management Discussion and Analysis)?

11

The Statement of Cash Flows

After studying Chapter 11, you should be able to:

1. Explain the purpose of a statement of cash flows.

2. Identify and classify business activities that produce cash inflows and outflows.

3. Understand the relationship between changes in cash and the changes in the balance sheet accounts.

4. Prepare the cash flows from operating activities section of a statement of cash flows using the indirect method.

5. Prepare the cash flows from investing activities section of a statement of cash flows.

6. Prepare the cash flows from financing activities section of a statement of cash flows.

7. Analyze information contained in the statement of cash flows.

8. *(Appendix 11A)* Prepare the cash flows from operating activities section of a statement of cash flows using the direct method.

9. *(Appendix 11B)* Use a spreadsheet to prepare the statement of cash flows.

Daniel Acker/Bloomberg/Getty Images

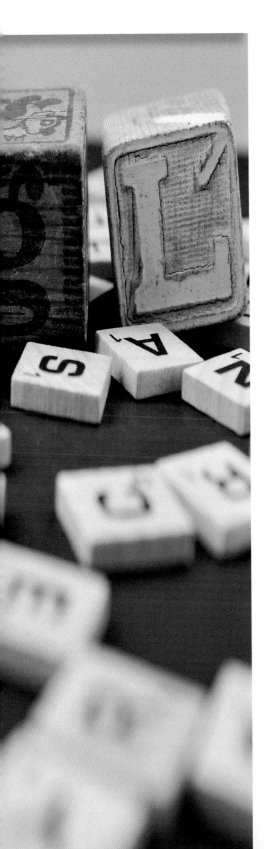

with Alphabet

In 1988, Larry Page and Sergey Brin, two Ph.D. students at Stanford University, founded Google in an attempt to build a better Internet search engine. Over the next two decades, Google became one of the world's leading technology companies, offering services such as Google Docs, Gmail, and Google Drive that extend beyond its technology roots. After a corporate restructuring in 2015, Google became the largest subsidiary of a holding company, Alphabet Inc. With cash of over $18 billion and marketable securities of over $101 billion, Alphabet is considered a "cash king" among the S&P 500.

In addition to the income statement, balance sheet, and retained earnings statement, companies are also required to provide a statement of cash flows. The statement of cash flows measures a company's inflows (sources) and outflows (uses) of cash during a period of time. While net income provides important information, the recognition of revenues and expenses can occur at different times than the related cash inflow or outflow. Therefore, a company's net income does not always equal the amount of cash that it received and spent. In addition to providing important information that aids in understanding how a company generates and uses cash, the statement of cash flows also allows users to identify differences between net income and cash flow.

Cash is the lifeblood of any business. A healthy cash flow is required if a company is to meet its current operating obligations, replace its worn machinery and equipment, pursue profitable new opportunities, or provide dividends to its stockholders. With operating cash flow of more than $54 billion, it's easy to see why many consider Alphabet cash royalty.

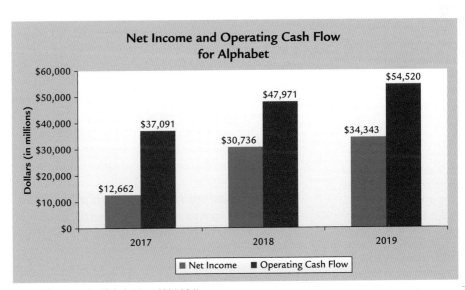

Net Income and Operating Cash Flow for Alphabet

	2017	2018	2019
Net Income	$12,662	$30,736	$34,343
Operating Cash Flow	$37,091	$47,971	$54,520

Source: Company for Alphabet Inc. 2016 10-K

OBJECTIVE

Explain the purpose of a statement of cash flows.

ROLE OF THE STATEMENT OF CASH FLOWS

In addition to being interested in the information in accrual-based financial statements such as the balance sheet and income statement, most financial statement users also want to know how a company obtained and used its cash. The purpose of the **statement of cash flows** is to provide relevant information about a company's cash receipts (inflows of cash) and cash payments (outflows of cash) during an accounting period.

The statement of cash flows is one of the primary financial statements. Because the other financial statements—the income statement, balance sheet, and statement of retained earnings—provide only limited information about a company's cash flows, the statement of cash flows can be viewed as a complement to these other financial statements. That is, while the income statement provides information about the company's performance on an accrual basis, it does not tell how much cash was generated or used as a result of the company's operations. Similarly, the balance sheet provides information on the changes in net assets, but it doesn't provide information on how much cash was used or received in relation to these changes. The statement of cash flows fills this void by explaining the sources from which a company has acquired cash (inflows of cash) and the uses to which the business has applied cash (outflows of cash).

The information in a statement of cash flows helps investors, creditors, and others in the following ways.

Assessing a company's ability to produce future net cash inflows One goal of financial reporting is to provide information that is helpful in predicting the amounts, timing, and uncertainty of a company's future cash flows. While net income is generally viewed to be the best single predictor of future cash flows, information about cash receipts and cash payments can, along with net income, allow users to predict future cash flows better than net income alone.

Judging a company's ability to meet its obligations and pay dividends As a company performs its business activities, it will incur various obligations. For example, suppliers want to know if the company can pay for the goods purchased on credit. Employees want to assess the company's ability to pay larger salaries and fringe benefits. Lenders are interested in the company's ability to repay the principal and interest on amounts borrowed. Similarly, investors often wish to know if a company is generating enough cash to be able to pay dividends and expand its productive capacity. In addition, success or failure in business often depends on whether a company has enough cash to meet unexpected obligations and take advantage of unexpected opportunities. Information about cash receipts and cash payments helps financial statement users make these important judgments.

Estimating the company's needs for external financing As companies operate, various expenditures can be financed through either internally generated funds or by external financing (debt or equity). Knowing the amount of cash that a company generates internally helps financial statement users assess whether a company will have to borrow additional funds from creditors or seek additional cash from investors.

Understanding the relationship between net income and cash flows The amount of a company's net income and the amount of cash generated from operations are often different amounts due to the application of accrual accounting concepts. Because of the judgments and estimates involved in accrual accounting, many financial statement users question the usefulness of reported income. However, when provided with cash flow information, these users can gain insights into the quality and reliability of the reported income amounts.

Evaluating the balance sheet effects of both cash and noncash investing and financing transactions Not all changes in cash are directly related to a company's

Next Level

If we already have the balance sheet and income statement, why is a statement of cash flows so important?

ANSWER:
The statement of cash flows provides information about a company's sources and uses of cash. Knowing how companies obtain and use cash provides users with a good idea of a company's financial strength and its long-term viability. The decision to invest in a company is much safer if a potential investor—be it a bank or stockholder—knows how much cash is being produced and where it is coming from.

day-to-day operations. Instead, a company may make investments in productive assets as it expands its operations or upgrades its facilities. In addition, a company may seek sources of cash by issuing debt or equity. These activities can be just as crucial to a company's long-term success as its current operations.

In summary, information about a company's cash receipts and cash payments, along with information contained in the balance sheet and the income statement, is critical to understanding and analyzing a company's operations.

In this chapter, we will explain how a statement of cash flows is prepared from the information contained in the balance sheet and the income statement. We will explore the measurement, presentation, and analysis of cash flow information and address the following questions:

- What are the principal sources and uses of cash?
- How is the statement of cash flows prepared and reported to external users?
- How is the statement of cash flows used by investors, creditors, and others?

CASH FLOW CLASSIFICATIONS

OBJECTIVE 2

Identify and classify business activities that produce cash inflows and outflows.

Because our focus is on cash flows, it is important to have a clear understanding of what is included in the term *cash*. For purposes of the statement of cash flows, cash includes both funds on hand (coins and currency) and cash equivalents. Recall from Chapter 4 that cash equivalents are short-term, highly liquid investments that are readily convertible to cash and have original maturities of 3 months or less. Because of their high liquidity or nearness to cash, cash equivalents are treated as cash in the statement of cash flows.

During an accounting period, a company engages in the three fundamental business activities discussed in Chapter 1—operating activities, investing activities, and financing activities. Each of these activities can increase (a cash inflow) or decrease (a cash outflow) a company's cash balance. Therefore, the statement of cash flows reconciles the beginning and ending balances of cash by describing the effects of business activities on a company's cash balance. This relationship is shown in Exhibit 11.1.

How the Statement of Cash Flows Links the Two Balance Sheets   **EXHIBIT 11.1**

Balance Sheet Jan. 1			Statement of Cash Flows For the year ended Dec. 31		Balance Sheet Dec. 31	
Assets			Operating activities	$ 3,400	**Assets**	
Cash	$1,800		Investing activities	(5,100)	Cash	$2,400
Other	6,300		Financing activities	2,300	Other	7,100
Total	$8,100				Total	$9,500
			Net change in cash	$ 600		
Liabilities and					**Liabilities and**	
Equity					**Equity**	
Liabilities	$4,200		Beginning cash	1,800	Liabilities	$4,400
Equity	3,900		Ending cash	$ 2,400	Equity	5,100
Total	$8,100				Total	$9,500

CASH FLOWS FROM OPERATING ACTIVITIES

Cash flows from operating activities (or operating cash flows) are the cash inflows and outflows that relate to acquiring (purchasing or manufacturing), selling, and delivering goods or services. Cash inflows from operating activities include:

- cash sales to customers
- collection of accounts receivable arising from credit sales
- cash dividends received
- interest received on investments in equity and debt securities

Cash outflows from operating activities include payments:

- to suppliers for goods and services
- to employees for wages and salaries
- to governments for taxes
- to lenders for interest on debt

Operating cash flows correspond to the *types* of items that determine net income (revenues and expenses). However, the *amounts* are different because the income statement is accrual-based while the statement of cash flows is cash-based. Therefore, to isolate the current period operating cash flow, companies must adjust the current period income statement items for any related noncash items, which can be determined by examining the changes in the related current assets and current liabilities.

Alphabet reported operating cash flow of $54,520 million compared to net income of $34,343 million (see Exhibit 11.5, p. 631). While various reasons exist for this difference, two major factors include adjustments for noncash items (such as depreciation and amortization) and accrual accounting adjustments of current assets and liabilities. The adjustments needed to reconcile net income with operating cash flow are discussed later in the chapter.

CASH FLOWS FROM INVESTING ACTIVITIES

Cash flows from investing activities (or investing cash flows) are the cash inflows and outflows that relate to acquiring and disposing of operating assets and investments in other companies (current and long-term), lending money, and collecting loans. Cash inflows from investing activities include cash received from the:

- sale of property, plant, and equipment
- collection of the principal amount of a loan (a note receivable)
- sale of investments in other companies

Cash outflows from investing activities include payments made to:

- acquire property, plant, and equipment
- purchase debt or equity securities of other companies as an investment
- loan money to others (notes receivable)

In general, investing cash flows relate to increases or decreases of long-term assets and investments.

Alphabet reported a $29,491 million cash outflow related to investing activities. Its major investing activities were related to the purchase and sale of marketable securities (investments), as well as purchases of property and equipment.

CASH FLOWS FROM FINANCING ACTIVITIES

Cash flows from financing activities (or financing cash flows) relate to obtaining resources from creditors and owners, providing owners a return on their investment, and repaying creditors. Cash inflows from financing activities include cash received from the:

- issuance of stock
- issuance of debt (bonds or notes payable)

Cash outflows from financing activities include cash payments to:

- repay the principal amount borrowed (bonds or notes payable)
- repurchase a company's own stock (treasury stock)
- pay dividends

In general, financing cash flows involve cash receipts and payments that affect long-term liabilities and stockholders' equity.

Alphabet reported a cash inflow of $18,498 million related to financing activities. Its major source of funds was from the issuance of long-term debt, and its major use of funds related to repurchases of stock.

NONCASH INVESTING AND FINANCING ACTIVITIES

Occasionally, investing and financing activities take place without affecting cash. For example, a company may choose to acquire an operating asset (such as a building) by issuing long-term debt. Alternatively, a company may acquire one asset by exchanging it for another. These types of activities are referred to as **noncash investing and financing activities**. Because these activities do not involve cash, they are not reported on the statement of cash flows. However, these transactions still provide useful information about a company's overall investing and financing activities. Any significant noncash investing and financing activities are required to be reported in a supplementary schedule that is shown either at the bottom of the statement of cash flows or in the notes to the financial statements. This requirement to disclose any significant noncash investing and financing activities is consistent with the full-disclosure principle—any information that would make a difference to financial statement users should be made known.

Exhibit 11.2 summarizes the classification of business activities as either operating, investing, or financing activities. Two particular activities—interest and dividends—are often misclassified by students. Interest (received or paid) and cash dividends received are classified as operating activities because they go into the determination of income. Cash dividends paid, on the other hand, are not an expense but are a reduction of retained earnings. Therefore, cash dividends paid are classified as a financing activity.

Classification of Cash Flows   **EXHIBIT 11.2**

Cash Inflows

Operating Activities
Cash received from:
- Customers for cash sales
- Collections of accounts receivable
- Dividends from investments
- Interest

Investing Activities
Cash received from the:
- Sale of property, plant, and equipment
- Collection of principal on a loan
- Sale or maturity of investments

Financing Activities
Cash received from:
- Issuing stock to owners
- Issuing notes or bonds (debt) to creditors
- Selling treasury stock

Cash Outflows

Operating Activities
Cash paid to:
- Suppliers of goods and services
- Employees for salaries and wages
- Governments for taxes
- Lenders for interest

Investing Activities
Cash paid to:
- Purchase property, plant, and equipment
- Make loans to other companies
- Purchase investments

Financing Activities
Cash paid to:
- Repay principal of long-term debt
- Owners as dividends
- Purchase treasury stock

EXAMPLE 11.1 shows how business activities can be classified as either operating, investing, financing, or noncash activities.

EXAMPLE 11.1   CLASSIFYING BUSINESS ACTIVITIES

Moore Inc. engaged in the following activities during the current year:

a. Payment of wages to employees	f. Retirement of debt by issuing stock
b. Issuance of common stock	g. Purchase of inventory
c. Purchase of property, plant, and equipment	h. Sale of property, plant, and equipment
d. Collection of cash from customers	i. Payment of dividends
e. Issuance of bonds	j. Payment of interest

Required:
Classify each of the above activities as an operating, investing, or financing activity and indicate whether the activity involved a cash receipt or cash payment. If the transaction does not involve cash, classify it as a noncash investing and financing activity.

Solution:

a. Because wages are an expense on the income statement, the payment of wages is classified as a cash payment for an operating activity.

b. The issuance of common stock results in an increase of stockholders' equity and cash. Therefore, it is classified as a cash receipt from a financing activity.

c. The purchase of property, plant, and equipment results in an increase to a long-term asset and a decrease of cash. Therefore, it is classified as a cash payment for an investing activity.

d. The collection of cash from customers relates to sales revenue on the income statement and is classified as a cash receipt from an operating activity.

e. Issuing bonds results in an increase to long-term liabilities and cash. Therefore, it is classified as a cash receipt from a financing activity.

f. The retirement of debt by issuing stock is a financing activity that does not involve cash. It is classified as a noncash investing and financing activity.

g. Because inventory is a component of cost of goods sold on the income statement, the purchase of inventory is classified as a cash payment for an operating activity.

h. The sale of property, plant, and equipment results in a decrease in a long-term asset and an increase in cash. Therefore, it is classified as a cash receipt from an investing activity.

i. The payment of dividends is a reduction in retained earnings, which is a part of stockholders' equity. Therefore, the payment of dividends is classified as a cash payment for a financing activity.

j. Interest is an expense on the income statement. Therefore, the payment of interest is classified as a cash payment for an operating activity.

FORMAT OF THE STATEMENT OF CASH FLOWS

Once a company has properly classified its cash inflows and outflows as operating, investing, or financing activities, it reports each of these three categories as shown in Exhibit 11.3. Note that the three cash flow categories are summed to obtain the net increase or decrease in cash. This change in cash reconciles the beginning and ending balances of cash as noted in Exhibit 11.1 (p. 623).

Format of the Statement of Cash Flows

EXHIBIT 11.3

Brooke Sportswear Inc.
Statement of Cash Flows
For the year ended December 31

Cash flows from operating activities

Cash inflows	$ xxx	
Cash outflows	(xxx)	
Net cash provided (used) by operating activities		$xxx

Cash flows from investing activities

Cash inflows	$ xxx	
Cash outflows	(xxx)	
Net cash provided (used) by investing activities		xxx

Cash flows from financing activities

Cash inflows	$ xxx	
Cash outflows	(xxx)	
Net cash provided (used) by financing activities		xxx
Net increase (decrease) in cash and cash equivalents		$xxx
Cash and cash equivalents at beginning of year		xxx
Cash and cash equivalents at end of year		$xxx

Schedule or note disclosure of noncash investing and financing activities

 YOUDECIDE **Statement of Cash Flow Classifications**

You are preparing the statement of cash flows for Sienna Corporation and consult the CFO about how to properly classify the cash paid for interest. The CFO states that the company chose to finance its recent expansion activities with large amounts of debt. Because the interest payments resulted from this financing decision, he believes that the cash paid for interest should be classified as a financing activity. In addition, the CFO points out that you shouldn't waste any more time on this since it's simply a classification issue. No matter where the interest payment is reported, the total change in cash will be the same and no one will care.

How should you classify the cash paid for interest?

The CFO certainly makes a good argument to classify interest payments as a financing cash flow. Similar to dividend payments (which are paid for the use of equity capital), interest is paid for the use of debt capital. However, the FASB states that operating cash flows should reflect the cash effects of transactions that enter into the determination of income. Because interest is an expense, it should be classified as an operating activity. While this is a classification issue, the CFO's assertion that the proper classification makes no difference is incorrect. The various classifications on a statement of cash flows provide insights into how a company generated and used its cash.

The proper classification of items in the statement of cash flows is critical for financial statement users.

ANALYZING THE ACCOUNTS FOR CASH FLOW DATA

Unlike the balance sheet and the income statement, the statement of cash flows cannot be prepared by simply using information obtained from an adjusted trial balance prepared using the accrual basis of accounting. Instead, each item on the balance sheet and the income statement must be analyzed to *explain* why cash changed by the amount that it did. In other words, the accrual-basis numbers in the balance sheet and the income statement must be adjusted to a cash basis.

The recording of any business activity creates two types of financial measures—*balances* and *changes*. Balances measure the dollar amount of an account at a given time. Changes measure the increases or decreases in account balances over a period of time. For example, consider the following T-account:

Accounts Receivable			
Balance, Jan. 1	11,000		
Credit sales	90,000	92,000	Cash collections
Balance, Dec. 31	9,000		

This T-account shows two balances and two changes. The beginning and ending balances ($11,000 and $9,000) measure accounts receivable at January 1 and December 31, respectively. The credit sales ($90,000) and cash collections ($92,000) are changes that measure the effects of selling goods and collecting cash. Like accounts receivable, every balance sheet account can be described in terms of balances and changes.

To understand a company's cash flows, the relationships between the *changes* in balance sheet accounts and the company's cash flows need to be analyzed. We will begin our analysis with the fundamental accounting equation:

$$\text{Assets} = \text{Liabilities} + \text{Stockholders' Equity}$$

Next, we will restate this equation in terms of changes (Δ):

$$\Delta \text{ Assets} = \Delta \text{ Liabilities} + \Delta \text{ Stockholders' Equity}$$

Separating assets into cash and noncash accounts:

$$\Delta \text{ Cash} + \Delta \text{ Noncash Assets} = \Delta \text{ Liabilities} + \Delta \text{ Stockholders' Equity}$$

Finally, moving the changes in noncash assets to the right side:

$$\Delta \text{ Cash} = \Delta \text{ Liabilities} + \Delta \text{ Stockholders' Equity} - \Delta \text{ Noncash Assets}$$

Where:

> Increases in Cash = Increases in Liabilities + Increases in Stockholders' Equity + Decreases in Noncash Assets

> Decreases in Cash = Decreases in Liabilities + Decreases in Stockholders' Equity + Increases in Noncash Assets

This analysis reveals that **all cash receipts or cash payments are associated with changes in other balance sheet accounts**. EXAMPLE 11.2 illustrates how to classify specific balance sheet accounts as increases in cash or decreases in cash.

Next Level

Why do we analyze changes in the balance sheet accounts to determine the inflows and outflows of cash? Wouldn't it be easier to simply look at the Cash account in the general ledger?

ANSWER:

It is correct that the Cash account in the general ledger will contain all cash inflows and cash outflows and a statement of cash flows could be prepared by analyzing this account. However, this would require individuals to identify, understand, and classify every single cash receipt or cash payment. With the large volume of cash transactions, this would be an extremely timeconsuming and inefficient task. It is much easier to determine cash flows by analyzing the changes in the balance sheet accounts.

EXAMPLE 11.2   CLASSIFYING CHANGES IN BALANCE SHEET ACCOUNTS

The following changes in the balance sheet accounts have been observed for the current period:

Account	Jan. 1	Dec. 31	Change
a. Accounts receivable	$ 25,000	$ 18,000	$ (7,000)
b. Bonds payable	400,000	300,000	(100,000)
c. Equipment	145,000	175,000	30,000
d. Inventory	15,000	18,000	3,000
e. Common stock	150,000	175,000	25,000
f. Retained earnings	75,000	95,000	20,000
g. Accounts payable	12,000	10,000	(2,000)
h. Unearned revenue	17,000	19,000	2,000

Required:
Classify each change as either an increase in cash or a decrease in cash.

Solution:

a.	Increase in cash		e.	Increase in cash
b.	Decrease in cash		f.	Increase in cash
c.	Decrease in cash		g.	Decrease in cash
d.	Decrease in cash		h.	Increase in cash

Exhibit 11.4 integrates the analysis of the relationships between the *changes* in balance sheet accounts and the company's cash flows with the cash flow classifications discussed in the previous section.

Cash Flow Classifications and Changes in Balance Sheet Accounts   EXHIBIT 11.4

Classification	Cash Effect	Balance Sheet Items Affected	Example
Operating	Inflow (+)	Decreases in current assets Increases in current liabilities Increases in retained earnings	Collecting an account receivable Receipt of revenue in advance Making a cash sale
	Outflow (−)	Increases in current assets Decreases in current liabilities Decreases in retained earnings	Purchasing inventory Paying an account payable Paying interest
Investing	Inflow (+)	Decreases in long-term assets	Selling equipment
	Outflow (−)	Increases in long-term assets	Buying equipment
Financing	Inflow (+)	Increases in long-term liabilities Increases in stockholders' equity	Issuing long-term debt Issuing stock
	Outflow (−)	Decreases in long-term liabilities Decreases in stockholders' equity	Retiring long-term debt Paying dividends

Examining Exhibit 11.4, several items are of interest:

- Cash flows from operating activities generally involve income statement items (which are reflected in retained earnings) and changes in current assets or liabilities.
- Investing activities are related to changes in long-term assets.
- Financing activities are related to changes in long-term liabilities and stockholders' equity.
- Retained earnings affects both cash flows from operating activities (for example, revenues, expenses, net income, or a net loss) and cash flows from financing activities (for example, payment of dividends).
- Each item on the balance sheet and the income statement must be analyzed to explain the change in cash.

PREPARING A STATEMENT OF CASH FLOWS

After the accounts have been analyzed to identify cash inflows and outflows, a statement of cash flows can be prepared. To prepare a statement of cash flows, you need:

- *Comparative balance sheets*: Used to determine the changes in assets, liabilities, and stockholders' equity during a period
- *A current income statement*: Used to determine cash flows from operating activities
- *Additional information about selected accounts*: Used to determine the reason why cash was received or paid

Using this information, there are five basic steps in preparing the statement of cash flows.

Step 1. **Compute the net cash flow from operating activities.** This involves adjusting the amounts on the income statement for noncash changes reflected in the balance sheet. Two methods, the indirect or direct method (explained in the next section), may be used to determine this amount.

Step 2. **Compute the net cash flow from investing activities.** Information from the balance sheet as well as any additional information provided will need to be analyzed to identify the cash inflows and outflows associated with long-term assets.

Step 3. **Compute the net cash flow from financing activities.** Information from the balance sheet as well as any additional information provided will need to be analyzed to identify the cash inflows and outflows associated with long-term liabilities and stockholders' equity.

Step 4. **Combine the net cash flows from operating, investing, and financing activities to obtain the net increase (decrease) in cash for the period.**

Step 5. **Compute the change in cash for the period and compare this with the change in cash from Step 4.** The change in cash, computed from the beginning balance of cash and the ending balance of cash as shown on the balance sheet, should reconcile with the net cash flow computed in Step 4.

The statement of cash flows for Alphabet is shown in Exhibit 11.5.

OBJECTIVE 4

Prepare the cash flows from operating activities section of a statement of cash flows using the indirect method.

PREPARING CASH FLOWS FROM OPERATING ACTIVITIES

The cash flows from operating activities section of the statement of cash flows may be prepared using either of two methods: the direct method or the indirect method. Both methods arrive at an identical amount—the net cash provided (used) by operating activities. The two methods differ only in how this amount is computed.

Statement of Cash Flows for Alphabet

EXHIBIT 11.5

Alphabet Inc. Statement of Consolidated Cash Flows* For the Year Ended December 31 (in millions of dollars)		
Cash Flows from Operating Activities		
Net income	$ 34,343	
Adjustments:		
Depreciation	10,856	
Amortization	925	
Other noncash items	7,577	
Changes in assets and liabilities:		
Accounts receivable	(4,340)	
Income taxes	(3,128)	
Accounts payable	428	
Accrued expenses and other liabilities	7,170	
Accrued revenue	1,273	
Other	(584)	
Net cash provided by operating activities		$54,520
Cash Flows from Investing Activities		
Purchases of property and equipment	$ (23,548)	
Purchases of marketable securities	(100,315)	
Maturities and sales of marketable securities	97,825	
Purchases of nonmarketable investments	(1,932)	
Maturities and sales of nonmarketable investments	405	
Acquisitions and purchases of intangible assets	(2,515)	
Other	(589)	
Net cash used for investing activities		(29,491)
Cash Flows from Financing Activities		
Net payments related to stock-based award activities	$ (4,765)	
Repurchases of stock	(18,396)	
Proceeds from issuance of debt	317	
Repayments of debt	(585)	
Other	(220)	
Net cash provided by financing activities		(23,209)
Effect of exchange rate changes on cash and cash equivalents		(23)
Net increase (decrease) in cash and cash equivalents		$ 1,797
Cash and cash equivalents at beginning of year		16,701
Cash and cash equivalents at end of year		$18,498

*The statement of cash flows information has been summarized and reformatted by the authors.

Source: Alphabet Inc. Form 10-K.

THE DIRECT METHOD

In the **direct method**, cash inflows and cash outflows are listed for each type of operating activity that a company performs. These cash flows are computed by adjusting *each item* on the income statement by the changes in the related current asset or liability accounts. Typical cash flow categories reported are cash collected from customers, cash paid to suppliers, cash paid to employees, cash paid for interest, and cash paid for taxes. The cash outflows are subtracted from the cash inflows to determine the net cash flow from operating activities. If the direct method is used, companies must also provide a supplementary schedule that shows the reconciliation of net income with operating cash flow. While the FASB prefers the use of the direct method because it is more consistent with the purpose of the statement of cash flows, it is not widely used.

THE INDIRECT METHOD

The indirect method does not report individual cash inflows and outflows. Instead, it focuses on the *differences* between net income and operating cash flow. The **indirect method** begins with net income and then adjusts it for noncash items to produce net cash flow from operating activities. These adjustments to net income are necessary for two reasons:

- to eliminate income statement items that do not affect cash (such as depreciation and gains/losses on sales of assets)
- to adjust accrual-basis revenues and expenses to cash receipts and cash payments

The changes in the related current asset and current liability accounts contain the information necessary to make the adjustments to revenue and expense accounts. Generally, companies prefer the indirect method because it is easier and less costly to prepare.

ETHICAL DECISIONS   By highlighting the differences between operating cash flows and net income, financial statement users may be able to more easily see attempts at earnings management. If managers try to manage earnings by manipulating the accrual accounting process (for example, increase revenues or decrease expenses on the income statement to increase income), these actions will often have no cash flow effect but will instead reveal themselves through changes in the accrual-basis accounts. When there are growing differences between operating cash flow and net income, the indirect method highlights the changes in the accrual accounts and allows users to judge the cause of these differences. ●

APPLYING THE INDIRECT METHOD

We will illustrate the preparation of cash flows from operating activities for Brooke Sportswear using the more popular indirect method. The direct method is illustrated in Appendix 11A. However, remember two important points:

- Cash flow from operating activities is the same under either method.
- The indirect and direct methods only apply to the operating activities section of the statement of cash flows. The investing and financing sections will be prepared the same way regardless of which method is used to prepare the operating activities section.

The income statement and comparative balance sheets for Brooke Sportswear are shown in Exhibit 11.6.

Because income statements are prepared on an accrual basis, the revenues and expenses recognized on the income statement are not necessarily the same as the cash receipts and cash payments for a period. For example, revenues may include credit sales for which the company has not collected cash and exclude collections of cash from credit sales made in a previous

Financial Statements for Brooke Sportswear

EXHIBIT 11.6

Brooke Sportswear
Balance Sheets

ASSETS	Jan. 1	Dec. 31
Current assets:		
Cash	$ 13,000	$ 15,000
Accounts receivable	46,000	53,000
Prepaid insurance	2,000	1,000
Inventory	51,000	63,000
Total current assets	$ 112,000	$ 132,000
Long-term investments	41,000	53,000
Property, plant, and equipment:		
Land	325,000	325,000
Equipment	210,000	243,000
Accumulated depreciation	(150,000)	(178,000)
Total assets	$ 538,000	$ 575,000
LIABILITIES AND EQUITY		
Current liabilities:		
Accounts payable	$ 17,000	$ 13,000
Wages payable	2,000	3,500
Interest payable	1,000	1,500
Income taxes payable	6,000	3,000
Total current liabilities	$ 26,000	$ 21,000
Long-term liabilities:		
Notes payable	115,000	109,000
Total liabilities	$ 141,000	$ 130,000
Equity:		
Common stock	$ 151,000	$ 165,000
Retained earnings	246,000	280,000
Total equity	$ 397,000	$ 445,000
Total liabilities and equity	$ 538,000	$ 575,000

Brooke Sportswear
Income Statement
For the year ended December 31

Sales revenue	$ 472,000
Less: Cost of goods sold	(232,000)
Gross margin	$ 240,000
Less operating expenses:	
Wages expense	(142,000)
Insurance expense	(15,000)
Depreciation expense	(40,000)
Income from operations	$ 43,000
Other income and expenses:	
Loss on disposal of property, plant, and equipment	(6,000)
Gain on sale of investments	15,000
Interest expense	(5,000)
Income before taxes	$ 47,000
Less: Income taxes expense	(8,000)
Net income	$ 39,000

Additional Information:

1. Equipment with a cost of $20,000 and accumulated depreciation of $12,000 was sold for $2,000 cash. Equipment was purchased for $53,000 cash.
2. Long-term investments with a cost of $16,000 were sold for $31,000 cash. Additional investments were purchased for $28,000 cash.
3. Notes payable in the amount of $35,000 were repaid, and new notes payable in the amount of $29,000 were issued for cash.
4. Common stock was issued for $14,000 cash.
5. Cash dividends of $5,000 were paid (obtained from the retained earnings statement).

period. Similarly, expenses may have been incurred for which no cash has been paid, or cash may have been paid related to expenses incurred in a previous period. Therefore, net income must be adjusted for these timing differences between the recognition of net income and the receipt or payment of cash.

Under the indirect method, four types of adjustments must be made to net income to adjust it to net cash flow from operating activities:

1. Add to net income any noncash expenses and subtract from net income any noncash revenues.

2. Add to net income any losses and subtract from net income any gains.

Next Level

Why are there differences between net income and net cash flow from operating activities?

ANSWER:
Net income is prepared under the accrual basis of accounting which records business activities when they occur instead of when cash is received or paid. Therefore, all of the adjustments that are made to net income reflect timing differences between the reporting of revenues and expenses and the related inflow or outflow of cash.

3. Add to net income any decreases in current assets or increases in current liabilities that are related to operating activities.
4. Subtract from net income any increases in current assets and decreases in current liabilities that are related to operating activities.

These adjustments and the computation of net cash flow from operating activities are illustrated in EXAMPLE 11.3 and explained below.

Adjustment of Noncash Revenues and Expenses The income statement often includes various noncash items such as depreciation expense, amortization expense, and bad debt expense.

- Noncash expenses reduce net income but do not reduce cash. Therefore, under the indirect method, **noncash expenses are added back to net income**.
- Noncash revenues increase income but do not increase cash. Therefore, under the indirect method, **noncash revenues are subtracted from net income**.

EXAMPLE 11.3   CALCULATING NET CASH FLOW FROM OPERATING ACTIVITIES: INDIRECT METHOD

Refer to the income statement and the current assets and current liabilities sections of Brooke Sportswear's balance sheets found in Exhibit 11.6 (p. 633).

Required:
Compute the net cash flow from operating activities using the indirect method.

Solution:

Net income	$ 39,000
Adjustments to reconcile net income to net cash flow from operating activities:*	
Depreciation expense	$ 40,000
Loss on disposal of equipment	6,000
Gain on sale of long-term investments	(15,000)
Increase in accounts receivable	(7,000)
Decrease in prepaid insurance	1,000
Increase in inventory	(12,000)
Decrease in accounts payable	(4,000)
Increase in wages payable	1,500
Increase in interest payable	500
Decrease in income taxes payable	(3,000)
Net cash provided by operating activities	$47,000

* The explanation of these adjustments is given in the text of this section.

Adjustment of Gains and Losses The sale of a long-term asset or the extinguishment of a long-term liability often produces either a gain or loss that is reported on the income statement. However, the gain or loss does not affect cash flow and should, therefore, not be included as an operating activity. Furthermore, the gain or loss does not reveal the total amount of cash received or paid. Instead, it only gives the amount received or paid in excess of the book value of the asset or liability. The correct procedure is to eliminate the gain or loss from net income and record the full amount of the cash flow as either an investing activity or a financing activity.

- Because gains increase net income, under the indirect method, **gains are subtracted from net income**.
- Because losses decrease net income, under the indirect method, **losses are added back to net income**.

Adjustments for Changes in Current Assets and Current Liabilities   As discussed earlier in the chapter, all cash receipts or cash payments are associated with changes in one or more balance sheet accounts. Generally, current assets and liabilities are related to the operating activities of a company, and changes in these accounts cause a difference between net income and cash flows from operating activities. Based on the earlier analysis of the balance sheet accounts, two general rules emerge:

- **Increases in current assets and decreases in current liabilities are subtracted from net income.**
- **Decreases in current assets and increases in current liabilities are added to net income.**

The adjustments to net income required to calculate cash flow from operating activities are summarized in Exhibit 11.7.

Adjustments Required to Calculate Cash Flow from Operating Activities   **EXHIBIT 11.7**

+ Add to Net Income	**− Subtract from Net Income**
• Noncash expenses	• Noncash revenues
• Losses	• Gains
• Decreases in current assets	• Increases in current assets
• Increases in current liabilities	• Decreases in current liabilities

The explanations of these adjustments for Brook Sportswear are shown below.

Accounts Receivable   The Accounts Receivable account increases when credit sales are recorded and decreases when cash is collected from customers.

Accounts Receivable			
Balance, Jan. 1	46,000		
Credit sales	xxx	xxx	Cash collections
Balance, Dec. 31	53,000		

The increase of accounts receivable implies that credit sales were $7,000 greater than the cash collected from customers. This is consistent with the results of our earlier analysis indicating that increases in noncash assets are related to decreases in cash. Because sales reported on the income statement were greater than the cash collections, the company would need to subtract the increase in accounts receivable from net income when computing net cash flow from operating activities. (A decrease in accounts receivable would be added to net income when computing net cash flow from operating activities.)

Prepaid Insurance   The Prepaid Insurance account increases when cash prepayments are made and decreases when expenses are incurred.

Prepaid Insurance			
Balance, Jan. 1	2,000		
Cash prepayments	xxx	xxx	Expense incurred
Balance, Dec. 31	1,000		

The decrease in prepaid insurance indicates that expenses incurred and recorded on the income statement were $1,000 higher than the cash payments. Because more expenses were incurred than were paid in cash, the company actually has more cash available at the end of the period than at the beginning of the period (because less cash was paid). This is consistent with the results of our earlier analysis indicating that decreases in noncash assets are related to increases in cash. The decrease in the Prepaid Insurance account needs to be added to net income when computing net cash flow from operating activities. (Increases in prepaid insurance would be subtracted from net income.)

Inventory   The Inventory account increases when inventory is purchased and decreases as inventory is sold.

Inventory			
Balance, Jan. 1	51,000		
Purchases	XXX	XXX	Cost of goods sold
Balance, Dec. 31	63,000		

The increase in inventory implies that purchases of inventory exceeded the cost of the inventory sold reported on the income statement by $12,000. Therefore, the company made "extra" cash purchases that were not included in cost of goods sold. To adjust net income to net cash flow from operating activities, the increase in the Inventory account, which represents the extra cash purchases, needs to be subtracted from net income. (Decreases in inventory would be added to net income.)

Accounts Payable   The Accounts Payable account increases when credit purchases are made and decreases when cash payments are made to suppliers.

Accounts Payable			
		17,000	Balance, Jan. 1
Cash payments	XXX	XXX	Credit purchases
		13,000	Balance, Dec. 31

The decrease in accounts payable indicates that the cash payments to suppliers exceeded the credit purchases of inventory by $4,000. Because the purchase of inventory is part of cost of goods sold, this implies that more cash was paid than was reflected in expenses. This is consistent with the results of our earlier analysis indicating that decreases in liabilities are related to decreases in cash. Therefore, the decrease in accounts payable needs to be subtracted from net income when computing the net cash flow from operating activities. (Increases of accounts payable are added to net income.)

Wages Payable   The Wages Payable account increases when wages are accrued (incurred but not yet paid) and decreases when wages are paid.

Wages Payable			
		2,000	Balance, Jan. 1
Cash payments	XXX	XXX	Wages expense
		3,500	Balance, Dec. 31

The increase in wages payable indicates that wages expense recorded on the income statement was greater than the cash paid for wages by $1,500. Because less cash was paid than expensed, the company actually has more cash available. This is consistent with the results of our earlier analysis indicating that increases in liabilities are related to increases in cash. Therefore, the increase in wages payable is added to net income when computing the net cash flow from operating activities. (Decreases in wages payable are subtracted from net income.)

Interest Payable   Interest payable increases when interest expense is recorded and decreases when interest is paid.

Interest Payable

		1,000	Balance, Jan. 1
Cash payments	xxx	xxx	Interest expense
		1,500	Balance, Dec. 31

The increase in interest payable implies that interest expense recorded on the income state-ment was $500 greater than the cash paid for interest. This is consistent with the results of our earlier analysis indicating that increases in liabilities are related to increases in cash. Therefore, the increase in interest payable is added to net income when computing the net cash flow from operating activities. (Decreases in interest payable are subtracted from net income.)

Income Taxes Payable The Income Taxes Payable account increases when income tax expense is incurred and decreases when income taxes are paid.

Income Taxes Payable

		6,000	Balance, Jan. 1
Cash payments	xxx	xxx	Income tax expense
		3,000	Balance, Dec. 31

The decrease in income taxes payable implies that the cash payments for income taxes were $3,000 greater than the income tax expense reported on the income statement. This is consis-tent with the results of our earlier analysis indicating that decreases in liabilities are related to decreases in cash. Therefore, less cash is available at the end of the period and the decrease in income taxes payable is subtracted from net income when computing the net cash flow from operating activities. (Increases in income taxes payable are added to net income.)

 YOUDECIDE Operating Cash Flow and the Quality of Earnings

You are analyzing the financial statements of Slater Inc., a retail company that operates primarily in the southeastern United States. While Slater has reported increasing net income, you notice that its operating cash flow has been declining. Further investigation reveals increasing accounts receivable and inventory balances.

What inferences can you make about the quality of Slater's earnings?

Many analysts will compare net income to operating cash flow as a means of assessing the quality of a company's earnings. All other things equal, the higher a company's operating cash flow relative to its net income, the greater the quality of the company's earnings. In Slater's situation, increasing income with declining operating cash flow is a warning sign that requires closer scrutiny.

The increasing accounts receivable balances could simply signal rapidly growing operations. However, it may also signal that a company is attempting to boost sales by allowing customers to take longer to pay or lending to riskier customers. Similarly, increasing inventory balances may be due to seasonal factors (for example, the normal inventory growth during a "slow" quarter) or could signal that the company was not able to sell its merchandise as it had planned. When differences between net income and operating cash flow are noted, it is critical to fully understand their implications for the company's prospects.

Understanding the differences between net income and operating cash flow can provide useful insights into the quality of a company's earnings.

PREPARING CASH FLOWS FROM INVESTING ACTIVITIES

OBJECTIVE 5

Prepare the cash flows from investing activities section of a statement of cash flows.

The second major section of the statement of cash flows reports the net cash flow from invest-ing activities. Information for preparing the investing activities portion of the statement of cash flows is obtained from the investment and long-term asset accounts. Because all of these accounts are assets, increases that were financed by cash would be treated as outflows of cash. Decreases in the assets that produced cash receipts would be treated as inflows of cash.

Although the beginning and ending balance sheets are useful sources for identifying changes in these accounts, you must refer to any additional data provided to determine the actual amount of investing cash inflows and outflows. For example, a company might purchase land at a cost of $200,000 and, during the same accounting period, sell land that had a cost of $145,000. If only the beginning and ending amounts for land are examined, one would erroneously conclude that there had been a single cash outflow of $55,000 for land, instead of two separate cash flows—a cash outflow for the purchase of land and a cash inflow related to the sale of land.

ANALYZING INVESTING ACTIVITIES

To analyze investing activities, follow the three basic steps outlined in Exhibit 11.8.

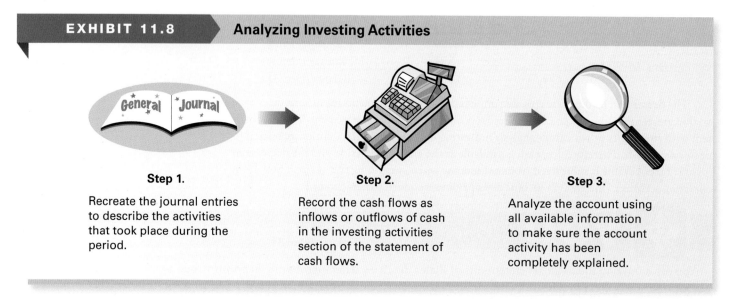

EXHIBIT 11.8 **Analyzing Investing Activities**

Step 1.
Recreate the journal entries to describe the activities that took place during the period.

Step 2.
Record the cash flows as inflows or outflows of cash in the investing activities section of the statement of cash flows.

Step 3.
Analyze the account using all available information to make sure the account activity has been completely explained.

To illustrate the analysis of the relevant accounts and the recreation of the journal entries, consider the information in Brooke Sportswear's financial statements in Exhibit 11.6 (p. 633).

Land Notice that no change occurred in the Land account, nor was any additional information given concerning this account. Therefore, you may conclude that there was no cash flow associated with land for the year.

Property, Plant, and Equipment To get a full picture of the Equipment account you must examine both the equipment and the related Accumulated Depreciation account. (For any operating asset that depreciates, you will need to analyze the two related accounts together.) Using the information from the financial statements and the additional information in Exhibit 11.6 (p. 633), you can recreate the activity in these accounts by making the following journal entries:

				Assets	=	Liabilities	+	Stockholders' Equity
Sale of Equipment	Cash	2,000		▲				
	Accumulated Depreciation	12,000		▲				
	Loss on Disposal of Property, Plant, and Equipment	6,000						▼
	Equipment		20,000	▼				

					Assets	=	Liabilities	+	Stockholders' Equity
Purchase of Equipment	Equipment	53,000			▲				
	Cash		53,000		▼				

Notice that the there are only two cash flows related to investing activities:

- a $2,000 cash inflow associated with the disposal of equipment
- a $53,000 cash outflow associated with the purchase of equipment

The loss on the disposal of equipment does not involve cash and is included as an adjustment in the operating section of the statement of cash flows. The analysis performed above is used to reconcile the change in the Equipment and Accumulated Depreciation accounts as shown in the following T-accounts:

Equipment

Balance, Jan. 1	210,000		
Purchase	53,000	20,000	Disposal
Balance, Dec. 31	243,000		

Accumulated Depreciation

		150,000	Balance, Jan. 1
Disposal	12,000	40,000	Depreciation expense
		178,000	Balance, Dec. 31

Investments Using the information in Exhibit 11.6 (p. 633), you can recreate the activity in the Investments account by making the following journal entries:

					Assets	=	Liabilities	+	Stockholders' Equity
Sale of Investment	Cash	31,000			▲				
	Investments		16,000		▼				
	Gain on Sale of Investments		15,000						▲

					Assets	=	Liabilities	+	Stockholders' Equity
Purchase of Investment	Investments	28,000			▲				
	Cash		28,000		▼				

Again, notice that two cash flows were related to investing activities:

- a $31,000 inflow of cash related to the sale of an investment
- a $28,000 outflow of cash related to the purchase of an investment

The gain on the sale of the investment does not involve cash and is included as an adjustment in the operating section of the statement of cash flows. The analysis performed above is used to reconcile the change in the Investments account as shown in the following T-account.

Investments			
Balance, Jan. 1	41,000		
Purchase	28,000	16,000	Sale
Balance, Dec. 31	53,000		

EXAMPLE 11.4 shows how to compute the investing activities section of the statement of cash flows for Brooke Sportswear.

EXAMPLE 11.4   REPORTING NET CASH FLOW FROM INVESTING ACTIVITIES

Refer to the income statement, the long-term assets sections of Brooke Sportswear's balance sheets, and the first two items of additional information in Exhibit 11.6 (p. 633).

Required:
Compute the net cash flow from investing activities.

Solution:

Cash flows from investing activities:	
Cash received from sale of equipment	$ 2,000
Purchase of equipment	(53,000)
Cash received from sale of investments	31,000
Purchase of investments	(28,000)
Net cash used for investing activities	$(48,000)

OBJECTIVE 6

Prepare the cash flows from financing activities section of a statement of cash flows.

PREPARING CASH FLOWS FROM FINANCING ACTIVITIES

The intent of the financing activities section of the statement of cash flows is to identify inflows and outflows of cash arising from business activities that either produced capital (long-term debt or stockholders' equity) for the company or repaid capital supplied to the company. Information for preparing the financing activities portion of the statement of cash flows is obtained from the Long-Term Debt and Stockholders' Equity accounts. Increases in these accounts suggest that cash has been received and decreases suggest that cash has been paid. (Because Treasury Stock is a contra-equity account, increases indicate cash outflows and decreases indicate cash inflows.)

ANALYZING FINANCING ACTIVITIES

To analyze financing activities, the same basic steps used to analyze investing activities (see Exhibit 11.8, p. 638) are followed:

Step 1. Recreate the journal entries to describe the activities that took place during the period.
Step 2. Record the cash flows as inflows or outflows of cash in the financing activities section of the statement of cash flows.
Step 3. Analyze the account to make sure the account activity has been completely explained.

   To illustrate the analysis of the relevant accounts and the recreation of the journal entries, consider the information in Brooke Sportswear's balance sheet.

Notes Payable Using information in Exhibit 11.6 (p. 633), you can recreate the activity in the Notes Payable account by making the following journal entries:

				Assets	=	Liabilities	+	Stockholders' Equity
Repayment of Principal	Notes Payable	35,000				▼		
	Cash		35,000	▼				

				Assets	=	Liabilities	+	Stockholders' Equity
Issuance of Note	Cash	29,000		▲				
	Notes Payable		29,000			▲		

Notice that there are two cash flows related to financing activities:

- a $35,000 cash outflow associated with the repayment of principal
- a $29,000 cash inflow associated with issuing the note

The payment of interest is considered an operating activity and is not relevant to this analysis. The analysis performed above is used to reconcile the change in the Notes Payable account as shown in the following T-account:

Notes Payable			
		115,000	Balance, Jan. 1
Repaid principal	35,000	29,000	Issued note
		109,000	Balance, Dec. 31

Common Stock Using information in Exhibit 11.6 (p. 633), you can recreate activity in the common stock account by making the following journal entry:

				Assets	=	Liabilities	+	Stockholders' Equity
Issuance of Stock	Cash	14,000		▲				
	Common Stock		14,000					▲

One cash inflow ($14,000) has caused the change in common stock. The credit entry to the Common Stock account is used to reconcile the change in the Common Stock account, as shown in the following T-account:

Common Stock			
		151,000	Balance, Jan. 1
Retired stock	0	14,000	Issued stock
		165,000	Balance, Dec. 31

Retained Earnings Using information in Exhibit 11.6 (p. 633), you can recreate the activity in the Retained Earnings account by making the following journal entry:

				Assets	=	Liabilities	+	Stockholders' Equity
Payment of Dividends	Dividends	5,000						▼
	Cash		5,000	▼				

The only cash flow, the payment of dividends, is a financing activity. The following T-account summarizes the activity in the Retained Earnings account:

	Retained Earnings		
		246,000	Balance, Jan. 1
Dividends	5,000	39,000	Net income
		280,000	Balance, Dec. 31

Note that retained earnings is increased by net income and decreased by the payment of dividends.[1] Net income does not affect cash flow from financing activities but is considered an operating activity.

EXAMPLE 11.5 shows how to compute the financing activities section of the statement of cash flows for Brooke Sportswear.

EXAMPLE 11.5   REPORTING NET CASH FLOW FROM FINANCING ACTIVITIES

Refer to the income statement, long-term assets, liabilities, and equity sections of Brooke Sportswear's balance sheet, and Items 3–5 of additional information in Exhibit 11.6 (p. 633).

Required:
Compute the net cash flow from financing activities.

Solution:

Cash flows from financing activities:	
Cash paid to retire principal on notes payable	$(35,000)
Cash received from issuing notes payable	29,000
Cash received from issuance of common stock	14,000
Cash paid for dividends	(5,000)
Net cash provided by financing activities	$ 3,000

Combining Examples 11-3 through 11-5, a complete statement of cash flows is presented in Exhibit 11.9. This exhibit presents cash flows from operating activities using the indirect method. Notice that the statement of cash flows explains the change in cash shown on the balance sheet of Brooke Sportswear in Exhibit 11.6 (p. 633).

 YOUDECIDE   Understanding Patterns in the Statement of Cash Flows

During a recent conference call with analysts, the CEO of Waggoner Inc. said that the company expects future sales growth as it expands into several new geographical markets. To corroborate the CEO's statements, you examine the statement of cash flows and find that the company reported negative operating cash flows, positive investing cash flows, and positive financing cash flows.

Does the statement of cash flows support the CEO's statements?

It does not appear that the CEO's statements are supported by the company's cash flows. An expanding company should exhibit negative investing cash flows as it invests in the long-term assets necessary for expansion. The positive investing cash flows shown by Waggoner indicate that it is a net seller of its fixed assets—not a purchaser. In addition, one would like to see any expansion supported by positive operating cash flows. Instead of being an expanding company, the pattern of cash flows exhibited by Waggoner suggests a company that is experiencing problems in generating operating cash flows. Further, it appears the company may be selling its fixed assets and obtaining capital through borrowing or stockholder contributions in order to cover the operating cash flow shortfall.

Careful analysis of the patterns and interrelationships of a company's cash flows can provide users with insights into a company's operations.

---

1 Dividends declared but not paid also reduce retained earnings but are classified as a noncash activity.

Statement of Cash Flows for Brooke Sportswear

EXHIBIT 11.9

Brooke Sportswear
Statement of Cash Flows
For the year ended December 31

Cash flows from operating activities		
Net income	$ 39,000	
Adjustments to reconcile net income to net cash flow from operating activities:		
Depreciation expense	40,000	
Loss on disposal of equipment	6,000	
Gain on sale of long-term investments	(15,000)	
Increase in accounts receivable	(7,000)	
Decrease in prepaid insurance	1,000	
Increase in inventory	(12,000)	
Decrease in accounts payable	(4,000)	
Increase in wages payable	1,500	
Increase in interest payable	500	
Decrease in income taxes payable	(3,000)	
Net cash provided by operating activities		$ 47,000
Cash flows from investing activities		
Cash received from sale of equipment	$ 2,000	
Purchase of equipment	(53,000)	
Cash received from sale of investments	31,000	
Purchase of investments	(28,000)	
Net cash used for investing activities		(48,000)
Cash flows from financing activities		
Cash paid to retire principal on notes payable	$(35,000)	
Cash received from issuing notes payable	29,000	
Cash received from issuance of common stock	14,000	
Cash paid for dividends	(5,000)	
Net cash provided by financing activities		3,000
Net increase (decrease) in cash		$ 2,000
Cash and cash equivalents, 1/1/2023		13,000
Cash and cash equivalents, 12/31/2023		$ 15,000

USING THE STATEMENT OF CASH FLOWS

OBJECTIVE 7

Analyze information contained in the statement of cash flows.

Effective analysis of the statement of cash flows requires:

- an examination of the statement of cash flows itself
- a comparison of the information on the current statement of cash flows with earlier statements
- a comparison of the information in the current statement of cash flows with information from other companies' statements of cash flow

EXAMINING THE STATEMENT OF CASH FLOWS

One of the most important insights that can be gained by inspecting the current period's statement of cash flows is an estimate of how long it will take to recover the cash outflow associated with long-term uses of cash (such as purchase of property, plant, and equipment or payment of dividends). Investments in property, plant, and equipment are likely to require several profitable years before the investment is completely recovered through the sale of goods or services.

Therefore, prudent managers will seek long-term sources of cash, such as long-term debt or equity, which will not need to be repaid before the original investment has been recovered through profitable operations.

The sources most frequently used to provide long-term cash inflows are operations, the sale of long-term debt, and the sale of stock. Of these three, operations is generally considered the least risky, or the most controllable. The sale of debt or equity requires that investors or creditors make sizable commitments to the company. Although cash inflows from operations also require that an outsider (the customer) make a commitment, the size and timing of a customer's cash commitments are more flexible. Thus, it is more likely that the company can produce cash inflows from customers on a regular basis. For this reason, most companies attempt to secure a sizable portion of their total cash inflows from operations. Generally, analysts view cash flows from operations as the most important section of the statement of cash flows because, in the long-run, this will be the company's source of cash used to provide a return to investors and creditors.

Because the cost of selling large debt or equity issues in the public capital markets is high, most large companies sell debt or equity in relatively large amounts. They also make smaller long-term or short-term borrowings directly from banks, insurance companies, and other financial intermediaries. Many businesses arrange a "pre-approved" line of credit that can be used, up to some limit, for borrowing whenever cash is needed. Sales of small amounts of stock to employees through stock option and stock bonus plans also help increase cash inflows.

COMPARING THE STATEMENT OF CASH FLOWS FROM SEVERAL PERIODS

An analysis of the statement of cash flows also requires a comparison of the company's current statement of cash flows with earlier statements of cash flow. Typically, several consecutive years should be analyzed in order to determine trends in cash inflows and cash outflows. The following questions may be helpful in beginning the analysis of a series of cash flow statements:

- What proportions of cash have come from operating, financing, and investing activities?
- Are there discernible trends in these proportions?
- What proportions of long-term uses of cash are financed by long-term sources of cash?
- How has the company financed any permanent increases in current assets?
- Has the company begun any investment programs that are likely to require significant cash outflows in the future?
- What are the probable sources for the cash inflows the company will need in the near future?
- Are these sources likely to be both able and willing to provide the cash that is needed?
- If the company is unable to secure all the cash it needs, could cash outflows be restricted to the available supply of cash without seriously affecting operations?

Financial statement users will rely on summary cash flow measures to help them make these assessments. Two such measures are a company's free cash flow and its cash flow adequacy ratio.

Free Cash Flow   A company's **free cash flow** represents the cash flow that a company is able to generate after considering the maintenance or expansion of its assets (capital expenditures) and the payment of dividends. Free cash flow is computed as:

$$\text{Free Cash Flow} = \text{Net Cash Flow from Operating Activities} - \text{Capital Expenditures} - \text{Cash Dividends}$$

Having positive free cash flow allows a company to pursue profit-generating opportunities. However, negative free cash flow is not necessarily a bad thing. For example, a company making large investments in productive assets (large capital expenditures) may show negative free cash flow. If these investments provide a high rate of return, this strategy will be good for the company in the long run.

Cash Flow Adequacy Ratio A second useful measure is the **cash flow adequacy ratio**. The cash flow adequacy ratio provides a measure of the company's ability to meet its maturing debt obligations with its operating cash flow. This ratio is calculated as:

$$\text{Cash Flow Adequacy} = \frac{\text{Free Cash Flow}}{\text{Average Amount of Debt Maturing over the Next 5 Years}}$$

The cash flow adequacy ratio is also an indicator of the company's credit quality. Generally, a higher cash flow adequacy ratio signals that a company is a better credit risk than a company that must seek outside sources of capital to repay its obligations.

EXAMPLE 11.6 illustrates the computation and analysis of these ratios for **John Deere** and **Caterpillar**.

EXAMPLE 11.6   ANALYZING FREE CASH FLOW AND CASH FLOW ADEQUACY

The following information was obtained from recent Form 10-K reports of **John Deere** and **Caterpillar**.

(amounts in millions)	John Deere	Caterpillar
Operating cash flows	$3,412	$6,912
Capital expenditures	1,120	1,056
Cash dividends	943	2,132
Average maturities of long-term debt over the next 5 years	473.2	4,258.8

Required:
Compute John Deere's and Caterpillar's free cash flow and cash flow adequacy ratios.

Solution:
Free Cash Flow = Net Cash from Operating Activities − Capital Expenditures − Cash Dividends

John Deere	Caterpillar
$3,412 − $1,120 − $943 = **$1,349**	$6,912 − $1,056 − $2,132 = **$3,724**

$$\text{Cash Flow Adequacy} = \frac{\text{Free Cash Flow}}{\text{Average Amount of Debt Maturing over the Next 5 Years}}$$

John Deere	Caterpillar
$\dfrac{\$1,349}{\$473.2} = 285.1\%$	$\dfrac{\$3,724}{\$4,258.8} = 87.4\%$

Source: Deere & Company and Caterpillar Form 10-Ks.

As you can see in Example 11.6, both John Deere and Caterpillar, with over $1.3 billion and $3.7 billion in free cash flow, respectively, have the financial flexibility to take advantage of profit-generating opportunities and internally finance its expansion needs. However, Caterpillar has a cash flow adequacy ratio of less than one. This implies that it may have to seek outside sources of capital in order to repay their maturing debt obligations. On the other hand, John Deere, with a cash flow adequacy ratio of almost 300%, is well-equipped to repay their maturing debt obligations.

COMPARING THE STATEMENT OF CASH FLOWS TO SIMILAR COMPANIES

Finally, the analysis of the statement of cash flows requires comparing information from similar companies. Such comparisons provide good reference points because similar companies generally secure cash from similar sources and are likely to spend cash for similar activities. Comparative analysis can reveal significant deviations in the:

- amounts of cash inflows
- sources of those inflows
- types of activities to which cash is applied

When significant differences are found among similar companies, an explanation should be sought in the other financial statements, in the notes accompanying the statements, or from management.

OBJECTIVE

(Appendix 11A) Prepare the cash flows from operating activities section of a statement of cash flows using the direct method.

APPENDIX 11A: THE DIRECT METHOD

In the direct method of computing net cash flow from operating activities, inflows and outflows of cash are listed for each type of operating activity that a company performs. This involves adjusting *each item* on the income statement by the changes in the related current asset or liability accounts. Typical operating cash flows and the adjustments necessary to compute them are given below. All numbers are taken from the financial statements for Brooke Sportswear given in Exhibit 11.6 (p. 633).

CASH COLLECTED FROM CUSTOMERS

Sales revenue includes both cash sales and credit sales. When all sales are for cash, the cash collected from customers equals sales. However, when credit sales are made, the amount of cash that was collected during a period must be determined by analyzing the Sales and Accounts Receivable accounts. The Accounts Receivable account increases when credit sales are recorded and decreases when cash is collected from customers.

Accounts Receivable			
Balance, Jan. 1	46,000		
Credit sales	xxx	xxx	Cash collections
Balance, Dec. 31	53,000		

The increase of accounts receivable implies that credit sales were $7,000 greater than the cash collected from customers. This is consistent with increases in noncash assets reflecting decreases in cash. Because cash collections were less than reported sales ($472,000), Brooke Sportswear would subtract the increase in accounts receivable from sales when computing cash collected from customers. A general formula to compute cash collections from customers is:

$$\text{Cash Collected from Customers} = \text{Sales} \begin{cases} + \text{ Decrease in Accounts Receivable} \\ - \text{ Increase in Accounts Receivable} \end{cases}$$

OTHER CASH COLLECTIONS

If other revenues exist (such as interest or rent), similar adjustments are made to determine the cash collections. For example, interest revenue is adjusted for any change in interest receivable as follows:

$$\text{Cash Collected for Interest} = \text{Interest Revenue} \begin{cases} + \text{ Decrease in Interest Receivable} \\ - \text{ Increase in Interest Receivable} \end{cases}$$

CASH PAID TO SUPPLIERS

A company pays its suppliers for inventory which it later sells to customers, as represented by cost of goods sold. These purchases of inventory from suppliers may be either cash purchases or credit purchases, reflected as accounts payable. To compute cash paid to suppliers, it is necessary to analyze two accounts—Inventory and Accounts Payable—and make two adjustments.

	Inventory		
Balance, Jan. 1	51,000		
Purchases	xxx	xxx	Cost of goods sold
Balance, Dec. 31	63,000		

	Accounts Payable		
		17,000	Balance, Jan. 1
Cash payments	xxx	xxx	Credit purchases
		13,000	Balance, Dec. 31

The increase in inventory implies that purchases of inventory exceeded the cost of goods sold by $12,000. (A decrease in inventory would imply that purchases of inventory were less than cost of goods sold.) Therefore, cost of goods sold needs to be increased to reflect the "extra" cash purchases that were not included as an expense. A general formula to capture this relationship is:

$$\text{Cost of Purchases} = \text{Cost of Goods Sold} \begin{cases} + \text{ Increases in Inventory} \\ - \text{ Decreases in Inventory} \end{cases}$$

Next, the cost of purchases must be adjusted by the change in accounts payable to compute the cash paid to suppliers. The decrease in accounts payable implies that the cash payments to suppliers exceeded the purchases of inventory by $4,000. (An increase in accounts payable would imply that cash payments were less than the cost of purchases.) Therefore, Brooke Sportswear would add the increase in accounts payable to the cost of purchases to compute the cash paid to suppliers. A general formula that captures this relationship is:

$$\text{Cash Paid to Suppliers} = \text{Cost of Purchases} \begin{cases} + \text{ Decreases in Accounts Payable} \\ - \text{ Increases in Accounts Payable} \end{cases}$$

Combining this adjustment with the first adjustment, the cash paid to suppliers is computed as:

$$\text{Cash Paid to Suppliers} = \begin{cases} + \text{ Increases in Inventory} \\ - \text{ Decreases in Inventory} \end{cases} \begin{cases} + \text{ Decreases in Accounts Payable} \\ - \text{ Increases in Accounts Payable} \end{cases}$$

CASH PAID FOR OPERATING EXPENSES

Recall that operating expenses are the expenses the business incurs in selling goods or providing services and managing the company. These are usually divided into selling and administrative expenses and include items such as advertising expense, salaries and wages, insurance expense, utilities expense, property tax expense, and depreciation. These expenses are recognized when goods and services are used, not when cash is paid. Therefore, the expense amounts reported on the income statement will probably not equal the amount of cash actually paid during the period. Some expenses are paid before they are actually recognized (such as prepaid insurance); other expenses are paid for after they are recognized, creating a payable account at the time of the cash payment (such as salaries payable).

To determine the amount of cash payments for operating expenses, it is necessary to analyze the changes in the balance sheet accounts that are related to operating expenses—prepaid expenses and accrued liabilities. A prepaid expense increases when cash prepayments are made and decreases when expenses are incurred. An accrued liability increases when expenses are accrued (incurred but not yet paid) and decreases when cash payments are made. Brooke Sportswear has two balances that need to be analyzed—prepaid insurance and wages payable.

Prepaid Insurance

Balance, Jan. 1	2,000		
Cash prepayments	xxx	xxx	Expense incurred
Balance, Dec. 31	1,000		

Wages Payable

		2,000	Balance, Jan. 1
Cash payments	xxx	xxx	Wages expense
		3,500	Balance, Dec. 31

The decrease in prepaid insurance indicates that expenses recorded on the income statement were $1,000 higher than the cash payments. Because more expenses were incurred than were paid in cash, the company actually has more cash available at the end of the period than at the beginning of the period. (An increase in prepaid expenses means that cash payments were higher than the expenses recognized on the income statement and a company would have less cash available at the end of the period.) Therefore, Brooke Sportswear should add the increase in prepaid insurance ($1,000) to insurance expense ($15,000) to compute the cash paid for insurance.

The increase in wages payable indicates that wages expense recorded on the income statement was greater than the cash paid for wages by $1,500. Because less cash was paid than expensed, the company actually has more cash available. (A decrease in wages payable would imply that cash payments were greater than the expense recorded on the income statement.) Therefore, Brooke Sportswear should subtract the increase in wages payable ($1,500) from wages expense to compute cash paid for wages.

Combining these two adjustments, a general formula to compute cash paid for operating expenses is:

$$\text{Cash Paid for Operating Expenses} = \text{Operating Expenses} \begin{cases} + \text{ Increases in Prepaid Expenses} \\ - \text{ Decreases in Prepaid Expenses} \\ + \text{ Decrease in Accrued Liabilities} \\ - \text{ Increase in Accrued Liabilities} \end{cases}$$

CASH PAID FOR INTEREST AND INCOME TAXES

Computing cash paid for interest and income taxes is similar to that for operating expenses. Interest payable increases when interest expense is recorded and decreases when interest is paid.

Interest Payable

		1,000	Balance, Jan. 1
Cash payments	xxx	xxx	Interest expense
		1,500	Balance, Dec. 31

The increase in interest payable implies that interest expense recorded on the income statement was $500 greater than the cash paid for interest. (A decrease in interest expense indicates that the cash paid for interest is greater than the interest expense recorded on the income statement.) Therefore, Brooke Sportswear would subtract the $500 increase in interest payable from interest expense ($5,000) to compute the cash paid for interest. A general formula to capture this relationship is:

$$\text{Cash Paid for Interest} = \text{Interest Expense} \begin{cases} + \text{ Decreases in Interest Payable} \\ - \text{ Increases in Interest Payable} \end{cases}$$

The Income Taxes Payable account increases when income tax expense is incurred and decreases when income taxes are paid.

Income Taxes Payable			
		6,000	Balance, Jan. 1
Cash payments	xxx	xxx	Income tax expense
		3,000	Balance, Dec. 31

The decrease in income taxes payable implies that the cash payments for income taxes were $3,000 greater than the income tax expense reported on the income statement. (An increase in income taxes payable implies that income tax expense reported on the income statement is greater than the cash paid for income taxes.) Therefore, Brooke Sportswear would add the increase in income taxes payable ($3,000) to income taxes expense ($8,000) to compute cash paid for income taxes. A general formula to capture this relationship is:

$$\text{Cash Paid for Income Taxes} = \text{Income Tax Expense} \begin{cases} + \text{ Decrease in Income Taxes Payable} \\ - \text{ Increase in Income Taxes Payable} \end{cases}$$

OTHER ITEMS

Noncash Revenues and Expenses The income statement often includes various noncash items such as depreciation expense, amortization expense, and bad debt expense. Noncash items do not affect cash flow. Therefore, under the direct method, **noncash items are not reported on the statement of cash flows**. Sometimes, depreciation expense (or some other noncash expense) is included as part of operating expenses. In this case, depreciation expense must be subtracted from operating expenses to compute the cash paid for operating expenses.

Gains and Losses The sale of a long-term asset or the extinguishment of a long-term liability often produces either a gain or loss that is reported on the income statement. However, the gain or loss does not affect cash flow and should not be included as an operating activity. Furthermore, the gain or loss does not reveal the total amount of cash received or paid. Instead, it only gives the amount received or paid in excess of the book value of the asset or liability. Therefore, **gains and losses are not reported on the statement of cash flows under the direct method**.

APPLYING THE DIRECT METHOD

EXAMPLE 11.7 (p. 650) illustrates and summarizes the computation of the net cash flow from operating activities using the direct method. Because each item on the income statement is adjusted under the direct method, it is common to begin the analysis with the first item on the income statement (sales) and proceed down the income statement in the order that the accounts are listed.

It is important to note that both the indirect and direct methods arrive at the identical amount for the net cash provided (used) by operating activities. Therefore, the net cash

EXAMPLE 11.7   CALCULATING NET CASH FLOWS FROM OPERATING ACTIVITIES: DIRECT METHOD

Refer to the financial statements for Brooke Sportswear in Exhibit 11.6 (p. 633).

Required:
Compute the net cash flow from operating activities using the direct method.

Solution:

Cash flows from operating activities		
Cash collected from customers[a]		$ 465,000
Cash paid:		
To suppliers of merchandise[b]	(248,000)	
For wages[c]	(140,500)	
For insurance[d]	(14,000)	
For interest[e]	(4,500)	
For income taxes[f]	(11,000)	
Total cash paid		(418,000)
Net cash provided by operating activities		$ 47,000

[a] $472,000 sales − $7,000 change in accounts receivable = $465,000
[b] $232,000 cost of goods sold + $12,000 change in inventory + $4,000 change in accounts payable = $248,000
[c] $142,000 wages expense − $1,500 change in wages payable = $140,500
[d] $15,000 insurance expense − $1,000 change in prepaid insurance = $14,000
[e] $5,000 interest expense − $500 change in interest payable = $4,500
[f] $8,000 income taxes expense + $3,000 change in income taxes payable = $11,000

provided by operating activities of $47,000 computed above is the same as the net cash flow from operating activities computed under the indirect method shown in Example 11.3 (p. 634). The two methods differ only in how this amount is computed and the presentation of the details on the statement of cash flows. In addition, if the direct method is used, companies must also provide a supplementary schedule that shows the reconciliation of net income with net cash flow from operating activities. This supplementary schedule is, in effect, the presentation shown under the indirect method in Example 11.3.

OBJECTIVE

(Appendix 11B) Use a spreadsheet to prepare the statement of cash flows.

APPENDIX 11B: USING A SPREADSHEET TO PREPARE THE STATEMENT OF CASH FLOWS

The use of a spreadsheet provides a means of systematically analyzing changes in the balance sheet amounts, along with the information from the income statement and any additional information, to produce a statement of cash flows. This approach produces spreadsheet entries (made only on the spreadsheet and not in the general ledger) that simultaneously reconstruct and explain the changes in the balance sheet account balances and identify the cash inflows and outflows. The spreadsheet is based on the same underlying principles as discussed in the chapter. Its primary advantage is that it provides a systematic approach to analyze the data, which is helpful in complex situations.

To construct the spreadsheet, follow these steps:

Step 1.   Construct five columns. The first column will contain the balance sheet account titles. Immediately beneath the balance sheet accounts, set up the three sections of the statement of cash flows. The second column will contain the beginning balances of the balance sheet accounts (enter the amounts at this time). The third and fourth column will contain the debit and credit adjustments, respectively. The fifth column will contain the ending balances of the balance sheet accounts (enter the amounts at this time).

Step 2. Analyze each change in the balance sheet accounts in terms of debits and credits. Enter the effects in the adjustments column. Note that each entry will adjust both the balance sheet account being considered and either a statement of cash flows section of the spreadsheet or another balance sheet account (other than cash). Note that all inflows of cash are recorded as debits and all outflows of cash are recorded as credits.

Step 3. Prepare the statement of cash flows from the information contained in the statement of cash flows section of the spreadsheet.

Exhibit 11.10 (p. 652) illustrates how to use a spreadsheet to prepare the statement of cash flows for Brooke Sportswear. The required adjustments, labeled as (a) - (r) in Exhibit 11.10 are explained below. Refer to the information given earlier in the chapter regarding the logic behind the analysis of these changes.

NET INCOME

a. Net income is listed as a cash inflow in the operating activities section. Because net income flows into retained earnings during the closing process, a credit to retained earnings reflects the effect of the closing entry.

ADJUSTING FOR NONCASH ITEMS

b. For Brooke Sportswear, the only noncash item was depreciation expense, which is added back to net income in the operating activities section and is reflected as a credit to accumulated depreciation.

ADJUSTING FOR GAINS AND/OR LOSSES DUE TO INVESTING AND FINANCING ACTIVITIES

c. The actual proceeds from the sale of equipment are shown as a cash inflow in the investing activities section. The loss on the disposal of equipment is added back to net income in the operating activities section. In addition, both equipment and accumulated depreciation should be adjusted to reflect the sale.

d. The cash paid to purchase equipment is shown as a cash outflow in the investing activities section. At this point, note that the beginning and ending balances of the Equipment and Accumulated Depreciation accounts are reconciled.

e. The actual proceeds from the sale of the investment are shown as a cash inflow in the investing activities section. The gain on the sale of the investment is subtracted from net income in the operating activities section. In addition, the Investments account should be adjusted to reflect the sale.

f. The cash paid to purchase the investment is shown as a cash outflow in the investing activities section. At this point, note that the beginning and ending balances of the Investments account are reconciled.

ADJUSTING FOR CHANGES IN CURRENT ASSETS AND CURRENT LIABILITIES

g. The increase in accounts receivable is subtracted from net income and reconciles the change in the Accounts Receivable account.

EXHIBIT 11.10 Spreadsheet to Prepare Statement of Cash Flows

	A	B	C	D	E	F	G
1		Brooke Sportswear					
2		Spreadsheet to Prepare the Statement of Cash Flows					
3		For the year ended December 31					
4							
5		Beginning		Adjustments			Ending
6		Balance		Debit		Credit	Balance
7	**Balance Sheet Accounts**						
8	Cash	13,000	(r)	2,000			15,000
9	Accounts Receivable	46,000	(g)	7,000			53,000
10	Prepaid Insurance	2,000			1,000	(h)	1,000
11	Inventory	51,000	(i)	12,000			63,000
12	Land	325,000					325,000
13	Equipment	210,000	(d)	53,000	20,000	(c)	243,000
14	Accumulated Depreciation	150,000	(c)	12,000	40,000	(b)	178,000
15	Investments	41,000	(f)	28,000	16,000	(e)	53,000
16							
17	Accounts Payable	17,000	(j)	4,000			13,000
18	Wages Payable	2,000			1,500	(k)	3,500
19	Interest Payable	1,000			500	(l)	1,500
20	Income Taxes Payable	6,000	(m)	3,000			3,000
21	Notes Payable	115,000	(n)	35,000	29,000	(o)	109,000
22	Common Stock	151,000			14,000	(p)	165,000
23	Retained Earnings	246,000	(q)	5,000	39,000	(a)	280,000
24							
25	**Statement of Cash Flows**						
26	Cash flow from operating activities						
27	Net income		(a)	39,000			
28	Adjustments to reconcile net						
29	income to net cash flow from						
30	operating activities						
31	Depreciation expense		(b)	40,000			
32	Loss on disposal of equipment		(c)	6,000			
33	Gain on sale of investments				15,000	(e)	
34	Increase in accounts receivable				7,000	(g)	
35	Decrease in prepaid insurance		(h)	1,000			
36	Increase in inventory				12,000	(i)	
37	Decrease in accounts payable				4,000	(j)	
38	Increase in wages payable		(k)	1,500			
39	Increase in interest payable		(l)	500			
40	Decrease in income taxes payable				3,000	(m)	
41							
42	Cash flows from investing activities						
43	Sale of equipment		(c)	2,000			
44	Purchase equipment				53,000	(d)	
45	Sale of investments		(e)	31,000			
46	Purchase of investment				28,000	(f)	
47							
48	Cash flows from financing activities						
49	Repaid note payable				35,000	(n)	
50	Issued note payable		(o)	29,000			
51	Issued common stock		(p)	14,000			
52	Paid dividend				5,000	(q)	
53							
54	Net change in cash				2,000	(r)	
55							
56				325,000	325,000		

h. The decrease in prepaid insurance is added to net income and reconciles the change in the Prepaid Insurance account.

i. The increase in inventory is subtracted from net income and reconciles the change in the Inventory account.

j. The decrease in accounts payable is subtracted from net income and reconciles the change in the Accounts Payable account.

k. The increase in wages payable is added to net income and reconciles the change in the Wages Payable account.

l. The increase in interest payable is added to net income and reconciles the change in the Interest Payable account.

m. The decrease in income taxes payable is subtracted from net income and reconciles the change in the Income Taxes Payable account.

ADJUSTING FOR CASH INFLOWS AND OUTFLOWS ASSOCIATED WITH FINANCING ACTIVITIES

n. The repayment of the notes payable is a cash outflow from a financing activity and adjusts the Notes Payable account.

o. The issuance of a notes payable is a cash inflow from a financing activity and reconciles the change in the Notes Payable account.

p. The issuance of common stock is a cash inflow from a financing activity and reconciles the change in the Common Stock account.

q. The payment of dividends is a cash outflow from a financing activity and, together with the first entry, Item a, reconciles the change in retained earnings. The final entry reconciles the cash balance.

r. The summation of the three sections of the statement of cash flows equals the change in cash for the period. This amount can be checked by summing the net cash flows from operating, investing, and financing activities computed in the previous steps.

COMPLETING THE STATEMENT OF CASH FLOWS

The statement of cash flows can now be prepared from the information developed in the statement of cash flows portion of the spreadsheet. The statement of cash flows for Brooke Sportswear is shown in Exhibit 11.9 (p. 643).

REVIEW CENTER

LO1. Explain the purpose of a statement of cash flows.

KEY TAKEAWAYS

- The purpose of the statement of cash flows is to provide information about a company's cash receipts (inflows of cash) and cash payments (outflows of cash) during an accounting period.
- The information in the statement of cash flows is complementary to the information contained in the income statement and the balance sheet and is critical to understanding and analyzing a company's operations.

KEY TERM

Statement of cash flows, 622

LO2. Identify and classify business activities that produce cash inflows and outflows.

KEY TAKEAWAYS

- The statement of cash flows is divided into three main sections based on the fundamental business activities that a company engages in during a period:
  - cash flows from operating activities, which encompass the cash inflows and outflows that relate to the determination of net income
  - cash flows from investing activities, which are related to acquisitions and disposals of long-term assets and investments
  - cash flows from financing activities, which are related to the external financing of the company (debt or stockholders' equity)
- Some business activities take place without affecting cash and are referred to as noncash investing and financing activities.

KEY TERMS

Cash flows from financing activities, 624
Cash flows from investing activities, 624
Cash flows from operating activities, 623
Noncash investing and financing activities, 625

EXAMPLE

Example 11.1   Classifying business activities, page 626

LO3. Understand the relationship between changes in cash and the changes in the balance sheet accounts.

KEY TAKEAWAYS

- Because of timing issues between the recognition of revenues and expenses and the inflows and outflows of cash, information about a company's cash flows can be obtained by examining the changes in the balance sheet account balances over a period.

- Increases in cash result from increases in liabilities, increases in stockholders' equity, and decreases in noncash assets.
- Decreases in cash result from decreases in liabilities, decreases in stockholders' equity, and increases in noncash assets.

KEY CALCULATIONS

Increases in Cash = Increases in Liabilities + Increases in Stockholders' Equity
            + Decreases in Noncash Assets

Decreases in Cash = Decreases in Liabilities + Decreases in Stockholders' Equity
            + Increases in Noncash Assets

EXAMPLE

| **Example 11.2** | Classifying changes in balance sheet accounts, page 629 |

KEY TAKEAWAYS

- The indirect method for reporting cash flows from operating activities begins with net income and adjusts it for noncash items to produce net cash flow from operating activities.
- The adjustments to net income are necessary to eliminate income statement items that do not affect cash and to adjust accrual-basis revenues and expenses to cash receipts and cash payments.
- Four types of adjustments are necessary:
  o add to net income any noncash expenses and subtract from net income any non-cash revenues
  o add to net income any losses and subtract from net income any gains
  o add to net income any decreases in current assets or increases in current liabilities that are related to operating activities
  o subtract from net income any increases in current assets and decreases in current liabilities that are related to operating activities

LO4. Prepare the cash flows from operating activities section of a statement of cash flows using the indirect method.

KEY TERMS

Direct method, 632
Indirect method, 632

EXAMPLE

| **Example 11.3** | Calculating net cash flow from operating activities: indirect method, page 634 |

LO5. Prepare the cash flows from investing activities section of a statement of cash flows.

KEY TAKEAWAYS

- The cash flows from the investing activities section reports the net cash flow related to buying and selling property, plant, and equipment or other operating assets, purchasing and selling investments in other companies, and lending and collecting the principal amount of loans from borrowers.
- The preparation of the investing activities section of a statement of cash flows involves a careful analysis of the information in the financial statements as well as a recreation of the journal entries that describe the activities that took place during a period.

EXAMPLE

Example 11.4	Reporting net cash flow from investing activities, page 640

LO6. Prepare the cash flows from financing activities section of a statement of cash flows.

KEY TAKEAWAYS

- The cash flows from financing activities section reports the net cash flow related to the borrowing and repayment of the principal amount of long-term debt, sale of common or preferred stock, payment of dividends, and purchase and sale of treasury stock.
- The preparation of the financing activities section of a statement of cash flows involves a careful analysis of the information in the financial statements as well as a recreation of the journal entries that describe the activities that took place during a period.

EXAMPLE

Example 11.5	Reporting net cash flow from financing activities, page 642

LO7. Analyze information contained in the statement of cash flows.

KEY TAKEAWAYS

- Effective analysis of the statement of cash flows requires an examination of the statement of cash flows itself, a comparison of the information on the current statement of cash flows with earlier statements, and a comparison of the information in the current statement of cash flows with information from other companies' statements of cash flow.
- Financial statement users may also rely on summary cash flow measures such as free cash flow (the cash flow that a company is able to generate after considering the maintenance or expansion of its assets) and the cash flow adequacy ratio (a measure of a company's ability to meet its debt obligations with its operating cash flow).

KEY TERMS

Cash flow adequacy ratio, 645
Free cash flow, 644

EXAMPLE

Example 11.6 Analyzing free cash flow and cash flow adequacy, page 645

KEY CALCULATIONS

$$\text{Free Cash Flow} = \text{Net Cash Flow from Operating Activities} - \text{Capital Expenditures} - \text{Cash Dividends}$$

$$\text{Cash Flow Adequacy} = \frac{\text{Free Cash Flow}}{\text{Average Amount of Debt Maturing over the Next 5 Years}}$$

KEY TAKEAWAYS

- The direct method for reporting cash flows from operating activities lists cash inflows and cash outflows for each type of operating activity that a company performs.
- Cash flows from operating activities are generally computed by adjusting each item on the income statement by the changes in the related current asset or current liability accounts.
- Typical cash flow categories reported under the direct method include cash collected from customers, cash paid to suppliers, cash paid to employees, cash paid for interest, and cash paid for taxes.

LO8. (Appendix 11A) Prepare the cash flows from operating activities section of a statement of cash flows using the direct method.

KEY CALCULTIONS

$$\text{Cash Collected from Customers} = \text{Sales} \begin{cases} + \text{ Decrease in Accounts Receivable} \\ - \text{ Increase in Accounts Receivable} \end{cases}$$

$$\text{Cash Collected for Interest} = \text{Interest Revenue} \begin{cases} + \text{ Decrease in Interest Receivable} \\ - \text{ Increase in Interest Receivable} \end{cases}$$

$$\text{Cash Paid to Suppliers} = \begin{cases} + \text{ Increases in Inventory} \\ - \text{ Decreases in Inventory} \end{cases} \begin{cases} + \text{ Decreases in Accounts Payable} \\ - \text{ Increases in Accounts Payable} \end{cases}$$

$$\text{Cash Paid for Operating Expenses} = \text{Operating Expenses} \begin{cases} + \text{ Increases in Prepaid Expenses} \\ - \text{ Decreases in Prepaid Expenses} \\ + \text{ Decrease in Accrued Liabilities} \\ - \text{ Increase in Accrued Liabilities} \end{cases}$$

$$\text{Cash Paid for Interest} = \text{Interest Expense} \begin{cases} + \text{ Decreases in Interest Payable} \\ - \text{ Increases in Interest Payable} \end{cases}$$

$$\text{Cash Paid for Income Taxes} = \text{Income Tax Expense} \begin{cases} + \text{ Decrease in Income Taxes Payable} \\ - \text{ Increase in Income Taxes Payable} \end{cases}$$

EXAMPLE

Example 11.7	Calculating net cash flows from operating activities: direct method, page 650

LO9. (Appendix 11B) Use a spreadsheet to prepare the statement of cash flows.

KEY TAKEAWAYS

- A spreadsheet provides a means of systematically analyzing changes in the balance sheet amounts, along with the information from the income statement and any additional information, to produce a statement of cash flows.
- The spreadsheet approach produces spreadsheet entries that simultaneously reconstruct and explain the changes in the balance sheet account balances and identify the cash inflows and outflows.

REVIEW PROBLEM

The income statement and comparative balance sheet for Solar System Company are shown below.

Solar System Company
Balance Sheets

	Jan. 1	Dec. 31
ASSETS		
Current assets:		
Cash	$ 47,000	$ 56,000
Accounts receivable	107,000	123,000
Prepaid expenses	9,000	10,000
Inventory	46,000	52,000
Total current assets	$ 209,000	$ 241,000
Property, plant, and equipment:		
Equipment	262,000	270,000
Accumulated depreciation	(109,000)	(118,000)
Total assets	$ 362,000	$ 393,000
LIABILITIES AND EQUITY		
Current liabilities:		
Accounts payable	$ 11,000	$ 18,000
Salaries payable	9,000	5,000
Income taxes payable	5,000	7,000
Total current liabilities	$ 25,000	$ 30,000
Long-term liabilities:		
Notes payable	130,000	120,000
Total liabilities	$ 155,000	$ 150,000
Equity:		
Common stock	$ 200,000	$ 213,000
Retained earnings	7,000	30,000
Total equity	$ 207,000	$ 243,000
Total liabilities and equity	$ 362,000	$ 393,000

Solar System Company
Income Statement
For the year ended December 31

Sales revenue	$1,339,000
Less: Cost of goods sold	(908,000)
Gross margin	$ 431,000
Less operating expenses:	
Salaries expense	(230,000)
Depreciation	(24,000)
Other operating expenses	(116,000)
Income from operations	$ 61,000
Other income and expenses:	
Gain on disposal of equipment	3,000
Interest expense	(14,000)
Income before taxes	$ 50,000
Less: Income taxes expense	(12,000)
Net income	$ 38,000

Additional Information for 2023:

1. Equipment with a cost of $24,000 and accumulated depreciation of $15,000 was sold for $12,000 cash. Equipment was purchased for $32,000 cash.
2. Notes payable in the amount of $10,000 were repaid.
3. Common stock was issued for $13,000 cash during the year.
4. Cash dividends of $15,000 were paid during the year.

Required:

Prepare a statement of cash flows for Solar System Company using the indirect method.

Solution:

Solar System Company Statement of Cash Flows For the year ended December 31, 2023		
Cash flows from operating activities		
Net income	$ 38,000	
Adjustments to reconcile net income to		
net cash flow from operating activities:		
Depreciation expense	24,000	
Gain on disposal of equipment	(3,000)	
Increase in accounts receivable	(16,000)	
Increase in prepaid expenses	(1,000)	
Increase in inventory	(6,000)	
Increase in accounts payable	7,000	
Decrease in salaries payable	(4,000)	
Increase in income taxes payable	2,000	
Net cash provided by operating activities		$ 41,000
Cash flows from investing activities		
Cash received from sale of equipment	$ 12,000	
Purchase of equipment	(32,000)	
Net cash used by investing activities		$(20,000)
Cash flows from financing activities		
Cash paid to retire notes payable	$(10,000)	
Cash received from issuance of common stock	13,000	
Cash paid for dividends	(15,000)	
Net cash used by financing activities		(12,000)
Net increase (decrease) in cash		$ 9,000
Cash and cash equivalents, 1/1/2023		47,000
Cash and cash equivalents, 12/31/2023		$ 56,000

APPLYING KNOWLEDGE

DISCUSSION QUESTIONS

1. What is a statement of cash flows?

   OBJECTIVE 1

2. How do investors, creditors, and others typically use the information in the statement of cash flows?

3. How is a statement of cash flows different from an income statement?

4. What are cash equivalents? How are cash equivalents reported on the statement of cash flows?

   OBJECTIVE 2

5. What are the three categories into which inflows and outflows of cash are divided? Be sure to describe what is included in each of these three categories.

6. Why are companies required to report noncash investing and financing activities? How are these activities reported?

7. Why are direct exchanges of long-term debt for items of property, plant, and equipment included in supplementary information for the statement of cash flows even though the exchanges do not affect cash?

OBJECTIVE 3
8. Describe the relationship between changes in cash and changes in noncash assets, liabilities, and stockholders' equity.

OBJECTIVE 4
9. What are two ways to report a company's net cash flow from operating activities? Briefly describe each method.

10. Why are depreciation, depletion, and amortization added to net income when the indirect method is used to report net cash flows from operating activities?

11. What does an increase in inventory imply? How would this increase in inventory be reported under the indirect method?

12. What does an increase in accounts payable imply? How would this increase in accounts payable be reported under the indirect method?

13. Does the fact that the cash flow from operating activities is normally positive imply that cash and cash equivalents usually increase each year?

OBJECTIVE 5
14. How is the sale of equipment at a loss reported on the statement of cash flows? Assume the indirect method is used to prepare the statement of cash flows.

OBJECTIVE 6
15. Where do the components of the changes in retained earnings appear in the statement of cash flows? Assume the indirect method is used to prepare the statement of cash flows.

OBJECTIVE 2 5 6
16. What are the most common sources of cash inflows from financing and investing activities?

17. What are the most common cash outflows related to investing and financing activities?

OBJECTIVE 7
18. What balance sheet account changes might you expect to find for a company that must rely on sources other than operations to fund its cash outflows?

19. From what source(s) should most companies secure the majority of cash inflows? Why?

20. Why should companies attempt to secure cash for investment in property, plant, and equipment from long-term or permanent sources?

OBJECTIVE 8
21. *(Appendix 11A)* When using the direct method, which items usually constitute the largest components of cash inflows from operating activities?

22. *(Appendix 11A)* Describe how to compute each of the cash inflows and cash outflows from operating activities under the direct method.

23. *(Appendix 11A)* Why is depreciation expense not generally reported on the statement of cash flows when using the direct method?

OBJECTIVE 9
24. *(Appendix 11B)* Why do companies often use a spreadsheet to prepare the statement of cash flows?

MULTIPLE-CHOICE QUESTIONS

OBJECTIVE 1
11-1 Which of the following is *not* a use of the statement of cash flows?
a. Aids in the prediction of future cash flow.
b. Provides a measure of the future obligations of the company.
c. Helps estimate the amount of funds that will be needed from creditors or stockholders.
d. Provides insights into the quality and reliability of reported income.

11-2 Which of the following would be classified as a cash outflow from an operating activity? **OBJECTIVE 2**
  a. Purchase of an investment
  b. Payment of dividends
  c. Purchase of equipment
  d. Payment of goods purchased from suppliers

11-3 Which of the following is an example of a cash inflow from an operating activity?
  a. Collection of cash relating to a note receivable
  b. Sale of property, plant, and equipment
  c. Collection of an account receivable from a credit sale
  d. None of these

11-4 Which of the following is an example of a cash outflow from a financing activity?
  a. Payment of cash dividends to stockholders
  b. Payment of interest on a note payable
  c. Payment of wages to employees
  d. Issuance of common stock for cash

11-5 Which of the following is true? **OBJECTIVE 3**
  a. An increase in cash may result from an increase in liabilities.
  b. An increase in cash may result from a decrease in stockholders' equity.
  c. An increase in cash may result from an increase in noncash assets.
  d. A decrease in cash may result from an increase in liabilities.

11-6 Which of the following statements is true? **OBJECTIVE 4**
  a. Net cash flow from operating activities must be determined using the indirect method.
  b. The indirect method adjusts sales for changes in noncash items to produce net cash flow from operating activities.
  c. Many companies prefer the indirect method because it is easier and less costly to prepare.
  d. The FASB prefers the indirect method.

11-7 Mullinix Inc. reported the following information: net income, $55,000; decrease in accounts receivable, $12,000; decrease in accounts payable, $6,500; and depreciation expense, $10,000. What amount did Mullinix report as cash flow from operating activities on its statement of cash flows?
  a. $50,500
  b. $59,500
  c. $70,500
  d. $83,500

11-8 Which item is added to net income when computing cash flows from operating activities?
  a. Gain on the disposal of property, plant, and equipment
  b. Increase in wages payable
  c. Increase in inventory
  d. Increase in prepaid rent

Use the following information for Multiple-Choice Questions 11-9 and 11-10:
Cornett Company reported the following information: cash received from the issuance of common stock, $150,000; cash received from the sale of equipment, $14,800; cash paid to purchase an investment, $20,000; cash paid to retire a note payable, $50,000; and cash collected from sales to customers, $225,000.

11-9 Refer to the information for Cornett Company above. What amount should Cornett **OBJECTIVE 5** report on its statement of cash flows as net cash flows provided by investing activities?
  a. $(5,200)
  b. $55,200
  c. $144,800
  d. None of these

11-10 Refer to the information for Cornett Company above. What amount should Cornett **OBJECTIVE 6** report on its statement of cash flows as net cash flows from financing activities?
  a. $65,200
  b. $94,800
  c. $100,000
  d. None of these

OBJECTIVE

11-11 Chasse Building Supply Inc. reported net cash provided by operating activities of $243,000, capital expenditures of $112,900, cash dividends of $35,800, and average maturities of long-term debt over the next 5 years of $122,300. What is Chasse's free cash flow and cash flow adequacy ratio?

a. $94,300 and 0.77, respectively

c. $130,100 and 1.06, respectively

b. $94,300 and 0.82, respectively

d. $165,900 and 1.36, respectively

OBJECTIVE

11-12 Smoltz Company reported the following information for the current year: cost of goods sold, $252,500; increase in inventory, $21,700; and increase in accounts payable, $12,200. What is the amount of cash paid to suppliers that Smoltz would report on its statement of cash flows under the direct method?

a. $218,600

c. $262,000

b. $243,000

d. $286,400

11-13 Romo Inc. reported the following information for the current year: operating expenses, $325,000; increase in prepaid expenses, $6,200; and decrease in accrued liabilities, $8,800. What is the amount of cash paid for operating expenses that Romo would report on its statement of cash flows under the direct method?

a. $310,000

c. $327,600

b. $322,400

d. $340,000

BRIEF EXERCISES

OBJECTIVE

Brief Exercise 11-14 Uses of the Statement of Cash Flows

Listed below are the three major financial statements and some of the ways in which they are used by investors, creditors and others.

Use		Financial Statement
a.	Aids in understanding the differences between net income and cash flow.	1. Balance Sheet
b.	Helps to assess a company's ability to produce future cash flows.	2. Income Statement 3. Statement of Cash Flows
c.	Assists in judging a company's ability to meets its obligations.	
d.	Helps in estimating the need for external financing.	

Required:

Match each financial statement with its use. (Each use may be related to more than one financial statement, and financial statements may be used more than one time.)

OBJECTIVE 2

EXAMPLE 11.1

Brief Exercise 11-15 Classification of Cash Flows

Foster Company reported the following items in its statement of cash flows presented using the indirect method.

a. Cash paid for interest

b. Proceeds from sale of building

c. Purchase of supplies on account

d. Issuance of common stock

e. Cash dividend paid to stockholders

f. Taxes paid to the federal government

g. Sale of inventory

h. Purchased equipment for cash

i. Issued long-term debt

j. Recording of depreciation expense

k. Repayment of principal on long-term debt

i. Loss on disposal of equipment

Required:

Indicate whether each item should be classified as a cash flow from operating activities, a cash flow from investing activities, or a cash flow from financing activities.

Brief Exercise 11-16 Analyzing Balance Sheet Accounts

OBJECTIVE 2 3

EXAMPLES 11.1 AND 11.2

A review of the balance sheet of Dixon Company revealed the following changes in the account balances:

a. Increase in retained earnings
b. Increase in equipment
c. Increase in interest receivable
d. Decrease in bonds payable

e. Increase in unearned rent revenue
f. Decrease in prepaid insurance
g. Decrease in long-term investment
h. Increase in accounts payable

Required:

1. Classify each change in the balance sheet account as a cash flow from operating activities, a cash flow from investing activities, a cash flow from financing activities, or a noncash investing and financing activity.
2. Indicate whether each of the changes in the balance sheet accounts produces an increase in cash, produces a decrease in cash, or is a noncash activity.

Brief Exercise 11-17 Determining Net Cash Flow from Operating Activities

OBJECTIVE 4

EXAMPLE 11.3

An analysis of the balance sheet and income statement of Sanchez Company revealed the following: net income, $12,750; depreciation expense, $32,600; decrease in accounts receivable, $21,500; increase in inventory, $18,300; increase in accounts payable, $19,800; and decrease in interest payable of $1,200.

Required:
Compute the net cash flows from operating activities using the indirect method.

Brief Exercise 11-18 Determining Net Cash Flow from Operating Activities

OBJECTIVE 4

EXAMPLE 11.3

Presented below are selected balance sheet information and the income statement for Burch Company.

Selected Balance Sheet Information			Burch Company Income Statement For the year ended December 31	
	Jan. 1	Dec. 31		
Cash	$17,500	$20,000	Sales	$250,000
Accounts receivable	8,000	10,500	Cost of goods sold	(160,000)
Inventory	21,000	18,000	Depreciation expense	(15,000)
Accounts payable	10,000	15,000	Other expenses	(35,000)
Income taxes payable	2,500	1,000	Income tax expense	(12,000)
			Net income	$ 28,000

Required:
Compute the net cash flows from operating activities using the indirect method.

Brief Exercise 11-19 Determining Net Cash Flow from Investing Activities

OBJECTIVE 5

EXAMPLE 11.4

Orlando Inc. reported the following information:

	Jan. 1	Dec. 31
Equipment	$32,000	$46,000
Accumulated depreciation	12,500	15,900
Investment (long-term)	50,000	38,000

In addition, Orlando sold equipment costing $8,000 with accumulated depreciation of $5,000 for $3,500. Orlando also reported a $3,000 gain on the sale of long-term investments.

Required:
Compute net cash flow from investing activities.

OBJECTIVE 6

EXAMPLE 11.5

Brief Exercise 11-20 Determining Net Cash Flow from Financing Activities

Madison Company reported the following information:

	12/31/2023	12/31/2022
Notes payable	$ 95,000	$75,000
Common stock	120,000	80,000
Retained earnings	20,000	36,000

Madison reported net income of $26,000 for the year ended December 31. In addition, Madison repaid $35,000 of the notes payable during the year.

Required:

Compute net cash flow from financing activities.

OBJECTIVE 7

EXAMPLE 11.6

Brief Exercise 11-21 Analyzing the Statement of Cash Flows

Manning Company reported the following information: cash provided by operating activities, $425,000; cash used by investing activities, $200,000; average debt maturing over the next 5 years, $80,000; capital expenditures, $275,000; cash dividends, $60,000.

Required:

Compute free cash flow and the cash flow adequacy ratio. (*Note:* Round ratios to two decimal places.) Comment on each ratio.

OBJECTIVE 8

EXAMPLE 11.7

Brief Exercise 11-22 *(Appendix 11A)* Cash Receipts from Customers

Singleton Inc. had accounts receivable of $22,150 at January 1 and $26,850 at December 31. Net income was $125,300 and sales revenue was $1,240,000.

Required:

Compute the amount of cash collected from customers using the direct method.

OBJECTIVE 8

EXAMPLE 11.7

Brief Exercise 11-23 *(Appendix 11A)* Cash Payments to Suppliers

Blackmon Company reported net income of $805,000 and cost of goods sold of $1,525,000 on its income statement. In addition, Blackmon reported an increase in inventory of $65,410, a decrease in prepaid insurance of $12,800, and a decrease in accounts payable of $43,190.

Required:

Compute the amount of cash payments to suppliers using the direct method.

OBJECTIVE 8

EXAMPLE 11.7

Brief Exercise 11-24 *(Appendix 11A)* Cash Payments for Operating Expenses

Luna Inc. reported operating expenses of $174,500, excluding depreciation expense of $36,200. During the year, Luna reported a decrease in prepaid expenses of $8,500 and a decrease in accrued liabilities of $18,200.

Required:

Compute the amount of cash payments for operating expenses using the direct method.

OBJECTIVE 8

EXAMPLE 11.7

Brief Exercise 11-25 *(Appendix 11A)* Determining Net Cash Flow from Operating Activities—Direct Method

Presented below are selected balance sheet information and the income statement for Burch Company.

Selected Balance Sheet Information			Burch Company Income Statement For the year ended December 31	
	Jan. 1	**Dec. 31**		
Cash	$17,500	$20,000	Sales	$ 250,000
Accounts receivable	8,000	10,500	Cost of goods sold	(160,000)
Inventory	21,000	18,000	Depreciation expense	(15,000)
Accounts payable	10,000	15,000	Other expenses	(35,000)
Income taxes payable	2,500	1,000	Income tax expense	(12,000)
			Net income	$ 28,000

Required:

Compute the net cash flows from operating activities using the direct method.

EXERCISES

Exercise 11-26 Classification of Cash Flows

OBJECTIVE ◀ 2

A review of the financial records for Rogers Inc. uncovered the following items:

a. Collected accounts receivable
b. Paid cash to purchase equipment
c. Received cash from the issuance of bonds
d. Paid interest on long-term debt
e. Sold equipment at book value
f. Depreciation on equipment
g. Issued common stock for land
h. Paid rent on building for the current period

i. Paid cash to settle an account payable
j. Declared and paid dividends to stockholders
k. Received cash dividend on investment
l. Repaid the principal amount of long-term debt
m. Amortization of a copyright
n. Sold a long-term investment at a gain

Rogers uses the indirect method to prepare the operating activities of its statement of cash flows.

Required:

Indicate whether each item should be classified as a cash flow from operating activities, cash flow from investing activities, cash flow from financing activities, or noncash investing and financing activity.

Exercise 11-27 Classification of Cash Flows

OBJECTIVE ◀ 2

The following are several items that might be disclosed on a company's statement of cash flows presented using the indirect method.

a. Net income
b. Depreciation expense
c. Issuance of common stock
d. Loss on disposal of equipment
e. Purchase of a building

f. Decrease in accounts payable
g. Converted bonds into common stock
h. Sale of long-term investment
i. Payment of interest
j. Increase in inventory

Required:

1. Indicate whether each item should be classified as a cash flow from operating activities, cash flow from investing activities, cash flow from financing activities, or noncash investing and financing activity.
2. **CONCEPTUAL CONNECTION** Why is the proper classification of cash flows important?

OBJECTIVE 3

Exercise 11-28 Analyzing Changes in Balance Sheet Accounts

A review of the balance sheet of Mathews Company revealed the following changes in the account balances:

a. Increase in accounts receivable
b. Increase in retained earnings
c. Decrease in salaries payable
d. Increase in common stock

e. Decrease in inventory
f. Increase in accounts payable
g. Decrease in long-term debt
h. Increase in property, plant, and equipment

Required:
1. For each of the above items, indicate whether it produces a cash inflow or a cash outflow.
2. Classify each change as a cash flow from operating activities (indirect method), cash flow from investing activities, or cash flow from financing activities.

OBJECTIVE 3

Exercise 11-29 Analyzing the Accounts

Casey Company uses a perpetual inventory system and engaged in the following transactions:

a. Made credit sales of $825,000. The cost of the merchandise sold was $560,000.
b. Collected accounts receivable in the amount of $752,600.
c. Purchased goods on credit in the amount of $574,300.
d. Paid accounts payable in the amount of $536,200.

Required:
Prepare the journal entries necessary to record the transactions. Indicate whether each transaction increased cash, decreased cash, or had no effect on cash.

OBJECTIVE 3

Exercise 11-30 Analyzing the Accounts

The controller for Summit Sales Inc. provides the following information on transactions that occurred during the year:

a. Purchased supplies on credit, $18,600
b. Paid $14,800 cash toward the purchase in Transaction a
c. Provided services to customers on credit, $46,925
d. Collected $39,650 cash from accounts receivable
e. Recorded depreciation expense, $8,175
f. Employee salaries accrued, $15,650
g. Paid $15,650 cash to employees for salaries earned
h. Accrued interest expense on long-term debt, $1,950

i. Paid a total of $25,000 on long-term debt, which includes $1,950 interest from Transaction h
j. Paid $2,220 cash for 1 years insurance coverage in advance
k. Recognized insurance expense, $1,340, that was paid in a previous period
l. Sold equipment with a book value of $7,500 for $7,500 cash
m. Declared cash dividend, $12,000
n. Paid cash dividend declared in Transaction m
o. Purchased new equipment for $28,300 cash
p. Issued common stock for $60,000 cash
q. Used $10,700 of supplies to produce revenues

Summit Sales uses the indirect method to prepare its statement of cash flows.

Required:
1. Construct a table similar to the one shown at the top of the next page. Analyze each transaction and indicate its effect on the fundamental accounting equation. If the transaction increases a financial statement element, write the amount of the increase preceded by a plus sign (+) in the appropriate column. If the transaction decreases a financial statement element, write the amount of the decrease preceded by a minus sign (−) in the appropriate column.
2. Indicate whether each transaction results in a cash inflow or a cash outflow in the "Effect on Cash Flows" column. If the transaction has no effect on cash flow, then indicate this by placing "none" in the "Effect on Cash Flows" column.

3. For each transaction that affected cash flows, indicate whether the cash flow would be classified as a cash flow from operating activities, cash flow from investing activities, or cash flow from financing activities. If there is no effect on cash flows, indicate this as a noncash activity.

	Effect on Accounting Equation					Effect on Cash
	Assets		Liabilities and Equity			
Transaction	Current	Noncurrent	Current Liabilities	Noncurrent Liabilities	Equity	Flows

Exercise 11-31 Reporting Net Cash Flow from Operating Activities

OBJECTIVE 4

The following information is available for Cornelius Inc.:

Selected Income Statement Information	Amount
Net income	$52,000
Depreciation expense	11,300

Selected Balance Sheet Information	Beginning Balance	Ending Balance
Accounts receivable	$11,500	$17,650
Inventory	33,800	27,825
Accounts payable	15,900	24,600

Required:
1. Compute the net cash flows from operating activities using the indirect method.
2. **CONCEPTUAL CONNECTION** Explain why Cornelius was able to report net cash flow from operating activities that was higher than net income.
3. **CONCEPTUAL CONNECTION** What could the difference between net income and cash flow from operating activities signal to financial statement users?

Exercise 11-32 Reporting Net Cash Flow from Operating Activities

OBJECTIVE 4

The following information is available for Bernard Corporation:

Net income	$185,200	Decrease in income taxes payable	$ 3,870
Decrease in accounts receivable	8,300	Increase in notes payable (due in 5 years)	50,000
Increase in inventory	19,900	Depreciation expense	52,700
Decrease in prepaid rent	4,410	Loss on disposal of equipment	6,450
Increase in salaries payable	7,100		

Required:
1. Compute the net cash flows from operating activities using the indirect method.
2. **CONCEPTUAL CONNECTION** What are the causes of the major differences between net income and net cash flow from operating activities?

Exercise 11-33 Determining Cash Flows from Investing Activities

OBJECTIVE 5

Burns Company's 2019 and 2018 balance sheets presented the following data for equipment:

	Jan. 1	Dec. 31
Equipment	$262,000	$325,000
Accumulated depreciation	108,000	133,900
Book value	$154,000	$191,100

During the year, equipment costing $41,000 with accumulated depreciation of $36,700 was sold for cash, producing a $3,200 gain.

Required:
1. Calculate the amount of depreciation expense.
2. Calculate the amount of cash spent for equipment.
3. Calculate the amount that should be included as a cash inflow from the disposal of equipment.

Exercise 11-34 Determining Cash Flows from Investing Activities

Airco owns several aircraft and its balance sheet indicated the following amounts for its aircraft accounts:

	Jan. 1	Dec. 31
Equipment, aircraft	$22,250,000	$32,700,000
Accumulated depreciation	13,125,000	13,900,000
Book value	$ 9,125,000	$18,800,000

Required:

1. Assume that Airco did not sell any aircraft during the year. Determine the amount of depreciation expense and the cash spent for aircraft purchases for the year.
2. If Airco sold for cash aircraft that cost $4,100,000 with accumulated depreciation of $3,825,000 producing a gain of $193,000, determine (a) the amount of depreciation expense, (b) the cash paid for aircraft purchases, and (c) the cash inflow from the disposal of aircraft.

OBJECTIVE 6

Exercise 11-35 Determining Cash Flows from Financing Activities

Solomon Construction Company reported the following amount on its balance sheet for notes payable:

	Jan. 1	Dec. 31
Notes payable	$120,000	$200,000

Required:

1. If Solomon did not repay any notes payable during the year, determine how much cash Solomon received from the issuance of notes payable.
2. If Solomon repaid $40,000 of notes payable during the year, determine what amounts Solomon would report in the financing activities section of the statement of cash flows.

OBJECTIVE 6

Exercise 11-36 Determining Cash Flows from Financing Activities

Nichols Inc. reported the following amounts on its balance sheet for equity:

	Jan. 1	Dec. 31
Common stock	$135,000	$210,000
Retained earnings	412,800	495,300

Required:

Assume that, for the current year, Nichols did not retire any stock, it reported $105,610 of net income for 2019, and any dividends declared were paid in cash. Determine the amounts Nichols would report in the financing section of the statement of cash flows.

Exercise 11-37 Partial Statement of Cash Flows

Service Company had net income during the current year of $65,800. The following information was obtained from Service's balance sheet:

Accounts receivable	$26,540 increase
Inventory	32,180 increase
Accounts payable	9,300 decrease
Interest payable	2,120 increase
Accumulated depreciation (Building)	14,590 increase
Accumulated depreciation (Equipment)	32,350 increase

Additional Information:

1. Equipment with accumulated depreciation of $18,000 was sold during the year.
2. Cash dividends of $29,625 were paid during the year.

Required:

1. Prepare the net cash flows from operating activities using the indirect method.
2. **CONCEPTUAL CONNECTION** How would the cash proceeds from the sale of equipment be reported on the statement of cash flows?
3. **CONCEPTUAL CONNECTION** How would the cash dividends be reported on the statement of cash flows?
4. **CONCEPTUAL CONNECTION** What could the difference between net income and cash flow from operating activities signal to financial statement users?

Exercise 11-38 Analyzing the Statement of Cash Flows

OBJECTIVE ◄ 7

Information for Ditka Inc. and McMahon Company is given below:

	Ditka Inc.	McMahon Company
Cash provided by operating activities	$2,475,000	$1,639,000
Capital expenditures	1,157,000	748,000
Dividends	285,000	189,000
Average debt maturity over next 5 years	985,000	1,212,000

Required:

1. Compute Ditka's and McMahon's free cash flow and cash flow adequacy ratio. (*Note:* Round ratio to two decimal places.)
2. **CONCEPTUAL CONNECTION** What information do these cash-based performance measures provide with regard to the two companies?

Exercise 11-39 Preparing the Statement of Cash Flows

OBJECTIVE ◄ 4 5 6 7

Balance sheet information for Beckwith Products Company is presented below.

	Jan. 1	Dec. 31
Assets:		
Cash	$ 25,000	$ 36,950
Accounts receivable	78,000	75,100
Inventory	36,000	45,300
Property, plant, and equipment	153,000	256,400
Accumulated depreciation	20,000	38,650
Total assets	$272,000	$375,100
Liabilities and Equity:		
Accounts payable	$ 11,000	$ 13,100
Interest payable	8,000	11,500
Wages payable	9,000	8,100
Notes payable	90,000	105,000
Common stock	50,000	100,000
Retained earnings	104,000	137,400
Total liabilities and equity	$272,000	$375,100

Additional Information:

1. Net income for the year was $58,400.
2. Cash dividends of $25,000 were declared and paid during the year.

(*Continued*)

3. During the year, Beckwith issued $50,000 of notes payable and repaid $35,000 principal relating to notes payable.
4. Common stock was issued for $50,000 cash.
5. Depreciation expense was $18,650, and there were no disposals of equipment.

Required:
1. Prepare a statement of cash flows (indirect method) for Beckwith Products.
2. Compute the following cash-based performance measures: (a) free cash flow and (b) cash flow adequacy. (*Note:* Assume that the average amount of debt maturing over the next 5 years is $85,000. Round ratio to two decimal places.)
3. **CONCEPTUAL CONNECTION** What can you conclude by examining the patterns in Beckwith's cash flows?

OBJECTIVE 8

Exercise 11-40 *(Appendix 11A)* Preparing Net Cash Flows from Operating Activities—Direct Method

Colassard Industries has the following data available for preparation of its statement of cash flows:

Sales revenue	$385,800	Inventory, increase	$ 8,710
Cost of goods sold	203,100	Prepaid insurance, increase	1,550
Wages expense	62,400	Accounts payable, increase	3,680
Insurance expense	13,780	Notes payable, increase	40,000
Interest expense	15,150	Interest payable, increase	1,240
Income taxes expense	27,400	Wages payable, decrease	6,700
Accounts receivable, decrease	15,600		

Required:
Prepare the cash flows from operating activities section of the statement of cash flows using the direct method.

OBJECTIVE 8

Exercise 11-41 *(Appendix 11A)* Preparing a Statement of Cash Flows—Direct Method

The controller of Newstrom Software Inc. provides the following information as the basis for a statement of cash flows:

Cash collected from customers	$785,400	Income taxes paid	$ 58,300
Cash paid for interest	22,100	Payment of dividends	35,000
Cash paid to employees and other		Principal payments on mortgage	
suppliers of goods and services	221,750	payable	60,000
Cash paid to suppliers of		Principal payments on long-term	
merchandise	395,540	debt	22,000
Cash received from the issuance of		Proceeds from the issuance of	
long-term debt	40,000	common stock	85,000
Cash received from disposal of		Purchase of equipment	120,000
equipment	42,500	Purchase of long-term investments	75,800
Cash received from sale of			
long-term investments	71,400		

Required:
1. Calculate the net cash provided (used) by operating activities.
2. Calculate the net cash provided (used) by investing activities.
3. Calculate the net cash provided (used) by financing activities.

Exercise 11-42 *(Appendix 11A)* **Preparing a Statement of Cash Flows—Direct Method**

Financial statements for Rowe Publishing Company are presented below.

Rowe Publishing Company Balance Sheets		
	Jan. 1	Dec. 31
ASSETS		
Current assets:		
Cash	$ 66,000	$ 85,000
Accounts receivable	231,000	240,000
Inventory	170,000	190,000
Total current assets	$467,000	$515,000
Property, plant, and equipment:		
Building	$ 400,000	$ 400,000
Equipment	130,000	155,000
	$ 530,000	$ 555,000
Accumulated depreciation	(350,000)	(375,000)
Net property, plant, and equipment	180,000	180,000
Total assets	$647,000	$695,000
LIABILITIES AND EQUITY		
Current liabilities:		
Accounts payable	$ 121,000	$ 133,000
Salaries payable	11,000	15,000
Income taxes payable	17,000	10,000
Total current liabilities	$149,000	$158,000
Long-term liabilities:		
Notes payable	$ 150,000	$ 115,000
Bonds payable	0	50,000
Total long-term liabilities	150,000	165,000
Total liabilities	$299,000	$323,000
Equity:		
Common stock	$ 300,000	$ 300,000
Retained earnings	48,000	72,000
Total equity	348,000	372,000
Total liabilities and equity	$647,000	$695,000

Rowe Publishing Company Income Statement For the year ended December 31		
Sales		$1,051,000
Less: Cost of goods sold		(578,000)
Gross margin		$ 473,000
Less operating expenses:		
Salaries	$(351,000)	
Depreciation	(25,000)	(376,000)
Income from operations		$ 97,000
Less: Interest expense		(16,000)
Income before taxes		$ 81,000
Less: Income taxes expense		(22,000)
Net income		$ 59,000

Additional Information:

1. No buildings or equipment were sold during the year. Equipment was purchased for $25,000 cash.
2. Notes payable in the amount of $35,000 were repaid during the year.
3. Bonds payable of $50,000 were issued for cash during the year.
4. Rowe Publishing declared and paid dividends of $35,000 during the year.

Required:

Prepare a statement of cash flows using the direct method to determine net cash flow from operating activities.

Exercise 11-43 *(Appendix 11B)* Using a Spreadsheet to Prepare a Statement of Cash Flows

Comparative balance sheets for Cincinnati Health Club are presented below.

Cincinnati Health Club Balance Sheets		
	Jan. 1	Dec. 31
ASSETS		
Current assets:		
Cash	$ 9,200	$ 5,300
Accounts receivable	8,900	10,500
Inventory	18,600	19,800
Total current assets	$ 36,700	$ 35,600
Property, plant, and equipment:		
Building	$ 490,000	$ 490,000
Equipment	270,000	280,000
	$ 760,000	$ 770,000
Accumulated depreciation	(120,000)	(148,000)
Net property, plant, and equipment	640,000	622,000
Total assets	$676,700	$657,600
LIABILITIES AND EQUITY		
Current liabilities:		
Accounts payable	$ 36,100	$ 55,300
Salaries payable	11,700	9,500
Income taxes payable	9,900	1,100
Total current liabilities	$ 57,700	$ 65,900
Long-term liabilities:		
Bonds payable	400,000	350,000
Total liabilities	$457,700	$415,900
Equity:		
Common stock	$ 150,000	$ 180,000
Retained earnings	69,000	61,700
Total equity	219,000	241,700
Total liabilities and equity	$676,700	$657,600

Additional Information:

1. Cincinnati Health Club reported net income of $2,700 for the year.
2. No buildings or equipment were sold during the year. Equipment was purchased for $10,000 cash.
3. Depreciation expense was $28,000.
4. Bonds payable of $50,000 were issued for cash during the year.
5. Common stock of $30,000 was issued during the year.
6. Cash dividends of $10,000 were declared and paid.

Required:

Using a spreadsheet, prepare a statement of cash flows. Assume Cincinnati Health Club uses the indirect method.

PROBLEM SET A

Problem 11-44A Classifying and Analyzing Business Activities

OBJECTIVE ▶2 3

CTT Inc. reported the following business activities:

a. Purchased property, plant, and equipment for cash

b. Purchased merchandise inventory for cash

c. Recorded depreciation on property, plant, and equipment

d. Issued common stock for cash

e. Purchased merchandise inventory on credit

f. Collected cash sales from customers

g. Paid cash dividends

h. Purchased a 2-year insurance policy for cash

i. Paid salaries of employees

j. Borrowed cash by issuing a note payable

k. Sold property, plant, and equipment for cash

l. Paid cash for principal amount of mortgage

m. Paid interest on mortgage

Required:

1. Indicate whether each activity should be classified as a cash flow from operating activities, cash flow from investing activities, cash flow from financing activities, or noncash investing and financing activity. Assume that CTT uses the indirect method.

2. For each activity that is reported on the statement of cash flows, indicate whether it produces a cash inflow, cash outflow, or no cash effect.

Problem 11-45A Reporting Net Cash Flow from Operating Activities

OBJECTIVE ◀4

The income statement for Granville Manufacturing Company is presented below.

Granville Manufacturing Company Income Statement For the year ended December 31	
Sales	$4,199,830
Cost of goods sold	(2,787,210)
Gross margin	$1,412,620
Operating expenses:	
Salaries expense	$ (831,800)
Depreciation expense	(246,100)
Administrative expense	(131,000)
Bad debt expense	(51,700)
Other expenses	(43,900)
Net income	$ 108,120

The following balance sheet changes occurred during the year:

- Accounts receivable increased by $182,400.
- Inventory increased by $98,725.
- Prepaid expenses decreased by $64,100.
- Accounts payable increased by $43,850.
- Salaries payable increased by $54,900.

Required:

1. Prepare the net cash flows from operating activities using the indirect method.

2. **CONCEPTUAL CONNECTION** What are the causes of the major differences between net income and net cash flow from operating activities?

OBJECTIVE ▶ 2 3 4▶

Problem 11-46A Classification of Cash Flows

Rolling Meadows Country Club Inc. is a privately owned corporation that operates a golf club. Rolling Meadows reported the following inflows and outflows of cash during the year:

Net income	$125,800	Cash received from sale of used golf carts	$12,700
Decrease in accounts receivable	7,175	Depreciation expense (buildings)	35,100
Increase in pro shop inventory	23,300	Depreciation expense (golf carts)	21,250
Increase in prepaid insurance	12,600	Proceeds from issuance of note payable	60,000
Increase in accounts payable	13,210	Payment on mortgage payable	42,000
Decrease in wages payable	7,400	Cash received from issuance of common stock	41,375
Increase in income taxes payable	2,125	Payment of cash dividends	40,000
Cash paid for new golf carts	85,000		

Rolling Meadows had cash on hand at Jan. 1 (the beginning of the year) of $8,500.

Required:

1. Prepare a properly formatted statement of cash flows using the indirect method.
2. **CONCEPTUAL CONNECTION** What can you conclude by examining the patterns in Rolling Meadow's cash flows?

OBJECTIVE ▶ 4 5 6▶

Problem 11-47A Preparing a Statement of Cash Flows

Erie Company reported the following comparative balance sheets:

	Jan. 1	Dec. 31
Assets:		
Cash	$ 12,750	$ 33,200
Accounts receivable	44,800	53,000
Inventory	27,500	29,500
Prepaid rent	6,200	2,200
Investments (long-term)	31,800	17,600
Property, plant, and equipment	149,450	162,000
Accumulated depreciation	(56,200)	(61,600)
Total assets	$216,300	$235,900
Liabilities and Equity:		
Accounts payable	$ 19,500	$ 16,900
Interest payable	4,800	3,500
Wages payable	7,100	9,600
Income taxes payable	3,600	5,500
Notes payable	53,000	28,000
Common stock	68,500	100,000
Retained earnings	59,800	72,400
Total liabilities and equity	$216,300	$235,900

Additional Information:

1. Net income was $20,500.
2. Cash dividends of $7,900 were declared and paid.
3. Long-term investments with a cost of $28,600 were sold for cash at a gain of $4,100. Additional long-term investments were purchased for $14,400 cash.
4. Equipment with a cost of $14,800 and accumulated depreciation of $13,500 was sold for $3,800 cash. New equipment was purchased for $27,350 cash.
5. Depreciation expense was $18,900.
6. A principal payment of $25,000 was made on long-term notes.
7. Common stock was sold for $31,500 cash.

Required:

Prepare a statement of cash flows for Erie using the indirect method to compute net cash flow from operating activities.

Problem 11-48A Preparing a Statement of Cash Flows

OBJECTIVE ◄ 4 5 6

Monon Cable Television Company reported the following financial information:

Monon Cable Television Company Balance Sheet Information		
	Jan. 1	**Dec. 31**
ASSETS		
Current assets:		
Cash	$ 8,000	$ 2,000
Accounts receivable	6,000	11,300
Supplies	1,700	1,200
Total current assets	$ 15,700	$ 14,500
Property, plant, and equipment:		
Equipment (antenna)	$ 35,000	$ 60,000
Buildings	190,000	210,000
Trucks	75,000	81,000
	$ 300,000	$351,000
Accumulated depreciation	(131,000)	(125,000)
Net property, plant, and equipment	169,000	226,000
Total assets	$184,700	$240,500
LIABILITIES AND EQUITY		
Current liabilities:		
Accounts payable	$ 8,000	$ 6,500
Rent payable	13,600	4,900
Royalties payable	3,100	3,300
Total current liabilities	$ 24,700	$ 14,700
Long-term liabilities:		
Notes payable (long-term)	0	40,000
Total liabilities	$ 24,700	$ 54,700
Equity:		
Common stock	$ 100,000	$100,000
Retained earnings	60,000	85,800
Total equity	160,000	185,800
Total liabilities and equity	$184,700	$240,500

Monon Cable Television Company Income Statement For the year ended December 31		
Sales		$519,000
Less operating expenses:		
Royalties expense	$240,000	
Salaries expense	26,000	
Utilities expense	83,000	
Supplies expense	13,000	
Rent expense	79,000	
Depreciation expense	28,000	469,000
Income from operations		$ 50,000
Other income (expenses):		
Gain on disposal of property, plant, and equipment	$ 800	
Interest expense	(1,800)	(1,000)
Income before taxes		$ 49,000
Less: Income taxes expense		(9,000)
Net income		$ 40,000

Additional Information:

1. Equipment (an old antenna) with a cost of $35,000 and accumulated depreciation of $34,000 was taken down and sold as scrap for $1,800 cash. A new antenna was purchased for cash at an installed cost of $60,000.
2. A building was purchased for $20,000 cash.
3. Trucks were purchased for $6,000 cash.
4. Depreciation expense was $28,000.
5. A long-term note payable was issued for $40,000 cash.
6. Dividends of $14,200 were paid.

(Continued)

Required:

1. Prepare a statement of cash flows using the indirect method to compute net cash flow from operating activities.
2. **CONCEPTUAL CONNECTION** Explain what has been responsible for the decrease in cash.

OBJECTIVE 8 **Problem 11-49A** *(Appendix 11A)* **Preparing Net Cash Flows from Operating Activities—Direct Method**

Yogurt Plus, a restaurant, collected the following information on inflows and outflows:

Inflows		Outflows	
Sales (all for cash)	$334,500	Cash payments made for merchandise sold	$176,450
Cash received from sale of common stock	72,000	Cash payments for operating expenses	115,210
Proceeds from issuance of long-term notes payable	50,000	Cash payments for interest	24,600
Proceeds from sale of used restaurant furniture	11,300	Cash payments for income taxes	9,475
Proceeds from issuance of short-term note payable	15,000	Purchase of restaurant furniture for cash	108,800
Notes payable issued in exchange for kitchen		Principal payment on mortgage	35,000
equipment	30,000	Payment of dividends	10,000
		Cost of kitchen equipment acquired in exchange for note payable	30,000

Yogurt Plus had a cash balance of $21,800 at January 1 (the beginning of the year).

Required:

1. Prepare a statement of cash flows using the direct method to determine net cash flow from operating activities.
2. **CONCEPTUAL CONNECTION** What can you conclude by examining the patterns in Yogurt Plus's cash flows?

OBJECTIVE 8 **Problem 11-50A** *(Appendix 11A)* **Preparing Net Cash Flows from Operating Activities—Direct Method**

Refer to the information for Granville Manufacturing Company in **Problem 11-45A**.

Required:

Prepare the cash flows from operating activities section of the statement of cash flows using the direct method.

OBJECTIVE 9 **Problem 11-51A** *(Appendix 11B)* **Using a Spreadsheet to Prepare a Statement of Cash Flows**

Jane Bahr, a controller of Endicott & Thurston, provided the following balance sheet information:

Endicott & Thurston Associates Balance Sheet			Additional Information:

	Jan. 1	Dec. 31
ASSETS		
Current assets:		
Cash	$ 17,000	$ 2,000
Accounts receivable	219,000	78,000
Prepaid rent	104,000	29,000
Total current assets	$340,000	$109,000
Long-term investments	40,000	51,000
Property, plant, and equipment:		
Equipment, computing	$ 362,000	$ 488,000
Furniture	365,000	400,000
	$ 727,000	$ 888,000
Accumulated depreciation	(554,000)	(366,000)
Net property, plant, and equipment	173,000	522,000
Total assets	$553,000	$682,000
LIABILITIES AND EQUITY		
Current liabilities:		
Accounts payable	$ 58,000	$ 56,000
Salaries payable	105,000	89,000
Total current liabilities	$163,000	$145,000
Long-term liabilities:		
Notes payable	105,000	80,000
Bonds payable	0	140,000
Total liabilities	$268,000	$365,000
Equity:		
Common stock	$ 225,000	$ 225,000
Retained earnings	60,000	92,000
Total equity	285,000	317,000
Total liabilities and equity	$553,000	$682,000

Additional Information:

1. Computing equipment with a cost of $250,000 and accumulated depreciation of $230,000 was sold for $5,000. New computing equipment was purchased for $376,000.
2. New office furniture was purchased at a cost of $35,000.
3. Depreciation expense was $42,000.
4. Investments costing $20,000 were sold for cash at a loss of $2,000. Additional investments were purchased for $31,000 cash.
5. A $25,000 principal payment on the long-term note was made.
6. A portion of the cash needed to purchase computing equipment was secured by issuing bonds payable for $140,000 cash.
7. Net income was $70,000 and dividends were $38,000.

Required:

1. Using a spreadsheet, prepare a statement of cash flows. Assume Endicott & Thurston use the indirect method.
2. **CONCEPTUAL CONNECTION** Discuss whether Endicott & Thurston appear to have matched the timing of inflows and outflows of cash.

PROBLEM SET B

OBJECTIVE ▸ 2 ▸ 3 ▸

Problem 11-44B Classifying and Analyzing Business Activities

Cowell Company had the following business activities:

a. Paid cash dividend to stockholders
b. Paid cash for inventory
c. Purchased equipment for cash
d. Paid interest on long-term debt
e. Acquired land in exchange for common stock
f. Issued common stock for cash

g. Paid salaries to employees
h. Received cash from the sale of merchandise
i. Recorded amortization related to an intangible asset
j. Issued bonds payable in exchange for cash
k. Sold equipment for cash
l. Purchased inventory on account

Cowell Company uses the indirect method to prepare its statement of cash flows.

Required:

1. Indicate whether each activity should be classified as a cash flow from operating activities, cash flow from investing activities, cash flow from financing activities, or noncash investing and financing activity.
2. For each activity that is reported on the statement of cash flows, indicate whether each activity produces a cash inflow, cash outflow, or no cash effect.

OBJECTIVE ▸ 4 ▸

Problem 11-45B Reporting Net Cash Flow from Operating Activities

The income statement for Dunn Products Inc. is presented below.

Dunn Products Inc. Income Statement For the year ended December 31	
Sales	$ 3,584,600
Cost of goods sold	(2,557,500)
Gross margin	$ 1,027,100
Other expenses:	
Salaries expense	$ (455,100)
Administrative expense	(247,000)
Depreciation expense	(214,500)
Bad debt expense	(37,000)
Income taxes expense	(28,200)
Net income	$ 45,300

The following balance sheet changes occurred during the year:

- Accounts receivable decreased by $85,150.
- Inventory decreased by $138,620.
- Prepaid expenses increased by $112,400.
- Accounts payable decreased by $67,225.
- Salaries payable increased by $18,300.

Required:

1. Prepare the net cash flows from operating activities using the indirect method.
2. **CONCEPTUAL CONNECTION** What are the causes of the major differences between net income and net cash flow from operating activities?

Problem 11-46B Classification of Cash Flows

OBJECTIVE ▸ 2 3 4

Fannin Company is a manufacturer of premium athletic equipment. Fannin reported the following inflows and outflows of cash during the year.

Net income	$594,600	Cash received from sale of investment	$ 22,850
Increase in accounts receivable	23,400	Cash paid for property, plant, and equipment	101,325
Decrease in inventory	61,250	Depreciation expense	93,410
Decrease in prepaid insurance	47,600	Proceeds from issuance of note payable	50,000
Decrease in accounts payable	31,550	Payment on bonds payable	200,000
Decrease in income taxes payable	7,600	Cash received from issuance of common stock	20,000
Increase in wages payable	18,200	Payment of cash dividends	30,000

Fannin had cash on hand at January 1 (the beginning of the year) of $118,250.

Required:

1. Prepare a properly formatted statement of cash flows using the indirect method.
2. **CONCEPTUAL CONNECTION** What can you conclude by examining the patterns in Fannin's cash flows?

Problem 11-47B Preparing a Statement of Cash Flows

OBJECTIVE ▸ 4 5 6

Volusia Company reported the following balance sheet information:

Volusia Company Balance Sheet			Additional Information:
	Jan. 1	Dec. 31	1. Net income was $18,300.
ASSETS			2. Cash dividends of $13,500 were declared and paid.
Cash	$ 16,300	$ 28,100	3. Long-term investments with a cost of $21,200 were sold for cash at a loss of $1,500. Additional long-term investments were purchased for $32,900 cash.
Accounts receivable	32,725	26,500	
Inventory	28,200	24,100	
Prepaid rent	1,800	3,900	4. Equipment with a cost of $25,000 and accumulated depreciation of $16,300 was sold for $4,500 cash. New equipment was purchased for $37,025 cash.
Investments, long-term	25,500	37,200	
Property, plant, and equipment	102,975	115,000	
Accumulated depreciation	(38,600)	(47,100)	5. Depreciation expense was $24,800.
Total assets	$168,900	$187,700	6. A principal payment of $15,000 was made on long-term notes. Volusia issued notes payable for $20,000 cash.
LIABILITIES AND EQUITY			
Accounts payable	$ 21,200	$ 24,900	7. Common stock was sold for $7,900 cash.
Interest payable	3,300	4,700	
Wages payable	6,900	4,600	
Income taxes payable	5,200	3,500	
Notes payable	30,000	35,000	
Common stock	65,000	72,900	
Retained earnings	37,300	42,100	
Total liabilities and equity	$168,900	$187,700	

Required:

Prepare a statement of cash flows for Volusia using the indirect method to compute net cash flow from operating activities.

OBJECTIVE 4 5 6 ▶   **Problem 11-48B Preparing a Statement of Cash Flows**

SDPS Inc. provides airport transportation services in southern California. An income statement and balance sheet appear below.

SDPS Inc. Balance Sheets				SDPS Inc. Income Statement For the year ended December 31			
		Jan. 1	Dec. 31				
ASSETS				Sales			$937,000
Current assets:				Less operating expenses:			
Cash		$ 82,000	$ 40,000	Wages expense		$278,000	
Accounts receivable		109,000	126,000	Rent expense		229,000	
Supplies, fuel		25,000	11,000	Supplies expense		83,000	
Total current assets		$216,000	$177,000	Maintenance			
Property, plant, and equipment:				expense		138,000	
Equipment, vehicles	$ 409,000		$ 524,000	Depreciation			
Accumulated				expense		215,000	943,000
depreciation	(136,000)		(174,000)	Income (loss) from			
Net property, plant,				operations			$ (6,000)
and equipment		273,000	350,000	Other income (expenses):			
Total assets		$489,000	$527,000	Loss on disposal of			
LIABILITIES AND EQUITY				property, plant,			
Current liabilities:				and equipment		$ (3,000)	
Accounts payable	$ 58,000		$ 103,000	Interest expense		(14,000)	(17,000)
Wages payable	29,000		22,000	Net loss			$ (23,000)
Repair and maintenance							
payable	34,000		41,000				
Rent payable	51,000		92,000				
Total current liabilities		$172,000	$258,000				
Long-term liabilities:							
Notes payable		125,000	100,000				
Total liabilities		$297,000	$358,000				
Equity:							
Common stock	$ 150,000		$ 150,000				
Retained earnings	42,000		19,000				
Total equity		192,000	169,000				
Total liabilities and equity		$489,000	$527,000				

Additional Information:

1. Vehicles with a cost of $310,000 and accumulated depreciation of $177,000 were sold for $130,000 cash. New vehicles were purchased for $425,000 cash.
2. A $25,000 principal payment on the long-term note was made.
3. No dividends were paid.

Required:

1. Prepare a statement of cash flows using the indirect method to compute net cash flow from operating activities.
2. **CONCEPTUAL CONNECTION** Explain what has been responsible for the decrease in cash.
3. **CONCEPTUAL CONNECTION** Determine how SDPS financed its increase in net property, plant, and equipment during a period in which it had a substantial net loss.

Problem 11-49B *(Appendix 11A)* Preparing Net Cash Flows from Operating Activities—Direct Method

OBJECTIVE 8

Befuddled Corporation collected the following information on inflows and outflows:

Inflows		Outflows	
Cash collections from sales	$956,500	Cash payments for cost of goods sold	$534,900
Proceeds from disposal of equipment	11,250	Cash payments for operating expenses	193,200
Proceeds received from issuance of notes payable	30,000	Cash payments for interest	36,400
		Cash payments for income taxes	21,300
		Cash payments for purchases of equipment	217,150
		Repayment of short-term notes payable	20,000
		Payment of cash dividends	38,000

Befuddled had a cash balance of $89,200 on January 1 (the beginning of the year).

Required:

1. Prepare a statement of cash flows using the direct method to determine net cash flow from operating activities.
2. **CONCEPTUAL CONNECTION** What can you conclude by examining the patterns in Befuddled's cash flows?

Problem 11-50B *(Appendix 11A)* Preparing Net Cash Flows from Operating Activities—Direct Method

OBJECTIVE 8

Refer to the information for Dunn Products Inc. in **Problem 11-45B**.

Required:

Prepare the cash flows from operating activities section of the statement of cash flows using the direct method.

OBJECTIVE 9   **Problem 11-51B** *(Appendix 11B)* **Using a Spreadsheet to Prepare a Statement of Cash Flows**

Fleet Limousine Service Inc. began operations on January 1. At the end of the year, the following balance sheet was prepared for Fleet.

Fleet Limousine Service Inc. Balance Sheets December 31		
ASSETS		
Current assets:		
Cash	$ 7,200	
Accounts receivable	15,900	
Supplies	3,100	
Total current assets		$ 26,200
Long-term investments		15,000
Property, plant, and equipment:		
Land	$ 11,000	
Building	175,000	
Equipment	233,400	
	$419,400	
Accumulated depreciation	(35,500)	
Net property, plant, and equipment		383,900
Total assets		$425,100
LIABILITIES AND EQUITY		
Current liabilities:		
Accounts payable	$ 12,700	
Unearned service revenue	21,800	
Salaries payable	4,600	
Rent payable	8,200	
Total current liabilities		$ 47,300
Long-term liabilities:		
Notes payable		95,000
Total liabilities		$142,300
Equity:		
Common stock	$300,000	
Retained earnings	(17,200)	
Total equity		282,800
Total liabilities and equity		$425,100

Additional Information:

1. During the year, land was purchased for $11,000, a building was purchased for $175,000, and equipment was purchased for $233,400.
2. Depreciation expense was $35,500.
3. The long-term note was issued for $100,000, and a principal payment of $5,000 was made.
4. Common stock was issued for $300,000 cash.
5. During the year, there was a net loss of $17,200, and no dividends were paid.

Required:

1. Using a spreadsheet, prepare a statement of cash flows. Assume Fleet Limousine uses the indirect method.
2. **CONCEPTUAL CONNECTION** Discuss whether Fleet Limousine appears to have matched the timing of inflows and outflows of cash.

CASES

Case 11-52 The Statement of Cash Flows and Credit Analysis

June's Camera Shop sells cameras and photographic supplies of all types to retail customers. June's also repairs cameras and provides color prints. To compete with other camera departments, June's offers fast, efficient, and effective repairs and photographic processing. For the last 2 years (Year 1 and Year 2), June's accountant prepared the following statements of cash flows:

June's Camera Shop Statements of Cash Flows For the years ended January 31, Year 2 and Year 1				
		Year 2		Year 1
Cash flows from operating activities				
Net income		$ 87,000		$ 63,000
Adjustments to reconcile net income to net cash provided by operating activities:				
Depreciation expense	$ 41,000		$ 37,000	
Increase in accounts receivable	(17,000)		(12,000)	
Increase in inventory	(19,000)		(11,000)	
Increase in accounts payable	15,000		14,000	
Increase in wages payable	11,000		5,000	
Increase in income taxes payable	6,000		3,000	
Total adjustments		37,000		36,000
Net cash provided by operating activities		$124,000		$ 99,000
Cash flows from investing activities				
Purchase of long-term investments	$(15,000)		$(10,000)	
Purchase of equipment	(45,000)		(40,000)	
Net cash used by investing activities		(60,000)		(50,000)
Cash flows from financing activities				
Principal payments on mortgage	$(15,000)		$(15,000)	
Payment of dividends	(12,000)		(10,000)	
Net cash used by financing activities		(27,000)		(25,000)
Net increase in cash and cash equivalents		$ 37,000		$ 24,000
Cash and cash equivalents at beginning of year		158,000		134,000
Cash and cash equivalents at end of year		$195,000		$158,000

Required:

1. Does June's Camera Shop appear to have grown (in terms of property, plant, and equipment) during the past 2 years?
2. June's president, June Smith, would like to open a second store. Smith believes that $225,000 is needed to equip the facility properly. The business has $100,000 of cash and liquid investments to apply toward the $225,000 required. Do the data in Year 1 and Year 2 statements of cash flow suggest whether or not June's Camera Shop is likely to be able to secure a loan for the remaining $125,000 needed for the expansion?
3. How long should it take June's Camera Shop to pay back the $125,000?

Case 11-53 Profitability Declines and the Statement of Cash Flows

The Bookbarn Inc. is a retail seller of new books in a moderate-sized city. Although initially very successful, The Bookbarn's sales volume has declined since the opening of two competing bookstores 2 years ago. The accountant for The Bookbarn prepared the following statement of cash flows at the end of the current year:

The Bookbarn Inc. Statement of Cash Flows For the year ended December 31		
Cash flows from operating activities		
Net income	$ 26,500	
Adjustments to reconcile net income to net cash provided by operating activities:		
Depreciation expense	$ 38,500	
Loss on disposal of property, plant, and equipment	2,100	
Increase in accounts receivable	(1,200)	
Increase in inventory	(3,800)	
Increase in accounts payable	6,700	
Decrease in wages payable	(1,200)	
Total adjustments		
Net cash provided by operating activities		$ 67,600
Cash flows from investing activities		
Purchase of equipment	$(12,000)	
Proceeds from disposal of equipment	2,300	
Net cash used by investing activities		(9,700)
Cash flows from financing activities		
Payment of dividends	$ (4,000)	
Repayment of mortgage	(10,000)	
Net cash used by financing activities		(14,000)
Net increase in cash		$ 43,900

Your analysis suggests that The Bookbarn's net income will continue to decline by $8,000 per year to $18,500 as sales continue to fall. Thereafter, you expect sales to stabilize.

Required:

1. What will happen to the amount of cash provided by operations as net income decreases?
2. Assume that equipment is nearly fully depreciated but that it will be fully serviceable for several years. What will happen to cash flows from operations as depreciation declines?
3. Do the operations of businesses experiencing declining sales volumes always consume cash? Explain your answer.
4. Can current assets and current liabilities buffer operating cash flows against the impact of declines in sales volume in the short run? In the long run? Explain your answer.

Case 11-54 Preparing a Prospective Statement of Cash Flows

Jane and Harvey Wentland have decided to open a retail athletic supply store, Fitness Outfitters Inc. They will stock clothing, shoes, and supplies used in running, swimming, bicycling, weight lifting, and other exercise and athletic activities. During their first year of operations, they expect the following results. (Subsequent years are expected to be more successful.)

Sales revenue	$ 629,000
Less: Cost of goods sold	(291,000)
Gross margin	$ 338,000
Less: Operating expenses	(355,000)
Net loss	$ (17,000)

By the end of the year, Fitness Outfitters needs to have a cash balance of $5,000 and is expected to have the following partial balance sheet:

ASSETS

Inventory		$ 53,000
Equipment	$97,000	
Accumulated depreciation, equipment	15,000	82,000

LIABILITIES AND EQUITY

Accounts payable		$ 37,000
Common stock		100,000
Retained earnings		(17,000)

Assume that all sales will be for cash and that equipment will be acquired for cash.

Required:

1. Prepare as much of the statement of cash flows for the year ending December 31 as you can. Use the direct method to determine cash flows from operations.
2. In the statement that you prepared for Requirement 1, by how much does the prospective cash balance exceed or fall short of the desired cash balance? If a shortfall occurs, where would you suggest that Jane and Harvey seek additional cash?
3. Does the preparation of a prospective statement of cash flows seem worthwhile for an ongoing business? Why?

Case 11-55 Income, Cash Flow, and Future Losses

On January 1, Year 1, Cermack National Bank loaned $5,000,000 under a 2-year, zero coupon note to a real estate developer. The bank recognized interest revenue on this note of approximately $400,000 per year. Due to an economic downturn, the developer was unable to pay the $5,800,000 maturity amount on December 31, Year 2. The bank convinced the developer to pay $800,000 on December 31, Year 2, and agreed to extend $5,000,000 credit to the developer despite the gloomy economic outlook for the next several years. Thus, on December 31, Year 2, the bank issued a new 2-year, zero coupon note to the developer to mature on December 31, Year 4, for $6,000,000. The bank recognized interest revenue on this note of approximately $500,000 per year.

The bank's external auditor insisted that the riskiness of the new loan be recognized by increasing the allowance for uncollectible notes by $1,500,000 on December 31, Year 2, and $2,000,000 on December 31, Year 3. On December 31, Year 4, the bank received $1,200,000 from the developer and learned that the developer was in bankruptcy and that no additional amounts would be recovered.

Required:

1. Prepare a schedule showing annual cash flows for the two notes in each of the 4 years.
2. Prepare a schedule showing the effect of the notes on net income in each of the 4 years.

(Continued)

3. Which figure, net income or net cash flow, does the better job of telling the bank's stockholders about the effect of these notes on the bank? Explain by reference to the schedules prepared in Requirements 1 and 2.

4. A commonly used method for predicting future cash flows is to predict future income and adjust it for anticipated differences between net income and net cash flow. Does the Cermack National Bank case shed any light on the justification for using net income in this way rather than simply predicting future cash flows by reference to past cash flows?

Case 11-56 Researching Accounting Standards: Dissenting Views and the Statement of Cash Flows

The preparation of cash flow statements is required by generally accepted accounting principles. This accounting standard was initially adopted by a four-to-three vote of the FASB. Several members of the Board took exception to various aspects of the statement including (1) the classification of interest and dividends received and interest paid as cash flows from operations and (2) the use of the indirect method.

Required:

Obtain the *Statement of Financial Accounting Standards No. 95 (FAS 95)* from the FASB website. Go to www.fasb.org, highlight the "Standards" tab, select "Pre-Codification Standards," select "Statement of Financial Accounting Standards No. 95," and click on the "As Issued" link.

1. How did dissenting members of the FASB prefer that interest and dividends received and interest paid be classified? (See the section following paragraph 34 of the full text of *Statement No. 95*.) How did the FASB justify classifying these items as cash flows from operations? (See paragraph 90 of *Statement No. 95*.)

2. Why did dissenting members of the FASB take exception to the indirect method? (See the section following paragraph 34 of the full text of *Statement No. 95*.) How did the FASB justify permitting use of the indirect method? (See paragraphs 108, 109, and 119 of *Statement No. 95*.)

Case 11-57 Research and Analysis Using the Annual Report

Obtain **Alphabet**'s 2019 annual report either through the "Investor Relations" portion of their website (do a web search for Alphabet investor relations) or go to www.sec.gov and click "Company Filings Search" under "Filings."

Required:

1. What method of computing net cash flow from operating activities did Alphabet use?

2. What was the amount of net cash provided by operating activities for the 2 most current years? What were the most significant adjustments that caused a difference between net income and net cash provided by operating activities?

3. What amount did the company pay for taxes during the most current year?

4. Why was the provision for depreciation and amortization added to net income to compute the net cash provided by operating activities?

5. Refer to Alphabet's investing and financing activities. What were some of Alphabet's significant uses of cash? What were some of Alphabet's significant sources of cash?

6. What was the amount of cash dividends paid by Alphabet for the most current year?

7. Are the time commitments of inflows and outflows well matched by Alphabet?

8. Are debt and equity likely to be available as inflows of cash in the near future?

Case 11-58 Comparative Analysis: Kroger versus Sprouts

Refer to the 10-K reports of **Kroger** and **Sprouts** that are available for download from the companion website at Cengage.com.

Required:

1. What method of computing net cash flow from operating activities did Kroger use? What method of computing net cash flow from operating activities did Sprouts use? Would you expect these to be the same? Why or why not?

2. Find net cash provided by operating activities for each company:
   a. What was the amount of cash provided by operating activities for the most recent fiscal year for Kroger? What was the amount of cash provided by operating activities for the most recent fiscal year for Sprouts?
   b. What was the most significant adjustment that caused a difference between net income and net cash provided by operating activities?
   c. Comparing net income to net cash provided by operating activities, can you draw any conclusions as to the quality of each company's earnings?

3. Refer to each company's investing and financing activities. What were some of the more significant uses of cash? What were some of the more significant sources of cash?

4. Does each company match the time commitments of inflows and outflows of cash well?

5. Are debt and equity likely to be available as inflows of cash in the near future?

ANNUAL REPORT PROBLEM

HOME DEPOT

Download the 10-K for **Home Depot** from the companion website at Cengage.com.

Required:

1. What does Home Depot report for the following accounts for the most current fiscal year?
   - Accounts receivable
   - Inventory
   - Property, plant, and equipment, net
   - Accounts payable and short-term debt
   - Long-term debt
   - Depreciation and amortization expense
   - Net income

2. Assume that Home Depot projects the following:
   - Accounts receivable will decrease by 2%.
   - Inventory will increase by 1%.
   - Property, plant and equipment will increase by 3%.
   - Short-term debt will decrease by 4%.
   - Long-term debt will increase by 4%.
   - Depreciation expense will increase by 2%.
   - Net income will increase by 20%.

Assume all other items remain unchanged from the prior year. Provide the forecasted balances for the next fiscal year for the above accounts.

3. Using only the information given above, what is the forecasted amount for cash flows from operating activities?

4. What is the largest source of cash in the investing section of the statement of cash flows for Home Depot?

5. What is largest use of cash in the investing section of the statement of cash flows for Home Depot?

6. What is the largest source of cash in the financing section of the statement of cash flows for Home Depot?

7. What is largest use of cash in the financing section of the statement of cash flows for Home Depot?

Note: *While the Annual Report problems in the textbook are static, when assigned in CNOW, these activities are algorithmic and the answers may vary from what appears in the Solutions Manual.*

CONTINUING PROBLEM

FRONT ROW ENTERTAINMENT

The income statement and comparative balance sheet for Front Row Entertainment are shown below:

Front Row Entertainment Inc. Balance Sheets December 31, 2024 and 2023		
	2024	**2023**
ASSETS		
Current assets:		
Cash	$ 30,322	$ 9,005
Accounts receivable, net	98,250	17,000
Prepaid expenses	133,400	57,200
Supplies	2,200	3,700
Inventory	61,380	2,850
Total current assets	$ 325,552	$89,755
Property, plant, and equipment:		
Building	1,857,250	0
Equipment	27,350	7,000
Accumulated depreciation	(53,835)	(2,160)
Trademark	25,000	—
Total assets	$2,181,317	$94,595
LIABILITIES AND EQUITY		
Current liabilities:		
Accounts payable	$ 2,450	$12,240
Salaries payable	2,500	3,690
Interest payable	40,917	2,250
Unearned sales revenue	1,780	28,650
Income taxes payable	550	2,180
Notes payable (short-term)	8,000	0
Total current liabilities	$ 56,197	$49,010
Long-term liabilities:		
Notes payable	$ 405,000	$25,000
Bonds payable, net	1,500,000	0
Less: Discount on bond payable	(109,530)	
Total long-term liabilities	$1,795,470	$25,000
Equity:		
Preferred stock	$ 150,000	$ 0
Common stock	18,000	16,000
Paid-in capital in excess of par:		
Preferred stock	75,000	0
Common stock	38,000	0
Treasury stock	1,800	0
Retained earnings	53,250	4,585
Less: Treasury stock	(6,400)	0
Total equity	$ 329,650	$20,585
Total liabilities and equity	$2,181,317	$94,595

(Continued)

Front Row Entertainment Inc. Income Statement For the year ended December 31, 2024	
Revenues:	
Sales revenue	$3,142,800
Service revenue	636,000
Total revenues	$3,778,800
Expenses:	
Artist fee expense	$2,134,260
Rent expense	952,663
Cost of goods sold	74,800
Salaries and wages expense	345,100
Depreciation expense	51,675
Interest expense	98,087
Income taxes expense	22,000
Other expenses	26,550
Total expenses	$3,705,135
Net income	$ 73,665

Additional Information:

1. Bonds payable of $1,500,000 were issued for $1,378,300 on July 1, 2024. During 2024, $12,170 of the discount on the bonds payable was amortized.
2. In January 2024, a $380,000 long-term note payable was issued in exchange for a building. No buildings were sold during the year.
3. On February 29, 2024, an $8,000 short-term note payable was issued in exchange for equipment. No equipment was sold during the year.
4. Cash dividends of $25,000 were declared and paid during 2024.
5. Common stock was issued for $40,000 cash during 2024.
6. Preferred stock was issued for $225,000 cash during 2024.
7. Treasury stock was purchased for $11,200 during 2024. Front Row reissued $4,800 of treasury stock in December 2024 for $6,600.

Required:

1. Prepare a statement of cash flows using the indirect method.
2. What conclusions can you draw about Front Row from the observed pattern of cash flows?

Financial Statement Analysis

After studying Chapter 12, you should be able to:

1. Explain how creditors, investors, and others use financial statements in their decisions.

2. Describe the most important SEC filings.

3. Discuss the difference between cross sectional and time series analysis.

4. Analyze financial statements using horizontal and vertical analysis.

5. Calculate and use financial statement ratios to evaluate a company.

Patrick T. Fallon/Bloomberg/Getty Images

EXPERIENCE FINANCIAL ACCOUNTING

with Sprouts Farmers Market

Stan Boney's father, Henry, opened his first fruit stand in San Diego in 1943. From there, the Boneys eventually opened four more fruit stands, and then some grocery stores. Stan grew up working in the family businesses. In 2002, Stan and his son, Shan, opened the first **Sprouts Farmers Market** in Chandler, Arizona. Their goal was to make natural foods easier to find and less expensive. Much to the bemusement of their competition, the Boneys refused to sell mass marketed sodas, snacks, and candy. However, Stan and Shan believed eating natural foods was healthier and more than just a fad.

Sprouts Farmers Market is a blend of farmers' markets, conventional supermarkets, natural food stores, and smaller specialty markets. It provides a complete offering of fresh, natural, and organic food at a great value. Further, Sprouts is on Fortune's Most Admired Companies List for 2019 in part for programs related to animal welfare, ethical food sourcing, eliminating food waste, and fighting hunger. For example, Sprouts employees gather food that is no longer in a retail condition but remains wholesome to consume through their Food Rescue Program. While much of this food is distributed to local farmers as a source of low-cost feed for their livestock, over 27 million pounds was provided to hunger relief agencies that provide food for needy people in their local communities.

Growing from that single store in 2002, Sprouts operated over 150 stores in eight states when it went public in 2013. By 2019, Sprouts had grown to 340 stores across 22 states, with more than 30,000 employees. As shown in the accompanying chart, net sales has grown from approximately $1.1 billion in 2011 to over $5.6 billion in 2019, while net income has grown from a loss of $27 million to a gain of almost $150 million over that same period of time. Further, according to its 2019 10-K (p. 9), "For 51 consecutive quarters, stores under our management have achieved positive comparable store sales growth." Clearly, Sprouts is a very successful company. Yet, how do we know whether Sprouts is a good company in which to invest? In reading this chapter, you will learn about a number of tools used by investors and creditors to analyze the financial status of Sprouts and other companies.

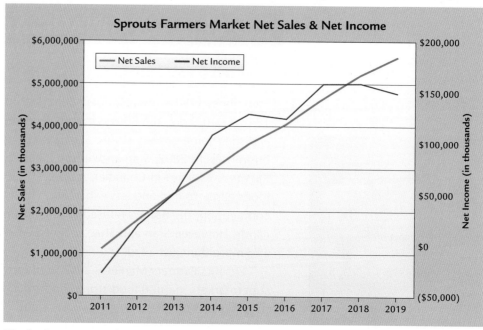

Taken from Sprouts Farmers Market 10-K's.

Throughout this book, you have learned how to use debits and credits to record many of the most common transactions in which companies engage. You have also studied how these debits and credits are summarized in the financial statements and how this information is useful to those interested in the company. In this chapter, we review, extend, and summarize the role of financial statements in business decision-making. The types of decisions facing customers, suppliers, employees, creditors, and investors are discussed. However, we concentrate primarily on investment and credit decisions and the techniques used for comparison to other companies or previous years.

Reading this chapter will help you answer the following questions:

- What decision-making groups use financial statements and what questions are they able to answer by analyzing the financial statements?
- What information can be found in SEC filings?
- Where can various information be found in the Form 10-K?
- How are financial statements analyzed?

USE OF FINANCIAL STATEMENTS IN DECISIONS

As we discussed in Chapter 1, the role of financial statements is to provide information that will help creditors, investors, and others make judgments which serve as the foundation for various decisions. While customers, suppliers, employees, creditors, and investors all use financial statement data to make decisions, as shown in Exhibit 12.1, each group uses the accounting information to answer different questions.

CUSTOMER DECISIONS

Customers want to buy from companies that will:

- continue to produce goods or provide services in the future
- provide repair or warranty service if required

The financial statements contain data describing the profitability and efficiency of a company's operations which customers can use to estimate the likelihood that a supplier will be able to deliver goods or services now and in the future.

Users of Financial Statements and Typical Questions

EXHIBIT 12.1

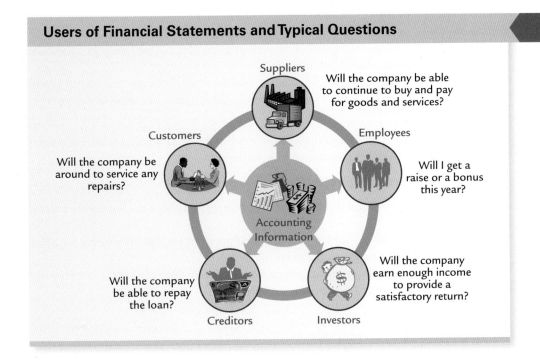

SUPPLIER DECISIONS

A company that is considering selling goods or providing services to another company wants to know whether its customer will be able to:

- pay for the purchase as agreed
- continue to purchase and pay for goods and services

Suppliers can use balance sheet data to estimate the likelihood that a customer will be able to pay for current purchases. They can use income statement data to analyze whether a customer will be able to continue purchasing and paying for goods or services in the future.

EMPLOYMENT DECISIONS

When you select an employer, you want to be sure that the company will provide:

- competitive salary and benefits
- experiences that will prepare you to assume increased responsibility
- a secure position for the foreseeable future

Income statement data can help a prospective employee assess the likelihood that a company will provide the growth and profits necessary to support a successful career. For example, examining a company's return on assets and sales growth can help prospective employees determine a company's profitability and growth.

In related decisions, unions representing employees use the financial statements. For example, when the employer's income statement suggests the employer is performing very well, the union will seek greater wages and benefits. Conversely, when the income statement suggests the employer is performing poorly (such as in the airline industry), unions may accept lower wages and benefits to help the employer stay in operation.

CREDIT DECISIONS

An individual or an organization that is considering making a loan needs to know whether the borrower will be able to repay the loan and its interest. For short-term loans (those of 1 year or less), the principal and interest will be repaid from current assets—cash on hand and cash that can be secured by selling inventory and collecting accounts receivable. A short-term lender, then, is most interested in the composition and amounts of a borrowing company's current assets and current liabilities. The excess of the current assets over current liabilities, an amount called *working capital*, is particularly important.

For a long-term loan, the principal and interest will be repaid from cash provided by profits earned over the period of the loan. A long-term lender, then, is most interested in estimating:

- future profits of the enterprise
- amounts of other claims against those profits, such as dividends to stockholders, payments to other lenders, and future investments by the firm

Information from three different statements is useful in making credit decisions:

- An analysis of the balance sheet can provide information about the borrower's current liquidity.
- Profitability data developed from current and previous income statements are often helpful in forecasting future profitability.
- Sources and uses of cash presented in the statement of cash flows are helpful in forecasting the amount and timing of future claims against profits.

INVESTMENT DECISIONS

Investors who buy stock in a corporation expect to earn returns on their investment from:

- dividends
- increases in the value of the stock (capital gains)

Both dividends and increases in the value of the stock depend on the future profitability of the company. The larger the profits, the more resources the company has available for payment of dividends and for investment in new assets to use in creating additional profits.

Although detailed analysis of the corporation is where you find the best information for predicting (or forecasting) future profits, this cannot be done in a vacuum. You must also understand economic and industry factors. For example, if you ignore how economic factors such as rising interest rates affect home construction (it slows it down), then forecasts of corporations whose performances are tied to this industry, such as **Lowe's** or **Home Depot**, may be overly optimistic. As such, most analysts take a top-down approach when trying to predict future profits. This approach starts with gathering economic and industry data. In fact, professional analysts typically specialize in certain industries so that their knowledge of how the economy and industry interact will be applicable to all the corporations they analyze (or "follow"). Yet, at some point, you must begin to analyze the corporation itself.

OBJECTIVE 2
Describe the most important SEC filings.

SEC FILINGS

Publicly traded corporations must file a variety of financial information, including audited financial statements, with the Securities and Exchange Commission (SEC) on an ongoing basis. For example, annual reports on **Form 10-K**, quarterly reports on **Form 10-Q**, and current reports for numerous specified events on **Form 8-K**, as well as many other disclosure requirements must be submitted to the SEC in a timely manner. These filings are the most important and complete source of financial information about the corporation and are the major source of information about the business for most investors (and creditors). A summary of the most important SEC filings is provided in Exhibit 12.2. A complete list of mandatory filings with more detailed descriptions is provided at www.sec.gov/about/forms/secforms.htm.

The Most Important SEC Filings

EXHIBIT 12.2

Filing	Description*
Form 10-K	The annual report on Form 10-K provides a comprehensive overview of the corporation's business and financial condition and includes *audited* financial statements. Although similarly named, the annual report on Form 10-K is distinct from the "annual report to shareholders," which a corporation must send to its stockholders when it holds an annual meeting to elect directors. For larger filers, the 10-K must be filed within 60 days of their fiscal year end.
Form 10-Q	The Form 10-Q includes *unaudited* financial statements and provides a continuing view of the corporation's financial position during the year. The report must be filed for each of the first three fiscal quarters of the corporation's fiscal year. For larger filers, this must be done within 40 days of the end of the quarter.
Form 8-K	In addition to filing Forms 10-K and 10-Q, public corporations must report material corporate events on a more current basis. Form 8-K is the "current report" companies must file with the SEC to announce major events that are important to investors and creditors.
Form DEF 14A (Proxy Statement)	The Proxy Statement notifies stockholders of issues that will be voted on at the annual stockholders' meeting. For example, stockholders commonly vote on the audit firm, executive compensation issues, and representation on the Board of Directors.
Forms 3, 4, and 5	Corporate officers, directors, and 10+ percent stockholders are collectively known as "insiders." Form 3 must be filed upon becoming an officer, director, or 10+ percent stockholders. Insiders must file Form 4 within 2 business days of buying or selling the corporation's stock. Form 5 is a special annual filing.
Forms S-1 and S-2 (Registration Statements) Rule 424 (Prospectus)	Corporations must file these forms to "register" their securities with the SEC prior to offering them to investors. Each form contains information for potential investors related to the sale of stock by the corporation. When the corporation sells stock to the public for the first time, it is called an "Initial Public Offering" or IPO. Subsequent offerings are referred to as Secondary Offerings.

*Descriptions taken from the SEC website.

FORMAT AND CONTENT OF FORM 10-K

The most useful filing is Form 10-K, which is filed after each fiscal year end. We provide **Kroger's** and **Sprouts Farmers Market's** financial statements at the end of the book in Appendices 5 and 6, respectively, and the full 10-Ks are on our companion website at Cengage.com. The 10-K includes audited financial statements, but there is also a wealth of additional information. Although 10-Ks are quite long (frequently well over 100 pages), all 10-Ks must follow a format mandated by the SEC. If you familiarize yourself with the mandated format, you will be able to find information of interest more efficiently.

Item 1 outlines the history of the company, discusses recent developments, and provides an overview of its industry and competitors. There is a detailed discussion of such things as major products, major suppliers and sources of raw materials, key customers, seasonalities, government regulations, and risk factors. A thorough read of this section is a good way to better understand the business and determine whether the company has a good strategy for creating profits.

Typically there is little important information in Items 2, 3, and 4. However, you should scan these items for anything of interest. **Item 2** describes the property holdings of the company; **Item 3** discusses lawsuits in which the company is involved; **Item 4** discusses anything brought to a stockholder vote in the fourth quarter (the 10-Qs handle this matter for the first three quarters). Item 3 is likely the most important of these items, as you will want to be aware of any serious litigation facing the company. However, most companies are parties to multiple lawsuits at any point in time, and a vast majority of these lawsuits will not materially affect the company.

Item 5 provides a summary of recent stock price and dividend activity, while **Item 6** summarizes financial data for the last 5 years. There is not much detail to these sections, but they do provide a nice overview. Further, Item 6 often provides information about key performance indicators, such as sales per square foot in the retail industry or revenues per passenger mile in the airline industry, which are not included in the financial statements.

Item 7 is Management's Discussion and Analysis, more frequently referred to as **MD&A**. This is one of the key parts of the 10-K. In this section, management discusses its views of the financial condition and performance of the company. Management is required to disclose trends, events, or known uncertainties that would materially affect the company. Included in this section are many statements about what will likely happen in the future. Although there is obviously uncertainty about whether these future events will happen, this information is designed to provide investors with information management believes necessary to understand the company and predict, or forecast, future performance. Item 7A is where the effect of market risk factors, such as fluctuating interest rates or currency exchange rates, on the company's financial performance is discussed. It is important to read the MD&A.

Item 8 contains the corporation's balance sheets for the last 2 years and income statements and statements of cash flows for the last 3 years. These three financial statements are the primary sources of information for analysts. Specifically, as discussed in other chapters and later in this chapter, financial statement ratio analysis provides analysts with a wealth of information to evaluate such things as the corporation's profitability, asset and debt management, and short-term liquidity. One part of Item 8 that should not be ignored is the footnotes provided as a supplement to the financial statements. This is where you will find information about the corporation's accounting policies (such as, does the company use LIFO or FIFO?) as well as disclosures providing additional detail about various accounts listed on the financial statements.

Finally, Item 8 also includes the auditor's opinions on (1) the effectiveness of the corporation's system of internal controls over financial reporting and (2) the fairness of presentation of the financial statements and accompanying footnotes. Although these opinions are typically "unqualified," indicating no major problems, you should definitely look at these opinions to ensure this is true. Auditing financial statements is one of the primary services provided by CPAs and is the focus of multiple courses for accounting majors.

Item 9 is reserved for changes in or disagreements with the auditors. This item also rarely indicates a problem, but you should look at it just in case. Item 9A is a recent addition to 10-Ks in response to requirements made by the passage of the Sarbanes–Oxley Act. Here management acknowledges its responsibility for establishing and maintaining a system of internal controls over financial reporting, its testing of this system's effectiveness, and its opinion of its effectiveness. It is this system of internal controls on which the auditors provide an opinion, although as discussed in the previous paragraph, the opinion is frequently included in Item 8.

Items 10 through 14 provide information that is usually provided in the proxy statement (see Form DEF 14A in Exhibit 12.2, p. 695) because stockholders typically vote on whether to retain directors and auditors (or principal accountants). Of course, the names of the parties are disclosed, as are their business experience or any family relationships with other directors or officers. Finally, **Item 15** is a listing of the financial statements (discussed as part of Item 8) and other required filings.

ANALYZING FINANCIAL STATEMENTS WITH CROSS SECTIONAL AND TIME SERIES ANALYSIS

OBJECTIVE ◄ 3

Discuss between cross sectional and time series analysis.

As with many things in life, context is important in financial statement analysis. For example, how well do you believe a corporation with $3.3 billion in net sales is performing? Your answer should be that it depends. That is, if net sales for the previous 2 years were $4.5 billion and $3.9 billion, respectively, you would say the trend is negative. However, if net sales for the previous 2 years were $2.0 billion and $2.8 billion, respectively, then you would conclude the trend is positive. Or, to make the judgment, you could see how this corporation's sales growth stacks up against a major competitor's.

The context with which we placed our hypothetical corporation's net sales and sales growth demonstrates the two general comparisons we make when analyzing financial statements—cross sectional analysis and time series (or trend) analysis.

CROSS SECTIONAL ANALYSIS

Cross sectional analysis compares one corporation to another corporation and to industry averages. Although this method is useful, it is often difficult to find a good comparison corporation, and even corporations classified in the same industry frequently have different aspects to their operations. For example, both Kroger and Sprouts Farmers Market are in the Grocery Stores Industry. However, many Kroger stores also have a pharmacy, in-store banking, video rental, and so on, while Sprouts stores do not provide these other services. Nonetheless, it is useful to highlight similarities, differences, strengths, and weaknesses of the corporation as compared to the competition and the industry as a whole. For example, for fiscal year 2019:

- Kroger's gross profit margin percentage was 22.07%.
- Sprouts' gross profit margin percentage was 33.63%.
- The Grocery Stores industry had gross profit margin percentages of 27.40%.

While Sprouts' gross margin percentage is well above the industry average, Kroger's is below the industry average. As we will discuss in more detail later in the chapter, this reflects more of a difference in strategy than an indication that Sprouts is outperforming Kroger.

TIME SERIES ANALYSIS

Time series (or trend) analysis compares a single corporation across time. For example, if you look at **Kroger**'s income statement in Appendix 4, you see that its net sales were:

- $123.280 billion in 2017
- $121.852 billion in 2018
- $122.286 billion in 2019

This shows a slightly declining trend from 2017 to 2019.

Year-to-year comparisons of important accounts and account groups help to identify the causes of changes in a company's income or financial position. Knowing the causes of these changes is helpful in forecasting a company's future profitability and financial position. In fact, the SEC requires comparative financial statements (2 years for the balance sheet and 3 years for both the income statement and statement of cash flows) in the 10-K, which facilitates trend analysis.

CROSS SECTIONAL AND TIME SERIES ANALYSIS ILLUSTRATED

Cross sectional and time series analysis are demonstrated in EXAMPLE 12.1.

EXAMPLE 12.1   INTERPRETING CROSS SECTIONAL AND TIME SERIES (OR TREND) ANALYSIS

Information from **Kroger's** and **Sprouts'** financial statements follows.

Kroger (in millions)

	2019	2018	2017
Net sales	$122,286	$121,852	$123,280
Cost of goods sold	95,294	95,103	95,811
Gross profit	$ 26,992	$ 26,749	$ 27,469

Sprouts (in thousands)

	2019	2018	2017
Net sales	$5,634,835	$5,207,336	$4,664,612
Cost of goods sold	3,740,017	3,459,861	3,097,582
Gross profit	$1,894,818	$1,747,475	$1,567,030

Required:

1. Using time series analysis, comment on the trend of Sprouts' cost of goods sold and gross profit.

2. What is the primary weakness of using raw financial statement numbers in cross sectional and time series analysis? What can you do about it?

3. Using cross sectional analysis, compare Sprouts' gross profit to that of Kroger's.

Solution (all $ are in thousands):

When analyzing a company's financial statements, cross sectional analysis compares the company's financial statements to a competitor or industry averages, and time series analysis compares specific line items of the financial statements over multiple years.

1. Sprouts' cost of goods sold increased by $362,279 ($3,459,861 − $3,097,582) from 2017 to 2018 and by $280,156 between 2018 and 2019. In isolation this may seem bad, but the primary reason for this increase is that sales were also increasing. In fact, Sprouts' gross profit increased by $180,445 between 2017 and 2018 and by $147,343 between 2018 and 2019.

2. The primary weakness is that raw financial statement numbers can be difficult to compare. For example, Sprouts' net sales increased by almost $1 billion from 2017 to 2019, while its gross profit only increased by about $328 million. However, if you look at the percentage change, net sales and gross profit increased by approximately 20.80% and 20.92%, respectively. Further, when comparing two competitors—like Sprouts and Kroger—making comparisons with raw financial statement numbers is difficult because they are often vastly different in size. Using percentage changes from year to year or between two financial statement line items helps overcome the differences in the relative sizes of items of interest.

3. When we look at the percentage change in gross profit from year to year we discover the following:

Growth in Gross Profit:	2018 to 2019*	2017 to 2018**
Sprouts	8.43%	11.52%
Kroger	0.91%	−2.62%

* (2019 Gross Profit − 2018 Gross Profit) ÷ 2018 Gross Profit
** (2018 Gross Profit − 2017 Gross Profit) ÷ 2017 Gross Profit

This analysis suggests that Sprouts is growing much faster than is Kroger. And, when we think about it, it's probably not surprising. Sprouts is in an expansion phase, where they are opening a relatively high percentage of new stores (over 5% per year), while Kroger is well established in most markets in the United States and is expanding at a much slower rate.

Source: Kroger 2019 10-K and Sprouts Farmers Market 2019 10-K.

ANALYZING THE FINANCIAL STATEMENTS WITH HORIZONTAL AND VERTICAL ANALYSIS

OBJECTIVE ◀ 4

Analyze financial statements using horizontal and vertical analysis.

The comparative financial statements included in the 10-K report the results in dollar amounts. This makes it easy to detect large changes between years in accounts or groups of accounts. These changes may indicate that the corporation is changing or that the conditions under which the corporation operates are changing. However, while comparative financial statements show changes in the amounts of financial statement items, analysts often prefer to restate the financial statements in percentages using common size statements. **Common size statements** express each financial statement line item in percentage terms, which highlights differences. Typically, this conversion from dollar amounts to percentages is done with horizontal or vertical analysis.

HORIZONTAL ANALYSIS

In **horizontal analysis**, each financial statement line item is expressed as a percent of the base year (typically the first year shown). EXAMPLE 12.2 shows how to prepare a common size income statement for horizontal analysis.

EXAMPLE 12.2 PREPARING COMMON SIZE STATEMENTS FOR HORIZONTAL ANALYSIS

Sprouts' income statement from its 2019 10-K follows.

Sprouts Farmers Markets, Inc.
Consolidated Income Statements
(In thousands, except per share amounts)

	Dec. 29, 2019	Dec. 30, 2018	Dec. 31, 2017
NET SALES	$5,634,835	$5,207,336	$4,664,612
Cost of Sales	3,740,017	3,459,861	3,097,582
GROSS PROFIT	1,894,818	1,747,475	1,567,030
Selling, general, and administrative expenses	1,549,707	1,404,443	1,245,640
Depreciation and amortization	120,491	108,045	94,194
Store closure and other costs	7,260	12,076	1,126
OPERATING INCOME	217,360	222,911	226,070
Interest expense, net	(21,192)	(27,435)	(21,177)
Other income	0	320	625
INCOME BEFORE INCOME TAXES	196,168	195,796	205,518
Income tax provision	(46,539)	(37,260)	(47,078)
NET INCOME	$ 149,629	$ 158,536	$ 158,440
NET INCOME PER BASIC SHARE	$ 1.25	$ 1.23	$ 1.17
NET INCOME PER DILUTED SHARE	$ 1.25	$ 1.22	$ 1.15
WEIGHTED AVERAGE SHARES OUTSTANDING (BASIC)	119,368	128,827	135,169
WEIGHTED AVERAGE SHARES OUTSTANDING (DILUTED)	119,742	129,776	137,884

CONTINUED

EXAMPLE 12.2 PREPARING COMMON SIZE STATEMENTS FOR HORIZONTAL ANALYSIS *(CONTINUED)*

Required:
Prepare a common size income statement to be used for horizontal analysis for Sprouts using 2017 as the base year.

Solution:
Horizontal analysis expresses each financial statement line item as a percentage of the base year.

Sprouts Farmers Markets, Inc.
Consolidated Income Statements
(In thousands, except per share amounts)

	Dec. 29, 2019	Dec. 30, 2018	Dec. 31, 2017
NET SALES	120.80%	111.63%	100.00%
Cost of sales	120.74%	111.70%	100.00%
GROSS PROFIT	120.92%	111.52%	100.00%
Selling, general, and administrative expenses	124.41%	112.75%	100.00%
Depreciation and amortization	127.92%	114.70%	100.00%
Store closure and other costs	644.76%	1,072.47%	100.00%
OPERATING INCOME	96.15%	98.60%	100.00%
Interest expense, net	100.07%	129.55%	100.00%
Other income	0.00%	51.20%	100.00%
INCOME BEFORE INCOME TAXES	95.45%	95.27%	100.00%
Income tax provision	98.86%	79.15%	100.00%
NET INCOME	94.44%	100.06%	100.00%

Source: Sprouts 2019 10-K.

Horizontal analysis is good for highlighting the growth (or shrinkage) in financial statement line items from year to year and is particularly useful for trend analysis. For example, looking at Sprouts' common size income statement in Example 12.2, we see that selling, general, and administrative expenses (SG&A) has grown faster than sales, and cost of sales when comparing 2017 through 2019. This has resulted in operating income declining by almost 4% despite an over 20% growth in sales revenue.

VERTICAL ANALYSIS

Vertical analysis, on the other hand, expresses each financial statement line item as a percent of the largest amount on the statement. On the income statement, this is net sales and on the balance sheet it is total assets. Vertical analysis helps distinguish between changes in account balances that result from growth and changes that are likely to have arisen from other causes. EXAMPLE 12.3 shows how to prepare a common size income statement and balance sheet for vertical analysis.

EXAMPLE 12.3 PREPARING COMMON SIZE STATEMENTS FOR VERTICAL ANALYSIS

Concept:
Vertical analysis expresses each financial statement line item as a percent of the largest amount on the statement.

Information:
Sprouts' balance sheets and income statements for the fiscal years 2017–2019 follow.

Sprouts Farmers Markets, Inc.
Consolidated Balance Sheets
(In thousands, except share and per share amounts)

	Dec. 29, 2019	Dec. 30, 2018	Dec. 31, 2017
ASSETS			
CURRENT ASSETS:			
Cash and cash equivalents	$ 85,314	$ 1,588	$ 19,479
Marketable securities	–	–	–
Accounts receivable, net	15,713	40,564	25,893
Inventories	275,979	264,366	229,542
Prepaid and other current assets	10,833	27,323	24,593
TOTAL CURRENT ASSETS	387,839	333,841	299,507
PROPERTY AND EQUIPMENT, NET	741,508	766,429	713,031
OPERATING LEASE ASSETS, NET	1,028,436.00	–	–
INTANGIBLE ASSETS, NET OF ACCUMULATED AMORTIZATION	185,395	194,803	196,205
GOODWILL	368,078	368,078	368,078
OTHER ASSETS	11,727	12,463	4,782
TOTAL ASSETS	$ 2,722,983	$1,675,614	$1,581,603
LIABILITIES AND SHAREHOLDERS' EQUITY			
CURRENT LIABILITIES			
Accounts payable and accrued liabilities	$ 261,326	$ 253,969	$ 244,853
Accrued salaries and benefits	48,579	48,603	45,623
Current portion of capital and financing lease obligations	0	7,428	9,283
Current portion of operating lease liabilities	106,153	0	0
Current portion of finance lease liabilities	754	0	0
TOTAL CURRENT LIABILITIES	416,812	310,000	299,759
LONG-TERM LIABILITIES			
Long-term capital and financing lease obligations	0	119,642	125,489
Long-term operating lease liabilities	1,078,927	0	0
Long-term debt and finance lease liabilities	549,419	453,000	348,000
Other long-term liabilities	41,517	153,377	130,640
Deferred income tax liability	54,356	50,399	27,066
TOTAL LONG-TERM LIABILITIES	1,724,219	776,418	631,195
TOTAL LIABILITIES	2,141,031	1,086,418	930,954

CONTINUED

EXAMPLE 12.3   PREPARING COMMON SIZE STATEMENTS FOR VERTICAL ANALYSIS *(CONTINUED)*

SHAREHOLDERS' EQUITY			
Preferred stock	0	0	0
Common stock	117	124	132
Additional paid-in capital	670,966	657,140	620,788
Accumulated other comprehensive income (loss)	(4,682)	1,134	(784)
(Accumulated deficit) retained earnings	(84,449)	(69,202)	30,558
Treasury stock	—	—	—
TOTAL SHAREHOLDERS' EQUITY	581,952	589,196	650,694
TOTAL LIABILITIES & SHAREHOLDERS' EQUITY	$ 2,722,983	$1,675,614	$1,581,648

Sprouts Farmers Markets, Inc.
Consolidated Income Statements
(In thousands, except per share amounts)

	Dec. 29, 2019	Dec. 30, 2018	Dec. 31, 2017
NET SALES	$5,634,835	$5,207,336	$4,664,612
Cost of sales	3,740,017	3,459,861	3,097,582
GROSS PROFIT	1,894,818	1,747,475	1,567,030
Selling, general, and administrative expenses	1,549,707	1,404,443	1,245,640
Depreciation and amortization	120,491	108,045	94,194
Store closure and other costs	7,260	12,076	1,126
OPERATING INCOME	217,360	222,911	226,070
Interest expense, net	(21,192)	(27,435)	(21,177)
Other income	0	320	625
INCOME BEFORE INCOME TAXES	196,168	195,796	205,518
Income tax provision	(46,539)	(37,260)	(47,078)
NET INCOME	$ 149,629	$ 158,536	$ 158,440
NET INCOME PER BASIC SHARE	$ 1.25	$ 1.23	$ 1.17
NET INCOME PER DILUTED SHARE	$ 1.25	$ 1.22	$ 1.15
WEIGHTED AVERAGE SHARES OUTSTANDING (BASIC)	119,368	128,827	135,169
WEIGHTED AVERAGE SHARES OUTSTANDING (DILUTED)	119,742	129,776	137,884

Source: Sprouts Farmers Market 2018 and 2019 10-K.

Required:
Prepare common size balance sheets and income statements to be used in vertical analysis for Sprouts.

Solution:
Vertical analysis expresses each financial statement line item as a percentage of the largest amount on the statement.

Sprouts Farmers Markets, Inc.
Consolidated Balance Sheets
(In thousands, except share and per share amounts)

	Dec. 29, 2019	Dec. 30, 2018	Dec. 31, 2017
ASSETS			
CURRENT ASSETS:			
Cash and cash equivalents	3.13%	0.09%	1.23%
Marketable securities	0.00%	0.00%	0.00%
Accounts receivable, net	0.58%	2.42%	1.64%
Inventories	10.14%	15.78%	14.51%
Prepaid and other current assets	0.40%	1.63%	1.55%
TOTAL CURRENT ASSETS	14.24%	19.92%	18.94%
PROPERTY AND EQUIPMENT, NET	27.23%	45.74%	45.08%
OPERATING LEASE ASSETS, NET	37.77%	0.00%	0.00%
INTANGIBLE ASSETS, NET OF ACCUMULATED AMORTIZATION	6.81%	11.63%	12.41%
GOODWILL	13.52%	21.97%	23.27%
OTHER ASSETS	0.43%	0.74%	0.30%
TOTAL ASSETS	100.00%	100.00%	100.00%
LIABILITIES AND SHAREHOLDERS' EQUITY			
CURRENT LIABILITIES			
Accounts payable and accrued liabilities	9.60%	15.16%	15.48%
Accrued salaries and benefits	1.78%	2.90%	2.88%
Current portion of capital and financing lease obligations	0.00%	0.44%	0.59%
Current portion of operating lease liabilities	3.90%	0.00%	0.00%
Current portion of finance lease liabilities	0.03%	0.00%	0.00%
TOTAL CURRENT LIABILITIES	15.31%	18.50%	18.95%
LONG-TERM LIABILITIES			
Long-term capital and financing lease obligations	0.00%	7.14%	7.93%
Long-term operating lease liabilities	39.62%	0.00%	0.00%
Long-term debt and finance lease liabilities	20.18%	27.03%	22.00%
Other long-term liabilities	1.52%	9.15%	8.26%
Deferred income tax liability	2.00%	3.01%	1.71%
TOTAL LONG-TERM LIABILITIES	63.32%	46.34%	39.91%
TOTAL LIABILITIES	78.63%	64.84%	58.86%
SHAREHOLDERS' EQUITY			
Preferred stock	0.00%	0.00%	0.00%
Common stock	0.00%	0.01%	0.01%
Additional paid-in capital	24.64%	39.22%	39.25%
Accumulated other comprehensive income (loss)	−0.17%	0.07%	−0.05%
(Accumulated deficit) retained earnings	−3.10%	−4.13%	1.93%
Treasury stock	0.00%	0.00%	0.00%
TOTAL SHAREHOLDERS' EQUITY	21.37%	35.16%	41.14%
TOTAL LIABILITIES & SHAREHOLDERS' EQUITY	100.00%	100.00%	100.00%

Source: Sprouts Farmers Market 2018 and 2019 10-K.

CONTINUED

EXAMPLE 12.3   PREPARING COMMON SIZE STATEMENTS FOR VERTICAL ANALYSIS *(CONTINUED)*

Sprouts Farmers Markets, Inc.
Consolidated Income Statements
(In thousands, except per share amounts)

	Dec. 29, 2019	Dec. 30, 2018	Dec. 31, 2017
NET SALES	100.00%	100.00%	100.00%
Cost of sales	66.37%	66.44%	66.41%
GROSS PROFIT	33.63%	33.56%	33.59%
Selling, general, and administrative expenses	27.50%	26.97%	26.70%
Depreciation and amortization	2.14%	2.07%	2.02%
Store closure and other costs	0.13%	0.23%	0.02%
OPERATING INCOME	3.86%	4.28%	4.85%
Interest expense, net	−0.38%	−0.53%	−0.45%
Other income	0.00%	0.01%	0.01%
INCOME BEFORE INCOME TAXES	3.48%	3.76%	4.41%
Income tax provision	−0.83%	−0.72%	−1.01%
NET INCOME	2.66%	3.04%	3.40%

Source: Sprouts Farmers Market 2018 and 2019 10-K.

Identifying non-growth changes and their causes can help forecast a company's future profitability or its future financial position. For example, in Example 12.3, **Sprouts**' selling, general, and administrative (SG&A) expense increased from 26.70% of net sales in 2017 to 27.50% in 2019. This may not seem like much of a change, but if cost of sales had remained at 26.70% of net sales, then gross profit would be over $12.37 million higher. Further, because many of the SG&A expenses are fixed (i.e., do not increase just because net sales increase), we would hope this percentage would actually decrease as net sales increase. Determining whether this negative trend in SG&A percentage can be turned around will have a significant effect on forecasting the future. The vertical analysis of the balance sheet is made more difficult by an accounting standard change moving an operating lease asset and significantly more long-term lease obligations onto the balance sheet. Obviously, adjustments for these standard changes are needed.

Further, you can, and should, get much more depth with such analysis. A careful horizontal and vertical analysis serves as a starting point for an inquiry into the causes of these changes, with the objective being forecasting the corporation's future financial statements.

ANALYZING THE FINANCIAL STATEMENTS WITH RATIO ANALYSIS

OBJECTIVE

Calculate and use financial statement ratios to evaluate a company.

Ratio analysis is an examination of financial statements conducted by preparing and evaluating a series of ratios. **Ratios** (or **financial ratios**), like other financial analysis data, normally provide meaningful information only when compared with ratios from previous periods for the same firm (i.e., time series, or trend, analysis) or similar firms (i.e., cross sectional analysis). Ratios help by removing most of the effects of size differences. When dollar amounts are used, size differences between firms may make a meaningful comparison impossible. However, properly constructed financial ratios permit the comparison of firms regardless of size.

We discuss six categories of ratio analysis:

- *Short-term liquidity ratios* are particularly helpful to short-term creditors, but all investors and creditors have an interest in these ratios.
- *Debt management ratios* and *profitability ratios* provide information for long-term creditors and stockholders.
- *Asset efficiency (or operating) ratios* help management operate the firm and indicate to outsiders the efficiency with which certain of the company's activities are performed.
- *Stockholder ratios* are of interest to a corporation's stockholders.
- *Dupont analysis* decomposes return on equity into margin, turnover, and leverage.

All these ratios are shown and defined in Exhibit 12.4 at the conclusion of this section (pp. 726–727). We will use data from **Sprouts**' financial statements in Appendix 5 to illustrate each of these types of financial statement ratios. Also note that in the following discussion all dollar amount are in thousands, except per share data, to match up with the financial statements.

SHORT-TERM LIQUIDITY RATIOS

Analysts want to know the likelihood that a company will be able to pay its current obligations as they come due. Failure to pay current liabilities can lead to suppliers refusing to sell needed inventory and employees leaving. As such, even companies with good business models can be forced into bankruptcy by their inability to pay current liabilities.

The cash necessary to pay current liabilities will come from existing cash or from receivables and inventory, which should turn into cash approximately at the same time the current liabilities become due. Property, plant, and equipment and other long-lived assets are much more difficult to turn into cash in time to meet current obligations without harming future operations. Accordingly, the **short-term liquidity ratios** compare some combination of current assets or operations to current liabilities.

Current Ratio Since a company must meet its current obligations primarily by using its current assets, the current ratio is especially useful to short-term creditors. The **current ratio** is expressed as follows:

$$\text{Current Ratio} = \frac{\text{Current Assets}}{\text{Current Liabilities}}$$

Using information from **Sprouts**' 2019 balance sheet, the current ratio for Sprouts is calculated as:

	2019	2018
Total current assets	$387,839	$333,841
Total current liabilities	$416,812	$310,000
Current ratio	**0.93**	**1.08**

Source: Sprouts Farmers Market 2019 10-K.

Sprouts' current liabilities increased at a much greater rate (34.46%) than did their current assets (16.17%). Consequently, Sprouts' short-term liquidity appears to have deteriorated.

There are no absolute standards for ratios, so a company's ratios are typically compared to the industry averages and/or competitors. The average for the Grocery Store industry is 0.84. By these standards, Sprouts' current ratio was relatively strong in both years.

Quick Ratio   Some analysts believe that the current ratio overstates short-term liquidity. They argue that prepaid expenses (expenses for which payments are made before consumption) often cannot be converted into cash. Further, inventories must be sold and receivables collected from those sales before cash is obtained to pay maturing current liabilities. Both the sale of inventory and collection of receivables can require a lengthy period. Conservative analysts argue that only those current assets that can be turned into cash almost immediately should be used to measure short-term liquidity.

A more conservative measure of short-term liquidity is based on *quick assets* (usually cash, receivables, and short-term investments) and current liabilities. The **quick ratio** (or *acid test ratio*) is expressed as follows:

$$\text{Quick Ratio} = \frac{\text{Cash} + \text{Short-Term Investment} + \text{Receivables}}{\text{Current Liabilities}}$$

Looking at the detail of **Sprouts'** current assets, the quick ratio is calculated as follows:

	2019	2018
Current assets:		
Cash and equivalents	$ 85,314	$ 1,588
Marketable securities	0	0
Receivables, net	15,713	40,564
Inventories	275,979	264,366
Prepaid expenses and other current assets	10,833	27,323
Total current assets	$387,839	$333,841
Quick assets	$101,027	$ 42,152
Total current liabilities	$416,812	$310,000
Quick ratio	**0.24**	**0.14**

Source: Sprouts Farmers Market 2019 10-K.

A quick ratio above 1.0 is considered adequate because there are enough liquid assets available to meet current obligations. Using this guideline, we see that Sprouts is incapable of meeting its current obligations with quick assets. Fortunately, groceries are relatively easy to sell (it's much harder to sell a car or jewelry, for example), so a low quick ratio is not a big problem in the Grocery Store Industry. Further, the Sprouts quick ratio is well above the industry average of 0.06.

Cash Ratio   An even more conservative short-term liquidity ratio is the cash ratio. Specifically, while the current and quick ratios assume that receivables will be collected, the cash ratio does not make this assumption. This ratio may be more appropriate for industries in which collectability is uncertain or for corporations with high credit risk receivables. The **cash ratio** is expressed as:

$$\text{Cash Ratio} = \frac{\text{Cash} + \text{Short-Term Investment}}{\text{Current Liabilities}}$$

Although **Sprouts** does not have high credit risk receivables, the cash ratio is calculated as:

	2019	2018
Current assets:		
Cash and equivalents	$ 85,314	$ 1,588
Marketable securities	–	–
Receivables	15,713	40,564
Inventories	275,979	264,366
Prepaid and other current assets	10,833	27,323
Total current assets	387,839	333,841
Liquid assets	$ 85,314	$ 1,588
Total current liabilities	$416,812	$310,000
Cash ratio	**0.20**	**0.01**

Source: Sprouts Farmers Market 2019 10-K.

The cash ratio indicates that Sprouts does not have enough cash and marketable securities to pay off its current liabilities in either 2018 or 2019. However, a cash ratio below 1.0 only indicates liquidity issues if you do not believe in Sprouts' ability to sell its inventories or collect its receivables.

Operating Cash Flow Ratio The operating cash flow ratio takes a slightly different approach. This ratio looks at the ability of operations to generate cash, which recognizes the more general concept that current obligations will be paid through operations (after all, selling inventory and collecting receivables is a big part of operations). The **operating cash flow ratio** is expressed as:

$$\text{Operating Cash Flow Ratio} = \frac{\text{Cash Flows from Operating Activities}}{\text{Current Liabilities}}$$

Looking at **Sprouts'** statement of cash flows and balance sheet, the operating cash flow ratio is calculated as follows:

	2019	2018
Cash flows from operating activities	$355,210	$294,379
Total current liabilities	$416,812	$310,000
Operating cash flow ratio	**0.85**	**0.95**

Source: Sprouts Farmers Market 2019 10-K.

In 2018 and 2019, Sprouts' operations did not generate enough cash to meet the current obligations due at the end of the year. Obviously, this is not ideal, but by looking more closely at Statement of Cash Flows in the Grocery Store Industry, you will discover that this is the norm in the industry. This means that grocery stores finance themselves, in part, by "borrowing" from its suppliers (by incurring an Accounts Payable rather than paying Cash it doesn't have), customers (e.g., gift cards), and so on.

Overview of Short-Term Liquidity Ratios While Sprouts' current and operating cash flow ratios declined in 2019, its cash and quick ratios improved. Because we have some confidence that Sprouts will be able to sell their inventory, collect their receivables and continue operations, the decline in the current and operating cash flow ratios should probably attract more of our attention. However, because Sprouts' ratios are so much better than industry averages, this doesn't yet warrant immediate concern with short-term liquidity. Nonetheless, for creditors, generally this is not good news. Creditors typically prefer all these measures of short-term liquidity be as high as possible. However, because investments in current assets (especially cash, receivables, and inventory) earn very small returns compared with the returns on investments in noncurrent assets, management must minimize the proportion of capital invested in current assets if it is to maximize profit. Using the income statement and balance sheet shown in Exhibit 12.3, EXAMPLE 12.4 illustrates how to calculate and interpret short-term liquidity ratios for **Kroger**.

EXHIBIT 12.3 ▶ **The Kroger Co. Income Statement and Balance Sheet**

The Kroger Co.
Consolidated Balance Sheets

(in millions)	FISCAL 2019 Feb. 1, 2020	2018 Feb. 2, 2019	2017 Feb. 2, 2018
ASSETS			
CURRENT ASSETS:			
Cash and cash equivalents	$ 399	$ 429	$ 347
Store deposits in-transit	1,179	1,181	1,161
Receivables	1,706	1,589	1,637
Inventories (FIFO)	8,464	8,123	7,781
LIFO reserve	(1,380)	(1,277)	(1,248)
Assets held for sale	0	166	835
Prepaid and other current assets	522	592	604
TOTAL CURRENT ASSETS	10,890	10,803	11,117
Property, plant, and equipment, net	21,871	21,635	21,071
Operating lease assets	6,814	0	0
Intangibles, net	1,066	1,258	1,100
Goodwill	3,076	3,087	2,925
Other assets	1,539	1,335	984
TOTAL ASSETS	$45,256	$38,118	$37,197
LIABILITIES AND SHAREHOLDERS' EQUITY			
CURRENT LIABILITIES			
Current portion long-term debt, including obligations under finance leases	$ 1,965	$ 3,157	$ 3,560
Current portion of operating lease liabilities	$ 597		
Trade accounts payable	6,349	6,059	5,858
Accrued salaries and wages	1,168	1,227	1,099
Liabilities held for sale	0	51	259
Other current liabilities	4,164	3,780	3,421
TOTAL CURRENT LIABILITIES	14,243	14,274	14,197
LONG-TERM LIABILITIES			
Long-term debt, including obligations under finance leases	12,111	12,072	12,029
Noncurrent operating lease liabilities	6,505	0	0
Deferred income taxes	1,466	1,562	1,568
Pension and postretirement benefit obligations	608	494	792
Other long-term liabilities	1,750	1,881	1,706
TOTAL LONG-TERM LIABILITIES	22,440	16,009	16,095
TOTAL LIABILITIES	36,683	30,283	30,292

Source: The Kroger Co. 2018 and 2019 10-K.

CONTINUED

The Kroger Co. Income Statement and Balance Sheet (CONTINUED)   **EXHIBIT 12.3**

SHAREHOLDERS' EQUITY

Preferred stock	0	0	0
Common stock	1,918	1,918	1,918
Additional paid-in capital	3,337	3,245	3,161
Accumulated other comprehensive loss	(640)	(346)	(471)
Accumulated earnings	20,978	19,681	17,007
Treasury stock	(16,991)	(16,612)	(14,684)
TOTAL SHAREHOLDERS' EQUITY	8,602	7,886	6,931
Noncontrolling interests	(29)	(51)	(26)
TOTAL EQUITY	8,573	7,835	6,905
TOTAL LIABILITIES & SHAREHOLDERS' EQUITY	$ 45,256	$ 38,118	$ 37,197

The Kroger Co.
Consolidated Income Statement

(in millions)	FISCAL 2019 Feb. 1, 2020	2018 Feb. 2, 2019	2017 Feb. 2, 2018
SALES	$122,286	$121,852	$123,280
OPERATING EXPENSES			
Cost of goods sold	95,294	95,103	95,811
Operating, general, and administrative	21,208	20,786	21,510
Rent	884	884	911
Depreciation and amortization	2,649	2,465	2,436
OPERATING PROFIT	2,251	2,614	2,612
OTHER INCOME (EXPENSE)			
Interest expense	(603)	(620)	(601)
Nonservice component of company-sponsored pension plan costs	–	(26)	(527)
Mark to market gain on Ocado securities	157	228	–
Gain on sale of businesses	176	1,782	–
NET EARNINGS BEFORE INCOME TAX (BENEFIT) EXPENSE	1,981	3,978	1,484
Income tax (benefit) expense	469	900	(405)
NET EARNINGS INCLUDING NONCONTROLLING INTERESTS	1,512	3,078	1,889
Net loss attributable to noncontrolling interests	(147)	(32)	(18)
NET EARNINGS ATTRIBUTABLE TO THE KROGER CO.	1,659	3,110	1,907

Source: The Kroger Co. 2018 and 2019 10-K.

EXAMPLE 12.4   CALCULATING AND INTERPRETING SHORT-TERM LIQUIDITY RATIOS

Refer to the information in **Kroger**'s income statement and balance sheet in Exhibit 12.3 (pp. 708–709). Kroger's cash flows from operations were (in millions) $4,164 and $4,664 in 2018 and 2019, respectively.

Required:
Calculate the following short-term liquidity ratios for Kroger for 2018 and 2019: (1) current ratio, (2) quick ratio, (3) cash ratio, and (4) operating cash flow ratio (operating cash flows are provided in the Information section).

Note: Treat "Store Deposits in-Transit" as Cash. These amounts are primarily funds deposited to Kroger's bank accounts for which it does not have immediate access—a majority are related to sales paid for with credit cards and checks.

CONTINUED

EXAMPLE 12.4	CALCULATING AND INTERPRETING SHORT-TERM LIQUIDITY RATIOS *(CONTINUED)*

Solution:

Short-term liquidity ratios assess the company's ability to meet its current obligations.

		2019 (in millions)	2018 (in millions)
1. Current Ratio $= \dfrac{\text{Current Assets}}{\text{Current Liabilities}}$		$\dfrac{\$10,890}{\$14,243} = \underline{0.76}$	$\dfrac{\$10,803}{\$14,274} = \underline{0.76}$
2. Quick Ratio $= \dfrac{\text{Cash} + \text{Short-Term Investments} + \text{Receivables}}{\text{Current Liabilities}}$		$\dfrac{(\$399 + \$1,179) + \$0 + \$1,706}{14,243} = \underline{0.23}$	$\dfrac{((\$429 + \$1,181) + \$0 + \$1,589)}{\$14,274} = \underline{0.22}$
3. Cash Ratio $= \dfrac{\text{Cash} + \text{Short-Term Investments}}{\text{Current Liabilities}}$		$\dfrac{((\$399 + \$1,179) + \$0)}{\$14,243} = \underline{0.11}$	$\dfrac{((\$429 + \$1,181) + \$0)}{\$14,274} = \underline{0.11}$
4. Operating Cash Flow Ratio $= \dfrac{\text{Cash Flow from Operating Activities}}{\text{Current Liabilities}}$		$\dfrac{\$4,664^*}{\$14,243} = \underline{0.33}$	$\dfrac{\$4,164^*}{\$14,274} = \underline{0.29}$

*Taken from the statement of cash flows. The numbers were provided in the Information section of this Example.

Source: The Kroger Co. 2019, 10-K

From Example 12.4, you can see that **Kroger**'s current, quick, and cash ratios are well below 1.0, which indicates Kroger will need to obtain cash from someplace other than current assets to pay off their current liabilities. This will entail some combination of (1) generating cash through operations or (2) obtaining additional financing, or, if things get really bad, (3) selling off noncurrent assets. Some comfort is provided by realizing that the grocery store industry averages for all three of these ratios are below 1.0, suggesting Kroger isn't dangerously below other companies in its industry.

However, compared to **Sprouts**' short term liquidity ratios shown previously in the text, Kroger's short-term liquidity ratios are generally weaker. This suggests that Kroger's risk of short-term insolvency is higher although neither corporation is in significant danger relative to industry averages.

DEBT MANAGEMENT RATIOS

Debt management ratios provide information on two aspects of debt. First, they provide information on the relative mix of debt and equity financing (often referred to as its capital structure). The primary advantages of debt over equity are:

- Interest payments are tax-deductible.
- Creditors do not share in profits.

Debt, however, is riskier than equity, because, unless the interest and principal payments are made when due, the firm may fall into bankruptcy. In most corporations, management attempts to achieve an appropriate balance between the cost advantage of debt and its extra risk.

Second, debt management ratios also try to show the corporation's ability to meet or cover its debt obligations through operations because interest and principal payments must be made as scheduled or a company can be declared bankrupt. The times interest earned ratio is an example of the latter type of measurement.

Times Interest Earned Ratio Some liabilities, like accounts payable, have flexible payment schedules that can be modified when necessary. Other liabilities—primarily short-term and long-term debt—have specific payment schedules that must be met. The cash used to make these payments must come from operations. Analysts use the times interest earned ratio to gauge a firm's ability to repay its debt from recurring operations. This ratio can focus either on accrual-basis interest expense or the cash-basis interest payments and are typically measured pre-tax because interest expense is tax deductible. The **times interest earned ratio** is expressed as:

$$\text{Times Interest Earned }(\textit{Accrual Basis}) = \frac{\text{Operating Income}}{\text{Interest Expense}}$$

$$\text{Times Interest Earned }(\textit{Cash Basis}) = \frac{\text{Cash Flows from Operations} + \text{Income Tax Payments} + \text{Interest Payments}}{\text{Interest Payments}}$$

The times interest earned ratios for **Sprouts** are calculated as:

	2019	2018
Cash flows from operating activities	$355,210*	$294,379*
Operating income	217,360	222,911
Interest payments	20,293*	27,086*
Interest expense	21,192	27,435
Income tax payments	44,637*	15,527*
Times interest earned (cash)	**20.70**	**12.44**
Times interest earned (accrual)	**10.26**	**8.13**

*Taken from the statement of cash flows.
Source: Sprouts Farmers Market 2019 10-K.

Sprouts appears to have an easy time covering its interest expense/payments. While the times interest earned ratios provide information on the company's ability to meet, or cover, its debt obligations, other debt management ratios assess the relative mix of debt and equity financing. We will consider four different ways of measuring the proportion of debt within a corporation's capital structure.

Long-Term Debt to Equity Ratio Despite its apparent misnomer, we prefer to define long-term debt as the sum of long-term debt and the debt-like obligations in current liabilities (notes or short-term loans). It is called the long-term debt to equity ratio because historically when corporations borrowed money, they locked themselves into long-term debt contracts. The long-term debt to equity ratio provides information on the proportion of capital provided by creditors and by stockholders. Of course, this type of debt also includes any current portion (i.e., long-term debt principal that must be repaid within the next 12 months). Additionally, it can include more flexible borrowing arrangements, such as lines of credit, that may be classified as current liabilities. The **long-term debt to equity ratio** is expressed as:

$$\text{Long-Term Debt to Equity Ratio} = \frac{\text{Long-Term Debt (including current portion)}}{\text{Total Equity}}$$

Sprouts has a long-term debt to equity ratio of 0.77 and 0.95 in 2018 and 2019, respectively, based on long-term debt of $453,000 in 2018 and $550,173 in 2019. These amounts are found by combining "long-term debt and finance lease liabilities" and "current portion of finance lease liabilities." As it turns out, Sprouts does not have any current portion of long-term debt.[1]

Debt to Equity Ratio Debt is also occasionally defined as all liabilities. This is a more inclusive view of debt recognizing that if corporations did not have current liabilities such as accounts payable, they would have to take out other borrowings or sell stock to finance its assets. The **debt to equity ratio** is expressed as:

$$\text{Debt to Equity Ratio} = \frac{\text{Total Liabilities}}{\text{Total Equity}}$$

Sprouts' debt to equity ratio was 3.68 in 2019 and 1.84 in 2018. Such a dramatic increase warrants some investigation. However, in this case, the increase is due to the change in lease accounting in 2019 virtually doubling total liabilities.

Long-Term Debt or Debt to Total Assets The proportion of total capital provided by creditors is also shown by the **long-term debt to total assets ratio** and the **debt to total assets ratio**. These measures are more useful when equity is negative, small, or subject to substantial changes. These ratios are expressed as:

$$\text{Long-Term Debt to Total Assets Ratio} = \frac{\text{Long-Term Debt (including current portion)}}{\text{Total Assets}}$$

$$\text{Debt to Total Assets Ratio} = \frac{\text{Total Liabilities}}{\text{Total Assets}}$$

Overview of Debt Management Ratios   EXAMPLE 12.5 demonstrates how to calculate and interpret debt management ratios.

---

1 Because many financial statement users view leases as unavoidable obligations, the FASB now requires companies to report virtually all of its lease obligations on the face of the balance sheet. This makes it difficult to compare 2019 (using ASC 842) to prior years (using ASC 840)—note the relatively large amounts in "current portion of operating lease liabilities" and "long-term operating lease liabilities" for 2019. For simplicity, we exclude these lease obligations from this long-term debt calculations, although many financial statement users will include it.

EXAMPLE 12.5   CALCULATING AND INTERPRETING DEBT MANAGEMENT RATIOS

Refer to the information in **Kroger's** income statement and balance sheet in Exhibit 12.3 (pp. 708–709). Additional financial statement information follows.

	2019 (in millions)	2018 (in millions)
Cash flows from operations*	$4,664	$4,164
Interest payments*	523	614
Income tax payments*	706	600

*Taken from the statement of cash flows.

Required:

Calculate the following debt management ratios for Kroger for 2018 and 2019: (1) times interest earned ratio (both cash and accrual), (2) long-term debt to equity ratio, (3) debt to equity ratio, (4) long-term debt to total assets ratio, and (5) debt to total assets ratio.

Solution:

Debt management ratios provide information on the company's ability to meet its debt obligations through operations.

		2019 (in millions)	2018 (in millions)
1.	Times Interest Earned (*Accrual Basis*) $= \dfrac{\text{Operating Income}}{\text{Interest Expense}}$	$\dfrac{\$2,251}{\$603} = \underline{3.73}$	$\dfrac{\$2,614}{\$620} = \underline{4.22}$
	Times Interest Earned (*Cash Basis*) $= \dfrac{\text{Cash Flows from Operations + Income Tax Payments + Interest Payments}}{\text{Interest Payments}}$	$\dfrac{\$4,664 + \$706 + \$523}{\$523} = \underline{11.27}$	$\dfrac{\$4,164 + \$600 + \$614}{\$614} = \underline{8.76}$
2.	Long-Term Debt to Equity $= \dfrac{\text{Long-Term Debt (including current portion)}}{\text{Total Equity}}$	$\dfrac{\$12,111 + \$1,965}{\$8,573} = \underline{1.64}$	$\dfrac{\$12,072 + \$3,157}{\$7,835} = \underline{1.94}$
3.	Debt to Equity $= \dfrac{\text{Total Liabilities}}{\text{Total Equity}}$	$\dfrac{\$36,683}{\$8,573} = \underline{4.28}$	$\dfrac{\$30,283}{\$7,835} = \underline{3.87}$
4.	Long-Term Debt to Total Assets $= \dfrac{\text{Long-Term Debt (including current portion)}}{\text{Total Assets}}$	$\dfrac{\$12,111 + \$1,965}{\$45,256} = \underline{0.31}$	$\dfrac{\$12,072 + \$3,157}{\$38,118} = \underline{0.40}$
5.	Debt to Total Assets $= \dfrac{\text{Total Liabilities}}{\text{Total Assets}}$	$\dfrac{\$36,683}{\$45,256} = \underline{0.81}$	$\dfrac{\$30,283}{\$38,118} = \underline{0.79}$

Source: The Kroger Co. 2019 10-K.

From the times interest earned ratios in Example 12.5, you can see that **Kroger** produced sufficient operating income and cash flows from operations to easily meet its interest expense in both years.

The long-term debt to equity, debt to equity, long-term debt to total assets, and debt to total asset ratios suggest a company financed mostly with debt. While the trend is difficult to evaluate because of the change in lease accounting that only affected 2019, it may be wise to attempt to remove the effects of the lease accounting change using the footnotes when evaluating any trends involving liabilities.

YOUDECIDE Credit Analysis

You are a loan officer at First National Bank. Your assistant has prepared the following financial statement and debt management ratio information to help you evaluate Carmody Manufacturing's loan application:

	2023	2022	2021	Industry (2021–2023)
Sales	171.2%	131.9%	100%	183.2%
Gross margin	168.7%	129.4%	100%	184.6%
Operating expenses	180.3%	134.7%	100%	160.5%
Operating income	160.5%	124.3%	100%	202.4%
Net income	162.2%	125.7%	100%	201.7%

You also have the following data for the year ended December 31, 2023:

For the Years 2021–2023	Carmody Manufacturing	Industry
Average current ratio	2.06	1.55
Average debt to equity ratio	19.47	80.14
Average long-term debt to equity ratio	17.23	49.83
Average times interest earned (accrual)	9.55	3.87

Carmody has asked First National for a long-term loan that will double its long-term debt.

Should you approve the loan for Carmody?

The data you have is somewhat mixed. The debt management ratios are outstanding for the industry. Even after doubling the amount of long-term debt, it is apparent that Carmody will remain better than the industry averages for the debt to equity, long-term debt to equity, and times interest earned ratios. The operating results, however, are not as encouraging. Carmody's growth is somewhat below industry averages. Further, the growth in operating expenses signals a problem—especially when you consider that many operating expenses are fixed (such as salaries).

Although you probably want to follow up with Carmody regarding its projected results of operations, given its low debt burden, First National should probably grant the loan.

ASSET EFFICIENCY RATIOS

Asset efficiency ratios (or **operating ratios**) are measures of how efficiently a company uses its assets. The principal asset efficiency ratios are measures of **turnover**, that is, the average length of time required for assets to be consumed or replaced. The faster an asset is turned over, the more efficiently it is being used. These ratios provide managers and other users of a corporation's financial statements with easily interpreted measures of the time required to turn receivables into cash, inventory into cost of goods sold, or total assets into sales.

But managers are not the only people interested in asset efficiency ratios. Since well-managed efficiently operated companies are usually among the most profitable, and since profits are the sources of cash from which long-term creditors receive their interest and principal payments, creditors seek information about the corporation's profit prospects from asset efficiency ratios. And stockholders find that larger profits are usually followed by increased dividends and higher stock prices, so they, too, are concerned with indicators of efficiency.

Accounts Receivable Turnover Ratio The length of time required to collect the receivable from a credit sale is the time required to "turn over" accounts receivable. The accounts receivable turnover ratio indicates how many times accounts receivable is turned over each year. The more times accounts receivable turns over each year, the more efficient are the firm's credit-granting and credit-collection activities. The **accounts receivable turnover ratio** is expressed as:

$$\text{Accounts Receivable Turnover Ratio} = \frac{\text{Net Credit Sales or Net Sales}}{\text{Average Accounts Receivable}}$$

While some firms make all their sales on credit, many also make a substantial proportion of their sales for cash (or on credit cards, which are essentially cash sales). It is unusual for a company making cash and credit sales to report the proportion that is credit sales. For that reason, the accounts receivable turnover ratio is often computed using whatever number the firm reports for sales. In addition, to find the average balance for any financial statement account, like average accounts receivable, divide the sum of the beginning and ending balances by two.

Using net sales, **Sprouts**' receivables turnover ratios were 156.71 and 200.25 for 2018 and 2019, respectively. This is far better than the 2019 industry average of 63.2, so Sprouts is very efficient at collecting cash from its sales.

Careful analysts examine quarterly or monthly financial statements, when available, to determine whether the amount of receivables recorded in the annual statements is representative of the receivables carried during the year. For example, businesses in the apparel industry often have much larger receivables after the Christmas selling season than during other parts of the year.

Inventory Turnover Ratio Inventory turnover is the length of time required to sell inventory to customers. The more efficient a firm, the more times inventory will be turned over. The **inventory turnover ratio** indicates the number of times inventory is sold during the year and is expressed as:

$$\text{Inventory Turnover Ratio} = \frac{\text{Cost of Goods Sold}}{\text{Average Inventory}}$$

Average inventory is beginning inventory plus ending inventory divided by 2.

Sprouts' inventory turnover ratios were 14.01 and 13.84 for 2018 and 2019, respectively. This means that Sprouts turns over its inventory about 14 times per year or about once every 4 weeks. Remember that inventory sitting in the warehouse or on the shelf is not earning a return. The weakening inventory turnover may deserve some minor attention, but it's not a drastic decrease. For example, does the slower moving inventory indicate weakening sales? Further, the industry average is 12.5, so Sprouts is relatively efficient with its inventory.

Now that we have examined both receivables and inventory turnover, let us combine these measurements to approximate the length of the operating cycle (the length of time required for an investment in inventory to produce cash). **Sprouts**' 2019 operating cycle can be estimated by adding the number of days needed to turn over both receivables and inventory. The inventory turns over in approximately 26 days (365 days ÷ 13.84 inventory turnover ratio) and the receivables turn over in approximately 2 days (365 days ÷ 200.25 receivables turnover ratio), which gives an operating cycle of approximately 28 days.

The longer the operating cycle, the larger the investment necessary in receivables and inventory. When assets are larger, more liabilities and equity are required to finance them. Large amounts of capital negatively affect net income and cash flows for dividends. Therefore, firms attempt to maintain as short an operating cycle as possible. The grocery store industry has a relatively short operating cycle because much of its inventory turns over relatively quickly (e.g., fruits, vegetable, and milk) and a vast majority of its customers pay with cash or credit card.

Asset Turnover Ratio Another measure of the efficiency of a corporation's operations is the **asset turnover ratio**. This ratio measures the efficiency with which a corporation's assets are used to produce sales revenues. The more sales dollars produced by each dollar invested in assets, the more efficiently a firm is considered to be operating. The asset turnover ratio is expressed as:

$$\text{Asset Turnover Ratio} = \frac{\text{Net Sales}}{\text{Average Total Assets}}$$

Average total assets equals beginning total assets plus ending total assets divided by 2.

Sprouts' asset turnover ratios were 3.20 and 2.56 in 2018 and 2019, respectively, which means about every 143 days (365 ÷ 2.56) in 2016. The asset turnover average for the industry is 2.69, so Sprouts is slightly below the industry average.

Care must be exercised when evaluating the asset turnover ratio. Some industries (such as electric utilities and capital intensive manufacturers) require a substantially larger investment in assets to produce a sales dollar than do other industries (such as fast-food restaurants, footwear stores or online merchants). And obviously, a company's total assets turn over much more slowly than its inventories and receivables.

Overview of Asset Efficiency Ratios   EXAMPLE 12.6 illustrates how to calculate and interpret asset efficiency ratios.

EXAMPLE 12.6   CALCULATING AND INTERPRETING ASSET EFFICIENCY RATIOS

Refer to the information in **Kroger**'s income statements and balance sheet in Exhibit 12.3 (pp. 708–709).

Required:
Calculate the following asset efficiency ratios for Kroger for 2018 and 2019: (1) accounts receivable turnover ratio, (2) inventory turnover ratio, and (3) asset turnover ratio.

Solution:
Asset efficiency ratios are a measure of how efficiently a company uses its assets.

			2019 (in millions)		2018 (in millions)	
1.	Accounts Receivable Turnover Ratio	= $\dfrac{\text{Net Sales}}{\text{Average Accounts Receivable*}}$	$\dfrac{\$122{,}286}{[(\$1{,}706 + \$1{,}589) \div 2]}$	= 74.23	$\dfrac{\$121{,}852}{[(\$1{,}589 + \$1{,}637) \div 2]}$	= 75.54
2.	Inventory Turnover Ratio	= $\dfrac{\text{Cost of Goods Sold}}{\text{Average Inventories}}$	$\dfrac{\$95{,}294}{[(\$8{,}464 + \$8{,}123) \div 2]}$	= 13.68	$\dfrac{\$95{,}103}{[(\$8{,}123 + \$7{,}781) \div 2]}$	= 14.22
3.	Asset Turnover Ratio	= $\dfrac{\text{Net Sales}}{\text{Average Total Assets}}$	$\dfrac{\$122{,}286}{[(\$45{,}256 + \$38{,}118) \div 2]}$	= 2.93	$\dfrac{\$121{,}852}{[(\$38{,}118 + \$37{,}197) \div 2]}$	= 3.24

*Note: Average Balance = $\dfrac{\text{Beginning Balance} + \text{Ending Balance}}{2}$

Source: The Kroger Co. 2018 and 2019 10-K.

Sprouts' accounts receivable turnover ratio is significantly stronger than Kroger's. This results in an operating cycle of approximately 28.19 days for Sprouts and 31.6 days for Kroger. This may not sound like a significant difference, but Kroger's operating cycle is 12% longer than Sprouts'.

It is important to note that turnover ratios must be interpreted carefully. A company's ability to increase its receivables turnover is limited by competitive considerations. If competitors allow customers a lengthy period before payment is expected, then the firm must offer similar credit terms or lose customers. In periods of high interest rates, the cost of carrying customers' receivables should not be underestimated. For example, Kroger's average receivables for the year were $1,647.5 million. If, on average, it takes Kroger 3 extra days before collecting its receivables (receivables turnover of 4.92 days versus 1.82 days for Sprouts) with a borrowing rate of 6%, Kroger will incur over $812,000 more in interest per year.

Additionally, a company's ability to increase its inventory turnover is also affected by its strategy and what the competition is doing. For example, if its strategy is to offer a wide selection or if its competitors stock large quantities of inventory, a corporation will be forced to keep more inventory on hand. This, of course, leads to lower inventory turnover.

Asset efficiency ratios measure the efficiency of a corporation's operations—a factor ultimately related to the corporation's profits. Let us now examine some direct measures of a corporation's profitability.

PROFITABILITY RATIOS

Profitability ratios measure two aspects of a corporation's profits:

- elements of operations that contribute to profit
- the relationship of profit to total investment and investment by stockholders

The first group of profitability ratios, which includes gross profit (or gross margin) percentage, operating margin percentage, and net profit margin percentage, expresses income statement elements as percentages of net sales. The second group of profitability ratios, which includes return on assets and return on equity, divides measures of income by measures of investment.

Gross Profit (or Gross Margin) Percentage **Gross profit percentage** is a measurement of the proportion of each sales dollar that is available to pay other expenses and provide profit for owners. It indicates the effectiveness of pricing, marketing, purchasing, and production decisions. Gross profit percentage is expressed as:

$$\text{Gross Profit Percentage} = \frac{\text{Gross Profit}}{\text{Net Sales}}$$

Sprouts' gross profit percentage was 33.56% in 2018 and 33.63% in 2019. This means that for every dollar in sales the merchandise costs approximately 66 or 67 cents, which results in 33 or 4 cents in gross profit. This is far above the industry average of 22.24%.

Operating Margin Percentage The operating margin percentage measures the profitability of a company's operations in relation to its sales. All operating revenues and expenses are included in income from operations, but expenses, revenues, gains, and losses that are unrelated to operations are excluded. For example, a retailer would exclude interest revenues produced by its credit activities from income from operations. The **operating margin percentage** is expressed as:

$$\text{Operating Margin Percentage} = \frac{\text{Income from Operations}}{\text{Net Sales}}$$

Sprouts' operating margin percentage was 4.28% in 2018 and 3.86% in 2019. The difference between the gross profit and operating margin percentage of approximately 30% in 2019 (33.63% gross margin percentage − 3.86% operating margin percentage) means that approximately 30 cents of every dollar of sales were spent on operating expenses in 2019. Although an operating margin of 3.63% may not sound very good, it is well above the industry average of 2.02% for the year.

Net Profit Margin Percentage The net profit margin percentage measures the proportion of each sales dollar that is profit. The **net profit margin percentage** is expressed as:

$$\text{Net Profit Margin Percentage} = \frac{\text{Net Income}}{\text{Net Sales}}$$

Sprouts' net profit margin percentage was 3.04% in 2018 and 2.66% in 2019. The 2019 figure is above the industry average of 1.49%.

In evaluating the gross profit, operating margin, and net profit margin percentage, it is important to recognize that there is substantial variation in profit margins from industry to industry. While retail grocery stores, such as **Sprouts** and **Kroger**, earn a relatively small amount of gross profit, operating margin, and net income per sales dollar. Pharmaceutical manufacturers, such as **Pfizer** and **Eli Lilly**, on the other hand, earn much more per sales dollar. Since the magnitude of these percentages is affected by many factors, changes from period to period must be investigated to determine the cause.

Return on Assets The return on assets ratio measures the profit earned by a corporation through use of all its capital, or the total of the investment by both creditors and owners. The **return on assets ratio** is expressed as:

$$\text{Return on Assets} = \frac{\text{Net Income} + [\text{Interest Expense} \times (1 - \text{Tax Rate})]}{\text{Average Total Assets}}$$

Profit, or return, is determined by adding interest expense net of tax to net income. Interest expense net of tax is expressed as:

$$\text{Interest Net of Tax} = \text{Interest Expense} \times (1 - \text{Tax Rate})$$

Interest expense is added to net income because it is a return to creditors for their capital contributions. Because the actual capital contribution made by creditors is included in the denominator (average total assets), the numerator must be computed on a comparable basis.

Sprouts return on assets was 11.10% in 2018 and 7.54% in 2019. As with the percentages discussed above, appropriate values for this ratio vary from industry to industry because of differences in risk. Over a several-year period, the average return on assets for an electric utility ought to be smaller than the average return on assets for a company that makes and sells home appliances. Companies in the home appliance industry, such as **Whirlpool Corporation**, have a much larger variability of net income because their operations are more sensitive to economic conditions. The average for the grocery store industry is 4%, so Sprouts is well above the mean in 2019 for this ratio.

Return on Equity The return on equity ratio measures the profit earned by a firm through the use of capital supplied by stockholders. Return on equity is similar to return on assets, except that the payments to creditors are removed from the numerator and the creditors' capital contributions are removed from the denominator. The **return on equity ratio** is expressed as:

$$\text{Return on Equity} = \frac{\text{Net Income}}{\text{Average Equity}}$$

One of the primary objectives of the management of a firm is to maximize returns for its stockholders. Although the link between a corporation's net income and increases in dividends and share price return is not perfect, the return on equity ratio is still an effective measure of management's performance for the stockholders. As is the case with return on assets, firms often differ in return on equity because of differences in risk. For example, the average several-year return on equity for a grocery store should be lower than the average return on equity for a retail department store because of the lower sensitivity to economic conditions.

The return on equity for **Sprouts** was 25.57% and 25.55% in 2018 and 2019, respectively, which is also significantly greater than the industry average of 18.9% in 2019.

Overview of Profitability Ratios EXAMPLE 12.7 demonstrates how to calculate and interpret profitability ratios.

EXAMPLE 12.7 CALCULATING AND INTERPRETING PROFITABILITY RATIOS

Refer to the information in **Kroger**'s income statement and balance sheet in Exhibit 12.3 (pp. 708–709).

Required:
Calculate the following profitability ratios for Kroger for 2018 and 2019: (1) gross profit percentage, (2) operating margin percentage, (3) net profit margin percentage, (4) return on assets, and (5) return on equity.

Solution:
Profitability ratios measure elements of operations that contribute to profit and the relationship of profit to total investment and investment by stockholders.

		2019 (in millions)	**2018** (in millions)
1.	Gross Profit Percentage $= \dfrac{\text{Gross Profit}}{\text{Net Sales}}$	$\dfrac{\$26{,}992}{\$122{,}286} = 22.07\%$	$\dfrac{\$26{,}749}{\$121{,}852} = 21.95\%$
2.	Operating Margin Percentage $= \dfrac{\text{Income from Operations}}{\text{Net Sales}}$	$\dfrac{\$2{,}251}{\$122{,}286} = 1.84\%$	$\dfrac{\$2{,}614}{\$121{,}852} = 2.15\%$
3.	Net Profit Margin Percentage $= \dfrac{\text{Net Income}}{\text{Net Sales}}$	$\dfrac{\$1{,}659}{\$122{,}286} = 1.36\%$	$\dfrac{\$3{,}110}{\$121{,}852} = 2.55\%$

4. Return on Assets $= \dfrac{\text{Net Income} + [\text{Interest Expense} \times (1 - \text{Tax Rate*})]}{\text{Average Total Assets**}}$

2019	**2018**
$\dfrac{\$1{,}659 + [603 \times (1 - 23.67\%)]}{[(\$45{,}256 + \$38{,}118) \div 2]} = 5.08\%$	$\dfrac{\$3{,}110 + [620 \times (1 - 22.62\%)]}{[(\$38{,}118 + \$37{,}197) \div 2]} = 9.53\%$

Note: $\left(\text{Tax Rate} = \dfrac{\text{Income Tax Expense}}{\text{Income before Income Taxes}} \right)$

**Note:* Average Total Assets $= \dfrac{\text{Beginning Total Assets} + \text{Ending Total Assets}}{2}$

5. Return on Equity $= \dfrac{\text{Net Income}}{\text{Average Equity*}}$

2019	**2018**
$\dfrac{\$1{,}659}{[(\$8{,}573 + \$7{,}835) \div 2]} = 20.22\%$	$\dfrac{\$3{,}110}{[(\$7{,}835 + \$6{,}905) \div 2]} = 42.20\%$

Note: Average Equity $= \dfrac{\text{Beginning Equity} + \text{Ending Equity}}{2}$

Source: The Kroger Co. 2018 and 2019 10-K.

As you can see in Example 12.7, Kroger had better profitability ratios in 2018. This is consistent with Sprouts, which showed deterioration in three of the five ratios, with the other two ratios staying relatively stable. However, the return on equity is concerning for Kroger. A little investigation shows that this disparity is due to the large gain on sale of businesses in 2018 ($1,782 million in 2018 and $176 million in 2019). Without the gain on sale of business, the return on equity was 18.02% in 2018 and 18.08% in 2019. These are much better indicators of future return on equity because Kroger cannot, and should not, count on creating earnings by selling businesses each and every year.

STOCKHOLDER RATIOS

Stockholders are primarily interested in two things:

- the creation of value
- the distribution of value

Stockholder ratios such as earnings per share and return on common equity provide information about the creation of value for stockholders. As discussed in Chapter 10, value is distributed to stockholders in one of two ways. Either the corporation issues dividends or repurchases stock. The remainder of the stockholder ratios—dividend yield, dividend payout, stock repurchase payout, and total payout—address this distribution of value.

Earnings per Share (EPS) Earnings per share ratio (EPS) measures the income available for common stockholders on a per-share basis and is examined by nearly all statement users. **Earnings per share ratio (EPS)** is expressed as:

$$\text{Earnings per Share Ratio} = \frac{\text{Net Income} - \text{Preferred Dividends}}{\text{Average Number of Common Shares Outstanding}}$$

For the average number of common shares outstanding, remember that treasury shares are not considered to be outstanding. Preferred dividends are subtracted from net income because those payments are a return to holders of shares other than common stock. In fact, the numerator, net income minus preferred dividends, is often called *income available for common shareholders*.

Although this formula allows you to calculate EPS on your own, corporations are also required to disclose EPS on the income statement. Sprouts reports EPS of $1.23 and $1.25 per share in 2018 and 2019, respectively.

Return on Common Equity The return on common equity ratio is arguably the most important ratio for investors. It's similar to the return on equity discussed in the profitability ratio section, but it uses the return on *common* equity rather than equity. Common equity is expressed as:

$$\text{Common Equity} = \text{Total Equity} - \text{Preferred Stock}$$

The **return on common equity ratio** is expressed as:

$$\text{Return on Common Equity} = \frac{\text{Net Income}}{\text{Average Common Equity}}$$

When there is no preferred stock, as is the case for **Sprouts**, return on common equity will equal traditional return on equity (ROE) because common equity will equal total equity —25.57% in 2018 and 22.55% in 2019.

Dividend Yield Ratio The dividend yield ratio measures the rate at which dividends provide a return to stockholders by comparing dividends with the market price of a share of stock. This ratio is conceptually similar to an interest rate on debt where the dividend is like the interest payment and the cost of the share of stock is the principal. The **dividend yield ratio** is expressed as:

$$\text{Dividend Yield Ratio} = \frac{\text{Dividends per Common Share}}{\text{Closing Market Price per Share for the Year}}$$

Dividend yield is affected by both the corporation's dividend policy and the behavior of its stock price. Because stock prices often change by substantial amounts over short periods, the dividend yield ratio is not stable. In fact, when a stock is traded regularly, the market price is likely to change many times each day. For this reason, some analysts compute dividend yield based on the average stock price for a given period. Others use the highest and the lowest prices for a period and present the dividend yield as a range. For ease, we calculate dividend yield using the closing market price for the year. Of course, in the case of Sprouts, it doesn't make any difference, because no dividends were declared or paid. The dividend yield of 0% is below the industry average of 31.63%. Interestingly, Sprouts states in its 2019 10-K (Item 5, p. 32), "Since we became a publicly traded company on August 1, 2013, we have not declared or paid, and do not anticipate declaring or paying in the foreseeable future, any cash dividends on our capital stock."

Dividend Payout Ratio The dividend payout ratio measures the proportion of a corporation's profits that are returned to the stockholders immediately as dividends. The **dividend payout ratio** is expressed as:

$$\text{Dividend Payout Ratio} = \frac{\text{Common Dividends}}{\text{Net Income}}$$

You could also calculate dividend payout using per share amounts (Dividends per Share ÷ EPS). You can find the dividends paid in the retained earnings column of the statement of stockholders' equity.

As stated above, Sprouts did not pay dividends in 2019, which also means its dividend payout ratio is 0%.

The dividend payout ratio varies from corporation to corporation, even within a given industry. Many corporations attempt to pay some stable proportion of earnings as dividends, while others never pay a dividend. Corporations are reluctant to reduce dividends unless absolutely necessary. The result of these two tendencies is that dividends per share are usually increased only when management is confident that higher earnings per share can be sustained. An increase in the dividend payout ratio is usually a signal that management expects future net income to be larger and sustainable.

Stock Repurchase Payout Ratio The **stock repurchase payout ratio** is expressed as:

$$\text{Stock Repurchase Payout Ratio} = \frac{\text{Common Stock Repurchases}}{\text{Net Income}}$$

You can find stock repurchases by looking at the Treasury Stock column of the statement of stockholders' equity or in the financing activities section of the Statement of Cash Flows.

Sprouts spent more money repurchasing stock in 2018 and 2019 than it earned in net income, resulting in stock repurchase payout ratios of 162.93% and 117.83% in 2018 and 2019, respectively. Over the last 30 years, it has become more and more common for companies to use stock repurchases rather than dividends to distribute cash to shareholders. As discussed in Chapter 10, this strategy has the benefit allowing individual shareholders to decide whether to incur the tax consequences of selling the stock, as opposed to dividends that impose tax consequences on all shareholders.

Total Payout Ratio The **total payout ratio** is expressed as:

$$\text{Total Payout Ratio} = \frac{\text{Common Dividends} + \text{Common Stock Repurchases}}{\text{Net Income}}$$

This ratio can also be calculated indirectly as:

$$\text{Total Payout Ratio} = \text{Dividend Payout Ratio} + \text{Stock Repurchase Payout Ratio}$$

Of course, the total payout ratio for Sprouts is also 162.93% in 2018 and 117.83% in 2019.

Overview of Stockholder Ratios   EXAMPLE 12.8 demonstrates how to calculate and interpret the stockholder ratios.

EXAMPLE 12.8   CALCULATING AND INTERPRETING STOCKHOLDER RATIOS

Stockholder ratios measure the creation of value and the distribution of value to stockholders.

Refer to the information for **Kroger**'s income statement and balance sheet in Exhibit 12.3 (pp. 708–709).

In millions, except per share amounts	2019	2018
Average common shares*	$ 799	$ 810
Dividends per common share**	$ 0.620	$ 0.545
Common dividends**	$ 486	$ 437
Repurchase of common shares**	$ 465	$ 2,010
Closing stock price for the year	$ 26.86	$ 28.07

*Typically disclosed near the bottom of the Income Statement

**Typically found in the Statement of Stockholders' Equity and/or the Statement of Cash Flows

Note: When calculating EPS for Kroger, you will need to subtract $34 and $19 from Net Income for 2018 and 2019, respectively. These amounts are the combined distributed and undistributed earnings to participating securities as mentioned in the Earnings per Common Share footnote (Note 11). Such adjustments are very unusual, but in this case are necessary to calculate the EPS shown on the Income Statement. Ignore this adjustment when calculating the other ratios.

Required:
Calculate the following stockholder ratios for Kroger for 2018 and 2019: (1) earnings per share, (2) return on common equity, (3) dividend yield, (4) dividend payout, (5) total payout, and (6) share repurchase payout.

Solution:

	2019	2018

1. $\text{EPS} = \dfrac{\text{Net Income**** - Preferred Dividends}}{\text{Average Number of Common Shares Outstanding}}$ $\dfrac{(\$1,659 - \$19^{***}) - \$0}{799} = \$2.05$ $\dfrac{(\$3,110 - \$34^{***}) - \$0}{810} = \$3.80$

2. $\text{Return on Common Equity} = \dfrac{\text{Net Income****}}{\text{Average Common Equity*****}}$

2019	2018
$1,659	$3,110
$[((\$8,573 - \$0) + (\$7,835 - \$0)) \div 2] = 20.22\%$	$[((\$7,835 - \$0) + (\$6,905 - \$0)) \div 2] = 42.20\%$

	2019	2018

3. $\text{Dividend Yield Ratio} = \dfrac{\text{Dividends per Common Share}}{\text{Closing Market Price per Share for the Year}}$ $\dfrac{\$0.62}{\$26.86} = 2.31\%$ $\dfrac{\$0.545}{\$28.07} = 1.94\%$

	2019	2018

4. $\text{Dividend Payout Ratio} = \dfrac{\text{Common Dividends}}{\text{Net Income****}}$ $\dfrac{\$486}{\$1,659} = 29.29\%$ $\dfrac{\$437}{\$3,110} = 14.05\%$

	2019	2018

5. $\dfrac{\text{Stock Repurchase}}{\text{Payout Ratio}} = \dfrac{\text{Common Stock Repurchases}}{\text{Net Income****}}$ $\dfrac{\$465}{\$1,659} = 28.03\%$ $\dfrac{\$2,010}{\$3,110} = 64.63\%$

***See Note above

*****Common Equity = Total Shareholders' Equity − Non-Controlling Interest = Total Shareholders' Equity

		2019		**2018**	
6. Total Payout Ratio	$= \dfrac{\text{Common Dividends + Common Stock Repurchases}}{\text{Net Income****}}$	$\dfrac{\$486 + \$465}{\$1,659} =$	57.32%	$\dfrac{\$437 + \$2,010}{\$3,110} =$	78.68%

****Non-controlling interest represents the portion of our subsidiaries owned by those outside the company. For example, we may own 80% of the stock of another company. In this case, 100% of the subsidiary's income statement is included (or consolidated) into Kroger's income statement because although Kroger only owns 80% of the stock, it controls 100% of the company. Then as can be seen, the portion of the Net Income attributable to the shareholders holding the other 20% of the subsidiary's stock is removed, leaving the Net Income attributable to Kroger. When calculating ROE, it is most important to be consistent. Either remove the non-controlling interest in both the numerator and denominator or leave it in for both. Here we choose to remove non-controlling interest.

Source: The Kroger Co. 2019 10-K.

As you can see in Example 12.8, **Kroger**'s 2018 and 2019 EPS of $3.80 and $2.05, respectively, are much higher than **Sprouts'** EPS of $1.23 and $1.25 in 2018 and 2019, respectively.

As for stockholder payout, the firms pursued quite different strategies. Sprouts did not pay dividends but had an aggressive stock repurchase program. Kroger, on the other hand, paid dividends of $0.545 per share and $0.62 per share in 2018 and 2019, respectively. This represents approximately 14% of Kroger's net income in 2018 and almost 30% in 2019 (see dividend payout ratio). Additionally, Kroger used almost 65% of its net income to repurchase shares in 2018 and just over 28% in 2019.

DUPONT ANALYSIS

Return on common equity (or return on equity, hereafter abbreviated as ROE) is the most important measure of profitability for investors. It represents the amount of income generated per dollar of book value of equity or common equity. In that way, it is conceptually similar to an interest rate. Recall that ROE is calculated as:

$$\text{ROE} = \frac{\text{Net Income}}{\text{Average Equity}}$$

Dupont analysis recognizes that ROE can be broken down into three important aspects of return—net profit margin, asset turnover, and leverage.

$$\text{ROE} = \frac{\text{Net Income}}{\text{Sales}} \times \frac{\text{Sales}}{\text{Average Total Assets}} \times \frac{\text{Average Total Assets}}{\text{Average Equity}}$$
$$= \text{Net Profit Margin} \times \text{Asset Turnover} \times \text{Total Leverage}$$

The logic of this breakdown is compelling. First, profitability requires that the corporation is able to earn an adequate gross profit margin. That is, **Sprouts** and **Kroger** must be able to sell their products for more than it costs to produce them. Net profit margin carries this idea down the income statement from gross profit to net income. As we learned earlier in the chapter, the net profit margin represents how many cents of profit there are on every sales dollar.

Second, how efficient is the corporation with its net assets? The desire for asset efficiency is obvious. Everyone knows that you would rather earn $1,000,000 on an investment of $5,000,000 than an investment of $50,000,000. Before discussing leverage, we will focus a little more closely on net profit margin and asset turnover, which taken together, give us return on assets (Net Income ÷ Average Total Assets), albeit ignoring the after-tax effect of interest expense in the numerator (see p. 718). To illustrate, consider **Sprouts** and **Kroger** for 2018. Their net profit margins and asset turnovers were:

	Net Profit Margin	Asset Turnover	Return on Assets
Sprouts	3.04%	3.20	9.73%*
Kroger	2.55%	3.24	8.26%*

*This differs from the return on assets shown on p. 719 for Sprouts and in Part 4 of Example 12.7 for Kroger because a Dupont analysis does not add back the after-tax effect of interest expense to net income (see discussion on p. 719).

This breakdown demonstrates that at least in 2018 Sprouts achieved a higher return on assets than Kroger through higher profit margins. Further, this breakdown highlights different strategies for achieving profitability. Companies that compete on price (i.e., lower margins) gain a competitive advantage by being more efficient with their assets. Companies with higher margins, on the other hand, are product differentiators. A successful product differentiator, like Sprouts, can earn higher margins on its products because customers view the products as sufficiently different from the competition's to warrant paying higher prices.

Most product differentiators experience lower asset turnover. You can probably think of these distinctions within and between industries. For example, **Wal-Mart** is a low-cost leader. Wal-Mart has very low margins but makes up for it by being extremely efficient with assets. **Nordstrom**, on the other hand, has much higher margins, but this is offset by lower turnover. Taken as a whole, grocery stores have low margins and high turnover; auto dealers and jewelry stores, such as **Toyota** and **Tiffany & Co.**, have high margins and low turnover. Further, the trade-off between margins and turnover is evident in a number of decisions. For example, if a store puts an item on sale, it sacrifices margins and hopes to make up for it with higher turnover.

Notice that 2018 ROE of 42.20% for **Kroger** and 25.57% for **Sprouts** is higher than their respective returns on assets. Return on *equity* can be made larger than return on *assets* by leveraging these assets through the use of debt. The idea of leverage is simple. For example, if you can borrow at 8% and earn 10% (assuming the same tax rates on the interest and return), then you win. If you could guarantee these two figures after taxes, you should borrow all you can because you are netting 2% on every dollar. That is, if you borrow $1,000,000, you will make $20,000 (a $100,000 return minus $80,000 in interest). If you can borrow $1,000,000,000, then you will make $20,000,000.

This effect is captured by the total leverage component of the Dupont analysis. Recall that a company can obtain money to finance its business by either selling stock or borrowing. If it chooses to sell stock, then stockholders are entitled to their share of the returns. If it borrows the money, on the other hand, the creditors do not share in the returns. So why don't all corporations use debt instead of equity? There are two reasons:

- They may not be able to find a low enough interest rate.
- While interest is guaranteed, returns are not. That is, while the returns may seem better than the interest right now, in a few years it may not be so. For evidence of this, consider stories of people who borrowed money at 15% on credit cards to invest in the stock market in the late 1990s.

EXAMPLE 12.9 illustrates how to perform and interpret a Dupont analysis.

EXAMPLE 12.9 PERFORMING AND INTERPRETING A DUPONT ANALYSIS

Refer to the information for **Kroger's** income statement and balance sheet in Exhibit 12.3 (pp. 708–709) in addition to the following information for **Sprouts** (all dollar amounts are in thousands):

Net income	$ 149,629	Ending total assets	$2,722,983
Sales	5,634,835	Beginning stockholders' equity	589,196
Beginning total assets	1,675,614	Ending stockholders' equity	581,952

Source: The Kroger Co. 2019 10-K and Sprouts Farmers Market 2019 10-K.

Required:
Perform a Dupont analysis for both corporations for 2019.

Solution:
A Dupont analysis decomposes a company's ROE into net profit margin, asset turnover, and total leverage.

Kroger (in millions)

$$\text{Dupont Analysis: ROE} = \left(\frac{\text{Net Income}}{\text{Sales}}\right) \times \left(\frac{\text{Sales}}{\text{Average Total Assets}}\right) \times \left(\frac{\text{Average Total Assets}}{\text{Average Equity}}\right)$$

$$= \left(\frac{\$1,659}{\$122,286}\right) \times \left[\frac{\$122,286}{(\$45,256 + \$38,118) \div 2}\right] \times \left[\frac{(\$45,256 + \$38,118) \div 2}{(\$8,573 + \$7,835) \div 2}\right]$$

$$= 1.36\% \times 2.93 \times 5.08$$

$$= \underline{20.22\%}^*$$

Sprouts (in thousands)

$$= \left(\frac{\$149,629}{\$5,634,835}\right) \times \left[\frac{\$5,634,835}{(\$2,722,983 + \$1,675,614) \div 2}\right] \times \left[\frac{(\$2,722,983 + \$1,675,614) \div 2}{(\$581,952 + \$589,196) \div 2}\right]$$

$$= 2.66\% \times 2.56 \times 3.76$$

$$= \underline{25.55\%}^*$$

Source: The Kroger Co. 2019 10-K and Sprouts Farmers Market 2019 10-K.

*Answers may differ slightly depending upon whether you round individual components of the Dupont Analysis.

The Dupont analysis in Example 12.9 shows that while Sprouts' ROE was very stable in 2018 and 2019, Kroger's ROE dropped significantly. Looking at 2019 alone, we see that Sprouts had a significantly better net profit margin (by almost double). However, Kroger utilized better turnover and higher leverage to produce an ROE that was only about 20% worse than Sprouts', despite the huge difference in margins.

SUMMARY OF FINANCIAL RATIOS

Exhibit 12.4 (pp. 726–727) summarizes the financial ratios presented in this chapter. More advanced accounting texts may present additional ratios; however, those introduced here are among the most widely used.

| **EXHIBIT 12.4** | **Summary of Financial Ratios** |

Short-Term Liquidity Ratios

1. Current Ratio $= \dfrac{\text{Current Assets}}{\text{Current Liabilities}}$

2. Quick Ratio $= \dfrac{\text{Cash + Short-Term Investments + Receivables}}{\text{Current Liabilities}}$

3. Cash Ratio $= \dfrac{\text{Cash + Short-Term Investments}}{\text{Current Liabilities}}$

4. Operating Cash Flow Ratio $= \dfrac{\text{Cash Flows from Operating Activities}}{\text{Current Liabilities}}$

Debt Management Ratios

5a. Times Interest Earned (*Accrual Basis*) $= \dfrac{\text{Operating Income}}{\text{Interest Expense}}$

5b. Times Interest Earned (*Cash Basis*) $= \dfrac{\text{Cash Flows from Operations + Income Tax Payments + Interest Payments}}{\text{Interest Expense}}$

6. Long-Term Debt to Equity Ratio $= \dfrac{\text{Long-Term Debt (including current portion)}}{\text{Total Equity}}$

7. Debt to Equity Ratio $= \dfrac{\text{Total Liabilities}}{\text{Total Equity}}$

8. Long-Term Debt to Total Assets Ratio $= \dfrac{\text{Long-Term Debt (including current portion)}}{\text{Total Assets}}$

9. Debt to Total Assets Ratio $= \dfrac{\text{Total Liabilities}}{\text{Total Assets}}$

Asset Efficiency Ratios

10. Accounts Receivable Turnover Ratio $= \dfrac{\text{Net Credit Sales or Net Sales}}{\text{Average Accounts Receivable}}$

11. Inventory Turnover Ratio $= \dfrac{\text{Cost of Goods Sold}}{\text{Average Inventory}}$

12. Asset Turnover Ratio $= \dfrac{\text{Net Sales}}{\text{Average Total Assets}}$

Profitability Ratios

13. Gross Profit Percentage $= \dfrac{\text{Gross Profit}}{\text{Net Sales}}$

14. Operating Margin Percentage $= \dfrac{\text{Income from Operations}}{\text{Net Sales}}$

15. Net Profit Margin Percentage $= \dfrac{\text{Net Income}}{\text{Net Sales}}$

16. Return on Assets $= \dfrac{\text{Net Income + [Interest Expense} \times (1 - \text{Tax Rate})]}{\text{Average Total Assets}}$

17. Return on Equity $= \dfrac{\text{Net Income}}{\text{Average Equity}}$

Summary of Financial Ratios *(CONTINUED)* | **EXHIBIT 12.4**

Stockholder Ratios

18. Earnings per Share (EPS) Ratio $= \dfrac{\text{Net Income} - \text{Preferred Dividends}}{\text{Average Number of Common Shares Outstanding}}$

19. Return on Common Equity $= \dfrac{\text{Net Income}}{\text{Average Common Equity}}$

20. Dividend Yield Ratio $= \dfrac{\text{Dividends per Common Share}}{\text{Closing Market Price per Share for the Year}}$

21. Dividend Payout Ratio $= \dfrac{\text{Common Dividends}}{\text{Net Income}}$

22. Stock Repurchase Payout Ratio $= \dfrac{\text{Common Stock Repurchases}}{\text{Net Income}}$

23. Total Payout Ratio $= \dfrac{\text{Common Dividends} + \text{Common Stock Repurchases}}{\text{Net Income}}$

Dupont Analysis

24. Return on Equity $= \dfrac{\text{Net Income}}{\text{Sales}} \times \dfrac{\text{Sales}}{\text{Average Total Assets}} \times \dfrac{\text{Average Total Assets}}{\text{Average Equity}}$

$= \text{Net Profit Margin} \times \text{Asset Turnover} \times \text{Total Leverage}$

DATA FOR RATIO COMPARISONS

As we pointed out earlier in the chapter, developing information from financial ratios requires that comparisons be made among the ratios of:

- the same corporation over time
- similar corporations over time
- similar corporations at the present time

Analysts rely on several sources to fulfill their need for a broad range of data for individual corporations as well as for industries and the economy.

We believe the best source of information about a corporation starts with the investor relations section of its website. This part of the website should contain links to the corporation's 10-K (and other SEC filings), analyst conference calls, and press releases. You can also gain information through the financial press (*The Wall Street Journal*, etc.) and investor discussion boards, although the latter must be evaluated with a critical eye.

Information on the industry can be obtained from industry guides such as **Standard & Poor's** and **IBISWorld**. These are often available through your university library website or in hard copy at the library. Also helpful are websites like **Google Finance**, **Yahoo! Finance**, **BizStats**, and **MSN**.

LO1. Explain how creditors, investors, and others use financial statements in their decisions.

KEY TAKEAWAYS

- The role of financial statements is to provide information for the following:
  - Creditors
  - Investors
  - Customers
  - Suppliers
  - Employees
- This information will help these groups form judgments, which will serve as the foundation for various decisions.

LO2. Describe the most important SEC filings.

KEY TAKEAWAYS

- Publicly traded corporations must file a variety of financial information, including audited annual financial statements, with the Securities and Exchange Commission (SEC) on an ongoing basis. For example:
  - Annual reports on Form 10-K
  - Quarterly reports on Form 10-Q
  - Current reports for numerous specified events on Form 8-K
- The annual report on Form 10-K provides a comprehensive overview of the corporation's business and financial condition and includes audited financial statements.
- Although similarly named, the annual report on Form 10-K is distinct from the "annual report to shareholders," which a corporation must send to its stockholders when it holds an annual meeting to elect directors.
- For larger filers, the 10-K must be filed within 60 days of the corporation's fiscal year end.

KEY TERMS

Form 8-K, 694
Form 10-K, 694
Form 10-Q, 694
MD&A, 696

LO3. Discuss the difference between cross sectional and time series analysis

KEY TAKEAWAYS

- Cross sectional analysis entails comparing a corporation's financial statements to its primary competitors and industry averages.
- Time series (or trend) analysis involves comparisons of the current year with previous years.
- Differences may exist in the size of two corporations or even in the same corporation from year to year (perhaps due to the acquisition of another corporation). Analysts address this problem by restating the financial statements in percentage terms.

KEY TERMS

Cross sectional analysis, 697
Time series (or trend) analysis, 697

EXAMPLE

EXAMPLE 12.1	Interpreting cross sectional and time series (or trend) analysis, page 698

KEY TAKEAWAYS

- In horizontal analysis, each financial statement line item is expressed as a percentage of the base year (typically the least recent year shown).
- In vertical analysis, each financial statement line item is expressed as a percentage of the largest statement amount—net sales on the income statement and total assets on the balance sheet.

LO4. Analyze financial statements using horizontal and vertical analysis.

KEY TERMS

Common size statements, 699
Horizontal analysis, 699
Vertical analysis, 700

EXAMPLES

EXAMPLE 12.2	Preparing common size statements for horizontal analysis, page 699
EXAMPLE 12.3	Preparing common size statements for vertical analysis, page 701

KEY TAKEAWAYS

- Ratios help remove the effects of size differences (as measured in dollars).
- Six categories of ratios are discussed:
  - Short-term liquidity
  - Debt management
  - Profitability
  - Asset efficiency (or operating)
  - Stockholder
  - Dupont
- More advanced accounting and finance texts may present additional ratios; however, those introduced here are among the most widely used.

LO5. Calculate and use financial statement ratios to evaluate a company.

KEY TERMS

Accounts receivable turnover ratio, 715
Asset efficiency ratios (or operating ratios), 714
Asset turnover ratio, 715
Cash ratio, 706
Current ratio, 705
Debt management ratios, 710
Debt to equity ratio, 712
Debt to total assets ratio, 712
Dividend payout ratio, 721
Dividend yield ratio, 720
Dupont analysis, 723
Earnings per share ratio (EPS), 720
Gross profit percentage, 717
Inventory turnover ratio, 715
Long-term debt to equity ratio, 711
Long-term debt to total assets ratio, 712

Net profit margin percentage, 718
Operating cash flow ratio, 707
Operating margin percentage, 717
Profitability ratios, 717
Quick ratio, 706
Ratio analysis, 705
Ratios (or financial ratios), 705
Return on assets ratio, 718
Return on common equity ratio, 720
Return on equity ratio, 718
Short-term liquidity ratios, 705
Stock repurchase payout ratio, 721
Stockholder ratios, 720
Times interest earned ratio, 711
Total payout ratio, 721
Turnover, 714

KEY CALCULATION

See Exhibit 12.4 for a summary of all the financial ratios, 710

EXAMPLES

EXAMPLE 12.4	Calculating and interpreting short-term liquidity ratios, page 709–710	
EXAMPLE 12.5	Calculating and interpreting debt management ratios, page 712–713	
EXAMPLE 12.6	Calculating and interpreting asset efficiency ratios, page 716	
EXAMPLE 12.7	Calculating and interpreting profitability ratios, page 719	
EXAMPLE 12.8	Calculating and interpreting stockholder ratios, page 722–723	
EXAMPLE 12.9	Performing and interpreting a Dupont analysis, page 725	

REVIEW PROBLEM

RATIO ANALYSIS

Following are consolidated balance sheets and income statements for Kellman Company:

Kellman Company and Subsidiaries
Consolidated Balance Sheets
(in thousands)

	December 31,		
	2022	**2021**	**2020**
ASSETS			
Current assets:			
Cash and cash equivalents	$ 40,588	$ 70,655	$ 62,977
Accounts receivable, net	93,515	71,867	53,132
Inventories	166,082	81,031	53,607
Income taxes receivable	614	4,310	0
Other current assets	11,028	8,944	5,252
Deferred income taxes	10,418	8,145	6,822
Total current assets	**$322,245**	**$244,952**	**$181,790**
Property and equipment, net	52,332	29,923	20,865
Intangible assets, net	6,470	7,875	0
Deferred income taxes	8,173	5,180	0
Other noncurrent assets	1,393	1,438	1,032
Total assets	**$390,613**	**$289,368**	**$203,687**
LIABILITIES AND STOCKHOLDERS' EQUITY			
Current liabilities:			
Accounts payable	$ 55,012	$ 42,718	$ 31,699
Accrued expenses	36,111	25,403	11,449
Income taxes payable	0	0	716
Current maturities of long-term debt	4,111	2,648	1,967
Current maturities of capital lease obligations	465	794	1,841
Total current liabilities	**$ 95,699**	**$ 71,563**	**$ 47,672**
Long-term debt, net of current maturities	9,298	1893	2 868
Capital lease obligations, net of current maturities	458	922	1,715
Deferred income taxes	0	0	330
Other long-term liabilities	4,673	602	272
Total liabilities	**$110,128**	**$ 74,980**	**$ 52,857**
Stockholders' equity:			
Class A common stock	$ 12	$ 12	$ 10
Class B common stock	4	4	5
Additional paid-in capital—common stock	162,362	148,562	124,803
Retained earnings	117,782	66,376	28,067
Unearned compensation	(182)	(463)	(1,889)
Notes receivable from stockholders	0	0	(163)
Accumulated other comprehensive income	507	(103)	(3)
Total stockholders' equity	**$280,485**	**$214,388**	**$150,830**
Total liabilities and stockholders' equity	**$390,613**	**$289,368**	**$203,687**

(Continued)

Kellman Company and Subsidiaries Consolidated Income Statements (in thousands)			
	December 31,		
	2022	**2021**	**2020**
Net sales	$ 606,561	$ 430,689	$ 281,053
Cost of goods sold	301,517	215,089	145,203
Gross profit	**$305,044**	**$215,600**	**$135,850**
Operating expenses			
Selling, general, and administrative expenses	218,779	158,682	100,040
Income from operations	**$ 86,265**	**$ 56,918**	**$ 35,810**
Interest income	1,549	2,231	273
Interest expense	(800)	(774)	(3,188)
Other income, net	2,029	712	79
Income before income taxes	**$ 89,043**	**$ 59,087**	**$ 32,974**
Income tax expense	36,485	20,108	13,255
Net income	**$ 52,558**	**$ 38,979**	**$ 19,719**
Cumulative preferred dividends on preferred stock	0	0	5,307
Net income available to common stockholders	**$ 52,558**	**$ 38,979**	**$ 14,412**

Additionally, you will need the following information:

Weighted average common shares outstanding	48,021	46,983	37,199
Cash flows from operating activities	$(14,628)	$10,701	$15,795
Dividends per share	$0	$0	$0
Dividends	$0	$0	$0
Stock repurchases	$0	$0	$0
Market price per share at year end	$43.67	$50.45	$38.31

Required:
1. Calculate the short-term liquidity ratios for Kellman Company for 2021 and 2022.
2. Calculate the debt management ratios for Kellman Company for 2021 and 2022.
3. Calculate the asset efficiency ratios for Kellman Company for 2021 and 2022.
4. Calculate the profitability ratios for Kellman Company for 2021 and 2022.
5. Calculate the stockholder ratios for Kellman Company for 2021 and 2022.
6. Perform a Dupont analysis for Kellman Company for 2021 and 2022.

Solution:
1. Short-term liquidity ratios:

$$\text{Current Ratio} = \frac{\text{Current Assets}}{\text{Current Liabilities}}$$

	2022	**2021**
Current assets	$322,245	$244,952
Current liabilities	95,699	71,563
Current ratio	**3.37**	**3.42**

$$\text{Quick Ratio} = \frac{\text{Cash + Short-Term Investments + Receivables}}{\text{Current Liabilities}}$$

	2022	2021
Cash	$40,588	$70,655
Short-term investments	0	0
Accounts receivable	93,515	71,867
Current liabilities	95,699	71,563
Quick ratio	**1.40**	**1.99**

$$\text{Cash Ratio} = \frac{\text{Cash + Short-Term Investments}}{\text{Current Liabilities}}$$

	2022	2021
Cash	$40,588	$70,655
Short-term investments	0	0
Current liabilities	95,699	71,563
Cash ratio	**0.42**	**0.99**

$$\text{Operating Cash Flow Ratio} = \frac{\text{Cash Flows from Operating Activities}}{\text{Current Liabilities}}$$

	2022	2021
Cash flows from operating activities	$(14,628)*	$10,701*
Current liabilities	95,699	71,563
Operating cash flow ratio	**(0.15)**	**0.15**

*Provided in the Information section.

2. Debt management ratios:

$$\text{Times Interest Earned} = \frac{\text{Operating Income}}{\text{Interest Expense}}$$

	2022	2021
Operating income	$86,265	$56,918
Interest expense	800	774
Times interest earned (accrual)	**107.83**	**73.54**

$$\text{Long-Term Debt to Equity Ratio} = \frac{\text{Long-Term Debt (including current portion)}}{\text{Total Equity}}$$

	2022	2021
Long-term debt	$ 9,298	$ 1,893
Current portion of long-term debt	4,111	2,648
Total equity	280,485	214,388
Long-term debt to equity	**0.05**	**0.02**

$$\text{Debt to Equity Ratio} = \frac{\text{Total Liabilities}}{\text{Total Equity}}$$

	2022	2021
Total liabilities	$110,128	$ 74,980
Total equity	280,485	214,388
Debt to equity	**0.39**	**0.35**

$$\text{Long-Term Debt to Total Assets Ratio} = \frac{\text{Long-Term Debt (including current portion)}}{\text{Total Assets}}$$

(*Continued*)

	2022	2021
Long-term debt	$ 9,298	$ 1,893
Current portion of long-term debt	4,111	2,648
Total assets	390,613	289,368
Long-term debt to total assets	**0.03**	**0.02**

$$\text{Debt to Total Assets Ratio} = \frac{\text{Total Liabilities}}{\text{Total Equity}}$$

	2022	2021
Total liabilities	$110,128	$ 74,980
Total assets	390,613	289,368
Debt to total assets	**0.28**	**0.26**

3. Asset efficiency ratios:

$$\text{Accounts Receivable Turnover Ratio} = \frac{\text{Net Sales}}{\text{Average Accounts Receivable*}}$$

$$\text{*Average Balance} = \frac{(\text{Beginning Balance} + \text{Ending Balance})}{2}$$

	2022	2021	2020
Net sales	$606,561	$430,689	$281,053
Receivables	93,515	71,867	53,132
Accounts receivable turnover ratio	**7.34**	**6.89**	

$$\text{Inventory Turnover Ratio} = \frac{\text{Cost of Goods Sold}}{\text{Average Inventories}}$$

	2022	2021	2020
Cost of goods sold	$301,517	$215,089	$145,203
Inventories	166,082	81,031	53,607
Inventory turnover ratio	**2.44**	**3.20**	

$$\text{Asset Turnover Ratio} = \frac{\text{Net Sales}}{\text{Average Total Assets}}$$

	2022	2021	2020
Net sales	$606,561	$430,689	$281,053
Total assets	390,613	289,368	203,687
Asset turnover ratio	**1.78**	**1.75**	

4. Profitability ratios:

$$\text{Gross Profit Percentage} = \frac{\text{Gross Profit}}{\text{Net Sales}}$$

	2022	2021
Net sales	$606,561	$430,689
Gross profit	305,044	215,600
Gross profit percentage	**50.29%**	**50.06%**

$$\text{Operating Margin Percentage} = \frac{\text{Income from Operations}}{\text{Net Sales}}$$

	2022	2021
Net sales	$606,561	$430,689
Income from operations	86,265	56,918
Operating margin percentage	**14.22%**	**13.22%**

$$\text{Net Profit Margin Percentage} = \frac{\text{Net Income}}{\text{Net Sales}}$$

	2022	2021
Net sales	$606,561	$430,689
Net income	52,558	38,979
Net profit margin percentage	**8.67%**	**9.05%**

$$\text{Return on Assets} = \frac{\text{Net Income} + [\text{Interest Expense} \times (1 - \text{Tax Rate})]}{\text{Average Total Assets}^*}$$

$$^*\text{Average Balance} = \frac{(\text{Beginning Balance} + \text{Ending Balance})}{2}$$

	2022	2021	2020
Total assets	$390,613	$289,368	$203,687
Income taxes expense	36,485	20,108	
Net income	52,558	38,979	
Interest expense	800	774	
Income before taxes	89,043	59,087	
Tax rate*	40.97%	34.03%	
Return on assets	**15.60%**	**16.02%**	

*Income Taxes Expense ÷ Income before Taxes

$$\text{Return on Equity} = \frac{\text{Net Income}}{\text{Average Equity}^*}$$

$$^*\text{Average Balance} = \frac{(\text{Beginning Balance} + \text{Ending Balance})}{2}$$

	2022	2021	2020
Net income	$ 52,558	$ 38,979	
Stockholders' equity	280,485	214,388	$150,830
Return on equity	**21.24%**	**21.35%**	

5. Stockholder ratios:

$$\text{Earnings per Share Ratio} = \frac{\text{Net Income} - \text{Preferred Dividends}}{\text{Average Number of Common Shares Outstanding}}$$

	2022	2021
Net income	$52,558	$38,979
Preferred dividends	0	0
Average common shares*	48,021	46,983
EPS	**1.09**	**0.83**

*Provided in the Information section.

$$\text{Return on Common Equity} = \frac{\text{Net Income}}{\text{Average Common Equity}^*}$$

*Common Equity = Total Equity − Preferred Stock − Additional Paid-In Capital—Preferred Stock

(*Continued*)

	2022	2021	2020
Net income	$ 52,558	$ 38,979	
Stockholders' equity	280,485	214,388	$150,830
Preferred stock	0	0	0
Additional paid-in capital—preferred stock	0	0	0
Return on common equity	**21.24%**	**21.35%**	

$$\text{Dividend Yield Ratio} = \frac{\text{Dividends per Common Share}}{\text{Closing Market Price per Share for the Year}}$$

	2022	2021
Dividends per share*	$ 0	$ 0
Closing market price for year*	43.67	50.45
Dividend yield ratio	**0.0%**	**0.0%**

*Provided in the Information section.

$$\text{Dividend Payout Ratio} = \frac{\text{Common Dividends}}{\text{Net Income}}$$

	2022	2021
Common dividends*	$ 0	$ 0
Net income	52,558	38,979
Dividend yield ratio	**0.0%**	**0.0%**

*Provided in the Information section.

$$\text{Total Payout Ratio} = \frac{\text{Common Dividends} + \text{Common Stock Repurchases}}{\text{Net Income}}$$

	2022	2021
Common dividends*	$ 0	$ 0
Common stock repurchases*	0	0
Net income	52,558	38,979
Total payout ratio	**0%**	**0%**

*Provided in the Information section.

6. Dupont analysis:

$$\text{ROE} = \frac{\text{Net Income}}{\text{Sales}} \times \frac{\text{Sales}}{\text{Average Total Assets}} \times \frac{\text{Average Total Assets}}{\text{Average Equity}}$$

$$= \text{Net Profit Margin} \times \text{Asset Turnover} \times \text{Total Leverage}$$

2022:

$$= \frac{\$52,558}{\$606,561} \times \frac{\$606,561}{(\$390,613 + \$289,368) \div 2} \times \frac{(\$390,613 + \$289,368) \div 2}{(\$280,485 + \$214,388) \div 2}$$

$$= 8.67\% \times 1.78 \times 1.37$$

$$= \underline{21.14\%}^*$$

*Does not equal ROE of 21.24% shown in Parts 4 and 5 because of rounding in the individual components.

2021:

$$= \frac{\$38,979}{\$430,689} \times \frac{\$430,689}{(\$289,368 + \$203,687) \div 2} \times \frac{(\$289,368 + \$203,687) \div 2}{(\$214,388 + \$150,830) \div 2}$$

$$= 9.05\% \times 1.75 \times 1.35$$

$$= \underline{21.38\%}^*$$

*Does not equal ROE of 21.35% shown in Parts 4 and 5 because of rounding in the individual components.

APPLYING KNOWLEDGE

DISCUSSION QUESTIONS

1. Describe how some of the primary groups of users use financial statements.
2. What is a 10-K?
3. How does the 10-K differ from the 10-Q?
4. Describe the information provided in Item 1 of the 10-K.
5. Describe the information provided in Item 7 of the 10-K.
6. Describe the information provided in Item 8 of the 10-K.
7. What is the difference between time series and cross sectional analysis?
8. What is the difference between horizontal and vertical analysis?
9. How do the current and quick ratios differ? Which is a more conservative measure of short-term liquidity? Support your answer.
10. How does the operating cash flow ratio differ from the current, quick, and cash ratios?
11. What are you trying to learn by calculating debt management ratios?
12. Why are higher asset turnover ratios considered to be better than lower turnover ratios?
13. What two aspects of a company's profitability are measured by profitability ratios?
14. What are the two major categories of stockholder ratios?
15. A Dupont analysis breaks down return on equity into what three components?
16. Why must you analyze the accounting policies of a company when performing financial statement analysis? Provide an example of how knowledge of accounting policies would affect your analysis of inventory.

MULTIPLE-CHOICE QUESTIONS

12-1 Which of the following use financial statement data to make decisions?   OBJECTIVE ◄ 1
   a. customers   c. suppliers
   b. investors   d. all of these

12-2 Which statement would best provide information about a company's current liquidity?
   a. income statement   c. statement of cash flows
   b. balance sheet   d. none of these

12-3 A banker is analyzing a company that operates in the petroleum industry. Which of the following might be a major consideration in determining whether the company should receive a loan?
   a. The petroleum industry suffers from political pressures concerning the selling price of its products.
   b. All companies in the petroleum industry use the same accounting principles.
   c. The company has a large amount of interest payments related to many outstanding loans.
   d. Inflation has been high for several years in a row.

12-4 Which of the following filings includes unaudited financial statements, provides a   OBJECTIVE ◄ 2
continuing view of the corporation's financial position during the year, and must be filed for each of the first three fiscal quarters of the corporation's fiscal year?
   a. 10-Q   c. 8-K
   b. 10-K   d. Form 13F

12-5   Which of the following filings is known as the "current report" that companies must file with the SEC to announce major events that are important to investors and creditors?

a. 10-Q   c. 8-K
b. 10-K   d. Form 13F

12-6   Which section of the Form 10-K includes an analysis of the company's financial condition and performance of the company?

a. Item 4—Submission of Matters to Vote   c. Item 6—Selected Financial Data
b. Item 5—Market for Common Stock   d. Item 7—Management Discussion and Analysis

12-7   Which of the following are required to be included in the Form 10-K?

a. the name of every person or group who owns more than 5% of a class of stock
b. a list of all financial statements and exhibits required to be filed
c. information on the salary and other forms of compensation paid to executive officers and directors
d. all of the above

OBJECTIVE 3   **12-8**   Which type of analysis compares a single corporation across time?

a. timetable analysis   c. company analysis
b. time series analysis   d. cross sectional analysis

12-9   Which of the following types of analysis compares one corporation to another corporation and to industry averages?

a. timetable analysis   c. company analysis
b. time series analysis   d. cross sectional analysis

OBJECTIVE 4   **12-10**   Which of the following types of analysis is particularly useful for trend analysis?

a. vertical analysis   c. trend-setting analysis
b. horizontal analysis   d. timetable analysis

12-11   Vertical analysis expresses each financial statement line item as a percent of the:

a. smallest statement amount.   c. average statement amount.
b. largest statement amount.   d. mean statement amount.

12-12   Horizontal analysis expresses each financial statement line item as a percent of:

a. base year.   c. net income.
b. total assets.   d. stockholders' equity.

OBJECTIVE 5   **12-13**   How is the current ratio calculated?

a. Cash Flows from Operating Activities ÷ Current Liabilities
b. (Cash + Marketable Securities + Accounts Receivable) ÷ Current Liabilities
c. Current Assets ÷ Current Liabilities
d. (Cash + Marketable Securities) ÷ Current Liabilities

12-14   Partial information from Fabray Company's balance sheet is:

Current Assets:		**Current Liabilities:**	
Cash	$ 1,200,000	Notes payable	$ 750,000
Marketable securities	3,750,000	Accounts payable	9,750,000
Accounts receivable	28,800,000	Accrued expenses	6,250,000
Inventories	33,150,000	Income taxes payable	250,000
Prepaid expenses	600,000	Total current liabilities	$17,000,000
Total current assets	$67,500,000		

What is Fabray's current ratio?

a. 0.25   c. 3.0
b. 1.8   d. 3.97

12-15 Hummel Inc. has $30,000 in current assets and $15,000 in current liabilities. What is Hummel's current ratio?

a. 3

b. 2

c. 1

d. 0.5

12-16 How is the cash ratio calculated?

a. (Cash + Marketable Securities) ÷ Current Liabilities

b. (Cash + Marketable Securities + Accounts Receivable) ÷ Current Liabilities

c. Current Assets ÷ Current Liabilities

d. Cash Flows from Operating Activities ÷ Current Liabilities

12-17 A firm's quick ratio is typically computed as:

a. (Cash + Marketable Securities + Accounts Receivable) ÷ Current Liabilities.

b. Total Liabilities ÷ Total Assets.

c. Current Liabilities ÷ Current Assets.

d. Current Assets ÷ Current Liabilities.

12-18 Schuester Company has $40,000 in current liabilities, $20,000 in cash, and $25,000 in marketable securities. What Schuester's cash ratio?

a. 0.625

b. 0.889

c. 1.125

d. 1.6

12-19 What ratio is used to measure a firm's liquidity?

a. current ratio

b. debt ratio

c. asset turnover

d. return on equity

12-20 Which of the following transactions could increase a firm's current ratio?

a. purchase of inventory for cash

b. purchase of temporary investments for cash

c. collection of accounts receivable

d. payment of accounts payable

12-21 Total Liabilities ÷ Total Equity equals:

a. Receivables Turnover Ratio

b. Accounts Payable Turnover Ratio

c. Debt to Equity Ratio

d. Times Interest Earned Ratio

12-22 Which of the following ratios is *not* a debt management ratio?

a. return on equity ratio

b. debt to equity ratio

c. long-term debt to equity ratio

d. times interest earned

12-23 The balance sheet for Sylvester Inc. at the end of the first year of operations indicates the following:

Total current assets	$600,000	Total long-term liabilities	$350,000
Total investments	85,000	Common stock, $10 par	600,000
Total property, plant, and equipment	900,000	Additional paid-in capital— common stock	60,000
Current portion of long-term debt	250,000	Retained earnings	325,000

What is the long-term debt to total assets ratio for the year (rounded to one decimal place)?

a. 22.1%

b. 37.9%

c. 40.0%

d. 41.7%

12-24 When analyzing a company's debt to equity ratio, if the ratio has a value that is greater than one, then the company has:

a. equal amounts of debt and equity.

b. more debt than equity.

c. less debt than equity.

d. none of these.

12-25 Cost of goods sold divided by average inventory is the formula to compute:
a. gross profit percentage.
b. return on sales percentage.
c. inventory turnover.
d. accounts receivable turnover.

12-26 A firm's asset turnover ratio is typically computed as:
a. Operating Income ÷ Net Sales.
b. Gross Profit ÷ Net Sales.
c. Net Sales ÷ Average Total Assets.
d. Net Income + [Interest Expense × (1 − Tax Rate)] ÷ Average Total Assets.

12-27 Which of the following ratios is used to measure a firm's efficiency at using its assets?
a. asset turnover ratio
b. current ratio
c. return on sales ratio
d. return on equity

12-28 Which of the following ratios is used to measure a firm's efficiency?
a. Net Income ÷ Equity
b. Assets ÷ Equity
c. Net Income ÷ Sales
d. Net Sales ÷ Average Total Assets

12-29 Pillsbury Corporation has $65,000 of cost of goods sold and average inventory of $30,000. What is Pillsbury's inventory turnover ratio?
a. 2.17
b. 1.46
c. 1.17
d. 0.46

12-30 If Abrams Company has an inventory turnover of 7.3 and a receivables turnover of 9.6, approximately how long is its operating cycle?
a. 95 days
b. 88 days
c. 72 days
d. There is not enough information to calculate the operating cycle.

12-31 Which of the following ratios is used to measure the profit earned on each dollar invested in a firm?
a. return on sales ratio
b. return on equity
c. current ratio
d. asset turnover ratio

12-32 Which of the following is the formula to compute the net profit margin percentage?
a. Operating Income ÷ Net Sales
b. Net Income ÷ Net Sales
c. Net Income ÷ Average Equity
d. Net Income + [Interest Expense × (1 − Tax Rate)] ÷ Average Total Assets

12-33 Selected information for Berry Company is as follows:

Average common stock	$600,000
Average additional paid-in capital	250,000
Average retained earnings	370,000
Sales revenue for year	915,000
Net income for year	240,000

Berry's return on equity, rounded to the nearest percentage point, is:
a. 20%.
b. 21%.
c. 28%.
d. 40%.

12-34 Which of the following ratios is used to measure a firm's profitability?
a. Liabilities ÷ Equity
b. Assets ÷ Equity
c. Sales ÷ Assets
d. Net Income ÷ Net Sales

12-35 Why might an industry group have higher 5-year average returns on equity than do other industries?
a. It is a lower-risk industry.
b. It is a higher-risk industry.
c. It is a high-growth industry.
d. None of these.

12-36 The dividend yield ratio measures the:
   a. income available for common stockholders on a per-share basis.
   b. profit earned by a firm through the use of capital supplied by stockholders.
   c. proportion of a corporation's profits that are returned to the stockholders immediately as dividends.
   d. rate at which dividends provide a return to stockholders.

12-37 Corporations are required to disclose earnings per share on which of the following statements?
   a. statement of cash flows   c. income statement
   b. balance sheet   d. all of these

12-38 Hudson Company has preferred dividends of $15,000, a net income of $40,000, and average common shares outstanding of 8,000. What is Hudson's earnings per share?
   a. $2.13   c. $3.13
   b. $2.67   d. $5.00

12-39 Which of the following are *not* part of common equity?
   a. preferred stock   c. retained earnings
   b. common stock   d. treasury stock

12-40 A Dupont analysis recognizes that return on equity can be broken down into three important aspects of return, which are:
   a. net profit margin, asset turnover, and leverage
   b. net profit margin, asset turnover, and average assets
   c. sales, income, and leverage
   d. sales, income, and equity

12-41 If a company has a higher net profit margin than most of its competitors, this means that the company:
   a. has a lower proportion of debt financing.
   b. has more loyal customers.
   c. is more efficient with its assets.
   d. has a higher proportion of each sales dollar that is profit.

12-42 Which of the following ratios is decomposed using the Dupont framework?
   a. assets-to-equity ratio   c. return on equity
   b. asset turnover   d. return on sales

12-43 Which of the following is *not* included in the Dupont framework?
   a. a measure of profitability   c. a measure of leverage
   b. a measure of efficiency   d. a measure of market share

12-44 When a Dupont analysis reveals that a company has much higher than average asset turnover and much lower than average profit margin, what can be concluded about the company's strategy?
   a. It is a product differentiator. c. It has no strategy.
   b. It needs to concentrate on   d. It is a low-cost provider.
      improving its profit margins.

12-45 Which of the following questions would be appropriate for an analyst to investigate regarding a company's liabilities?
   a. Are the liabilities properly   c. Are the liabilities reported?
      classified?   d. All of these would be appropriate.
   b. Are estimated liabilities large
      enough?

BRIEF EXERCISES

OBJECTIVE 3

Brief Exercise 12-46 Cross Sectional Analysis

Cross sectional analysis entails comparing a company to its competitors.

Required:

Indicate one of the biggest weaknesses of using cross sectional analysis when analyzing a company.

OBJECTIVE 3

Brief Exercise 12-47 Time Series Analysis

Time series analysis involves comparing a company's income statement and balance sheet for the current year to its previous years' income statements and balance sheets.

Required:

CONCEPTUAL CONNECTION Explain whether it is always bad if a company's cost of goods sold is increasing from year to year.

OBJECTIVE 4

Brief Exercise 12-48 Horizontal and Vertical Analysis

Plato Clothing Company specializes in selling apparel for special occasions. In 2022 and 2023, Plato's account balances were as follows:

	2023	2022
Accounts receivable	$ 60,000	$ 42,000
Merchandise inventory	16,000	19,000
Total assets	345,000	310,000
Net sales	420,000	385,000
Cost of goods sold	135,000	165,000

Required:

1. Calculate the change in each of the Plato's accounts from 2022 to 2023.
2. Indicate what happened from 2022 to 2023 to accounts receivable and merchandise inventory as a percentage of total assets. Indicate what happened from 2022 to 2023 to cost of goods sold as a percentage of net sales.

OBJECTIVE 3

Brief Exercise 12-49 Short-Term Liquidity Ratios

Larry, Curly, and Moe companies operate in the same industry. Each company provided financial information to the public containing three ratios for 2022 and 2023.

(in millions)		Larry	Curly	Moe
Current ratio	12/31/23	2.2 to 1	1.7 to 1	1.8 to 1
	12/31/22	2.0 to 1	1.5 to 1	2.3 to 1
Inventory turnover ratio	12/31/23	5.7 times	4.5 times	6.0 times
	12/31/22	7.6 times	5.8 times	9.8 times
Quick ratio	12/31/23	2.1 to 1	1.6 to 1	0.7 to 1
	12/31/22	1.0 to 1	1.4 to 1	1.1 to 1

Required:

Explain which company appears to be the most liquid at December 31, 2023.

Brief Exercise 12-50 Debt Management Ratios   OBJECTIVE ◀ 5

Rocky Corporation provides annual and quarterly financial data to the public. For the years of 2022 and 2023, Rocky's financial data included the following account balances:

	2023	2022
Total liabilities	$2,020,000	$1,580,000
Common stock ($25 par)	360,000	335,000
Paid-in capital in excess of par—common stock	190,000	155,000
Retained earnings	201,000	180,000

Required:

Determine whether the debt to equity ratio is increasing or decreasing and whether Rocky should be concerned.

Brief Exercise 12-51 Debt Management and Short-Term Liquidity Ratios   OBJECTIVE ◀ 5

Duffy Company is an international travel agency providing travel planning services to customers in over 20 countries. Recently, the travel industry has been experiencing volatility as a result of increases in oil prices. Duffy's investors have been following its financial information closely to determine its ability to continue as a going concern. Its investors have used the following information to determine financial ratios:

	2023	2022
Current assets	$11,000	$9,600
Long-term assets	8,000	6,600
Current liabilities	1,500	3,200
Long-term liabilities	5,000	0
Stockholders' equity	4,800	4,800

Required:

Between 2022 and 2023, indicate whether Duffy's debt to equity ratio increased or decreased. Also, indicate whether Duffy's current ratio increased or decreased. Interpret these ratios.

Brief Exercise 12-52 Asset Efficiency Ratios   OBJECTIVE ◀ 5

Sammy Inc.'s financial statements for 2023 indicate the following account balances:

Net sales	$422,596
Cost of goods sold	211,000
Average accounts receivable	17,380
Average inventory	3,845
Average property, plant, and equipment	77,565
Average total assets	132,116

Required:

1. Using this information, calculate Sammy's receivable turnover ratio. (*Note:* Round to two decimal places.)
2. Using this information, calculate Sammy's asset turnover ratio and also convert the ratio into days.

Brief Exercise 12-53 Profitability Ratios   OBJECTIVE ◀ 5

Vanderwood Publications is a magazine publisher established in Southern California. Financial analysts are concerned about Vanderwood's ability to generate positive returns as printed material becomes less popular than digital material. Financial analysts observe the following account balances from Vanderwood to determine financial ratios:

Revenue	$2,300,000
Expenses	1,100,000
Net income	425,000
Assets	760,000
Liabilities	275,000
Average equity	800,000

(Continued)

Required:

Compute Vanderwood's return on equity.

OBJECTIVE 5

Brief Exercise 12-54 Profitability Ratios

Bell Corporation operates in the highly competitive consulting industry. Bell's balance sheet indicates the following balances as of December 31, 2023.

Cash	$ 120,000
Accounts receivable	113,000
Inventory	77,000
Property, plant, and equipment	525,000
Accounts payable	86,000
Bonds payable (due in 2025)	140,000
Common stock (12/31/2022)	270,000
Common stock (12/31/2023)	280,000
Retained earnings (12/31/2022)	205,000
Retained earnings (12/31/2023)	245,000

Required:

Calculate Bell's return on equity if Bell's 2023 net income is $115,000.

OBJECTIVE 5

Brief Exercise 12-55 Profitability Ratios

Blake Corp. is a publicly traded company on a large stock exchange. Blake's financial statement for 2023 and 2022 included the following data:

	2023	2022
Net income	$230,000	$195,000
Cash dividends paid on preferred stock	11,000	11,000
Cash dividends paid on common stock	38,000	34,000
Weighted average number of preferred shares outstanding	29,000	29,000
Weighted average number of common shares outstanding	108,000	104,000

Required:

Calculate Blake's earnings per share as it would be reported on the 2023 income statement.

OBJECTIVE 5

Brief Exercise 12-56 Stockholder Ratios

Harden Corp.'s financial data for 2023 and 2022 included the following:

	2023	2022
Net income	$210,000	$195,000
Cash dividends paid on common stock	64,000	42,000
Market price per share of common stock at the end of the year	26.00	21.00
Shares of common stock outstanding	150,000	150,000

Required:

Calculate Harden's dividend payout ratio for 2023.

EXERCISES

Exercise 12-57 SEC Filings

OBJECTIVE ◀ 2

The SEC requires publicly traded companies to file many different forms.

Required:

Describe the Form 10-Q.

Exercise 12-58 Form 10-K

OBJECTIVE ◀ 2

Form 10-K has many different items.

Required:

1. Indicate what is included in the Management's Discussion and Analysis section of the 10-K.
2. List five important things that are included in the Form 10-K.

Exercise 12-59 Getting Familiar with the Format of the 10-K

OBJECTIVE ◀ 2

Look up **Columbia Sportswear**'s 10-K for 2019 (filed February 20, 2020). It can be found online (which allows you to search and reference the entire 10-K) by searching for "Columbia Sportswear investor relations." Once at that site click on "Financial Information" then "SEC Filings," move the "View" pull down menu to "Annual Filings," and click the "Search" button.

Required:

Answer the following questions and include in which item number of the 10-K the information was found:

1. Where are Columbia 's Apparel items manufactured?
2. Name Columbia 's four primary brands.
3. How many employees did Columbia have on December 31, 2019?
4. Is Columbia involved in any litigation that may materially affect its financial position?
5. 2019 net sales were $3,042.5 million. How much of these sales are attributable to the Wholesale and the Direct to Consumer (DTC) channels, respectively (in dollars)?
6. What method of depreciation does Columbia use? What is the range of useful lives for furniture and fixtures?
7. Who audits Columbia, and what date was the audit opinion signed?

Exercise 12-60 Financial Statement Users

OBJECTIVE ◀ 3

Many groups analyze financial statements to make decisions.

Required:

1. **CONCEPTUAL CONNECTION** Explain why a person who is selecting an employer should be sure to view and analyze the company's financial statements.
2. **CONCEPTUAL CONNECTION** Explain why a business that is considering selling goods or providing services to another business should review the company's financial statements.

OBJECTIVE 3 4

Exercise 12-61 Horizontal Analysis of Income Statements

Consolidated income statements for Cooper Manufacturing follow.

Cooper Manufacturing Consolidated Income Statements (in thousands except per share amounts)			
	Three fiscal years ended December 31		
	2023	**2022**	**2021**
Sales	$10,088,322	$ 7,976,954	$7,086,542
Costs and expenses:			
Cost of goods sold	$ 6,844,915	$ 5,107,113	$4,003,989
Research and development	592,001	664,564	602,135
Selling, general, and administrative	1,384,111	1,550,857	1,642,770
Restructuring costs and other	(126,855)	320,856	50,000
	$ 8,694,172	$ 7,643,390	$6,298,894
Operating income	$ 1,394,150	$ 333,564	$ 787,648
Interest and other income, net	(21,988)	29,321	49,634
Income before income taxes	$ 1,372,162	$ 362,885	$ 837,282
Provision for income taxes	381,525	70,104	285,430
Net income	$ 990,637	$ 312,781	$ 551,852
Earnings per common and common equivalent share	$ 3.43	$ 1.18	$ 2.06
Common and common equivalent shares used in the calculations of earnings per share	288,740	264,985	268,110

Required:

1. Prepare common size income statements for horizontal analysis (in percentage terms, rounded to two decimal places). You do not need to include the actual dollar amounts shown above.
2. **CONCEPTUAL CONNECTION** Explain why net income decreased in 2022 and increased in 2023.

OBJECTIVE 3

Exercise 12-62 Vertical Analysis of Balance Sheets

Consolidated balance sheets for Winged Manufacturing follow.

Winged Manufacturing Consolidated Balance Sheets (dollars in thousands)		
	December 31	
	2023	**2022**
ASSETS		
Current assets:		
Cash and cash equivalents	$1,203,488	$ 676,413
Short-term investments	54,368	215,890
Accounts receivable, net of allowance for doubtful accounts of $90,992 ($83,776 in 2022)	1,581,347	1,381,946
Inventories	1,088,434	1,506,638
Deferred tax assets	293,048	268,085
Other current assets	255,767	289,383
Total current assets	$4,476,452	$4,338,355

Property, plant, and equipment:		
Land and buildings	$ 484,592	$ 404,688
Machinery and equipment	572,728	578,272
Office furniture and equipment	158,160	167,905
Leasehold improvements	236,708	261,792
	$1,452,188	$1,412,657
Accumulated depreciation and amortization	(785,088)	(753,111)
Net property, plant, and equipment	$ 667,100	$ 659,546
Other assets	159,194	173,511
Total assets	$5,302,746	$5,171,412

LIABILITIES AND STOCKHOLDERS' EQUITY

Current liabilities:		
Short-term borrowings	$ 292,200	$ 823,182
Accounts payable	881,717	742,622
Accrued compensation and employee benefits	136,895	144,779
Accrued marketing and distribution	178,294	174,547
Accrued restructuring costs	58,238	307,932
Other current liabilities	396,961	315,023
Total current liabilities	$1,944,305	$2,508,085
Long-term debt	304,472	7,117
Deferred tax liabilities	670,668	629,832
Total liabilities	$2,919,445	$3,145,034
Stockholders' equity:		
Common stock, no par value: 320,000,000 shares authorized; 119,542,527 shares issued and outstanding in 2023 (116,147,035 shares in 2022)	$ 297,929	$ 203,613
Retained earnings	2,096,206	1,842,600
Accumulated translation adjustment	(10,834)	(19,835)
Total stockholders' equity	$2,383,301	$2,026,378
Total liabilities and stockholders' equity	$5,302,746	$5,171,412

Required:
1. Prepare common size balance sheets for vertical analysis (in percentage terms, rounded to two decimal places). You do not need to include the actual dollar amounts shown above.
2. Indicate from what sources Winged appears to have secured the resources for its asset increase.

Exercise 12-63 Horizontal Analysis Using Income Statements   OBJECTIVE ▶ 3 4

The consolidated 2023, 2022, and 2021 income statements for Butler Corporation follow.

Butler Corporation Consolidated Income Statements (in millions except per share amounts)			
		December 31,	
	2023	2022	2021
Net sales	$26,130.0	$24,780.0	$19,292.2
Costs and expenses:			
Cost of goods sold	(11,946.1)	(10,611.7)	(9,876.2)
Selling, general, and administrative	(9,864.4)	(8,721.2)	(7,605.9)
Amortization of intangible assets	(408.0)	(265.9)	(208.3)
Operating income	$ 3,911.5	$ 5,181.2	$ 1,601.8

(*Continued*)

	December 31,		
	2023	2022	2021
Interest expense	(572.7)	(586.1)	(613.7)
Interest income	88.7	113.7	161.6
Income before income taxes	$ 3,427.5	$ 4,708.8	$1,149.7
Provision for income taxes	834.6	597.1	597.5
Net income	$ 2,592.9	$ 4,111.7	$ 552.2

Required:

1. Prepare common size income statements for horizontal analysis (in percentage terms, rounded to two decimal places). You do not need to include the actual dollar amounts shown above.
2. Indicate what Butler's 2023, 2022, and 2021 tax rates were on its income before taxes (in percentage terms, rounded to two decimal places).
3. **CONCEPTUAL CONNECTION** Explain why net income increased by a larger percentage than sales in 2023 and 2022.

OBJECTIVE 3 4

Exercise 12-64 Horizontal Analysis Using Balance Sheets

The consolidated 2023 and 2022 balance sheets for Butler Corporation follow.

Butler Corporation Consolidated Balance Sheets (in millions except per share amounts)		
	December 31	
	2023	2022
ASSETS		
Current assets:		
Cash and cash equivalents	$ 226.9	$ 169.9
Short-term investments at cost which approximates market	1,629.3	1,888.5
Accounts and notes receivable, less allowance:		
$128.3 in 2023 and $112.0 in 2022	1,883.4	1,588.5
Inventories	924.7	768.8
Prepaid expenses, taxes, and other current assets	499.8	426.6
Total current assets	$ 5,164.1	$ 4,842.3
Investments in affiliates and other assets	1,756.6	1,707.9
Property, plant, and equipment, net	8,855.6	7,442.0
Intangible assets, net	7,929.5	6,959.0
Total assets	$23,705.8	$20,951.2
LIABILITIES AND STOCKHOLDERS' EQUITY		
Current liabilities:		
Short-term borrowings	$ 2,191.2	$ 706.8
Accounts payable	1,390.0	1,164.8
Income taxes payable	823.7	621.1
Accrued compensation and benefits	726.0	638.9
Accrued marketing	400.9	327.0
Other current liabilities	1,043.1	1,099.0
Total current liabilities	$ 6,574.9	$ 4,557.6
Long-term debt	7,442.6	7,964.8
Other liabilities	1,342.0	1,390.8
Deferred income taxes	2,007.6	1,682.3
Total liabilities	$17,367.1	$15,595.5

Stockholders' equity:		
Capital stock, par value $1 per share: authorized 1,800.0 million shares, 14.4 million and 7.4 million shares issued at December 31, 2023 and 2022, respectively	$ 14.4	$ 7.4
Capital in excess of par value	879.5	674.6
Retained earnings	6,541.9	5,439.7
Other comprehensive income (loss)	(183.9)	(99.0)
Less: Treasury stock, at cost: 64.3 shares in 2023 and 2022	(913.2)	(667.0)
Total stockholders' equity	$ 6,338.7	$ 5,355.7
Total liabilities and stockholders' equity	$23,705.8	$20,951.2

Required:
1. Calculate the percentage that Butler's total assets increased by during 2023 (in percentage terms, rounded to one decimal place). You do not need to include the actual dollar amounts shown above.
2. Determine whether any of the asset categories experienced larger increases than others.
3. Indicate where Butler acquired the capital to finance its asset growth.
4. Indicate whether any of the individual liability or equity items increased at a rate different from the rate at which total liabilities and equity increased.

Exercise 12-65 Preparation of Common Size Statements for Vertical Analysis

OBJECTIVE ◀ 3 4

Financial statements for Steele Inc. follow.

Steele Inc.
Consolidated Income Statements
(in thousands except per share amounts)

	2023	2022	2021
Net sales	$ 7,245,088	$ 6,944,296	$ 6,149,218
Cost of goods sold	(5,286,253)	(4,953,556)	(4,355,675)
Gross margin	$ 1,958,835	$ 1,990,740	$ 1,793,543
General and administrative expenses	(1,259,896)	(1,202,042)	(1,080,843)
Special and nonrecurring items	2,617	0	0
Operating income	$ 701,556	$ 788,698	$ 712,700
Interest expense	(63,685)	(62,398)	(63,927)
Other income	7,308	10,080	11,529
Gain on sale of investments	0	9,117	0
Income before income taxes	$ 645,179	$ 745,497	$ 660,302
Provision for income taxes	(254,000)	(290,000)	(257,000)
Net income	$ 391,179	$ 455,497	$ 403,302

Steele Inc.
Consolidated Balance Sheets
(in thousands)

ASSETS	Dec. 31, 2023	Dec. 31, 2022
Current assets:		
Cash and equivalents	$ 320,558	$ 41,235
Accounts receivable	1,056,911	837,377
Inventories	733,700	803,707
Other	109,456	101,811
Total current assets	$2,220,625	$1,784,130

(Continued)

Property and equipment, net	1,666,588	1,813,948
Other assets	247,892	248,372
Total assets	$4,135,105	$3,846,450
LIABILITIES AND STOCKHOLDERS' EQUITY		
Current liabilities:		
Accounts payable	$ 250,363	$ 309,092
Accrued expenses	347,892	274,220
Other current liabilities	15,700	0
Income taxes	93,489	137,466
Total current liabilities	$ 707,444	$ 720,778
Long-term debt	650,000	541,639
Deferred income taxes	275,101	274,844
Other long-term liabilities	61,267	41,572
Total liabilities	$1,693,812	$1,578,833
Stockholders' equity:		
Preferred stock	$ 100,000	$ 100,000
Common stock	89,727	89,727
Additional paid-in capital—common stock	128,906	127,776
Retained earnings	2,397,112	2,136,794
	$2,715,745	$2,454,297
Less: Treasury stock, at cost	(274,452)	(186,680)
Total stockholders' equity	$2,441,293	$2,267,617
Total liabilities and stockholders' equity	$4,135,105	$3,846,450

Required:

1. Prepare common size income statements and balance sheets for Steele to be used in vertical analysis (in percentage terms, rounded to two decimal places). You do not need to include the actual dollar amounts shown above.
2. **CONCEPTUAL CONNECTION** Indicate whether gross margin grew as much as sales between 2021 and 2022 and between 2022 and 2023, and, if so, why it grew.
3. **CONCEPTUAL CONNECTION** Indicate whether the relative proportion of Steele's assets changed between 2022 and 2023, and, if so, explain the change.
4. **CONCEPTUAL CONNECTION** Indicate whether the relative proportion of Steele's liabilities and equity changed between 2022 and 2023, and, if so, explain the change.
5. **CONCEPTUAL CONNECTION** Explain how Steele appears to have financed the 7.5% increase in assets that occurred between 2022 and 2023.

OBJECTIVE **3** **4** **Exercise 12-66 Common Size Statements for Vertical Analysis**

The following consolidated income statements and balance sheets are available for Azure Inc.:

Azure Inc.						
Consolidated Income Statements						
	Year ended December 31,					
	2023		**2022**		**2021**	
	Amount	**%**	**Amount**	**%**	**Amount**	**%**
Revenues	$901,170	100.0	$728,035	100.0	$661,850	100.0
Costs and expenses:						
Cost of goods sold	$539,801	59.9	$439,005	60.3	$401,743	60.7
Selling and administrative	318,113	35.3	206,034	28.3	176,052	26.6
Interest	17,122	1.9	18,201	2.5	17,208	2.6
Other expenses (income)	9,913	1.1	2,912	0.4	(1,324)	(0.2)
Total costs and expenses	$884,949	98.2	$666,152	91.5	$593,679	89.7

	Amount	%	Amount	%	Amount	%
Income before provision for income taxes	$ 16,221	1.8	$ 61,883	8.5	$ 68,171	10.3
Provision for income taxes	4,506	0.5	22,569	3.1	23,827	3.6
Net income	$ 11,715	1.3	$ 39,314	5.4	$ 44,344	6.7

Azure Inc.
Consolidated Income Statements

	December 31,					
	2023		**2022**		**2021**	
	Amount	%	Amount	%	Amount	%
ASSETS						
Current assets	$147,129	31.4	$ 62,417	14.3	$ 66,927	16.1
Investment	30,925	6.6	95,589	21.9	91,453	22.0
Property, plant, and equipment (net)	270,831	57.8	261,015	59.8	241,519	58.1
Other assets	19,680	4.2	17,459	4.0	15,796	3.8
Total assets	$468,565	100.0	$436,480	100.0	$415,695	100.0
LIABILITIES AND STOCKHOLDERS' EQUITY						
Current liabilities	$ 68,410	14.6	$ 29,244	6.7	$ 28,683	6.9
Long-term debt	152,284	32.5	162,807	37.3	152,976	36.8
Total liabilities	$220,694	47.1	$192,051	44.0	$181,659	43.7
Common stock	$183,209	39.1	$182,332	41.8	$171,266	41.2
Retained earnings	64,662	13.8	62,097	14.2	62,770	15.1
Total stockholders' equity	$247,871	52.9	$244,429	56.0	$234,036	56.3
Total liabilities and stockholders' equity	$468,565	100.0	$436,480	100.0	$415,695	100.0

Required:

1. **CONCEPTUAL CONNECTION** Explain why income from operations decreased in 2022 and 2023 while sales increased.
2. Determine whether the proportion of resources invested in the various asset categories changed from 2021 to 2023.
3. Determine whether the proportion of capital supplied by creditors changed.
4. Indicate from what sources Azure secured the capital to finance its increase in current assets in 2023.

Exercise 12-67 Short-Term Liquidity Ratios

OBJECTIVE ◀ 5

The financial statements for Puck Enterprises, a retailer, follow.

Puck Enterprises
Consolidated Income Statements
(millions of dollars except per share data)

	December 31		
	2023	**2022**	**2021**
Revenues	$19,233	$17,927	$16,115
Costs and expenses:			
Cost of retail sales, buying, and occupancy	$14,164	$13,129	$11,751
Selling, publicity, and administration	3,175	2,978	2,801
Depreciation	498	459	410
Interest expense, net	446	437	398
Taxes other than income taxes	343	313	283
Total costs and expenses	$18,626	$17,316	$15,643

(*Continued*)

Earnings before income taxes	$ 607	$ 611	$ 472
Provision for income taxes	232	228	171
Net earnings	$ 375	$ 383	$ 301

Puck Enterprises Consolidated Balance Sheets (millions of dollars)		
	December 31,	
	2023	**2022**
ASSETS		
Current assets:		
Cash and cash equivalents	$ 521	$ 117
Accounts receivable	1,536	1,514
Merchandise inventories	2,497	2,618
Other	267	165
Total current assets	$ 4,821	$ 4,414
Property and equipment:		
Land	$ 2,480	$ 998
Buildings and improvements	4,753	4,342
Fixtures and equipment	1,982	2,197
Construction-in-progress	248	223
Accumulated depreciation	(2,336)	(2,197)
Net property and equipment	$ 7,127	$ 5,563
Other	320	587
Total assets	$12,268	$10,564
LIABILITIES AND STOCKHOLDERS' EQUITY		
Current liabilities:		
Notes payable	$ 200	$ 23
Accounts payable	1,654	1,347
Accrued liabilities	903	849
Income taxes payable	145	160
Current portion of long-term debt	173	371
Total current liabilities	$ 3,075	$ 2,750
Long-term debt	4,279	5,038
Deferred income taxes and other	536	450
Loan to ESOP	(217)	(267)
Total liabilities	$ 7,673	$ 7,971
Stockholders' equity:		
Preferred stock	368	374
Common stock	72	71
Additional paid-in capital—common	73	58
Retained earnings	4,082	2,357
Total stockholders' equity	$ 4,595	$ 2,860
Total liabilities and stockholders' equity	$ 12,268	$ 10,564

Required:

1. Compute the four short-term liquidity ratios (rounded to two decimal places) for 2022 and 2023, assuming operating cash flows are $394 million and $501 million, respectively.
2. **CONCEPTUAL CONNECTION** Indicate which ratios appear to be most appropriate for a retail organization. Indicate what other information you would like to know to comment on Puck's short-term liquidity.

Exercise 12-68 Debt Management Ratios

OBJECTIVE ◄ 5

Refer to Steele's financial statements in **Exercise 12-65**.

Required:

1. Compute the five debt management ratios for 2022 and 2023 (rounded to two decimal places).
2. **CONCEPTUAL CONNECTION** Indicate whether the ratios have changed and whether the ratios suggest that Steele is more or less risky for long-term creditors at December 31, 2023, than at December 31, 2022.

Exercise 12-69 Asset Efficiency Ratios

OBJECTIVE ◄ 5

Refer to Steele's financial statements in **Exercise 12-65** and the information below.

Statement Item	January 1, 2022 (in thousands)
Accounts receivable	$ 752,945
Inventories	698,604
Total assets	3,485,233

Required:

1. Compute the three asset efficiency ratios (rounded to two decimal places) for 2022 and 2023.
2. Indicate the length of Steele's operating cycle in days (rounded to two decimal places) for the years ended December 31, 2023, and December 31, 2022.

Exercise 12-70 Profitability Ratios

OBJECTIVE ◄ 5

Refer to Steele's financial statements in **Exercise 12-65** and the information below.

Statement Item	January 1, 2022 (in thousands)
Total assets	$3,485,233
Total stockholders' equity	2,083,122

Required:

1. Compute the five profitability ratios (in percentage terms, rounded to two decimal places) for 2022 and 2023.
2. **CONCEPTUAL CONNECTION** Explain what these ratios suggest about Steele's profitability. Indicate what other information you would like to know to further assess Steele's profitability.

Exercise 12-71 Stockholder Ratios

OBJECTIVE ◄ 5

Refer to Steele's financial statements in **Exercise 12-65** and the information below.

	Year ended December 31,	
Item	2023	2022
Average number of common shares outstanding (thousands)	362,202	364,398
Preferred dividends (thousands)	$ 24,000	$ 24,000
Dividends per common share	0.36	1.54
Common dividends (thousands)	130,861.00	561,172.30
Common stock repurchases	0	0
Market price per share:		
High	83.25	79.10
Low	63.25	59.00
Close	78.42	66.36

At January 1, 2022, total stockholders' equity was $2,083,122 and there was no preferred stock.

(Continued)

Required:

1. Compute the earnings per share, return on common equity, dividend yield ratio, and dividend payout ratio (in percentage terms, rounded to two decimal places except for EPS, which should be rounded to nearest cent) for 2022 and 2023.
2. **CONCEPTUAL CONNECTION** Indicate whether there were significant changes in these ratios between the years ended December 31, 2023, and December 31, 2022. Determine whether the stockholder ratios suggest that Steele was a better investment at December 31, 2023, or December 31, 2022.

OBJECTIVE 5

Exercise 12-72 Dupont Analysis

Refer to Steele's financial statements in **Exercise 12-65** and the information below.

Statement Item	January 1, 2022 (in millions)
Total assets	$3,485,233
Total stockholders' equity	2,083,122

Industry Averages	Year ended December 31,	
	2023	2022
Return on equity	5.31%	12.54%
Profit margin	4.00	6.21
Asset turnover	0.83	1.96
Leverage	1.60	1.03

Required:

1. Perform a Dupont analysis (in percentage terms, rounded to two decimal places) for 2022 and 2023.
2. **CONCEPTUAL CONNECTION** Explain what you learn about Steele's trends from 2022 to 2023 by comparing its performance to the industry averages.

PROBLEM SET A

OBJECTIVE 3 4

Problem 12-73A Using Common Size Data for Credit Analysis

You are the credit manager for London Supplies. One of your sales staff has made a $50,000 credit sale to Bing Company, an electronics manufacturer. Your responsibility is to decide whether to approve the sale. You have the following data for the electronics industry and Bing:

For the Years 2019–2023	Industry	Bing Company
Average annual sales growth	13.4%	17.6%
Average annual operating income growth	10.8%	9.7%
Average annual net income growth	14.4%	9.9%
Average annual asset growth	10.3%	14.2%
Average debt to equity ratio	0.32	0.26
Average current ratio	4.04	3.71
Average inventory turnover ratio	2.53	2.06
Average accounts receivable turnover ratio	3.95	4.18

For Bing, you have the following data for the year ended December 31, 2023:

Sales revenue	$3,908,000
Net income	$359,000
Total assets	$3,626,000
Current ratio	1.82
Debt to equity ratio	0.37
Inventory turnover ratio	1.79
Accounts receivable turnover ratio	3.62

The salesperson believes that Bing would order about $200,000 per year of materials that would provide a gross margin of $35,000 to London if reasonable credit terms could be arranged.

Required:

CONCEPTUAL CONNECTION State whether you would grant authorization for Bing to purchase on credit and support your decision.

Problem 12-74A Using Common Size Data for Investment Analysis

OBJECTIVE ◀ 3 4

Assume that you are a trust officer for the Joss Bank. You are attempting to select a pharmaceutical manufacturer's stock for a client's portfolio. You have secured the following data:

	5-Year Averages				
	Industry Average	Opal	Main	Darcy	Hunt
Sales growth	8.3%	9.8%	7.9%	7.2%	10.1%
Net income growth	13.0	12.0	10.7	4.2	16.1
Asset growth	5.0	6.1	4.6	4.4	6.2

	Current Year				
	Industry Average	Opal	Main	Darcy	Hunt
Return on equity	16.2%	17.5%	17.5%	19.4%	21.6%
Return on assets	8.5	7.8	12.7	8.4	11.4
Dividend payout	43.0	40.0	23.0	31.0	31.0

Required:

CONCEPTUAL CONNECTION Comment on the relative performance of these firms.

Problem 12-75A Using Common Size Income Statement Data

OBJECTIVE ◀ 3 4

The income statements for Jolly Fun Inc. follow.

Jolly Fun Inc. Consolidated Income Statements			
	Year ended December 31,		
	2023	2022	2021
Revenues:			
Theme parks and resorts	$3,440.7	$3,306.9	$2,794.3
Filmed entertainment	3,673.4	3,115.2	2,593.7
Consumer products	1,415.1	1,081.9	724.0
	$8,529.2	$7,504.0	$6,112.0
Costs and expenses:			
Theme parks and resorts	$2,693.8	$2,662.9	$2,247.7
Filmed entertainment	3,051.2	2,606.9	2,275.6
Consumer products	1,059.7	798.9	494.2
	$6,804.7	$6,068.7	$5,017.5
Operating income:			
Theme parks and resorts	$ 746.9	$ 644.0	$ 546.6
Filmed entertainment	622.2	508.3	318.1
Consumer products	355.4	283.0	229.8
	$1,724.5	$1,435.3	$1,094.5
Corporate activities:			
General and administrative expenses	$ 164.2	$ 148.2	$ 160.8
Interest expense	157.7	126.8	105.0
Investment and interest income	(186.1)	(130.3)	(119.4)
	$ 135.8	$ 144.7	$ 146.4
Income (loss) on investment in Asian theme park	$ (514.7)	$ 11.2	$ 63.8
Income before income taxes	$1,074.0	$1,301.8	$1,011.9
Income taxes	402.7	485.1	375.3
Net income	$ 671.3	$ 816.7	$ 636.6

(Continued)

Required:

1. Calculate how much each of the revenues and expenses changed from 2021 through 2023 (in percentage terms, rounded to two decimal places). Utilize 2021 as the base year for both 2022 and 2023. You do not need to include the actual dollar amounts shown above.
2. **CONCEPTUAL CONNECTION** Explain the primary causes of Jolly's increase in net income in 2022 and the decrease in 2023.

OBJECTIVE 3 4

Problem 12-76A Using Common Size Statements

The following income statement and vertical analysis data are available for Riley Manufacturing:

	Riley Manufacturing Consolidated Income Statements					
	Year ended June 30,					
	2023		**2022**		**2021**	
(in thousands)	Amount	%	Amount	%	Amount	%
Sales	$2,970.0	100.0	$3,465.0	100.0	$3,960.0	100.0
Other income, net	23.7	0.8	34.6	1.0	39.6	1.0
Total revenues	$2,993.7	100.8	$3,499.6	101.0	$3,999.6	101.0
Costs and expenses:						
Cost of goods sold	$1,303.8	43.9	$1,566.2	45.2	$1,920.6	48.5
Selling and administrative	1,571.1	52.9	1,593.9	46.0	1,564.2	39.5
Interest	62.4	2.1	65.8	1.9	59.4	1.5
Total costs and expenses	$2,937.3	98.9	$3,225.9	93.1	$3,544.2	89.5
Income before income taxes	$ 56.4	1.9	$ 273.7	7.9	$ 455.4	11.5
Income taxes expense	14.8	0.5	107.4	3.1	182.2	4.6
Net income	$ 41.6	1.4	$ 166.3	4.8	$ 273.2	6.9

Required:

1. **CONCEPTUAL CONNECTION** Suggest why net income declined from $273,200 to $41,600 while the cost of goods sold percentage decreased each year and selling and administrative expenses remained nearly constant.
2. **CONCEPTUAL CONNECTION** Determine what could cause sales to decline while the gross margin percentage increases.

OBJECTIVE 3 4

Problem 12-77A Using Common Size Statements

Twisted Company owns and operates a small chain of pretzel stands located near colleges and universities. Twisted has experienced significant growth in recent years. The following data are available for Twisted:

	Twisted Company Consolidated Income Statements (in thousands)		
	Year ended December 31,		
	2023	**2022**	**2021**
Sales	$51,638	$41,310	$34,425
Cost of goods sold	31,050	24,840	20,700
Gross margin	$20,588	$16,470	$13,725
Other income, net	383	426	405
	$20,971	$16,896	$14,130
Costs and expenses:			
Selling and administrative	$16,570	$13,465	$11,350
Interest	1,237	765	554
Total costs and expenses	$17,807	$14,230	$11,904
Income before income taxes	$ 3,164	$ 2,666	$ 2,226
Provision for income taxes	885	746	623
Net income	$ 2,279	$ 1,920	$ 1,603

Twisted Company
Consolidated Balance Sheets
(in thousands)

	December 31,		
	2023	**2022**	**2021**
ASSETS			
Current assets:			
Cash	$ 360	$ 293	$ 236
Accounts receivable	4,658	3,690	3,285
Inventories	6,064	4,478	3,442
Total current assets	$11,082	$ 8,461	$ 6,963
Property, plant, and equipment (net)	4,860	3,600	2,756
Other assets	574	585	562
Total assets	$16,516	$12,646	$10,281
LIABILITIES AND STOCKHOLDERS' EQUITY			
Current liabilities:			
Short-term notes payable	$ 4,230	$ 1,620	$ 450
Accounts payable	1,147	1,013	720
Total current liabilities	$ 5,377	$ 2,633	$ 1,170
Long-term debt	3,150	3,150	3,150
Total liabilities	$ 8,527	$ 5,783	$ 4,320
Common stock & additional paid-in capital	$ 4,725	$ 4,725	$ 4,725
Retained earnings	3,264	2,138	1,236
Total stockholders' equity	$ 7,989	$ 6,863	$ 5,961
Total liabilities and stockholders' equity	$16,516	$12,646	$10,281

Required:

1. Determine how much Twisted's sales, net income, and assets have grown during these 3 years.
2. Explain how Twisted has financed the increase in assets.
3. Determine whether Twisted's liquidity is adequate.
4. **CONCEPTUAL CONNECTION** Explain why interest expense is growing.
5. If Twisted's sales grow by 25% in 2024, what would you expect net income to be?
6. If Twisted's assets must grow by 25% to support the 25% sales increase and if 50% of net income is paid in dividends, how much capital must Twisted raise in 2024?

Problem 12-78A Preparing Common Size Statements

OBJECTIVE ◄ 3 4

The financial statements for Venus Industries follow:

Venus Industries
Consolidated Income Statement
(in thousands, except per share data)

	Year ended December 31,		
	2023	**2022**	**2021**
Revenues	$4,578,041	$3,864,324	$3,003,610
Costs and expenses:			
Cost of goods sold	$2,227,189	$2,089,089	$2,005,691
Selling and administrative	922,261	836,212	664,061
Interest	29,744	32,966	30,472
Other expenses (income)	1,475	2,141	(43)
Total costs and expenses	$3,180,669	$2,960,408	$2,700,181

(Continued)

Income before income taxes	$1,397,372	$ 903,916	$ 303,429
Income taxes	229,500	192,600	174,700
Net income	$1,167,872	$ 711,316	$ 128,729

Venus Industries
Consolidated Balance Sheets (in thousands)

	December 31,	
	2023	2022
ASSETS		
Current assets:		
Cash and equivalents	$ 291,284	$ 260,050
Accounts receivable, less allowance for doubtful accounts		
of $19,447 and $20,046	807,530	596,018
Inventories	592,986	512,917
Deferred income taxes	26,378	28,355
Prepaid expenses	40,663	32,977
Total current assets	$1,778,288	$1,450,363
Property, plant, and equipment	$ 571,032	$ 497,795
Less accumulated depreciation	(193,037)	(151,758)
Net property, plant, and equipment	$ 377,995	$ 346,037
Goodwill	174,326	110,363
Other assets	30,927	24,701
Total assets	$2,361,536	$1,931,464
LIABILITIES AND STOCKHOLDERS' EQUITY		
Current liabilities:		
Current portion of long-term debt	$ 52,985	$ 3,652
Notes payable	108,165	105,696
Accounts payable	135,701	134,729
Accrued liabilities	138,563	134,089
Income taxes payable	17,150	42,422
Total current liabilities	$ 452,564	$ 420,588
Long-term debt	15,033	77,022
Noncurrent deferred income taxes	29,965	27,074
Other noncurrent liabilities	43,575	23,728
Commitments and contingencies	0	0
Redeemable preferred stock	300	300
Total liabilities	$ 541,437	$ 548,712
Stockholders' equity:		
Common stock at stated value:		
Class A convertible—26,691 and 26,919 shares outstanding	$ 155	$ 161
Class B—49,161 and 48,591 shares outstanding	2,720	2,716
Capital in excess of stated value	108,451	93,799
Treasury stock (common at cost)	(7,790)	(6,860)
Retained earnings	1,716,563	1,292,936
Total stockholders' equity	$1,820,099	$1,382,752
Total liabilities and stockholders' equity	$2,361,536	$1,931,464

Required:

1. Prepare common size income statements to be used for horizontal analysis for Venus for 2021 to 2023 (in percentage terms, rounded to two decimal places). Utilize 2021 as the base year for both 2022 and 2023. You do not need to include the actual dollar amounts shown above.

2. **CONCEPTUAL CONNECTION** Indicate why Venus' net income increased between 2021 and 2023.

3. Prepare common size balance sheets to be used for vertical analysis for 2023 and 2022 (in percentage terms, rounded to two decimal places). You do not need to include the actual dollar amounts shown above.

4. Indicate whether the proportion of dollars invested in the various categories of assets has changed significantly between 2022 and 2023.

5. Indicate whether the proportion of capital raised from the various liability categories and common stockholders' equity has changed significantly between 2022 and 2023.

6. **CONCEPTUAL CONNECTION** Describe Venus' performance and financial position.

Problem 12-79A Preparation of Ratios

OBJECTIVE ◀ 5

Refer to the financial statements for Twisted Company in **Problem 12-77A**.

Required:

1. **CONCEPTUAL CONNECTION** Compute the asset efficiency ratios for Twisted for 2023 and 2022 (in percentage terms, rounded to two decimal places). Indicate whether efficiency has changed.

2. **CONCEPTUAL CONNECTION** Compute the profitability ratios (rounded to two decimal places) for Twisted for 2023 and 2022. Determine by how much Twisted's profitability ratios have changed (in percentage terms, rounded to two decimal places) for the 2-year period.

3. **CONCEPTUAL CONNECTION** Compute the debt management ratios (in percentage terms, rounded to two decimal places) for Twisted for 2022 and 2023. Discuss whether creditors are as secure in 2023 as they were in 2022.

Problem 12-80A Comparing Financial Ratios

OBJECTIVE ◀ 5

Presented below are selected ratios for four firms. Badgley is a heavy equipment manufacturer, Reagan is a newspaper publisher, Klein is a food manufacturer, and Taylor is a grocery chain.

	Badgley	Reagan	Klein	Taylor
Short-term liquidity ratio				
Current ratio	1.3	1.7	1.0	1.6
Debt management ratio				
Long-term debt to equity	1.81	0.45	0.30	0.09
Asset efficiency ratios				
Accounts receivable turnover	4.66	8.28	11.92	116.15
Inventory turnover	6.26	40.26	7.29	8.43
Profitability ratios				
Operating income	12.6%	25.4%	21.2%	3.8%
Net income	5.9	10.9	10.8	1.9
Return on assets	4.7	10.6	16.8	10.3
Return on equity	36.0	22.6	38.0	21.2

Required:

1. Which firm has the weakest current ratio?

2. **CONCEPTUAL CONNECTION** Explain why the turnover ratios vary so much among the four firms.

(Continued)

3. **CONCEPTUAL CONNECTION** Explain why the return on equity ratio is larger than the return on asset ratio for all four firms.
4. **CONCEPTUAL CONNECTION** Discuss whether the large differences in the return on equity ratios can exist over long periods of time.

OBJECTIVE 5

Problem 12-81A Preparation of Ratios

Refer to the financial statements for Burch Industries in **Problem 12-78A** and the following data.

	2023	2022	2021
Average number of common shares outstanding	77,063	76,602	76,067
Accounts receivable, net	$ 667,547	$ 596,018	$ 521,588
Inventories	592,986	471,202	586,594
Total assets	2,187,463	1,872,861	1,708,430
Stockholders' equity	1,646,026	1,324,149	1,032,789
Stock repurchases	930,111	581,134	288,320
Cash flows from operating activities	190,000	150,000	137,000
Common dividends paid	$ 57,797	$ 45,195	$ 39,555
Dividends per common share	0.75	0.59	0.52
Market price per share:			
High	90.25	77.45	54.50
Low	55.00	35.12	26.00
Close	86.33	71.65	43.22

	Year ended December 31,	
Industry Averages	**2023**	**2022**
Return on equity	25.98%	23.04%
Profit margin	0.05	0.04
Asset turnover	2.24	2.56
Leverage	2.32	2.25

Required:
1. Prepare all the financial ratios for Burch for 2023 and 2022 (using percentage terms where appropriate and rounding all answers to two decimal places).
2. **CONCEPTUAL CONNECTION** Explain whether Burch's short-term liquidity is adequate.
3. **CONCEPTUAL CONNECTION** Discuss whether Burch uses its assets efficiently.
4. **CONCEPTUAL CONNECTION** Determine whether Burch is profitable.
5. **CONCEPTUAL CONNECTION** Discuss whether long-term creditors should regard Burch as a high-risk or a low-risk firm.
6. Perform a Dupont analysis (rounding to two decimal places) for 2022 and 2023.

OBJECTIVE 5

Problem 12-82A Accounting Alternatives and Financial Analysis

Lime Automobiles has asked your bank for a $125,000 loan to expand its sales facility. Lime provides you with the following data:

	2023	2022	2021
Sales revenue	$7,100,000	$6,300,000	$5,400,000
Net income	119,000	113,000	104,000
Ending inventory (FIFO)*	525,000	495,000	450,000
Purchases	5,370,000	5,105,000	4,770,000
Depreciable assets	1,450,000	1,330,000	1,240,000

*The 2020 ending inventory was $420,000 (FIFO).

Your inspection of the financial statements of other automobiles sales firms indicates that most of these firms adopted the LIFO method in the late 1970s. You further note that Lime has used 5% of depreciable asset cost when computing depreciation expense and that other automobile dealers use 10%. Assume that Lime's effective tax rate is 21% of income before tax. Also assume the following:

	2023	2022	2021
Ending inventory (LIFO)*	$328,000	$310,000	$280,000

* The 2020 ending inventory was $260,000 (LIFO).

Required:
1. Compute cost of goods sold for 2021–2023, using both the FIFO and the LIFO methods.
2. Compute depreciation expense for Lime for 2021–2023, using both 5% and 10% of the cost of depreciable assets.
3. Recompute Lime's net income for 2021–2023, using LIFO and 10% depreciation. (Don't forget the tax impact of the increases in cost of goods sold and depreciation expense.)
4. **CONCEPTUAL CONNECTION** Explain whether Lime appears to have materially changed its financial statements by the selection of FIFO (rather than LIFO) and 5% (rather than 10%) depreciation.

CASES

Case 12-83 Ethics and Equity

Kelsey Calhoun is employed as a financial analyst at a large brokerage house. Her job is to follow companies in the computer hardware sector and issue reports that will be used by her firm's brokers in making recommendations to the brokerage house's clients. Her reports are summarized by her ratings of the company—strong buy, buy, hold, sell, or strong sell. She is in frequent contact with the top management of the companies she follows.

After a thorough investigation, she believes she should downgrade Protech from a "strong buy" to a "hold." However, when she informs Protech's CFO, the CFO threatens to call her boss. Later that week, her boss calls her to request that she reconsider her downgrade and states that her cooperation will be "greatly appreciated."

Required:
How should Kelsey respond to her boss? Are there any other steps she should consider taking?

Case 12-84 Assessing the Effects of the "Clean Air" Legislation

Congress is considering legislation that would require significant reductions over a several-year period in the quantity of emissions that electric utilities will be allowed to discharge into the air. Electric utilities that generate their electricity by burning inexpensive, but relatively high-sulfur, coal will be most affected by this legislation. Some utilities plan to comply with this legislation by burning coal with a lower sulfur content. Other utilities plan to comply with this legislation by installing devices on power plant smokestacks that would filter emissions before it is discharged into the air.

Required:
1. In what places on the financial statements of coal-dependent electric utilities do you expect to observe the effects of this legislation?
2. In what places on the financial statements of companies that mine coal do you expect to observe the effects of this legislation?

Case 12-85 Changes in the Price of Fuel for Aircraft

The cost of fuel is reported to be about 20% of the total operating cost for a major airline. Events in the Middle East caused jet fuel costs to nearly double from 2008 to 2011.

Required:

1. If you were the CEO of a major airline, how would you suggest that the airline respond to the fuel price increase?
2. How would you expect the financial statements of major airlines to be affected by the fuel price increase and the actions that the airlines would take in response?

Case 12-86 Analyzing Growth

Consolidated financial statements for Initech Corporation follow.

Initech Corporation
Consolidated Income Statements
(in millions except per share amounts)

	Three years ended December 31,		
	2023	**2022**	**2021**
Net revenues	$8,782	$5,844	$4,779
Cost of goods sold	$3,252	$2,557	$2,316
Research and development	970	780	618
Marketing, general, and administrative expenses	1,168	1,017	765
Operating costs and expenses	$5,390	$4,354	$3,699
Operating income	$3,392	$1,490	$1,080
Interest expense	(50)	(54)	(82)
Interest income and other, net	188	133	197
Income before taxes	$3,530	$1,569	$1,195
Provision for taxes	1,235	502	376
Net income	$2,295	$1,067	$ 819

Initech Corporation
Consolidated Balance Sheets
(in millions except per share amounts)

	December 31,	
ASSETS	**2023**	**2022**
Current assets:		
Cash and cash equivalents	$ 1,659	$ 1,843
Short-term investments	1,477	993
Accounts and notes receivable, net of allowance		
for doubtful accounts of $22 ($26 in 2022)	1,448	1,069
Inventories	838	535
Deferred tax assets	310	205
Other current assets	70	46
Total current assets	$ 5,802	$ 4,691
Property, plant, and equipment:		
Land and buildings	$ 1,848	$ 1,463
Machinery and equipment	4,148	2,874
Construction in progress	317	311
	$ 6,313	$ 4,648
Less accumulated depreciation	(2,317)	(1,832)
Property, plant, and equipment, net	$ 3,996	$ 2,816
Long-term investments	1,416	496
Other assets	130	86
Total assets	$11,344	$ 8,089

| | December 31, | |
	2023	2022
LIABILITIES AND STOCKHOLDERS' EQUITY		
Current liabilities:		
Short-term debt	$ 399	$ 202
Long-term debt redeemable within 1 year	98	110
Accounts payable	427	281
Deferred income on shipments to distributors	200	149
Accrued compensation and benefits	544	435
Other accrued liabilities	374	306
Income taxes payable	391	359
Total current liabilities	$ 2,433	$ 1,842
Long-term debt	426	249
Deferred tax liabilities	297	180
Other long-term liabilities	688	373
Total liabilities	$ 3,844	$ 2,644
Stockholders' equity:		
Preferred stock, $0.001 par value, 50 shares authorized; none issued	$ 0	$ 0
Common stock, $0.001 par value, 1,400 shares authorized, issued, and outstanding in 2023 and 2022	1	1
Additional paid-in capital—common stock	2,193	1,775
Retained earnings	5,306	3,669
Total stockholders' equity	$ 7,500	$ 5,445
Total liabilities and stockholders' equity	$11,344	$ 8,089

Required:

1. Prepare common size income statements to be used for both vertical and horizontal analysis for 2021–2023 (in percentage terms, rounded to two decimal places). You do not need to include the actual dollar amounts shown above.

2. Using the common size income statements for both vertical and horizontal analysis prepared in Requirement 1, indicate why Initech's profits increased more rapidly than sales for 2022 and 2023.

3. Prepare common size balance sheets for vertical analysis for 2022 and 2023 (in percentage terms, rounded to two decimal places). You do not need to include the actual dollar amounts shown above.

4. Did the proportion of assets invested in the various classes of assets change significantly from 2022 to 2023?

5. How has Initech financed its growth in assets?

6. Did the income statement change as much between 2022 and 2023 as the balance sheet?

Case 12-87 Identifying the Causes of Profitability Changes

The consolidated financial statements for Dowsett Shipping Corporation and Subsidiaries follow.

Dowsett Shipping Corporation and Subsidiaries
Consolidated Income Statements
(in thousands, except per share amounts)

	Fiscal year ended May 31,		
	2023	2022	2021
Revenues	$7,808,043	$7,550,060	$7,688,296
Operating expenses:			
Salaries and employee benefits	$3,807,493	$3,637,080	$3,438,391
Rentals and landing fees	658,138	672,341	650,001
Depreciation and amortization	579,896	577,157	562,207
Fuel	495,384	508,386	663,327
Maintenance and repairs	404,639	404,311	449,394
Restructuring charges	(12,500)	254,000	121,000
Other	1,497,820	1,473,818	1,551,850
	$7,430,870	$7,527,093	$7,436,170
Operating income	$ 377,173	$ 22,967	$ 252,126
Other income (expenses):			
Interest, net	$ (160,923)	$(164,315)	$ (181,880)
Gain on disposition of aircraft and related equipment	4,633	2,832	11,375
Other, net	(17,307)	(8,312)	(8,679)
Payroll tax loss	0	0	(32,000)
Other income (expenses), net	$ (173,597)	$ (169,795)	$ (211,184)
Income (loss) before income taxes and extraordinary loss	$ 203,576	$ (146,828)	$ 40,942
Provision (credit) for income taxes	93,767	(33,046)	35,044
Income (loss) before extraordinary loss	$ 109,809	$ (113,782)	$ 5,898
Extraordinary loss, net of tax benefit of $34,287	(55,943)	0	0
Net income (loss)	$ 53,866	$ (113,782)	$ 5,898

Dowsett Shipping Corporation and Subsidiaries Consolidated Balance Sheets (in thousands)		
	May 31,	
	2023	**2022**
ASSETS		
Current assets:		
Cash and cash equivalents	$ 155,456	$ 78,177
Receivable, less allowance for doubtful accounts of $31,308 and $32,074	922,727	899,773
Spare parts, supplies and fuel	164,087	158,062
Prepaid expenses and other	63,573	69,994
Deferred income taxes	133,875	0
Total current assets	$ 1,439,718	$ 1,206,006
Property and equipment, at cost		
Flight equipment	$ 2,843,253	$ 2,540,350
Package handling and ground support equipment	1,413,793	1,352,659
Computer and electronic equipment	947,913	851,686
Other	1,501,250	1,433,212
	$ 6,706,209	$ 6,177,907
Less accumulated depreciation and amortization	(3,229,941)	(2,766,610)
Net property and equipment	$ 3,476,268	$ 3,411,297
Other assets:		
Goodwill	$ 432,215	$ 487,780
Equipment deposits and other assets	444,863	358,103
Total other assets	$ 877,078	$ 845,883
Total assets	$ 5,793,064	$ 5,463,186
LIABILITIES AND STOCKHOLDERS' EQUITY		
Current liabilities:		
Current portion of long-term debt	$ 133,797	$ 155,257
Accounts payable	554,111	430,130
Accrued expenses	761,357	799,468
Total current liabilities	$ 1,449,265	$ 1,384,855
Long-term debt, less current portion	1,882,279	1,797,844
Deferred income taxes	72,479	123,715
Other liabilities	717,660	577,050
Total liabilities	$ 4,121,683	$ 3,883,464
Common stockholders' equity:		
Common stock, $0.10 par value, 100,000 shares authorized, 54,743 and 54,100 shares issue	$ 5,474	$ 5,410
Additional paid-in capital—common stock	699,385	672,727
Retained earnings	969,515	906,555
	$ 1,674,374	$ 1,584,692
Less treasury stock and deferred compensation related to stock plans	(2,993)	(4,970)
Total common stockholders' equity	$ 1,671,381	$ 1,579,722
Total liabilities and stockholders' equity	$ 5,793,064	$ 5,463,186

(*Continued*)

Required:
1. Evaluate Dowsett's performance in 2023.
2. What were the primary factors responsible for Dowsett's loss in 2022 and return to profitability in 2023?
3. How did Dowsett finance the $329,878,000 increase in assets in 2023?

CONTINUING PROBLEM

FRONT ROW ENTERTAINMENT

The income statement and consolidated balance sheets for Front Row Entertainment follow.

Front Row Entertainment Inc.
Consolidated Balance Sheets

	December 31	
ASSETS	**2024**	**2023**
Current assets:		
Cash	$ 30,322	$ 9,005
Accounts receivable, net	98,250	17,000
Prepaid expenses	133,400	57,200
Supplies	2,200	3,700
Inventory	61,380	2,850
Total current assets	$ 325,552	$89,755
Property, plant, and equipment:		
Building	1,857,250	0
Equipment	27,350	7,000
Accumulated depreciation	(53,835)	(2,160)
Trademark	25,000	0
Total assets	$2,181,317	$94,595
LIABILITIES AND EQUITY		
Current liabilities:		
Accounts payable	$ 2,450	$12,240
Salaries payable	2,500	3,690
Interest payable	40,917	2,250
Unearned sales revenue	1,780	28,650
Income taxes payable	550	2,180
Notes payable (short-term)	8,000	0
Total current liabilities	$ 56,197	$49,010
Long-term liabilities:		
Notes payable	$ 405,000	$25,000
Bonds payable, net	1,500,000	0
Less: Discount on bond payable	(109,530)	
Total long-term liabilities	$1,795,470	$25,000
Equity:		
Preferred stock	$ 150,000	$ 0
Common stock	18,000	16,000
Additional paid-in capital:		
Preferred stock	75,000	0
Common stock	38,000	0
Treasury stock	1,800	0
Retained earnings	53,250	4,585
Less: Treasury stock	(6,400)	0
Total stockholders' equity	$ 329,650	$20,585
Total liabilities and equity	$2,181,317	$94,595

Front Row Entertainment Inc. Income Statement For the year ended December 31, 2024	
Revenues:	
Sales revenue	$3,142,800
Service revenue	636,000
Total revenues	$3,778,800
Expenses:	
Artist Fee expense	$2,134,260
Rent expense	952,663
Cost of goods sold	74,800
Salaries and wages expense	345,100
Depreciation expense	51,675
Interest expense	98,087
Income taxes expense	22,000
Other expenses	26,550
Total expenses	$3,705,135
Net income	$ 73,665

Additional information:

- The market price of the common shares at the end of the year is $17.55 per share.
- The average number of common shares outstanding for 2024 is 16,400.
- The dividends per common share for 2024 were $25,000, which is approximately $1.45 per share ($25,000/17,300 common shares). The 17,300 shares can be calculated from information in Chapter 10 (16,000 shares at Jan. 1, 2024 + 2,000 shares issued on June 15, 2024 – 700 shares repurchased on July 10, 2024).
- Common stock repurchases for 2024 were $11,200. This is taken from Chapter 10 as 700 common shares were repurchased as treasury stock at a cost of $16 per share.
- Cash flows used in operating activities for 2024 were ($77,783).
- Preferred dividends for 2020 were $0.

Note: Round all answers to two decimal places.

Required:

1. Calculate the short-term liquidity ratios for Front Row for 2024.
2. Calculate the debt management ratios for Front Row for 2024.
3. Calculate the asset efficiency ratios for Front Row for 2024.
4. Calculate the profitability ratios for Front Row for 2024.*
5. Calculate the stockholder ratios for Front Row for 2024.

*In computing gross margin, include only the expenses of Cost of Goods Sold and Artist Fee Expense.

1
Appendix

Data Analytics and Accounting Information

All companies collect data and use data analytics to make business decisions.

Every time you perform a Google search, share a photo on Snapchat, or stream a movie on Netflix, data are created. In fact, some people believe that we are at the start of a data revolution, which could be even more transformative for business than the Industrial Revolution. This is because of great advances in machine learning and artificial intelligence. In this new environment, a company's success increasingly depends on its ability to collect, interpret, and generate insights from massive amounts of data.

Because accounting's role is to provide useful information to internal and external users, it is well positioned to use data analytics to help companies gain valuable insights. These insights can help to improve financial reports, identify opportunities for increased operational efficiency, or better manage risks. By interpreting vast amounts of available data, accountants can help managers, investors, creditors, and others make critical business decisions.

WHAT IS DATA ANALYTICS?

Data analytics is the process of analyzing data so that businesses can make decisions more efficiently. It is used in all sorts of businesses and settings. For example, the executive VP and CEO of the Boston Red Sox uses data analytics to increase profits and optimize the sports fan experience.[1] Data analytics is important for accountants because in accounting, our goal is to make business decisions. Data analytics includes many techniques that can be used to learn about the risks and opportunities that businesses face.

Data analytics is helpful only if it can be used to answer important questions. For example, identifying the historical frequencies of uncollectable accounts is important because managers need this information to estimate the allowance for doubtful accounts. Similar questions that managers could answer using data analytics include the following: How much of this month's sales are customers likely to return? And how much is the company likely to spend on warranty repairs? What is the return on investment from a recent marketing campaign? How will upgrading the machines on a production line affect company profits?

In order to successfully use data analytics, accountants need to:

1. understand when and how data analytics can be used to answer business questions;

2. determine whether the data need to be corrected or transformed prior to use;

3. assess the data's reliability, relevance, and completeness;

4. manipulate the data so they are useful;

5. perform data analysis (e.g., look for trends, identify correlations, use data mining or machine learning techniques) to answer questions and draw conclusions; and

6. communicate the results in a timely and useful way.

Data analytics can be descriptive, diagnostic, predictive, or prescriptive. The chart below provides a description and example of each type.

Type	Description	Example
Descriptive	Describes what has happened or summarizes outcomes	Did we meet our sales quota for the month?
Diagnostic	Explains why things happened by trying to understand how variables are related	Is there a relation between the volume of product sold and its appearance in a video with a popular YouTuber?
Predictive	Attempts to predict what will happen in the future	What is the probability of the video going viral, and is this likely to lead to increased product demand?
Prescriptive	Recommends a possible course of action	If the video has a 70% probability of going viral, we should increase production.

1 To learn about the Red Sox's data analytics experience, you can watch the video "Hitting a Home Run with Data Analytics" at https://www.facebook.com/watch/live/?v=467463257216993&ref=watch_permalink.

DATA ANALYTICS EXAMPLE

Managers can use computer systems to collect data about customers, suppliers, and competitors. Large databases containing many customer orders, returns, and payment histories are only helpful when managers can learn something useful from the data. For example, a manager may want to know how much sales will increase if the company allows customers to purchase goods for credit (on account). She may also want to know how frequently customers fail to pay their debts on time and what a customer's payment history can tell the company about the likelihood that the customer will pay in the future.

To answer questions like these, managers need a way to identify how different pieces of information are related. In Chapter 5, we learned how to use the accounts receivable aging method to estimate the allowance for doubtful accounts. For example, managers could estimate that 1% of accounts overdue for less than 15 days would be expected to default. The probability of default would grow as accounts become more overdue, say until at 61 days, when it would be estimated that 30% of the accounts will default. In textbook examples, the default percentages are given, but in the real world, the company's managers need to estimate these percentages. Here, the manager needs to know the relation between the age of an account receivable and the probability of ultimate repayment.

A manager can use data analytics to help make good estimates. For example, she could look back over the past 5 years and identify all cases where customer payments were less than 15 days overdue. Using these cases, she could compute how frequently customers defaulted. She could also perform this process for accounts that were late by different amounts—for example, 16–30 days late, 31–60 days late, and more than 60 days late. The manager could then use these historical frequencies to estimate uncollectable accounts.

More sophisticated data analytics should lead to even more precise estimates. For example, the manager could look at a specific customer's repayment history or at the customer's credit score and use these as additional signals about the collectability of that customer's overdue accounts.

Because large companies can have millions of customers, it's not feasible to manually look through years of sales data, identify cases where customers were late making payments, and review each customer's repayment history. But with a good data analytics system, this information could be available in minutes.

Analysis Using Excel to Calculate FIFO and LIFO Cost

For the following case study problem, students may access the necessary spreadsheets at cengage.com, under the student resources for Financial Accounting, 5e.

LEARNING OBJECTIVES

After completing this case, you should be able to:

1. Analyze the cost of inventory items using the LIFO and FIFO methods.

2. Create "intermediate calculation columns" in Excel to facilitate complex calculations.

3. Create Excel spreadsheets using calculations with absolute references.

4. Create Excel spreadsheets that sort data according to business assumptions.

Summary: In this hands-on case, you will use Excel to analyze inventory cost using the first-in, first-out (FIFO) and last-in, first-out (LIFO) methods.

Case Scenario: You work for an online retail business, Jage's Pages, that purchases and sells Keto cookbooks. Because the company does not have a big warehouse, it does not acquire a large inventory all at once. Instead, it buys more inventory as units are sold. At the end of the month, you need to calculate the inventory cost and the month's cost of goods sold. You can estimate the inventory cost and the cost of goods sold using FIFO or LIFO and decide to figure out what these figures would be using both methods. To do this, you should first create an Excel spreadsheet that can calculate the inventory cost and the cost of goods sold using the FIFO method. Next, do the same thing using the LIFO method, and compare the outcomes from using the two methods.

REQUIREMENTS

CONCEPT QUESTIONS

1. Explain the FIFO and LIFO methods.

2. Explain how you create an "intermediate column" to keep track of numbers such as cumulative numbers needed in further calculations.

3. Explain how to set up Excel calculations using cell references so that you can populate a spreadsheet efficiently. What happens when you copy and paste cell references from one row to the next row?

4. Explain why you may sometimes not want to use relative cell references when copying and pasting but instead use an absolute reference to a specific cell.

5. Explain how to sort a date data field in Excel.

ACTIVITY

You are to build a spreadsheet that can calculate the inventory cost and the cost of goods sold.

Hint: This is a challenging, complex task. No one function in Excel allows you to accomplish this task directly but by working through this case, you will learn how to accomplish this complex task by breaking the problem down into smaller steps. This case will guide you through the steps.

1. In business, you are likely to have so many transactions that you cannot simply calculate everything manually. Using an Excel spreadsheet will allow you to automate the calculations. Before you create calculations in Excel, you should think about the inputs that you will need to solve this problem. You should also list the major steps that you need Excel to perform. After you have thought through the steps, go to cengage.com and locate the student resources for this title. Open the Excel file FIFO_LIFOCaseData.xlsx. Save the file as Lastname_Firstname_FIFO_ LIFOSolution.xlsx (where "Lastname" is your actual last name and "Firstname" is your actual first name). To help you get started, the file already has a list of columns for you to fill out. To accomplish this task, complete the following steps.

2. Perform FIFO analysis: the purchases in the file were entered according to their purchase dates, from oldest to newest.

   a. Sort the layers according to their purchase dates: for FIFO, the oldest purchases should be listed first; for LIFO, the newest purchases should be listed first.

   b. Calculate the purchase cost for each layer.

   c. Calculations using an "intermediate column": to find the cumulative units in inventory, calculate the total number of units purchased up to that purchase date from column D.

   d. Calculations using absolute references and the Excel max function: In column F, calculate the number of units remaining at the end of the month. When the total number of units purchased is less than the number of units sold, the company has sold the entire inventory layer and no more units remain from this layer.

   e. Calculate how many units remain from each layer after the sale.

   f. Calculate the number of units sold from each layer.

   g. Calculate the inventory cost from each layer.

   h. Calculate the cost of goods sold from each layer.

   i. Cost calculations: find total purchase cost, units on hand, total inventory cost, and cost of goods sold. (*Hint:* cost of goods sold = total purchase cost – total inventory cost.)

3. After you complete FIFO, perform LIFO analysis. (*Hint:* You need to sort the data by date first. Then you can perform the same steps as in FIFO.)

4. Compare the results using FIFO and LIFO. What happens to the relative inventory costs and costs of goods sold if the unit cost increases over time?

Analysis Using the Accounts Receivable Aging Method

For the following case study problem, students may access the necessary spreadsheets at cengage.com, under the student resources for Financial Accounting, 5e.

LEARNING OBJECTIVES

After completing this case, you should be able to:

1. Estimate the bad debt expense for the month using the aging method.

2. Create Excel formulas using conditional logic.

3. Create Excel calculations using cell references based on an aging schedule of accounts receivable.

Summary: In this hands-on case, you will use Excel to analyze an aging schedule of accounts receivable. You will use the accounts receivable aging method to find the bad debt expense for the month.

Case scenario: You are working at a gardening center, Payton's Potted Plants, that sells live plants and plant care items to customers on credit and tracks the status of the accounts receivable every month. In order to calculate the ending allowance for doubtful accounts for the month of April, you decide to prepare a spreadsheet. It must estimate the total dollar amount of uncollectible accounts using an analysis of the accounts receivable balance so that you can determine the bad debt expense for April. To understand the receivables' current payment status, you decide to classify the accounts as current, 1–30 days past due, 31–60 days past due, or 60+ days past due. Because there are many customers and you want to be able to reuse and update the spreadsheet in the future, you decide to create a reusable Excel spreadsheet.

REQUIREMENTS

CONCEPT QUESTIONS

1. Explain what bad debt expense is and how it is determined.

2. Explain the aging method for estimating bad debt expense.

3. Explain how to set up Excel calculations using cell references so that you can populate a spreadsheet efficiently. What happens when you copy and paste cell references from one row to the next row?

4. Explain why you may sometimes not want to use Excel cell references to update when copying and pasting but instead have the cell reference remain fixed at a specific cell.

5. Explain conditional logic and provide an example of how to apply it.

6. Explain what to do when you need to combine two conditions in a criterion.

ACTIVITY

Build a spreadsheet that will: (i) show whether each account is current (i.e., not past due) or past due 1–30 days, 31–60 days, or by more than 60 days; (ii) calculate the total for each category; and (iii) calculate the estimated amount of uncollectible accounts for each category.

1. In business, you are likely to have so many transactions that you cannot calculate everything manually. Using an Excel spreadsheet will allow you to automate the calculations. Before you create calculations in Excel, you should think about the inputs that you will need to solve this

problem. You should also list the major steps that you need Excel to perform. After you have thought through the steps, go to cengage.com and locate the student resources for this title. Open the Excel file ARAgingSchedule_CaseData.xlsx. Save the file as Lastname_Firstname_ ARAgingScheduleSolution.xlsx (where "Lastname" is your actual last name and "Firstname" is your actual first name). To help you get started, the file already has a list of columns for you to fill out. To accomplish this task, complete the following steps.

2. Create formulas to find the number of days that each account is past due, where a negative number means that an account is not past due.

3. For each age category, show the customer's account if it is in that category, and show a blank if it is not in that category. As a reminder, the categories are as follows:

   a. Not past due

   b. 1–30 days past due

   c. 31–60 days past due

   d. 61+ days past due

4. Find the total dollar value of accounts receivable for each age category.

5. For each age category, estimate the uncollectible amount.

6. Find the total estimated uncollectible amount.

7. Using this information, calculate the bad debt expense for April.

8. What is the journal entry to record the bad debt expense?

2
Appendix

Investments

After studying Appendix 2, you should be able to:

1. Explain the accounting for debt investments.

2. Explain the accounting for equity investments.

3. Describe accounting for business combinations.

Khakimullin Aleksandr/Shutterstock.com

Although companies can invest in virtually any asset (such as land), we will concentrate on the most common investments—buying equity or debt securities.

- *Equity Securities*: An **equity security** represents an ownership interest in another company. Although most equity securities are common stock, preferred stock is also an equity security.
- *Debt Securities*: A **debt security** represents a creditor relationship with another company. Debt securities include corporate bonds, U.S. treasury securities, and municipal bonds.

A company buys debt or equity securities with either short- or long-term investment horizons. As discussed in Chapter 4, short-term investment horizons are typically attempts to earn greater returns with cash that is not immediately needed for operations. Such "excess cash" results when cash inflows are not evenly distributed throughout the year. For example, many retail businesses, such as **Best Buy**, **American Eagle Outfitters**, and **Nordstrom**, collect significantly more cash around Christmas than during other times of the year. Consequently, they may need to save some of the cash collected at Christmas to meet operational needs during times of lower cash inflows. Other companies, such as banks, mutual funds, and insurance companies, buy and sell securities to profit from day-to-day changes in security prices.

Companies also attempt to maximize returns over long-term investment horizons. For insurance companies, such as **State Farm**, and mutual funds, such as **Fidelity**, for example, long-term investment income generated from debt and equity securities is a core part of operations. Or, companies may accumulate capital for future expansion to avoid having to borrow or sell additional stock. Companies may also invest in equity securities to establish long-term relationships, obtain significant influence, or control the other company. For example, to assure itself of access to high quality raw materials, a company may purchase the common stock of a supplier—the more common stock purchased, the more influence that can be exerted.

CLASSIFYING AND ACCOUNTING FOR DEBT INVESTMENTS

OBJECTIVE 1

Explain the accounting for debt investments.

At acquisition, a company classifies debt securities into one of the following three categories:

- **Held-to-maturity securities** are debt investments that management intends to hold until the debt contract requires the borrower to repay the debt in its entirety. These securities are valued at an amortized cost basis.
- **Trading securities** are debt investments that management intends to sell in the near term. Trading securities are bought and sold frequently with the intent to profit on short-term changes in price. They are valued using the fair value method, with any changes in fair value recognized in income. Trading securities are always classified as current assets on the balance sheet.
- **Available-for-sale securities** are debt investments that management intends to sell in the future, but not necessarily in the near term. Therefore, debt investments that don't warrant inclusion as trading securities or held-to-maturity securities are considered available-for-sale. These investments are valued using the fair value method; however, any changes in fair value are recognized in other comprehensive income. On the balance sheet, available-for-sale securities are classified as current or noncurrent assets depending on whether they expect to be sold within 1 year or one operating cycle, whichever is longer.

The accounting for debt investments is discussed in the following sections.

AMORTIZED COST METHOD

Investments in debt securities that are classified as held-to-maturity are accounted for by the **amortized cost method** (also called *the cost method*). Investments are recorded at cost when acquired, and interest income is recognized with appropriate amortization of premiums and discounts. In other words, the amortized cost method closely parallels accounting for long-term liabilities, which is described in Chapter 9. EXAMPLE A2.1 illustrates the accounting for investments in held-to-maturity investments.

EXAMPLE A2.1   ACCOUNTING FOR HELD-TO-MATURITY INVESTMENTS

On January 1, Redbird Corporation purchases 10-year, 5% bonds with a face value of $100,000 for $96,000 cash. Any discounts or premiums are amortized on a straight-line basis. The fair value of the investment at December 31 is $98,000.

Required:

1. Prepare the journal entry to record the purchase of the investment.

2. Prepare the journal entry to record the receipt of the first two interest payments.

Solution:

1.

				Assets	= Liabilities +	Stockholders' Equity
Jan. 1	Investments—Held to Maturity	96,000		▲		
	Cash		96,000	▼		

2. The investment pays interest of $2,500 ($100,000 × 5% × 6/12) every 6 months, and the amortization of the discount is $200 {[($100,000 − $96,000)/10 years] × 6/12} every 6 months. The following entries would be made to record receipt of the first two interest payments:

				Assets	= Liabilities +	Stockholders' Equity
June 30	Cash	2,500		▲		
	Investments—Held-to-Maturity	200		▲		
	Interest Income		2,700			▲

				Assets	= Liabilities +	Stockholders' Equity
Dec. 31	Cash	2,500		▲		
	Investments—Held-to-Maturity	200		▲		
	Interest Income		2,700			▲

Reporting in the Financial Statements On the balance sheet, held-to-maturity securities are classified as noncurrent assets unless the date of maturity is within 1 year or one operating cycle, whichever is longer. Any interest income is reported in the "Other Income and Expenses" section of the income statement.

As shown in Example A2.1, at December 31, Redbird's investment account is $96,400 ($96,000 + $400 amortized discount). The financial statements would report this investment as:

Redbird Corporation Partial Balance Sheet December 31	
Noncurrent assets:	
Investments (held-to-maturity), net of unamortized discount	$96,400

Redbird Corporation Partial Income Statement For the year ended December 31	
Other Income and Expenses	
Interest income	$5,400

Because the market value of Redbird's investment is $1,600 ($98,000 − $96,400) more than its book value, there is an unrealized gain of $1,600. The rationale for not recognizing unrealized gains or losses on held-to-maturity investments is that changes in market value do not affect the amount that is realized from such investments. If securities are held to maturity, the amount that is realized is the face value—as determined by the debt agreement.

FAIR VALUE METHOD

For all debt investments classified as trading or available-for-sale securities, the initial purchase of the investment is recorded at cost. At each subsequent reporting date, the **fair value method** is used to account for the investment. This means the investment is valued at the price for which the investor could sell the asset in an orderly transaction between market participants. For most investments, this price is a quoted price in an active market, but if no active market exists, other techniques are used to estimate the fair market value. EXAMPLE A2.2 illustrates the accounting for investments in trading and available-for-sale securities.

EXAMPLE A2.2 ACCOUNTING FOR TRADING AND AVAILABLE-FOR-SALE INVESTMENTS

On August 1, Redbird Corporation made the following purchases of securities:

Security	Type	Classification	Cost
Metzler Design	Debt	Trading	5,000
IMG	Debt	Trading	15,000
Total Trading Securities			**$20,000**
Alabama Co.	Debt	AFS	$ 8,000
Mutare Inc.	Debt	AFS	7,000
Total Available-for-Sale Securities			**$15,000**

During the remainder of the year, the following occurred:

- On December 20, Redbird sold the IMG investment for $15,600 cash.
- On December 31, interest of $1,500 was received from the remaining investments.

CONTINUED

EXAMPLE A2.2   ACCOUNTING FOR TRADING AND AVAILABLE-FOR-SALE INVESTMENTS *(CONTINUED)*

Requirement

1. Prepare the journal entry to record the purchase of the investment.

2. Prepare the journal entry to record the sale of the investment.

3. Prepare the journal entry to record the receipt of interest.

Solution

1.

Date	Account and Explanation	Debit	Credit	Assets	= Liabilities +	Stockholders' Equity
Aug. 1	Investments—Trading Securities	20,000		▲		
	Investments—Available-for-Sale					
	Securities	15,000		▲		
	Cash		35,000	▼		

2.

Date	Account and Explanation	Debit	Credit	Assets	= Liabilities +	Stockholders' Equity
Dec. 20	Cash	15,600		▲		
	Investments—Trading Securities		15,000	▼		
	Gain on Sale of Investments		600			▲

3.

Date	Account and Explanation	Debit	Credit	Assets	= Liabilities +	Stockholders' Equity
Dec. 31	Cash	1,500		▲		
	Interest Income		1,500			▲

Recognition of Fair Value   On the balance sheet, both trading and available-for-sale securities are recorded at fair value. The investments must be written up or down to fair value at the balance sheet date (often called "marking to market"). The change in fair value results in **unrealized gains** and/or **unrealized losses**. EXAMPLE A2.3 illustrates the recognition of fair value trading and available-for-sale investments.

EXAMPLE A2.3   RECOGNIZING CHANGES IN FAIR VALUE

Assume that Redbird reports the following information at December 31:

Security	Classification	Acquisition Cost	Market Value at 12/31	Difference
Metzler Design	Trading	5,000	4,200	
Total Trading Securities		**$ 5,000**	**$ 4,200**	(800)
Alabama Co.	AFS	$ 8,000	$ 8,600	
Mutare Inc.	AFS	7,000	6,500	
Total Available-for-Sale Securities		**$15,000**	**$15,100**	100

Required

1. Prepare the journal entry to record the fair value of the available-for-sale investments.

2. Prepare the journal entry to record the fair value of the trading investments.

Solution

Date	Account and Explanation	Debit	Credit	Assets	= Liabilities +	Stockholders' Equity
Dec. 31	Allowance to Adjust Available-for-Sale Securities to Market	100		▲		
	Unrealized Gain (Loss) on Available-for-Sale Securities		100			▲

The unrealized gain or loss related to the investment in available-for-sale securities is reported in the "Accumulated Other Comprehensive Income" portion of stockholders' equity.

Date	Account and Explanation	Debit	Credit	Assets	= Liabilities +	Stockholders' Equity
Dec. 31	Unrealized Gain (Loss) on Trading Securities	800				▼
	Allowance to Adjust Trading Securities to Market		800	▼		

The unrealized gain or loss related to the investment in trading securities is reported on the income statement.

The allowance accounts are valuation accounts containing the unrealized gains and losses for the Available-for-Sale and Trading investment portfolios, respectively. Valuation accounts are used to record changes in the fair values of the investments so that the investment accounts (both Available-for-Sale and Trading investments) reflect the original cost. At the balance sheet date, the allowance accounts are adjusted to reflect the current amount of unrealized gain or loss in the investment portfolio. On the balance sheet, the allowance accounts are netted with the respective investment accounts (added if the allowance has a debit balance and subtracted if it has a credit balance) to report the investments at fair value as:

Redbird Corporation Partial Balance Sheet December 31		
Current assets:		
Trading securities, at cost	$ 5,000	
Less: Allowance to adjust trading securities to market	(800)	
Trading securities, at market*		$ 4,200
Noncurrent assets:		
Available-for-sale securities, at cost	$15,000	
Add: Allowance to adjust available-for-sale securities to market	100	
Available-for-sale securities, at market*		$15,100
Stockholders' equity:		
Accumulated other comprehensive income		$ 100

* While trading securities will always be classified as current assets, available-for-sale securities are classified as current or noncurrent assets depending on whether they will be sold within 1 year or one operating cycle, whichever is longer.

Redbird Corporation Partial Income Statement For the year ended December 31	
Other income:	
Interest income	$1,500
Other loss:	
Unrealized loss on trading securities	$ 100

To summarize, the only difference in the accounting for trading and available-for-sale securities is that unrealized gains and losses affect the financial statements differently:

- Unrealized gains and losses for investments in trading securities are included on the income statement and, thus, flow into retained earnings.
- Unrealized gains and losses for investments in available-for-sale securities, on the other hand, are *not* included on the income statement. Instead, they are included as part of "accumulated other comprehensive income," a separate account in stockholders' equity.

OBJECTIVE **2**

Explain the accounting for equity investments.

ACCOUNTING FOR EQUITY INVESTMENTS

Accounting for investments in equity securities differs depending upon the amount of common stock owned. The difference exists because of the nature of the ownership interest.

- *Passive*: If an investor owns less than 20% of the common stock, the investment is generally considered to be passive; that is, the investor is not attempting to exert influence over the operating and financial policies of the investee. In this case, the *fair value method* is used.
- *Significant Influence*: If the investor owns 20% to 50% of the outstanding common stock, then the investor is assumed to possess significant influence over the operating and financial policies of the investee. In this case, the *equity method* is used to account for the investment.

- *Control*: If the investor owns over 50% of the outstanding common stock, the investor is deemed to have control over the operating and financial policies of the investee. The investor is then called the **parent** and the investee is called a **subsidiary**. In these cases, the subsidiary's financial statements are combined with the parent's into a single set of **consolidated financial statements**.

Each of the methods for accounting for equity investments in will be discussed in the sections that follow.

PASSIVE INVESTMENTS: FAIR VALUE METHOD

Passive equity investments are accounted for using the fair value method. The accounting for these investments mirrors the accounting for trading securities. That is, the investment is initially recorded at cost and subsequently written up or down to fair value with any unrealized gains or unrealized losses included in income. EXAMPLE A2.4 illustrates the accounting for passive equity investments.

EXAMPLE A2.4   RECORDING PASSIVE EQUITY INVESTMENTS

On January 1, Bluebird Company purchased the following equity securities:

- 100 shares of common stock of Aaron Inc. for $5,000
- 500 shares of common stock of Goldman Company for $10,000

These investments are considered passive. In addition, on August 30, Bluebird received cash dividends of $300. The fair value of the investments at December 31 is: Aaron Inc.—$55 per share; Goldman Company—$18 per share.

Required:
1. Prepare the journal entry to record the purchase of the equity investments.
2. Prepare the journal entry to record the receipt of dividends.
3. Prepare the journal entry to record the fair value of the equity investments at December 31.

Solution:
1.

Date	Account and Explanation	Debit	Credit	Assets	= Liabilities +	Stockholders' Equity
Jan. 1	Investment in Equity Securities	15,000		▲		
	Cash		15,000	▼		

2.

Date	Account and Explanation	Debit	Credit	Assets	= Liabilities +	Stockholders' Equity
Aug. 30	Cash	300		▲		
	Dividend Income		300			▲

3. The fair value of the equity investments at December 31 is $13,500 [(100 shares + $45 per share) + (500 shares + $18 per share)]. The decrease in fair value of $1,500 ($15,000 − $13,500) is recorded as follows:

Date	Account and Explanation	Debit	Credit	Assets	= Liabilities +	Stockholders' Equity
Dec. 31	Unrealized Gain (Loss) on Equity Securities	1,500		▲		
	Investment in Equity Securities		1,500			▲

Note that the investment account is adjusted directly to fair value and no valuation account is used.

Passive equity investments are reported at fair value on the balance sheet. Any unrealized gains or losses are reported in "Other Income and Expenses" on the income statement.

Bluebird Company Partial Balance Sheet December 31	
Current assets:	
Investment in equity securities, at fair value	$13,500

Bluebird Company Partial Income Statement For the year ending December 31	
Other income and expenses:	
Dividend income	$ 300
Unrealized gain (loss) on equity securities	1,500

SIGNIFICANT INFLUENCE: EQUITY METHOD

The fair value method should be used when equity investments are considered passive. However, when the investor possesses significant influence over the operating and financial policies of the investee (20% to 50% common stock ownership), the investor must use the *equity method* to account for the investment. The **equity method** requires an investor to recognize income when it is reported as earned by the investee, rather than when dividends accrue. The earlier recognition of investment income and loss under the equity method is consistent with the close relationship between the investor and investee. EXAMPLE A2.5 illustrates the accounting for investments under the equity method.

EXAMPLE A2.5   APPLYING THE EQUITY METHOD

On January 1, Romanov Inc. purchased 25% of the common stock of on its major suppliers—Korsgard Mining—for $4,000,000 cash. On November 1, Korsgard declared and paid a cash dividend of $60,000. For the year ending December 31, Korsgard reported net income of $440,000.

Required:
1. Prepare the entry that Romanov should make to record its purchase of Korsgard common stock.
2. Prepare the entry that Romanov should make to record the receipt of dividends.
3. Prepare the entry that Romanov should make to record its share of Korsgard's net income.

Solution:
1. The investment is recorded at cost as follows:

Date	Account and Explanation	Debit	Credit	Assets	= Liabilities +	Stockholders' Equity
Jan. 1	Investments—Equity Method	4,000,000		▲		
	Cash		4,000,000	▼		

2. Dividends received are treated as a return of investment. Therefore, the investment account is reduced for Romanov's proportionate share of the dividend, which is $15,000 ($60,000 × 25%).

Date	Account and Explanation	Debit	Credit	Assets	=	Liabilities	+	Stockholders' Equity
Nov. 1	Cash	15,000		▲				
	Investments—Equity Method		15,000	▼				

3. Under the equity method, the investor recognizes income when income is earned by the investee. Thus, Romanov's proportionate share of Korsgard's net income is $110,000 ($440,0000 × 25%).

Date	Account and Explanation	Debit	Credit	Assets	=	Liabilities	+	Stockholders' Equity
Dec. 31	Investments—Equity Method	110,000		▲				
	Investment Income—Equity Method		110,000	▼				

Equity method investments are carried on the balance sheet as:

Acquisition Cost + Investor's Share of the Investee's Income (Loss)
− Investor's Share of the Investee's Dividends

Notice that the investment account is *not* adjusted for changes in the fair market value of the common stock. Romanov would account for its investment in Korsgard as follows:

Investments—Equity Method (Korsgard Mining)

Purchase of Korsgard stock, Jan. 1	4,000,000		Receipt of Korsgard
		15,000	dividends, Nov. 1
Redbird's share of Korsgard net income, Dec. 31	110,000		
	4,095,000		

Romanov Corporation
Partial Balance Sheet
December 31

Noncurrent assets:	
Investments—equity method (Korsgard)	$4,095,000

Romanov Corporation
Partial Income Statement
For the year ending December 31

Investment income—equity method (Korsgard)	$110,000

One advantage of the equity method over the fair value method is that it prevents an investor from manipulating its own income by exerting influence over the amount and timing of investee dividends.

CONTROL: CONSOLIDATED FINANCIAL STATEMENTS

If the investor holds enough common stock to control the investee (50% or more common stock ownership), then the two corporations are no longer separate reporting entities. In such cases, the investor (referred to as the parent) must prepare consolidated financial statements, which combine its financial statements with those of the investee (referred to as the subsidiary) of the two corporations as if they were a single company.

To prepare consolidated financial statements, the separate financial statements of the parent and subsidiary are combined as follows:

- The effect of any intercompany transactions are eliminated. Intercompany transactions are transactions between the parent and the subsidiary. These must be eliminated because the consolidated financial statements are, in effect, the financial statements of a single entity.
- The parent's investment account is eliminated against the subsidiary's equity accounts.

To illustrate the preparation of consolidated balance sheets, consider the following situation in which a parent owns all the outstanding stock of its subsidiary.[1]

Exhibit A2.1 presents a **consolidation worksheet** that is used to prepare the consolidated balance sheet. The individual balance sheets for the parent and subsidiary are listed in the two left columns of the worksheet. Consolidation adjustments are entered into the third column. The amounts in the fourth column can be computed by adding the first two columns and the adjustments. For purposes of this illustration, it is assumed that there are no intercompany transactions.

EXHIBIT A2.1	Worksheet for Preparing the Consolidated Balance Sheet				

| | | | Adjustments | | |
	Parent	Subsidiary	Debit	Credit	Consolidated
Assets:					
Current assets	$ 9,250,000	$ 700,000			$ 9,950,000
Investment in subsidiary	2,750,000			2,750,000	—
Property, plant, and equipment	68,000,000	2,300,000			70,300,000
Total assets	$80,000,000	$3,000,000			$80,250,000
Liabilities	$10,000,000	$ 250,000			$10,250,000
Stockholders' equity:					
Common stock	40,000,000	1,000,000	1,000,000		40,000,000
Retained earnings	30,000,000	1,750,000	1,750,000		30,000,000
Total liabilities and stockholders' equity	$80,000,000	$3,000,000			$80,250,000

As you can see in Exhibit A2.1, the consolidation of these two balance sheets eliminates the parent's Investment in Subsidiary account, as well as eliminating the subsidiary's Common Stock and Retained Earnings accounts.

Just as a consolidation worksheet was used to prepare the consolidated balance sheet, a similar worksheet is prepared for the consolidated income statement. The preparation of a consolidated income statement is discussed in advanced accounting texts.

---

1   Many large corporations have a complex network of many subsidiaries. However, for the sake of simplicity, the examples here discuss a two-corporation structure involving one parent and one subsidiary.

Reporting a Noncontrolling Interest Consolidation is required when a parent acquires between 50% and 100% of the subsidiary's stock. Any voting stock not held by the parent is called the **noncontrolling interest**, and the holders of such shares are called noncontrolling stockholders (or minority stockholders). However, even when the parent owns less than 100% of the subsidiary's stock, 100% of the subsidiary's assets and liabilities are included in the consolidated balance sheet. In other words, if the parent controls the subsidiary, it controls *all* of the subsidiary's assets and liabilities.

For example, assume that the parent had acquired only 80% of the subsidiary. The consolidated total assets still would have been $80,250,000 because the parent controls all of the assets of the subsidiary. However, the noncontrolling interest would have been $550,000 [20% × ($1,000,000 + $1,750,000)], and this amount must be shown as a component of stockholders' equity on the consolidated balance sheet. Further, the consolidated income statement would show 100% of Sub's revenues and expenses, but 20% of net income would be deducted as belonging to the noncontrolling interest.

SUMMARY

Exhibit A2.2 provides a summary of accounting for debt and equity investments.

Accounting for Investments in Debt and Equity Securities			EXHIBIT A2.2

Investments in Debt Securities	Method	Reporting of Interest Income	Reporting of Unrealized Gains and Losses
1. Held-to-maturity	Amortized cost	Net Income	Not recognized
2. Trading	Fair value	Net Income	Net income
3. Available-for-sale	Fair value	Net Income	Other comprehensive income

Investments in Equity Securities	Method	Reporting of Dividends	Reporting of Unrealized Gains and Losses
1. Passive (own <20% of the stock)	Fair value	Net Income	Net income
2. Significant influence (own 20% to 50% of the stock)	Equity	Reduces investment account	Not recognized
3. Control (own >50% of the stock)	Equity plus consolidation	Eliminated	Not recognized

BUSINESS COMBINATIONS

OBJECTIVE 3

Describe accounting for business combinations.

Any transaction or set of transactions that brings together two or more previously separate entities to form a single accounting entity is called a **business combination**. Business combinations take many forms. Some, like parent–subsidiary relationship described in the previous section, involve the acquisition of another corporation's stock in exchange for cash. Others involve the acquisition of another corporation's stock with the parent's own common stock. In either case, these are called **stock acquisitions** because the stock of the other corporation is being acquired. The parent could also purchase some or all of the assets of the other corporation. This is referred to as an **asset acquisition**. In this case, the two entities actually become a single legal entity.

Business combinations usually, but not always, transfer ownership of the acquired business entity from one stockholder group to another. In general, purchased assets are recorded at current cost, which is measured as the fair value of the cash and other consideration given up to acquire the asset. Thus, a purchased asset is recorded at its current value to the purchaser, without regard to its recorded value to the seller. Applying this logic to a business combination, a purchased company must be recorded at the value of the cash and other consideration given by the acquiring company.

To illustrate, consider the acquisition of all the assets and liabilities (i.e., an asset acquisition) of Landron Bottling Works by CactusCo for $12,000,000. With the approval of Landron's stockholders and creditors, Landron transfers all of its assets and liabilities to CactusCo and distributes the cash to Landron's stockholders. On the acquisition date, Landron's stockholders' equity was $6,500,000. CactusCo determines that Landron's liabilities of $1,000,000 are correctly valued, but its identifiable assets have a fair value of $3,800,000 more than their book value of $7,500,000. Thus, the acquisition cost exceeds the fair value of the net assets (assets minus liabilities) acquired by $1,700,000:

Acquisition cost			$12,000,000
Current value of identifiable net assets acquired:			
Book value of assets acquired	$7,500,000		
Adjustment to current value	3,800,000	$11,300,000	
Less:			
Book value of liabilities acquired	$1,000,000		
Adjustment to current value	0	(1,000,000)	(10,300,000)
Excess of acquisition cost over current value (goodwill)			$ 1,700,000

The excess of acquisition cost over the fair value of Landron's identifiable net assets is recorded as goodwill. **Goodwill** is an intangible asset arising from attributes that are not separable from the business—such as customer satisfaction, product quality, skilled employees, and business location. CactusCo's recording of the acquisition would be recorded with following journal entry:

Account and Explanation	Debit	Credit	Assets	=	Liabilities	+	Stockholders' Equity
Assets (various accounts)	11,300,000		▲				
Goodwill	1,700,000		▲				
Liabilities (various accounts)		1,000,000			▲		
Cash		12,000,000	▼				

This entry assumes that Landron goes out of existence as a corporation. If, instead of selling its net assets to CactusCo, Landron stockholders sell all their stock (as in a stock acquisition) to CactusCo, Landron will continue as a legal entity and the journal entry would be as follows:

Account and Explanation	Debit	Credit	Assets	=	Liabilities	+	Stockholders' Equity
Investments—Equity Method	12,000,000		▲				
Cash		12,000,000	▼				

In this case, CactusCo must also consolidate Landron's financial statements, substituting the detailed assets (including goodwill) and liabilities for the investment account. The financial statements for a 100% asset acquisition will be identical to the consolidated financial statements for a 100% stock acquisition.

REVIEW CENTER

KEY TAKEAWAYS

- Investments in debt securities are classified three ways:
  - Held-to-maturity securities are those investments that management intends to hold until the maturity date of the debt.
  - Trading securities are those investments that management intends to sell in the near term.
  - Available-for-sale investments are all securities that don't warrant inclusion as trading securities or available for sale securities.
- Held-to-maturity securities are accounted for at amortized cost.
- Trading and available-for-sale securities are accounted for at fair value.
  - For trading securities, any unrealized gain or loss is recognized in income.
  - For available-for-sale securities, any unrealized gain or loss is recognized in other comprehensive income.

LO1. Explain the accounting for debt investments.

KEY TERMS

Amortized cost method, 778
Available-for-sale securities, 779
Debt security, 777
Equity security, 777
Fair value method, 779

Held-to-maturity securities, 777
Trading securities, 777
Unrealized gains, 780
Unrealized losses, 780

EXAMPLES

EXAMPLE A2.1 Accounting for held-to-maturity investments, page 778

EXAMPLE A2.2 Accounting for trading and available-for-sale investments, page 779–780

EXAMPLE A2.3 Recognizing changes in fair value, page 781

KEY TAKEAWAYS

- All equity investments in which the investee owns less than 20% of the common stock are accounted for using the fair value method. Under this method, any unrealized gains or losses are recognized in income.
- The equity method is used for equity securities in which 20% or more of the outstanding common stock is owned. Under this method, an investor recognizes income as it is earned by the investee, and any dividends received are treated as a return of investment.
- Investments in equity securities in which more than 50% of the outstanding common stock is owned are required to issue consolidated financial statements.

LO2. Explain the accounting for equity investments.

KEY TERMS

Consolidated financial statements, 783   Noncontrolling interest, 787
Consolidation worksheet, 786   Parent, 783
Equity method, 784   Subsidiary, 783

EXAMPLES

> **EXAMPLE A2.4**   Recording passive equity investments, page 783
>
> **EXAMPLE A2.5**   Applying the equity method, page 784–785

LO3. Describe the accounting for business combinations.

KEY TAKEAWAYS

- Business combinations can occur through either an asset or stock acquisition.
- A business combination is recorded at the cost of the acquisition, without regard to the seller's book value.
- The excess of acquisition cost over the current value of identifiable net assets is recorded as goodwill.

KEY TERMS

Asset acquisition, 787   Goodwill, 788
Business combination, 787   Stock acquisition, 788

APPLYING KNOWLEDGE

DISCUSSION QUESTIONS

OBJECTIVE 1

1. Describe the three classifications that are possible for investments in debt securities.
2. Describe the amortized cost method of accounting for investments. Under which circumstances should it be used?
3. What event triggers the recognition of investment income under the amortized cost method? Under the fair value method? Under the equity method?

OBJECTIVE 1 2

4. Describe the fair value method of accounting for investments. Under which circumstances should it be used?
5. How do available-for-sale securities differ from trading securities?
6. What is the allowance to adjust short-term investments to market, and why is it used?

OBJECTIVE 2

7. Describe the equity method of accounting for investments. Under which circumstances should it be used?
8. How does the equity method discourage the manipulation of net income by investors?
9. Define the terms *parent* and *subsidiary*.
10. What is noncontrolling interest and where is it reported on the consolidated balance sheet?

11. How does the consolidated balance sheet differ from the balance sheet of the parent?

12. Why is it necessary to eliminate transactions between the parent and subsidiary in consolidation?

13. What is the difference between an asset acquisition and a stock acquisition?

OBJECTIVE 3

14. What is goodwill, and how is it calculated?

MULTIPLE-CHOICE QUESTIONS

A2-1 Investments in equity securities are deemed to be "passive" if:
 a. less than 20% of the firm's stock is owned.
 b. between 20% and 50% of the firm's stock is owned.
 c. between 50% and 100% of the firm's stock is owned.
 d. 100% of the firm's stock is owned.

OBJECTIVE 2

A2-2 Debt investments that management intends to sell in the future, but not necessarily in the near term, are called:
 a. available-for-sale securities.
 b. trading securities.
 c. debt securities.
 d. stock securities.

OBJECTIVE 1

A2-3 Which of the following is a reason businesses purchase securities?
 a. To save (and earn returns on) money from uneven cash flows
 b. To diversify risk
 c. To profit from changes in day-to-day security prices
 d. All of the above

A2-4 Which of the following terms is not used for debt securities?
 a. Trading securities
 b. Held-to-maturity securities
 c. Available-for-sale securities
 d. Fair value securities

A2-5 How are held-to-maturity securities valued?
 a. Historical cost
 b. Amortized cost
 c. Fair market value
 d. Amortized fair value

A2-6 The Boss Inc. reported an unrealized gain *on its income statement* due to appreciation in the stock price of AMW Corp. How much of AMW does The Boss own, and how has The Boss classified this investment?
 a. Owns 35%, trading security
 b. Owns 18%, available-for-sale security
 c. Owns 9%, trading security
 d. Owns 12%, equity security

OBJECTIVE 2

A2-7 EMK Corp. is holding two bonds to maturity, both of which have a book value of $132,000. At the end of the fiscal year, the fair market value of Bond A is $118,000, and the fair market value of Bond B is $136,000. What is the unrealized gain or loss reported on the financial statements on these two bonds?
 a. Unrealized gain of $4,000
 b. Unrealized loss of $10,000
 c. Unrealized loss of $14,000
 d. No unrealized gain or loss is reported

OBJECTIVE 1

Refer to the following information for Multiple-Choice Questions A2-8 and A2-9:
Shackley Inc. owns three available-for-sale debt securities which have yielded the following fiscal year end results:
A. Interest income: $350
B. Gain on sale: $2,000
C. Unrealized loss: $600

A2-8   Refer to the information for Shackley above. Which of these are reported on
Shackley's income statement?

a. B only
b. A and B

c. A and C
d. B and C

A2-9   Refer to the information for Shackley above. Assume that one of the securities was
solely responsible for the $600 unrealized loss and was responsible for $150 of the
interest income. If Shackley bought that security for $3,500, what is the value of the
security on the year end balance sheet?

a. $2,900
b. $3,050

c. $3,500
d. $3,650

OBJECTIVE ▶2◀   **A2-10** JFK Inc. buys 30% of the shares outstanding for KLN Company. What account will
JFK debit?

a. Investments—Equity Method
b. Investments

c. Trading Securities
d. Available-for-Sale Securities

A2-11 Whopper Corporation owns a 40% interest in BigMac Corporation, which it
purchased for $2.5 million. During fiscal year 2020, BigMac paid cash dividends
of $50,000 and reported net income of $700,000. What is the value of Whopper's
investment in BigMac reported on its 2020 balance sheet?

a. $3,150,000
b. $2,760,000

c. $2,500,000
d. $2,450,000

OBJECTIVE ▶1◀   **A2-12** When the market value of a company's available-for-sale securities is lower than its
cost, the difference should be:

a. shown as a liability.
b. shown as a valuation allowance added to the historical cost of the investments.
c. shown as a valuation allowance subtracted from the historical cost of the
investments.
d. No entry is made, the securities are shown at historical cost.

OBJECTIVE ▶2◀   **A2-13** What account title will *not* appear on consolidated financial statements?

a. Investment in MJK Corporation (35% ownership)
b. Inventory
c. Investment in EBL Corporation (80% ownership)
d. Common Stock

A2-14 Consolidated financial statements are required:

a. only when 100% of the common stock of another corporation is owned.
b. when over 50% of the common stock of another corporation is owned.
c. only when significant influence or control can be exerted over another company.
d. whenever the commons stock of another corporation is owned.

A2-15 Assume a parent has total assets of $6,000,000 and a subsidiary has total assets of
$4,000,000. If the parent owns 70% of the subsidiary's common stock, what amount
of total assets will be reported on the consolidated balance sheet?

a. $10,000,000
b. $7,000,000

c. $6,000,000
d. $0, consolidation is not necessary

OBJECTIVE ▶3◀   **A2-16** Goodwill is calculated as the excess of the cost of an acquired company over the:

a. book value of net assets acquired.
b. fair value of assets acquired.
c. book value of identifiable net assets acquired.
d. fair value of identifiable net assets acquired.

EXERCISES

Exercise A2-17 Matching Accounting Methods and Investments

OBJECTIVE ‹2›

Consider the following accounting methods for long-term investments:

a. Amortized cost method

c. Equity method

b. Fair value method

d. Consolidation of parent and subsidiary

Required:

Match one or more of these methods with each of the investments described below:

1. Mueller Inc. owns 75% of Johnston Corporation's outstanding common stock.
2. Anderson Inc. owns 25% of Peterson Corporation's outstanding common stock.
3. Wixon Corporation owns 12% of the outstanding common stock of Gilman Inc.
4. Kohler Corporation holds a $40,000 long-term note receivable from Bennett Inc., a major customer. Kohler expects to sell the note within the next 2 or 3 years.
5. Janis Products Inc. holds $200,000 in Gibson Manufacturing bonds. Janis plans to hold these until they mature.

Exercise A2-18 Equity Securities

OBJECTIVE ‹2›

Pear Investments invests in securities classified as trading securities. During the year, it entered into the following transactions:

Purchased 20,000 shares of ABC common stock at $38 per share
Purchased 32,000 shares of XYZ common stock at $17 per share

At December 31, ABC common stock was trading at $39.50 per share and XYZ common stock was trading at $16.50 per share.

Required:

1. Prepare the necessary adjusting entry to value the equity securities at fair market value at December 31.
2. **CONCEPTUAL CONNECTION** What is the income statement effect of this adjusting entry?

Exercise A2-19 Available-for-Sale Securities

OBJECTIVE ‹1›

Tolland Financial invests in securities classified as available-for- sale. During the year, it entered into the following available-for-sale security transactions:

Purchased debt securities of DTR for $500,000
Purchased debt securities of MJO for $968,000

At December 31, the DTR debt securities were trading at $520,000 and the MJO debt securities are trading for $950,000.

Required:

1. Prepare the necessary adjusting entry to value the available-for-sale securities at fair market value.
2. **CONCEPTUAL CONNECTION** What is the income statement effect of this adjusting entry?

Exercise A2-20 Allowance for Available-for-Sale Securities

OBJECTIVE ‹1›

McCarthy Corporation's allowance to reduce available-for-sale securities to market has a $7,200 credit balance on January 1. The market value of the available-for-sale portfolio at January 1 and December 31, are $120,000 and $117,000, respectively.

Required:

Prepare the adjusting entry, if any, to adjust the allowance at year end.

OBJECTIVE **1**

Exercise A2-21 Adjusting the Allowance to Adjust Trading Securities to Market

Caesar Corporation has the following information for its portfolio of trading securities at the end of the past 4 years:

Date	Portfolio Cost	Portfolio Market Value
12/31/2021	$162,300	$153,800
12/31/2022	109,600	106,200
12/31/2023	148,900	151,300
12/31/2024	139,000	138,700

Required:

1. Prepare the journal entries, if necessary, to adjust the allowance account at the end of 2022, 2023, and 2024.
2. **CONCEPTUAL CONNECTION** What is the income statement effect of the 2024 entry?
3. **CONCEPTUAL CONNECTION** How would your answer to Requirement 2 change if this was an available-for-sale portfolio?

OBJECTIVE **2**

Exercise A2-22 Investments in Equity Securities

Williams Corporation acquired the following equity securities during the year:

April 9: 200 shares of Southwestern Company common stock	$14,600
June 30: 500 shares of Montgomery Products common stock	14,500

Williams's investment in both of these companies is passive. On August 30, Williams received a dividend of $1.20 per share from the Southwestern Company, Williams also received a dividend of $1.80 per share from Montgomery Products on October 10. At December 31, the Southwestern stock has a market value of $75 per share, and the Montgomery stock has a market value of $25 per share.

Required:

1. Prepare entries for Williams's journal to record these two investments and the receipt of the dividends.
2. Calculate the market value of Williams's short-term investment portfolio at December 31.
3. Prepare the necessary adjusting entry at December 31.
4. How would these securities be disclosed on the December 31 balance sheet? Assume that Williams expects to sell the investment in the next year.

OBJECTIVE **2**

Exercise A2-23 Fair Value and Equity Methods

Nadal Corporation purchased 10,000 shares of Cutler Inc.'s common stock, on January 1, for $100,000. During the year, Cutler declared and paid cash dividends to Nadal in the amount of $8,000. Nadal's share of Cutler's net income for the year was $12,400. At December 31, the fair value of 10,000 shares of Cutler's common stock was $120,000. This is Nadal's only investment.

Required:

1. Assume that Cutler has 75,000 shares of common stock outstanding. What journal entries will Nadal make during the year relative to this investment?
2. Assume that Cutler has 40,000 shares of common stock outstanding. What journal entries will Nadal make during the year relative to this investment?

OBJECTIVE **2**

Exercise A2-24 Fair Value Method

On January 1, Miller Inc. acquired 1,500 shares of the outstanding common stock of Graceland Industries for $16 per share, or $24,000. On that date, Graceland had 10,000 shares of common stock outstanding. On October 1, Graceland declared and paid a cash dividend of $2 per share. On November 13, Miller sold 300 shares of Graceland for $5,000. Graceland reported net income of $36,000. Graceland's stock sold for $15 per share at December 31. This is Miller's only investment, and Miller plans on remaining invested in Graceland for a number of years.

Required:

1. Prepare Miller's journal entries to record the transactions related to its investment in Graceland.
2. Give the title and amount of each item (except Cash) related to this investment on the December 31, balance sheet. Name the balance sheet section in which each item appears.

Exercise A2-25 Equity Method

OBJECTIVE ◀ 2

On January 1, Hill Corporation acquired 40% of the outstanding common stock (400 of 1,000 outstanding shares) of Valley Manufacturing Inc. for $60,000, which equals the book value of Valley. On December 31, Valley reported net income of $30,000 and declared and paid a cash dividend of $11,500.

Required:

1. Prepare the journal entries made by Hill to record the transactions related to its investment in Valley.
2. Give the title and amount of each item (except Cash) related to the investment on the December 31, balance sheet. Name the balance sheet section in which each item appears.

Exercise A2-26 Accounting for Investments in Equity Securities

OBJECTIVE ◀ 1

On January 1, Stern Corporation purchased 100 shares of common stock issued by Milstein Inc. (representing 12% of the total shares outstanding) for $6,000 and 500 shares of Heifetz Inc. (representing 25% of the total shares outstanding) for $20,000. Assume that the acquisition cost of each investment equals the book value of the related stockholders' equity on the records of the investee. During the year, Milstein declared and paid cash dividends to Stern of $500, and Heifetz declared and paid cash dividends to Stern of $1,700. Milstein reported net income of $12,000, and Heifetz reported net income of $15,000. On December 31, the market value of 100 shares of Milstein was $6,450, and the market value of 500 shares of Heifetz was $19,720.

Required:

Answer the following questions for both investments:

	Milstein	Heifetz
1. Which accounting method is applicable?		
2. What amount is recorded in the investment account on the date of acquisition?		
3. What amount is recorded in Stern's net income from the investment?		
4. What amount is reported for the investment on the balance sheet at December 31?		

Exercise A2-27 Investments in Trading Securities

OBJECTIVE ◀ 1

Maxwell Company engaged in the following transactions involving short-term investments:
a. Purchased bonds of Bartco Inc. for $12,800.
b. Received cash for interest of $320.
c. Sold $2,560 of the bonds for $2,440 cash.
d. Purchased debt of Newton Company for $20,900.
e. Received cash for interest of $380 on the Newton debt.

At December 31, the Bartco bonds have a market value of $9,600, and the Newton debt has a market value of $22,420.

Required:

1. Prepare entries for Maxwell's journal to record these transactions assuming they are trading securities.
2. Prepare the necessary adjusting entry at December 31.

(*Continued*)

3. **CONCEPTUAL CONNECTION** What is the income statement effect of the adjusting entry?

4. How would these investments be reported on the December 31 balance sheet?

OBJECTIVE 2 3

Exercise A2-28 Consolidated Balance Sheet

Augusta Inc. acquired 100% of the outstanding common stock of Dear Corporation in a business combination. Immediately before the business combination, the two businesses had the following balance sheets:

Augusta		Dear	
Cash	$ 3,100	Cash	$ 180
Equipment (net)	9,500	Equipment (net)	930
Total assets	$12,600	Total assets	$1,110
Common stock	$ 9,100	Common stock	$ 700
Retained earnings	3,500	Retained earnings	410
Total liabilities & equity	$12,600	Total liabilities & equity	$1,110

Augusta agreed to give Dear's stockholders $1,500 cash in exchange for all their Dear common stock. Dear's equipment has a fair value of $1,100.

Required:

1. Prepare the entries for Augusta and Dear to record the business combination.
2. Prepare the balance sheet of Augusta immediately after the business combination.
3. Prepare the balance sheet of Dear immediately after the business combination.
4. Calculate the amount of the adjustment to the book value of Dear's equity and the amount of goodwill.
5. Prepare a consolidated balance sheet immediately after the combination.

OBJECTIVE 3

Exercise A2-29 Goodwill

Pindar Corporation acquired all the outstanding stock of Strauss Company for $23,000,000 on January 1. On the date of acquisition, Strauss had the following balance sheet:

Strauss Company
Balance Sheet
January 1

Assets		Liabilities	
Accounts receivable	$ 6,800,000	Accounts payable	$ 2,000,000
Inventory	4,700,000	Notes payable	8,000,000
Property, plant & equipment (net)	16,300,000	Total liabilities	$10,000,000
		Stockholders' Equity	
		Common stock	$ 2,000,000
		Additional paid-in capital—	
		common stock	8,000,000
		Retained earnings	7,800,000
		Total stockholders' equity	$17,800,000
		Total liabilities & stockholders'	
Total assets	$27,800,000	equity	$27,800,000

All Strauss' assets and liabilities have book values equal to their fair values except for equipment, which has a fair value of $20,700,000.

Required:

1. Calculate the amount of goodwill.
2. Prepare the journal entry by Pindar to record the acquisition.
3. Assume that instead of acquiring all the outstanding common stock of Strauss, Pindar acquired 100% of Strauss' net assets. What would Pindar's journal entry be in this case?

3
Appendix

Time Value of Money

After studying Appendix 3, you should be able to:

1 Explain how compound interest works.

2 Use future value and present value tables to apply compound interest to accounting transactions.

Time value of money is widely used in business to measure today's value of future cash outflows or inflows and the amount to which liabilities (or assets) will grow when compound interest accumulates.

In transactions involving the borrowing and lending of money, the borrower usually pays *interest*. In effect, interest is the **time value of money**. The amount of interest paid is determined by the length of the loan and the interest rate.

However, interest is not restricted to loans made to borrowers by banks. Investments (particularly, investments in debt securities and savings accounts), installment sales, and a variety of other contractual arrangements all include interest. In all cases, the arrangement between the two parties—the note, security, or purchase agreement—creates an asset in the accounting records of one party and a corresponding liability in the accounting records of the other. All such assets and liabilities increase as interest is earned by the asset holder and decrease as payments are made by the liability holder.

COMPOUND INTEREST CALCULATIONS

OBJECTIVE ◀ **1**

Explain how compound interest works.

Compound interest is a method of calculating the time value of money in which interest is earned on the previous periods' interest. That is, interest for the period is added to the account balance and interest is earned on this new balance in the next period. In computing compound interest, it's important to understand the difference between the *interest period* and the *interest rate*:

- The **interest period** is the time interval between interest calculations.
- The **interest rate** is the percentage that is multiplied by the beginning-of-period balance to yield the amount of interest for that period.

The interest rate must agree with the interest period. For example, if the interest period is 1 month, then the interest rate used to calculate interest must be stated as a percentage "per month."

When an interest rate is stated in terms of a time period that differs from the interest period, the rate must be adjusted before interest can be calculated. For example, suppose that a bank advertises interest at a rate of 12% per year compounded monthly. Here, the interest period would be 1 month. Since there are 12 interest periods in 1 year, the interest rate for 1 month is one-twelfth the annual rate, or 1%. In other words, if the *rate statement period* differs from the *interest period*, the stated rate must be divided by the number of interest periods included in the rate statement period. A few examples of adjusted rates follow:

Stated Rate	Adjusted Rate for Computations
12% per year compounded semiannually	6% per 6-month period (12% ÷ 2)
12% per year compounded quarterly	3% per quarter (12% ÷ 4)
12% per year compounded monthly	1% per month (12% ÷ 12)

If an interest rate is stated without reference to a rate statement period or an interest period, assume that the period is 1 year. For example, both "12%" and "12% per year" should be interpreted as 12% per year compounded annually.

Compound interest means that interest is computed on the original amount plus undistributed interest earned in previous periods. The simplest compound interest calculation involves putting a single amount into an account and adding interest to it at the end of each period. EXAMPLE A3.1 shows how to compute future values using compound interest.

EXAMPLE A3.1   COMPUTING FUTURE VALUES USING COMPOUND INTEREST

An investor deposits $20,000 in a savings account on January 1, 2024. The bank pays interest of 6% per year compounded monthly.

Required:
Assuming that the only activity to the account is the deposit of interest at the end of each month, how much money will be in the account after the interest payment on March 31, 2024?

Solution:
Interest represents the time value of money. When deposits earn simple interest, interest is only earned on the principal (the amount deposited). When deposits earn compound interest, interest is also earned on the any interest earned in prior periods. Monthly interest will be ½% (6% per year ÷ 12 months).

Account balance, 1/1/24	$20,000.00
January interest ($20,000.00 × ½%)	100.00
Account balance, 1/31/24	$20,100.00
February interest ($20,100.00 × ½%)	100.50
Account balance, 2/28/24	$20,200.50
March interest ($20,200.50 × ½%)	101.00
Account balance, 3/31/24	$20,301.50

Note: Here, interest was the only factor that altered the account balance after the initial deposit. In more complex situations, the account balance is changed by subsequent deposits and withdrawals as well as by interest. Withdrawals reduce the balance and, therefore, the amount of interest in subsequent periods. Additional deposits have the opposite effect, increasing the balance and the amount of interest earned.

As you can see in Example A3.1, the balance in the account continues to grow each month by an increasing amount of interest. The amount of monthly interest increases because interest is *compounded,* In other words, interest is computed on accumulated interest as well as on principal. For example, February interest of $100.50 consists of $100 interest on the $20,000 principal and 50¢ interest on the $100 January interest ($100 × 0.005 = 50¢).

In Example A3.1, the compound interest only amounts to 25¢. That might seem relatively insignificant, but if the investment period is sufficiently long, the amount of compound interest grows large even at relatively small interest rates. For example, suppose your parents invested $1,000 at ½% per month when you were born with the objective of giving you a college graduation present at age 21. How much would that investment be worth after 21 years? The answer is $3,514. In 21 years, the compound interest is $2,514—more than 2½ times the original principal. Without compounding, interest over the same period would have been only $1,260.

The amount to which an account will grow when interest is compounded is the **future value** of the account. Compound interest calculations can assume two fundamentally different forms:

- calculations of future values
- calculations of present values

As shown, calculations of future values are projections of future balances based on *past* and *future* cash flows and interest payments. In contrast, calculations of present values are determinations of present amounts based on *expected* future cash flows.

PRESENT VALUE OF FUTURE CASH FLOWS

Whenever a contract establishes a relationship between an initial amount borrowed or loaned and one or more future cash flows, the initial amount borrowed or loaned is the **present value** of those future cash flows. The present value can be interpreted in two ways:

- From the borrower's viewpoint, it is the liability that will be exactly paid by the future payments.
- From the lender's viewpoint, it is the receivable balance that will be exactly satisfied by the future receipts.

In understanding cash flows, cash flow diagrams that display both the amounts and the times of the cash flows specified by a contract can be quite helpful. In these diagrams, a time line runs from left to right. Inflows are represented as arrows pointing upward and outflows as arrows pointing downward. For example, suppose that the Hilliard Corporation borrows $100,000 from Citizens Bank of New Hope on January 1, 2025. The note requires three $38,803.35 payments, one each at the end of 2025, 2026, and 2027, and includes interest at 8% per year. The cash flows for Hilliard are shown in Exhibit A3.1.

Cash Flow Diagram   **EXHIBIT A3.1**

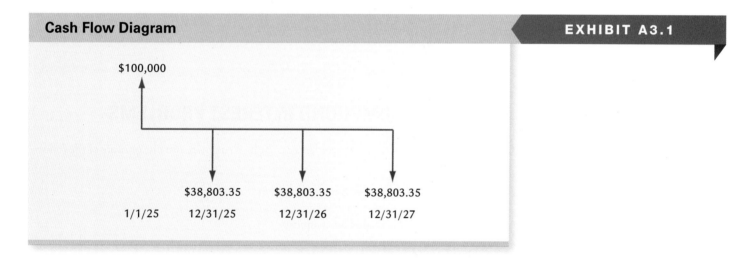

The calculation that follows shows, from the borrower's perspective, the relationship between the amount borrowed (*the present value*) and the future payments (*future cash flows*) required by Hilliard's note.

Amount borrowed, 1/1/25	$100,000.00
Add: 2025 interest ($100,000.00 × 0.08)	8,000.00
Subtract payment on 12/31/25	(38,803.35)
Liability at 12/31/25	$ 69,196.65
Add: 2026 interest ($69,196.65 × 0.08)	5,535.73
Subtract payment on 12/31/26	(38,803.35)
Liability at 12/31/26	$ 35,929.03
Add: 2027 interest ($35,929.03 × 0.08)	2,874.32
Subtract payment on 12/31/27	(38,803.35)
Liability at 12/31/27	$ 0.00

Present value calculations like this one are future value calculations in reverse. Here, the three payments of $38,803.35 exactly pay off the liability created by the note. Because the reversal of future value calculations can present a burdensome and sometimes difficult algebraic problem, shortcut methods using tables have been developed (see Exhibits A3.7, A3.8, A3.9, and A3.10, discussed later in this appendix).

INTEREST AND THE FREQUENCY OF COMPOUNDING

The number of interest periods into which a compound interest problem is divided can make a significant difference in the amount of compound interest. For example, assume that you are evaluating four 1-year investments, each of which requires an initial $10,000 deposit. All four investments earn interest at a rate of 12% per year, but they have different compounding periods. The data in Exhibit A3.2 show the impact of compounding frequency on future value. Investment D, which offers monthly compounding, accumulates $68 more interest by the end of the year than Investment A, which offers only annual compounding.

EXHIBIT A3.2   **Effect of Interest Periods on Compound Interest**

Investment	Interest Period	I	N	Calculation of Future Amount in One Year*
A	1 year	12%	1	($10,000 × 1.12000) = $11,200
B	6 months	6%	2	($10,000 × 1.12360) = 11,236
C	1 quarter	3%	4	($10,000 × 1.12551) = 11,255
D	1 month	1%	12	($10,000 × 1.12683) = 11,268

* The multipliers (1.12000 for Investment A, 1.12360 for Investment B, etc.) are taken from the future value table in Exhibit A3.7 (p.819).

OBJECTIVE
Use future value and present value tables to apply compound interest to accounting transactions.

FOUR BASIC COMPOUND INTEREST PROBLEMS

Any present value or future value problems can be broken down into one or more of the following four basic problems:

- computing the future value of a single amount
- computing the present value of a single amount
- computing the future value of an annuity
- computing the present value of an annuity

COMPUTING THE FUTURE VALUE OF A SINGLE AMOUNT

In computing the future value of a single amount, the following elements are used:

- f: the cash flow
- FV: the future value
- n: the number of periods between the cash flow and the future value
- i: the interest rate per period

To find the future value of a single amount, establish an account for f dollars and add compound interest at i % to that account for n periods:

$$FV = (f)(1 + i)^n$$

The balance of the account after n periods is the future value.

Because people frequently need to compute the future value of a single amount, tables have been developed to make it easier. Therefore, instead of using the formula above, you could use the future value table in Exhibit A3.7 (p. 819), where M_1 is the multiple that corresponds to the appropriate values of n and i:

$$FV = (f)(M_1)$$

For example, suppose Allied Financial loans $200,000 at a rate of 6% per year compounded annually to an auto dealership for 4 years. Exhibit A3.3 shows how to compute the future value (FV) at the end of the 4 years—the amount that will be repaid.

Future Value of a Single Amount: An Example

EXHIBIT A3.3

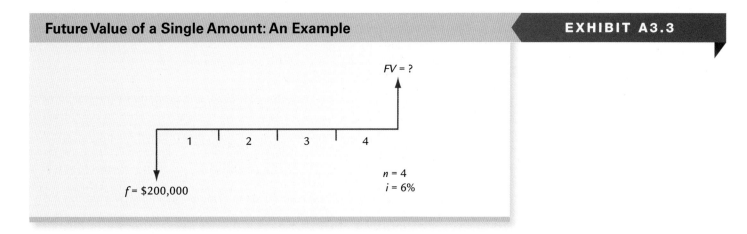

Assuming Allied's viewpoint (the lender's), using a compound interest calculation, the unknown future value (FV) would be found as follows:

Amount loaned	$200,000.00
First year's interest ($200,000.00 × 0.06)	12,000.00
Loan receivable at end of first year	$212,000.00
Second year's interest ($212,000.00 × 0.06)	12,720.00
Loan receivable at end of second year	$224,720.00
Third year's interest ($224,720.00 × 0.06)	13,483.20
Loan receivable at end of third year	$238,203.20
Fourth year's interest ($238,203.20 × 0.06)	14,292.19
Loan receivable at end of the fourth year	$252,495.39

As you can see, the amount of interest increases each year. This growth is the effect of computing interest for each year based on an amount that includes the interest earned in prior years (i.e., compounding interest).

The shortcut calculation, using the future value table (Exhibit A3.7, p. 819), would be:

$$FV = (f)(M_1)$$
$$= (\$200,000)(1.26248)$$
$$= \$252,496$$

You can find M_1 at the intersection of the 6% column ($i = 6\%$) and the fourth row ($n = 4$) or by calculating 1.06^4. This multiple is the future value of the single amount after having been borrowed (or invested) for 4 years at 6% interest. The future value of $200,000 is 200,000 times the multiple.

Note that there is a difference between the answer ($252,495.39) developed in the compound interest calculation and the answer ($252,496) determined using the future value table. This is because the numbers in the table have been rounded to five decimal places. If they were taken to eight digits ($1.06^4 = 1.26247696$), the two answers would be equal. EXAMPLE A3.2 shows how to compute the future value of a single amount.

EXAMPLE A3.2   COMPUTING FUTURE VALUE OF A SINGLE AMOUNT

The Kitchner Company sells an unneeded factory site for $200,000 on July 1, 2024. Kitchner expects to purchase a different site in 18 months so that it can expand into a new market. Meanwhile, Kitchner decides to invest the $200,000 in a money market fund that is guaranteed to earn 6% per year compounded semiannually (3% per 6-month period).

Required:

1.   Draw a cash flow diagram for this investment from Kitchner's perspective.

2.   Calculate the amount of money in the money market fund on December 31, 2024, and prepare the journal entry necessary to recognize interest income.

3.   Calculate the amount of money in the money market fund on December 31, 2025, and prepare the journal entry necessary to recognize interest i.

Solution:

Interest represents the time value of money. The future value of a single amount is the original cash flow plus compound interest as of a specified future date.

1.

2.   Because we are calculating the value at 12/31/24, there is only one period:

$FV = (f)(FV$ of a Single Amount, 1 period, 3%)
    $= (\$200,000)(1.03)$
    $= \underline{\$206,000}$

The excess of the amount of money over the original deposit is the interest earned from July 1 through December 31, 2024.

					Assets	=	Liabilities	+	Stockholders' Equity
Dec. 31, 2024	Cash		6,000		▲				
	Interest Income			6,000					▲

3. $FV = (f)(FV$ of a Single Amount, 3 period, 3%)
    $= (\$200,000)(1.09273)$
    $= \underline{\$218,546}$

The interest income for the year is the increase in the amount of money during 2025, which is $12,546 ($218,546 − $206,000). The journal entry to record interest income would be:

					Assets	=	Liabilities	+	Stockholders' Equity
Dec. 31, 2025	Cash		12,546		▲				
	Interest Income			12,546					▲

COMPUTING THE PRESENT VALUE OF A SINGLE AMOUNT

In computing the present value of a single amount, the following elements are used:

- f: the future cash flow
- PV: the present value
- n: the number of periods between the present time and the future cash flow
- i: the interest rate per period

In present value problems, the interest rate is sometimes called the *discount rate*.

To find the present value of a single amount, use the following equation:

$$PV = \frac{f}{(1 + i)^n}$$

You could use the present value table in Exhibit A3.8 (p. 820), where M_2 is the multiple from Exhibit A3.8 that corresponds to the appropriate values of n and i:

$$PV = (f)(M_2)$$

Suppose **Marathon Oil** has purchased property on which it plans to develop oil wells. The seller has agreed to accept a single $150,000,000 payment 3 years from now, when Marathon expects to be selling oil from the field. Assuming an interest rate of 7% per year, the (PV) at the end of the 3 years from the borrower's perspective can be calculated as shown in Exhibit A3.4.

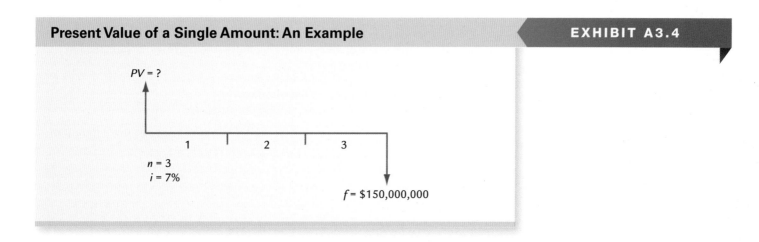

Present Value of a Single Amount: An Example

EXHIBIT A3.4

The shortcut calculation, using the present value table (Exhibit A3.8, p. 820), would be:

$$PV = (f)(M_2)$$
$$= (\$150,000,000)(0.81630)$$
$$= \underline{\$122,445,000}$$

You can find M_2 at the intersection of the 7% column ($i = 7\%$) and the third row ($n = 3$) in Exhibit A3.8 or by calculating $[1/(1.07)^3]$. This multiple is the present value of a $1 cash inflow or outflow in 3 years at 7%. Thus, the present value of $150,000,000 is 150,000,000 times the multiple.

Although the future value calculation cannot be used to determine the present value, it can be used to verify that the present value calculated by using the table is correct. The following calculation is proof for the present value problem:

Calculated present value (*PV*)	$122,445,000
First year's interest ($122,445,000 × 0.07)	8,571,150
Loan payable at end of first year	$131,016,150
Second year's interest ($131,016,150 × 0.07)	9,171,131
Loan payable at end of second year	$140,187,281
Third year's interest ($140,187,281 × 0.07)	9,813,110
Loan payable at end of the third year (*f*)	$150,000,391

Again, the $391 difference between the amount here and the assumed $150,000,000 cash flow is due to rounding.

When interest is compounded on the calculated present value of $122,445,000, then the present value calculation is reversed, and we return to the future cash flow of $150,000,000. This reversal proves that $122,445,000 is the correct present value. EXAMPLE A3.3 shows how to compute the present value of a single amount.

EXAMPLE A3.3　COMPUTING PRESENT VALUE OF A SINGLE AMOUNT

On October 1, 2024, Adelsman Manufacturing Company sold a new machine to Randell Inc. The machine represented a new design that Randell was eager to place in service. Since Randell was unable to pay for the machine on the date of purchase, Adelsman agreed to defer the $60,000 payment for 15 months. The appropriate rate of interest in such transactions is 8% per year compounded quarterly (2% per 3-month period).

Required:
1. Draw the cash flow diagram for this deferred-payment purchase from Randell's (the borrower's) perspective.

2. Calculate the present value of this deferred-payment purchase.

3. Prepare the journal entry necessary to record the acquisition of the machine.

Solution:
Interest expense represents the time value of money. The present value of a single cash flow is a specified amount of money at a specified future date discounted back to today at a specified compound interest rate.

1.

2. The present value of the $60,000 payment.

$$PV = (f)(PV \text{ of a Single Amount, } 5 \text{ period, } 2\%)$$
$$= (\$60,000)(0.90573)$$
$$= \underline{\$54,344}$$

3.

		Assets	=	Liabilities	+	Stockholders' Equity
Oct. 1, 2024　Equipment	54,344	▲				
Notes Payable		54,344		▲		

COMPUTING THE FUTURE VALUE OF AN ANNUITY

So far, we have been discussing problems that involve a single cash flow. However, there are also instances of multiple cash flows one period apart. An **annuity** is a number of equal cash flows; one to each interest period. For example, an investment in a security that pays $1,000 to an investor every December 31 for 10 consecutive years is an annuity. A loan repayment schedule that calls for a payment of $367.29 on the first day of each month can also be considered an annuity. (Although the number of days in a month varies from 28 to 31, the interest period is defined as 1 month without regard to the number of days in each month.)

In computing the future value of an annuity, the following elements are used:

- f: the amount of each repeating cash flow
- FV: the future value after the last (n^{th}) cash flow
- n: the number of cash flows
- i: the interest rate per period

To find the future value of an annuity, use the following equation:

$$FV = (f)\left[\frac{(1+i)^n - 1}{i}\right]$$

Alternatively, you could use the future value table in Exhibit A3.9 (p. 821), where M_3 is the multiple from Exhibit A3.9 that corresponds to the appropriate values of n and i compound interest calculations:

$$FV = (f)(M_3)$$

Assume that **Chase** wants to advertise a new savings program to its customers. The savings program requires the customers to make four annual payments of $5,000 each, with the first payment due 3 years before the program ends. Chase advertises a 6% interest rate compounded annually. The future value of this annuity immediately after the fourth cash payment from the investor's perspective is shown in Exhibit A3.5.

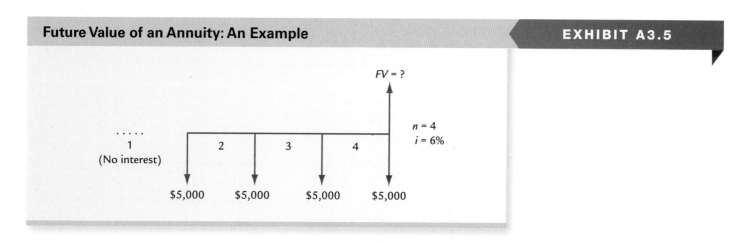

Future Value of an Annuity: An Example   **EXHIBIT A3.5**

Note that the first period in Exhibit A3.5 is drawn with a dotted line. When using annuities, the time-value-of-money model assumes that all cash flows occur at the end of a period. Therefore, the first cash flow in the future value of an annuity occurs at the end of the first period. However, since interest cannot be earned until the first deposit has been made, the first period is identified as a no-interest period.

The future value (FV) can be computed as:

Interest for first period ($0 × 6%)	$ 0.00
First deposit	5,000.00
Investment balance at end of first year	$ 5,000.00
Second year's interest ($5,000.00 × 0.06)	300.00
Second deposit	5,000.00
Investment balance at end of second year	$10,300.00
Third year's interest ($10,300.00 × 0.06)	618.00
Third deposit	5,000.00
Investment balance at end of third year	$15,918.00
Fourth year's interest ($15,918.00 × 0.06)	955.08
Fourth deposit	5,000.00
Investment at end of the fourth year	$21,873.08

This calculation shows that the lender has accumulated a future value (FV) of $21,873.08 by the end of the fourth period, immediately after the fourth cash investment.

The shortcut calculation, using the future value table (Exhibit A3.9, p. 821), would be:

$$FV = (f)(M_3)$$
$$= (\$5,000)(4.37462)$$
$$= \$21,873$$

You can find M_3 at the intersection of the 6% column ($i = 6\%$) and the fourth row ($n = 4$) in the Exhibit A3.9 (p. 821) or by calculating $(1.06^4 - 1) \div 0.06$. This multiple is the future value of an annuity of four cash flows of $1 each at 6%. The future value of an annuity of $5,000 cash flows is 5,000 times the multiple. Thus, the table allows us to calculate the future value of an annuity by a single multiplication, no matter how many cash flows are involved. EXAMPLE A3.4 shows how to compute the future value of an annuity.

EXAMPLE A3.4   COMPUTING FUTURE VALUE OF AN ANNUITY

Greg Smith is a lawyer and CPA specializing in retirement and estate planning. One of Greg's clients, the owner of a large farm, wants to retire in 5 years. To provide funds to purchase a retirement annuity from New York Life at the date of retirement, Greg asks the client to give him annual payments of $170,000, which Greg will deposit in a special fund that will earn 7% per year.

Required:
1. Draw the cash flow diagram for the fund from Greg's client's perspective.

2. Calculate the future value of the fund immediately after the fifth deposit.

3. If Greg's client needs $1,000,000 to purchase the annuity, how much must be deposited every year?

Solution:
Interest represents the time value of money. The future value of an annuity is the value of a series of equal cash flows made at regular intervals with compound interest at a specified future date.

1.

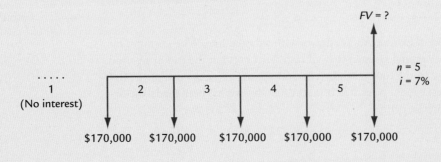

2. $FV = (f)(FV \text{ of an Annuity}, 5 \text{ period}, 7\%)$
   $= (\$170,000)(5.75074)$
   $= \underline{\$977,626}$

3. In this case, the future value is known, but the annuity amount (f) is not:

$\$1,000,000 = (f)(FV \text{ of an Annuity}, 5 \text{ periods}, 7\%)$
$\$1,000,000 = (f)(5.75074)$
$\qquad f = \$1,000,000/5.75074$
$\qquad f = \underline{\$173,890.66}$

PRESENT VALUE OF AN ANNUITY

In computing the present value of an annuity, the following elements are used:

- f: the amount of each repeating cash flow
- PV: the present value of the n future cash flows
- n: the number of cash flows and periods
- i: the interest (or discount) rate per period

To find the present value of an annuity, use the following equation:

$$PV = (f)\frac{1 - \dfrac{1}{(1 + i)^n}}{i}$$

You could also use the present value table in Exhibit A3.10 (p. 822), where M_4 is the multiple from Exhibit A3.10 that corresponds to the appropriate values of n and i:

$$PV = (f)(M_4)$$

For example, assume that **Xerox Corporation** purchased a new machine for its manufacturing operations. The purchase agreement requires Xerox to make four annual payments of $24,154 each. The interest rate is 8% compounded annually and the first cash flow occurs 1 year after the purchase. Exhibit A3.6 shows how to determine the present value of this annuity from Xerox's (the borrower's) perspective. Note that the same concept applies to both the lender's and borrower's perspectives.

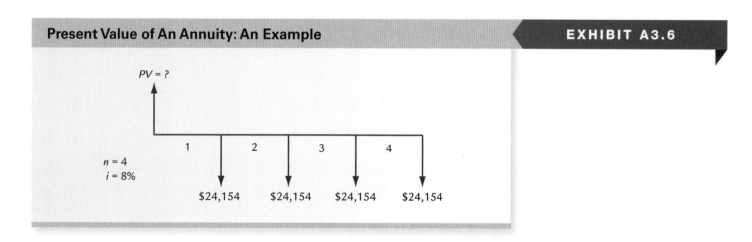

Present Value of An Annuity: An Example

EXHIBIT A3.6

The shortcut calculation, using the present value table (Exhibit A3.10, p. 822), would be:

$$PV = (f)(M_4)$$
$$= (\$24{,}154)(3.31213)$$
$$= \$80{,}001.19$$

You can find M_4 at the intersection of the 8% column ($i = 8\%$) and the fourth row ($n = 4$) in Exhibit A3.10 or by solving for $[1 - (1 \div 1.08^4)] \div 0.08$. This multiple is the present value of an annuity of four cash flows of $1 each at 8%. The present value of an annuity of four $24,154 cash flows is 24,154 times the multiple.

Again, although the compound interest calculation is not used to determine the present value, it can be used to prove that the present value found using the table is correct. The following calculation verifies the present value in the problem:

Calculated present value (PV)	$ 80,001.19
Interest for first year ($80,001.19 $\times$ 0.08)	6,400.10
Less: First cash flow	(24,154.00)
Balance at end of first year	$ 62,247.29
Interest for second year ($62,247.29 $\times$ 0.08)	4,979.78
Less: Second cash flow	(24,154.00)
Balance at end of second year	$ 43,073.07
Interest for third year ($43,073.07 $\times$ 0.08)	3,445.85
Less: Third cash flow	(24,154.00)
Balance at end of third year	$ 22,364.92
Interest for fourth year ($22,364.92 $\times$ 0.08)	1,789.19
Less: Fourth cash flow	(24,154.00)
Balance at end of fourth year	$ 0.11

This proof uses a compound interest calculation that is the reverse of the present value formula. If the present value (PV) calculated with the formula is correct, then the proof should end with a balance of zero immediately after the last cash flow. This proof ends with a balance of $0.11 because of rounding in the proof itself and in the table in Exhibit A3.10 (p. 822).
EXAMPLE A3.5 shows how to compute the present value of an annuity.

EXAMPLE A3.5   COMPUTING PRESENT VALUE OF AN ANNUITY

Bates Builders purchased a subdivision site from the Second National Bank and Trust Co. on January 1, 2024. Bates gave the bank an installment note. The note requires Bates to make four annual payments of $600,000 each on December 31 of each year, beginning in 2024. Interest is computed at 9%.

Required:
1.   Draw the cash flow diagram for this purchase from Bates' perspective.

2.   Calculate the cost of the land as recorded by Bates on January 1, 2024.

3.   Prepare the journal entry that Bates will make to record the purchase of the land.

Solution:
Interest represents the time value of money. The present value of an annuity is the value of a series of equal future cash flows at regular intervals with compound interest discounted back to today.

1.

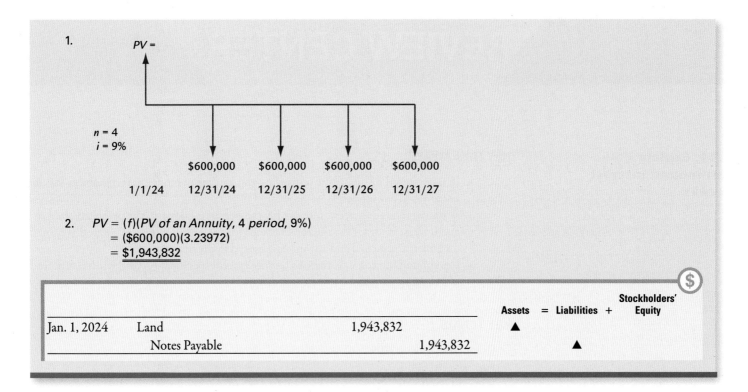

$PV =$

$n = 4$
$i = 9\%$

| | $600,000 | $600,000 | $600,000 | $600,000 |
| 1/1/24 | 12/31/24 | 12/31/25 | 12/31/26 | 12/31/27 |

2. $PV = (f)(PV \text{ of an Annuity, 4 period, 9\%})$
   $= (\$600,000)(3.23972)$
   $= \underline{\$1,943,832}$

			Assets	=	Liabilities	+	Stockholders' Equity
Jan. 1, 2024	Land	1,943,832	▲				
	Notes Payable		1,943,832		▲		

REVIEW CENTER

LO1. Explain how compound interest works.

KEY TAKEAWAYS

- In transactions involving the borrowing and lending of money, it is customary for the borrower to pay interest.
- With compound interest, interest for the period is added to the principal amount, and interest is earned on the total balance for the next period (i.e., interest is earned on both the principal and any interest earned in previous periods).
- Compound interest calculations require careful specification of the interest period and the interest rate.

KEY TERMS

Compound interest, 799
Future value, 800
Interest period, 799
Interest rate, 799
Present value, 801
Time value of money, 799

EXAMPLE

> **EXAMPLE A3.1**   Computing future values using compound interest, page 800

LO2. Use future and present value tables to apply compound interest to accounting transactions.

KEY TAKEAWAYS

- Cash flows are described as either:
  - single cash flows or
  - annuities
- An annuity is a number of equal cash flows made at regular intervals.
- All other cash flows are a series of one or more single cash flows.
- Accounting for such cash flows may require the following:
  - Calculation of the amount to which a series of cash flows will grow when interest is compounded (i.e., the future value)
  - The amount a series of future cash flows is worth today after taking into account compound interest (i.e., the present value)

KEY TERM

Annuity, 807

KEY CALCULATIONS

Future Value of a Single Amount $=$ Cash Flow $(1 + i)^n$
Present Value of a Single Amount $=$ Cash Flow $\div (1 + i)^n$
Future Value of an Annuity $=$ Cash Flow $[((1 + i)^n - 1) \div i]$
Present Value of an Annuity $=$ Cash Flow $[(1 - (1 \div (1 + i)^n)) \div i]$

EXAMPLES

EXAMPLE A3.2	Computing future value of a single amount, page 804
EXAMPLE A3.3	Computing present value of a single amount, page 806
EXAMPLE A3.4	Computing future value of an annuity, page 808
EXAMPLE A3.5	Computing present value of an annuity, page 810

APPLYING KNOWLEDGE

DISCUSSION QUESTIONS

1. Why does money have a time value?
2. Describe the four basic time-value-of-money problems.
3. How is compound interest computed? What is a future value? What is a present value?
4. Define an annuity in general terms. Describe the cash flows related to an annuity from the viewpoint of the lender in terms of receipts and payments.
5. Explain how to use time-value-of-money calculations to measure an installment note liability.

BRIEF EXERCISES

Brief Exercise A3-1 Explain How Compound Interest Works

OBJECTIVE ◀ 1

EXAMPLE A3.1

Jim Emig has $6,000.

Required:
Calculate the future value of the $6,000 at 12% compounded quarterly for 5 years. (*Note:* Round answers to two decimal places.)

Brief Exercise A3-2 Use Future Value and Present Value Tables to Apply Compound Interest to Accounting Transactions

OBJECTIVE ◀ 2

EXAMPLE A3.2

Cathy Lumbattis inherited $140,000 from an aunt.

Required:
If Cathy decides not to spend her inheritance but to leave the money in her savings account until she retires in 15 years, how much money will she have, assuming an annual interest rate of 8%, compounded semiannually? (*Note:* Round answers to two decimal places.)

OBJECTIVE `2`

EXAMPLE A3.3

Brief Exercise A3-3 Use Future Value and Present Value Tables to Apply Compound Interest to Accounting Transactions

LuAnn Bean will receive $7,000 in 7 years.

Required:

What is the present value at 7% compounded annually? (*Note:* Round answers to two decimal places.)

OBJECTIVE `2`

EXAMPLE A3.3

Brief Exercise A3-4 Use Future Value and Present Value Tables to Apply Compound Interest to Accounting Transactions

A bank is willing to lend money at 6% interest, compounded annually.

Required:

How much would the bank be willing to loan you in exchange for a payment of $600 4 years from now? (*Note:* Round answers to two decimal places.)

OBJECTIVE `2`

EXAMPLE A3.4

Brief Exercise A3-5 Use Future Value and Present Value Tables to Apply Compound Interest to Accounting Transactions

Ed Walker wants to save some money so that he can make a down payment of $3,000 on a car when he graduates from college in 4 years.

Required:

If Ed opens a savings account and earns 3% on his money, compounded annually, how much will he have to invest now? (*Note:* Round answers to two decimal places.)

OBJECTIVE `2`

EXAMPLE A3.4

Brief Exercise A3-6 Use Future Value and Present Value Tables to Apply Compound Interest to Accounting Transactions

Kristen Quinn makes equal deposits of $500 semiannually for 4 years.

Required:

What is the future value at 8%? (*Note:* Round answers to two decimal places.)

OBJECTIVE `2`

EXAMPLE A3.4

Brief Exercise A3-7 Use Future Value and Present Value Tables to Apply Compound Interest to Accounting Transactions

Chuck Russo, a high school math teacher, wants to set up an IRA account into which he will deposit $2,000 per year. He plans to teach for 20 more years and then retire.

Required:

If the interest on his account is 7% compounded annually, how much will be in his account when he retires? (*Note:* Round answers to two decimal places.)

OBJECTIVE `2`

EXAMPLE A3.4

Brief Exercise A3-8 Use Future Value Tables to Apply Compound Interest to Accounting Transactions

Larson Lumber makes annual deposits of $500 at 6% compounded annually for 3 years.

Required:

What is the future value of these deposits? (*Note:* Round answers to two decimal places.)

OBJECTIVE `2`

EXAMPLE A3.5

Brief Exercise A3-9 Use Future Value and Present Value Tables to Apply Compound Interest to Accounting Transactions

Michelle McFeaters can earn 6%.

Required:

How much would have to be deposited in a savings account in order for Michelle to be able to make equal annual withdrawals of $200 at the end of each of 10 years? (*Note:* Round answers to two decimal places.) The balance at the end of the last year would be zero.

Brief Exercise A3-10 Use Future Value and Present Value Tables to Apply Compound Interest to Accounting Transactions

OBJECTIVE 2

EXAMPLE A3.5

Barb Muller wins the lottery. She wins $20,000 per year to be paid for 10 years. The state offers her the choice of a cash settlement now instead of the annual payments for 10 years.

Required:

If the interest rate is 6%, what is the amount the state will offer for a settlement today? (*Note:* Round answers to two decimal places.)

EXERCISES

Exercise A3-11 Practice with Tables

OBJECTIVE 2

Refer to the appropriate tables on pages 819–822.

Required:

Note: Round answers to two decimal places. Determine the:

a. future value of a single cash flow of $5,000 that earns 7% interest compounded annually for 10 years.

b. future value of an annual annuity of 10 cash flows of $500 each that earns 7% compounded annually.

c. present value of $5,000 to be received 10 years from now, assuming that the interest (discount) rate is 7% per year.

d. present value of an annuity of $500 per year for 10 years for which the interest (discount) rate is 7% per year and the first cash flow occurs 1 year from now.

Exercise A3-12 Practice with Tables

OBJECTIVE 2

Refer to the appropriate tables on pages 819–822.

Required:

Note: Round answers to two decimal places. Determine the:

a. present value of $1,200 to be received in 7 years, assuming that the interest (discount) rate is 8% per year.

b. present value of an annuity of seven cash flows of $1,200 each (one at the end of each of the next 7 years) for which the interest (discount) rate is 8% per year.

c. future value of a single cash flow of $1,200 that earns 8% per year for 7 years.

d. future value of an annuity of seven cash flows of $1,200 each (one at the end of each of the next 7 years), assuming that the interest rate is 8% per year.

Exercise A3-13 Future Values

OBJECTIVE 2

Refer to the appropriate tables on pages 819–822.

Required:

Note: Round answers to two decimal places. Determine the:

a. future value of a single deposit of $15,000 that earns compound interest for 4 years at an interest rate of 10% per year.

b. annual interest rate that will produce a future value of $13,416.80 in 6 years from a single deposit of $8,000.

c. size of annual cash flows for an annuity of nine cash flows that will produce a future value of $79,428.10 at an interest rate of 9% per year.

d. number of periods required to produce a future value of $17,755.50 from an initial deposit of $7,500 if the annual interest rate is 9%.

OBJECTIVE `2`

Exercise A3-14 Future Values and Long-Term Investments

Portman Corporation engaged in the following transactions during 2024:

a. On January 1, 2024, Portman deposited $12,000 in a certificate of deposit paying 6% interest compounded semiannually (3% per 6-month period). The certificate will mature on December 31, 2027.

b. On January 1, 2024, Portman established an account with Lee County Bank. Portman will make quarterly payments of $2,500 to Lee beginning on March 31, 2024, and ending on December 31, 2025. Lee guarantees an interest rate of 8% compounded quarterly (2% per 3-month period).

Required:

1. Prepare the cash flow diagram for each of these two investments.
2. Calculate the amount to which each of these investments will accumulate at maturity. (*Note:* Round answers to two decimal places.)

OBJECTIVE `2`

Exercise A3-15 Future Values

On January 1, Beth Woods made a single deposit of $8,000 in an investment account that earns 8% interest.

Required:

Note: Round answers to two decimal places.

1. Calculate the balance in the account in 5 years assuming the interest is compounded annually.
2. Determine how much interest will be earned on the account in 7 years if interest is compounded annually.
3. Calculate the balance in the account in 5 years assuming the 8% interest is compounded quarterly.

OBJECTIVE `2`

Exercise A3-16 Future Values

Palmer Transit Company invested $70,000 in a tax-anticipation note on June 30, 2024. The note earns 12% interest compounded monthly (1% per month) and matures on March 31, 2025.

Required:

Note: Round answers to two decimal places.

1. Prepare the cash flow diagram for this investment.
2. Determine the amount Palmer will receive when the note matures.
3. Determine how much interest Palmer will earn on this investment from June 30, 2024, through December 31, 2024.

OBJECTIVE `2`

Exercise A3-17 Present Values

Refer to the appropriate tables on pages 819–822.

Required:

Note: Round answers to two decimal places. Determine the:

a. present value of a single $14,000 cash flow in 7 years if the interest (discount) rate is 8% per year.

b. number of periods for which $5,820 must be invested at an annual interest (discount) rate of 7% to produce an investment balance of $10,000.

c. size of the annual cash flow for a 25-year annuity with a present value of $49,113 and an annual interest rate of 9%. One payment is made at the end of each year.

d. annual interest rate at which an investment of $2,542 will provide for a single $4,000 cash flow in 4 years.

e. annual interest rate earned by an annuity that costs $17,119 and provides 15 payments of $2,000 each, one at the end of each of the next 15 years.

Exercise A3-18 Present Values

OBJECTIVE ▸ 2

Phillips Enterprises signed notes to make the following two purchases on January 1, 2024:

a. new piece of equipment for $60,000, with payment deferred until December 31, 2025. The appropriate interest rate is 9% compounded annually.

b. small building from Richter Construction. The terms of the purchase require a $75,000 payment at the end of each quarter, beginning March 31, 2024, and ending June 30, 2026. The appropriate interest rate is 2% per quarter.

Required:

Note: Round answers to two decimal places.

1. Prepare the cash flow diagrams for these two purchases.
2. Prepare the entries to record these purchases in Phillips' journal.
3. Prepare the cash payment and interest expense entries for Purchase b at March 31, 2024, and June 30, 2024.
4. Prepare the adjusting entry for Purchase a at December 31, 2024.

Exercise A3-19 Present Values

OBJECTIVE ▸ 2

Krista Kellman has an opportunity to purchase a government security that will pay $200,000 in 5 years.

Required:

Note: Round answers to two decimal places.

1. Calculate what Krista would pay for the security if the appropriate interest (discount) rate is 6% compounded annually.
2. Calculate what Krista would pay for the security if the appropriate interest (discount) rate is 10% compounded annually.
3. Calculate what Krista would pay for the security if the appropriate interest (discount) rate is 6% compounded semiannually.

Exercise A3-20 Future Values of an Annuity

OBJECTIVE ▸ 2

On December 31, Natalie Livingston signs a contract to make annual deposits of $4,200 in an investment account that earns 10%. The first deposit is made that day.

Required:

Note: Round answers to two decimal places.

1. Calculate what the balance in this investment account will be just after the seventh deposit has been made if interest is compounded annually.
2. Determine how much interest will have been earned on this investment account just after the seventh deposit has been made if interest is compounded annually.

Exercise A3-21 Future Values of an Annuity

OBJECTIVE ▸ 2

Devon National Bank pays 8% interest compounded weekly (0.154% per week) on savings accounts. The bank has asked your help in preparing a table to show potential customers the number of dollars that will be available at the end of 10-, 20-, 30-, and 40-week periods during which there are weekly deposits of $1, $5, $10, or $50. The following data are available:

Length of Annuity	Future Value of Annuity at an Interest Rate of 0.154% per Week
10 weeks	10.0696
20 weeks	20.2953
30 weeks	30.6796
40 weeks	41.2250

(Continued)

Required:

Complete a table similar to the one below. (*Note:* Round answers to two decimal places.)

			Amount of Each Deposit		
Number of Deposits	**$1**	**$5**	**$10**	**$50**
10				
20				
30				
40				

Exercise A3-22 Future Value of a Single Cash Flow

Jenkins Products has just been paid $25,000 by Shirley Enterprises, which has owed Jenkins this amount for 30 months but been unable to pay because of financial difficulties. Had it been able to invest this cash, Jenkins assumes that it would have earned an interest rate of 12% compounded monthly (1% per month).

Required:

Note: Round answers to two decimal places.
1. Prepare a cash flow diagram for the investment that could have been made if Shirley had paid 30 months ago.
2. Determine how much Jenkins has lost by not receiving the $25,000 when it was due 30 months ago.
3. **CONCEPTUAL CONNECTION** Indicate whether Jenkins would make an entry to account for this loss. Why or why not?

Exercise A3-23 Installment Sale

Wilke Properties owns land on which natural gas wells are located. Cincinnati Gas Company signs a note to buy this land from Wilke on January 1, 2024. The note requires Cincinnati to pay Wilke $775,000 per year for 25 years. The first payment is to be made on December 31, 2024. The appropriate interest rate is 9% compounded annually.

Required:

Note: Round answers to two decimal places.
1. Prepare a diagram of the appropriate cash flows from Cincinnati Gas's perspective.
2. Determine the present value of the payments.
3. Indicate what entry Cincinnati Gas should make at January 1, 2024.

Exercise A3-24 Installment Sale

Bailey's Billiards sold a pool table to Sheri Sipka on October 31, 2024. The terms of the sale are no money down and payments of $50 per month for 30 months, with the first payment due on November 30, 2024. The table they sold to Sipka cost Bailey's $800, and Bailey uses a perpetual inventory system. Bailey's uses an interest rate of 12% compounded monthly (1% per month).

Required:

Note: Round answers to two decimal places.
1. Prepare the cash flow diagram for this sale.
2. Calculate the amount of revenue Bailey's should record on October 31, 2024.
3. Prepare the journal entry to record the sale on October 31. Assume that Bailey's records cost of goods sold at the time of the sale (perpetual inventory accounting).
4. Determine how much interest income Bailey's will record from October 31, 2024, through December 31, 2024.
5. Determine how much Bailey's 2024 income before taxes increased by this sale.

OBJECTIVE 2

OBJECTIVE 2

EXAMPLE A3.5

OBJECTIVE 2

EXAMPLE A3.5

Future Value of a Single Amount

EXHIBIT A3.7

$$FV = 1(1 + i)^n$$

n/i	1%	2%	3%	4%	5%	6%	7%	8%	9%	10%	12%	14%	16%	18%	20%	25%	30%
1	1.01000	1.02000	1.03000	1.04000	1.05000	1.06000	1.07000	1.08000	1.09000	1.10000	1.12000	1.14000	1.16000	1.18000	1.20000	1.25000	1.30000
2	1.02010	1.04040	1.06090	1.08160	1.10250	1.12360	1.14490	1.16640	1.18810	1.21000	1.25440	1.29960	1.34560	1.39240	1.44000	1.56250	1.69000
3	1.03030	1.06121	1.09273	1.12486	1.15763	1.19102	1.22504	1.25971	1.29503	1.33100	1.40493	1.48154	1.56090	1.64303	1.72800	1.95313	2.19700
4	1.04060	1.08243	1.12551	1.16986	1.21551	1.26248	1.31080	1.36049	1.41158	1.46410	1.57352	1.68896	1.81064	1.93878	2.07360	2.44141	2.85610
5	1.05101	1.10408	1.15927	1.21665	1.27628	1.33823	1.40255	1.46933	1.53862	1.61051	1.76234	1.92541	2.10034	2.28776	2.48832	3.05176	3.71293
6	1.06152	1.12616	1.19405	1.26532	1.34010	1.41852	1.50073	1.58687	1.67710	1.77156	1.97382	2.19497	2.43640	2.69955	2.99598	3.81470	4.82681
7	1.07214	1.14869	1.22987	1.31593	1.40710	1.50363	1.60578	1.71382	1.82804	1.94872	2.21068	2.50227	2.82622	3.18547	3.58318	4.76837	6.27485
8	1.08286	1.17166	1.26677	1.36857	1.47746	1.59385	1.71819	1.85093	1.99256	2.14359	2.47596	2.85259	3.27841	3.75886	4.29982	5.96046	8.15731
9	1.09369	1.19509	1.30477	1.42331	1.55133	1.68948	1.83846	1.99900	2.17189	2.35795	2.77308	3.25195	3.80296	4.43545	5.15978	7.45058	10.60450
10	1.10462	1.21899	1.34392	1.48024	1.62889	1.79085	1.96715	2.15892	2.36736	2.59374	3.10585	3.70722	4.41144	5.23384	6.19174	9.31323	13.78585
11	1.11567	1.24337	1.38423	1.53945	1.71034	1.89830	2.10485	2.33164	2.58043	2.85312	3.47855	4.22623	5.11726	6.17593	7.43008	11.64153	17.92160
12	1.12683	1.26824	1.42576	1.60103	1.79586	2.01220	2.25219	2.51817	2.81266	3.13843	3.89598	4.81790	5.93603	7.28759	8.91610	14.55192	23.29809
13	1.13809	1.29361	1.46853	1.66507	1.88565	2.13293	2.40985	2.71962	3.06580	3.45227	4.36349	5.49241	6.88579	8.59936	10.69932	18.18989	30.28751
14	1.14947	1.31948	1.51259	1.73168	1.97993	2.26090	2.57853	2.93719	3.34173	3.79750	4.88711	6.26135	7.98752	10.14724	12.83918	22.73737	39.37376
15	1.16097	1.34587	1.55797	1.80094	2.07893	2.39656	2.75903	3.17217	3.64248	4.17725	5.47357	7.13794	9.26552	11.97375	15.40702	28.42171	51.18589
16	1.17258	1.37279	1.60471	1.87298	2.18287	2.54035	2.95216	3.42594	3.97031	4.59497	6.13039	8.13725	10.74800	14.12902	18.48843	35.52714	66.54166
17	1.18430	1.40024	1.65285	1.94790	2.29202	2.69277	3.15882	3.70002	4.32763	5.05447	6.86604	9.27646	12.46768	16.67225	22.18611	44.40892	86.50416
18	1.19615	1.42825	1.70243	2.02582	2.40662	2.85434	3.37993	3.99602	4.71712	5.55992	7.68997	10.57517	14.46251	19.67325	26.62333	55.51115	112.45541
19	1.20811	1.45681	1.75351	2.10685	2.52695	3.02560	3.61653	4.31570	5.14166	6.11591	8.61276	12.05569	16.77652	23.21444	31.94800	69.38894	146.19203
20	1.22019	1.48595	1.80611	2.19112	2.65330	3.20714	3.86968	4.66096	5.60441	6.72750	9.64629	13.74349	19.46076	27.39303	38.33760	86.73617	190.04946
21	1.23239	1.51567	1.86029	2.27877	2.78596	3.39956	4.14056	5.03383	6.10881	7.40025	10.80385	15.66758	22.57448	32.32378	46.00512	108.42022	247.06453
22	1.24472	1.54598	1.91610	2.36992	2.92526	3.60354	4.43040	5.43654	6.65860	8.14027	12.10031	17.86104	26.18640	38.14206	55.20614	135.52527	321.18389
23	1.25716	1.57690	1.97359	2.46472	3.07152	3.81975	4.74053	5.87146	7.25787	8.95430	13.55235	20.36158	30.37622	45.00763	66.24737	169.40659	417.53905
24	1.26973	1.60844	2.03279	2.56330	3.22510	4.04893	5.07237	6.34118	7.91108	9.84973	15.17863	23.21221	35.23642	53.10901	79.49685	211.75824	542.80077
25	1.28243	1.64061	2.09378	2.66584	3.38635	4.29187	5.42743	6.84848	8.62308	10.83471	17.00006	26.46192	40.87424	62.66863	95.39622	264.69780	705.64100
26	1.29526	1.67342	2.15659	2.77247	3.55567	4.54938	5.80735	7.39635	9.39916	11.91818	19.04007	30.16658	47.41412	73.94898	114.47546	330.87225	917.33330
27	1.30821	1.70689	2.22129	2.88337	3.73346	4.82235	6.21387	7.98806	10.24508	13.10999	21.32488	34.38991	55.00038	87.25980	137.37055	413.59031	1192.53329
28	1.32129	1.74102	2.28793	2.99870	3.92013	5.11169	6.64884	8.62711	11.16714	14.42099	23.88387	39.20449	63.80044	102.96656	164.84466	516.98788	1550.29328
29	1.33450	1.77584	2.35657	3.11865	4.11614	5.41839	7.11426	9.31727	12.17218	15.86309	26.74993	44.69312	74.00851	121.50054	197.81359	646.23485	2015.38126
30	1.34785	1.81136	2.42726	3.24340	4.32194	5.74349	7.61226	10.06266	13.26768	17.44940	29.95992	50.95016	85.84988	143.37064	237.37631	807.79357	2619.99564

Present Value of a Single Amount

$$PV = \frac{1}{(1+i)^n}$$

EXHIBIT A3.8

n/i	1%	2%	3%	4%	5%	6%	7%	8%	9%	10%	12%	14%	16%	18%	20%	25%	30%
1	0.99010	0.98039	0.97087	0.96154	0.95238	0.94340	0.93458	0.92593	0.91743	0.90909	0.89286	0.87719	0.86207	0.84746	0.83333	0.80000	0.76923
2	0.98030	0.96117	0.94260	0.92456	0.90703	0.89000	0.87344	0.85734	0.84168	0.82645	0.79719	0.76947	0.74316	0.71818	0.69444	0.64000	0.59172
3	0.97059	0.94232	0.91514	0.88900	0.86384	0.83962	0.81630	0.79383	0.77218	0.75131	0.71178	0.67497	0.64066	0.60863	0.57870	0.51200	0.45517
4	0.96098	0.92385	0.88849	0.85480	0.82270	0.79209	0.76290	0.73503	0.70843	0.68301	0.63552	0.59208	0.55229	0.51579	0.48225	0.40960	0.35013
5	0.95147	0.90573	0.86261	0.82193	0.78353	0.74726	0.71299	0.68058	0.64993	0.62092	0.56743	0.51937	0.47611	0.43711	0.40188	0.32768	0.26933
6	0.94205	0.88797	0.83748	0.79031	0.74622	0.70496	0.66634	0.63017	0.59627	0.56447	0.50663	0.45559	0.41044	0.37043	0.33490	0.26214	0.20718
7	0.93272	0.87056	0.81309	0.75992	0.71068	0.66506	0.62275	0.58349	0.54703	0.51316	0.45235	0.39964	0.35383	0.31393	0.27908	0.20972	0.15937
8	0.92348	0.85349	0.78941	0.73069	0.67684	0.62741	0.58201	0.54027	0.50187	0.46651	0.40388	0.35056	0.30503	0.26604	0.23257	0.16777	0.12259
9	0.91434	0.83676	0.76642	0.70259	0.64461	0.59190	0.54393	0.50025	0.46043	0.42410	0.36061	0.30751	0.26295	0.22546	0.19381	0.13422	0.09430
10	0.90529	0.82035	0.74409	0.67556	0.61391	0.55839	0.50835	0.46319	0.42241	0.38554	0.32197	0.26974	0.22668	0.19106	0.16151	0.10737	0.07254
11	0.89632	0.80426	0.72242	0.64958	0.58468	0.52679	0.47509	0.42888	0.38753	0.35049	0.28748	0.23662	0.19542	0.16192	0.13459	0.08590	0.05580
12	0.88745	0.78849	0.70138	0.62460	0.55684	0.49697	0.44401	0.39711	0.35553	0.31863	0.25668	0.20756	0.16846	0.13722	0.11216	0.06872	0.04292
13	0.87866	0.77303	0.68095	0.60057	0.53032	0.46884	0.41496	0.36770	0.32618	0.28966	0.22917	0.18207	0.14523	0.11629	0.09346	0.05498	0.03302
14	0.86996	0.75788	0.66112	0.57748	0.50507	0.44230	0.38782	0.34046	0.29925	0.26333	0.20462	0.15971	0.12520	0.09855	0.07789	0.04398	0.02540
15	0.86135	0.74301	0.64186	0.55526	0.48102	0.41727	0.36245	0.31524	0.27454	0.23939	0.18270	0.14010	0.10793	0.08352	0.06491	0.03518	0.01954
16	0.85282	0.72845	0.62317	0.53391	0.45811	0.39365	0.33873	0.29189	0.25187	0.21763	0.16312	0.12289	0.09304	0.07078	0.05409	0.02815	0.01503
17	0.84438	0.71416	0.60502	0.51337	0.43630	0.37136	0.31657	0.27027	0.23107	0.19784	0.14564	0.10780	0.08021	0.05998	0.04507	0.02252	0.01156
18	0.83602	0.70016	0.58739	0.49363	0.41552	0.35034	0.29586	0.25025	0.21199	0.17986	0.13004	0.09456	0.06914	0.05083	0.03756	0.01801	0.00889
19	0.82774	0.68643	0.57029	0.47464	0.39573	0.33051	0.27651	0.23171	0.19449	0.16351	0.11611	0.08295	0.05961	0.04308	0.03130	0.01441	0.00684
20	0.81954	0.67297	0.55368	0.45639	0.37689	0.31180	0.25842	0.21455	0.17843	0.14864	0.10367	0.07276	0.05139	0.03651	0.02608	0.01153	0.00526
21	0.81143	0.65978	0.53755	0.43883	0.35894	0.29416	0.24151	0.19866	0.16370	0.13513	0.09256	0.06383	0.04430.	0.03094	0.02174	0.00922	0.00405
22	0.80340	0.64684	0.52189	0.42196	0.34185	0.27751	0.22571	0.18394	0.15018	0.12285	0.08264	0.05599	0.03819	0.02622	0.01811	0.00738	0.00311
23	0.79544	0.63416	0.50669	0.40573	0.32557	0.26180	0.21095	0.17032	0.13778	0.11168	0.07379	0.04911	0.03292	0.02222	0.01509	0.00590	0.00239
24	0.78757	0.62172	0.49193	0.39012	0.31007	0.24698	0.19715	0.15770	0.12640	0.10153	0.06588	0.04308	0.02838	0.01883	0.01258	0.00472	0.00184
25	0.77977	0.60953	0.47761	0.37512	0.29530	0.23300	0.18425	0.14602	0.11597	0.09230	0.05882	0.03779	0.02447	0.01596	0.01048	0.00378	0.00142
26	0.77205	0.59758	0.46369	0.36069	0.28124	0.21981	0.17220	0.13520	0.10639	0.08391	0.05252	0.03315	0.02109	0.01352	0.00874	0.00302	0.00109
27	0.76440	0.58586	0.45019	0.34682	0.26785	0.20737	0.16093	0.12519	0.09761	0.07628	0.04689	0.02908	0.01818	0.01146	0.00728	0.00242	0.00084
28	0.75684	0.57437	0.43708	0.33348	0.25509	0.19563	0.15040	0.11591	0.08955	0.06934	0.04187	0.02551	0.01567	0.00971	0.00607	0.00193	0.00065
29	0.74934	0.56311	0.42435	0.32065	0.24295	0.18456	0.14056	0.10733	0.08215	0.06304	0.03738	0.02237	0.01351	0.00823	0.00506	0.00155	0.00050
30	0.74192	0.55207	0.41199	0.30832	0.23138	0.17411	0.13137	0.09938	0.07537	0.05731	0.03338	0.01963	0.01165	0.00697	0.00421	0.00124	0.00038

Future Value of an Annuity

$$FVA = \frac{(1+i)^n - 1}{i}$$

n/i	1%	2%	3%	4%	5%	6%	7%	8%	9%	10%	12%	14%	16%	18%	20%	25%	30%
1	1.00000	1.00000	1.00000	1.00000	1.00000	1.00000	1.00000	1.00000	1.00000	1.00000	1.00000	1.00000	1.00000	1.00000	1.00000	1.00000	1.00000
2	2.01000	2.02000	2.03000	2.04000	2.05000	2.06000	2.07000	2.08000	2.09000	2.10000	2.12000	2.14000	2.16000	2.18000	2.20000	2.25000	2.30000
3	3.03010	3.06040	3.09090	3.12160	3.15250	3.18360	3.21490	3.24640	3.27810	3.31000	3.37440	3.43960	3.50560	3.57240	3.64000	3.81250	3.99000
4	4.06040	4.12161	4.18363	4.24646	4.31013	4.37462	4.43994	4.50611	4.57313	4.64100	4.77933	4.92114	5.06650	5.21543	5.36800	5.76563	6.18700
5	5.10101	5.20404	5.30914	5.41632	5.52563	5.63709	5.75074	5.86660	5.98471	6.10510	6.35285	6.61010	6.87714	7.15421	7.44160	8.20703	9.04310
6	6.15202	6.30812	6.46841	6.63298	6.80191	6.97532	7.15329	7.33593	7.52333	7.71561	8.11519	8.53552	8.97748	9.44197	9.92992	11.25879	12.75603
7	7.21354	7.43428	7.66246	7.89829	8.14201	8.39384	8.65402	8.92280	9.20043	9.48717	10.08901	10.73049	11.41387	12.14152	12.91590	15.07349	17.58284
8	8.28567	8.58297	8.89234	9.21423	9.54911	9.89747	10.25980	10.63663	11.02847	11.43589	12.29969	13.23276	14.24009	15.32700	16.49908	19.84186	23.85769
9	9.36853	9.75463	10.15911	10.58280	11.02656	11.49132	11.97799	12.48756	13.02104	13.57948	14.77566	16.08535	17.51851	19.08585	20.79890	25.80232	32.01500
10	10.46221	10.94972	11.46388	12.00611	12.57789	13.18079	13.81645	14.48656	15.19293	15.93742	17.54874	19.33730	21.32147	23.52131	25.95868	33.25290	42.61950
11	11.56683	12.16872	12.80780	13.48635	14.20679	14.97164	15.78360	16.64549	17.56029	18.53117	20.65458	23.04452	25.73290	28.75514	32.15042	42.56613	56.40535
12	12.68250	13.41209	14.19203	15.02581	15.91713	16.86994	17.88845	18.97713	20.14072	21.38428	24.13313	27.27075	30.85017	34.93107	39.58050	54.20766	74.32695
13	13.80933	14.68033	15.61779	16.62684	17.71298	18.88214	20.14064	21.49530	22.95338	24.52271	28.02911	32.08865	36.78620	42.21866	48.49660	68.75958	97.62504
14	14.94742	15.97394	17.08632	18.29191	19.59863	21.01507	22.55049	24.21492	26.01919	27.97498	32.39260	37.58107	43.67199	50.81802	59.19592	86.94947	127.91255
15	16.09690	17.29342	18.59891	20.02359	21.57856	23.27597	25.12902	27.15211	29.36092	31.77248	37.27971	43.84241	51.65951	60.96527	72.03511	109.68684	167.28631
16	17.25786	18.63929	20.15688	21.82453	23.65749	25.67253	27.88805	30.32428	33.00340	35.94973	42.75328	50.98035	60.92503	72.93901	87.44213	138.10855	218.47220
17	18.43044	20.01207	21.76159	23.69751	25.84037	28.21288	30.84022	33.75023	36.97370	40.54470	48.88367	59.11760	71.67303	87.06804	105.93056	173.63568	285.01386
18	19.61475	21.41231	23.41444	25.64541	28.13238	30.90565	33.99903	37.45024	41.30134	45.59917	55.74971	68.39407	84.14072	103.74028	128.11667	218.04460	371.51802
19	20.81090	22.84056	25.11687	27.67123	30.53900	33.75999	37.37896	41.44626	46.01846	51.15909	63.43968	78.96923	98.60323	123.41353	154.74000	273.55576	483.97343
20	22.01900	24.29737	26.87037	29.77808	33.06595	36.78559	40.99549	45.76196	51.16012	57.27500	72.05244	91.02493	115.37975	146.62797	186.68800	342.94470	630.16546
21	23.23919	25.78332	28.67649	31.96920	35.71925	39.99273	44.86518	50.42292	56.76453	64.00250	81.69874	104.76842	134.84051	174.02100	225.02560	429.68087	820.21510
22	24.47159	27.29898	30.53678	34.24797	38.50521	43.39229	49.00574	55.45676	62.87334	71.40275	92.50258	120.43600	157.41499	206.34479	271.03072	538.10109	1067.27963
23	25.71630	28.84496	32.45288	36.61789	41.43048	46.99583	53.43614	60.89330	69.53194	79.54302	104.60289	138.29704	183.60138	244.48685	326.23686	673.62636	1388.46351
24	26.97346	30.42186	34.42647	39.08260	44.50200	50.81558	58.17667	66.76476	76.78981	88.49733	118.15524	158.65862	213.97761	289.49448	392.48424	843.03295	1806.00257
25	28.24320	32.03030	36.45926	41.64591	47.72710	54.86451	63.24904	73.10594	84.70090	98.34706	133.33387	181.87083	249.21402	342.60349	471.98108	1054.79118	2348.80334
26	29.52563	33.67091	38.55304	44.31174	51.11345	59.15638	68.67647	79.95442	93.32398	109.18177	150.33393	208.33274	290.08827	405.27211	567.37730	1319.48898	3054.44434
27	30.82089	35.34432	40.70963	47.08421	54.66913	63.70577	74.48382	87.35077	102.72313	121.09994	169.37401	238.49933	337.50239	479.22109	681.85276	1650.36123	3971.77764
28	32.12910	37.05121	42.93092	49.96758	58.40258	68.52811	80.69769	95.33883	112.96822	134.20994	190.69889	272.88923	392.50277	566.48089	819.22331	2063.95153	5164.31093
29	33.45039	38.79223	45.21885	52.96629	62.32271	73.63980	87.34653	103.96594	124.13536	148.63093	214.58275	312.09373	456.30322	669.44745	984.06797	2580.93941	6714.60421
30	34.78489	40.56808	47.57542	56.08494	66.43885	79.05819	94.46079	113.28321	136.30754	164.49402	241.33268	356.78685	530.31173	790.94799	1181.88157	3227.17427	8729.98548

EXHIBIT A3.10

Present Value of an Annuity

$$PVA = \frac{1 - \frac{1}{(1+i)^n}}{i}$$

n/i	1%	2%	3%	4%	5%	6%	7%	8%	9%	10%	12%	14%	16%	18%	20%	25%	30%
1	0.99010	0.98039	0.97087	0.96154	0.95238	0.94340	0.93458	0.92593	0.91743	0.90909	0.89286	0.87719	0.86207	0.84746	0.83333	0.80000	0.76923
2	1.97040	1.94156	1.91347	1.88609	1.85941	1.83339	1.80802	1.78326	1.75911	1.73554	1.69005	1.64666	1.60523	1.56564	1.52778	1.44000	1.36095
3	2.94099	2.88388	2.82861	2.77509	2.72325	2.67301	2.62432	2.57710	2.53129	2.48685	2.40183	2.32163	2.24589	2.17427	2.10648	1.95200	1.81611
4	3.90197	3.80773	3.71710	3.62990	3.54595	3.46511	3.38721	3.31213	3.23972	3.16987	3.03735	2.91371	2.79818	2.69006	2.58873	2.36160	2.16624
5	4.85343	4.71346	4.57971	4.45182	4.32948	4.21236	4.10020	3.99271	3.88965	3.79079	3.60478	3.43308	3.27429	3.12717	2.99061	2.68928	2.43557
6	5.79548	5.60143	5.41719	5.24214	5.07569	4.91732	4.76654	4.62288	4.48592	4.35526	4.11141	3.88867	3.68474	3.49760	3.32551	2.95142	2.64275
7	6.72819	6.47199	6.23028	6.00205	5.78637	5.58238	5.38929	5.20637	5.03295	4.86842	4.56376	4.28830	4.03857	3.81153	3.60459	3.16114	2.80211
8	7.65168	7.32548	7.01969	6.73274	6.46321	6.20979	5.97130	5.74664	5.53482	5.33493	4.96764	4.63886	4.34359	4.07757	3.83716	3.32891	2.92470
9	8.56602	8.16224	7.78611	7.43533	7.10782	6.80169	6.51523	6.24689	5.99525	5.75902	5.32825	4.94637	4.60654	4.30302	4.03097	3.46313	3.01900
10	9.47130	8.98259	8.53020	8.11090	7.72173	7.36009	7.02358	6.71008	6.41766	6.14457	5.65022	5.21612	4.83323	4.49409	4.19247	3.57050	3.09154
11	10.36763	9.78685	9.25262	8.76048	8.30641	7.88687	7.49867	7.13896	6.80519	6.49506	5.93770	5.45273	5.02864	4.65601	4.32706	3.65640	3.14734
12	11.25508	10.57534	9.95400	9.38507	8.86325	8.38384	7.94269	7.53608	7.16073	6.81369	6.19437	5.66029	5.19711	4.79322	4.43922	3.72512	3.19026
13	12.13374	11.34837	10.63496	9.98565	9.39357	8.85268	8.35765	7.90378	7.48690	7.10336	6.42355	5.84236	5.34233	4.90951	4.53268	3.78010	3.22328
14	13.00370	12.10625	11.29607	10.56312	9.89864	9.29498	8.74547	8.24424	7.78615	7.36669	6.62817	6.00207	5.46753	5.00806	4.61057	3.82408	3.24867
15	13.86505	12.84926	11.93794	11.11839	10.37966	9.71225	9.10791	8.55948	8.06069	7.60608	6.81086	6.14217	5.57546	5.09158	4.67547	3.85926	3.26821
16	14.71787	13.57771	12.56110	11.65230	10.83777	10.10590	9.44665	8.85137	8.31256	7.82371	6.97399	6.26506	5.66850	5.16235	4.72956	3.88741	3.28324
17	15.56225	14.29187	13.16612	12.16567	11.27407	10.47726	9.76322	9.12164	8.54363	8.02155	7.11963	6.37286	5.74870	5.22233	4.77463	3.90993	3.29480
18	16.39827	14.99203	13.75351	12.65930	11.68959	10.82760	10.05909	9.37189	8.75563	8.20141	7.24967	6.46742	5.81785	5.27316	4.81219	3.92794	3.30369
19	17.22601	15.67846	14.32380	13.13394	12.08532	11.15812	10.33560	9.60360	8.95011	8.36492	7.36578	6.55037	5.87746	5.31624	4.84350	3.94235	3.31053
20	18.04555	16.35143	14.87747	13.59033	12.46221	11.46992	10.59401	9.81815	9.12855	8.51356	7.46944	6.62313	5.92884	5.35275	4.86958	3.95388	3.31579
21	18.85698	17.01121	15.41502	14.02916	12.82115	11.76408	10.83553	10.01680	9.29224	8.64869	7.56200	6.68696	5.97314	5.38368	4.89132	3.96311	3.31984
22	19.66038	17.65805	15.93692	14.45112	13.16300	12.04158	11.06124	10.20074	9.44243	8.77154	7.64465	6.74294	6.01133	5.40990	4.90943	3.97049	3.32296
23	20.45582	18.29220	16.44361	14.85684	13.48857	12.30338	11.27219	10.37106	9.58021	8.88322	7.71843	6.79206	6.04425	5.43212	4.92453	3.97639	3.32535
24	21.24339	18.91393	16.93554	15.24696	13.79864	12.55036	11.46933	10.52876	9.70661	8.98474	7.78432	6.83514	6.07263	5.45095	4.93710	3.98111	3.32719
25	22.02316	19.52346	17.41315	15.62208	14.09394	12.78336	11.65358	10.67478	9.82258	9.07704	7.84314	6.87293	6.09709	5.46691	4.94759	3.98489	3.32861
26	22.79520	20.12104	17.87684	15.98277	14.37519	13.00317	11.82578	10.80998	9.92897	9.16095	7.89566	6.90608	6.11818	5.48043	4.95632	3.98791	3.32970
27	23.55961	20.70690	18.32703	16.32959	14.64303	13.21053	11.98671	10.93516	10.02658	9.23722	7.94255	6.93515	6.13636	5.49189	4.96360	3.99033	3.33054
28	24.31644	21.28127	18.76411	16.66306	14.89813	13.40616	12.13711	11.05108	10.11613	9.30657	7.98442	6.96066	6.15204	5.50160	4.96967	3.99226	3.33118
29	25.06579	21.84438	19.18845	16.98371	15.14107	13.59072	12.27767	11.15841	10.19828	9.36961	8.02181	6.98304	6.16555	5.50983	4.97472	3.99381	3.33168
30	25.80771	22.39646	19.60044	17.29203	15.37245	13.76483	12.40904	11.25778	10.27365	9.42691	8.05518	7.00266	6.17720	5.51681	4.97894	3.99505	3.33206

International Financial Reporting Standards

After studying Appendix 4, you should be able to:

1 Understand and describe some of the important aspects of international financial reporting standards.

2 Understand key differences between IFRS and U.S. GAAP.

INTERNATIONAL FINANCIAL REPORTING

OBJECTIVE 1

Understand and describe some of the important aspects of international financial reporting standards.

Business is becoming an increasingly global activity as companies conduct operations across national boundaries. Not only are more and more companies engaging in international transactions, they are also seeking capital from foreign stock exchanges. Due to a variety of factors (such as differences in culture, legal systems, and business environments), the historical development of accounting standards on a country-by-country basis has led to considerable diversity in financial accounting practices. To facilitate the conduct of business in an international environment, there has been heightened interest in the development of international accounting standards. This appendix will address some of the more frequently asked questions with regard to **international financial reporting standards (IFRS)**.

WHAT ARE IFRS?

IFRS have both a narrow and a broad meaning. Narrowly, IFRS refer to the accounting standards issued by the International Accounting Standards Board after 2001. More broadly, IFRS describe the entire international set of generally accepted accounting standards. IFRS encompass:

- international accounting standards (IAS) issued prior to 2001
- international financial reporting standards (IFRS) issued after 2001
- interpretations of these standards

IFRS are generally considered less detailed and more concept-based than U.S. GAAP. Over the last 20 years, IFRS have assumed the role as the common language of financial reporting in much of the world.

WHO DEVELOPS IFRS?

The following bodies play an instrumental role in the development of IFRS.

International Accounting Standards Board (IASB) IFRS are developed by the **International Accounting Standards Board (IASB)**, which is headquartered in London. The IASB is an independent, privately funded accounting standard-setting body that consists of 14 members from nine countries. To ensure geographical diversity, members of the IASB normally include four members from the Asia/Oceania region, four members from Europe, four members from the Americas, one from Africa, and one from any area. The goal of the IASB is to develop a single set of high-quality accounting standards that result in transparent and comparable information reported in general purpose financial statements. The general structure of the IASB is shown in Exhibit A4.1.

Monitoring Board The Monitoring Board's purpose is to enhance public accountability of the IFRS Foundation through oversight of the IFRS Foundation Trustees. Its main responsibilities are to participate in the trustee nomination process, approve appointments to the trustees, and ensure that the trustees continue to discharge their duties according to their mandate.

International Financial Reporting Standards (IFRS) Foundation The IASB is overseen by the International Financial Reporting Standards Foundation. The IFRS Foundation is a not-for-profit organization that funds, appoints the members of, and oversees the IASB. The IFRS Foundation is composed of 22 trustees who possess a wide degree of professional experience—including auditors, preparers, users, academics, and others.

IFRS Interpretations Committee The IFRS Interpretations Committee interprets the application of and provides guidance on financial reporting issues not specifically addressed in IFRS. Any interpretations must be reported to the IASB for approval.

IFRS Advisory Council The IFRS Advisory Council advises the IASB and the IFRS Foundation on a number of issues, such as items that should be on the IASB agenda, input on the timetable of the various IASB projects, and advice on various aspects of these projects.

Accounting Standards Advisory Forum The Accounting Standards Advisory Forum (ASAF) advises the IASB on its technical standard-setting activities.

EXHIBIT A4.1   **Structure of the IASB**

Source: Based on information found at www.iasplus.com.

HOW LONG HAS THE IASB BEEN ISSUING STANDARDS?

International standard setting began in 1973 with the formation of the International Accounting Standards Committee (IASC). Between 1973 and 1998, the IASC completed a set of core standards, which began to gain global acceptance. In all, the IASC issued 41 International Accounting Standards (IAS).

In 2001, the IASB was established as the successor organization of the IASC and assumed the standard-setting responsibilities from the IASC. The IASB endorsed the standards of the IASC and began issuing its own standards, which are called International Financial Reporting Standards (IFRS). At this point, with support from the Securities and Exchange Commission (SEC), the Financial Accounting Standards Board (FASB), the European Union (EU), and others, the movement to a single set of high-quality international accounting standards began to pick up considerable momentum. Therefore, IFRS represent a relatively young body of accounting literature. Exhibit A4.2 outlines key dates in the development of IFRS.

EXHIBIT A4.2   **Key Dates in the Development of IFRS**

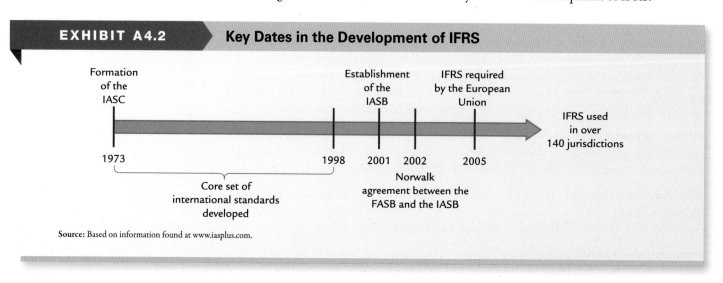

Source: Based on information found at www.iasplus.com.

WHAT ORGANIZATIONS HAVE PLAYED A ROLE IN THE DEVELOPMENT OF IFRS?

In 2002, the FASB and the IASB reached an agreement, known as the Norwalk Agreement, in which both standard setters formalized their commitment to develop "as quickly as practicable" a common set of accounting standards. This process, commonly referred to as **convergence** or **harmonization** of U.S. GAAP and IFRS, involves removing existing differences between the two sets of accounting standards and working together on future accounting standards. The FASB and the IASB are currently involved in several joint standard setting projects aimed at reducing the differences between U.S. GAAP and IFRS.

The Securities and Exchange Commission (SEC) has long supported (as early as 1988) the development of an internationally acceptable set of accounting standards, and it publicly supported the Norwalk Agreement. Statements by the SEC have reiterated its support for a single set of high-quality globally accepted accounting standards and encouraged continued convergence of U.S. GAAP and IFRS.

The EU has been instrumental to the global acceptance of IFRS. In a pivotal event for the use of IFRS, the EU, in 2002, required its member countries to use IFRS by 2005. With the EU adoption of IFRS, the number of countries using IFRS more than doubled between 2003 and 2006.

WHO USES IFRS?

IFRS have gained global acceptance and are currently used in over 140 jurisdictions, including over 30 member-states of the European Union, Australia, and Israel. Exhibit A4.3 highlights the use of IFRS around the world.

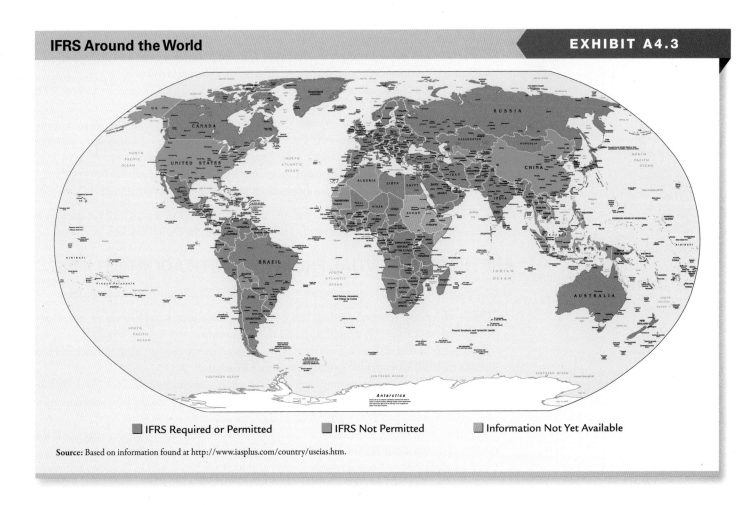

IFRS Around the World   **EXHIBIT A4.3**

■ IFRS Required or Permitted   ■ IFRS Not Permitted   ■ Information Not Yet Available

Source: Based on information found at http://www.iasplus.com/country/useias.htm.

WHEN ARE IFRS EXPECTED TO BE USED IN THE UNITED STATES?

With the majority of companies throughout the world following IFRS, there is considerable pressure for the United States to adopt IFRS. The United States currently allows foreign companies who trade on U.S. stock exchanges to use IFRS without reconciliation to U.S. GAAP. While the SEC had originally envisioned 2015 as the earliest possible date for the mandatory adoption of IFRS by U.S. companies, a 2012 SEC staff paper on incorporating IFRS into U.S. financial reporting is widely viewed as advocating a "go-slow" approach. In considering the adoption of IFRS, the SEC has identified several key issues that will be considered in transitioning to IFRS, including:

- determining whether IFRS are sufficiently developed and applied consistently enough to be used in the United States
- understanding the impact of IFRS adoption on companies
- evaluating whether the financial statement preparers and auditors are sufficiently prepared to convert to IFRS
- determining if investors have adequate preparation and understanding of IFRS and how they differ from U.S. GAAP

At the time of this writing, it does not appear that U.S. adoption of IFRS will occur in the foreseeable future. Factors often cited for this lack of enthusiasm for IFRS relate to the litigious environment in the United States, disagreements between the IASB and the FASB, and the reluctance of U.S. political leaders to give up standard-setting authority to an international organization.

WHAT ARE THE ADVANTAGES OF IFRS?

Proponents of IFRS cite the following four major advantages of using IFRS:

- The use of IFRS should increase the comparability and transparency of financial information between companies that operate in different countries. Thus, use of IFRS should enable investors and other users to more readily assess performance and to make comparisons among companies that currently use different accounting standards.
- IFRS will allow companies and investors to more easily access foreign capital markets. This ease of access is expected to be a stimulus for economic growth.
- IFRS should allow for a more efficient use of company resources as companies streamline their financial reporting processes. Thus, there is an opportunity for companies to lower costs by standardizing and centralizing the financial reporting function.
- IFRS generally require more judgments than the strict application of rules. The use of judgment is seen as a means of preventing the financial abuses that have occurred under U.S. GAAP.

Overall, the reduction in complexities from the use of a single set of high-quality standards is expected to have major benefits for investors, companies, and the capital markets in general.

ARE THERE POTENTIAL PROBLEMS WITH ADOPTING IFRS?

The movement toward IFRS presents many challenges as well as opportunities, including:

- IFRS, which are relatively young, may be viewed as a lower quality set of standards compared to U.S. GAAP, which has stood the test of time.
- There are inherent difficulties involved with integrating worldwide cultural differences to ensure that IFRS are applied and interpreted consistently.
- IFRS generally require more judgment and less reliance on rules than U.S. GAAP. While this exercise of judgment can be a positive aspect of IFRS, many see the potential abuses of judgment as a key problem with IFRS.
- Not all countries will use the same version of IFRS. Many countries that currently use IFRS have selectively modified (or carved out) certain standards with which they do not agree. Such modification will reduce comparability and increase complexity in financial reporting.
- Companies will incur significant transition costs in creating new accounting policies, modifying their accounting systems, and training their employees with regard to IFRS.

WHAT DO FINANCIAL STATEMENTS LOOK LIKE UNDER IFRS?

While the details of preparing financial statements under IFRS is a topic more appropriately covered in intermediate accounting courses, it is helpful to identify a few of the major differences between financial statements prepared under U.S. GAAP and those prepared under IFRS. As an example of financial statements prepared according to IFRS, Exhibit A4.4 shows the income statement and balance sheet of

Financial Statements Prepared Under IFRS   **EXHIBIT A4.4**

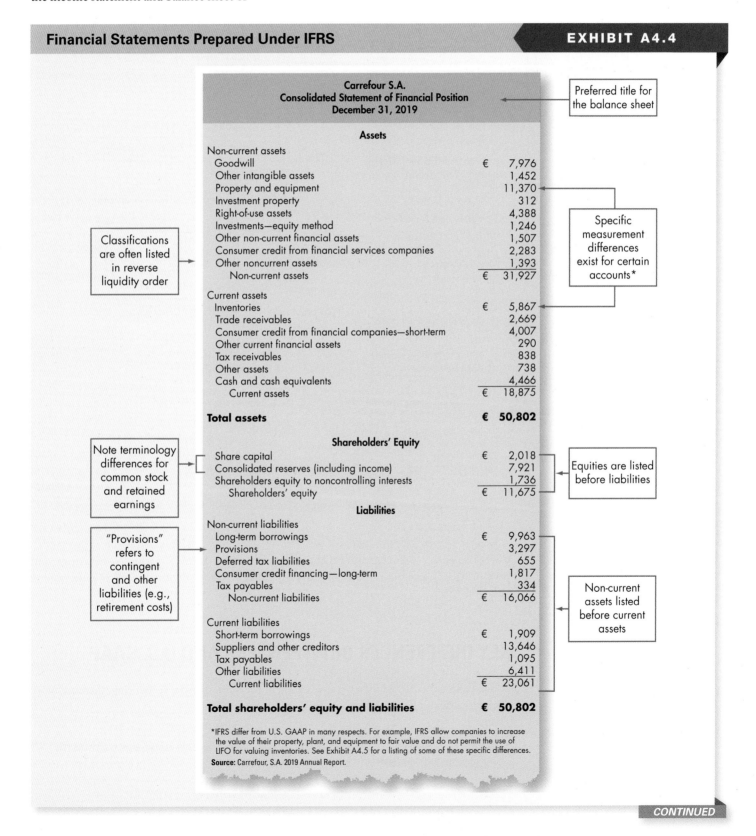

Carrefour S.A.
Consolidated Statement of Financial Position
December 31, 2019

Preferred title for the balance sheet

Assets

Non-current assets
Goodwill	€	7,976
Other intangible assets		1,452
Property and equipment		11,370
Investment property		312
Right-of-use assets		4,388
Investments—equity method		1,246
Other non-current financial assets		1,507
Consumer credit from financial services companies		2,283
Other noncurrent assets		1,393
Non-current assets	€	31,927

Current assets
Inventories	€	5,867
Trade receivables		2,669
Consumer credit from financial companies—short-term		4,007
Other current financial assets		290
Tax receivables		838
Other assets		738
Cash and cash equivalents		4,466
Current assets	€	18,875

Total assets   **€   50,802**

Classifications are often listed in reverse liquidity order

Specific measurement differences exist for certain accounts*

Shareholders' Equity

Share capital	€	2,018
Consolidated reserves (including income)		7,921
Shareholders equity to noncontrolling interests		1,736
Shareholders' equity	€	11,675

Note terminology differences for common stock and retained earnings

Equities are listed before liabilities

Liabilities

Non-current liabilities
Long-term borrowings	€	9,963
Provisions		3,297
Deferred tax liabilities		655
Consumer credit financing—long-term		1,817
Tax payables		334
Non-current liabilities	€	16,066

Current liabilities
Short-term borrowings	€	1,909
Suppliers and other creditors		13,646
Tax payables		1,095
Other liabilities		6,411
Current liabilities	€	23,061

Total shareholders' equity and liabilities   **€   50,802**

"Provisions" refers to contingent and other liabilities (e.g., retirement costs)

Non-current assets listed before current assets

*IFRS differ from U.S. GAAP in many respects. For example, IFRS allow companies to increase the value of their property, plant, and equipment to fair value and do not permit the use of LIFO for valuing inventories. See Exhibit A4.5 for a listing of some of these specific differences.
Source: Carrefour, S.A. 2019 Annual Report.

CONTINUED

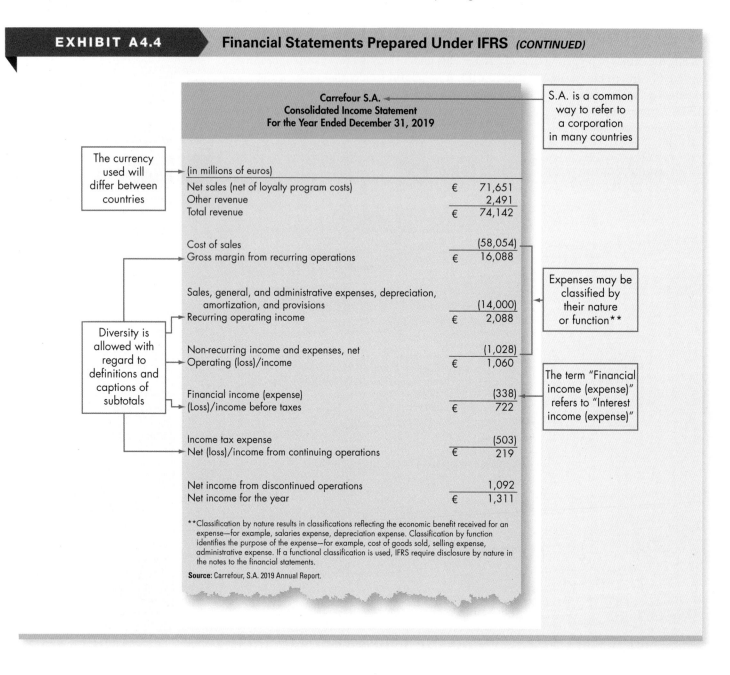

EXHIBIT A4.4   **Financial Statements Prepared Under IFRS** *(CONTINUED)*

Carrefour S.A.
Consolidated Income Statement
For the Year Ended December 31, 2019

S.A. is a common way to refer to a corporation in many countries

The currency used will differ between countries

(in millions of euros)

Net sales (net of loyalty program costs)	€	71,651
Other revenue		2,491
Total revenue	€	74,142
Cost of sales		(58,054)
Gross margin from recurring operations	€	16,088
Sales, general, and administrative expenses, depreciation, amortization, and provisions		(14,000)
Recurring operating income	€	2,088
Non-recurring income and expenses, net		(1,028)
Operating (loss)/income	€	1,060
Financial income (expense)		(338)
(Loss)/income before taxes	€	722
Income tax expense		(503)
Net (loss)/income from continuing operations	€	219
Net income from discontinued operations		1,092
Net income for the year	€	1,311

Diversity is allowed with regard to definitions and captions of subtotals

Expenses may be classified by their nature or function**

The term "Financial income (expense)" refers to "Interest income (expense)"

**Classification by nature results in classifications reflecting the economic benefit received for an expense—for example, salaries expense, depreciation expense. Classification by function identifies the purpose of the expense—for example, cost of goods sold, selling expense, administrative expense. If a functional classification is used, IFRS require disclosure by nature in the notes to the financial statements.

Source: Carrefour, S.A. 2019 Annual Report.

Carrefour S.A., a French retailer that operates in Europe, South America, North Africa, and parts of Asia.[1] Carrefour is the second largest retailer in the world in terms of revenue, trailing only **Wal-Mart**.

OBJECTIVE 2
Understand key differences between IFRS and U.S. GAAP.

KEY DIFFERENCES BETWEEN IFRS AND U.S. GAAP

While IFRS are expected to have far-reaching impacts on financial accounting, there are more similarities than differences between IFRS and U.S. GAAP.

---

1 The differences between the retained earnings statement and the statement of cash flows under U.S. GAAP and IFRS are relatively minor, so we will focus on the balance sheet and income statement here.

WHAT SIMILARITIES AND DIFFERENCES EXIST?

To aid in understanding the impact of IFRS on financial accounting, review Exhibit A4.5. As you can see, the topics covered in this text will provide you with a solid foundation for your study of accounting.

| **Comparison of IFRS and U.S. GAAP** | **EXHIBIT A4.5** |

Chapter	Comparison

1	• The fundamental accounting equation is the same under IFRS and U.S. GAAP.
	• Balance Sheet:
	  ○ IFRS uses the same balance sheet classifications as U.S. GAAP, although terminology differences exist. For example, stockholders' equity may be called "capital and reserves."
	  ○ IFRS do not specify a particular balance sheet format. International balance sheets are often listed in reverse order as compared to U.S. GAAP. For example, IFRS often present noncurrent assets first, followed by current assets. Additionally, stockholders' equity is often presented first, followed by noncurrent liabilities, and then current liabilities.
	• Income Statement:
	  ○ Similar to U.S. GAAP, IFRS do not prescribe a specific format (single-step or multiple-step) for the income statement.
	  ○ IFRS allow income statement items to be classified either by their nature or their function. U.S. GAAP classifies income statement items by their function (e.g., cost of goods sold).
	  ○ Terminology differences do exist. For example, sales may be referred to as "turnover," or interest expense may be referred to as "finance costs."
	• Retained Earnings Statement:
	  ○ IFRS do not specify the retained earnings statement as a required financial statement. Instead, IFRS require the change in retained earnings be shown on the statement of changes in equity.
	  ○ Terminology differences often exist. For example, retained earnings is often called "accumulated profits and losses."
	• Statement of Cash Flow:
	  ○ IFRS require the presentation of a statement of cash flows whose format is similar to the one required under U.S. GAAP. However, some items (described in Chapter 11) may be classified differently.

2	• The IASB and the FASB are developing a joint conceptual framework. The first phase of this framework that describes the objective of financial accounting and the qualitative characteristics of accounting information has been completed and is discussed in Chapter 2. • In general, IFRS are considered more "principles-based" than U.S. GAAP. Conversely, U.S. GAAP is considered more "rules-based" than IFRS. • IFRS and U.S. GAAP use the identical double-entry accounting system. • Under IFRS, transactions are analyzed, journalized, and posted in the same manner as under U.S. GAAP.
3	• The IASB and FASB contain almost identical revenue recognition standards. Similarly, the expense recognition principle under IFRS is similar to that of U.S. GAAP. • The adjustment process under IFRS is the same as the adjustment process under U.S. GAAP.
4	• Internal control issues are company and financial accounting system-specific, and the issues would be similar in an international environment. • The documentation and assessment requirements of Section 404 of the Sarbanes–Oxley Act (SOX) impose a much greater burden on U.S. companies compared to international companies. • The management, control, and accounting for cash are the same under IFRS as under U.S. GAAP.
5	• The IASB and FASB contain almost identical revenue recognition standards. • The recognition and valuation of receivables under IFRS is generally the same as U.S. GAAP.
6	• The purchase and sale of inventory is generally the same under IFRS as under U.S. GAAP. • IFRS do not allow the use of LIFO for determining the cost of inventory.

CONTINUED

EXHIBIT A4.5	Comparison of IFRS and U.S. GAAP *(CONTINUED)*

7	• While the accounting for an asset's initial cost is similar under IFRS and U.S. GAAP, IFRS allow for companies to increase the value of their property, plant, equipment, and intangible assets up to fair value. This is not permitted under U.S. GAAP. • While similar depreciation methods are used, IFRS allow the depreciation of each component of an asset separately (component depreciation); this is permitted, but not required, by U.S. GAAP. • Generally, the accounting for intangible assets under IFRS is similar to U.S. GAAP. However, under IFRS, research costs are expensed while development costs are capitalized as an intangible asset if it is probable that future benefits will be generated. • The impairment model under IFRS is a single-step process rather than the two-step process used in U.S. GAAP. In addition, IFRS allow recovery of impairment losses, which is not allowed under U.S. GAAP.
8	• The accounting for current liabilities is generally the same under IFRS and U.S. GAAP. • IFRS commonly report liabilities on the balance sheet in reverse order relative to U.S. GAAP—from least liquid to most liquid. • IFRS refer to loss contingencies that are recognized in the financial statements as "provisions." Loss contingencies that are not recognized in the financial statements are referred to as "contingencies." • Similar to U.S. GAAP, IFRS recognize provisions when the contingent event is probable. However, IFRS define probable as "more likely than not," while U.S. GAAP defines probable as "likely." Therefore, more events will be recognized as provisions under IFRS.
9	• The accounting for bonds and notes payable is generally the same under IFRS as under U.S. GAAP.
10	• The accounting for equity is generally the same under IFRS as under U.S. GAAP. • Some terminology differences exist. For example, under IFRS, stockholders' equity is often called "capital and reserves." The use of the term "reserves" has generally been discouraged under U.S. GAAP.

11	• The classification of certain business activities differs under IFRS relative to U.S. GAAP.
	  o IFRS allow companies to report taxes paid as an operating, investing, or financing transaction. Under U.S. GAAP, taxes paid are classified as an operating activity.
	  o IFRS allow companies to report the payment of dividends and interest as either an operating or a financing activity. Under U.S. GAAP the payment of dividends is a financing activity, while payment of interest is an operating activity.
	  o Interest or dividends received may be reported as either operating or investing cash inflows under IFRS. These are both operating activities under U.S. GAAP.

12	• The analysis of financial statements is the same under IFRS as it is under U.S. GAAP.

WHERE CAN I GO TO FIND OUT MORE ABOUT IFRS?

IFRS Foundation website:
www.ifrs.org

American Institute of Certified Public Accountants (AICPA) website for IFRS Resources:
www.IFRS.com

Ernst & Young IFRS page:
www.ey.com/GL/en/Issues/IFRS

Deloitte IFRS page:
www.iasplus.com

International Association for Accounting Education & Research:
www.iaaer.org/resources

PricewaterhouseCoopers IFRS page:
www.pwc.com/gx/en/ifrs-reporting/index.jhtml

KPMG IFRS page:
www.kpmg-institutes.com/institutes/ifrs-institute.htm

SUMMARY OF LEARNING OBJECTIVES

- International financial reporting standards (IFRS) are an international set of generally accepted accounting standards.
- IFRS are developed by the International Accounting Standards Board (IASB), an independent, privately funded standard-setting body consisting of 14 members from nine countries.
- International standard setting began in 1973; however, the development of a single-set of high quality international accounting standards accelerated in 2001 with the establishment of the IASB and the European Union's requirement of the use of IFRS.
- IFRS are currently used in over 140 jurisdictions and are currently being considered in the United States.
- The reduction in complexities from the use of a single set of high-quality standards is expected to have major benefits for investors, companies and capital markets in general. However, the movement toward IFRS presents many challenges as well.
- A familiarity with financial statements prepared under IFRS is useful for financial statement users.

LO1. Understand and describe some of the important aspects of international financial reporting standards.

KEY TERMS

Convergence (harmonization), 827
International Accounting Standards
  Board (IASB), 825

International financial reporting standards
  (IFRS), 825

- IFRS are expected to have far-reaching impacts on financial accounting; however, an understanding of the basics of U.S. generally accepted accounting principles will provide a strong foundation for the study of international accounting standards.
- Within each topical area of accounting, financial statement users need to be able to identify key differences between U.S. GAAP and IFRS.

LO2. Understand key differences between IFRS and U.S. GAAP.

APPLYING KNOWLEDGE

MULTIPLE-CHOICE QUESTIONS

A4-1 Which of the following best describes international financial reporting standards?
  a. IFRS describe the generally accepted accounting principles that are currently used by all companies in the United States.
  b. IFRS consist only of standards that have been issued since the IASB was formed in 2001.
  c. IFRS are considered to be more concept-based than U.S. GAAP.
  d. IFRS will be required to be used in the United States beginning in 2020.

A4-2 Which of the following statements is true?
   a. The FASB has consistently resisted the adoption of IFRS in the United States for fear that it will lose its standard-setting authority.
   b. The requirement to use IFRS by the European Union led to a significant increase in the global acceptance of IFRS.
   c. IFRS have existed for nearly as long as U.S. GAAP; however, it only recently began to gain acceptance as a body of high-quality accounting standards.
   d. The SEC is considering allowing foreign companies who trade stock on the U.S. stock exchanges to use IFRS.

A4-3 Convergence of U.S. GAAP and IFRS is best described as:
   a. the replacement of U.S. GAAP by IFRS.
   b. the replacement of IFRS by U.S. GAAP.
   c. changing existing U.S. GAAP so that any differences in IFRS will be insignificant.
   d. changing both existing U.S. GAAP and IFRS to reduce differences and developing new GAAP through a joint standard-setting process.

A4-4 Which of the following organizations has the responsibility to create IFRS?
   a. Financial Accounting Standards Board
   b. International Financial Reporting Standards Foundation
   c. International Accounting Standards Board
   d. Securities and Exchange Commission

A4-5 Which of the following is *not* an advantage of IFRS?
   a. The use of IFRS should increase the comparability and transparency of financial information.
   b. The use of IFRS will make it easier to access foreign capital markets.
   c. IFRS require more judgments than U.S. GAAP.
   d. IFRS are less conservative than U.S. GAAP, so net income under IFRS will generally be higher than net income under U.S. GAAP.

A4-6 Which of the following is *not* a disadvantage of IFRS?
   a. The use of IFRS will lead to an outflow of capital from the U.S. to foreign countries.
   b. The use of IFRS could be viewed as adopting a lower quality standard.
   c. Due to cultural differences among countries, it will be difficult to ensure consistent application and interpretation of IFRS.
   d. Different versions of IFRS exist that may cause confusion for users of financial statements.

A4-7 With regard to the presentation of financial information under IFRS, which of the following is true?
   a. The terminology on the balance sheet and the income statement is the same under IFRS and U.S. GAAP.
   b. Under IFRS, the elements of the balance sheet are often presented in reverse order relative to U.S. GAAP, with noncurrent assets presented before current assets and stockholders' equity presented before liabilities.
   c. Under IFRS, the elements of the income statement are often presented in reverse order, with expenses presented first followed by revenues.
   d. IFRS do not require the presentation of a statement of cash flows.

A4-8 Which of the following inventory costing methods is *not* allowed under IFRS?
   a. FIFO   c. average cost
   b. specific identification   d. LIFO

A4-9   Which of the following is true?

    a. IFRS allow property, plant, and equipment to be revalued upward if fair value is higher than historical cost.

    b. IFRS contain more extensive guidance on revenue recognition than U.S. GAAP.

    c. IFRS have a much more broad definition of cash than U.S. GAAP.

    d. The accounting for research and development costs is identical under IFRS and U.S. GAAP.

A4-10   Which of the following is true with regard to contingent liabilities?

    a. IFRS and U.S. GAAP use the same terminology to refer to contingent liabilities.

    b. A contingent liability is recognized under IFRS when it is more likely than not that the contingent event will occur.

    c. Fewer events will be recognized as contingent liabilities under IFRS than under U.S. GAAP.

    d. Provisions are contingent liabilities that are not recognized in the financial statements.

THE KROGER CO.

FORM 10-K

(Annual Report)

For the fiscal year ended February 1, 2020

Address	1014 Vine Street
	Cincinnati, OH 45202
Telephone	(513) 762-4000
CIK	0000056873
Symbol	KR
SIC Code	5411 - Supermarkets and Other Grocery (except Convenience) Stores
Industry	Food Retail
Sector	Retail Trade
Fiscal Year	01/31

For the complete text of the Form10-K for the Kroger Co., please go to cengage.com.

ITEM 8.   FINANCIAL STATEMENTS AND SUPPLEMENTARY DATA

Consolidated Financial Statements of the Kroger Co.
For the Fiscal Year Ended February 1, 2020
Table of Contents

REPORT OF INDEPENDENT REGISTERED PUBLIC ACCOUNTING FIRM

To the Board of Directors and Shareholders of The Kroger Co.

OPINIONS ON THE FINANCIAL STATEMENTS AND INTERNAL CONTROL OVER FINANCIAL REPORTING

We have audited the accompanying consolidated balance sheets of The Kroger Co. and its subsidiaries (the "Company") as of February 1, 2020, and February 2, 2019, and the related consolidated statements of operations, of comprehensive income, of changes in shareholders' equity, and of cash flows for each of the 3 years in the period ended February 1, 2020, including the related notes (collectively referred to as the "consolidated financial statements"). We also have audited the Company's internal control over financial reporting as of February 1, 2020, based on criteria established in *Internal Control—Integrated Framework* (2013) issued by the Committee of Sponsoring Organizations of the Treadway Commission (COSO).

In our opinion, the consolidated financial statements referred to above present fairly, in all material respects, the financial position of the Company as of February 1, 2020, and February 2, 2019, and the results of its operations and its cash flows for each of the 3 years in the period ended February 1, 2020, in conformity with accounting principles generally accepted in the United States of America. Also in our opinion, the Company maintained, in all material respects, effective internal control over financial reporting as of February 1, 2020, based on criteria established in *Internal Control—Integrated Framework* (2013) issued by the COSO.

Changes in Accounting Principles

As discussed in Note 18 to the consolidated financial statements, the Company changed the manner in which it accounts for leases in 2019 and the manner in which it accounts for revenues from contracts with customers in 2018.

BASIS FOR OPINIONS

The Company's management is responsible for these consolidated financial statements, for maintaining effective internal control over financial reporting, and for its assessment of the effectiveness of internal control over financial reporting, included in Management's Report on Internal Control Over Financial Reporting appearing under Item 9A. Our responsibility is to express opinions on the Company's consolidated financial statements and on the Company's internal control over financial reporting based on our audits. We are a public accounting firm registered with the Public Company Accounting Oversight Board (United States) (PCAOB) and are required to be independent with respect to the Company in accordance with the U.S. federal securities laws and the applicable rules and regulations of the Securities and Exchange Commission and the PCAOB.

We conducted our audits in accordance with the standards of the PCAOB. Those standards require that we plan and perform the audits to obtain reasonable assurance about whether the consolidated financial statements are free of material misstatement, whether due to error or fraud, and whether effective internal control over financial reporting was maintained in all material respects.

Our audits of the consolidated financial statements included performing procedures to assess the risks of material misstatement of the consolidated financial statements, whether due to error or fraud, and performing procedures that respond to those risks. Such procedures included examining, on a test basis, evidence regarding the amounts and disclosures in the consolidated financial statements. Our audits also included evaluating the accounting principles used and significant estimates made by management, as well as evaluating the overall presentation of the consolidated financial statements. Our audit of internal control over financial reporting included obtaining an understanding of internal control over financial reporting, assessing the risk that a material weakness exists, and testing and evaluating the design and operating effectiveness of internal control based on the assessed risk. Our audits also included performing such other procedures as we considered necessary in the circumstances. We believe that our audits provide a reasonable basis for our opinions.

DEFINITION AND LIMITATIONS OF INTERNAL CONTROL OVER FINANCIAL REPORTING

A company's internal control over financial reporting is a process designed to provide reasonable assurance regarding the reliability of financial reporting and the preparation of financial statements for external purposes in accordance with generally accepted accounting principles. A company's internal control over financial reporting includes those policies and procedures that (i) pertain to the maintenance of records that, in reasonable detail, accurately and fairly reflect the transactions and dispositions of the assets of the company; (ii) provide reasonable assurance that transactions are recorded as necessary to permit preparation of financial statements in accordance with generally accepted accounting principles and that receipts and expenditures of the company are being made only in accordance with authorizations of management and directors of the company; and (iii) provide reasonable assurance regarding prevention or timely detection of unauthorized acquisition, use, or disposition of the company's assets that could have a material effect on the financial statements.

Because of its inherent limitations, internal control over financial reporting may not prevent or detect misstatements. Also, projections of any evaluation of effectiveness to future periods are subject to the risk that controls may become inadequate because of changes in conditions or that the degree of compliance with the policies or procedures may deteriorate.

CRITICAL AUDIT MATTERS

The critical audit matter communicated below is a matter arising from the current period audit of the consolidated financial statements that was communicated or required to be communicated to the audit committee and that (i) relates to accounts or disclosures that are material to the consolidated financial statements and (ii) involved our especially challenging, subjective, or complex judgments. The communication of critical audit matters does not alter in any way our opinion on the consolidated financial statements, taken as a whole, and we are not, by communicating the critical audit matter below, providing a separate opinion on the critical audit matter or on the accounts or disclosures to which it relates.

Goodwill Impairment Assessment—Kroger Specialty Pharmacy ("KSP") Reporting Unit

As described in Notes 1 and 3 to the consolidated financial statements, the Company's consolidated goodwill balance was $3.1 billion as of February 1, 2020, and the goodwill associated with the KSP reporting unit was $243 million. Management reviews goodwill annually for impairment in the fourth quarter of each year and also upon the occurrence of triggering events. The fair value of a reporting unit is compared to its carrying value for purposes of identifying potential impairment. Goodwill impairment is recognized for any excess of the reporting unit's carrying value over its fair value, not to exceed the total amount of goodwill allocated to the reporting unit. As disclosed by management, the fair value of the Company's KSP reporting unit was estimated using multiple valuation techniques, a discounted cash flow model (income approach), a market multiple model and comparable mergers and acquisition model (market approaches), with each method weighted in the calculation. The income approach relies on management's estimates of revenue growth rates, margin assumptions, and discount rate to estimate future cash flows. The market approaches require the determination of an appropriate peer group, which is utilized to derive estimated fair values based on selected market multiples.

The principal considerations for our determination that performing procedures relating to the goodwill impairment assessment of the KSP reporting unit is a critical audit matter are there was significant judgment by management when developing the fair value measurement of the reporting unit. This in turn led to a high degree of auditor judgment, subjectivity, and effort in performing procedures to evaluate management's cash flow projections and significant assumptions, including revenue growth rates, margin assumptions, discount rate, peer group determination, and market multiple selection. In addition, the audit effort involved the use of professionals with specialized skill and knowledge to assist in performing these procedures and evaluating the audit evidence obtained.

Addressing the matter involved performing procedures and evaluating audit evidence in connection with forming our overall opinion on the consolidated financial statements. These procedures included testing the effectiveness of controls relating to management's goodwill impairment assessment, including controls over the valuation of the Company's KSP reporting unit. These procedures also included, among others, testing management's process for developing the fair value estimate, evaluating the appropriateness of the income and market approach models, testing the completeness, accuracy, and relevance of the underlying data used in the models, and evaluating the significant assumptions used by management, including the revenue growth rates, margin assumptions, discount rate, peer group determination, and market multiple selection. Evaluating management's assumptions relating to revenue growth rates and margin assumptions involved evaluating whether the assumptions used by management were reasonable considering (i) the current and past performance of the reporting unit, (ii) the consistency with external market and industry data, and (iii) whether these assumptions were consistent with evidence obtained in other areas of the audit. Evaluating the Company's peer group determinations included evaluating the appropriateness of the identified peer companies. Professionals with specialized skill and knowledge were used to assist in the evaluation of the Company's discounted cash flow and market models, and certain significant assumptions, including the discount rate, peer group determination, and market multiples.

/s/ PricewaterhouseCoopers LLP
Cincinnati, Ohio
April 1, 2020

We have served as the Company's auditor since 1929.

THE KROGER CO.
CONSOLIDATED BALANCE SHEETS

(In millions, except par amounts)	February 1, 2020	February 2, 2019
ASSETS		
Current assets		
Cash and temporary cash investments	$ 399	$ 429
Store deposits in-transit	1,179	1,181
Receivables	1,706	1,589
FIFO inventory	8,464	8,123
LIFO reserve	(1,380)	(1,277)
Assets held for sale	—	166
Prepaid and other current assets	522	592
Total current assets	10,890	10,803
Property, plant and equipment, net	21,871	21,635
Operating lease assets	6,814	—
Intangibles, net	1,066	1,258
Goodwill	3,076	3,087
Other assets	1,539	1,335
Total Assets	$ 45,256	$ 38,118
LIABILITIES		
Current liabilities		
Current portion of long-term debt including obligations under finance leases	$ 1,965	$ 3,157
Current portion of operating lease liabilities	597	—
Trade accounts payable	6,349	6,059
Accrued salaries and wages	1,168	1,227
Liabilities held for sale	—	51
Other current liabilities	4,164	3,780
Total current liabilities	14,243	14,274
Long-term debt including obligations under finance leases	12,111	12,072
Noncurrent operating lease liabilities	6,505	—
Deferred income taxes	1,466	1,562
Pension and postretirement benefit obligations	608	494
Other long-term liabilities	1,750	1,881
Total Liabilities	36,683	30,283
Commitments and contingencies see Note 13		
SHAREHOLDERS' EQUITY		
Preferred shares, $100 par per share, 5 shares authorized and unissued	—	—
Common shares, $1 par per share, 2,000 shares authorized; 1,918 shares issued in 2019 and 2018	1,918	1,918
Additional paid-in capital	3,337	3,245
Accumulated other comprehensive loss	(640)	(346)
Accumulated earnings	20,978	19,681
Common shares in treasury, at cost, 1,130 shares in 2019 and 1,120 shares in 2018	(16,991)	(16,612)
Total Shareholders' Equity—The Kroger Co.	8,602	7,886
Noncontrolling interests	(29)	(51)
Total Equity	8,573	7,835
Total Liabilities and Equity	$ 45,256	$ 38,118

The accompanying notes are an integral part of the consolidated financial statements.

THE KROGER CO.
CONSOLIDATED STATEMENTS OF OPERATIONS

Years Ended February 1, 2020, February 2, 2019, and February 3, 2018

(In millions, except per share amounts)	2019 (52 weeks)	2018 (52 weeks)	2017 (53 weeks)
Sales	$ 122,286	$ 121,852	$ 123,280
Operating expenses			
Merchandise costs, including advertising, warehousing, and transportation, excluding items shown separately below	95,294	95,103	95,811
Operating, general, and administrative	21,208	20,786	21,510
Rent	884	884	911
Depreciation and amortization	2,649	2,465	2,436
Operating profit	2,251	2,614	2,612
Other income (expense)			
Interest expense	(603)	(620)	(601)
Non-service component of company-sponsored pension plan costs	—	(26)	(527)
Mark to market gain on Ocado securities	157	228	—
Gain on sale of businesses	176	1,782	—
Net earnings before income tax (benefit) expense	1,981	3,978	1,484
Income tax (benefit) expense	469	900	(405)
Net earnings including noncontrolling interests	1,512	3,078	1,889
Net loss attributable to noncontrolling interests	(147)	(32)	(18)
Net earnings attributable to The Kroger Co.	$ 1,659	$ 3,110	$ 1,907
Net earnings attributable to The Kroger Co. per basic common share	$ 2.05	$ 3.80	$ 2.11
Average number of common shares used in basic calculation	799	810	895
Net earnings attributable to The Kroger Co. per diluted common share	$ 2.04	$ 3.76	$ 2.09
Average number of common shares used in diluted calculation	805	818	904

The accompanying notes are an integral part of the consolidated financial statements.

THE KROGER CO.
CONSOLIDATED STATEMENTS OF COMPREHENSIVE INCOME

Years Ended February 1, 2020, February 2, 2019, and February 3, 2018

(In millions)	2019 (52 weeks)	2018 (52 weeks)	2017 (53 weeks)
Net earnings including noncontrolling interests	$ 1,512	$ 3,078	$ 1,889
Other comprehensive income (loss)			
Realized gains on available for sale securities, net of income tax[1]	—	(4)	4
Change in pension and other postretirement defined benefit plans, net of income tax[2]	(105)	147	214
Unrealized gains and losses on cash flow hedging activities, net of income tax[3]	(47)	(23)	23
Amortization of unrealized gains and losses on cash flow hedging activities, net of income tax[4]	4	5	3
Cumulative effect of accounting change[5]	(146)	—	—
Total other comprehensive income (loss)	(294)	125	244
Comprehensive income	1,218	3,203	2,133
Comprehensive loss attributable to noncontrolling interests	(147)	(32)	(18)
Comprehensive income attributable to The Kroger Co.	$ 1,365	$ 3,235	$ 2,151

(1) Amount is net of tax expense (benefit) of ($1) in 2018 and $1 in 2017.

(2) Amount is net of tax expense (benefit) of ($33) in 2019, $45 in 2018, and $83 in 2017.

(3) Amount is net of tax expense (benefit) of ($17) in 2019, ($8) in 2018, and $0 in 2017.

(4) Amount is net of tax expense of $3 in 2019, $3 in 2018, and $3 in 2017.

(5) Related to the adoption of Accounting Standards Update ("ASU") 2018-02, "Income Statement—Reporting Comprehensive Income (Topic 220): Reclassification of Certain Tax Effects from Accumulated Other Comprehensive Income," (see Note 18 for additional details).

The accompanying notes are an integral part of the consolidated financial statements.

THE KROGER CO.
CONSOLIDATED STATEMENTS OF CASH FLOWS

Years Ended February 1, 2020, February 2, 2019, and February 3, 2018

(In millions)	2019 (52 weeks)	2018 (52 weeks)	2017 (53 weeks)
Cash Flows from Operating Activities:			
Net earnings including noncontrolling interests	$ 1,512	$ 3,078	$ 1,889
Adjustments to reconcile net earnings including noncontrolling interests to net cash provided by operating activities:			
Depreciation and amortization	2,649	2,465	2,436
Asset impairment charge	120	56	71
Operating lease asset amortization	640	—	—
LIFO charge (credit)	105	29	(8)
Stock-based employee compensation	155	154	151
Expense for company-sponsored pension plans	39	76	591
Goodwill impairment charge	—	—	110
Deferred income taxes	(56)	(45)	(694)
Gain on sale of businesses	(176)	(1,782)	—
(Gain) loss on the sale of assets	(158)	2	(31)
Mark to market gain on Ocado securities	(157)	(228)	—
Loss on deconsolidation and impairment of Lucky's Market	412	—	—
Other	(109)	58	39
Changes in operating assets and liabilities net of effects from mergers and disposals of businesses:			
Store deposits in-transit	3	(20)	(265)
Receivables	(36)	(208)	61
Inventories	(351)	(354)	(23)
Prepaid and other current assets	(33)	244	41
Trade accounts payable	342	213	158
Accrued expenses	302	416	(40)
Income taxes receivable and payable	(142)	289	(96)
Contribution to company-sponsored pension plan	—	(185)	(1,000)
Operating lease liabilities	(639)	—	—
Proceeds from contract associated with sale of business	295	—	—
Other	(53)	(94)	23
Net cash provided by operating activities	4,664	4,164	3,413
Cash Flows from Investing Activities:			
Payments for property and equipment, including payments for lease buyouts	(3,128)	(2,967)	(2,809)
Proceeds from sale of assets	273	85	138
Proceeds on settlement of financial instrument	—	235	—
Payments for acquisitions, net of cash acquired	—	(197)	(16)
Purchases of stores	—	(44)	
Net proceeds from sale of businesses	327	2,169	—
Purchases of Ocado securities	—	(392)	—
Other	(83)	(75)	(20)
Net cash used by investing activities	(2,611)	(1,186)	(2,707)

Cash Flows from Financing Activities:	813	2,236	1,523
Proceeds from issuance of long-term debt	(2,304)	(1,372)	(788)
Payments on long-term debt including obligations under finance leases	350	(1,321)	696
Net proceeds (payments) on commercial paper	(486)	(437)	(443)
Dividends paid	55	65	51
Proceeds from issuance of capital stock	(465)	(2,010)	(1,633)
Treasury stock purchases	(46)	(57)	(87)
Other			
Net cash used by financing activities	(2,083)	(2,896)	(681)
Net (decrease) increase in cash and temporary cash investments	(30)	82	25
Cash and temporary cash investments:			
Beginning of year	429	347	322
End of year	$ 399	$ 429	$ 347
Reconciliation of capital investments:			
Payments for property and equipment, including payments for lease buyouts	$ (3,128)	$ (2,967)	$ (2,809)
Payments for lease buyouts	82	5	13
Changes in construction-in-progress payables	2	(56)	(188)
Total capital investments, excluding lease buyouts	$ (3,044)	$ (3,018)	$ (2,984)
Disclosure of cash flow information:			
Cash paid during the year for interest	$ 523	$ 614	$ 656
Cash paid during the year for income taxes	$ 706	$ 600	$ 348

The accompanying notes are an integral part of the consolidated financial statements.

THE KROGER CO.
CONSOLIDATED STATEMENT OF CHANGES IN SHAREHOLDERS' EQUITY

Years Ended February 1, 2020, February 2, 2019, and February 3, 2018

(In millions, except per share amounts)	Common Stock Shares	Common Stock Amount	Additional Paid-In Capital	Treasury Stock Shares	Treasury Stock Amount	Accumulated Other Comprehensive Income (Loss)	Accumulated Earnings	Noncontrolling Interest	Total
Balances at January 28, 2017	1,918	$ 1,918	$ 3,070	994	$ (13,118)	$ (715)	$ 15,543	$ 12	$ 6,710
Issuance of common stock:									
Stock options exercised	—	—	—	(4)	51	—	—	—	51
Restricted stock issued	—	—	(119)	(2)	85	—	—	—	(34)
Treasury stock activity:									
Treasury stock purchases, at cost	—	—	—	58	(1,567)	—	—	—	(1,567)
Stock options exchanged	—	—	—	2	(66)	—	—	—	(66)
Share-based employee compensation	—	—	151	—	—	—	—	—	151
Other comprehensive income net of tax of $87	—	—	—	—	—	244	—	—	244
Other	—	—	59	—	(69)	—	—	(20)	(30)
Cash dividends declared ($0.495 per common share)	—	—	—	—	—	—	(443)	—	(443)
Net earnings (loss) including noncontrolling interests	—	—	—	—	—	—	1,907	(18)	1,889
Balances at February 3, 2018	1,918	$ 1,918	$ 3,161	1,048	$ (14,684)	$ (471)	$ 17,007	$ (26)	$ 6,905
Issuance of common stock:									
Stock options exercised	—	—	—	(4)	65	—	—	—	65
Restricted stock issued	—	—	(119)	(3)	74	—	—	—	(45)
Treasury stock activity:									
Treasury stock purchases, at cost	—	—	—	76	(1,927)	—	—	—	(1,927)
Stock options exchanged	—	—	—	3	(83)	—	—	—	(83)
Share-based employee compensation	—	—	154	—	—	—	—	—	154
Other comprehensive income net of tax of $39	—	—	—	—	—	125	—	—	125
Other	—	—	49	—	(57)	—	—	7	(1)
Cash dividends declared ($0.545 per common share)	—	—	—	—	—	—	(436)	—	(436)
Net earnings (loss) including noncontrolling interests	—	—	—	—	—	—	3,110	(32)	3,078
Balances at February 2, 2019	1,918	$ 1,918	$ 3,245	1,120	$ (16,612)	$ (346)	$ 19,681	$ (51)	$ 7,835
Issuance of common stock:									
Stock options exercised	—	—	—	(3)	55	—	—	—	55
Restricted stock issued	—	—	(128)	(3)	92	—	—	—	(36)

Treasury stock activity:

Treasury stock purchases, at cost	—	—	—	14	(400)	—	—	—	(400)
Stock options exchanged	—	—	—	2	(65)	—	—	—	(65)
Share-based employee compensation	—	—	155	—	—	—	—	—	155
Other comprehensive loss net of tax of ($47)	—	—	—	—	—	(294)	—	—	(294)
Cumulative effect of accounting change (see Note 18)	—	—	—	—	—	—	146	—	146
Deconsolidation of Lucky's Market	—	—	—	—	—	—	—	168	168
Other	—	—	65	—	(61)	—	(5)	1	—
Cash dividends declared ($0.62 per common share)	—	—	—	—	—	—	(503)	—	(503)
Net earnings (loss) including noncontrolling interests	—	—	—	—	—	—	1,659	(147)	1,512
Balances at February 1, 2020	1,918	$ 1,918	$ 3,337	1,130	$ (16,991)	$ (640)	$ 20,978	$ (29)	$ 8,573

The accompanying notes are an integral part of the consolidated financial statements.

SPROUTS FARMERS MARKET, INC.

FORM 10-K
(Annual Report)

For the fiscal year ended December 29, 2019

Address	5455 East High Street, Suite 111
	Phoenix, Arizona 85054
Telephone	(480) 814-8016
CIK	0001575515
Symbol	SFM
SIC Code	5411-Retail-Grocery Stores
Industry	Grocery store, Health food store
Sector	Consumer Defensive
Fiscal Year	12/31

For the complete Form 10-K of Sprouts Farmers Market, Inc., please go to Cengage.com.

ITEM 8.   FINANCIAL STATEMENTS AND SUPPLEMENTARY DATA

Index to Financial Statements
Consolidated Financial Statements for
Sprouts Farmers Market, Inc. and Subsidiaries:

REPORT OF INDEPENDENT REGISTERED PUBLIC ACCOUNTING FIRM

To the Board of Directors and Stockholders of Sprouts Farmers Market, Inc.

OPINIONS ON THE FINANCIAL STATEMENTS AND INTERNAL CONTROL OVER FINANCIAL REPORTING

We have audited the accompanying consolidated balance sheets of Sprouts Farmers Market, Inc. and its subsidiaries (the "Company") as of December 29, 2019, and December 30, 2018, and the related consolidated statements of income, of comprehensive income, of stockholders' equity and of cash flows for each of the 3 years in the period ended December 29, 2019, including the related notes (collectively referred to as the "consolidated financial statements"). We also have audited the Company's internal control over financial reporting as of December 29, 2019, based on criteria established in *Internal Control—Integrated Framework* (2013) issued by the Committee of Sponsoring Organizations of the Treadway Commission (COSO).

In our opinion, the consolidated financial statements referred to above present fairly, in all material respects, the financial position of the Company as of December 29, 2019, and December 30, 2018, and the results of its operations and its cash flows for each of the 3 years in the period ended December 29, 2019, in conformity with accounting principles generally accepted in the United States of America. Also in our opinion, the Company maintained, in all material respects, effective internal control over financial reporting as of December 29, 2019, based on criteria established in *Internal Control—Integrated Framework* (2013) issued by the COSO.

Change in Accounting Principle

As discussed in Note 3 to the consolidated financial statements, the Company changed the manner in which it accounts for leases in 2019. This matter is also discussed below as a critical audit matter.

BASIS FOR OPINIONS

The Company's management is responsible for these consolidated financial statements, for maintaining effective internal control over financial reporting, and for its assessment of the effectiveness of internal control over financial reporting, included in Management's Annual Report on Internal Control Over Financial Reporting appearing under Item 9A. Our responsibility is to express opinions on the Company's consolidated financial statements and on the Company's internal control over financial reporting based on our audits. We are a public accounting firm registered with the Public Company Accounting Oversight Board (United States) (PCAOB) and are required to be independent with respect to the Company in accordance with the U.S. federal securities laws and the applicable rules and regulations of the Securities and Exchange Commission and the PCAOB.

We conducted our audits in accordance with the standards of the PCAOB. Those standards require that we plan and perform the audits to obtain reasonable assurance about whether the consolidated financial statements are free of material misstatement, whether due to error or fraud, and whether effective internal control over financial reporting was maintained in all material respects.

Our audits of the consolidated financial statements included performing procedures to assess the risks of material misstatement of the consolidated financial statements, whether due to error or fraud, and performing procedures that respond to those risks. Such procedures included examining, on a test basis, evidence regarding the amounts and disclosures in the consolidated financial statements. Our audits also included evaluating the accounting principles used and significant estimates made by management, as well as evaluating the overall presentation of the consolidated financial statements. Our audit of internal control over financial reporting included obtaining an understanding of internal control over financial reporting, assessing the risk that a material weakness exists, and testing and evaluating the design and operating effectiveness of internal control based on the assessed risk. Our audits also included performing such other procedures as we considered necessary in the circumstances. We believe that our audits provide a reasonable basis for our opinions.

DEFINITION AND LIMITATIONS OF INTERNAL CONTROL OVER FINANCIAL REPORTING

A company's internal control over financial reporting is a process designed to provide reasonable assurance regarding the reliability of financial reporting and the preparation of financial statements for external purposes in accordance with generally accepted accounting principles. A company's internal control over financial reporting includes those policies and procedures that (i) pertain to the maintenance of records that, in reasonable detail, accurately and fairly reflect the transactions and dispositions of the assets of the company; (ii) provide reasonable assurance that transactions are recorded as necessary to permit preparation of financial statements in accordance with generally accepted accounting principles and that receipts and expenditures of the company are being made only in accordance with authorizations of management and directors of the company; and (iii) provide reasonable assurance regarding prevention or timely detection of unauthorized acquisition, use, or disposition of the company's assets that could have a material effect on the financial statements.

Because of its inherent limitations, internal control over financial reporting may not prevent or detect misstatements. Also, projections of any evaluation of effectiveness to future periods are subject to the risk that controls may become inadequate because of changes in conditions or that the degree of compliance with the policies or procedures may deteriorate.

CRITICAL AUDIT MATTERS

The critical audit matters communicated below are matters arising from the current period audit of the consolidated financial statements that were communicated or required to be communicated to the audit committee and that (i) relate to accounts or disclosures that are material to the consolidated financial statements and (ii) involved our especially challenging, subjective, or complex judgments. The communication of critical audit matters does not alter in any way our opinion on the consolidated financial statements, taken as a whole, and we are not, by communicating the critical audit matters below, providing separate opinions on the critical audit matters or on the accounts or disclosures to which they relate.

Impairment of Store-level Long-lived Assets
As described in Notes 3, 6, and 7 to the consolidated financial statements, the Company's property and equipment, net of accumulated depreciation, was $741.5 million as of December 29, 2019. Additionally, the Company had $1.0 billion of operating and finance lease assets as of December 29, 2019. During 2019, the Company recorded an impairment charge of $4.1 million on store-level long-lived assets. Management assesses its long-lived assets, including property and equipment, right-of-use assets and finite-lived intangible assets, for potential impairment whenever events or changes in circumstances indicate that the carrying value of an asset group may not be recoverable. Management groups and evaluates long-lived assets for impairment at the individual store level, which is the lowest level at which independent identifiable cash flows are available. Recoverability of assets to be held and used is measured by a comparison of the carrying amount of an asset group to the future undiscounted cash flows expected to be generated by that asset. The impairment analysis contains management assumptions about key variables including sales growth rate, gross margin, payroll, and other

controllable expenses. If impairment is indicated, a loss is recognized for any excess of the carrying value over the estimated fair value of the asset group. The fair value is estimated based on the discounted future cash flows using a discount rate commensurate with the related risk or comparable market values, if available.

The principal considerations for our determination that performing procedures relating to the impairment of store-level long-lived assets is a critical audit matter are there was significant judgment by management in developing the estimated future undiscounted cash flows expected to be generated by the asset. This in turn led to a high degree of auditor judgment, subjectivity, and effort in performing procedures and evaluating the undiscounted cash flows, including the significant assumptions for sales growth rate and gross margin.

Addressing the matter involved performing procedures and evaluating audit evidence in connection with forming our overall opinion on the consolidated financial statements. These procedures included testing the effectiveness of controls relating to the impairment of long-lived assets, including controls over the development of assumptions used in the valuation of the asset groups. These procedures also included, among others, testing management's process for developing the undiscounted cash flows, evaluating the appropriateness of the undiscounted cash flow model, testing the completeness, accuracy and relevance of underlying data used in the valuation, and evaluating the significant assumptions used by management, including sales growth rate and gross margin. Evaluating management's assumptions related to sales growth rate and gross margin involved evaluating whether the assumptions used by management were reasonable considering (i) current and past performance of each asset group, (ii) consistency with external market and industry data, and (iii) consistency with evidence obtained in other areas of the audit.

Adoption of Accounting Standard on Leases

As described above and in Note 3 to the consolidated financial statements, the Company adopted the accounting standard on leases in 2019, which resulted in the recognition of operating lease assets and liabilities of approximately $1.0 billion and $1.1 billion, respectively, as of December 31, 2018, the first day of fiscal year 2019. Additionally, the Company recognized a cumulative effect adjustment, which increased retained earnings by $11.4 million, net of tax. Management elected the package of practical expedients permitted under the transition guidance within the new standard, which among other things, permits companies not to reassess prior conclusions on lease identification, lease classification and initial direct costs. Management did not elect the hindsight practical expedient. In addition, the Company derecognized approximately $114.0 million of lease obligations and $102.6 million of net assets related to leases that had been classified as financing lease obligations under the former failed-sale leaseback guidance and are now classified as operating leases as of the transition date.

The principal considerations for our determination that performing procedures relating to the adoption of accounting standard on leases is a critical audit matter are there was significant judgment by management in the interpretation and application of the leasing transition guidance. This in turn led to a high degree of auditor judgment, subjectivity, and effort in performing procedures and evaluating the reasonableness of management's judgments related to the leasing transition guidance, specifically related to the derecognition of financing lease obligations and the recognition of the operating lease assets and liabilities. In addition, the audit effort involved the use of professionals with specialized skill and knowledge to assist in performing these procedures and evaluating the evidence obtained.

Addressing the matter involved performing procedures and evaluating audit evidence in connection with forming our overall opinion on the consolidated financial statements. These procedures included testing the effectiveness of controls relating to the adoption of accounting standard on leases, including controls related to the application of the transition guidance. These procedures also included, among others, (i) examining the executed lease agreements, (ii) evaluating the significant judgments used by management in the interpretation and application of the leasing transition guidance, specifically related to the derecognition of financing lease obligations and the recognition of operating lease assets and liabilities, and (iii) calculating the operating lease asset and liability based on the terms and conditions of each lease. In evaluating the judgments used in the derecognition of financing lease obligations and recognition of operating lease assets and liabilities, management's analysis and conclusions were obtained and the applicability of the transition guidance was evaluated. Professionals with specialized skill and knowledge were used to assist in evaluating the reasonableness of management's judgments, including interpretation and application of the leasing transition guidance.

/s/ PricewaterhouseCoopers LLP
Phoenix, Arizona
February 20, 2020

We have served as the Company's auditor since 2011.

SPROUTS FARMERS MARKET, INC. AND SUBSIDIARIES
CONSOLIDATED BALANCE SHEETS
(IN THOUSANDS, EXCEPT SHARE AND PER SHARE AMOUNTS)

	December 29, 2019	December 30, 2018
ASSETS		
Current assets:		
Cash and cash equivalents	$ 85,314	$ 1,588
Accounts receivable, net	15,713	40,564
Inventories	275,979	264,366
Prepaid expenses and other current assets	10,833	27,323
Total current assets	387,839	333,841
Property and equipment, net of accumulated depreciation	741,508	766,429
Operating lease assets, net	1,028,436	—
Intangible assets, net of accumulated amortization	185,395	194,803
Goodwill	368,078	368,078
Other assets	11,727	12,463
Total assets	$ 2,722,983	$ 1,675,614
LIABILITIES AND STOCKHOLDERS' EQUITY		
Current liabilities:		
Accounts payable and accrued liabilities	261,326	$ 253,969
Accrued salaries and benefits	48,579	48,603
Current portion of capital and financing lease obligations	—	7,428
Current portion of operating lease liabilities	106,153	—
Current portion of finance lease liabilities	754	—
Total current liabilities	416,812	310,000
Long-term capital and financing lease obligations	—	119,642
Long-term operating lease liabilities	1,078,927	—
Long-term debt and finance lease liabilities	549,419	453,000
Other long-term liabilities	41,517	153,377
Deferred income tax liability	54,356	50,399
Total liabilities	2,141,031	1,086,418
Commitments and contingencies (Note 19)		
Stockholders' equity:		
Undesignated preferred stock; $0.001 par value; 10,000,000 shares authorized, no shares issued and outstanding	—	—
Common stock, $0.001 par value; 200,000,000 shares authorized, 117,543,668 shares issued and outstanding, December 29, 2019; 124,975,691 shares issued and outstanding, December 30, 2018	117	124
Additional paid-in capital	670,966	657,140
Accumulated other comprehensive income (loss)	(4,682)	1,134
Accumulated deficit	(84,449)	(69,202)
Total stockholders' equity	581,952	589,196
Total liabilities and stockholders' equity	$ 2,722,983	$ 1,675,614

The accompanying notes are an integral part of these consolidated financial statements.

SPROUTS FARMERS MARKET, INC. AND SUBSIDIARIES
CONSOLIDATED STATEMENTS OF INCOME
(IN THOUSANDS, EXCEPT PER SHARE AMOUNTS)

	Year Ended		
	December 29, 2019	December 30, 2018	December 31, 2017
Net sales	$ 5,634,835	$ 5,207,336	$ 4,664,612
Cost of sales	3,740,017	3,459,861	3,097,582
Gross profit	1,894,818	1,747,475	1,567,030
Selling, general and administrative expenses	1,549,707	1,404,443	1,245,640
Depreciation and amortization (exclusive of depreciation included in cost of sales)	120,491	108,045	94,194
Store closure and other costs	7,260	12,076	1,126
Income from operations	217,360	222,911	226,070
Interest expense, net	21,192	27,435	21,177
Other income	—	320	625
Income before income taxes	196,168	195,796	205,518
Income tax provision	46,539	37,260	47,078
Net income	$ 149,629	$ 158,536	$ 158,440
Net income per share:			
Basic	$ 1.25	$ 1.23	$ 1.17
Diluted	$ 1.25	$ 1.22	$ 1.15
Weighted average shares outstanding:			
Basic	119,368	128,827	135,169
Diluted	119,742	129,776	137,884

The accompanying notes are an integral part of these consolidated financial statements.

SPROUTS FARMERS MARKET, INC. AND SUBSIDIARIES
CONSOLIDATED STATEMENTS OF COMPREHENSIVE INCOME
(IN THOUSANDS)

	Year Ended		
	December 29, 2019	December 30, 2018	December 31, 2017
Net income	$ 149,629	$ 158,536	$ 158,440
Other comprehensive income (loss), net of tax			
Unrealized gain (losses) on cash flow hedging activities, net of income tax of ($2,012), $663, and ($271)	(5,816)	1,918	(784)
Total other comprehensive income (loss)	$ (5,816)	$ 1,918	$ (784)
Comprehensive income	$ 143,813	$ 160,454	$ 157,656

The accompanying notes are an integral part of these consolidated financial statements.

SPROUTS FARMERS MARKET, INC. AND SUBSIDIARIES
CONSOLIDATED STATEMENTS OF STOCKHOLDERS' EQUITY
(IN THOUSANDS, EXCEPT SHARE AMOUNTS)

	Shares	Common Stock	Additional Paid-in Capital	(Accumulated Deficit) Retained Earnings	Accumulated Other Comprehensive Income (Loss)	Total Stockholders' Equity
Balances at January 1, 2017	140,002,242	$ 140	$ 597,269	$ 75,500	$ —	$ 672,909
Net income	—	—	—	158,440	—	158,440
Other comprehensive income (loss)	—	—	—	—	(784)	(784)
Issuance of shares under stock plans	2,144,669	2	9,298	—	—	9,300
Repurchase and retirement of common stock	(9,696,819)	(10)	—	(203,382)	—	(203,392)
Share-based compensation	—	—	14,221	—	—	14,221
Balances at December 31, 2017	132,450,092	$ 132	$ 620,788	$ 30,558	$ (784)	$ 650,694
Net income	—	—	—	158,536	—	158,536
Other comprehensive income (loss)	—	—	—	—	1,918	1,918
Issuance of shares under stock plans	3,227,693	3	21,840	—	—	21,843
Repurchase and retirement of common stock	(11,096,595)	(11)	—	(258,296)	—	(258,307)
Share-based compensation	—	—	14,512	—	—	14,512
Balances at December 30, 2018	124,581,190	$ 124	$ 657,140	$ (69,202)	$ 1,134	$ 589,196
Net income	—	—	—	149,629	—	149,629
Other comprehensive income (loss)	—	—	—	—	(5,816)	(5,816)
Issuance of shares under stock plans	822,586	1	4,877	—	—	4,878
Repurchase and retirement of common stock	(7,950,858)	(8)	—	(176,302)	—	(176,310)
Share-based compensation	—	—	8,949	—	—	8,949
Impact of adoption of ASC 842 related to leases	—	—	—	11,426	—	11,426
Balances at December 29, 2019	117,452,918	$ 117	$ 670,966	$ (84,449)	$ (4,682)	$ 581,952

The accompanying notes are an integral part of these consolidated financial statements.

SPROUTS FARMERS MARKET, INC. AND SUBSIDIARIES
CONSOLIDATED STATEMENTS OF CASH FLOWS
(IN THOUSANDS)

	Year Ended		
	December 29, 2019	December 30, 2018	December 31, 2017
Cash flows from operating activities			
Net income	$ 149,629	$ 158,536	$ 158,440
Adjustments to reconcile net income to net cash provided by operating activities:			
Depreciation and amortization expense	122,804	110,749	96,987
Operating lease asset amortization	81,842	—	—
Store closure and other costs	4,113	4,115	—
Share-based compensation	8,949	14,512	14,221
Deferred income taxes	(216)	23,333	7,803
Other noncash items	4,136	1,482	2,086
Changes in operating assets and liabilities:			
Accounts receivable	36,062	(7,666)	(4,920)
Inventories	(11,612)	(34,824)	(25,079)
Prepaid expenses and other current assets	19,208	(2,908)	(2,733)
Other assets	(1,275)	(5,086)	(114)
Accounts payable and other accrued liabilities	28,699	4,366	39,244
Accrued salaries and benefits	295	3,039	12,764
Operating lease liabilities	(88,002)	—	—
Other long-term liabilities	578	24,731	10,868
Cash flows from operating activities	355,210	294,379	309,567
Cash flows from investing activities			
Purchases of property and equipment	(183,232)	(177,083)	(198,624)
Proceeds from sale of property and equipment	—	1	30
Cash flows used in investing activities	(183,232)	(177,082)	(198,594)
Cash flows from financing activities			
Proceeds from revolving credit facilities	265,405	233,000	153,000
Payments on revolving credit facilities	(180,405)	(128,000)	(60,000)
Payments on capital and financing lease obligations	—	(4,517)	(4,192)
Payments on finance lease liabilities	(690)	—	—
Payments of deferred financing costs	—	(2,131)	—
Cash from landlord related to capital and financing lease obligations	—	3,643	1,325
Repurchase of common stock	(176,310)	(258,307)	(203,392)
Proceeds from exercise of stock options	4,878	21,843	9,300
Other	(319)	(59)	—
Cash flows used in financing activities	(87,441)	(134,528)	(103,959)
Increase / (Decrease) in cash, cash equivalents, and restricted cash	84,537	(17,231)	7,014
Cash, cash equivalents, and restricted cash at beginning of the period	2,248	19,479	12,465
Cash, cash equivalents, and restricted cash at the end of the period	$ 86,785	$ 2,248	$ 19,479
Supplemental disclosure of cash flow information			
Cash paid for interest	$ 20,293	$ 27,086	$ 20,759
Cash paid for income taxes	44,637	15,527	33,475
Supplemental disclosure of noncash investing and financing activities			
Property and equipment in accounts payable	$ 18,515	$ 12,001	$ 17,869
Property acquired through capital and financing lease obligations	—	9,081	23,882

The accompanying notes are an integral part of these consolidated financial statements.

GLOSSARY

A

account a record of increases and decreases in each of the basic elements of the financial statements (each of the company's asset, liability, stockholders' equity, revenue, expense, gain, and loss items).

account payable an obligation that arises when a business purchases goods or services on credit.

account receivable money due from another business or individual as payment for services performed or goods delivered. Payment is typically due in 30 to 60 days and does not involve a formal note between the parties, nor does it include interest.

accounting the process of identifying, measuring, recording, and communicating financial information about a company's activities so decision-makers can make informed decisions.

accounting cycle the procedures that a company uses to transform the results of its business activities into financial statements.

accounting system the methods and records used to identify, measure, record, and communicate financial information about a business.

accounts receivable turnover ratio net credit sales or net sales divided by average accounts receivable.

accrual-basis accounting a method of accounting in which revenues are generally recorded when earned (rather than when cash is received) and expenses are matched to the periods in which they help produce revenues (rather than when cash is paid).

accrued expenses previously unrecorded expenses that have been incurred, but not yet paid in cash.

accrued liabilities liabilities that usually represent the completed portion of activities that are in process at the end of the period.

accrued revenues previously unrecorded revenues that have been earned but for which no cash has yet been received.

accumulated depreciation the total amount of depreciation expense that has been recorded for an asset since the asset was acquired. It is reported on the balance sheet as a contra-asset.

accumulated other comprehensive income the total of comprehensive income for all periods and conveys the changes in assets and liabilities resulting from all transactions with nonowners.

additional paid-in capital the amount received in excess of the par value.

adjusted trial balance an updated trial balance that reflects the changes to account balances as the result of adjusting entries.

adjusting entries journal entries that are made at the end of an accounting period to record the completed portion of partially completed transactions.

aging method a method in which bad debt expense is estimated indirectly by determining the ending balance desired in the allowance for doubtful accounts and then computing the necessary adjusting entry to achieve this balance; the amount of this adjusting entry is also the amount of bad debt expense.

allowance for doubtful accounts a contra-asset account that is established to "store" the estimate of uncollectible accounts until specific accounts are identified as uncollectible.

amortization the process whereby companies systematically allocate the cost of their intangible operating assets as an expense among the accounting periods in which the asset is used and the benefits are received.

amortized cost method a method of accounting for held-to-maturity investment securities in which the security is recorded at cost when acquired, and interest income is recognized with appropriate amortization of discounts and premiums.

annuity a series of equal cash flows at regular intervals.

articles of incorporation a document that authorizes the creation of the corporation, setting forth its name, purpose, and the names of the incorporators.

articulation describes the linkages between the financial statements. Specifically, the income statement links the beginning and ending balance sheet through retained earnings; the statement of shareholders' equity links the beginning and ending balances of equity; and the statement of cash flows links the beginning and ending balances of cash.

asset acquisition a business combination in which a parent company purchases some or all of the assets of a subsidiary company.

asset turnover ratio a ratio that measures the efficiency with which a corporation's assets (usually accounts receivable or inventory) are used to produce sales revenues.

assets economic resources representing expected future economic benefits controlled by the business (e.g., cash, accounts receivable, inventory, land, buildings, equipment, and intangible assets).

authorized shares the maximum number of shares a company may issue in each class of stock.

available-for-sale securities debt investments that management intends to sell in the future, but not necessarily in the near term.

average age of fixed assets a rough estimate of the age of fixed assets that can be computed by dividing accumulated depreciation by depreciation expense.

average cost method an inventory costing method that allocates the cost of goods available for sale between ending inventory and cost of goods sold based on a weighted average cost per unit.

average days to sell inventory an estimate of the number of days it takes a company to sell its inventory. It is found by dividing 365 days by the inventory turnover ratio.

B

bad debt expense the expense that results from receivables that are not paid.

balance sheet a financial statement that reports the resources (assets) owned by a company and the claims against those resources (liabilities and stockholders' equity) at a specific point in time.

bank reconciliation the process of reconciling any differences between a company's accounting records and the bank's accounting records.

bond a type of note that requires the issuing entity to pay the face value of the bond to the holder when it matures and, usually, periodic interest at a specified rate.

book value (carrying value) the value of an asset or a liability as it appears on the balance sheet. Book value is calculated as the cost of the asset or liability minus the balance in its related contra account (e.g., cost of equipment less accumulated depreciation; notes payable less discount on notes payable).

business combination   a transaction or set of transactions that brings together two or more previously separate entities to form a single accounting entity.

business process risks   threats to the internal processes of a company.

C

callable bonds   bonds that give the borrower the right to pay off (or call) the bonds prior to their due date. The borrower typically "calls" debt when the interest rate being paid is much higher than the current market conditions.

capital   a company's assets less its liabilities. Capital is also known as stockholders' equity.

capital expenditures   expenditures to acquire long-term assets or extend the life, expand the productive capacity, increase the efficiency, or improve the quality of existing long-term assets.

capital stock   the portion of a corporation's stockholders' equity contributed by investors (owners) in exchange for shares of stock.

cash-basis accounting   a method of accounting in which revenue is recorded when cash is received, regardless of when it is actually earned. Similarly, an expense is recorded when cash is paid, regardless of when it is actually incurred. Cash-basis accounting does not tie recognition of revenues and expenses to the actual business activity but rather to the exchange of cash.

cash equivalents   short-term, highly liquid investments that are readily convertible to cash and have original maturities of three months or less.

cash flow adequacy ratio   the cash flow adequacy ratio provides a measure of the company's ability to meet its debt obligations and is calculated as: Cash Flow Adequacy = Free Cash Flow ÷ Average Amount of Debt Maturing over the Next Five Years.

cash flows from financing activities   any cash flow related to obtaining resources from creditors or owners, which includes the issuance and repayment of debt, common and preferred stock transactions, and the payment of dividends.

cash flows from investing activities   the cash inflows and outflows that relate to acquiring and disposing of operating assets, acquiring and selling investments (current and long-term), and lending money and collecting loans.

cash flows from operating activities   any cash flows directly related to earning income, including cash sales and collections of accounts receivable as well as cash payments for goods, services, salaries, and interest.

cash over and short   an account that records the discrepancies between deposited amounts of actual cash received and the total of the cash register tape.

cash ratio   a short-term liquidity ratio that is calculated as: (Cash+ Short-Term Investments) ÷ Current Liabilities.

chart of accounts   the list of accounts used by a company.

common size statements   financial statements that express each financial statement line item in percentage terms.

common stock   the basic ownership interest in a corporation. Owners of common stock have the right to vote in the election of the board of directors, share in the profits and dividends of the company, keep the same percentage of ownership if new stock is issued (preemptive right), and share in the distribution of assets in liquidation.

comparability   one of the four qualitative characteristics that useful information should possess. Information has comparability if it allows comparisons to be made between companies.

compound interest   a method of calculating the time value of money in which interest is earned on the previous periods' interest.

conservatism principle   a principle which states that when more than one equally acceptable accounting method exists, the method that results in the lower assets and revenues or higher liabilities and expenses should be selected.

consignment   an arrangement where goods owned by one party are held and offered for sale by another.

consistency   one of the four qualitative characteristics that useful information should possess. Consistency refers to the application of the same accounting principles by a single company over time.

consolidated financial statements   financial statements which combine the financial statements of a parent and subsidiary company or companies as if they were a single company.

consolidation worksheet   a worksheet used to prepare consolidated financial statements.

contingent liability   an obligation whose amount or timing is uncertain and depends on future events. For example, a firm may be contingently liable for damages under a lawsuit that has yet to be decided by the courts.

contract rate   see *interest rate*

contributed capital   the owners' contributions of cash and other assets to the company (includes the common stock of a company).

control activities   the policies and procedures that top management establishes to help insure that its objectives are met.

convertible bonds   bonds that allow the bondholder to convert the bond into another security—typically common stock.

corporate charter   see *articles of incorporation*

corporation   a company chartered by the state to conduct business as an "artificial person" and owned by one or more stockholders.

cost   any expenditure necessary to acquire the asset and to prepare the asset for use.

cost constraint   qualitative characteristic of useful information that states that the benefit received from accounting information should be greater than the cost of providing that information.

cost of goods available for sale   the sum of the cost of beginning inventory and the cost of purchases.

cost of goods sold (cost of sales)   an expense that represents the outflow of resources caused by the sale of inventory. This is often computed as the cost of goods available for sale less the cost of ending inventory.

coupon rate   see *interest rate*

credit   the right side of a T-account; alternatively, credit may refer to the act of entering an amount on the right side of an account.

credit cards   a card that authorizes the holder to make purchases up to some limit from retailers. Credit cards are a special form of factoring in which the issuer of the credit card pays the seller the amount of each sale less a service charge and then collects the full amount of the sale from the buyer at some later date.

creditor   the person to whom money is owed.

cross sectional analysis   a type of analysis that compares one corporation to another corporation and to industry averages.

cumulative dividend preference   a provision that requires the eventual payment of all preferred dividends—both dividends in arrears and current dividends—to preferred stockholders before any dividends are paid to common stockholders.

current assets cash and other assets that are reasonably expected to be converted into cash within one year or one operating cycle, whichever is longer.

current dividend preference a provision that requires that current dividends must be paid to preferred stockholders before any dividends are paid to common stockholders.

current liabilities obligations that require a firm to pay cash or another current asset, create a new current liability, or provide goods or services within one year or one operating cycle, whichever is longer.

current ratio a measure of liquidity that is computed as: Current Assets ÷ Current Liabilities.

D

date of record the date on which a stockholder must own one or more shares of stock in order to receive the dividend.

debenture bonds another name for unsecured bonds.

debit the left side of a T-account; alternatively, debit may refer to the act of entering an amount on the left side of an account.

debit card a card that authorizes a bank to make an immediate electronic withdrawal (debit) from the holder's bank account and a corresponding deposit to another party's account.

debt management ratios a type of ratio that provides information on two aspects of debt: (1) the relative mix of debt and equity financing (often referred to as its capital structure) and (2) the corporation's ability to meet its debt obligations through operations because interest and principal payments must be made as scheduled, or a company can be declared bankrupt.

debt security a financial instrument that exists when one entity owes another entity some combination of interest and principal.

debt to equity ratio a measure of the proportion of capital provided by creditors relative to that provided by stockholders. This ratio is calculated as: Total Liabilities ÷ Total Equity.

debt to total assets ratio a measure of the proportion of capital provided by creditors. This ratio is calculated as: Total Liabilities ÷ Total Assets.

declaration date the date on which a corporation announces its intention to pay a dividend on common stock.

declining balance depreciation method an accelerated depreciation method that produces a declining amount of depreciation expense each period by multiplying the declining book value of an asset by a constant depreciation rate. Declining balance depreciation expense for each period of an asset's useful life equals the declining balance rate times the asset's book value (cost less accumulated depreciation) at the beginning of the period.

depletion the process of allocating the cost of a natural resource to each period in which the resource is removed from the earth.

deposit in transit an amount received and recorded by a company, but which has not been recorded by the bank in time to appear on the current bank statement.

depreciable cost depreciable cost is calculated as the cost of the asset less its residual (or salvage) value. This amount will be depreciated (expensed) over the asset's useful life.

depreciation the process whereby companies systematically allocate the cost of their tangible operating assets (other than land) as an expense in each period in which the asset is used.

depreciation expense the amount of depreciation recorded on the income statement.

direct method a method of computing net cash flow from operating activities by adjusting each item on the income statement by the changes in the related current asset or liability accounts. Typical cash flow categories reported are cash collected from customers, cash paid to suppliers, cash paid to employees, cash paid for interest, and cash paid for taxes.

discount when a bond sells at a price below face value, due to the yield being greater than the stated rate of interest.

discount period the reduced payment period associated with purchase discounts.

dividend amounts paid periodically by a corporation to its stockholders as a return of their invested capital. Dividends represent a distribution of retained earnings, not an expense.

dividend payout ratio a ratio that measures the proportion of a corporation's profits that are returned to the stockholders immediately as dividends. It is calculated as: Common Dividends ÷ Net Income.

dividend yield ratio a ratio that measures the rate at which dividends provide a return to stockholders, by comparing dividends with the market price of a share of stock. It is calculated as: Dividends per Common Share ÷ Closing Market Price per Share for the Year.

dividends in arrears cumulative preferred stock dividends remaining unpaid for one or more years are considered to be in arrears.

Dupont analysis a type of analysis that recognizes that ROE can be broken down into three important components—net profit margin, asset turnover, and leverage.

E

earnings per share (EPS) a ratio that measures the income available for common stockholders on a per-share basis. EPS is calculated as net income less preferred dividends divided by the average number of common shares outstanding.

economic entity assumption one of the four basic assumptions that underlie accounting that assumes each company is accounted for separately from its owners.

equity see *stockholders' equity*

equity method a method of accounting for investments in which the investor possesses significant influence over the operating and financial policies of the investee.

equity security a financial instrument that represents an ownership interest in a corporation.

events events make up the multitude of activities in which companies engage. External events result from an exchange between the company and another outside entity, and internal events result from a company's own actions that do not involve other companies.

exercise (or strike) price the price at which employees can buy stock when their employer grants stock options.

expense recognition principle this principle requires that an expense be recorded and reported in the same period as the revenue it helped generate.

expenses the cost of assets used, or the liabilities created, in the operation of the business.

F

face value the amount of money that a borrower must repay at maturity; also called par value or principal.

factor   a method of handling receivables in which the seller receives an immediate cash payment reduced by the factor's fees. The factor, the buyer of the receivables, acquires the right to collect the receivables and the risk of uncollectibility. In a typical factoring arrangement, the sellers of the receivables have no continuing responsibility for their collection.

fair value method   a method of accounting for passive equity and debt investments that are classified as trading or available for sale. Under this method, the investment is valued at the price for which the investor could sell the asset (the fair value).

faithful representation   qualitative characteristic of information stipulating it should be complete, neutral, and free from error.

FIFO   see *first-in, first-out method*

financial accounting   accounting and reporting to satisfy the outside demand (primarily investors and creditors) for accounting information.

Financial Accounting Standards Board (FASB)   the primary accounting standard-setter in the United States which has been granted this power to set standards by the Securities and Exchange Commission.

financial statements   a set of standardized reports in which the detailed transactions of a company's activities are reported and summarized so they can be communicated to decision-makers.

finished goods inventory   the account in manufacturing firms that represents the cost of the final product that is available for sale.

first-in, first-out (FIFO) method   an inventory costing system in which the earliest (oldest) purchases (the first in) are assumed to be the first sold (the first out) and the more recent purchases are in ending inventory.

fiscal year   an accounting period that runs for one year.

fixed asset turnover ratio   a ratio that indicates how efficiently a company uses its fixed assets. This ratio is calculated by dividing net sales by average fixed assets.

F.O.B. destination   means free-on-board until the goods reach the destination. This is a shipping arrangement in which ownership of inventory passes from the seller to the buyer at the destination and, therefore, the seller pays for shipping.

F.O.B. shipping point   means free-on-board until shipping begins. This is a shipping arrangement in which ownership of inventory passes from the seller to the buyer at the shipping point and, therefore, the buyer pays for shipping.

Form 8-K   the "current report" companies must file with the SEC to announce major events that are important to investors and creditors.

Form 10-K   the annual report on Form 10-K provides a comprehensive overview of the corporation's business and financial condition and includes *audited* financial statements. Although similarly named, the annual report on Form 10-K is distinct from the "annual report to shareholders," which a corporation must send to its shareholders when it holds an annual meeting to elect directors. For larger filers, the 10-K must be filed within 60 days of their fiscal year end.

Form 10-Q   the Form 10-Q includes *unaudited* financial statements and provides a continuing view of the corporation's financial position during the year. The report must be filed for each of the first three fiscal quarters of the corporation's fiscal year. For larger filers, this must be done within 40 days of the end of the quarter.

free cash flow   the cash flow that a company is able to generate after considering the maintenance or expansion of its assets (capital expenditures) and the payment of dividends. Free cash flow is calculated as Net Cash Flow from Operating Activities – Capital Expenditures – Cash Dividends.

freight-in   the transportation costs that are normally paid by the buyer under F.O.B. shipping point terms.

freight-out   the transportation costs that the seller is usually responsible for paying under F.O.B. destination shipping terms.

full disclosure   a policy that requires any information that would make a difference to financial statement users to be revealed.

fundamental accounting equation   Assets = Liabilities + Stockholders' Equity. The left side of the accounting equation shows the assets, or economic resources, of a company. The right side of the accounting equation indicates who has a claim on the company's assets.

future value   the amount to which money will grow in the future when compound interest is applied.

G

gains   increases in net assets that occur from peripheral or incidental transactions.

general ledger   a collection of all the individual financial statement accounts that a company uses in its financial statements.

generally accepted accounting principles (GAAP)   the rules and conventions used to prepare financial statements. By following these rules and conventions financial statements users are able to compare performance over time and across companies.

goodwill   an unidentifiable intangible asset that arises from factors such as customer satisfaction, quality products, skilled employees, and business location.

gross margin (gross profit)   a key performance measure that is computed as sales revenue less cost of goods sold.

gross profit percentage   a measurement of the proportion of each sales dollar that is available to pay other expenses and provide profit for owners.

gross profit ratio   a measurement of the proportion of each sales dollar that is available to pay other expenses and provide profit for owners; it is computed by dividing gross margin by net sales.

H

held-to-maturity securities   debt investments that management intends to hold until the debt contract requires the borrower to repay the debt in its entirety.

historical cost principle   a principle that requires the activities of a company to be initially measured at their cost—the exchange price at the time the activity occurs.

horizontal analysis   a type of analysis in which each financial statement line item is expressed as a percent of the base year (typically the first year shown).

I

impairment   a permanent decline in the future benefits or service potential of an asset.

income from operations   gross margin less operating expenses. This represents the results of the core operations of the business.

income statement   a financial statement that reports the profitability of a business over a specific period of time.

indirect method   a method that computes operating cash flows by adjusting net income for items that do not affect cash flows.

intangible assets   intangible assets are similar to property, plant, and equipment in that they provide a benefit to a company over a number of years; however, these assets lack physical substance.

intangible operating assets   assets that provide a benefit to a company over a number of years but lack physical substance. Examples of intangible assets include patents, copyrights, trademarks, and good will.

interest   the excess of the total amount of money paid to a lender over the amount borrowed.

interest period the time interval between interest calculations.

interest rate a percentage of the principal that must be paid in order to have use of the principal. It is multiplied by the beginning-of-period balance to yield the amount of interest for the period.

internal control system the policies and procedures established by top management and the board of directors to provide reasonable assurance that the company's objectives are being met in three areas: (1) effectiveness and efficiency of operations, (2) reliability of financial reporting, and (3) compliance with applicable laws and regulations.

International Accounting Standards Board (IASB) an independent, privately funded accounting standard-setting body with the goal of developing a single set of high-quality accounting standards that result in transparent and comparable information reported in general purpose financial statements.

international financial reporting standards (IFRS) a general term that describes an international set of generally accepted accounting standards.

inventory products held for resale that are classified as current assets on the balance sheet.

inventory turnover ratio a ratio that describes how quickly inventory is purchased (or produced) and sold. It is calculated as cost of goods sold divided by average inventory.

involuntary disposal a type of disposal that occurs when assets are lost or destroyed through theft, acts of nature, or by accident.

issued shares the number of shares actually sold to stockholders.

J

journal a chronological record showing the debit and credit effects of transactions on a company.

journal entry a record of a transaction that is made in a journal so that the entire effect of the transaction is contained in one place.

junk bonds unsecured bonds where the risk of the borrower failing to make the payments is relatively high.

L

last-in, first-out (LIFO) method an inventory costing system that allocates the cost of goods available for sale between ending inventory and cost of goods sold based on the assumption that the most recent purchases (the last in) are the first to be sold (the first out).

lease an agreement that enables a company to use property without legally owning it.

leverage the use of borrowed capital to produce more income than needed to pay the interest on a debt.

liabilities probable future sacrifices of economic benefits; liabilities usually require the payment of cash, the transfer of assets other than cash, or the performance of services.

LIFO reserve the amount that inventory would increase (or decrease) if the company had used FIFO.

liquidating dividends dividends that return paid-in capital to stockholders; liquidating dividends occur when retained earnings has been reduced to zero.

liquidity a company's ability to pay obligations as they become due.

long-term debt obligations that extend beyond one year.

long-term debt to equity ratio a ratio that provides information on the proportion of capital provided by this type of debt and by stockholders. It is calculated as: Long-Term Debt (including current portion) ÷ Total Equity.

long-term debt to total assets ratio a measure of the proportion of capital provided by long-term creditors which is calculated as: Long-Term Debt (including current portion) ÷ Total Assets.

long-term investments investments that the company expects to hold for longer than one year. This includes land or buildings that a company is not currently using in operations, as well as debt and equity securities.

long-term liabilities the obligations of the company that will require payment beyond one year or the operating cycle, whichever is longer.

losses decreases in net assets that occur from peripheral or incidental transactions.

lower of cost or net realizable (LCNRV) value the value at which inventory is reported under GAAP, where cost is the historical cost of the inventory and net realizable value is the estimated selling price minus the costs of disposal.

M

management's discussion and analysis (MD&A) a section of the annual report that provides a discussion and explanation of various items reported in the financial statements. Management uses this section to highlight favorable and unfavorable trends and significant risks facing the company.

manufacturers companies that buy and transform raw materials into a finished product which is then sold.

market rate the market rate of interest demanded by creditors.

maturity the date on which a borrower agrees to pay the creditor the face (or par) value.

merchandise inventory the inventory held by merchandisers.

merchandisers companies, either retailers or wholesalers, that purchase inventory in a finished condition and hold it for resale without further processing.

mortgage bonds bonds that are secured by real estate.

N

natural resources resources, such as coal deposits, oil reserves, and mineral deposits, that are physically consumed as they are used by a company and that can generally be replaced or restored only by an act of nature.

net income the excess of a company's revenue over its expenses during a period of time.

net loss the excess of a company's expenses over its revenues during a period of time.

net profit margin a useful measure of a company's ability to generate profit.

net profit margin percentage a measure of the proportion of each sales dollar that is profit, determined by dividing net income by net sales.

no-par stock stock without a par value.

non-sufficient funds (NSF) check a check that has been returned to the depositor because funds in the issuer's account are not sufficient to pay the check (also called a "bounced" check).

noncash investing and financing activities investing and financing activities that take place without affecting cash. For example, a company may choose to acquire an operating asset (e.g., building) by issuing long-term debt.

noncontrolling interest voting stock of a subsidiary that is not held by the parent company.

nonoperating activities revenues and expenses from activities other than the company's principal operations.

nontrade receivables   receivables that arise from transactions not involving inventory (e.g., interest receivable or cash advances to employees).

normal balance   the type of balance expected of an account based on its effect on the fundamental accounting equation. Assets, expenses, and dividends have normal debit balances while liabilities, stockholders' equity, and revenues have normal credit balances.

note(s) payable   a payable that arises when a business borrows money or purchases goods or services from a company that requires a formal agreement or contract.

note(s) receivable   receivables that generally specify an interest rate and a maturity date at which any interest and principal must be repaid.

O

operating assets   the long-lived assets that are used by the company in the normal course of operations.

operating cash flow ratio   a ratio that looks at the ability of operations to generate cash, which recognizes the more general concept that current obligations will be paid through operations (after all, selling inventory and collecting receivables is a big part of operations). This ratio is calculated as Cash Flows from Operating Activities ÷ Current Liabilities.

operating cycle   the average time that it takes a company to purchase goods, resell them, and collect the cash from customers.

operating expenses   the expenses the business incurs in selling goods or providing services and managing the company.

operating margin percentage   a measure of the profitability of a company's operations in relation to its sales that is calculated as Income from Operations ÷ Net Sales.

organizational costs   significant costs such as legal fees, stock issue costs, accounting fees, and promotional fees that a company may incur when it is formed.

outstanding check   a check that has been issued and recorded by the business but that has not been "cashed" by the recipient of the check.

outstanding shares   the number of issued shares actually in the hands of stockholders.

P

par value   for stock, it is an arbitrary monetary amount printed on each share of stock that establishes a minimum price for the stock when issued, but does not determine its market value. For debt, par value is the amount of money the borrower agrees to repay at maturity.

parent   an investor company that owns over 50% of the outstanding stock of an investee company.

participating dividend preference   a provision allowing preferred shareholders to share in amounts available for distribution to common shareholders. This is over and above the preferred dividend preference.

partnership   a business owned jointly by two or more individuals.

payment date   the date on which the dividend will actually be paid.

payroll taxes   taxes that businesses must pay based on employee payrolls; these amounts are not withheld from employee pay, rather they are additional amounts that must be paid over and above gross pay.

percentage of credit sales method   a method of determining bad debt expense whereby past experience and management's view of how the future may differ from the past are used to estimate the percentage of the current period's credit sales that will eventually become uncollectible.

periodic inventory system   an inventory system that records the cost of purchases as they occur (in an account separate from the Inventory account), takes a physical count of inventory at the end of the period, and applies the cost of goods sold model to determine the balances of ending inventory and cost of goods sold. The Inventory account reflects the correct inventory balance only at the end of each accounting period.

permanent accounts   accounts of asset, liability, and stockholders' equity items whose balances are carried forward from the current accounting period to future accounting periods.

perpetual inventory system   an inventory system in which balances for inventory and cost of goods sold are continually (perpetually) updated with each sale or purchase of inventory. The accounts reflect the correct inventory and cost of goods sold balances throughout the period.

petty cash   a fund used to pay for small dollar amounts.

posting   the process of transferring information from journalized transactions to the general ledger.

preferred stock   a class of stock that generally does not give voting rights, but grants specific guarantees and dividend preferences.

premium   when a bond's selling price is above face value.

prepaid expenses   asset arising from the payment of cash which has not been used or consumed by the end of the period.

present value   determinations of present amounts based on expected future cash flows.

principal   the amount of money borrowed and promised to be repaid (usually with interest).

prior period adjustment   the correction of an error made in the financial statements of a prior period. The adjustment is entered as a direct adjustment to retained earnings.

profitability ratios   ratios that measure two aspects of a corporation's profits: (1) those elements of operations that contribute to profit and (2) the relationship of profit to total investment and investment by stockholders.

property, plant, and equipment   the tangible, long-lived, productive assets used by a company in its operations to produce revenue. This includes land, buildings, machinery, manufacturing equipment, office equipment, and furniture.

purchase allowance   a situation in which the purchaser chooses to keep the merchandise if the seller is willing to grant a deduction (allowance) from the purchase price.

purchase discounts   price reductions (usually expressed as a percentage of the purchase price) that companies offer their customers to encourage prompt payment.

purchase returns   the cost of merchandise returned to suppliers.

purchases   the cost of merchandise acquired for resale during the accounting period.

Q

quick ratio   a measure of a company's short-term liquidity that is calculated as follows: (Cash + Short-Term Investments + Receivables) ÷ Current Liabilities.

R

ratio analysis   an examination of financial statements conducted by preparing and evaluating a series of ratios.

ratios (financial ratios)   data that provide meaningful information only when compared with ratios from previous periods for the same firm or similar firms; they help by removing most of the effects of size differences.

raw materials inventory   the account in manufacturing firms that includes the basic ingredients to make a product.

relevance one of the four qualitative characteristics that useful information should possess. Accounting information is said to be relevant if it is capable of making a difference in a business decision by helping users predict future events or by providing feedback about prior expectations. Relevant information must also be provided in a timely manner.

research and development (R&D) expense the cost of internal development of intangible assets that is expensed as incurred.

residual value (salvage value) the amount of cash or trade-in consideration that the company expects to receive when an asset is retired from service.

retailers merchandisers that sell directly to consumers.

retained earnings (or deficit) the accumulated earnings (or losses) over the entire life of the corporation that have not been paid out in dividends.

retained earnings statement a financial statement that reports how much of the company's income was retained in the business and how much was distributed to owners for a period of time.

return on assets ratio a ratio that measures the profit earned by a corporation through use of all its capital, or the total of the investment by both creditors and owners. Return on assets is calculated as: [Net Income + Interest (1 – Tax Rate)]/Average Total Assets.

return on common equity ratio a ratio that is basically the same as the return on equity ratio. It is calculated as: Net Income/(Total Equity + Preferred Stock + Paid-In Capital – Preferred Stock).

return on equity ratio a ratio that measures the profit earned by a firm through the use of capital supplied by stockholders. Return on equity is computed as net income divided by average equity.

revenue the increase in assets that results from the sale of products or services.

revenue expenditures expenditures that do not increase the future economic benefits of the asset. These expenditures are expensed as they are incurred.

revenue recognition principle a principle that requires revenue to be recognized or recorded in the period in which it is earned and the collection of cash is reasonably assured.

S

safeguarding the physical protection of assets through, for example, fireproof vaults, locked storage facilities, keycard access, and anti-theft tags on merchandise.

sales discount a price reduction (usually expressed as a percentage of the selling price) that companies may offer to encourage prompt payment.

sales taxes money collected from the customer for the governmental unit levying the tax.

secured a term used for a bond that has some collateral pledged against the corporation's ability to pay.

Securities and Exchange Commission (SEC) the federal agency established by Congress to regulate securities markets and ensure effective public disclosure of accounting information. The SEC has the power to set accounting rules for publicly traded companies.

securitization a process in which large businesses and financial institutions frequently package factored receivables as financial instruments or securities and sell them to investors.

segregation of duties the idea that accounting and administrative duties should be performed by different individuals, so that no one person has access to the asset and prepares all the documents and records for an activity.

service charges fees charged by the bank for services provided. Examples include annual maintenance, minimum balance, and foreign transaction fees.

shareholders see *stockholders*

short-term liquidity ratios a type of ratio that compares some combination of current assets or operations to current liabilities.

sole proprietorship a business owned by one person.

specific identification method an inventory costing method that determines the cost of ending inventory and the cost of goods sold based on the identification of the actual units sold and in inventory. This method does not require an assumption about the flow of costs but actually assigns cost based on the actual flow of inventory.

stated capital (legal capital) the amount of capital that, under law, cannot be returned to the corporation's owners unless the corporation is liquidated.

stated rate see *interest rate*

statement of cash flows a financial statement that provides relevant information about a company's cash receipts (inflows of cash) and cash payments (outflows of cash) during an accounting period.

stock acquisitions a business combination in which a parent company acquires the stock of a subsidiary company's stock with the parent's own common stock.

stock dividend a dividend paid to stockholders in the form of additional shares of stock (instead of cash).

stock options the right to buy stock at a set price. Stock options are frequently given to employees and executives as compensation for their services.

stock repurchase payout ratio a ratio that addresses the distribution of company value and can be calculated directly as Common Stock Repurchase ÷ Net Income, or indirectly as Stock Repurchase Payout Ratio = Total Payout Ratio – Dividend Payout Ratio.

stock split a stock issue that increases the number of outstanding shares of a corporation without changing the balances of its equity accounts.

stock warrant the right granted by a corporation to purchase a specified number of shares of its capital stock at a stated price and within a stated time period.

stockholder payout the amounts distributed (paid out) to owners through dividends and/or stock repurchases (treasury stock). Analysts typically evaluate these amounts as a percentage of Net Income.

stockholder ratios ratios such as earnings per share and return on common equity that provide information about the creation of value for shareholders.

stockholders the owners of a corporation who own its shares in varying numbers.

stockholders' equity the owners' claims against the assets of a corporation after all liabilities have been deducted.

straight-line depreciation method a depreciation method that allocates an equal amount of an asset's cost to depreciation expense for each year of the asset's useful life. Straight-line depreciation expense for each period is calculated by dividing the depreciable cost of an asset by the asset's useful life.

strategic risks possible threats to the organization's success in accomplishing its objectives that are external to the organization.

subsidiary an investee company in which an investor company owns over 50% of the outstanding stock.

T

T-account a graphical representation of an account that gets its name because it resembles the capital letter T. A T-account is a two-column record that consists of an account title and two sides divided by a vertical line—the left side is called the debit side and the right side is called the credit side.

temporary accounts the accounts of revenue, expense, and dividend items that are used to collect the activities of only one period.

time-period assumption one of the four basic assumptions that underlie accounting that allows the life of a company to be divided into artificial time periods so net income can be measured for a specific period of time (e.g., monthly, quarterly, annually).

time series (or trend) analysis a type of analysis that compares a single corporation across time.

time value of money the idea that a cash flow in the future is less valuable than a cash flow at present.

timeliness quality of information where it is available to users before it loses its ability to influence decisions.

times interest earned ratio a ratio that measures the excess of net income over interest to gauge a firm's ability to repay its debt. It is calculated as: Income from Operations ÷ Interest Expense.

total payout ratio a ratio that adds stock repurchases to common dividends and compares this to net income. It is calculated as: Total Payout Ratio = (Common Dividends + Common Stock Repurchases)/ Net Income.

trade receivable an account receivable that is due from a customer purchasing inventory in the ordinary course of business.

trading securities equity or debt investments that management intends to sell in the near term.

transaction any event, external or internal, that is recognized in the financial statements.

transaction analysis the process of determining the economic effects of a transaction on the elements of the accounting equation.

treasury stock previously issued stock that is repurchased by the issuing corporation.

trial balance a list of all active accounts and each account's debit or credit balance.

turnover the average length of time required for assets to be consumed or replaced.

U

understandability quality of information whereby users with a reasonable knowledge of accounting and business can comprehend the meaning of that information.

unearned revenue a liability that occurs when a company receives payment for goods that will be delivered or services that will be performed in the future.

units-of-production depreciation method a depreciation method that allocates the cost of an asset over its expected life in direct proportion to the actual use of the asset; depreciation expense is computed by multiplying an asset's depreciable cost by a usage ratio.

unrealized gains an increase in the fair value of an investment security.

unrealized losses a decrease in the fair value of an investment security.

unsecured a term used for bonds in which the lender is relying on the general credit of the borrowing corporation rather than on collateral.

useful life the period of time over which the company anticipates deriving benefit from the use of the asset.

V

verifiability quality of information indicating the information is verifiable when independent parties can reach a consensus on the measurement of the activity.

vertical analysis a type of analysis that expresses each financial statement line item as a percent of the largest amount on the statement.

voluntary disposal a type of disposal that occurs when a company determines that the asset is no longer useful; the disposal may occur at the end of the asset's useful life or at some other time.

W

warranty a guarantee to repair or replace defective goods during a period (ranging from a few days to several years) following the sale.

wholesalers merchandisers that sell to other retailers.

withholding taxes businesses are required to withhold taxes from employees' earnings; standard withholdings include federal, state, and possibly city or county income taxes, as well as Social Security and Medicare. Employees may also have amounts withheld for such things as retirement accounts and health insurance.

work-in-process inventory the account in manufacturing firms that consists of the raw materials that are used in production, as well as other production costs such as labor and utilities.

working capital a measure of liquidity computed as: Current Assets – Current Liabilities.

worksheet an informal schedule that accountants use to assist them in organizing and preparing the information necessary to perform the end-of-period steps in the accounting cycle—namely the preparation of adjusting entries, financial statements, and closing entries.

Y

yield the market rate of interest demanded by creditors; yield may differ from stated rate because the underwriter disagrees with the borrower as to the correct yield or because of changes in the economy or creditworthiness of the borrower between the setting of the stated rate and the date of issue.

INDEX

TYPICAL CHART OF ACCOUNTS

ASSETS

Accounts Receivable
Accumulated Depletion
Accumulated
  Depreciation
Allowance for Doubtful
  Accounts
Allowance to Adjust
  Available-for-Sale
  Securities to Market
Allowance to Adjust
  Trading Securities to
  Market
Buildings
Cash
Copyright
Equipment
Finished Goods
  Inventory
Franchise
Furniture
Goodwill
Interest Receivable
Inventory
Investments
Investments—Available-
  for-Sale Securities
Investments—Equity
  Method
Investments—Trading
  Securities
Land
Leasehold Improvements
Natural Resources
Notes Receivable
Other Assets
Patent
Petty Cash
Prepaid Advertising
Prepaid Insurance
Prepaid Rent
Prepaid Repairs &
  Maintenance
Prepaid Security Services
Raw Materials Inventory
Rent Receivable
Supplies
Tax Refund Receivable
Trademark
Trucks
Work-in-Process Inventory

LIABILITIES

Accounts Payable
Bonds Payable
Capital Lease Liability
Charitable
  Contributions
Commissions Payable
Discount on Bonds
  Payable
Discount on Notes
  Payable
Dividends Payable
Excise Taxes Payable
Income Taxes Payable
Interest Payable
Lawsuit Payable
Lease Liability
Leased Assets
Medicare Taxes
  Payable
Notes Payable
Premium on Bonds
  Payable
Premium on Notes
  Payable
Property Taxes Payable
Rent Payable
Repair & Maintenance
  Payable
Royalties Payable
Salaries Payable
Sales Taxes Payable
Social Security Taxes
  Payable
Unearned Rent
  Revenue
Unearned Sales
  Revenue
Unearned Service
  Revenue
Unemployment Taxes
  Payable
Union Dues Payable
Utilities Payable
Wages Payable
Warranty Liability

STOCKHOLDERS' EQUITY

Accumulated Other
  Comprehensive
  Income
Additional Paid-In
  Capital—Common
  Stock
Additional Paid-In
  Capital—Preferred
  Stock
Additional Paid-In
  Capital—Treasury
  Stock
Common Stock
Preferred Stock
Retained Earnings
Treasury Stock
Unrealized Gain (Loss)
  on Available-for-Sale
  Securities

EQUITY-RELATED ACCOUNTS

Dividends
Income Summary

REVENUES/GAINS

Dividend Income
Interest Income
Investment Income—
  Equity Method
Rent Revenue
Sales Revenue
Service Revenue

Gain on Disposal of
  Property, Plant, &
  Equipment
Gain on Sale of
  Intangibles
Gain on Sale of
  Investments
Gain on Settlement of
  Lawsuit
Unrealized Gain (Loss) on
  Trading Securities

EXPENSES/LOSSES

Advertising Expense
Amortization Expense
Artist Fee Expense
Bad Debt Expense
Bank Service Charge
  Expense
Cash Over and Short
Commissions Expense
Cost of Goods Sold
Delivery Expense
Depreciation Expense
Income Taxes Expense
Insurance Expense
Interest Expense
Legal Expense
Medicare Taxes Expense
Miscellaneous Expense
Organizational Costs
Other Expense
Postage Expense
Property Taxes Expense

Purchase Allowances
Purchase Discounts
Purchase Returns
Purchases
Rent Expense
Repairs & Maintenance
  Expense
Research and
  Development Expense
Royalties Expense
Salaries Expense
Security Services Expense
Service Charge Expense
Social Security Taxes
  Expense
Supplies Expense
Transportation-In
Unemployment Taxes
  Expense
Utilities Expense
Wages Expense
Warranty Expense

Loss from Impairment
Loss on Disposal of
  Property, Plant, &
  Equipment
Loss on Sale of
  Intangibles
Loss on Sale of
  Investments

Note:

The Chart of Accounts for this edition of Financial Accounting: The Cornerstone of Business Decision Making has been simplified and standardized throughout all hypothetical in-chapter examples and end-of-chapter assignments in order to strengthen the pedagogical structure of the book. Account titles for real company financial statements will vary. Common alternate account titles are given in the textbook where the account is introduced, as appropriate, and real financial statement excerpts are included to help familiarize readers with alternate account titles.

When additional information is needed for an account title, it will be shown in parenthesis after the title [e.g., Accumulated Depreciation (Equipment), Excise Taxes Payable (State), Social Security Taxes Payable (Employer), etc.]

This Chart of Accounts is listed alphabetically by category for ease of reference. However, accounts in the textbook and in real financial statements are listed in order of liquidity.